IMPORTANT

HERE IS YOUR REGISTRATION CODE TO ACCESS MCGRAW-HILL PREMIUM CONTENT AND MCGRAW-HILL ONLINE RESOURCES

For key premium online resources you need THIS CODE to gain access. Once the code is entered, you will be able to use the web resources for the length of your course.

Access is provided only if you have purchased a new book.

If the registration code is missing from this book, the registration screen on our website, and within your WebCT or Blackboard course will tell you how to obtain your new code. Your registration code can be used only once to establish access. It is not transferable

To gain access to these online resources

1. USE your web browser to go to: **www.mhhe.com/timmons7e**
2. CLICK on "First Time User"
3. ENTER the Registration Code printed on the tear-off bookmark on the right
4. After you have entered your registration code, click on "Register"
5. FOLLOW the instructions to setup your personal UserID and Password
6. WRITE your UserID and Password down for future reference. Keep it in a safe place.

If your course is using WebCT or Blackboard, you'll be able to use this code to access the McGraw-Hill content within your instructor's online course.
To gain access to the McGraw-Hill content in your instructor's WebCT or Blackboard course simply log into the course with the user ID and Password provided by your instructor. Enter the registration code exactly as it appears to the right when prompted by the system. You will only need to use this code the first time you click on McGraw-Hill content.

These instructions are specifically for student access. Instructors are not required to register via the above instructions.

The McGraw-Hill Companies
McGraw-Hill Irwin

Thank you, and welcome to your McGraw-Hill/Irwin Online Resources.

Timmons/Spinelli
t/a New Venture Creation
ISBN-13: 978-0-07-327066-1
ISBN-10: 0-07-327066-0

GPQQ-9CVY-XVTN-D443-D87N

REGISTRATION CODE
REGISTRATION CODE

The McGraw-Hill Companies
McGraw-Hill Irwin

New Venture Creation

ENTREPRENEURSHIP FOR THE 21st CENTURY

SEVENTH EDITION

New Venture Creation

ENTREPRENEURSHIP FOR THE 21st CENTURY

Jeffry A. Timmons, A.B., M.B.A., D.B.A.
Franklin W. Olin Distinguished Professor of Entrepreneurship
Director, Price Babson College Fellows Program
Babson College
Babson Park, Massachusetts

and

Stephen Spinelli, Jr., B.A., M.B.A., Ph.D.
John H. Muller, Jr. Chair, Entrepreneurship
Director, Arthur M. Blank Center for Entrepreneurship
Chairman, Entrepreneurship Division
Babson College
Babson Park, Massachusetts

McGraw-Hill Irwin

Boston Burr Ridge, IL Dubuque, IA Madison, WI New York San Francisco St. Louis
Bangkok Bogotá Caracas Kuala Lumpur Lisbon London Madrid Mexico City
Milan Montreal New Delhi Santiago Seoul Singapore Sydney Taipei Toronto

The McGraw·Hill Companies

McGraw-Hill Irwin

NEW VENTURE CREATION: ENTREPRENEURSHIP FOR THE 21st CENTURY

Published by McGraw-Hill/Irwin, a business unit of The McGraw-Hill Companies, Inc., 1221 Avenue of the Americas, New York, NY, 10020.

Some ancillaries, including electronic and print components, may not be available to customers outside the United States.

This book is printed on acid-free paper.

1 2 3 4 5 6 7 8 9 0 QPD/QPD 0 9 8 7 6

ISBN-13: 978-0-07-310279-5
ISBN 0-07-310279-2

Editorial director: *John E. Biernat*
Senior sponsoring editor: *Ryan Blankenship*
Editorial coordinator: *Allison J. Belda*
Associate marketing manager: *Margaret A. Beamer*
Media producer: *Benjamin Curless*
Project manager: *Bruce Gin*
Production supervisor: *Gina Hangos*
Designer: *Cara David*
Senior media project manager: *Susan Lombardi*
Cover design: *Cara David*
Interior design: *Cara David*
Typeface: *10.5/12 New Caledonia*
Compositor: *TechBooks/GTS, New Delhi, India Campus*
Printer: *Quebecor World Dubuque Inc.*

Library of Congress Cataloging-in-Publication Data

Timmons, Jeffry A.
New venture creation : entrepreneurship for the 21st century / Jeffry A. Timmons and Stephen Spinelli, Jr.–7th ed.
p. cm.
Includes bibliographical references and index.
ISBN-13: 978-0-07-310279-5 (alk. paper)
ISBN-10: 0-07-310279-2 (alk. paper)
1. New business enterprises–Handbooks, manuals, etc. 2. Entrepreneurship–Handhooks, manuals, etc. I. Spinelli, Stephen. II. Title.
HD62.5.T55 2007
658.1'141–dc22

2005056238

www.mhhe.com

DEDICATED TO

Ralph "Bud" Sorenson, *Babson's seventh president, and our dear friend and mentor. Ralph was the very first college or university president in the world to create a vision and make a strategic commitment to entrepreneurship as a field of education, research, and community outreach.*

—Jeff and Steve

ABOUT THE AUTHORS

Jeffry A. Timmons

Franklin W. Olin Distinguished Professor of Entrepreneurship and director, Price-Babson College Fellows Program at Babson College.

AB, Colgate University; MBA, DBA, Harvard University Graduate School of Business.

Since the late 1960s, Jeffry A. Timmons has been one of the pioneers in the development of entrepreneurship education and research in America. He is recognized as a leading authority internationally for his research, innovative curriculum development, and teaching in entrepreneurship, new ventures, entrepreneurial finance, and venture capital. Babson College is recognized as a world leader in entrepreneurship education. *U. S. News and World Report* has ranked the F. W. Olin Graduate School of Business the number one school in entrepreneurship 12 years in a row, *Success* magazine rated Babson the number one school for entrepreneurs, and the *Financial Times* ranked Babson number one in entrepreneurship in the world in 2001.

Professor Timmons is somewhat of an academic heretic—having resigned tenure twice, as well as resigning two endowed chairs. In 1994, he resigned the Harvard endowed professorship he had held since 1989 to return to Babson College, which he had joined in 1982, and in 1995 was named the first Franklin W. Olin Distinguished Professor of Entrepreneurship. Earlier he had been the first to hold the Paul T. Babson Professorship for two years and, subsequently, became the first named to the Frederic C. Hamilton Professorship in Free Enterprise Studies, from which he resigned in 1989 to accept the Harvard chair. Earlier at Northeastern University in 1973, he launched what is believed to be the first undergraduate major in new ventures and entrepreneurship in the country, and later created and led the Executive MBA program. Both of these programs exist today. *BusinessWeek's 1995 Guide to Graduate Business Schools* rated Timmons as the "best bet" and among the top 10 professors at Harvard Business School. A September 1995 *Success* magazine feature article called him "one of the two most powerful minds in entrepreneurship in the nation." Michie P. Slaughter, former president of the Kauffman Center for Entrepreneurial Leadership at the Ewing Marion Kauffman Foundation, calls him "the premier entrepreneurship educator in America." Before her death in January 2001, Gloria Appel, as president of the Price Institute for Entrepreneurial Studies, noted, "He has done more to advance entrepreneurship education than any other educator in America." In 1995, the Price Institute and Babson College faculty and friends chose to honor Dr. Timmons by endowing The Jeffry A. Timmons Professorship in recognition of his contributions to Babson and to the field.

In 1985, he designed and launched the Price-Babson College Fellows Program, aimed at improving teaching and research by teaming highly successful entrepreneurs with experienced faculty. This unique initiative was in response to a need to create a mechanism enabling colleges and universities to attract and support entrepreneurship educators and entrepreneurs with "an itch to teach". There is now a core group of over 1,100 entrepreneurship educators and entrepreneurs from approximately 300 colleges and universities in the United States and 32 foreign countries, who are alumni of the Price-Babson College Fellows Program. In May 1995, *INC.* magazine's "Who's Who" special edition on entrepreneurship called him "the Johnny Appleseed of entrepreneurship education" and concluded that this program had "changed the terrain of entrepreneurship education." The program was the winner of two national awards, has been replicated outside the United States, and has now been expanded to PriceBabson at Berkeley. In 1998, Dr. Timmons led an initiative now funded by the Kauffman Center for Entrepreneurial Leadership to create Lifelong Learning for Entrepreneurship Education Professionals (LLEEP), which in addition to Price-Babson at Berkeley offers a series of training clinics for entrepreneurship educators. With the Price Babson College Fellow Program's Symposium for Entrepreneurship Educators (SEE) as its flagship program, LLEEP now has as its partners leading faculty members from Stanford University, University of California at Berkeley, University of Colorado at Boulder, Syracuse University, Umass Online, and Rensselaer Polytechnic Institute.

In 2003 Dr. Timmons worked with Professor Steve Spinelli to conceive a sister program to the SEE program that would be available for engineering schools with an interest in entrepreneurship. They partnered with colleagues at the new Olin College of Engineering on the Babson campus—President Rick Miller, Provost David Kerns, Dean Michael Moody, and Professors John Bourne, Ben Linder, Heidi Neck, and Stephen Schiffman—to win a three-year National Science Foundation grant to design, develop, and deliver such a program. The first pilot was done is June 2005 with significant success, and will now be offered on the Babson/Olin Campus in 2006 and 2007.

During the past decades, Dr. Timmons has helped launch several new initiatives at Babson, including the Babson-Kauffman Entrepreneurship Research Conference, the Kauffman Foundation/CEL Challenge Grant, the Price Challenge Grant, business plan competitions, and a president's seminar. In 1997 he led an initiative to create the first need-based full-tuition scholarship for MBA students with a $900,000 matching grant from the Price Institute for Entrepreneurial Studies. Each year one of the recipients of this Price-Babson Alumni Scholarship is named the Gloria Appel Memorial Scholar in honor of this long-time benefactor, colleague, and friend. In addition to teaching, Professor Timmons devotes a major portion of his efforts at Babson to the Price-Babson programs and to joint initiatives funded by the Kauffman Center for Entrepreneurial Leadership and Babson, including new research and curriculum development activities. He has provided leadership in developing and teaching in initiatives that assist Native Americans seeking economic self-determination and community development most notably through entrepreneurship education programs at the nation's several Tribal Colleges. In April 2001, Professor Timmons was recognized for these efforts in a citation voted by the legislature of the State of Oklahoma naming him Ambassador for Entrepreneurship. Currently he is helping replicate these efforts for other minority communities, most notably an initiative to support the development of a consortium of entrepreneurship education programs at the historically black colleges.

Since 1999, he has served as special advisor to the National Commission on Entrepreneurship. The work of the commission culminated in a national conference held in April 2001 that was jointly sponsored by the John F. Kennedy School of Government at Harvard University, the National Commission of Entrepreneurship, and the Kauffman Center for Entrepreneurial Leadership. Professor Timmons served as a lead moderator at conference sessions.

A prolific researcher and writer, he has written nine books, including this textbook first published in 1974. *New Venture Creation* has been rated by *INC.*, *Success*, and *The Wall Street Journal* as a "classic" in entrepreneurship, and has been translated into both Japanese and Chinese. In 1996 and 1998, *INC.* featured the book's fourth edition as one of the top eight "must read" books for entrepreneurs. *Venture Capital at the Crossroads* written with Babson colleague William Bygrave (1992) is considered the seminal work on the venture capital industry and is also translated into Japanese. Earlier, Dr. Timmons wrote *The Entrepreneurial Mind* (1989), *New Business Opportunities* (1990), *The Insider's Guide to Small Business Resources* (1984), *The Encyclopedia of Small Business Resources* (1984), and his contributed chapters to other books including *The Portable MBA in Entrepreneurship* (1994, 1997, 2003). More recently, he has co-authored *How to Raise Capital*, with Babson Professor Andrew Zacharakis (2005), and *Business Plans That Work*, with Steve Spinelli (2004). Timmons has authored over 100 articles and papers, which have appeared in numerous leading publications, such as *Harvard Business Review* and *Journal of Business Venturing*, along with numerous teaching case studies. In 1995, he began to develop a new audiotape series on entrepreneurship, working with Sam Tyler, producer of the *In Search of Excellence* series for PBS with Tom Peters. He has also appeared in the national media in the United States and numerous other countries and has been quoted in *INC.*, *Success*, *The Wall Street Journal*, *The New York Times*, *Los Angeles Times*, *BusinessWeek*, *Working Woman*, *Money*, *USA Today*, and has had feature articles written about him in *The Rolling Stone* (1997), *The Boston Globe* (1997), and *Success* (1994).

Dr. Timmons has earned a reputation for "practicing what he teaches." One former graduate and software entrepreneur interviewed for the *Rolling Stone* article put it succinctly: "When going to his classes I couldn't wait to get there; and when I got there I didn't ever want to leave!" For over 35 years he has been immersed in the world of entrepreneurship as an investor, director, and/or advisor in private companies and investment funds including Cellular One in Boston, New Hampshire, and Maine; the Boston Communications Group; BCI Advisors, Inc.; Spectrum Equity Investors; Internet Securities, Inc.; Chase Capital Partners; Color Kinetics, Inc.; and others. He also served since 1991 as founding member of the board of directors of the Kauffman Center for Entrepreneurial Leadership at the Ewing Marion Kauffman Foundation. For the next 10 years he served as a special advisor to the president and board of directors of the Kauffman Center, where he conceived of the Kauffman Fellows Program and served as its dean of faculty. In 2003 he worked closely with the president and alumni of the Kauffman Fellows Program to successfully spin the program out of the Kauffman Foundation into an independent entity as the Center for Venture Management, and continues as dean, chairman of the Educational Advisory Committee, and on the board of directors. The aim of this innovative program is to create for aspiring venture capitalists and entrepreneurs what the Rhodes scholarship and White House Fellows programs are to politics and public affairs. In 2001, Dr. Timmons joined the President's Council at the newly formed Franklin W. Olin College of Engineering. In 1994 and 1996, he served as a national judge for the Ernst & Young Entrepreneur of the Year Awards.

Dr. Timmons received his MBA and DBA from Harvard Business School, where he was a National Defense Education Act fellow, and is a graduate of Colgate University, where he was a Scott Paper Foundation Scholar. He served as a trustee of Colgate from 1991 to 2000. He lives on his 500+ acre farm in New Hampshire with his wife of 40 years, Sara, and winters at Brays Island Plantation near Savannah, Georgia. He enjoys the outdoors: fly-fishing, hunting with his Elhew pointer Breeze, and golf. He is one of the founders of the Wapack Highlands Greenway Initiative in New Hampshire, is active in the Henry's Fork Foundation and Wildlife Conservation Trust of New Hampshire, and serves as a director of Timber Owners of New England. He is a member of numerous other wildlife and nature organizations, including The Monadnock Conservancy, The Harris Center, The Nature Conservancy, The Moosehead Region Futures Committee, Atlantic Salmon Federation, and Ruffed Grouse Society.

Stephen Spinelli, Jr.

Director, Arthur M. Blank Center for Entrepreneurship, and chairman, Entrepreneurship Division at Babson College.

Vice provost for Entrepreneurship and Global Management at Babson College.

Paul T. Babson Chair in Entrepreneurship at Babson College.

Alan Lewis Chair in Global Management.

B.A., McDaniel College (formerly Western Maryland College); MBA, Babson Graduate School of Business; and PhD (Economics), Imperial College, University of London.

The majority of Dr. Spinelli's professional experience has been in entrepreneurship. He was a founding shareholder, director, and manager of Jiffy Lube International. He was also founder, chairman, and CEO of American Oil Change Corporation. In 1991, he completed a sale of Jiffy Lube to Pennzoil Company. Although Dr. Spinelli now heads the Entrepreneurship Division at Babson and teaches full-time, he has not abandoned his business roots. He continues to consult with regional, national, and international companies; serves as a director at several corporations including Keystone Automotive, Tencorp, Inc., and Alco Equipment; and participates as an angel investor with investments in more than a dozen start-ups.

Dr. Spinelli is the quintessential "pracademic"—a business practitioner turned academic. Having successfully harvested Jiffy Lube, Dr. Spinelli was invited to attend the Price Babson College Fellows Program and his career in academia was launched. After several years of part-time teaching, he joined the ranks of full-time faculty after receiving his PhD in October 1995 from the University of London. Dr. Spinelli's expertise is in start-up and growth management. His research has focused on an understanding of strategic entrepreneurial relationships. He is the author of more than two dozen journal articles, book chapters, academic papers, and teaching case studies. He is also the author of *Franchising: Pathway to Entrepreneurship* (Prentice-Hall; 2003). His latest book, *Never Bet the Farm*, is co-authored with Anthony Iaquinto. A superb educator, he is now a key member of the faculty of the Price Babson College Fellows Program's Symposium for Entrepreneurship Educators, in addition to his teaching in the undergraduate, graduate, and executive education programs, and is a shining example of the many contributions that entrepreneurs can make to an academic institution. In 2003 Dr. Spinelli founded the Babson-Historically Black Colleges and Universities case writing consortium. This group is dedicated to writing entrepreneurship teaching cases focused on African-American entrepreneurs.

In 1998–1999, the Arthur M. Blank Center for Entrepreneurship began a national search for a Dr. Spinelli proved the best candidate by far, and he now leads Babson College's Entrepreneurship Division (perhaps the first such autonomous academic division in the country) as well as the center, a 16,000-square-foot building, which houses the largest dedicated entrepreneurship faculty in the world, as well as numerous research and outreach programs. The center includes hatchery space for student entrepreneurs, teleconferencing facilities, and a resource/archival space for visiting research scholars. He is a leading force in curriculum innovation at Babson and, with his colleagues in the Entrepreneurship Division, continually defines and delivers new initiatives. In 1999, he led the design and implementation of an entrepreneurship intensity track for MBAs seeking to launch new business ventures upon graduation. Building on this highly successful initiative, he led the design and development of ACE, an accelerated honors curriculum for aspiring entrepreneurs in Babson's undergraduate program. Dr. Spinelli's presentation to the United States Association for Small Business and Entrepreneurship (USASBE) resulted in the naming of the F. W. Olin Graduate School of Business as the 2002 National Model MBA program. Babson currently offers 15 undergraduate courses in entrepreneurship and 20 courses at the graduate level.

Dr. Spinelli has been a strong voice for entrepreneurship outside the Babson community as well. He has been a keynote speaker for Advent International's CEO Conference, the MCAA National Convention, and Allied Domecq International's Retailing Conference; has been called to testify before the U.S. Senate Subcommittee on Small Business and Entrepreneurship; and is often quoted as an expert in the field in such leading publications as *The Wall Street Journal, Forbes, Financial Times,* and *INC.*

Dr. Spinelli continues to give back to his community, especially in his boyhood hometown of Springfield, Massachusetts. He and his wife, Carol, maintain their home in western Massachusetts. He is the current chairman of Western Massachusetts Entrepreneurship Consortium (and EntreNet.com), a not-for-profit consortium of organizations seeking to advance entrepreneurship in western Massachusetts. He also serves as a director for several local, regional, and national not-for-profits or community-based associations, including the National Foundation for Teaching Entrepreneurship (NFTE), Visiting Nurses Association of Western Massachusetts, and UNICO International.

Jeffry A. Timmons *timmons@babson.edu*
Stephen Spinelli, Jr. *spinelli@babson.edu*
Arthur M. Blank Center for Entrepreneurship
Babson College
Babson Park, MA 02457 *USA*
781-239-4420
781-239-4178 (fax)
www.babson.edu/entrep

PREFACE

A Book for the Next Generation of Entrepreneurial Leaders—Worldwide

The evolution of entrepreneurship in America over the past 35 years has had an extraordinary impact on the cultural and economic landscape in the United States. While there will always be opportunities for improvement and innovation, America's entrepreneurial revolution has become a model for business people, educators, and policymakers around the globe.

People in every nation have enormous entrepreneurial qualities and aspirations, and that spirit is finding its way into nearly all world markets. Entrepreneurship is exploding in countries like India, China, and in the former Soviet bloc—and affecting positive social and economic change in such diverse countries as Korea, Mexico, South Africa, El Salvador, and Ireland. The 2004 Global Entrepreneurship Monitor (GEM) study found that in the 34 countries surveyed, 9.3 percent (73 million) of the 784 million people comprising the population of 18- to 64-year-olds were either nascent entrepreneurs or the owner/manager of a new business. Significantly, 41 percent of these entrepreneurs were women.

In our roles as student, teacher, researcher, observer, and participant in this revolution, we can honestly say that global adoption of the entrepreneurial mindset appears to be growing exponentially larger and faster. That mindset, while informed by new venture experiences, affects larger corporations and the not-for-profit world as well. In our assessment, we are at the dawn of a new age of entrepreneurial reasoning, equity creation, and philanthropy, whose impact in the coming years will dwarf what we experienced over the last century.

An Edition for an Era of Uncertainty and Extraordinary Opportunity

The new millennium is being defined as much by worldwide challenges and uncertainty as it is from the enormous opportunities afforded by technology, global communications, and the increasing drive to develop socially, economically, and environmentally sane and sensible new ventures. As with past generations, entrepreneurs in this arena face the ultimate and most demanding juggling act: how to simultaneously balance the insatiable requirements of marriage, family, new venture, service to community, and still have time for one's own pleasure and peace.

A Book about the Entrepreneurial Process: The Basis for a Curriculum as Well as a Course!

New Venture Creation **is about the actual process of getting a new venture started, growing the venture, successfully harvesting it, and starting again.**

There is a substantial body of knowledge, concepts, and tools that entrepreneurs need to know—before taking the startup plunge, during, and after—if they are to get the odds in their favor. Accompanying the explosion in entrepreneurship has been a significant increase in research and knowledge about the entrepreneurial process. Much of what was known previously has been reinforced and refined, while some has been challenged. Numerous new insights have emerged. *New Venture Creation* continues to be the product of experience and considerable research in this field, rooted in real-world application and refined in the classroom.

As with previous editions, the design and flow of this book are aimed at creating knowledge, skills, and awareness. In a pragmatic way—through text, case studies, and hands-on exercises—students are engaged to discover critical aspects of entrepreneurship, and what level of competencies, know-how, experience, attitudes, resources, and networks is required to pursue different entrepreneurial opportunities. No doubt about it: There is no substitute for the real thing—actually starting a company. But short of that, it is possible to expose students to many of the vital issues and immerse them in key learning experiences, such as critical self-assessment and the development of a business plan.

This book is divided into five parts. Parts I through IV detail the driving forces of entrepreneurship—opportunity recognition, the business plan, the founder and the team, and resource requirements. Part I describes the global entrepreneurial revolution and addresses the mindset required to tackle this tremendously challenging and rewarding pursuit. Part II lays out the process by which real opportunities—not just ideas—can be discovered and selected. This section examines the type of opportunity around which higher potential ventures can be built (with acceptable risks and trade-offs), and how entrepreneurs can exit their businesses profitably—when they want to—rather than when they have to—or worse, not at all. Part III concerns entrepreneurial leadership, team creation, and personal ethics. Part IV addresses franchising as an entrepreneurial vehicle, marshaling resources, entrepreneurial finance, and fund-raising. The book concludes with a section dealing with strategies for success, managing rapid growth, and harvest issues.

Once the reader understands how winning entrepreneurs think, act, and perform, he or she can then establish goals to practice emulating those actions, attitudes, habits, and strategies. *New Venture Creation* challenges readers to think about the process of becoming an entrepreneur, and seeks to enable entrepreneurs to immerse themselves in the dynamics of launching and growing a company. The book addresses practical issues such as the following:

- What are my real talents, strengths, and weaknesses, and how can I exploit those talents and strengths, and minimize my weaknesses?
- How can I recognize when an opportunity is more than just another good idea, and whether it's one that fits with my personal mindset, capabilities, and life goals?
- Why do some firms grow quickly to several million in sales, but then stumble, never growing beyond a single-product firm?
- What are the critical tasks and hurdles in seizing an opportunity and building the business?
- How much money do I need, and when, where, and how can I get it—on acceptable terms?
- What financing sources, strategies, and mechanisms can I bring to bear throughout the process—from pre-start, through the early growth stage, to the harvest of my venture?
- What are the minimum resources I need to gain control over the opportunity, and how can I do this?
- Is a business plan needed? If so, what kind is required and how and when should I develop one?
- Who are the constituents for whom I must create or add value to achieve a positive cash flow, and to develop harvest options?
- What is my venture worth, and how do I negotiate what to give up?
- What are the critical transitions in entrepreneurial management as a firm grows from $1 million, to $5 million, to over $25 million in sales?
- What are some of the pitfalls, minefields, and hazards I need to anticipate, prepare for, and respond to?
- What are the contacts and networks I need to access and develop?
- Do I know what I do and do not know, and do I know what to do about it?
- How can I develop a personal "entrepreneurial game plan" to acquire the experience I need to succeed?
- How critical and sensitive is the timing in each of these areas?
- Why do entrepreneurship and entrepreneurial management seem surrounded by paradoxes, well-known to entrepreneurs, such as:

  Ambiguity and uncertainty versus planning and rigor?
  Creativity versus disciplined analysis?
  Patience and perseverance versus urgency?
  Organization and management versus flexibility?
  Innovation and responsiveness versus systemization?
  Risk avoidance versus risk management?
  Current profits versus long-term equity?

The *New Venture Creation* models are useful not only as a comprehensive textbook for a course in entrepreneurship, but also as a road map for a curriculum or departmental major in entrepreneurship. Since the late 1990s, for example, Babson College has been setting the standard for management education in the 21st century with a new approach based on the model of the entrepreneurial process in this text. This integrative program has been a major factor in keeping Babson College in the top spot among entrepreneurship schools in America and, now, around the world.

A Summary of Changes in the 7th Edition: New Cases, New Chapters, New Data, and Major Revisions

This edition is a significant update from the 6th edition. New cases, exercises, updated Web sites, and textural material have been added to capture the current financial, economic, technological, and globally competitive environment of this first half-decade of the new century. A special effort has been made to include cases that capture the dynamic ups and downs new firms experience over an extended period of time. By grappling with decisions faced by entrepreneurs—from startup to harvest—this text offers a broad and rich perspective on the often turbulent and unpredictable nature of the entrepreneurial process.

This edition features major changes and additions:

- There has been a major restructuring and reordering of the flow of the book, which now begins with a focus on the reader as the aspiring entrepreneur.
- Eight new cases—nearly half of the total—and two revised cases have been added to this edition.
- This 7th edition contains the latest updates, including examples of entrepreneurs in action, coping with the post-Internet bubble era.
- Internet Impacts: brief, focused reports relating to the Timmons Model on how the Internet has fundamentally changed the business landscape forever. These are concrete, current examples of how entrepreneurs use the Internet to their advantage in every aspect of their venture from launch to growth and renewal.
- For the first time, we have included a dynamic financial planning model that can be a breakthrough tool for entrepreneurs evaluating or planning a venture.
- Further refinements of the Timmons Model of the entrepreneurial process, including the addition of social, economic, and environmental sustainability factors.
- We have included the latest data and updates on the significant changes in the whole new world of capital markets, the economy, and the banking environment that are relevant to entrepreneurs.
- Our classic business plan guide has been updated with new material on social and environmental sustainability.
- We have added a new exercise that will challenge students to research, brainstorm, and identify what are likely to be the upcoming "sea changes" that will drive the next growth industries.
- Professor Tim Habbershon, director of the Institute for Family Enterprise at Babson College, has contributed a dynamic new chapter on family enterprising.

Chapter 1, "The Entrepreneurial Mind: Crafting a Personal Entrepreneurial Strategy"—a Major Rewrite

This chapter looks at the entrepreneurial founder and the unique qualities of that mindset. The Crafting a Personal Entrepreneurial Strategy exercise toward the end of the 6th edition has been brought forward so students can get started on it right away. There is also an updated and broader discussion and data on the importance of women and minorities in the entrepreneurial economy.

In the new case film *October Sky*, NASA engineer Homer H. Hickam, Jr.'s autobiography provides the basis for this movie set in the late 1950s about a teenager from a coal mining town who overcomes enormous obstacles in his quest to design and launch homemade rockets. *October Sky* is a dramatic mix of traditional family conflicts, supportive mentoring, and a young man's entrepreneurial passion and drive. The Instructor's Manual provides a detailed note for use with the film. Students can view the film in or outside of class, and then use it as a basis for class discussion of the entrepreneurial mind in action: thought processes, principles of entrepreneurial thinking and reasoning, entrepreneurial practices, strategies, and the like.

Chapter 2, "America's Entrepreneurial Revolution Goes Global"—a Significant Rewrite with New Material

Chapter 2 represents a major revision from the previous edition and presents updated empirical evidence of how America's entrepreneurial drive has sparked a worldwide entrepreneurial revolution. In this edition we include updated and new data on the entrepreneurial economy by incorporating the latest findings of Babson's Global Entrepreneurship Monitor (GEM) report. This chapter also addresses the lessons learned from the recent Internet bubble and subsequent recession, and introduces the following relational formula that began in America and is now seen worldwide:

Innovation + Entrepreneurship = Prosperity & Philanthropy

The new case about Roxanne Quimby tells the remarkable story of a young woman, living at a subsistence level in the backwoods of Maine, who sees an opportunity and grows it in a few years into a multi-million-dollar venture. What begins as a lifestyle business doesn't stay that way for long. This case replaces PC-Build, which will revert to the NVC/McGraw Web site.

Exercise: Visit with an Entrepreneur: Most students will know at least several entrepreneurs, but few will have explored with them in depth the carefully thought through questions in this exercise. It establishes important benchmarks, role models, and comparisons that are referenced throughout the course.

Chapter 3, "The Entrepreneurial Process"—New and Updated Material

This is an update on what was a major revision in the previous edition of *New Venture Creation.* It further develops the Timmons Model framework for the entrepreneurial process and offers a new "real world" example that illustrates the conceptual model. One significant change in the model is the inclusion of the concept of "sustainability," for the community and the environment.

New in this edition is a discussion of how the new entrepreneurial paradigm has permeated the not-for-profit world via venture philanthropy, how corporations are embracing and inventing their own versions of entrepreneurial management, and how the e-society is being embraced by government and becoming more central to policy debates.

Revised Case: Kurt and John Bauer: This case series follows an about-to-graduate MBA and his brother as they explore the idea of turning Kurt's second-year field project into a business magazine in Eastern Europe focusing on Poland.

Chapter 4, "The Opportunity: Creating, Shaping, Recognizing, and Seizing"—Revisions and Updated Material

This chapter had been significantly revised in the previous edition. The material focuses on opportunity assessment and due diligence strategies. The criteria for evaluating venture opportunities have been refined further, and new Web-based resources and tools have been added.

Case: Securities Online, Inc.: This is the second case in the series that concludes the Bauer brothers' saga. It's a year later, and the brothers have a significantly redefined opportunity, strategy, and business plan. They are seeking venture capital to grow, not a magazine publishing arm as they had originally set out to do but instead, an online financial and economic information service that will provide data to investment banks, consulting firms, and banks. The case captures the dynamic creation and shaping of an Internet-based higher-potential venture.

New Exercise: The Next Sea-Changes: Students are challenged to research, brainstorm, and identify new technologies and discoveries that will drive the next growth industries, just as the integrated circuit drove the evolution from mainframe computers to personal computers and PDAs.

Chapter 5, "Screening Venture Opportunities"—New and Updated Material

This chapter was substantially enhanced in the previous edition and builds on the drivers and criteria in Chapter 4. The classic screening guide has been fine-tuned to include sustainability points.

Exercises: QuickScreen and Venture Opportunity Screening Exercises (VOSE) provide valuable formats to guide the initial evaluation of an idea and the due diligence needed to determine its profit potential, probable risk/reward, and impact on the sustainability of the enterprise. The VOSE was simplified and segmented in the last edition into discrete exercises that can be used separately or in total. This change allows for maximum flexibility in the syllabus and when counseling individual students or mentoring field study projects.

The QuickScreen, a dehydrated version of the VOSE, helps students to quickly cut through to the core characteristics of an opportunity.

Case: Burt's Bees: This case follows the Roxanne Quimby story begun earlier. Roxanne is a remarkable entrepreneur, whose creative ideas and entrepreneurial spirit lead her to create a new business around bee's wax products and derivatives. With her company experiencing profitable growth, Roxanne faces a major issue of re-location to North Carolina and the offer of a significant strategic sale.

Chapter 6, "The Business Plan"—Updated Material and a New Case

This important chapter has been moved up in the text to enhance the flow of practical tools and to expose students earlier to the process of developing a business plan. The biggest change is the incorporation of sustainability aspects into the opportunity and business plan development.

New Case: Newland Medical Technologies: It had all seemed like a perfect plan. With two assertive angel investors guiding her medical device company on what seemed to be an acquisition fast track, young entrepreneur Sarah Foster and her husband decided that the time was right to start a family. However, by the middle of her first trimester, everything had changed. As co-founder and president, Sarah was now compelled to seriously reconsider the course she'd set for her medical device venture. In doing so, she was going to have to make some tough choices in order to strike a balance between motherhood and her professional passions.

Chapter 7, "The Entrepreneurial Manager"—Updated Material and a New Case

Chapter 7 discusses the skills and requirements of the founder as the company grows through various stages. It looks at the leadership issues inherent in building a company from scratch. The chapter emphasizes that the ability to shape and guide a cohesive team is particularly critical in high-tech firms, where the competitive landscape can shift dramatically in the face of disruptive technologies. Exhibits have been further refined.

Exercise: Management Skills and Know-How Assessment: An organized inventory of management skills enables students to obtain feedback and to assess their skills, know-how, and competencies, and the relevant experience that is necessary to pursue the opportunity they are developing.

New Case: Jim Poss: Jim Poss's enterprise, Seahorse Power Company, is an engineering startup that encourages the adoption of environmentally friendly methods of power generation by designing products that are cheaper and more efficient than 20th century technologies. Poss is sure that his first product, a patent-pending, solar-powered trash compactor, could make a real difference. This case chronicles the evolution of this green venture and places Poss at the critical juncture of deciding how best to deal with potential investors and funding alternatives.

Chapter 8, "The New Venture Team"—Revisions and a New Case

This chapter puts the zoom lens on the "people" portion of the Timmons Model—the entrepreneurial team. The issues of building the team, leading the team, the delicate allocation of equity and compensation, and critical issues and pitfalls faced in the process are discussed. Some new Web sites and information on compensation patterns in higher potential ventures are included.

New Case: Maclean Palmer: Palmer, an African American, is the founder of a new private equity fund in 2000. The case details his meticulous and thoughtful approach to putting a team together from scratch for a potential lifelong partnership.

Exercise: Rewards: This carefully structured exercise guides students through the issues, trade-offs, and decisions that are confronted in determining equity ownership and compensation in the team.

Chapter 9, "Personal Ethics and the Entrepreneur"—New and Updated Material

Chapter 9 addresses the complex and thorny issues of ethics and integrity for the entrepreneur and the implications for future success. It seeks to build understanding of the critical importance of high ethical standards and awareness in the team and the company.

Case: Wayne Postoak: This is the story of a highly successful basketball coach and teacher who becomes an entrepreneur. It is a short but rich case, particularly since it involves a Native American who builds a successful company with sales in excess of $10 million.

Exercise: Ethics: This short exercise compels students to make various ethical choices and utilizes their answers to focus discussion on the issues raised by the assignment and in the chapter.

Chapter 10, "Resource Requirements"—New and Updated Material, plus a New Financial Planning Template

The zoom lens now focuses on the third element of the Timmons Model, managing the resources. This chapter examines strategies and techniques used by entrepreneurs to identify and marshal resources. Frugal bootstrapping strategies are discussed, as well as the implications of the Sarbanes-Oxley Act of 2002—a sweeping financial disclosure law that is having an affect even on small ventures.

New Financial Tool: The Shad Business Planning Model: An interactive financial tool that can be used and modified to develop financial projections for the income statement, balance sheet, and cash flow statement, this template can save entrepreneurs dozens, if not hundreds, of hours. The model is fully integrated so that any change in, for example, revenue, margins, or capital raised (both debt and equity) will immediately be calculated and shown on each of the three statements. Available for download through the NVC/McGraw Web site.

Exercise: Build Your Brain Trust: This exercise is modeled after the Babson Brain Trust, a program at Babson College designed to create collisions and networking opportunities for student entrepreneurs as they seek to identify significant venture opportunities.

Exercise: How Entrepreneurs Turn Less into More: A short field project requiring students to identify and interview—in depth—entrepreneurs who have created companies with sales over $3 million, having started with less than $50,000 of seed capital. This can be a powerful and revealing exercise for students.

Case: Quick Lube Franchise Company: This case examines how one of the original founders of the Jiffy Lube franchise becomes a leading franchisee and is then faced with harvesting issues. The complex valuation, timing, deal structuring, and negotiating issues are an important aspect of the case.

Chapter 11, "Franchising"—Revised with Updated Material

Chapter 11 examines franchising as an opportunity and as a risk-reward management strategy. It examines the entrepreneurial aspects of franchising—including structural and strategic alternatives available to entrepreneurs, selection criteria, resource and experience requirements, and the building and managing of the franchise system—as well as the complex set of relationships that can evolve.

Case: Mike Bellobuono: This case follows the story of an undergraduate who becomes enamored with a bagel shop concept and chooses franchising to grow his concept.

Chapter 12, "Entrepreneurial Finance"—Revised Material with an Updated Case

This chapter discusses what entrepreneurs need to know about entrepreneurial finance, such as determining capital requirements, the free cash flow format, and developing financial and fund-raising strategies.

Revised Case: Midwest Lighting: Always a favorite, this is a classic partners-in-conflict case. The valuation, the future estimates of the business's potential, and a mechanism for getting one of the partners out are embedded in the case. The teaching note shares the methodology that breaks the logjam and the subsequent success stories of each. This is the 2005 version, with totally updated numbers that bring it into the current period. The fundamental content, issues, and lessons from the case are timeless.

Chapter 13, "Obtaining Venture and Growth Capital"—a Significant Revision with Updated Exhibits, New Material, and a New Case

This chapter discusses sources of informal angel equity and venture capital, how angels and venture capital investors evaluate deals, and how to deal with investors. Included are significant new and updated materials such as data and exhibits on capital markets, discussion of the venture capital environment in the aftermath of the dot.com mania and subsequent recession, and new Web site resources. The concept and framework for a capital markets food chain remain a chapter anchor.

New Case: Forte Ventures chronicles the development and fund-raising challenges of Maclean Palmer (see Chapter 8) as he attempts to create his own private equity firm during the worst period in the history of the U.S. venture capital industry: 2000–2001.

Chapter 14, "The Deal: Valuation, Structure, and Negotiation"—a Rewrite with New Material

Chapter 14 lays out in detail the various valuation methodologies used by entrepreneurs and venture capitalists, pre- and post-money, deal structuring principles, and negotiation issues faced by entrepreneurs. It also discusses the pitfalls and sand traps encountered by entrepreneurs.

Case: Paul J. Tobin: This is the story of an Army private who rises to be the president of Cellular One in Boston. The case examines Tobin's strategies to build and finance a growing telecommunications business. The case describes his journey, how he identified opportunities, developed strategies, and raised venture capital to build the business. Unfortunately, the strategy is flawed, and now the company must be re-created or go under.

Chapter 15, "Obtaining Debt Capital"—Revised Material with a New Case

The various sources of debt capital are discussed in detail, including the managing and orchestrating of the banking relationship—before and after the loan. The chapter examines how the bank looks at a loan proposal, including criteria, covenants, and personal guarantees, and what to do when the bank declines the loan. The tar pits and time bombs awaiting the unwary borrower are also covered.

New Case: Bank Documents: "The Devil Is in the Details": Based on an actual bank loan and review by a lending institution, this case provides students with an intimate journey through the financial statements and money flows of the company. It examines how and why the bank considers such a loan, the issues of whether to renew the credit line, and the thinking and perspective of both the company and the bank. Developed by Professor Leslie Charm at Babson College, this is the best case we have ever seen on the subject.

Chapter 16, "Managing Rapid Growth"—New and Updated Material

This chapter places a zoom lens on the unique issues and demands of managing rapid growth in entrepreneurial companies. The role of leadership, culture, and current climate are discussed. Three entrepreneurial leadership models for the 21st century are examined.

Case: EverNet Corporation: Jim Kenefick is facing a major crisis. While his $20 million telecommunications business is doing very well, he is out of cash and out of prospects for securing vital additional funding. Vendors are demanding to be paid, and Kenefick must act quickly and decisively in order to save his company.

Chapter 17, "The Family as Entrepreneur"—New Chapter by Tim Habbershon, Director of the Institute for Family Enterprise at Babson College; a New Case

This new chapter, which is based on Professor Habbershon's model and his extensive research, outlines the significant economic and entrepreneurial contribution families make to communities and countries worldwide, and examines the different roles families play in the entrepreneurial process. The chapter describes the six dimensions for family enterprising, provides a model to assess a family's relative mindset for enterprising, and identifies key issues for family dialogue.

New Exercises: Mindset and Methods Continua: The mindset continuum establishes the family's financial risk and return expectations and their competitive posture in relation to the marketplace. The methods continuum establishes the organization's entrepreneurial orientation and actions. It reflects the beliefs of the shareholders and stakeholders on how the leaders incite entrepreneurship in the organization. The point of these assessments is to surface family members' beliefs and fuel the family dialogue. Plotting these scores into the Family Enterprising Model provides a visual tool for constructive family dialogue.

New Case: Indulgence Spa Products: Robert and Ulissa Dawson had become role models in the African-American community. Their family enterprise, Dawson Products, was one of the last remaining privately held black enterprises in the personal care products industry. They had taught their daughters, Angela, 39, and Jimella, 32, to be self-sufficient at a young age. Bright, energetic, and independent, the talented young women have become key figures in the growth trajectory of this family enterprise. Now Jimella wants to strike out on her own rather than stay and grow the core family business. This case is loaded with classic issues facing a family firm.

Chapter 18, "The Entrepreneur and the Troubled Company"—New and Updated Material

This chapter addresses the signs and symptoms that are indicative of companies heading for trouble, what the turnaround experts look for, and the strategies and approaches of resuscitating stalled or disintegrating ventures.

New Case: Lightwave: In the mid-1990s, seasoned entrepreneurs George Kinson and Dr. Schyler Weiss shocked the staid lighting industry with their full spectrum digital lighting prototypes. After taking the award for Product of the Year at a major trade show, their company rapidly evolved from a fledgling startup to one of the most talked-about companies in the industry. Then the Internet bubble burst, and Lightwave was forced to abandon its plans for going public. By 2003, however, the company was back on track. The question for the team now was whether to move ahead with an additional round of financing in anticipation of an IPO, and how to price and structure that deal.

Chapter 19, "The Harvest and Beyond"—Revised Material

New Venture Creation concludes by looking at the entrepreneurial process as a journey and not a destination, harvest options and their consequences, and beyond the harvest.

Case: Boston Communications Group, Inc., picks up the story of Paul Tobin and examines the orchestrating and managing of an eventual harvest in the mid-1990s, through either a strategic sale to the likes of GTE or an initial public offering (IPO). The case provides an intimate look at the anatomy of valuation and pricing of an IPO, the role and selection of underwriters, and the nature of the robust and tumultuous capital markets in mid-1996.

OF SPECIAL INTEREST TO ENTREPRENEURSHIP EDUCATORS

We believe that we can positively change the world through entrepreneurship education. In 1984, we launched the Symposia for Entrepreneurship Educators (SEE) to teach educators from institutions around the globe. Since then, we have trained over 1,150 academics and entrepreneurs from 355 different academic institutions, government organizations, and foundations in 48 countries to teach entrepreneurship in a way that combines theory and practice to tens of thousands of students each year. We are committed to helping colleges and universities develop creative and innovative entrepreneurship curricula, to increase teaching effectiveness, and to develop the teaching skills of entrepreneurs who are interested in engaging in full- or part-time teaching.

Our Symposia for Entrepreneurship Educators program include:

Price-Babson Symposium for Entrepreneurship Educators: Our flagship program, created in partnership with the Price Institute for Entrepreneurial Studies, is held each spring on our campus to build an international cadre of educators who understand the importance of combining entrepreneurship theory and practice in teaching. Cross-disciplinary educators from around the world attend Price-Babson SEE.

Babson-Olin Symposium for Engineering Entrepreneurship Educators (SyE^3): Designed and delivered in partnership with Olin College of Engineering and funded through a grant from the NSF Partnerships for Innovation program, this special-focus program is offered to engineering educators who want to incorporate entrepreneurship content and pedagogy into their engineering courses and curricula. Babson-Olin SyE^3 alumni will develop engineering graduates who can successfully transform innovations into the products, systems, services, and companies that drive economic growth.

Babson Symposium for Entrepreneurship Educators: Our customized programs are hosted on multiple occasions throughout the year at institutions around the world. Babson SEE programs foster global entrepreneurial growth and economic development through entrepreneurship education.

REFLECT: Our reunion program is hosted for all SEE alumni. REFLECT provides an opportunity to network and share lessons learned in entrepreneurship education.

For more information on any of these SEE programs, go to http://www3.babson.edu/ESHIP/outreach-events/symposia/.

ACKNOWLEDGMENTS

The seventh edition of the original manuscript for the book celebrates over 35 years of intellectual capital acquired through research, case development, course development, teaching, and practice. The latter has included risking both reputation and wallet in a wide range of ventures, involving both former students and others. All of this was possible only because of Jeff's wife, Sara, and their full-grown daughters, and Steve's wife, Carol, and their grown son and daughter. It has also been made possible by the support, encouragement, thinking, and achievements of many people: colleagues at Babson and Harvard, former professors and mentors, associates, entrepreneurs, former students, and our many friends who till this soil.

This edition was possible because of the tremendous effort of our colleague, friend, and former Babson MBA student, Carl Hedberg, who took complete charge of the editing, project management, much of the research, and much of the writing and revising of various cases and other materials. All of this was accomplished on schedule, with the most cheerful mindset, and during a period of enormous other distractions in Carl's life. We are extremely grateful for your Herculean effort, Carl, and for all your work and contributions to Babson and the Arthur M. Blank Center for Entrepreneurship. The major upgrades in earlier editions were made possible in large part by the superb assistance of my research assistants, Christy Remey Chin and Rebecca Voorheis—both of whom have since gone on to complete MBAs at Harvard Business School and Duke, respectively.

The original book (1977) stemmed from research and concepts developed in Jeff's doctoral dissertation at Harvard. Later work with various co-authors from earlier editions, his course development work and research in new ventures at Northeastern University in the 1970s, and in new ventures and financing entrepreneurial ventures at Babson College in the 1980s contributed heavily to the evolution of this text. From 1989 to 1995, Jeff's research in venture capital and his course development work in the course electives at Harvard have enabled him to make major additions and improvements in many of the chapters.

Once again, Jeff has found it an absolute delight and rewarding experience to work with Steve Spinelli. This is the second edition he has joined as co-author, and his ideas and insights, disciplined work style, and great collegial approach to everything make him a world-class colleague. Since the last edition Steve has been promoted to the newly created position of vice provost for entrepreneurship at Babson College. He was a co-founder of Jiffy Lube International and largest franchisee in the nation, and a franchising expert.

We have drawn on intellectual capital from many roots and contributors, and have received support and encouragement, as well as inspiration. To list them all might well take a full chapter by itself, but we wish to offer special thanks to those who have been so helpful in recent years, especially Jeff's former colleagues from Harvard Business School, who have been a constant source of encouragement, inspiration, and friendship. Thanks to William Sahlman for his superb work in entrepreneurial finance, much of which is evident in this text, and Howard Stevenson for his tremendous support and encouragement over many years.

The seventh edition was made possible by the tremendous support of Babson College and the wonderful $30 million gift by the Franklin W. Olin Foundation to build the F.W. Olin Graduate School of Business and to fund the chair now held by Jeff Timmons. Special thanks to William F. Glavin, former president at Babson, for convincing Jeff to return to Babson College full time, and for always providing complete support for his work. Other key supporters at Babson include our president, Brian Barefoot; Michael Fetters, our provost; Mark P. Rice, the Murata Dean of the MBA program and first Jeffry A. Timmons professor of entrepreneurial studies;

Patricia Greene, dean of the undergraduate school; and Fritz Fleischman, dean of faculty, for his support for entrepreneurship at Babson College and this project vis-à-vis a sabbatical for Professor Timmons.

We are extremely appreciative of Professor Timothy Habbershon for his contribution of the new chapter on family enterprising. Tim is doing groundbreaking work on family enterprises and at Babson College. Readers will find this chapter the most useful material on the subject that they have seen. Thanks to our other colleagues in Babson's Entrepreneurship Division, especially long time partner Bill Bygrave, for continuing friendship and support. And a special thank you to Arthur M. Blank for his generous support and gift that provided for our wonderful facility, the Arthur M. Blank Center for Entrepreneurship. Thanks to Julian E. Lange for his original contribution of the chapter on the Internet, and for his ongoing council and advice on Internet-related issues. The adjunct faculty members at Babson College—whom we call our entrepreneur faculty—continually share their expertise with their academic colleagues and our students. Leslie Charm and Edward Marram have each contributed significantly to the chapters on debt equity, managing rapid growth, and managing the troubled company. They are fabulous teachers and colleagues, while still remaining active in the business world. We are also very grateful to colleagues and friends Fred Alper, Michael Gordon, Elizabeth Riley, and Ernie Parizeau for sharing their insights with this seventh edition of *New Venture Creation.* All these colleagues continue to be an immensely valuable resource! Thanks also to Steve Spinelli's able MBA assistant, Jeffrey Palter.

Cases in this and previous editions would not be possible without the collaboration and support of sharing entrepreneurs. We wish to thank Mike Healey; Gary and George Mueller; Roxanne Quimby; Paul Tobin; Wayne Postoak; Jim Kenefick; Mike Bellobuono; Thomas Darden, Jr.; Jim Poss; Gloria Ro Kolb; Joe, Eunice, and Ursula Dudley; and case writer Sandra Sowell-Scott, who have all given of their time and talent. In addition to sharing their stories for the cases, they continue to make class visits at Babson as well as other academic institutions across the country, enriching the educational experience of our students.

One of the most inspiring and rewarding sources of our energy for this project and the entire entrepreneurial mission is the nearly 1,150 alumni (from over 355 institutions and 48 countries) who are our partners and colleagues in the Price Babson Fellows program. In 2006 we will celebrate the twenty-second year of our annual Symposium for Entrepreneurship Educators (SEE). Gloria Appel, the late president of the Price Institute for Entrepreneurial Studies, was a phenomenal partner, friend, mentor, and supporter from the beginning and, despite her passing, continues to be an inspiration for my work.

In 2004, we partnered with our neighbors at Olin College of Engineering on the Babson College campus to create a sister program to SEE for engineering colleges and received a three-year National Science Foundation grant to design, develop, and deliver this program. The first highly successful pilot program of the Babson-Olin Symposium for Engineering Entrepreneurship Educators was held in June 2005. This program, which will now be held annually at Babson and Olin Colleges, is aimed at increasing the entrepreneurship literacy of engineering faculty and students, and the technology literacy of business faculty and students, and thereby improving prosperity in America.

Since 1991, Jeff's colleagues and dear friends at the Ewing Marion Kauffman Foundation in Kansas City have continued to be a source of both support and inspiration. Their important work in accelerating entrepreneurship in America has made important strides in so many arenas. It is a joy to have colleagues who share our passion for entrepreneurship: the late Mr. K (Ewing Marion Kauffman), Michie Slaughter (retired), Kurt Mueller, Bob Rogers, Bert Berkeley, Pat Cloherty, Bob Compton, Willie Davis, Jeff's fishing-buddy Mike Herman, Tony Maier, Judith Cone, and Jim McGraw. We can think of no other organization in America that has done more to advance education, research, public policy, entrepreneurial thinking, and practice than the Kauffman Center.

We continue to derive great inspiration from our Native American colleagues who were the very first to create entrepreneurship curricula and centers in America's trial colleges and institutions. Michele Lansdowne at Salish Kootenai College and Lisa Little Chief Bryan from Rosebud Reservation, and now teaching at Black Hills State University, have both worked tirelessly to write and produce two sets of case studies and case videos based on Native American entrepreneurs. With support from the Kauffman Center and the Theodore R. and Vivian M. Johnson Scholarship Foundation they have worked to build an American Indian entrepreneurship curriculum. The Johnson Foundation has also provided ongoing support of training for tribal college faculty in this curriculum to ensure its continued use. Florence Stickney from San Francisco State University has led groundbreaking efforts at Pine Ridge Reservation. For the Cherokee Nation, Charles Gourd continues his strong efforts to bring entrepreneurship education to rural Oklahoma. In 2004, Jeff worked closely with Dwight Gourneau, a founder and past-president of the American Indian Society for Engineers and Scientists, to present a day-long workshop on entrepreneurship at their annual meeting in Anchorage, Alaska, along with Charlie Gourd and Lisa Little Chief Bryan.

The relevance and richness of the cases and materials in this text can be traced in considerable measure to Jeff's involvement with both ventures and venture funds. His colleagues at BCI Growth Capital (Don Remey, Hoyt Goodrich, Steve Ely, and Ted Horton) have contributed ideas and cases, and Brion Applegate, Bill Collatos, and Bob Nicholson and their associates at Spectrum Equity Investors have been generous with their time and ideas in contributing to cases and by coming to Jeff's classes.

In addition to all those acknowledged and thanked in previous editions, a special thanks and debt of appreciation is due to all our current and former students from whom we learn, and by whom we are inspired with each encounter. We marvel at your accomplishments, and sigh in great relief at how little damage we have imparted—usually!

We would like to extend a special thanks to those professors who have reviewed previous editions of *New Venture Creation*, as they have helped to shape the direction of the text.

Finally, I want to express a very special thank-you to Bruce Gin, Allison Belda, and Ryan Blankenship at Irwin/McGraw-Hill for their highly competent and professional effort in advancing this revision.

J.A.T. and S.S.

BRIEF CONTENTS

TABLE OF CONTENTS

PART I
The Entrepreneurial Mind for an Entrepreneurial Society

PART II

The Opportunity

PART III

The Founder and Team

PART V

Startup and Beyond

I

PART ONE

The Entrepreneurial Mind for an Entrepreneurial Society

At the heart of the entrepreneurial process is the founder: the opportunity seeker, the creator and initiator; the leader, problem solver, and motivator; the strategizer and guardian of the mission, values, and culture of the venture. Without this human energy, drive, and vitality, the greatest ideas—even when they are backed by an overabundance of resources and staff—will fail, grossly underperform, or simply never get off the ground. Brilliant musical, scientific, or athletic aptitude and potential do not equal the great musician, the great scientist, or the great athlete. The difference lies in the intangibles: creativity and ingenuity, commitment, tenacity and determination, a passion to win and excel, and leadership and team-building skills.

Think of the number of first-round draft picks who never made the grade in professional sports—even without suffering a career-ending injury. Then consider the many later-round picks who became Superstars, like Tom Brady, the 199th pick in the twelfth round by the New England Patriots, who has quarterbacked the team to three Super Bowl Championships—in his first four years!

So what is it that an aspiring young entrepreneur needs to know, and what habits, attitudes, and mind-sets can be learned, practiced, and developed—and thereby improve the odds of success? We begin this seventh edition with a focus on you—the lead entrepreneur. We examine the mind-sets, the learnable and acquirable attitudes and habits that lead to entrepreneurial success—and failure. By examining patterns and practices of entrepreneurial thinking and reasoning, and the entrepreneurial mind in action, you can begin your own assessment and planning process to get you headed where you want to go. This personal entrepreneurial strategy will evolve into your personal business plan—a blueprint to help you learn, grow, attract mentors who can change your life and your ventures, and pursue the opportunities that best suit you.

Survival odds for a venture go up once you reach the benchmark of $1 million in sales and 20 employees. Launching or acquiring and then building a business that will exceed these levels is more fun and more challenging than being involved in the vast majority of small one- or two-person operations. But perhaps most important, a business of this magnitude achieved the critical mass necessary to attract good people and, as a result, significantly enhances the prospects of realizing a harvest. An entrepreneur isn't simply creating a job; he or she can build a business that can lift a community.

A leader who thinks and acts with an "entrepreneurial mind" can make a critical difference as to whether a business is destined to be a traditional, very small lifestyle firm, a stagnant or declining large one, or a higher potential venture. Practicing certain mental attitudes and actions can stimulate, motivate, and reinforce the kind of zest and entrepreneurial culture whose self-fulfilling prophecy is success.

It is almost impossible to take a number of people, give them a single test, and determine who possess entrepreneurial minds and those who do not. Rather, it is useful for would-be entrepreneurs and others involved in entrepreneurship to study how successful entrepreneurs think, feel, and respond and how those factors that are significant can be developed and strengthened—as a decathlete develops and strengthens certain muscles to compete at a certain level.

Entrepreneurs who create or recognize opportunities and then seize and shape them into higher potential ventures think and do things differently. They operate in an entrepreneurial domain, a place governed by certain modes of action and dominated by certain driving forces.

Take for example, Rick Adam, who by the late 1990s had made millions as a software entrepreneur. He had also spotted a compelling opportunity in the general aviation industry. As an avid pilot, Adam knew firsthand how few new aircraft designs were available—at any price. The reason was that the cost to design, engineer, and bring to market an FAA certified general aviation product was estimated by industry veterans to be in the neighborhood of $250 million, and a minimum of 10 years. Despite having no previous experience in manufacturing, Adam put up tens of millions of his own money (and raised tens of millions more) to start up Adam Aircraft. Using sophisticated model-fabrication technology, and by applying design and engineering practices Adam had mastered in software development, his company spent under $60 million to develop the A-500—a sleek, pressurized twin-engine design that achieved FAA certification in just five years. Their A-700 prototype—a personal jet that utilized the same airframe structure—was flying for another $20 million, and was expected to be certified by the end of 2006. Rick Adam commented on the endeavor:

> I've done a lot of entrepreneurial things, and when you think there is a big opportunity, you look at it thoughtfully and you say, well, if this is such a big opportunity, why isn't anybody taking it? What do I know, or what do I see that nobody else is seeing? So, very often, entrepreneurial opportunities occur because a series of events come together—particularly with technology—and you suddenly have all the ingredients you need to be successful at something that just moments ago was impossible. Then, assuming you are a good business person and a good executer, you can get there if you focus, and keep at it.

It makes a lot of sense for entrepreneurs to pay particular attention to picking partners, key business associates, and managers with an eye for complementing the entrepreneurs' own weaknesses and strengths and the needs of the venture. As will be seen, they seek people who fit. Not only can an entrepreneur's weakness be an Achilles' heel for new ventures, but also the whole is almost always greater than the sum of its parts.

Finally, ethics are terribly important in entrepreneurship. In highly unpredictable and fragile situations, ethical issues cannot be handled according to such simplistic notions as "always tell the truth." It is critical that an entrepreneur understands, develops, and implements an effective integrity strategy for the business.

1

Chapter One

The Entrepreneurial Mind: Crafting a Personal Entrepreneurial Strategy

Who can be an entrepreneur you ask? Anyone who wants to experience the deep, dark canyons of uncertainty and ambiguity; and who wants to walk the breathtaking highlands of success. But caution, do not plan to walk the latter until you have experienced the former.

An Entrepreneur

Results Expected

Upon completion of this chapter, you will have:

1. Examined ways to help you discover whether being an entrepreneur gives you sustaining energy, rather than takes it away.
2. Explored the entrepreneurial mind—the strategies, habits, attitudes, and behaviors that work for entrepreneurs who build higher potential ventures.[1]
3. Examined the characteristics of various entrepreneurial groups.
4. Developed concepts for evaluating a personal entrepreneurial strategy and an apprenticeship, and an entrepreneur's creed.
5. Examined a framework for self-assessment and developed a personal entrepreneurial strategy.
6. Initiated a self-assessment and goal-setting process that can become a lifelong habit of entrepreneurial thinking and action.
7. Watched the film *October Sky*.

Three Principles for Achieving Entrepreneurial Greatness

One of the most extraordinary entrepreneurial success stories of our time is that of the late Ewing Marion Kauffman, who founded and built Marion Labs, a company with over $1 billion in sales, and then founded the Ewing Marion Kauffman Foundation. Kauffman started his pharmaceutical company, now one of the leading companies in the world, in 1950 with $5,000 in the basement of his Kansas City home. Previously, he had been very successful at another company. Kauffman (or "Mr. K." as he preferred) recalled, "The president first cut back my sales commission, then he cut back my territory. So, I quit and created Marion Labs."

The authors would like to thank Frederic M. Alper, a longtime friend and colleague and adjunct professor at Babson College, for his insights and contributions to this chapter, in particular the graphic representation of entrepreneurial attributes and the development of the QuickLook exercise to develop a personal entrepreneurial strategy.

[1] Jeffry A. Timmons, *The Entrepreneurial Mind* (Acton, MA: Brick House Publishing, 1989).

With the acquisition of the company by Merrell-Dow in 1989 (becoming Marion, Merrell Dow, Inc.), more than 300 people became millionaires. Thirteen foundations have been created by former Marion associates, and the Ewing Marion Kauffman Foundation is one of only a dozen or so foundations in America with assets of over $1 billion. The two-pronged mission of the foundation is to make a lasting difference in helping youths at risk and encouraging leadership in all areas of American life.

Having had the great privilege and honor of knowing and working with Mr. K., from 1991 until his death in 1993, and continuing the relationship with the Marion Labs management team and now Ewing Marion Kauffman Foundation team, Jeff Timmons came to appreciate more each passing year the three core principles that are the cornerstone of the values, philosophy, and culture of Marion Labs and now of the Kauffman Foundation.

- Treat others as you would want to be treated.
- Share the wealth that is created with all those who have contributed to it at all levels.
- Give back to the community.

There are many legendary examples of Mr. K. practicing these principles while growing Marion Labs. There was the time when he had sent his young chief financial officer to Europe to negotiate a supply contract with a major German company. When the CFO returned, he proudly showed Mr. K. the incredibly favorable terms he had extracted from the supplier—who he had determined badly needed the business. From his point of view, he had "cleverly won" the contract by being a sharp and tough negotiator.

After reviewing the situation and the agreement, Mr. K. blasted the CFO: "This is a totally one-sided contract—in our favor—and it is terribly unfair. They won't be able to make any money on this, and that's not how we treat our suppliers, or our customers. You get back on that plane tomorrow, apologize to them, and then create a deal that works for us—and lets them make a reasonable return as well."

Stunned, the CFO sheepishly returned to Germany to work out a contract that met with Mr. K.'s approval. Less than two years later, a worldwide supply crisis forced that German supplier to reduce its customer shipments by over 90 percent. Mr. K.'s fairness principle had not been forgotten; Marion Labs was the only American company that continued to have its requirements filled.

As simple as these principles may be, few organizations truly, sincerely, and consistently practice them. It takes a lot more than lip service or a stand-alone profit-sharing plan to create an entrepreneurial culture like this. Consider the following unique characteristics at Marion Labs and the Ewing Marion Kauffman Foundation:

- No one is an employee; everyone is an associate.
- Even at $1 billion in sales, there are no formal organizational charts.
- Everyone who meets or exceeds high performance goals participates in a companywide bonus, profit-sharing, and stock option plan.
- Benefit programs treat all associates the same, even top management.
- Managers who attempt to develop a new product and fail are not punished with lateral promotions or geographic relocation to Timbuktu, nor are they ostracized. Failures are gateways to learning and continual improvement.
- Those who will not or cannot practice these core principles are not tolerated.

The ultimate message is clear: Great companies can be built upon simple but elegant principles, and all the capital, technology, service management, and latest information available cannot substitute for these principles, nor will they cause such a culture to happen. These ideals are at the very heart of the difference between good and great companies.

Leadership and Human Behavior

A single psychological model of entrepreneurship has not been supported by research. However, behavioral scientists, venture capitalists, investors, and entrepreneurs share the opinion that the eventual success of a new venture will depend a great deal upon the talent and behavior of the lead entrepreneur and of his or her team.

A number of myths still persist about entrepreneurs. Foremost among these myths is the belief that leaders are born, not made. The roots of much of this thinking reflect the assumptions and biases of an earlier era, when rulers were royal and leadership was the prerogative of the aristocracy. Fortunately, such notions have not withstood the tests of time or the inquisitiveness of researchers of leadership and management. Consider recent research, which distinguishes managers from leaders, as summarized in Exhibit 1.1. It is widely accepted today that leadership is an extraordinarily complex subject, depending more on the interconnections among the leader, the task, the situation, and those being led than on inborn or inherited characteristics alone.

There are numerous ways of analyzing human behavior that have implications in the study of entrepreneurship. For example, for over 35 years Dr.

EXHIBIT 1.1

Comparing Management and Leadership

	Management	Leadership
Creating an Agenda	Planning and budgeting—establishing detailed steps and timetables for achieving needed results, and then allocating the resources necessary to achieve these results	Establishing direction—developing a vision of the future, often the distant future, and strategies for producing the changes needed to achieve that vision
Developing a Human Network for Achieving the Agenda	Organizing and staffing—establishing some structure for accomplishing plan requirements, staffing that structure with individuals, delegating responsibility and authority for carrying out the plan, providing policies and procedures to help guide people, and creating methods or systems to monitor implementation	Aligning people—communicating the direction by words and deeds to all those whose cooperation may be needed to influence the creation of teams and coalitions that understand the vision and strategies, and accept their validity
Execution	Controlling and problem solving—monitoring results versus plan in some detail, identifying deviations, and then planning and organizing to solve these problems	Motivating and inspiring—energizing people to overcome major political, bureaucratic, and resource barriers to change by satisfying very basic, often unfulfilled human needs
Outcomes	Producing a degree of predictability and order, and having the potential of consistently producing key results expected by various stakeholders	Producing change, often to a dramatic degree, and having the potential of producing extremely useful change

Source: Reprinted with the permission of The Free Press, a Division of Simon & Schuster Adult Publishing Group, from *A Force for Change: How Leadership Differs from Management* by John P. Kotter, Copyright © 1990 by John P. Kotter, Inc. All rights reserved.

David C. McClelland of Harvard University and Dr. John W. Atkinson of the University of Michigan and their colleagues sought to understand individual motivation.[2] Their theory of psychological motivation is a generally accepted part of the literature on entrepreneurial behavior. The theory states that people are motivated by three principal needs: (1) the need for achievement, (2) the need for power, and (3) the need for affiliation. The *need for achievement* is the need to excel and for measurable personal accomplishment. A person competes against a self-imposed standard that does not involve competition with others. The individual sets realistic and challenging goals and likes to get feedback on how well he or she is doing in order to improve performance. The *need for power* is the need to influence others and to achieve an "influence goal." The *need for affiliation* is the need to attain an "affiliation goal"—the goal to build a warm relationship with someone else and/or to enjoy mutual friendship.

Research

Other research focused on the common attitudes and behaviors of entrepreneurs. A 1983 study found a relationship between attitudes and behaviors of successful entrepreneurs and various stages of company development.[3] A year later, another study found that entrepreneurs were unique individuals; for instance, this study found that "what is characteristic is not so much an overall type as a successful, growth-oriented entrepreneurial type. . . . It is the company builders who are distinctive."[4] More recently, a study of 118 entrepreneurs revealed that "those who like to plan are much more likely to be in the survival group than those who do not."[5] Clearly, the get-rich-quick entrepreneurs are not the company builders, nor are they the planners of successful ventures. Rather it is the visionary who participates in the day-to-day routine to achieve a long-term objective and who is generally passionate and not exclusively profit-oriented.

[2] See John W. Atkinson, *An Introduction to Motivation* (Princeton, NJ: Van Nostrand, 1964); J. W. Atkinson, *Motives in Fantasy, Action and Society* (Princeton, NJ: Van Nostrand, 1958); D. C. McClelland, *The Achieving Society* (Princeton, NJ: Van Nostrand, 1961); J. W. Atkinson and N. T. Feather, eds., *A Theory of Achievement Motivation* (New York: John Wiley & Sons, 1966); and D. C. McClelland and D. G. Winter, *Motivating Economic Achievement* (New York: Free Press, 1969).

[3] Neil Churchill, "Entrepreneurs and Their Enterprises: A Stage Model," *Frontiers of Entrepreneurship Research: 1983*, ed. J. A. Hornaday et al. (Babson Park, MA: Babson College, 1983), pp. 1–22.

[4] N. R. Smith and John B. Miner, "Motivational Considerations in the Success of Technologically Innovative Entrepreneurs," in *Frontiers of Entrepreneurship Research: 1984*, ed. J. Hornaday et al. (Babson Park, MA: Babson College, 1984), pp. 448–95.

[5] John B. Miller, Norman R. Smith, and Jeffrey S. Bracker, "Entrepreneur Motivation and Firm Survival among Technologically Innovative Companies," ed. Neil C. Churchill et al., *Frontiers of Entrepreneurship Research: 1991* (Babson Park, MA: Babson College, 1992), p. 31.

EXHIBIT 1.2

Characteristics of Entrepreneurs

Date	Authors	Characteristics	Normative	Empirical
1848	Mill	Risk bearing	X	
1917	Weber	Source of formal authority	X	
1934	Schumpeter	Innovation; initiative	X	
1954	Sutton	Desire for responsibility	X	
1959	Hartman	Source of formal authority	X	
1961	McClelland	Risk taking; need for achievement		X
1963	Davids	Ambition; desire for independence, responsibility, self-confidence		X
1964	Pickle	Drive/mental; human relations; communication ability; technical knowledge		X
1971	Palmer	Risk measurement		X
1971	Hornaday and Aboud	Need for achievement; autonomy; aggression; power; recognition; innovative/independent		X
1973	Winter	Need for power	X	
1974	Borland	Internal locus of power	X	

Academics have continued to characterize the special qualities of entrepreneurs. (See Exhibit 1.2 for a summary of this research.) As a participant in this quest to understand the entrepreneurial mind, in January 1983, Howard H. Stevenson and Jeffry Timmons spoke with 60 practicing entrepreneurs.[6] One finding was that entrepreneurs felt they had to concentrate on certain fundamentals: responsiveness, resiliency, and adaptiveness in seizing new opportunities. These entrepreneurs spoke of other attitudes, including an ability "to activate vision" and a willingness to learn about and invest in new techniques, to be adaptable, to have a professional attitude, and to have patience. They talked about the importance of "enjoying and being interested in business," as well as the business as "a way of life." Other attitudes they spoke of included a willingness to learn about and invest in new techniques, to be adaptable, to have a professional attitude, and to have patience.

Many of the respondents recognized and endorsed the importance of human resource management; one entrepreneur said that one of the most challenging tasks was playing "a leadership role in attracting high-quality people, imparting your vision to them, and holding and motivating them." Other entrepreneurs focused on the importance of building an organization and teamwork. For example, the head of a manufacturing firm with $10 million in sales said, "Understanding people and how to pull them together toward a basic goal will be my main challenge in five years." The head of a clothing manufacturing business with 225 employees and $6 million in sales shared a view of many that one of the most critical areas where an entrepreneur has leverage and long-term impact is in managing employees. He said, "Treating people honestly and letting them know when they do well goes a long way."

A number of respondents believed that the ability to conceptualize their business and do strategic planning would be of growing importance, particularly when thinking five years ahead. Similarly, the ageless importance of sensitivity to and respect for employees was stressed by a chief executive officer of a firm with $40 million in sales and 400 employees: "It is essential that the separation between management and the average employee should be eliminated. Students should be taught to respect employees all the way down to the janitor and accept them as knowledgeable and able persons." One company that has taken this concept to heart is Ben & Jerry's Homemade Ice Cream Inc. The company began operations with a covenant that "no boss got more than five times the compensation, including both pay and benefits, of the lowest-paid worker with at least one year at the company."[7] Since its inception, the covenant has been modified to seven to one, while the company reported $63.2 million in revenue in the first half of 1992.[8]

A consulting study by McKinsey & Co. of medium-size growth companies (i.e., companies with sales between $25 million and $1 billion and with

[6] J. A. Timmons and H. H. Stevenson, "Entrepreneurship Education in the *80s*: What Entrepreneurs Say," in *Entrepreneurship: What It Is and How to Teach It*, ed. J. Kao and H. H. Stevenson (Boston: Harvard Business School, 1985), pp. 115–34.
[7] Floyd Norris, "Low-Fat Problem at Ben & Jerry's," *The New York Times*, September 9, 1992, p. D6.
[8] Ibid.

sales or profit growth of more than 15 percent annually over five years) confirms that the chief executive officers of winning companies were notable for three common traits: perseverance, a builder's mentality, and a strong propensity for taking calculated risks.[9]

Converging on the Entrepreneurial Mind

Desirable and Acquirable Attitudes, Habits, and Behaviors

Many successful entrepreneurs have emphasized that while their colleagues have initiative and a take-charge attitude, are determined to persevere, and are resilient and able to adapt, it is not just a matter of personality. It is what they *do* that matters most.[10]

While there is an undeniable core of such inborn characteristics as energy and raw intelligence, which an entrepreneur either has or does not, it is becoming apparent that possession of these characteristics does not necessarily an entrepreneur make. There is also a good deal of evidence that entrepreneurs are born and made better and that certain attitudes and behaviors can be acquired, developed, practiced, and refined through a combination of experience and study.[11]

While not all attitudes, habits, and behaviors can be acquired by everyone at the same pace and with the same proficiency, entrepreneurs are able to significantly improve their odds of success by concentrating on those that work, by nurturing and practicing them, and by eliminating, or at least mitigating, the rest. Painstaking effort may be required, and much will depend upon the motivation of an individual to grow, but it seems people have an astounding capacity to change and learn if they are motivated and committed to do so.

Testimony given by successful entrepreneurs also confirms attitudes and behaviors that successful entrepreneurs have in common. Take, for instance, the first 21 inductees into Babson College's Academy of Distinguished Entrepreneurs,[12] including such well-known entrepreneurs as Ken Olsen of DEC, An Wang of Wang Computers, Wally Amos of Famous Amos' Chocolate Chip Cookies, Bill Norris of Control Data, Sochiro Honda of Honda Motors, and the late Ray Kroc of McDonald's. All 21 of the inductees mentioned the possession of three attributes as the principal reasons for their successes: (1) the ability to respond positively to challenges and learn from mistakes, (2) personal initiative, and (3) great perseverance and determination.[13]

"Themes" have emerged from what successful entrepreneurs do and how they perform. Undoubtedly many attitudes and behaviors characterize the entrepreneurial mind, and there is no single set of attitudes and behaviors that every entrepreneur must have for every venture opportunity. Further, the *fit* concept argues that what is required in each situation depends on the mix and match of the key players and how promising and forgiving the opportunity is, given the founders' strengths and shortcoming. A team might collectively show many of the desired strengths, but even then there is no such thing as a perfect entrepreneur—as yet.

Six Dominant Themes

Nothing that sends you to the grave with a smile on your face comes easy. Work hard doing what you love. Find out what gives you energy and improve on it.

Betty Coster, Entrepreneur

A consensus has emerged around six dominant themes, shown in Exhibits 1.3 and 1.4.

Commitment and Determination Commitment and determination are seen as more important than any other factor. With commitment and determination, an entrepreneur can overcome incredible obstacles and also compensate enormously for other weaknesses. For 16 long years following his graduation from Babson College, Mario Ricciardelli worked to create a travel agency that catered to students. He endured lean personal finances and countless setbacks, including several near bankruptcies, the sudden failure of a charter airline that left his young clients stranded in Mexico, and a stock-swap deal with a high-profile Internet venture that fell to earth after two difficult years when the bubble burst. Mario and Jacqui Lewis, his partner acquired in a subsequent acquisition, convinced the troubled parent

[9] Donald K. Clifford, Jr., and Richard E. Cavanagh, *The Winning Performance* (New York: Bantam Books, 1985), p. 3.

[10] Determining the attitudes and behaviors in entrepreneurs that are "acquirable and desirable" represents the synthesis of over 50 research studies compiled for the first and second editions of this book. See extensive references in J. A. Timmons, L. E. Smollen, and A. L. M. Dingee, Jr., *New Venture Creation*, 2nd ed. (Homewood, Ill.: Richard D. Irwin, 1985), pp. 139–69.

[11] David C. McClelland, "Achievement Motivation Can Be Developed," *Harvard Business Review*, November–December 1965; David C. McClelland and David G. Winter, *Motivating Economic Achievement* (New York: Free Press, 1969); and Jeffry A. Timmons, "Black Is Beautiful—Is It Bountiful?" *Harvard Business Review*, November–December 1971, p. 81.

[12] By 2005 a total of 85 inductees had joined the Academy of Distinguished Entrepreneurs, including founders as Paul Fireman of Reebok International Ltd.; Arthur M. Blank of The Home Depot; Richard Branson of Virgin Group; Ely R. Callaway of Callaway Golf; Leo Gorman of L.L. Bean, Inc.; Robert A. Swanson of Genentech, Inc.; Tom Stemberg of Staples; and Leonard Riggio of Barnes and Noble.

[13] John A. Hornaday and Nancy B. Tieken, "Capturing Twenty-One Heffalumps," in *Frontiers of Entrepreneurship Research: 1983*, ed. J. A. Hornaday et al. (Babson Park, MA: Babson College, 1983), pp. 23–50.

EXHIBIT 1.3

Six Themes of Desirable and Acquirable Attitudes and Behaviors

Theme	Attitude or Behavior
Commitment and Determination	Tenacious and decisive, able to recommit/commit quickly Intensely competitive in achieving goals Persistent in solving problems, disciplined Willing to undertake personal sacrifice Immersed
Leadership	Self-starter; high standards but not perfectionist Team builder and hero maker; inspires others Treats others as you want to be treated Shares the wealth with all the people who helped create it Honest and reliable; builds trust; practices fairness Not a lone wolf Superior learner and teacher; courage Patient and urgent
Opportunity Obsession	Has intimate knowledge of customers' needs and wants Market driven Obsessed with value creation and enhancement
Tolerance of Risk, Ambiguity, and Uncertainty	Calculated risk taker Risk minimizer Risk sharer Manages paradoxes and contradictions Tolerates uncertainty and lack of structure Tolerates stress and conflict Able to resolve problems and integrate solutions
Creativity, Self-Reliance, and Adaptability	Nonconventional, open-minded, lateral thinker Restless with status quo Able to adapt and change; creative problem solver Quick learner No fear of failure Able to conceptualize and "sweat details" (helicopter mind)
Motivation to Excel	Goal-and-results oriented; high but realistic goals Drive to achieve and grow Low need for status and power Interpersonally supporting (versus competitive) Aware of weaknesses and strengths Has perspective and sense of humor

company to let them turn in their shares in exchange for their cash-strapped online travel portal. Having no money to expand into other markets, in 2003, the team refocused their efforts on building the most comprehensive and exciting online spring break travel program anywhere. By pouring all of their attention into that narrow space, the company was able to dramatically increase bookings and profitability. In their first season as a newly independent venture, they generated just under a million in free cash flow. In early 2004, with year-over-year growth in bookings of 100 percent, the partners decided to look for a buyer. Ninety days later, Mario and Jacqui joined the ranks of American millionaires when their company, StudentCity.com, was acquired by First Choice Holidays, a $5 billion tour operator in Europe.

Total commitment is required in nearly all entrepreneurial ventures. Almost without exception, entrepreneurs live under huge, constant pressures—first for their firms to survive startup, then for them to stay alive, and, finally, for them to grow. A new venture demands top priority for the entrepreneur's time, emotions, and loyalty. Thus, commitment and determination usually require personal sacrifice. An

EXHIBIT 1.4

Core and Desirable Entrepreneurial Attributes

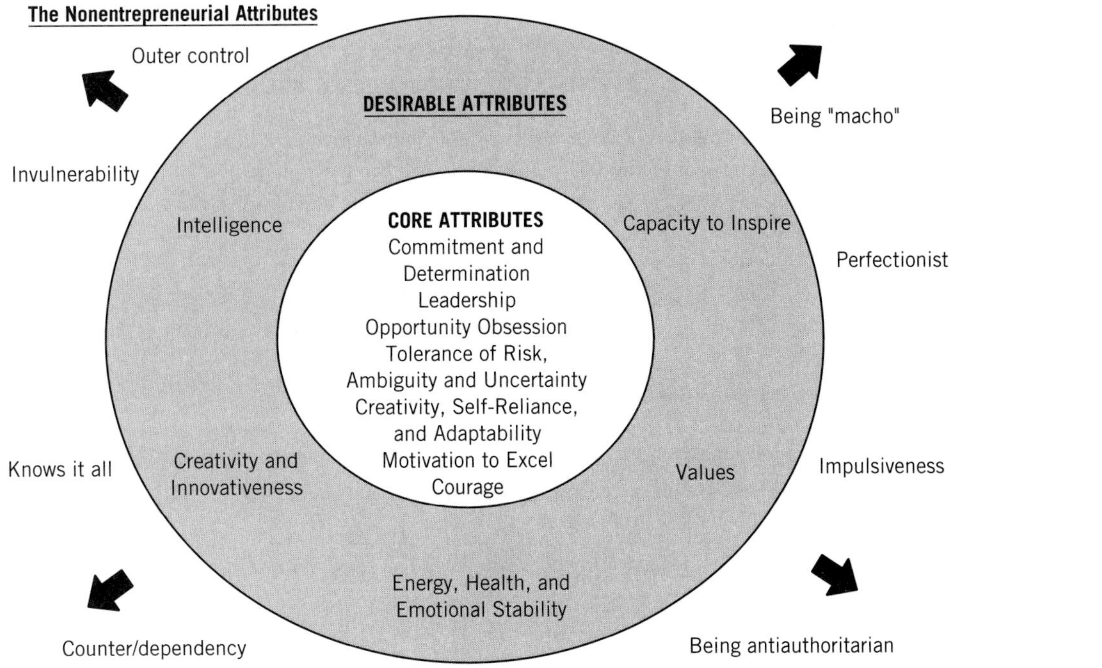

entrepreneur's commitment can be measured in several ways—through a willingness to invest a substantial portion of his or her net worth in the venture, through a willingness to take a cut in pay because he or she will own a major piece of the venture, and through other major sacrifices in lifestyle and family circumstances.

The desire to win does not equal the will to never give up. This is a critically important distinction. Countless would-be entrepreneurs (and lots of other types of people for that matter) say that they really want to win. But few have the dogged tenacity and unflinching perseverance to make it happen. Take a young entrepreneur we shall call Stephen. One of the authors introduced him to a potentially invaluable lead—a brain trust prospect and mega-angel investor. Stephen placed several phone calls to the investor, but none were returned. He made a few more calls, each time leaving a message with the referral information. Still, no response.

Over the next week the young entrepreneur made yet another series of over two dozen calls that once again received no response. At that point, what would you have done? Have you ever called anyone that many times and not gotten any sort of reply? Would you keep trying, or decide to move on and not waste any more time? Feeling that this individual was a potentially invaluable contact, Stephen refused to give up. He would make 12 more calls before finally getting a response. In the luncheon meeting that followed soon after, the mega-angel agreed to invest $1 million in Stephen's startup, and serve as chairman of the board. The company became successful, and was sold four years later for $55 million.

Entrepreneurs are intensely competitive: they love to win and love to compete—at anything! The best of them direct all this competitive energy toward the goal and toward their external competitors. This is critical; founders who get caught up in competing with peers in the company invariably destroy team cohesion and spirit and, ultimately, the team.

Entrepreneurs who successfully build new enterprises seek to overcome hurdles, solve problems, and complete the job; they are disciplined, tenacious, and persistent. They are able to commit and recommit quickly. They are not intimidated by difficult situations; in fact, they seem to think that the impossible just takes a little longer. However, they are neither aimless nor foolhardy in their relentless attack on a problem or obstacle that can impede their business. If a task is unsolvable, an entrepreneur will actually give up sooner than others. Most researchers share the opinion that while entrepreneurs are extremely persistent, they are also realistic in recognizing what they can and cannot do, and where they can get help to solve a very difficult but necessary task.

EXHIBIT 1.5

The Entrepreneurial Leadership Paradigm

The Lead Entrepreneur	
Self-concept	Has a realist's attitude rather than one of invincibility
Intellectually honest	Trustworthy, his/her word is his/her contract
	Admits what and when he/she does not know
Pace maker	Displays a high energy level and a sense of urgency
Courage	Capable of making hard decisions: setting and beating high goals
Communication skills	Maintains an effective dialogue with the venture team, in the marketplace, and with other venture constituents
Team player	Competent in people management and team-building skills
The Venture Team	
Organizational style	The lead entrepreneur and the venture team blend their skills to operate in a participative environment
Ethical behavior	Practices strong adherence to ethical business practices
Faithfulness	Stretched commitments are consistently met or bettered
Focus	Long-term venture strategies are kept in focus but tactics are varied to achieve them
Performance/reward	High standards of performance are created and superior performance is rewarded fairly and equitably
Adaptability	Responsive to rapid changes in product/technological cycles
External Environmental Influences	
Constituent needs	Organization needs are satisfied, in parallel with those of the other publics the enterprise serves
Prior experience	Extensive prior experiences are effectively applied
Mentoring	The competencies of others are sought and used
Problem resolution	New problems are immediately solved or prioritized
Value creation	High commitment is placed on long-term value creation for backers, customers, employees, and other stakeholders
Skill emphasis	Marketing skills are stressed over technical ones

Source: Adapted from Alan J. Grant, "The Development of an Entrepreneurial Leadership Paradigm for Enhancing Venture Capital Success," *Frontiers of Entrepreneurship Research, 1992,* ed. J. Hornaday, et. al. (Babson Park, MA: Babson College, 1992).

Leadership Successful entrepreneurs are experienced, possessing intimate knowledge of the technology and marketplace in which they will compete, sound general management skills, and a proven track record. They are self-starters and have an internal locus of control with high standards. They are patient leaders, capable of installing tangible visions and managing for the longer haul. The entrepreneur is at once a learner and a teacher, a doer and a visionary. The vision of building a substantial enterprise that will contribute something lasting and relevant to the world while realizing a capital gain requires the patience to stick to the task for 5 to 10 years or more.

Work by Dr. Alan Grant lends significant support to the fundamental "driving forces" theory of entrepreneurship that will be explored in Chapter 4. Grant surveyed 25 senior venture capitalists to develop an entrepreneurial leadership paradigm. Three clear areas evolved from his study: the lead entrepreneur, the venture team, and the external environment influences, which are outlined in further detail in Exhibit 1.5. Furthermore, Grant suggested that to truly understand this paradigm, it should be "metaphorically associated with a *troika,* a Russian vehicle pulled by three horses of *equal* strength. Each horse represents a cluster of the success factors. The troika was driven toward success by the visions and *dreams* of the founding entrepreneurs."[14]

Successful entrepreneurs possess a well-developed capacity to exert influence *without* formal power. These people are adept at conflict resolution. They know when to use logic and when to persuade, when to make a concession, and when to exact one. To run a successful venture, an entrepreneur learns to get along with many different constituencies—the customer, the supplier, the financial backer, the creditor, as well as the partners and others on the inside—often with conflicting aims. Success comes when the entrepreneur is a mediator, a negotiator rather than a dictator.

[14] Alan Grant. "The Development of an Entrepreneurial Leadership Paradigm for Enhancing New Venture Success," *Frontiers of Entrepreneurship Research: 1992,* ed. J. Hornaday et al. (Babson Park, MA: Babson College, 1992).

Successful entrepreneurs are interpersonally supporting and nurturing—not interpersonally competitive. When a strong need to control, influence, and gain power over others characterizes the lead entrepreneur, or where he or she has an insatiable appetite for putting an associate down, the venture usually gets into trouble. Entrepreneurs should treat others as they want to be treated; they should share the wealth with those who contributed. A dictatorial, adversarial, and domineering management style makes it very difficult to attract and keep people who thrive on a thirst for achievement, responsibility, and results. Compliant partners and managers often are chosen. Destructive conflicts often erupt over who has the final say, who is right, and whose prerogatives are what.

Entrepreneurs who create and build substantial enterprises are not lone wolves and super-independent. They do not need to collect all the credit for the effort. They not only recognize the reality that it is rarely possible to build a substantial business working all alone, but also actively build a team. They have an uncanny ability to make heroes out of the people they attract to the venture by giving responsibility and sharing credit for accomplishments.

In the corporate setting, this "hero-making" ability is identified as an essential attribute of successful entrepreneurial managers.[15] These hero makers, of both the independent and corporate varieties, try to make the pie bigger and better, rather than jealously clutching and hoarding a tiny pie that is all theirs. They have a capacity for objective interpersonal relationships as well, which enables them to smooth out individual differences of opinion by keeping attention focused on the common goal to be achieved.[16]

Opportunity Obsession Successful entrepreneurs are obsessed first with opportunity—not with the money, the resources, the contacts and networking, and not with image or appearances. While some of these latter items have a place and time in the entrepreneurial process, they are not the source and driver for new ventures. Entrepreneurs, in their best creative mode, are constantly thinking of new ideas for businesses by watching trends, spotting patterns, and connecting the dots to shape and mold a unique enterprise.

Take Tom Stemberg, for example. After business school—and after over 15 years in the supermarket business—he began to look for major new opportunities. He researched and rejected many decent ideas that were either not good "big" opportunities, or not the right fit for him. He then noted a recurring pattern with profound economic implications; every Main Street shop in America was selling ballpoint pens (wholesale cost: about 30 cents) for $2, $3, and more. He soon learned that these very large gross margins were common for a wide range of products used by small businesses and the self-employed: copy paper, writing and clerical supplies, calculators, and other electronics. Stemberg believed there was a new business model underlying this opportunity pattern—which, if well-developed and executed, could revolutionize the office supply business and become a major enterprise. He and Leo Kahn founded Staples, and they were certainly right.

Entrepreneurs realize good ideas are a dime a dozen, but good opportunities are few and far between. Fortunately, a great deal is now known about the criteria, the patterns, and the requirements that differentiate the good idea from the good opportunity. Entrepreneurs rely heavily on their own previous experiences (or their frustrations as customers) to come up with their breakthrough opportunities. Kurt Bauer, for instance, had no prior business training or experience before he headed for Eastern Europe in 1990 on a Fulbright Scholarship to work on privatization in Poland and Russia. In fact, he postponed his acceptances to top medical schools in order to go east. He was so impressed with the seemingly endless stream of new business opportunities in the old eastern bloc countries that upon his return two years later, he decided to go to business school and try to figure out how to recognize and pursue the best of these opportunities. We will study his venture here from its roots and conception, to business plan development, to fund-raising and launch. Kurt and his brother John, and their venture, are a classic example of a pattern of opportunity obsession.

In Chapters 2, 3, and 4, we will examine in great detail how entrepreneurs and investors are "opportunity obsessed." We will see their ingenious, as well as straightforward, ways and patterns of creating, shaping, molding, and recognizing opportunities that are not just another good idea, and then transforming these "caterpillars into butterflies." These practices, strategies, and habits are part of the entrepreneurial mind-set, and are skills and know-how that are learnable and acquirable.

The entrepreneur's credo is to think opportunity first and cash last. Time and again—even after harvesting a highly successful venture—lead entrepreneurs will start up another company. They possess all the money and material wealth anyone would ever

[15] 14 David L. Bradford and Allan R. Cohen, *Managing for Excellence: The Guide to Developing High Performance in Contemporary Organizations* (New York: John Wiley & Sons, 1984).

[16] Churchill, "Entrepreneurs and Their Enterprises: A Stage Model," pp. 1–22.

hope for, yet it is not enough. Like the artist, scientist, athlete, or musician who, at great personal sacrifice, strives for yet another breakthrough discovery, new record, or masterpiece, the greatest entrepreneurs are similarly obsessed with what they believe is the next breakthrough opportunity.

An excellent example of this pattern is David Neeleman, founder of the new discount airline Jet Blue. Having created the first electronic airline ticket a few years earlier while at Morris Air (later sold to Southwest Airlines), he was a wealthy man. And yet, along the way, he had developed a unique vision for a new airline. In 1998, he was having dinner with his longtime backer and friend Michael Lazarus, founding partner of Weston-Presidio Capital Partners. Michael asked, "Why do you want to start a new airline—what is the big opportunity you see?" Neeleman replied, "I'm going to fly people where they want to go!!" This simple but brilliant concept saw an opportunity in what all other would-be airline entrepreneurs saw as a barrier to entry; the entrenched, massive hub system of large, established airlines.

Entrepreneurs like Stemberg and Neeleman think big enough about opportunities. They know that a mom-and-pop business can often be more exhausting and stressful, and much less rewarding, than a high-potential business. Their opportunity mind-set is how to create it, shape it, mold it, or fix it so that the customer/end-user will respond: Wow! Their thinking habits focus on what can go right here, what and how can we change the product or service to make it go right? What do we have to offer to become the superior, dominant product or service?

Tolerance of Risk, Ambiguity, and Uncertainty Because high rates of change and high levels of risk, ambiguity, and uncertainty are almost a given, successful entrepreneurs tolerate risk, ambiguity, and uncertainty. They manage paradoxes and contradictions.

Entrepreneurs risk money, but they also risk reputation. Successful entrepreneurs are not gamblers; they take calculated risks. Like the parachutist, they are willing to take a risk; however, in deciding to do so, they calculate the risk carefully and thoroughly and do everything possible to get the odds in their favor. Entrepreneurs get others to share inherent financial and business risks with them. Partners put up money and put their reputations on the line, and investors do likewise. Creditors also join the party, as do customers who advance payments and suppliers who advance credit. For example, one researcher studied three very successful entrepreneurs in California who initiated and orchestrated actions that had risk consequences.[17] It was found that while they shunned risk, they sustained their courage by the clarity and optimism with which they saw the future. They limited the risks they initiated by carefully defining and strategizing their ends and by controlling and monitoring their means—and by tailoring them both to what they saw the future to be. Further, they managed risk by transferring it to others.

In 1990, John B. Miner proposed his concept of motivation-organizational fit, within which he contrasted a hierarchic (managerial) role with a task (entrepreneurial) role.[18] This study of motivational patterns showed that those who are task oriented (i.e., entrepreneurs) opt for the following roles because of the corresponding motivations:

Role	Motivation
1. Individual achievement.	A desire to achieve through one's own efforts and to attribute success to personal causation.
2. Risk avoidance.	A desire to avoid risk and leave little to chance.
3. Seeking results of behavior.	A desire for feedback.
4. Personal innovation.	A desire to introduce innovative solutions.
5. Planning and setting goals.	A desire to think about the future and anticipate future possibilities.

Entrepreneurs also tolerate ambiguity and uncertainty and are comfortable with conflict. Ask someone working in a large company how sure they are about receiving a paycheck this month, in two months, in six months, and next year. Invariably, they will say that it is virtually certain and will muse at the question. Startup entrepreneurs face just the opposite situation; there may be no revenue at the beginning, and if there is, a 90-day backlog in orders would be quite an exception. To make matters worse, lack of organization, structure, and order is a way of life. Constant changes introduce ambiguity and stress into every part of the enterprise. Jobs are undefined and changing continually, customers are new, co-workers are new, and setbacks and surprises are inevitable. And there never seems to be enough time.

Successful entrepreneurs maximize the good "higher performance" results of stress and minimize the negative reactions of exhaustion and frustration. Two surveys have suggested that very high levels of

[17] Daryl Mitton, "No Money, Know-How, Know-Who: Formula for Managing Venture Success and Personal Wealth," *Frontiers of Entrepreneurship Research: 1984,* ed. J. Hornaday et al. (Babson Park, MA: Babson College, 1984), p. 427.

[18] John B. Miner, "Entrepreneurs, High Growth Entrepreneurs and Managers: Contrasting and Overlapping Motivational Patterns," *Journal of Business Venturing 5,* p. 224.

both satisfaction and stress characterize founders, to a greater degree than managers, regardless of the success of their ventures.[19]

Creativity, Self-Reliance, and Ability to Adapt The high levels of uncertainty and very rapid rates of change that characterize new ventures require fluid and highly adaptive forms of organization that can respond quickly and effectively.

Successful entrepreneurs believe in themselves. They believe that their accomplishments (and setbacks) lie within their own control and influence and that they can affect the outcome. Successful entrepreneurs have the ability to see and "sweat the details" and also to conceptualize (i.e., they have "helicopter minds"). They are dissatisfied with the status quo and are restless initiators.

The entrepreneur has historically been viewed as an independent, a highly self-reliant innovator, and the champion (and occasional villain) of the free enterprise economy. More modern research and investigation have refined the agreement among researchers and practitioners alike that effective entrepreneurs actively seek and take initiative. They willingly put themselves in situations where they are personally responsible for the success or failure of the operation. They like to take the initiative to solve a problem or fill a vacuum where no leadership exists. They also like situations where personal impact on problems can be measured. Again, this is the action-oriented nature of the entrepreneur expressing itself.

Successful entrepreneurs are adaptive and resilient. They have an insatiable desire to know how well they are performing. They realize that to know how well they are doing and how to improve their performance, they need to actively seek and use feedback. Seeking and using feedback is also central to the habit of learning from mistakes and setbacks, and of responding to the unexpected. For the same reasons, these entrepreneurs often are described as excellent listeners and quick learners.

Entrepreneurs are not afraid of failing; rather, they are more intent on succeeding, counting on the fact that "success covers a multitude of blunders,"[20] as George Bernard Shaw eloquently stated. People who fear failure will neutralize whatever achievement motivation they may possess. They will tend to engage in a very easy task, where there is little chance of failure, or in a very difficult situation, where they cannot be held personally responsible if they do not succeed.

Further, successful entrepreneurs learn from failure experiences. They better understand not only their roles but also the roles of others in causing the failure, and thus are able to avoid similar problems in the future. There is an old saying to the effect that the cowboy who has never been thrown from a horse undoubtedly has not ridden too many! The iterative, trial-and-error nature of becoming a successful entrepreneur makes serious setbacks and disappointments an integral part of the learning process.

Motivation to Excel Successful entrepreneurs are motivated to excel. Entrepreneurs are self-starters who appear driven internally by a strong desire to compete against their own self-imposed standards and to pursue and attain challenging goals. This need to achieve has been well established in the literature on entrepreneurs since the pioneering work of McClelland and Atkinson on motivation in the 1950s and 1960s. Seeking out the challenge inherent in a startup and responding in a positive way, noted by the distinguished entrepreneurs mentioned above, is achievement motivation in action.

Conversely, these entrepreneurs have a low need for status and power, and they derive personal motivation from the challenge and excitement of creating and building enterprises. They are driven by a thirst for achievement, rather than by status and power. Ironically, their accomplishments, especially if they are very successful, give them power. But it is important to recognize that power and status are a result of their activities. Setting high but attainable goals enables entrepreneurs to focus their energies, be very selective in sorting out opportunities, and know what to say no to. Having goals and direction also helps define priorities and provides measures of how well they are performing. Possessing an objective way of keeping score, such as changes in profits, sales, or stock price, is also important. Thus, money is seen as a tool, and a way of keeping score, rather than the object of the game by itself.

Successful entrepreneurs insist on the highest personal standards of integrity and reliability. They do what they say they are going to do, and they pull for the long haul. These high personal standards are the glue and fiber that bind successful personal and business relationships and make them endure.

A study involving 130 members of the Small Company Management Program at Harvard Business School confirmed how important this issue is. Most simply said it was the single most important factor in their long-term successes.[21]

[19] D. Boyd and D. E. Gumpert, "Loneliness of the Start-Up Entrepreneur," *in Frontiers of Entrepreneurship Research: 1982 and 1983*, ed. J. A. Hornaday et al. (Babson Park, MA: Babson College, 1983), pp. 478–87.

[20] Cited in Royal Little, *How to Lose $100,000,000 and Other Valuable Advice* (Boston: Little, Brown and Company, 1979), p. 72.

[21] Timmons and Stevenson, "Entrepreneurship Education in the 80s: What Entrepreneurs Say," pp. 115–34.

EXHIBIT 1.6

Opportunity Knocks—Or Does It Hide? An Examination of the Role of Opportunity Recognition in Entrepreneurship

Number (and Proportion) of Opportunities of Various Sources and Types

Sources of Opportunities	Entrepreneurs	Nonentrepreneurs
Prior work	67 (58.3%)	13 (48.2%)
Prior employment	36	6
Prior consulting work	11	4
Prior business	20	2
Network	25 (21.7%)	8 (29.6%)
Social contact	7	6
Business contact	18	2
Thinking by analogy	13 (11.3%)	6 (22.2%)
Partner	10 (8.7%)	—
Types of Opportunities	**Entrepreneurs**	**Nonentrepreneurs**
Niche expansion/ underserved niche	29 (25.2%)	7 (29.2%)
Customer need	34 (29.6%)	6 (25.0%)
Own firm's need	6 (5.2%)	1 (4.2%)
Better technology	46 (40.0%)	10 (41.7%)

Source: Zeitsma, Charlene (1999). Opportunity Knocks–Or Does it Hide? An Examination of the Role of Opportunity Recognition in Entrepreneurship. In P.D. Reynolds, W.D. Bygrave, S. Maaigart, C.M. Mason, G.D. Meyer, H.J. Sapienza & K.G. Shaver (Eds.), *Frontiers of Entrepreneurship Research 1999,* Babson Park MA: Babson College. Used by permission of the author.

Note: Numbers equal total people in the sample allocated to each category. Numbers in parentheses equal percentage of total surveyed.

The best entrepreneurs have a keen awareness of their own strengths and weaknesses and those of their partners and of the competitive and other environments surrounding and influencing them. They are coldly realistic about what they can and cannot do and do not delude themselves; that is, they have "veridical awareness" or "optimistic realism." It also is worth noting that successful entrepreneurs believe in themselves. They do not believe that fate, luck, or other powerful, external forces will govern the success or failure of their venture. They believe they personally can affect the outcome. This attribute is also consistent with achievement motivation, which is the desire to take personal responsibility, and self-confidence.

This veridical awareness often is accompanied by other valuable entrepreneurial traits—perspective and a sense of humor. The ability to retain a sense of perspective, and to "know thyself" in both strengths and weaknesses, makes it possible for an entrepreneur to laugh, to ease tensions, and to get an unfavorable situation set in a more profitable direction.

Entrepreneurial Reasoning: The Entrepreneurial Mind[22] in Action

How do successful entrepreneurs think, what actions do they initiate, and how do they start and build businesses? By understanding the attitudes, behaviors, management competencies, experience, and know-how that contribute to entrepreneurial success, one has some useful benchmarks for gauging what to do. Exhibit 1.6 examines the role of opportunity in entrepreneurship.

Successful entrepreneurs have a wide range of personality types. Most research about entrepreneurs has focused on the influences of genes, family, education, career experience, and so forth, but no psychological model has been supported. Studies have shown that an entrepreneur does not need specific inherent traits, but rather a set of acquired skills.[23] Perhaps one Price-Babson College fellow phrased it best when he said, "One does not want to overdo the personality stuff, but there is a certain ring to it."[24]

[22] See Timmons, *The Entrepreneurial Mind* (1989).
[23] William Lee, "What Successful Entrepreneurs *Really* Do," Lee Communications, 2001.
[24] Comment made during a presentation at the June 1987 Price-Babson College Fellows Program by Jerry W Gustafson, Coleman-Fannie May Candies Professor of Entrepreneurship, Beloit College, at Babson College.

EXHIBIT 1.7

Who Is the Entrepreneur?

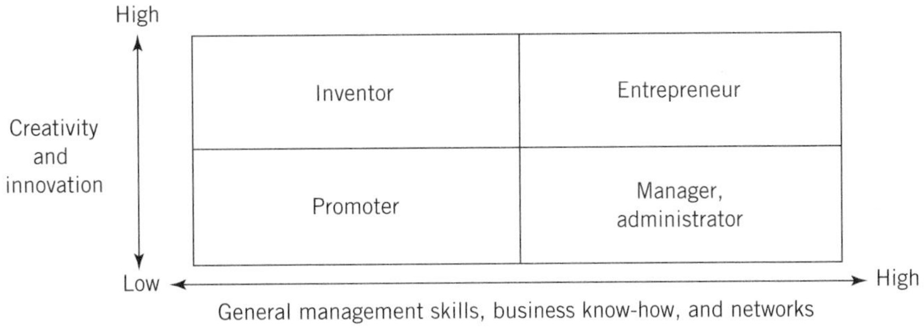

"There is no evidence of an ideal entrepreneurial personality. Great entrepreneurs can be either gregarious or low key, analytical or intuitive, charismatic or boring, good with details or terrible, delegators or control freaks. What you need is a capacity to execute in certain key ways."[25] Successful entrepreneurs share common attitudes and behaviors. They work hard and are driven by an intense commitment and determined perseverance; they see the cup half full, rather than half empty; they strive for integrity; they thrive on the competitive desire to excel and win; they are dissatisfied with the status quo and seek opportunities to improve almost any situation they encounter; they use failure as a tool for learning and eschew perfection in favor of effectiveness; and they believe they can personally make an enormous difference in the final outcome of their ventures and their lives.

Those who have succeeded speak of these attitudes and behaviors time and again.[26] For example, two famous entrepreneurs have captured the intense commitment and perseverance of entrepreneurs. Wally Amos, famous for his chocolate chip cookies, said, "You can do anything you want to do."[27] John Johnson of Johnson Publishing Company (publisher of *Ebony*) expressed it this way: "You need to think yourself out of a corner, meet needs, and never, never accept no for an answer."[28]

Successful entrepreneurs possess not only a creative and innovative flair, but also solid management skills, business know-how, and sufficient contacts. Exhibit 1.7 demonstrates this relationship.

Inventors, noted for their creativity, often lack the necessary management skills and business know-how. Promoters usually lack serious general management and business skills and true creativity. Managers govern, police, and ensure the smooth operation of the status quo; their management skills, while high, are tuned to efficiency as well, and creativity is usually not required. Although the management skills of the manager and the entrepreneur overlap, the manager is more driven by conservation of resources and the entrepreneur is more opportunity-driven.[29]

The Concept of Apprenticeship

Shaping and Managing an Apprenticeship

When one looks at successful entrepreneurs, one sees profiles of careers rich in experience. Time and again there is a pattern among successful entrepreneurs. They have all acquired 10 or more years of substantial experience, built contacts, garnered the know-how, and established a track record in the industry, market, and technology niche within which they eventually launch, acquire, or build a business. Frequently, they have acquired intimate knowledge of the customer, distribution channels, and market through direct sales and marketing experience. The more successful ones have made money for their employer before doing it for themselves. Consider the following examples:

- Apple Computer founders Steve Jobs and Steve Wozniak were computer enthusiasts as preteens and had accumulated a relatively lengthy amount of experience by the time they started the company in their mid-20s. In entirely new industries such as microcomputers, a few years can be a large amount of experience.

[25] William Lee, "What Successful Entrepreneurs *Really* Do," Lee Communications, 2001.
[26] See the excellent summary of a study of the first 21 inductees into Babson College's Academy of Distinguished Entrepreneurs by John A. Hornaday and Nancy Tieken, "Capturing Twenty-One Heffalumps," in *Frontiers of Entrepreneurship Research: 1983*, pp. 23, 50.
[27] Made during a speech at his induction in 1982 into the Academy of Distinguished Entrepreneurs, Babson College.
[28] Made during a speech at his induction in 1979 into the Academy of Distinguished Entrepreneurs, Babson College.
[29] Timmons, Muzyka, Stevenson, and Bygrave, "Opportunity Recognition: The Core of Entrepreneurship," pp. 42–49.

- Paul Tobin had no prior cellular phone experience when he was picked up by John Kluge to launch Cellular One of eastern Massachusetts—but neither did anyone else! He had had six years of experience at Satellite Business Systems in marketing and had previously spent over five years launching and building his own company in a nontechnology business. His learning curves as an entrepreneur were invaluable in the next startup.
- Jeff Parker had worked for 10 years in the bond-trading business at three major investment banks; he had sold, managed, and built a substantial trading business at one of the investment banks. His technical and computer background enabled him to write programs to assist bond traders on the first Apple Computers. He launched Technical Data Corporation with $100,000, and built the first online computer system for bond traders. A few years later, his company was sold to Telerate for more than $20 million.[30]

Tens of thousands of similar examples exist. There are always exceptions to any such pattern, but if you want the odds in your favor, get the experience first. Successful entrepreneurs are likely to be older and to have at least 8 to 10 years of experience. They are likely to have accumulated enough net worth to contribute to funding the venture or to have a track record impressive enough to give investors and creditors the necessary confidence. Finally, they usually have found and nurtured relevant business and other contacts and networks that ultimately contribute to the success of their ventures.

The first 10 or so years after leaving school can make or break an entrepreneur's career in terms of how well he or she is prepared for serious entrepreneuring. Evidence suggests that the most durable entrepreneurial careers, those found to last 25 years or more, were begun across a broad age spectrum, but after the person selected prior work or a career to prepare specifically for an entrepreneurial career.

Having relevant experience, know-how, attitudes, behaviors, and skills appropriate for a particular venture opportunity can dramatically improve the odds for success. The other side of the coin is that if an entrepreneur does not have these, then he or she will have to learn them while launching and growing the business. The tuition for such an approach is often greater than most entrepreneurs can afford.

Since entrepreneurs frequently evolve from an entrepreneurial heritage or are shaped and nurtured by their closeness to entrepreneurs and others, the concept of an apprenticeship can be a useful one. Much of what an entrepreneur needs to know about entrepreneuring comes from learning by doing. Knowing what to prepare for, where the windows for acquiring the relevant exposure lie, how to anticipate these, where to position oneself, and when to move on can be quite useful.

As Howard Stevenson of the Harvard Business School has often reminded us when teaching in the Price Babson College Fellows Program, and elsewhere:

> You have to approach the world as an equal. There is no such thing as being supplicant. You are trying to work and create a better solution by creating action among a series of people who are relatively equal. We destroy potential entrepreneurs by putting them in a velvet-lined rut, by giving them jobs that pay too much, and by telling them they are too good, before they get adequate intelligence, experience, and responsibility.

Windows of Apprenticeship

Exhibit 1.8 summarizes the key elements of an apprenticeship and experience curve and relates these to age windows.[31] Age windows are especially important because of the inevitable time it takes to create and build a successful activity, whether it is a new venture or within another organization.

There is a saying in the venture capital business that the "lemons," or losers, in a portfolio ripen in about two and one-half years and that the "pearls," or winners, usually take seven or eight years to come to fruition. Therefore, seven years is a realistic time frame to expect to grow a higher potential business to a point where a capital gain can be realized. Interestingly, presidents of large corporations, presidents of colleges, and self-employed professionals often describe years as the time it takes to do something significant.

The implications of this are quite provocative. First, time is precious. Assume an entrepreneur spends the first five years after college or graduate school gaining relevant experience. He or she will be 25 to 30 years of age (or maybe as old as 35) when launching a new venture. By the age of 50, there will have been time for starting, at most, three successful new ventures. What's more, entrepreneurs commonly go through false starts or even a failure at first in the trial-and-error process of learning the entrepreneurial ropes. As a result, the first venture may not be launched until later (i.e., in the entrepreneur's mid- to

[30] This example is drawn from "Technical Data Corporation," HBS Cases 283-072, 283-073, Harvard Business School, 198-1.
[31] The authors wish to acknowledge the contributions to this thinking by Harvey "Chet" Krentzman, entrepreneur, lecturer, author, and nurturer of at least three dozen growth-minded ventures over the past 20 years.

EXHIBIT 1.8

Windows of Entrepreneurial Apprenticeship

Elements of the Apprenticeship and Experience Curve	Age 20s	30s	40s	50s
1. Relevant Business Experience	Low	Moderate to high	Higher	Highest
2. Management Skills and Know-How	Low to moderate	Moderate to high	High	High
3. Entrepreneurial Goals and Commitment	Varies widely	Focused high	High	High
4. Drive and Energy	Highest	High	Moderate	Lowest
5. Wisdom and Judgment	Lowest	Higher	Higher	Highest
6. Focus of Apprenticeship	Discussing what you enjoy; key is learning business, sales, marketing; profit and loss responsibility	General management Division management Founder	Growing and harvesting	Reinvesting
7. Dominant Life-Stage Issues*	Realizing your dream of adolescence and young adulthood	Personal growth and new directions and ventures	Renewal, regeneration, reinvesting in the system	

*From The Seasons of a Man's Life by Daniel Levinson, copyright © 1978 by Daniel J. Levinson. Used by permission of Alfred A. Knopt, a division of Random House, Inc.

late 30s). This would leave time to grow the current venture and maybe one more. (There is always the possibility of staying with a venture and growing it to a larger company of $50 million or more in sales.)

Reflecting on Exhibit 1.8 will reveal some other paradoxes and dilemmas. For one thing, just when an entrepreneur's drive, energy, and ambition are at a peak, the necessary relevant business experience and management skills are least developed, and those critical elements, wisdom and judgment, are in their infancy. Later, when an entrepreneur has gained the necessary experience in the "deep, dark canyons of uncertainty" and has thereby gained wisdom and judgment, age begins to take its toll. Also, patience and perseverance to relentlessly pursue a long-term vision need to be balanced with the urgency and realism to make it happen. Flexibility to stick with the moving opportunity targets and to abandon some and shift to others is also required. However, flexibility and the ability to act with urgency disappear as the other commitments of life are assumed.

The Concept of Apprenticeship: Acquiring the 50,000 Chunks

During the past several years, studies about entrepreneurs have tended to confirm what practitioners have known all along: that some attitudes, behaviors, and know-how can be acquired and that some of these attributes are more desirable than others.

Increasingly, research studies on the career paths of entrepreneurs and the self-employed suggest the role of experience and know-how is central in successful venture creation. Many successful entrepreneurs do not have prior industry experience. More critical to the entrepreneur is the ability to gain information and act on it.[32] Evidence also suggests that success is linked to preparation and planning.[33] This is what getting 50,000 chunks of experience is all about.

Although formal market research may provide useful information, it is also important to recognize the entrepreneur's collective, qualitative judgment must be weighted most heavily in evaluating opportunities. One study found that entrepreneurs view believing in the idea, and experimenting with new venture ideas that result in both failures and successes as the most important components of opportunity recognition.[34]

Most successful entrepreneurs follow a pattern of apprenticeship, where they prepare for becoming entrepreneurs by gaining the relevant business experiences from parents who are self-employed or through job experiences. They do not leave acquisition of experience to accident or osmosis. As entrepreneur

[32] Karl H. Vesper, "New Venture Ideas: Don't Overlook the Experience Factor," *Harvard Business Review*, reprinted in *Growing Concerns: Building and Managing the Smaller Business*, ed. D. E. Gumpert (New York: John Wiley & Sons, 1984), pp. 28–55.

[33] See Robert Ronstadt's and Howard Stevenson's studies reported in *Frontiers of Entrepreneurship Research: 1983*.

[34] "Successful Entrepreneurs' Insights into Opportunity Recognition," Gerald Hills & Rodney Shrader, University of Illinois, Chicago, 2000.

Harvey "Chet" Krentzman has said, "Know what you know and what you *don't* know."

Role Models

Numerous studies show a strong connection between the presence of role models and the emergence of entrepreneurs. For instance, an early study showed that more than half of those starting new businesses had parents who owned businesses.[35] Likewise, 70 percent of MIT graduates who started technology businesses had entrepreneurial parents.[36] The authors summarized it this way:

> Family firms spawn entrepreneurs. Older generations provide leadership and role modeling. This phenomenon cuts across industries, firm size and gender.

Myths and Realities

Folklore and stereotypes about entrepreneurs and entrepreneurial success are remarkably durable, even in these informed and sophisticated times. More is known about the founders and the process of entrepreneurship than ever before.

However, certain myths enjoy recurring attention and popularity, in part because while generalities may apply to certain types of entrepreneurs and particular situations, the great variety of founders tend to defy generalization. Exhibit 1.9 lists myths about entrepreneurs that have persisted and realities that are supported by research.

Studies have indicated that 90 percent or more of founders start their companies in the same marketplace, technology, or industry they have been working in.[37] Others have found that entrepreneurs are likely to have role models, have 8 to 10 years of experience, and be well educated. It also appears that successful entrepreneurs have a wide range of experiences in products/markets and across functional areas.[38] Studies also have shown that most successful entrepreneurs start companies in their 30s. One study of founders of high-tech companies on Route 128 in Boston from 1982 to 1984 showed that the average age of the founders was 40.

It has been found that entrepreneurs work both more and less than their counterparts in large organizations, that they have high degrees of satisfaction with their jobs, and that they are healthier.[39] Another study showed that nearly 21 percent of the founders were over 40 when they embarked on their entrepreneurial career, the majority were in their 30s, and just over one-quarter did so by the time they were 25.

What Can Be Learned?

For nearly 30 years, the authors have been engaged as educators, cofounders, investors, advisors, and directors of new, higher potential ventures. Many of these have been launched by former students, and most of the cases in this book are about those founders. A vivid memory of one of the authors is when the great Texas real estate entrepreneur Trammel Crow was inducted into Babson College's Academy of Distinguished Entrepreneurs. The instant we met, he put his arm around me and said, "Perfesser, do you mean to tell me you think you can actually teach someone to be an on-tree-pre-newer!" My response was straightforward, "Mr. Crow, what I think you are really asking me is, 'Am I preposterous enough to believe that in 35 to 40 hours of class time, during a single semester, I can convert the average student into the economic equivalent of a Picasso or a Beethoven!?' Mr. Crow, I think we both know the answer to that question." He laughed and smiled, and said he reckoned he did.

New Venture Creation immerses you in the dynamics and realities of launching and growing lifestyle to higher potential ventures. Throughout the text are multipart cases about real, young entrepreneurs, including some college and graduate students. You will face the same situations these aspiring entrepreneurs faced as they sought to turn dreams into reality. The cases and text, combined with other online resources, will enable you to grapple with all of the conceptual, practical, financial, and personal issues entrepreneurs encounter. This book will help you get the odds of success in your favor. It will focus your attention on developing answers for the most important of these questions, including:

- What does an entrepreneurial career take?
- What is the difference between a good opportunity and just another idea?
- Is the opportunity I am considering the right opportunity for me now?

[35] A. Cooper and W. Dunkelberg, *A New Look at Business Entry* (San Mateo, CA: National Federation of Independent Businesses, March 1984).
[36] *Fortune*, June 7, 1999.
[37] A good summary of some of these studies is provided by Robert H. Brockhaus, "The Psychology of the Entrepreneur," in *Encyclopedia of Entrepreneurship*, ed. C. Kent, D. Sexton, and K. Vesper (Englewood Cliffs, NJ: Prentice-Hall, 1982), pp. 50, 55.
[38] Over 80 studies in this area have been reported in *Frontiers of Entrepreneurship Research* (Babson Park, MA: Babson College) for the years 1981 through 1997.
[39] Stevenson, "Who Are the Harvard Self-Employed?" p. 233.

EXHIBIT 1.9

Myths and Realities about Entrepreneurs

Myth 1—Entrepreneurs are born, not made.

Reality—While entrepreneurs are born with certain native intelligence, a flair for creating, and energy, these talents by themselves are like unmolded clay or an unpainted canvas. The making of an entrepreneur occurs by accumulating the relevant skills, know-how, experiences, and contacts over a period of years and includes large doses of self-development. The creative capacity to envision and then pursue an opportunity is a direct descendant of at least 10 or more years of experience that lead to pattern recognition.

Myth 2—Anyone can start a business.

Reality—Entrepreneurs who recognize the difference between an idea and an opportunity, and who think big enough, start businesses that have a better chance of succeeding. Luck, to the extent it is involved, requires good preparation. And the easiest part is starting. What is hardest is surviving, sustaining, and building a venture so its founders can realize a harvest. Perhaps only one in 10 to 20 new businesses that survive five years or more results in a capital gain for the founders.

Myth 3—Entrepreneurs are gamblers.

Reality—Successful entrepreneurs take very careful, calculated risks. They try to influence the odds, often by getting others to share risk with them and by avoiding or minimizing risks if they have the choice. Often they slice up the risk into smaller, quite digestible pieces; only then do they commit the time or resources to determine if that piece will work. They do not deliberately seek to take more risk or to take unnecessary risk, nor do they shy away from unavoidable risk.

Myth 4—Entrepreneurs want the whole show to themselves.

Reality—Owning and running the whole show effectively puts a ceiling on growth. Solo entrepreneurs usually make a living. It is extremely difficult to grow a higher potential venture by working single-handedly. Higher potential entrepreneurs build a team, an organization, and a company. Besides, 100 percent of nothing is nothing, so rather than taking a large piece of the pie, they work to make the pie bigger.

Myth 5—Entrepreneurs are their own bosses and completely independent.

Reality—Entrepreneurs are far from independent and have to serve many masters and constituencies, including partners, investors, customers, suppliers, creditors, employees, families, and those involved in social and community obligations. Entrepreneurs, however, can make free choices of whether, when, and what they care to respond to. Moreover, it is extremely difficult, and rare, to build a business beyond $1 million to $2 million in sales single-handedly.

Myth 6—Entrepreneurs work longer and harder than managers in big companies.

Reality—There is no evidence that all entrepreneurs work more than their corporate counterparts. Some do, some do not. Some actually report that they work less.

Myth 7—Entrepreneurs experience a great deal of stress and pay a high price.

Reality—Being an entrepreneur is stressful and demanding. But there is no evidence that it is any more stressful than numerous other highly demanding professional roles, and entrepreneurs find their jobs very satisfying. They have a high sense of accomplishment, are healthier, and are much less likely to retire than those who work for others. Three times as many entrepreneurs as corporate managers say they plan to never retire.

Myth 8—Start a business and fail and you'll never raise money again.

Reality—Talented and experienced entrepreneurs—because they pursue attractive opportunities and are able to attract the right people and necessary financial and other resources to make the venture work—often head successful ventures. Further, businesses fail, but entrepreneurs do not. Failure is often the fire that tempers the steel of an entrepreneur's learning experience and street savvy.

Myth 9—Money is the most important startup ingredient.

Reality—If the other pieces and talents are there, the money will follow, but it does not follow that an entrepreneur will succeed if he or she has enough money. Money is one of the least important ingredients in new venture success. Money is to the entrepreneur what the paint and brush are to the artist—an inert tool that in the right hands, can create marvels.

Myth 10—Entrepreneurs should be young and energetic.

Reality—While these qualities may help, age is no barrier. The average age of entrepreneurs starting high potential businesses is in the mid-30s, and there are numerous examples of entrepreneurs starting businesses in their 60s. What is critical is possessing the relevant know-how, experience, and contacts that greatly facilitate recognizing and pursuing an opportunity.

Myth 11—Entrepreneurs are motivated solely by the quest for the almighty dollar.

Reality—Entrepreneurs seeking high potential ventures are more driven by building enterprises and realizing long-term capital gains than by instant gratification through high salaries and perks. A sense of personal achievement and accomplishment, feeling in control of their own destinies, and realizing their vision and dreams are also powerful motivators. Money is viewed as a tool and a way of keeping score, rather than an end in itself. Entrepreneurs thrive on the thrill of the chase; and, time and again, even after an entrepreneur has made a few million dollars or more, he or she will work on a new vision to build another company.

(Continued)

EXHIBIT 1.9 (concluded)

Myths and Realities about Entrepreneurs

Myth 12—Entrepreneurs seek power and control over others.

Reality—Successful entrepreneurs are driven by the quest for responsibility, achievement, and results, rather than for power for its own sake. They thrive on a sense of accomplishment and of outperforming the competition, rather than a personal need for power expressed by dominating and controlling others. By virtue of their accomplishments, they may be powerful and influential, but these are more the by-products of the entrepreneurial process than a driving force behind it.

Myth 13—If an entrepreneur is talented, success will happen in a year or two.

Reality—An old maxim among venture capitalists says it all: The lemons ripen in two and a half years, but the pearls take seven or eight. Rarely is a new business established solidly in less than three or four years.

Myth 14—Any entrepreneur with a good idea can raise venture capital.

Reality—Of the ventures of entrepreneurs with good ideas who seek out venture capital, only 1 to 3 out of 100 are funded.

Myth 15—If an entrepreneur has enough startup capital, he or she can't miss.

Reality—The opposite is often true; that is, too much money at the outset often creates euphoria and a spoiled-child syndrome. The accompanying lack of discipline and impulsive spending usually lead to serious problems and failure.

Myth 16—Entrepreneurs are lone wolves and cannot work with others.

Reality—The most successful entrepreneurs are leaders who build great teams and effective relationships working with peers, directors, investors, key customers, key suppliers, and the like.

Myth 17—Unless you attained 600+ on your SATs or GMATs, you'll never be a successful entrepreneur.

Reality—Entrepreneurial IQ is a unique combination of creativity, motivation, integrity, leadership, team building, analytical ability, and ability to deal with ambiguity and adversity.

- Why do some firms grow quickly to several million dollars in sales but then stumble, never growing beyond a single-product firm?
- What are the critical tasks and hurdles in seizing an opportunity and building the business?
- How much money do I need and when, where, and how can I get it—on acceptable terms?
- What financing sources, strategies, and mechanisms can I use from prestart, through meaningful careers in new and growing firms, and in the early growth stage to the harvest of my venture?
- What are the minimum resources I need to gain control over the opportunity, and how can I do this?
- Is a business plan needed? If so, what kind is needed and how and when should I develop one?
- Who are the constituents for whom I must create or add value to achieve a positive cash flow and to develop harvest options?
- What is my venture worth and how do I negotiate what to give up?
- What are the critical transitions in entrepreneurial management as a firm grows from $1 million to $5 million to $25 million in sales?
- What is it that entrepreneurial leaders do differently which enables them to achieve such competitive breakthroughs and advantages, particularly over conventional practices, but also so-called best practices?
- What are the opportunities and implications for 20th century entrepreneurs and the Internet, and how can these be seized and financed?
- What do I need to know and practice in entrepreneurial reasoning and thinking to have a competitive edge?
- What are some of the pitfalls, minefields, and hazards I need to anticipate, prepare for, and respond to?
- What are the contacts and networks I need to access and to develop?
- Do I know what I do and do not know, and do I know what to do about it?
- How can I develop a personal "entrepreneurial game plan" to acquire the experience I need to succeed?
- How critical and sensitive is the timing in each of these areas?
- Why do entrepreneurs who succeed in the long term seek to maintain reputations for integrity and ethical business practices?

We believe that we can significantly improve the quality of decisions students make about entrepreneurship and thereby also improve the fit between what they aspire to do and the requirements of the particular opportunity. In many cases, those choices lead to self-employment or meaningful careers in new and growing firms and, increasingly, in large firms that "get it." In other cases, students join larger firms whose customer base and/or suppliers are principally the entrepreneurial sector. Still others seek careers in the financial institutions and professional services firms that are at the vortex of the entrepreneurial economy: venture capital, private equity, investment banks, commercial banks, consulting, accounting, and the like.

Our view of entrepreneurship is that it need not be an end in itself. Rather, it is a pathway that leads to innumerable ideas and opportunities, and opens visions of what young people can become. You will learn skills, and how to use those skills appropriately. You will learn how to tap your own and others' creativity, and to apply your new energy. You will learn the difference between another good idea and a serious opportunity. You will learn the power and potential of the entrepreneurial team. You will learn how entrepreneurs finance and grow their companies, often with ingenious bootstrapping strategies that get big results with minimal resources. You will learn the joy of self-sufficiency and independence. You will learn how entrepreneurial leaders make this happen, and give back to society. You will discover anew what it is about entrepreneurship that gives you sustaining entrepreneurial reasoning and thinking in order to fuel your dreams. One of the best perspectives on this comes from Professor Jerry Gustafson, Coleman-Fannie May Chair, Beloit College, Beloit, Wisconsin, who was probably the first professor at a liberal arts college to create an entrepreneurship course:

> Entrepreneurship is important for its own sake. The sub ject frames an ideal context for students to address perennial questions concerning their identity, objectives, hopes, relation to society, and the tension between thought and action. Entrepreneurship concerns thinking of what we are as persons. . . . Furthermore, of its nature, entrepreneurship is about process. One cannot discuss entrepreneurship without encountering the importance of goal-setting, information gathering, persistence, resourcefulness, and resiliency. It is not lost on students that the behaviors and styles of entrepreneurs tend to be socially rewarded, and these are precisely the behaviors we wish to see the students exhibit in the classroom.[40]

A Word of Caution: What SATs, IQ Tests, GMATs, and Others Don't Measure

> *Nothing in the world can take the place of persistence. Talent will not; nothing is more common than unsuccessful men with talent. Genius will not; unrewarded genius is almost a proverb. Education will not; the world is full of educated derelicts. Persistence and determination alone are omnipotent. The slogan "Press on" has solved and solved and always will solve the problems of the human race.*
>
> President Calvin Coolidge

The following data about alumni whose careers were followed for nearly 25 years has always shocked second-year Harvard MBA students. Regardless of the measure one applies, among the very top of the class were graduates who were both highly successful and not very successful. At the bottom of the class were alumni who became outrageously successful, and others who accomplished little with their lives and exceptional education. The middle of the class achieved all points on the continuum of success. How could this be?

America's brightest fared poorly in the Third International Mathematics and Science Study comparing high school seniors from 20 nations, according to the *New York Times.* In a competition between the world's most precocious seniors, those taking physics and advanced math, the Americans performed at the bottom. The article noted:

> After decades of agonizing over the fairness of SAT scores, the differences between male and female mathematical skills, and gaps in IQ between various racial and ethnic groups, the notion of intelligence and how to measure it remains more a political than scientific, and as maddenly elusive as ever.[41]

In short, there are many different kinds of intelligence, a much greater bandwidth than most researchers and test architects ever imagined. The dynamic and subtle complexities of the entrepreneurial task require its own special intelligences. How else would one explain the enormous contradiction inherent in business and financially failed geniuses?

One only need consider the critical skills and capacities that are at the heart of entrepreneurial leadership and achievement, yet are not measured by the IQ tests, SATs, GMATs, and the like that grade and sort young applicants with such imprecision. Consider the skills and capacities not measured by these tests:

- ✓ Leadership skills.
- ✓ Interpersonal skills.
- ✓ Team building and team playing.
- ✓ Creativity and ingenuity.
- ✓ Motivation.
- ✓ Learning skills (versus knowledge).
- ✓ Persistence and determination.
- ✓ Values, ethics, honesty, and integrity.

[40] Professor Jerry Gustafson, "SEEing Is Not Only about Business," *PULSE*, 1988 (Babson Park, MA: Price-Babson Fellows Program).
[41] "Tests Show Nobody's Smart about Intelligence," *The New York Times*, March 1, 1998, p. 4–1.

- ✓ Goal-setting orientation.
- ✓ Self-discipline.
- ✓ Frugality.
- ✓ Resourcefulness.
- ✓ Resiliency and capacity to handle adversity.
- ✓ Ability to seek, listen, and use feedback.
- ✓ Reliability.
- ✓ Dependability.
- ✓ Sense of humor.

It is no wonder that a number of excellent colleges and universities eliminated these measures or placed them in a proper perspective. Obviously, this should not be construed to mean entrepreneurship is for dummies. Quite the opposite is true. Indeed, intelligence is a very valuable and important asset for entrepreneurs, but by itself is woefully inadequate.

Clearly, just being very smart won't help much if one doesn't possess numerous other qualities (see Chapters 7, 8, and 9: "The Entrepreneurial Manager," "The New Venture Team," and "The Personal Ethics and the Entrepreneur," respectively, for an elaboration on these other qualities). A fascinating article by Chris Argyris, "Teaching Smart People How to Learn," is well worth reading to get some powerful insights into why it is often *not* the class genius who becomes most successful.[42]

A Personal Strategy

An apprenticeship can be an integral part of the process of shaping an entrepreneurial career. One principal task is to determine what kind of entrepreneur he or she is likely to become, based on background, experience, and drive. Through an apprenticeship, an entrepreneur can shape a strategy and action plan to make it happen. The "Crafting a Personal Entrepreneurship Strategy" exercise at the end of this chapter addresses this issue more fully. For a quick inventory of your entrepreneurial attributes, do the "QuickLook: The Personal Entrepreneurial Strategy" exercise at the end of this chapter.

Despite all the work involved in becoming an entrepreneur, the bottom line is revealing. Evidence about careers and job satisfaction of entrepreneurs all points to the same conclusion: If they had to do it over again, not only would more of them become entrepreneurs again, but also they would do it sooner.[43] They report higher personal satisfaction with their lives and their careers than their managerial counterparts. Nearly three times as many say they plan never to retire, according to Stevenson. Numerous other studies show that the satisfaction from independence and living and working where and how they want to is a source of great satisfaction.[44] Financially, successful entrepreneurs enjoy higher incomes and a higher net worth than career managers in large companies. In addition, the successful harvest of a company usually means a capital gain of several million dollars or more and, with it, a new array of very attractive options and opportunities to do whatever they choose to do with the rest of their lives.

Entrepreneur's Creed

So much time and space would not be spent on the entrepreneurial mind if it were just of academic interest. But they are, entrepreneurs themselves believe, in large part responsible for success. When asked an open-ended question about what entrepreneurs believed are the most critical concepts, skills, and know-how for running a business—today and five years hence—their answers were very revealing. Most mentioned mental attitudes and philosophies based on entrepreneurial attributes, rather than specific skills or organizational concepts. These answers are gathered together in what might be called an entrepreneur's creed:

- Do what gives you energy—have fun.
- Figure out what can go right and make it.
- Say "can do," rather than "cannot" or "maybe."
- *Illegitimi non carborundum:* tenacity and creativity will triumph.
- Anything is possible if you believe you can do it.
- If you don't know it can't be done, then you'll go ahead and do it.
- The cup is half-full, not half-empty.
- Be dissatisfied with the way things are—and look for improvement.
- Do things differently.
- Don't take a risk if you don't have to—but take a calculated risk if it's the right opportunity for *you*.

[42] Chris Argyris, "Teaching Smart People to Learn," *Harvard Business Review*, May–June 1991.
[43] Stevenson, "Who Are the Harvard Self-Employed?" *Frontiers of Entrepreneurship Research: 1983*, ed. J. A. Hornaday et al. (Babson Park, MA: Babson College, 1983), pp. 233–54.
[44] Robert C. Ronstadt, "The Decision Not to Become an Entrepreneur," in *Frontiers of Entrepreneurship Research: 1983*, ed. J. Hornaday et al. (Babson Park, MA: Babson College, 1983), pp. 192–212; and Robert C. Ronstadt, "Ex-Entrepreneurs and the Decision to Start an Entrepreneurial Career," in *Frontiers of Entrepreneurship Research: 1983*, pp. 437–60.

- Businesses fail; successful entrepreneurs learn—but keep the tuition low.
- It is easier to beg for forgiveness than to ask for permission in the first place.
- Make opportunity and results your obsession—not money.
- Money is a tool and a scorecard available to the right people with the right opportunity at the right time.
- Making money is even more fun than spending it.
- Make heroes out of others—a team builds a business; an individual makes a living.
- Take pride in your accomplishments—it's contagious!
- Sweat the details that are critical to success.
- Integrity and reliability equal long-run oil and glue.
- Accept the responsibility, less than half the credit, and more than half the blame.
- Make the pie bigger—don't waste time trying to cut smaller slices.
- Play for the long haul—it is rarely possible to get rich quickly.
- Don't pay too much—but don't lose it!
- Only the lead dog gets a change of view.
- Success is getting what you want: Happiness is wanting what you get.
- Give back.
- Never give up.

Chapter Summary

1. Entrepreneurs are men and women of all sizes, ages, shapes, religions, colors, and backgrounds. There is no one single profile or psychological template.
2. Successful entrepreneurs share six common themes that describe their attitudes and ways of thinking and acting.
3. Rather than being inborn, the behaviors inherent in these six attributes can be nurtured, learned, and encouraged, which successful entrepreneurs model for themselves and those with whom they work.
4. Entrepreneurs love competition and actually avoid risks when they can, preferring carefully calculated risks.
5. Entrepreneurship can be learned; it requires an apprenticeship.
6. Most entrepreneurs gain the apprenticeship over 10 years or more after the age of 21 and acquire networks, skills, and the ability to recognize business patterns.
7. The entrepreneurial mind-set can benefit large, established companies today just as much as smaller firms.
8. Many myths and realities about entrepreneurship provide insights for aspiring entrepreneurs.
9. A word of caution: IQ tests, SATs, GMATs, LSATs, and others do not measure some of the most important entrepreneurial abilities and aptitudes.
10. Most successful entrepreneurs have had a personal strategy to help them achieve their dreams and goals, both implicitly and explicitly.
11. The principal task for the entrepreneur is to determine what kind of entrepreneur he or she wants to become based on his or her attitudes, behaviors, management competencies, experience, and so forth.
12. Self-assessment is the hardest thing for entrepreneurs to do, but if you don't do it, you will really get into trouble. If you don't do it, who will?

Study Questions

1. Who was Ewing Marion Kauffman, what did he do, and what was his philosophy of entrepreneurial leadership?
2. What is the difference between a manager and a leader?
3. Define the six major themes that characterize the mind-sets, attitudes, and actions of a successful entrepreneur. Which are most important, and why? How can they be encouraged and developed?
4. Entrepreneurs are made, not born. Why is this so? Do you agree, and why or why not?
5. Explain what is meant by the apprenticeship concept, and why is it so important to young entrepreneurs?
6. What is your personal entrepreneurial strategy? How should it change?
7. "What is one person's ham is another person's poison." What does this mean?
8. Can you evaluate thoroughly your attraction to entrepreneurship?
9. Who should be an entrepreneur and who should not?

MIND STRETCHERS

Have you considered?

1. Who can be an entrepreneur, and who cannot? Why?
2. Why has there been a 30-year brain drain of the best entrepreneurial talent in America away from the largest established companies? Can this be reversed? How?
3. How do you personally stack up against the six entrepreneurial mind-sets? What do you need to develop and improve?
4. If you work for a larger company, what is it doing to attract and keep the best entrepreneurial talent?
5. How would you describe and evaluate your own apprenticeship? What else has to happen?
6. Is Bill Gates an entrepreneur, a leader, a manager? How can we know?
7. How will you personally define success in 5, 10, and 25 years? Why?
8. Assume that at age 40 to 50 years, you have achieved a net worth of $25 million to $50 million in today's dollars. So what? Then what?
9. David Neeleman, founder of Jet Blue, was already very wealthy from his success at Morris Air and Southwest Air. So why did he start Jet Blue, and what might he revolutionize next?
10. Great athletic talent is not equal to a great athlete. Why? How does this apply to entrepreneurship?

Exercise

Crafting a Personal Entrepreneurial Strategy

If you don't know where you're going, any path will take you there.

From *The Wizard of Oz*

Crafting a personal entrepreneurial strategy can be viewed as the personal equivalent of developing a business plan. As with planning in other situations, the process itself is more important than the plan.

The key is the process and discipline that put an individual in charge of evaluating and shaping choices and initiating action that makes sense, rather than letting things just happen. Having a longer-term sense of direction can be highly motivating. It also can be extremely helpful in determining when to say no (which is much harder than saying yes) and can temper impulsive hunches with a more thoughtful strategic purpose. This is important because today's choices, whether or not they are thought out, become tomorrow's track record. They may end up shaping an entrepreneur in ways that he or she may not find so attractive 10 years hence and, worse, may also result in failure to obtain just those experiences needed in order to have high-quality opportunities later on.

Therefore, a personal strategy can be invaluable, but it need not be a prison sentence. It is a point of departure, rather than a contract of indenture, and it can and will change over time. This process of developing a personal strategy for an entrepreneurial career is a very individual one and, in a sense, one of self-selection. One experienced venture capital investor in small ventures, Louis L. Allen, shares this view of the importance of the role of self-selection:

> Unlike the giant firm which has recruiting and selection experts to screen the wheat from the chaff, the small business firm, which comprises the most common economic unit in our business systems, cannot afford to employ a personnel manager. . . . More than that, there's something very special about the selection of the owners: they have selected themselves. . . . As I face self-selected top managers across my desk or visit them in their plants or offices I have become more and more impressed with the fact that this self-selection process is far more important to the success or failure of the company than the monetary aspects of our negotiations.

Reasons for planning are similar to those for developing a business plan (see Chapter 6). Planning helps an entrepreneur to manage the risks and uncertainties of the future; helps him or her to work smarter, rather than simply harder; keeps him or her in a future-oriented frame of mind; helps him or her to develop and update a keener strategy by testing the sensibility of his or her ideas and approaches with others; helps motivate; gives him or her a "results orientation"; helps be effective in managing and coping with what is by nature a stressful role; and so forth.

Rationalizations and reasons given for not planning, like those that will be covered in Chapter 6, are that plans are out of date as soon as they are finished and that no one knows what tomorrow will bring and, therefore, it is dangerous to commit to uncertainty. Further, the cautious, anxious person may find that setting personal goals creates a further source of tension and pressure and a heightened fear of failure. There is also the possibility that future or yet unknown options, which actually might be more attractive than the one chosen, may become lost or be excluded.

Commitment to a career-oriented goal, particularly for an entrepreneur who is younger and lacks much real-world experience, can be premature. For the person who is inclined to be a compulsive and obsessive competitor and achiever, goal setting may add gasoline to the fire. And, invariably, some events and environmental factors beyond one's control may boost or sink the best-laid plans.

Personal plans fail for the same reasons as business plans, including frustration when the plan appears not to work immediately and problems of changing behavior from an activity-oriented routine to one that is goal-oriented. Other problems are developing plans that are based on admirable missions, such as improving performance, rather than goals, and developing plans that fail to anticipate obstacles, and those that lack progress milestones, reviews, and so forth.

A Conceptual Scheme for Self-Assessment

Exhibit 1.10 shows one conceptual scheme for thinking about the self-assessment process called the Johari Window. According to this scheme, there are two sources of information about the self: the individual and others. According to the Johari Window, there are three areas in which individuals can learn about themselves.

There are two potential obstacles to self-assessment efforts. First, it is hard to obtain feedback; second, it is hard to receive and benefit from it. Everyone possesses a personal frame of reference, values, and so forth, which influence first impressions. It is, therefore, almost impossible for an individual to obtain an unbiased view of himself or herself from someone else. Further, in most social situations, people usually present self-images that they want to preserve, protect, and defend, and behavioral norms usually exist that prohibit people from telling a person that he or she is presenting a face or impression that differs from what the person thinks is being presented. For example, most people will not point out to a stranger during a conversation that a piece of spinach is prominently dangling from between his or her front teeth.

The first step for an individual in self-assessment is to generate data through observation of his or her thoughts and actions and by getting feedback from others for the purposes of (1) becoming aware of blind spots and (2) reinforcing or changing existing perceptions of both strengths and weaknesses.

Once an individual has generated the necessary data, the next steps in the self-assessment process are to study the data generated, develop insights, and then establish apprenticeship goals to gain any learning, experience, and so forth.

Finally, choices can be made in terms of goals and opportunities to be created or seized.

Crafting an Entrepreneurial Strategy

Profiling the Past

One useful way to begin the process of self-assessment and planning is for an individual to think about his or her entrepreneurial roots (what he or she has done, his or her preferences in terms of lifestyle and work style, etc.) and couple this with a look into the future and what he or she would like most to be doing and how he or she would like to live.

In this regard, everyone has a personal history that has played and will continue to play a significant role in influencing his or her values, motivations, attitudes, and behaviors. Some of this history may provide useful insight into prior entrepreneurial inclinations, as well as into his or her future potential fit with an entrepreneurial role. Unless an entrepreneur is enjoying what he or she is doing for work most of the time, when in his or her 30s, 40s, or 50s, having a great deal of money without enjoying the journey will be a very hollow success.

Profiling the Present

It is useful to profile the present. Possession of certain personal entrepreneurial attitudes and behaviors (i.e., an "entrepreneurial mind") has been linked to successful careers in entrepreneurship. These attitudes and behaviors deal with such factors as commitment, determination, and perseverance; the drive to achieve and grow; an orientation toward goals; the taking of initiative and personal responsibility; and so forth.

In addition, various role demands result from the pursuit of opportunities. These role demands are external in the

EXHIBIT 1.10

Peeling the Onion

	Known to Entrepreneur and Team	**Not Known to Entrepreneur and Team**
Known to Prospective Investors and Stakeholders	Area 1 *Known area:* (what you see is what you get)	Area 2 *Blind area:* (we do not know what we do not know, but you do)
Not Known to Prospective Investors and Stakeholders	Area 3 *Hidden area:* (unshared—you do not know what we do, but the deal does not get done until we find out)	Area 4 *Unknown area:* (no venture is certain or risk free)

Source: McIntyre, James; Rubin, Irwin M.; Kolb, David A, Organizational Psychology: Experiential Approach 2nd Edition, © 1974. Adapted by permission of Pearson Education, Inc., Upper Saddle River, NJ.

sense that they are imposed upon every entrepreneur by the nature of entrepreneurship. As will be discussed in Chapter 6, the external business environment is given, the demands of a higher potential business in terms of stress and commitment are given, and the ethical values and integrity of key actors are given. Required as a result of the demands, pressures, and realities of starting, owning, and operating a substantial business are such factors as accommodation to the venture, toleration of stress, and so forth. A realistic appraisal of entrepreneurial attitudes and behaviors in light of the requirements of the entrepreneurial role is useful as part of the self-assessment process.

Also, part of any self-assessment is an assessment of management competencies and what "chunks" of experience, know-how, and contacts need to be developed.

Getting Constructive Feedback

A Scottish proverb says, "The greatest gift that God hath given us is to see ourselves as others see us." One common denominator among successful entrepreneurs is a desire to know how they are doing and where they stand. They have an uncanny knack for asking the right questions about their performance at the right time. This thirst to know is driven by a keen awareness that such feedback is vital to improving their performance and their odds for success.

Receiving feedback from others can be a most demanding experience. The following list of guidelines in receiving feedback can help:

- Feedback needs to be solicited, ideally, from those who know the individual well (e.g., someone he or she has worked with or for) and who can be trusted. The context in which the person is known needs to be considered. For example, a business colleague may be better able to comment upon an individual's managerial skills than a friend. Or a personal friend may be able to comment on motivation or on the possible effects on the family situation. It is helpful to chat with the person before asking him or her to provide any specific written impressions and to indicate the specific areas he or she can best comment upon. One way to do this is to formulate questions first. For example, the person could be told, "I've been asking myself the following question . . . and I would really like your impressions in that regard."
- Specific comments in areas that are particularly important either personally or to the success of the venture need to be solicited and more detail probed if the person giving feedback is not clear. A good way to check if a statement is being understood correctly is to paraphrase the statement. The person needs to be encouraged to describe and give examples of specific situations or behaviors that have influenced the impressions he or she has developed.
- Feedback is most helpful if it is neither all positive nor all negative.
- Feedback needs to be obtained in writing so that the person can take some time to think about the issues, and so feedback from various sources can be pulled together.
- The person asking for feedback needs to be honest and straightforward with himself or herself and with others.
- Time is too precious and the road to new venture success too treacherous to clutter this activity with game playing or hidden agendas. The person receiving feedback needs to avoid becoming defensive and taking negative comments personally.
- It is important to listen carefully to what is being said and think about it. Answering, debating, or rationalizing should be avoided.
- An assessment of whether the person soliciting feedback has considered all important information and has been realistic in his or her inferences and conclusions needs to be made.
- Help needs to be requested in identifying common threads or patterns, possible implications of self-assessment data and certain weaknesses (including alternative inferences or conclusions), and other relevant information that is missing.
- Additional feedback from others needs to be sought to verify feedback and to supplement the data.
- Reaching final conclusions or decisions needs to be left until a later time.

Putting It All Together

Exhibit 1.11 shows the relative fit of an entrepreneur with a venture opportunity, given his or her relevant attitudes and behaviors and relevant general management skills, experience, know-how, and contacts, and given the role demands of the venture opportunity. A clean appraisal is almost impossible. Self-assessment just is not that simple. The process is cumulative, and what an entrepreneur does about weaknesses, for example, is far more important than what the particular weaknesses might be. After all, everyone has weaknesses.

Thinking Ahead

As it is in developing business plans, goal setting is important in personal planning. Few people are effective goal setters. Perhaps fewer than 5 percent have ever committed their goals to writing, and perhaps fewer than 25 percent of adults even set goals mentally.

Again, goal setting is a process, a way of dealing with the world. Effective goal setting demands time, self-discipline, commitment and dedication, and practice. Goals, once set, do not become static targets.

A number of distinct steps are involved in goal setting, steps that are repeated over and over as conditions change:

- Establishment of goals which are specific and concrete (rather than abstract and out of focus), measurable, related to time (i.e., specific about what will be accomplished over a certain time period), realistic, and attainable.

EXHIBIT 1.11

Fit of the Entrepreneur and the Venture Opportunity

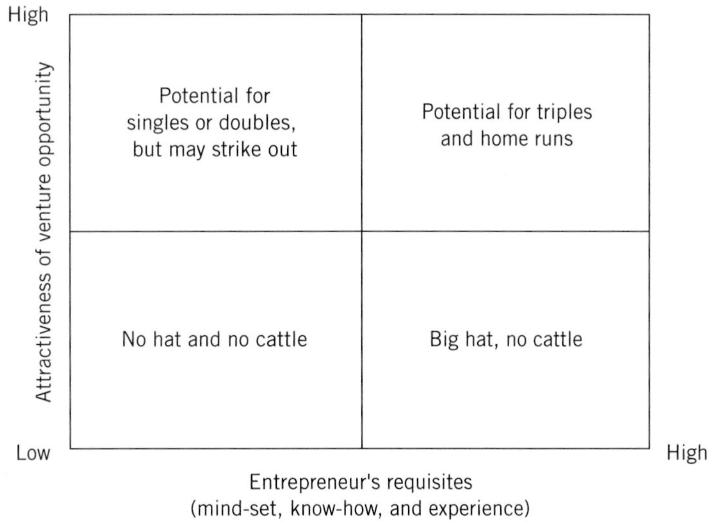

- Establishment of priorities, including the identification of conflicts and trade-offs and how these can be resolved.
- Identification of potential problems and obstacles that could prevent goals from being attained.
- Specification of action steps that are to be performed to accomplish the goal.
- Indication of how results will be measured.
- Establishment of milestones for reviewing progress and tying these to specific dates on a calendar.
- Identification of risks involved in meeting the goals.
- Identification of help and other resources that may be needed to obtain goals.
- Periodic review of progress and revision of goals.

Exercise

Personal Entrepreneurial Strategy

The exercise that follows will help you gather data, both from yourself and from others, evaluate the data you have collected, and craft a personal entrepreneurial strategy.

The exercise requires active participation on your part. The estimated time to complete the exercise is 1.5 to 3 hours. Those who have completed the exercise—students, practicing entrepreneurs, and others—report that the self-assessment process was worthwhile and it was also demanding. Issues addressed will require a great deal of thought, and there are, of course, no wrong answers.

Although this is a self-assessment exercise, it is useful to receive feedback. Whether you choose to solicit feedback and how much, if any, of the data you have collected you choose to share with others is your decision. The exercise will be of value only to the extent that you are honest and realistic in your approach.

A complex set of factors clearly goes into making someone a successful entrepreneur. No individual has all the personal qualities, managerial skills, and the like, indicated in the exercise. And, even if an individual did possess most of these, his or her values, preferences, and such may make him or her a very poor risk to succeed as an entrepreneur.

The presence or absence of any single factor does not guarantee success or failure as an entrepreneur. Before proceeding, remember, it is no embarrassment to reach for the stars and fail to reach them. It is a failure not to reach for the stars.

Name:

Date:

Part I: Profile of the Past

STEP 1

Examine Your Personal Preferences.

What gives you energy, and why? These are things from either work or leisure, or both, that give you the greatest amount of personal satisfaction, sense of enjoyment, and energy.

Source of Energy	Reason

What takes away your energy, and why? These create for you the greatest amount of personal dissatisfaction, anxiety, or discontent and take away your energy and motivation.

Source of Energy	Reason

Rank (from the most to the least) the items you have listed above:

Gives Energy	Takes Energy

In 20 to 30 years, how would you like to spend an ideal month? Include in your description your desired lifestyle, work style, income, friends, and so forth, and a comment about what attracts you to, and what repels you about, this ideal existence.

Review the idea generation guide you completed in Chapter 4 and list the common attributes of the 10 businesses you wanted to enter and the 10 businesses you did not:

Attributes—Would Energize	**Attributes—Would Turn Off**

Which of these attributes would give you energy and which would take it away, and why?

Attribute	**Give or Take Energy**	**Reason**

Complete this sentence: "I would/would not like to start/acquire my own business someday because . . ."

Discuss any patterns, issues, insights, and conclusions that have emerged:

Rank the following in terms of importance to you:

	Important	←	———	→	Irrelevant
Location	5	4	3	2	1
Geography (particular area)	5	4	3	2	1
Community size and nature	5	4	3	2	1
Community involvement	5	4	3	2	1
Commuting distance (one way):					
20 minutes or less	5	4	3	2	1
30 minutes or less	5	4	3	2	1
60 minutes or less	5	4	3	2	1
More than 60 minutes	5	4	3	2	1
Lifestyle and Work Style					
Size of business:					
Less than $1 million sales or under 5–10 employees	5	4	3	2	1
More than $1 million sales or 5–10 employees	5	4	3	2	1
More than $10 million sales and 40–50 employees	5	4	3	2	1
Rate of real growth:					
Fast (over 25%/year)	5	4	3	2	1
Moderate (10% to 15%/year)	5	4	3	2	1
Slow (less than 10%/year)	5	4	3	2	1
Workload (weekly):					
Over 70 hours	5	4	3	2	1
55 to 60 hours	5	4	3	2	1
40 hours or less	5	4	3	2	1
Marriage	5	4	3	2	1
Family	5	4	3	2	1
Travel away from home:					
More than 60%	5	4	3	2	1
30% to 60%	5	4	3	2	1
Less than 30%	5	4	3	2	1
None	5	4	3	2	1
Standard of Living					
Tight belt/later capital gains	5	4	3	2	1
Average/limited capital gains	5	4	3	2	1
High/no capital gains	5	4	3	2	1
Become very rich	5	4	3	2	1
Personal Development					
Utilization of skill and education	5	4	3	2	1
Opportunity for personal growth	5	4	3	2	1
Contribution to society	5	4	3	2	1
Positioning for opportunities	5	4	3	2	1
Generation of significant contacts, experience, and know-how	5	4	3	2	1
Status and Prestige	5	4	3	2	1
Impact on Ecology and Environment: Sustainability	5	4	3	2	1
Capital Required					
From you	5	4	3	2	1
From others	5	4	3	2	1
Other Considerations	5	4	3	2	1

Imagine you had $1,000 with which to buy the items you ranked on the previous page. Indicate below how you would allocate the money. For example, the item that is most important should receive the greatest amount. You may spend nothing on some items, you may spend equal amounts on some, and so forth. Once you have allocated the $1,000, rank the items in order of importance, the most important being number 1.

Item	Share of $1,000	Rank
Location		
Lifestyle and work style		
Standard of living		
Personal development		
Status and prestige		
Ecology and environment		
Capital required		
Other considerations		

STEP 2

Examine Your Personal History

List activities (1) that have provided you financial support in the past (e.g., a part-time or full-time job, a paper route), (2) that have contributed to your well-being (e.g., financing your education or a hobby), and (3) that you have done on your own (e.g., building something).

Discuss why you became involved in each of the activities above and what specifically influenced each of your decisions.

Discuss what you learned about yourself, about self-employment, about managing people, and about making money.

List and discuss your full-time work experience, including descriptions of specific tasks for which you had responsibility, specific skills you used, the number of people you supervised, whether you were successful, and so forth.

Discuss why you became involved in each of the employment situations above and what specifically influenced each of your decisions.

Discuss what you learned about yourself, about employment, about managing people, and about making money.

List and discuss other activities, such as sports, in which you have participated and indicate whether each activity was individual (e.g., chess or tennis) or team (e.g., football).

What lessons and insights emerged, and how will these apply to life as an entrepreneur?

If you have ever been fired from or quit either a full-time or part-time job, indicate the job, why you were fired or quit, the circumstances, and what you have learned and what difference this has made.

If you changed jobs or relocated, indicate the job, why the change occurred, the circumstances, and what you have learned from those experiences.

Among those individuals who have influenced you most, do any own and operate their own businesses or engage independently in a profession (e.g., certified public accountant)?

How have the people above influenced you? How do you view them and their roles? What have you learned from them about self-employment? Include a discussion of the things that attract or repel you, the trade-offs they have had to consider, the risks they have faced and rewards they have enjoyed, and entry strategies that have worked for them.

If you have ever started a business of any kind or worked in a small company, list the things you liked most and those you liked least, and why.

Like Most	**Reason**	**Like Least**	**Reason**

If you have ever worked for a larger company (over 500 employees or about $50 million to $60 million in sales), list the things you liked most and those you liked least about your work, and why.

Like Most	**Reason**	**Like Least**	**Reason**

Summarize those factors in your history that you believe are entrepreneurial strengths or weaknesses.

Strengths	**Weaknesses**

Part II: Profile of the Present: Where You Are

STEP 1

Examine Your "Entrepreneurial Mind."

Examine your attitudes, behaviors, and know-how. Rank yourself (on a scale of 5 to 1)

	Strongest	←	———	→	**Weakest**
Commitment and Determination					
Decisiveness	5	4	3	2	1
Tenacity	5	4	3	2	1
Discipline	5	4	3	2	1
Persistence in solving problems	5	4	3	2	1
Willingness to sacrifice	5	4	3	2	1
Total immersion	5	4	3	2	1
Opportunity Obsession					
Having knowledge of customers' needs	5	4	3	2	1
Being market driven	5	4	3	2	1
Obsession with value creation and enhancement	5	4	3	2	1
Tolerance of Risk, Ambiguity, and Uncertainty					
Calculated risk-taker	5	4	3	2	1
Risk minimizer	5	4	3	2	1
Risk sharer					
Tolerance of uncertainty and lack of structure	5	4	3	2	1
Tolerance of stress and conflict	5	4	3	2	1
Ability to resolve problems and integrate solutions	5	4	3	2	1

	Strongest	←	———	→	Weakest
Creativity, Self-Reliance, and Ability to Adapt					
Nonconventional, open-minded, lateral thinker	5	4	3	2	1
Restlessness with status quo	5	4	3	2	1
Ability to adapt	5	4	3	2	1
Lack of fear of failure	5	4	3	2	1
Ability to conceptualize and to "sweat details" (helicopter mind)	5	4	3	2	1
Motivation to Excel					
Goal and results orientation	5	4	3	2	1
Drive to achieve and grow (self-imposed)	5	4	3	2	1
Low need for status and power	5	4	3	2	1
Ability to be interpersonally supporting (versus competitive)	5	4	3	2	1
Awareness of weaknesses (and strengths)	5	4	3	2	1
Having perspective and sense of humor	5	4	3	2	1
Leadership					
Being self-starter	5	4	3	2	1
Having internal locus of control	5	4	3	2	1
Having integrity and reliability	5	4	3	2	1
Having patience	5	4	3	2	1
Being team builder and hero maker	5	4	3	2	1

Summarize your entrepreneurial strengths.

Summarize your entrepreneurial weaknesses.

STEP 2

Examine Entrepreneurial Role Requirements.

Rank where you fit in the following roles.

	Strongest	←	———	→	Weakest
Accommodation to Venture					
Extent to which career and venture are No. 1 priority	5	4	3	2	1
Stress					
The cost of accommodation	5	4	3	2	1
Values					
Extent to which conventional values are held	5	4	3	2	1
Ethics and Integrity	5	4	3	2	1

Summarize your strengths and weaknesses.

STEP 3

Examine Your Management Competencies.
Rank your skills and competencies below.

	Strongest	←	———	→	Weakest
Marketing					
Market research and evaluation	5	4	3	2	1
Marketing planning	5	4	3	2	1
Product pricing	5	4	3	2	1
Sales management	5	4	3	2	1
Direct mail/catalog selling	5	4	3	2	1
Telemarketing	5	4	3	2	1
Customer service	5	4	3	2	1
Distribution management	5	4	3	2	1
Product management	5	4	3	2	1
New product planning	5	4	3	2	1
Operations/Production					
Manufacturing management	5	4	3	2	1
Inventory control	5	4	3	2	1
Cost analysis and control	5	4	3	2	1
Quality control	5	4	3	2	1
Production scheduling and flow	5	4	3	2	1
Purchasing	5	4	3	2	1
Job evaluation	5	4	3	2	1
Finance					
Accounting	5	4	3	2	1
Capital budgeting	5	4	3	2	1
Cash flow management	5	4	3	2	1
Credit and collection management	5	4	3	2	1
Managing relations with financial sources	5	4	3	2	1
Short-term financing	5	4	3	2	1
Public and private offerings	5	4	3	2	1
Administration					
Problem solving	5	4	3	2	1
Communications	5	4	3	2	1
Planning	5	4	3	2	1
Decision making	5	4	3	2	1
Project management	5	4	3	2	1
Negotiating	5	4	3	2	1
Personnel administration	5	4	3	2	1
Management information systems	5	4	3	2	1
Computer/IT/www	5	4	3	2	1
Interpersonal/Team					
Leadership/vision/influence	5	4	3	2	1
Helping and coaching	5	4	3	2	1

	Strongest	←	———	→	Weakest
Marketing					
Feedback	5	4	3	2	1
Conflict management	5	4	3	2	1
Teamwork and people management	5	4	3	2	1
Law					
Corporations	5	4	3	2	1
Contracts	5	4	3	2	1
Taxes	5	4	3	2	1
Securities	5	4	3	2	1
Intellectual property rights and patents	5	4	3	2	1
Real estate law	5	4	3	2	1
Bankruptcy	5	4	3	2	1
Unique Skills	5	4	3	2	1

STEP 4

Based on an Analysis of the Information Given in Steps 1–3, Indicate the Items You Would Add to a "Do" List.

Part III: Getting Constructive Feedback

Part III is an organized way for you to gather constructive feedback. (If you choose not to get constructive feedback at this time, proceed to Part IV.)

STEP 1

(Optional) Give a Copy of Your Answers to Parts I and II to the Person Designated to Evaluate Your Responses. Ask Him or Her to Answer the Following:
Have you been honest, objective, hard-nosed, and complete in evaluating your skills?

Are there any strengths and weaknesses you have inventoried incorrectly?

Are there other events or past actions that might affect this analysis and that have not been addressed?

STEP 2

Solicit Feedback.
Give one copy of the feedback form (begins on the next page) to each person who has been asked to evaluate your responses.

Feedback Form

Feedback for:

Prepared by:

STEP 1

Please Check the Appropriate Column Next to the Statements about the Entrepreneurial Attributes, and Add Any Additional Comments You May Have:

	Strong	Adequate	Weak	No Comment
Commitment and Determination				
Decisiveness	S	A	W	NC
Tenacity	S	A	W	NC
Discipline	S	A	W	NC
Persistence in solving problems	S	A	W	NC
Willingness to sacrifice	S	A	W	NC
Total immersion	S	A	W	NC
Opportunity Obsession				
Having knowledge of customer's needs	S	A	W	NC
Being market driven	S	A	W	NC
Obsession with value creation and enhancement	S	A	W	NC
Tolerance of Risk, Ambiguity, and Uncertainty				
Calculated risk-taker	S	A	W	NC
Risk minimizer	S	A	W	NC
Risk sharer	S	A	W	NC
Tolerance of uncertainty and lack of structure	S	A	W	NC
Tolerance of stress and conflict	S	A	W	NC
Ability to resolve problems and integrate solutions	S	A	W	NC
Creativity, Self-Reliance, and Ability to Adapt				
Nonconventional, open-minded, lateral thinker	S	A	W	NC
Restlessness with status quo	S	A	W	NC
Ability to adapt	S	A	W	NC
Lack of fear of failure	S	A	W	NC
Ability to conceptualize and to "sweat details" (helicopter mind)	S	A	W	NC
Motivation to Excel				
Goal and results orientation	S	A	W	NC
Drive to achieve and grow (self-imposed standards)	S	A	W	NC
Low need for status and power	S	A	W	NC
Ability to be interpersonally supportive (versus competitive)	S	A	W	NC
Awareness of weaknesses (and strengths)	S	A	W	NC
Having perspective and sense of humor	S	A	W	NC
Leadership				
Being self-starter	S	A	W	NC
Having internal locus of control	S	A	W	NC
Having integrity and reliability	S	A	W	NC
Having patience	S	A	W	NC
Being team builder and hero maker	S	A	W	NC

Please make any comments that you can on such matters as my energy, health, and emotional stability; my creativity and innovativeness; my intelligence; my capacity to inspire; my values; and so forth.

STEP 2

Please Check the Appropriate Column Next to the Statements about Entrepreneurial Role Requirements to Indicate My Fit and Add Any Additional Comments You May Have.

	Strong	Adequate	Weak	No Comment
Accommodation to venture	S	A	W	NC
Stress (cost of accommodation)	S	A	W	NC
Values (conventional economic and professional values of free enterprise system)	S	A	W	NC
Ethics and integrity	S	A	W	NC

Additional Comments:

STEP 3

Please Check the Appropriate Column Next to the Statements about Management Competencies, and Add Any Additional Comments You May Have.

	Strong	Adequate	Weak	No Comment
Marketing				
Market research and evaluation	S	A	W	NC
Marketing planning	S	A	W	NC
Product pricing	S	A	W	NC
Sales management	S	A	W	NC
Direct mail/catalog selling	S	A	W	NC
Telemarketing	S	A	W	NC
Customer service	S	A	W	NC
Distribution management	S	A	W	NC
Product management	S	A	W	NC
New product planning	S	A	W	NC
Operations/Production				
Manufacturing management	S	A	W	NC
Inventory control	S	A	W	NC
Cost analysis and control	S	A	W	NC
Quality control	S	A	W	NC
Production scheduling and flow	S	A	W	NC
Purchasing	S	A	W	NC
Job evaluation	S	A	W	NC
Finance				
Accounting	S	A	W	NC
Capital budgeting	S	A	W	NC
Cash flow management	S	A	W	NC
Credit and collection management	S	A	W	NC
Managing relations with financial sources	S	A	W	NC
Short-term financing	S	A	W	NC
Public and private offerings	S	A	W	NC
Administration				
Problem solving	S	A	W	NC
Communications	S	A	W	NC
Planning	S	A	W	NC
Decision making	S	A	W	NC
Project management	S	A	W	NC
Negotiating	S	A	W	NC
Personnel administration	S	A	W	NC
Management information systems	S	A	W	NC
Computer/IT/www	S	A	W	NC

	Strong	Adequate	Weak	No Comment
Interpersonal/Team				
Leadership/vision/influence	S	A	W	NC
Helping and coaching	S	A	W	NC
Feedback	S	A	W	NC
Conflict management	S	A	W	NC
Teamwork and people management	S	A	W	NC
Law				
Corporations	S	A	W	NC
Contracts	S	A	W	NC
Taxes	S	A	W	NC
Securities	S	A	W	NC
Intellectual property rights and patents	S	A	W	NC
Real estate law	S	A	W	NC
Bankruptcy	S	A	W	NC
Unique Skills	S	A	W	NC

Additional Comments:

STEP 4

Please Evaluate My Strengths and Weaknesses.

In what area or areas do you see my greatest potential or existing strengths in terms of the venture opportunity we have discussed, and why?

Area of Strength	Reason

In what area or areas do you see my greatest potential or existing weaknesses in terms of the venture opportunity we have discussed, and why?

Area Weakness	Reason

If you know my partners and the venture opportunity, what is your evaluation of their fit with me and the fit among them?

Given the venture opportunity, what you know of my partners, and your evaluation of my weaknesses, should I consider any additional members for my management team? If so, what should be their strengths and relevant experience?

Please make any other suggestions that would be helpful for me to consider (e.g., comments about what you see that I like to do, my lifestyle, work style, patterns evident in my skills inventory, the implications of my particular constellation of management strengths and weaknesses and background, the time implications of an apprenticeship).

Part IV: Putting It All Together

STEP 1

Reflect on Your Previous Responses and the Feedback You Have Solicited or Have Received Informally (from Class Discussion or from Discussions with Friends, Parents, Etc.).

STEP 2

Assess Your Entrepreneurial Strategy.

What have you concluded at this point about entrepreneurship and you?

How do the requirements of entrepreneurship—especially the sacrifices, total immersion, heavy workload, and long-term commitment—fit with your own aims, values, and motivations?

What specific conflicts do you anticipate between your aims and values, and the demands of entrepreneurship?

How would you compare your entrepreneurial mind, your fit with entrepreneurial role demands, your management competencies, and so forth, with those of other people you know who have pursued or are pursuing an entrepreneurial career?

Think ahead 5 to 10 years or more, and assume that you would want to launch or acquire a higher potential venture. What "chunks" of experience and know-how do you need to accumulate?

What are the implications of this assessment of your entrepreneurial strategy in terms of whether you should proceed with your current venture opportunity?

What is it about the specific opportunity you want to pursue that will provide you with sustained energy and motivation? How do you know this?

At this time, given your major entrepreneurial strengths and weaknesses and your specific venture opportunity, are there other "chunks" of experience and know-how you need to acquire or attract to your team? (Be specific!)

What other issues or questions have been raised for you at this point that you would like answered?

What opportunities would you most want to be in a position to create/pursue in 5 to 10 years? What are the implications for new skills, know-how, mentors, team members, and resources?

Part V: Thinking Ahead

Part V considers the crafting of your personal entrepreneurial strategy. Remember, goals should be specific and concrete, measurable, and, except where indicated below, realistic and attainable.

STEP 1

List, in Three Minutes, Your Goals to Be Accomplished by the Time You Are 70.

STEP 2

List, in Three Minutes, Your Goals to Be Accomplished over the Next Seven Years. (If You Are an Undergraduate, Use the Next Four Years.)

STEP 3

List, in Three Minutes, the Goals You Would Like to Accomplish If You Have Exactly One Year from Today to Live. Assume You Would Enjoy Good Health in the Interim but Would Not Be Able to Acquire Any More Life Insurance or Borrow an Additional Large Sum of Money for a "Final Fling." Assume Further That You Could Spend That Last Year of Your Life Doing Whatever You Want to Do.

STEP 4

List, in Six Minutes, Your Real Goals and the Goals You Would Like to Accomplish over Your Lifetime.

STEP 5

Discuss the List from Step 4 with Another Person and Then Refine and Clarify Your Goal Statements.

STEP 6

Rank Your Goals According to Priority.

STEP 7

Concentrate on the Top Three Goals and Make a List of Problems, Obstacles, Inconsistencies, and So Forth, That You Will Encounter in Trying to Reach Each of These Goals.

STEP 8

Decide and State How You Will Eliminate Any Important Problems, Obstacles, Inconsistencies, and So Forth.

STEP 9

For Your Top Three Goals, Write Down All the Tasks or Action Steps You Need to Take to Help You Attain Each Goal and Indicate How Results Will Be Measured.
It is helpful to organize the goals in order of priority.

Goal	Task/Action Step	Measurement	Rank

STEP 10

Rank Tasks/Action Steps in Terms of Priority.

To identify high-priority items, it is helpful to make a copy of your list and cross off any activities or task that cannot be completed, or at least begun, in the next seven days, and then identify the single most important goal, the next most important, and so forth.

STEP 11

Establish Dates and Durations (and, If Possible, a Place) for Tasks/Action Steps to Begin.

Organize tasks/action steps according to priority. If possible, the date should be during the next seven days.

Goal	Task/Action Step	Measurement	Rank

STEP 12

Make a List of Problems, Obstacles, Inconsistencies, and So Forth.

STEP 13

Decide How You Will Eliminate Any Important Problems, Obstacles, Inconsistencies, and So Forth, and Adjust the List in Step 12.

STEP 14

Identify Risks Involved and Resources and Other Help Needed.

2

Chapter Two

America's Entrepreneurial Revolution Goes Global

We are in the midst of a silent revolution—a triumph of the creative and entrepreneurial spirit of humankind throughout the world.

I believe its impact on the 21st century will equal or exceed that of the Industrial Revolution in the 19th and 20th.

Jeffry A. Timmons
The Entrepreneurial Mind, 1989

Results Expected

Upon completion of this chapter, you will have:

1. Examined how the entrepreneurial revolution in the United States is beginning to have a profound impact on the rest of the world.
2. Learned how entrepreneurs, innovators, and their growing companies are the engine of wealth and job creation, innovation, and new industries, and how venture and risk capital fuels that engine.
3. Discovered how entrepreneurship is the principal source of philanthropy in America.
4. Learned why the American Dream is more alive and well than ever in our nation's history and is ready for the e-generation now.
5. Discovered how this revolution will drive future economic prosperity worldwide.

Entrepreneurship: A Global Movement

The evolution of entrepreneurship in America over the past 35 years has had an extraordinary impact on the cultural and economic landscape in the United States. While there will always be opportunities for improvement and innovation, America's entrepreneurial revolution has become a model for business people, educators, and policymakers around the globe. For example, as part of a goal to "make the EU the most competitive economy in the world by 2010," in 2000, an action plan was derived with the following broad objectives:

1. Fueling entrepreneurial mind-sets.
2. Encouraging more people to become entrepreneurs.
3. Gearing entrepreneurs for growth and competitiveness.
4. Improving the flow of finance.
5. Creating a more entrepreneurial-friendly regulatory and administrative framework.

These goals mirror the factors that have been critical in advancing entrepreneurship in the United States. In July 2004, an EU commission followed up on these goals with recommendations for fostering entrepreneurial mind-sets through school education. These too are reflective of the American experience:

- Introduce entrepreneurship into the national (or regional) curriculum at all levels of formal education (from primary school to university), either as a horizontal aspect or as a specific topic.
- Train and motivate teachers to engage in entrepreneurial education.
- Promote the application of programs based on "learning by doing," for instance, by means of project work, virtual firms, and mini-companies, etc.
- Involve entrepreneurs and local companies in the design and running of entrepreneurship courses and activities.
- Increase the teaching of entrepreneurship within higher education outside economic and business courses, notably at scientific and technical universities, and place emphasis on setting up companies in the curricula of business-type studies at universities.

Entrepreneurship is exploding in countries like India, China, and in the former Soviet bloc—and affecting positive social and economic change in such diverse countries as Korea, Mexico, South Africa, and Ireland. The Global Entrepreneurship Monitor (GEM) 2004 study found that in the 34 countries surveyed, 9.3 percent (73 million) of the 784 million people composing the population of 18- to 64-year-olds either were nascent entrepreneurs or were the owner/manager of a new business.[1] Significantly, 41 percent of these entrepreneurs were women.

In our roles as student, researcher, observer, and participant in this revolution, we can honestly say that global adoption of the entrepreneurial mind-set appears to be growing exponentially larger and faster. In our assessment, we are at the dawn of a new age of entrepreneurial reasoning, equity creation, and philanthropy, whose impact in the coming years will dwarf what we experienced over the last century.

Entrepreneurship: Innovation + Entrepreneurship = Prosperity and Philanthropy

Surely one of the most promising recent developments in the entrepreneurial revolution is entrepreneurship becoming a central, nonpartisan cornerstone in America's policy debates. Beyond the political rhetoric, which exploited the e-word in the last three presidential elections, the relevance and economic import of the entrepreneurial phenomenon have recently legitimized entrepreneurship as vital to any debate on our social economic policies. The creation of the National Commission on Entrepreneurship in 1999 launched an awareness of building educational initiative to assist legislators, governors, and policymakers to understand the contributions and potential of the entrepreneurial economy.

In addition to its numerous white papers and gatherings, the commission's efforts culminated in the Policy and Entrepreneurship Conference at the John F. Kennedy School of Government at Harvard University in April 2001. There was consensus among the attendees and speakers, including governors, congressmen, senators, entrepreneurs/CEOs, and academics, that entrepreneurship deserves a central presence in the policy agenda. Even more encouraging, in June 2001, the long-standing U.S. Senate Committee on Small Business changed its name to Small Business and Entrepreneurship, sending a very significant message. The National Governor's Association is also including entrepreneurship in its meetings and policy discussions.

The formidable link between public policy and entrepreneurial activity in the United States has become increasingly important. Politicians are now aware of this link and have begun to emphasize the ways entrepreneurship leads to greater national and global prosperity.

> *In every neighborhood in my hometown of Memphis, and all across America, I see young people tutoring and mentoring, building homes, caring for seniors, and feeding the hungry. I also see them using their entrepreneurial spirit to build companies, start non-profits, and drive our new economy.*
>
> Harold Ford, Jr., United States Representative
> 2000 Democratic National Convention Speech

Job Creation Twenty years ago, MIT researcher David Birch began to report his landmark findings that defied all previous notions that large established businesses were the backbone of the economy and the generator of new jobs. In fact, one Nobel Prize–winning economist gained his award by "proving" that any enterprise with fewer than 100 employees was irrelevant to the study of economics and policymaking! Birch stunned researchers, politicians, and the business world with just the opposite conclusion: New and growing smaller firms created 81.5 percent of the net new jobs in the economy from 1969 to 1976.[2] This general pattern has been repeated yearly. Since 1980,

[1] Z. J. Acs, P. Arenius, M. Hay, and M. Minniti, Babson College, London Business School, *Global Entrepreneurship Monitor, 2004 Executive Report*, p. 16.
[2] David L. Birch, 1979, The Job Creation Process, unpublished report, MIT Program on Neighborhood and Regional Change prepared for the Economic Development Administration, U.S. Department of Commerce, Washington, DC.

for instance, America has created over 34 million new jobs, while the Fortune 500 lost over 5 million jobs! Who creates these jobs? According to the U.S. Small Business Administration's Office of Advocacy, small businesses (those with fewer than 500 employees) represent more than 99 percent of all employers and provide about 75 percent of all new net jobs. *Inc.* magazine estimates that small companies employ somewhat more than half of the U.S. workforce. Entrepreneurial firms account for a significant amount of employment growth (defined by at least 20 percent a year for four years, from a base of at least $100,000 in revenues). These "gazelles," as David Birch calls them, make up only 3 percent of all firms but added 5 million jobs from 1994 to 1998. When one considers the history of Microsoft, a startup in the late 1970s, these job creation findings are not quite so surprising. In 1980, for instance, Microsoft had just $8 million in revenue and 38 employees. By the end of 2004, its sales were $21.8 billion, it had over 31,000 employees, and the total market value of its stock was $362.3 billion.

One can readily see the far-reaching change in employment patterns caused by this explosion of new companies. In the 1960s, about 1 in 4 persons worked for a Fortune 500 company. As recently as 1980, the Fortune 500 employed 20 percent of the workforce. Yet by the late 1990s, that number is just 1 in 14! This same pattern tells the story of the explosive growth of new regions and centers of technology and entrepreneurship throughout the country. It is impossible to name a new high growth area—starting with Silicon Valley and Boston, and extending to the Research Triangle of North Carolina; Austin, Texas; Denver/Boulder, Colorado; Indianapolis, Columbus, and Ann Arbor; or Atlanta, Georgia—without observing this same job-creation phenomenon from new and growing smaller companies.[3]

Twenty years later, innumerable research studies have examined and reexamined the job-creation statistics. The ultimate conclusion is the same, as reported in the most comprehensive study as recent as 1997:

> Small firms are generally the creators of jobs, as almost all firms begin small (because of resource constraints) and often need to grow to compete. Small firms create about 75 percent of the new net jobs.[4]

New Venture Formation

Classical entrepreneurship means new venture creation. But it is much more, as you shall discover throughout this chapter and book. It is arguably the single most powerful force to create economic and social mobility. Because it is opportunity-centered and rewards only for talent and performance—and could care less about religion, gender, skin color, social class, national origin, and the like—it enables people to pursue and realize their dreams, to falter and to try again, and to seek opportunities that match who they are, what they want to be, and how and where they want to live. No other employer can make this claim.

The role of *women and entrepreneurship* is particularly noteworthy. Consider what has happened in only one generation. In 1970, women-owned businesses were limited mainly to small service businesses and employed less than 1 million persons nationwide. They represented only 4 percent of all businesses. Analyzing data provided by the U.S. Bureau of the Census, the Center for Women's Business Research (www.nfwbo.org) projected that as of 2004, there were an estimated 10.6 million privately held, 50 percent or more women-owned firms in the United States, accounting for nearly half (47.7 percent) of all privately held firms in the country. These firms generated $2.46 trillion in sales and employed 19.1 million people nationwide. Between 1997 and 2002, the number of privately held majority or 50 percent women-owned businesses grew by 11 percent, or more than 1½ times the rate of all privately held firms (6 percent).[5]

Increasingly, women start businesses at a faster pace than men, and a growing portion are high-potential, higher growth companies. Pick up any issue of some of the leading business magazines, including *Fortune, BusinessWeek, Forbes, Inc., Success, or Fast Company,* and you will read eye-popping stories of remarkable women—and men—who are creating, reinventing, and transforming companies of all kinds into multi-million-dollar successes. Women entrepreneurs are without a doubt crucial to continued economic expansion.

A similar pattern can be seen for a variety of ethnic and racial groups (Exhibit 2.1). According to 1997 U.S. Census statistics, the number of African American–owned nonfarm businesses in the United States totaled 823,500 (4% of nonfarm businesses); they employed 718,300 people and generated $71.2 billion in revenues (compared to $1 million in 1990). Asian and Pacific Islander–owned businesses in the United States totaled about 913,000 (4% of the nation's nonfarm businesses), employed more than 2.2

[3] "The Valley of Money's Delight," *The Economist,* March 29, 1997, pp. 5–20.
[4] U.S. Small Business Administration Office of Advocacy, http://www.sba.gov, Small Business FAQ.
[5] *Completing the Picture: Equally-Owned Firms in 2002,* underwritten by Pitney Bowes Inc., Wells Fargo, NAWBO, Philadelphia Chapter, April 2003.

EXHIBIT 2.1

Growth of Entrepreneurship among Ethnic and Racial Groups

Ownership	Number of Firms Owned			Sales and Receipts (billion $)			Number of Employees (millions)		
	1992	1997+	% Increase	1992	1997+	% Increase	1992	1997+	% Increase
African American	620,912	780,770	25.7%	$32.2	$42.7	32.5%	.34	.71	108%
Hispanic	862,605	1,120,000	30.0	76.8	114.0	48.9	.69	1.30	88
Asian/ Pacific Islander	603,426	785,480	30.2	95.7	161.0	68.4	*	2.20	
American Indian/ Alaska Native	102,271	187,921	83.7	8.1	22.0	178.5	*	.30	

*Data unavailable as these two groups were combined in 1992 Census. Total employees for these groups combined in 1992 was 860,408.
+ Due to methodological variations, 1997 statistics have been adjusted to compare with 1992 data.
Source: U.S. Census Bureau 1997 and 1992 Economic Census.

million people, and generated $306.9 billion in revenues in 1997. American Indian and Alaska Native–owned businesses in the United States totaled 197,300 (0.9% of total nonfarm businesses), employed 298,700 people, and generated $34.3 billion in revenues in 1997. Hispanic-owned businesses totaled 1.2 million firms (6% of nonfarm businesses), employed over 1.3 million people, and generated $186.3 billion (1% of the $18.6 trillion for all businesses) in 1997.

American Dream: For the Young at Start!

Aspiring to work for oneself is deeply embedded in American culture, and has never been stronger. A 1994 Gallup Poll survey (crafted by Dr. Marilyn Kourilsky and sponsored by the Kauffman Center for Entrepreneurial Leadership, Ewing Marion Kauffman Foundation in Kansas City, showed just how lively and robust the American Dream is today. A national random sample of high school seniors were asked a number of questions about their future career aspirations. A stunning 70 percent said they wanted to own their own business! A generation earlier this would have been less than 10 percent. Further, 86 percent said they wanted to know more about entrepreneurship. Reflective of today's transformed economy, half of their parents said they would like to own their own business. In a 2004 Gallup Poll, 90 percent of American parents said they would approve if one or more of their children pursued entrepreneurship.

Also in 2004, *USA Today* asked a national sample of men and women if for one year they could take any job they wanted, what would that job be? The results reveal how ingrained the entrepreneurial persona has become in society; 47 percent of the women and 38 percent of the men said they would want to run their own company. Surprisingly, for the men, this was a higher percentage than those who said "professional athlete"!

Among corporate managers laid off as a result of downsizing, 70 percent are over 40 years of age and one-fifth of them are starting their own company. Other recent studies show that at any one time about 10% of the adult population is attempting to start a business of some kind.

Roper Starch polled the founders of *Inc.* magazine's 500 fastest growing firms in America between 1992 and 1996, and compared their responses with 200 high-level executives of Fortune 500 companies. Among the survey's conclusions:

- More than 90 percent of the *Inc.* 500 founders and 80 percent of the executives said smaller entrepreneurial companies have become role models for the way business should operate.
- Sixty-nine percent of the entrepreneurs, but only 40 percent of the executives, agreed with the statement "I love what I do for a living."
- Asked what would they do if they could live their lives over, more than one-third of the corporate executives said they would choose to run their own company.
- Employees seem to win more respect at young growing companies.[6]

Uniformly, the self-employed report the highest levels of personal satisfaction, challenge, pride, and

[6] *Fast Track*, "Building a Company Is the new American Dream," *The Boston Globe*, Oct. 1, 1997, p. D4.

EXHIBIT 2.2

Mega-Entrepreneurs Who Started in Their 20s

Entrepreneurial Company	Founder(s)
Microsoft	Bill Gates and Paul Allen
Netscape	Marc Andressen
Dell Computers	Michael Dell
Gateway 2000	Ted Waitt
McCaw Cellular	Craig McCaw
Apple Computers	Steve Jobs and Steve Wozniak
Digital Equipment Corporation	Ken and Stan Olsen
Federal Express	Fred Smith
Google	Larry Page Sergey Brin
Genentech	Robert Swanson
Polaroid	Edward Land
Nike	Phil Knight
Lotus Development Corporation	Mitch Kapor
Ipix.com	Kevin McCurdy
Yahoo!	David Filo Jerry Yang

remuneration. They seem to love the entrepreneurial game for its own sake. They love their work because it is invigorating, energizing, and meaningful. Entrepreneurs, as they invent, mold, recognize, and pursue opportunities, are the genius and energy behind this extraordinary value and wealth creation phenomenon: *the entrepreneurial process*.

Sir Winston Churchill probably was not thinking about the coming entrepreneurial generation when he wrote in his epic book *While England Slept*, "The world was meant to be wooed and won by youth." Yet this could describe perfectly what has transpired over the past 30 years as young entrepreneurs in their 20s conceived of, launched, and grew new companies that, in turn, spawned entirely new industries. Consider just a few of these twenty-something entrepreneurs (see Exhibit 2.2).

There are many more, lesser known, but just as integral a part of the entrepreneurial revolution as these exceptional founders. You will come to know and appreciate some of them in this book.

Take, for example, Doug Ranalli and Shae Plimley, who along with technical expert Tom Sosnowski created UNIFI in 1991. Still in their twenties, Doug, one of the author's formers students, and his wife conducted research to identify opportunities for high growth. As a result, they created a company in 1991 that would become the MCI of international faxing. By 1999 they had raised $270 million in 13 rounds of financing, had grown company revenues beyond $100 million, and were heading for $200 million.

Roxanne Quimby is a very different but extraordinary entrepreneur. Enjoying basic subsistence living on a small farm in the backwoods of Maine, she conceived of an idea to develop natural products from bee's wax and other natural things. Her new business began slowly and was very fragile, but today is a thriving business relocated to North Carolina and exceeding $30 million in annual sales.

Jack Staack had worked his way up, after dropping out of school, to the mail room and the factory floor at an International Harvester Plant in Springfield, Missouri, in the early 1980s, when it was announced that the plant would likely close. He and a handful of colleagues pooled $100,000 of their own money and borrowed $8.9 million from a local bank—note the 89 to 1 leverage!—and bought the plant for 10 cents a share to try to save the business and their jobs. The plant was failing, with $10 million in revenues. Today the business does nearly $150 million, is quite profitable, and has a share price over $40. It rebuilds engines shipped to the United States by Mercedes and has led to the startup of over 30 additional businesses.

Michael Healey and Bob Loftblad, also former students, were in their 20s and second-year MBA students at Babson College in 1990–1991 when they began work on a business plan to create a new do-it-yourself computer kit venture. Their plan won the annual Douglass Prize as the best in the competition in 1991, and became the basis for launching the company. Today the company exceeds $15 million in sales.

Nineteen years ago, Patricia Gallup and David Hall decided there must be a better way to buy information technology products, so they established PC Connection. Seeing a significant business opportunity in the emerging personal computer industry, the two entrepreneurs launched their direct computer supply business with the philosophy that providing technical advice and focusing on customer service was as important as low prices. Since 1995, the company has grown at compound annual growth rate of nearly 40 percent. PC Connection currently has 1,300 employees and in 1999 purchased ComTez Federal (re-christened GovConnection in 2001) to handle all government and education accounts.[7]

Paul J. Tobin also began his entrepreneurial career while in his 20s after completing his MBA. His first venture, U.S. Glass, a glass replacement business in New England, was moderately successful, but taught him many lessons and only whetted his appetite to be

[7] Source: http://www.pcconnection.com.

on his own. After selling his company to his partners, he became a marketing manager for a major satellite communications company. A few years later John Kluge selected him as CEO to launch Cellular One in Boston. Kluge's Metro Media Corporation had won the first cellular license for eastern Massachusetts. This became a launching pad to raise venture capital to acquire his own cellular licenses in Maine and New Hampshire, which became Cellular One. The company acquired its licenses at $9 per capita, and was sold in 1989 for $147 per capita—for a 132 percent internal rate of return for the venture capital investors, and an infinite return for him and his cofounders as they invested their time and talent only. This team founded Boston Communications Group, Inc., to create roaming and other services for the cellular industry and had an initial public offering in June 1996 (NASDAQ: BCGI). Today the company exceeds $100 million in profitable revenue.

Another former MBA candidate at Babson, Ann Stockbridge Sullivan, developed a business plan while still a student to build a retirement community in Kennebunk, Maine. She succeeded in raising $6 million of capital, achieved a 97 percent occupancy rate in the first year, and has had a two-year wait list since 1993!

Wayne Postoak, a Native American, was a young professor and highly successful basketball coach at Haskell Indian Nations University, in Lawrence, Kansas, in the 1970s. Haskell is the only national four-year university for Native Americans, enrolling students from nearly 200 tribes throughout North America. Haskell also launched the first Center for Tribal Entrepreneurial Studies in 1995. Postoak's children had aspirations for a college education and medical school, which he knew he could not afford on his coaching and teaching salary. He decided to launch his own construction firm, which today employs nearly 100 people and has sales above $10 million. (Only about 3 percent of all businesses in the country exceed $10 million in annual sales.)

Another demonstration of young entrepreneurial success includes two Babson College alumni, Kevin McCurdy and Howard Field, who started bamboo.com in 1995. McCurdy admits his strength is in turning an idea into a business opportunity. By the year 2000, bamboo.com, which developed Internet imaging technology, had 400 employees, had gone public on NASDAQ, and merged with the company's primary competitor, Interactive Pictures, in a deal worth more than $1 billion.

In 1982, John Coleman, a weather forecaster for ABC-TV, was frustrated that weather coverage was so brief during a typical news show. How could such a complex and dynamic phenomenon affecting every person on the planet be given in three minutes! He thought the weather could be covered continuously on a dedicated TV channel—a radical idea at the time. The Weather Channel was born. It lost $6 million the first year and, typical of the entrepreneurial process, it took six years to turn a profit. Today the Weather Channel is seen in more than 84 million homes nationwide. Its Web site, weather.com, attracts over 450 million page views per month, and is consistently ranked among the top TV-related Web sites by Nielsen/NetRatings.

Formation of New Industries This e-generation of economic revolutionaries has become the creators and leaders of entire new industries, not just a few outstanding new companies. From among the staggering raw number of startups emerge the lead innovators and creators that often become the dominant firms in new industries. This is evident from the 20-something list above. Exhibit 2.3 is a partial list of entirely new industries, not in existence a generation ago, that are today major sectors in the economy.

These new industries have transformed the economy. In the true creative birth and destruction process first articulated by Joseph Schumpeter, these new industries replace and displace older ones. David Birch has reported how this pace has accelerated. In the 1960s to the 1990s, it took 20 years to replace 35 percent of the companies then on the list of Fortune 500 companies. By the late 1980s, that replacement took place every five years (e.g., nearly 30 new faces each year), and in the 1990s, it occurred in three to four years. This outcome is the downsizing and right sizing of large companies we commonly hear about today. A generation earlier virtually no one predicted such a dramatic change. How could this happen so quickly? How could huge, cash-rich, dominant firms of the 1960s and 1970s get toppled from their perch by newcomers!

Consider the following example, which is typical of how this has occurred. One of the authors, in 1984,

EXHIBIT 2.3

New Industries Launched by the E-Generation

Personal computers	Voice mail information technology services
Biotechnology	Cellular phone services
Wireless cable TV	CD-ROM
Fast oil changes	Internet publishing and shopping
PC software	Desktop computing
Desktop information	Virtual imaging
Wireless communications/handheld devices/PDAs	Convenience foods superstores
Healthy living products	Digital media and entertainment
Electronic paging	Pet care services
CAD/CAM	

became the first outside member of the partner's committee (effectively, the board of directors) at the launch of Cellular One in Boston and eastern Massachusetts. We had one competitor: NYNEX, the cash-rich, multi-billion-dollar phone giant. The Federal Communications Commission (FCC) ruled that both firms could initiate service on January 1, 1985, which they did. Compare the strategies of the two firms. NYNEX built twice as many microwave transmission towers at a cost of $500,000 each, and it is estimated spent two to three times more on advertising and promotion of their new service as did Cellular One. NYNEX also had a substantially larger staff.

But what Cellular One lacked in size, cash, towers, and marketing budget they made up for in entrepreneurial ingenuity and strategies. For instance, NYNEX initially had one service and installation center, near their headquarters in the center of downtown Boston (noted for its narrow, one-way streets with very limited and expensive parking). Cellular One opened multiple service and installation centers on the famous Route 128, America's technology highway, which circumscribes the greater Boston area. It was a marketing and service battle, not a hardware (translate to "more towers") battle. This pattern repeated itself for each of the next five years, as NYNEX replaced its Mobile Communications president each year. And each year *Cellular One won three customers for each one that NYNEX gained.*

This pattern continues to repeat itself time and again in industry after industry, which accounts for the pace and magnitude of the demolition of the old Fortune 500 group of yesteryear.

The capital markets note the future value of these up-and-comers, compared to the old giants. Take, for instance, the Big Three automakers, giants of the prior generation of the 1950s and 1960s. By year-end 2004, they had combined sales of $542.8 billion, employed 1,034,200, but had a year-ending market capitalization (total value of all shares of the company) of $97.2 billion, or just 18 cents per dollar of revenue. Intel, Microsoft, and Cisco had 2004 total sales of $96 billion, employed just 176,000, but enjoyed a market cap of $564.5 billion! That's 5.8 times the value of the Big Three, and $5.90 per dollar of revenue, or nearly 33 times the Big Three!

This pattern of high market value characterizes virtually every new industry that has been—and continues to be—created by the new e-generation. This is also the case when entrepreneurs compete directly with industry stalwarts. Airlines Delta, American, and Continental employed 205,000 employees and had combined sales in 2004 of $43 billion. Their market capitalization was $7.8 billion, about 18 cents per dollar of revenue. In contrast, with a total of 41,000 employees, Jet Blue, Southwest, and AirTran had 2004 sales of $8 billion and a combined market capitalization of $16 billion—$2 per dollar of revenue. Exhibit 2.4 shows these relationships.

EXHIBIT 2.4

The Impact of Entrepreneurship on American Giants Old and New

	Sales in 2004 ($billion)	Employees in 2004 (000s)	Market Capitalization in Late December 2004 ($billion)
Ford	193.5	323.0	26.6
GM	170.8	327.5	22.6
Chrysler	177.5	383.7	48.5
Total	**541.8**	**1,034.2**	**97.7**
Intel	34.2	85.0	147.3
Microsoft	38.5	57.0	290.4
Cisco	22.9	34.0	126.7
Total	**95.6**	**176.0**	**564.5**
Delta	14.9	70.6	5.1
American	18.5	96.4	1.8
Continental	9.6	37.7	0.9
Total	**43.0**	**204.7**	**7.8**
Jet Blue	1.3	4.7	2.4
Southwest	5.8	31.0	12.7
AirTran	1.0	5.3	0.9
Total	**8.1**	**41.0**	**16.0**

Source: Capital IQ, via Yahoo! Finance. Used by permission of Capital IQ.

Innovation At the heart of the entrepreneurial process is the innovative spirit. After all, from Ben Franklin to Thomas Edison to Steve Jobs and Bill Gates, the history of the country shows a steady stream of brilliant entrepreneurs and innovators. For years it was believed by the press, the public, and policymakers that research and development occurring in large companies after World War II and driven by the birth of the space age after Sputnik in 1957 was the main driver of innovation in the nation.

This belief turned to myth—similar to the earlier beliefs about job creation—as the National Science Foundation, U.S. Department of Commerce, and others began to report research in the 1980s and 1990s that surprised many. They found that since World War II, *small entrepreneurial firms have been responsible for half of all innovation and 95 percent of all radical innovation in the United States!* Other studies showed that research and development at smaller entrepreneurial firms was more productive and robust than at large firms: smaller firms generated twice as many innovations per R&D dollar spent as the giants; twice as many innovations per R&D scientist as the giants; and 24 times as many innovations per R&D dollar versus those mega-firms with more than 10,000 employees!

EXHIBIT 2.5

Major Inventions by U.S. Small Firms in the 20th Century

Acoustical suspension speakers	Aerosol can	Air conditioning
Airplane	Artificial skin	Assembly line
Audiotape recorder	Automatic fabric cutting	Automatic transfer equipment
Bakelite	Biosynthetic insulin	Catalytic petroleum cracking
Continuous casting	Cotton picker	Fluid flow meter
Fosin fire extinguisher	Geodesic dome	Gyrocompass
Heart valve	Heat sensor	Helicopter
Heterodyne radio	High-capacity computer	Hydraulic brake
Leaning machine	Link trainer	Nuclear magnetic resonance
Pacemaker	Personal computer	Prefabricated housing
Piezo electrical devices	Polaroid camera	Pressure-sensitive cellophane
Quick-frozen foods	Rotary oil drilling bit	Safety razor
Six-axis robot arm	Soft contact lens	Sonar fish monitoring
Spectrographic grid	Stereographic image sensoring	Zipper

Source: Office of Advocacy of the U.S. Small Business Administration.

Clearly, smaller entrepreneurial firms do things differently when it comes to research and development activities. This innovative environment accounted for the development of the transistor and then the semiconductor. Today, Moore's Law—the power of the computer chip will double every 18 months at constant price—is actually being exceeded by modern chip technology. Combine this with management guru Peter Drucker's Postulate: a 10-fold increase in the productivity of any technology results in economic discontinuity. Thus, every five years there will be a 10-fold increase in productivity. Author George Gilder recently argued that communications bandwidth doubles every 12 months, creating an economic discontinuity every three to four years.[8] It does not take a lot of imagination to see the profound economic impact of such galloping productivity on every product use and application one can envision. The explosion in a vast array of opportunities is imminent.

This innovation cylinder of the entrepreneurial engine of America's economy has led to the creation of major new inventions and technologies. Exhibit 2.5 summarizes some of these in the 20th century.

Today, the fast pace of innovation is actually accelerating. New scientific breakthroughs in biotechnology and nanotechnology are driving the next great waves of innovation. *Nano* means one-billionth, so a nanometer is one-billionth of a meter or 1/80,000 the diameter of a human hair. A new class of nano-size products in drugs, optical-network devices, and bulk materials is attracting substantial research funding and private equity.[9] The e-generation, the next generation of entrepreneurs, will create leading ventures and wealth in these and other applications of nanotechnology.

Venture and Growth Capital Venture capital has deep roots in our history, and the evolution to today's industry is uniquely American. This private risk capital is the rocket fuel of America's entrepreneurial engine. Classic venture capitalists work as coaches and partners with entrepreneurs and innovators at a very early stage to help shape and accelerate the development of the company.[10] The fast growth, highly successful companies backed by venture capital investors read like a "Who's Who of the Economy": Apple Computer, Intuit, Compaq Computer, Staples, Intel, Federal Express, Cisco, e-Bay, Starbucks Coffee, Nextel Communication, Juniper Networks, Yahoo, Sun Microsystems, Amazon, Genetech, Google, Blackberry, Microsoft, and thousands of others. Typical of these legendary investments that both created companies and lead their new industry are the following:

- In 1957, General George Doriot, father of modern American venture capital, and his young associate Bill Congelton at American Research & Development (ARD) invested $70,000 for 77 percent of the founding stock of a new company created by four MIT graduate students, lead by Kenneth Olsen. By the time their investment was sold in 1971, it was worth

[8] Jeffry Timmons is indebted to Robert Compton, a colleague on the board of directors of the Kauffman Center for Entrepreneurial Leadership, for bringing his attention to these economic discontinuities arguments.
[9] Red Herring, "Nanotech Grows Up," June 15 & July 1, 2001, pp. 47–58.
[10] William D. Bygrave and Jeffry A. Timmons, Ibid., Chapter 1.

EXHIBIT 2.6

SEMICONDUCTOR INDUSTRY: Cumulative Number of Venture Capital Investments and Industry Shipments

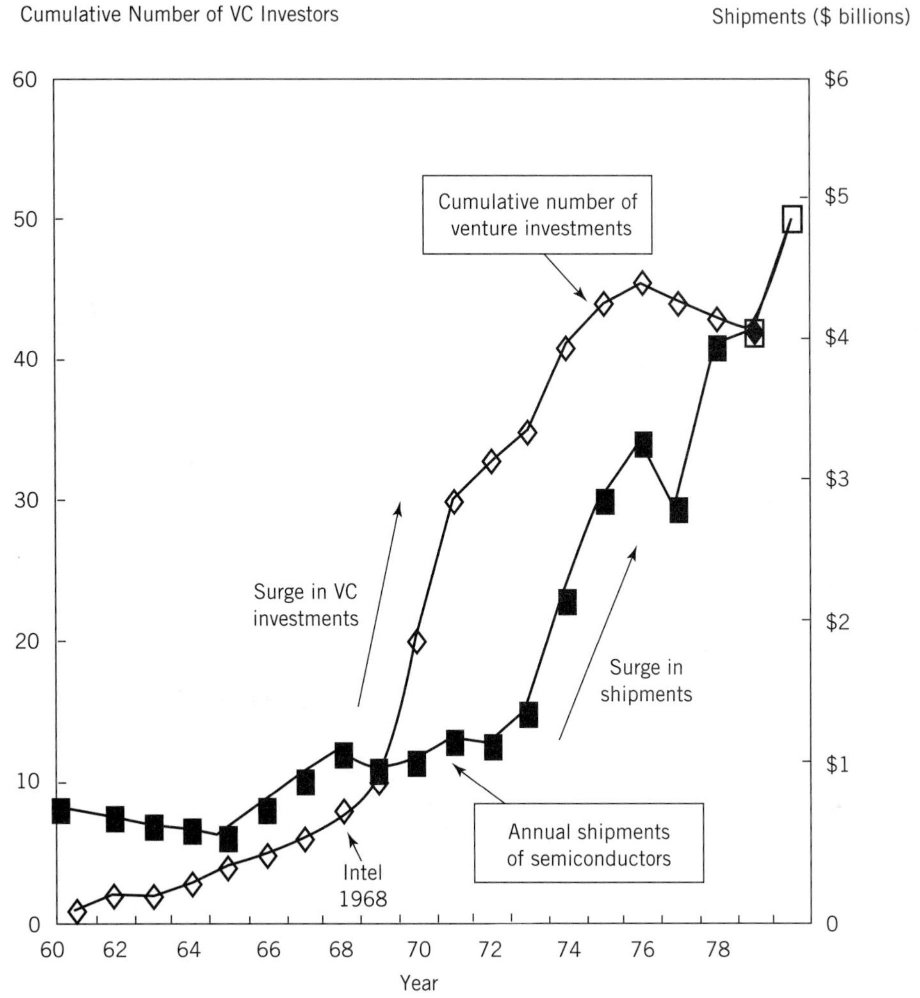

Source: Reprinted by permission of Harvard Business School Press. From *Venture Capital at the Crossroads* by W. D. Bygrave, J. A. Timmons. Boston, MA 1992, p. 101. Copyright © 1992 by the Harvard Business School Publishing Corporation; all rights reserved.

$355 million. The company was Digital Equipment Corporation and became the world leader in microcomputers by the 1980s.

- In 1968, Gordon Moore and Robert Noyce teamed with Arthur Rock to launch Intel Corporation with $2.5 million, and $25,000 from each of the founders. Intel is the leader in semiconductors today.
- In 1975, Arthur Rock, in search of concepts "that change the way people live and work," invested $1.5 million in the startup of Apple Computer, Inc. The investment was valued at $100 million at Apple's first public stock offering in 1978.
- After monthly losses of $1 million and more for 29 consecutive months, a new company that launched the overnight delivery of small packages turned the corner. The $25 million invested in Federal Express was worth $1.2 billion when the company issued stock to the public.

A good depiction of the long gestation period for upstart companies like these, whose collective expansions blossom into entire new industries, is shown in Exhibit 2.6 (the semiconductor industry) and in Exhibit 2.7 (the microcomputer industry). Even with these fast-paced, emerging technologies—funded early on by venture capitalists—it took nearly 10 years before either industry really took off. Virtually every other new industry since, from biotechnology to personal computers to PC software to wireless communications to the Internet, would follow this pattern.

EXHIBIT 2.7

MICROCOMPUTER INDUSTRY: Cumulative Number of Startup Companies and Industry Shipments

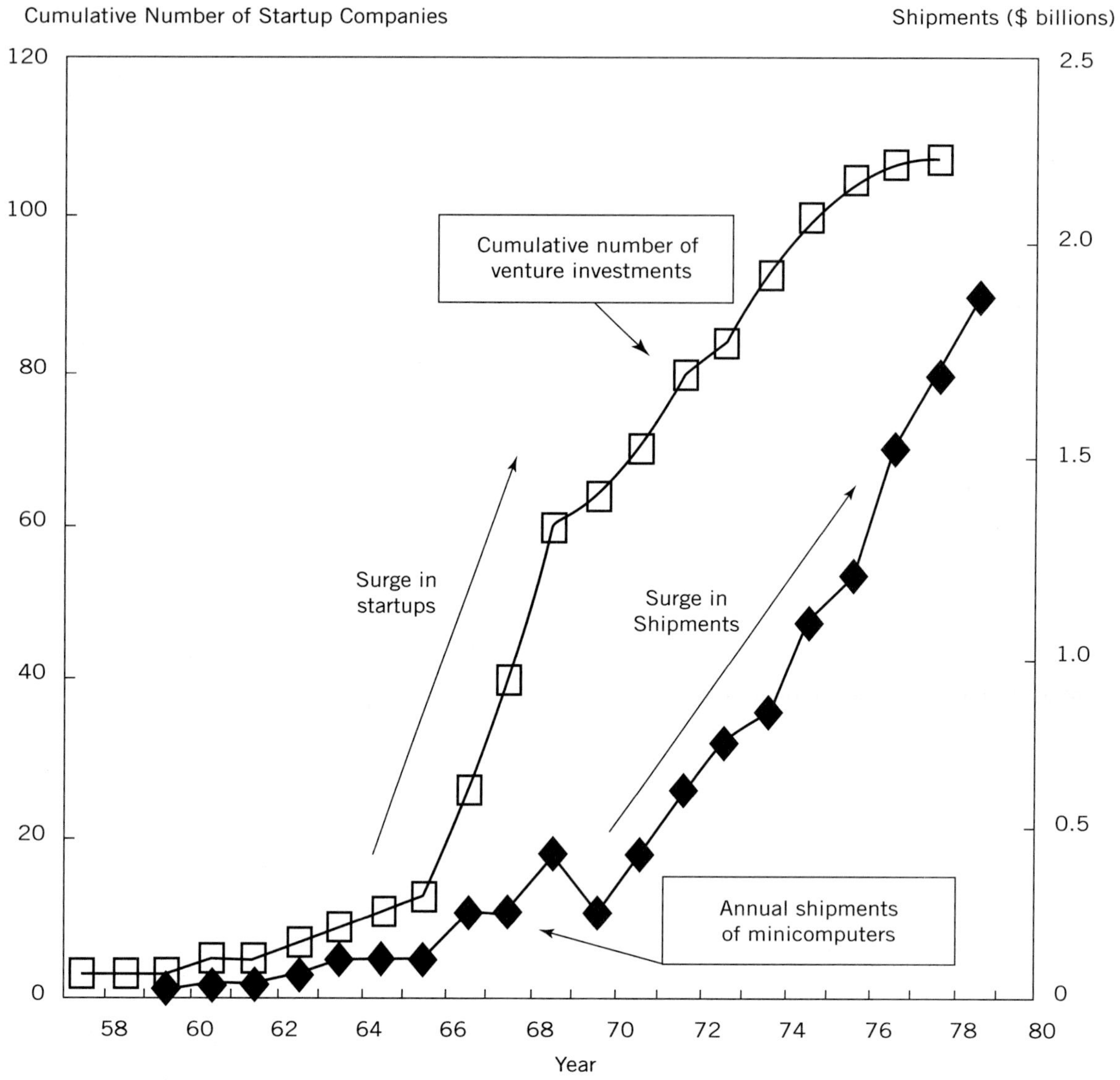

Source: Reprinted by permission of Harvard Business School Press. From *Venture Capital at the Crossroads* by W. D. Bygrave, J. A. Timmons. Boston, MA 1992, p. 107. Copyright © 1992 by the Harvard Business School Publishing Corporation; all rights reserved.

The U.S. venture capital industry has accounted for thousands of such investments over the years, and this value creation has had a hugely disproportionate impact on the formation of new industries and the economy. In Chapter 13, on obtaining venture and growth capital, we will examine in detail investing characteristics and performance since 2000, and describe in detail pertinent aspects and current practices in venture capital investing.

In addition to the $15 billion to $20+ billion of venture capital, moderately wealthy to very wealthy individuals represent a total annual pool of about $108 billion, which they invest in new ventures. So-called angel investors represent a seasoned subset of these individuals. The Center for Venture Research at the University of New Hampshire reported that in 2004, roughly 48,000 ventures received angel financing. Total investment reached $22.5 billion, an increase from the previous year's total of $18.1 billion.

Similar to the venture capitalists, these angels bring far more than money to the entrepreneurial process. As successful entrepreneurs themselves, they bring experience, learning curves, networks, wisdom, and maturity to the fledgling companies in which they invest. As directors and advisors, they function as coach, confidant, mentor, and cheerleader. Given the explosion of the entrepreneurial economy in the past 25 years, there is now a cadre of harvested entrepreneurs in the nation that is 20 to 30 times larger than that of the past generation. This pool of talent, know-how, and money continues to play an enormously important role in cultivating and accelerating e-generation capabilities.

Philanthropy and Leadership: Giving Back to the Community Another lesser known and largely ignored role of American entrepreneurs is that of philanthropists and creative community leaders. A majority of new buildings, classrooms, athletic facilities, and endowed professorships at universities across the nation have been funded by a harvested company founder who wants to give back. The largest gifts and the greatest proportion of donors among any groups giving to university capital campaigns are successful entrepreneurs. At one time, half of the total MIT endowment was attributed to gifts of founders' stock.

This same pattern also characterizes local churches, hospitals, museums, orchestras, and schools. The bulk of the financial gifts to these institutions are from successful entrepreneurs, such as Ted Turner's $1 billion gift over 10 years to the United Nations, which he announced in 1997. The time and creative leadership the entrepreneurs devote to these community institutions are as important as their money. Talk with any person from another country who has spent enough time in America to come to see these entrepreneurial leaders active in their communities, and they will convince you just how truly unique this is. America's leading foundations were all created by gifts of the founders of great companies: Ford, Carnegie, Kellogg, Mellon, Kauffman.

It has been one of Jeff Timmons's greatest honors and privileges to have known and worked with Ewing Marion Kauffman and his team in the creation and development of the Kauffman Center for Entrepreneurial Leadership in Kansas City, at the Ewing Marion Kauffman Foundation—now among the 15 largest foundations in the country with approximately $2 billion in assets. Their vision is clear: self-sufficient people in healthy communities. The Kauffman Center's mission is at the core of the entrepreneurial revolution: *accelerating entrepreneurship in America.*

Mr. K., as he was affectionately known, was probably best known outside Kansas City as owner of the Kansas City Royals (which he later gifted to the city). In 1950, he quit his top sales job because of his treatment by the president of the company. "The year before," Mr. K. says, "I made more money than the president, so he cut back my commission. The next year I made more money than he did again, so he cut back my territory. So I quit and started Marion Labs in my basement." His entrepreneurial genius created Marion Laboratories, Inc., which grew to $1 billion in revenues, $6.5 billion in market capitalization, and had more than 300 millionaires among its 3,400 staff. Mr. K. grew the company on three principles: (1) treat people as you would want to be treated, (2) those who produce should share the rewards, and (3) give back to the community. You will hear more about the remarkable success of Mr. K. in subsequent chapters, but the following quotes best sum Mr. K.'s entrepreneurial spirit and life philosophy:

> Live what you talk, make your actions match your words. You must live what you preach and do it right and do it often. Day after day.
>
> As an entrepreneur, you really need to develop a code of ethics, a code of relationships with your people, because it's the people who come and join you. They have dreams of their own. You have your dream of the company. They must mesh somewhat.

These sentiments are mirrored time and again by highly successful mega-entrepreneurs who have created America's leading foundations: Carnegie, Olin, Ford, Kellogg, Lilly, Gates, and Blank, to name a few. What is much less known and appreciated by the general public is the extent to which this giving-back-to-the-community ethic of philanthropy is repeated by entrepreneurs at the local community level. Take, for example, the Varney family of Antrim, New Hampshire. Their Monadnock Paper Mills company, a multi-generational firm, is the largest employer in the area. They have been industry leaders in environmentally clean papermaking. In fact, the major river for miles downstream from their mill has some of the best catch-and-release trophy trout water in the state. They also support many community causes, from the local hospital, to the arts center, to the leading conservation organizations, and many more, to which the family has generously contributed time and money. The extent of this volunteerism and generosity in communities across America often surprises European visitors.

One cannot find a building, a stadium, science or arts center at both private and public universities in America that has not come from the wealth creation and gift of a highly successful entrepreneur.

Franklin W. Olin (1860–1951)—engineer, entrepreneur, and professional baseball player—epitomizes the "innovation + entrepreneurship = prosperity and philanthropy" process of wealth creation and giving back to the community. In 1938, Olin transferred a large part of this personal wealth to a private philanthropic foundation. In the 60 years since then, the New York–based Olin Foundation has awarded grants totaling more than $300 million to construct and fully equip 72 buildings on 57 independent college campuses.

The Franklin W. Olin College of Engineering received its educational charter from the Commonwealth of Massachusetts in 1997, the same year the Foundation announced its ambitious plans for the college. By the end of 1999, the new institution's leadership team had been hired, and site development work commenced on 70 acres adjacent to Babson College.

Despite their stellar backgrounds, the faculty could not invent the new curriculum alone. As a college that intended to be unusually student-centric, student feedback and assistance in curriculum development would be imperative. The college decided to recruit student "partners" for a special pre-freshman year in which they would work closely with the faculty to develop the curriculum and student life programs.

These 30 "Olin Partners" were an exceptional group of fearless, enterprising students. Recruited from around the country, they received offers of admission from the top universities and engineering programs, such as Harvard, MIT, and Cal Tech. They chose Olin—despite its lack of a track record—for the unprecedented opportunity to shape their own college experience. "Other colleges may offer credentials," said Olin Partner Que Anh Nguyen. "We have the chance to make history."

In August 2002, the Olin Partners were joined by equally well-qualified classmates to form Olin's inaugural freshman class of 75 students. The aim of the school is to foster the development of technological leaders who are well-rounded "Renaissance engineers" in the tradition of Leonardo da Vinci—and Franklin Olin.

Another example of philanthropic entrepreneurs is Babson alumnus Arthur M. Blank, co-founder of The Home Depot and owner of the Atlanta Falcons. As a way of giving back to the community, he funded the Arthur M. Blank Center for Entrepreneurship at Babson College, which opened in 1998, and created the Arthur Blank Family Foundation to support innovative endeavors leading to better circumstances for low-income youth and their families.

At the colleges and universities, hospitals, churches and synagogues, private schools, museums, and the like, the boards of directors and trustees who lead, fund, and help perpetuate these institutions are, more often than not, entrepreneurs. As in their own companies, their creative, entrepreneurial leadership is their most valuable contribution.

The Entrepreneurial Revolution: A Decade of Acceleration and Boom

A "revolution" in higher education has played a critical role in the steady growth of entrepreneurship. Today well over 2,000 colleges, universities, and community colleges offer such courses and many of them offer majors in entrepreneurship or entrepreneurial studies. In the last 10 years alone, American universities have invested over $1 billion in creating entrepreneurship education and research capacity. There are over 44 academic journals and over 100 entrepreneurship centers. The number of endowed professorships has grown from the very first (the Paul T. Babson Professorship at Babson College in 1980) to nearly 400 today in the United States, and another 150-plus in the rest of the world. Below is a sampling of the many indicators—including innumerable entrepreneurial initiatives among not-for-profit foundations and organizations—that point to an ever-expanding culture of entrepreneurship.

Education

- In 2005, the National Science Foundation awarded a three-year grant to Babson College to partner with the new Olin College of Engineering to create a new program for engineering faculty. The Babson-Olin Program—sister program of the longtime successful Price-Babson Program—will educate engineering faculty to bring entrepreneurship into their curricula, to build their own teaching capacities, and thereby improve prosperity in America.
- In 2004, the Ewing Marion Kauffman Foundation of Kansas City—America's leading foundation in entrepreneurship—made $25 million in grants to eight major universities to create entrepreneurship education across life sciences, medicine, and engineering.
- The Kauffman Foundation has been joined by other new and established foundations in supporting entrepreneurship, including the Franklin W. Olin Foundation, the Reynolds Foundation, the Ted & Vivian Johnson Foundation, the Koch Foundation, the Manchester Craftsman's Guild in Pittsburgh, and others.
- Haskell Indian Nations University in Lawrence, Kansas, created the first Center for Tribal Entrepreneurial Studies, and is now partnering with numerous tribal colleges around the nation to develop appropriate entrepreneurship curricula.
- In Salt Lake City, the University of Utah began a venture fund in 2002 with a $500,000 gift from local businessman James Sorenson and his son Jim. The fund, which had raised $5 million by 2005, will utilize five teams of five students to each consider 80 deals a week. Many of the potential deals will come from VC firms working with the university.

Policy

- To credit the entrepreneurs who create more than 75 percent of the net new jobs nationwide, and generate more than 50 percent of the nation's gross domestic product, President Bush declared May 6–12, 2001, Small Business Week.
- The National Commission on Entrepreneurship (NCOE) was launched in February 1999. As a nonpartisan organization, the goal of NCOE is to serve as a necessary bridge between entrepreneurs and lawmakers. In April 2001, the Center for Business and Government, John F. Kennedy School of Government, and the NCOE hosted a conference on Entrepreneurship and Public Policy in the 21st Century. Conference attendees consisted of policymakers, academicians, and entrepreneurs from around the country.

Women

- Between 1997 and 2004, the number of privately held firms owned by women of color in the United States grew 54.6 percent, while the overall number of firms in the United States grew by only 9 percent over the same period. These firms appear to be prospering as both employment (up 61.8 percent) and sales (up 73.6 percent) also grew during this period. Women's business ownership is up among all groups, but the number of Hispanic (up 63.9 percent) and Asian-owned firms (up 69.3 percent) has grown especially fast.
- A 2003 Babson College/MassMutual report on women in family-owned businesses found that female-owned family firms are nearly two times as productive as male-owned family enterprises. With average revenues of $26.9 million, firms run by women were somewhat smaller in size compared to their male-owned counterparts ($30.4 million average revenues). Allowing for that, however, the women generated their sales with far fewer median employees—26 individuals compared with 50 at male-owned firms. Conclusion: women in business typically do more with less.

Minority Groups

- In 2003, African-American self-employment reached its highest levels in both number, at 710,000, and rate, at 5.2 percent (calculated as the number of African-American self-employed divided by the number of African Americans in the labor force).
- The *2002 Panel Study of Entrepreneurial Dynamics* (Babson College, Ewing Marion Kauffman Foundation) reported that African Americans are 50 percent more likely to start a business than whites. This difference is even more noticeable among populations with advanced degrees: African-American males with graduate degrees are 2.6 times more likely to start a business than their white counterparts.
- Latino self-employment increased significantly, from 241,000 in 1979 to 1 million in 2003. The Latino self-employment rate was 7 percent (calculated as the number of Latino self-employed divided by the number of Latinos in the labor force) in 2003.
- Data from the 2000 census shows that since 1997 the number of Native American–owned businesses has risen by 84 percent to 197,300, and that their gross incomes have increased by 179 percent to $34.3 billion. Asian Americans and Pacific Islanders constitute a little more than 3 percent of the population and own nearly 4.5 percent of businesses.
- While efforts to promote entrepreneurship among low-income communities have expanded over the years, only recently have Native American communities begun to benefit from these programs and services. The Corporation for Enterprise Development and Native American Entrepreneurship Development has been created to strengthen the supports for Native American entrepreneurship across the country.

Youth Entrepreneurship

- Entrepreneurship education is now gaining a foothold in elementary through high schools in at least 30 states. At least eight states have passed legislation requiring such education, and the federal Department of Education has approved the first curriculum, YESS/Mini-Society, created by the Kauffman Center.
- The National Foundation for Teaching Entrepreneurship (NFTE) has significantly expanded its out-of-school educational programs in the inner cities to help youths seeking self-sufficiency and self-respect through entrepreneurship. NFTE now teaches 10,000 students per year.
- The national Girls Scouts and Boys Scouts in 1997 created, with the help and support of the Kauffman Center, the very first Scout Merit Badges in Entrepreneurship. The badge symbol: a hand reaching for a star!

Entrepreneurs: America's Self-Made Millionaires

The founders of great companies such as Apple Computer, Federal Express, Staples, Intuit, and Lotus Development Corporation become millionaires when their companies become publicly traded. But the vast majority of the new generation of millionaires are invisible to most Americans, and do not at all fit the stereotype one derives from the press and media. The authors of *The Millionaire Next Door,* Thomas J. Stanley and William D. Danko, share some new insights into this group:

> . . . the television image of wealthy Americans is false: The truly wealthy are not by and large ostentatious but, rather, are very persistent and disciplined people running ordinary businesses.[11]

The profile of these 3.5 million—out of 100 million households in the nation—millionaires (defined as having a net worth of $1 million or more) is revealing: they accumulated their wealth through hard work, self-discipline, planning, and frugality—all very entrepreneurial virtues. Two-thirds of them still working are self-employed. They are not descendants of the Rockefellers or Vanderbilts. Instead, they are truly self-made: more than 80 percent are ordinary people who have accumulated their wealth in one generation. They live below their means, would rather be financially independent than display high social status, and don't look like most people's stereotype of millionaires. They get rich slowly: The average millionaire is 57 years old. Their businesses are not the sexy, high-tech, Silicon Valley variety; rather they have created and own such businesses as ambulance services, citrus farming, cafeteria service, diesel engine re-building, consulting services, janitorial service, job training school, meat processor, mobile home parks, pest controller, newsletter publisher, rice farmer, and sandblasting contractor![12]

The implications of this new study are quite significant and encouraging for the vast majority of entrepreneurs. Clearly, the American Dream is more alive and well than ever, and more accessible than ever. One does not have to be born to wealth, attend prep school, and go to an elite Ivy League school to become successful. Further, the study seems to confirm what has been articulated in all editions of *New Venture Creation:* A combination of talent and skills plus opportunity matched with the needed resources and applied with the entrepreneurial mind-set is key. And there have never been more opportunities to pursue an entrepreneurial dream.

Dawn of the New Age of Equity Creation

Value creation is not a linear process; it requires a long-term perspective. While the U.S. investment and capital markets have been an integral part of this revolution in entrepreneurship, it is more important to recognize the long-term resilience of the system. Despite a recession in the late 1980s, and a downturn in the first years of the new century (precipitated by the tragic events of 9/11), the capital markets have continued to trend upward.

The venture capital industry has closely mirrored these overall economics. During the late 1990s the venture capital industry nearly quadrupled in size, with a staggering surge to $103 billion in 2000 alone. Between 1998 and 2002, $223 billion was committed by limited partners to the U.S. venture capital industry. Predictably, this spike in the supply of venture capital resulted in extremely disappointing returns, with substantial losses, and a major shake-out in the industry beginning in 2001—similar to what had occurred between 1988 and 1993.

This most recent downturn in the venture capital industry culminated in 2003 with a six-year aggregate investment low of $18.9 billion. According to the National Venture Capital Association, the industry rebounded in 2004 with aggregate investments of $21 billion into 2,873 deals (Exhibit 2.8). Although this increase was largely related to later stage investments, there were 841 early stage deals that year—accounting for $3.9 billion, or 29 percent of all investments. This represented a slightly greater percentage of all venture capital activity that year, an indication that venture capitalists would continue to invest for the longer term.

In 2001, the Dow Jones Industrial Average—the nation's oldest and most recognizable stock barometer—set a bear market low of 7,286. By the end of 2003, the Dow had recovered to 10,454—just about 9 percent less than what the Dow was at the height of the stock market bubble (Exhibit 2.9). Average daily trading in shares increased between 2000 and 2003, but the value of those shares (especially NASDAQ issues—many of which were associated with the Internet boom) was still lagging (Exhibit 2.10).

Not surprisingly, initial public offerings (IPOs) and all equity values in 2003 were below their 1999 highs (Exhibit 2.11). What is important to note, however, is that total underwritings had recovered, and that in 2003, IPOs and all equity had gained over 400 and 600 percent in value, respectively, since 1990.

The implications of all this are profound for aspiring entrepreneurs and the nation. The overall wealth

[11] "The Millionaire Next Door," *Success Magazine,* March 1997, pp. 45–51.
[12] Ibid., pp. 46–48.

EXHIBIT 2.8

U.S. Venture Capital Investment by Year (1990–2004)

Time Period	Number of Companies	Average per Company ($mils)	Sum Investment ($millions)
1990	1,433	1.9	2,767.1
1991	1,231	1.8	2,241.7
1992	1,345	2.6	3,511.1
1993	1,161	3.2	3,708.1
1994	1,197	3.4	4,120.6
1995	1,776	4.4	7,853.5
1996	2,464	4.5	10,992.9
1997	3,084	4.8	14,646.9
1998	3,557	5.9	20,899.8
1999	5,403	9.9	53,579.6
2000	7,832	13.4	104,827.4
2001	4,451	9.2	40,798.4
2002	3,042	7.1	21,579.3
2003	2,825	6.7	18,911.0
2004	2,873	7.3	21,004.4

Source: PricewaterhouseCoopers/Venture Economics/National Venture Capital Association/ Money Tree™ Survey of 3/28/05. Used by permission of PricewaterhouseCoopers.

EXHIBIT 2.9

The Stock Market Metrics

	1985	1990	1999	2003
Dow Jones Industrial Average (at year-end)	1,546.67	2,633.66	11,497.12	10,453.92
Equity mutual fund assets	$116.9 billion	$245.6 billion	$4,041.9 billion	$3,684.8 billion
Net cash flows into mutual funds	$68.2 billion	$44.4 billion	$363.4 billion	−$42.5 billion

Source: *2004 Securities Industries Factbook;* Securities Industry Association.

EXHIBIT 2.10

U.S. Stock Markets Average Daily Trading

	Number of Shares (in millions)				$ Value (in billions)			
	1980	1990	2000	2003	1980	1990	2000	2003
NYSE	44.9	156.8	1,041.60	1,398.40	$1.5	$5.2	$43.9	$35.5
NASDAQ	26.4	131.9	1757.0	1,685.50	$0.3	$1.8	$80.9	$28.0

Source: *Securities Industry Association Research Reports,* Vol. V, No. 6, June 25, 2004.

EXHIBIT 2.11

U.S. Stock Markets Total Value

	1980 (in billions)	1990 (in billions)	2000 (in billions)	2003 (in billions)
IPOs	1.4	10.1	66.8	43.7
Total underwritings	57.6	312.3	1,959.8	2,889.9
All equity	13	23.9	191.7	156.3

Source: *2004 Securities Industry Factbook; Securities Industry Association.*

of the nation, expressed as a U.S. household balance sheet, grew from $550 billion in 1970 to about $9 trillion by the end of 1997. What may astonish some is that over 95 percent of the nation's wealth has been created since 1980, a direct result of this entrepreneurial revolution. We are now beginning to see this result culminate in the rest of the world.

Building an Entrepreneurial Society

The Poorer Get Richer More than any other aspect of our society and economy, entrepreneurship is the great equalizer and mobilizer of opportunity. It is indifferent to race, religion, sex, or geography. It rewards performance and punishes shabbiness and ineptness. No other institutional process offers the chance for self-sufficiency, self-determination, and economic improvement as the entrepreneurial process. We saw earlier the stunning profile of America's millionaires, who by and large are self-made entrepreneurs. Even the Forbes 400 wealthiest persons are self-made: in 2004, 61 percent, and 7 out of the top 10, were self-made.

Yet, one of the most durable debates in American society is our love-hate relationship with wealth and income distribution. Our immigrant heritage as a land of opportunity came to be known as "Horatio Alger Stories" as these 120 novels after the Civil War portrayed ordinary boys rising from rags to riches in a generation. All too often, however, one hears the notion that "the rich get richer" and, by implication, the poor must be getting poorer. But if this is true, and the middle class is eventually encroached upon, the political repercussions will be heard round the world.

Create Equal Opportunities, Not Equal Incomes What has been lost historically in this debate is that equal incomes are neither desirable nor possible. Most important is that opportunities are available for anyone who wants to prepare and to compete. The entrepreneurial process will take over and result in economic expansion and accompanying social mobility. A recent study at the Federal Reserve Bank of Dallas sheds valuable insight.[13] In one experiment in the 1970s, for instance, three groups of Canadians, all in their 20s, all with at least 12 years of schooling, volunteered to work in a simulated economy where the only employment was making woolen belts on small hand looms. They could work as much or as little as they liked, earning $2.50 for each belt. After 98 days, the results were anything but equal: 37.2 percent of the economy's income went to the 20 percent with the highest earnings. The bottom 20 percent received only 6.6 percent.[14]

Entrepreneurship = Economic and Social Mobility The authors of the Federal Reserve study would agree with the earlier case presented here showing the radical transformation of the American economy as a result of the entrepreneurial revolution. Their data also show this is still the land of opportunity. Income mobility in America from 1975 to 1991 shows that a significant portion of those in the lowest quintile in 1975 had moved up, including 29 percent all the way to the top quintile (see Exhibit 2.12). In terms of absolute gain, the data, adjusted for inflation, showed the poor are getting richer faster (see Exhibit 2.13). The study concluded with this important summation:

> Striving to better oneself isn't just private virtue. It sows the seeds of economic growth and technical advancement. There's no denying that the system allows some Americans to become richer than others. We must accept that. Equality of income is not what has made the U.S. economy grow and prosper. It's opportunity. . . . Our proper cultural icon is not the common man. It's the *self-made* man or woman.[15]

EXHIBIT 2.12

Moving on Up

Income Quintile in 1975	Percent in Each Quintile in 1991				
	1st	*2nd*	*3rd*	*4th*	*5th*
5th (highest)	.9%	2.8%	10.2%	23.6%	62.5%
4th	1.9	9.3	18.8	32.6	37.4
3rd (middle)	3.3	19.3	28.3	30.1	19.0
2nd	4.2	23.5	20.3	25.2	26.8
1st (lowest)	5.1	14.6	21.0	30.0	29.0

[13] W. Michael Cox and Richard Aim, "By Our Own Bootstraps: Economic Opportunity and the Dynamics of Income Distribution," *1995 Annual Report* (Dallas, TX: The Federal Reserve Bank), pp. 2–23.
[14] Ibid., p. 5.
[15] Ibid., p. 18.

EXHIBIT 2.13

The Poor Are Getting Richer Faster

Income Quintile in 1975	*Average Income in 1975**	*Average Income in 1991**	*Absolute Gain*
5th (highest)	$45,704	$49,678	$ 3,974
4th	22,423	31,292	8,869
3rd (middle)	13,030	22,304	9,274
2nd	6,291	28,373	22,082
1st (lowest)	1,153	26,475	25,322

*Figures are in 1993 dollars.

In another comparison, the standard of living of the bottom 10 percent of American families in 1995 was actually higher than the average family in 1970. It is clear that America's success is becoming a global success story. Just as this nation has created and encouraged policies and priorities to support the entrepreneurial process, countries around the world are following that lead, and in doing so, they are fostering and ensuring the mobility of opportunity just described.

Internet Impact: Resources

Communication Goes Global

The ever-expanding number of devices designed to exploit Internet accessibility is having a profound impact on global communications. As a pervasive global network, the Internet provides a means for geographically disbursed parties to work from the same system, using the same information, in a real-time environment.

Using Web-based communications, organizations can now quickly and effectively keep value chain participants in the loop—from concept through design and delivery—without ever meeting in the same physical space. This includes the ability to utilize external systems such as cooperative research databases, property databases, road databases that include information relevant to routing, and demographic databases for marketing purposes.

The Internet also has become an effective tool for collaborative design, development, and data maintenance. Internet-based collaboration not only can nullify a development team's physical separation, enhance productivity, and shorten design cycles, but also opens up the talent base to include special application freelancers, as well as engineers under the employ of consultants, vendors, clients, and business partners.

Chapter Summary

This chapter has set the stage for the remainder of the book. We have seen that:

- Entrepreneurs are the creators, the innovators, and the leaders who give back to society, as philanthropists, directors, and trustees, and who, more than any others, change the way people live, work, learn, play, and lead.
- Entrepreneurs create new technologies, products, processes, and services that become the next wave of new industries, and these in turn drive the economy.
- Entrepreneurs create value with high potential, high growth companies, which are the job creation engines of the U.S. economy.
- Venture capital provides the fuel for the high potential, high growth companies.
- America and the world are at the dawn of a new age of equity creation as evidenced by a 10- to 30-fold increase in our capital markets in just 20 years.
- Entrepreneurs are realizing the value they have created; more than 95 percent of the wealth America has today has been created since 1980.
- America's 2.5 million millionaires are mostly self-made entrepreneurs.
- In America, the poor get richer as a result of the entrepreneurial process.
- Building an entrepreneurial society for the 21st century and beyond is the highest priority for the new e-generation.

Study Questions

Can you answer the following?

1. How has America's and the world's economy changed over the past generation? Why?
2. How has the number of new venture formations in the United States changed in the past 30 years? Why has this happened? Why will this pattern continue?
3. From where do the new jobs in America derive? Why?
4. Explain the extent to which large versus new and emerging companies contribute to all innovations. To radical innovations.
5. When was the vast majority of wealth created in America, and by whom? *(a)* Carnegies, Vanderbilts, and Rockefellers before 1990. *(b)*Automobile, food, and real estate magnates after 1900 but before 1970. *(c)* Founders of companies since 1970.
6. Who are the millionaires today?
7. Name some exceptional companies whose founders were in their 20s when they launched their company.
8. What role has venture capital played in this economic transformation?
9. It is often argued that "the rich get richer and the poor get poorer." How and why has the entrepreneurial revolution affected this old stereotype? What are its implications?
10. What has happened to large and established companies of yesteryear as a result of this surge by entrepreneurial upstarts?

Internet Resources for Chapter 2

http://www3.babson.edu/Eship *The Arthur M. Blank Center for Entrepreneurship*

http://www.benlore.com *The Entrepreneur's Mind*

http://www.inc.com *Inc. magazine*

http://www.nvca.org *National Venture Capital Association*

http://www.sba.gov *Small Business Administration*

http://www.ventureeconomics.com *Venture Economics*

http://www.ventureone.com *Venture One*

http://www.venturesource.com *Database on venture-backed companies and investors*

http://www.womensbusinessresearch.org *Center for Women's Business Research*

http://www.ncaied.org *The National Center for American Indian Enterprise Development*

MIND STRETCHERS

Have you considered?

1. As a citizen, what policies are needed to encourage and build an entrepreneurial society?
2. How will opportunities and the availability of capital change in this new century as a result of this economic and social revolution? How can one be best prepared for this?
3. Many, if not most, people prefer predictability to unpredictability. Yet, the entrepreneurial process is inherently chaotic, unpredictable, and unplannable. Who will succeed and who will falter in this dynamic process? What skills and mind-sets are required?
4. If this revolution continues at its pace of the past 25 years (e.g., a 10- to 15-fold increase) at your 25th college or graduate school reunion, what will be the Dow Jones Industrial and the NASDAQ Average? How many businesses and jobs will there be? How many new industries that no one has thought of today? What if this pace is 50 percent faster or slower?

Exercise

Visit with an Entrepreneur and Create a Lifelong Learning Log

Through an interview with entrepreneurs who have, within the past 5 to 10 years, started firms whose sales now exceed $2 million to $3 million and are profitable, you can gain insight into an entrepreneur's reasons, strategies, approaches, and motivations for starting and owning a business. Gathering information through interviewing is a valuable skill to practice. You can learn a great deal in a short time through interviewing if you prepare thoughtfully and thoroughly.

The Visit with an Entrepreneur Exercise has helped students interview successful entrepreneurs. While there is no right way to structure an interview, the format in this exercise has been tested successfully on many occasions. A breakfast, lunch, or dinner meeting is often an excellent vehicle.

Select two entrepreneurs and businesses about which you would like to learn. This could be someone you see as an example or role model to which you aspire, or which you know the least about but are eager to learn. Interview at least two entrepreneurs with differing experiences, such as a high potential (e.g., $5 million revenue plus) and a lifestyle business (usually much smaller, but not necessarily).

Create a Lifelong Learning Log

Create a computer file or acquire a notebook or binder in which you record your goals, triumphs and disappointments, and lessons learned. This can be done as key events happen or on some other frequent basis. You might make entries during times of crisis and at year's end to sum up what you accomplished and your new goals. The record of personal insights, observations, and lessons learned can provide valuable anchors during times of difficult decisions as well as interesting reading—for you at least.

A Visit with an Entrepreneur

STEP 1

Contact the Person You Have Selected and Make an Appointment.

Be sure to explain why you want the appointment and to give a realistic estimate of how much time you will need.

STEP 2

Identify Specific Questions You Would Like to Have Answered and the General Areas about Which You Would Like Information. (See the Interview In Step 3.)

Using a combination of open-end questions, such as general questions about how the entrepreneur got started, what happened next, and so forth, and closed-end questions, such as specific questions about what his or her goals were, if he or she had to find partners, and so forth, will help keep the interview focused and yet allow for unexpected comments and insights.

STEP 3

Conduct the Interview.

Recording this interview on audiotape can be helpful and is recommended unless you or the person being interviewed objects. Remember, too, that you most likely will learn more if you are an interested listener.

The Interview

Questions for Gathering Information

- Would you tell me about yourself before you started your first venture?

  Who else did you know while you were growing up who had started or owned a business, and how did they influence you? Anyone later, after you were 21 years old?

  Were your parents, relatives, or close friends entrepreneurial? How so?

  Did you have role models?

  What was your education/military experience? In hindsight, was it helpful? In what specific ways?

  Did you have a business or self-employment during your youth?

  In particular, did you have any sales or marketing experience? How important was it, or a lack of it, to starting your company?

  When, under what circumstances, and from whom did you become interested in entrepreneurship and learn some of the critical lessons?

- Describe how you decided to create a job by starting your venture instead of taking a job with someone else.

  How did you spot the opportunity? How did it surface?

  What were your goals? What were your lifestyle needs or other personal requirements? How did you fit these together?

  How did you evaluate the opportunity in terms of the critical elements for success? The competition? The market? Did you have specific criteria you wanted to meet?

Did you find or have partners? What kind of planning did you do? What kind of financing did you have?

Did you have a startup business plan of any kind? Please tell me about it.

How much time did it take from conception to the first day of business? How many hours a day did you spend working on it?

How much capital did it take? How long did it take to reach a positive cash flow and break-even sales volume? If you did not have enough money at the time, what were some ways in which you bootstrapped the venture (bartering, borrowing, and the like)? Tell me about the pressures and crises during that early survival period.

What outside help did you get? Did you have experienced advisors? lawyers? accountants? tax experts? patent experts? How did you develop these networks and how long did it take?

How did any outside advisors make a difference in your company?

What was your family situation at the time?

What did you perceive to be the strengths of your venture? Weaknesses?

What was your most triumphant moment? Your worst moment?

Did you want to have partners or do it solo? Why?

- Once you got going:

What were the most difficult gaps to fill and problems to solve as you began to grow rapidly?

When you looked for key people as partners, advisors, or managers, were there any personal attributes or attitudes you were particularly seeking because you knew they would fit with you and were important to success? How did you find them?

Are there any attributes among partners and advisors that you would definitely try to avoid?

Have things become more predictable? Or less?

Do you spend more time, the same amount of time, or less time with your business now than in the early years?

Do you feel more managerial and less entrepreneurial now?

In terms of the future, do you plan to harvest? To maintain? To expand?

In your ideal world, how many days a year would you want to work? Please explain.

Do you plan ever to retire? Would you explain?

Have your goals changed? Have you met them?

Has your family situation changed?

What do you learn from both success and failure?

What were/are the most demanding conflicts or trade-offs you face (e.g., the business versus personal hobbies or a relationship, children, etc.)?

Describe a time you ran out of cash, what pressures this created for you, the business, your family, and what you did about it. What lessons were learned?

Can you describe a venture that did not work out for you and how this prepared you for your next venture?

Questions for Concluding

- What do you consider your most valuable asset, the thing that enabled you to make it?
- If you had it to do over again, would you do it again, in the same way?
- As you look back, what do you believe are the most critical concepts, skills, attitudes, and know-how you needed to get your company started and grown to where it is today? What will be needed for the next five years? To what extent can any of these be learned?
- Some people say there is a lot of stress being an entrepreneur. What have you experienced? How would you say it compares with other "hot seat" jobs, such as the head of a big company, or a partner in a large law or accounting firm?
- What things do you find personally rewarding and satisfying as an entrepreneur? What have been the rewards, risks, and trade-offs?
- Who should try to be an entrepreneur? And who should not?
- What advice would you give an aspiring entrepreneur? Could you suggest the three most important lessons you have learned? How can I learn them while minimizing the tuition?
- Would you suggest any other entrepreneur I should talk to?
- Are there any other questions you wished I had asked, from which you think I could learn valuable lessons?

STEP 4

Evaluate What You Have Learned.
Summarize the most important observations and insights you have gathered from these interviews. Contrast especially what patterns, differences, and similarities exist between lifestyle and high potential entrepreneurs. Who can be an entrepreneur? What surprised you the most? What was confirmed about entrepreneurship? What new insights emerged? What are the implications for you personally, your goals, career aspirations?

STEP 5

Write a Thank You Note.
This is more than a courtesy; it will also help the entrepreneur remember you favorably should you want to follow up on the interview.

Case

Roxanne Quimby

Preparation Questions

1. Who can be an entrepreneur?
2. What are the risks, rewards, and trade-offs of a lifestyle business vs. a high potential business—one that will exceed $5 million in sales and grow substantially?
3. What is the difference between an idea and an opportunity? For whom? What can be learned from Exhibits C and D?
4. Why has the company succeeded so far?
5. What should Roxanne and Burt do, and why?

> *Our goal for the first year was $10,000 in total sales. I figured if I could take home half of that, it would be more money than I'd ever seen.*
>
> Roxanne Quimby

Introduction

Roxanne Quimby sat in the president's office of Burt's Bees' newly relocated manufacturing facility in Raleigh, North Carolina. She was surrounded by unpacked boxes and silence from the unmoving machines with no one there to operate them. Quimby looked around and asked herself, "Why did I do this?" She felt lonely and missed Maine, Burt's Bees' previous home. Quimby had founded and built Burt's Bees, a manufacturer of beeswax-based personal care products and handmade crafts, in central Maine and was not convinced she shouldn't move it back there. She explained:

> When we got to North Carolina, we were totally alone. I realized how much of the business existed in the minds of the Maine employees. There, everyone had their mark on the process. That was all lost when we left Maine in 1994. I just kept thinking "Why did I move Burt's Bees?" I thought I would pick the company up and move it and everything would be the same. Nothing was the same except that I was still working 20-hour days.

Quimby had profound doubts about this move to North Carolina and was seriously considering moving back to Maine. She needed to make a decision quickly because Burt's Bees was in the process of hiring new employees and purchasing a great deal of manufacturing equipment. If she pulled out now, losses could be minimized and she could hire back each of the 44 employees she had left back in Maine, since none of them had found new jobs yet. On the other hand, it would be hard to ignore all the reasons she had decided to leave Maine in the first place. If she moved Burt's Bees back, she would face the same problems that inspired this move. In Maine, Burt's Bees would probably never grow over $3 million in sales, and Quimby felt it had potential for much more.

Roxanne Quimby

The Black Sheep

"I was a real black sheep in my family," Quimby said. She had one sister who worked for AMEX, another sister who worked for Charles Schwab, and her father worked for Merrill Lynch. She was not interested in business at all, though, and considered it dull. Quimby attended the San Francisco Art Institute in the late 1960s and "got radicalized out there," she explained. "I studied, oil painted, and graduated without any job prospects. I basically dropped out of life. I moved to central Maine where land was really cheap—$100 an acre—and I could live removed from society."

Personal politics wasn't the only thing that pushed Quimby below the poverty line. While in college, Roxanne's father discovered she was living with her boyfriend and disowned her, severing all financial and familial ties. Her father, a Harvard Business School graduate and failed entrepreneur, did give her one gift—an early entrepreneurial education. At the age of five, Roxanne Quimby's father told her he wouldn't give her a cent for college but would match every dollar she earned herself. By her high school graduation Quimby had banked $5,000 by working on her father's numerous entrepreneurial projects and selling her own handmade crafts.

In 1975 Quimby and her boyfriend married and moved to Guilford, Maine—an hour northwest of Bangor. They bought 30 acres of land at $100 an acre and built a two-room house with no electricity, running water, or phone. In 1977 Quimby had twins and her lifestyle became a burden. She washed diapers in pots of boiling water on a wood-burning stove and struggled constantly to make ends meet with minimum wage jobs. Her marriage broke apart when the twins were four. Quimby packed up everything she owned on a toboggan and pulled the load across the snow to a friend's house.

The money-making skills her father forced her to develop allowed Quimby to survive. She and her children

 Funding provided by the Ewing Marion Kauffman Foundation.

lived in a small tent and Quimby made almost $150 a week by working local flea markets—buying low and selling high. She also held jobs waitressing. Quimby described, "I always felt I had an entrepreneurial spirit. Even as a waitress I felt entrepreneurial because I had control. I couldn't stand it when other people controlled my destiny or performance. Other jobs didn't inspire me to do my best, but waitressing did because I was accountable to myself. Eventually I got fired from these jobs because I didn't hesitate to tell the owners what I thought. I had a bit of an attitude."

In 1984 Quimby began to question her lifestyle and realized she had to make a change. She explained, "I decided I had to make a real income. I started to feel the responsibility of having kids. I had waitressing jobs but there were only three restaurants in town and I had been fired from all three. That's when I hooked up with Burt."

A Kindred Spirit

Like Roxanne Quimby, Burt Shavitz had also dropped out of life in the early 70s. A New York native and ex-photographer for *Life* and *New York* magazines, Shavitz lived in an 8′ by 8′ house (previously a turkey coop) on a 20-acre farm in Dexter, Maine, which he purchased in 1973. Shavitz, a beekeeper with 30 hives, sold honey off the back of his truck during hunting season. He earned maybe $3,000 a year, which was exactly enough to pay property taxes and buy gas for his pickup truck.

When Roxanne first saw Burt, who she described as a "good-looker," she knew she had to meet him. In an article in *Lear's* magazine Quimby said, "I pretended I was interested in the bees, but I was really interested in Burt. Here was this lone beekeeper. I wanted to fix him, to tame the wild man."[1] When Quimby and Shavitz met in 1984, the bond was immediate. Quimby talked about Shavitz's role at Burt's Bees:

> I convinced Burt into this enterprise. He has always believed in my vision, but unlike me he's emotionally detached and uninvolved. Therefore, he has some great ideas and is more likely to take risks. He's my main sounding board and gives me a lot of moral and psychological support. I never could have done this without him. In all this time, there's never been a conflict between us. The chemistry has always been there. We're just really on the same wavelength. We've been through a lot together that would have broken other relationships. I've always been the motivator and the one involved in day-to-day operations, but very rarely does he disagree with me. He's kind of my guru.

In the beginning of their fast friendship, Burt taught Roxanne about beekeeping and Roxanne discovered Burt's large stockpile of beeswax. Quimby suggested making candles with the beeswax. She took her hand-dipped and sculpted candles to a crafts fair at a local high school and brought home $200. She remembers, "I had never held that much money in my hand." Burt's Bees was born.

Quimby and Shavitz pooled $400 from their savings to launch a honey and beeswax business. They purchased some household kitchen appliances for mixing, pouring, and dipping. A friend rented them an abandoned one-room schoolhouse with no heat, running water, windows, or electricity for $150 a year—the cost of the fire insurance. Neither of them had a phone so they convinced the local health food store to take messages for Burt's Bees. Quimby traveled to fair after fair around the region, sleeping in the back of a pickup truck and making a few hundred dollars a day. She set what seemed like an impossible goal for the first year's sales—$10,000. That year, 1987, Burt's Bees made $81,000 in sales.

Burt's Bees' Early Success

Burt's Bees' big break came in 1989 at a wholesale show in Springfield, Massachusetts. The owner of an upscale boutique in Manhattan bought a teddy bear candle and put it in the window of his store. The candle was a hit and the boutique owner barraged the health food store with messages asking for new shipments. Quimby began hiring employees to help with production and expanded the product line to include other handmade crafts and beeswax-based products like lip balm. In 1993, Burt's Bees had 44 employees.

Quimby explained her transformation into a businessperson:

> After a while, I realized I just liked it. I liked buying and selling things well, adding value. I had no security issues because I'd been living at the bottom for so many years. I knew if worse came to worse and the business failed, I could survive. I'd seen the worst and knew I could handle it. I'd never been trapped by the need for security or a regular paycheck. I loved the freedom of starting a business, of not knowing how it would turn out. It was this big experiment and whether it succeeded or failed totally depended on me. I realized the goal was not the most interesting part; the problems along the way were. I found business was the most incredibly liberating thing. I never would have thought that before. The only rule is that you have to make a little bit more than you spend. As long as you can do that, anything else you do is OK. There are no other opportunities that have as few rules.

Not only did Roxanne Quimby have a passion for business, but she also had a talent. Since the beginning of Burt's Bees in 1987, the company had never once dipped into the red, had always turned a profit, and its profits had always increased [see *Exhibit A*]. A number of large national retailers stocked Burt's Bees' products including L.L. Bean, Macy's, and Whole Foods Market Company. By 1993, Burt's Bees had sales representa-

[1] John Bentham, "Enterprise," *Lear's*, March 1994, pp. 20–21.

EXHIBIT A

Burt's Bees Sales, 1987–1993

Year	Sales
1987	$81,000
1988	$137,779
1989	$180,000
1990	$500,000
1991	$1,500,000
1992	$2,500,000
1993	$3,000,000

tives across the country and sold its products in every state. By all accounts, Burt's Bees' products were a success. Quimby explained their appeal:

> We sell really well in urban areas. People in urban areas need us more because they can't step out the front door and get freshness or simplicity. Our products aren't sophisticated or sleek. They're down-home and basic. Everyone has an unconscious desire for more simplicity and our products speak to that need.

The company was not only profitable, it was totally debt-free. Burt's Bees had never taken out a loan. Quimby didn't even have a credit card. When she applied for one in 1993, by then a millionaire, she had to get her sister to co-sign because she had no credit history. She was strongly averse to going into debt. Quimby explained:

> I've never taken on debt because I don't ever want to feel like I can't walk away from it this afternoon. That's important to me. A monthly payment would trap me into having to explain my actions. I love being on the edge with no predictability, no one to report to. Anyway, there was no way a bank would have given me the money to start Burt's Bees. I could just see myself with some banker trying to explain, "I've never had a job or anything but could you give me some money because I have this idea about beeswax."

Quimby was so debt-averse and cash-aware, she refused to sell products to any retailer that didn't pay its bill within the required 30 days. This meant turning down orders from retailing powerhouses like I. Magnin and Dean & Deluca. In 1993, with about $3 million in sales, the company wrote off only $2,500 in uncollected debts. In the same year, Burt's Bees had $800,000 in the bank, and pretax profits were 35 percent of sales.

The Move

The Costs of Doing Business in Maine

The main impetus for the move was the excessive costs associated with Burt's Bees' location in northern Maine. These costs were:

1. *High transport costs:* "Our transport costs were ridiculously high," said Quimby. Because of its vast distance from any metropolitan areas, shipping products to distributors and receiving materials were astronomically expensive. Burt's Bees was almost always the last stop on truckers' routes.
2. *High payroll taxes:* Burt's Bees was being taxed about 10 percent of its payroll by the state of Maine. Payroll taxes were so high because unemployment in Maine hovered around 20 percent.
3. *Lack of expertise:* In 1993, Burt's Bees had 44 employees who were all "welfare moms." Quimby said, "They brought a set of hands and a good attitude to work, but no skills." Everything was made by hand. Burt's Bees' most popular product, lip balm, was mixed with a household blender then poured from teapots into metal tins. "When we received a shipment of containers or labels, we had to break down the pallets inside the truck because no one knew how to operate a forklift. Everything was inefficient and costly. There weren't any people with expertise in Maine," Quimby explained. For a while, Quimby aggressively recruited managers from around New England. When they came up to Guilford to interview and realized how isolated the town was, though, they would turn down any offer Quimby made.

Roxanne Quimby moved the company to free Burt's Bees from these constraints and liberate it to grow. Since beginning operations in 1987, Burt's Bees struggled to keep up with demand. Quimby had no time to focus on broad management issues since she spent most of her time pouring beeswax along with the other 44 employees in order to fill distributors' unceasing orders. She explained:

> The business had developed a life of its own and it was telling me it wanted to grow. But it was growing beyond me, my expertise, my goals, and definitely beyond Maine. If I kept it in northern Maine, I would have stunted its growth. But the business was my child in a way and as its mother I wanted to enable it to grow. The business provided a great income and I could have gone on like that for a while. But I knew it had a lot more potential than $3 million. At the same time, I knew $3 million was the most I could do on my own. I was working all of the time and there was no one to lean on or delegate to. My lack of formal business training really began to bite me. I didn't even know about payroll taxes. We would get fined for missing tax deadlines we didn't even know existed.

Why North Carolina?

Roxanne Quimby felt she had to move the company away from Maine. But to where? She didn't want to live in a big, bustling city, but the new location had to be central. Quimby explained how she finally chose North Carolina as Burt's Bees' new home:

> I had a map of the United States in my office with pins where all of our sales reps were. I used to always look at that map—when I was on the phone, doing paperwork, or just sitting at my desk—until one day I noticed North Carolina. It just seemed central, well placed. And, it turned out, a large percentage of the country's population lives within a 12-hour drive of North Carolina. One of my biggest worries about moving was telling Burt. I said to Burt one day, "We need to move and it looks like North Carolina is the place to go." Burt said, "OK, Roxy" and I thought to myself, "Thank God Burt is always on my wavelength."

Burt got on the phone with a representative at the North Carolina Department of Commerce and told him about Burt's Bees. Burt and Roxanne were pleasantly surprised to learn North Carolina was extremely aggressive about recruiting new companies to the state and was eager to attract Burt's Bees, even though it was quite a bit smaller than other companies locating in the "Triangle"[2] The North Carolina Department of Commerce sent Burt's Bees a software program which Quimby used to plug in financial information and calculate the estimated taxes Burt's Bees would pay in North Carolina. The estimated taxes were significantly less than those they were paying in Maine.

Perhaps more compelling, though, was the large supply of skilled labor in North Carolina. If Burt's Bees moved, it would be able to hire an ex-Revlon plant engineer to establish and operate its manufacturing processes. Quimby also had a lead on a marketing manager in North Carolina with experience at Lancome, Vogue, and Victoria's Secret's personal care products division.

As a next step, the North Carolina Department of Commerce invited Roxanne and Burt to visit North Carolina for a three-day tour of the Triangle area and available manufacturing facilities. "You should have seen the look on the representative's face when he picked us up from the airport," Quimby laughed. "Burt has this deep, gruff voice, so he must have sounded very different on the phone than he looks. Burt is 62, has crazy white hair to his shoulders and a long white beard, is really tall, and pretty much looks like he just walked out of the woods of Maine." She continued to say, "The representative recovered really well, though, and took us around the whole area for three days. He showed us tons of plants and real estate. He made us a great offer and we were impressed."

When they got back to Maine, Quimby called the Maine Department of Commerce to give it a chance to keep Burt's Bees in the state. "If they had offered us half the deal North Carolina did," Quimby said, "I would have taken it." The Maine Department of Commerce asked Roxanne to call back in a couple of months because the person in charge of business recruiting was out on maternity leave. Quimby marveled, "We were the second largest employer in the town and they didn't respond to us at all. We finally heard from the Governor of Maine when he read an article about us in *Forbes*[3] which mentioned we were leaving the state. By then it was too late. The move was only a few days away and we had already signed a lease on the new manufacturing facility."

Trimming the Azalea Bush: The Economics of the Move

Roxanne Quimby likened Burt's Bees' move to transplanting an azalea bush in full bloom. She said, "I realized I had to trim and prune radically to allow it to survive." In Maine, Burt's Bees biggest resource was cheap labor—people on the production line were paid $5 an hour. Therefore, most of Burt's Bees products were very labor-intensive and production was totally unautomated. All of its products, from birdhouses to candles to baby clothes, were handmade.

In North Carolina, though, the company's biggest resource was skilled labor. But skilled labor is expensive and Burt's Bees wouldn't be able to keep making its labor-intensive handmade items. Quimby would have to automate everything and change Burt's Bees' whole product line to focus on skincare products [see *Exhibit B*, for industry employment statistics]. She explained, "Our products in Maine were totally unrelated production-wise, but they were related in the sense that each product communicated down-home values and simplicity. In North Carolina, though, we would have to get rid of all the handmade products and that was pretty much everything. We had to automate."

When Quimby arrived in North Carolina she sat down to evaluate the product line and decided to focus on skincare [for general industry statistics, see *Exhibit C* and *D*]. Skincare products require only blending and filling, which is very straightforward, and machinery can do almost everything. "To justify the move to North Carolina from a cost- and manufacturing-perspective, we would have to make more 'goop,'" Quimby stated. "I looked at my list of prospective new products and there wasn't anything on the list that we made in 1988."

Quimby planned on retaining Burt's Bees environmental ethic by excluding any chemical preservatives and using primarily all-natural ingredients in its skincare products. Still, though, Burt's Bees would have to become an entirely new company and abandon the product line responsible for the company's early success.

Not only would the product line have to be overhauled, but Roxanne realized she and Burt couldn't re-

[2]The "Triangle" area in North Carolina includes Chapel Hill, Raleigh, and Durham and is the home of Research Triangle Park, a large high-tech business park similar to Silicon Valley in California or Route 128 in Massachusetts.

[3]Dana Wechsler Linder, "Dear Dad," *Forbes*, December 6, 1993, pp. 98–99.

EXHIBIT B

Occupations Employed by Standard Industrial Classification (SIC) 284: Soap, Cleaners, and Toilet Goods

Occupation	% of Industry Total, 1994	% Change to 2005 (projected)
Packaging & filling machine operators	8.5	−30.1
Hand packers & packagers	6.3	−20.1
Assemblers, fabricators, & hand workers	5.7	16.5
Sales & related workers	4.9	16.5
Freight, stock & material movers, hand	3.6	−6.8
Secretaries, ex legal & medical	3.5	6.0
Chemical equipment controllers, operators	3.0	4.8
Industrial machinery mechanics	2.7	28.1
Machine operators	2.6	2.6
Industrial truck & tractor operators	2.6	16.5
Chemists	2.5	28.1
Crushing & mixing machine operators	2.5	16.4
General managers & top executives	2.5	10.5
Traffic, shipping & receiving clerks	2.2	12.1
Marketing, advertising & PR managers	2.0	16.5
Science & mathematics technicians	1.8	16.5
Bookkeeping, accounting & auditing clerks	1.8	16.5
Maintenance repairers, general utility	1.7	4.8
Inspectors, testers & graders, precision	1.6	16.5
General office clerks	1.6	−.7
Order clerks, materials, merchandise & service	1.5	13.9
Machine feeders & offbearers	1.5	4.8
Clerical supervisors & managers	1.5	19.1
Professional workers	1.4	39.7
Industrial production managers	1.4	16.4
Stock clerks	1.4	−5.3
Managers & administrators	1.3	16.4
Adjustment clerks	1.2	39.8
Accountants & auditors	1.2	16.5
Management support workers	1.1	16.4
Engineering, mathematical & science managers	1.1	32.2
Truck drivers light & heavy	1.0	20.1

Source: *Manufacturing USA: Industry Analyses, Statistics, and Leading Companies, 5th ed., Vol 1*, ed. Arsen J. Darnay, Gale Research Inc. (1996), p. 837.

main the sole owners of the company if she wanted it to grow. Since the inception of Burt's Bees, Roxanne and Burt held 70 percent and 30 percent of its stock, respectively. The truly talented employees Quimby hoped to attract would want shared ownership of the company and would be highly motivated by stock rewards. Quimby knew sharing ownership would mean feeling accountable to others and having to justify her sometimes unorthodox decisions. Accountability was exactly what she had fought so hard to avoid her whole life, and Quimby's autonomy was partly a cause of her success.

EXHIBIT C

General Industry Statistics for SIC 2844: Toilet Preparations*

	Establishments		Employment			Compensation		Production ($million)			
Year	Total	With 20≤ Employees	Total (000)	Production Workers (000)	Production Hours (mill)	Payroll ($mill)	Wages ($/hour)	Cost of Materials	Value Added by Manufacture	Value of Shipments	Capital Investment
1988	687	277	64.9	40.5	78.1	1,551.3	9.08	4,445.1	12,053.2	16,293.6	292.6
1989	676	282	63.6	39.4	75.4	1,615.5	9.69	4,758.2	11,979.2	16,641.9	313.7
1990	682	284	63.6	38.1	74.3	1,620.6	10.14	4,904.6	12,104.2	17,048.4	280.4
1991	674	271	57.4	35.6	69.8	1,616.3	10.81	5,046.3	12,047.4	18,753.5	299.5
1992	756	305	60.1	37.2	75.6	1,783.3	10.82	5,611.3	13,167.2	19,706.4	507.3
1993	778	299	61.7	38.6	79.7	1,857.8	10.59	6,152.6	13,588.8	19,736.0	472.6

**Manufacturing USA: Industry Analyses, Statistics, and Leading Companies*, 5th ed., Vol. 1, ed. Arsen J. Darnay, Gale Research Inc. (1996), p. 833.
Source: 1982, 1987, 1992 *Economic Census; Annual Survey of Manufactures*, 83–86, 88–91, 93–94. Establishment counts for noncensus years are from *County Business Patterns*.

EXHIBIT D

Comparison of Toilet Preparations Industry (SIC 2844) to the Average of All U.S. Manufacturing Sectors, 1994*

Selected Measurement	All Manufacturing Sectors Average	SIC 2844 Average	Index
Employees per establishment	49	77	157
Payroll per establishment	$1,500,273	$ 2,397,065	160
Payroll per employee	$ 30,620	$ 31,191	102
Production workers per establishment	34	47	137
Wages per establishment	$ 853,319	$ 1,061,646	124
Wages per production worker	$ 24,861	$ 22,541	91
Hours per production worker	2,056	2,062	100
Wages per hour	$ 12.09	$ 10.93	90
Value added per establishment	$4,602,255	$17,781,454	386
Value added per employee	$ 93,930	$ 231,375	246
Value added per production worker	$ 134,084	$ 377,541	282
Cost per establishment	$5,045,178	$ 8,648,566	171
Cost per employee	$ 102,970	$ 112,536	109
Cost per production worker	$ 146,988	$ 183,629	125
Shipments per establishment	9,576,895	26,332,221	275
Shipments per employee	195,460	342,639	175
Shipments per production worker	279,017	559,093	200
Investment per establishment	$ 321,011	$ 654,570	204
Investment per employee	$ 6,552	$ 8,517	130
Investment per production worker	$ 9,352	$ 13,898	149

**Manufacturing USA: Industry Analyses, Statistics, and Leading Companies*, 5th ed., Vol. 1, ed. Arsen J. Darnay, Gale Research Inc. (1996), p. 833.

Conclusion

Quimby walked around the empty North Carolina factory. She tried to imagine the empty space filled with machinery and workers, humming with activity and production. Her mind kept reflecting back to the old schoolhouse in Maine, though. Was her ambiguity about this move merely a temporary sentimentality or should she listen to her instinct, which hadn't failed her to date? She had to make a decision soon. As she saw it, Quimby had three choices:

1. *Stay in North Carolina:* Quimby could mentally and financially commit to the North Carolina move and try to get over her doubts. Burt's Bees had promising leads in North Carolina on a plant manager from Revlon and a sales and marketing manager with experience at Lancome, Vogue, and Victoria's Secret. Quimby's expertise deficit could largely be solved with these two experts.
2. *Move back to Maine:* Quimby could halt all purchasing and hiring and move back to Maine where most of her ex-employees could be hired back. There would be some sunk costs involved, but they could be minimized if she acted quickly. Additionally, Burt's Bees could keep its original product line that made the company so successful in the first place. The governor of Maine said to call him if she changed her mind about North Carolina. She could pursue a deal with the state of Maine to mitigate Burt's Bees' tax, transport, and employment costs.
3. *Sell the Company:* Although it might be difficult to attract a buyer at only $3 million in sales, Burt's Bees had received quite a bit of attention in the industry and would be an enticing purchase to many prospective buyers. Quimby knew she didn't want to be at Burt's Bees forever and said, "I feel like at some point, this business isn't going to need me anymore. My child will grow up and want to move away from its mother. There are other things I want to do which are next on my list." Quimby dreamed about living in India and working with rural women on product design, production, and marketing of their handmade crafts. If she sold Burt's Bees, this dream could become an immediate reality.

II

PART TWO

The Opportunity

One often hears, especially from younger, newer entrepreneurs, the exhortation: "Go for it! You have nothing to lose now. So what if it doesn't work out. You can do it again. Why wait?" While the spirit this reflects is commendable and there can be no substitute for doing, such itchiness can be a mistake unless it is focused on a solid opportunity.

Most entrepreneurs launching businesses, particularly the first time, run out of cash quicker than they bring in customers and profitable sales. While there are many reasons for this, the first is that they have not focused on the *right* opportunities. Unsuccessful entrepreneurs usually equate an idea with an opportunity; successful entrepreneurs know the difference!

Successful entrepreneurs know that it is important to "think big enough." They understand that they aren't simply creating a job for themselves and a few employees; they are building a business that can create value for themselves and their community.

While there are boundless opportunities for those with entrepreneurial zest, a single entrepreneur will likely be able to launch and build only a few good businesses—probably no more than three or four—during his or her energetic and productive years. (Fortunately, all you need to do is grow and harvest one quite profitable venture whose sales have exceeded several million dollars. The result will be a most satisfying professional life, as well as a financially rewarding one.)

How important is it, then, that you screen and choose an opportunity with great care? Very important! It is no accident that venture capital investors have consistently invested in no more than 1 or 2 percent of all the ventures they review.

As important as it is to find a good opportunity, even good opportunities have risks and problems. The perfect deal has yet to be seen. Identifying risks and problems before the launch while steps can be taken to eliminate them or reduce any negative effect early is another dimension of opportunity screening.

3

Chapter Three

The Entrepreneurial Process

"I don't make movies to make money. I make money to make movies."

—Walt Disney

Results Expected

Upon completion of this chapter, you will have:

1. Developed a definition of entrepreneurship and the entrepreneurial process that spans lifestyle to high potential ventures.
2. Examined the practical issues you will address and explore throughout the book.
3. Learned how entrepreneurs and their financial backers get the odds for success in their favor, defying the pattern of disappointment and failure experienced by many.
4. Examined the Timmons Model of the entrepreneurial process, how it can be applied to your entrepreneurial career aspirations and ideas for businesses, and how recent research confirms its validity.
5. Analyzed the Kurt and John Bauer case study.

Demystifying Entrepreneurship

Entrepreneurship is a way of thinking, reasoning, and acting that is opportunity obsessed, holistic in approach, and leadership balanced.[1] Entrepreneurship results in the creation, enhancement, realization, and renewal of value, not just for owners, but for all participants and stakeholders. At the heart of the process is the creation and/or recognition of opportunities,[2] followed by the will and initiative to seize these opportunities. It requires a willingness to take risks—both personal and financial—but in a very calculated fashion in order to constantly shift the odds of success, balancing the risk with the potential reward. Typically, entrepreneurs devise ingenious strategies to marshall their limited resources.

Today, entrepreneurship has evolved beyond the classic startup notion to include companies and organizations of all types, in all stages. Thus, *entrepreneurship can occur—and fail to occur—in firms that are old and new; small and large; fast and slow growing; in the private, not-for-profit, and public sectors; in all geographic points; and in all stages of a nation's development, regardless of politics.*

Entrepreneurial leaders inject imagination, motivation, commitment, passion, tenacity, integrity, teamwork, and vision into their companies. They face dilemmas and must make decisions despite ambiguity and contradictions. Very rarely is entrepreneurship a get-rich-quick proposition. On the contrary, it is one of continuous renewal, as entrepreneurs are never satisfied with the nature of their opportunity.

[1] This definition of entrepreneurship has evolved over the past two decades from research at Babson College and the Harvard Business School and has recently been enhanced by Stephen Spinelli, Jr., the John Muller Chairholder at Babson College.

[2] J. A. Timmons, D. F. Muzyka, H. H. Stevenson, and W. D. Bygrave, "Opportunity Recognition: The Core of Entrepreneurship," in *Frontiers of Entrepreneurship Research* (Babson Park, MA: Babson College, 1987), p. 409.

The result of this value creation process, as we saw in Chapter 2, is that the total economic pie grows larger and society benefits.

Classic Entrepreneurship: The Startup

The classic expression of entrepreneurship is the raw startup company, an innovative idea that develops into a high growth company. The best of these become entrepreneurial legends: Microsoft, Netscape, Amazon.com, Sun Microsystems, Home Depot, McDonald's, Compaq Computer, Intuit, Staples, and hundreds of others are now household names. Success, in addition to the strong leadership from the main entrepreneur, almost always involves building a team with complementary talents. The ability to work as a team and sense an opportunity where others see contradiction, chaos, and confusion are critical elements of success. Entrepreneurship also requires the skill and ingenuity to find and control resources, often owned by others, in order to pursue the opportunity. It means making sure the upstart venture does not run out of money when it needs it the most. Most highly successful entrepreneurs have held together a team and acquired financial backing in order to chase an opportunity others may not recognize.

Entrepreneurship in Post-Brontosaurus Capitalism: Beyond Startups

As we saw in Chapter 2, the upstart companies of the 1970s and 1980s have had a profound impact on the competitive structure of the United States and world industries. Giant firms, such as IBM (knocked off by Apple Computer and then Microsoft), Digital Equipment Corporation (another victim of Apple Computer and acquired by Compaq Computer Corporation), Sears (demolished by upstart Wal-Mart and recently merged with Kmart), and AT&T (knocked from its perch first by MCI, and then by cellular upstarts McCaw Communications, Inc., CellularOne, and others), once thought invincible, have been dismembered by the new wave of entrepreneurial ventures. The resulting downsizing during the 1980s[3] was still going strong by the end of 2001, with Fortune 500 companies cutting more than 900,000 jobs by October. While large companies shrank payrolls, new ventures added jobs. According to a 2000 study, 4.3 million jobs and $736 billion in annual revenues were created by venture capital investments.[4] As autopsy after autopsy was performed on failing large companies, a fascinating pattern emerged, showing, at worst, a total disregard for the winning entrepreneurial approaches of their new rivals and, at best, a glacial pace in recognizing the impending demise and the changing course.

"People Don't Want to Be Managed. They Want to Be Led!"[5]

These giant firms can be characterized, during their highly vulnerable periods, as hierarchical in structure with many layers of reviews, approvals, and vetoes. Their tired executive blood conceived of leadership as *managing and administering* from the top down, in stark contrast to Ewing M. Kauffman's powerful insight, "People don't want to be managed. They want to be led!" These stagnating giants tended to reward people who accumulated the largest assets, budgets, number of plants, products, and head count, rather than rewarding those who created or found new business opportunities, took calculated risks, and occasionally made mistakes, all with bootstrap resources. While very cognizant of the importance of corporate culture and strategy, the corporate giants' pace was glacial: The research on dozens of giant companies in the 1970s and 1980s concludes that it typically took six years for a large firm to change its strategy and 10 to 30 years to change its culture. Meanwhile, the median time it took startups to accumulate the necessary capital was one month, but averaged six months.[6]

To make matters worse, these corporate giants had many bureaucratic tendencies, particularly arrogance. They shared a blind belief that if they followed the almost sacred best-management practices of the day, they could not help but prevail. During the 1970s and 1980s, these best-management practices did not include entrepreneurship, entrepreneurial leadership, and entrepreneurial reasoning. If anything, these were considered dirty words in corporate America. Chief among these sacred cows was staying close to your customer. What may shock you is the conclusion of two Harvard Business School professors:

> One of the most consistent patterns in business is the failure of leading companies to stay at the top of their industries when technologies or markets change. . . . But a more fundamental reason lies at the heart of the paradox: Leading companies succumb to one of the

[3] Edward J. Mathias, *Economic & Investment Environment—1997* (Washington, DC: The Carlyle Group, January 1998), p. 119.
[4] Ellen Florian, "Layoff Count," http://www.fortune.com/indexw.jhtml?channel=artcol.jhtml&doc id=205433, December 10, 2001.
[5] The authors' favorite quote from Ewing M. Kauffman, founder of Marion Laboratories, Inc., the Ewing Marion Kauffman Foundation, Kansas City, Missouri.
[6] W. J. Dennis, Jr., "Wells Fargo/NFIB Series on Business Starts and Stops," November 1999.

> most popular, valuable management dogmas. They stay close to their customers.[7]
>
> When they do attack, the [new] entrant companies find the established players to be easy and unprepared opponents because the opponents have been looking up markets themselves, discounting the threat from below.[8]

One gets further insight into just how vulnerable and fragile the larger, so-called well-managed companies can become, and why it is the newcomers who pose the greatest threats. This pattern also explains why there are tremendous opportunities for the coming e-generation even in markets that are currently dominated by large players. Professors Bower and Christensen summarize it this way:

> The problem is that managers keep doing what has worked in the past: serving the rapidly growing needs of their current customers. The processes that successful, well-managed companies have developed to allocate resources among proposed investments are incapable of funneling resources in programs that current customers explicitly don't want and whose profit margins seem unattractive.[9]

Coupled with what we saw in Chapter 2 regarding how many new innovations, firms, and industries have been created in the past 30 years, it is no wonder that brontosaurus capitalism has found its ice age.

Signs of Hope in a Corporate Ice Age

Fortunately, for many giant firms, the entrepreneurial revolution may spare them from their own ice age. One of the most exciting developments of the decade is the response of some large, established U.S. corporations to the revolution in entrepreneurial leadership. After nearly three decades of experiencing the demise of giant after giant, corporate leadership, in unprecedented numbers, is launching experiments and strategies to recapture entrepreneurial spirit and to instill the culture and practices we would characterize as entrepreneurial reasoning. The e-generation has too many attractive opportunities in truly entrepreneurial environments. They do not need to work for a brontosaurus that lacks spirit.

Increasingly, we see examples of large companies adopting principles of entrepreneurship and entrepreneurial leadership in order to survive and to renew. Researchers document how large firms are applying entrepreneurial thinking, in pioneering ways, to invent their futures, including companies such as GE, Corning, and Motorola,[10] Harley-Davidson Motorcycles ($1.35 billion in revenue), Marshall Industries ($2.2 billion), and Science Applications International Corporation (SAIC) in San Diego. Most large brontosaurus firms could learn valuable lessons on how to apply entrepreneurial thinking from companies such as these.

Metaphors

Improvisational, quick, clever, resourceful, and inventive all describe good entrepreneurs. Likewise, innumerable metaphors from other parts of life can describe the complex world of the entrepreneur and the entrepreneurial process. From music it is jazz, with its uniquely American impromptu flair. From sports many metaphors exist: LeBron James's agility, the broken-field running of Curtis Martin, the wizardry on ice of Wayne Gretzky, or the competitiveness of Tiger Woods. Even more fascinating are the unprecedented comebacks of athletic greats such as Michael Jordan, Picabo Street, and Lance Armstrong.

Perhaps the game of golf, more than any other, replicates the complex and dynamic nature of managing risk and reward, including all the intricate mental challenges faced in entrepreneuring. No other sport, at one time, demands so much physically, is so complex, intricate, and delicate, and is simultaneously so rewarding and punishing; and none tests one's will, patience, self-discipline, and self-control like golf. Entrepreneurs face these challenges and remunerations as well. If you think that the team concept isn't important in golf, remember the 2004 American Ryder Cup team, which failed to work together and lost to the Europeans. And what about the relationship between the caddy and golfer?

An entrepreneur also faces challenges like a symphony conductor or a coach who must blend and balance a group of diverse people with different skills, talents, and personalities into a superb team. On many occasions it demands all the talents and agility of a juggler who must, under great stress, keep many balls in the air at once, making sure if one comes down it belongs to someone else.

The complex decisions and numerous alternatives facing the entrepreneur also have many parallels with the game of chess. As in chess, the victory goes to the most creative player, who can imagine several alternate moves in advance and anticipate possible defenses.

[7] Joseph L. Bower and Clayton M. Christensen, "Disruptive Technologies: Catching the Wave," *Harvard Business Review*, January–February 1995, p. 43.
[8] Ibid., p. 47.
[9] Ibid.
[10] *Fast Company*, June–July 1997, pp. 32, 79, 104; and U. Srinivasa Rangan, "Alliances Power Corporate Renewal," Babson College, 2001.

This kind of mental agility is frequently demanded in entrepreneurial decision making.

Still another parallel can be drawn from the book, *The Right Stuff,* by Tom Wolfe, later made into a movie. The first pilot to break the sound barrier, Chuck Yeager, describes what it was like to be at the edge of both the atmosphere and his plane's performance capability, a zone never before entered—a vivid metaphor for the experience of a first-time entrepreneur:

> In the thin air at the edge of space, where the stars and the moon came out at noon, in an atmosphere so thin that the ordinary laws of aerodynamics no longer applied and a plane could skid into a flat spin like a cereal bowl on a waxed Formica counter and then start tumbling, end over end like a brick . . . you had to be "afraid to panic." In the skids, the tumbles, the spins, there was only one thing you could let yourself think about: what do I do next?[11]

This feeling is frequently the reality on earth for entrepreneurs who run out of cash! Regardless of the metaphor or analogy you choose for entrepreneurship, each is likely to describe a creative, even artistic, improvised act. The outcomes are often either highly rewarding successes or painfully visible misses. Always, urgency is on the doorstep.

Entrepreneurship = Paradoxes

One of the most confounding aspects of the entrepreneurial process is its contradictions. Because of its highly dynamic, fluid, ambiguous, and chaotic character, the process's constant changes frequently pose paradoxes. A sampling of entrepreneurial paradoxes follows. Can you think of other paradoxes that you have observed or heard about?

An opportunity with no or very low potential can be an enormously big opportunity. One of the most famous examples of this paradox is Apple Computer Inc. Founders Steve Jobs and Steve Wozniak approached their employer, Hewlett-Packard Corporation (HP), with the idea for a desktop, personal computer and were told this was not an opportunity for HP. Hence, Jobs and Wozniak started their own company. Frequently, business plans rejected by some venture capitalists become legendary successes when backed by another investor. Intuit, maker of Quicken software, for example, was rejected by 20 venture capitalists before securing backing.

To make money you have to first lose money. It is commonly said in the venture capital business that the lemons, or losers, ripen in two-and-a-half years, while the plums take seven or eight years. A startup, venture-backed company typically loses money, often \$10 million to \$25 million or more, before sustaining profitability and going public, usually at least five to seven years later.

To create and build wealth one must relinquish wealth. Among the most successful and growing companies in the United States, the founders aggressively dilute their ownership to create ownership throughout the company. By rewarding and sharing the wealth with the people who contribute significantly to its creation, owners motivate stakeholders to make the pie bigger.

To succeed, one first has to experience failure. It is a common pattern that the first venture fails, yet the entrepreneur learns and goes on to create a highly successful company. Jerry Kaplan teamed with Lotus Development Corporation founder Mitch Kapor to start the first pen-based computer. After \$80 million of venture capital investment, the company was shut down. Kaplan went on to launch On-Sale, Inc., an Internet Dutch-auction, which experienced explosive growth and went public in 1996.

Entrepreneurship requires considerable thought, preparation, and planning, yet is basically an unplannable event. The highly dynamic, changing character of technology, markets, and competition make it impossible to know all your competitors today, let alone five years from now. Yet great effort is invested in attempting to model and envision the future. The resulting business plan is inevitably obsolete when it comes off the printer. This is a creative process—like molding clay. You need to make a habit of planning and reacting as you constantly reevaluate your options, blending the messages from your head and your gut, until this process becomes second nature.

For creativity and innovativeness to prosper, rigor and discipline must accompany the process. For years, hundreds of thousands of patents for new products and technologies lay fallow in government and university research labs because there was no commercial discipline.

Entrepreneurship requires a bias toward action and a sense of urgency, but also demands

[11] Tom Wolfe, *The Right Stuff* (New York: Bantam Books, 1980), pp. 51–52.

patience and perseverance. While his competitors were acquiring and expanding rapidly, one entrepreneur's management team became nearly outraged at his inaction. This entrepreneur reported he saved the company at least $50 million to $100 million during the prior year by just sitting tight. He learned this lesson from the Jiffy Lube case series from *New Venture Creation,* which he studied during a weeklong program for the Young Presidents Organization (YPO), at Harvard Business School in 1991.

The greater the organization, orderliness, discipline, and control, the less you will control your ultimate destiny. Entrepreneurship requires great flexibility and nimbleness in strategy and tactics. One has to play with the knees bent. Overcontrol and an obsession with orderliness are impediments to the entrepreneurial approach. As the great race car driver Mario Andretti said, "If I am in total control, I know I am going too slow!"

Adhering to management best practice, especially staying close to the customer that created industry leaders in the 1980s, became a seed of self-destruction and loss of leadership to upstart competitors. We discussed earlier the study of "disruptive technologies."

To realize long-term equity value, you have to forgo the temptations of short-term profitability. Building long-term equity requires large, continuous reinvestment in new people, products, services, and support systems, usually at the expense of immediate profits.

The world of entrepreneurship is not neat, tidy, linear, consistent, and predictable, no matter how much we might like it to be that way.[12] In fact, it is from the collisions inherent in these paradoxes that value is created as illustrated in Exhibit 3.1. These paradoxes illustrate just how contradictory and chaotic this world can be. To thrive in this environment, one needs to be very adept at coping with ambiguity, chaos, and uncertainty, and at building management skills that create predictability. Exhibit 3.2 exemplifies this ambiguity and need for patience.

EXHIBIT 3.1

Entrepreneurship IS a Contact Sport

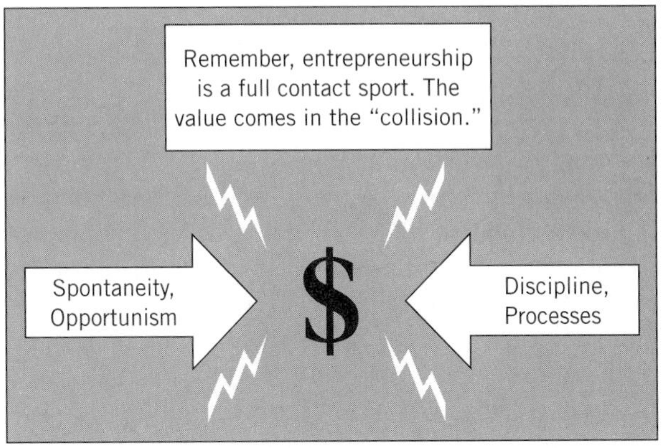

EXHIBIT 3.2

Time for New Technologies to Reach 25% of the U.S. Population

Household electricity (1873)	46 years
Telephone (1875)	35 years
Automobile (1885)	55 years
Airplane travel (1903)	54 years
Radio (1906)	22 years
Television (1925)	26 years
Videocassette recorder (1952)	34 years
Personal computer (1975)	15 years
Cellular phone	13years
Internet	**7 years**

Source: From *The Wall Street Journal,* 1997. Used by permission of Dow Jones & Co. Inc. via The Copyright Clearance Center.

The Higher Potential Venture: Think Big Enough

One of the biggest mistakes aspiring entrepreneurs make is strategic. They think too small. Sensible as it may be to think in terms of a very small, simple business as being both more affordable, more manageable, less demanding, and less risky, the opposite is true. The chances of survival and success are lower in these small, job-substitute businesses, and even if they do survive, they are less financially rewarding. As one founder of numerous businesses put it: Unless this business can pay you at least five times your present salary, the risk and wear and tear won't be worth it.

Consider one of the most successful venture capital investors ever, Arthur Rock. His criterion for searching for opportunities is very simple: *look for business concepts that will change the way people live or work.* His home-run investments are legendary, including Intel, Apple Computer, Teledyne, and dozens of others. Clearly, his philosophy is to think

[12] See Howard H. Stevenson. *Do Lunch or Be Lunch* (Cambridge, MA: Harvard Business School Press, 1998) for a provocative argument for predictability as one of the most powerful of management tools.

big. Today an extraordinary variety of people, opportunities, and strategies characterize the approximately 30 million proprietorships, partnerships, and corporations in the country. Remember, high potential ventures become high impact firms that often make the world a better place!

Eleven percent of the U.S. population is actively working toward starting a new venture.[13] More than 90 percent of startups have revenues of less than $1 million annually, while 863,505 reported revenues of $1 million to $25 million—just over 9 percent of the total. Of these, only 296,695 grew at a compounded annual growth rate of 30 percent or more for the prior three years, or about 3 percent. Similarly, just 3 percent—1 in 33—exceeded $10 million in revenues, and only 0.3 percent exceeded $100 million in revenues.

Not only can nearly anyone start a business, but also a great many can succeed. While it certainly might help, a person does not have to be a genius to create a successful business. As Nolan Bushnell, founder of Atari, one of the first desktop computer games in the early 1980s, and Pizza Time Theater, said, "If you are not a millionaire or bankrupt by the time you are 30, you are not really trying!"[14] It is an entrepreneur's preparedness for the entrepreneurial process that is important. Being an entrepreneur has moved from cult status in the 1980s to rock star infamy in the 1990s to become de rigueur at the turn of the century. Amateur entrepreneurship is over. The professionals have arrived.[15]

A stunning number of mega-entrepreneurs launched their ventures during their 20s. While the rigors of new ventures may favor the "young at start," age is *not* a barrier to entry. One study showed that nearly 21 percent of founders were over 40 when they embarked on their entrepreneurial careers, the majority were in their 30s, and just over one-quarter did so by the time they were 25. Further, numerous examples exist of founders who were over 60 at the time of launch, including one of the most famous seniors, Colonel Harland Sanders, who started Kentucky Fried Chicken with his first Social Security check.

Smaller Means Higher Failure Odds

Unfortunately, the record of survival is not good among all firms started. One of the most optimistic research firm estimates the failure rate for startups is 46.4 percent. While government data, research, and business mortality statisticians may not agree on the precise failure and survival figures for new businesses, they do agree that failure is the rule, not the exception.

Complicating efforts to obtain precise figures is the fact that it is not easy to define and identify failures, and reliable statistics and databases are not available. However, the Small Business Administration determined that in 1999 there were 588,900 startups, while 528,600 firms closed their doors.[16]

Failure rates also vary widely across industries. In 1991, for instance, retail and services accounted for 61 percent of all failures and bankruptcies in that year.[17]

The following discussion provides a distillation of a number of failure-rate studies over the past 50 years.[18] These studies illustrate that (1) failure rates are high, and (2) although the majority of the failures occur in the first two to five years, it may take considerably longer for some to fail.[19]

While government data, research, and business mortality statisticians may not always agree on the precise failure and survival figures for new businesses, they do agree that startups run a high risk of failure. Another study outlined in Exhibit 3.3 found that of 565,812 firms one year old or less in the first quarter of 1998 only 303,517 were still alive by the first quarter of 2001. This is an average failure rate of 46.4 percent.

Failure rates across industries vary as seen in Exhibit 3.3. The real estate industry, with a 36.8 percent rate of startup failure, is the lowest. The technology sector has a high rate of failure at 53.9 percent. The software and services segment of the technology industry has an even higher failure rate; 55.2 percent of startups tracked closed their doors. Unfortunately, the record of survival is not good among all firms started.

---

[13] *The Global Entrepreneurship Monitor,* Babson College and the London Business School, May 2004.
[14] In response to a student question at Founder's Day, Babson College, April 1983.
[15] *INC.,* May 15, 1997.
[16] *The State of Small Business: A Report of the President, Transmitted to the Congress,* 1999 (Washington, DC: Small Business Administration, 1999).
[17] *The State of Small Business,* 1992, p. 128.
[18] Information has been culled from the following studies: David L. Birch, MIT Studies, 1979–1980; Michael B. Teitz et al., "Small Business and Employment Growth in California," Working Paper No. 348, University of California at Berkeley, March 1981, table 5, p. 22; U.S. Small Business Administration, August 29, 1988; B. D. Phillips and B. A. Kirchhoff, "An Analysis of New Firm Survival and Growth," *Frontiers in Entrepreneurship Research: 1988,* ed. B. Kirchhoff et al. (Babson Park, MA: Babson College, 1988), pp. 266–67; and *BizMiner 2002 Startup Business Risk Index: Major Industry Report,* Brandow Co., Inc., 2002.
[19] Summaries of these are reported by Albert N. Shapero and Joseph Gigherano, "Exits and Entries: A Study in Yellow Pages Journalism," in *Frontiers of Entrepreneurship Research: 1982,* ed. K. Vesper et al. (Babson Park, MA: Babson College, 1982), pp. 113–41, and Arnold C. Cooper and Carolyn Y. Woo, "Survival and Failure: A Longitudinal Study," in *Frontiers of Entrepreneurship Research: 1988,* ed. B. Kirchhoff et al. (Babson Park, MA: Babson College, 1988), pp. 225–37.

EXHIBIT 3.3

Overall Startup Failure Rates

	Startups* Tracked			
Industry	**Startups 1998 Q1**	**Survivors 2002 Q1**	**Survival (percent)**	**Failure (percent)**
Total for all industries	565,812	303,517	53.6%	46.4%
Agriculture	15,564	9,239	59.4	40.6
Finance	14,899	8,005	53.7	46.3
Manufacturing	32,236	18,921	58.7	41.3
Real estate	16,229	10,261	63.2	36.8
Retail	142,504	72,512	50.9	49.1
Wholesale	37,307	19,171	51.4	48.6
Technology	28,575	13,159	46.1	53.9
Computer Hardware	485	221	45.6	54.4
Computer Software/Services	18,733	8,387	44.8	55.2

Source: *BizMiner 2002 Startup Business Risk Index: Major Industry Report,* © 2002 BizMiner. Reprinted by permission.

*Startups are defined as firms that are one year old or less.

To make matters worse, most people think the failure rates are actually much higher. Since actions often are governed by perceptions rather than facts, this perception of failure, in addition to the dismal record, can be a serious obstacle to aspiring entrepreneurs.

Still other studies have shown significant differences in survival rates among Bradstreet industry categories: retail trade, construction, and small service businesses accounted for 70 percent of all failures and bankruptcies. One study calculates a risk factor or index for startups by industry, which sends a clear warning signal to the would-be entrepreneur.[20] At the high end of risk is tobacco products and at the low end you find the affinity and membership organizations such as AAA or Welcome Wagon. "The fishing is better in some streams versus others," is a favorite saying of the authors. Further, 99 percent of these failed companies had fewer than 100 employees. Through observation and practical experience one would not be surprised by such reports. The implications for would-be entrepreneurs are important: Knowing the difference between a good idea and a real opportunity is vital. This will be addressed in detail in Chapter 4.

A certain level of failure is part of the "creative self-destruction" described by Joseph Schumpeter in his numerous writings, including *Business Cycles* (1939) and *Capitalism.* It is part of the dynamics of innovation and economic renewal, a process that requires both births and deaths. More important, it is also part of the learning process inherent in gaining an entrepreneurial apprenticeship. If a business fails, no other country in the world has laws, institutions, and social norms that are more forgiving. Firms go out of existence, but entrepreneurs survive and learn.

The daunting evidence of failure poses two important questions for aspiring entrepreneurs. First, are there any exceptions to this general rule of failure, or are we faced with a punishing game of entrepreneurial roulette? Second, if there is an exception, how does one get the odds for success in one's favor?

Getting the Odds in Your Favor

Fortunately, there is a decided pattern of exceptions to the overall rate of failure among the vast majority of small, marginal firms created each year. Most smaller enterprises that cease operation simply do not meet our notion of entrepreneurship. They do not create, enhance, or pursue opportunities that realize value. They tend to be job substitutes in many instances. Undercapitalized, undermanaged, and often poorly located, they soon fail.

Threshold Concept

Who are the survivors? The odds for survival and a higher level of success change dramatically if the venture reaches a critical mass of at least 10 to 20 people with \$2 million to \$3 million in revenues and is currently pursuing opportunities with growth potential.

[20] *BizMiner 2002 Startup Business Risk Index.*

EXHIBIT 3.4

One-Year Survival Rates by Firm Size

Firm Size (employees)	Survival Percent
1–24	53.6%
25–49	68.0
50–99	69.0
100–249	73.2

Source: *BizMiner 2002 Startup Business Risk Index: Major Industry Report,* © 2002 BizMiner. Reprinted by permission.

Exhibit 3.4 shows that based on a cross-section of all new firms, one-year survival rates for new firms increase steadily as the firm size increases. The rates jump from approximately 54 percent for firms having up to 24 employees to approximately 73 percent for firms with between 100 and 249 employees.

One study found that empirical evidence supports the liability of newness and liability of smallness arguments and suggests that newness and small size make survival problematic. The authors inferred, "Perceived satisfaction, cooperation, and trust between the customer and the organization [are] important for the continuation of the relationship. High levels of satisfaction, cooperation, and trust represent a stock of goodwill and positive beliefs which are critical assets that influence the commitment of the two parties to the relationship."[21] The authors of this study noted, "Smaller organizations are found to be more responsive, while larger organizations are found to provide greater depth of service. . . . The entrepreneurial task is to find a way to either direct the arena of competition away from the areas where you are at a competitive disadvantage, or find some creative way to develop the required competency."[22]

After four years, the survival rate jumps from approximately 35 to 40 percent for firms with fewer than 19 employees to about 55 percent for firms with 20 to 49 employees. Although any estimates based on sales per employee vary considerably from industry to industry, this minimum translates roughly to a threshold of $50,000 to $100,000 of sales per employee annually. But highly successful firms can generate much higher sales per employee. According to several reports, the service industry has the most closed businesses (38.6 percent), distribution (28.7 percent), and production (17.8 percent) after four to five years.

Promise of Growth

The definition of entrepreneurship implies the promise of expansion and the building of long-term value and durable cash flow streams as well.

However, as will be discussed later, it takes a long time for companies to become established and grow. Historically, two of every five small firms founded survive six or more years but few achieve growth during the first four years.[23] The study also found that survival rates more than double for firms that grow, and the earlier in the life of the business that growth occurs, the higher the chance of survival.[24] The 2000 INC. 500 exemplify this, with a five-year growth rate of 1,933 percent.[25]

Some of the true excitement of entrepreneurship lies in conceiving, launching, and building firms such as these.

Venture Capital Backing

Another notable pattern of exception to the failure rule is found for businesses that attract startup financing from successful private venture capital companies. While venture-backed firms account for a very small percentage of new firms each year, in 2000, 238 of 414 IPOs, or 57 percent, had venture backing.[26]

Venture capital is not essential to a startup, nor is it a guarantee of success. Of the companies making the 2001 INC. 500, only 18 percent raised venture capital and only 3 percent had venture funding at startup.[27] Consider, for instance, that in 2000 only 5,557 companies received venture capital.[28] However, companies with venture capital support fare better overall. Only 46 companies with venture capital declared bankruptcy or became defunct in 2000.[29] This is less than 1 percent of companies that received venture capital in 2000.

These compelling data have led some to conclude a threshold core of 10 to 15 percent of new companies

[21] S. Venkataraman and Murray B. Low, "On the Nature of Critical Relationships: A Test of the Liabilities and Size Hypothesis," in *Frontiers in Entrepreneurship Research: 1991* (Babson Park, MA: Babson College, 1991), p. 97.
[22] Ibid., pp. 105–6.
[23] Bruce D. Phillips and Bruce A. Kirchhoff, "An Analysis of New Firm Survival and Growth," in *Frontiers in Entrepreneurship Research: 1988* (Babson Park, MA: Babson College, 1988), pp. 266–67.
[24] This reaffirms the exception to the failure rule noted above and in the original edition of this book in 1977.
[25] Susan Greco, "The INC. 500 Almanac," *INC,* October 2001, p. 80.
[26] "Aftermarket at a Glance," *The IPO Reporter,* December 10, 2001; and "IPO Aftermarket," *Venture Capital Journal,* December 2001.
[27] "The INC. 500 Almanac."
[28] Venture Economics, http://www.ventureeconomics.com/vec/stats/2001q2/us.html, July 30, 2001.
[29] *VentureXpert,* Thompson Financial Data Services, 2001.

will become the winners in terms of size, job creation, profitability, innovation, and potential for harvesting (and thereby realize a capital gain).

Private Investors Join Venture Capitalists

As noted in Chapter 2, harvested entrepreneurs by the tens of thousands have become "angels" as private investors in the next generation of entrepreneurs. Many of the more successful entrepreneurs have created their own investment pools and are competing directly with venture capitalists for deals. Their operating experiences and successful track records provide a compelling case for adding value to an upstart company. Take, for example, highly successful Boston entrepreneur Jeff Parker. His first venture, Technical Data Corporation, enabled Wall Street bond traders to conduct daily trading with a desktop computer. Parker's software on the Apple II created a new industry in the early 1980s.

After harvesting this and other ventures, he created his own private investment pool in the 1990s. As the Internet explosion occurred, he was one of the early investors to spot opportunities in startup ventures. In one case, he persuaded the founders of a new Internet firm to select him as lead investor instead of accepting offers from some of the most prestigious venture capital firms in the nation. According to the founders, it was clear that Parker's unique entrepreneurial track record and his understanding of their business would add more value than the venture capitalists at startup.

Private investors and entrepreneurs such as Parker have very similar selection criteria to the venture capitalists: They are in search of the high potential, higher growth ventures. Unlike the venture capitalists, however, they are not constrained by having to invest so much money in a relatively short period that they must invest it in minimum chunks of $3 million to $5 million or more. Private investors, therefore, are prime sources for less capital-intensive startups and early-stage businesses.

This overall search for higher potential ventures has become more evident in recent years. The new e-generation appears to be learning the lessons of these survivors, venture capitalists, private investors, and founders of higher potential firms. Hundreds of thousands of college students now have been exposed to these concepts for more than two decades, and their strategies for identifying potential businesses are mindful of and disciplined about the ingredients for success. Unlike 20 years ago, it is now nearly impossible not to hear and read about these principles whether on television, in books, on the Internet, or in a multitude of seminars, courses, and programs for would-be entrepreneurs of all types.

Find Financial Backers and Associates Who Add Value

One of the most distinguishing disciplines of these higher potential ventures is how the founders identify financial partners and key team members. They insist on backers and partners who do more than bring just money, friendship, commitment, and motivation to the venture. They surround themselves with backers who can add value to the venture through their experience, know-how, networks, and wisdom. Key associates are selected because they are smarter and better at what they do than the founder; and they raise the overall average of the entire company. This theme will be examined in detail in later chapters.

Option: The Lifestyle Venture

For many aspiring entrepreneurs, issues of family roots and location take precedence. Accessibility to a preferred way of life, whether it is access to fishing, skiing, hunting, hiking, music, surfing, rock climbing, canoeing, a rural setting, the mountains, can be more important than how large a business one has or the size of one's net worth. Others vastly prefer to be with and work with their family or spouse. They want to live in a nonurban area that they consider very attractive. Take Jake and Diana Bishop, for instance. Both have advanced degrees in accounting. They gave up six-figure jobs they both found rewarding and satisfying on the beautiful coast of Maine to return to their home state of Michigan for several important lifestyle reasons. They wanted to work together again in a business, which they had done successfully earlier in their marriage. It was important to be much closer than the 14-hour drive to Diana's aging parents. They also wanted to have their children—then in their 20s—join them in the business. Finally, they wanted to live in one of their favorite areas of the country, Harbor Spring on Lake Michigan in the northwest tip of the state. They report never to have worked harder in their 50 years, nor have they been any happier. They are growing their rental business more than 20 percent a year, making an excellent living, and creating equity value. If done right, one can have a lifestyle business and actually realize higher potential.

Yet, couples who give up successful careers in New York City to buy an inn in Vermont to avoid the rat race generally last only six to seven years. They discover the joys of self-employment, including seven-day, 70- to 90-hour workweeks, chefs and day help that do not show up, roofs that leak when least expected, and the occasional guests from hell. The grass is always greener, so they say.

The Timmons Model: Where Theory and Practice Collide in the Real World

How can aspiring entrepreneurs—and the investors and associates who join the venture—get the odds of success on their side? What do these talented and successful high potential entrepreneurs, their venture capitalists, and their private backers do differently? What is accounting for their exceptional record? Are there general lessons and principles underlying their successes that can benefit aspiring entrepreneurs, investors, and those who would join a venture? If so, can these lessons be learned?

These are the central questions of our lifetime work. We have been immersed as students, researchers, teachers, and practitioners of the *entrepreneurial process.* As founding shareholders and investors of several high potential ventures (some of which are now public), directors and advisors to ventures and venture capital funds, a charter director and advisor to the Kauffman Center for Entrepreneurial Leadership at the Ewing Marion Kauffman Foundation, and as director of the Arthur M. Blank Center for Entrepreneurship at Babson College, we have each applied, tested, refined, and tempered academic theory as fire tempers iron into steel: in the fire of practice.

Intellectual and Practical Collisions with the Real World

Throughout this period of evolution and revolution, *New Venture Creation* has adhered to one core principle: In every quest for greater knowledge of the entrepreneurial process and more effective learning, there must be intellectual and practical collisions between academic theory and the real world of practice. The standard academic notion of something being all right in practice but not in theory is unacceptable. This integrated, holistic balance is at the heart of what we know about the entrepreneurial process and getting the odds in your favor.

Value Creation: The Driving Forces

A core, fundamental entrepreneurial process accounts for the substantially greater success pattern among higher potential ventures. Despite the great variety of businesses, entrepreneurs, geographies, and technologies, central themes or driving forces dominate this highly dynamic entrepreneurial process.

- It is *opportunity* driven.
- It is driven by a *lead entrepreneur* and an *entrepreneurial team.*
- It is *resource parsimonious and creative.*
- It depends on the *fit and balance* among these.
- It is *integrated and holistic.*
- It is *sustainable.*

These are the controllable components of the entrepreneurial process that can be assessed, influenced, and altered. Founders and investors focus on these forces during their careful due-diligence process to analyze the risks and determine what changes can be made to improve a venture's chances of success.

First, we will elaborate on each of these forces to provide a blueprint and a definition of what each means. Then using the early years of Netscape as an example, we will illustrate how the holistic, balance, and fit concepts pertain to a startup.

Change the Odds: Fix It, Shape It, Mold It, Make It

The driving forces underlying successful new venture creation are illustrated in Exhibit 3.5. The process starts with opportunity, not money, strategy, networks, team, or the business plan. Most genuine opportunities are much bigger than either the talent and capacity of the team or the initial resources available to the team. The role of the lead entrepreneur and the team is to juggle all these key elements in a changing environment. Think of a juggler bouncing up and down on a trampoline that is moving on a conveyor belt at unpredictable speeds and directions, while trying to keep all three balls in the air. That is the dynamic nature of an early-stage startup. The business plan provides the language and code for communicating the quality of the three driving forces of the Timmons Model and of their fit and balance.

In the entrepreneurial process depicted in the Timmons Model, the shape, size, and depth of the opportunity establishes the required shape, size, and depth of both the resources and the team. We have found that many people are a bit uncomfortable viewing the opportunity and resources somewhat precariously balanced by the team. It is especially disconcerting to some because we show the three key elements of the entrepreneurial process as circles, and thus the balance appears tenuous. These reactions are justified, accurate, and realistic. The entrepreneurial process is dynamic. Those who recognize the risks better manage the process and garner more return.

EXHIBIT 3.5

The Timmons Model of the Entrepreneurial Process

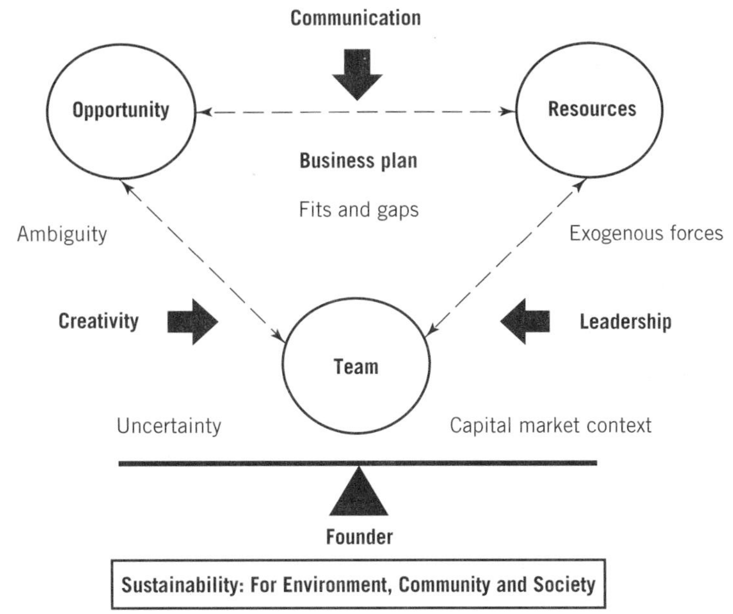

The lead entrepreneur's job is simple enough. He or she must carry the deal by *taking charge of the success equation.* In this dynamic context, ambiguity and risk are actually your friends. Central to the homework, creative problem solving and strategizing, and due diligence that lies ahead is analyzing the fits and gaps that exist in the venture. What is wrong with this opportunity? What is missing? What good news and favorable events can happen, as well as the adverse? What has to happen to make it attractive and a fit for me? What market, technology, competitive, management, and financial risks can be reduced or eliminated? What can be changed to make this happen? Who can change it? What are the least resources necessary to grow the business the farthest? Is this the right team? By implication, if you can determine these answers and make the necessary changes by figuring out how to fill the gaps and improve the fit and attract key players who can add such value, then the odds for success rise significantly. In essence, the entrepreneur's role is to manage and redefine the risk–reward equation—all with an eye towards **sustainability.** Since part of the entrepreneur's legacy is to create positive impact without harming the environment, the community, or society, the concept of sustainability appears as the underlying foundation in the model.

The Opportunity At the heart of the process is the opportunity. Successful entrepreneurs and investors know that a good idea is not necessarily a good opportunity. For every 100 ideas presented to investors in the form of a business plan or proposal, usually fewer than 4 get funded. More than 80 percent of those rejections occur in the first few hours; another 10 to 15 percent are rejected after investors have read the business plan carefully. Less than 10 percent attract enough interest to merit a more due diligence thorough review that can take several weeks or months. These are very slim odds. Countless hours and days have been wasted by would-be entrepreneurs chasing ideas that are going nowhere. An important skill for an entrepreneur or an investor is to be able to quickly evaluate whether serious potential exists, and to decide how much time and effort to invest.

John Doerr is a senior partner at one of the most famous and successful venture capital funds ever, Kleiner, Perkins, Caulfield & Byers, and is considered by some to be the most influential venture capitalist of his generation. During his career, he has been the epitome of the revolutionaries described earlier, who have created new industries as lead investors in such legends as Sun Microsystems, Compaq Computer, Lotus Development Corporation, Intuit, Genentech, Millennium, Netscape, and Amazon.Com. Regardless of these past home runs, Doerr insists, "There's never been a better time than now to start a company. In the past, entrepreneurs started businesses. Today they invent new business models. That's a big difference, and it creates huge opportunities."[30]

[30] "John Doerr's Start-Up Manual," *Fast Company,* February–March 1997, pp. 82–84.

EXHIBIT 3.6

The Entrepreneurial Process Is Opportunity Driven*

Market demand is a key ingredient to measuring an opportunity:

- Is customer payback less than one year?
- Do market share and growth potential equal 20 percent annual growth and is it durable?
- Is the customer reachable?

Market structure and size help define an opportunity:

- Emerging and/or fragmented?
- $50 million or more, with a $1 billion potential?
- Proprietary barriers to entry?

Margin analysis helps differentiate an opportunity from an idea:

- Low cost provider (40 percent gross margin)?
- Low capital requirement versus the competition?
- Break even in 1–2 years?
- Value added increase of overall corporate P/E ratio?

*Durability of an opportunity is a widely misunderstood concept. In entrepreneurship, durability exists when the investor gets her money back plus a market or better return on investment.

Another venture capitalist recently stated, "After the irrational exuberance of the late 90s, it is again a great time to start a business. Venture capital is plentiful, valuations make sense and venture capitalists are anxious for high potential ventures."[31]

Exhibit 3.6 summarizes the most important characteristics of good opportunities. Underlying market demand—because of the value-added properties of the product or service, the market's size and 20-plus percent growth potential, the economics of the business, particularly robust margins (40 percent or more), and free cash flow characteristics—drives the value creation potential.

We build our understanding of opportunity by first focusing on market readiness: the consumer trends and behaviors that seek new products or services. Once these emerging patterns are identified, the aspiring entrepreneur develops a service or product concept and, finally, the service or product delivery system is conceived. We then ask the questions articulated in the exhibit.

These criteria will be described in great detail in Chapter 4 and can be applied to the search and evaluation of any opportunity. In short, the greater the growth, size, durability, and robustness of the gross and net margins and free cash flow, the greater the opportunity. The more *imperfect* the market, the greater the opportunity. The greater the rate of change, the discontinuities, and the chaos, the greater is the opportunity as we saw with Moore's Law and Drucker's Postulate in Chapter 2. The greater the inconsistencies in existing service and quality, in lead times and lag times, and the greater the vacuums and gaps in information and knowledge, the greater is the opportunity.

EXHIBIT 3.7

Understand and Marshall Resources, Don't Be Driven by Them

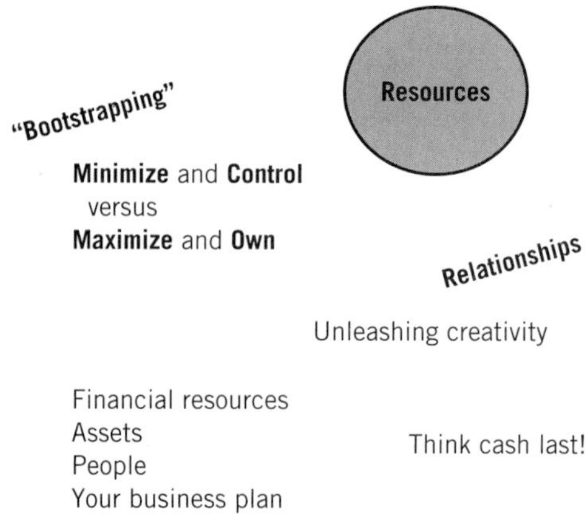

Resources: Creative and Parsimonious

One of the most common misconceptions among untried entrepreneurs is that you first need to have all the resources in place, especially the money, to succeed with a venture. Thinking money first is a big mistake. Money follows high potential opportunities conceived of and led by a strong management team. Investors have bemoaned for years that there is too much money chasing too few deals. In other words, there is a shortage of quality entrepreneurs and opportunities, not money. Successful entrepreneurs devise ingeniously creative and stingy strategies to marshal and gain control of resources (Exhibit 3.7). Surprising as it may sound, investors and successful entrepreneurs often say one of the worst things that can happen to an entrepreneur is to have *too much money too early.*

Howard Head is a wonderful, classic example of succeeding with few resources. He developed the first metal ski, which became the market leader, and then the oversize Prince tennis racket—developing two totally unrelated technologies is a rare feat. Head

[31]Ernie Parizeau, Partner, Norwest Venture Partners, June 2001.

left his job at a large aircraft manufacturer during World War II and worked in his garage on a shoestring budget to create his metal ski. It took more than 40 versions before he developed a ski that worked and could be marketed. He insisted that one of the biggest reasons he finally succeeded is that he had so little money. He argued that if he had complete financing he would have blown it all long before he evolved the workable metal ski.

Bootstrapping is a way of life in entrepreneurial companies and can create a significant competitive advantage. Doing more with less is a powerful competitive weapon, as we saw in Chapter 2 as upstart Cellular One outperformed NYNEX three-to-one with one-half to one-third the resources. Each company's approach was to minimize and control the resources, but not necessarily own them. Whether it is assets for the business, key people, the business plan, or startup and growth capital, successful entrepreneurs *think cash last.* Such strategies encourage a discipline of leanness, where everyone knows that every dollar counts, and the principle "conserve your equity" (CYE) becomes a way of maximizing shareholder value.

The Entrepreneurial Team There is little dispute today that the entrepreneurial team is a key ingredient in the higher potential venture. Investors are captivated "by the creative brilliance of a company's head entrepreneur: A Mitch Kapor, a Steve Jobs, a Fred Smith . . . and bet on the superb track records of the management team working as a group."[32] Venture capitalist John Doerr reaffirms General George Doriot's dictum: I prefer a Grade A entrepreneur and team with a Grade B idea, over a Grade B team with a Grade A idea. Doerr stated, "In the world today, there's plenty of technology, plenty of entrepreneurs, plenty of money, plenty of venture capital. What's in short supply is great teams. Your biggest challenge will be building a great team."[33]

Famous investor Arthur Rock articulated the importance of the team more than a decade ago. He put it this way: "If you can find good people, they can always change the product. Nearly every mistake I've made has been I picked the wrong people, not the wrong idea."[34] Finally, as we saw earlier, the ventures with more than 20 employees and $2 million to $3 million in sales were much more likely to survive and prosper than smaller ventures. In the vast majority of cases, it is very difficult to grow beyond this without a team of two or more key contributors.

Clearly, a new venture requires a lead entrepreneur that has personal characteristics described in

EXHIBIT 3.8

An Entrepreneurial Team Is a Critical Ingredient for Success

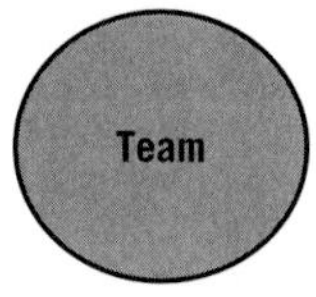

An entrepreneurial leader
- Learns and teaches—faster, better
- Deals with adversity, is resilient
- Exhibits integrity, dependability, honesty
- Builds entrepreneurial culture and organization

Quality of the team

"Passion"
- Relevant experience and track record
- Motivation to excel
- Commitment, determination, and persistence
- Tolerance of risk, ambiguity, and uncertainty
- Creativity
- Team locus of control
- Adaptability
- Opportunity obsession
- Leadership and courage
- Communication

Exhibit 3.8. But the high potential venture also requires interpersonal skills to foster communications and, therefore, team building.

Exhibit 3.8 summarizes the important aspects of the team. These teams invariably are formed and led by a very capable entrepreneurial leader whose track record exhibits both accomplishments and several qualities that the team must possess. A pacesetter and culture creator, the lead entrepreneur is central to the team as both a player and a coach. The ability and skill in attracting other key management members and then building the team is one of the most valued capabilities investors look for. The founder who becomes the leader does so by building heroes in the team. A leader adapts a philosophy that rewards success and supports honest failure, shares the wealth with those who help create it, and sets high standards for both performance and conduct. We will examine in detail the entrepreneurial leader and the new venture team in Chapters 7 and 8.

Importance of Fit and Balance Rounding out the model of the three driving forces is the concept of fit and balance between and among these forces. Note that the team is positioned at the bottom of the triangle in the Timmons Model (Exhibit 3.5). Imagine the founder, the entrepreneurial leader of the venture, standing on a large ball, balancing the triangle over her head. This imagery is helpful in

[32] William D. Bygrave and Jeffry A. Timmons, *Venture Capital at the Crossroads* (Boston: Harvard Business School Press, 1992), p. 8.
[33] *Fast Company*, February–March 1997, p. 84.
[34] Arthur Rock, "Strategy vs. Tactics from a Venture Capitalist," *Harvard Business Review*, November–December 1987, pp. 63–67.

appreciating the constant balancing act since opportunity, team, and resources rarely match. When envisioning a company's future, the entrepreneur can ask: What pitfalls will I encounter to get to the next boundary of success? Will my current team be large enough, or will we be over our heads if the company grows 30 percent over the next two years? Are my resources sufficient (or too abundant)? Vivid examples of the failure to maintain a balance are everywhere, such as when large companies throw too many resources at a weak, poorly defined opportunity. For example, Lucent Technologies' misplaced assumption slowness to react to bandwidth demand resulted in an almost 90 percent reduction in market capitalization.

Exhibit 3.9 shows how this balancing act evolved for Netscape from inception through the initial public offering to just before its merger with AOL Time Warner. While the drawings oversimplify these incredibly complex events, they help us to think conceptually—an important entrepreneurial talent—about the company building process, including the strategic and management implications of striving to achieve balance and the inevitable fragility of the process.

The Internet was a huge, rapidly growing, but elusive opportunity. Mark Andressen had no significant capital or other resources to speak of. There was no team. Such a mismatch of ideas, resources, and talent could quickly topple out of the founder's control and fall into the hands of someone who could turn it into a real opportunity. Visually, the process can be appreciated as a constant balancing act, requiring continual assessment, revised strategies and tactics, an experimental approach. By addressing the types of questions necessary to shape the opportunity, the resources, and the team, the founder begins to mold the idea into an opportunity, and the opportunity into a business, just as you would mold clay from a shapeless form into a piece of artwork.

At the outset, founder Marc Andressen would have seen something like the first figure, Exhibit 3.9(a), with the huge Internet opportunity far outweighing the team and resources. The gaps were major. Enter venture capitalist John Doerr, the first venture capitalist to vividly see the size and potential of the opportunity. He had great faith in Andressen and knew he could fill the resource gaps and help build the team, both with inside management and outside directors and professional advisors. This new balance in Exhibit 3.9(b) creates a justifiable investment. The opportunity is still huge and growing, and competitors are inevitable (see Exhibit 3.9(c)). To fully exploit this opportunity, attract a large and highly talented group of managers and professionals, and create even greater financial strength than competitors, the company must complete an initial public stock offering (IPO). Strategic investors can greatly enhance the balance of the driving forces. Strategic investors, or partners, are defined as

EXHIBIT 3.9(a)

Netscape—Journey through the Entrepreneurial Process: At Startup, a Huge Imbalance

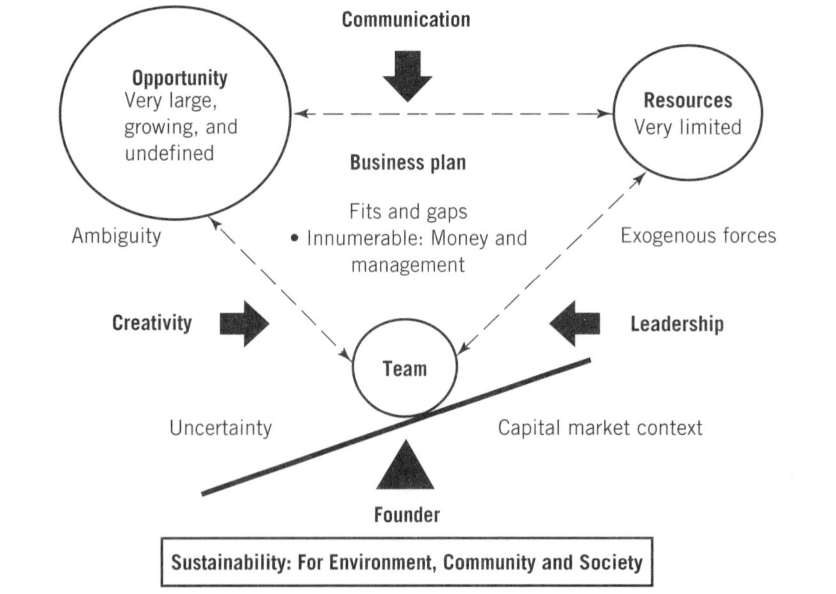

EXHIBIT 3.9(b)

Netscape—Journey through the Entrepreneurial Process: At Venture Capital Funding, toward New Balance

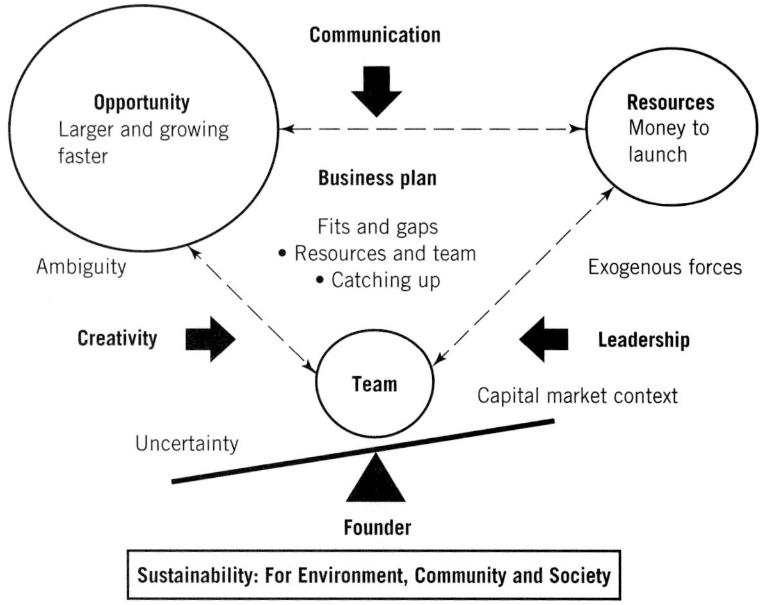

EXHIBIT 3.9(c)

Netscape—Journey through the Entrepreneurial Process: At IPO, a New Balance

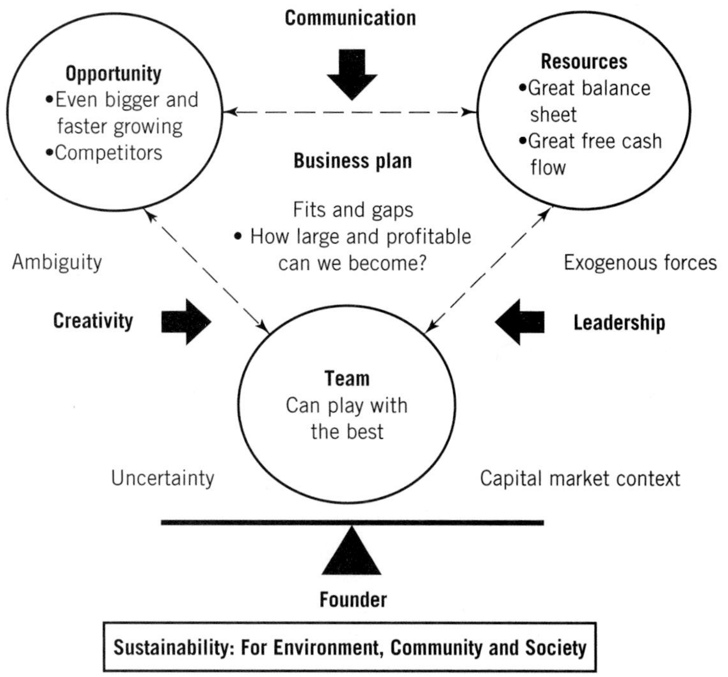

EXHIBIT 3.9(d)

Netscape—Journey through the Entrepreneurial Process: Today, toward a New Imbalance

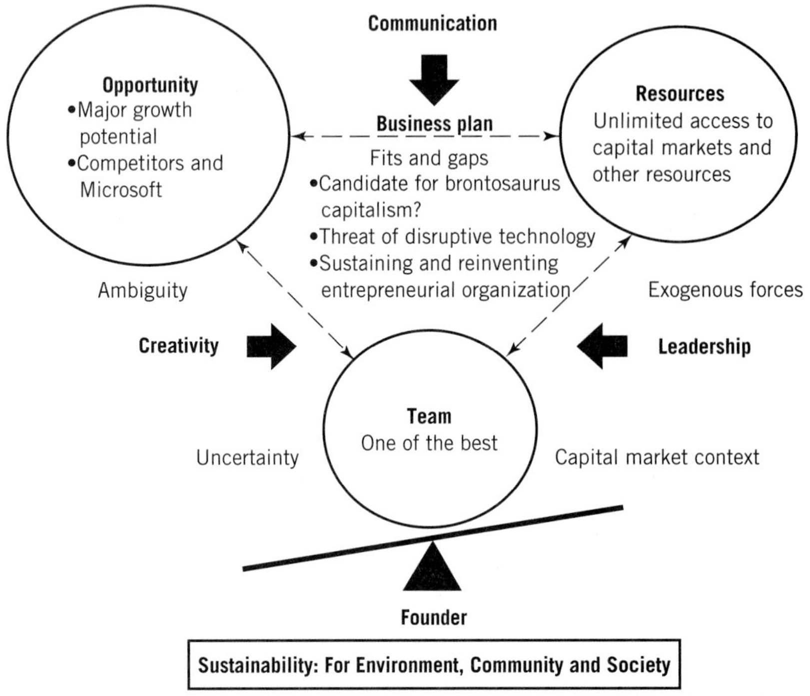

people who can fill gaps left by other members of the team. They create balance where imbalance exists. The role of the strategic investor differs according to the needs of a venture.

Netscape emerged (see Exhibit 3.9(d)) larger and stronger in people and resources but faced new challenges. Even the best and brightest of new ventures tend to erode over two or more decades into slow-moving, reactive firms. Could Netscape sustain and reinvent its entrepreneurial roots and organization as the opportunity continued to mushroom and competition for markets, people, and technology were greater than ever? Would it become blindsided and eclipsed by a new disruptive technology, just as Apple Computer and Microsoft bludgeoned IBM and Digital Equipment? Netscape was acquired by AOL (.45 shares in AOL for every share of Netscape) in 1998. This all-stock deal valued Netscape at $4.2 billion. In effect, AOL acquired Netscape so that AOL would *not* become a brontosaurus!

This iterative entrepreneurial process is based on both logic and trial and error. It is both intuitive and consciously planned. It is a process not unlike what the Wright brothers originally engaged in while creating the first self-propelled airplane. They conducted more than 1,000 glider flights before succeeding. These trial-and-error experiments led to the new knowledge, skills, and insights needed to actually fly. Entrepreneurs have similar learning curves.

The fit issue can be appreciated in terms of a question: This is a fabulous opportunity, but for whom? Some of the most successful investments ever were turned down by numerous investors before the founders received backing. Intuit received 20 rejections for startup funding by sophisticated investors. One former student, Ann Southworth, was turned down by 24 banks and investors before receiving funding for an elderly extended-care facility. Ten years later, the company was sold for an eight-figure profit. Time and again, there can be a mismatch between the type of business and investors, the chemistry between founders and backers, or a multitude of other factors that can cause a rejection. Thus, how the unique combination of people, opportunity, and resources come together at a particular time may determine a venture's ultimate chance for success.

The potential for attracting outside funding for a proposed venture depends on this overall fit and how the investor believes he or she can add value to this fit and improve the fit, risk–reward ratio, and odds for success. Exhibit 3.10 shows the possible outcomes.

EXHIBIT 3.10

Fit of Entrepreneur and Venture Capital

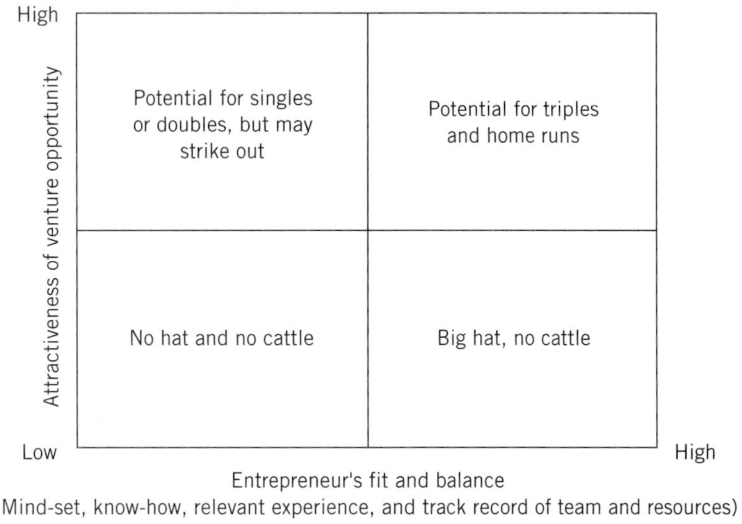

Importance of Timing Equally important is the timing of the entrepreneurial process. Each of these unique combinations occurs in real time, where the hourglass drains continually and may be friend, foe, or both. Decisiveness in recognizing and seizing the opportunity can make all the difference. Don't wait for the perfect time to take advantage of an opportunity; there is no perfect time. Most new businesses run out of money before they can find enough customers and the right team for their great idea. Opportunity is a moving target.

Recent Research Supports the Model

The Timmons Model originally evolved from doctoral dissertation research at the Harvard Business School, about new and growing ventures. Over nearly three decades, the model has evolved and been enhanced by ongoing research, case development, teaching, and experience in high potential ventures and venture capital funds. The fundamental components of the model have not changed, but their richness and relationships of each to the whole have been steadily enhanced as they have become better understood. Numerous other researchers have examined a wide range of topics in entrepreneurship and new venture creation. The bottom line is that the model, in its simple elegance and dynamic richness, harnesses what you need to know about the entrepreneurial process in order to get the odds in your favor. As each of the chapters and accompanying cases, exercises, and issues expand on the process, addressing individual dimensions, a detailed framework with explicit criteria will emerge. If you engage this material fully, you cannot help but improve your chances of success.

The 2001 INC. 500 companies had on average a five-year growth rate of 1,933 percent, 2000 sales of \$25 million, and 160 employees.[35] Similar to the INC. 500 companies, the Ernst & Young LLP Entrepreneur of the Year winners were the basis of a major research effort conducted by the National Center for Entrepreneurship Research at the Kauffman Center for Entrepreneurial Leadership, with a specific focus on 906 high growth companies.[36] These findings provide important benchmarks of the practices in a diverse group of industries, among a high performing group of companies.

Most significantly, these results reconfirm the importance of the model and its principles: the team, the market opportunity, the resource strategies, most of the individual criteria, the concept of fit and balance, and the holistic approach to entrepreneurship.

Exhibit 3.11 summarizes the 26 leading practices identified in four key areas: marketing, finances, management, and planning. (A complete version of the study is available from the National Center for Entrepreneurship Research, Kauffman Center for Entrepreneurial Leadership, Kansas City, MO 64112.)

[35] Susan Greco, "INC. 500 Almanac," *INC.*, October 2001, pp. 74–84.

[36] Donald L. Sexton and Forrest I. Seale, *Leading Practices of Fast Growth Entrepreneurs: Pathways to High Performance* (Kansas City, MO: Kauffman Center for Entrepreneurial Leadership, 1997).

EXHIBIT 3.11

Leading Practices

Leading marketing practices of fast growth firms

- Deliver products and services that are perceived as highest quality to expanding segments.
- Cultivate pacesetting new products and services that stand out in the market as best of the breed.
- Deliver product and service benefits that demand average or higher market pricing.
- Generate revenue flows from existing products and services that typically sustain approximately 90% of the present revenue base, while achieving flows from new products and services that typically expand revenue approximately 20% annually.
- Generate revenue flows from existing customers that typically sustain approximately 80% of the ongoing revenue base, while achieving flows from new customers that typically expand revenue flows by about 30% annually.
- Create high impact, new product and service improvements with development expenditures that typically account for no more than approximately 6% of revenues.
- Utilize a high yield sales force that typically accounts for approximately 60% of marketing expenditures.
- Rapidly develop broad product and service platforms with complementary channels to help expand a firm's geographic marketing area.

Leading financial practices of fast growth firms

- Anticipate multiple rounds of financing (on average every 2.5 years).
- Secure funding sources capable of significantly expanding their participation amounts.
- Utilize financing vehicles that retain the entrepreneur's voting control.
- Maintain control of the firm by selectively granting employee stock ownership.
- Link the entrepreneur's long-term objectives to a defined exit strategy in the business plan.

Leading management practices of fast growth firms

- Use a collaborative decision-making style with the top management team.
- Accelerate organizational development by assembling a balanced top management team with or without prior experience of working together.
- Develop a top management team of three to six individuals with the capacity to become the entrepreneur's entrepreneurs. Align the number of management levels with the number of individuals in top management.
- Establish entrepreneurial competency first in the functional areas of finance, marketing, and operations. Assemble a balanced board of directors comprised of both internal and external directors.
- Repeatedly calibrate strategies with regular board of directors meetings.
- Involve the board of directors heavily at strategic inflection points.

Leading planning practices of fast growth firms

- Prepare detailed written monthly plans for each of the next 12 to 24 months and annual plans for three or more years.
- Establish functional planning and control systems that tie planned achievements to actual performance and adjust management compensation accordingly.
- Periodically share with employees the planned versus actual performance data directly linked to the business plan.
- Link job performance standards that have been jointly set by management and employees to the business plan.
- Prospectively model the firm based on benchmarks that exceed industry norms, competitors, and the industry leader.

Chapter Summary

1. We began to demystify entrepreneurship by examining its classic startup definition and a broader, holistic way of thinking, reasoning, and acting that is opportunity obsessed and leadership balanced.
2. Entrepreneurship has many metaphors and poses many paradoxes.
3. Getting the odds in your favor is the entrepreneur's perpetual challenge, and the smaller the business the poorer are the odds of survival.
4. Thinking big enough can improve the odds significantly. Higher potential ventures are sought by successful entrepreneurs, venture capitalists, and private investors.
5. The Timmons Model is at the heart of spotting and building the higher potential venture and understanding its three driving forces: opportunity, the team, and resources. The concept of fit and balance is crucial.
6. Recent research on CEOs of fast-growth ventures nationwide adds new validity to the model.

Study Questions

1. Can you define what is meant by classic entrepreneurship and the high potential venture? Why and how are threshold concepts, cover your equity, bootstrapping of resources, fit, and balance important?
2. How many additional metaphors and paradoxes about entrepreneurship can you write down?
3. "People don't want to be managed, they want to be led." Explain what this means and its importance and implications for developing your own style and leadership philosophy.
4. What are the most important determinants of success and failure in new businesses? Who has the best and worst chances for success, and why?
5. What are the most important things you can do to get the odds in your favor?
6. What criteria and characteristics do high growth entrepreneurs, venture capitalists, and private investors seek in evaluating business opportunities? How can these make a difference?
7. Define and explain the Timmons Model. Apply it and graphically depict, as in the Netscape example, the first five years or so of a new company with which you are familiar.
8. What are the most important skills, values, talents, abilities, and mind-sets one needs to cultivate as an entrepreneur?

Internet Resources for Chapter 3

http://www.entreworld.com *Resources for the Entrepreneur (The Kauffman Foundation)*

http://www.entrepreneur.com *Entrepreneur Magazine*

http://www.ey.com *Ernst & Young*

http://www.pwcglobal.com *PricewaterhouseCoopers*

http://www.yeo.org *Young Entrepreneurs' Organization*

http://www.startupjournal.com *The Wall Street Journal Center for Entrepreneurs*

MIND STRETCHERS

Have you considered?

1. Who can be an entrepreneur? When?
2. More than 80 percent of entrepreneurs learn the critical skills they need after age 21. What does this mean for you?
3. In your lifetime, the odds are that leading firms today such as Microsoft, Netscape, Dell Computer, American Airlines, McDonald's, and American Express will be knocked off by upstarts. How can this happen? Why does it present an opportunity, and for whom?
4. What do you need to be doing now, and in the next 12 months, to get the odds in your favor?
5. List 100 ideas and then pick out the best 5 that might be an opportunity. How can these become opportunities? Who can make them opportunities?

Case

Kurt and John Bauer

Preparation Questions

1. Evaluate the opportunity facing Kurt Bauer in 1994 and his business plan.
2. What fund-raising strategy would you recommend?
3. How would you value a startup company?
4. What should the professor say? What should Kurt do?

Kurt Bauer sat in his usual seat in the sky deck of his Entrepreneurial Finance class. The last class of his career at a rather well-known East Coast business school had just ended and his professor, who had just received a standing ovation amid calls of "O Captain, My Captain,"[1] left the room for the final time. In addition to Entrepreneurial Finance, Kurt had conducted an independent study project with this professor, who had heard about his job search many times: He would probably hear about it again.

Kurt had come to business school to figure out how to recognize great business opportunities. His family background predisposed him to entrepreneurship; Kurt had fond memories of wandering around his grandfather's manufacturing business, visiting his dad's packing plant in Pennsylvania, and working in his mother's store. These experiences not only made him feel comfortable with the risk of entrepreneurship, but were also a source of passion for becoming an entrepreneur.

The quest for a golden opportunity seemed within reach. Kurt had evaluated numerous opportunities and had narrowed the field to two. Now it was time to graduate and decide which life to live next.

Privatizing Eastern Europe

Before business school, Kurt spent two years working on privatization and economic reform in Eastern Europe and the former Soviet Union. This work made him realize the potential of setting up a business in Russia. He recalled discussing business ideas while having dinner with a reporter for the *Financial Times* who said, "Every sentence written about Eastern Europe contains clues to a business opportunity."

Toward the end of his work in Eastern Europe, Kurt looked into several startup possibilities. He spent two months researching the possibility of setting up a food packaging company in Russia. The company would be a subsidiary of his father's packaging company in Pennsylvania. The dearth of packaging in Russia, the potential market, the availability of supplies, and the cost structure of the business made the idea appealing. They pursued the opportunity further, even entering talks with a partner, but ultimately decided that the risk of investment in Russia at that time was too high. Instead of setting up a business, Kurt returned to the States to attend business school.

Kurt remained intrigued by business opportunities in Eastern Europe. He closely followed business development in the region and continued to explore business ideas. For summer employment after his first year in graduate school, he looked for positions with small companies or startups in Eastern Europe, eventually joining a group doing privatization in Poland. This gave him a chance to get a good overview of the region's economic transformation and establish contacts for the future.

In addition to working on the privatization of several companies, Kurt looked at possible investments for a $100 million fund the company was setting up in Poland. He had meetings with representatives from a wide array of industries and prepared extensive investment memoranda on these opportunities. The summer experience further convinced him that the timing was right for entrepreneurship in Eastern Europe.

The Final Year

During Kurt's second year, he invested most of his job search time looking at opportunities in Eastern Europe. An offer to go back to his summer employer was his fallback option in case he did not pursue an entrepreneurial opportunity.

His search in the fall was wide ranging, from working with owners of newly established firms in Eastern Europe to startup ideas. In terms of new businesses, he looked into setting up a bottled water company in Poland, but quickly realized that the business was too capital intensive. From the bottled water idea, he developed the following criteria for business opportunities in emerging economies:

1. Low fixed costs.
2. Low variable costs going forward.
3. Low asset intensity.
4. Quick to break even.
5. Proven business rather than completely new idea.
6. High market potential.

 This case was written by Kurt Bauer. For purposes of class discussion, it has been edited by Dan D'Heilly and Andrea Alyse under the direction of Jeffry A. Timmons, Franklin W. Olin Distinguished Professor of Entrepreneurship, Babson College. Funding provided by the Ewing Marion Kauffman Foundation.

[1] From "O Captain, My Captain!" by Walt Whitman.

Ventures that met these criteria would be far more attractive for a young entrepreneur. With low fixed costs, it would be possible to get startup capital from friends and family. It also limited any venture's downside. Low variable costs going forward would keep the burn rate low in the critical early stages and give the company more financial flexibility. Also, a company with low asset intensity, such as publishing or online services, would require less cash to fuel its growth. As Kurt's uncle said, such companies have the potential to "mint money."

Kurt also wanted a business where he could quickly tell how things were going. Any business that entailed setting up a manufacturing facility, for example, would not only involve high fixed costs, but may also take a year before starting production and a longer time before reaching breakeven. In an uncertain environment such as Eastern Europe, Kurt wanted to know as soon as possible if the business was going poorly. He also felt that a shorter time to breakeven would make it easier to adapt and change business focus if it was necessary.

Kurt thought it was important to look for proven businesses. It is usually easier to transplant a business idea from one place to another, rather than starting something completely new. Kurt had been impressed by several cases and examples he studied where entrepreneurs in other countries had simply mimicked what worked in developed countries. For example, in Eastern Europe successful startups included English-language publications, restaurant franchises, and copy centers.

Finally, Kurt wanted a business with a large market potential. While a bagel shop in Prague might be a successful business, he felt that such an idea did not have the potential upside to make it interesting.

These criteria made it easier for Kurt to screen possible opportunities as he headed into his final semester at business school. One by one he had eliminated possibilities. In January, two new opportunities arose.

Opportunity Knocks

Kurt had dinner with a fellow second-year student who told him that his dad, Ludwig Schmitt had recently launched a magazine in Eastern Europe. He thought there might be an opportunity for Kurt with this startup operation. Kurt called Ludwig the next day, and they talked about his magazine and the possibility of working together.

Born in Poland, Ludwig emigrated to America as a youth. When the Soviet Union loosened its grip on Eastern Europe in the early 1980s, Ludwig had been one of the first wave of entrepreneurs back into Poland. He had run an export-import business since 1986, and in 1991 he cofounded the magazine, *What, Where, When* in Warsaw.

After several telephone conversations, Kurt flew to New York for a meeting. They discussed the magazine and a variety of other business opportunities in the eastern bloc. At the end of the day, Ludwig asked Kurt to put his ideas in writing.

On the plane back to Boston, Kurt thought about the opportunity to work with Ludwig Schmitt. They got along well during this visit, and Kurt thought that he would probably be a valuable mentor in Eastern Europe. This was particularly important because his friend had described his father as "difficult." Kurt also liked the publishing business, and thought the *What, Where, When* magazine niche might be a good entry point into Eastern European markets. Kurt had a rough draft for Ludwig (see *Exhibit A*) before the plane touched down.

Ludwig responded to Kurt's letter (see *Exhibit B*) saying he wanted Kurt to work for him full-time; half as general manager of the magazine, and half on new business opportunities. He suggested Prague as a base, which Kurt found very appealing. Ludwig also included his thoughts about compensation and suggested they arrange a trip to Eastern Europe to visit his operations.

What, Where, When Magazine

After the fall of the wall, Ludwig had noticed a dearth of periodicals in Poland (see *Exhibit C*). He also realized that it was a struggle for a Westerner to obtain basic information about what was going on in Warsaw. Even for him, someone who spoke fluent Polish, it was not easy to navigate in the new climate.

One night in the fall of 1990, while he was in his room at the Warsaw Marriott, Ludwig thought of the idea to start a magazine aimed at Western businesspersons which would provide an assortment of information about what to do in Warsaw. He talked to a friend, Nicholas Andrechevski, the publisher of the second largest Polish daily newspaper, and Nicholas said he would look into it. A month later, Ludwig and Nicholas met again and decided to launch the *What, Where, When* magazine. They formed a joint venture, with each party owning 50 percent of the equity.

The magazine was put together based on the model of similar magazines in the West, such as *New York Magazine,* the *Where* magazines, or *Time Out* in London. It served as a combination business directory, arts and entertainment guide, restaurant directory, and tourist guide. Articles were written about Polish culture, upcoming events, and other interesting features about the city or the people. Articles and information were featured in English, Polish, and German.

Revenue was 100 percent advertising driven, compared to industry standards of 80 percent advertising and 20 percent subscription/newsstand sales. This revenue came from targeting businesses that wanted to reach Western businesspersons and tourists. The primary advertisers were restaurants, professional service firms, hotels, airlines, car rentals, and other companies catering to affluent travelers in Poland.

EXHIBIT A

Kurt Bauer
90 Putnam St. #2
Cambridge, MA 02139
Tel/Fax: 617-497-7673

March 8, 1994

Ludwig Schmitt
Crystal Publishing

Dear Ludwig:

I hope you've enjoyed your trip to Poland and Russia. No lost limbs, I trust.

On this side of the ocean I have been thinking about our conversations and feel that the opportunity to work for you in some capacity is very appealing. I see several options (and combinations of options):

1. Manager Role. I could serve as an on-the-ground manager/overseer for your publishing company. Areas of focus would include improving cash flow, expanding the advertising base (especially from German and other international companies looking to advertise across your network of magazines), and expanding the business. In this position I would also help with long-term strategy.

2. Business Development Role. I would help you look for business opportunities that complement your existing operations. This could include looking for other publishing or business opportunities that could be started up with little or no capital and benefit from the network of offices you have developed.

One such idea I mentioned when we talked on the phone was to become the eastern European sales representative for a telephone company called Telegroup, a leading international phone service repackager. It is possible to use their service from anywhere in the world, including Eastern Europe. Their price from the Czech Republic to the States, for example, is about 40 percent cheaper than that of the Czech phone company, or AT&T direct. They also offer lower rates to any country you dial, such as Germany or Japan. Our cut would be 10 percent of revenues we generate in an annuity form. So if we signed up people who made a total of $100K worth of phone calls to the United States per month (the office in Warsaw I worked in had only six U.S. professionals who made about $10K worth of phone calls to the United States monthly), we would make $10K per month. The representative in France now makes about $30K/month, and Paris has the same number of U.S. ex-pats as Prague—40,000. Apparently the best way to get ex-pats to sign up is to advertise in English publications. In France, single full-page ads in the English dailies each generated about 300 customers (at an average revenue per month of $150). Your magazine might be the perfect way to reach such customers and it's an easy sell if you can publish rates 40 percent below AT&T or the local carrier.

3. Advisor Role. As you know I have several other offers to work in privatization or investment management in Eastern Europe. It may be possible to negotiate an offer with one of these companies whereby I'm able to spend time working for you. I could serve as an advisor/consultant who helps with the items mentioned above, but still work for another company.

There are certainly more options and combinations of options, but I think that this would be a good starting point. All have their appeal. If I were to work in more of a "full-time" role for you, you would have a man on the ground to devote his energy to increasing revenue and profitability, expanding the business, and looking for other opportunities. In the other options where I do not work for you full time, your current business would not have me as a full-time expense, but would still get some of the benefits of me working for you.

In terms of remuneration, for an option where I work for you full-time, I think the following might serve as a starting point:

- Salary: $35–40K
- Profit sharing: 5–10 percent (depending on the current numbers)
- Options: A fair percentage vested quarterly (depends on current numbers)
- Commissions: The amount above a fair price per page (say $1,300 for Poland)
- New business: Sharing of revenue or profit or equity of new businesses

The cash flow characteristics of the Telegroup idea are extremely appealing. For essentially no additional fixed costs, we may be able to develop say $5–10K cash flow per month. An option for remuneration of this idea, based on my time invested and using your office as the base, might be that we split the revenue between us.

For the more part-time option, we could use commissions and some small remuneration as a basis. The upside could be in the form of profit sharing or options if certain profit levels or targets are passed.

These are my initial thoughts. I look forward to talking to you further about them. I hope things went well in LA.

Sincerely,

Kurt

EXHIBIT B

March 19, 1994

Kurt Bauer
Cambridge, MA
Via FAX 1 617 497 7673

Dear Kurt:

Thanks for your fax of March 8th. In fact, things in LA went rather poorly. Hopefully, just another demonstration of the cyclical nature of that business.

I am very pleased at your interest in working with me in Eastern Europe. I thought we got along well during our meeting in February, and believe that working as a team would have interesting possibilities.

I have tried to combine the ideas you put forward with some of my own thoughts, and want to make you the following proposal:

1) I would prefer to have you working with me in a full-time capacity. Thus, the Manager Role you suggest could be a good start. However, as you know, I already have a number of other business activities and projects. I am always seeking to leverage my time and situation, so, a Business Development Role would certainly be a part of your activities. Let me advance some specifics . . .

A) You would be headquartered in Prague

- It is more centrally located
- I have access to an apartment there
- It is the site of the magazine which I believe will be the most profitable in the group, but also one where the most managerial and sales help is needed right now.

B) You would act as my associate vis-à-vis the magazine operations. I would want some type of commitment, e.g., a one year contract. Your activities would include . . .

- Assist in organizing and improving local sales
- Major focus on group and international marketing
- Review feasibility of international distribution
- Participate in organizing new magazines in places like Budapest, Sofia, etc.

C) My long-term strategy 2 to 3 years down the road is either to sell out to a larger publishing group, or bring our own group public. It will be your task to analyze the possibilities and to begin our preparation in this direction.

2) As mentioned above, leveraging my time is always on my mind. I am ready to work with you on any new business ideas, and am prepared to design a suitable generous, profit sharing plus equity structure.

As I mentioned in our discussions I am very interested in learning more about the specifics and technical aspects of the Telegroup deal. Clearly using our magazines and offices, in terms of direct advertising, barter possibilities, contracts, etc., would give us a low cost entry into this field, and, if the projections can be even partially realized, it would be a sorely needed cash generator.

Here are some potential problems to be addressed in this project.

- I am only a, plus/minus, 50 percent owner of the magazines. While I have no obligation to share my other initiatives with my magazine partners, I cannot take advantage of them either. We would have to devise a fair, arm's-length, compensation system for the local offices.
- Since the majors are already advertising with us, or will be sooner or later, we cannot become so identified with one service provider as to lose those revenues.

3) As far as your entrepreneurial interests are concerned, I am more than willing to allow those full scope. I too have some ideas which I have not had the time and/or funds to pursue, and would see our association as useful in this regard.

One of your first entrepreneurial tasks might well be the raising of some debt or equity capital to allow us to take advantage of opportunities, and grow the business in a faster and more effective manner.

4) Compensation, given my present cash-flow situation, I must limit my fixed cash obligations as much as possible. Here are my thoughts:

- Basic salary: 25K

  Plus reasonable travel expenses, and possibly an apartment in Prague.

- Assuming the "Telegroup" project materializes, a division of profits 50/50. Always keeping Number 2 above in mind.
- Commissions: 10 percent of international sales
- Profit sharing: 10 percent of my share
- Options/equity: To be discussed, but available

(Continued)

EXHIBIT B (continued)

- New business: Sharing of revenue, profit, or equity of new business on equal terms.
- Finders fee: 5 percent in cash or equity for any initial funds raised.

Clearly there will be many details and much planning to be done. We must agree on the broad principles first, but I am prepared to do what I can to get you on board quickly. Please let me know what you think of the above, and how you wish to proceed.

I am leaving for Europe Tuesday evening. My itinerary covers Prague, Warsaw, Sofia, and Bucharest, with a possible stop in Budapest. I will be back in the New York area on the evening of April 10th (another auction) and will stay until April 15th.

Monday, the 11th, will be an all-day inspection as this is to be a big auction. I am likely to be free Tuesday, but my friend/client from Central America will be arriving Tuesday evening, so the balance of the week is tied up.

However, I will certainly be available by phone, both these next two weeks and in New York. And I can always stay over a day or two after the 15th if necessary. Perhaps we can meet in New York again. Depending on the state of affairs in Europe I will probably be going back there, perhaps as soon as April 20th. If your schedule permits it, and our talks have advanced sufficiently, you may want to join me then for say 7 to 10 days.

Regards,

Ludwig

P. S. Enclosed is an unaudited balance sheet from Warsaw for the calendar year ending 12/31/93. I hope you can make some sense of these numbers, as they are Polish accounting principles. For example, we are apparently allowed to amortize all of our "Startup costs/losses" pre-tax.

EXHIBIT C

The Publishing Opportunity in Eastern Europe

I. Overview

The upheaval in Eastern Europe over the previous four years has spawned a flurry of free-market activity. Across industries, formerly state-owned companies, after rounds of privatization, now operate in the private sector. Foreign companies have entered the market, launching joint ventures or wholly owned subsidiaries. And entrepreneurial ventures have sprung up to take advantage of the new opportunities.

Within this context of rapid change, the publishing industry, like most other industries, has undergone a tremendous transformation. Before the fall of the Communist regimes, publishing was extensively controlled—even more so than most industries because of its political importance. But the fall of the wall launched the political and economic transformations in the east. The formerly state-owned and controlled publishing industry was liberalized. New publishing companies emerged—some entrepreneurial startups, other subsidiaries or joint ventures of western companies. As a result, new publications of all sorts sprung up across the former Eastern Bloc.

Now newsstands and bookstores in Eastern Europe are beginning to resemble those in the West. Newspapers are no longer controlled by the state—they are published by independent, privately held companies. Foreign books, which used to circulate in limited numbers in the Communist regimes, are now ubiquitous. Shakespeare and Stephen King are readily available. Magazine proliferation is similar—customers can choose from *BusinessWeek* to local versions of *People,* from children's magazines to *Playboy.*

While the size of the publishing market in Eastern Europe is about the same size now as it was just before the revolutions, the growth in the share of that market held by new private sector ventures has been phenomenal.

II. The Publishing Industry in Eastern Europe—History

In the former Eastern Bloc, publishing was tightly controlled by the state. Usually the State Media Ministry or Cultural Ministry would select appropriate material for the population to read, and the state-controlled companies (cooperatives) would publish only that material. Supply was regulated by the central ministry, distribution was through state-owned channels, and for books, the final point of sale was almost invariably at state-owned bookstores.

Most Eastern bloc countries had far fewer publishers than western countries, and advertising agencies were virtually nonexistent. In Poland, for example, prior to 1989 a total of only 60 publishers, printers, and distributors existed and only one advertising agency served the entire industry ("The Demand for Money, Theory, Evidence & Problems" D. Laidler 1993, Harper Collins College Publishers, NY).

The breadth of publication was also extremely limited. This was especially true in magazines and newspapers. Typically only a handful of newspapers existed for the entire country. Nearly all western newspapers and magazines were banned. Even western scientific publications took years to receive. In book publishing, breadth was also more limited than in the West.

EXHIBIT C (continued)

The Publishing Opportunity in Eastern Europe

Distribution was through a central subscription and distribution monopoly. The government distribution office would tell the publisher how many subscribers it had, and thus how many issues to print. It would not tell the publisher who its actual readers were or where they lived (Evans Identifying the Basis of Party Competition in Eastern Europe, G Evans, S Whitefield-British Journal of Political Science, 1993). In Poland, for example, all authorized publishers were required to send their print runs to one of two distributors, Skladnica Ksiegarska for books or Ruch for magazines and newspapers. For books, the distributor would supply the 18 wholesalers who, in turn, supplied the state-owned retail bookstores (Laidler, 1993).

High literacy coupled with extensive bans formed the basis for the dramatic change in the publishing industry after the revolutions swept eastern Europe in 1989 and 1990.

III. Publishing in Eastern Europe

1. The Market in the West The publishing industry covers the actual putting together of a book or magazine or other publication. Publishers guide the publishing process, taking the editorial content and advertising, if any, through the editing, layout, and other stages, and are usually the company which markets the final product. The veritable printing of the pages, though, is part of the printing industry. Advertising is often considered a separate industry from publishing.

The size of these industries is considerable. The world printing industry, for example, is $400 billion; the U.S. share of the industry is $117 billion, or 2 percent of GNP; and Europe is $74 billion. The publishing industry in the United States is smaller, and its size depends on what is included in the figure. The book, magazine, and newspaper publishing industry, for example, represents about $60 billion, or 1 percent of GNP. Print advertising is about a $63 billion industry, or 1 percent of GNP (U.S. Statistical Abstracts, 1993).

2. Market Size and Growth in Eastern Europe It is difficult to get exact figures for the publishing and printing industries in Eastern Europe, but estimates put the publishing industry at just over $1 billion and the printing industry around $2.7 billion (Simpson, 1992; figures do not include the former Soviet Union). The size of the print advertising industry is difficult to determine, but is probably between one and three billion dollars.

A comparison of the size of the printing and publishing markets in the three leading Eastern European countries with the size in the United States reveals that Poland and Hungary are still far below the United States in terms of percent of GNP for those industries. In the United States, printing and publishing represent 2 percent and 1 percent of GNP, respectively. In Poland, they represent 0.9 percent and 0.5 percent, respectively—about half the level in the United States. In Hungary, printing represents 0.7 percent and publishing 0.6 percent of GNP. This gap represents potential for further growth for these industries in Hungary and Poland, if development in these countries mirrors that in the States.

TABLE 1

Country Analysis

	Growth	Market Publishing	Size Printing	Private Sector % GNP	Political Stability	Assoc. of Printers
Poland	5%	$350 Mil.	$615 Mil.	60%	High	8
Hungary	0%M	$250 Mil.	$263 Mil.	45%	High	9
Czech	2%	$300 Mil.	$ 1 Bil.	40%	High	7
Russia	−20%	−$500 Mil.	$ 16 Bil.	20%	Low	8
Bulgaria	−10%	−$ 50 Mil.	$360 Mil.	Low	Med	6
Romania	−15%	−$ 50 Mil.	$465 Mil.	Low	Med	4

TABLE 2

Segment Analysis

	Seg Size	Grow	Cmpt'n	Distrib Ease	Pub. Power	New Title Intro Ease	Cust Loyalty	Ad Rev % of Rev
Magazines	Lg	H	M–H	L–M	M	H	M–H	80%
Newspapers	Lg	L	H	H	H	L	H	50–90%
Newsletters	Sm	H	L	L	H	L	H	Varies
Other	Sm	H	L–M	L–M	H	L–H	L–H	Varies

(Continued)

EXHIBIT C (continued)

The Publishing Opportunity in Eastern Europe

As noted above, the growth since the beginning of the transition has come from the new private-sector companies. While in most Eastern European countries the size of the publishing and printing markets are about the same size they were at the beginning of the transformation, private companies now predominate in the market. As mentioned above, in Poland, the growth in book volume of the private sector between 1990 and 1992 was nearly 1,000 percent. Growth in the private sector will most likely continue, though probably at rates of 25 percent to 50 percent during the next few years (various conversations).

3. Newspaper and Magazine Markets in Eastern Europe As in the West, the market may be broken down into five major segments: (1) books, (2) magazines, (3) newspapers, (4) newsletters, (5) other specialty publications. In the U.S. publishing industry, book publishing totals $24 billion, magazines about $10 billion, and newspapers about $35 billion (Halverson, 1993). The size of the other segments are difficult to determine.

It is also difficult to determine the exact size of the periodical industry in Eastern Europe. In Poland, the size of the newspaper and magazine market is probably about $150 million, not including advertising. As in the West, advertising usually makes up between 30 percent and 90 percent of the revenues of the periodical. Thus, in Poland the advertising associated with periodical publishing is probably around $250 million.

In Poland, over 4,000 periodical titles exist ("Polish Press Market," *PAP Newswire,* 1992). Over 70 dailies and 20 national newspapers are in circulation ("Polish Press Market," *PAP Newswire,* 1992). The market, though, is still highly fragmented. *Wprost* and *Polityka,* weeklies in Poland whose formats resemble *Newsweek* and *Time,* are among the 10 most popular magazines, but their regular readers represent only 2 percent of the total number of people reading Polish periodicals, according to the Pentor Institute. Throughout Eastern Europe, only about half the magazines launched then are still being published, according to Chicago-based international publishing consultant Lee B. Hall (Johnson, 1993).

The range of newspapers is also considerable and has begun to resemble the range in the West. In Poland, for example, newsstands typically have between 10 and 20 newspapers. The variety is also extensive, from the serious, a la the *Wall Street Journal,* to the tabloids, similar to the *National Enquirer* in the United States. The two largest dailies, *Gazata Wybczal* and *Rzeczpospolita,* are serious, traditional newspapers. Many of the most popular weekly newspapers are tabloids, such as *Nie* (No), *Skandale* (Scandals), *Super Skandale bez kurtyny* (Super-scandals without a curtain), and *Noweskandale* (New scandals).

Just as entry into the market has been extensive during the last four years, so has exit. Similar to the western periodical market, most new entrants actually fail. In the West, the failure rate is well over 70 percent, and while it is unclear what the exact percentage is in Eastern Europe, the figure is likely just as high. An example of a high profile failure was the first Polish daily in color, *Glob 24.* After just months of publication, the newspaper went bankrupt.

The market for newspapers also mirrors that in the West in terms of its generally regional basis, except for a few leading national newspapers. Most newspapers are based in the city where they have their largest circulation. Describing the regional nature of the Polish newspaper market, one article notes: "Poland is a country of regional newspapers. . . . Polls indicate that 40 percent of readers read regional newspapers more or less regularly, while little more than 20 percent are regular readers of nationwide newspapers" (Bartyzel, 1993).

As with books, the periodical market has seen extensive western entrance. German Publishers, for example, translated about 7 million copies per month of German publications for the Polish market in late 1992 (Bartyzel, 1993). The most popular were the biweeklies *Tina* and *Bravo* and the monthlies *Dziewczyna* (Girl) and *Popcorn.* Their cheap price, their target marketing to specific audiences (young people, women, narrow groups of hobbyists), and their simple formulas made them quite successful (Bartyzel, 1993). Even though German publishers were discouraged from buying periodicals during the privatization process (largely because of historical reasons), they now own a substantial number of newspapers and magazines.

The one Polish magazine publisher of magazines able to keep up with the westerners is Prozynski and Co. It sells nine periodicals, most of which are monthlies such as *Poradnik domowy* (Household Guidebook), *Cztery kety* (Four Corners), and periodicals for children (Bartyzel, 1993).

Other western publishers have come into Eastern Europe in full force. *BusinessWeek, PC World, PC Magazine, Scientific American, Playboy, Cosmopolitan,* and numerous other western periodicals are now published across Eastern Europe. They are published under a variety of arrangements, including licensing agreements, joint ventures, and wholly owned subsidiaries. The section that follows on western houses in Eastern Europe will feature some of those companies and publications.

Distribution The current distribution system still suffers because the inadequate system during the command era has yet to be replaced by a well-functioning western-style distribution system. While it is getting better in Eastern Europe, especially Poland, the Czech Republic, and Hungary, it is still a problem. In order to reach subscribers of magazines, for example, it is necessary to use the postal service. The post, though, remains unreliable and many issues never end up where they are sent.

It is estimated that hundreds of distributors and dozens of book wholesalers operate today in the new market economies of Eastern Europe. In Poland, hundreds exist, but of those, 18 wholesale centers have 90 percent of the book trade market. The publisher still has little power in the value chain. Distributors in Poland mark up the price by 30 percent to 40 percent. In Hungary about 10–12 major distributors exist and had a total turnover of about HUF 200 million in 1992.

The situation in other Eastern European countries is similar, although as one heads further east, distribution becomes even more difficult. In Russia, for example, periodical publishers have no subscriber lists to rent out because the formerly state-owned distribution monopoly owned the lists, and at the present time the government monopoly will not rent them out. Part of the delivery monopoly has been privatized, but even with this change the Russian mail service is so inadequate that distribution remains a major obstacle.

EXHIBIT C (continued)

The Publishing Opportunity in Eastern Europe

In Poland, the formerly state-owned distributor Ruch is still responsible for the sale of most periodicals, but has been overwhelmed organizationally by the flood of new titles. Under the law, and unlike private distributors, Ruch is forced to accept all periodicals for distribution. As of 1993 about 10 other periodical distribution firms had strong market presence. They usually refuse to distribute less popular periodicals, and as a result, they have fewer and fewer Polish publishers as preferred suppliers.

Market information from distributors is still difficult to obtain, but the situation is getting better. Macek Machnacz, director of Jard Press, the largest private distribution firm in Poland, noted that substantial information is now available for the publisher about the publication. He stated, though, that too few publishers make use of this information. He also discussed the nature of the increasingly competitive market: "It's true that this market is very cramped but it doesn't mean that all vacancies are already occupied."

Price and Costs Coupled with the increase in new publishers and the availability of an array of new titles and publications, prices have increased dramatically. Book prices in Poland, for example, have tripled. But even though they have tripled, Polish books are still less expensive than books in the West, where paperbacks cost from 5 to 10 dollars. The average price for a paperback in Poland is 50,000 to 100,000 zlotys (about two and a half to five dollars).

During the initial part of the transition, much of the printing, especially of western authors and new publishing companies, was done in the West. Phantom Press in Poland, for example, initially sent its books to be printed in the United Kingdom. It did so because its unit cost of $0.17 per book (on orders averaging 40,000) was cheaper than having the books printed in Poland. And the quality was better. Ludwig Schmitt, who started International Publishing and the magazine *What, Where, When* (see below), initially sent the magazine to be printed in Berlin. In Germany, his unit costs were about $0.40 for his 48-page glossy magazine, to which he had to add transportation and tariffs. Harlequin had its books printed in either Germany or the United Kingdom. Total unit costs (printing, transportation, distribution, tariffs, etc.) for Harlequin were about $0.40 in 1991, when they printed abroad.

Now publications in Poland, Hungary, and the Czech Republic are increasingly printed in Eastern Europe. In general, because of lower labor and transportation costs, printing in Eastern Europe is about 25 to 40 percent less expensive than in the West (Schmitt, conversations; Wotjak, conversations). For Harlequin, when they started to print in Poland in 1992, unit costs dropped to $0.33. Ludwig's glossy 48-page magazine cost about $0.30 per unit to print in Poland.

IV. Western Houses in Eastern Europe

Western publishing houses have become dominant, if not the dominant, players in Eastern Europe. While many hesitated at first, they are now heading full-force into the former Eastern Bloc. Some, such as IDG, Robert Hersant, Ringier, Gannett, and Maxwell now own several publications. The following, while by no means exhaustive, gives a broad overview of western houses' activities in Eastern Europe:

- **IDG Communications.** IDG launched a Russian edition of *PC World* in 1988 in a joint venture with Radio iSviaz, a state-owned publishing company. The company now publishes 18 magazines in the former East Bloc. But problems abound. IDG often has problems getting paper. According to one IDG executive: "In some countries, we were limited to 50,000 copies because of paper allocations. For us, it was not hard to distribute, but to distribute for the demand that was there" (Johnson, 1993). One amusing problem happened with the premier issue of *PC World* in Russia. The issue had 30 advertising pages. But when the first issue came back from the press, only three of the 30 ad pages were actually in the issue. The "technical problem" was with the Russian editor, who had cut out the ads to make room for more substance. He thought the ads were "unattractive and unnecessary" (Johnson, 1993).
- **McGraw-Hill, *Business Week* International.** The Polish edition of *BusinessWeek*, launched in April 1992 with an initial circulation of 10,000, was at 25,000 by July 1993. The Russian edition was launched in September 1990 with an initial circulation of 50,000, and is now at 60,000. However, parent company McGraw-Hill stopped publishing the Hungarian edition last year because of lack of advertising and problems with its publishing partner. Ad revenue is now $600,000 per year for the Russian edition.
- **Publisher Jurg Marquard Group** (JMG) of Zug, Switzerland, acquired majority ownership in the second largest Polish newspaper, *Express Wieczorny,* in 1993. Jurg Marquard, owner and founder of the publishing group, commented on the acquisition: "This acquisition provides us with the opportunity to participate in the most significant moment in recent history, the opening of Eastern Europe to open and free publishing." *Express Wieczorny* is published in Warsaw and is considered one of the most influential daily newspapers in Poland ("Jurg Marquard," *Business Wire,* 1993).

  JMG formed a 50/50 joint venture in Poland called Fibak Marquard Press with Wojtek Fibak's Noma Press. The joint venture now operates a printing plant in Katowice which prints 19 newspapers and 17 other publications, including *Sports, Panorama,* and *Nowe Echo.* The plant employs approximately 1,000 workers ("Jurg Marquard," *Business Wire,* 1993).

  JMG has had publishing operations in Eastern Europe for many years. In Hungary, the company is the majority stockholder in *Magyar Hirlap,* the second largest daily newspaper. In addition, the company owns possibly the most modern newspaper printing plant in Hungary, Marquard Color Print. The Jurg Marquard Group also has operations in the Czech and Slovak Republics, Romania, Bulgaria, and Russia ("Jurg Marquard," *Business Wire,* 1993).
- **Ringier.** Swiss media giant Ringier AG launched a new daily in Czech called *Blesk* after extensive market research and a $500,000 promotional campaign. *Blesk* was launched in 1992 and within one year had become the number-one daily with sales of 500,000 copies.

(Continued)

EXHIBIT C (concluded)

The Publishing Opportunity in Eastern Europe

- **Playboy.** One of the most successful magazines in Eastern Europe is *Playboy.* It currently licenses to publishers in Hungary and the Czech Republic and has a joint venture in Poland. In the licensing deals, Playboy International provides the structure and the foreign publishers provide the time, energy, and capital. Advertising is done at both levels. The Eastern European editions sell on average between 275 and 300 ad pages per year, and circulation ranges from 40,000 to 80,000.
- **General Media International.** Another company using the licensing approach, General Media International publishes *Penthouse* in Eastern Europe. The magazine was launched in Russia in 1992 with an initial circulation of 300,000. Amusingly, a dual pricing structure was established by newsstands: one to look and one to buy. GMI has launched a Czech edition and is in discussions about Polish and Hungarian versions. In contrast to the success of *Penthouse,* GM's launch of *Omni* in Russia in 1990 was a complete failure; *Omni* is no longer published in Russia.
- **Rodale Press.** The U.S. company Rodale Press was one of the first publishers in post-Communist Russia with the farming magazine *Novii Fermer.* But because of a complicated way to earn hard currency to support the magazine which involved setting up a meat processing plant, the venture ran into problems. Distribution was also extremely difficult. From an initial circulation of 50,000, production was cut back in 1993 to a circulation of 40,000. Currently, Rodale is working with a number of private distribution companies to develop more efficient distribution systems in Russia.
- **Ziff.** *PC Magazine,* published by Ziff, now has Russian, Czech, Hungarian, and Polish editions. The magazine is widely distributed and is in a niche that has grown quickly over the past three years.
- **Maxwell.** Maxwell owns a number of dailies in Hungary. One of the most successful, the newspaper *Magyar Hirlap,* was sold to the Swiss publisher Marquard in 1992.

These advertisers were reached by a direct sales force in each city, who received up to 10 percent commission. The sales force had expanded dramatically in the past year, and now totaled eight in Warsaw, six in Prague, five in Bucharest, three in Lodz, and three in Krakow.

The production process of the magazine included three main steps: (1) design and layout; (2) printing; and (3) distribution. For the first part, design and layout, much of the magazine stayed the same from issue to issue. The centerfold was always a map of the city, and several pages contained the same information about the city from issue to issue. Advertising was then allotted the appropriate number of pages. Other pages were filled with stories or features that fit the style of the magazine.

Layout for the first magazine was done in the United States. Ludwig brought the relevant information and advertisements, and a layout company prepared the films. The films were taken to Germany for printing. The initial run was 35,000 copies. The magazines were then trucked to Warsaw for local distribution.

Once in-house design and layout was completed, disks were sent to the printer. Printing had originally been done in Germany, but was now done locally. Print runs were 50,000 for the Warsaw and Prague issues, and 35,000 for the other cities.

Distribution was through hotels, airline offices, travel agents, tourist offices and directories, and car rental agencies. Ludwig managed to convince nearly every prominent hotel in Warsaw to put the magazine in their hotel rooms, so that visitors would have a readily accessible city guide. It was not a difficult sell: the magazine was, after all, free to the hotels, and gave their guests relevant information. Ludwig hired one person to ensure that distribution was taken care of properly.

EXHIBIT D

Annotated Income Statement for Warsaw Magazine

($000s)	1993	1994*
Revenue	350	500
COGS		
Labor	100	130
Printing	150	165
Rent/Office	30	40
Gross margin	70	165
Depreciation	20	20
General Administration	40	45
	==	==
Net Income	10	100
	==	==

*Estimated.

The basic financials for the Warsaw magazine are shown in *Exhibit D.* Net profit of only $10K for 1993 was partly due to the fact that the Warsaw office absorbed many of the startup costs for the other magazines, such as initial layout work and administration. For the first months of 1994, the Warsaw magazine was running a net income of just under $10K per month.

As far as the other magazines were concerned, the two other Polish magazines and the Bucharest magazine had reached positive cash flow. Prague was still a net consumer of cash, but was projected to reach positive cash flow in the summer of 1994.

For major cities, the advertising price per pages was about $1,200 for local advertisers, and about $2,000 for international advertisers. The inside covers were $3,000 and the back cover was $5,000. Based on Ludwig's initial expenses, this gave him a breakeven of 12 to 14 pages. By the third issue, the magazine had reached positive cash flow. Warsaw currently had about 30 pages of advertising per issue, yielding revenues of $45K per month. Based on this recent performance, Ludwig expected yearly revenues of slightly over $500K. He expected net income to be around $100K. Ludwig thought that the other magazines had the potential to follow Warsaw's path.

One of the problems the startup faced was currency devaluation. Inflation in Poland was well over 50 percent, but it was difficult to constantly raise prices. The value of his advertising revenues one year down the road would amount to about half the present value in real terms, and several customers had prepaid for an entire year. What made the issue particularly troublesome was that his printing bills were paid in German marks.

Despite this problem, the magazine continued to operate with a positive cash flow during the first year. Ludwig improved and expanded the magazine. He quickly increased the number of pages to 48, and professionalized the layout. He moved the production to Poland and bought a Macintosh II to do layout in-house. His staff had grown to 12 people by the end of 1993.

Ludwig also launched the *What, Where, When* magazine in other Polish cities and Eastern European countries. In 1993, he moved forward with two new Polish offices, Krakow and Lodz. Both were funded by the flagship Warsaw office. Also, cash from the Warsaw magazine funded the first issues of the Prague and Bucharest versions of the magazine, which were launched in the beginning of 1994.

Ludwig planned to continue expanding his business. He set up a joint venture in Sofia with the intention of publishing the first magazine by the fall of 1994. He also pursued negotiations with a potential partner in Budapest. In the established cities, his goal was to improve cash flow and leverage *What, Where, When* into other magazine publishing opportunities.

The Eastern European Operations

After negotiating a more specific understanding, Kurt flew to Eastern Europe for a tour of Ludwig's operation. Kurt thought that a business trip to Eastern Europe would allow them to become better acquainted, in addition to providing insight into the nature of the publishing opportunity. As the overnight train from Munich pulled into Prague, Kurt found himself awash in memories of his adventures in the former Eastern Bloc. The spires of Prague also rekindled pleasant thoughts about this city. Getting off the train, he changed money and took the subway to the Forum Hotel to meet Ludwig.

At the Forum, Ludwig welcomed him and they discussed the coming day's events. On the agenda was a trip to the lawyer's office, visiting the magazine's office, a meeting with a layout editor, and a visit with one of Ludwig's customers from his export-import business. The day went quickly, a series of meetings and glimpses into the workings of his business in Prague. Before long, they had boarded the 9:20 PM train to Warsaw.

The two days in Warsaw followed a similar pattern. Most of his time was spent in the magazine office, and Kurt had an opportunity to talk with staff members: the general manager, the production manager, the layout staff, the advertising manager and several advertising reps. He saw the production of the magazine, and had a chance to review financial statements. He also had a chance to attend the semiannual board meeting and meet Ludwig's Polish partner, Nicholas. Kurt observed that although Ludwig was always a powerful man, he was even more so when in his own element.

At the end of two days, Ludwig flew on to Bucharest. Kurt spent one more day in Warsaw before flying back to the States. That day he met with several other people about another business opportunity he had been exploring. Most important, he met Rafal Sokól, a broker and analyst who had previously worked on the Warsaw Stock Exchange.

An Online Financial Information Service for Eastern Europe

It was also in late January that a second serious business idea began to gather momentum. In the fall, he had thought about the opportunity to set up some type of online service for Eastern Europe. But he felt his initial idea, to start a Polish information service covering business opportunities, had limited potential. After his first entrepreneurial finance class, though, he revisited the idea. The case that day had been about an online financial service company called Technical Data Corp. The second case was about another online company called BRC. Kurt decided to reevaluate the opportunity for an online financial information service in Eastern Europe (see *Exhibit E*).

The recent growth in the Eastern European stock markets made the idea attractive. In Poland, total capitalization was now $3 billion and daily volume had reached $200 million. In the Czech Republic, total capitalization was a spectacular $15 billion, with daily volume at $15 million. This was coupled with the fact that a total of $6 billion in foreign investment had poured into the two countries.[2] Into Czech equities alone, $350 million had moved eastward.[3] In Poland, Pioneer Mutual now had a $1 billion fund. An array of other funds had been set up in the two countries in the $100 million range. The growth in the

[2] Sosnowski, *Warsaw Voice*, May 8, 1994.
[3] Mastrini, Reuters, May 2, 1994.

private sector, about 12 percent in Poland, and the returns in the stock markets, over 700 percent in Poland, were additional reasons for the rush into these countries.

Reuters and Telerate had entered into the Eastern European markets, but they only provided real-time stock quotes and limited news stories. These companies viewed themselves more as wire services and had historically focused on real-time information. No one provided a comprehensive online financial information service for the Eastern Bloc. In fact, no database service existed which had information on the publicly traded companies in the Czech Republic or Poland. Kurt thought a need existed for a Bloomberg-style information service.

Kurt contacted several fund managers and analysts whose portfolios included companies in the Eastern Bloc. They all indicated that most of their information came from daily newspapers and word of mouth. Some said that they would pay for information about the Eastern Bloc online. In the future such information would become increasingly necessary. Others indicated that most of the investing in Czech and Polish equities was speculative by unsophisticated investors. As such, they thought an online information service was not needed, yet it might be needed in the future.

While his background was not in information services, Kurt thought he had the background to set up a business in Eastern Europe. He had helped set up an office in Moscow, and was even entrusted to run the company's office in Poland during the summer when the managers were traveling.

In part due to his lack of experience, he felt the most important aspect would be team building and marshaling human resources. He had seen how important this was in his family's entrepreneurial ventures. So from the beginning he sought to build a team that would bring together players with the right experience, skills, and attitudes.

The first person he called was his brother, John, who was a research engineer at Carnegie Mellon University and had extensive experience with advanced systems integration and programming. John, who had expressed entrepreneurial yearnings in the past, was intrigued. After looking into the idea, his brother said that it was feasible from the hardware and software perspectives. Because of recent strides in the computer technology and the dramatic decrease in price, it should be possible to get the hardware for around $25K, and the software could be developed by adapting an off-the-shelf database program for about $4K.

Kurt also pursued contacts with individuals who had experience in the online financial information industry. Fortuitously, the father of a fellow business school friend had just retired from Reuters. Kurt did a Nexis search on Robert Reid and learned that he had been a senior VP in charge of Instinet, an off-the-big-board trading service that Reuters offered. Before that, he was a Senior VP at the NYSE. His friend put Kurt in touch with his father, and Reid helped Kurt think through the idea. He said he thought the idea was a good one, and that he certainly could envision the upside of such a service. He also said that while Reuters was in the market, they were not in the database business. They would not likely compete in the intended niche.

Most important to Kurt, Reid indicated his willingness to serve as an advisor to the company, and potentially as a director. Their conversations were long and involved, and Reid seemed excited about the idea. During the course of the following weeks, Reid sent Kurt a couple of packets of pertinent information in the mail.

Kurt talked to others in the online industry, such as Jerome Rubin, the founder of Lexis/Nexis, who was now the head of the News in the Future Project at MIT. He confirmed that the technology these days was "cheap and simple." He said it was possible to get a standard retrieval program inexpensively and have a programmer adapt it. Several others in the online industry who he talked to were basically in agreement with Rubin.

A key part of the team would be a Polish partner. During Kurt's April trip to Poland with Ludwig, he dedicated his last day to meetings for the online service. In addition to meeting with the head of the trading system at the stock exchange and analysts at one of the funds in Poland, he also met with potential partners. In his last meeting he met the cousin of a former Polish colleague, Rafal Sokól. Sokól was formerly at the Warsaw Stock Exchange, and now in a financial consulting partnership. The partners produced a daily column on the Polish Stock Market for the most popular financial daily.

Kurt was impressed with Sokól, and his partner Szafirowski. They were smart, knowledgeable, young, ambitious, and they spoke good English. It was decided that they should continue to talk, to fax each other additional information about themselves and the opportunity, and to meet again in three weeks in Poland.

When Kurt got back home, he talked to Reid and his brother John about Sokól and Szafirowski. John had done more research on the technical side of the business. He had spoken at length with friends who worked in the Real-time Financial Information Lab which had been endowed by Reuters, Bloomberg, Knight-Ridder, and others. He talked to another friend who owned his own database consulting company and ordered sample kits from several database companies. After these talks and research, John had put together a summary of the technical requirements of the business based on several different options.

John had also talked to one of the programmers working for him, Jae Chang, who was one of the best programmers John had ever known. Chang was excited about the startup idea and said that he would be willing to work for next to nothing, in exchange for equity. John even managed to get him a job for the summer programming the interface of a new Internet node at Carnegie Mellon, an experience which would be directly applicable to the online service—the Internet would be one of the channels of information dissemination for the service.

Kurt realized business school would soon come to an end. Since returning from Warsaw he had written an outline and an executive summary of the business plan. He had talked extensively to his uncle, who had launched or owned seven different businesses, and now was a substantial supporter of new ventures and young entrepreneurs. After looking at the outline, his uncle said that Kurt had his first $50K if he needed it. His parents would put in another $50K. Kurt and his brother could add $30K together. Based on his projections, he thought that this amount could get him up and running for at least nine months. Kurt wondered if he was crazy to even consider going into business in competition with billion dollar firms like Bloomberg and Reuters, but he had done his homework and he didn't see a fatal flaw—yet.

Commencement

As the clapping in class came to an end, Kurt's thoughts turned again to what lay ahead. It was time to make a decision. Kurt felt that he could develop the financial information service idea further without additional capital investment. But was he being unrealistic about his ability to create a world-class service when he was a rookie in the industry? On the other hand, Ludwig had an opportunity at the magazine that was ready to grow, and he was also eager to support Kurt in developing new ventures. Ludwig was expecting a call within the next few days; Kurt wondered what he should do.

EXHIBIT E

Emerging Markets Online—Financial Information

A. Strategy

Emerging Markets Online will provide financial information covering the Polish and Czech stock markets and public companies. The target market will be domestic and international brokers, traders, investors, and others working with Eastern European equity markets. Information will be available online, on diskette, on CD-ROM, and via fax.

Emerging Markets Online's (EMO) strategy and focus will be similar to Bloomberg in the United States. EMO will target analysts, brokers, and institutional investors by providing a database of fundamentals, news, press releases, and analyst reports. Fundamental information (Income Statement, Balance Sheet, Ratios, etc.) will come mainly from public sources, such as monthly and quarterly reports, which are readily available in Poland and the Czech Republic. EMO will include news stories from Polish and Czech daily newspapers and newsletters in the database. In other countries, news stories from daily and weekly sources are included in databases in exchange for commission. Analyst reports will also be put online in a similar exchange for commission. EMO will avoid direct competition with Reuters and Telerate in the real-time stock quote arena. The service will be similar to Bloomberg in developed markets.

Even though EMO will offer a service similar to Bloomberg, emerging markets are perceived to be an area of weakness for Bloomberg.* Bloomberg currently has a relative dearth of information on emerging market equities because they are focused on developed markets. As one venture capitalist who covers the online industry said, "Bloomberg right now has so much on their plate; they are concerned with the big markets like Japan and London." The markets EMO will cover, while large for an entrepreneurial venture, are too small for a company like Bloomberg to warrant attention at this time.

EMO will have an additional advantage because the expensive human capital will be working primarily for equity. EMO will have a much lower breakeven than established online companies, permitting it to reach positive cash flow before the industry becomes more competitive in three years.

B. Opportunity

- **Volume explosion:** Daily stock market volume in Poland up to $200 million. Currently, the daily volume of the Polish stock exchange has surpassed many Western European exchanges and is almost as large as the Toronto exchange. The total capitalization is larger than China and approaching smaller, more developed markets. The following provides an overview of the two main markets:

	Total Cap	Daily Vol.	Number of Cos.	1993 Perform.	1993 GNP
Czech	$14 bil.	$ 15 mil.	1330	97%	+5%
Poland	$6 bil.	$200 mil.	27	783%	+3%

This leap in the size of the Eastern European markets mirrors the growth in the capital flows to emerging market stock markets in general:

- International portfolio investment in emerging markets is now $56 billion, up 56 percent from the year before, and up from $7.5 billion in 1989 (Austin, 1994).
- 9.5 percent of international equity assets allocated to emerging markets in 1993, up from 2.5 percent in 1989 (survey of 30 international institutional investors, IFC, 1993).
- Total market cap of $740 billion in 1992 for group of 25 emerging markets (IFC, 1993).

*"Technology: Reuters vs. Bloomberg," *Asia Money and Finance,* March, 1993, pp. 63–64.

(Continued)

EXHIBIT E (continued)

Emerging Markets Online—Financial Information

- Number of companies listed on emerging stock markets now represents roughly 40 percent of the world total (IFC, 1993).
- Pension funds, endowments, and foundations now own global equities worth $170 billion, and plan to raise this to $300 billion in the next three years (Financial Times, 1993).
- All 24 emerging stock markets tracked by the World Bank's International Finance Corp. showed greater returns in 1993 than the Standard & Poor's 500 Index (Bailey, 1994).
- **Total capitalization growth:** Poland now $6 billion and Czech $14 billion. The Polish market now has about $200 million in daily volume and the Czech market should grow considerably in volume this year. The total capitalization of the two markets is about $21 billion. Over the course of the next two to three years, about 400 Polish companies should be privatized and listed on the Polish stock exchange. This will tremendously increase the total capitalization of the market and the inflow of capital into the market.
- **No online database service provides in-depth financial information:** The demand for financial information in the United States had driven tremendous industry growth over the past 10 years. The market for online services in the United States is now between $15 billion and $35 billion, depending on the estimate, of which one-third to one-half is financial online services.[†] The industry has been growing at 30 percent annually and is expected to continue to grow at 20[†] percent per year in the future. The demand for such information is evident by the growth in demand in the investment community for services such as Reuters, Dow Jones, Telerate, Bloomberg, Knight-Ridder, and a slew of smaller companies. The number of online financial information services in the United States now totals 160, up 30 from last year alone.[‡] The growth in the size of the market is also partly due to price insensitive customers. Investment managers will readily pay $80K per month each for a broad range of services.

  Poland and the Czech Republic are still low on the online information curve. Analysts now mostly glean information from newspapers and publicly released financial information. This is similar to Mexico before the late 1980s and developed countries before the 1980s. Eastern Europe is on the cusp of the development of the online information industry; it should follow a similar trend as more capital flows into the country and as the equity markets become more sophisticated.
- **Relatively price-insensitive customers:** 200 licensed Polish brokers each trade about $6 million per month; Pioneer in Poland has a $1 billion equity fund. Brokers, institutional investors, and related business are typically price insensitive with respect to critical information. Revenues of more than $250 per month for an information service should be readily achievable.
- **Success of comparables in other emerging markets:** Emerging markets have followed the same trend in the financial information market. As capital flowed into the country, and as the market became more sophisticated, demand for information increased, and online financial information services grew tremendously. In Mexico in 1985, for example, a newspaper, *El Norte*, set up one of the first online information services covering Mexican financial information. That company now has 2,200 customers and averages about $2K in revenue from each customer, or $4.4 million per month. This is despite the fact the Reuters and Telerate were already in the market when the company started, and that several other domestic and international providers, such as Bloomberg, are now on the scene. Other emerging markets such as Hong Kong have followed a similar trend of moving from relatively low sophistication of information provision to higher sophistication.
- **Quick to positive cash flow:** Low asset intensity (typically 0.15); quick to break even.
- **Easily technologically feasible:** Compare to accessibility of Internet around the world. In terms of software, it is now possible to adapt an off-the-shelf database program in a matter of a couple of months with one or two programmers. The program will be configured so that fundamental information may be accessed and graphed in a manner similar to Bloomberg. The program will also be able to run text searches for news items, and retrieve analyst reports. Because of our technical team's extensive involvement in programmer circles, it will be possible to minimize the costs of the adaptation by hiring the top undergraduate programmers during the summer inexpensively.

  Software program: $2,000
  Programmer adaptation: $3,000
  Total software costs: $5,000

C. Basic Financials

The online industry, like the software industry, is characterized by low asset intensity, typically in the range of 0.1 to 0.2. Once an online service is up and running, the cost of adding an additional customer is low. After breakeven is reached, then such companies have great free cash flow characteristics, often with over 50 percent of additional revenue flowing through to the bottom line (see *Table 3*).

Startup costs are also relatively low, as outlined above. Hardware and software should cost under $30K if purchased. "Loaned" or leased equipment will lower hardware costs even more. Other startup costs will be kept below $20K, keeping the total up-front costs below $50K.

†"Multimedia," *The Economist*, October 16, 1993; Booker Ellis, "Online Services," *Computerworld*, August 24, 1992.
‡Jayne Levin, "Online Investment Services Are Exploding," *The Washington Post*, April 11, 1993.

(Continued)

EXHIBIT E (concluded)

Emerging Markets Online—Financial Information

Initial capitalization for hardware, software and 6 mo. working capital:	$100K
Burn rate for one year:	$5K/mo.
Revenue projections for end of year one: 20 customers @ $250/Mo.	$5K/mo.
Revenue projections for year 5 based on comparable countries: (based on a conservative 500 customers @ $1,000/Mo.	$6 million

Thus, the company's minimum burn rate in the first 6 months will be $3,750. Even with a higher burn rate of $6,000 per month, the company will be able to operate about nine months without revenue until it is out of cash.

In terms of revenue, it is assumed that the company will have no revenue for the first six months. After that point, the company expects to add 10 customers per month. Customers will be given one month of free usage to try the system. After this period, it is expected that 50 percent will retain the service, with an average monthly bill of $250. With these conservative projections, both cash flow and EBIT will turn positive in month 12. The total operating cash outflow will have been less than $45K.

After one year, the company should show excellent cash flow characteristics. In year two, an estimated average of 50 customers at $500 per month will generate $25K per month in revenue, or $300K per year. Of that, it is estimated that about 20 percent should flow through to the bottom line. In year three, an average of 200 customers at $500 per month will generate $1.2 million in sales, with a net income of $220K. A 20x multiple would put the value of the company at $4.4 million.

- **Exit Strategy.** EMO will be set up with an exit strategy of three to five years in mind. By ensuring that the system remains flexible and compatible with other services, EMO will be a prime acquisition target for any of the larger online services. Reuters, for example, has a business development department which focuses on such acquisitions. One individual in the department, a graduate of the Harvard Business School, said that $5 million to $10 million acquisitions are common in his department.

D. Prospective Management Team

Kurt Bauer worked on privatization in Poland and Russia; attended Harvard Business School and Harvard College.

Robert Reid, former Sr. VP, Reuter's; head of Instinet, an online NYSE equities trading system; former Sr. VP, NYSE.

John Bauer, Research Engineer, Carnegie Mellon University; extensive experience in advanced system integration and software engineering.

Jae Chang, extensive programming experience; rewrote Carnegie Mellon's Internet interface; Carnegie Mellon University computer and electrical engineer.

Rafal Sokól, Partner, Conmar Investors. Worked on Polish Stock Exchange. Extensive experience as analyst of Polish equities. Publishes column in leading financial newspaper.

Krzysztof Szafirowski, Partner, Conmar Investors. Investment advisor on Polish equities. Publishes column in leading Polish financial newspaper.

Jeff Grady, Manager, Copernicus Fund in Poland. Manager, first western consulting company in Poland. Four years work experience in Poland.

Walter Wilkie, founder and owner of seven companies. Board Member, various companies.

TABLE 3

Emerging Markets Online—Proforma Income Statement

	Sept '94	Oct	Nov	Dec	Jan '95	Feb	Mar	Apr	May	Jun	Jul	Aug
Rev	0	0	0	0	0	0	0	1250	2500	3750	5000	6250
COGS												
Programmer	625	625	625	625	625	625	625	625	625	625	625	625
Data Entry	1960	1960	1960	1960	1960	1960	1960	1960	1960	1960	1960	1960
Expenses	1200	1200	1200	1200	1200	1200	1200	1200	1200	1200	1200	1200
Office	500	500	500	500	500	500	500	500	500	500	500	500
Other	300	300	300	300	300	300	300	300	300	300	300	300
Total	4585	4585	4585	4585	4585	4585	4585	4585	4585	4585	4585	4585
Gross	−4585	−4585	−4585	−4585	−4585	−4585	−4585	−3335	−2085	−835	415	1665
Depreciation	833	833	833	833	833	833	833	833	833	833	833	833
SGA	500	500	500	500	500	500	500	500	500	500	500	500
EBIT	−5918	−5918	−5918	−5918	−5918	−5918	−5918	−4668	−3418	−2168	−918	332
Cash Flow												
EBIT	−5918	−5918	−5918	−5918	−5918	−5918	−5918	−4668	−3418	−2168	−918	332
+Depr	833	833	833	833	833	833	833	833	833	833	833	833
+ NWC	0	0	0	0	0	0	0	0	0	0	0	0
−CapEx	0	0	0	0	0	0	0	0	0	0	0	0
FCF	−5085	−5085	−5085	−5085	−5085	−5085	−5085	−3835	−2585	−1335	−85	1165
Total Cash	−5085	−10170	−15255	−20340	−25425	−30510	−35595	−39430	−42015	−43350	−43435	−42270

Assumptions:

Costs		
Programmer Wages		500/mo
Programmer: Total Cost		625/mo
Data Entry		4 people
DE Wages		350/mo
Total DE Cost		1,400/mo
	Office	500/mo
	Phone	300/mo
	Supplies	400/mo
	Travel	500/mo
	Other	300/mo
Total Other		$2,000/mo
SGA		$500/mo

Revenues	
Months until customers	6
New customers/month	10
Months free usage	1
Retention of free customers	50%
Avg. Monthly rev/customer	$250
Depreciation	
Total fixed costs	$30,000
Deprec period	3 years
Deprec/mo—straight line	$833

4

Chapter Four

The Opportunity: Creating, Shaping, Recognizing, Seizing

I was seldom able to see an opportunity, until it ceased to be one.

Mark Twain

Results Expected

At the conclusion of this chapter, you will have:

1. Examined the importance of "think big enough" and the realities that accompany most new ventures.
2. Examined how the most successful ventures track a "circle of ecstasy" and match investors' appetites in "the food chain" for ventures.
3. Defined the differences between an idea and an opportunity.
4. Examined opportunity via a zoom lens on the criteria used by successful entrepreneurs, angels, and venture capital investors in evaluating potential ventures.
5. Examined the role of ideas, pattern recognition, and the creative process in entrepreneurship.
6. Identified sources of information for finding and screening venture opportunities.
7. Generated some new venture ideas and your personal criteria using the three idea generation exercises.
8. Considered the "next sea-changes" related to recent advances in technology.
9. Analyzed the Securities Online, Inc. case.

Think Big Enough

Since its inception, *New Venture Creation* has attempted to inspire aspiring entrepreneurs to "think big enough." Time and again the authors have observed the classic small business owner who, almost like a dairy farmer, is enslaved by and wedded to the business. Extremely long hours of 70, 80, or even 100 hours a week, and rare vacations, are often the rule rather than the exception. And these hardworking owners rarely build equity, other than in the real estate they may own for the business. One of the big differences between the growth- and equity-minded entrepreneur and the traditional small business owners that the entrepreneur thinks *bigger.* Longtime good friend Patricia Cloherty puts it this way: "It is critical to think big enough. If you want to start and build a company, you are going to end up exhausted. So you might as well think about creating a BIG company. At least you will end up exhausted and *rich,* not just exhausted!"

Pat has a wealth of experience as a venture capitalist and is past president of Patrioff & Company in New York City. She also served as the first female president of the National Venture Capital Association. In these capacities, she has been a lead investor, board member, and creator of many highly successful high-technology and biotechnology ventures, many of which were acquired or achieved an initial public offering (IPO). Her theme of thinking bigger is embedded throughout this book. How can you engage in a "think big" process that takes you on a journey treading the fine line between high ambitions and being totally out of your mind? How do you know whether the idea you are chasing is just another rainbow or has a bona fide pot of gold at the end? You can never know which side of the line you are on—and can stay on—until you try and until you undertake the journey.

Opportunity through a Zoom Lens

The original proposal by founder Scott Cook to launch a new software company called Intuit was turned down by many venture capital investors before it was funded! Thousands of similar examples illustrate just how complex, subtle, and situational (at the time, in the market space, the investor's other alternatives, etc.) is the opportunity recognition process. If the brightest, most knowledgeable, and most sophisticated investors in the world miss opportunities such as Intuit, we can conclude that the journey from idea to high potential opportunity is illusive, contradictory, and perilous. Think of this journey as a sort of road trip through varied terrain and weather conditions. At times, the journey consists of full sunshine and straight, smooth superhighways, as well as twisting, turning, narrow one-lane passages that can lead to breathtaking views. Along the way you also will unexpectedly encounter tornadoes, dust storms, hurricanes, and volcanoes. All too often you seem to run out of gas with none in sight, and flat tires come when you least expect them. This is the entrepreneur's journey.

Transforming Caterpillars into Butterflies

This chapter is dedicated to making that journey friendlier by focusing a zoom lens on the opportunity. It shares the road maps and benchmarks used by successful entrepreneurs, venture capitalists, angels, and other private equity investors in their quest to transform the often-shapeless caterpillar of an idea into a spectacularly handsome butterfly of a venture. These criteria comprise the core of their due diligence to ascertain the viability and profit potential of the proposed business, and therefore, the balance of risk and reward. It will examine the role of ideas and pattern recognition in the creative process of entrepreneurship.

You will come to see the criteria used to identify higher potential ventures as jumping-off points at this rarefied end of the opportunity continuum, rather than mere endpoints. One to 10 out of 100 entrepreneurs create ventures that emerge from the pack. Examined through a zoom lens, these ventures reveal a highly dynamic, constantly molding, shaping, and changing work of art, rather than a product of a formula or a meeting of certain items on a checklist. This highly organic and situational character of the entrepreneurial process underscores the criticality of determining *fit* and balancing *risk and reward*. As the authors have argued for three decades: The business plan is obsolete as soon as it comes off the printer! It is in this shaping process that the best entrepreneurial leaders and investors add the greatest value to the enterprise and creatively transform an idea into a venture.

New Venture Realities

It is useful to put the realities faced by Scott Cook and millions of others in perspective. Consider the following fundamental realities as normal as you seek to convert your caterpillar into a gorgeous butterfly:

New Ventures: Fundamental Realities

Most new ventures are works in process and works of art. What you start out to do is not what you end up doing.

Most business plans are obsolete at the printer.

Onset Venture Partners found that 91 percent of portfolio companies that followed their business plans failed!

Speed, adroitness of reflex, and adaptability are crucial. Keep the knees bent!

The key to succeeding is failing quickly and recouping quickly, and keeping the tuition low.

Success is highly situational, depending on time, space, context, and stakeholders.

The best entrepreneurs specialize in making "new mistakes" only.

Starting a company is a lot harder than it looks, or you think it will be; but you can last a lot longer and do more than you think if you do not try to do it solo, and you don't give up prematurely.

These realities are intended to convey the highly dynamic, at times chaotic, nature of this beast, and the highly dynamic context within which most new ventures evolve. Such realities present so much room for the unexpected and the contradictory that it places a premium on thinking big enough and doing everything you can to make sure your idea becomes an opportunity. Therefore, how can the aspiring entrepreneur think about this complex, even daunting challenge?

The Circle of Ecstasy and the Food Chain for Ventures

What most small businesses do not know, but what is a way of life in the world of high potential ventures, is what we will call the "circle of venture capital ecstasy" (Exhibit 4.1) and "the food chain for entrepreneurial ventures" (Exhibit 4.2). These concepts enable the entrepreneur to visualize how the company building-investing-harvesting cycle works. Understanding this cycle and the appetites of different suppliers in the capital markets food chain enables you to answer the questions for *what* reason does this venture exist and for *whom*? Knowing the answers to these questions has profound implications for fund-raising, team building, and growing and harvesting the company—or coming up short in any of these critical entrepreneurial tasks.

Exhibit 4.1 shows that the key to creating a company with the highest value (e.g., market capitalization) begins with identifying an opportunity in the "best technology and market space," which creates the attraction for the "best management team." Speed and agility to move quickly attracts the "best venture capitalists, board members, and other mentors and advisors" who can add value to the venture.

Exhibit 4.2 captures the food chain concept, which will be discussed again in greater detail in Chapter 13. Different players in the food chain have very different capacities and preferences for the kind of venture in which they want to invest. The vast majority of startup entrepreneurs spend inordinate amounts of time chasing the wrong sources with the wrong venture. One goal in this chapter, and again in Chapter 13, is to provide a clear picture of what those criteria are and to grasp what "think big enough" means to the players in the food chain. This is a critical early

EXHIBIT 4.1

Circle of Venture Capital Ecstasy

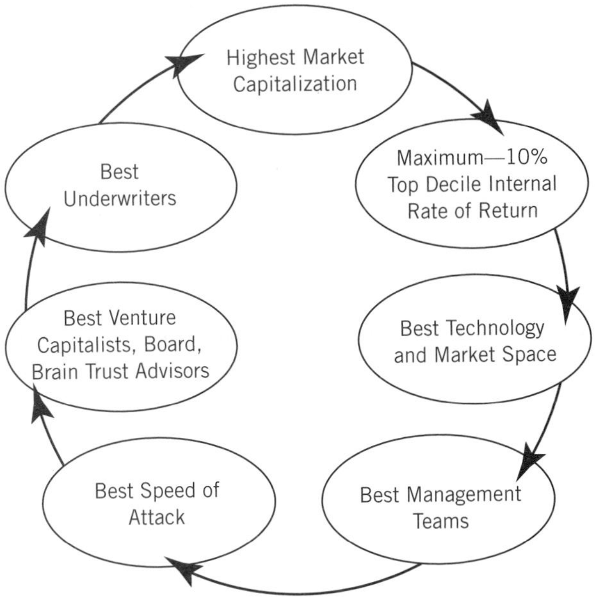

EXHIBIT 4.2

The Capital Markets Food Chain for Entrepreneurial Ventures

Stage of Venture	R&D	Seed	Launch	High Growth
Company Enterprise Value at Stage	Less than $1 million	$1–$5 million	>$1–$50 million-plus	More than $100 million
Sources	Founders High net worth individuals FFF* SBIR**	FFF* Angel funds Seed funds SBIR	Venture capital series A, B, C . . .† Strategic partners Very high net worth individuals Private equity	IPOs Strategic acquirers Private equity
Amount of Capital Invested	Up to $200,000	$10,000–$500,000	$500,000–$20 million	$10–$50 million-plus
% Company Owned at IPO	10–25%	5–15%	40–60% by prior investors	15–25% by public
Share Price and Number‡	$.01–$.50 1–5 million	$.50–$1.00 1–3 million	$1.00–$8.00+/− 5–10 million	$12–$18+ 3–5 million

* Friends, Families, and Fools

† Venture Capital Series A, B, C . . . (Average Size of Round)

	A	@ $5.1 million—startup
Round	B	@ $8.1 million—product development
(Q4 2004)	C+	@ $11.3 million—shipping product

Valuations vary markedly by industry (e.g., $2x^s$)

Valuations vary by region and VC cycle

‡ At Post–IPO

** Small Business Innovation Research, a N&F Program

step to avoid wasting time chasing venture capitalists, angels, and others when there is a misfit from the outset. As one CEO put it, "There are so many investors out there that you could spend the rest of your career meeting with them and still not get all of them." In fact, the problem is compounded when seeking angel or informal investors since there are a hundred times more of them than there are venture capitalists.

Why waste time thinking too small and on ventures for which there is no appetite in the financial marketplace? Knowing how capital suppliers and entrepreneurs think about the opportunity creation and recognition process, their search and evaluation strategies, and what they look for is a key frame of reference.

When Is an Idea an Opportunity?

The Essence: Four Anchors If an idea is not an opportunity, what is an opportunity? Superior business opportunities have the following four fundamental anchors:

1. They create or add significant value to a customer or end-user.
2. They do so by solving a significant problem, removing a serious pain-point, or meeting a significant want or need—for which someone is willing to pay a premium.
3. They have robust market, margin, and money-making characteristics that will allow the entrepreneur to estimate and communicate sustainable value to potential stakeholders: large enough ($50 million +), high growth (20 percent +), high gross margins (40 percent +), strong and early free cash flow (recurring revenue, low assets, and working capital), high profit potential (10 to 15 percent + after tax), and attractive, realizable returns for investors (25 to 30 percent + IRR).
4. They are a good *fit* with the founder(s) and management team at the time and marketplace—along with an attractive *risk-reward* balance.

For an opportunity to have these qualities, the "window of opportunity" is opening and will remain open long enough. Further, entry into a market with the right characteristics is feasible, and the management team is able to achieve it. The venture has or is able to achieve a competitive advantage (i.e., to achieve leverage). Finally, the economics of the venture are rewarding and forgiving enough to allow for significant profit and growth potential.

To summarize: *A superior opportunity has the qualities of being attractive, durable, and timely and is anchored in a product or service which creates or adds value for its buyer or end-user—usually by solving a very painful, serious problem.*[1] The most successful entrepreneurs, venture capitalists, and private investors are opportunity-focused; that is, they start with what customers and the marketplace want, and do not lose sight of this.

The Real World

Opportunities are created, or built, using ideas and entrepreneurial creativity. Yet, while the image of a carpenter or mason at work is useful, in reality the process is more like the collision of particles in a nuclear reaction or like the spawning of hurricanes over the ocean. Ideas interact with real-world conditions and entrepreneurial creativity at a point in time. The product of this interaction is an opportunity around which a new venture can be created.

The business environment in which an entrepreneur launches his or her venture cannot be altered significantly. Despite assumptions often made concerning social and nonprofit organizations, they also are subject to market forces and economic constraints. Consider, for instance, what would happen to donations if it were perceived that a nonprofit organization was not reinvesting its surplus returns, but instead was paying management excessive salaries. Or what if a socially oriented organization concentrated all its efforts on the social mission, while neglecting revenues? Clearly, dealing with suppliers, production costs, labor, and distribution is critical to the health of these social corporations. Thus, social and nonprofit organizations are just as concerned with positive cash flow and generating sufficient cash flows, even though they operate in a different type of market than for-profit organizations. For-profit businesses operate in a free enterprise system characterized by private ownership and profits.

Spawners and Drivers of Opportunities

In a free enterprise system, changing circumstances, chaos, confusion, inconsistencies, lags or leads, knowledge and information gaps, and a variety of

[1] See Jeffry A. Timmons, *New Business Opportunities* (Acton, MA: Brick House Publishing, 1989).

other vacuums in an industry or market spawn opportunities.

Changes in the business environment and the ability to anticipate these changes are so critical in entrepreneurship that constant vigilance for changes is a valuable habit. An entrepreneur with credibility, creativity, and decisiveness can seize an opportunity while others study it.

Opportunities are situational. Some conditions under which opportunities are spawned are idiosyncratic, while at other times they are generalizable and can be applied to other industries, products, or services. In this way, cross-association can trigger in the entrepreneurial mind the crude recognition of existing or impending opportunities. It is often assumed that a marketplace dominated by large, multibillion-dollar players is impenetrable by smaller, entrepreneurial companies. You can't possibly compete with entrenched, resource-rich, established companies. The opposite can be true for several seasons. A number of research projects have shown that it can take years or more for a large company to change its strategy and even longer to implement the new strategy, since it can take 10 years or more to change the culture enough to operate differently. For a new or small company, 10 or more years is forever. When Cellular One was launched in Boston, giant NYNEX was the sole competitor. It is estimated NYNEX built twice as many towers (at $400,000 each), spent two to three times as much on advertising and marketing, and had a larger head count. Yet, Cellular One grew from scratch to $100 million in sales in five years and won three customers for every one that NYNEX won. What made this substantial difference? It was an entrepreneurial management team at Cellular One.

Some of the most exciting opportunities have come from fields the conventional wisdom said are the domain of big business: technological innovation. The performance of smaller firms in technological innovation is remarkable—95 percent of the radical innovations since World War II have come from new and small firms, not the giants. A National Science Foundation study found that smaller firms generated 24 times as many innovations per research and development dollar versus firms with 10,000 or more employees.[2]

There can be exciting opportunities in plain vanilla businesses that might never get the attention of venture capital investors. The revolution in microcomputers, management information systems (MIS), and computer networking had a profound impact on a number of businesses that had changed little in decades. The used-auto-parts business has not changed in decades. Yet, the team at Pintendre Auto, Inc., saw a new opportunity in this field by applying the latest computer and information technology to a traditional business that relied on crude, manual methods to track inventory and find parts for customers.[3] In just three years, Pintendre Auto grew to $16 million in sales.

Technology and regulatory changes have profoundly altered and will continue to alter the way we conceive of opportunities. Cable television with its hundreds of channels came of age in the 1990s and brought with it new opportunities in the sale and distribution of goods from infomercials to shopping networks to pay-per-view. The Internet has created an even more diverse set of opportunities in sales and distribution, most notably Amazon.com, Priceline, and eBay.

Consider the following broad range of examples that illustrate the phenomenon of vacuums in which opportunities are spawned:

- Deregulation of telecommunications and the airlines led to the formation of tens of thousands of new firms in the 1980s, including Cellular One (now Cingular) and Federal Express.
- Microcomputer hardware in the early 1980s far outpaced software development. The industry was highly dependent on the development of software, leading to aggressive efforts by IBM, Apple, and others to encourage software entrepreneurs to close this gap.
- Fragmented, traditional industries that have a craft or mom-and-pop character may have little appreciation or know-how in marketing and finance. Such possibilities can range from fishing lodges, inns, and hotels to cleaners/laundries, hardware stores, pharmacies, waste management plants, flower shops, nurseries, tents, and auto repairs.
- In our service-dominated economy (70 percent of businesses are service businesses, versus 30 percent just 30 years ago), customer service, rather than the product itself, can be the critical success factor. One study by the Forum Corporation in Boston showed that 70 percent of customers leave because of poor service and only 15 percent because of price or product quality. Can you think of your last "wow" experience with exceptional customer service?

[2] Leifer, McDermott, O'Connor, Peters, Rice, and Veryzer, *Radical Innovation: How Mature Companies Can Outsmart Upstarts,* HBS Press, 2000.
[3] Barrie McKenna, "More Than the Sum of Its Parts," *Globe and Mail,* February 23, 1993, p. B24.

EXHIBIT 4.3

Summary of Opportunity Spawners and Drivers

Root of Change/Chaos/Discontinuity	Opportunity Creation
Regulatory changes	Cellular, airlines, insurance, telecommunications, medical, pension fund management, financial services, banking, tax and SEC laws
10-fold change in 10 years or less	Moore's Law—computer chips double productivity every 18 months: financial services, private equity, consulting, Internet, biotech, information age, publishing
Reconstruction of value chain and channels of distribution	Superstores—Staples, Home Depot; all publishing; autos; Internet sales and distribution of all services
Proprietary or contractual advantage	Technological innovation: patent, license, contract, franchise, copyrights, distributorship
Existing management/investors burned out/undermanaged	Turnaround, new capital structure, new breakeven, new free cash flow, new team, new strategy; owners' desires for liquidity, exit; telecom, waste management service, retail businesses
Entrepreneurial leadership	New vision and strategy, new team equals secret weapon; organization thinks, acts like owners
Market leaders are customer obsessed or customer blind	New, small customers are low priority or ignored: hard disk drives, paper, chemicals, mainframe computers, centralized data processing, desktop computers, corporate venturing, office superstores, automobiles, software, most services

- Sometimes existing competitors cannot, or will not, increase capacity as the market is moving. For example, in the late 1970s, some steel firms had a 90-week delivery lag, with the price to be determined, and foreign competitors took notice.
- The tremendous shift to offshore manufacturing of labor-intensive and transportation-intensive products in Asia, Eastern Europe, and Mexico, such as computer-related and microprocessor-driven consumer products, is an excellent example.
- In a wide variety of industries, entrepreneurs sometimes find that they are the only ones who can perform. Such fields as consulting, software design, financial services, process engineering, and technical and medical products and services abound with examples of know-how monopolies. Sometimes a management team is simply the best in an industry and irreplaceable in the near term, just as is seen with great coaches with winning records.

Exhibit 4.3 summarizes the major types of discontinuities, asymmetries, and changes that can result in high potential opportunities. Creating such changes through technical innovation (PCs, wireless telecommunications, Internet servers, software), influencing and creating the new rules of the game (airlines, telecommunications, financial services and banking, medical products), and anticipating the various impacts of such changes is central to recognizing opportunities.

Search for Sea-Changes

A simple criterion for the highest potential ventures comes from famed venture capitalist Arthur Rock: "We look for ideas that will change the way people live or work." As a lead investor in Apple Computer and a host of other world-class startups, he knows of what he speaks. The best place to start in seeking to identify such ideas in a macro sense is to identify significant sea-changes that are occurring or will occur. Think of the profound impact that personal computing, biotechnology, and the Internet have had on the past generation. The great new ventures of the next generation will come about by the same process and will define these next great sea-changes. Exhibit 4.4 summarizes some categories for thinking about such changes. These include technology, market and societal shifts, and even opportunities spawned from the excesses produced by the Internet boom. Moore's Law (the computing power of a chip doubles every 18 months) has been a gigantic driver of much of our technological revolution over the past 30 years. Breakthroughs in gene mapping and cloning, biotechnology, and nanotechnology and changes brought about by the Internet will continue to create huge opportunities for the next generation. Beyond the macro view of sea-changes, how can one think about opportunities in a more practical, less abstract sense? What are some parameters of business/revenue models that increase the odds of thinking big enough and therefore appeal to the food chain? At the end of Chapter 5 is the

EXHIBIT 4.4

Ideas versus Opportunities: Search for Sea-Changes

Where Are Opportunities Born?

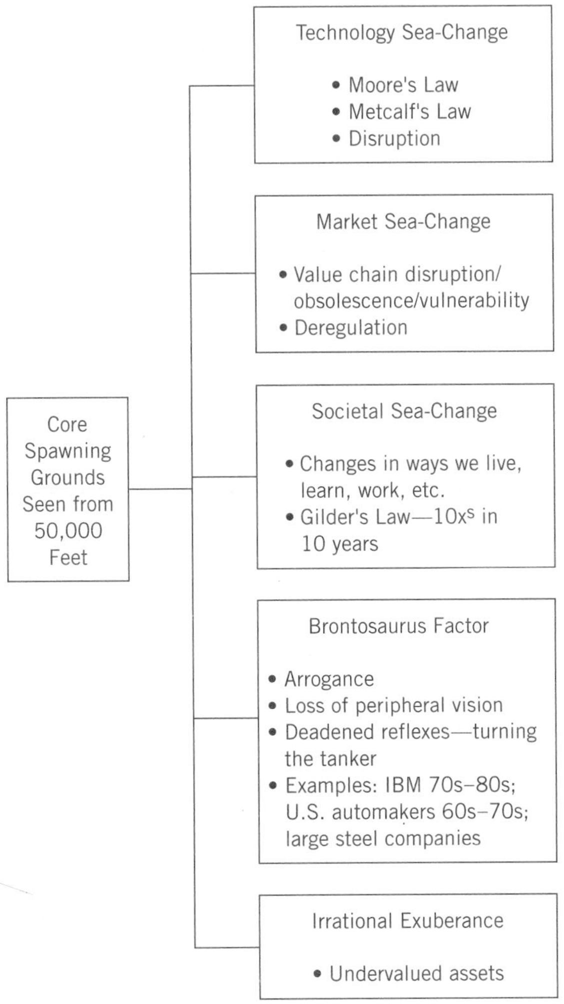
Core Spawning Grounds Seen from 50,000 Feet
Technology Sea-Change
• Moore's Law
• Metcalf's Law
• Disruption
Market Sea-Change
• Value chain disruption/ obsolescence/vulnerability
• Deregulation
Societal Sea-Change
• Changes in ways we live, learn, work, etc.
• Gilder's Law—10x^{s} in 10 years
Brontosaurus Factor
• Arrogance
• Loss of peripheral vision
• Deadened reflexes—turning the tanker
• Examples: IBM 70s–80s; U.S. automakers 60s–70s; large steel companies
Irrational Exuberance
• Undervalued assets

Sea-Change Exercise which will challenge you to think creatively and expansively about how new technology discoveries will drive the next new industries. This pattern continues to this day.

Desirable Business/Revenue Model Metrics

We will emphasize time and again in *New Venture Creation* that *happiness is a positive cash flow!—but think cash last.* You don't have an entry strategy until you have said no to lots of ideas; ideas that just come to you aren't usually opportunities; and the numbers don't matter but the economics really do matter.

The Role of Ideas

Ideas as Tools

A good idea is nothing more than a tool in the hands of an entrepreneur. Finding a good idea is the *first* step in the process of converting an entrepreneur's creativity into an opportunity.

The importance of the idea is often overrated at the expense of underemphasizing the need for products or services, or both, that can be sold in enough quantity to real customers.

Further, the new business that simply bursts from a flash of brilliance is rare. Usually a series of trial-and-error iterations, or repetitions, is necessary before a crude and promising product or service fits with what the customer is willing to pay for. Howard Head made 40 different metal skis before he finally made the model that worked consistently. With surprising frequency, major businesses are built around totally different products than those originally envisioned. Consider these examples:

> When 3-M chemist Spence Silver invented a new adhesive that would not dry or permanently bond to things, he had no idea what to do with it. It wasn't until another 3-M chemist, Arthur Fry, needed a bookmark for his choir book that the idea for applying the glue to small pieces of paper was found, and Post-it Notes were born.[4]
>
> Polaroid Corporation was founded with a product based on the principle of polarized light. It was thought that polarized lamps would prevent head-on collisions between cars by preventing the "blinding" glare of oncoming headlights. But the company grew to its present size based on another application of the same technology: instant photography.
>
> William Steere, CEO of Pfizer, described the discovery of Viagra, the fastest selling drug in history, as having "a certain serendipity" behind it. The drug was originally developed by Pfizer to treat angina–its real "potency" was discovered as a side effect.[5]

As one entrepreneur expressed it:

> Perhaps the existence of business plans and the language of business give a misleading impression of business

[4] P. R. Nayak and J. M. Ketterman, *Breakthroughs: How the Vision and Drive of Innovators in Sixteen Companies Created Commercial Breakthroughs That Swept the World* (New York: Rawson Associates, 1986), chap. 3.

[5] Tracy Corrigan, "Far More Than the Viagra Company: Essential Guide to William Steere," *Financial Times (London)*, August 31, 1998, p. 7.

building as a rational process. But, as any entrepreneur can confirm, starting a business is very much a series of fits and starts, brainstorms and barriers. Creating a business is a round of chance encounters that leads to new opportunities and ideas, mistakes that turn into miracles.[6]

The Great Mousetrap Fallacy

Perhaps no one did a greater disservice to generations of would-be entrepreneurs than Ralph Waldo Emerson in his oft-quoted line: "If a man can make a better mousetrap than his neighbor, though he builds his house in the woods the world will make a beaten path to his door."

What can be called the great mousetrap fallacy was thus spawned. It is often assumed that success is possible if an entrepreneur can just come up with a new idea. In today's changing world, if the idea has anything to do with technology, success is certain—or so it would seem.

But the truth is that ideas are inert and, for all practical purposes, worthless. Further, the flow of ideas is phenomenal. Venture capital investors, for instance, during the investing boom of the late 1990s, received as many as 100 to 200 proposals and business plans each month. Only 1 percent to 3 percent of these actually received financing, however.

Yet the fallacy persists despite the lessons of practical experience noted long ago in the insightful reply to Emerson by O.B. Winters: "The manufacturer who waits for the world to beat a path to his door is a great optimist. But the manufacturer who shows this 'mousetrap' to the world keeps the smoke coming out his chimney."

Contributors to the Fallacy

One cannot blame it all on Ralph Waldo Emerson. There are several reasons for the perpetuation of the fallacy. One is the portrayal in oversimplified accounts of the ease and genius with which such ventures as Xerox, IBM, and Polaroid made their founders wealthy. Unfortunately, these exceptions do not provide a useful rule to guide aspiring entrepreneurs.

Another is that inventors seem particularly prone to mousetrap myopia. Perhaps, like Emerson, they are substantially sheltered in viewpoint and experience from the tough, competitive realities of the business world. Consequently, they may underestimate, if not seriously downgrade, the importance of what it takes to make a business succeed. Frankly, inventing and brainstorming may be a lot more fun than the diligent observation, investigation, and nurturing of customers that are often required to sell a product or service.

Contributing also to the great mousetrap fallacy is the tremendous psychological ownership attached to an invention or to a new product. This attachment is different from attachment to a business. While an intense level of psychological ownership and involvement is certainly a prerequisite for creating a new business, the fatal flaw in attachment to an invention or product is the narrowness of its focus. The focal point needs to be the building of the business, rather than just one aspect of the idea.

Another source of mousetrap fallacy myopia lies in a technical and scientific orientation, that is, a desire to do it better. A good illustration of this is the experience of a Canadian entrepreneur who with his brother founded a company to manufacture truck seats. The entrepreneur's brother had developed a new seat for trucks that was a definite improvement over other seats. The entrepreneur knew he could profitably sell the seat his brother had designed, and they did so. When they needed more manufacturing capacity, one brother had several ideas on how to improve the seat. The first brother stated: "If I had listened to him, we probably would be a small custom shop today, or out of business. Instead, we concentrated on making seats that would sell at a profit, rather than just making a better and better seat. Our company has several million dollars of sales today and is profitable."

Related to "doing it better" is the idea of doing it first. Having the best idea first is by no means a guarantee of success. Just ask the creators of the first spreadsheet software, VisiCalc, what being first did for them. They would describe a painful downside to being first. Sometimes the first ones merely prove to the competition that a market exists to be snared. Therefore, unless having the best idea also includes the capacity to preempt other competitors by capturing a significant share of the market or by erecting insurmountable barriers to entry, first does not necessarily mean most viable.

Spotting an opportunity within an existing market was a key aspect in the development of a mass-produced rotary electric toothbrush. The founding entrepreneur had noted a large pricing spread among retail products. At the low end were devices in the range of $5. There was then a jump to the $60 to $80 range, and then another jump to products that were selling for well over $100. His research showed that new battery technology, plus outsourcing and a new rotary design, could result in a disposable product

[6] Joline Godfrey, *Our Wildest Dreams: Women Entrepreneurs, Making Money, Having Fun, Doing Good* (New York: Harper Business, 1992), p. 27.

that would fill the gaps, steal market share, and yield substantial profits. His $1.75 million business turned into $475 million when his company was sold to Procter & Gamble. This is an excellent example of a clear pricing pattern that can be applied elsewhere.[7]

Pattern Recognition

The Experience Factor

One cannot build a successful business without ideas, just as one could not build a house without a hammer. In this regard, experience is vital in looking at new venture ideas.

Time after time, experienced entrepreneurs exhibit an ability to recognize quickly a pattern—and an opportunity—while it is still taking shape. The late Herbert Simon, Nobel laureate and Richard King, Mellon University Professor of Computer Science and Psychology at Carnegie-Mellon University, wrote extensively about pattern recognition. He described the recognition of patterns as a creative process that is not simply logical, linear, and additive but intuitive and inductive as well. It involves, he said, the creative linking, or cross-association, of two or more in-depth "chunks" of experience, know-how, and contacts.[8] Simon contended that it takes 10 years or more for people to accumulate what he called the "50,000 chunks" of experience that enable them to be highly creative and recognize patterns—familiar circumstances that can be translated from one place to another.

Thus, the process of sorting through ideas and recognizing a pattern can also be compared to the process of fitting pieces into a three-dimensional jigsaw puzzle. It is impossible to assemble such a puzzle by looking at it as a whole unit. Rather, one needs to see the relationships between the pieces and be able to fit together some that are seemingly unrelated before the whole is visible.

Recognizing ideas that can become entrepreneurial opportunities stems from a capacity to see what others do not—that one plus one equals three. Consider the following examples of the common thread of pattern recognition and new business creation by linking knowledge in one field or marketplace with quite different technical, business, or market know-how:

> In 1973, Thomas Stemberg worked for Star Market in Boston where he became known for launching the first line of low-priced generic foods. Twelve years later, he applied the same low-cost, large-volume supermarket business model to office supplies. The result was Staples, the first office superstore and today a multibillion-dollar company.[9]
>
> During travel throughout Europe, the eventual founders of Crate & Barrel frequently saw stylish and innovative products for the kitchen and home that were not yet available in the United States. When they returned home, the founders created Crate & Barrel to offer these products for which market research had, in a sense, already been done. In Crate & Barrel, the knowledge of consumer buying habits in one geographical region, Europe, was transferred successfully to another, the United States.
>
> When Sycamore Systems went public in October 1999 its founders, Desh Deshpande and Daniel Smith, became multibillionaires—on paper, at least. But the success of Sycamore and its founders did not come about by chance. The pair had prior experience founding Cascade Communications Corp., one of the most touted telecommunications startups in the 1990s. That company delivered switches and accompanying software to handle the increasing demand for data over conventional phone lines. In Sycamore, Deshpande and Smith used their experience at Cascade to anticipate the need for similar switches and software that would increase the data-carrying efficiency of the nation's new fiber-optic networks. One idea led to the birth of two giant telecommunications companies.[10]

Enhancing Creative Thinking

The creative thinking described above is of great value in recognizing opportunities, as well as other aspects of entrepreneurship. The notion that creativity can be learned or enhanced holds important implications for entrepreneurs who need to be creative in their thinking. Most people can certainly spot creative flair. Children seem to have it, and many seem to lose it. Several studies suggest that creativity actually peaks around the first grade because a person's life tends to become increasingly structured and defined by others and by institutions. Further, the development of intellectual discipline and rigor in

[7] This example was provided by Harvard Business School professor William A. Sahlman during a session of the 2004 Symposium for Entrepreneurship Educators (SEE) at Babson College.

[8] Herbert A. Simon, "What We Know about the Creative Process" in ed. R. L. Kuhn, *Frontiers in Creative and Innovative Management* (Cambridge, MA: Ballinger Publishing Co., 1985), pp. 3–20.

[9] Joseph Pereira, "Focus, Drive and an Eye for Discounts: Staples of Stemberg's Business Success," *The Wall Street Journal*, September 6, 1996, p. A9B. Used by permission of Dow Jones & Co. Inc. via The Copyright Clearance Center.

[10] Paul C. Judge, "Can Even a Proven Team Deliver on This Switchmaker's Astonishing IPO?" *BusinessWeek*, December 20, 1999, pp. 150–56.

thinking takes on greater importance in school than during the formative years, and most of our education beyond grade school stresses a logical, rational mode of orderly reasoning and thinking. Finally, social pressures may tend to be a taming influence on creativity.

Evidence suggests that one can enhance creative thinking in later years. The Eureka! Ranch (www.eurekaranch.com) business was founded on the principle that creativity is inherent in most people and can be unleashed by freeing them from convention. Often, executives will be doused with water as they step out of their vehicles onto the ranch.

One of the authors participated in one of these training sessions, and it became evident during the sessions that the methods did unlock the thinking process and yielded very imaginative solutions.

Approaches to Unleashing Creativity

Since the 1950s, much has been learned about the workings of the human brain. Today, there is general agreement that the two sides of the brain process information in different ways. The left side performs rational, logical functions, while the right side operates the intuitive and nonrational modes of thought. A person uses both sides, actually shifting from one mode to the other (see Exhibit 4.5). Approaching ideas creatively and maximizing the control of these modes of thought can be of value to the entrepreneur.

More recently, professors have focused on the creativity process. For instance, Michael Gordon stressed the importance of creativity and the need for brainstorming in a presentation on the elements of personal power. He suggested that using the following 10 brainstorming rules could enhance creative visualization.

1. Define your purpose.
2. Choose participants.
3. Choose a facilitator.
4. Brainstorm spontaneously, copiously.
5. No criticisms, no negatives.
6. Record ideas in full view.
7. Invent to the "void."
8. Resist becoming committed to one idea.
9. Identify the most promising ideas.
10. Refine and prioritize.

Team Creativity

Teams of people can generate creativity that may not exist in a single individual. The creativity of a team of people is impressive, and comparable or better creative solutions to problems evolving from the collective interaction of a small group of people have been observed.

A good example of the creativity generated by using more than one head is that of a company founded by a Babson College graduate with little technical training. He teamed up with a talented inventor, and the entrepreneurial and business know-how of the founder complemented the creative and technical skills of the inventor. The result has been a rapidly growing multi-million-dollar venture in the field of video-based surgical equipment.

EXHIBIT 4.5

Comparison of Left-Mode and Right-Mode Brain Characteristics

L-Mode	R-Mode
Verbal: Using words to name, describe, and define.	*Nonverbal:* Awareness of things, but minimal connection with words.
Analytic: Figuring things out step-by-step and part-by-part.	*Synthetic:* Putting things together to form wholes.
Symbolic: Using a symbol to *stand for* something. For example, the sign + stands for the process of addition.	*Concrete:* Relating to things as they are at the present moment.
Abstract: Taking out a small bit of information and using it to represent the whole thing.	*Analogic:* Seeing likenesses between things; understanding metaphoric relationships!
Temporal: Keeping track of time, sequencing one thing after another, doing first things first, second things second, etc.	*Nontemporal:* Without a sense of time.
Rational: Drawing conclusions based on *reason* and *facts.*	*Nonrational:* Not requiring a basis of reason or facts; willingness to suspend judgment.
Digital: Using numbers as in counting.	*Spatial:* Seeing where things are in relation to other things, and how parts go together to form a whole.
Logical: Drawing conclusions based on logic; one thing following another in logical order—for example, a mathematical theorem or a well-stated argument.	*Intuitive:* Making leaps of insight, often based on incomplete patterns, hunches, feelings, or visual images.
Linear: Thinking in terms of linked ideas, one thought directly following another, often leading to a convergent conclusion.	*Holistic:* Seeing whole things all at once; perceiving the overall patterns and structures, often leading to divergent conclusions.

Source: "A Comparison of Left-Mode and Right-Mode Characteristics," from Drawing on the Right Side of the Brain by Betty Edwards, copyright © 1979, 1989, 1999 by Betty Edwards. Used by permission of Jeremy P. Tarcher, an imprint of Penguin Group (USA) Inc.

Students interested in exploring this further may want to do the creative squares exercise at the end of the chapter.

Big Opportunities with Little Capital

Within the dynamic free enterprise system, opportunities are apparent to a limited number of individuals—and not just to the individuals with financial resources. Ironically, successful entrepreneurs such as Howard Head attribute their success to the discipline of limited capital resources. Thus, in the 1990s, many entrepreneurs learned the key to success is in the art of bootstrapping, which "in a startup is like zero inventory in a just-in-time system: it reveals hidden problems and forces the company to solve them."[11] Consider the following:

- A 1991 study revealed that of the 110 startups researched, 77 had been launched with $50,000 or less; 46 percent were started with $10,000 or less as seed capital. Further, the primary source of capital was, overwhelmingly, personal savings (74 percent), rather than outside investors with deep pockets.[12]
- In the 1930s, Josephine Esther Mentzer assisted her uncle by selling skin care balm and quickly created her own products with $100 initial investment. After convincing the department stores rather than the drugstores to carry her products, Estee Lauder was on its way to becoming a $4 billion corporation.[13]
- Putting their talents (cartooning and finance) together, Roy and Walt Disney moved to California and started their own film studio—with $290 in 1923. By mid-2001, the Walt Disney Co. had a market capitalization exceeding $40 billion.[14]
- While working for a Chicago insurance company, a 24-year-old sent out 20,000 inquiries for a black newsletter. With 3,000 positive responses and $500, John Harold Johnson published *Jet* for the first time in 1942. In the 1990s, Johnson Publishing publishes various magazines, including *Ebony*.[15]
- With $100 Nicholas Graham, age 24, went to a local fabric store, picked out some fabrics, and made $100 worth of ties. Having sold the ties to specialty shops, Graham was approached by Macy's to place his patterns on men's underwear. So Joe Boxer Corporation was born and "six months into Joe Boxer's second year, sales had already topped $1 million."[16]

Real Time

Opportunities exist or are created in real time and have what we call a window of opportunity. For an entrepreneur to seize an opportunity, the window must be open and remain open long enough to achieve market-required returns.

Exhibit 4.6 illustrates a window of opportunity for a generalized market. Markets grow at different rates over time and as a market quickly becomes larger, more and more opportunities are possible. As the market becomes established, conditions are not as favorable. Thus, at the point where a market starts to become sufficiently large and structured (e.g., at five years in Exhibit 4.6), the window opens; the window begins to close as the market matures (e.g., at 12–13 years in the exhibit).

The curve shown describes the rapid growth pattern typical of such new industries as microcomputers and software, cellular phones, quick oil changes, and biotechnology. For example, in the cellular phone industry, most major cities began service between 1983 and 1984. By 1989, there were more than 2 million subscribers in the United States, and the industry continued to experience significant growth. In other industries where growth is not so rapid, the slope of a curve would be less steep and the possibilities for opportunities fewer.

In considering the window of opportunity, the length of time the window will be open is important. It takes a considerable length of time to determine whether a new venture is a success or a failure. And, if it is to be a success, the benefits of that success need to be harvested.

Exhibit 4.7 shows that for venture-capital-backed firms, the lemons (i.e., the losers) ripen in about two and a half years, while the pearls (i.e., the winners) take seven or eight years. An extreme example of the length of time it can take for a pearl to be harvested is the experience of a Silicon Valley venture capital firm that invested in a new firm in 1966 and was finally able to realize a capital gain in early 1984.

Another way to think of the process of creating and seizing an opportunity in real time is to think of it

[11] Amar Bhide, "Bootstrap Finance," *Harvard Business Review*, November–December 1992, p. 112.
[12] Edward B. Roberts, *Entrepreneurs in High Technology: Lessons from MIT and Beyond* (New York: Oxford University Press, 1991), p. 144, Table 5–2.
[13] Teri Lammers and Annie Longsworth, "Guess Who? Ten Big-Timers Launched from Scratch," *INC.*, September 1991, p. 69.
[14] Financial data from Dow Jones Interactive, http://www.djnr.com.
[15] Ibid.
[16] Robert A. Mamis, "The Secrets of Bootstrapping," *INC.*, September 1991, p. 54.

EXHIBIT 4.6

Changes in the Placement of the Window of Opportunity

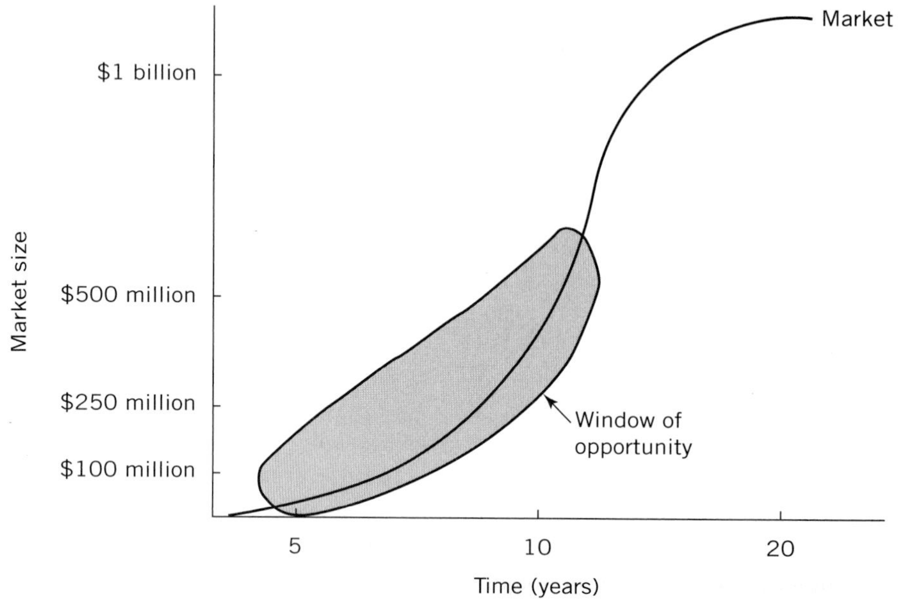

EXHIBIT 4.7

Lemons and Pearls

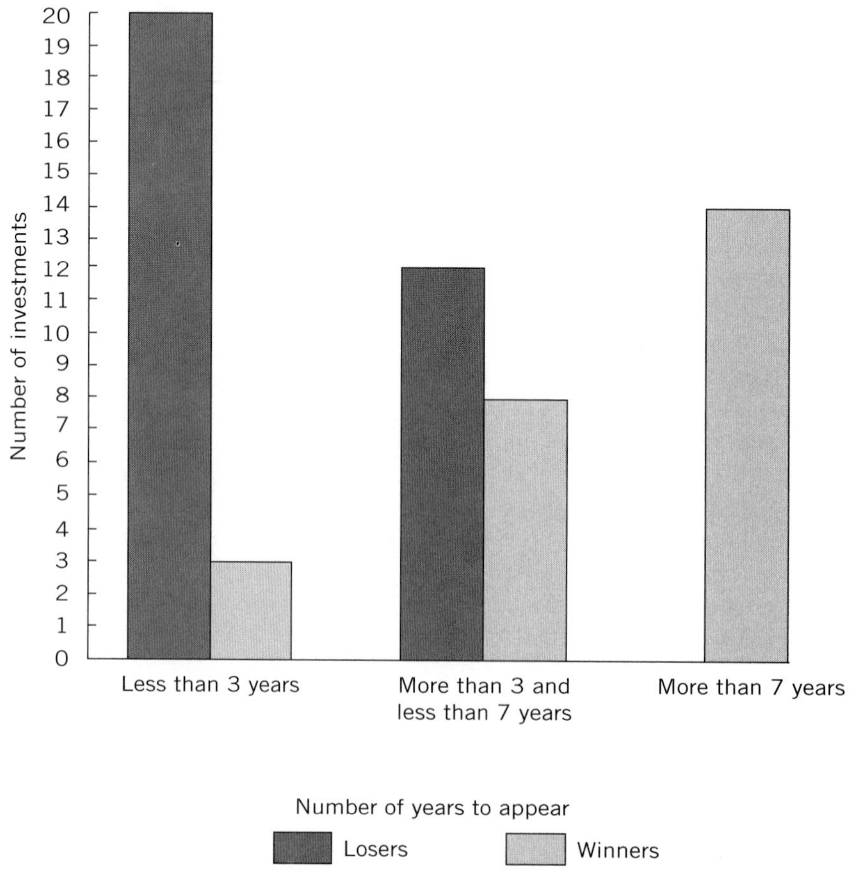

as a process of selecting objects (opportunities) from a conveyor belt moving through an open window, the window of opportunity. The speed of the conveyor belt changes, and the window through which it moves is constantly opening and closing. The continually opening and closing window and the constantly changing speed of the conveyor belt represent the volatile nature of the marketplace and the importance of timing. For an opportunity to be created and seized, it needs to be selected from the conveyor belt before the window closes.

The ability to recognize a potential opportunity when it appears and the sense of timing to seize that opportunity, as the window is opening, rather than slamming shut, are critical. That opportunities are a function of real time is illustrated in a statement made by Ken Olsen, then president and founder of Digital Equipment Corporation, in 1977: "There is no reason for any individual to have a computer in their home." It is not easy for even the world's leading experts to predict just which innovative ideas and concepts for new business will evolve into the major industries of tomorrow. This is vividly illustrated by several quotations from very famous innovators. In 1901, two years before the famous flight, Wilbert Wright said, "Man will not fly for 50 years." In 1910, Thomas Edison said, "The nickel-iron battery will put the gasoline buggy . . . out of existence in no time." And in 1932, Albert Einstein made it clear: "[There] is not the slightest indication that nuclear energy will ever be obtainable. It would mean that the atom would have to be shattered at will."

Relation to the Framework of Analysis

Successful opportunities, once recognized, fit with the other forces of new venture creation. This iterative process of assessing and reassessing the fit among the central driving forces in the creation of a new venture were shown in Chapter 3. Of utmost importance is the fit of the lead entrepreneur and the management team with an opportunity. Good opportunities are both desirable to and attainable by those on the team using the resources that are available.

To understand how the entrepreneurial vision relates to the analytical framework, it may be useful to look at an opportunity as a three-dimensional relief map with its valleys, mountains, and so on, all represented. Each opportunity has three or four critical factors (e.g., proprietary license, patented innovation, sole distribution rights, an all-star management team, breakthrough technology). These elements pop out at the observer; they indicate huge possibilities where others might see obstacles. Thus, it is easy to see why there are thousands of exceptional opportunities that will fit with a wide variety of entrepreneurs but that might not fit neatly into the framework outlines in Exhibit 4.8.

Screening Opportunities

Opportunity Focus

Opportunity focus is the most fruitful point of departure for screening opportunities. The screening process should not begin with strategy (which derives from the nature of the opportunity), nor with financial and spreadsheet analysis (which flow from the former), nor with estimations of how much the company is worth and who will own what shares.[17]

These starting points, and others, usually place the cart before the horse. Perhaps the best evidence of this phenomenon comes from the tens of thousands of tax-sheltered investments that turned sour in the mid-1980s. Also, many entrepreneurs who start businesses—particularly those for whom the ventures are their first—run out of cash at a faster rate than they bring in customers and profitable sales. There are lots of reasons why this happens, but one thing is certain: These entrepreneurs have not focused on the right opportunity.

Over the years, those with experience in business and in specific market areas have developed rules to guide them in screening opportunities. For example, during the initial stages of the irrational exuberance about the dot.com phenomenon, number of "clicks" changed to attracting "eyeballs," which changed to page view. Many investors got caught up in false metrics. Those who survived the NASDAQ crash of 2000–2001 understood that dot.com survivors would be the ones who executed transactions. Number of customers, amount of the transaction, and repeat transactions became the recognized standards.[18]

Screening Criteria: The Characteristics of High Potential Ventures

Venture capitalists, savvy entrepreneurs, and investors also use this concept of boundaries in screening ventures. Exhibit 4.8 summarizes criteria used by venture capitalists to evaluate opportunities: opportunities,

[17] See J. A. Timmons, D. F. Muzyka, H. H. Stevenson, and W. D. Bygrave, "Opportunity Recognition: The Core of Entrepreneurship" in *Frontiers of Entrepreneurship Research*, ed. Neil Churchill et al. (Babson Park, MA: Babson College, 1987), p. 409.
[18] Ernie Parizeau, partner, Norwest Venture Partners, in a speech to Babson College MBAs, December 2000.

EXHIBIT 4.8

Criteria for Evaluating Venture Opportunities

	Attractiveness	
Criteria	**Highest Potential**	**Lowest Potential**
Industry and Market	Changes way people live, work, learn, etc.	Incremental improvement only
Market:	Market driven; identified; recurring revenue niche	Unfocused; onetime revenue
Customers	Reachable; purchase orders Remove serious pain-point	Loyal to others or unreachable
User benefits	Less than one-year payback Solves a very important problem/need	Three years plus payback
Value added	High; advance payments	Low; minimal impact on market
Product life	Durable	Perishable
Market structure	Imperfect, fragmented competition or emerging industry	Highly concentrated or mature or declining industry
Market size	$100+ million to $1+ billion sales potential	Unknown, less than $20 million or multibillion sales
Growth rate	Growth at 30–50% or more	Contracting or less than 10%
Market capacity	At or near full capacity	Undercapacity
Market share attainable (Year 5)	20% or more; leader	Less than 5%
Cost structure	Low-cost provider; cost advantages	Declining cost
Economics		
Time to break even/positive cash flow	Under 1½–2 years	More than 4 years
ROI potential	25% or more; high value	Less than 15–20%; low value
Capital requirements	Low to moderate; fundable/bankable	Very high; unfundable or unbankable
Internal rate of return potential	25% or more per year	Less than 15% per year
Free cash flow characteristics:	Favorable; sustainable; 20–30% or more of sales	Less than 10% of sales
Sales growth	Moderate to high (+15% to +20%)	Less than 10%
Asset intensity	Low/sales $	High
Spontaneous working capital	Low, incremental requirements	High requirements
R&D/capital expenditures	Low requirements	High requirements
Gross margins	Exceeding 40% and durable	Under 20%
After-tax profits	High; greater than 10%; durable	Low
Time to break-even profit and loss	Less than two years; breakeven not creeping or leaping	Greater than four years; breakeven creeping or leaping up
Harvest Issues		
Value-added potential	High strategic value	Low strategic value
Valuation multiples and comparables	Price/earnings = +20x; +8 − 10x EBIT; +1.5 − 2x revenue: Free cash flow +8 − 10x	Price/earnings ≤ 5x, EBIT ≤ 3 − 4x; revenue ≤ .4
Exit mechanism and strategy	Present or envisioned options	Undefined; illiquid investment
Capital market context	Favorable valuations, timing, capital available; realizable liquidity	Unfavorable; credit crunch
Competitive Advantage Issues		
Fixed and variable costs	Lowest; high operating leverage	Highest
Control over costs, prices, and distribution	Moderate to strong	Weak
Barriers to entry:	Knowledge to overcome	
Proprietary protection	Have or can gain	None
Response/lead time	Competition slow; napping	Unable to gain edge
Legal, contractual advantage	Proprietary or exclusivity	None
Contracts and networks	Well-developed; accessible	Crude; limited
Key people	Top talent; an A team	B or C team

EXHIBIT 4.8 (concluded)

Management Team		
Entrepreneurial team	All-star combination; free agents	Weak or solo entrepreneur; not free agents
Industry and technical experience	Top of the field; super track record	Underdeveloped
Integrity	Highest standards	Questionable
Intellectual honesty	Know what they do not know	Do not want to know what they do not know
Fatal-Flaw Issue	Nonexistent	One or more
Personal Criteria		
Goals and fit	Getting what you want; but wanting what you get	Surprises; only making money
Upside/downside issues	Attainable success/limited risks	Linear; on same continuum
Opportunity costs	Acceptable cuts in salary, etc.	Comfortable with status quo
Desirability	Fits with lifestyle	Simply pursuing big money
Risk/reward tolerance	Calculated risk; low risk/reward ratio	Risk averse or gambler
Stress tolerance	Thrives under pressure	Cracks under pressure
Strategic Differentiation		
Degree of fit	High	Low
Team	Best in class; excellent free agents	B team; no free agents
Service management	Superior service concept	Perceived as unimportant
Timing	Rowing with the tide	Rowing against the tide
Technology	Groundbreaking; one of a kind	Many substitutes or competitors
Flexibility	Able to adapt; commit and decommit quickly	Slow; stubborn
Opportunity orientation	Always searching for opportunities	Operating in a vacuum; napping
Pricing	At or near leader	Undercut competitor; low prices
Distribution channels	Accessible; networks in place	Unknown; inaccessible
Room for error	Forgiving and resilient strategy	Unforgiving, rigid strategy

many of which tend to have a high-technology bias. As will be seen later, venture capital investors reject 60 percent to 70 percent of the new ventures presented to them very early in the review process, based on how the entrepreneurs satisfy these criteria.

However, these criteria are not the exclusive domain of venture capitalists. The criteria are based on good business sense that is used by successful entrepreneurs, angels, private investors, and venture capitalists. Consider the following examples of great small companies built without a dime of professional venture capital.

- Paul Tobin, who built Cellular One in eastern Massachusetts from the ground up to $100 million in revenue in five years, started Roamer Plus with less than $300,000 of internally generated funds from other ventures. Within two years, it grew to a $15 million annual sales rate and was very profitable.
- Mark Nelson started Ovid Technologies in the late 1980s in a one-bedroom apartment in Manhattan's Spanish Harlem. Unable to find investors, his company grew while he rented more and more apartments in his building until computer network wires ran in and out of windows. Salaries for his employees were low, but at least Nelson allowed them to live rent-free in their office spaces! It was not until 1994, when Ovid had 150 employees, that Ovid went public and raised $10 million. In 1999, he sold his company for $200 million.[19]
- In 1986 Pleasant Rowland founded the Pleasant Company as a mail order catalog company selling the American Girls Collection of historical dolls. She had begun the company with the modest royalties she received from writing children's books and did not have enough capital to compete in stores with the likes of Mattel's Barbie.[20] By 1992 she had grown the company to $65 million in sales. Mattel acquired it in 1998 for $700 million, and under Rowland's continued management, the company had sales of $300 million in 1999 and 2000.[21]

[19] Sarah Schafer, "Start-Up Sizzled without Venture Capital," *Washington Post*, June 27, 1999, p. H7.
[20] Mollie Neal, "Cataloger Gets Pleasant Results," *Direct Marketing*, May 1992, p. 33.
[21] Brian Dumaine, "How to Compete with a Champ," *Fortune*, January 10, 1994, p. 106.

- In 1983, Charlie Butcher, at age 66, had to decide whether to buy out an equal partner in his 100-year-old industrial polish and wax business (Butcher Polish) with less than $10 million in sales. This niche business had high gross margins, very low working capital and fixed-asset requirements for increased sales, substantial steady growth of more than 18 percent per year, and excellent products. The result was a business with very high free cash flow and potential for growth. He acquired the company with a bank loan and seller financing, and then he increased sales to over $50 million by 1993. The company continues to be highly profitable. Butcher vows never to utilize venture capital money or to take the company public.

The point of departure here is opportunity and, implicitly, the customer, the marketplace, and the industry. Exhibit 4.8 shows how higher and lower potential opportunities can be placed along an attractiveness scale. The criteria provide some quantitative ways in which an entrepreneur can make judgments about industry and market issues, competitive advantage issues, economic and harvest issues, management team issues, and fatal flaw issues and whether these add up to a compelling opportunity. For example, *dominant* strength in any one of these criteria can readily translate into a winning entry, whereas a flaw in any one can be fatal.

Entrepreneurs contemplating opportunities that will yield attractive companies, not high potential ventures, can also benefit from paying attention to these criteria. These entrepreneurs will then be in a better position to decide how these criteria can be compromised. As outlined in Exhibit 4.8, business opportunities with the greatest potential will possess many of the following, or they will dominate in one or a few for which the competition cannot come close.

Industry and Market Issues

Market. *Higher potential* businesses can identify a market niche for a product of service that meets an important customer need and provides high value-added or value-created benefits to customers. This invariably means the product or service eliminates or drastically reduces a major pain-point for a customer or end-user, or solves a major problem/bottleneck for which the customer is willing to pay a premium. Customers are reachable and receptive to the product or service, with no brand or other loyalties. The potential payback to the user or customer of a given product or service through cost savings or other value-added or valued-created properties is one year or less and is identifiable, repeatable, and verifiable. Further, the life of the product or service exists beyond the time needed to recover the investment, plus a profit. And the company is able to expand beyond a one-product company. Take, for example, the growing success of cellular phone service. At prevailing rates, one can talk for about $25 an hour, and many providers of professional services can readily bill more than the $25 an hour for what would otherwise be unused time. If benefits to customers cannot be calculated in such dollar terms, then the market potential is far more difficult and risky to ascertain.

Lower potential opportunities are unfocused regarding customer need, and customers are unreachable and/or have brand or other loyalties to others. A payback to the user of more than three years and low value-added or value-created properties also makes an opportunity unattractive. Being unable to expand beyond a one-product company can make for a lower potential opportunity. The failure of one of the first portable computer companies, Osborne Computer, is a prime example of this.

Market Structure. Market structure, such as evidenced by the number of sellers, size distribution of sellers, whether products are differentiated, conditions of entry and exit, number of buyers, cost conditions, and sensitivity of demand to changes in price, is significant.

A fragmented, imperfect market or emerging industry often contains vacuums and asymmetries that create unfilled market niches—for example, markets where resource ownership, cost advantages, and the like can be achieved. In addition, those where information or knowledge gaps exist and where competition is profitable, but not so strong as to be overwhelming, are attractive. An example of a market with an information gap is that experienced by a Boston entrepreneur who encountered a large New York company that wanted to dispose of a small, old office building in downtown Boston. This office building, because its book value was about $200,000, was viewed by the financially oriented firm as a low-value asset, and the company wanted to dispose of it so the resulting cash could be put to work for a higher return. The buyer, who had done more homework than the out-of-town sellers, bought the building for $200,000 and resold it in less than six months for more than $8 million.

Industries that are highly concentrated, that are perfectly competitive, or that are mature or declining are typically unattractive. The capital requirements and costs to achieve distribution and marketing presence can be prohibitive, and price-cutting and other competitive strategies in highly concentrated markets can be a significant barrier to entry. (The most blatant example is organized crime and its life-threatening actions when territories are invaded.) Revenge by normal competitors who are well positioned through product strategy, legal tactics, and the like, also can be punishing to the pocketbook.

The airline industry, after deregulation, is an example of a perfectly competitive market and one where many of the recent entrants will have difficulty. The unattractiveness of perfectly competitive industries is captured by the comment of prominent Boston venture capitalist William Egan, who put it this way: "I want to be in a nonauction market."[22]

Market Size. An attractive new venture sells to a market that is large and growing (i.e., one where capturing a small market share can represent significant and increasing sales volume). A minimum market size of more than $100 million in sales is attractive. In the medical and life sciences today, this target boundary is more like $500 million. Such a market size means it is possible to achieve significant sales by capturing roughly 5 percent or less and thus not threatening competitors. For example, to achieve a sales level of $1 million in a $100 million market requires only 1 percent of the market. Thus, a recreational equipment manufacturer entered a $60 million market that was expected to grow at 20 percent per year to over $100 million by the third year. The founders were able to create a substantial smaller company without obtaining a major market share and possibly incurring the wrath of existing companies.

However, such a market can be too large. A multi-billion-dollar market may be too mature and stable, and such a level of certainty can translate into competition from Fortune 500 firms and, if highly competitive, into lower margins and profitability. Further, an unknown market or one that is less than $10 million in sales also is unattractive. To understand the disadvantages of a large, more mature market consider the entry of a firm into the microcomputer industry today versus the entry of Apple Computer into that market in 1975.

Growth Rate. An attractive market is large and growing (i.e., one where capturing a good share of the increase is less threatening to competitors and where a small market share can represent significant and increasing sales volume). An annual growth rate of 30 percent to 50 percent creates niches for new entrants, and such a market is a thriving and expansive one, rather than a stable or contracting one, where competitors are scrambling for the same niches. Thus, for example, a $100 million market growing at 50 percent per year has the potential to become a $1 billion industry in a few years, and if a new venture can capture just 2 percent of sales in the first year, it can attain sales in the first year of $1 million. If it just maintains its market share over the next few years, sales will grow significantly.

Market Capacity. Another signal of the existence of an opportunity in a market is a market at full capacity in a growth situation—in other words, a demand that the existing suppliers cannot meet. Timing is of vital concern in such a situation, which means the entrepreneur should be asking, Can a new entrant fill that demand before the other players can decide to and then actually increase capacity?

Market Share Attainable. The potential to be a leader in the market and capture at least a 20 percent share can create a very high value for a company that might otherwise be worth not much more than book value. For example, one such firm, with less than $15 million in sales, became dominant in its small market niche with a 70 percent market share. The company was acquired for $23 million in cash.

A firm that will be able to capture less than 5 percent of a market is unattractive in the eyes of most investors seeking a higher potential company.

Cost Structure. A firm that can become the low-cost provider is attractive, but a firm that continually faces declining cost conditions is less so. Attractive opportunities exist in industries where economies of scale are insignificant (or work to the advantage of the new venture). Attractive opportunities boast of low costs of learning by doing. Where costs per unit are high when small amounts of the product are sold, existing firms that have low promotion costs can face attractive market opportunities.

For instance, consider the operating leverage of Johnsonville Sausage. Its variable costs were 6 percent labor and 94 percent materials. What aggressive incentives could management put in place for the 6 percent to manage and to control the 94 percent? Imagine the disasters that would occur if the scenario were reversed!

A word of caution from Scott W. Kunkel and Charles W. Hofer, who observed:

> Overall, industry structure . . . had a much smaller impact on new venture performance than has previously been suggested in the literature. This finding could be the result of one of several possibilities:
>
> 1. Industry structure impacts the performance of established firms, but does NOT have a significant impact on new venture performance.
> 2. The most important industry structural variables influencing new ventures are different from those which impact established firms and thus

[22] Comment made during a presentation at Babson College, May 1985.

research has yet to identify the industry structural variables that are most important in the new venture environment.

3. Industry structure does NOT have a significant DIRECT impact on firm performance, as hypothesized by scholars in the three fields of study. Instead, the impact of industry structure is strongly mitigated by other factors, including the strategy selected for entry.[23]

Economics

Profits After Tax. High and durable gross margins usually translate into strong and durable after-tax profits. Attractive opportunities have potential for durable profits of at least 10 percent to 15 percent and often 20 percent or more. Those generating after-tax profits of less than 5 percent are quite fragile.

Time to Breakeven and Positive Cash Flow. As mentioned above, breakeven and positive cash flow for attractive companies are possible within two years. Once the time to breakeven and positive cash flow is greater than three years, the attractiveness of the opportunity diminishes accordingly.

ROI Potential. An important corollary to forgiving economics is reward. Very attractive opportunities have the potential to yield a return on investment of 25 percent or more per year. During the 1980s, many venture capital funds achieved only single-digit returns on investment. High and durable gross margins and high and durable after-tax profits usually yield high earnings per share and high return on stockholders' equity, thus generating a satisfactory "harvest" price for a company. This is most likely true whether the company is sold through an initial public offering or privately, or whether it is acquired. Given the risk typically involved, a return on investment potential of less than 15 percent to 20 percent per year is unattractive.

Capital Requirements. Ventures that can be funded and have capital requirements that are low to moderate are attractive. Realistically, most higher potential businesses need significant amounts of cash—several hundred thousand dollars and up—to get started. Businesses that can be started with little or no capital are rare, but they do exist. One such venture was launched in Boston in 1971 with $7,500 of the founder's capital and grew to over $30 million in sales by 1989. In today's venture capital market, the first round of financing is typically $1 million to $2 million or more for a startup.[24] Some higher potential ventures, such as those in the service sector or "cash sales" businesses, have lower capital requirements than do high-technology manufacturing firms with large research and development expenditures.

If the venture needs too much money or cannot be funded, it is unattractive. An extreme example is a venture that a team of students recently proposed to repair satellites. The students believed that the required startup capital was in the $50 million to $200 million range. Projects of this magnitude are in the domain of the government and the very large corporation, rather than that of the entrepreneur and the venture capitalist.

Internal Rate of Return Potential. Is the risk–reward relationship attractive enough? The response to this question can be quite personal, but the most attractive opportunities often have the promise of—and deliver on—a very substantial upside of 5 to 10 times the original investment in 5 to 10 years. Of course, the extraordinary successes can yield 50 to 100 times or more, but these are exceptions. A 25 percent or more annual compound rate of return is considered very healthy. In the early 1990s, those investments considered basically risk free had yields of 3 percent to 8 percent.

Free Cash Flow Characteristics. Free cash flow is a way of understanding a number of crucial financial dimensions of any business: the robustness of its economics; its capital requirements, both working and fixed assets; its capacity to service external debt and equity claims; and its capacity to sustain growth.[25] We define unleveraged free cash flow (FCF) as earnings before interest but after taxes (EBIAT) *plus* amortization (A) and depreciation (D) *less* spontaneous working capital requirements (WC) *less* capital expenditures (CAPex), or FCF = EBIAT + [A+D] −[+ or − WC] − CAPex. EBIAT is driven by sales, profitability, and asset intensity. Low-asset-intensive, high-margin businesses generate the highest profits and sustainable growth.[26] We will explore this in detail in Chapter 12, Entrepreneurial Finance.

Gross Margins. The potential for high and durable gross margins (i.e., the unit selling price less all direct and variable costs) is important. Gross margins

[23] Scott W. Kunkel and Charles W. Hofer, "The Impact of Industry Structure on New Venture Performance," *Frontiers of Entrepreneurship Research, 1993* (Babson Park, MA: Babson College, 1993).

[24] J. A. Timmons, W. Bygrave, and N. Fast, "The Flow of Venture Capital to Highly Innovative Technology Ventures," a study for the National Science Foundation, reported in *Frontiers of Entrepreneurship Research: 1984* (Babson Park, MA: Babson College, 1984).

[25] For a more detailed description of free cash flow, see "Note on Free Cash Flow Valuation Models" by William Sahlman, HBS 9-288-023, Harvard Business School, 1987.

[26] William A. Sahlman, "Sustainable Growth Analysis," HBS 9-284-059, Harvard Business School, 1984.

exceeding 40 percent to 50 percent provide a tremendous built-in cushion that allows for more error and more flexibility to learn from mistakes than do gross margins of 20 percent or less. High and durable gross margins, in turn, mean that a venture can reach breakeven earlier, preferably within the first two years. Thus, for example, if gross margins are just 20 percent, for every $1 increase in fixed costs (e.g., insurance, salaries, rent, and utilities), sales need to increase $5 just to stay even. If gross margins are 75 percent, however, a $1 increase in fixed costs requires a sales increase of just $1.33. One entrepreneur, who built the international division of an emerging software company to $17 million in highly profitable sales in just five years (when he was 25 years old), offers an example of the cushion provided by high and durable gross margins. He stresses there is simply no substitute for outrageous gross margins by saying, "It allows you to make all kinds of mistakes that would kill a normal company. And we made them all. But our high gross margins covered all the learning tuition and still left a good profit."[27] Gross margins of less than 20 percent, particularly if they are fragile, are unattractive.

Time to Breakeven—Cash Flow and Profit and Loss (P&L). New businesses that can quickly achieve a positive cash flow and become self-sustaining are highly desirable. It is often the second year before this is possible, but the sooner the better. Obviously, simply having a longer window does not mean the business will be lousy. Two great companies illustrate that a higher potential business can have a longer window. Pilkington Brothers, an English firm that developed plate glass technology, ran huge losses for over 2½ years before it was regarded as a great company. Similarly, Federal Express went through an early period of enormous negative cash flows of $1 million a month.

Harvest Issues

Value-Added Potential. New ventures that are based on strategic value in an industry, such as valuable technology, are attractive, while those with low or no strategic value are less attractive. For example, most observers contend that a product technology of compelling strategic value to Xerox was owned, in the mid-1980s, by a small company with about $10 million in sales and showing a prior-year loss of $1.5 million. Xerox purchased the company for $56 million. Opportunities with extremely large capital commitments, whose value on exit can be severely eroded by unanticipated circumstances, are less attractive. Nuclear power is a good example.

Thus, one characteristic of businesses that command a premium price is that they have high value-added strategic importance to their acquirer, such as distribution, customer base, geographic coverage, proprietary technology, contractual rights, and the like. Such companies might be valued at four, five, or even six times (or more) last year's *sales*, whereas perhaps 60 percent to 80 percent of companies might be purchased at .75 to 1.25 times sales.

Valuation Multiples and Comparables. Consistent with the above point, there is a large spread in the value the capital markets place on private and public companies. Part of your analysis is to identify some historical boundaries for valuations placed on companies in the market/industry/technology area you intend to pursue. The rules outlined in Exhibit 4.8 are variable and should be thought of as a boundary and a point of departure.

Exit Mechanism and Strategy. Businesses that are eventually sold—privately or to the public—or acquired, usually are started and grown with a harvest objective in mind. Attractive companies that realize capital gains from the sale of their businesses have, or envision, a harvest or exit mechanism. Unattractive opportunities do not have an exit mechanism in mind. Planning is critical because, as is often said, it is much harder to get out of a business than to get into it. Giving some serious thought to the options and likelihood that the company can eventually be harvested is an important initial and ongoing aspect of the entrepreneurial process.

Capital Market Context. The context in which the sale or acquisition of the company occurs is largely driven by the capital markets at that particular time. Timing can be a critical component of the exit mechanism because, as one study indicated, since World War II, the average bull market on Wall Street has lasted just six months. For a keener appreciation of the critical difference the capital markets can make, one only has to recall the stock market crash of October 19, 1987, the bank credit crunch of 1990–1992, or the bear market of 2001–2003. By the end of 1987, the valuation of the Venture Capital 100 index dropped 43 percent and private company valuations followed. Initial public offerings are especially vulnerable to the vicissitudes of the capital markets; here the timing is vital. Some of the most successful companies seem to have been launched when debt and equity capital were most available and relatively cheap.

[27] R. Douglas Kahn, president, Interactive Images, Inc., speaking at Babson College about his experiences as international marketing director at McCormack & Dodge from 1978 through 1983.

Competitive Advantages Issues

Variable and Fixed Costs. An attractive opportunity has the potential for being the lowest-cost producer and for having the lowest marketing and distribution costs. For example, Bowmar was unable to remain competitive in the market for electronic calculators after the producers of large-scale integrated circuits, such as Hewlett-Packard, entered the business. Being unable to achieve and sustain a position as a low-cost producer shortens the life expectancy of a new venture.

Degree of Control. Attractive opportunities have potential for moderate-to-strong degree of control over prices, costs, and channels of distribution. Fragmented markets where there is no dominant competitor—no IBM—have this potential. These markets usually have a market leader with a 20 percent market share *or less*. For example, sole control of the source of supply of a critical component for a product or of channels of distribution can give a new venture market dominance even if other areas are weak.

Lack of control over such factors as product development and component prices can make an opportunity unattractive. For example, in the case of Viatron, its suppliers were unable to produce several of the semiconductors the company needed at low enough prices to permit Viatron to make the inexpensive computer terminal that it had publicized extensively.

A market where a major competitor has a market share of 40 percent or more usually implies a market where power and influence over suppliers, customers, and pricing create a serious barrier and risk for a new firm. Such a firm will have few degrees of freedom. However, if a dominant competitor is at full capacity, is slow to innovate or to add capacity in a large and growing market, or routinely ignores or abuses the customer (remember "Ma Bell"), there may be an entry opportunity. However, entrepreneurs usually do not find such sleepy competition in dynamic, emerging industries dense with opportunity.

Entry Barriers. Having a favorable window of opportunity is important. Having or being able to gain proprietary protection, regulatory advantage, or other legal or contractual advantage, such as exclusive rights to a market or with a distributor, is attractive. Having or being able to gain an advantage in response/lead times is important because these can create barriers to entry or expansion by others. For example, advantages in response/lead times in technology, product innovation, market innovation, people, location, resources, or capacity make an opportunity attractive. Possession of well-developed, high-quality, accessible contacts that are the product of years of building a top-notch reputation and that cannot be acquired quickly is also advantageous. Sometimes this competitive advantage may be so strong as to provide dominance in the marketplace, even though many of the other factors are weak or average. An example of how quickly the joys of startup may fade if others cannot be kept out is the experience of firms in the hard disk industry that were unable to erect entry barriers into the U.S. markets in the early to mid-1980s. By the end of 1983, some 90 hard disk drive companies were launched, and severe price competition led to a major industry shakeout.

If a firm cannot keep others out or if it faces already existing entry barriers, it is unattractive. An easily overlooked issue is a firm's capacity to gain distribution of its product. As simple as it may sound, even venture-capital-backed companies fall victim to this market issue. Air Florida apparently assembled all the right ingredients, including substantial financing, yet was unable to secure sufficient gate space for its airplanes. Even though it sold passenger seats, it had no place to pick the passengers up or drop them off.

Management Team Issues

Entrepreneurial Team. Attractive opportunities have existing teams that are strong and contain industry superstars. The team has proven profit and loss experience in the same technology, market, and service area, and members have complementary and compatible skills. An unattractive opportunity does not have such a team in place or has no team.

Industry and Technical Experience. A management track record of significant accomplishment in the industry, with the technology, and in the market area, with a proven profit and lots of achievements where the venture will compete is highly desirable. A top-notch management team can become the most important strategic competitive advantage in an industry. Imagine relocating the Chicago Bulls or the Phoenix Suns to Halifax, Nova Scotia. Do you think you would have a winning competitor in the National Basketball Association?

Integrity. Trust and integrity are the oil and glue that make economic interdependence possible. Having an unquestioned reputation in this regard is a major long-term advantage for entrepreneurs and should be sought in all personnel and backers. A shady past or record of questionable integrity is for B team players only.

Intellectual Honesty. There is a fundamental issue of whether the founders know what they do and do not know, as well as whether they know what to do about shortcomings or gaps in the team and the enterprise.

Fatal-Flaw Issues. Basically, attractive ventures have no fatal flaws; an opportunity is rendered unattractive if it suffers from one or more fatal flaws. Usually, these relate to one of the above criteria, and examples abound of markets that are too small, that have overpowering competition, where the cost of entry is too high, where an entrant is unable to produce at a competitive price, and so on. An example of a fatal-flaw entry barrier was Air Florida's inability to get flights listed on reservation computers.

Personal Criteria

Goals and Fit. Is there a good match between the requirements of business and what the founders want out of it? Dorothy Stevenson pinpointed the crux of it with this powerful insight: "Success is *getting* what you want. Happiness is *wanting* what you get."

Upside/Downside Issues An attractive opportunity does not have excessive downside risk. The upside and the downside of pursuing an opportunity are not linear, nor are they on the same continuum. The upside is easy, and it has been said that success has a thousand sires. The downside is another matter; it has also been said that failure is an orphan. An entrepreneur needs to be able to absorb the financial downside in such a way that he or she can rebound without becoming indentured to debt obligations. If an entrepreneur's financial exposure in launching the venture is greater than his or her net worth—the resources he or she can reasonably draw upon, and his or her alternative disposable earnings stream if it does not work out—the deal may be too big. While today's bankruptcy laws are generous, the psychological burdens of living through such an ordeal are infinitely more painful than the financial consequences. An existing business needs to consider if a failure will be too demeaning to the firm's reputation and future credibility, aside from the obvious financial consequences.[28]

Opportunity Cost. In pursuing any venture opportunity, there are also opportunity costs. An entrepreneur who is skilled enough to grow a successful, multi-million-dollar venture has talents that are highly valued by medium- to large-size firms as well. While assessing benefits that may accrue in pursuing an opportunity, an entrepreneur needs to heed other alternatives, including potential "golden handcuffs," and account honestly for any cut in salary that may be involved in pursuing a certain opportunity.

Further, pursuing an opportunity can shape an entrepreneur in ways that are hard to imagine. An entrepreneur will probably have time to execute between two and four multi-million-dollar ventures between the ages of 25 and 50. Each of these experiences will position him or her, *for better or for worse*, for the next opportunity. Since an entrepreneur in the early years needs to gain relevant management experience and since building a venture (either one that works or one that does not) takes more time than is commonly believed, it is important to consider alternatives while assessing an opportunity.

Desirability. A good opportunity is not only attractive but also desirable (i.e., good opportunity fits). An intensely personal criterion would be the desire for a certain lifestyle. This desire may preclude pursuing certain opportunities that may be excellent for someone else. The founder of a major high-technology venture in the Boston area was asked why he located the headquarters of his firm in downtown Boston, while those of other such firms were located on the famous Route 128 outside the city. His reply was that he wanted to live in Boston because he loved the city and wanted to be able to walk to work. He said, "The rest did not matter."

Risk/Reward Tolerance. Successful entrepreneurs take calculated risks or avoid risks they do not need to take; as a country-western song puts it: "You have to know when to hold 'em, know when to fold 'em, know when to walk away, and know when to run." This is not to suggest that all entrepreneurs are gamblers or have the same risk tolerance; some are quite conservative while others actually seem to get a kick out of the inherent danger and thrill in higher risk and higher stake games. The real issue is fit—recognizing that gamblers and overly risk-averse entrepreneurs are unlikely to sustain any long-term successes.

Stress Tolerance. Another important dimension of the fit concept is the stressful requirements of a fast-growth high-stakes venture. Or as President Harry Truman said so well: "If you can't stand the heat, get out of the kitchen."

Strategic Differentiation

Degree of Fit. To what extent is there a good fit among the driving forces (founders and team, opportunity, and resource requirements) and the timing given the external environment?

Team. There is no substitute for an absolutely top quality team. The execution of and the ability to adapt and to devise constantly new strategies is vital to survival and success. A team is nearly unstoppable

[28] This point was made by J. Willard Marriott, Jr., at Founder's Day at Babson College, 1988.

if it can inculcate into the venture a philosophy and culture of superior learning, as well as teaching skills, an ethic of high standards, delivery of results, and constant improvement. Are they free agents—clear of employment, noncompete, proprietary rights, and trade secret agreements—who are able to pursue the opportunity?

Service Management. Several years ago, the Forum Corporation of Boston conducted research across a wide range of industries with several hundred companies to determine why customers stopped buying these companies' products. The results were surprising: 15 percent of the customers defected because of quality and 70 percent stopped using a product or service because of bad customer service. Having a "turbo-service" concept that can be delivered consistently can be a major competitive weapon against small and large competitors alike. Home Depot, in the home supply business, and Lexus, in the auto industry, have set an entirely new standard of service for their respective industries.

Timing. From business to historic military battles to political campaigns, timing is often the one element that can make a significant difference. Time can be an enemy or a friend; being too early or too late can be fatal. The key is to row with the tide, not against it. Strategically, ignoring this principle is perilous.

Technology. A breakthrough, proprietary product is no guarantee of success, but it creates a formidable competitive advantage (see Exhibit 4.9).

Flexibility. Maintaining the capacity to commit and uncommit quickly, to adapt, and to abandon if necessary is a major strategic weapon, particularly when competing with larger organizations. Larger firms can typically take 6 years or more to change basic strategy and 10 to 20 years or more to change the culture.

Opportunity Orientation. To what extent is there a constant alertness to the marketplace? A continual search for opportunities? As one insightful entrepreneur put it, "Any opportunity that just comes in the door to us, we do not consider an opportunity. And we do not have a strategy until we are saying no to lots of opportunities."

Pricing. One common mistake of new companies, with high-value-added products or services in a growing market, is to underprice. A price slightly below to as much as 20 percent below competitors is rationalized as necessary to gain market entry. In a 30 percent gross margin business, a 10 percent price increase results in a 20 percent to 36 percent increase in gross margin and will lower the break-even sales level for a company with $900,000 in fixed costs to $2.5 million from $3 million. At the $3 million sales level, the company would realize an extra $180,000 in pre-tax profits.

Distribution Channels. Having access to the distribution channels is sometimes overlooked or taken for granted. New channels of distribution can leapfrog and demolish traditional channels; for example, direct mail, home shopping networks, infomercials, and the coming revolution in interactive television in your own home.

Room for Error. How forgiving is the business and the financial strategy? How wrong can the team be in estimates of revenue costs, cash flow, timing, and capital requirements? How bad can things get,

EXHIBIT 4.9

Major Inventions by U.S. Small Firms in the 20th Century

Acoustical suspension speakers	Fluid flow meter	Nuclear magnetic resonance
Aerosol can	Fosin fire extinguisher	Plezo electronic devices
Air-conditioning	Geodesic dome	Polaroid camera
Airplane	Gyrocompass	Prefabricated housing
Artificial skin	Heart valve	Pressure-sensitive cellophane
Assembly line	Heat sensor	Quick frozen foods
Automatic fabric cutting	Helicopter	Rotary oil drilling bit
Automatic transfer equipment	Heterodyne radio	Safety razor
Bakelite	High capacity computer	Six-axis robot arm
Biosynthetic insulin	Hydraulic brake	Soft contact lens
Catalytic petroleum cracking	Learning machine	Sonar fish monitoring
Continuous casting	Link trainer	Spectographic grid
Cotton picker		Stereographic image sensoring

Source: Small Business Association.

yet be able to survive? If some single-engine planes are more prone to accidents, by 10 or more times, which plane do you want to fly in? High leverage, lower gross margins, and lower operating margins are the signals in a small company of flights destined for fatality.

Gathering Information

Finding Ideas

Factors suggest that finding a potential opportunity is most often a matter of being the right person, in the right place, at the right time. How can you increase your chances of being the next Anita Roddick of The Body Shop? Numerous sources of information can help generate ideas.

Existing Businesses Purchasing an ongoing business is an excellent way to find a new business idea. Such a route to a new venture can save time and money and can reduce risk as well. Investment bankers and business brokers are knowledgeable about businesses for sale, as are trust officers. However, brokers do not advertise the very best private businesses for sale, and the real gems are usually bought by the individuals or firms closest to them, such as management, directors, customers, suppliers, or financial backers. Bankruptcy judges have a continual flow of ventures in serious trouble. Excellent opportunities may be buried beneath all the financial debris of a bankrupt firm.

Franchises Franchising is another way to enter an industry, by either starting a franchise operation or becoming a franchisee. This is a fertile area. The number of franchisors nationally stands at more than 4,000, according to the International Franchise Association and the Department of Commerce, and franchisors account for well over $600 billion in sales annually and nearly one-third of all retail sales.[29] See Chapter 6 for a fuller discussion of franchises, including resource information.

Patents Patent brokers specialize in marketing patents that are owned by individual inventors, corporations, universities, or other research organizations to those seeking new commercially viable products. Some brokers specialize in international product licensing, and occasionally a patent broker will purchase an invention and then resell it. Although, over the years, a few unscrupulous brokers have tarnished the patent broker's image, acquisitions effected by reputable brokers have resulted in significant new products. Notable among these was Bausch & Lomb's acquisition, through National Patent Development Corporation, of the U.S. right to hydron, a material used in contact lenses. Some patent brokers are:

- MGA Technology, Inc., Chicago.
- New Product Development Services, Inc., Kansas City, Missouri.
- University Patents, Chicago.
- Research Corporation, New York.
- Pegasus Corporation, New York.
- National Patent Development Corporation, New York.

Product Licensing A good way to obtain exposure to many product ideas available from universities, corporations, and independent investors is to subscribe to information services such as the *American Bulletin of International Technology, Selected Business Ventures* (published by General Electric), *Technology Mart, Patent Licensing Gazette,* and the National Technical Information Service. In addition, corporations, not-for-profit research institutions, and universities are sources of ideas.

Corporations. Corporations engaged in research and development often develop inventions or services that they do not exploit commercially. These inventions either do not fit existing product lines or marketing programs or do not represent sufficiently large markets to be interesting to large corporations. A good number of corporations license these kinds of inventions, either through patent brokers, product-licensing information services, or their own patent-marketing efforts. Directly contacting a corporation with a licensing program may prove fruitful. Among the major corporations known to have active internal patent-marketing efforts are the following:

- Gulf and Western Invention Development Corporation
- Kraft Corporation, Research and Development
- Pillsbury Company, Research and Development Laboratories
- Union Carbide Corporation, Nuclear Division
- RCA Corporation, Domestic Licensing
- TRW Corporation, System Group
- Lockheed Corporation, Patent Licensing

[29] See also "Economic Impact of Franchised Businesses," International Franchise Association, IFA Educational Foundation, 2004.

Not-for-Profit Research Institutes. These nonprofit organizations do research and development under contract to the government and private industry as well as some internally sponsored research and development of new products and processes that can be licensed to private corporations for further development, manufacturing, and marketing. One example of how this works is Battelle Memorial Institute's participation in the development of xerography and the subsequent license of the technology to the Haloid Corporation, now Xerox Corporation. Some nonprofit research institutes with active licensing programs are:

- Battelle Memorial Institute
- ITT Research Institute
- Stanford Research Institute
- Southwest Research Institute

Universities. A number of universities are active in research in the physical sciences and seek to license inventions that result from this research either directly or through an associated research foundation that administers its patent program. Massachusetts Institute of Technology and the California Institute of Technology publish periodic reports containing abstracts of inventions they own that are available for licensing. In addition, since a number of very good ideas developed in universities never reach formal licensing outlets, another way to find these ideas is to become familiar with the work of researchers in your area of interest. Among universities that have active licensing programs are:

- Massachusetts Institute of Technology
- California Institute of Technology
- University of Wisconsin
- Iowa State University
- Purdue University
- University of California
- University of Oregon

Industry and Trade Contacts

Trade Shows and Association Meetings. Trade shows and association meetings in a number of industries can be an excellent way to examine the products of many potential competitors, meet distributors and sales representatives, learn of product and market trends, and identify potential products. The American Electronics Association is a good example of an association that holds such seminars and meetings.

Customers. Contacting potential customers of a certain type of product can identify a need and where existing products might be deficient or inadequate. Discussions with doctors who head medical services at hospitals might lead to product ideas in the biomedical equipment business.

Distributors and Wholesalers. Contacting people who distribute a certain type of product can yield extensive information about the strengths and weaknesses of existing products and the kinds of product improvements and new products that are needed by customers.

Competitors. Examining products offered by companies competing in an industry can show whether an existing design is protected by patent and whether it can be improved or imitated.

Former Employers. A number of businesses are started with products or services, or both, based on technology and ideas developed by entrepreneurs while others employed them. In some cases, research laboratories were not interested in commercial exploitation of technology, or the previous employer was not interested in the ideas for new products, and the rights were given up or sold. In others, the ideas were developed under government contract and were in the public domain. In addition, some companies will help entrepreneurs set up companies in return for equity.

Professional Contact. Ideas can also be found by contacting such professionals as patent attorneys, accountants, commercial bankers, and venture capitalists who come into contact with those seeking to license patents or to start a business using patented products or processes.

Consulting. A method for obtaining ideas that has been successful for technically trained entrepreneurs is to provide consulting and one-of-a-kind engineering designs for people in fields of interest. For example, an entrepreneur wanting to establish a medical equipment company can do consulting or can design experimental equipment for medical researchers. These kinds of activities often lead to prototypes that can be turned into products needed by a number of researchers. For example, this approach was used in establishing a company to produce psychological testing equipment that evolved from consulting done at the Massachusetts General Hospital and, again, in a company to design and manufacture oceanographic instruments that were developed from consulting done for an oceanographic institute.

Networking. Networks can be a stimulant and source of new ideas, as well as a source of valuable contacts with people. Much of this requires personal initiative on an informal basis, but around the country, organized networks can facilitate and accelerate the process of making contacts and finding new business ideas. Near Boston, a high-density area of exceptional entrepreneurial activity, several networks have emerged, including the Babson Entrepreneurial Exchange, the Smaller Business Association of New England (SBANE), the MIT Enterprise Forum, the 128 Venture Group, and the Boston Computer Society. Similar organizations can be found across the United States. A sampling includes the American Women's Economic Development Corporation in New York City; the Association of Women Entrepreneurs; the Entrepreneur's Roundtable of the UCLA Graduate Student Association; and the Association of Collegiate Entrepreneurs at Wichita State University.

Shaping Your Opportunity

You will need to invest in thorough research to shape your idea into an opportunity. *Data available about market characteristics, competitors, and so on, are frequently inversely related to the real potential of an opportunity;* that is, if market data are readily available and if the data clearly show significant potential, then a large number of competitors will enter the market and the opportunity will diminish.

The good news: Most data will be incomplete, inaccurate, and contradictory, and their meaning will be ambiguous. For entrepreneurs, gathering the necessary information and seeing possibilities and making linkages where others see only chaos are essential.

Leonard Fuld defined competitor intelligence as highly specific and timely information about a corporation.[30] Finding out about competitors' sales plans, key elements of their corporate strategies, the capacity of their plants and the technology used in them, who their principal suppliers and customers are, and what new products rivals have under development is difficult, but not impossible, even in emerging industries, when talking to intelligence sources.[31]

Using published resources is one source of such information. Interviewing people and analyzing data are also critical. Fuld believes that because business transactions generate information, which flows into the pubic domain, one can locate intelligence sources by understanding the transaction and how intelligence behaves and flows.[32]

This can be done legally and ethically. There are, of course, less-than-ethical (not to mention illegal) tactics, which include conducting phony job interviews, getting customers to put out phony bid requests, and lying, cheating, and stealing. Entrepreneurs need to be very careful to avoid such practices and are advised to consult legal counsel when in doubt.

The information sources given below are just a small start. Much creativity, work, and analysis will be involved to find intelligence and to extend the information obtained into useful form. For example, a competitor's income statement and balance sheet will rarely be handed out. Rather, this information must be derived from information in public filings or news articles or from credit reports, financial ratios, and interviews.[33]

Published Sources

The first step is a complete search of materials in libraries and on the Internet. You can find a huge amount of published information, databases, and other sources about industries, markets, competitors, and personnel. Some of this information will have been uncovered when you search for ideas. Listed below are additional sources that should help get you started.

Guides and Company Information

Valuable information is available in special issues and the Web sites of *BusinessWeek, Forbes, INC., The Economist, Fast Company,* and *Fortune* and online, in the following:

Hoovers.com
ProQuest.com
Bloomberg.com
Harrisinfo.com

Valuable Sites on the Internet

- Entreworld (http://www.entreworld.org), the Web site of the Kauffman Center for Entrepreneurial Leadership, Ewing Marion Kauffman Foundation
- *Fast Company* (http://www.fastcompany.com)
- Ernst & Young (http://www.ey.com)
- *INC.* magazine (http://www.inc.com)
- Entrepreneur.com & magazine (http://www.entrepreneur.com)
- EDGAR Database (http://www.sec.gov) Note that subscription sources, such as ThomsonResearch

[30] Leonard M. Fuld, *Competitor Intelligence: How to Get It: How to Use It* (New York: John Wiley & Sons, 1985), p. 9.
[31] Ibid. See also "How to Snoop on Your Competitors," *Fortune,* May 14, 1984, pp. 28–33; and also information published by accounting firms such as *Sources of Industry Data,* published by Ernst & Young.
[32] Fuld, *Competitor Intelligence,* pp. 12–17.
[33] Ibid., p. 325.

(http://www.thomsonfinancial.com), provide images of other filings as well.
- Venture Economics (http://www.ventureeconomics.com)

Journal Articles via Computerized Indexes

- Factiva with Dow Jones, *Reuters, The Wall Street Journal*
- EBSCOhost
- FirstSearch
- Ethnic News Watch
- LEXIS/NEXIS
- New York Times
- InfoTrac from Gale Group
- ABI/Inform and other ProQuest databases
- RDS Business Reference Suite
- The Wall Street Journal

Statistics

- Stat-USA (http://www.stat-usa.gov)—U.S. government subscription site for economic, trade and business data, and market research
- U.S. Census Bureau (http://www.census.gov)—the source of many statistical data including:
  - Statistical Abstract of the United States
  - American FactFinder—population data
  - Economic Programs (http://www.census.gov/econ/www/index.html)—data by sector
  - County Business Patterns
  - Zip Code Business Patterns
  - Knight Ridder . . . CRB Commodity Year Book
- Manufacturing USA, Service Industries USA and other sector compilations from Gale Group
- Economic Statistics Briefing Room (http://www.whitehouse.gov/fsbr/esbr.html)
- Federal Reserve Bulletin
- Survey of Current Business
- FedStats (http://www.fedstats.gov/)
- Global Insight (http://www.globalinsight.com)
- International Financial Statistics—International Monetary Fund
- World Development Indicators—World Bank
- Bloomberg Database

Consumer Expenditures

- New Strategist Publications
- Consumer Expenditure Survey
- Euromonitor

Projections and Forecasts

- ProQuest
- InfoTech Trends
- Guide to Special Issues and Indexes to Periodicals (*Grey House Directory of Special Issues*)
- RDS Business Reference Suite
- Value Line Investment Survey

Market Studies

- LifeStyle Market Analyst
- MarketResearch.com
- Scarborough Research
- Simmons Market Research Bureau

Other Sources

- Wall Street Transcript
- Brokerage House reports from Investext, Multex, etc.
- Company annual reports and websites

Other Intelligence

Everything entrepreneurs need to know will not be found in libraries because this information needs to be highly specific and current. This information is most likely available from people—industry experts, suppliers, and the like. Summarized below are some useful sources of intelligence.

Trade Associations Trade associations, especially the editors of their publications and information officers, are good sources of information.[34] Trade shows and conferences are prime places to discover the latest activities of competitors.

Employees Employees who have left a competitor's company often can provide information about the competitor, especially if the employee departed on bad terms. Also, a firm can hire people away from a competitor. While consideration of ethics in this situation is very important, the number of experienced people in any industry is limited, and competitors must prove that a company hired a person intentionally to get specific trade secrets in order to challenge any hiring legally. Students who have worked for competitors are another source of information.

Consulting Firms Consulting firms frequently conduct industry studies and then make this information available. Frequently, in such fields as computers

[34] Ibid., pp. 46, 48.

or software, competitors use the same design consultants, and these consultants can be sources of information.

Market Research Firms Firms doing market studies, such as those listed under published sources above, can be sources of intelligence.

Key Customers, Manufacturers, Suppliers, Distributors, and Buyers These groups are often a prime source of information.

Public Filings Federal, state, and local filings, such as filings with the Securities and Exchange Commission (SEC), Patent and Trademark Office, or Freedom of Information Act filings, can reveal a surprising amount of information. There are companies that process inquiries of this type.

Reverse Engineering Reverse engineering can be used to determine costs of production and sometimes even manufacturing methods. An example of this practice is the experience of Advanced Energy Technology, Inc., of Boulder, Colorado, which learned firsthand about such tactics. No sooner had it announced a new product, which was patented, when it received 50 orders, half of which were from competitors asking for only one or two of the items.

Networks The networks mentioned in Chapter 3 as sources of new venture ideas also can be sources of competitor intelligence.

Other Classified ads, buyers guides, labor unions, real estate agents, courts, local reporters, and so on, can all provide clues.[35]

Internet Impact: Resources

Learning and Research

E-learning as a supplement to the traditional classroom experience is having an increasing impact on the educational experience of millions of people. By being part of a networked learning environment, students can contact subject matter authorities; access articles that are out of print; view simulations, multimedia, and interactive course materials; and easily connect—outside of class—with the instructor and fellow students.

The Internet has also become a tremendous resource for entrepreneurial research and opportunity exploration. The rapid growth of data sources, Web sites, sophisticated search engines, and consumer response forums allows for up-to-date investigations of business ideas, competitive environments, and value chain resources.

Pro-active, low- or no-cost research can now be conducted using e-mailed questionnaires, or by directing potential subjects to a basic Web site set up to collect responses. And as it does for students, the Internet provides entrepreneurs with the extraordinary capability to tap wisdom and advice from experts on virtually anything—anywhere in the world.

Chapter Summary

1. Ideas are a dime a dozen. Perhaps one out of a hundred becomes a truly great business, and one in 10 to 15 becomes a higher potential business. The complex transformation of an idea into a true opportunity is akin to a caterpillar becoming a butterfly.
2. High potential opportunities invariably solve an important problem, want, or need that someone is willing to pay for now. In renowned venture capitalist Arthur Rock's words: "I look for ideas that will change the way people live and work."
3. There are decided patterns in superior opportunities, and recognizing these patterns is an entrepreneurial skill aspiring entrepreneurs need to develop.
4. Rapid changes and disruptions in technology, regulation, information flows, and the like cause opportunity creation. The journey from idea to high potential opportunity requires navigating an undulating, constantly changing, three-dimensional relief map while inventing the vehicle and road map along the way.
5. Some of the best opportunities actually require some of the least amount of capital, especially via the Internet.
6. The best opportunities often don't start out that way. They are crafted, shaped, molded, and reinvented in real time and market space. Fit with the entrepreneur and resources, the timing, and the balance of risk and reward govern the ultimate potential.
7. The highest potential ventures are found in high growth markets, with high gross margins, and robust free cash flow characteristics, because their underlying products or services add significantly greater value to the customer, compared with the next best alternatives.
8. Trial and error. Learning-by-doing alone is not enough for developing breakthrough ventures, which require experience, creativity, and conceptualizing.

[35] Fuld, *Competitor Intelligence*, pp. 369–418.

Study Questions

1. What is the difference between an idea and a good opportunity?
2. Why is it said that ideas are a dime a dozen?
3. What role does experience play in the opportunity creation process, and where do most good opportunities come from? Why is trial-and-error learning not good enough?
4. List the sources of ideas that are most relevant to your personal interests, and conduct a search using the Internet.
5. What conditions and changes that may occur in society and the economy spawn and drive future opportunities? List as many as you can think of as you consider the next 10 years.
6. Evaluate your best idea against the summary criteria in Exhibit 4.8. What appears to be its potential? What has to happen to convert it into a high potential business?
7. Draw a value chain and free cash flow chain for an existing business dominated by a few large players. How can you use the Internet, desktop computer, and other information technology to capture (save) a significant portion of the margins and free cash flows?

MIND STRETCHERS

Have you considered?

1. Steve Jobs, founder of Apple Computer, was 10 years old when he built his first computer. Colonel Sanders was 65 years old when he started Kentucky Fried Chicken. What is an opportunity for whom?
2. Most successful existing businesses are totally preoccupied with their most important, existing customers and therefore lack the peripheral opportunity vision to spot new products and services. How is this happening where you work? Is this an opportunity for you?
3. The most successful ventures have leadership and people as the most important competitive advantage. How does this change the way you think about opportunities?
4. Who can you work with during the next few years to learn a business and have the chance to spot new opportunities outside the weak peripheral vision of an established business?
5. Barriers to entry can create opportunities for those with the right knowledge and experience. Why is this so? Can you find some examples?

Case
Securities Online, Inc.*

A former MBA student turns a second year field project into a new venture which provides financial and market information on Russia and Poland to investment banks, consulting firms, banks, venture funds, and others.

Preparation Questions:

1. Evaluate Securities Online, Inc. as of 1995.
2. How have the opportunities changed over the past year? Why?
3. What fund-raising strategy would you recommend?
4. What should the professor say? What should Kurt and John Bauer do?

June 1994 graduation was less than two months away as Kurt Bauer put the finishing touches on his second-year independent research report at the Harvard Business School. In early February 1994, he and his brother John identified several ideas for entrepreneurial businesses in Eastern Europe, such as food packaging in Russia and acquiring a publishing business in Poland, and were discussing which, if any, might make sense for them. At the time, John was with the Field Robotics Center at Carnegie Mellon University, in Pittsburgh. With his dual engineering degree he had a sharp picture of the technological aspects, while Kurt saw emerging opportunities in international information arbitrage. John had been attending Carnegie Mellon business school classes at night in entrepreneurship, so he and Kurt decided to develop a business plan together as part of their MBA studies.

*© Copyright Jeffry A. Timmons, 1996. This case was written by Kurt Bauer. For purposes of class discussion, it has been edited by Dan D'Heilly and Andrea Alyse under the direction of Jeffry A. Timmons, Franklin W. Olin Distinguished Professor of Entrepreneurship, Babson. Funding provided by the Ewing Marion Kauffman Foundation.

The conclusions Kurt and his brother John (see Appendix A) were coming to were mind-boggling: There appeared to be so many entrepreneurial opportunities in Eastern Europe and the old Soviet bloc that it was hard to know where to begin. On the surface at least, it also looked like it would be hard to miss. But the lessons he had learned working both in Eastern Europe and in taking the entrepreneurial finance course were sobering: slam dunks are few and far between.

By spring 1995, they had made some progress with their business idea and had raised $135,000 of their own capital, as well as from family and friends and also invested a lot of sweat equity all in their attempt to launch the venture. One thing was clear: The business plan that had evolved over the past several months showed promising opportunities in the business publishing and information field (see Appendix A for the Securities Online Business Plan).

Kurt was now contemplating the next phase of the company's financing and development. It appeared that for as little as $300,000 to $400,000, Securities Online could achieve its ambitious growth objectives. He was about to meet with his professor who had supervised the project and wanted to make sure he had the right questions. Is this a real opportunity? What will it take? How can it be financed? What is the company worth? What should the two founders be prepared to give up to attract outside capital? How might a deal be structured? What if it doesn't work? These and myriad related issues made for a head-spinning morning as the office door opened. "Good morning, Kurt!"

Background

Following his 1988 graduation from Harvard College, summa cum laude in biology, Kurt went on to a Fulbright Scholarship to travel and work in Germany and Eastern Europe. Subsequently, he turned down admission to the medical schools at Harvard, Yale, Stanford, and others to instead join Graham Allison at the John F. Kennedy School of Government at Harvard to work on privatization projects in Eastern Europe. These were heady days following the fall of the Berlin Wall and the subsequent liberation from 75 years of centralized, government-mandated, and (mis)managed economies throughout the Eastern bloc. With market-based economies springing up, enabling democracy to bloom, the opportunities for new ventures seemed endless. Not a day went by without hearing of a new company, a new idea, and another entrepreneur taking the plunge. Early success stories fueled the flames of excitement, possibilities, and entrepreneurial dreams. Kurt imagined this must have been what it was like 100 years ago in America as a new nation began to acquire its entrepreneurial and industrial legs. He knew that after obtaining his MBA he wanted to be part of this renewal in Eastern Europe.

The area of keenest interest to the Bauers was the business data and information vacuum that existed in the emerging capital markets and free market economies, particularly in Poland and Russia. Much of this opportunity stemmed from Kurt's firsthand experience and knowledge of these two countries. As the Eastern bloc embarked upon privatization and market economies, foreign capital, large corporations seeking to establish market access, newcomers, financial institutions, professional services, and consulting organizations all converged on these countries. Whether providing or using capital, or having clients that did so, these players faced serious data and knowledge gaps, adversely affecting the risk-reward ratio in accepting and serving client companies, making investments, and backing entrepreneurs trying to gain market entry.

The Bauers' field research had explored a wide range of business publishing ideas that might fill the many gaps that existed. Many of these seemed plausible, particularly since little or no competition existed. Yet, Kurt was constantly aware of other would-be entrepreneurs doing market research, exploring alliances, and searching for the concept that could become a major business in Eastern Europe. It seemed that legions of the wanna-bes of the entrepreneurial world were flocking to the same opportunities the Bauers had set their sights on.

Internet Use Explodes

Since 1980, John was intimately involved in the use of a personal computer, and then the Internet. He continued to focus his interests in this area at Carnegie Mellon. He and Kurt were keenly aware that the Internet was beginning to experience explosive growth in the United States and worldwide. The rate of growth only seemed to be exceeded by the optimism and frenzy among corporations and venture capital investors alike to get in on the ground floor. Many sensed that this could be the next big technology breakthrough, similar to the explosion in microcomputers in the early 1980s, and biotechnology in the early 1990s.

These discussions in the spring of 1994 led to a clear sense that there was an opportunity to exploit commercial technology. At this point, hardware prices had been falling 40 percent per annum, making it possible to launch an information technology firm at extremely low cost. Herein was a technology strategy that they concluded could give a significant competitive edge to a new entrant: rapidly integrate off-the-shelf personal computer technology rather than spend large sums of money and time to research and develop their own proprietary systems and graphical user interface. John explained:

> We are betting on low-cost computers with off-the-shelf products and shareware. Our server technology, Linux, will provide the same functionality and power as very expensive server systems. Jae Chang, our key technical

person, has convinced us that this is the technical way to go. It is open to the public, yet, there are perhaps 50,000 to 200,000 users or more of this operating system now (spring of 1994). We believe this would allow us to expand in an incredibly cheap manner. It looks like we could open an office for under $10,000 in hardware and software costs.

Most corporate competitors would think they had to spend $150,000 to $200,000 for a complete system with hardware, database, distribution and file server, and software.

Jae was key to the success of the new company. John reflected on what he called Jae's "incredible startup mentality":

> He is one of the most frugal and hardworking people I had ever met. He had a monthly budget of $426 in living expenses, of which $330 went for rent! He did this for six months. He is very hard working: 24 hours a day, seven days a week. He would sleep in his office five days in a row if he had to.

John noted how important this was since their startup budget did not include salaries for the founders for the first 13 months.

Venture Capital Frenzy

It was well known in the venture capital and entrepreneurial communities that such breakthrough opportunities as envisioned by the Bauers were the fountainhead of early stage investments that would become industry legends: DEC in the 50s; Apple Computer in the 70s; Lotus Development in the 80s; biotechnology and telecommunications in the 90s. Careers and fortunes were made and lost on such spectacular investment opportunities. Every venture capital investor knew it, and it only made the race between greed and fear more intriguing and exciting. After all, if you found the equivalent of the next Apple Computer at startup, you would become a venture capital legend at warp speed, not to mention wealthy as well.

Such a climate fueled both ambition and speculation. Valuations for Internet companies were showing a rapid increase in the early 1990s (see Exhibit A). The capital markets were signaling a clear bet: Some major companies will be built and major fortunes won—and lost—around the emergence of the Internet. What was not so clear was just what those businesses would be, and how entrepreneurs would capture the potential revenue streams and rents. Yet, for those with a recent memory, the frenzy sounded like the familiar ring in the hard-disk drive industry in the early and mid-1980s. While downright scary for private equity investors, this was purely good news for entrepreneurs such as Kurt and John. This could not be a better time to find capital in search of the next mega home-run investment.

Life Is Trade-Offs

With his track record and experience in Eastern Europe and his excellent performance in the MBA program, Kurt was a very attractive candidate for the both the consulting and investment banking industries, and he had been contacted by some of the leaders. Classmates' stories of six-figure starting salaries and substantial starting bonuses made these jobs look virtually risk-free, com-

EXHIBIT A

H&Q Internet Index

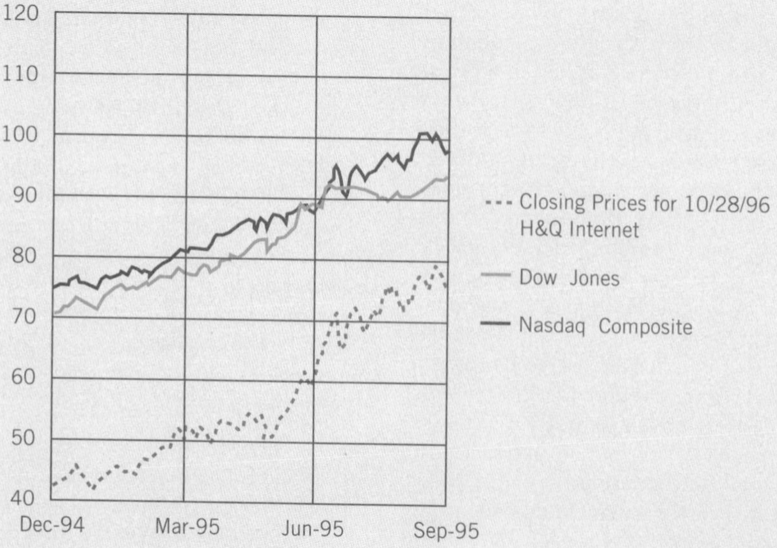

(Continued)

Index Components

Ticker	Company	Ticker	Company	Ticker	Company
COMS	3Com	EDFY	Edify	OMKT	Open Market
ADBE	Adobe Systems	EXCA	Excalibur Technologies	OTEXF	Open Text
AOL	America Online	XCIT	Excite	PRMO	Premenos Technology
ASND	Ascend Communications	FFOX	Firefox Communications	PSIX	PSINet
BBN	Bolt Beranek & Newman	FTPS	FTP Software	QDEK	Quarterdeck
BBTK	Broadband Technologies	FULCF	Fulcrum Technologies	RAPT	Raptor Systems
BVSN	Broad VSOlon	GANF	Gandalf Technologies	SCUR	Secure Computing
CNWK	C:Net, Inc.	GVIL	Global Village Communication	SGI	Silicon Graphics
CAML	Camelot	INDV	Individual	SWEBF	SoftQuad International
CSCC	Cascade Communications	INFO	Infonautics	SPYG	Spyglass
CKFR	Checkfree	SEEK	Infoseek	SSW	Sterling Software
CHKPF	Check Point Software Technologies	INTU	Intuit	SUNW	Sun Microsystems
CSCO	Cisco Systems	LCOS	Lycos	SRVC	SunRiver
CMGI	CMG Information Service	MAIDY	M.A.I.D. PLC	USRX	U.S. Robotics
CSRV	CompuServe	MACR	Macromedia	USOR	U.S. Order
CU	CUC International	MECK	Mecklermedia Corp.	VRTY	Verity
CYCH	Cybercash	NETC	Netcom On-line Com.-Services	VOCLF	VocalTec
DWTI	Dataware Technologies	NETM	Netmanage, Inc.	YHOO	Yahoo
DTOP	Desktop Data	NSCP	Netscape Communications		

Source: Used by permission of JP Morgan.

pared to the risk of a startup, right out of school. Time had run out on the four excellent offers he had secured, and he had to turn them down when the hope and promise for his new venture far outweighed tangible results.

Both John and Jae Chang faced equally difficult choices. John would have to give up his well-paid, prestigious position at one of the world's leading robotics centers. To make matters worse, he was more than halfway toward completion of his MBA, but he could not realistically attempt to complete the program and do what was necessary to be a major equity holder and cofounder of the new business. Jae was "the most talented programmer I had encountered at Carnegie Mellon," according to John, "and had other very attractive offers." He too decided to take the plunge with the Bauers.

As the door opened to the office, Kurt wondered what advice his professor might have. He also pondered whether he could really pull this off:

> Do I really want to ask my family and some friends to put their own *after-tax*, hard-won cash into my startup company nearly halfway around the globe? I feel a tremendous commitment to John and Jae, given what they have had to sacrifice.

Other conflicting demands raced through his mind as he had a flashback to one of the professor's favorite John Bauer Bernard Shaw quotes: "Any darned fool can start a love affair; but it takes a real genius to end one successfully!" He reflected that getting started may well be the easiest part of the journey.

Appendix A

EXCERPTS FROM THE SECURITIES ONLINE BUSINESS PLAN

I. Executive Summary

Securities Online Incorporated ("SOI") offers a truly unique opportunity to invest simultaneously in the tremendous growth of Emerging Markets and the Information Revolution. SOI is an electronic content provider offering financial and business information on Poland and Russia. The SOI service is available via both the Internet and direct dial-up. The content on the service includes news, corporate financials, prospectuses, and analyst reports, as well as industry, money market, fixed income, and macroeconomic information. Currently, SOI's database is the most comprehensive source of information covering the Polish markets; a majority of the information is available *only* via SOI online.

Investment Highlights

- *Prominent, Enthusiastic Customers and Suppliers.* Large multinational investment banks already use the product regularly. Only two months after the launch of the service in March 1995, major customers include Citibank, CS First Boston, and the European Bank for Reconstruction and Development. These customers have responded enthusiastically, with comments such as "This is what we are looking for . . . an outstanding resource."[1] And "This service is excellent!"[2] Suppliers also include highly regarded firms, such as *The Financial Times.*
- *Internet Information Revolution.* The Information Revolution is here now on the Internet, which is growing in number of users and overall revenues at well over 100 percent annually.[3] In this rapidly growing industry, content providers are considered to occupy the highest value-added segment. One expert summed up the general sentiment: "Content is king."[4] As a content provider on the Internet, SOI is well-poised to be at the forefront of this revolution and bring it to emerging markets.
- *Emerging Market Information.* The SOI service covers the fast-growing emerging market segment of the financial services industry—private capital inflows to emerging markets have grown annually at 45 percent, from $40 billion to $175 billion, during the last four years.[5]
- *Leading-Edge Service and Technology.* SOI delivers, around the world in seconds, documents in their original format, complete with graphics, charts, and corporate logos. The unique SOI service is extremely user-friendly, fully searchable, based on an open architecture, and compatible with all the major computer operating systems.
- *First-Mover Advantage.* SOI already has the most comprehensive financial and business information service in Poland and it will be the first such service to cover Central and Eastern Europe and Russia.
- *Low-Cost Model.* Securities Online can produce a superior product while operating on a significantly lower cost structure than competing services (such as Bloomberg, Investext, or First-Call) by leveraging the Internet, off-the-shelf software, and recent hardware developments.

The Securities Online Product

SOI offers a unique online financial and business information service, which currently covers Poland and Russia. The information on the service includes news, company financials, prospectuses, industry data, macroeconomic information, and analyst reports. In Poland, the IS service is the most comprehensive of its kind.

The SOI service is based on advanced technology that enables immediate worldwide retrieval of documents in their original format, including graphics, charts, and corporate logos. The service is extremely user-friendly and requires no technical expertise. The entire database of text, spreadsheets, and graphics is searchable in both English and the local languages. SOI employs an open architecture enabling users to download items directly from the service to their personal computer. Access to the service is via either direct dial-up or the Internet.

---

[1] Dr. Frank Ryan, head of research, the European Bank for Reconstruction and Development, 1995.
[2] Douglass Craig, International Finance Corporation, comment sent by e-mail, 1995.
[3] *BusinessWeek,* 1994.
[4] Richard Patterson, *Wired,* May 1995.
[5] Godel Aksa, March 3, 1995.

The Company

SOI was founded in June 1994 by Kurt and John Bauer (brothers) to exploit the opportunities for content providers on the Internet. With the idea of providing an emerging market financial and business information service, the company initially focused on one specific emerging market—Poland. During the course of the following year, the company created the service, signed its first customers, became operational in three countries, and grew to a team of 16 full-time and part-time employees/consultants in its Warsaw, London, and Pittsburgh offices.

Mission

SOI's mission is to be the premier provider of online financial and business information on selected emerging markets.

Strategy

SOI's strategy is to:

- Provide in-depth financial and business information.
- Focus on specific emerging markets.
- Exploit the worldwide scope of the Internet.
- Deliver a more powerful and user-friendly service.

Management and Advisors

- Kurt Bauer. Over four years' experience in privatization, transactions, and private enterprise in Poland and Russia. Received both a BA and MBA, Harvard University.
- John Bauer. Three years' experience in advanced systems integration as a robotics engineer. Received a BS in Electrical and Computer Engineering from Carnegie Mellon University.
- Jeffry A. Timmons. Currently holds the MBA Class of 1954 Professor of New Ventures chair at Harvard University, and the Frederic C. Hamilton Professor of Free Enterprise Studies at Babson College. Internationally recognized for his work in entrepreneurship, new ventures, and venture capital.
- Robert Reid. Over 16 years' experience in the online financial information industry. Senior vice president, Reuters, head of Instinet; senior vice president, NYSE; vice president, Bridge, Inc.
- Rafal Sokol. Four years' experience with the Polish capital markets at the Polish Stock Exchange and a private financial services consultancy. Undergraduate economics, Warsaw School of Economics.
- Jae Chang. Experience in networking software development at Intel and Carnegie Mellon University's Robotics Institute. BS, Computer and Electrical Engineering, Carnegie Mellon University.
- Mike Hayward. Experience with Unix, databases, networking, and security at ConnectSoft and Intel. BS, Mathematics and Computer Science from Carnegie Mellon University.

Customers

- Citibank
- CS First Boston
- Kleinwort Bensen
- EBRD
- KPMG
- Goldman Sachs

Financials

SOI revenues are from:

- Selling the service to customers on a subscription or usage basis.
- Selling advertising on its service.

Currently, SOI charges $500 per month for a fixed-rate subscription and has two variable rate options. SOI charges $1,000 per month for a full advertisement on the service.

	Actual	Projections			
	Q1 1995	1995	1996	1997	1998
Sales	$3,550	$227,000	$1,330,000	$2,853,000	$5,388,000
Net Profit	(48,005)	(406,000)	(121,000)	620,000	1,044,000
Subscriptions	10	135	375	577	897
Avg. Monthly Revenue/ Subscription	$255.00	$312.50	$375.00	$437.50	$500.00
Advertisements	1	6	12	18	20
Avg. Monthly Revenue/ Advertisement	$1000	$750	$1250	$1750	$2250
Employees	7	18	24	27	30
Offices	3	6	8	9	10

Statistics

	April 1995
# Data Providers	31
# Documents on Service	16,250
# Files/Week Added (avg)	750
# Server Hits/Month	49,840
# Unique User Visits/Month	834
# Mirrored Servers	3

SOI has a low break-even of 40 accounts per country. SOI has another very attractive financial feature—low asset intensity. Thus, similar to magazines, increasing the top line substantially impacts the bottom line.

Investment Opportunity

SOI is offering equity participation for an investment of $500,000 with an option for an additional $500,000 to be used for geographic expansion and working capital.

SOI intends to sell the business to a strategic investor in three to five years.

II. Mission and Strategy

A. Mission

SOI aims to be the premier provider of online financial and business information on selected emerging markets.

B. Strategy

The Securities Online Incorporated (SOI) strategy is to:

1. Provide In-Depth Information Reliable information is notoriously scarce in emerging markets. SOI fills an unoccupied niche by providing customers with

(1) A unique assortment of difficult-to-find primary and secondary emerging market data in a centralized, proprietary online database service.
(2) "Exclusives"—data which are available in either online format *only* from SOI and/or translations or presentations available only from SOI.

2. Focus on Specific Emerging Markets SOI will focus on particular emerging markets where data are difficult to obtain and demand for such information is high. SOI will initially focus on Central and Eastern Europe and Russia, and will eventually expand to other selected markets.

3. Move Early into Selected Markets SOI seeks to move quickly into emerging markets to build up first-mover advantages. Early entrance will make SOI known as the leading (or a leading) provider of online financial and business information in the selected markets. In Poland, SOI now has the most in-depth service, with over three-quarters of its material not available on any other online service.

Relatively few online financial services exist in emerging markets. Reuters, Bloomberg, Telerate, and Disclosure all have information on emerging markets, but the amount of in-depth information is limited. SOI will fill the niche of an in-depth source of financial and business information in these markets. In Poland, for example, no other service fills such a niche. In the words of one Polish broker, "You have no competition."[6]

4. Exploit the Worldwide Scope of the Internet SOI is a business conceived to exploit the worldwide scope of the Internet. SOI uses the latest commercially available networking technologies along with the Internet infrastructure to deliver information to customers around the world, to develop and maintain its service, and to run its own internal operations. In this way, SOI does not need expensive proprietary networks relied upon by established information providers.

At the same time, SOI sells its service via direct dial-up, which allows customers to avoid using the Internet to access the service. Thus, while SOI uses the Internet, it does not rely on the Internet.

5. Deliver a More Powerful and User-Friendly Service SOI's unique service makes information retrieval easy by means of its extremely user-friendly interface, easy-to-use tools, comprehensive searching ability, and open architecture. The system is capable of delivering information in a format identical to its printed version, including text, charts, graphs, logos, pictures, and even video.

III. The Product

The following section describes the SOI product and service in detail. However, words cannot compare to an actual demonstration.

A. Overview

SOI provides a unique, proprietary, online data product for users of Polish and Russian financial and business information. The SOI service offers users instant access to corporate financial statements, business and financial news, brokerage reports, money market and fixed-income information, macroeconomic data, prospectuses, and a range of other financial and business information on these selected emerging markets. Currently, the SOI service in Poland is the most in-depth of its kind, with over 75 percent of the information available online only via SOI.

[6] Rafal Lys, BGZ, 1995.

The SOI service is based on advanced technology. SOI delivers, in seconds around the globe, documents in their original format. Brokerage research reports, for example, are available in a format identical to their printed version, including graphics, charts, and corporate logos. All of this is within an extremely user-friendly, easy-to-use point-and-click system. The database consists of text, spreadsheets, graphs, logos, and pictures, all of which is searchable in both English and the local languages. The open architecture of the service enables users to download text and spreadsheet documents directly to their own computer.

Users may access the service via either direct dial-up or the Internet. For direct dial-up, SOI installs software (which is fully Windows, Macintosh, or Unix compatible) on the end user's computer. The user then simply "points and clicks" to access the service. On the Internet, users go to the SOI World Wide Web address (www.securitiesonline.com) and then access the service in the same manner.

SOI intends to expand its business model to additional selected emerging markets. The geographic scope of SOI could range from Central and Eastern Europe and the Commonwealth of Independent States or extend to countries in Latin America, Asia, and Africa as well.

B. The Product's Content

Types of Information SOI's goal is to provide a deeper and broader assortment of up-to-date information from selected emerging markets than is available from any other information service. The broad categories of information include:

- *Company Financial Information.* Basic financial statements (income statement, balance sheet, ratios, etc.) for public companies from both pubic and private sources. Data for unlisted companies and select private companies will also be provided as available. Much of this information is made available to the user in spreadsheet format.
- *Newspaper and Other Periodical Articles.* SOI has signed agreements with nearly all the leading news periodicals in Poland, including the most highly respected business, financial, and economic newspaper (*Nowa Europa,* the Polish equivalent of the *Financial Times*) and the leading investor's newspaper. Stories from these periodicals are gathered and posted to the SOI database on a daily or weekly basis. (In the case of *Nowa Europa,* English articles are now put in the evening before they are published.)
- *Analyst Reports.* Agreements (seven as of April 10, 1995) have been made with leading brokerages covering the geographic focus markets. These brokerages include their company, market, and other reports on the SOI service in exchange for an advertisement, a commission, or a discount on the service. Users can perform keyword searches on analyst reports just as on any information on the service. The most significant data-provider agreement is with CS First Boston, the leading investment bank in the Eastern and Central European and Russian markets.
- *Macroeconomic Data.* Spreadsheet or tabular formatted basic economic statistics, cross-sectional and historical, acquired from government and private sources.
- *Prospectuses.* Live and historical prospectuses for offerings within the geographic focus areas are posted for online perusal. The SEC regulations now allow U.S. customers to access live prospectuses online.
- *Fixed-Income.* Daily updates of the bill and the bond market, as well as the commercial paper market. Sources include the top banks, such as ING and Bank Handlowy.
- *Surveys, General Reports, and Other Useful Resources.* General reports on countries and industries from supranational organizations or major financial market press such as the *Financial Times.*

Data Providers Data providers include the press, government bodies, banks and financial institutions, private companies, and research organizations that are capable of supplying the types of data described above.

Data providers are recruited both from the geographic focus areas ("in-country") and in the developed financial markets. In-country data providers are particularly important in that they are difficult to access from Western financial centers, such as London and New York, and represent opportunities for SOI to gain exclusive agreements. Developed market data providers provide summary analysis and "brand name" credibility.

C. The Product's Features

Benefits to Data Users The SOI service currently provides unique benefits and features, which are not available from other information services. They are as follows:

- *Deep and Broad Assortment of Relevant Data.* As with any distribution channel, one of the primary services rendered by SOI is the assembly of goods and services specific to a set of customer interests. SOI is the first and only online information service that specializes in financial data for the emerging markets of Eastern and Central Europe and Russia. No other information provides such a centralized compilation of relevant data.
- *Exclusive Content.* As of March 28, 1995, for three-quarters of its data providers, the SOI service is the only online channel. SOI plans to increase both the amount of information available only through SOI and the number of exclusive providers. The CS First Boston arrangement may represent a very significant exclusive arrangement.
- *Presentation.* The SOI service has a leading-edge, easy-to-use, graphical user interface. Windows, Mac, or Unix compatible, the software offers "point and click" navigation, and an intuitive search mechanism for conducting keyword searches of the entire database.

Compared to other systems (such as Lexis/Nexis) the SOI system is very easy to learn and use, even for infrequent users.

- *Original Format.* Information on the SOI service is available in a format identical to the printed version, including graphs, charts, and corporate logos. Thus, research reports, corporate information, and even the *Financial Times* survey on Poland are presented in a format as they appear in print.
- *Open Architecture.* The service is on an "open system" platform that features automatic downloading of data into spreadsheets and word processing programs on the user's computer. Many other financial information services either do not permit manipulation (e.g., Bloomberg) or do not offer such extensive data downloading.
- *Searchability.* The service enables users to search the entire database of text, spreadsheets, graphs, and other files to locate information of interest. The search engine was developed in-house to provide users with an easy-to-use means of searching, pulling up, printing, and saving articles from the service.
- *Native Language Support.* SOI offers data users the ability to find material both in English and in native languages. This enables users to get a variety of information, including information from local sources not available in English.
- *Flexible Access.* Because the SOI service does not require dedicated terminals, leased lines, or special equipment, the customer can access the service from any computer, modem, and telephone line. Clients may even dial in from their portables when traveling. This presents a significant cost and flexibility advantage over fixed-terminal services. This feature also has kept costs low during the growth phase of the company.
- *Relatively Inexpensive.* Relatively means both in comparison to traditional data sources (periodicals, fax services, primary data-gathering) and in comparison to other less-focused information services, where the customer would have to pay for the entire service just to gain access to the small fraction of the data relevant to their interests.

Benefits to Data Providers

- *Wide, Inexpensive, Fast Distribution over a New Channel.* Internet distribution reaches customers that data providers would not ordinarily reach. The online format further amortizes their fixed investment in assembling data without incurring significant variable costs (printing, etc.). Distribution via the Internet also enables the information to be disseminated much faster; in the case of some information, such as prospectuses, the information can be available one week before it is available in printed form.
- *Presentation/Exact Reproduction.* The SOI service enables data providers to distribute their information electronically in the same visual format that it would be distributed on paper. This is the primary reason why CS First Boston has decided to include its reports on the service. The quality of the printouts and the presentation of the service is shown later in the business plan.
- *Marketing Services.* Data providers can "piggyback" on SOI's marketing efforts, in that they are listed in the SOI marketing materials and promoted as part of the SOI service.
- *Subscription/Advertising Revenues.* Several data providers have cited the possibility of obtaining advertisements and additional subscriptions from SOI's users as one reason to put their information on the service.
- *Data and Electronic Archiving.* In many cases, including prominent Western sources such as CS First Boston, the data provider does not have adequate electronic storage of its own information. Even when electronic archives are kept, they are often not searchable or readily accessible. SOI enables data providers to access their archival information readily and easily.

Differentiation Although SOI will enjoy a first-mover advantage in its market niche, SOI anticipates that as these financial markets develop, the challenge to differentiate versus competitors will increase. SOI anticipates that the "Assortment" advantage will likely diminish, especially if there are any new entrants to the market. Similarly, the "Presentation" and "Data Manipulation" advantages are imitable. In order to preserve its first-mover advantage, SOI will differentiate itself by (1) moving faster than competitors into new markets in order to continue being regarded as the leading emerging markets information source, and (2) adding "exclusives," with the following priority:

- New information not available anywhere else, in any media.
- Formats or translations not available from sources other than the SOI service.
- Information not available online except through the SOI service.

Note that not all the information needs to be exclusive—just a large enough fraction of the total material to create a barrier to switching away from SOI to a competing service.

D. Supply Agreement with CS First Boston (Pending Legal Approval)

CS First Boston CS First Boston is ranked by *Institutional Investor* magazine as the number one broker and provider of research and services in Eastern Europe (here, this includes Russia). It is considered to be the "brand leader" for advice. For Eastern European activities alone, it markets in-house research and brokerage services to 1,400 companies worldwide.

Proposed Terms The terms of the arrangement between SOI and CS First Boston currently pending legal approval are as follows:

- CS First Boston will list its Eastern European (Poland, Czech, Hungary, and Russia) emerging markets reports on the IS service. There are three types of reports: industry reports, company reports, and market overviews. Reports will be available online at the same time as they are published in other formats.
- The relationship is for two years with a 12-month notice of termination.
- SOI is the exclusive Internet source, although not the only online source. CS First Boston also lists its reports on First Call and MAID.
- The reports will only be available to CS First Boston clients. General SOI subscribers will not be able to access the reports until their status as a CS First Boston client has been confirmed.

Implications for Subscriptions Sales SOI also stands to benefit from increased subscription sales as CS First Boston intends to market SOI to its customer list. CS First Boston plans to add the current copy to upcoming reports:

CS First Boston East European Research Available on the Internet:

> From this week, we are making our research available to those of our clients who use "Securities Online," a new information service specializing in providing information on East European markets, through the Internet.
>
> This service will allow clients to download the research at will, in an almost identical form to that in which it is printed, including all graphs and tables. The service will also allow subscribers to send messages to CS First Boston research staff, and to search the reports for key words. We consider that "Securities Online" is an excellent information service for Eastern Europe, and are pleased to add distribution via this service to our list of client services.

CS First Boston estimates that, of its 1,400 corporate customers who have an active interest in SOI's geographic focus area, 200 may be interested in subscribing to the IS service. Based on this estimate, the revenue potential for SOI at current subscription rates (excluding set-up fee) is approximately $1.2 million.

Even though the CS First Boston material is available only to CS First Boston clients, the presence of the name on SOI screens and menus will help market the service more generally. Having the imprimatur of a highly respected (market leading) financial institution is likely to have a positive impact on subscription sales.

E. Distribution

Distribution to the SOI information service is primarily online. The SOI service is made available to customers through direct dial-up or via the Internet, using standard desktop computing equipment. The Internet currently extends to each of the Eastern European countries. An Internet node will be established in each SOI sales, technical, and geographic focus market location to host the service in local areas, maximizing network speed and reducing downtime.

The Internet is also instrumental for maintaining SOI's product. SOI collects data from its data providers both over the Internet and through direct dial-up. The data are assembled at SOI's headquarters in Pittsburgh, Pennsylvania, and then mirrored back to each location via the Internet. SOI employees, located in various countries, use the Internet (e-mail and Internet "chat" sessions) as the primary vehicle for intracompany communications and file transfer.

The Internet dramatically decreases the costs of SOI's operations. As an example, SOI has had conference "chat sessions" on the Internet that have included Poland, the United States, and the United Kingdom. An hourlong conference costs SOI a few dollars.

Reliable Internet access is a critical success factor for SOI. In order to function smoothly, SOI must be confident that the local Internet access providers in every relevant market have minimal downtime (i.e., the time in which the local service is not accessible).

In Poland, SOI has entered into a joint venture (Internet Technologies, Inc.) to ensure that Internet access will be adequate. In exchange for assistance in setting up the necessary network, SOI has a majority equity stake (35 percent) in Internet Technologies, Inc. Without a capital contribution on the part of SOI, the joint venture enables SOI to control the reliability of access to the Internet and to run its service locally on the Internet Technologies server. This is a very attractive arrangement for SOI, for which reliable Internet access is reason enough to enter into such an arrangement.

F. The Product's Geographic Focus

Securities Online currently provides an extensive service covering financial data in one market, Poland. It has begun operations in Russia and currently offers one of the leading providers of Russian financial information. SOI's development will continue in selected geographic focus markets, as follows:

- Phase I: Poland and Russia, with special emphasis on Poland (January 1995–June 1995).
- Phase II: Deeper Russian coverage; inclusion of Czech Republic and Hungary (June 1995–December 1995).
- Phase III: Expansion to other emerging markets (January 1996 and onwards).

SOI's business model is transferable across many emerging markets. In a conservative scenario, expansion may be limited to Eastern and Central Europe and the Commonwealth of Independent States. Or, SOI's scope could include countries in Latin America, Asia, and Africa.

Geographic Focus Market Selection: Phase 1 The focus on Poland in Phase I is for the following reasons: (1) increasing investor interest in the Polish market; (2) growth of the Polish economy and relative stability of the Polish government; (3) familiarity of SOI principals with the Polish privatization and capital markets development process; (4) manageable size of the business model for Poland.

After a period of depressed interest, Poland is gaining favor with investors. A recent United Nations study indicates that Poland attracts 24 percent of "initial" foreign direct investment (FDI) to Central and Eastern Europe and the Commonwealth of Independent States, accounting for $4.1 billion at the end of 1994. Poland is second only to Hungary (attracting 27 percent) and ahead of Russia (15 percent), Kazakhstan (14 percent), and the Czech Republic (8 percent). Recent leadership changes indicate that privatization activity is likely to accelerate in mid- to late 1995,[7] and bullish reports on the Polish economy are appearing more frequently.[8]

SOI's prioritization of Russia over Hungary and the Czech Republic reflects investor interest in a potentially large, volatile (and unstable) market, and that information on Russia is extremely difficult to find. The aforementioned UN study indicates that Russia draws 31 percent of total foreign investment for "long-term" projects worth more than $10 million, second only to Kazakhstan (39 percent) and far outstripping Hungary, which draws 8 percent.[9]

Geographic Focus Market Selection: Phases 2 and 3 SOI will balance customer demand with available resources (in particular, useful in-country contacts and staff availability) to determine markets suitable for expansion. After Poland and Russia, SOI plans to expand to the Czech Republic and Hungary.

Long-term non-European targets include India, Turkey, and East Asian countries.

IV. Customers

Overview

SOI's customers consist of sophisticated players in the worldwide capital markets. Information is a key component to the success of investment and business strategy no matter where in the value chain a customer is participating: sales, origination, trading, venture capital, consulting, or fund management. Price is not a primary concern of these customers; pertinent, timely data is.

Capital flows to emerging markets have grown considerably over the past few years. For example, international portfolio investment in emerging markets has grown at 65.3 percent (CAGR) over the last four years.[10] Overall private capital flows to emerging markets have increased 45 percent (CAGR) per year over the last four years.[11] Developing markets often offer higher yield, but they are also riskier as well. In such an environment, timely information is imperative to achieve higher returns. SOI provides information on emerging markets in an easy-to-use format using technologically advanced systems. Target customers are a diverse group of brokers, traders, corporate finance professionals, institutional investors, venture capitalists, management consultants, and corporate executives. Ancillary customers include corporate advertisers who may purchase advertising space on the system. Initial customer feedback has been exceedingly positive, and each customer group's diverse characteristics have been addressed by SOI's capabilities.

A. Customers

Since its initial launch in February 1995, SOI has had a very strong response from prominent customers. As of April 20, 1995, major customers include:

- CS First Boston
- Citibank
- Kleinwort Bensen
- KPMG
- European Bank for Reconstruction and Development

Preliminary feedback has been exceedingly positive. Customers generally feel that SOI is providing a valuable service as demonstrated in Table V. Customer references are available upon request.

Market Segmentation The IS service is targeted toward domestic and international brokers, traders, fund managers, other investors, consultants, and businesspersons who use financial, market, and business information in the geographic focus areas.

In Phase 1 the primary emphasis will be on customers in London and Warsaw.

In the future, SOI will target customers in the other emerging market capitals, as well as in developed market financial centers such as New York, Frankfurt, Zurich, Geneva, and Vienna. Those cities are the Western centers for Central/Eastern European and Russian financial activities. Also, SOI will target large companies and other investors in Central/Eastern Europe and Russia.

SOI's primary target markets include:

- Brokers
- Institutional investor/fund managers
- Traders
- Corporate finance professionals
- National investment fund managers in Poland
- Consultants
- Venture capitalists

[7] "Pole Leadership Changes Clear Privatization Path," *The Wall Street Journal* (Europe), March 27, 1995.
[8] *Financial Times Survey: Poland, Financial Times,* March 28, 1995.
[9] "Kazakhstan, Russia First for Investment," *Financial Times,* March 24, 1995.
[10] Austin et al., 1994.
[11] Godel Aksa, 1995.

TABLE V

SOI's Target Customers

What SOI's Target Customers Are Saying

"This is what we are looking for . . . an outstanding resource."
—Frank Ryan, head of research, EBRD

"The economist saw these reports on the service and were simply amazed."
—Peter Johnson, Researcher, CS first Boston

"This service is unique. You have no competition. This service is needed here for investment."
—Rafal Lys, chief investment advisor, BGZ

"This is impressive. I installed the software in no time, used it for half an hour, then had a partner check it out. When he looked at the information on the service, he said, 'This is the most comprehensive information I have encountered since working in the region.'"
—David Saef, analyst, Schooner Capital

"I log in about twice per day. The service is great. It gives me up-to-date financial and I can do searches on various topics."
—Mariusz Kolecki, analyst, Kleinwort Bensen

"You will have users in the bank."
—Anna Oakeshout, researcher, EBRD

"This service is excellent! It's precisely the sort of real content service which the Internet needs."
—Douglass Craig, International Finance Corporation (sent by e-mail)

"[A Service covering Central and Eastern Europe] would be of great use. Information is scanty."
—Douglass Polunin, manager, Pictet Emerging Market Fund

"Getting information is a very slow process. I have to go to the exchange in person for information, and even then it is not readily available."
—Mark Seasholes, former Poland analyst, Baring Securities

"With respect to an online information service, because of the need, we may even be prepared to invest money. There is a real need for more information."
—David Mathews, manager, Fleming Investment

In addition to targeting groups as users, SOI sells advertising space on its service.

Primary Targets

Brokers. In Poland, a total of 48 brokerage houses exist, each of which has actively traded an average of about $10 million to $50 million per month on the exchange over the past year. In addition to the array of Polish brokers, four Western brokerages (Creditanstalt, Citibank, Raiffeisen, and CS First Boston) are licensed in Poland. Other Western investment houses use Polish or the local Western brokerages.

Brokers in London also sell Polish securities to London-based and other international investment funds, and to other investors. They, just like Polish brokers, are in need of in-depth information on the Polish market. Because of the distance from the market, it is even more difficult for them to get information.

Brokerage house analysts use information to help clients with investment questions. In most markets, premium information and analysis are key components to the success of a full-service brokerage house.

One aspect of this segment worth noting is that overall volume of foreign securities is growing rapidly. The total volume of foreign equities was $3.8 trillion in 1993, up from $73 billion in 1979, or cumulative annual growth of 33 percent per year. Of this, fixed income volume was $1.8 trillion in 1993, compared to $36.4 billion in1974, or annual growth of 23 percent per year.[12]

Institutional Investors. Many institutional investors now place a percentage of international or emerging market fund capital in Central/Eastern Europe, especially in Poland, Hungary, and the Czech Republic. Furthermore, several institutional investors have set up funds, which invest solely in Eastern Europe or are based locally. Pioneer, for example, has a $500 million equity fund in Poland, and numerous other funds that invest in the region are in the $50 million-plus range.

Fund managers and analysts also lack information and analysis in the Polish, Czech, Russian, and other Central/Eastern European markets. Fund managers demand information about the markets and the equities they invest in. Some managers actively seek out information themselves, while others tend to rely on brokers for their information. Fund managers that rely mostly on their own information sources are prime candidates for subscribing to the service. Others may be able to get brokers to use soft commissions to pay for the service.

SOI has identified a list of funds that each have positions in Central and Eastern European and Russia. These fund managers will be a major target in London and elsewhere.

[12] *The Economist,* December 17, 1994.

Proprietary Traders. Proprietary traders are individuals who trade on the accounts of large banks and financial institutions. They usually have at their disposal a large amount of cash to invest. Many of these individuals focus on emerging markets and are always looking for new opportunities or interesting vehicles. They scan a wide array of information sources to look for such opportunities.

Corporate Finance Professional. Both Western and local banks are at the heart of transactions in Central and Eastern Europe. Because of the transformations of these economies, there is extensive privatization, merger, and acquisition activity. Bankers involved in these transactions require extensive information about the company, the industry, and the country when preparing for the transaction.

New Investment Funds. The Polish government has just recently established 15 mutual funds to manage 444 companies. These funds, managed by teams of Western and Polish companies, will control over $200 million in assets each. As investors and asset managers themselves, they will need company, industry, macroeconomic, market, and country information. The teams invariably include Western partners who, because they are not as familiar with Poland (but are used to online services), are a prime target for the SOI service. The 15 funds chosen by the government should be operational by spring/summer 1995.

Management Consultants. Many industries and companies in SOI's geographic focus are undergoing major reorganization and restructuring, providing management consultants with demand that is estimated to be growing at over 30 percent per year.

Consultants require company, industry, market, and economic information for client analysis. Access to information drives their business. Also similar to financial service professionals, consultants have high bill rates and are usually under significant time pressure.

Western consultancies are prevalent in SOI's first geographic focus. Each of the "Big Five" accountancies (KPMG, Price Waterhouse, Coopers & Lybrand, Deloitte & Touche, and Ernst & Young), for example, has on average over 100 professionals in their Warsaw office. The "Big Five" have large consulting departments, and along with the traditional strategic consultancies are increasing their staffing in Warsaw.

Venture Capitalists. In scouting for deals, venture capitalists scan a wide array of information. They read extensively about and do research on various companies and industries. In order to make educated investment decisions, they need access to the right information.

The venture capital industry in Central and Eastern Europe has grown from nonexistent to considerable size in the last five years. Major venture firms, such as Advent International and Schooner Capital, have set up funds focused solely on the region. Others, backed with funds from the EBRD, are moving in quickly.

Additional Targets

Corporate Advertisers. SOI is using a newsletter or magazine model to approach banks and companies to include information about their companies in a "service" section of the database. Just as many industry newsletters and "trade" magazines have advertisements in addition to in-depth information, SOI is making it possible for companies to advertise on the service.

Hotel Business Centers. Hotels play a central role in business activity in Poland. Most top hotels offer clients a business center which provides a range of business services. As a means of reaching hotel guests, SOI is offering business centers the opportunity to put the service in the center and to advertise the service to clients by placing a brochure in each hotel room.

B. Characteristics of Target Market

Online financial and business information service customers are characteristically:

- Information dependent.
- Time-sensitive.
- Multiple source users.
- Frustrated with existing sources (for Eastern and Central Europe and Russia).

Information Dependence Information and analysis drive the business of SOI's target customers. They are critical to the $10 million to $50 million per month in turnover for each licensed Polish brokerage. Information is behind each investment decision of the regular million-dollar investments that fund managers make. It forms the basis of consulting studies for companies investing in the region. Pertinent information is of high value to these customers; it is the lifeblood of their business.

Time Sensitivity In addition to the importance of the information, SOI's target customers are extremely time-sensitive. Usually they need the information immediately (or sometimes, yesterday). Mailing or even express courier service does not suffice. They also are often under significant time pressure to gather information. They will pay a premium to have the information at their fingertips.

Multiple Information Source Usage Members of SOI's target market do not limit themselves to one information source. They typically use information from a wide range of sources to drive their analysis and provide depth to their accumulation of information. Multiple subscriptions to online services or databases mirror subscription to a variety of newspapers and newsletters.

Frustration with Current Sources In developed countries, financial service professionals and consultants usually have access to several online information providers and databases. With emerging markets, use of online services is less ubiquitous. But if these countries follow the development path of more advanced countries, use should parallel the dramatic increase in such services.

The combination of the growth in stock market volume and total capitalization, the development of the bond market, the increasing amount of foreign direct investment, and a dramatic rise in funds poised for investment in these markets has pushed demand for financial information.

At the same time inefficient and insufficient information flow impedes investment. Investors report that lack of quality information on which to base decisions is the single greatest factor holding back investment in Eastern and Central European economies. Customer interviews reveal a great deal of frustration regarding data availability and enthusiasm for the type of service SOI supplies.

C. Sales and Marketing Agreements

Direct Sales SOI's sales approach is currently largely via direct sales ("accounts"). SOI's financial model calls for an average of only 7.5 accounts per month for the first year. In both London and in Poland, SOI is located very close to most of its target market (SOI is in the Marriott/LIM center, which is the heart of business activity in Warsaw, and is in the middle of the City of London, where most of the banks are situated), thereby enabling sales staff to readily and quickly reach the target customers.

Targeted Advertising Offered by Partners

SOI has approached a number of companies to discuss arrangements that will help to promote the SOI service and link SOI with recognized industry leaders. In doing so, SOI looks for free advertising space or promotion of the SOI service by well-known, well-respected firms.

Financial Times. SOI has an arrangement with the *Financial Times* to promote its service. The agreement is as follows:

- SOI received a 12- inch advertisement in the Poland Country Survey published on March 28, 1995.
- SOI included the survey (with graphs and photographs) in its service. The survey was available for no charge on the Securities Online Internet Server for one week. After the first week, it was available to subscribers at the usual billing rates.
- SOI and the *Financial Times* are currently working to include future surveys and other publications on the service.

The benefits for SOI include:

- Credibility—association with one of the leading worldwide financial newspapers and a recognized name.
- Promotion—advertising to a readership directly in line with SOI's target customers.
- Sales material—promotional material to include in future sales and marketing material.

CS First Boston. See earlier for a description of the agreement terms with CS First Boston to promote the service.

Local Advertising SOI also has agreements with other data providers to obtain free advertising space in their publications. For example, in Poland SOI currently has an agreement with the *Central European Business Weekly, Capital, Gazeta Bankowa,* and others for free advertising.

D. Pricing Schedule

SOI has three different pricing options for the service:

Fixed-Price Introductory Offer:

$500 per month per country.

Initial three-month period.

Unlimited usage.

Option 1: Fixed Plus Variable Pricing

$200 per month per country.

Usage costs approximately $0.10 per line ($2–$4 per page).

Direct dial-up costs of about $20 per hour.

Option 2: Variable Pricing

No monthly charge.

Usage costs approximately $0.20 per line ($4–$8 per page).

Direct dial-up costs of about $20 per hour.

Advertising Pricing Pricing for advertisements starts with a basic listing of the company for $200 per month. A multiple-page listing costs $1,000 per month.

Payment Terms For both pricing methods, SOI offers discounts for longer payment periods and usage prepayments. This also benefits SOI's short-term cash position.

V. Industry Overview

Business Information Services Market Segmentation

The business information services market ($27 billion in sales in the United States in1993) can be segmented in two ways: (1) by type of data provided and (2) by the industry that uses the data. By combining these two segmentation schemes, the size of SOI's target market may be estimated. SOI participates in this market using advanced technology to provide economic and financial data to clients in the professional services industry (particularly the "Wall Street" customer segment, including investment bankers, fund managers, and brokers). The following analysis characterizes the global opportunity since information technology adoption globally follows directions set in the United States. Because SOI focuses on geographic markets where the "digital transformation" is by no means nature, SOI can realistically expect to grow considerably faster than the market in developed countries.

Industry Segmentation

There are five major industry segments, which are further subdivided. SOI provides data to the second largest industry segment, the professional and intermediate services market. This was the fastest growing segment over the five-year historical period, and growth in this segment has also been accelerating whereas growth in all other segments is slowing down. Table VIa summaries the size and growth of the major industry segments in the United States alone.[13]

The professional and intermediate services industry segment is subdivided into five major customer submarkets. Table VIb shows the size and growth of each of these submarkets in the United States. The three financial submarkets (Wall Street, banks, and insurance) represent nearly 80 percent of the intermediate and professional services market.

Within this segment, the largest submarket (Wall Street) was primarily responsible for the strong segment growth, accelerating its spending 12.4 percent over 1992. Spending was largely a consequence of the increase in transaction activity and underlying growth in the securities markets.

Data Segmentation

The business information services market can also be segmented by the type of data provided. Table VIc shows how the entire $27 billion U.S. market is broken down.

Economic and financial data was the second-fastest growing segment in the first-year historical period. It is projected to be the fastest growing segment in the entire business information market through 1998, at 10 percent per year on average.

[13] "Business Information Services," in the Veronis, Suhler & Associates' *Communications Industry Report,* November 1994.

TABLE VIa

1993 Business Information Services Market by Industry in the United States

Industry	$ Millions in 1993	% of Market	% CAGR, 1988–93	% Change, 1992–93
Consumer Goods and Services	$8,995	33.2%	6.1%	5.4%
Professional and Intermediate Services (Financial, Legal, Business Data Services) (Wall Street, Banks, Insurance)	7,911	29.2	7.7	8.0
Basic Industry (Construction, Agriculture, Industrial)	4,631	17.1	6.1	5.5
Distribution (Wholesale, Retail, Related Services)	4,441	16.4	6.1	3.9
Government and Nonprofit	1,089	4.0	6.2	4.0
TOTAL	$27,067	100.0%	6.5%	5.9%

TABLE VIb

Intermediate and Professional Industry Submarkets in the United States

Submarkets	$ Millions in 1993	% of Market	% CAGR, 1988–93	% Change, 1992–93
Wall Street	$2,667	33.7%	9.8%	12.4%
Banks	1,792	22.7	6.7	8.1
Insurance	1,509	19.1	5.9	5.9
Business Data Services	858	10.8	6.7	4.6
Legal	1,085	13.8	7.8	3.3
TOTAL	$7,911	100.0%	7.7%	8.0%

TABLE VIc

1993 Business Information Services Market by Type of Data in the United States

Data Type Segment	$ Millions in 1993	% of Market	% CAGR, 1988–93	% CAGR, 1993–98
Marketing	$8,998	33.2%	5.5%	7.0%
Economic and Financial	5,301	19.6	8.5	10.0
Credit Data	3,122	11.5	5.3	6.3
Payroll and Human Resources	3,246	12.0	6.6	7.0
Product and Price Data	1,756	6.5	5.4	5.4
Legal and Regulatory	2,113	7.8	8.7	6.9
Scientific and Technical	1,117	4.1	9.6	7.0
General Business	1,414	5.2	5.2	5.8
TOTAL	$27,067	100.0%	6.5%	7.4%

TABLE VId

Business Information Services Market in the United States

Intermediate and Professional Industry Segmented by Type of Data ($ millions, 1993)

Submarket	Marketing Information Services	Economic and Financial	Credit	Payroll and Human Resource	Product and Pricing	Legal and Regulatory	General Business	Total
Wall Street	$194	$2,213	$58	$50	$39	$47	$66	$2,667
Banks	594	363	584	97	26	58	70	1,792
Insurance	599	215	420	97	47	63	68	1,509
Business Data Services	185	168	100	163	37	168	37	858
Legal	10	10	30	100	5	915	15	1,085
TOTAL	$1,582	$2,969	$1,192	$507	$154	$1,251	$256	$7,911

Cross-Segmentation

Combining these two types of segmentation (industry and type of data) allows us to size the market in which SOI participates. Table VId shows spending in 1993 in the intermediate and professional markets by type of data. Within the Wall Street customer submarket, economic and financial data alone represent over $2.2 billion in spending in the United States.

Online Information Services in SOI's Geographic Scope

SOI participates in a geographic segment of the industry that is considerably underdeveloped compared to the United States. Central and Eastern European and Russian databases accounted for only 12 of 660, or less than 2 percent of databases in one comprehensive list. In its first target market, Poland, SOI is the only service of its kind. In Russia, one service exists, which is considerably inferior to the SOI service.

VI. Competitive Advantages and Risks

A. Sources of Competitive Advantage

SOI has several sustainable competitive advantages:

- *First-Mover Advantage.* SOI is the first such service to cover Poland and it will be the first such service to cover Central and Eastern Europe. The SOI service is based on proprietary code, which took nine months to develop and is continually improving. Relationships with data providers were developed concurrently and SOI currently has contracts ranging from three months to 10 years in duration. To create a salable product required the input of five years of full-time equivalents.
- *Unique Team.* The SOI management and employee team has significant accumulated experience in financial information services, computer programming, and knowledge of and contacts in Poland. This combination of business understanding, Harvard Business School network, and Carnegie Mellon technical expertise gives SOI the ability to understand

both the target financial industry and the technology to provide a leading-edge service.

- *Strong Understanding of the Geographic Focus Markets.* SOI has considerable experience in Poland and Russia and the target customers of emerging market financial and business information.
- *Technological Basis.* SOI draws on top talent from one of the leading technology universities in the world and already has in place sophisticated software and systems that enable it to deliver its service at a low cost. SOI is also extremely quick to respond to the explosive growth and development of the Internet.
- *Low-Cost Operating Model.* SOI uses the Internet for many aspects of its business to keep costs very low. SOI currently has "expensive" human capital working for equity; total current salary expenditures amount to $1,600 per month. SOI is extremely judicious about keeping costs to a minimum. For example, two partners in Poland currently share a small one-room apartment, which costs the company $200 per month. This is similar to the cost of a hotel room in Warsaw for one night.
- *Highly Trained Talent Pool.* SOI draws on talent from Carnegie Mellon University and Harvard Business School. SOI maintains relationships and contacts at both these institutions, and will use these contacts to further extend its staff in the future.

B. Risks

There are risks associated with the SOI business model. Many of the business characteristics are "double-edged swords" in that the benefits they provide to SOI are potentially appropriated by competitors and thus not sustainable advantages. However, being aware of these risks is the first step toward managing them and reducing the threat they pose. Following are the risks, in relative order of their "manageability":

Strategic Risk: Low Barriers to Entry. This is an example of a competitive advantage that "cuts both ways." If this niche turns out to be highly profitable, SOI could attract competitors. SOI can create barriers to entry by:

1. Using its position as first-mover to erect "intangible" barriers such as strong reputation with customers and data providers.
2. Continually improving the service in ways that increase the amount of time required to replicate it or create a competing service.
3. Entering into exclusive or semi-exclusive (i.e., SOI as the only online channel) relationships with data providers.

Strategic Risk: Low Barriers to Switching. Again, the low cost of the service to customers is a competitive advantage that "cuts both ways." By not requiring customers to invest in fixed hardware, SOI does not create a barrier to switching in the same way some other online services do. SOI will have to erect other barriers to switching, using means such as:

1. Signing long-term contracts with customers (and data providers).
2. Maximizing users' dependency on, familiarity with, and loyalty to SOI data, format, or tools.

Business Risk: Existence of Large Established Players with Infrastructure in Place. Information services have been largely fixed-cost businesses. The risk is that although large players such as Bloomberg are currently not prioritizing SOI's geographic focus market, they may do so in the future. This affects SOI's exit strategy: the risk is that the large financial services will attempt to provide similar data without purchasing SOI. SOI's best defense is to:

1. Build and maintain loyal and dependent customers.
2. Closely watch the moves of other online services.
3. Maintain good working relationships with data providers.
4. Rapidly expand the depth and breadth of the service.

Technology Risk. Security and integrity of data are the primary concerns of an information service company. While diligent hackers are nearly impossible to avoid, the concern is less that someone will "steal" data and use it, but rather a simple fear of vandalism. SOI's best defense is:

1. Good data hygiene and meticulous adherence to security procedures.
2. Constant monitoring of activity and password protection.

Market/Economic Risk: Upheaval in the Investment Community. In 1994 and early 1995, we have witnessed instability in the investment services market as have never been seen before. Layoffs at Goldman Sachs, JP Morgan's loss of its AAA debt rating, and speculation-driven financial crises at Baring Securities would have been unthinkable two years ago. These developments may lead to cost control measures or increased risk aversion in these markets that may affect price sensitivity and basic demand for SOI's service. While these risks are difficult to manage, SOI can address them by:

1. Marketing its service from a cost-benefit perspective.
2. Emphasizing efficiency in data gathering and productivity as major benefits that accrue to SOI customers.

Political Risk. Upheaval in the geographic focus markets could shift investment patterns away from SOI's focus market. (Frankly, it is exactly this risk and its associated returns that attracts investors to these markets, creating the niche opportunity for SOI.) The best "defense" for SOI is diversification across geographical focus markets, certainly within

Eastern/Central Europe and Russia, and eventually across other emerging markets. SOI's major concern here is operational: to ensure the safety of key personnel and to plan for the expatriation of equipment and documents if necessary.

VII. Management

A. Governance

The Board of Directors is currently composed of SOI's two largest shareholders, Mr. Kurt Bauer and Mr. John Bauer. The Board meets formally at least once a month, either in person or via conference call. Each Board member has an equal vote, but in cases of ties, Mr. Kurt Bauer has the deciding vote. These members are permanent members of the Board. In addition to the Board, the key management team (which includes Mr. Jae Chang, Mr. Mike Hayward, and Mr. Rafal Sokol) meets regularly to discuss the major management issues.

Upon receipt of external financing, SOI plans to expand Board membership to include a representative from each major source of capital. At that time, SOI may also bring in additional member(s) with no capital stake but with substantial expertise in the online business information industry.

The target for Board composition is management (2 with 4 votes) and external directors (3). After Board expansion, full Board meetings will occur quarterly, with monthly meetings or conference calls as needed.

B. Management Team

Kurt Bauer (Management). Mr. Bauer spent over two years working on privatization and fund formation in Poland and Russia. He also spent two years in Germany, actively studying the transformation of the former East bloc. He is a graduate of Harvard Business School (1994) and Harvard College (1988) and an alumnus of four family-owned businesses.

John Bauer (Management/Development). As an Electrical and Computer Engineer at Carnegie Mellon University (1992), Mr. Bauer has extensive experience in advanced systems integration. In his most recent position he oversaw a multi-million-dollar hardware and software project, involving 12 software programmers and hardware developers.

Dr. Jeffry A. Timmons (Business Advisor). Dr. Timmons currently holds the MBA Class of 1954 Professor of New Ventures chair at Harvard University and the Frederic C. Hamilton Professor of Free Enterprise Studies at Babson College. He is internationally recognized for his work in entrepreneurship, new ventures, and venture capital.

Robert Reid (Business Advisor). Mr. Reid has over 16 years' experience in the online financial information industry as senior vice president, Reuters, head of Instinet; senior vice president, NYSE; and vice president, Bridge, Inc.

Jae Chang (Management/Development). Mr. Chang, a BS, Computer and Electrical Engineering graduate of Carnegie Mellon University (1994), has experience in developing user interfaces and in computer networking. He previously worked as a developer at Intel Corporation and at Carnegie's Robotics Institute.

Mike Hayward (Management/Development). Mr. Hayward is a former software engineer at ConnectSoft and Intel with extensive experience with Unix, databases, networking, and security. He received his BS degree in Mathematics and Computer Science from Carnegie Mellon (1994).

Rafal Sokol (Management). Mr. Sokol, a former partner of Conmar Investors, has spent the past four years working in the financial markets in Poland. He was one of three partners at an investment advisory firm that among other things publishes a daily column in the leading financial newspaper in Poland. Prior to setting up his own company, Sokol worked on the Polish Stock Exchange and as an analyst of Polish equities.

Craig Lane (Management). Mr. Lane worked as an international consultant in Washington, D.C., and as an investment banker in Warsaw. He received his DBA from Duke University.

Melissa Burch (Operations/Logistics). Ms. Burch, formerly of Apple Computer, Inc., has extensive knowledge of online service marketing and data translation. She was the database administrator for both eWorld and AppleLink and worked with over 50 data providers.

Partnership agreements are currently in place for all stakeholder employees (Kurt Bauer, John Bauer, Robert Reid, Jae Chang, Mike Hayward, and Rafal Sokol). Employee work and confidentiality agreements are in place for all other employees.

C. Organizational Structure

Geography SOI is a decentralized organization with global operations. The corporate headquarters and technical center is in Pittsburgh, where most of the technical staff responsible for the design and smooth functioning of the SOI service are located.

SOI maintains satellite offices overseas in selected Eastern European capital cities (currently Warsaw) and major financial centers (currently London) where its customers and data providers are located. In the satellite offices, activities are divided between managing relationships with data providers and sales. In the major financial centers, the focus is on sales and marketing. Where necessary, SOI establishes subsidiaries or enters into joint venture arrangements to ensure compliance with local laws and to access local knowledge, language skills, and connections.

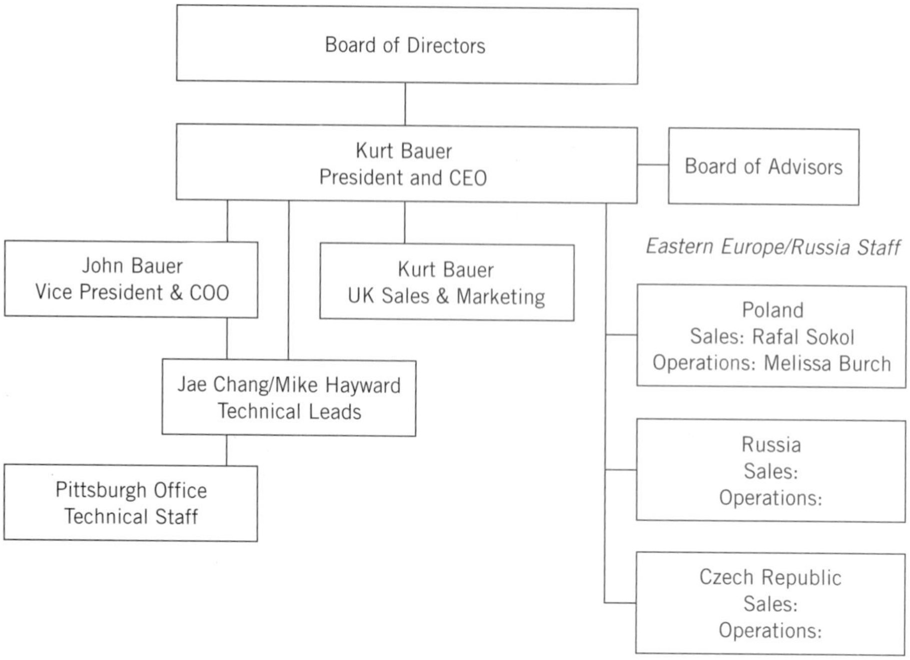

Reporting Relationships The above diagram illustrates current reporting relationships at SOI:

The hierarchical nature of organization charts is not very descriptive for SOI. SOI is a very flat, fluid organization, which has tremendous flexibility to quickly deploy technical, sales, and managerial resources to the places where they are most needed.

D. Revenue and Income Scenarios

Two primary scenarios:

Eastern Europe and Russia only—conservative.

Wider emerging markets—aggressive.

	Eastern Europe and Russia	Emerging Markets
Sales Year 3	$2.9 million	$5.0 million
Net Income Year 3	$0.7 million	$1.3 million

E. Cash Requirements

	Eastern Europe and Russia	Emerging Markets
Capital Requirement	$514,000	$508,000
Average Burn Rate (Year 1)	$34,000/month	$34,000/month
Month Cash Flow Positive	Month 14	Month 13

F. Valuation

	Eastern Europe and Russia	Emerging Markets
DCF Valuation	2.5 million	5.5 million
Sales Multiple (of 3 × on year 3)	8.7 million	15.0 million
EBIT Multiple (of 8 × on year 3)	5.4 million	16.8 million

VIII. Omitted from the Original Business Plan for Reasons of Confidentiality

IX. Exit Strategy

SOI's target is to exit the business in three to five years via sale to either one of the larger online providers or a strategic partner.

Acquisitions are commonplace in the online industry. Companies such as SOI bring larger players in the market new niches and customers, expanded content and product, and enhanced technical skills. For example, Reuters has a business development department that currently has $350 million for acquisitions. Acquisitions of $15 million to $20 million are not uncommon for companies with similar characteristics to SOI. In addition to Reuters, several other online financial information services, such as Telerate, Bloomberg, International Thomson, Maid, News Corp., are all potential buyers. This market suggests a liquid and attractive acquisition market.

In addition to the online service providers, SOI could also sell to a strategic investor. Recent purchases of "content providers" by communications companies, such as MCI agreeing to buy 13.5 percent of News Corp. for $2 billion,[14] gives SOI another large pool of potential investors. Acquisition activity in this area, like in the online industry, has been heavy in the past few years. Also, other companies seeking to understand online information services or electronic publishing are prime potential purchasers.

SOI may be a candidate for acquisition by one of its customers or suppliers as well. A supplier such as the *Financial Times* may acquire SOI for its technological abilities and understanding of the electronic publishing industry and the Internet. CS First Boston or ING could acquire SOI as a means of strengthening their position in emerging market financial services.

Such a wide array of potential buyers should enable investors to obtain liquidity within three to five years.

Business Plan Appendices

A. SOI Demonstration

There are two basic ways for a demo user to access the service: either by directly dialing one of our Points of Presence (POP) or via the Internet. Both methods require the appropriate software and hardware (computer, modem, and phone line); however, the difference is that direct dialing implies that the software is provided by Securities Online (we assume the user already has the hardware) while access via the Internet typically implies that the user already has the means of accessing the Internet and thus our service without our software.

Thus, for obvious reasons, the easiest and quickest way is via the Internet since the user already has access to our service. Access to the publicly viewable side of our service is open to everyone while access to the privileged side of the service is restricted until the user provides a valid user name and password, which we can provide with a simple phone call.

The other means—the most common—is by having us provide the user with the appropriate software and direct-dialing capabilities for use with a modem to connect to our POP. The installation software is mailed out on a couple of diskettes. The user simply runs a program, which performs the entire installation. If the hardware is correctly configured, a click of an icon will start the software and dial the modem to one of our POPs where users can finally access the service directly. For security, the direct-dial user must still provide a user name and password to access the service. We have mailed out dozens of installation disks in this way, and usually with a bit of extra help on the phone, our demo users have been able to access the service and also quickly and easily navigate through the service. Mastering the interface is as simple as a point and a click.

If you already have the installation software in front of you, then refer to the documentation that came with the software for more detailed instructions. If you would like access to the service, please call us.

B. Economic Opportunities in Eastern Europe and Russia

Various developments in the emerging markets of Eastern Europe and Russia provide opportunities for business in general, and specifically for firms catering to the emerging business-to-business sector in these markets. This includes firms offering administrative services and equipment, communications services, transactions support, and information services. Following are a few of the most important relevant trends:

- *GDP Growth.* Poland, the entrance market for SOI, experienced the highest growth in Europe in 1993. GDP rose 3.8 percent in real terms in 1993 and preliminary results for 1994 are even higher at 4.5 percent.[15] Private-sector growth is estimated to be 10 percent annually.
- *Stable Macroeconomics and Business Conditions.* Macroeconomic conditions in the three largest economies in eastern Europe—Poland, the Czech Republic, and Hungary—now approach their Western neighbors. Inflation is under control and decreasing, budget deficits are small, trade policy has been liberated, 60 percent of GNP is in private hands, and a solid legal framework is in place.
- *Foreign Capital Influx.* Foreign direct investment in short- and long-term projects in Eastern European and former Soviet economies totaled $118 billion at the end of 1994,[16] of which 70 percent was for oil and gas exploration in Russia and Kazakhstan. As the consumer markets develop, the proportion represented by petroleum will decrease.

	Market Capitalization (in billions)	Daily Volume (in billions)	Number of Companies	GNP, 1993	GNP, 1994	GNP, 1995 (estimate)
Poland	$ 4	$10	27	4.0%	5.5%	4.8%
Russia	$15	$ 7	80	−12.0%	−15.0%	−4.0%
Czech Republic	$15	$15	1,330	−1.0%	2.6%	4.3%
Hungary	$ 1.4	$40	40	−2.0%	2.7%	0.5%

[14] "MCI Agrees to Inject as Much as $2 Billion in News Corp in Data Highway Venture," *Wall Street Journal,* May 11, 1995.

[15] *Financial Times* "Survey: Poland," p. VII.

[16] "Kazakhstan, Russia First for Investment," *Financial Times,* March 24, 1995.

- *Development and Growth of Capital Markets.* The capital markets are developing quickly. Polish daily volume is now $200 million; total market capitalization in Poland is $6 billion and $14 billion in the Czech Republic. The daily volume of the Polish stock exchange rivals many Western European exchanges, such as Vienna and Helsinki, and is almost as large as the Toronto exchange. The total capitalization in both Poland and the Czech Republic is larger than China and approaching that of smaller, more developed markets. The following provides an overview of the two main markets:

Investment Flows to Emerging Markets
This leap in the size of the Eastern European markets mirrors the growth in the capital flows to emerging markets in general:

- International portfolio investment in emerging markets is now $56 billion, up 56 percent from the year before, and up from $7.5 billion in 1989.[17]
- Of international equity assets, 9.5 percent is allocated to emerging markets in 1993, up from 2.5 percent in 1989.[18]
- Total market capitalization is $740 billion in 1992 for the group of 25 emerging markets.[19]
- Number of companies listed on emerging stock markets now represents roughly 40 percent of the world total.[20]
- Pension funds, endowments, and foundations now own global equities worth $170 billion, and plan to raise this to $300 billion in the next three years.[21]
- All 24 emerging stock markets tracked by the World Bank's International Finance Corp. showed greater returns in 1993 than the Standard & Poor's 500 index.[22]
- Privatization of economy continues.
- Over the next two to three years, up to 400 Polish companies will be privatized and listed on the Polish stock exchange. Also, the 15 newly chosen mass privatization mutual funds will be listed on the stock exchange within the next six months. These new listings will tremendously increase the total capitalization of and capital inflow to the market.

C. About the Internet

What Is the Internet? The Internet is essentially thousands (upon thousands) of computers connected together via phone line, cable, or satellite. What began as a means of linking university researchers together has become the "information superhighway," connecting not only educational facilities but also service organizations, individuals, and businesses worldwide. Internet tools enable rapid transmission and retrieval of data at a very low cost. For example, a stock broker in Australia may order a magazine subscription from a company in the United States, send an electronic-mail message to a friend in Germany, gather statistics on a textile business in Malaysia, and at night browse a virtual art gallery in Prague all for the cost of a local phone call.

Growth on the Internet in terms of both connected users and networked computers is growing exponentially. Although there is no precise way to measure growth, some statistics indicate that Internet sites are added at the rate of 40,000 per month, while the number of users doubles every five months. By 1997, there will be approximately 175 million users on the Internet. In this climate of rapid expansion, the commercial segment has surpassed all other segments of the Internet market. Companies as diverse as JP Morgan, IBM, MCI, Federal Express, MTV, and LL Bean are now online.

Currently, 90 percent of all computers on the Internet are in the United States. Lower hardware costs and more fully developed Internet access technology can account for much of this activity. Within the diverse Internet corporate market, the U.S. companies predominate. But the market in Europe is on the verge of tremendous growth. Already in the United Kingdom, Internet growth statistics are following those in the United States, with users growing at over 10 percent to 20 percent per month.

Growth of the Internet Access Industry A simple hardware setup of a computer and modem is all that is necessary to dial up the Internet, but an Internet access provider is also required to connect to the online environment. These companies range from large long-distance carriers such as MCI and Sprint, to small, local-access providers. Some access companies only provide e-mail; others, such as startups America Online and CompuServe, offer complete commercial online services, while still others sell full-service Internet sites.

It is interesting to note that the new ventures, such as America Online and CompuServe, are growing faster than the larger conglomerates. Furthermore, despite the emergence of large providers, small companies continue to proliferate and prosper. In New York City, for example, six local providers exist with between 700 and 3,000 subscribers each. The total revenues for the six online access providers were $10 million in 1993. While revenues of consumer online services (such as e-mail) are growing at 35 percent a month, the average age of the companies is less than three years. Considering growth rates of over 150 percent annually for the industry, valuations of over $10 million seem reasonable.

Growth of the Internet in Europe These statistics reflect Internet access providers' growth in the United States; Europe, east and west, is expected to demonstrate similar patterns. Already in the United Kingdom, Internet

[17] Austin et al., 1994.
[18] IFC, "Survey of 30 international institutional investors," 1993.
[19] Ibid.
[20] Ibid.
[21] *Financial Times,* 1993.
[22] Bailey, 1994.

growth statistics are following those in the United States, with users growing at over 10 percent to 20 percent per month. Internet access providers in the United Kingdom are showing even greater growth than in the United States: the growth for three of the largest providers combined has been over 400 percent over the last year.

In Western Europe, Internet access providers charge up to five times more than in the United States. In Germany, for example, a survey of Internet access providers put the cost per month of basic e-mail services at about $60 and the cost of full Internet access at over $250 per month. The U.K. Internet price schedule is similar to that of Germany.

In Poland, the Czech Republic, and Hungary, no Western service providers are available locally and only a few domestic Internet access providers exist. In Poland, only one provider actively targets commercial users and its service is primarily in Polish. Without competition the costs for such services are high: with basic e-mail service running about $100 per month and full Internet access at about $400 per month.

Even with the higher Internet service costs and an overall lag in technological sophistication in Eastern Europe, international businesses with Eastern European offices are spurring the demand for e-mail and Internet access. With the influx of Western goods, the cost of hardware is beginning to drop to reasonable levels, any company can now have e-mail and Internet access for less than $1,000. International businesses are increasingly relying on Internet services as an inexpensive and efficient means of information transfer, and are able to provide the resources to establish the necessary Internet sites in Eastern Europe. Eastern Europe is expected to demonstrate a tremendous growth.

D. Joint Venture with Internet Technologies, Inc.

SOI has entered into a joint venture with former banker Rafal Plutecki, to form Internet Technologies (IT). This arrangement represents an ideal partnership for SOI.

The following are the relevant details:

- Plutecki puts up a total of $100,000, $30,000 up front and $7K per month for 10 months. The $30,000 is for equity, the $70,000 is in the form of a loan to be paid back only when Internet Technologies (IT) is cash flow positive. SOI receives 35 percent of the company.
- Plutecki manages, runs, and takes care of IT except for setting it up and training a systems operation person (to be done by Mike Hayward). SOI sets up the server and software, and this is limited to what SOI chooses to do.
- Plutecki buys a Cisco router and Sun Microsystems server in Poland, and obtains the necessary 64KB connection to Eunet (European Internet backbone).
- Plutecki obtains office space in the Warsaw Marriott. SOI sublets a portion of the space and pays for its phone lines.
- SOI puts the IS service on the IT server so that clients in Poland can dial up a local number and get the service directly. (This also allows SOI to do much of its internal operations activities in Warsaw instead of Pittsburgh if it so chooses.)
- SOI brings over (but Plutecki pays for) an undergraduate intern or two to come for the summer.
- If a major problem with the server comes up, SOI provides assistance, which can be in the form of e-mails to IT's system operations or other people. (This is in SOI's interest anyway, because if the service is "down," both SOI customers and SOI's data providers will be inconvenienced.)
- Exit is a buy-sell after three years. (If SOI wants to, after year 3 SOI can say it wants to sell its shares to Plutecki. Plutecki names a price, and SOI can either sell all its shares, or buy all of Plutecki's shares at that price; this ensures fair valuation of shares.)

Exercise

The Next Sea-Changes

The devastating tsunami in Asia in late December 2004 was a sobering reminder of the massive, life-changing impact that such an event can have. The "sea-change" metaphor is one we have used in earlier editions to urge aspiring entrepreneurs to research, brainstorm, and envision future quantum changes in technology and society. As we have seen, such sea-changes as electricity, the airplane, the integrated circuit (Moore's Law), and wireless communications have been the wellheads of new major industries. What will be the likely technology and societal changes during the next 20 to 30 years that will spawn the next generation of new industries? Entrepreneurs and innovators who anticipate the answers to this complex question will become the Gates, Jobs, Blank, and Stemberg of the next generation.

Purpose

The purpose of this exercise is to provide a pathway for exploring this question. We hope to broaden your horizon of technological literacy, and enrich your vision of the next quarter century—the window of your life when you have the best chance of creating and seizing the mega-opportunities that lie ahead.

We ask you to do some research and thinking about the future directions of technology, and how scientific inquiries which are under way today can lead to knowledge breakthroughs. This new scientific knowledge will, in turn, lead to innovations. When fueled, ignited, and driven by entrepreneurship, some of these innovations will become commercialized and in the process create entirely new industries.

The following steps will assist you in this research task, but you should not confine your efforts to these steps alone. You also need to pursue as many other sources as possible using Google and other resources. Be sure to "follow the data and your gut instinct." If you find an area of science and technology that excites you—or which you instinctively believe can change the way people will live, work, learn, or relax—then pursue it.

STEP 1

Go to the National Science Foundation summary of the 50 discoveries that the NSF believes have had the most impact on every American's life (www.nsf.gov/about/history/nifty50/index.jsp). You will find such breakthrough discoveries as bar codes, CAD/CAM, genomics, speech recognition, computer visualization techniques, and Web browsers. All of these are examples of "sea-changes"—the spawners and drivers of new industries that we discussed in this chapter and in Chapter 2.

STEP 2

Select one or two of the nifty 50 that interest you the most. Now examine number 10 on the list: "computer visualization techniques." Note the 11 industries and fields that have been significantly impacted by this basic discovery. Out of these 11 pick one or two you know the least about, but for which you have the most passion. Conduct some key word searches on Google and the like to identify products, companies, or market segments that are driven by the entrepreneurs behind these innovations. Repeat this process for all of the major discoveries you are attracted to. Once you have a good sense of how these linkages exist, go to Step 3.

STEP 3

Meet with two to five of your classmates over breakfast, lunch, dinner, and share what you have learned, your observations and insights about how industries are born, and what potential new fields might arise.

- What patterns and common characteristics did you find? What are the lead times and early indicators?
- What technologies have the most future potential impact on the way people live, work, learn?
- Who are the entrepreneurs who create the technology-based firms that utilize these discoveries? What is their background, preparation, skills, experience, and so forth? Any common denominators?
- Have any of your ideas, assumptions, and beliefs been altered about where and when the next biggest opportunities will emerge?

STEP 4

Visit the NSF home page (www.nsf.gov) and find the list of 11 different program areas, including geosciences, environmental research, engineering. Select one that interests you the most and you know the least about. Go into the Web site and identify the research grants awarded to this topic over the past few years.

- What topics and problems are attracting the most money and activity? Why is this so?
- What new scientific knowledge and/or breakthroughs might be expected and what are some of the potential "sea-change" impacts?
- What potential commercial applications can be envisioned from these new technologies?
- What existing technologies, products, and services are most likely to be disrupted and replaced by these innovations?
- What societal trends can be combined with these future technologies to create entire new industries?

STEP 5

In class, or in informal groups, discuss and explore the implications of your findings from the exercise.

- What are two or three future sea-changes you anticipate?
- What other exploration do you need to do?
- How can you better prepare yourself to be able to recognize and seize these future opportunities now, in 10 years, in 15 years?
- What implications do you see for your personal entrepreneurial strategy, which you began to develop in Chapter 1—especially with regard to projects to work on, next education and work experience, brain trust and mentor additions?

Exercise

Opportunity Creating Concepts and the Quest for Breakthrough Ideas

After you have fully digested the discussions in this chapter, you should aim to prepare an industry analysis utilizing the criteria listed in Exhibit 4.8. This should be a first cut analysis, and not an overly exhaustive effort. Your value chain should be mapped out on one to two pages maximum, with the other questions/issues answered in bullet points on one to two pages maximum. Rather than an exhaustive effort, this exercise is designed to get you to a specific way of thinking.

Your task is to complete a *simple, clear, and articulate value chain analysis* of an industry that is of interest to you. Analyze the value chain, as it *currently exists*. Next, complete an *information flow analysis* of that value chain, overlaying an analysis of the flow of information through the various stages of the value chain. Then broaden your thinking to *create a value cluster* of that industry. Make sure you are thinking multidimensionally, not just linearly. Describe or visually depict the impact of these multiple dimensions on the flow of both goods/services *and* information. Explain how this value cluster expansion adds or intensifies value for that industry, as compared to the linear chain. Finally, provide a *succinct analysis of the margins in this value cluster,* with particular emphasis on the extremes (highs/lows).

Also consider:

- What were the de-constructors and re-constructors that drive the value chain and opportunity in this industry?
- What is your best estimate of the composition of the free cash flow, profit, and value chains in a business in this industry?
- What prevailing industry practices, conventions, wisdom in marketing, distribution, outsourcing customer services, IT and capital investment are significant in this business?
- What new practices, conventions, and so forth are now in place, and what is their half-life?
- What are the growth segments?
- Where do the pundits (Forrester, IDG, Research Sources, and other Wall Street analysts) think the next growth market will be?
- What are the parameters and characteristics of that market?

If you are planning to bring a high-tech product to market, you might want to consider the framework discussed in *Crossing the Chasm: Marketing and Selling High-Tech Products to Mainstream Customers* by Geoffrey Moore and Regis McKenna and look at the value chain and the specific industry segment(s) you plan to focus on. You should also consider reviewing Clayton M. Christensen's writings on disruptive innovation in, among others, *The Innovators Dilemma.*

Exercise
Creative Squares

STEP 1
Divide Your Group by (1) Separating Into a Number of Groups of Three or More Persons Each and (2) Having at Least Five Individuals Work Alone

STEP 2
Show the Following Figure to Everyone and Ask the Groups and the Individuals to Count the Total Number of Squares in the Figure Assume that the figure is a square box on a single flat plane. In counting, angles of any square must be right angles, and the sides must be of equal length.

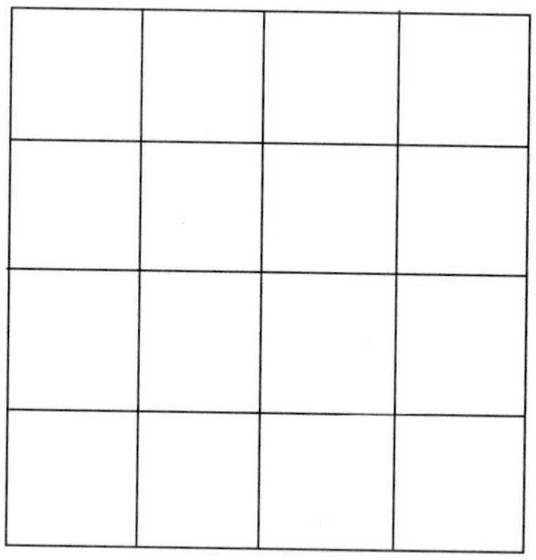

STEP 3
Discuss the Creative Process by Which the Groups and the Individuals Reached Their Answers

Exercise

Idea Generation Guide

Before beginning the process of generating ideas for new ventures, it is useful to reflect on an old German proverb that says, "Every beginning is hard." If you allow yourself to think creatively, you will be surprised at the number of interesting ideas you can generate once you begin.

The Idea Generation Guide is an exercise in generating ideas. The aim is for you to generate as many interesting ideas as possible. *While generating your ideas, do not evaluate them or worry about their implementation.* Discussion and exercises in the rest of the book will allow you to evaluate these ideas to see if they are opportunities and to consider your own personal entrepreneurial strategy.

And remember—in any creative endeavor there are no right answers.

Name:

Date:

STEP 1

Generate a List of as Many New Venture Ideas as Possible As a consumer or paid user, think of the biggest, most frustrating, and painful task or situation you continually must take, and one which would be worth a lot to eliminate or minimize. These are often the seeds of real opportunities. Thinking about any unmet or poorly filled customer needs you know of that have resulted from regulatory changes, technological changes, knowledge and information gaps, lags, asymmetries, inconsistencies, and so forth, will help you generate such a list. Also, think about various products and services (and their substitutes) and the providers of these products or services. If you know of any weaknesses or vulnerabilities, you may discover new venture ideas.

STEP 2

Expand Your List if Possible Think about your personal interests, your desired lifestyle, your values, what you feel you are likely to do very well, and contributions you would like to make.

STEP 3

Ask at Least Three People Who Know You Well to Look at Your List, and Revise Your List to Reflect Any New Ideas Emerging From This Exchange See discussion about getting feedback in Chapter 1.

STEP 4

Jot Down Insights, Observations, and Conclusions That Have Emerged About Your Business Ideas or Your Personal Preferences Which ones solve the greatest pain-point/aggravation/frustration for which you (and others you have spoken with) would pay a significant premium to eliminate?

5

Chapter Five

Screening Venture Opportunities

Entrepreneurs need to think big. You are going to end up exhausted in building a company. So you might as well end up exhausted and rich!

Patricia Cloherty
First Woman President of the National Venture Capital Association

Results Expected

At the conclusion of this chapter, you will have:

1. Examined two screening methodologies—QuickScreen and the Venture Opportunity Screening Exercises (VOSE)—that can help you to determine whether your ideas are potential opportunities.
2. Applied the opportunity criteria from Chapter 4 to your ideas and begun to assess the probable *fit* with you, your team, resources, and the *balance of risk and reward.*
3. Begun to consider with more creativity and depth what you need to do to improve both the *fit* and the *risk and reward relationship.*
4. Determined whether your best idea at this time has sufficient potential to pursue the development of a thorough business plan.
5. Concluded whether you believe you can sufficiently alter the idea and your strategy to create a *good fit* and an *attractive risk–reward balance* for you and your investors.
6. Analyzed the "Burt's Bees" case study.

Screening Venture Opportunities

Time is the ultimate ally and enemy of the entrepreneur. The harsh reality is that you will not have enough time in a quarter, a year, or a decade to pursue all the ideas for businesses you and your team can think of. Perhaps the cruelest part of the paradox is that you have to find and make the time for the good ones. To complicate the paradox, *you do not have a strategy until you are saying no to lots of opportunities!* This demand is part of the both punishing and rewarding Darwinian aspect of entrepreneurship: Many will try, many will fail, some will succeed, and a few will excel. While the number of new enterprises launched in the United States can vary widely from year to year, only 10 to 15 percent of those will ever prove to be opportunities that achieve sales of $1 million or more.

This chapter will put you in the trenches, engaging in the first of many titanic-like struggles to determine whether your good idea is truly a good opportunity. Ideas that turn into superior businesses are not accidents; they are consistent with the model portrayed in Chapter 3, and with these four anchors we introduced in Chapter 4:

1. They create or add significant value to a customer or end-user.
2. They do so by solving a significant problem, removing a serious pain-point, or meeting a significant want or need—for which someone is willing to pay a premium.

3. They have robust market, margin, and money-making characteristics that will allow the entrepreneur to estimate and communicate sustainable value to potential stakeholders: large enough ($50 million +), high growth (20 percent +), high gross margins (40 percent +), strong and early free cash flow (recurring revenue, low assets, and working capital), high profit potential (10 to 15 percent + after tax), and offer attractive realizable returns for investors (25 to 30 percent + IRR).
4. They are a good *fit* with the founder(s) and management team at the time and marketplace—along with an attractive *risk-reward* balance.

QuickScreen

If most sophisticated private equity investors and venture capitalists invest in only 2 to 3 out of 100 ideas, then one can see how important it is to focus on a few superior ideas. The ability to quickly and efficiently reject ideas is a very important entrepreneurial mindset. Saying no to lots of ideas directly conflicts with your passion and commitment for a particular idea. To make the struggle more manageable, this chapter provides two methodologies. The first, QuickScreen, should enable you to conduct a preliminary review and evaluation of an idea in an hour. Unless the idea has been, or you are confident it can be, molded and shaped so that it has the four anchors, you will waste a lot of time on a lower potential idea. The QuickScreen exercise can be reproduced for your own use.

Venture Opportunity Screening Exercises (VOSE)

The Venture Opportunity Screening Exercises are designed to segment the screening of ideas into manageable pieces. The QuickScreen provides a broad overview of an idea's potential. In a team effort, each member of the team should complete the exercise separately and then meet as a team to merge the results. After each VOSE, you should revisit the QuickScreen and reevaluate your scoring. When you are satisfied that all the exercises are complete, the combined documents will provide the substance needed to complete your business plan. It also provides an audit trail of your opportunity shaping activity. Not only does this help you memorialize your thinking, but it provides excellent articulation when explaining your thought process to sophisticated investors—many of whom will be asking probing questions to test your depth of knowledge.

Whether or not an entrepreneur plans to seek venture capital or an outside private investor to pursue an opportunity, it is vital to have a realistic view of the vulnerabilities and realities, as well as the opportunity's compelling strengths. Often, the iterative process of carefully examining different ideas through many eyes, within and outside your team, often *triggers creative ideas and insights about how the initial business concept and strategy can be altered and molded to significantly enhance the value chain, free cash flow characteristics, and risk–reward relationships and thus the fit.* This process is central to value creation and the development of higher potential ventures, but it is far from cut and dried.

This early seed stage is also a marvelous time for a "trial marriage" with prospective team members. This work can be detailed, tedious, and downright boring. Finding out now who can deliver what; who has the work ethic, consistency, and reliability; and whether you can work together will save a lot of money and headaches later. Ultimately, the *fit* issue boils down to this: Do the opportunity, the resources required (and their cost), the other team members (if any), the timing, and balance of risk and reward *work for me?*

Exercise
QuickScreen

I. Market and Margin Related Issues

Criterion	Higher Potential	Lower Potential
Need/want/problem/pain-point	Identified	Unfocused
Customers	Reachable and receptive	Unreachable/loyal to others
Payback to users	Less than one year	More than three years
Value added or created	IRR 40% +	IRR less than 20%
Market size	$50–100 million	Less than $10 million or + $1 billion
Market growth rate	More than 20%	Less than 20%, contracting
Gross margin	More than 40% and durable	Less than 20% and fragile

(continued)

Overall Potential:					
1. Market	higher	______	avg	______	lower
2. Margins	higher	______	avg	______	lower

II. Competitive Advantages: Relative to the Current and Evolving Set of Competitors

	Higher Potential	Lower Potential
Fixed and variable costs	Lowest	Highest
Degree of control	Stronger	Weaker
Prices and cost		
Channels of supply and distribution		
Barriers to competitor's entry	Can create	Weak/None
Proprietary advantage	Defensible	None
Lead time advantage (product, technology, people, resources, location)	Slow competition	None
Service chain	Strong edge	No edge
Contractual advantage	Exclusive	None
Contacts and networks	Key access	Limited

Overall potential					
1. Costs	higher	______	avg	______	lower
2. Channel	higher	______	avg	______	lower
3. Barriers to entry	higher	______	avg	______	lower
4. Timing	higher	______	avg	______	lower

III. Value Creation and Realization Issues

	Higher Potential	Lower Potential
Profit after tax	10–15% or more and durable	Less than 5%; fragile
Time to breakeven	Less than 2 years	More than 3 years
Time to positive cash flow	Less than 2 years	More than 3 years
ROI potential	40–70% +, durable	Less than 20%, fragile
Value	High strategic value[1]	Low strategic value
Capitalization requirements	Low-moderate; fundable	Very high; difficult to fund
Exit mechanism	IPO, acquisition	Undefined; illiquid investment

Overall value creation potential					
1. Timing	higher	______	avg	______	lower
2. Profit/free cash flow	higher	______	avg	______	lower
3. Exit/liquidity	higher	______	avg	______	lower

IV. Overall Potential

	Go	No Go	Go, if . . .
1. Margins and markets			
2. Competitive advantages			
3. Value creation and realization			
4. Fit: "O" + "R" + "T"			
5. Risk–reward balance			
6. Timing			
7. Other compelling issues: must know or likely to fail			
a.			
b.			
c.			
d.			
e.			

[1] "Strategic value" can have many meanings. In the context of opportunity recognition, strategic value exists when a company in the value chain you would enter could substantively benefit from the launch of your business.

Venture Opportunity Screening Exercises

The new venture creation process requires a due diligence. We recommend that the components of these exercises be used to channel your thought and data collection efforts toward creating the foundation for development of the complete business plan. Allow for a dynamic processing of each component and thereby the shaping of the opportunity and a plan to execute it. It is okay to be initially broad in your perspective and then become more focused in later iterations.

The VOSE is based on the criteria discussed in Chapter 4. At the end of each exercise, you should have a clearer idea of the relative attractiveness of your opportunity. Rarely is it simply cut and dried. Most of the time, there will be considerable uncertainty and numerous unknowns and risks. Completing these exercises can, however, help you understand those uncertainties and risks as you make a decision about the idea. The process will help you devise ways to make these uncertainties and risks more acceptable for you, and if not, then you know you need to keep searching.

Every venture is unique. Operations, marketing, cash flow cycles, and so forth vary a good bit from company to company, from industry to industry, from region to region, and from country to country. As a result, you may find that not every issue is pertinent to your venture, and perhaps some questions are irrelevant. Here and there you may need to add to these exercises or further tailor them to your circumstances.

Working through these exercises is a lengthy process. This is a map of how to think about the tough, dull legwork of good due diligence that should be done before launching into a venture. Completing these exercises will help you determine if your opportunity is attractive enough vis-à-vis the four anchors to develop a complete business plan. As you work through these exercises, you will find that much of the work of writing a business plan comes from your answers in the exercises. While you may decide to delay work on some of these exercises, eventually you will need to ask yourself and your "team" these questions.

Ideally, each member of your team will complete these exercises.

As with other exercises in this text, feel free to make as many copies of the VOSE as needed.

Exercise 1

Opportunity Concept and Strategy Statement

Briefly describe your vision, the opportunity concept, and your strategy. What is your vision for the business? What is the value creation proposition? What is the significant problem, want, or need that it will solve? Why is this problem/bottleneck/pain-point/aggravation/joy important enough that a customer or end-user will pay an above average to a premium price for it? Why does this opportunity exist, now, for you? Can you describe the concept and your entry strategy in 25 words or less?

Exercise 2
The Venture Opportunity Profile

Fill in this profile by indicating for each criterion where your venture is located on the ***potential*** continuum. Check off your best estimate of where your idea stacks up, being as specific as possible. If you are having trouble, information can be found in magazines and newsletters, from other entrepreneurs, from trade shows and fairs, or from online resources.

Venture Opportunity Profile

Criterion	**Highest Potential** ←	→ **Lowest Potential**
Industry and Market		
Market: Need	Market driven; identified; recurring revenue niche	Unfocused; onetime revenue
Customers	Reachable; purchase orders	Loyal to others or unreachable
User benefits	Less than one year payback	Three years plus payback
Value added	High; advance payments	Low; minimal impact on market
Product life	Durable	Perishable
Market structure	Imperfect, fragmented competition or emerging industry	Highly concentrated or mature or declining industry
Market size	\$100 + million to \$1 billion sales potential	Unknown, less than \$20 million or multibillion sales
Growth rate	Growth at 30% to 50% or more	Contracting or less than 10%
Market capacity	At or near full capacity	Undercapacity
Market share attainable (Year 5)	20% or more; leader	Less than 5%
Cost structure	Low-cost provider; cost advantages	Declining cost

Criterion	Highest Potential	Lowest Potential
Economics		
Profits after tax	10% to 15% or more; durable	Less than 15%; fragile
ROI potential	25% or more; high value	Less than 15% to 20%; low value
Capital requirements	Low to moderate; fundable	Very high; unfundable
Internal rate of return potential	25% or more per year	Less than 15% per year
Free cash flow characteristics	Favorable; sustainable; 20 to 30 + % of sales	Less than 10% of sales
Sales growth	Moderate to high (15 + % to 20 + %)	Less than 10%
Asset intensity	Low/sales $	High/sales $
Spontaneous working capital	Low, incremental requirements	High requirements
R&D/capital expenditures	Low requirements	High requirements
Gross margins	Exceeding 40% and durable	Under 20%
Time to breakeven—cash flow	Less than 2 years; breakeven not creeping	Greater than 4 years; breakeven creeping up
Time to breakeven—P&L	Less than 2 years; breakeven not creeping	Greater than 4 years; breakeven creeping up
Harvest Issues		
Value-added potential	High strategic value	Low strategic value
Valuation multiples and comparables	p/e = 20 + ×; 8–10 + × EBIT; 1.5–2 + × revenue free cash flow 8–10 + ×	p/e = 5 ×, EBIT = 3–4×; revenue = .4
Exit mechanism and strategy	Present or envisioned options	Undefined; illiquid investment
Capital market context	Favorable valuations, timing, capital available; realizable liquidity	Unfavorable; credit crunch
Competitive Advantage Issues		
Fixed and variable costs	Lowest; high operating leverage	Highest
Control over costs, prices, and distribution	Moderate to strong	Weak

Criterion	Highest Potential	Lowest Potential
Barriers to entry:		
Proprietary protection	Have or can gain	None
Response/lead time	Competition slow; napping	Unable to gain edge
Legal, contractual advantage	Proprietary or exclusivity	None
Contacts and networks	Well-developed; accessible	Crude; limited
Key people	Top talent; an A team	B or C team
Management Team		
Entrepreneurial team	All-star combination; free agents	Weak or solo entrepreneur
Industry and technical experience	Top of the field; super track record	Underdeveloped
Integrity	Highest standards	Questionable
Intellectual honesty	Know what they do not know	Do not want to know what they do not know
Fatal-Flaw Issue	Nonexistent	One or more
Personal Criteria		
Goals and fit	Getting what you want; but wanting what you get	Surprises
Upside/downside issues	Attainable success/limited risks	Linear; on same continuum
Opportunity costs	Acceptable cuts in salary, etc.	Comfortable with status quo
Desirability	Fits with lifestyle	Simply pursuing big money
Risk/reward tolerance	Calculated risk; low R/R ratio	Risk averse or gambler
Stress tolerance	Thrives under pressure	Cracks under pressure
Strategic Differentiation		
Degree of fit	High	Low
Team	Best in class; excellent free agents	B team; no free agents

Criterion	Highest Potential	Lowest Potential
Service management	Superior service concept	Perceived as unimportant
Timing	Rowing with the tide	Rowing against the tide
Technology	Groundbreaking; one-of-a-kind	Many substitutes or competitors
Flexibility	Able to adapt; commit and decommit quickly	Slow; stubborn
Opportunity orientation	Always searching for opportunities	Operating in a vacuum; napping
Pricing	At or near leader	Undercut competitor; low prices
Distribution channels	Accessible; networks in place	Unknown; inaccessible
Room for error	Forgiving strategy	Unforgiving, rigid strategy

Assess the external environment surrounding your venture opportunity, including the following:

- An assessment of the characteristics of the opportunity window, including its perishability:

- A statement of what entry strategy suits the opportunity, and why:

- A statement of evidence of and/or reasoning behind your belief that the external environment and the forces creating your opportunity, as described in Exercise 1 and the profile you just completed, fit:

- A statement of your exit strategy and an assessment of the prospects that this strategy can be met, including a consideration of whether the risks, rewards, and tradeoffs are acceptable:

Checkpoint

Before you proceed to further exercises, be sure the opportunity you have outlined is compelling and you can answer the question, "Why does the opportunity exist now?" It is possible you ought to abandon or alter the product or service idea behind your venture at this point. The amount of money and time needed to get the product or service to market, and to be open for business, may be beyond your limits. Beware the opportunity for which the potential rewards are too large compared to the risks and vulnerabilities to obsolescence and competition.

Exercise 3
Opportunity Shaping Research and Exercise

Articulate the reasons that make you believe your idea is an opportunity. This will likely affect or "shape" your opportunity. We have listed some important questions that you should address, but you might also want to add additional perspectives. The principle objective of this exercise is to focus the lens on the major components of your opportunity.

Assess the attractiveness of your venture opportunity by applying screening Criteria. Include the following:

- What is the critical problem, want, or need your product or service will solve?
- Why is this a critical problem or serious pain-point/aggravation that demands removal?
- Who will pay a premium price, compared with alternatives, if you can address this problem or want?
- What is the underlying value creation proposition: How and why will it pay for itself, yield major benefits/advantages, etc.?
- A brief description of the market(s) or market niche(s) you want to enter:
- An exact description of the product(s) or service(s) to be sold and, if a product, its eventual end-use(s). (If your product(s) or service(s) are already commercially available or exist as prototypes, attach specifications, photographs, samples of work, etc.)

- An estimate of how perishable the product(s) or service(s) are, including if it is likely to become obsolete and when:

- An assessment of whether there are substitutes for the product(s) or services(s):

- An assessment of the status of development and an estimate of how much time and money will be required to complete development, test the product(s) or service(s), and then introduce the product(s) or service(s) to the market:

Development Tasks		
Development Task	**Dollars Required**	**Months to Complete**

- An assessment of any major difficulties in manufacturing the product(s) or delivering the service(s) and how much time and money will be required to resolve them:

- An assessment of your primary customer group:
  —A description of the main reasons why your primary group of customers will buy your product or service, including whether customers in this group are reachable and receptive and how your product or service will add or create value, and what this means for your entry or expansion strategy:

- A description of the necessary customer support, such as warranty service, repair service, and training of technicians, salespeople, service people, or others:

- An assessment of the strengths and weaknesses, relative to the competition, of the product(s) or service(s) in meeting customer needs, including a description of payback of and value added by the product(s) or service(s):

—A list of 5 to 10 crucial questions you need to have answered and other information you need to know to identify good customer prospects:

—An indication of how customers buy products or services (e.g., from direct sales, either wholesale or retail; through manufacturers' representatives or brokers; through catalogs; via direct mail; on the Web; etc.):

—A description of the purchasing process (i.e., where it occurs and who is ultimately responsible for approving expenditures; what and who influence the sale; how long does it take from first contact to close, to delivery, and to cash receipt; and your conclusions about the competitive advantages you can achieve and how your product or service can add or create value):

- An assessment of the market potential for your venture's product or service, the competition, and what is required to bring and sell the product or service to the customer. (Such an analysis need not be precise or comprehensive but should eliminate from further consideration those ventures that have obvious market difficulties.) Include the following information:
—An estimate, for the past, present, and future, of the *approximate* size of the *total* potential market, as measured in units and in dollars or number of customers. In making your estimates, use available market data to estimate *ranges* of values and to identify the area (country, region, locality, etc.) and data for each segment if the market is segmented:

	Total Market Size				
	Year				
	20__	**20__**	**20__**	**20__**	**20__**
Sales of Units/ Number of Customers					
Sales in Dollars					

Sources of Data:

Researcher:

Confidence in Data:

—An assessment of the type of market in terms of price, quality, and service; degree of control, and so on; and your conclusions about what approaches are necessary to enter, survive, and win:

- What good news or information will arrive (or can you cause to arrive) that will enhance your opportunity?

- What are the odds for *(a)* implementation success or *(b)* sufficient magnitude of the new venture?

- What can you alter or add to enhance the opportunity?

- What can you do or learn to make *you* the most *knowledgeable* competitor in this industry?

- Other compelling issues:

Exercise 4

Customer Contact Research and Exercise

Entrepreneurship is a full-contact activity. That contact is first and foremost with potentially revenue-generating customers. It is ***essential*** that you communicate with customers and document their responses. Attempt to reconcile customer reactions in this section to the opportunity shaping research and exercise (Exercise 3). Please provide:

- An assessment, based on a survey of customers, of how your customers do business, and of what investigative steps are needed next:

	Customer Survey		
	Customer		
	No. 1	**No. 2**	**No. 3**
Nature of Customers			
Business or Role			
Reactions: Positive Negative Questions			

Specific Needs/Uses			
Acceptable Terms—Price, Support, etc.			
Basis of Purchase Decisions: Time Frame Who Makes Decision Dollar Limits			
Substitutes/Competitive Products or Services Used			

Names of Competitors			
Competitive Products			
Substitute Products			

Customers Surveyed	
No.	**Name**

Exercise 5

Mining the Value Chain—Defining the "White Space"[1]

Your opportunity must be placed in the context of both a competitive environment and an existing value chain that you believe can be improved upon and altered in a way that creates value. In addition to tracing the movement of physical goods, you should also map the flow of information and the resultant margins that "flow" to channel players. Please provide:

- An assessment of how your product or service will be positioned in the market, including:

  —A statement of any proprietary protection, such as patents, copyrights, or trade secrets, and what this means in the way of competitive advantage:

  —An assessment of any competitive advantages you can achieve in the level of quality, service, and so forth, including an objective description of any strengths (and weaknesses) of the product or service:

1 "White space" refers to those gaps in an industry or market into which your opportunity falls. When you complete the value chain exercise—looking at the flow of physical, informational, and financial margins—you will be able to see the market anomalies (positive or negative) that create space for your opportunity.

—An assessment of your pricing strategy versus those of competitors:

	Pricing Strategy[2]		
	Highest Price	**Average Price**	**Lowest Price**
Retail			
Wholesale			
Distributor			
Internet			
Manufacturing			
Other Channel			

[2] Consider the opportunity recognition process that led to the rotary electric toothbrush venture described in the previous chapter.

—An assessment of the competitors in your industry or market niche in terms of price versus performance/benefits/value added:[3]

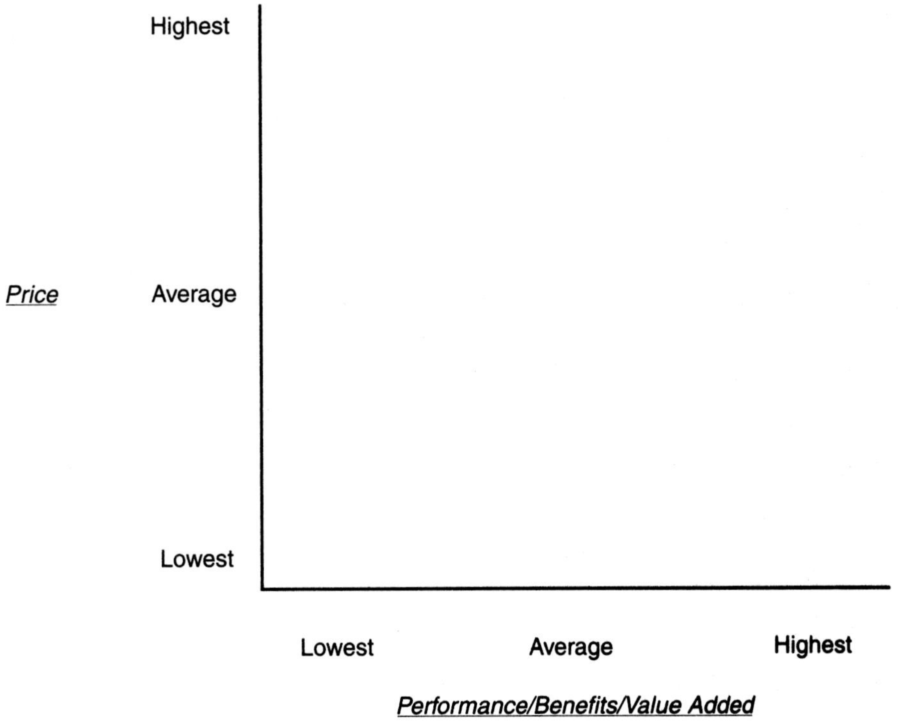

—An indication of how you plan to distribute and sell your product or services (e.g., through direct sales, mail order, manufacturers' representatives, etc.) and the likely sales, marketing, and advertising/trade promotion costs:

—A distribution plan for your product(s) or service(s), including any special requirements, such as refrigeration, and how much distribution costs will be as a percentage of sales and of total costs:

[3] Note: If there is a 10 to 30 times (or more) spread among competitive products, there is an opportunity lurking.

- Complete this chart of the three flows (physical, informational, and margin) to find the value chain for your product or service. Following the physical flow, map how your product or service will get to the end-user or consumer, the portion of the final selling price realized in each step, and the dollar and percentage markup and the dollar and percentage gross margin per unit. This exercise will help you identify the market anomalies (positive and negative) that can identify spaces in which you can create your opportunity. The value chain formed from these flows is constructed for a generalized consumer product and needs to be modified for your particular produce, service, industry, or region.

Mining the Value Chain

Physical Flow	Components Materials & Labor Raw Materials	Manufacturer or Service Provider	Distributor	Wholesaler	End-User or Customer
Margin Flow	Price/Unit: Dollars Percent	Price/Unit: Dollars Percent	Price/Unit: Dollars Percent	Price/Unit: Dollars Percent	Price/Unit: Dollars Percent
	Markup/Unit: Dollar Percent	Markup/Unit: Dollar Percent	Markup/Unit: Dollar Percent	Markup/Unit: Dollar Percent	Markup/Unit: Dollar Percent
	Gross Margin: Dollar Percent	Gross Margin: Dollar Percent	Gross Margin: Dollar Percent	Gross Margin: Dollar Percent	Gross Margin: Dollar Percent
Informational Flow	Key Data	Key Data	Key Data	Key Data	Key Data
	Mean of Data Transfer	Mean of Data Transfer	Mean of Data Transfer	Mean of Data Transfer	Mean of Data Transfer

Exercise 6

Economics of the Business—How Do You Make Money in the White Space?

Your mining of the value chain (Exercise 5) should present a view of the "white space" for your business. In this section, we ask you to begin to *quantify* the space and to estimate the time and resources it will take to fill that space. These preliminary assessments will provide the foundation for the development of your financial statements, including income statement, balance sheet, cash flow, and break-even point. Please provide:

- A realistic estimate of approximate sales and market share for your product or service in the market area which your venture can attain in each of your first five years:

Product/Service Sales and Market Share

	Year				
	1	**2**	**3**	**4**	**5**
Total Market: Units Dollars					
Est. Sales: Units Dollars					
Est. Market Share (percent):					
Est. Market Growth: Units Dollars					

Source of Data:

Researcher:

Confidence in Data:

Checkpoint

Consider whether you suffer from **mousetrap myopia** or whether you lack enough experience to tackle the venture at this stage. It is possible that if your venture does not stand up to this evaluation, you may simply not be as far along as you had thought. Remember, the single largest factor contributing to stillborn ventures and to those who will ripen as lemons is lack of opportunity focus. If you were unable to fill in the chart on Product/Service Sales and Market Share on the previous page, or do not have much of an idea of how to answer them, it is possible that you need to do more work before proceeding with this venture.

- An assessment of the costs and profitability of your product or service:

Product/Service Costs and Profitability

Product/Service:

Sales Price:

Sales Level:

	Dollars/Unit	Percent of Sales Price/Unit
Production Costs (i.e., labor and material costs) or Purchase Costs		
Gross Margin		
Fixed Costs		
Profit before Taxes		
Profit after Taxes		

- An assessment of the minimum resources required to "get the doors open and revenue coming in," the costs, dates required, alternative means of gaining control of (but not necessarily owning) these, and what this information tells you:

Resource Needs

	Minimum Needed	Cost ($)	Date Required	Probable Source
Plant, Equipment, and Facilities (remember, you only have to control the asset, not own it)				
Product/Service Development (include raw materials and other inventory)				
Market Research				
Setup of Sales and Distribution (e.g., brochures, demos, and mailers)				
One time Expenditures (e.g., legal costs)				
LeaseDeposits and Other Prepayments (e.g., utilities)				

Overhead (e.g., salaries, rent, and insurance)				
Sales Costs (e.g., trips to trade shows)				
Other Startup Costs				
TOTAL				
COMMENTS				

- A rough estimate of requirements for manufacturing and/or staff, operations, facilities, including:

  —An assessment of the major difficulties for such items as equipment, labor skills and training, and quality standards in the manufacture of your product(s) or the delivery of your service(s):

—An estimate of the number of people who will be required to launch the business and the key tasks they will perform:

—An assessment of how you will deal with these difficulties and your estimate of the time and money needed to resolve them and begin scalable production:

- An identification of the cash flow and cash conversion cycle for your business over the first 15 months (including a consideration of leads/lags in getting sales, producing your product or service, delivering your product or service, and billing and collecting cash). Show as a bar chart the timing and duration of each activity below:

Cash Flow, Conversion Cycle, and Timing of Key Operational Activities

Development of Forecasts

Manufacturing

Sales Orders

Billing:

Invoice

Collect

Selling Season

1 2 3 4 5 6 7 8 9 10 11 12 13 14 15

Months

- A preliminary, estimated cash flow statement for the first year, including considerations of resources needed for startup and your cash conversion cycle:

- An estimation of (1) the total amount of asset and working capital needed in peak months and (2) the amount of money needed to reach positive cash flow, the amount of money needed to reach breakeven, and an indication of the months when each will occur:

- Create a break-even chart similar to the following:

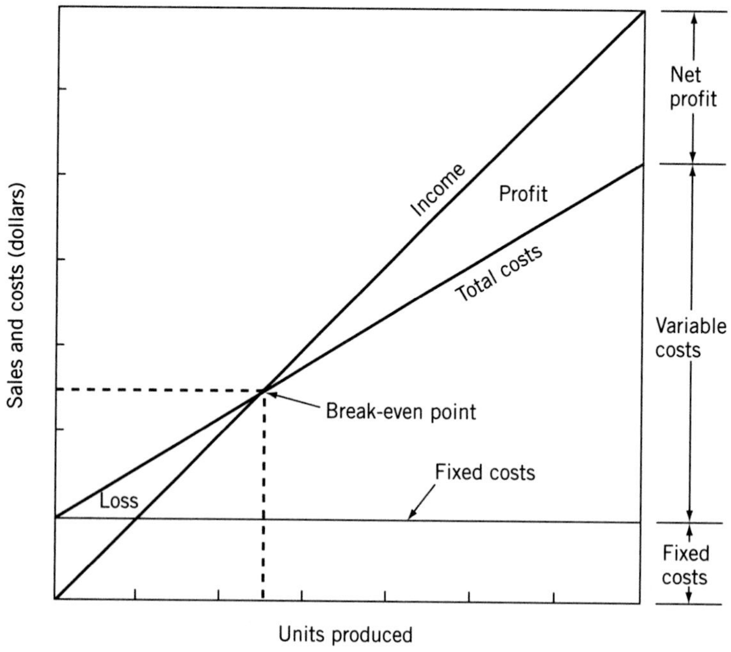

To calculate the number of units required to breakeven: \$ Selling Price − Variable Cost = \$ Contribution Margin/Unit Fixed Costs/\$ Contribution Margin = Units to Breakeven

- An estimate of the capital required for asset additions and operating needs (and the months in which these will occur) to attain the sales level projected in five years:

Exercise 7

Capital and Harvest—How Will You Realize Dollars from the Venture

The amount and nature of capital requirements for launching a new venture must be articulated in the context of the needs of the resource provider(s). In this section, you should purposefully link capital needs with the requirements of that provider(s). Specifically, the investor usually reaps a reward at harvest. The realistic timing and nature of the harvest will help define the logical investor or investors.

After reviewing both Chapter 4 and Chapter 13, think about your opportunity in the context of the capital markets food chain. Ask yourself:

Who is this opportunity for, and not for?

Who will, and will not, invest in this venture?

Who *should* invest?

Please provide:

- A statement of how you intend to raise capital, including all types (e.g., venture capital, financing raised through asset lenders, financing against inventory, receivables, equipment, and real estate), when, and from whom:

- A statement of whether you intend to harvest your venture, how and when this might occur, and the prospects. (If you do not intend to harvest the venture, include instead a statement of the prospects that profits will be both durable and large enough to be attractive.)

- An assessment of the sources of value, such as strategic, to another firm already in the market or one contemplating entry and an indication if there is a logical buyer(s) of your venture:

  —What do businesses similar to yours sell for as a multiple of sales, EBIT, cash flow, profits after taxes, and other metrics?

  —Who can help you find these answers?

- An assessment of how much it would take to liquidate the venture if you decided to exit and whether this is high:

Checkpoint

Reconsider if your venture opportunity is attractive. Beware of compromising on whether your opportunity has forgiving and rewarding economics. For example, are you convinced that the amount you need to raise is reasonable with respect to the venture's potential and risk? Are others convinced? If they are not, what do you know that they do not (and vice versa)? Most startups run out of cash before they secure enough profitable customers to sustain a positive cash flow. Your preliminary estimates of financial requirements need to be within the amount that an angel investor, venture capitalist, or other lender is willing to commit to a single venture or that you can personally raise. Even if your idea is not a candidate for venture capital financing, it is worth looking at your venture in this way.

Exercise 8

Competitive Landscape— Your Strategic Analysis

Every company has a competitor or substitute! Your customers were putting their money somewhere before you created your business. Look at both direct and indirect competitors. Who is the most knowledgeable person or competitor in this market? How does this affect you, your team, and your venture opportunity? Who can/should do this other than you? How do you become that person?

You may have acquired competitive information when you talked to potential customers in the customer contact research and exercise (Exercise 4). Estimates and relative position of the competitors is appropriate. When you have a relative understanding of the competitors, you should assess ***your*** position among these firms in terms of sustainable competitive advantages.

Please provide:

- An assessment of competitors in the market, including those selling substitute products:

Competitor No.	Name	Products/Services That Compete Directly	Substitutes

- A profile of the competition:

Competitor Profile

	Competitor No.			
	1	2	3	4
Estimated Sales/Year ($)				
Estimated Market Share (%)				
Description of Sales Force				

Marketing Tactics: Selling Terms Advertising/Promotion Distribution Channel Service/Training/Support Pricing					
Major Strengths					
Major Weaknesses					

- A ranking of major competitors by market share:

No.	**Competitor**	**Estimated Market Share**

- A Robert Morris Associates statement study:

RMA Study

RMA Data for Period Ending	**Estimates for Proposed Venture**				
Asset Size	**Under $250M**	**$250M to Less Than $1MM**	**$1MM to Less Than $10MM**	**$10MM to Less Than $50MM**	**All Sizes**
Number of Statements					
Assets:	%	%	%	%	%
Cash					
Marketable securities					
Receivables net					
Inventory net					
All other current					
Total current					
Fixed assets net					
All other noncurrent					
Total					
Liabilities:					
Due to banks—short-term					
Due to trade					
Income taxes					
Current maturities long-term debt					
All other current					
Total current debt					
Noncurrent debt, unsubordinated					
Total unsubordinated debt					
Subordinated debt					
Tangible net worth					
Total					
Income Data:					
Net sales					
Cost of sales					
Gross profit					
All other expense net					
Profit before taxes					
Ratios:					
Quick					
Current					
Fixed/worth					
Debt/worth					
Unsubordinated debt/capital funds					
Sales/receivables					
Cost sales/inventory					
Sales/working capital					
Sales/worth					
Percent profit before taxes/worth					
Percent profit before taxes/total assets					
Net sales/total asset					

M = thousand.
MM = million.

- An assessment of whether there are economies of scale in production and/or cost advantages in marketing and distribution:

- An assessment, for *each* competitor's product or service, of its costs and profitability:

	Competitor Costs and Profitability			
Product/Service				
Sales Price				
Sales Level				

For Each:

	Dollars/Unit	Percent of Sales Price/Unit
Production Costs (i.e., labor and material costs) or Purchase Costs		
Gross Margin		
Fixed Costs		
Profit before Taxes		
Profit after Taxes		

- An assessment of the history and projections of competitors' profits and industry averages:

Competitor Profits—Historical and Projected		Competitor			
	Industry Average	1	2	3	4
Profits (percent of sales)					
Past Two Years					
Current Year					
Projected Next Two Years					
Sales/Employee					
Profit/Employee					

- A ranking of competitors in terms of cost:

No.	Competitor

- A profile for the current year of your competitors in terms of price and quality and of market share and profitability. Place competitors (using small circles identified by names) in the appropriate locations in the boxes below:

Array of Competitors

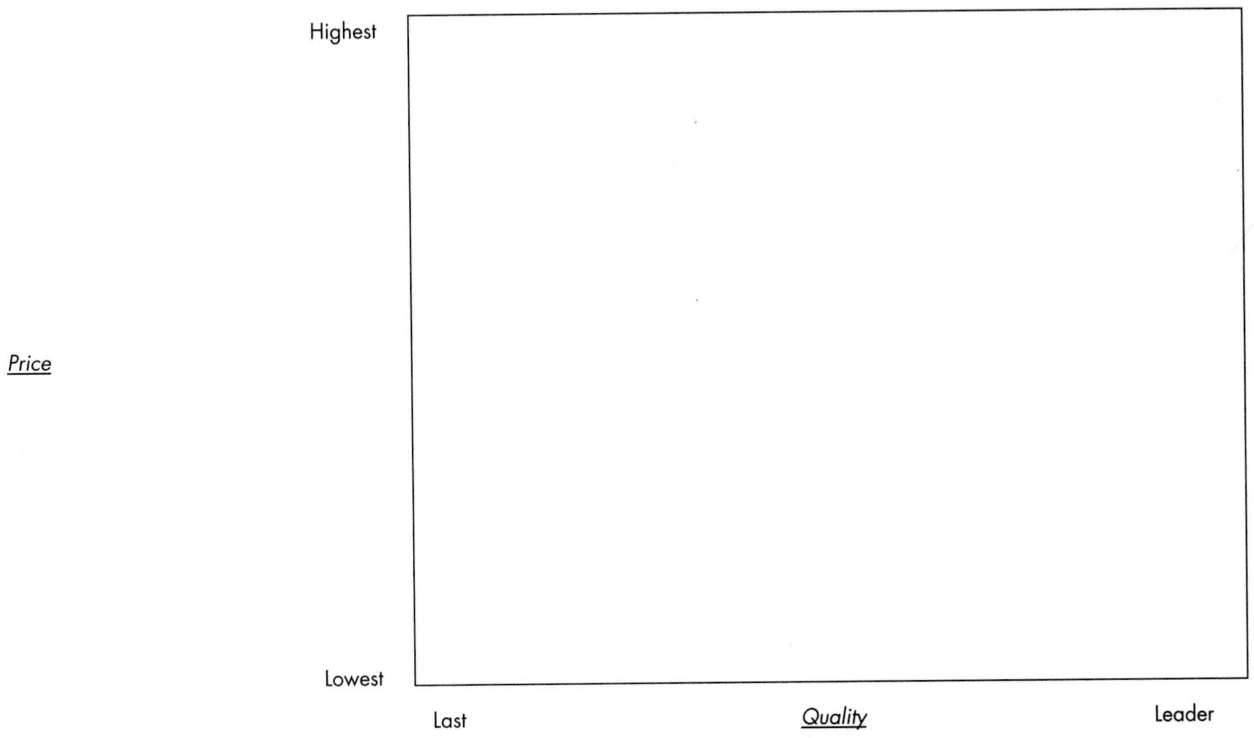

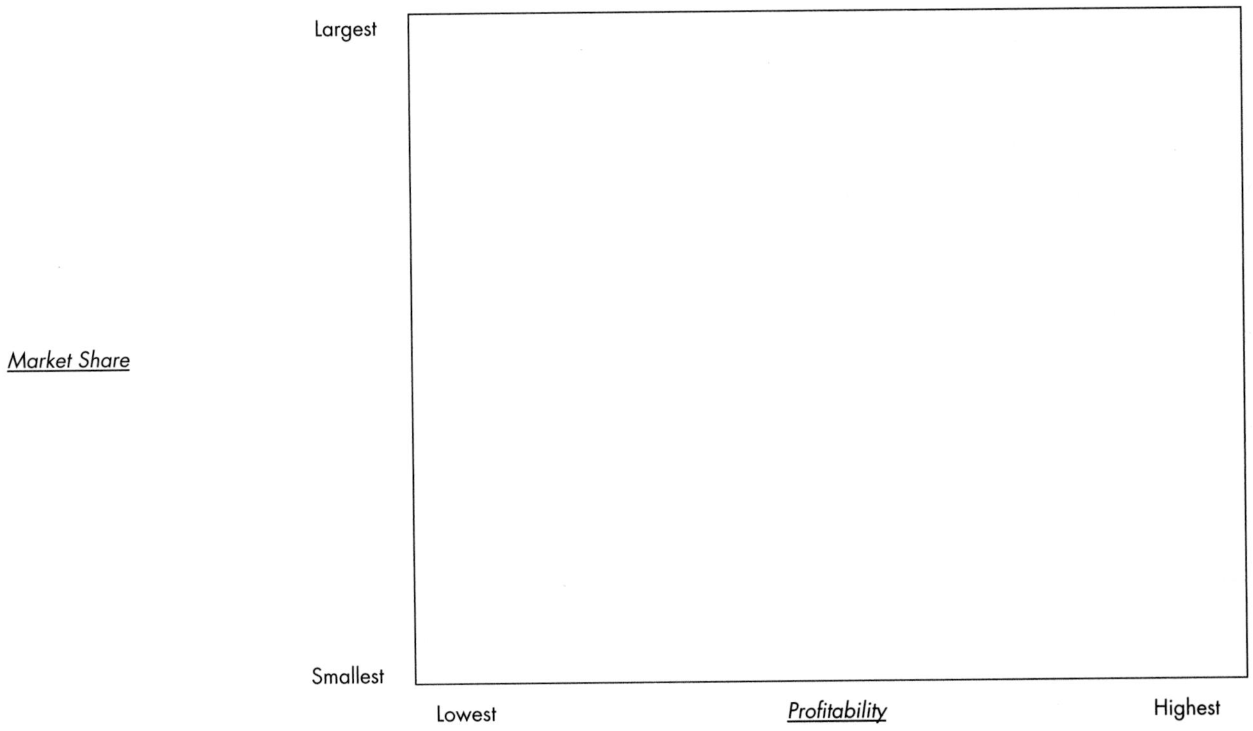

- An assessment of the degree of control in the market (including that over prices, costs, and channels of distribution and by suppliers, buyers, etc.) and the extent to which you can influence these or will be subject to influence by others:

- An assessment of current lead times for changes in technology, capacity, product and market innovation, and so forth:

- An assessment of whether your venture will enjoy cost advantages or disadvantages in production and in marketing and distribution, and an indication of whether your venture will have the lowest, average, or highest costs of production, marketing, and distribution:

- An assessment of other competitive advantages that you have or can gain, how you would secure these, and what time and money is required, including:

  —An indication of whether your product or service will benefit from, or be subject to, any regulations and of the status of any copyrights, trade secrets, or patents or licenses and distribution or franchise agreements:

—An indication if you enjoy advantages in response and lead times for technology, capacity changes, product and market innovation, and so forth:

—An indication if you enjoy other unfair advantage, such as a strategic advantage, people advantage, resource advantage, location advantage, and so on:

—An assessment of whether you think you can be price competitive and make a profit, or other ways, such as product differentiation, in which you can compete:

- A ranking of your venture in terms of price and quality and of market share and profitability relative to your competitors. Add your venture to the Arrays of Competitors above:

- An assessment of whether any competitors enjoy competitive advantages, such as legal or contractual advantages:

- An assessment of whether any competitors are vulnerable, the time period of this vulnerability, and the impact on market structure of their succumbing to vulnerabilities:

Checkpoint

Do you have sufficient competitive advantage? Remember, a successful company sells to a market that is large and growing, where capturing a small market share can bring significant sales volume, where it does not face significant barriers to entry, and where its competition is profitable but not so strong as to be overwhelming. Further, a successful company has a product or service that solves significant problems that customers have with competitive products, such as poor quality, poor service, poor delivery, and the like, and a sales price that will enable it to penetrate the market.

Exercise 9

Founder's Commitment

For the team to conclude that the idea is truly an opportunity, the founders must assess the commitment of their partners. There are many aspects of commitment, including but not limited to trust, an understanding and belief in responsibilities, financial contribution and extraction, and the overall belief in the team. Please provide:

- An assessment of your partners and/or management team, including:

  —An evaluation of whether the founders and/or the management team are sufficiently committed to the opportunity and how much they are personally willing to sacrifice, to invest in time, money, personal guarantees, and so forth:

  —An assessment of whether the founders and/or the management team possess the industry knowledge, experience, know-how, and skills required for the venture's success; if additional personnel is necessary and if these can be attracted to the venture; and if anyone on the team has managed previously what you are trying to undertake:

  —An assessment of whether the founders and/or management team have the necessary vision and entrepreneurial zest and whether they will be able to inspire this in others:

—An assessment of the level of trust felt among the founders and/or management team:

—A statement about who will do what—roles, responsibilities, and tasks:

—A statement about the contributions each founder and team member is expected to make:

—A statement about who will get what salary, what benefits, and what ownership share:

Checkpoint

Can do? Remember, the team is a primary force driving successful entrepreneurial ventures. It is important to question the assumptions on which your team has been shaped; for example, equal salaries and stock ownership can indicate that assumptions as to tasks, roles, and responsibilities are naive. Someone on your team needs to be experienced and competent in the areas of team dynamics and management, or the team needs to be able to attract someone who is.

If you have completed Exercises 1 through 9 and reviewed each checkpoint, you should have a fairly good handle on whether your idea is an opportunity and you will have completed most of the due diligence required to write a business plan. Completing the next two exercises will be very helpful as you build a strategy to launch time.

Exercise 10

Flaws, Assumptions, and Downside Consequences—Risk Reconsidered

Assess whether your venture opportunity has any fatal flaws:
List significant assumptions (assumptions about customer orders, sales projections, etc.), including:

- A consideration of significant tradeoffs that you have made:

- A consideration of the major risks (unreliability of customer orders; overoptimistic sales projections; inability to achieve cost and time estimates; underestimating the magnitude, intensity, and vindictiveness of competitors' responses; etc.):

- How far wrong can your revenue, cost, capital requirements, and time estimates be and still support a good business model?

Rank assumptions according to importance:

Evaluate the downside consequences, if any, when your assumptions are proved invalid; how severe the impact would be; and if and how these can be minimized, including:

- The cost and consequences of (1) lost growth opportunities and (2) liquidation or bankruptcy to the company, to you, and to other stakeholders:

Rate the risk of the venture as high, medium, or low:

Exercise 11

Action Steps—Setting a Week-by-Week Schedule

List chronologically the 10 to 15 most critical actions you need to take during the next six months and the hurdles that need to be overcome to convert your idea into a real opportunity. It is a good idea to have another person review what you have listed and adjust the list, if warranted.

Date	Action

Make a week-by-week schedule of key tasks to be performed, when they are to be performed, and by whom. Break larger tasks into their smallest possible components. Be alert for conflicts.

Week No.	Task	Date Completed	Person Responsible

Checkpoint

It is important to take a hard look at the assumptions you have made, both implicit and explicit, and to assess the risk of the venture. Time and again, first-time entrepreneurs overestimate sales and delivery dates and underestimate costs, effort, and time required to execute the opportunity and to reach a positive cash flow. Also, while each new business has its risks and problems, as well as its opportunities, difficulties need to be identified as soon as possible so they can be avoided or eliminated or their impact minimized.

Exercise 12
Four Anchors Revisited

Revisit Exercises 1 and 2.

A FINAL CHECKPOINT: Your responses to the VOSE will help you determine whether you want to continue with your venture and develop a completed business plan. If your venture has passed, a crucial question to consider before proceeding is, What do I want to get out of the business? You will want to think twice about whether the venture provides a strong fit with your personal goals, values, and needs; is what gives you energy; leads you down the path you want to be on and to further and even better opportunities. Remember, you are what you do. If you have been able to complete all the exercises, are satisfied that most of the results are positive, and if the answers to the personal issues are yes (see the ***QuickLook*** exercise in Chapter 7), then go for it!

After completing all the previous exercises, you should have a much sharper sense of the extent to which your good idea exhibits the four anchors described at the beginning of the chapter. Also ask yourself, who are the one or two *best* people on the planet to answer the following questions and what is their effect on me, my team, and this opportunity?

As you continue to work on your business you need to constantly consider the following questions, since creative insights that can make a significant difference can occur at any time:

1. How can the value proposition be enhanced and improved?
2. What can be changed, added, modified, or eliminated to improve the *fit*?
3. What can be done to improve the value chain and the free cash flow characteristics?
4. What can be done to enhance the risk–reward balance?

Case

Burt's Bees

The biggest businesses have revolutionized civilization, changed the way we live. That's my aspiration: to change the world for the better through my company.

Roxanne Quimby

Introduction

By April 1997, Burt's Bees had 20 employees and was on track to make between $6 million and $8 million in sales for the year. Burt's Bees margins were, on average, 35 percent of sales. A container of Burt's Bees lip balm, which cost 23 cents to make (including overhead), sold for $2.25–$2.50 in stores. The company distributed to every state in the country, could be found in more than 3,000 stores nationwide, and had just entered the European and Japanese markets. Burt's Bees products had also entered such conventional retailers' inventories as Eckerds, the Drug Emporium, and Fred Meyer. Roxanne Quimby, the president and founder of Burt's Bees, explained:

> It's not a lot of fun to go into these stores—it's a chore. They realize this and so they're looking for creative new products to liven things up, make shopping a more pleasant experience. We're starting to get a lot of inquiries from mainstream stores. They don't have an artistic inclination for merchandising, though, so we give them pre-made floor stands and displays to help with the backdrop and give meaning to the products for the consumer.

Pruning the Product Line

Burt's Bees' success was hard won through 18 to 24 months of pruning after the company's move from Guilford, Maine, in 1994. Production was extremely labor-intensive in Maine due to the large supply of low-paid unskilled labor. Burt's Bees had to automate production in North Carolina, though, to minimize the cost of its highly paid skilled labor. From 1994 to 1996, Roxanne Quimby cut products "like crazy." In 1994 alone, she took out $1.5 million in products including beeswax candles, the company's first and best-selling item. Every product Quimby cut was replaced with a skin care product since Burt's Bees had invested heavily in cosmetics manufacturing equipment, and the manufacturing processes involved in skin care were relatively straightforward. Quimby stated:

> We kept the lip balm, moisturizer, and baby powder, but that's it. There's not a single thing we made in 1987 that we still make today. We had to make more "goop" once we bought the blending and filling equipment. By the time we opened as a fully operational facility in North Carolina in 1994, we were still at $3 million but had totally different products. In terms of the marketing spin, that was predetermined by our environmental ethic [see Exhibit A for the company's Mission Statement]. We draw the line at chemical preservatives. Our products had to be all-natural. If we ever step over that line, we have a whole lot of competition. As long as we're in the all-natural niche, we're the only one who doesn't add stuff like petroleum-synthesized fillers or artificial preservatives.

Burt's Bees' corporate attorney, Lanny Hiday, added, "We just went through a long trademarking process so we had to compile product lists from 1987 on. It was amazing to see how different our products are now. Sometimes we joke that we'll be making diesel engines in five years. "By January 1997, Burt's Bees had over 70 "Earth Friendly, Natural Personal Care Products" [see Exhibit B].

Despite Burt's Bees' success as a manufacturer of personal care products, the company faced yet another dilemma: Should it enter the retail market? Walking through any mall in America today, you notice the market for retail personal care products is hardly vacant. How could Burt's Bees enter the retail market with the same success it had realized as a manufacturer only?

A Retail Experiment

In late 1996, Roxanne Quimby began what she called a "retail experiment." She opened a Burt's Bees retail store in Carrboro, North Carolina. While Burt's Bees had two other company-owned stores in Burlington, Vermont, and Ithaca, New York, the Carrboro store was established so that Quimby could develop a large-scale retail concept for the company. Quimby laughed:

> I worked at the Carrboro store for 10 hours the other day and sold only $400 worth of products while our Vice President of Marketing and Sales sold something like $30,000 worth of products in 15 minutes on QVC. But I'm testing a very valuable concept. I'm interested in controlling the whole chain from manufacturing to retail. I don't like being separated from the end-user. Our ultimate customers—the retailers—aren't interested in how the product works out for the person who takes it home.

EXHIBIT A

Burt's Bees' Mission Statement

Who We Are

We are Burt's Bees, a manufacturer of all-natural, Earth-friendly personal care products including:

herbal soaps

aromatherapy bath oils

powders

bath salts

salves

balms

We make these products in our facility in North Carolina, and sell them through more than 3,000 stores across the country, including three company-owned stores in Burlington, VT; Carrboro, NC; and Ithaca, NY.

What We Believe

We believe that work is a creative, sustaining and fulfilling expression of the Inner Being.

We believe that what is right is not always popular and what is popular is not always right.

We believe that no one can do everything but everyone can do something.

We believe that the most complicated and difficult problems we face as a civilization have the simplest solutions.

We believe that Mother Nature has the answers and She teaches by example.

We believe that by imitating Her economy, emulating Her generosity and appreciating Her graciousness, we will realize our rightful legacy on the magnificent Planet Earth.

What's In It?

Our ingredients are the best that Mother Nature has to offer: herbs, flowers, botanical oils, beeswax, essential oils and clay. Safe effective ingredients that have withstood the test of time.

What's Not In It?

We leave out the petroleum-synthesized fillers like mineral oil and propylene glycol. We don't use artificial preservatives such a methyl paraben or diazolidinyl urea. Take a closer look and read the label.

We Deliver What Others Only Promise!

What's It In?

Bottles, jars, tubes, caps, closures, bags, dispensers, containers, "convenient" throwaway plastic. Our planet is awash in trash!

How does Burt's Bees Reduce, Reuse & Recycle?

We Reduce. You'll find very little plastic here. We're exploring the use of simple, safe, effective and time-tested materials made of cotton, paper, metal and glass.

We Reuse. Many of our containers can be used again and again. Use our cotton bags to hold jewelry or other small items. Try our tins for pins, pills, tacks, clips, nails, screws, and nuts and bolts. Our canisters make attractive pencil holders and our glass jars will safely store your herbs and spices.

We Recycle. Bring back your empties. What we can't reuse we will recycle at our engineering recycling system at our plant in Raleigh, North Carolina.

WE LOOK DIFFERENT & WE ARE DIFFERENT

To me, the decision to buy is crucial. I like to just be in the store so I can observe customers and how they evaluate and respond to the products. I don't know whether we would open lots of company stores or start franchising or what, but that's what I'm trying to figure out.

The Market and Competition

Sales in the skin care and bath products industry demonstrated a distinct upward trend. Bath gels, washes, and scrubs, for example, increased 114 percent in dollar volume between 1994 and 1995—the largest category growth in the health and beauty market—while dollar volume of the entire health and beauty industry[1] increased only 64% in the same year.[2] Increased sales were partly aided by a virtual cut in half of prices. While the average bath gel debuted at around $10 in 1994, it cost $3.90 in 1996.[3] Skin care and bath products had developed into a major market niche over the past couple of years, accounting for $1.8 billion of the health and beauty market's $14.2 billion in sales for 1995.[4] Even though competition was fierce, the size of the pie had increased dramatically—sales had doubled between 1993 and 1995.

Market entrants were quick to try to capitalize on this growth. Companies such as The Body Shop, Bath & Body Works, Garden Botanika, and Origins were aggressively battling for market dominance. Most new skin care and

[1] Bath Gels, Washes, and Scrubs is a subset of the Bath Sundries product category, which is a subset of the overall Health & Beauty market. The Bath Sundries product category grew 32 percent in dollar volume between 1994 and 1995. The Health & Beauty category includes products such as meal supplements, tooth whiteners, thermometers, antacids, mouthwashes, razors, feminine hygiene, deodorant, acne preparations, and analgesics.

[2] "A Sofi Year for HBC." *Progressive Grocer*, May 1996, pp. 263–64.

[3] "Skincare: New Body Washes Make a Splash," *Progressive Grocer*, May 1996, p. 270.

[4] Ibid.

EXHIBIT B

Burt's Bees 1997 Product List

Product Collection	Product Name	Suggested Retail Price
Burt's Beeswax Collection	Beeswax Lip Balm (tin or tube)	$ 2.25–2.50
	Beeswax Face Soap 1.9 oz	$ 5.00
	Beeswax Moisturizing Creme 1 oz	$ 6.00
	Beeswax Moisturizing Creme 2 oz	$10.00
	Beeswax Pollen Night Creme 0.5 oz	$ 8.00
	Beeswax Royal Jelly Eye Creme 0.25 oz	$ 8.00
Wise Woman Collection	Comfrey Comfort Salve 1 oz	$ 4.00
	Calendula Massage Oil 4 fl oz	$ 8.00
	Mugwort & Yarrow Massage Oil 4 fl oz	$ 8.00
	Bladderwrack Massage Oil 4 fl oz	$ 8.00
	Comfrey Massage Oil 4 fl oz	$ 8.00
	Comfrey or Calendula Massage Oil 8 fl oz	$11.00
Ocean Potion Collection	Dusting Powder 5 oz	$14.00
	Dusting Powder Canister 3.5 oz	$ 6.00
	Emollient Bath & Body Oil 4 fl oz	$ 8.00
	Seaweed Soap 3.5 oz	$ 5.00
	Detox Dulse Bath 2 oz	$ 2.00
	Dead Sea Salts 25 oz	$12.00
	Sea Clay Mud Pack 6 oz	$10.00
Green Goddess Collection	Bath Salts 25 oz	$10.00
	Clay Mask 3 oz	$ 6.00
	Cleansing Gelee 4 oz	$ 8.00
	Beauty Bar 3.5 oz	$ 5.00
	Moisturizing Creme 2 oz	$10.00
	Dusting Powder 5 oz	$12.00
	Emollient Milk Bath 1 oz	$ 2.50
	Circulation Bath 1 oz	$ 2.50
	Foot Freshening Powder 3 oz	$ 8.00
	Flaxseed Eye Rest	$ 9.00
Farmer's Market Collection	Orange Essence Cleansing Creme 4 oz	$ 8.00
	Coconut Foot Creme 4 oz	$ 8.00
	Carrot Nutritive Creme 4 oz	$14.00
	Lemon Butter Cuticle Crème 1 oz	$ 5.00
	Citrus Facial Scrub 2 oz	$ 6.00
	Apple Cider Vinegar Toner 4 fl oz	$ 5.00
	Sunflower-Oatmeal Body Soak 1 oz	$ 2.50
	Avocado Hair Treatment 4 oz	$ 8.00
	Wheat Germ Bath & Body Oil 4 fl oz	$ 6.00
	Fruit Flavored Lip Gloss .25 oz	$ 3.50
Baby Dee Collection	Dusting Powder 5 oz	$ 12.00
	Dusting Powder Canister 2.5 oz	$ 8.00
	Skin Creme 2 oz	$10.00
	Buttermilk Soap 3.5 oz	$ 5.00
	Buttermilk Bath 1 oz	$ 3.00
	Apricot Baby Oil 4 fl oz	$ 6.00
	Apricot Baby Oil 8 fl oz	$10.00
Farmer's Friend Collection	Garden Soap 6 oz	$ 5.00
	Hand Salve 3 oz	$ 6.50

(continued)

EXHIBIT B (concluded)

Product Collection	Product Name	Suggested Retail Price
	Hand Salve .30 oz	$ 2.00
	Lemon Grass Insect Lotion 2 fl oz	$ 5.00
Furry Friends Collection	Oat Straw Pet Soap 3.5 oz	$ 6.00
	Rosemary & Nettles Coat Conditioner 4 oz	$ 8.00
	Lemon Oil Dry Shampoo 1.5 oz	$ 4.00
	Tea Tree Pest Powder 3 oz	$ 6.50
	Calendula Hot Spot Ointment 1.5 oz	$ 6.00
	Burt's Bones 5.5 oz	$ 5.00
	Wheat Grass Seeds 1 oz	$ 3.00
	Cat Nip Toy	TBD
Kitchen Cupboard Collection	Kitchen Soap 6 oz	$ 6.00
	Kitchen Crème 2 oz	$ 6.50
	Lemon Oil Cuticle & Nail Soak 1 oz	$ 3.00
Bay Rum Collection	Exfoliating Soap 3.5 oz	$ 5.00
	Shaving Soap 3 oz	$ 5.00
	Cologne 3.25 fl oz	$16.00
	Shave Brush	$ 6.50
	Razor	$ 5.00
Sugar Body Scrubs Collection	Lavender Sugar Body Scrub 1 oz	$ 3.00
	Rose Sugar Body Scrub 1 oz	$ 3.00
	Vanilla Sugar Body Scrub 1 oz	$ 3.00
Rebound Collection	Deodorizing Body Powder 3 oz	$ 6.00
	Invigorating Foot Bath 1 oz	$ 2.50
	Stimulating Massage Oil 4 fl oz	$ 8.00
	Therapeutic Bath Crystals 1 lb	$ 8.00

bath products claimed to be "all-natural" and appealed primarily to young women who didn't purchase traditional personal care products found in mainstream department stores. Donald A. David, the editor of *Drug and Cosmetic Industry* journal, wrote in late 1996:

> There is a "market glut" in the soaps and scents business stimulated by the competition between The Body Shop and Bath & Body Works. Indeed, the retail outlets out there under the banners of these two companies (and their hard-charging competitors Garden Botanika, Crabtree & Evelyn, Aveda, Nature's Elements and H_2O Plus) now number over 1,400 in the U.S. alone, a staggering number even if it isn't added to the ranks of scent-purveying store chains such as Victoria's Secret, Frederick's of Hollywood, The Gap, Banana Republic, and dozens more. . . . A shakeout seems inevitable. For example, when last heard from, Nature's Element was in Chapter 11, Garden Botanika's stock price plunged two-thirds in value three months after an initial public offering, and The Body Shop and H_2O Plus have been plagued by lagging profits. . . . Without having to deal with everyday product sales figures, this market watcher believes that the glut does not augur well for soaps and bath lines, wherever they are sold [see Exhibit C].[5]

EXHIBIT C

Retail Statistics for Cosmetic and Toiletry Sales (% of total sales by retail outlet)

Retail Outlet	1990	1994
Food stores	27%	25%
Drugstores	26%	23%
Mass merchandisers	16%	20%
Department stores	16%	17%
Direct sales	7%	8%
All other	8%	8%

Source: "Retail Statistics," *Stores,* October 1996, pp. 108–110. Courtesy of Stores Magazine/Deloitte.

Even if Burt's Bees stayed out of the retail market, competition was also fierce in manufacturing. The largest health and beauty products manufacturers [see Exhibits D and E], including Gillette, Lever Brothers, Chesebrough-Pond's, Jergens, Freeman, and St. Ives,

[5] Donald A. Davis, "Glut Indeed." *Drug and Cosmetic Industry,* November 1996, p. 22.

EXHIBIT D

50 Largest Manufacturers in the Toilet Preparations Industry (SIC 2844), 1996

Rank	Company Name	Sales ($ million)	Employees (000)
1	Johnson & Johnson	15,734	81.5
2	Colgate-Palmolive	7,588	28.0
3	Amway	4,500	10.0
4	Helene Curtis Industries Inc.	1,266	3.4
5	Alberto-Culver Co.	1,216	8.5
6	Cosmair Inc	1,000	0.4
7	Forever Living Products International	939	0.9
8	Perrigo Co.	669	3.9
9	Clairol Inc.	350	2.0
10	Freedom Chemical Co.	300	1.0
11	Neutrogena Corp.	282	0.8
12	Benckiser Consumer Products	230	1.5
13	John Paul Mitchell Systems	190	<0.1
14	Del Laboratories Inc.	167	1.1
15	Johnson Co.	140	0.9
16	Dep Corp.	138	0.4
17	Kolmar Laboratories	130	0.8
18	Guest Supply Inc.	116	0.7
19	Redmond Products Inc.	115	0.2
20	Cosmolab Inc.	110	0.7
21	Accra Pac Group Inc.	100	0.8
22	Sebastian International Inc.	100	0.4
23	Andrew Jergens Co.	97	0.6
24	Houbigant Inc.	97	0.6
25	Cumberland-Swan Inc.	80	0.8
26	Combe Inc.	70	0.4
27	BeautiControl Cosmetics Inc.	64	0.3
28	Sheseido Cosmetics	60	0.2
29	Jean Phillipe Fragrances Inc.	59	<0.1
30	NutraMax Products Inc.	56	0.5
31	Arthur Matney Company Inc.	55	0.5
32	Aramis Inc.	53	0.3
33	Luster Products Co.	53	0.3
34	Ranir Corp.	53	0.3
35	Aveda Corp.	50	0.3
36	DeMer and Dougherty Inc.	50	0.2
37	Russ Kalvin Inc.	49	0.3
38	Scott Chemical Co.	48	0.3
39	CCA Industries Inc.	48	0.1
40	Image Laboratories Inc.	47	0.3
41	Cosmyl Inc.	44	0.3
42	Pavion Ltd.	40	0.5
43	MEM Company Inc.	38	0.3
44	Pro-Line Corp.	38	0.3
45	Belcam Inc.	35	0.3
46	Penthouse Manufacturing	35	0.2

(continued)

EXHIBIT D (continued)

50 Largest Manufacturers in the Toilet Preparations Industry (SIC 2844), 1996

Rank	Company Name	Sales ($ million)	Employees (000)
47	Cosmar Corp.	33	<0.1
48	Megas Beauty Care Inc.	32	0.3
49	American International Industries	31	0.2
50	Aminco Inc.	31	0.2

Source: Arsen J. Damay, ed., *Manufacturing USA: Industry Analyses, Statistics, and Leading Companies*, 5th ed. Vol. (Farmington, MI: Gale Research Inc., 1996), p. 834.

EXHIBIT E

1995 Top 9 Hand & Body Lotions

Rank	Brand	1995 Sales ($ million)	1995 Market Share (%)	Manufacturer
1	Intensive Care	149.9	18.6	Chesebrough-Pond's
2	Jergens	89.9	11.2	Andrew Jergens
3	Lubriderm	77.9	9.7	Warner-Wellcome
4	Nivea	44.1	5.5	Beiersdorf
5	Suave	43.0	5.3	Helene Curits
6	Eucerin	41.1	5.1	Beiersdorf
7	Curel	36.8	4.6	Bausch & Lomb
8	Neutragena	34.5	4.3	Netragena
9	St. Ives	34.4	4.3	St. Ives

had been introducing their own "natural" skin care and bath products to ensure their continued market dominance.

Conclusion

Roxanne Quimby had always planned on selling Burt's Bees at some point, but she believed that no buyer would consider the company for purchase until it reached at least $25 million in sales. Quimby couldn't decide what the best route to $25 million was, though. Was it retail? If so, how could Burt's Bees establish a presence in such a crowded market? If retail wasn't a good move for the company, where did Burt's Bees' future lay? If Burt's Bees remained a manufacturer and direct seller, how could the company expand its product reach and close the gap between $6–$8 million and $25 million?

6

Chapter Six

The Business Plan

Madame, enclosed please find the novel you commissioned. It is in two volumes. If I had had more time I could have written it in one.

Voltaire

Results Expected

Upon completion of this chapter, you will have:

1. Examined a model of a business plan proven and refined over 35 years of actual use.
2. Determined what needs to be included in the plan, why, and for whom.
3. Identified some of the pitfalls in the business plan preparation process and how to avoid these.
4. Analyzed a complete business plan developed by a young entrepreneur to raise capital for a new medical device venture.
5. Concluded what has to be done to develop and complete a business plan for your proposed venture.
6. Analyzed the "Newland Medical Technologies" case study.
7. Understood the commitment necessary to turn your vision into a written document.
8. Realized that a well-articulated business plan is an important part of the entrepreneurial process, not an end in itself.

Developing the Business Plan

The business plan itself is the culmination of a usually lengthy, arduous, creative, and iterative process that, as we explored in Chapters 4 and 5, can transform the caterpillar of a raw idea into the magnificent butterfly of an opportunity. The plan will carefully articulate the merits, requirements, risks, and potential rewards of the opportunity and how it will be seized. It will demonstrate how the four anchors noted below (and in Chapter 5) reveal themselves to the founders and investors by converting all the research, careful thought, and creative problem solving from the Venture Opportunity Screening Exercises into a thorough plan. The business plan for a high potential venture reveals the business's ability to:

- Create or add significant value to a customer or end-user.
- Solve a significant problem, or meet a significant want or need for which someone will pay a premium.
- Have robust market, margin, and moneymaking characteristics: large enough ($50-plus million), high growth (20-plus percent), high margins (40-plus percent), strong and early free cash flow (recurring revenue, low assets, and working capital), high profit potential (10 to 15 percent after tax), and attractive realizable returns for investors (25 to 30 percent IRR).
- *Fit* well with the founder(s) and management team at the time, in the marketspace, and with the risk-reward balance.

The plan becomes the point of departure for prospective investors to begin their due diligence to ascertain potential and various risks of the venture: technology risks, market risks, management risks, competitive and strategic risks, and financial risks. Even if you do not intend to raise outside capital, this homework is vital. The collisions between founders and investors that occur during meetings, discussions, and investigations reveal a great deal to all parties and begin to set the code for their relationship and negotiations. Getting to know each other much more closely is a crucial part of the evaluation process. Everyone will be thinking: Are these intelligent people; can we work well with them during thick but especially thin times; are they creative; do they listen; can they add value to the venture; is this the right management; do I want them as business partners; are they honest; are we having fun yet?

The investors who can bring the most insight, know-how, and contacts to the venture, and thus add the greatest value, will reveal themselves as well. The most valuable investors will see weaknesses, even flaws, in how the market is viewed, the technology or service, the strategies, the proposed size and structure of the financing, and the team, and will propose strategies and people to correct these. If it is the right investor, it can make the difference between an average and a good or great venture.

The Plan Is Obsolete at the Printer

The authors have argued for three decades that the plan is obsolete the instant it emerges from the printer. In today's fast-paced climate, it is obsolete before it goes into the printer! The pace of technological and information-age change, and the dynamism of the global marketplace, shortened the already brief life expectancy of any business plan. It is nearly impossible to find a year-old venture today that is identical in strategy, market focus, products or services, and team as the original business plan described.

Work in Progress—Bent Knees Required

In such a rapidly changing environment, flexibility and responsiveness become critical survival skills. Developing an idea into a business, and articulating how this will be done via a business plan, requires an open mind and "bent knees," along with clear focus, commitment, and determination.

The business plan should be thought of as a work in progress. Though it must be completed if you are trying to raise outside capital, attract key advisors, directors, team members, or the like, it can never be finished. Like a cross-country flight plan, many unexpected changes can occur along the way: a thunderstorm, smoke-impaired visibility, fog, or powerful winds can develop. One has to be prepared to continually adjust course to minimize risk and ensure successful completion of the journey. Such risk-reward management is inherent in the business planning process.

The Plan Is Not the Business

Developing the business plan is one of the best ways to define the blueprint, strategy, resource, and people requirements for a new venture. It is this document that focuses and communicates the founder's vision. The vast majority of INC.'s 500 fastest growing companies had business plans at the outset. Without a business plan, it is exceedingly difficult to raise capital from informal or formal investors.

Too often first-time entrepreneurs jump to a simplistic conclusion: All that is needed is a fat, polished, and enticing business plan and the business will automatically be successful. They confuse the plan with building the business. Some of the most impressive business plans never become great businesses. And some of the weakest plans lead to extraordinary businesses. Mitch Kapor's original business plan for Lotus Development Corporation, creator of the 1-2-3 spreadsheet, was a brief letter, some descriptions of the personal computer market, a description of nearly 10 separate products, a one-year monthly startup budget, and a five-year goal of $30 million in revenue, which would require about $200,000 to $300,000 in capital. Venture capital backers Sevin-Rosen basically discarded the plan, the strategy, the product mix, the capital requirements, the launch plan, and the vision for the venture's first five years. These venture capitalists concluded the opportunity was much bigger, that $1 million of startup capital was required, that the company would either be several hundred million in revenue in five years, or would not be in business, even at $30 million in sales. The first-mover advantage of a warp-speed launch strategy was vital, and the rocket needed to be lit. The rest is history. Lotus Development reached $500 million in revenue in the first five years.

The message here is two-edged. The odds can be shaped in your favor through the development of a business plan. But just because you have a plan does not mean the business will be an automatic success. Unless the fundamental opportunity is there, along with the requisite resources and team needed to pursue it, the best plan in the world won't make much difference. Some helpful tips in preparing a business plan are summarized in Exhibit 6.1.

EXHIBIT 6.1

Do's and Don'ts for Preparing a Business Plan

Do

Involve all of the management team in the preparation of the business plan.

Make the plan logical, comprehensive, readable, and as short as possible.

Demonstrate commitment to the venture by investing a significant amount of time and some money in preparing the plan.

Articulate what the critical risks and assumptions are and how and why these are tolerable.

Disclose and discuss any current or potential problems in the venture.

Identify several alternative sources of financing.

Spell out the proposed deal—how much for what ownership share—and how investors will win.

Be creative in gaining the attention and interest of potential investors.

Remember that the plan is not the business and that an ounce of can-do implementation is worth two pounds of planning.

Accept orders and customers that will generate a positive cash flow, even if it means you have to postpone writing the plan.

Know your targeted investor group (e.g., venture capitalist, angel investor, bank, or leasing company) and what they really want and what they dislike, and tailor your plan accordingly.

Let realistic market and sales projections drive the assumptions underlying the financial spreadsheets, rather than the reverse.

Don't

Have unnamed, mysterious people on the management team (e.g., a "Mr. G" who is currently a financial vice president with another firm and who will join you later).

Make ambiguous, vague, or unsubstantiated statements, such as estimating sales on the basis of what the team would like to produce.

Describe technical products or manufacturing processes using jargon or in a way that only an expert can understand, because this limits the usefulness of the plan.

Spend money on developing fancy brochures, elaborate PowerPoint and Flash presentations, and other "sizzle"; instead, show the "steak."

Waste time writing a plan when you could be closing sales and collecting cash.

Assume you have a done deal when you have a handshake or verbal commitment but no money in the bank. (The deal is done when the check clears!)

Some Tips from the Trenches

The most valuable lessons about preparing a business plan and raising venture capital come from entrepreneurs who have succeeded in these endeavors. Tom Huseby[1] is founder and head of SeaPoint Ventures outside Seattle, a venture capital firm allied with Venrock Venture Capital, Oak Venture Partners, and Sevin-Rosen Venture Partners. An engineering graduate of Columbia University and a Stanford MBA, Huseby spent 18 years with Raychem Corporation of California, first working in sales, then developing and managing new businesses, and eventually running Raychem's businesses in several countries. Tom is a remarkable entrepreneur who has raised more than $80 million of venture capital as CEO of two telecommunications startup companies in the early and mid-1990s that subsequently became publicly traded companies: Innova Corporation (NASDAQ: INNV) and Metawave Corporation (NASDAQ: MWAV). Consider the following wisdom Tom gleaned from his own experience on both sides of the negotiating table: entrepreneur/CEO and venture capitalist.

RE: Venture Capitalists

- There are a lot of venture capitalists. Once you meet one you could end up meeting all 700-plus of them.
- Getting a no from venture capitalists is as hard as getting a yes; qualify your targets and force others to say no.
- Be vague about what other venture capitalists you are talking to.
- Don't ever meet with an associate or junior member twice without also meeting with a partner in that venture capital firm.

RE: The Plan

- Stress your business concept in the executive summary.
- The numbers don't matter; but the economics (e.g., value proposition and business model) really matter.

[1] The authors are extremely grateful to Tom Huseby, a longtime friend, fellow fly fisherman, and wilderness explorer, for sharing his extraordinary wit and insights over the years in classes at Babson College, Harvard Business School, and with the Kauffman Fellows Program, and for his contribution here.

- Make the business plan look and feel good.
- Prepare lots of copies of published articles, contracts, market studies, purchase orders, and the like.
- Prepare very detailed résumés and reference lists of key players in the venture.
- If you can't do the details, make sure you hire someone who can.

RE: The Deal

- Make sure your current investors are as desperate as you are.
- Create a market for your venture.
- Never say "no" to an offer price.
- Use a lawyer who is experienced at closing venture deals.
- Don't stop selling until the money is in the bank.
- Make it a challenge.
- Never lie.

RE: The Fund-Raising Process

- It is much harder than you ever thought it could be.
- You can last much longer than you ever thought you could.
- The venture capitalists have done this before and have to do this for the rest of their lives!

This is particularly valuable advice for any entrepreneur seeking outside capital and anticipating dealing with investors.[2]

How to Determine If Investors Can Add Value

One of the most frequently missed opportunities in the entire process of developing a business plan and trying to convince outside investors to part with their cash is a consequence of sell-sell-sell! myopia by the founders. Selling ability is one of the most common denominators among successful entrepreneurs.

Too often, however, entrepreneurs—typically out of cash, or nearly so—become so obsessed with selling to prospective investors that they fail to ask great questions and do little serious listening. As a result, these founders learn very little from these prospects, even though they probably know a great deal about the technology, market, and competitors. After all, that is the investor's business.

Entrepreneurs who not only succeed at developing a great business concept but also attract the right investors who can add a great deal of value to the venture through their experience, wisdom, and networks are usually very savvy listeners. They use the opportunity, beyond presenting their plan and selling themselves, to carefully query prospective investors: You've seen our concept, our story, and our strategies, what have we missed? Where are we vulnerable? How would you knock us off? Who will knock us off? How would you modify our strategy? What would you do differently? Who do we need with us to make this succeed? What do you believe has to happen to make this highly successful? Be as blunt as you wish.

Two powerful forces are unleashed in this process. First, as a founder, you will begin to discern just how smart, knowledgeable, and, most important, creative the investors are about the proposed business. Do they have creative ideas, insights, and alternative ways of thinking about the opportunity and strategy that you and your team may not have thought of? This enables you, the founder, to ascertain just what value the investors might add to the venture and whether their approach to telling you and your team that you are "all wet" on certain things is acceptable. Would the relationship be likely to wear you out over time and demoralize you? In the process you will learn a great deal about your plan and the investors.

The second powerful force is the message implicitly sent to the investors when you make such genuine queries and listen, rather than become argumentative and defensive (which they may try to get you to do): We have given this our best shot. We are highly committed to our concept and believe we have the right strategy, but our minds are open. We listen; we learn; we have bent knees; we adapt and change when the evidence and ideas are compelling; we are not granite heads. Investors are much more likely to conclude that you are a founder and a team that they can work with.

The Dehydrated Business Plan

A dehydrated business plan usually runs from 4 to10 pages, but rarely more. It covers key points, such as those suggested for the executive summary in the business planning guide that follows. Essentially, such a plan documents the analysis of and information about the heart of the business opportunity, competitive advantages the company will enjoy, and creative insights that an entrepreneur often has.

Since it can usually be prepared in a few hours, it is preferred by entrepreneurs who find it difficult to

[2] See also William A. Sahlman, "How to Write a Great Business Plan," *Harvard Business Review,* July–August 1997, pp. 98–108, for an excellent article on business plans.

find enough slack time while operating a business to write a complete plan. In many instances, investors prefer a dehydrated plan in the initial screening phase.

A dehydrated plan is not intended to be used exclusively in the process of raising or borrowing money; it can be a valuable compass to keep you on track. Consider it a map of the main battleground ahead, but remember that it will not provide the necessary details and tactical plans necessary to conduct the battle.

Who Develops the Business Plan?

Consideration often is given to hiring an outside professional to prepare the business plan, so the management team can use its time to obtain financing and start the business.

There are two good reasons it is *not* a good idea to hire outside professionals. First, in the process of planning and of writing the business plan, the consequences of different strategies and tactics and the human and financial requirements for launching and building the venture can be examined, before it is too late. For example, one entrepreneur discovered, while preparing his business plan, that the major market for his biomedical product was in nursing homes, rather than in hospital emergency rooms, as he and his physician partner had previously assumed. This realization changed the focus of the marketing effort. Had he left the preparation to an outsider, this might not have been discovered or, at the very least, it is unlikely he would have had the same sense of confidence and commitment to the new strategy.

A Closer Look at the What

The Relationship between Goals and Actions

Consider a team that is enthusiastic about an idea for a new business and has done a considerable amount of thinking and initial work evaluating the opportunity (such as thoroughly working through the Venture Opportunity Screening Exercises in Chapter 5). Team members believe the business they are considering has excellent market prospects and fits well with the skills, experience, personal goals, values, and aspirations of its lead entrepreneur and the management team. They now need to ask about the most significant risks and problems involved in launching the enterprise, the long-term profit prospects, and the future financing and cash flow requirements. The team must determine the demands of operating lead times, seasonality, facility location, marketing and pricing strategy needs, and so forth, so they can take action.

These questions now need to be answered convincingly with the evidence for them shown *in writing*. The planning and the development of such a business plan is neither quick nor easy. In fact, effective planning is a difficult process that demands time, discipline, commitment, dedication, and practice. However, it also can be stimulating and fun as innovative solutions and strategies to solve nagging problems are found.

The skills to write a business plan are not necessarily the ones needed to make a venture successful (although some of these skills are certainly useful). The best single point of departure for, and an anchor during, the planning process is the motto on a small plaque in the office of Paul J. Tobin, past president of Cellular One, a company that was a pioneer in the cellular phone business in America. The motto says "Can Do," and is an apt one for planning and for making sure that a plan serves the very practical purpose for which it is intended.

Further, if a venture intends to use the business plan to raise capital, it is important for the team to do the planning and write the plan itself. Investors attach great importance to the quality of the management team *and* to their complete understanding of the business they are preparing to enter. Thus, investors want to be sure that what they see is what they get—that is, the team's analysis and understanding of the venture opportunity and its commitment to it. Investors usually correlate a team's ability to communicate the vision with their ability to make it a reality. They are going to invest in a team and a leader, not in a consultant. Nothing less will do, and anything less is usually obvious.

Segmenting and Integrating Information

When planning and writing a business plan, it is necessary to organize information in a way that it can be managed and that is useful.

An effective way to organize information with the idea of developing a business plan is to segment the information into sections, such as the target market, the industry, the competition, the financial plan, and so on, and then integrate the information into a business plan.

This process works best if sections are discrete and the information within them digestible. Then the order in which sections are developed can vary, and different sections can be developed simultaneously. For example, since the heart and soul of a plan lies in the analysis of the market opportunity, of the competition, and of a resultant competitive strategy that can win, it is a good idea to start with these sections and integrate information along the way. Because the financial and operations aspects of the venture will be driven by the rate of growth and the magnitude and the specific substance of the market revenue plans, these can be developed later.

The information is then further integrated into the business plan. The executive summary is prepared last.

Establishing Action Steps

The following steps, centered around actions to be taken, outline the process by which a business plan is written. These action steps are presented in the exercise, "The Business Plan Guide."

- *Segmenting information.* An overall plan for the project, by section, needs to be devised and needs to include priorities—who is responsible for each section, the due date of a first draft, and the due date of a final draft.
- *Creating an overall schedule.* Next, create a more specific list of tasks, identify priorities and who is responsible for them. Determine when they will be started, and when they will be completed. This list needs to be as specific and detailed as possible. Tasks need to be broken down into the smallest possible component (e.g., a series of phone calls may be necessary before a trip). The list then needs to be examined for conflicts and lack of reality in time estimates. Peers and business associates can be asked to review the list for realism, timing, and priorities.
- *Creating an action calendar.* Tasks on the *do* list then need to be placed on a calendar. When the calendar is complete, the calendar needs to be reexamined for conflicts or lack of realism.
- *Doing the work and writing the plan.* The necessary work needs to be done and the plan written. Adjustments need to be made to the *do* list and the calendar, as necessary. As part of this process, it is important to have a plan reviewed by an attorney to make sure it contains no misleading statements, unnecessary information, and caveats. The plan also needs to be reviewed by an objective outsider, such as an entrepreneurially minded executive who has significant profit and loss responsibility, or a venture capitalist who would not be a potential investor. No matter how good the lead entrepreneur and his or her team are in planning, there will be issues that they will overlook and certain aspects of the presentation that are inadequate or less than clear. A good reviewer also can act as a sounding board in the process of developing alternative solutions to problems and answers to questions investors are likely to ask.

Preparing a Business Plan

A Complete Business Plan

It may seem to an entrepreneur who has completed the exercises in Chapter 5 and who has spent hours informally thinking and planning that jotting down a few things is all that needs to be done. *However, there is a great difference between screening an opportunity and developing a business plan.*

There are two important differences in the way these issues need to be addressed. First, a business plan can have two uses: (1) inducing someone to part with $500,000 to $10 million or more, and (2) guiding the policies and actions of the firm over a number of years. Therefore, strategies and statements need to be well thought out, unambiguous, and capable of being supported.

Another difference is that more detail is needed. (The exception to this is the dehydrated business plan discussed earlier in this chapter.) This means the team needs to spend more time gathering detailed data, interpreting it, and presenting it clearly. For example, for the purpose of screening an opportunity, it may be all right to note (if one cannot do any better) that the target market for a product is in the $30 million to $60 million range and the market is growing over 10 percent per year. For planning an actual launch, this level of detail is not sufficient. The size range would need to be narrowed considerably; if it were not narrowed, those reading or using the plan would have little confidence in this critical number. And saying the target market is growing at over 10 percent is too vague. Does that mean the market grew at the stated rate between last year and the year before, or does it mean that the market grew on average by this amount over the past three years? Also, a statement phrased in terms of "over 10 percent" smacks of imprecision. The actual growth rate needs to be known and needs to be stated. Whether the rate will or will not remain the same, and why, needs to also be explained.

Preparing an effective business plan for a startup can easily take 200 to 300 hours. Squeezing that amount of time into evenings and weekends can make the process stretch over 3 to 12 months.

EXHIBIT 6.2

Business Plan Table of Contents

I. EXECUTIVE SUMMARY
- Description of the Business Concept and the Business Opportunity and Strategy.
- Target Market and Projections.
- Competitive Advantages.
- Costs.
- Sustainability.
- The Team.
- The Offering.

II. THE INDUSTRY AND THE COMPANY AND ITS PRODUCT(S) OR SERVICE(S)
- The Industry.
- The Company and the Concept.
- The Product(s) or Service(s).
- Entry and Growth Strategy.

III. MARKET RESEARCH AND ANALYSIS
- Customers.
- Market Size and Trends.
- Competition and Competitive Edges.
- Estimated Market Share and Sales.
- Ongoing Market Evaluation.

IV. THE ECONOMICS OF THE BUSINESS
- Gross and Operating Margins.
- Profit Potential and Durability.
- Fixed, Variable, and Semivariable Costs.
- Months to Breakeven.
- Months to Reach Positive Cash Flow.

V. MARKETING PLAN
- Overall Marketing Strategy.
- Pricing.
- Sales Tactics.
- Service and Warranty Policies.
- Advertising and Promotion.
- Distribution.

VI. DESIGN AND DEVELOPMENT PLANS
- Development Status and Tasks.
- Difficulties and Risks.
- Product Improvement and New Products.
- Costs.
- Proprietary Issues.

VII. MANUFACTURING AND OPERATIONS PLAN
- Operating Cycle.
- Geographical Location.
- Facilities and Improvements.
- Strategy and Plans.
- Regulatory and Legal Issues.

VIII. MANAGEMENT TEAM
- Organization.
- Key Management Personnel.
- Management Compensation and Ownership.
- Other Investors.
- Employment and Other Agreements and Stock Option and Bonus Plans.
- Board of Directors.
- Other Shareholders, Rights, and Restrictions.
- Supporting Professional Advisors and Services.

IX. OVERALL SCHEDULE

X. CRITICAL RISKS, PROBLEMS, AND ASSUMPTIONS

XI. THE FINANCIAL PLAN
- Actual Income Statements and Balance Sheets.
- Pro Forma Income Statements.
- Pro Forma Balance Sheets.
- Pro Forma Cash Flow Analysis.
- Breakeven Chart and Calculation.
- Cost Control.
- Highlights.

XII. PROPOSED COMPANY OFFERING
- Desired Financing.
- Offering.
- Capitalization.
- Use of Funds.
- Investor's Return.

XIII. APPENDICES

A plan for a business expansion or for a situation such as a leveraged buyout typically takes half this effort because more is known about the business, including the market, its competition, financial and accounting information, and so on.

Exhibit 6.2 is a sample table of contents for a business plan. The information shown is included in most effective business plans and is a good framework to follow. Organizing the material into sections makes dealing with the information more manageable. Also, while the amount of detail and the order of presentation may vary for a particular venture according to its circumstances, most effective business plans contain this information in some form. (The amount of detail and the order in which information is presented is important. These can vary for each particular situation and will depend upon the purpose of the plan and the age and stage of the venture, among other factors.)

A Final Checklist*

This list will help you allocate your time and maintain your focus!
These points will also be important as you prepare for an
oral presentation of your business plan.

Make Your Point Quickly and Give Hierarchy to Your Data—The Details Matter!

✓ Hook the readers, especially in the executive summary, by having a compelling opportunity where you can:
- Identify a need or opportunity in a large and growing market.
- Conceptualize a business that will fill that need, or take advantage of that opportunity.
- Demonstrate that you have the know-how and the team to effectively build a profitable and sustainable business (or identify how you will create such a team).

✓ Prioritize the points you are making into three categories:
- Essential—without this the plan makes no sense.
- Good to know—directly supports and gives context to your essential points.
- Interesting—provides a higher level of understanding of market dynamics, industry, etc., but may not relate directly to the nuts and bolts of your business plan. Interesting information should be relegated to the appendix so it doesn't get in the way of the reader.

✓ Articulate the size of your market: who are your customers, why they will purchase your product or service, how much they will buy at what price.

✓ Include evidence of customers—this will increase your credibility.

✓ Discuss the competition, and why the customer will buy your product or service versus the alternatives.

✓ Articulate your marketing strategy. How will customers become aware of your product and service, and how will you communicate the benefits?

✓ Be specific when discussing your team. Articulate what relevant experience each brings to the business. If you can't identify key managers, you should outline the type of experience you want and a plan for recruiting that person.

✓ Edit for the details—clarity and typos—a sloppy presentation says a lot!

* The authors are grateful to Greg White of Chicago Venture Partners who developed this list and to longtime friend and entrepreneur Frederic Alper for sharing this with us. They use this approach in their work with the Denali Initiative, a national program that teaches entrepreneurship to leaders of nonprofit organizations from many parts of the country, and use *New Venture Creation* in its curriculum.

Internet Impact: Opportunity

Small Business Commerce

An eBay-commissioned telephone survey of companies with less than 100 full-time employees consisted of two sampling components: a random sample of 200 businesses that fit the target criteria, and a random sample of 200 similar businesses that had, in addition, used eBay for purchasing in the past 12 months.

Fifty-one percent of the respondents indicated that the Internet had improved their profitability, and 58 percent said the medium had helped their businesses to grow or expand. Fully one-third of the participants in the survey sold goods and services online, and 15 percent said the Internet was essential to their survival.

Not surprisingly, survey participants themselves were e-commerce consumers: 54 percent said that they've purchased computers and office technology online, 48 percent have acquired capital equipment and supplies, and 21 percent bought office furnishings. One-third purchased inventory to resell online and 59 percent used the Internet to purchase other business-related goods.

Source: AC Nielsen for eBay, 2004.

Chapter Summary

1. The business plan is more of a process and work in progress than an end in itself.
2. Given today's pace of change in all areas affecting an enterprise, the plan is obsolete the moment it emerges from the printer.
3. The business plan is a blueprint and flight plan for a journey that converts ideas into opportunities, articulates and manages risks and rewards, and articulates the likely flight and timing for a venture.

4. The numbers in a business plan don't matter, but the economics of the business model and value proposition matter enormously.
5. The plan is not the business; some of the most successful ventures were launched without a formal business plan or with one that would be considered weak or flawed.
6. Preparing and presenting the plan to prospective investors is one of the best ways for the team to have a trial marriage, to learn about the venture strategy, and to determine who can add the greatest value.
7. The dehydrated business plan can be a valuable shortcut in the process of creating, shaping, and molding an idea into a business.

Study Questions

1. What is a business plan, for whom is it prepared, and why?
2. What should a complete business plan include?
3. Who should prepare the business plan?
4. How is the plan used by potential investors, and what are the four anchors they are attempting to validate?
5. What is a dehydrated business plan, and when and why can it be an effective tool?
6. Please explain the expression: The numbers in the plan don't matter.
7. How can entrepreneurs use the business plan process to identify the best team members, directors, and value-added investors?
8. Prepare an outline of a business plan tailored to the specific venture you have in mind.

Internet Resources for Chapter 6

http://www.mitforumcambridge.org *Site of MIT's Enterprise Forum*

http://www.caseplace.org *Free online service for business school faculty, students, and businesses*

http://www.sba.gov/starting_business/planning/basic.html *Features a "Business Plan Road Map to Success" tutorial*

http://www.businessplans.org *Helpful resources c/o Business Resource Software, Inc.*

http://bus.colorado.edu/bplan *Includes sample plans and spreadsheet templates*

http://wsj.miniplan.com *The Wall Street Journal's 10-step miniplan*

http://www.entrepreneur.com/howto/bizplan *How to build a business plan*

http://www.inc.com/guides/write_biz_plan *Building a plan section by section*

MIND STRETCHERS

Have you considered?

1. You have sell-sell-sell mind-set myopia, but it has to be tempered with listening, inquiry, and learning. Can you think of a time when you have oversold? What did you learn from that experience?
2. Under what conditions and circumstances is it not to your advantage to prepare a business plan?
3. Identify three businesses that exceed $10 million in sales, are profitable, and did not have a business plan at launch. Why, and what did you learn from this?
4. Some of the most valuable critiques and inputs on your venture will come from outside your team. Who else should review your plan; who knows the industry/market/technology/competitors?
5. A good friend offers you a look at a business plan. You are a director of a company that is a potential competitor of the venture proposed in the plan. What would you do?

Exercise

The Business Plan Guide

An Exercise and Framework

This Business Plan Guide follows the order of presentation outlined in Exhibit 6.2. Based on a guide originally developed at Venture Founders Corporation by Leonard E. Smollen and the late Brian Haslett, and on more than 30 years of observing and working with entrepreneurs and actually preparing and evaluating hundreds of plans, it is intended to make this challenging task easier.

There is no single best way to write a business plan; the task will evolve in a way that suits you and your situation. While there are many ways to approach the preparation for and writing of a business plan, it is recommended that you begin with the market research and analysis sections. In writing your plan, you should remember that although one of the important functions of a business plan is to influence investors, rather than preparing a fancy presentation, you and your team need to prove to yourselves and others that your opportunity is worth pursuing, and to construct the means by which you will do it. Gathering information, making hard decisions, and developing plans comes first.

The Business Plan Guide shows how to present information succinctly and in a format acceptable to investors. While it is useful to keep in mind who your audience is and that information not clearly presented will most likely not be used, it also is important not to be concerned just with format. The Business Plan Guide indicates specific issues and shows you what needs to be included in a business plan and why.

You may feel as though you have seen much of this before. You should. The guide is based on the analytical framework described in the book and builds upon the Venture Opportunity Screening Exercises in Chapter 5. If you have not completed the Opportunity Screening Exercises, it is helpful to do so before proceeding. The Business Plan Guide will allow you to draw on data and analysis developed in the Venture Opportunity Screening Exercises as you prepare your business plan.

As you proceed through the Business Plan Guide, remember that statements need to be supported with data whenever possible. Note also that it is sometimes easier to present data in graphic, visual form. Include the source of all data, the methods and/or assumptions used, and the credentials of people doing research. If data on which a statement is based are available elsewhere in the plan, be sure to reference where.

Remember that the Business Plan Guide is just that—a guide. It is intended to be applicable to a wide range of product and service businesses. For any particular industry or market, certain critical issues are unique to that industry or market. In the chemical industry, for example, some special issues of significance currently exist, such as increasingly strict regulations at all levels of government concerning the use of chemical products and the operation of processes, diminishing viability of the high capital cost, special-purpose chemical processing plants serving a narrow market, and long delivery times of processing equipment. In the electronics industry, the special issues may be the future availability and price of new kinds of large-scale integrated circuits. Common sense should rule in applying the guide to your specific venture.

The Guide

Name:

Venture:

Data:

STEP 1

Segment Information into Key Sections

Establish priorities for each section, including individual responsibilities, due dates for drafts and the final version. When you segment your information, it is vital to keep in mind that the plan needs to be logically integrated and that information should be consistent. Because the market opportunity section is the heart and soul of the plan, it may be the most difficult section to write; but it is best to assign it a high priority and to begin working there first. Remember to include such tasks as printing in the list.

Section or Task	Priority	Person(s) Responsible	Date to Begin	First Draft Due Date	Date Completed or Final Version Due Date

STEP 2

List Tasks That Need to Be Completed

Devise an overall schedule for preparing the plan by assigning priority, persons responsible, and due dates to each task necessary to complete the plan. It is helpful to break larger items (fieldwork to gather customer and competitor intelligence, trade show visits, etc.) into small, more manageable components (such as phone calls required before a trip can be taken) and to include the components as a task. *Be as specific as possible.*

Task	Priority	Person Responsible	Date to Begin	Date of Completion

STEP 3

Combine the List of Segments and the List of Tasks to Create a Calendar

In combining your lists, consider if anything has been omitted and whether you have been realistic in what people can do, when they can do it, what needs to be done, and so forth. To create your calendar, place an X in the week when the task is to be started and an X in the week it is to be completed and then connect the Xs. When you have placed all tasks on the calendar, look carefully again for conflicts or lack of realism. In particular, evaluate if team members are overscheduled.

	Week														
Task	**1**	**2**	**3**	**4**	**5**	**6**	**7**	**8**	**9**	**10**	**11**	**12**	**13**	**14**	**15**

STEP 4

A Framework to Develop and Write a Business Plan

As has been discussed, the framework below follows the order of presentation of the table of contents shown in Exhibit 6.2. While preparing your own plan, you will most likely want to consider sections in a different order from the one presented in this exhibit. (Also, when you integrate your sections into your final plan, you may choose to present material somewhat differently.)

Cover

The cover page includes the name of the company, its address, its telephone number, the date, and the securities offered. Usually, the name, address, telephone number, and the date are centered at the top of the page and the securities offered are listed at the bottom. Also suggested on the cover page at the bottom is the following text:

> This business plan has been submitted on a confidential basis solely for the benefit of selected, highly qualified investors in connection with the private placement of the above securities and is not for use by any other persons. Neither may it be reproduced, stored, or copied in any form. By accepting delivery of this plan, the recipient agrees to return this copy to the corporation at the address listed above if the recipient does not undertake to subscribe to the offering. Do not copy, fax, reproduce, or distribute without permission.

Table of Contents

Included in the table of contents is a list of the sections, subsections, and any appendices, and the pages on which they can be found. (See Exhibit 6.2.)

I. Executive Summary The first section in the body of the business plan is usually an executive summary. The summary is usually short and concise (one or two pages). The summary articulates what the opportunity conditions are and why they exist, who will execute the opportunity and why they are capable of doing so, how the firm will gain entry and market penetration—it answers the questions we asked in Chapter 4: "for *what* reason does this venture exist and for *whom?*"

Essentially, the summary for your venture needs to mirror the criteria shown in Exhibit 4.8 and the Venture Opportunity Screening Exercises in Chapter 5. This is your chance to clearly articulate how your business is durable and timely, and how it will create or add value to the buyer or end-user.

The summary is usually prepared after the other sections of the business plan are completed. As the other sections are drafted, it is helpful to note one or two key sentences, and some key facts and numbers from each.

The summary is important for those ventures trying to raise or borrow money. Many investors, bankers, managers, and other readers use the summary to determine quickly whether they find the venture of interest. Therefore, unless the summary is appealing and compelling, it may be the only section read, and you may never get the chance to make a presentation or discuss your business in person.

Leave plenty of time to prepare the summary. (Successful public speakers have been known to spend an hour of preparation for each minute of their speech.)

The executive summary usually contains a paragraph or two covering each of the following:

A. *Description of the business concept and the business.* Describe the business concept for the business you are or will be in. Be sure the description of your concept explains how your product or service will fundamentally change the way customers currently do certain things. For example, Arthur Rock, the lead investor in Apple Computer and Intel, has stated that he focuses on concepts that will change the way people live and/or work. You need to identify when the company was formed, what it will do, what is special or proprietary about its product, service, or technology, and so forth. Include summary information about any proprietary technology, trade secrets, or unique capabilities that give you an edge in the marketplace. If the company has existed for a few years, a brief summary of its size and progress is in order. Try to make your description 25 words or less, and briefly describe the specific product or service.

B. *The opportunity and strategy.* Summarize what the opportunity is, why it is compelling, and the entry strategy planned to exploit it. Clearly state the main point or benefit you are addressing. This information may be presented as an outline of the key facts, conditions, competitors' vulnerabilities ("sleepiness," sluggishness, poor service, etc.), industry trends (is it fragmented or emerging?), and other evidence and logic that define the opportunity. Note plans for growth and expansion beyond the entry products or services and into other market segments (such as international markets) as appropriate.

C. *The target market and projections.* Identify and briefly explain the industry and market, who the primary customer groups are, how the product(s) or service(s) will be positioned, and how you plan to reach and service these groups. Include information about the structure of the market, the size and growth rate for the market segments or niches you are seeking, your unit and dollar sales estimates, your anticipated market share, the payback period for your customers, and your pricing strategy (including price versus performance/value/benefits considerations).

D. *The competitive advantages.* Indicate the significant competitive edges you enjoy or can create as a result of your innovative product, service, and strategy; advantages in lead time or barriers to entry; competitors' weaknesses and vulnerabilities; and other industry conditions.

E. Sustainability. Discuss the social, economic, and environmental sustainability of your business model. Summarize the employment opportunities that your business is likely to create, and describe any plans for outsourcing or using offshore labor and how that might impact the community and your labor pool. Briefly describe any environmental issues related to your business with regard to resources, waste generation, and legislative compliance.

F. *The team.* Summarize the relevant knowledge, experience, know-how, and skills of the lead entrepreneur and any team members, noting previous accomplishments, especially those involving profit and loss responsibility and general management and people management experience. Include significant information, such as the size of a division, project, or prior business with which the lead entrepreneur or a team member was the driving force.

G. *The offering.* Briefly indicate the dollar amount of equity and/or debt financing needed, how much of the company you are prepared to offer for that financing, what principal use will be made of the capital, and how the investor, lender, or strategic partner will achieve its desired rate of return. Remember, your targeting resource provider has a well-defined appetite and you must understand the "Circle of Venture Capital Ecstasy" (Chapter 4).

II. The Industry and the Company and Its Product(s) or Service(s) A major area of consideration is the company, its concept for its product(s) and service(s), and its interface with the industry in which it will be competing. This is the context into which the marketing information, for example, fits. Information needs to include a description of the industry, a description of the concept, a description of your company, and a description of the product(s) or service(s) you will offer, the proprietary position of these product(s) or service(s), their potential advantages, and entry and growth strategy for the product(s) or service(s).

A. *The industry.*

- Present the current status and prospects for the industry in which the proposed business will operate. Be sure to consider industry structure.
- Discuss briefly market size, growth trends, and competitors.
- Discuss any new products or developments, new markets and customers, new requirements, new entrants and exits, and any other national or economic trends and factors that could affect the venture's business positively or negatively.
- Discuss the environmental profile of the industry. Consider energy requirements, supply chain factors, waste generation, and recycling capabilities. Outline any new green technologies or trends that may have an impact on this opportunity.

B. *The company and the concept.*

- Describe generally the concept of the business, what business your company is in or intends to enter, what product(s) or service(s) it will offer, and who are or will be its principal customers.
- By way of background, give the date your venture was incorporated and describe the identification and development of its products and the involvement of the company's principals in that development.
- If your company has been in business for several years and is seeking expansion financing, review its history and cite its prior sales and profit performance, and if your company has had setbacks or losses in prior years, discuss these and emphasize current and future efforts to prevent a recurrence of these difficulties and to improve your company's performance.

C. *The product(s) or service(s).*

- Describe in some detail each product or service to be sold.
- Discuss the application of the product or service and describe the primary end use as well as any significant secondary applications. Articulate how you will solve a problem, relieve pain, or provide a benefit or needed service.
- Describe the service or product delivery system.
- Emphasize any unique features of the product or service and how these will create or add significant value; also, highlight any differences between what is currently on the market and what you will offer that will account for your market penetration. Be sure to describe how value will be added and the payback period to the customer—that is, discuss how many months it will take for the customer to cover the initial purchase price of the product or service as a result of its time, cost, or productivity improvements.
- Include a description of any possible drawbacks (including problems with obsolescence) of the product or service.
- Define the present state of development of the product or service and how much time and money will be required to fully develop, test, and introduce the product or service. Provide a summary of the functional specifications and photographs, if available, of the product.
- Discuss any head start you might have that would enable you to achieve a favored or entrenched position in the industry.
- Describe any features of the product or service that give it an "unfair" advantage over the competition. Describe any patents, trade secrets, or other proprietary features of the product or service.
- Discuss any opportunities for the expansion of the product line or the development of related products or services. (Emphasize opportunities and explain how you will take advantage of them.)

D. *Entry and growth strategy.*

- Indicate key success variables in your marketing plan (e.g., an innovative product, timing advantage, or marketing approach) and your pricing, channel(s) of distribution, advertising, and promotion plans.
- Summarize how fast you intend to grow and to what size during the first five years and your plans for growth beyond your initial product or service.
- Show how the entry and growth strategy is derived from the opportunity and value-added or other competitive advantages, such as the weakness of competitors.
- Discuss the overall environmental and social sustainability of your growth plan. Consider the effect on the community if the growth strategy involves offshore manufacturing or outsourced labor. Examine the potential environmental impact of your business as it grows.

III. Market Research and Analysis Information in this section needs to support the assertion that the venture can capture a substantial market in a growing industry and stand up to competition. Because of the importance of market analysis and the critical dependence of other parts of the plan on this information, you are advised to prepare this section of the business plan before any other. Take enough time to do this section very well and to check alternative sources of market data.

This section of the business plan is one of the most difficult to prepare, yet it is one of the most important. Other sections of the business plan depend on the market research and analysis presented here. For example, the predicted sales levels directly influence such factors as the size of the manufacturing operation, the marketing plan, and the amount of debt and equity capital you will require. Most entrepreneurs seem to have great difficulty preparing and presenting market research and analyses that show that their ventures' sales estimates are sound and attainable.

A. *Customers.*

- Discuss who the customers for the product(s) or service(s) are or will be. Note that potential customers need to be classified by relatively homogeneous groups having common, identifiable characteristics (e.g., by major market segment). For example, an automotive part might be sold to manufacturers and to parts distributors supplying the replacement market, so the discussion needs to reflect two market segments.
- Show who and where the major purchasers for the product(s) or service(s) are in each market segment. Include national regions and foreign countries, as appropriate.
- Indicate whether customers are easily reached and receptive, how customers buy (wholesale, through manufacturers' representatives, etc.), where in their organizations buying decisions are made, and how long decisions take. Describe customers' purchasing processes, including the bases on which they make purchase decisions (e.g., price, quality, timing, delivery, training, service, personal contacts, or political pressures) and why they might change current purchasing decisions.
- List any orders, contracts, or letters of commitment that you have in hand. These are *the most powerful data* you can provide. List also any potential customers who have expressed an interest in the product(s) or service(s) and indicate why; also list any potential customers who have shown no interest in the proposed product or service and explain why they are not interested and explain what you will do to overcome negative customer reaction. Indicate how fast you believe your product or service will be accepted in the market.
- If you have an existing business, list your principal current customers and discuss the trends in your sales to them.

B. *Market size and trends.*

- Show for five years the size of the current total market and the share you will have, by market segment, and/or region, and/or country, for the product or service you will offer, in units, dollars, and potential profitability.
- Describe also the potential annual growth for at least three years of the total market for your product(s) or service(s) for each major customer group, region, or country, as appropriate.
- Discuss the major factors affecting market growth (e.g., industry trends, socioeconomic trends, government policy, environmental impacts, and population shifts) and review previous trends in the market. Any differences between past and projected annual growth rates need to be explained.

C. *Competition and competitive edges.*

- Make a realistic assessment of the strengths and weaknesses of competitors. Assess the substitute and/or alternative products and services and list the companies that supply them, both domestic and foreign, as appropriate.
- Compare competing and substitute products or services on the basis of market share, quality, price, performance, delivery, timing, service, warranties, and other pertinent features.
- Compare the fundamental value that is added or created by your product or service, in terms of economic benefits to the customer and to your competitors.
- Discuss the current advantages and disadvantages of these products and services and say why they are not meeting customer needs.
- Indicate any knowledge of competitors' actions that could lead you to new or improved products and

an advantageous position. For example, discuss whether competitors are simply sluggish or nonresponsive or are asleep at the switch.

- Identify the strengths and weaknesses of the competing companies and determine and discuss each competitor's market share, sales, distribution methods, and production capabilities.
- Review the financial position, resources, costs, and profitability of the competition and their profit trend. Note that you can utilize Robert Morris Associates data for comparison.
- Indicate who are the service, pricing, performance, cost, and quality leaders. Discuss why any companies have entered or dropped out of the market in recent years.
- Discuss the three or four key competitors and why customers buy from them, and determine and discuss why customers leave them. Relate this to the basis for the purchase decision examined in IIIA.
- From what you know about the competitors' operations, explain why you think they are vulnerable and you can capture a share of their business. Discuss what makes you think it will be easy or difficult to compete with them. Discuss, in particular, your competitive advantages gained through such "unfair" advantage as patents.

D. *Estimated market share and sales.*

- Summarize what it is about your product(s) or service(s) that will make it salable in the face of current and potential competition. Mention, especially, the fundamental value added or created by the product(s) or service(s).
- Identify any major customers (including international customers) who are willing to make, or who have already made, purchase commitments. Indicate the extent of those commitments, and why they were made. Discuss which customers could be major purchasers in future years and why.
- Based on your assessment of the advantages of your product or service, the market size and trends, customers, competition and their products, and the trends of sales in prior years, estimate the share of the market and the sales in units and dollars that you will acquire in each of the next three years. Remember to show assumptions used.
- Show how the growth of the company sales in units and its estimated market share are related to the growth of the industry, the customers, and the strengths and weaknesses of competitors. Remember, the assumptions used to estimate market share and sales need to be clearly stated.
- If yours is an existing business, also indicate the total market, your market share, and sales for two prior years.

E. *Ongoing market evaluation.*

- Explain how you will continue to evaluate your target markets; assess customer needs and service; guide product improvement, pricing, and new product programs; plan for expansions of your production facility, and guide product/service pricing.

IV. The Economics of the Business The economic and financial characteristics, including the apparent magnitude and durability of margins and profits generated, need to support the fundamental attractiveness of the opportunity. The underlying operating and cash conversion cycle of the business, the value chain, and so forth need to make sense in terms of the opportunity and strategies planned.

A. *Gross and operating margins.*

- Describe the magnitude of the gross margins (i.e., selling price less variable costs) and the operating margins for each of the product(s) and/or service(s) you are selling in the market niche(s) you plan to attack. Include results of your contribution analysis.

B. *Profit potential and durability.*

- Describe the magnitude and expected durability of the profit stream the business will generate—before and after taxes—and reference appropriate industry benchmarks, other competitive intelligence, or your own relevant experience.
- Address the issue of how perishable or durable the profit stream appears to be. Provide reasons why your profit stream is perishable or durable, such as barriers to entry you can create, your technological and market lead time, and environmental sustainability, which in some cases can be a driver for cost reduction.

C. *Fixed, variable, and semivariable costs.*

- Provide a detailed summary of fixed, variable, and semivariable costs, in dollars and as percentages of total cost as appropriate, for the product or service you offer and the volume of purchases and sales upon which these are based.
- Show relevant industry benchmarks.

D. *Months to breakeven.*

- Given your entry strategy, marketing plan, and proposed financing, show how long it will take to reach a unit break-even sales level.
- Note any significant stepwise changes in your breakeven that will occur as you grow and add substantial capacity.

E. *Months to reach positive cash flow.*

- Given the above strategy and assumptions, show when the venture will attain a positive cash flow.

- Show if and when you will run out of cash. Note where the detailed assumptions can be found.
- Note any significant stepwise changes in cash flow that will occur as you grow and add capacity.

V. Marketing Plan The marketing plan describes how the sales projections will be attained. The marketing plan needs to detail the overall marketing strategy that will exploit the opportunity and your competitive advantages. Include a discussion of sales and service policies; pricing, distribution, promotion, and advertising strategies; and sales projections. The marketing plan needs to describe *what is* to be done, *how* it will be done, *when* it will be done, and *who* will do it.

A. *Overall marketing strategy.*

- Describe the specific marketing philosophy and strategy of the company, given the value chain and channels of distribution in the market niche(s) you are pursuing. Include, for example, a discussion of the kinds of customer groups that you already have orders from or that will be targeted for initial intensive selling effort and those targeted for later selling efforts; how specific potential customers in these groups will be identified and how they will be contacted; what features of the product or service, such as service, quality, price, delivery, warranty, or training, will be emphasized to generate sales; if any innovative or unusual marketing concepts will enhance customer acceptance, such as leasing where only sales were previously attempted; and so forth.
- Indicate whether the product(s) or service(s) will initially be introduced internationally, nationally, or regionally; explain why; and if appropriate, indicate any plans for extending sales at a later date.
- Discuss any seasonal trends that underlie the cash conversion cycle in the industry and what can be done to promote sales out of season.
- Describe any plans to obtain government contracts as a means of supporting product development costs and overhead.
- Describe any sustainability advantages you have or can develop, and how these aspects relate to building customer loyalty and community support for your product(s) or service(s).

B. *Pricing.*

- Discuss pricing strategy, including the prices to be charged for your product and service, and compare your pricing policy with those of your major competitors, including a brief discussion of payback (in months) to the customer.
- Discuss the gross profit margin between manufacturing and ultimate sales costs and indicate whether this margin is large enough to allow for distribution and sales, warranty, training, service, amortization of development and equipment costs, price competition, and so forth, and still allow a profit.
- Explain how the price you set will enable you (1) to get the product or service accepted, (2) to maintain and increase your market share in the face of competition, and (3) to produce profits.
- Justify your pricing strategy and differences between your prices and those for competitive or substitute products or services in terms of economic payback to the customer and value added through newness, quality, warranty, timing, performance, service, cost savings, efficiency, and the like.
- If your product is to be priced lower than those of the competition, explain how you will do this and maintain profitability (e.g., through greater value added via effectiveness in manufacturing and distribution, lower labor costs, lower material costs, lower overhead, or other cost component).
- Discuss your pricing policy, including a discussion of the relationship of price, market share, and profits.

C. *Sales tactics.*

- Describe the methods (e.g., own sales force, sales representatives, ready-made manufacturers' sales organizations, direct mail, or distributors) that will be used to make sales and distribute the product or service and both the initial plans and longer-range plans for a sales force. Include a discussion of any special requirements (e.g., refrigeration).
- Discuss the value chain and the resulting margins to be given to retailers, distributors, wholesalers, and salespeople and any special policies regarding discounts, exclusive distribution rights, and so on, given to distributors or sales representatives and compare these to those given by your competition. (See the Venture Opportunity Screening Guide Exercises.)
- Describe how distributors or sales representatives, if they are used, will be selected, when they will start to represent you, the areas they will cover and the head count of dealers and representatives by month, and the expected sales to be made by each.
- If a direct sales force is to be used, indicate how it will be structured and at what rate (a head count) it will be built up; indicate if it is to replace a dealer or representative organization and, if so, when and how.
- If direct mail, magazine, newspaper, or other media, telemarketing, or catalog sales are to be used, indicate the specific channels or vehicles, costs (per 1,000), expected response rates, and so on. Discuss how these will be built up.
- Show the sales expected per salesperson per year and what commission, incentive, and/or salary they are slated to receive, and compare these figures to the average for your industry.

- Present a selling schedule and a sales budget that includes all marketing promotion and service costs.

D. *Service and warranty policies.*

- If your company will offer a product that will require service, warranties, or training, indicate the importance of these to the customers' purchasing decisions and discuss your method of handling service problems.
- Describe the kind and term of any warranties to be offered, whether service will be handled by company service people, agencies, dealers and distributors, or returns to the factory.
- Indicate the proposed charge for service calls and whether service will be a profitable or break-even operation.
- Compare your service, warranty, and customer training policies and practices to those of your principal competitors.

E. *Advertising and promotion.*

- Describe the approaches the company will use to bring its product or service to the attention of prospective purchasers.
- For original equipment manufacturers and for manufacturers of industrial products, indicate the plans for trade show participation, trade magazine advertisements, direct mailings, the preparation of product sheets and promotional literature, and use of advertising agencies.
- For consumer products, indicate what kind of advertising and promotional campaign will introduce the product, including sales aids to dealers, trade shows, and so forth.
- Present a schedule and approximate costs of promotion and advertising (direct mail, telemarketing, catalogs, etc.), and discuss how these costs will be incurred.

F. *Distribution.*

- Describe the methods and channels of distribution you will employ. Discuss the availability and capacity of these channels.
- Indicate the sensitivity of shipping cost as a percent of the selling price.
- Note any special issues or problems that need to be resolved or present potential vulnerabilities.
- If international sales are involved, note how these sales will be handled, including distribution, shipping, insurance, credit, and collections.

VI. Design and Development Plans The nature and extent of any design and development work and the time and money required before a product or service is marketable need to be considered in detail. (Note that design and development costs are often underestimated.) Design and development might be the engineering work necessary to convert a laboratory prototype to a finished product; the design of special tooling; the work of an industrial designer to make a product more attractive and salable; or the identification and organization of employees, equipment, and special techniques, such as equipment, new computer software, and skills required for computerized credit checking, to implement a service business.

A. *Development status and tasks.*

- Describe the current status of each product or service and explain what remains to be done to make it marketable.
- Describe briefly the competence or expertise that your company has or will require to complete this development.
- List any customers or end-users who are participating in the development, design, and/or testing of the product or service. Indicate results to date or when results are expected.

B. *Difficulties and risks.*

- Identify any major anticipated design and development problems and define approaches to their solution.
- Discuss the possible effect on the cost of design and development, on the time to market introduction, and so forth, of such problems.

C. *Product improvement and new products.*

- In addition to describing the development of the initial products, discuss any ongoing design and development work that is planned to keep the product(s) or service(s) that can be sold to the same group of customers. Discuss customers who have participated in these efforts and their reactions, and include any evidence that you may have.
- With regard to ongoing product development, outline any compliance issues relating to new, pending, or potential environmental legislation. Discuss any green technologies or production capabilities that could enhance sustainability.

D. *Costs.*

- Present and discuss the design and development budget, including costs of labor, materials, consulting fees, and so on.
- Discuss the impact on cash flow projections of underestimating this budget, including the impact of a 15 percent to 30 percent contingency.

E. *Proprietary issues.*

- Describe any patent, trademark, copyright, or intellectual property rights you own or are seeking.
- Describe any contractual rights or agreements that give you exclusivity or proprietary rights.

- Discuss the impact of any unresolved issues or existing or possible actions pending, such as disputed rights of ownership, relating to proprietary rights on timing and on any competitive edge you have assumed.

VII. Manufacturing and Operations Plan

The manufacturing and operations plan needs to include such factors as plant location, the type of facilities needed, space requirements, capital equipment requirements, and labor force (both full- and part-time) requirements. For a manufacturing business, the manufacturing and operations plan needs to include policies on inventory control, purchasing, production control, and which parts of the product will be purchased and which operations will be performed by your workforce (called make-or-buy decisions). A service business may require particular attention to location (proximity to customers is generally a must), minimizing overhead, and obtaining competitive productivity from a labor force.

A. *Operating cycle.*

- Describe the lead/lag times that characterize the fundamental operating cycle in your business. (Include a graph similar to the one found in the Venture Opportunity Screening Exercises.)
- Explain how any seasonal production loads will be handled without severe dislocation (e.g., by building to inventory or using part-time help in peak periods).

B. *Geographical location.*

- Describe the planned geographical location of the business. Include any location analysis, and so on, that you have done.
- Discuss any advantages or disadvantages of the site location in terms of labor (including labor availability, whether workers are unionized, wage rates, and outsourcing), closeness to customers and/or suppliers, access to transportation, state and local taxes and laws (including zoning and environmental impact regulations), access to utilities (energy use and sustainability), and so forth.

C. *Facilities and improvements.*

- For an existing business, describe the facilities, including plant and office space, storage and land areas, special tooling, machinery, and other capital equipment currently used to conduct the company's business, and discuss whether these facilities are adequate and in compliance with health, safety, and environmental regulations. Discuss any economies of scale.
- For a startup, describe how and when the necessary facilities to start production will be acquired.
- Discuss whether equipment and space will be leased or acquired (new or used) and indicate the costs and timing of such actions and how much of the proposed financing will be devoted to plant and equipment.
- Explain future equipment needs in the next three years.
- For startups expecting to outsource manufacturing, indicate the location and size of the firm, and discuss the advantages, risks, and monitoring regime.
- Discuss how and when, in the next three years, plant space and equipment will be expanded and capacities required by future sales projections and any plans to improve or add existing plant space. Discuss any environmental impacts related to those expansion requirements. If there are any plans to move the facility, outsource labor, or move production overseas, discuss the impact on the local community. Indicate the timing and cost of such acquisitions.

D. *Strategy and plans.*

- Describe the manufacturing processes involved in production of your product(s) and any decisions with respect to subcontracting of component parts, rather than complete in-house manufacture.
- Justify your proposed make-or-buy policy in terms of inventory financing, available labor skills, and other nontechnical questions, as well as production, cost, and capability issues.
- Discuss who potential subcontractors and/or suppliers are likely to be and any information about, or any surveys that have been made of, these subcontractors and suppliers.
- Present a production plan that shows cost/volume/inventory level information at various sales levels of operation with breakdowns of applicable material, labor, purchased components, and factory overhead.
- Describe your approach to quality control, production control, and inventory control; explain what quality control and inspection procedures the company will use to minimize service problems and associated customer dissatisfaction.
- Describe the environmental sustainability of your operations, including the activities of your subcontractors and suppliers.

E. *Regulatory and legal issues.*

- Discuss any relevant state, federal, or foreign regulatory requirements unique to your product, process, or service such as licenses, zoning permits, health permits, and environmental approvals necessary to begin operation.
- Note any pending regulatory changes that can affect the nature of your opportunity and its timing.
- Discuss any legal or contractual obligations that are pertinent as well.

VIII. Management Team This section of the business plan includes a description of the functions that will need to be filled, a description of the key management personnel and their primary duties, an outline of the organizational structure for the venture, a description of the board of directors, a description of the ownership position of any other investors, and so forth. You need to present indications of commitment, such as the willingness of team members to initially accept modest salaries, and of the existence of the proper balance of technical, managerial, and business skills and experience in doing what is proposed.

A. *Organization.*

- Present the key management roles in the company and the individuals who will fill each position. (If the company is established and of sufficient size, an organization chart needs to be appended.)
- If it is not possible to fill each executive role with a full-time person without adding excessive overhead, indicate how these functions will be performed (e.g., using part-time specialists or consultants to perform some functions), who will perform them, and when they will be replaced by a full-time staff member.
- If any key individuals will not be on board at the start of the venture, indicate when they will join the company.
- Discuss any current or past situations where key management people have worked together that could indicate how their skills complement each other and result in an effective management team.

B. *Key management personnel.*

- For each key person, describe in detail career highlights, particularly relevant know-how, skills, and track record of accomplishments, that demonstrate his or her ability to perform the assigned role. Include in your description sales and profitability achievements (budget size, number of subordinates, new product introductions, etc.) and other prior entrepreneurial or general management results.
- Describe the exact duties and responsibilities of each of the key members of the management team.
- Complete résumés for each key management member need to be included here or as an exhibit and need to stress relevant training, experience, and concrete accomplishments, such as profit and sales improvement, labor management success, manufacturing or technical achievements, and meeting budgets and schedules.

C. *Management compensation and ownership.*

- State the salary to be paid, the stock ownership planned, and the amount of equity investment (if any) of each key member of the management team.
- Compare the compensation of each key member to the salary he or she received at his or her last independent job.

D. *Other investors.*

- Describe here any other investors in your venture, the number and percentage of outstanding shares they own, when they were acquired, and at what price.

E. *Employment and other agreements and stock option and bonus plans.*

- Describe any existing or contemplated employment or other agreements with key members.
- Indicate any restrictions on stock and investing that affect ownership and disposition of stock.
- Describe any performance-dependent stock option or bonus plans.
- Summarize any incentive stock option or other stock ownership plans planned or in effect for key people and employees.

F. *Board of directors.*

- Discuss the company's philosophy about the size and composition of the board.
- Identify any proposed board members and include a one- or two-sentence statement of each member's background that shows what he or she can bring to the company.

G. *Other shareholders, rights, and restrictions.*

- Indicate any other shareholders in your company and any rights, restrictions, or obligations, such as notes or guarantees, associated with these. (If they have all been accounted for above, simply note that there are no others.)

H. *Supporting professional advisors and services.*

- Indicate the supporting services that will be required.
- Indicate the names and affiliations of the legal, accounting, advertising, consulting, and banking advisors selected for your venture and the services each will provide.

IX. Overall Schedule A schedule that shows the timing and interrelationship of the major events necessary to launch the venture and realize its objectives is an essential part of a business plan. The underlying cash conversion and operating cycle of the business will provide key inputs for the schedule. In addition to being a planning aid, by showing deadlines critical to a venture's success, a well-presented schedule can be extremely valuable in convincing potential investors that the management team is able to plan for venture growth in a way that recognizes obstacles and minimizes investor risk. Since the time to do things tends to be underestimated in most business plans, it is important to demonstrate that you have correctly estimated these amounts in determining the schedule. Create your schedule as follows:

1. Lay out (use a bar chart) the cash conversion cycle of the business for each product or service expected, the lead and elapsed times from an order to the purchase of raw materials, or inventory to shipping and collection.
2. Prepare a month-by-month schedule that shows the timing of product development, market planning, sales programs, production, and operations, and that includes sufficient detail to show the timing of the primary tasks required to accomplish an activity.
3. Show on the schedule the deadlines or milestones critical to the venture's success, such as:
   - Incorporation of the venture.
   - Completion of design and development.
   - Completion of prototypes.
   - Obtaining of sales representatives.
   - Obtaining product display at trade shows.
   - Signing of distributors and dealers.
   - Ordering of materials in production quantities.
   - Starting of production or operation.
   - Receipt of first orders.
   - Delivery on first sale.
   - Receiving the first payment on accounts receivable.
4. Show on the schedule the "ramp up" of the number of management personnel, the number of production and operations personnel, and plant or equipment and their relation to the development of the business.
5. Discuss in a general way the activities most likely to cause a schedule slippage, what steps will be taken to correct such slippages, and the impact of schedule slippages on the venture's operation, especially its potential viability and capital needs.

X. Critical Risks, Problems, and Assumptions The development of a business has risks and problems, and the business plan invariably contains some implicit assumptions about them. You need to include a description of the risks and the consequences of adverse outcomes relating to your industry, your company and its personnel, your product's market appeal, and the timing and financing of your startup. Be sure to discuss assumptions concerning sales projections, customer orders, and so forth. If the venture has anything that could be considered a fatal flaw, discuss why it is not. The discovery of any unstated negative factors by potential investors can undermine the credibility of the venture and endanger its financing. Be aware that most investors will read the section describing the management team first and then this section.

Do not omit this section. If you do, the reader will most likely come to one or more of the following conclusions:

1. You think he or she is incredibly naive or stupid, or both.
2. You hope to pull the wool over his or her eyes.
3. You do not have enough objectivity to recognize and deal with assumptions and problems.

Identifying and discussing the risks in your venture demonstrate your skills as a manager and increase the credibility of you and your venture with a venture capital investor or a private investor. Taking the initiative on the identification and discussion of risks helps you to demonstrate to the investor that you have thought about them and can handle them. Risks then tend not to loom as large black clouds in the investor's thinking about your venture.

1. Discuss assumptions and risks implicit in your plan.
2. Identify and discuss any major problems and other risks, such as:
   - Running out of cash *before* orders are secured.
   - Potential price cutting by competitors.
   - Any potentially unfavorable industry trends.
   - Design or manufacturing costs in excess of estimates.
   - Sales projections not achieved.
   - An unmet product development schedule.
   - Difficulties or long lead times encountered in the procurement of parts or raw materials.
   - Difficulties encountered in obtaining needed bank credit.
   - Larger-than-expected innovation and development costs.
   - Running out of cash *after* orders pour in.
3. Indicate what assumptions or potential problems and risks are most critical to the success of the venture, and describe your plans for minimizing the impact of unfavorable developments in each case.

XI. The Financial Plan The financial plan is basic to the evaluation of an investment opportunity and needs to represent your best estimates of financial requirements. The purpose of the financial plan is to indicate the venture's potential and to present a timetable for financial viability. It also can serve as an operating plan for financial management using financial benchmarks. In preparing the financial plan, you need to look creatively at your venture and consider alternative ways of launching or financing it.

As part of the financial plan, financial exhibits need to be prepared. To estimate *cash flow needs,* use cash-based, rather than an accrual-based, accounting (i.e., use a real-time cash flow analysis of expected receipts and disbursements). This analysis needs to cover three years, including current- and prior-year income statements and balance sheets, if applicable; profit and loss forecasts for three years; pro forma income statements and balance sheets; and a break-even chart. On the appropriate exhibits, or in an attachment, assumptions behind such items as sales levels and growth, collections and payables periods, inventory requirements, cash balances, and cost of goods need to be specified. Your analysis of the operating and cash conversion cycle in the business will enable you to identify these critical assumptions.

Pro forma income statements are the plan-for-profit part of financial management and can indicate the potential financial feasibility of a new venture. Because usually the level of profits, particularly during the startup years of a venture, will not be sufficient to finance operating asset needs, and because actual cash inflows do not always match the actual cash outflows on a short-term basis, a cash flow forecast indicating these conditions and enabling management to plan cash needs is recommended. Further, pro forma balance sheets are used to detail the assets required to support the projected level of operations and, through liabilities, to show how these assets are to be financed. The projected balance sheets can indicate if debt-to-equity ratios, working capital, current ratios, inventory turnover, and the like are within the acceptable limits required to justify future financings that are projected for the venture. Finally, a break-even chart showing the level of sales and production that will cover all costs, including those costs that vary with production level and those that do not, is very useful.

A. *Actual income statements and balance sheets.* For an existing business, prepare income statements and balance sheets for the current year and for the prior two years.

B. *Pro forma income statements.*

- Using sales forecasts and the accompanying production or operations costs, prepare pro forma income statements for at least the first three years.
- Fully discuss assumptions (e.g., the amount allowed for bad debts and discounts, or any assumptions made with respect to sales expenses or general and administrative costs being a fixed percentage of costs or sales) made in preparing the pro forma income statement and document them.
- Draw on Section X of the business plan and highlight any major risks, such as the effect of a 20 percent reduction in sales from those projected or the adverse impact of having to climb a learning curve on the level of productivity over time, that could prevent the venture's sales and profit goals from being attained, plus the sensitivity of profits to these risks.

C. *Pro forma balance sheets.* Prepare pro forma balance sheets semiannually in the first year and at the end of each of the first three years of operation.

D. *Pro forma cash flow analysis.*

- Project cash flows monthly for the first year of operation and quarterly for at least the next two years. Detail the amount and timing of expected cash inflows and outflows. Determine the need for and timing of additional financing and indicate peak requirements for working capital. Indicate how necessary additional financing is to be obtained, such as through equity financing, bank loans, or short-term lines of credit from banks, on what terms, and how it is to be repaid. Remember they are based on cash, not accrual, accounting.
- Discuss assumptions, such as those made on the timing of collection of receivables, trade discounts given, terms of payments to vendors, planned salary and wage increases, anticipated increases in any operating expenses, seasonality characteristics of the business as they affect inventory requirements, inventory turnovers per year, capital equipment purchases, and so forth. Again, these are real time (i.e., cash), not accruals.
- Discuss cash flow sensitivity to a variety of assumptions about business factors (e.g., possible changes in such crucial assumptions as an increase in the receivable collection period or a sales level lower than that forecasted).

E. *Break-even chart.*

- Calculate breakeven and prepare a chart that shows when breakeven will be reached and any stepwise changes in breakeven that may occur.
- Discuss the breakeven shown for your venture and whether it will be easy or difficult to attain, including a discussion of the size of break-even sales volume relative to projected total sales, the size of gross margins and price sensitivity, and how the break-even point might be lowered in case the venture falls short of sales projections.

F. *Cost control.* Describe how you will obtain information about report costs and how often, who will be responsible for the control of various cost elements, and how you will take action on budget overruns.

G. *Highlights.* Highlight the important conclusions, including the maximum amount and timing of cash required, the amount of debt and equity needed, how fast any debts can be repaid, etc.

XII. Proposed Company Offering The purpose of this section of the plan is to indicate the amount of money that is being sought, the nature and amount of the securities offered to investors, a brief description of the uses that will be made of the capital raised, and a summary of how the investor is expected to achieve its targeted rate of return. It is recommended that you read the discussion about financing in Part IV.

The terms for financing your company that you propose here are the first steps in the negotiation process with those interested in investing, and it is very possible that your financing will involve different kinds of securities than originally proposed.

A. *Desired financing.* Based on your real-time cash flow projections and your estimate of how much money is required over the next three years to carry out the development and/or expansion of your business as described, indicate how much of this capital requirement will be obtained by this offering and how much will be obtained via term loans and lines of credit.

B. *Offering.*

- Describe the type (e.g., common stock, convertible debentures, debt with warrants, debt plus stock), unit price, and total amount of securities to be sold in this offering. If securities are not just common stock, indicate by type, interest, maturity, and conversion conditions.

- Show the percentage of the company that the investors of this offering will hold after it is completed or after exercise of any stock conversion or purchase rights in the case of convertible debentures or warrants.
- Securities sold through a private placement and that therefore are exempt from SEC registration should include the following statement in this part of the plan:

  The shares being sold pursuant to this offering are restricted securities and may not be resold readily. The prospective investor should recognize that such securities might be restricted as to resale for an indefinite period of time. Each purchaser will be required to execute a Non-Distribution Agreement satisfactory in form to corporate counsel.

C. *Capitalization.*

- Present in tabular form the current and proposed (postoffering) number of outstanding shares of common stock. Indicate any shares offered by key management people and show the number of shares that they will hold after completion of the proposed financing.
- Indicate how many shares of your company's common stock will remain authorized but unissued after the offering and how many of these will be reserved for stock options for future key employees.

D. *Use of funds.* Investors like to know how their money is going to be spent. Provide a brief description of how the capital raised will be used. Summarize as specifically as possible what amount will be used for such things as product design and development, capital equipment, marketing, and general working capital needs.

E. *Investors' return.* Indicate how your valuation and proposed ownership shares will result in the desired rate of return for the investors you have targeted and what the likely harvest or exit mechanism (IPO, outright sale, merger, MBO, etc.) will be.

XIII. Appendices Include pertinent information here that is too extensive for the body of the business plan but that is necessary (product specs or photos; lists of references, suppliers of critical components; special location factors, facilities, or technical analyses; reports from consultants or technical experts; and copies of any critical regulatory approval, licenses, etc).

STEP 5

Integrate Sections

Integrate the discrete sections you have created into a coherent business plan that can be used for the purpose for which it was created.

STEP 6

Get Feedback

Once written, it is recommended that you get the plan reviewed. No matter how good you and your team are, you will most likely overlook issues and treat aspects of your venture in a manner that is less than clear. A good reviewer can give you the benefit of an outside objective evaluation. Your attorney can make sure that there are no misleading statements in your plan and that it contains all the caveats and the like.

Case

Newland Medical Technologies

Preparation Questions

1. Discuss the process that Sarah and her partners have gone through to bring to market their medical device. How might they have avoided some of the pitfalls they have encountered?
2. Examine Newland's strategy in light of the special circumstances in this industry. What is your recommendation for moving the company forward?
3. In light of your strategic plan for Newland Medical, how can Sarah achieve a balance between her personal and professional objectives and commitments?

It had all seemed like a perfect plan. With two assertive angel investors guiding her medical device company on what seemed to be an acquisition fast track, Sarah Foster and her husband decided that the time was right to start a family. However, by the fall of 2005 (the middle of her first trimester), everything had changed.

Sarah, cofounder and president of Newland Medical Technologies, was now compelled to seriously reconsider the course she'd set for her company. In doing

This case was prepared by Carl Hedberg under the direction of Professor Stephen Spinelli. © Copyright Babson College, 2005.

so, she was going to have to make some tough choices in order to strike a balance between motherhood and her professional passions.

Opportunity Recognition

Sarah Foster had been working with hip implant designs for Johnson & Johnson in Massachusetts for two years when the corporate office announced they were moving her division out west to Iowa. Sarah loved the work, but she and her husband, a professor at a local college, also loved living in the Boston area. She passed on the offer and instead leveraged her engineering degrees from MIT and Stanford to secure employment close to home (see Exhibit 1). Still, the bright engineer never lost sight of her primary career objective:

> I had been looking for a medical device opportunity ever since I left Johnson & Johnson. Then a friend of mine—a urologist at the Brigham and Women's Hospital in Boston—told me how there was a need for better stents[1] in urology, since most of the industry focus has been in cardiac work. He pointed out that even though it was commonly known that the ureter naturally dilates in the presence of a foreign body, no stent products had taken full advantage of this fact. We felt that gently stimulating a wider dilation would improve urine flow and might even help pass kidney stones.

Kidney stones, or ureteral stones, were a debilitating malady that affected nearly 10 percent of the U.S. population. The pain of stone disease was most severe when the stone lodged in the ureter and obstructed urine flow.

A patient arriving with kidney stones was usually treated as an emergency. The Emergency Room physician would administer pain medication and almost always consult a urologist. The immediate and near-term treatment had to be safe, effective, and keep the patient's options open for later procedures.

By the late 1990s, most urologists were meeting these needs with the "Double-J"—a standard polyurethane stent inserted into the ureter to relieve pain by allowing urine to flow around the stone. With the Double-J, stones often remained in the ureter; the choice of procedure to remove such stones was related to the size and location of the stone, as well as access to sophisticated equipment.

Patients with stones less than 5 mm typically waited in pain a few days or up to several weeks for the stone to pass. Larger stones were broken up using ultrasound and laser technologies—leaving fragments too small to retrieve but plenty big enough to ensure a painful passing. Basketing was a secondary procedure that was very effective in removing individual stone fragments, but it required a skilled surgeon and an extended operating time (see Exhibit 2).

In the winter of 1999, Sarah and Dr. Grainer began brainstorming a sheath-covered stent that could be deployed in the same manner and with the same materials as the Double-J. Once inside the ureter, the sheath would be removed, and their stent would enlarge the passageway with a series of expansion bulbs along its length (see Exhibit 3). While their aim was to relieve urine flow to a greater degree than competitive products, during their initial trials on pigs they noticed that as the device was slowly withdrawn from the ureter, stones became trapped in the basket-like bulbs. Direct and atraumatic removal of stones from the ureter had never been done before; now they had their product.

The SRS

To emphasize what they now saw as the *primary* attribute, Sarah and Dr. Grainer named their device the Stone Removal Stent (SRS). A new series of animal trials led to the following procedure outline:

1. The ureter was located within the bladder using a cystoscope, and a guide wire was inserted up the ureter.
2. The SRS was slipped over the guide wire and pushed into place.
3. The sheath around the SRS was removed to open the baskets.
4. In one to two days, the SRS caused the ureter to passively dilate and enlarge the passageway.
5. The SRS was slowly withdrawn, whereby stones were either trapped in the baskets, fell into the baskets upon removal, or were merely swept alongside.

Throughout 2000 and into 2001, Sarah took charge of the effort as Dr. Grainer returned to his full-time practice. She raised money from friends and family to secure a patent on the unique-application stent. At the same time, she continued to examine various aspects of the opportunity in order to assemble the business plan she would need to attract professional investors.

Target Market

Sarah determined that the target market included kidney stones that received primary ureteroscopy and extracorporeal shock-wave lithotripsy (ESWL) therapy (the two most common procedures), as well as stenting to relieve urine flow. The price of ESWL machines ranged from \$500,000 to \$1.5 million, a prohibitive cost to all but the largest medical centers. Although these prices were coming down, there were only 400 units in the United

[1] A medical stent was an expandable wire mesh or polyurethane tube that was inserted into a hollow structure of the body to keep it open or to provide strength. Stents were used on diverse structures such as coronary arteries, other blood vessels, the common bile duct, the esophagus, the trachea, and the ureter—the tract that conducts urine flow from the kidney to the bladder.

EXHIBIT 1

Résumé: Sarah Choi Foster

Education

2002–2004 **F.W. OLIN BUSINESS SCHOOL AT BABSON COLLEGE** **Wellesley. MA**
M.B.A., May 2003, cum laude, Babson Fellow.
- Consulted with Boston Scientific, Inc.; competitive analysis and e-commerce initiatives.
- Entrepreneurship Intensity Track program, Hatchery company.

1996–1997 **STANFORD UNIVERSITY** **Stanford, CA**
M.S. degree in Mechanical Engineering, Design, June 1997.
Concentration: Mechatronics (Mechanical electronics) & Design for Manufacturability.
- Design projects: 3M-sponsored portable overhead projector, smart tag–playing robot, automated 3-D foam facsimile machine, automated paper palm-tree maker.

1992–1996 **MASSACHUSETTS INSTITUTE OF TECHNOLOGY** **Cambridge, MA**
B.S. degree in Mechanical Engineering, May 1996. Minor in Music.
- UTAP Full Scholarship

Experience

2003–present **NEWLAND MEDICAL TECHNOLOGIES, INC.** **Boston, MA**
President and Founder
- Raised $600K to bring an FDA-approved patented product to market
- Built team and running the business

2002 **PERCEPTION ROBOTICS, INC.** **Waltham, MA**
Kauffman Intern, Product Manager Intern
- Analyzed potential e-commerce partners for an interactive retail software system.
- Helped develop new product value proposition for Web cameras.

1999–2002 **THE GILLETTE COMPANY** **Boston, MA**
Design Engineer, Shaving and Technology Lab
- Managed design process and testing of high volume plastic packaging for various toiletries.
- Designed Economy Gel antiperspirant container from market requirement to mold production.

1998–1999 **JOHNSON & JOHNSON PROFESSIONAL, INC.** **Rayhnam, MA**
Project Engineer, Hip R&D
- Served as lead engineer to design hip implant products; two patents granted, three pending.
- Launched the Bipolar and Calcar Hip instrumentation systems, developed with customers.
- Worked with team of Japanese surgeons to design custom implants for Asian population.
- Analyzed structural integrity of various hip prostheses by Finite Element Analysis.

1997–1998 **DEFENSE INTELLIGENCE AGENCY / PENTAGON** **Washington, DC**
Analyst, Strategic Industries Branch
- Researched new technological developments in foreign countries, briefed division heads.
- Wrote articles in specialty field for internal publication to decision makers.

1995 **MISSILE & SPACE INTELLIGENCE CENTER** **Huntsville, AL**
Intern, Surface to Air Missile Division
- Researched modifications to a foreign missile and resulting impact on U.S. defense strategies.
- Served as co-liaison to White Sands Testing Range and Sandia National Lab for testing.

Other: Unigraphics, ProENGINEER, SolidWorks ANSYS, C, working knowledge of Korean and German.
Interests include symphony playing, triathlons, downhill skiing, cycling, and woodworking.

EXHIBIT 2

Anatomy and Stone Removal Procedures

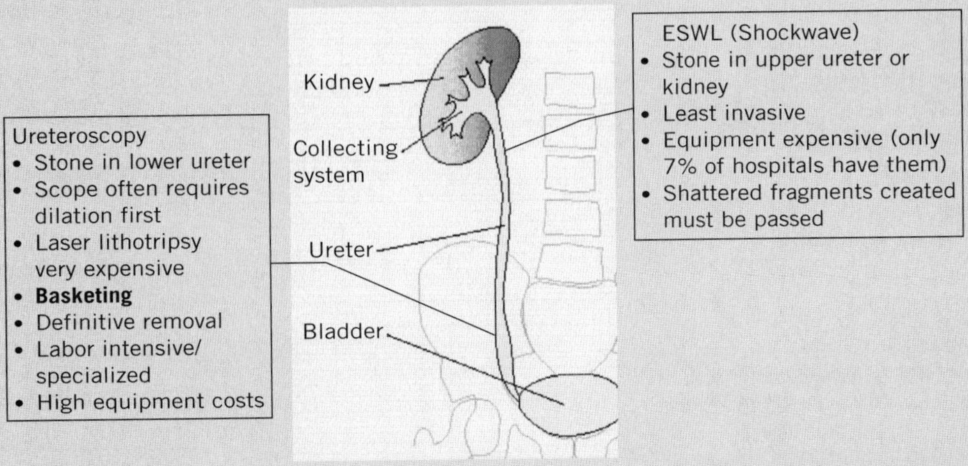
Ureteroscopy
• Stone in lower ureter
• Scope often requires dilation first
• Laser lithotripsy very expensive
• Basketing
• Definitive removal
• Labor intensive/ specialized
• High equipment costs
Kidney
Collecting system
Ureter
Bladder
ESWL (Shockwave)
• Stone in upper ureter or kidney
• Least invasive
• Equipment expensive (only 7% of hospitals have them)
• Shattered fragments created must be passed

EXHIBIT 3

The SRS: Insertion and Expanded Forms

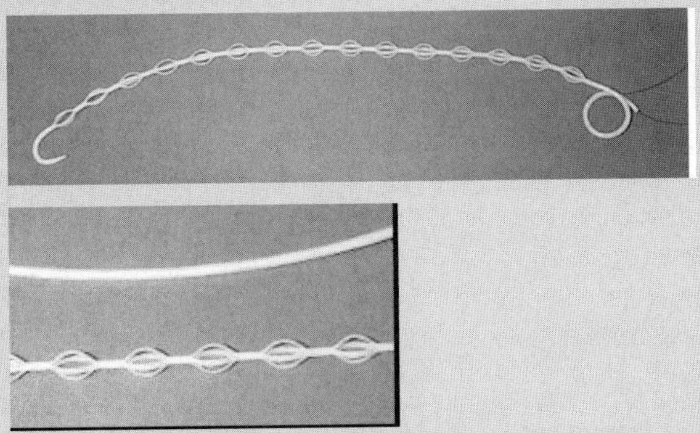

States, about 7 percent of all hospitals. Over $2 billion was spent every year on treating kidney stones. The average per patient annual expenditure was in the range of $7,000, excluding pharmaceuticals.

Sarah found that in the early 2000s there were approximately 260,000 primary and secondary procedures each year in the United States. Since the SRS had proven effective in capturing smaller stones that were currently left painfully untreated, she added in 75 percent of those for a total U.S. market of 800,000 target procedures (see Exhibit 4). At a price of $250 each, the SRS represented a $200 million opportunity.

Customers

The two main customers for this stent would be urologists and medical centers. The urologist determined the procedure and decided which device would be used. The actual buyer would be the hospital, where purchasing administrators kept an eagle eye on the costs, and were often strongly influenced by reimbursement procedure policies set by the Center for Medicare and by Medicaid Services. One method hospitals used to cut costs was to order aggregated packages of devices and services from highly diversified suppliers such as Johnson & Johnson.

Urologists were well educated, risk averse, and generally not keen on trying brand new devices and procedures. A physician's chief concerns would include patient comfort and safety, risk, and reimbursement. A decision to try an innovative device was most often prompted by a visit from a trusted sales representative. In making that decision, the urologist would be most influenced by endorsements from academically respected colleagues and from sound technical data from clinical studies. In 2001, there were just over 7,100 licensed urologists in the United States, with most treating stones. A typical urologist cared for a large patient population, averaging 140 stone patients per year.

EXHIBIT 4

Procedure Market Tree

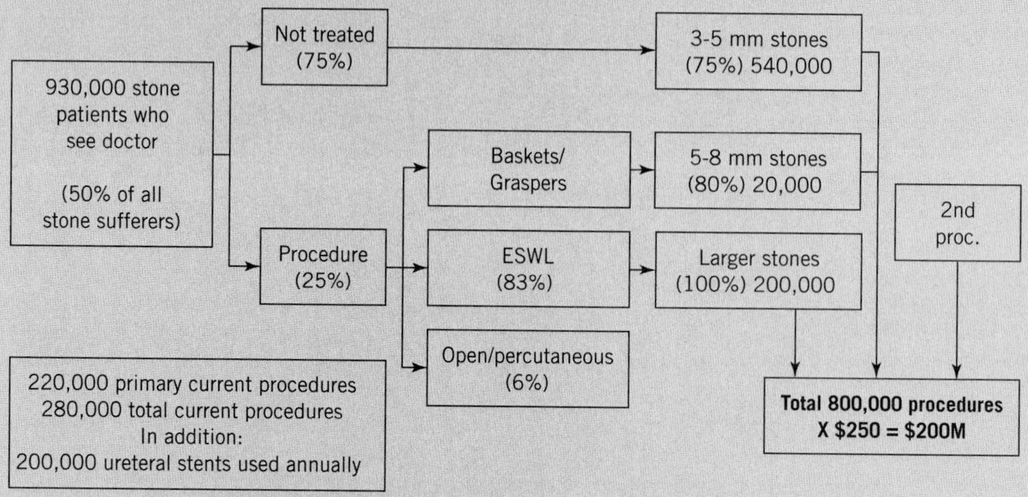

In the Internet age, patients were becoming more educated about options, and could therefore be strong influencers. Patient concerns included relieving immediate pain, avoiding invasive procedures, and the definitive removal of the stone. Kidney stone patients were most often Caucasians between the ages of 20 and 40. Eighty percent were likely to have a recurrence.

Attracting the Competition

The main competitors were those who had a leading market share in basket retrieval and ureteral stent devices (see Exhibit 5). Stents like the Double-J were simple devices, produced by many manufacturers, and were not purchased on the basis of any technological superiority.

EXHIBIT 5

Competitor Profiles

	Location	Employees	Revenues	Products	Price Points	Perception
Cook Urological private	Spencer, IN	300, incl mnf (4,000 all Cook)	$25.1M	Stents, baskets, wires, and other lithotripsers	Medium	Good products and innovative—strong company (esp. good #1 in biliary market)
BARD Urological	Covington, GA	8,100 (all BARD)	$95M w/out Foleys ($360M total) 1999	Stents, baskets, laser, and other lithotripsers	Low-end	Slow, no innovation
Microvasive (Boston Scientific)	Natick, MA	14,400 (all BSC)	$143M $133M (stones) 1999	Stents, baskets, laser, and other lithotripsers	High-end	Innovative (with acquisitions), good sales force, good products
Surgitek (ACMI) private	Southboro, MA (HQ); Racine, WI (Urology)		$17M stents	Stents, baskets, scopes, lasers	Low-end	Based on quantity, but no innovation, hungry for new products
Applied Medical	Rancho Santa Margarita, CA	375, incl mnf	$31M (all three divisions) 2001	Various dilators and specialty stuff	High-end	Interesting, good, clever products, not full product line

Revenue leader Boston Scientific had made many acquisitions. This suggested to Sarah that their internal R&D structure did not provide the company with sufficient numbers of new innovations. Unit leader ACMI was undergoing a restructuring and a change of leadership that seemed indicative of a lull in new innovations. Neither company had a presence in the ESWL market.

Makers of the ESWL machines and laser lithotripsers were also suppliers of ESWL accessories such as water bags and fluids. Sarah reasoned that large sellers like Dornier MedTech and Siemens Medical Systems might have an early-stage interest in a product like the SRS, since it worked in conjunction with ESWL. In a sense, though, every stent competitor in the space was a potential distributor—or a research and development partner or parent. Major players in the industry, with their established and credible sales and marketing capabilities, could significantly affect the speed of adoption of new devices.

Unlike most ventures, the strategy would not be to go up against top competitors, and investors would have little interest in closely monitoring the usual metrics such as sales revenues, gross margins, and projected net income. The objective would be to establish a following among the best medical practitioners in the world—even if that meant giving away the stents for free. Sarah felt that once the SRS had proven market demand, the company would then have an excellent chance of being acquired.

Startup

Working part time, Sarah completed the business plan in the late summer of 2001. Since an acquisition harvest could not be accurately timed or priced, financial projections for the company she had named Newland Medical Technologies followed a standard scenario of steady growth (see Exhibit 6). By the spring of the following year, she had raised just over $600,000 in seed

EXHIBIT 6

Newland Pro Forma Income Statement

	2004	2005	2006	2007	2008
Net Revenues	0	721,000	8,380,000	22,327,000	34,811,625
Total Cost of Goods Sold (see below)	0	335,160	2,692,135	6,620,487	9,434,219
Percent of Revenues		46.5%	32.1%	29.7%	27.1%
Gross Profit	0	385,840	5,687,865	15,706,513	25,377,406
Percent of Revenues		53.5%	67.9%	70.3%	72.9%
Operating Expenses					
Sales & Marketing	166,200	939,900	1,573,016	2,379,059	2,858,596
Research & Development	225,240	448,795	600,140	947,216	1,105,338
General & Administrative	153,800	315,700	680,055	1,057,531	1,398,100
Total Operating Expenses	545,240	1,704,395	2,853,211	4,383,806	5,362,034
Net Earnings before Taxes	(545,240)	(1,318,555)	2,834,654	11,322,707	20,015,372
Taxes	0	0	498,899	4,529,083	8,006,149
Net Earnings	(545,240)	(1,318,555)	2,335,755	6,793,624	12,009,223
Cost of Goods Sold Breakdown (e.g., 2005)					
Direct Costs					
Average Material Cost per Unit	8				
Average Labor Cost per Unit	14				
Sterilizing and Packaging per Unit	8				
Manufacturer per Unit Markup (20%)	6				
Total per Unit Direct Costs	36				
Direct Costs: 6,200 Units (2005)	223,200				
Indirect Costs					
Salaries and Benefits	84,750				
Facility; Shipping	7,210				
Depreciation	20,000				
Total Indirect Costs	111,960				
Cost of Goods & Services	335,160				

capital from friends, family, Dr. Grainer, and her own savings. When she began to discuss assembling a cohesive venture team, Sarah was surprised to learn that Dr. Grainer had been assuming all along that she would serve as president and CEO. While she was very excited about the opportunity, she also knew what she didn't know:

> To do it the right way, I was going to need some practical business education. In the fall of 2002, I was accepted into the MBA program at the F.W. Olin Graduate School of Business [at Babson College in Wellesley, Massachusetts]. I then switched jobs, to a position with a well-defined, short-range end point.

Patent work—mostly legal—took nearly a year and drained a third of the capital she had raised. After completing some additional R&D work on the stent, Sarah applied for Food and Drug Administration (FDA) approval. Given her past experience with Johnson & Johnson, and some good advice from an expert at Babson College, no one was surprised when the SRS sailed through the usually tough FDA process in just under three months. Sarah recalled the strategy:

> Professor Boulnois[2] had come up with the idea of taking a two-tiered approach. First we got the SRS approved as a basic drainage stent—no problem there. When we filed our follow-on application with a different indication—stone removal—we got lucky because we had the same reviewer for both applications. She saw that it was the identical device that she had just approved, with a new indication, and because of that, we received that next approval in less than 30 days. And because stents are an established category of medical devices, we got our reimbursement codes in far less time than it would normally take a company with a brand new technology.[3]

While attending the Olin School, Sarah spent much of her time looking for the $1.7 million in venture funding she estimated Newland would need to commercialize the SRS device. After pitching her plan to numerous investors, angel groups, and at business plan forums in the Boston area, Sarah came across a business development foundation in Rhode Island. They agreed to put up $65,000—as long as 20 percent was spent directly in Rhode Island. As a result, Sarah began working with a company in that state to produce prototypes in a manner that would satisfy the stringent FDA production and quality requirements. The company was also offering a total solution under one roof—from extrusion to packaging.

By the time she had graduated in January 2004, Sarah had attracted two additional team members—an engineer she had met at a previous job and a business development talent who had approached her at a business plan forum. Since she had no money to pay them, in both cases she offered to "back pay" their earned salaries from the next round of funding she expected to raise.

Even though the economy had substantially recovered following the 2001 recession, investors were still very cautious. Ever since they had received FDA approval, Sarah had been meeting with and receiving helpful feedback and additional contacts from numerous venture capitalists. She finally concluded, however, that Newland was at too early a stage for that type of investor.

At a business plan competition in spring 2004, a fellow Babson graduate recommended that she speak with his uncle, a local philanthropist and retired venture investor. Sarah recalled that at first the lead appeared to be yet another dead end:

> Peter Cunningham is in his seventies, and he had told his nephew Bill that he wasn't doing any more investments. But Bill said, "You've got to meet this woman and see what she is doing." So I met him in November, and soon after, he became our first angel investor.

Mr. Cunningham invested $250,000 and attracted two other local angels, who each invested $75,000. The capital was a long way from full funding, but it provided sustaining salaries for the team and a one-room incubator space in Boston's south end—halfway between two major medical research centers. Their proximity to those research labs would prove immediately critical.

Setbacks

By getting to know the researchers at the animal testing facilities at New England Medical, Sarah noted that they were able to further Newland's research at almost no cost:

> The labs were doing their cardio work on pigs in the morning and working with the urinary tract system most every afternoon. They were curious about the SRS capabilities and were willing to add our stent to their work with the ureters. It was great; we didn't have to hang around for it, and we could just walk over to discuss what sorts of indications and challenges they had identified.

[2] Dr. Jean-Luc Boulnois, an adjunct professor at Babson College, was founder and president of Interactive Consulting, Inc., a management consulting firm specializing in business development for European early-stage medical technology companies entering the U.S. market.

[3] By the early 2000s, the Centers for Medicare & Medicaid Services (CMS) had become a bottleneck challenge for many ventures seeking to commercialize a medical device product. The CMS was charged with the subjective task of evaluating the costs and benefits of particular technologies—an evolving field with plenty of room for debate. Reimbursement issues could be so complex and complicated that receiving payment for new products had become the greatest stumbling block for early entrants—and CMS was only one piece of the coverage approval puzzle. To achieve reimbursement coverage and payment throughout the country for a new technology, medical device ventures were required to weave their way through a maze of several hundred payers. Moreover, new products had to struggle to get assigned a unique code that would distinguish them from existing technologies. Even after that code was assigned, it might take several years for Medicare to recognize that device as a new cost. Since health care facilities wouldn't use products that had not received proper payment approvals, it was not unusual for reimbursement gaps to derail the implementation of viable, FDA approved medical device innovations.

While pre-FDA approval trials had confirmed that the SRS would perform as expected once the device was placed in the ureter, these latest tests brought to light some serious design flaws. Sarah explained:

> Back when we started, the first five stents we designed wouldn't fit in the ureter. So our focus became making the baskets small enough to fit inside a sheath. We made a bunch, and when 15 in a row deployed successfully and worked as expected, I immediately began to move forward on developing the business plan. Then when we got FDA approval and the reimbursement codes, I figured we were ready to go out into the market.
>
> The problem was Dr. Grainer and I hadn't talked to enough doctors early on when we were still in that design stage. For example, we chose an insertion guide wire that was larger than the standard—but one that an advisor said ought to be fine. We had created a device that worked—it could stay in the body, it dilated the ureter, patients didn't feel any pain, and it caught stones—but because our design was far more difficult to place than a standard stent, we had failed to create a salable product. When it became clear that this was never going to take off as a commercial venture, we went back to the drawing board.

Significantly compounding this challenge was that her chosen manufacturer had turned out to be not even remotely capable of being a one-stop shop. As a result, the team was compelled to assemble a supply chain of specialists: an extruder, a fine-tooling shop, a coating company, a sterilization expert, and a medical packager. While Sarah was pleased that this arrangement gave them more control over quality at each level of production, she understood that the need to pass off work-in-process between several companies would extend lead times and increase the possibility of communication challenges. From a strategy perspective, she explained that developing a single-site manufacturing capability may not have been the way to go anyway:

> I have found no consensus on whether medical device companies like ours should spend time and money perfecting a manufacturing capability. Some investors feel that having a production capacity would boost our appeal as an acquisition. Other investors feel just the opposite, that a big company like Boston Scientific would acquire Newland for the value of its patented devices, and would probably prefer to develop their own manufacturing systems.

Rebirth and Conception

In late 2004, the team—bolstered by 60 successful patient trials and very positive feedback from a range of physicians—began their full-scale effort to build a critical mass of advocates and attract at least one major distributor. They got a significant boost in March 2005, when Boston-based Taylor Medical Supply (TMS) agreed to test Newland's stent in a few of their major markets in the United States.

Meanwhile, Sarah focused on raising funds to restore coffers depleted from the struggle to get back to the point where they had thought they had been months earlier. At an angel investor breakfast in late May, she met a pair of harvested entrepreneurs looking for investment opportunities. Chris Fallon had made his money when his single-product banking software venture was acquired by a major financial corporation in New York. Claudia Grimes was the cofounder of an adventure sports vacation portal that was snapped up by a multinational travel agency—just eight months after her venture had proven sales and profitability.

Both investors expressed interest in Newland, particularly because they felt that the company was at an excellent point for a lucrative early-stage acquisition. Sarah explained:

> There are a few times when you can sell a medical device company like ours: after a product development milestone like proof of concept on animals, after FDA approval, after a series of successful clinical trials, and after your first million or so in sales.
>
> Chris and Claudia were certain that since we had a patented product that had FDA approval and payment codes, it was an excellent time for us to sell. They could see we were ready for market, and they were talking about putting up at least $200,000 apiece—as long as we pursued an acquisition strategy. Although an early-stage acquisition (pre-sales) was never in our plan, the more we thought about it, the more it sounded like an attractive option.

One constituent that was not pleased with what they saw as an abrupt shift in strategy was Taylor Medical Supply. Sarah thought that their displeasure was particularly acute because of the way they learned about the change:

> Things had started to move very fast. We chose an investment banker whose initial task was to act as an intermediary between Newland and potential buyers. He called TMS to let them know we were pursing an acquisition, and to ask if they wanted in on it. They were definitely taken aback. They told the investment banker that from their perspective we'd been moving toward a distribution deal. That was news to me; they had never seemed more than lukewarm about taking on our device. Not only did they decline to put in an offer, but they suspended their test marketing of the SRS. Still, they did indicate that initial feedback from their clients had been very positive.

With endorsements from two prominent medical centers, and a few promising acquisition prospects considering the possibilities, it seemed that momentum was building for a speedy harvest. Encouraged by Newland's progress, that summer, Sarah and her husband ran the numbers—with an allowance for misconceptions—and estimated that is was an excellent time to start a family. On paper, their planned parenthood coincided well with the harvest schedule that Newland's newest investors were espousing. The couple was a bit shocked, but thoroughly delighted, when Sarah became pregnant that very month. Well, she mused, maybe the acquisition strategy would continue to charge down a similar fast track. It didn't.

A Fork in the Road with a Baby on Board

Despite assurances that all was going according to their plan, by the fall, Sarah was having a hard time dealing with the aggressive angels she'd brought on. The nature of the relationship provided them with a good deal of latitude with regard to setting the pace and direction of the acquisition strategy that Sarah and her original investors had signed off on, and it wasn't long before Chris and Claudia began to demand changes in the deal structure that would provide them with better returns.

In mid-October 2005, their investment banker brought an offer to the table from a middle-tier medical supply distributor based in Florida. The $9.5 million term sheet provided a generous five-year earn-out for Sarah and her team—provided they stayed on in Boston to develop a line of innovative stents. The terms also required that Sarah serve as president, and it was contingent upon FDA approval of Newland's latest innovation—now in early trials.[4] The offer provided no funds to make that happen, and when Chris and Claudia said that any further capital would have to come with additional equity, Sarah finally decided to confide in her original investors:

> I had kept Chris Cunningham and his group apprised of our decision to seek an acquisition, and they had agreed with that. But these two entrepreneur angels were so difficult to work with, and neither of them had any experience in the medical industry. Maybe that's not a crucial requirement, but overall, they just didn't seem to get what we were about. Mr. Cunningham looked at me and said, "Well, if what has been stopping you from tossing these two aside was the money, you should have come to me earlier."

But for Sarah this wasn't just about the money, the equity split, or the harvest: it was about developing new and exciting medical products that could make a difference. Nevertheless, as president she felt that if Newland could strike a deal with a large company that would give current investors a decent return and provide Newland with a base of resources to further new product development, then that was the path she ought to pursue. On the other hand, staying the course and building a line of innovative products would significantly increase their acquisition value.

If not for her pregnancy, Sarah wouldn't hesitate for a moment; she'd return to their original strategy—and to her passion for building an innovative medical device enterprise. To pursue that course now, however, she would be facing the prospect of being a new mother *and* running a growing business. With an offer on the table and funds running short, she swallowed hard against a particularly acute bout of morning sickness. It was time to make some tough decisions.

[4] Newland Medical was working on a line of stents designed to hold the ureter open against, for example, external compression from a tumor. Newland's ureteral structural stents would be significantly more resistant to compression than any product that was currently on the market. These devices would allow patients with locally and regionally invasive tumors (typically end-stage and terminal) to survive longer with healthy kidney function. Taking into account national occurrence rates for diseases that tended to exert pressure on urinary passageways, the team estimated that this represented a $25 million market opportunity.

III

PART THREE

The Founder and Team

Entrepreneurial founders must take a personal role in attracting, motivating, inspiring, and retaining an effective team of both specialists and generalists. The quality of that team has never been more fundamental and important than it is now. The new millennium has ushered in a wave of new opportunities that will require nimble and creative teams. Some pundits have characterized this time as the communication era, characterized by galloping innovation—fueled by the ability of inventive engineers and creative entrepreneurs to instantly access and share information worldwide. Stung by the dot.com fallout and the recession that followed, private and venture capital investors have a renewed appreciation for the time-tested wisdom that successful new ventures are often all about the team. Chapter 7—The Entrepreneurial Manager—looks at the leadership issues inherent in building a company from scratch—and the significant recruiting, sales, and management skills the founder(s) must bring to bear as the enterprise grows through various stages.

Entrepreneurship titles now dominate the business sections at major booksellers like Barnes & Noble, and a growing number of students and professionals are seeking career opportunities in the entrepreneurial sector. While this has created a significant pool of talent to support the development of new ventures, one of the most critical aspects of entrepreneuring is in being able to attract the *right* people: team players whose skills and know-how are critical to the success of the enterprise. Ambiguity, risk, and the need to collectively turn on a dime in the face of shifting competitive landscapes require that entrepreneurial teams be greater than the sum of their parts. Like marriage, forming and building that team can be a rather unscientific, occasionally unpredictable, and frequently surprising experience. In Chapter 8, The New Venture Team, we put a zoom lens on the "people" portion of the Timmons model.

The solo entrepreneur may make a living, but it is the team builder who develops an organization and a company with sustainable value and attractive harvest options. The vision of what these founders are trying to accomplish provides the unwritten ground rules that become the fabric, character, and purpose behind the venture. Effective lead entrepreneurs are able to build a culture around the business mission and the brand by rewarding success, supporting honest failure, sharing the wealth with those who helped to create it, and setting high ethical standards of conduct. Chapter 9—Personal Ethics and the Entrepreneur—addresses the complex and thorny issues of ethics and integrity for the entrepreneur, and how those decisions and choices can have a significant impact on future success.

7

Chapter Seven

The Entrepreneurial Manager

It's rare to find a leader who can carry a growing company through all its phases. When you get into the $1-to-$2-billion range, then you may find leaders with entrepreneurial tendencies; but, in addition, they have real management and people skills.

Peter J. Sprague
Chairman of the Board, National Semiconductor Corporation

Results Expected

Upon completion of this chapter, you will have:

1. Studied different views about entrepreneurial managers and discovered that an individual can be both an entrepreneur and a manager.
2. Identified the stages of growth entrepreneurial ventures go through, the domain occupied, the venture modes characteristic of the entrepreneurial domain, and the principal forces acting in the domain.
3. Identified specific skills entrepreneurs need to know to manage startup, survival, and growth.
4. Analyzed the new "Dawson Products" case study.
5. Evaluated your own skills and developed an action plan.

The Entrepreneurial Domain

Converging on the Entrepreneurial Manager

There are convergent pressures on being an entrepreneur and being a manager as a venture accelerates and grows beyond founder-driven and founder-dominated survival. Key to achieving sustained growth, and an eventual harvest, is an entrepreneur's ability to have or develop competencies as an entrepreneurial manager.

In the past, those studying entrepreneurship and others active in starting new ventures, such as venture capitalists, professors, and researchers, have generally believed that the kind of person with the entrepreneurial spirit required to propel a new venture through startup to a multi-million-dollar annual sales level is different from the kind of person who has the capacity to manage the new firm as it grows from zero to $20 million or more in sales. Further, it has long been thought that the entrepreneur who clings to the lead role too long will limit or impede company growth.

As John Kenneth Galbraith explained in 1971, "The great entrepreneur must, in fact, be compared in life with the male *apis mellifera.* He accomplishes his act of conception at the price of his own extinction."[1] In short, conventional wisdom stated that a

[1] John Kenneth Galbraith, *The New Industrial State* (Boston: Houghton Mifflin, 1971).

good entrepreneur is usually not a good manager, since he or she lacks the necessary management skill and experience. Likewise, it is assumed that a manager is not an entrepreneur, since he or she lacks some intense personal qualities and the orientation required to launch a business from ground zero.

While results are mixed, some evidence suggests that new ventures that flourish beyond startup and grow to become substantial, successful enterprises can be headed by entrepreneurs who are also effective managers. Testing conventional wisdom, two researchers empirically studied the tenure of 54 Fortune 1,000 corporations' founders. They assumed that there are three ways founders have to adapt: (1) shift from creation to exploitation, (2) shift from passionate commitment to dispassionate objectivity, and (3) shift from direct personal control over organizational actions to indirect impersonal control. Taking into account the growth rate, the timing of the initial public offering, the founder's age, education, and other factors, this 1990 study found the following:

1. If the firm grows relatively slowly, and the founder is capable of some adaptation, then the firm can apparently become quite large.
2. Founders with scientific or engineering backgrounds remain in control of the companies they found for shorter periods than do founders whose academic focus was business.
3. The founder's tenure will typically be longer in family-dominated firms.[2]

More recently, researchers "observed that many founders can and do manage growth successfully. The applicability of conventional wisdom regarding the 'leadership crisis' in rapid-growth entrepreneurial firms may no longer be valid, if, in fact, it ever was."[3] Founder Bill Gates still heads Microsoft, founder; Steve Jobs is once again at the helm of Apple Computer, and founder Andy Grove is now the senior advisor to executive management at Intel. Numerous examples such as this clearly indicate founders can learn and grow faster than their companies do.

These and other data seem to defy the notion that entrepreneurs can start but cannot manage growing companies. While the truth is probably somewhere in between, one thing is apparent: Growing a higher potential venture requires management skills.

Clearly, a complex set of factors goes into making someone a successful entrepreneurial manager. Launching a new venture and then managing rapid growth involves managerial roles and tasks not found in most mature or stable environments. Further, one of the greatest strengths of successful entrepreneurs is that they know what they do and do not know. They have disciplined intellectual honesty, which prevents their optimism from becoming myopic delusion and their dreams from becoming blind ambition. No individual has all these skills, nor does the presence or absence of any single skill guarantee success or failure. That an entrepreneur knows that he or she needs a certain skill and knows where to get it is as valuable as knowing whether he or she already has it.

Principal Forces and Venture Models

Companies, whether they are new, growing, or mature, occupy a place in either an administrative or an entrepreneurial domain, an area influenced by certain principal forces and characterized by ways of acting, called venture modes. Exhibits 7.1 and 7.2 illustrate the entrepreneurial and administrative domains and the dynamic of the principal forces acting in the domains and the dominant venture modes that result.

In the exhibits, the four cells are defined by the stage of the venture (upper axis), the extent of change and uncertainty accompanying it (right axis), and the degree to which a venture is administrative (bottom axis) or entrepreneurial (left axis). Clearly, the entrepreneurial domain is the two upper cells in both exhibits, and the domains are functions of both the change and uncertainty facing a venture and the stage of growth of the venture.

Each venture mode (i.e., way of acting) for firms in each cell is driven by certain principal forces. These forces are shown in Exhibit 7.2. Shown in Exhibit 7.1 are dominant venture modes characteristic of firms in each cell. Organizations at different stages are characterized by differing degrees of change and uncertainty and are therefore more or less entrepreneurial or more or less administrative. Thus, for example, a new venture in the seed/startup stage, which is characterized by high change and uncertainty, is most entrepreneurial. These firms will be new, innovative, or backbone ventures; will be led by a team; will be driven by their founders' goals, values, commitment, and perceptions of the opportunities; and will minimize the use of resources. At the other extreme is a mature firm, one that is in the maturity stage and characterized by low change and uncertainty, is stable or contracting, is led by an administrator or custodian, is driven by resource ownership

[2] George C. Rubenson and Anil K. Gupta, "The Founder's Disease: A Critical Reexamination," *Frontiers of Entrepreneurship Research: 1990,* ed. Neil Churchill et al. (Babson Park, MA: Babson College, 1990), pp. 177–78.

[3] Gary E. Willard, David A. Krueger, and Henry R. Feeser, "In Order to Grow, Must the Founder Go: A Comparison of Performance between Founder and Non-Founder Managed High-Growth Manufacturing Firms," *Journal of Business Venturing* 7, 1996, p. 190.

EXHIBIT 7.1

Dominant Venture Modes

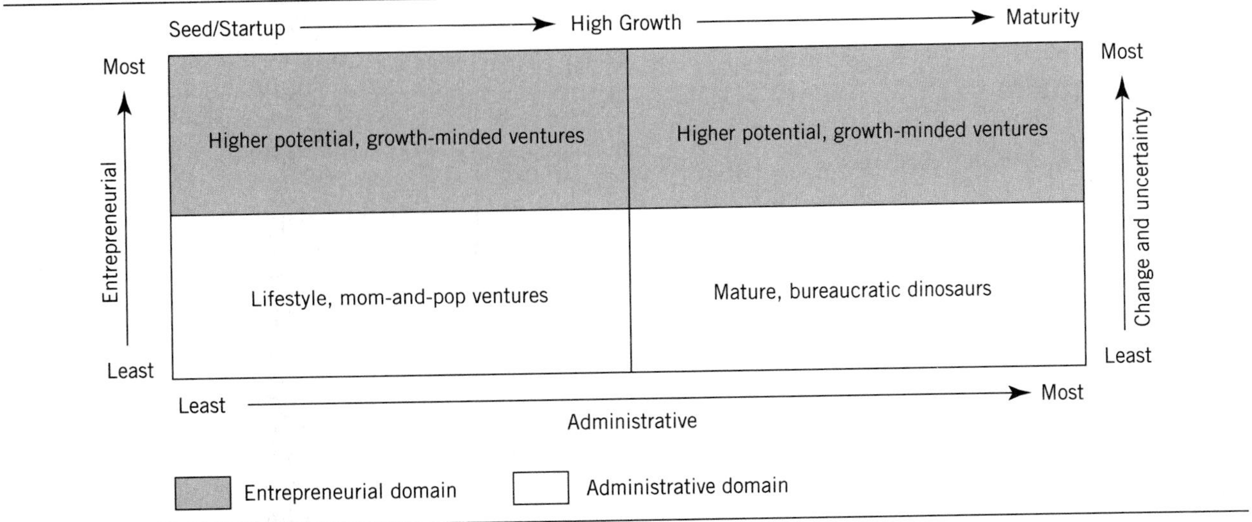

Source: These exhibits are built on work by Timmons and Stevenson: See Howard H. Stevenson, "A New Paradigm for Entrepreneurial Management," in *Entrepreneurship: What It Is and How to Teach It* (Harvard Business School, 1985), pp. 30–51; and Jeffry A. Timmons and Howard H. Stevenson, "Entrepreneurship Education in the 80s: What Entrepreneurs Say," in *Entrepreneurship: What It Is and How to Teach It*, pp. 115–34.

and administrative efficiency, and is reactive. Other firms fall in between.

The managerial skills required of the firms in each cell are more evident upon examination of these principal forces and dominant venture modes. For example, creativity and comprehensive managerial skills are required to manage firms in both cells in the entrepreneurial domain. In the upper-left-hand cell, entrepreneurial managers need to cope effectively with high levels of change and uncertainty, whether their management skills can be affectionately labeled MBWA (management by wandering around, of

EXHIBIT 7.2

Principal Driving Forces

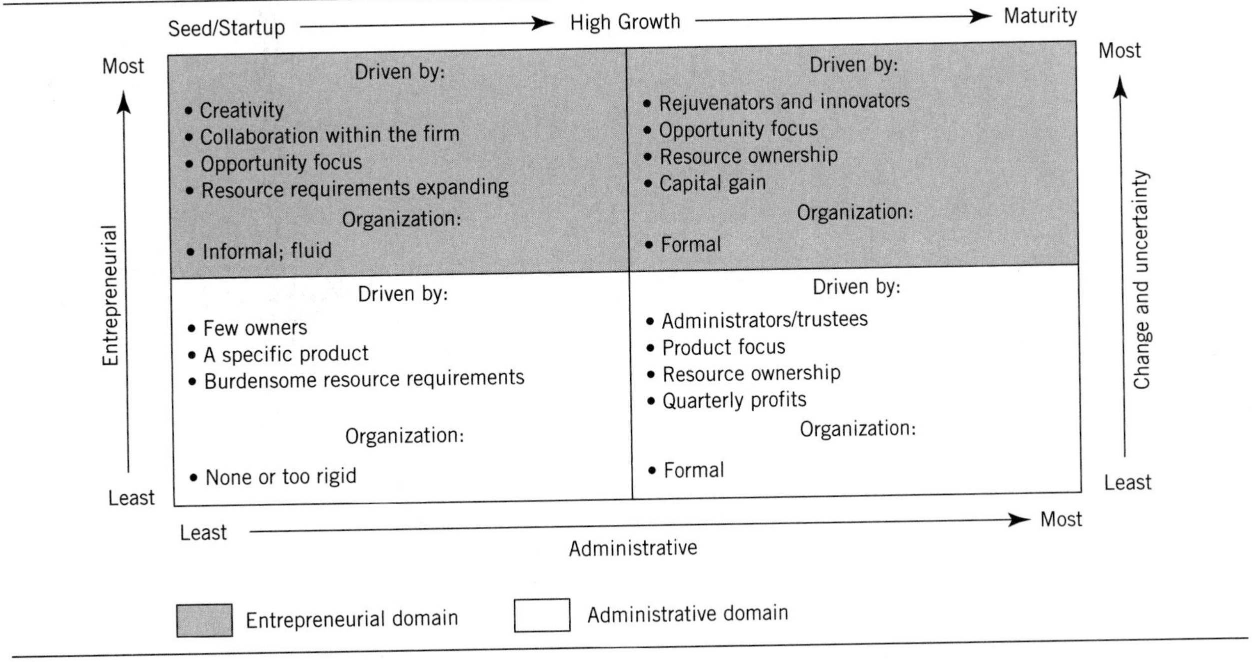

Hewlett-Packard fame) or management by muddling through. Certainly, as the firm enters the high-growth stage, this changes.

Stages of Growth

A Theoretical View

Clearly, entrepreneurship is not static. Exhibit 7.3 represents a *theoretical* view of the process of gestation and growth of new ventures and the transitions that occur at different "boundaries" in this process.[4] Ventures are sown, sprout, grown, and harvested. Even those successful ventures that are not grown to harvest (i.e., those that have been defined as "attractive") go through stages of growth.

This smooth, S-shape curve in the exhibit is rarely, if ever, replicated in the real world. If one actually tracked the progress of most emerging companies, the "curve" actually would be a ragged and jagged line with many ups and downs; these companies would experience some periods of rapid progress followed by setbacks and accompanying crises.

For the purposes of illustration, Exhibit 7.3 shows venture stages in terms of time, sales, and number of employees. It is at the boundaries between stages that new ventures seem to experience transitions. Several researchers have noted that the new venture invariably goes through transition and will face certain issues.[5] Thus, the exhibit shows the crucial transitions during growth and the key management tasks of the chief executive officer or founders. Most important and most challenging for the founding entrepreneur or a chief executive officer is coping with crucial transitions and the change in management tasks, going from managing to managing managers, as a firm grows to roughly 30 employees, to 50, to 75, and then up.

[4] For another useful view of the stages of development of a firm and required management capabilities, see Carroll V. Kroeger, "Management Development and the Small Firm," *California Management Review* 17, no. 1 (Fall 1974), pp. 41–47.

[5] L. A. Griener, "Evolution and Revolution as Organizations Grow," in *Trials and Rewards of the Entrepreneur* (Boston: Harvard Business Review, 1977), pp. 47–56; and H. N. Woodward, "Management Strategies for Small Companies," in *Trials and Rewards of the Entrepreneur* (Boston: Harvard Business Review, 1981), pp. 57–66.

EXHIBIT 7.3

Stages of Venture Growth, Crucial Transitions, and Core Management Mode

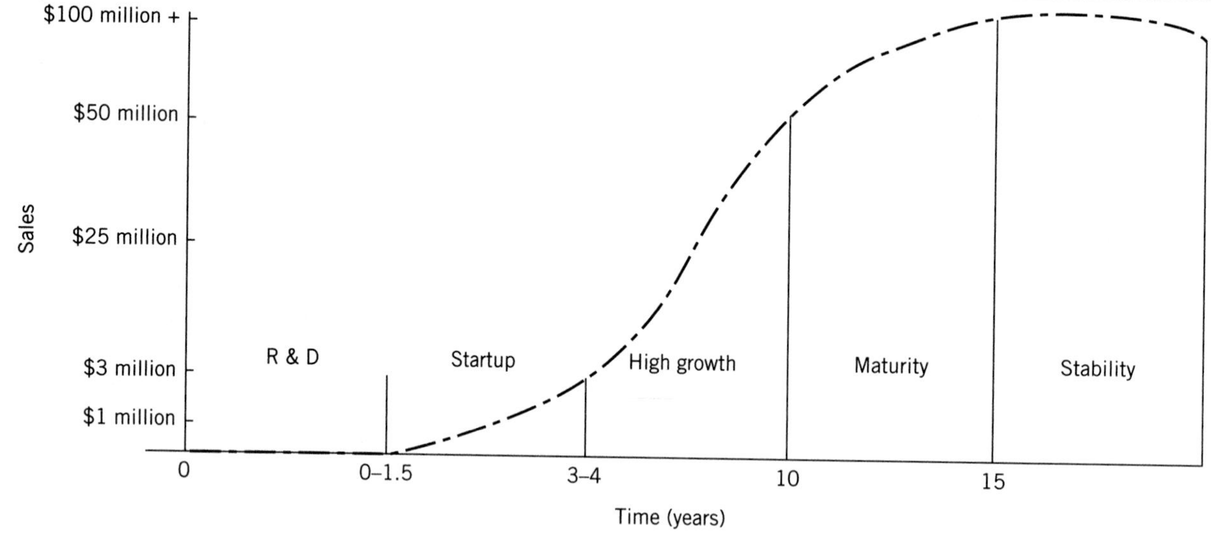

Crucial transitions:

Sales	0–$5 million	$5–$15 million	$10–$25 million+
Employees	0 to 20–25	25–75	75–100+
Core management mode	Doing	Managing	Managing managers

The *research and development stage*, sometimes referred to as the nascent stage, is characterized by a single aspiring entrepreneur, or small team, doing the investigation and due diligence for their business idea. The nascent stage can be as short as a few months or can last years. Research indicates that if an idea is not turned into a going concern within 18 months, the chances of a startup fall dramatically. Nascent entrepreneurs have many fits and starts, and the business model can change often in the process.

The *startup stage,* a stage that usually covers the first two or three years but perhaps as many as seven, is by far the most perilous stage and is characterized by the direct and exhaustive drive, energy, and entrepreneurial talent of a lead entrepreneur and a key team member or two. Here, the critical mass of people, market and financial results, and competitive resiliency are established, while investor, banker, and customer confidence is earned. The level of sales reached varies widely, but typically ranges between \$2 million and \$20 million. A new company then begins its high growth stage. The exact point at which this occurs can rarely be identified by a date on the calendar until well after the fact. It is in this stage that new ventures exhibit a failure rate exceeding 60 percent; that is, it is in this stage that the lemons ripen.

As with the other stages, the length of time it takes to go through the *high growth stage,* as well as the magnitude of change occurring during the period, varies greatly. Probably the most difficult challenge for the founding entrepreneur occurs during the high growth stage, when he or she finds it is necessary to let go of power and control (through veto) over key decisions that he or she has always had, and when key responsibilities need to be delegated without abdicating ultimate leadership and responsibility for results. But the challenges do not end there. For example, sales of Litton's microwave oven division had reached \$13 million, and it had 275 employees. The long-range plan called for building sales volume to \$100 million in five to seven years (i.e., growing at 40 percent per year, compounded). The head of the division said, "Having studied the market for the previous two years, I was convinced that the only limit on our growth was our organization's inability to grow as rapidly as the market opportunities."[6]

From the high growth stage, a company then moves to what is called the *maturity stage.* In this stage, the key issue for the company is no longer survival; rather, it is one of steady, profitable growth. The *stability stage* usually follows.

Managing for Rapid Growth

Managing for rapid growth involves a management orientation not found in mature and stable environments. (This topic will be addressed again in Chapter 16.) For one thing, the tenet that one's responsibility must equal one's authority is often very counterproductive in a rapid-growth venture. Instead, results usually require close collaboration of a manager with other people than his or her subordinates, and managers invariably have responsibilities far exceeding their authority. Politics and personal power can be a way of life in many larger and stagnant institutions, as managers jockey for influence and a piece of a shrinking pie in a zero-sum game; but in rapid-growth firms, power and control are delegated. Everyone is committed to making the pie larger, and power and influence are derived not only from achieving one's own goals but also from contributing to the achievements of others as well. Influence also is derived from keeping the overall goals in mind, from resolving differences, and from developing a reputation as a person who gets results, can manage others, and grows managerial talent as well.

Thus, among successful entrepreneurs and entrepreneurial managers, there is a well-developed capacity to exert influence *without* formal power. These people are adept at conflict resolution. They know when to use logic and when to persuade, when to make a concession and when to exact one. To run a successful venture, an entrepreneur learns to get along with many different constituencies, often with conflicting aims—the customer, the supplier, the financial backer, and the creditor, as well as the partners and others on the inside. Similarly, an entrepreneurial manager must operate in a world that is increasingly interdependent. Attempting to advise managers on how to exert "influence without authority," Allan R. Cohen and David L. Bradford assert, "If you are a manager, you not only need to exercise influence skills with your peers and your own boss, but also to help the people who work for you learn to be effective influencers—even of you—since that will free you to spend more of your time seeking new opportunities and working the organization above and around you."[7]

Whereas successful entrepreneurs are interpersonally supporting and nurturing—not interpersonally competitive—successful entrepreneurial managers understand their interdependencies and have learned to incorporate mutual respect, openness, trust, and mutual benefit into their management style. Fundamental to this progressive style of management is the

[6] William W. George, "Task Teams for Rapid Growth," *Harvard Business Review,* March–April 1977.

[7] David L. Bradford and Allan R. Cohen, *Power Up: Transforming Organizations through Shared Leadership* (New York: John Wiley & Sons, 1998).

EXHIBIT 7.4

Entrepreneurial Transitions

Modes/Stages	Planning	Doing	Managing	Managing Managers
Sales	$0	0–$5 million	$5–$15 million	$10 million or more
Employees	0–5	0–30	30–75	75 and up
Transitions	Characteristics: Founder-driven Wrenching changes Highly influential informal advisor Resource desperation Very quick or very slow decision making	Characteristics: Founder-driven creativity Constant change, ambiguity, and uncertainty Time compression Informal Communications Counterintuitive decision making and structure Relative inexperience	Probable crises: Erosion of creativity of founders Confusion over ambiguous roles, responsibilities, and goals Desire for delegation versus autonomy and control Need for organization and operating policies	Probable crises: Failure to clone founders Specialization/eroding of collaboration versus practice of power, information, and influence Need for operating controls and mechanisms Conflict among founders

awareness and practice of reciprocity for mutual gain.[8] When a strong need to control, influence, and gain power over others characterizes the lead entrepreneur or the entrepreneurial manager, or when he or she has an insatiable appetite for putting an associate down, more often than not the venture gets into trouble. A dictatorial, adversarial, and dominating management style makes it very difficult to attract and keep people who thirst for achievement, responsibility, and results. Compliant partners and managers are often chosen. Destructive conflicts often erupt over who has the final say, who is right, and whose prerogatives are what.

In the corporate setting, the "hero-making" ability is identified as an essential attribute of successful entrepreneurial managers.[9] These hero makers try to make the pie bigger and better, rather than jealously clutching and hoarding a tiny pie that is all theirs. They have a capacity for objective interpersonal relationships as well, which enables them to smooth out individual differences of opinion by keeping attention focused on the common goal to be achieved.[10]

Exhibit 7.4 characterizes probable crises that growing ventures will face, including erosion of creativity by founders and team members; confusion or resentment, or both, over ambiguous roles, responsibilities, and goals; failure to clone founders; specialization and eroding of collaboration; desire for autonomy and control; need for operating mechanisms and controls; and conflict and divorce among founders and members of the team. The exhibit further delineates issues that confront entrepreneurial managers.

Compounding of Time and Change In the high growth stage, change, ambiguity, and uncertainty seem to be the only things that remain constant. Change creates higher levels of uncertainty, ambiguity, and risk, which, in turn, compound to shrink time, an already precious commodity. One result of change is a series of shock waves rolling through a new and growing venture by way of new customers, new technologies, new competitors, new markets, and new people. In industries characterized by galloping technological change, with relatively minuscule lead and lag times in bringing new products to market and in weathering the storms of rapid obsolescence, the effects of change and time are extreme. For example, the president of a rapidly growing, small computer company said, "In our business it takes 6 to 12 months to develop a new computer, ready to bring to the market, and product technology obsolescence is running about 9 to 12 months." This time compression has been seen in such industries as electronics and aerospace in the 1960s; small computers, integrated circuits, and silicon chips in the 1970s; microcomputers in the 1980s; telecommunications, the Internet, and biotechnology in the 1990s; and nanotechnology in the 2000s.

[8] Ibid.

[9] David L. Bradford and Allan R. Cohen, *Power Up: Transforming Organizations through Shared Leadership* (New York: John Wiley & Sons, 1998).

[10] Neil C. Churchill, "Entrepreneurs and Their Enterprises: A Stage Model," in *Frontiers of Entrepreneurship Research: 1983,* ed J. A. Hornaday et al. (Babson Park, MA: Babson College, 1983), pp. 1–22.

Nonlinear and Nonparametric Events Entrepreneurial management is characterized by nonlinear and nonparametric events. Just as the television did not come about by a succession of improvements in the radio, and the jet plane did not emerge from engineers and scientists attempting to develop a better and better piston engine plane, so too events do not follow straight lines, progress arithmetically, or even appear related within firms. Rather, they occur in bunches and in stepwise leaps. For example, a firm may double its sales force in 15 months, rather than over eight years, while another may triple its manufacturing capacity and adopt a new materials resource planning system immediately, rather than utilizing existing capacity by increasing overtime, then adding a third shift nine months later, and finally adding a new plant three years hence.

Relative Inexperience In addition, the management team may be relatively inexperienced. The explosive birth and growth of these firms are usually unique events that cannot be replicated, and most of the pieces in the puzzle—technology, applications, customers, people, the firm itself—are usually new. Take Prime Computer as an example. Sales at this manufacturer of minicomputers grew rapidly in five years from $100 million per year to nearly $1.2 billion per year. The average age of all employees in the company was less than 29 years, and the firm was barely 10 years old.

Counterintuitive, Unconventional Decision Making Yet another characteristic of rapidly growing ventures in the entrepreneurial domain is counterintuitive, unconventional patterns of decision making. For example, a computer firm needed to decide what approach to take in developing and introducing three new products in an uncertain, risky marketplace. Each proposed new product appeared to be aimed at the same end-user market, and the person heading each project was similarly enthusiastic, confident, and determined about succeeding. A traditional approach to such a problem would have been to determine the size and growth rates of each market segment; evaluate the probable estimates of future revenue costs and capital requirements for their accuracy; compare the discounted, present-value cash flow that will emerge from each project; and select the project with the highest yield versus the required internal rate of return. Such an analysis sometimes overlooks the fact that most rapid growth companies have many excellent alternatives and, more commonly, the newness of technology, the immaturity of the marketplace, and the rapid discovery of further applications make it virtually impossible to know which of any product proposals is best. The computer firm decided to support all three new products at once, and a significant new business was built around each one. New market niches were discovered simultaneously and the unconventional approach paid.

Fluid Structures and Procedures Most rapid growth ventures also defy conventional organizational patterns and structures. It is common to find a firm that has grown $25 million, $50 million, or even $150 million per year in sales and that still has no formal organizational chart. If an organizational chart does exist, it usually has three distinguishing features: First, it is inevitably out of date. Second, it changes frequently. For example, one firm had eight major reorganizations in its first five years as it grew to $5 million. Third, the organizational structure is usually flat (i.e., it has few management layers), and there is easy accessibility to the top decision makers. But the informality and fluidity of organization structures and procedures do not mean casualness or sloppiness when it comes to goals, standards, or clarity of direction and purpose. Rather, they translate into responsiveness and readiness to absorb and assimilate rapid changes while maintaining financial and operational cohesion.

Entrepreneurial Culture There exists in growing new ventures a common value system, which is difficult to articulate, is even more elusive to measure, and is evident in behavior and attitudes. There is a belief in and commitment to growth, achievement, improvement, and success and a sense among members of the team that they are "in this thing together." Goals and the market determine priorities, rather than whose territory or whose prerogatives are being challenged. Managers appear unconcerned about status, power, and personal control. They are more concerned about making sure that tasks, goals, and roles are clear than whether the organizational chart is current or whether their office and rug reflect their current status. Likewise, they are more concerned about the evidence, competence, knowledge, and logic of arguments affecting a decision than the status given by a title or the formal position of the individual doing the arguing. Contrast this with a multi-billion-dollar, but stagnant, firm in England. Reportedly, 29 different makes and models of automobiles are used in the firm to signify one's position.

This entrepreneurial climate, or culture, exists in larger firms also. Such a climate attracts and encourages the entrepreneurial achievers, and it helps perpetuate the intensity and pace so characteristic of high growth firms. Exhibit 7.5 shows how five companies studied by Rosabeth Moss Kanter range from most to least entrepreneurial. Kanter, who has

EXHIBIT 7.5

Characteristics of Five Companies, Ranging from Most to Least Entrepreneurial

	Companies Studied				
	Chipco	**Radco**	**Medco**	**Finco**	**Utico**
Percent of effective managers with entrepreneurial accomplishments	71%	69%	67%	47%	33%
Economic trend	Steadily up	Trend up but now down	Upward trend	Mixed	Downward trend
Change issues	Change normal; constant change in product generation; proliferating staff and units.	Change normal in products, technologies; changeover to second management generation with new focus.	Reorganized 2–3 years ago to install matrix; normal product and technology changes.	Change a shock; new top management group from outside reorganizing and trying to add competitive market posture.	Change a shock; undergoing reorganization to install matrix and add competitive market posture and reducing staff.
Organization structure	Matrix	Matrix in some areas; product lines act as quasi divisions.	Matrix in some areas.	Divisional; unitary hierarchy within division; some central officers.	Functional organization; currently overlaying matrix of regions and markets.
Information flow	Decentralized	Mixed	Mixed	Centralized	Centralized
Communication emphasis	Free Horizontal	Free Horizontal	Moderately free Horizontal	Constricted Vertical	Constricted Vertical
Culture	Clear, consistent; favors individual initiative.	Clear, though in transition from invention emphasis to routinization and systems.	Clear; pride in company; belief that talent will be rewarded.	Idiosyncratic; depends on boss and area.	Clear but undergoing changes; favors security, maintenance, and protection.
Emotional climate	Pride in company, team feeling, some burnout.	Uncertainty regarding changes.	Pride in company; team feeling.	Low trust; high uncertainty.	High uncertainty, confusion.
Rewards	Abundant; visibility, chance to do more challenging work in the future, and get bigger budget projects.	Abundant; visibility, chance to do more challenging work in the future, and get bigger budget projects.	Moderately abundant; conventional.	Scarce; primarily monetary.	Scarce; promotion and salary freeze; recognition by peers grudging.

Source: Reprinted by permission of *Harvard Business Review*. From "Middle Managers as Innovators" by Rosabeth Moss Kanter, July-August 1982, p. 103. Copyright © 1982 by the Harvard Business School Publishing Corporation; all rights reserved.

been studying "intrapreneurship" since the 1980s, asserted that the global economy was experiencing the postentrepreneurial revolution, which "takes entrepreneurship a step further, applying entrepreneurial principles to the traditional corporation, creating a marriage between entrepreneurial creativity and corporate discipline, cooperation, and teamwork."[11] This revolution has not made managing any easier; in fact, Kanter suggests, "This constitutes the ultimate corporate balancing act. Cut back and grow. Trim down and build. Accomplish more, and do it in new areas, with fewer resources."[12] Clearly, some corporations will embrace these challenges with more success than others; the following section will shed some light on how "giants learn to dance."[13]

[11] Rosabeth Moss Kanter, *When Giants Learn to Dance* (New York: Simon & Schuster, 1989), pp. 9–10.
[12] Ibid., p. 31.
[13] Ibid.

What Entrepreneurial Managers Need to Know

Much of business education traditionally has emphasized and prepared students for life in the administrative domain. There is nothing wrong with that, but education preparing students to start and manage vibrant, growing new ventures cannot afford to emphasize administrative efficiency, maintenance tasks, resource ownership, and institutional formalization. Rather, such a program needs to emphasize skills necessary for life in the entrepreneurial domain. For example, effective entrepreneurial managers need to be especially skillful at managing conflict, resolving differences, balancing multiple viewpoints and demands, and building teamwork and consensus. These skills are particularly difficult when working with others outside one's immediate formal chain of command.

In talking of larger firms, Kanter identifies power and persuasion skills, skill in managing problems accompanying team and employee participation, and skill in understanding how change is designed and constructed in an organization as necessary. Kanter notes:

> In short, individuals do not have to be doing "big things" in order to have their cumulative accomplishments eventually result in big performance for the company. . . . They are only rarely the inventors of the "breakthrough" system. They are only rarely doing something that is totally unique or that no one, in any organization, ever thought of before. Instead, they are often applying ideas that have proved themselves elsewhere, or they are rearranging parts to create a better result, or they are noting a potential problem before it turns into a catastrophe and mobilizing the actions to anticipate and solve it.[14]

A study of midsized growth companies having sales between $25 million and $1 billion and a sales or profit growth of more than 15 percent annually over five years confirms the importance of many of these same fundamentals of entrepreneurial management.[15] For one thing, these companies practiced opportunity-driven management. According to the study, they achieved their first success with a unique product or distinctive way of doing business and often became leaders in market niches by delivering superior value to customers, rather than through low prices. They are highly committed to serving customers and pay very close attention to them. For another thing, these firms emphasize financial control and managing every element of the business.

In a book that follows up on the implementation issues of how one gets middle managers to pursue and practice entrepreneurial excellence (first made famous in *In Search of Excellence* by Tom Peters and Bob Waterman), two authors note that some of the important fundamentals practiced by team-builder entrepreneurs—who are more intent on getting results than just getting their own way—also are emulated by effective middle managers.[16] Or as John Sculley, of Apple Computers, explained:

> The heroic style—the lone cowboy on horseback—is not the figure we worship anymore at Apple. In the new corporation, heroes won't personify any single set of achievements. Instead, they personify the process. They might be thought of as gatekeepers, information carriers, and teams. Originally heroes at Apple were the hackers and engineers who created the products. Now, more teams are heroes.[17]

The ability to shape and guide a cohesive team is particularly critical in high-tech firms where the competitive landscape can shift dramatically in the face of disruptive technologies. In his book *The Innovator's Dilemma,* Clayton Christensen finds that even aggressive, innovative, and customer-driven organizations can been rendered nearly obsolete if they fail to take decisive, and at times radical, actions to stay competitive.[18] The point of greatest peril in the development of a high-tech market, writes Geoffrey Moore in his book *Crossing the Chasm,* lies in making the transition from an early market, dominated by a few visionary customers, to a mainstream market that is dominated by a large block of customers who are predominantly pragmatists in orientation.[19] In Exhibit 7.6, Babson entrepreneur in residence Ed Marram describes this as the "Blunder" stage of growth, perilously positioned between "Wonder" and Thunder."

Lead entrepreneurs whose companies successfully break into the mass market must then find a way to manage the hyper-growth and gigantic revenues that can result from an international surge in demand.[20] Several entrepreneurial managers who have skillfully negotiated these high-tech waters are as well-known as the companies they founded: think Dell, Gates, Jobs, and Ellison. What sort of skills and

[14] Rosabeth Moss Kanter, *The Change Masters* (New York: Simon & Schuster, 1983), pp. 354–55.
[15] The study was done by McKinsey & Company. See "How Growth Companies Succeed," reported in *Small Business Report,* July 1984, p. 9.
[16] David L. Bradford and Allan R. Cohen, *Managing for Excellence* (New York: John Wiley & Sons, 1984), pp. 3–4.
[17] John Sculley with John Byrne, *Odyssey: Pepsi to Apple . . . A Journey of Adventures, Idea, and the Future* (New York: HarperCollins Publishers Inc., 1987), p. 321.
[18] Clayton M. Christensen, *The Innovator's Dilemma* (Harvard Business School Press, 1997).
[19] Geoffrey Moore, *Crossing the Chasm* (New York: HarperCollins, 2002).
[20] Geoffrey Moore, *Inside the Tornado: Marketing Strategies from Silicon Valley's Cutting Edge* (New York: HarperCollins, 1999).

EXHIBIT 7.6

Stages of Growth

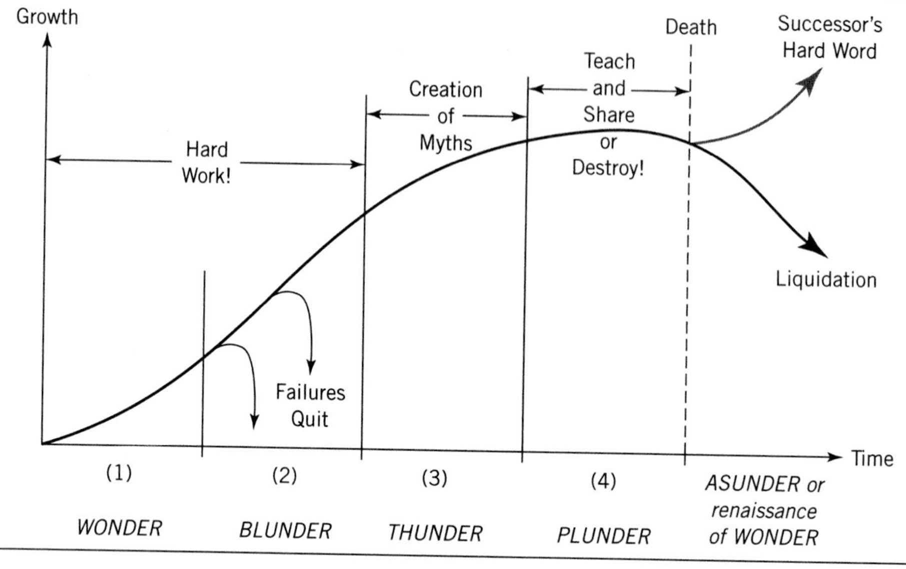

personality are required to achieve such high levels of performance in a dynamic and uncertain marketplace? As portrayed in Stephen Covey's classic work, *The 7 Habits of Highly Effective People*, these individuals are curious, proactive team builders who have a passion for continuous improvement and renewal in their lives and in their ventures. Maybe most important in this context: these leaders have "the ability to envision, to see the potential, to create with their minds what they cannot at present see with their eyes . . . "[21]

Management Competencies

Entrepreneurs who build substantial companies that grow to more than $10 million in sales and 75 to 100 employees are good entrepreneurs *and* good managers. Typically, they will have developed a solid base and a wide breadth of management skills and know-how over a number of years working in different areas (e.g., sales, marketing, manufacturing, and finance). It would be unusual for any single entrepreneur to be outstanding in all areas. More likely, a single entrepreneur will have strengths in one area, such as strong people management, conceptual and creative problem-solving skills, and marketing know-how, as well as some significant weaknesses. While it is risky to generalize, often entrepreneurs whose background is technical are weak in marketing, finance, and general management. Entrepreneurs who do not have a technical background are, as you might expect, often weakest in the technical or engineering aspects.

Throughout this book, the concept of fit has been stressed. Having a management team whose skills are complementary is important, not the possession by an individual of a single, absolute set of skills or a profile. The art and craft of entrepreneuring involves recognizing the skills and know-how needed to succeed in a venture, knowing what each team member does or does not know, and then compensating for shortcomings, either by getting key people on board to fill voids or by an individual accumulating the additional "chunks" before he or she takes the plunge. After all, the venture and the people area work in process.

Skills in Building Entrepreneurial Culture

Managers of entrepreneurial firms need to recognize and cope with innovation, taking risks, and responding quickly, as well as with absorbing major setbacks. The most effective managers seem to thrive on the hectic, and at times chaotic, pace and find it challenging and stimulating, rather than frustrating or overwhelming. They use a consensus approach to build a motivated and committed team, they balance conflicting demands and priorities, and they manage conflicts adroitly.

[21] Stephen R. Covey, *The 7 Habits of Highly Effective People* (New York: Simon and Schuster, 1989).

These managers thus need interpersonal/teamwork skills that involve (1) the ability to create, through management, a climate and spirit conducive to high performance, including pressing for performance while rewarding work well done and encouraging innovation, initiative, and calculated risk taking; (2) the ability to understand the relationships among tasks and between the leader and followers; and (3) the ability to lead in those situations where it is appropriate, including a willingness to manage actively, supervise and control activities of others through directions, suggestions, and the like.

These interpersonal skills can be called entrepreneurial influence skills, since they have a great deal to do with the way these managers exact influence over others.

Leadership, Vision, Influence These managers are skillful in creating clarity out of confusion, ambiguity, and uncertainty. These entrepreneurial managers are able to define adroitly and gain agreement on who has what responsibility and authority. Further, they do this in a way that builds motivation and commitment to cross-departmental and corporate goals, not just parochial interests. But this is not perceived by other managers as an effort to jealously carve out and guard personal turf and prerogatives. Rather, it is seen as a genuine effort to clarify roles, tasks, and responsibilities, and to make sure there is accountability and appropriate approvals. This does not work unless the manager is seen as willing to relinquish his or her priorities and power in the interest of an overall goal. It also requires skill in making sure the appropriate people are included in setting cross-functional or cross-departmental goals and in making decisions. When things do not go as smoothly as was hoped, the most effective managers work them through to an agreement. Managers who are accustomed to traditional line/staff or functional chains of command are often baffled and frustrated in their new role. While some may be quite effective in dealing with their own subordinates, it is a new task to manage and work with peers, the subordinates of others, and even superiors outside one's chain of command.

Helping, Coaching, and Conflict Management The most effective managers are very creative and skillful in handling conflicts, generating consensus decisions, and sharing their power and information. They are able to get people to open up, instead of clamming up; they get problems out on the table, instead of under the rug; and they do not become defensive when others disagree with their views. They seem to know that high-quality decisions require a rapid flow of information in all directions and that knowledge, competence, logic, and evidence need to prevail over official status or formal rank in the organization. The way they manage and resolve conflicts is intriguing. They can get potential adversaries to be creative and to collaborate by seeking a reconciliation of viewpoints. Rather than emphasizing differences and playing the role of hard-nose negotiator or devil's advocate to force their own solution, they blend ideas. They are more willing to risk personal vulnerability in this process—often by giving up their own power and resources—than are less-effective managers. They insist on fairness and integrity in the short and long term, rather than short term gain. The trade-offs are not easy: At the outset, such an approach involves more managers, takes more time, often appears to yield few immediate results, and seems like a more painful way to manage. Later, however, the gains from the motivation, commitment, and teamwork anchored in consensus are striking. For one thing, there is swiftness and decisiveness in actions and follow-through because the negotiating, compromising, and accepting of priorities is history. For another, new disagreements that emerge do not generally bring progress to a halt, since there is both high clarity and broad acceptance of the overall goals and underlying priorities. Without this consensus, each new problem or disagreement often necessitates a time-consuming and painful confrontation and renegotiation simply because it was not done initially. Apparently, the Japanese understand this quite well.

Teamwork and People Management Another form of entrepreneurial influence has to do with encouraging creativity and innovation, and with taking calculated risks. Entrepreneurial managers build confidence by encouraging innovation and calculated risk taking, rather than by punishing or criticizing whatever is less than perfect. They breed independent, entrepreneurial thinking by expecting and encouraging others to find and correct their own errors and to solve their own problems. This does not mean they follow a throw-them-to-the-wolves approach. Rather, they are perceived by their peers and other managers as accessible and willing to help when needed, and they provide the necessary resources to enable others to do the job. When it is appropriate, they go to bat for their peers and subordinates, even when they know they cannot always win. An ability to make heroes out of other team members and contributors and to make sure others are in the limelight, rather than accept these things oneself, is another critical skill.

The capacity to generate trust—the glue that binds an organization or relationship together—is critical. The most effective managers are perceived as trustworthy; they behave in ways that create trust. They do this by being straightforward. They do what they say they are going to do. They are not the corporate rumor carriers. They are open and spontaneous, rather than guarded and cautious with each word. And they are perceived as being honest and direct. They treat their associates with respect, as they would want to be treated. They share the wealth with those who help create it by their high performance. Also, it is easy to envision the kind of track record and reputation these entrepreneurial managers build for themselves. They have a reputation of getting results, because they understand that the task of managing in a rapid growth company usually goes well beyond one's immediate chain of command. They become known as the creative problem solvers who have a knack for blending and balancing multiple views and demands. Their calculated risk taking works out more often than it fails. And they have a reputation for developing human capital (i.e., they groom other effective growth managers by their example and their mentoring).

Other Management Competencies

Entrepreneurial managers need a sound foundation in what are considered traditional management skills. Interestingly, in the study of practicing entrepreneurs mentioned earlier, no one assigned much importance to capital asset-pricing models, beta coefficients, linear programming, and so forth, the prevailing and highly touted "new management techniques."[22]

The list below is divided into two cross-functional areas (administration and law and taxation) and four key functional areas (marketing, operations/production, finance, entrepreneurial management, law and taxes, and information technology). Technical skills unique to each venture are also necessary.

Marketing

- *Market research and evaluation.* Ability to analyze and interpret market research study results, including knowing how to design and conduct studies and to find and interpret industry and competitor information, and a familiarity with questionnaire design and sampling techniques. One successful entrepreneur stated that what is vital "is knowing where the competitive threats are and where the opportunities are and an ability to see the customers' needs."
- *Marketing planning.* Skill in planning overall sales, advertising, and promotion programs and in deciding on effective distributor or sales representative systems and setting them up.
- *Product pricing.* Ability to determine competitive pricing and margin structures and to position products in terms of price and ability to develop pricing policies that maximize profits.
- *Sales management.* Ability to organize, supervise, and motivate a direct sales force, and the ability to analyze territory and account sales potential and to manage a sales force to obtain maximum share of market.
- *Direct selling.* Skills in identifying, meeting, and developing new customers and in closing sales. Without orders for a product or service, a company does not really have a business.
- *Service management.* Ability to perceive service needs of particular products and to determine service and spare-part requirements, handle customer complaints, and create and manage an effective service organization.
- *Distribution management.* Ability to organize and manage the flow of product from manufacturing through distribution channels to ultimate customer, including familiarity with shipping costs, scheduling techniques, and so on.
- *Product management.* Ability to integrate market information, perceived needs, research and development, and advertising into a rational product plan, and the ability to understand market penetration and breakeven.
- *New product planning.* Skills in introducing new products, including marketing testing, prototype testing, and development of price/sales/merchandising and distribution plans for new products.

Operations/Production

- *Manufacturing management.* Knowledge of the production process, machines, personnel, and space required to produce a product and the skill in managing production to produce products within time, cost, and quality constraints.
- *Inventory control.* Familiarity with techniques of controlling in-process and finished goods inventories of materials.
- *Cost analysis and control.* Ability to calculate labor and materials costs, develop standard cost systems, conduct variance analyses, calculate overtime labor needs, and manage/control costs.

[22] Timmons and Stevenson, "Entrepreneurship Education in the 80s. What Entrepreneurs Say," pp. 115–34.

- *Quality control.* Ability to set up inspection systems and standards for effective control of quality of incoming, in-process, and finished materials. Benchmarking continuous improvement.
- *Production scheduling and flow.* Ability to analyze work flow and to plan and manage production processes, to manage work flow, and to calculate schedules and flows for rising sales levels.
- *Purchasing.* Ability to identify appropriate sources of supply, to negotiate supplier contracts, and to manage the incoming flow of material into inventory, and familiarity with order quantities and discount advantages.
- *Job evaluation.* Ability to analyze worker productivity and needs for additional help, and the ability to calculate cost-saving aspects of temporary versus permanent help.

Finance

- *Raising capital.* Ability to decide how best to acquire funds for startup and growth; ability to forecast funds needs and to prepare budgets; and familiarity with sources and vehicles of short- and long-term financing, formal and informal.
- *Managing cash flow.* Ability to project cash requirements, set up cash controls, and manage the firm's cash position, and the ability to identify how much capital is needed, when and where you will run out of cash, and breakeven.
- *Credit and collection management.* Ability to develop credit policies and screening criteria, and to age receivables and payables, and an understanding of the use of collection agencies and when to start legal action.
- *Short-term financing alternatives.* Understanding of payables management and the use of interim financing, such as bank loans, factoring of receivables, pledging and selling notes and contracts, bills of lading and bank acceptance; and familiarity with financial statements and budgeting/profit planning.
- *Public and private offerings.* Ability to develop a business plan and an offering memo that can be used to raise capital, a familiarity with the legal requirements of public and private stock offerings, and the ability to manage shareholder relations and to negotiate with financial sources.
- *Bookkeeping, accounting, and control.* Ability to determine appropriate bookkeeping and accounting systems as the company starts and grows, including various ledgers and accounts and possible insurance needs.
- *Other specific skills.* Ability to read and prepare an income statement and balance sheet, and the ability to do cash flow analysis and planning, including break-even analysis, contribution analysis, profit and loss analysis, and balance sheet management.

Entrepreneurial Management

- *Problem solving.* Ability to anticipate potential problems; ability to gather facts about problems, analyze them for real causes, and plan effective action to solve them; and ability to be very thorough in dealing with details of particular problems and to follow through.
- *Communications.* Ability to communicate effectively and clearly—orally and in writing—to media, public, customers, peers, and subordinates.
- *Planning.* Ability to set realistic and attainable goals, identify obstacles to achieving the goals, and develop detailed action plans to achieve those goals, and the ability to schedule personal time very systematically.
- *Decision making.* Ability to make decisions on the best analysis of incomplete data, when the decisions need to be made.
- *Project management.* Skills in organizing project teams, setting project goals, defining project tasks, and monitoring task completion in the face of problems and cost/quality constraints.
- *Negotiating.* Ability to work effectively in negotiations, and the ability to balance quickly value given and value received. Recognizing onetime versus ongoing relationships.
- *Managing outside professionals.* Ability to identify, manage, and guide appropriate legal, financial, banking, accounting, consulting, and other necessary outside advisors.
- *Personnel administration.* Ability to set up payroll, hiring, compensation, and training functions.

Law and Taxes

- *Corporate and securities law.* Familiarity with the Uniform Commercial Code, including forms of organization and the rights and obligations of officers, shareholders, and directors; and familiarity with Security and Exchange Commission, state, and other regulations concerning the securities of your firm, both registered and unregistered, and the advantages and disadvantages of different instruments.

- *Contract law.* Familiarity with contract procedures and requirements of government and commercial contracts, licenses, leases, and other agreements, particularly employment agreements and agreements governing the vesting rights of shareholders and founders.
- *Law relating to patent and proprietary rights.* Skills in preparation and revision of patent applications and the ability to recognize a strong patent, trademark, copyright, and privileged information claims, including familiarity with claim requirements, such as intellectual property.
- *Tax law.* Familiarity with state and federal reporting requirements, including specific requirements of a particular form of organization, of profit and other pension plans, and the like.
- *Real estate law.* Familiarity with leases, purchase offers, purchase and sale agreements, and so on, necessary for the rental or purchase and sale of property.
- *Bankruptcy law.* Knowledge of bankruptcy law, options, and the forgivable and nonforgivable liabilities of founders, officers, and directors.

Information Technology

- Information and management systems tools from laptop to Internet: sales, supply chain, inventory, payroll, etc.
- Business to business, business to consumer, business to government via the Internet.
- Sales, marketing, manufacturing, and merchandising tools.
- Financial, accounting, and risk analysis and management tools (e.g., Microsoft's Office platform).
- Telecommunications and wireless solutions for corporate information, data, and process management.

As has been said before, not all entrepreneurs will find they are greatly skilled in the areas listed above, and if they are not, they will most likely need to acquire these skills, either through apprenticeship, through partners, or through the use of advisors. However, while many outstanding advisors, such as lawyers and accountants, are of enormous benefit to entrepreneurs, these people are not always businesspeople and they often cannot make the best business judgments for those they are advising. For example, lawyers' judgments, in many cases, are so contaminated by a desire to provide perfect or fail-safe protection that they are totally risk averse.

Chapter Summary

1. The growing enterprise requires that the founder and team develop competencies as entrepreneurial leaders and managers.
2. Founders who succeed in growing their firms beyond $10 million in sales learn to adapt and grow quickly themselves as managers and leaders, or they do not survive.
3. Founders of rapidly growing firms defy the conventional wisdom that entrepreneurs cannot manage growing beyond the startup.
4. Ventures go through stages of growth from startup, through rapid growth, to maturity, to decline and renewal.
5. The largest single factor that increases the complexity and difficulty of managing a young company is its rate of growth in orders and revenue.
6. The faster the rate of growth, the more difficult and challenging are the management issues, and the more flexible, adaptive, and quick learning must be the organization.
7. Entrepreneurs create and invent new and unique approaches to organizing and managing work.
8. As ventures grow, the core management competencies need to be covered by the team.

Study Questions

1. What is the difference between an entrepreneurial manager and an administrator?
2. What do founders do to grow their ventures beyond $10 million in sales?
3. Define the stages that most companies experience as they grow, and explain the management issues and requirements anticipated at each stage.

4. What drives the extent of complexity and difficulty of management issues in a growing company?
5. List the main management competencies that need to be addressed as a company grows to exceed $10 million in revenue.
6. Can you compare and describe the principal differences in the leadership, management, and organization between the best growing companies of which you are aware, and large, established companies? Why are there differences?
7. What would be your strategy for changing and creating an entrepreneurial culture in a large, nonentrepreneurial firm? Is it possible? Why, or why not?

Internet Resources for Chapter 7

http://www.entreworld.org *A selective review guide to Web sources for the entrepreneur*

http://www.hbr.com *The Harvard Business Review*

http://www.fastcompany.com *Fast Company is a media company that chronicles how companies develop and compete in fast-paced, challenging business environments*

http://www.redherring.com *Red Herring is a media company covering innovation, technology, financing, and entrepreneurial activity*

http://www.business.gov *One-stop access to federal government information, services, and transactions on business development, financial assistance, taxes, laws and regulations, international trade, workplace issues, buying and selling*

http://edge.lowe.org *Peerspectives is a peer-learning community for growing companies that provides access to information that leads to solutions for the entrepreneur trying to grow his or her business*

http://emc.score.org *The SCORE Association is a national, nonprofit association and a resource partner with the SBA, with 11,500 volunteer members and 389 chapters throughout the United States*

MIND STRETCHERS

Have you considered?

1. It is often said, "You cannot hire an entrepreneur." What are the implications for large companies today?
2. How would you characterize the attitudes, behaviors, and mind-sets of the most effective leaders and managers you have worked for? The worst? What accounts for the difference?
3. Read recent issues of *Fast Company* magazine: What is happening in corporate America?
4. What should the president, the Congress, and governors do to encourage and accelerate entrepreneurship in America?

Exercise

Managerial Skills and Know-How Assessment

Name:

Venture:

Date:

Part I—Management Competency Inventory

Part I of the exercise involves filling out the Management Competency Inventory and evaluating how critical certain management competencies are either (1) for the venture or (2) personally over the next one to three years. *How you rank the importance of management competencies, therefore, will depend on the purpose of your managerial assessment.*

STEP 1

Complete the Management Competency Inventory on the following pages. For each management competency, place a check in the column that best describes your knowledge and experience. Note that a section is at the end of the inventory for **unique skills** required by your venture; for example, if it is a service or franchise business, there will be some skills and know-how that are unique. Then rank from 1 to 3 particular management competencies as follows:

1 = Critical

2 = Very Desirable

3 = Not Necessary

	Competency Inventory				
	Rank	Thorough Knowledge & Experience (Done Well)	Some Knowledge & Experience (So-So)	No Knowledge or Experience (New Ground)	Importance (1–3 Years)
Marketing					
Market Research and Evaluation *Finding and interpreting industry and competitor information; designing and conducting market research studies; analyzing and interpreting market research data; etc.*					

Market Planning *Planning overall sales, advertising, and promotion programs; planning and setting up effective distributor or sales representative systems; etc.*					
Product Pricing *Determining competitive pricing and margin structures and break-even analysis; positioning products in terms of price; etc.*					

Customer Relations Management (CRM)

Customer Service *Determining customer service needs and spare-part requirements; managing a service organization and warranties; training; technical backup, telecom and Internet systems and tools; etc.*					
Sales Management *Organizing, recruiting, supervising, compensating, and motivating a direct sales force; analyzing territory and account sales potential; managing sales force; etc.*					
Direct Selling *Identifying, meeting, and developing new customers, suppliers, investors, brain trust and team; closing sales; etc.*					

Direct Mail/ Catalog Selling *Identifying and developing appropriate direct mail and catalog sales and related distribution; etc.*				
Electronic and Telemarketing *Identifying, planning, implementing appropriate telemarketing programs; Internet-based programs; etc.*				

Supply Chain Management

Distribution Management *Organizing and managing the flow of product from manufacturing through distribution channels to customers, etc.*				
Product Management *Integrating market information, perceived needs, research and development, and advertising into a rational product plan; etc.*				
New Product Planning *Planning the introduction of new products, including marketing testing, prototype testing, and development of price, sales, merchandising, and distribution plans; etc.*				

Operations/ Production

Manufacturing Management *Managing production to produce products within time, cost, and quality constraints; knowledge of Manufacturing Resource Planning; etc.*				
Inventory Control *Using techniques of controlling in-process and finished goods inventories, etc.*				
Cost Analysis and Control *Calculating labor and materials costs; developing standard cost systems; conducting variance analyses; calculating overtime labor needs; managing and controlling costs; etc.*				
Quality Control *Setting up inspection systems and standards for effective control of quality in incoming, in-process, and finished goods; etc.*				
Production Scheduling and Flow *Analyzing work flow; planning and managing production processes; managing work flow; calculating schedules and flows for rising sales levels; etc.*				
Purchasing *Identifying appropriate sources of supply; negotiating supplier contracts; managing the incoming flow of material into inventory, etc.*				

Job Evaluation *Analyzing worker productivity and needs for additional help; calculating cost-saving aspects of temporary versus permanent help; etc.*				

Finance

Accounting *Determining appropriate bookkeeping and accounting systems; preparing and using income statements and balance sheets; analyzing cash flow, breakeven, contribution, and profit and loss; etc.*				
Capital Budgeting *Preparing budgets; deciding how best to acquire funds for startup and growth; forecasting funds needs; etc.*				
Cash Flow Management *Managing cash position, including projecting cash requirements; etc.*				
Credit and Collection Management *Developing credit policies and screening criteria, etc.*				
Short-Term Financing *Managing payables and receivables; using interim financing alternatives, managing bank and creditor relations; etc.*				

Public and Private Offering Skills *Developing a business plan and offering memo; managing shareholder relations; negotiating with financial sources deal structuring and valuation; etc.*				

Entrepreneurial Management

Problem Solving *Anticipating problems and planning to avoid them; analyzing and solving problems, etc.*				
Culture and Communications *Communicating effectively and clearly, both orally and in writing, to customers, peers, subordinates, and outsiders; etc. Treat others as you would be treated, share the wealth, give back.*				
Planning *Ability to set realistic and attainable goals, identify obstacles to achieving the goals, and develop detailed action plans to achieve those goals.*				
Decision Making *Making decisions based on the analysis of incomplete data, etc.*				
Project Management *Organizing project teams; setting project goals; defining project tasks; monitoring task completion in the face of problems and cost/quality constraints; etc.*				

Negotiating *Working effectively in negotiations; etc.*				
Personnel Administration *Setting up payroll, hiring, compensation, and training functions; identifying, managing, and guiding appropriate outside advisors; etc.*				
Management Information Systems *Knowledge of relevant management information systems available and appropriate for growth plans; etc.*				
Information Technology and the Internet *Using spreadsheet, word processing, and other relevant software; using e-mail, management tools, and systems*				

Interpersonal Team

Entrepreneurial Leadership/Vision/ Influence *Actively leading, instilling vision and passion in others, and managing activities of others; creating a climate and spirit conducive to high performance; etc.*				
Helping *Determining when assistance is warranted and asking for or providing such assistance.*				

Feedback *Providing effective feedback or receiving it; etc.*				
Conflict Management *Confronting differences openly and obtaining resolution; using evidence and logic; etc.*				
Teamwork and People Management *Working with others to achieve common goals; delegating responsibility and coaching subordinates, etc.*				
Build a Brain Trust				

Law

Corporations *Understanding the Uniform Commercial Code, including forms of organization and the rights and obligations of officers, shareholders, and directors; etc.*				
Contracts *Understanding the requirements of government and commercial contracts, licenses, leases, and other agreements; etc.*				

Taxes *Understanding state and federal reporting requirements; understanding tax shelters, estate planning, fringe benefits, and so forth; etc.*				
Securities *Understanding regulations of the Security and Exchange Commission and state agencies concerning the securities, both registered and unregistered; etc.*				
Patents and Proprietary Rights *Understanding the preparation and revision of patent applications; recognizing strong patent, trademark, copyright, and privileged information claims; etc.*				
Real Estate *Understanding agreements necessary for the rental or purchase and sale of property; etc.*				
Bankruptcy *Understanding options and the forgivable and nonforgivable liabilities of founders, officers, directors, and so forth; etc.*				
Unique Skills *List unique competencies required.* *1.* *2.* *3.*				

Part II—Managerial Assessment

Part II involves assessing management strengths and weaknesses, deciding which areas of competence are most critical, and developing a plan to overcome or compensate for any weaknesses and to capitalize on management strengths.

STEP 1

Assess management strengths and weaknesses:

- Which management skills are particularly strong?
- Which management skills are particularly weak?
- What gaps are evident? When?

STEP 2

Circle the areas of competence most critical to the success of the venture, and cross out those that are irrelevant.

STEP 3

Consider the implications for you and for developing the venture management team.

- What are the implications of this particular constellation of management strengths and weaknesses?
- Who in your team can overcome or compensate for each critical weakness?
- How can you leverage your critical strengths?
- What are the time implications of the above actions? For you? For the team?
- How will you attract and fill the critical gaps in your weaknesses?

STEP 4

Obtain feedback. If you are evaluating your management competencies as part of the development of a personal entrepreneurial strategy and planning your apprenticeship, refer back to "Crafting a Personal Entrepreneurial Strategy" in Chapter 1. Complete this exercise if you have not done so already.

Case

Jim Poss

Preparation Questions

1. Apply the Timmons entrepreneurship framework (entrepreneur-opportunity-resources) to analyze this case. Pay particular attention to the entrepreneur's traits and how he gathered resources for his venture.
2. Discuss Jim's fund-raising strategies. What other options might be considered for raising the funds SPC needs? Is this a good investment?
3. Discuss the growth strategy. What additional market(s) would you recommend pursuing as they move ahead?

On his way through Logan Airport, Jim Poss stopped at a newsstand to flip through the June 2004 *National Geographic* cover story that declared, "The End of Cheap Oil." Inside was a two-page spread of an American family sitting among a vast array of household possessions that were derived, at least in part, from petroleum-based products: laptops, cell phones, clothing, footwear, sports equipment, cookware, and containers of all shapes and sizes. Without oil, the world will be a very different place. Jim shook his head.

> . . . and here we are burning this finite, imported, irreplaceable resource to power three-ton suburban gas-guzzlers with "these colors don't run" bumper stickers!

Jim's enterprise, Seahorse Power Company (SPC), was an engineering startup that encouraged the adoption of environmentally friendly methods of power generation by designing products that were cheaper and more efficient than 20th century technologies. Jim was sure that his first product, a patent-pending solar-powered trash compactor, could make a real difference.

> In the United States alone, 180 million garbage trucks consume over a billion gallons of diesel fuel a year . . .

By compacting trash on-site and off-grid, the mailbox-sized "BigBelly" could cut pickups by 400 percent. The prototype—designed on the fly at a cost of $10,000—had been sold to Vail Ski Resorts in Colorado for $5,500. The green technology had been working as promised since February, saving the resort lots of time and money on round-trips to a remote lodge accessible only by snow machine.

Jim viewed the $4,500 loss on the sale as an extremely worthwhile marketing and proof-of-concept expense. Now that they were taking the business to the next level with a run of 20 machines, Jim and his SPC team had to find a way to reduce component costs and increase production efficiencies.

Jim returned the magazine to the rack and made his way to the New York Shuttle gate. An investor group in the City had called another meeting, and Jim felt that it was time for him to start asking the hard questions about the deal they were proposing. These investors in socially responsible businesses had to be given a choice: either write him the check they've been promising—and let him run SPC the way he saw fit—or decline to invest altogether so he could concentrate on locating other sources of funding to close this $250,000 seed round. So far, all Jim had received from this group were voices of concern and requests for better terms—it was time to do the deal or move on.

Green Roots

As a kid, Jim Poss was always playing with motors, batteries, and other electronics. He especially enjoyed fashioning new gadgets from components he had amassed by dismantling all manner of appliances and electronic devices. He also spent a lot of time out of doors cross-country skiing with his father. Jim said that by his senior year in high school, he knew where he was headed:

> I had read *Silent Spring*[1] and that got me thinking about the damage we are doing to the earth. And once I started learning about the severity of our problems—that was it. By the end of my first semester at Duke University, I had taken enough environmental science to see that helping businesses to go green was going to be a huge growth industry.

Jim felt that the best way to get businesses to invest in superior energy systems was to make it profitable for them to do so. In order to prepare himself for this path, Jim set up a double major in environmental science and policy, and geology—with a minor in engineering. He graduated in 1996 and found work as a hydrologist, analyzing soil and rock samples for a company that engineered stable parking lots for shopping malls. He didn't stay long:

> That certainly wasn't my higher calling. I poked around, and within six months I found a fun job redesigning the

This case was prepared by Carl Hedberg under the direction of Professor William Bygrave. © Copyright Babson College, 2004. Funding provided by the F. W. Olin Graduate School and a gift from the class of 2003.

[1] *Silent Spring*, written in 1962 by Rachel Carson, exposed the hazards of the pesticide DDT, eloquently questioned humanity's faith in technological progress, and helped set the stage for the environmental movement. Appearing on a CBS documentary shortly before her death from breast cancer in 1964, the author remarked, "Man's attitude toward nature is today critically important simply because we have now acquired a fateful power to alter and destroy nature. But man is a part of nature, and his war against nature is inevitably a war against himself. . . . [We are] challenged as mankind has never been challenged before to prove our maturity and our mastery, not of nature, but of ourselves."

production capabilities at a small electronics firm. Soon after that, I started working for this company called Solectria; that was right up my alley.

As a sales engineer at Solectria—a Massachusetts-based designer and manufacturer of sustainable transportation and energy solutions—Jim helped clients configure electric drive systems for a wide range of vehicles. He loved the work and developed an expertise in using spreadsheets to calculate the most efficient layout of motors, controllers, power converters, and other hardware. By 1999, though, he decided that it was once again time to move on:

> Solectria had a great group of people, but my boss was a micromanager and I wasn't going to be able to grow. I found an interesting job in San Francisco as a production manager for a boat manufacturing company—coordinating the flow of parts from seven or eight subcontractors. When the [Internet] bubble burst, the boat company wasn't able to raise capital to expand. My work soon became relatively mundane, so I left.

This time, though, Jim decided to head back to school:

> I had now worked for a bunch of different businesses and I had seen some things done well, but a lot of things done wrong. I knew that I could run a good company—something in renewable energy, and maybe something with gadgets. I still had a lot to learn, so I applied to the MBA program at Babson College. I figured that I could use the second-year EIT[2] module to incubate something.

Opportunity Exploration

Between his first and second year at Babson, Jim applied for a summer internship through the Kauffman Program. He sent a proposal to the Spire Corporation—a publicly traded manufacturer of highly engineered solar electric equipment—about investigating the market and feasibility of solar-powered trash compactors. Jim had discussed his idea with someone he knew on the board, and the same week that the HR department informed him that there were no openings, he got a call from the president of the company:

> Roger Little had talked with the board member I knew and said that while they weren't interested in having me write a case study on some solar whatever-it-was, he said they'd like me to write some business plans for Spire—based on their existing opportunities and existing operations. I said sure, I'll take it.

That summer, Jim worked with the executive team to complete three business plans. When they asked him to stay on, Jim agreed to work 15 hours per week—on top of his full-time MBA classes. Every month or so he would bring up his idea for a solar-powered trash compactor with the Spire executives, but their answer was always the same:

> I was trying to get them to invest in my idea or partner with me in some way, and these guys kept saying, "It'll never work." So I just kept working on them. I did the calculations to show them that with solar we could do 10 compactions a day and have plenty [of electric charge] on reserve for a run of cloudy weather. Finally, they just said that they don't get into end-user applications.

Early in his second year, Jim attended a product design fair featuring young engineers from Babson's new sister school, the Franklin W. Olin School of Engineering. He connected with Jeff Satwicz, an engineering student with extensive experience in remote vehicle testing for the Department of Defense. When Jim got involved with a project that required engineering capabilities, he knew whom to call:

> I went up the hill to Olin to ask Jeff if he'd like to help design a folding grill for tailgating—he said sure. It's funny, the two schools are always talking about working together like that, but it doesn't happen until the students sit in the café together and exchange ideas. That's how it works; the faculty wasn't involved—and they didn't really need to be.

Although Jim didn't stay with the grill team, the project had forged a link with an engineer with a penchant for entrepreneurship. Now certain of his trajectory, Jim incorporated the Seahorse Power Company (SPC)—a nod to his ultimate aspiration of developing power systems that could harness the enormous energy of ocean waves and currents.

Understanding that sea-powered generators were a long way off, Jim began to investigate ways to serve well-capitalized ventures that were developing alternative-energy solutions. One idea was to lease abandoned oil wells in California for the purpose of collecting and selling deep-well data to geothermal energy businesses that were prospecting in the area. When Jim sought feedback, he found that even people who liked his concept invariably pointed him in a different direction:

> Everybody kept telling me that wind was where it's at—and they were right; it's the fastest growing energy source in the world. All the venture capitalists are looking at wind power. I realized, though, that if I was going to make wind plants, I'd have to raise $200 million to $500 million—with no industry experience. Impossible. So instead, I started looking at what these [wind-plant ventures] needed.

[2] The Entrepreneurship Intensity Track (EIT) was a compressed and highly focused entrepreneurial curriculum for graduate students at Babson College. The program provided a select group of MBAs with the necessary skills to take a business idea through the critical stages of exploration, investigation, and refinement. The program's individual flexibility tailored each student's education to best fit their perceived market opportunity, and enabled them to fund and launch their business during the spring of their second year.

The DAQ Buoy

Jim discovered that The Cape Wind Project, a company working to build a wind farm on Nantucket Sound, had erected a $2.5 million, 200-foot monitoring tower to collect wind and weather data in the targeted area. Jim felt that there was a better way:

> Meteorological testing is a critical first step for these wind businesses. I thought, whoa, they've just spent a lot of money to construct a static tower that probably won't accurately portray the wind activity in that 25-square-mile area. And without good data, it's going to be really hard for them to get funding.
>
> My idea was to deploy data buoys that could be moved around a site to capture a full range of data points. I spent about six months writing a business plan on my data acquisition buoy—the DAQ. I figured that to get to the prototype stage I'd need between $5 million and $10 million. This would be a pretty sophisticated piece of equipment, and a lot of people worried that if a storm came up and did what storms typically do to buoys, we'd be all done. I was having a hard time getting much traction with investors.

EXHIBIT 1

Target Customers

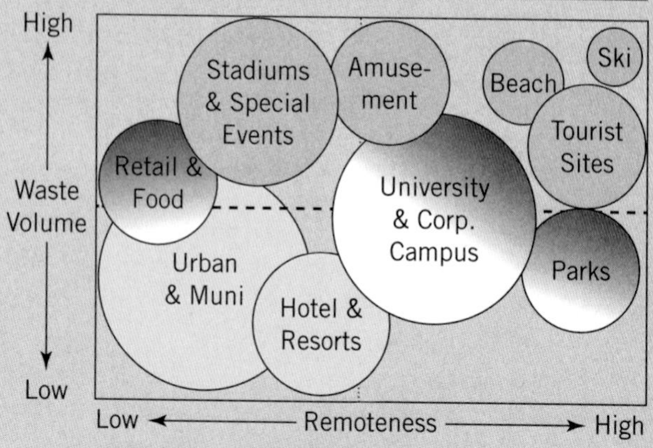

Finding the Waste

Even while he was casting about for a big-concept opportunity, Jim had never lost sight of his solar compactor idea. With the spring semester upon him, he decided to see if that business would work as an EIT endeavor. Although he was sure that such a device would be feasible—even easy—to produce, he didn't start to get excited about the project until he took a closer look at the industry:

> I did an independent study to examine the trash industry. I was about a week into that when I looked at the market size and realized that I had been messing around with expensive, sophisticated business models that didn't offer close to the payback as this compactor would.
>
> U.S. companies spent $12 billion on trash receptacles in 2000, and $1.2 billion on compaction equipment in 2001. The average trash truck gets less than three miles to the gallon and costs over $100 an hour to operate. There are lots of off-grid sites[3] that have high trash volumes—resorts, amusement parks, and beaches—and many are getting multiple pickups a day. That's a tremendous waste of labor and energy resources.

Joining him in the EIT module was first-year MBA candidate Alexander Perera. Alex had an undergraduate degree in environmental science from Boston University, as well as industry experience in renewable energy use and energy efficiency measures. The pair reasoned that if a solar-compactor could offer significant savings as a trash collection device, then the market could extend beyond the off-grid adopters to include retail and food establishments, city sidewalks, and hotels (see Exhibit 1).

Gearing Up

By the time the spring semester drew to a close, they had a clear sense of the market and the nature of the opportunity—in addition to seed funding of $22,500: $10,000 from Jim's savings, and $12,500 through the hatchery program at Babson College. Since solar power was widely perceived as a more expensive, more complex, and less efficient energy source than grid power, it was not surprising to discover that the competition—dumpster and compaction equipment manufacturers—had never introduced a system like this. Nevertheless, Jim and Alex were certain that if they could devise a reliable solar-powered compactor that could offer end-users significant cost savings, established industry players could be counted on to aggressively seek to replicate or acquire that technology.

Understanding that patent protections were often only as good as the legal minds that drafted them, Jim had sought out the best. The challenge was that most of the talented patent attorneys he met with were far outside of his meager budget. In May 2003, Jim got a break when he presented his idea at an investor forum:

> I won $1,500 in patent services from Brown and Rudnick.[4] That might not have taken me too far, but they have a very entrepreneurial mind-set. They gave me a flat rate for the patent—which is not something many firms will do. I paid the $7,800 up front, we filed a provisional patent in June, and they agreed to work with me as I continued to develop and modify the machine.

[3] Sites without electrical power.

[4] Brown Rudnick Berlack Israels, LLP, Boston, Massachusetts.

Jim's efforts had again attracted the interest of Olin engineer Jeff Satwicz, who in turn brought in Bret Richmond, a fellow student with experience in product design, welding, and fabrication. When the team conducted some reverse engineering to see if the vision was even feasible, Jim said they were pleasantly surprised:

> I found a couple of kitchen trash compactors in the want ads and bought them both for about 125 bucks. We took them apart, and that's when I realized how easy this was going to be . . . of course, nothing is ever as easy as you think it's going to be.

Pitching without Product

Figuring that it was time to conduct some hard field research, they decided to call on businesses that would be the most likely early adopters of an off-grid compactor. Alex smiled as he described an unexpected turn of events:

> We had a pretty simple client-targeting formula: remoteness, trash volume, financial stability, and an appreciation for the environmental cachet that could come with a product like this. Literally the first place I called was the ski resort in Vail, Colorado. Some eco-terrorists had recently burned down one of their lodges to protest their expansion on the mountain, and they were also dealing with four environmental lawsuits related to some kind of noncompliance.
>
> This guy Luke Cartin at the resort just jumped at the solar compactor concept. He said, "Oh, this is cool. We have a lodge at Blue Sky Basin that is an hour and a half round trip on a snow cat. We pick up the trash out there three or four times a week, sometimes every day. We could really use a product like that . . ." That's when you put the phone to your chest and think, *oh my gosh . . .*

Jim added that after a couple of conference calls, they were suddenly in business without a product:

> I explained that we were students and that we had not actually built one of these things yet (sort of). Luke asked me to work up a quote for three machines. They had been very open about their costs for trash pickup, and I figured that they'd be willing to pay six grand apiece. I also had a rough idea that our cost of materials would fall somewhat less than that.
>
> Luke called back and said that they didn't have the budget for three, but they'd take one. I was actually really happy about that, because I knew by then that making just one of these was going to be a real challenge.

In September, SPC received a purchase order from Vail Resorts. When Jim called the company to work out a payment plan with 25 percent up front, Luke surprised them again:

> He said, "We'll just send you a check for the full amount, minus shipping, and you get the machine here by Christmas." That was great, but now we were in real trouble because we had to figure out how to build this thing quickly, from scratch—and on a tight budget.

Learning by Doing

The team set out to design the system and develop the engineering plans for the machine that SPC had now trademarked as the "BigBelly Solar-Powered Trash Compactor." Although his Olin team was not yet versant with computer-aided design (CAD) software, Jim saw that as an opportunity:

> These guys were doing engineering diagrams on paper with pens and pencils—but now we were going to need professional stuff. I said that we could all learn CAD together, and if they made mistakes, great, that's fine; we'd work through it.

Concurrent to this effort was the task of crunching the numbers to design a machine that would work as promised. As they began to source out the internal components, they searched for a design, fabrication, and manufacturing subcontractor that could produce the steel cabinet on a tight schedule. Although the team had explained that SPC would be overseeing the entire process from design to assembly, quotes for the first box still ranged from $80,000 to $400,000. Jim noted that SPC had an even bigger problem to deal with:

> On top of the price, the lead times that they were giving me were not going to cut it; I had to get this thing to Colorado for the ski season!
>
> So, we decided to build it ourselves. I went to a local fabricator trade show and discovered that although they all have internal engineering groups, some were willing to take a loss on the research and development side in order to get the manufacturing contract.
>
> We chose Boston Engineering since they are very interested in developing a relationship with Olin engineers. They gave me a hard quote of $2,400 for the engineering assistance, and $2,400 for the cabinet. By this time we had sourced all the components we needed, and we began working with their engineer to size everything up. Bob Treiber, the president, was great. He made us do the work ourselves out at his facility in Hudson (Massachusetts), but he also mentored us, and his firm did a ton of work pro bono.

Fulfillment and Feedback

As the Christmas season deadline came and went, the days grew longer. By late January 2004, Jim was working through both of the shifts they had set up, from four in the morning to nearly eleven at night. In February, they fired up the device, tested it for three hours, and shipped it off to Colorado (see Exhibit 2). Jim met the device at their shipping dock, helped unwrap it, met the staff, and

EXHIBIT 2

The BigBelly Arrives in Vail

put a few finishing touches on the machine. Although it worked, even at zero degree temperatures, it had never been tested in the field. Jim left after a few days, and for two weeks, he endured a deafening silence.

Jim wrestled with how he could check in with SPC's first customer without betraying his acute inventor's angst about whether the machine was still working, and if it was, what Vail thought about it. Finally, when he could stand it no longer, he placed the call under the guise of soliciting satisfied-customer feedback. The news from Vail nearly stopped his heart:

> They said that they had dropped the machine off a forklift and it fell on its face. Oh man, I thought; if it had fallen on its back, that would have been okay, but this was bad—real bad. And then Luke tells me that it was a bit scratched—but it worked fine. He told me how happy they were that we had made it so robust. When I asked how heavy the bags were that they were pulling out of the thing, he said, "I don't know; we haven't emptied it yet . . ." I was astounded.

As it turned out, the Vail crew discovered that the single collection bag was indeed too heavy—a two-bin system would be more user-friendly. The resort also suggested that the inside cart be on wheels, that the access door be in the back, and that there be some sort of wireless notification when the compactor was full.

As the SPC team got to work incorporating these ideas into their next generation of "SunPack" compactors, they were also engineering a second product that they hoped would expand their market reach to include manufacturers of standard compaction dumpsters. The "SunPack Hippo" would be a solar generator designed to replace the 220-volt AC-power units that were used to run industrial compactors. The waste hauling industry had estimated that among commercial customers that would benefit from compaction, between 5 and 20 percent were dissuaded from adopting such systems because of the setup cost of electrical wiring. SPC planned to market the system through manufacturing and/or distribution partnerships.

Protecting the Property

While the interstate shipment of the BigBelly had give SPC a legal claim to the name and the technology, Jim made sure to keep his able patent attorneys apprised of new developments and modifications. SPC had applied for a provisional patent in June 2003, and they had one year to broaden and strengthen those protections prior to the formal filing. As that date approached, the attorneys worked to craft a document that protected the inventors from infringement, without being so broad that it could be successfully challenged in court.

The SPC patents covered as many aspects of Sun Pack products as possible, including energy storage, battery charging, energy draw cycle time, sensor controls, and wireless communication. The filing also specified other off-grid power sources for trash compaction such as foot pedals, windmills, and water wheels.

Even without these intellectual property protections, though, Jim felt that they had a good head start in an industry segment that SPC had created. Now they had to prove the business model.

The Next Generation

While the first machine had cost far more to build than the selling price, the unit had proven the concept and been a conduit for useful feedback. A production run of 20 machines, however, would have to demonstrate that the business opportunity was as robust as the prototype appeared to be. That would mean cutting the cost of materials by more than 75 percent to around $2,500 per unit. SPC estimated that although the delivered price of $5,000 was far more expensive than the cost of a traditional trash receptacle, the system could pay for itself by trimming the ongoing cost of collection (see Exhibit 3).

The team had determined that developing a lease option for the BigBelly would alleviate new-buyer jitters by having SPC retain the risk of machine ownership—a move that could increase margins by 10 percent. Over the next five years SPC expected to expand its potential customer pool by reducing the selling price to around $3,000—along with a corresponding drop in materials costs (see Exhibit 4).

With steel prices escalating, the SPC team designed their new machines with 30 percent fewer steel parts. They also cut the size of the solar panel and the two-week battery storage capacity in half, and replaced the expensive screw system of compaction with a simpler, cheaper, and more efficient sprocket and chain mechanism (see Exhibit 5).

EXHIBIT 3

Customer Economics

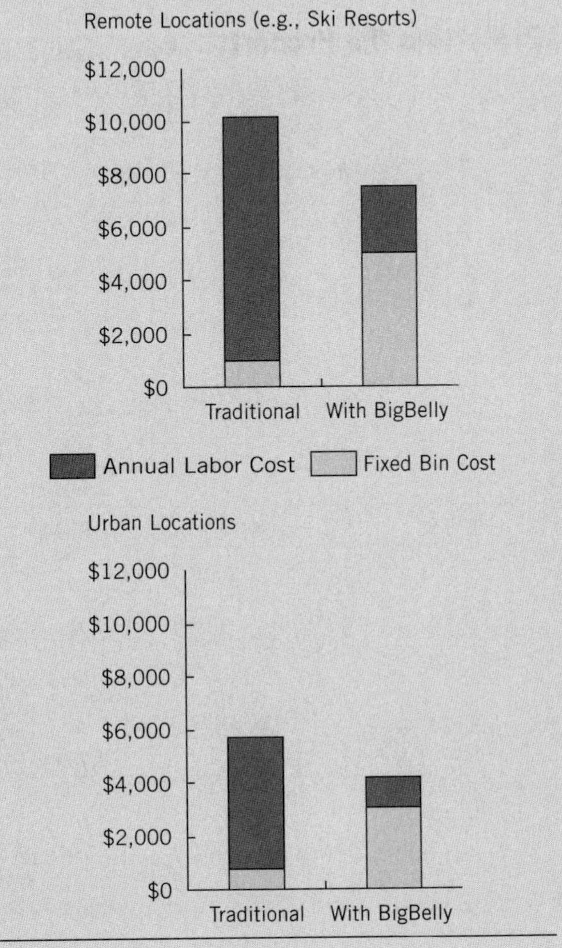

EXHIBIT 4

BigBelly Economics

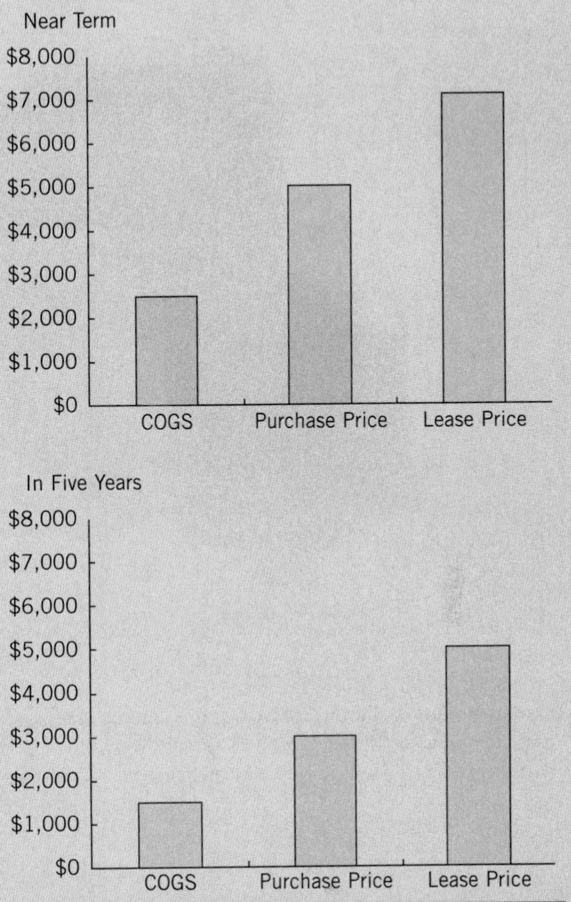

In order to offer an effective service response capability, the team tried to restrict their selling efforts to the New England area, although "a sale was a sale." One concern that kept cropping up was that this unique device would be a tempting target for vandals. Team members explained that the solar panel on top was protected by a replaceable sheet of Lexan,[5] that all mechanical parts were entirely out of reach, and that the unit had already proven to be quite solid. The general feeling, Jim noted, was that if the machine could be messed with, people would find a way:

> One state park ranger was worried that it would get tossed into the lake, so I assured him that the units would be very heavy. He said, "So they'll sink really fast . . ."

Jim added that the overall response had been very favorable—so much so that once again, there was a real need for speed:

> We have pre-sold nearly half of our next run to places like Acadia National Park in Maine, Six-Flags Amusement Park in Massachusetts, Harbor Lights in Boston,

[5] A clear, high-impact-strength plastic used in many security applications.

EXHIBIT 5

BigBelly CAD Schematic

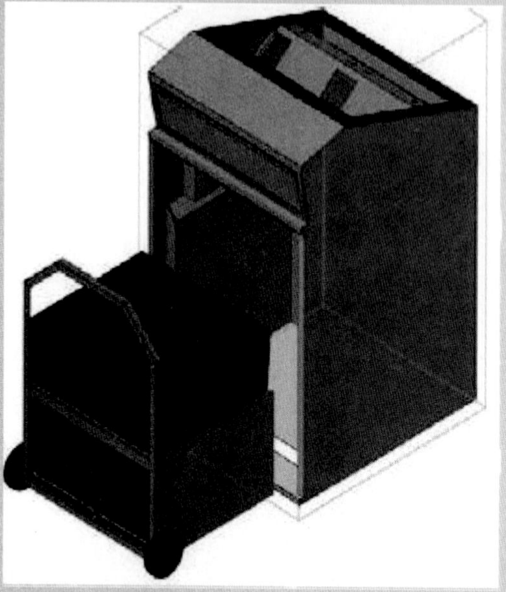

beaches on Nantucket, and Harvard University. Fifty percent down-payment deposits should be coming in soon, but that won't cover what we'll need to get this done.

Projections and Funding

During this "early commercialization period," Jim was committed to moderating investor risk by leveraging on-campus and contractor facilities as much as possible. The company was hoping to close on an A-round of $250,000[6] by early summer to pay for cost-reduction engineering, sales and marketing, and working capital. The following year the company expected to raise a B-round of between $700,000 and $1 million.

SPC was projecting a positive cash flow in 2006 on total revenues of just over $4.7 million (see Exhibit 6).

[6] Based on a pre-money valuation of $2.5 million. The principal and interest on this seed-round note would convert into equity at the A-round with an additional 30 percent discount to A-round investors. Seed-round investors would have the right to re-invest in the A-round to offset dilution.

EXHIBIT 6

SPC Financial Projections

	2004	2005	2006	2007	2008
BigBelly unit sales	50	300	1,200	3,600	9,000
BigBelly revenues	$225,000	$1,200,000	$4,200,000	$10,800,000	$22,500,000
Hippo royalty revenues	0	120,000	525,000	1,620,000	3,937,500
Total income	225,000	1,320,000	4,725,000	12,420,000	26,437,500
COGS	146,250	660,000	2,100,000	4,860,000	9,000,000
Gross income	78,750	660,000	2,625,000	7,560,000	17,437,500
SG&A	400,000	1,600,000	2,600,000	5,000,000	11,000,000
EBIT	($321,250)	($940,000)	$25,000	$2,560,000	$6,437,500

EXHIBIT 7

Market Size and Penetration

	2004	2005	2006	2007	2008
Top-Down					
SunPack market* (billion)	$1.0	$1.0	$1.0	$1.0	$1.0
SunPack % penetration	0.0%	0.1%	0.5%	1.2%	2.6%
Bottom-Up					
Total potential customers**	30,000	30,000	30,000	30,000	30,000
Potential units/customer	20	20	20	20	20
Total potential units	600,000	600,000	600,000	600,000	600,000
Cumulative units sold	50	350	1,550	5,150	14,150
Cumulative % penetration	0.0%	0.1%	0.3%	0.9%	2.4%

*Assume $600,000 BigBelly market (5% of $12 billion waste receptacles sold to target segments) plus a $400,000 power unit market ($1.2 billion compacting dumpsters sold/$12,000 average price × $4,000 per power unit).

**Assume 400 resorts, 600 amusement parks, 2,000 university campuses, 5,000 commercial campuses, 2,200 hotels, 4,000 municipalities, 57 National Parks, 2,500 state parks and forests, 3,700 RV parks and campgrounds, and 17,000 fast-food and retail outlets.

The team felt that if their products continued to perform well, their market penetration estimates would be highly achievable (see Exhibit 7). Jim estimated that by 2008, SPC would become an attractive merger or acquisition candidate.

In January 2004, as Jim began work on drafting an SBIR[7] grant proposal, his parents helped out by investing $12,500 in the venture. That same month, while attending a wind energy conference sponsored by Brown and Rudnick, Jim overheard an investor saying that he was interested in putting a recent entrepreneurial windfall to work in socially responsible ventures. Jim decided it was worth a try:

> I gave him my three-minute spiel on the compactor. He said that it sounded interesting, but that he was into wind power—after all, this *was* a wind-power conference. "Well then," I said, "have I got a business plan for you!"

That afternoon Jim sent the investor the most recent version of the data acquisition buoy business plan. That led to a three-hour meeting where the investor ended up explaining to Jim why the DAQ was such a good idea. Jim said that the investor also understood how difficult it would be to get the venture fully funded:

> [The investor] said, "Well, I sure wish you were doing the data acquisition buoy, but I can also see why you're not." I assured him that my passion was, of course, offshore wind, and that it was something I was planning to do in the future. So he agreed to invest $12,500 in the compactor—but only because he wanted to keep his foot in the door for what SPC was going to do later on.

In February, after the folks at Vail had come back with their favorable review, Jim called on his former internship boss at the Spire Corporation. Roger Little was impressed with Jim's progress, and his company was in for $25,000. In April, the team earned top honors in the 2004 Douglas Foundation Graduate Business Plan Competition at Babson College. The prize—$20,000 cash plus $40,000 worth of services—came with a good deal of favorable press as well. The cash, which Jim distributed evenly among the team members, was their first monetary compensation since they had begun working on the project.

Although SPC could now begin to move ahead on the construction of the next 20 cabinets, Jim was still focused on the search for a rather uncommon breed of investor:

> This is not a venture capital deal, and selling this idea to angels can be a challenge because many are not sophisticated enough to understand what we are doing. I had one group, for example, saying that this wouldn't work because most trash receptacles are located in alleys—out of the sun.
>
> Here we have a practical, commonsense business, but since it is a new technology, many investors are unsure of how to value it. How scalable is it? Will our patent filings hold up? Who will fix them when they break?

[7] The Small Business Innovation Research (SBIR) Program was a source of government grant funding driven by 10 federal departments and agencies that allocated a portion of their research and development capital for awards to innovative small businesses in the United States.

Earlier that spring Jim had presented his case in Boston to a gathering of angels interested in socially responsible enterprises. Of the six presenters that day, SPC was the only one offering products that were designed to lower direct costs. During the networking session that followed, Jim said that one group in particular seemed eager to move ahead:

> They liked that Spire had invested, and they seemed satisfied with our projections. When I told them that we had a $25,000 minimum, they said not to worry—they were interested in putting in $50,000 now and $200,000 later. In fact, they started talking about setting up funding milestones so that they could be our primary backers as we grew. They wanted me to stop fund-raising, focus on the business, and depend on them for all my near-term financing needs.
>
> At this point I felt like I needed to play hardball with these guys, show them where the line was. My answer was that I wasn't at all comfortable with that, and that I would be comfortable when I had $200,000 in the bank—my bank. They backed off that idea, and by the end of the meeting, they agreed to put in the $50,000; but first they said they had to perform some more due diligence.

Momentum

By May 2004, the Seahorse Power Company had a total of six team members.[8] All SPC workers had been given an equity stake in exchange for their part-time services. The investor group expressed deep concern with this arrangement, saying that the team could walk away when the going got tough—and maybe right when SPC needed them most. Jim explained that it wasn't a negotiable point:

> They wanted my people to have "skin in the game" because they might get cold feet and choose to get regular jobs. I told them that SPC workers are putting in 20 hours a week for free when they could be out charging consulting rates of $200 an hour. They have plenty of skin in this game, and I'm not going to ask them for cash. Besides, if we could put up the cash, we wouldn't need investors, right?

As Jim settled into his seat for the flight to New York, he thought some more about the investors' other primary contention: his pre-money valuation was high by a million:

> These investors—who still haven't given us a dime—are saying they can give me as much early-stage capital as SPC would need, but at a pre-money of $1.5 million and dependent on us hitting our milestones. With an immediate funding gap of about $50,000, it's tempting to move forward with these guys so we can fill current orders on time and maintain our momentum. On the other hand, I've already raised some money on the higher valuation, and maybe we can find the rest before the need becomes really critical.

[8] Three of the most recent equity partners were Richard Kennelly, a former director at Conservation Law Foundation where he concentrated on electric utility deregulation, renewable energy, energy efficiency, air quality, and global warming; Kevin Dutt, an MBA in operations management and quantitative methods from Boston University with extensive work experience in improving manufacturing and operational practices in a range of companies; and Steve Delaney, an MBA from The Tuck School at Dartmouth College with a successful track record in fund-raising, business development, market strategy, finance, and operations.

8

Chapter Eight

The New Venture Team

In the world today, there's plenty of technology, plenty of entrepreneurs, plenty of venture capital. What's in short supply is great teams. Your biggest challenge will be building a great team.

John Doerr,
Partner, Kleiner, Perkins, Caufield & Byers (*Fast Company*, February–March 1997)

Results Expected

Upon completion of the chapter, you will have:

1. Identified and examined the role and significance of teams in building successful new ventures.
2. Examined successful entrepreneurial philosophies and attitudes that can anchor vision in forming and developing effective new venture teams.
3. Identified the critical issues and hurdles, including common pitfalls, faced by entrepreneurs in forming and building new venture teams.
4. Examined issues of reward that new teams face in slicing the equity pie.
5. Analyzed the "Maclean Palmer" case study.
6. Developed a reward system for your own venture.

The Importance of the Team

The Connection to Success

Evidence suggests that a management team can make all the difference in venture success. There is a strong connection between the growth potential of a new venture (and its ability to attract capital beyond the founder's resources from private and venture capital backers) and the quality of its management team.

The existence of a quality management team is one of the major differences between a firm that provides its founder simply a job substitute, and the ability to employ perhaps a few family members and others, and a higher potential venture. The lone-wolf entrepreneur may make a living, but the team builder creates an organization and a company—a company where substantial value and harvest options are created.

Ventures that do not have teams are not necessarily predestined for the new venture graveyard. Yet, building a higher potential venture without a team is extremely difficult. Some entrepreneurs have acquired a distaste for partners, and some lead entrepreneurs can be happy only if they are in complete control; that is, they want employees, not partners, either internally or as outside investors. Take, for instance, an entrepreneur who founded a high-technology firm that grew steadily, but slowly, over 10 years to nearly $2 million in sales. As new patterns and technological advances in fiber optics drew much interest from venture capitalists, he had more than one offer of up to $5 million of funding, which he turned down because the investors wanted to own 51 percent or more of his venture. Plainly and simply, he said, "I do not want to give up control of what I have worked so long and hard to create." While clearly the exception to the rule, this entrepreneur has managed to grow his business to more than $20 million in sales.

Since the 1970s, numerous studies have pointed to the importance of a team approach to new venture creation. Solid teams are far more likely to attract venture capital, team-led startups have a greater chance of survival, and those enterprises often realize higher overall returns than ventures run by solo entrepreneurs.

Not only is the existence of a team important, but so too is the quality of that team. Because of this, venture capital investors are often very active in helping to shape—and reshape—management teams. A study in the late 1990s demonstrated the increasing importance of team formation, teamwork history, and cooperation between new venture teams and venture capitalists.[1] This is especially true today with highly technical ventures in areas such as biotechnology, nanotechnology, and photonics.

There is, then, a valuable role that the right partner(s) can play in a venture. In addition, mounting evidence suggests that entrepreneurs face loneliness, stress, and other pressures. At the very least, finding the right partner can mitigate these pressures.[2] The key is identifying and working with the right partner or partners. Getting the right partners and working with them successfully usually involves anticipating and dealing with some very critical issues and hurdles, when it is neither too early nor too late.

Forming and Building Teams

Anchoring Vision in Team Philosophy and Attitudes

The most successful entrepreneurs seem to anchor their vision of the future in certain entrepreneurial philosophies and attitudes (i.e., attitudes about what a team is, what its mission is, and how it will be rewarded). The soul of this vision concerns what the founder or founders are trying to accomplish and the unwritten ground rules that become the fabric, character, and purpose guiding how a team will work together, succeed and make mistakes together, and realize a harvest together. The rewards, compensation, and incentive structures rest on this philosophy and attitudes.

This fundamental mind-set is often evident in later success. The anchoring of this vision goes beyond all the critical nuts-and-bolts issues covered in the chapters and cases on the opportunity, the business plan, financing, and so forth. Each of these issues is vital, but each by itself may not lead to success. A single factor rarely, if ever, does.

The capacity of the lead entrepreneur to craft a vision and then to lead, inspire, persuade, and cajole key people to sign up for and deliver the dream makes an enormous difference between success and failure, between loss and profit, and between substantial harvest and "turning over the keys" to get out from under large personal guarantees of debt. Instilling a vision, and the passion to win, occurs very early, often during informal discussions, and seems to trigger a series of self-fulfilling prophecies that lead to success, rather than to "almosts" or to failure. In a study to determine the actual existence of lead entrepreneurs in INC. 500 firms, it was found that among macro-entrepreneurial teams, lead entrepreneurs do exist and they have stronger entrepreneurial vision and greater self-efficacy or self-confidence to act on their vision and make it real.[3]

Thus, lead entrepreneurs and team members who understand team building and teamwork have a secret weapon. Many with outstanding technical or other relevant skills, educational credentials, and so on, will be at once prisoners and victims of the highly individualistic competitiveness that got them to where they are. They may be fantastic lone achievers, and some may even "talk a good team game." But when it comes to how they behave and perform, their egos can rarely fit inside an airplane hangar. They simply do not have the team mentality.

What are these team philosophies and attitudes that the best entrepreneurs have and are able to identify or instill in prospective partners and team members? These can be traced to the entrepreneurial mind-set discussed in Chapter 1—a mind-set that can be seen actively at work around the team-building challenge. While there are innumerable blends and variations, most likely the teams of those firms that succeed in growing up big will share many of the following:

- *Cohesion.* Members of a team believe they are all in this together, and if the company wins, everyone wins. Members believe that no one can win unless everyone wins and, conversely, if anyone loses, everyone loses. Rewards, compensation, and incentive structures rest on building company value and return on capital invested, no matter how small or sizable.

[1] L. W. Busenitz, D. Moesel, and J. Fiet, "The Framing of Perceptions of Fairness in the Relationship between Venture Capitalists and New Venture Teams," *Entrepreneurship Theory and Practice* 21 (1997), pp. 5–21.

[2] David Boyd and David Gumpert, "The Loneliness of the Start-Up Entrepreneur," in *Frontiers of Entrepreneurship Research, 1982,* ed. J. A. Hornaday et al. (Babson Park, MA: Babson College, 1982), pp. 478–87.

[3] J. W. Carland and J. C. Carland, "Investigating the Existence of the Lead Entrepreneur," *Journal of Small Business Management* 38, no. 4 (2000), pp. 59–77.

- *Teamwork.* A team that works as a team, rather than one where individual heroes are created, may be the single most distinguishing feature of the higher-potential company. Thus, on these teams, efforts are made to make others' jobs easier, to make heroes out of partners and key people, and to motivate people by celebrating their successes. As Harold J. Seigle, the highly successful, now retired, president and chief executive officer of the Sunmark Companies, likes to put it, "High performance breeds strong friendships!"
- *Integrity.* Hard choices and trade-offs are made regarding what is good for the customer, the company, and value creation, rather than being based on purely utilitarian or Machiavellian ethics or narrow personal or departmental needs and concerns. There is a belief in and commitment to the notion of getting the job done without sacrificing quality, health, or personal standards.
- *Commitment to the long haul.* Like most organizations, new ventures thrive or wither according to the level of commitment of their teams. Members of a committed team believe they are playing for the long haul and that the venture is not a get-rich-quick drill. Rather, the venture is viewed as a delayed-gratification game in which it can take 5, 7, or even 10 or more years to realize a harvest. *No one gets a windfall profit by signing up now but bailing out early or when the going gets tough.* Stock vesting agreements reflect this commitment. For example, stock will usually be so vested over five or seven years that anyone who leaves early, for whatever reasons, can keep stock earned to date, but he or she is required to sell the remaining shares back to the company at the price originally paid. Of course, such a vesting agreement usually provides that if the company is unexpectedly sold or if a public offering is made long before the five-or-seven-year vesting period is up, then stock is 100 percent vested automatically with that event.
- *Harvest mind-set.* A successful harvest is the name of the game. This means that eventual capital gain is viewed as the scorecard, rather than the size of a monthly paycheck, the location and size of an office, a certain car, or the like.
- *Commitment to value creation.* Team members are committed to value creation—making the pie bigger for everyone, including adding value for customers, enabling suppliers to win as the team succeeds, and making money for the team's constituencies and various stakeholders.
- *Equal inequality.* In successful emerging companies, democracy and blind equality generally do not work very well, and diligent efforts are made to determine who has what responsibility for the key tasks. The president is the one to set the ground rules and to shape the climate and culture of the venture. Bill Foster, founder and president of Stratus Computer, was asked if he and his partners were all equal. He said, "Yes, we are, except I get paid the most and I own the most stock."[4] For example, stock is usually not divided equally among the founders and key managers. In one company of four key people, stock was split as follows: 34 percent for the president, 23 percent each for the marketing and technical vice presidents, and 6 percent for the controller. The remainder went to outside directors and advisors. In another company, seven founders split the company as follows: 22 percent for the president, 15 percent for each of the four vice presidents, and 9 percent for each of the two other contributors. An example of how failure to differentiate in terms of ownership impacts a business is seen in a third firm, where four owners each had equal share. Yet, two of the owners contributed virtually everything, while the other two actually detracted from the business. Because of this unresolved problem, the company could not attract venture capital and never was able to grow dramatically.
- *Fairness.* Rewards for key employees and stock ownership are based on contribution, performance, and results over time. Since these can only be roughly estimated in advance, and since there will invariably be surprises and inequities, both positive and negative, as time goes on, adjustments are made. One good example is a company that achieved spectacular results in just two years in the cellular phone business. When the company was sold, it was evident that two of the six team members had contributed more than was reflected in their stock ownership position. To remedy this, another team member gave one of the two team members stock worth several hundred thousand dollars. Since the team was involved in another venture, the president made adjustments in the various ownership positions in the new venture, with each member's concurrence, to adjust for past

[4] Remarks made at Babson College Venture Capital Conference, June 1985.

inequities. In addition, it was decided to set aside 10 percent of the next venture to provide some discretion in making future adjustments for unanticipated contributions to ultimate success.

- *Sharing of the harvest.* This sense of fairness and justness seems to be extended by the more successful entrepreneurs to the harvest of a company, even when there is no legal or ethical obligation to do so. For example, as much as 10 percent to 20 percent of the "winnings" is frequently set aside to distribute to key employees. In one such recent harvest, employees were startled and awash with glee when informed they would each receive a year's salary after the company was sold. However, this is not always the case. In another firm, 90 percent of which was owned by an entrepreneur and his family, the president, who was the single person most responsible for the firm's success and spectacular valuation, needed to expend considerable effort to get the owners to agree to give bonuses to other key employees of around $3 million, an amount just over 1 percent of the $250 million sale price. (It is worth considering how this sense of fairness, or lack of it, affects future flows of quality people and opportunities from which these entrepreneurs can choose new ventures.)

A Process of Evolution

An entrepreneur considering issues of team formation will rarely discover black-and-white, bulletproof answers that hold up over time. Nor is it being suggested that an entrepreneur needs answers to all questions concerning what the opportunity requires, and when, before moving ahead. Emphasis on the importance of new venture teams also does not mean every new venture must start with a full team that plunges into the business. It may take some time for the team to come together as a firm grows, and there will also always be some doubt, a hope for more than a prospective partner can deliver, and a constant recalibration. Again, creative acts, such as running a marathon or entrepreneuring, will be full of unknowns, new ground, and surprises. Preparation is an insurance policy, and thinking through these team issues and team building concepts in advance is very inexpensive insurance.

The combination of the right team of people and a right venture opportunity can be very powerful. The whole is, in such instances, greater than the sum of the parts. However, the odds for highly successful venture teams are rather thin. Even if a venture survives, the turnover among team members during the early years probably exceeds the national divorce rate. Studies of new venture teams seeking venture capital show many never get off the ground. These usually exhaust their own resources and commitment before raising the venture capital necessary to launch their ventures. Of those that are funded, about 1 in 20 becomes very successful in three to five years, in that it will return in excess of five times the original investment in realizable capital gains.

The formation and development of new venture teams seems to be idiosyncratic, and there seems to be a multitude of ways in which venture partners come together. Some teams form by accidents of geography, common interest, or working together. Perhaps the common interest is simply that the team members want to start a business, while in other cases the interest is an idea that members believe responds to a market need. Others form teams by virtue of past friendships. For example, roommates or close friendships in college or graduate school frequently lead to business partnerships. This was the case with two of Jeff Timmons's classmates in the MBA program at the Harvard Business School. Concluding that they would eventually go into business together after rooming together for a week, Leslie Charm and Carl Youngman have been partners for over 32 years as owners of three national franchise companies, an entrepreneurial advisory and troubled-business-management company, and a venture capital company, AIGIS Ventures, LLC. Jiffy Lube was founded by college football coach Jim Hindman and some of his coaches and players—including Steve Spinelli.

In the evolution of venture teams, two distinct patterns are identifiable. In the first, one person has an idea (or simply wants to start a business), and then three or four associates join the team over the next one to three years as the venture takes form. Alternatively, an entire team forms at the outset based on such factors as a shared idea, a friendship, an experience, and so forth.

Filling the Gaps

There is no simple cookbook solution to team formation; rather, there are as many approaches to forming teams as there are ventures with multiple founders.

Successful entrepreneurs search out people and form and build a team based on what the opportunity requires, and when.[5] Team members will contribute

[5] See J. A. Timmons, "The Entrepreneurial Team," *Journal of Small Business Management,* October 1975, pp. 36–37.

high value to a venture if they complement and balance the lead entrepreneur—and each other. Yet, ironically, while a substantial amount of thought usually accompanies the decision of people to go into business together, an overabundance of the thinking, particularly among the less experienced, can focus on less critical issues, such as titles, corporate name, letterhead, or what kind of lawyer or accountant is needed. Thus, teams are often ill-conceived from the outset and can easily plunge headlong into unanticipated and unplanned responses to crises, conflicts, and changes.

A team starts with a lead entrepreneur. In a startup situation, the lead entrepreneur usually wears many hats. Beyond that, comparison of the nature and demands of the venture and the capabilities, motivations, and interests of the lead entrepreneur will signal gaps that exist and that need to be filled by other team members or by accessing other outside resources, such as a board of directors, consultants, lawyers, accountants, and so on.

Thus, for example, if the strengths of the lead entrepreneur or a team member are technical in nature, other team members, or outside resources, need to fill voids in marketing, finance, and such. Realistically, there will be an overlapping and sharing of responsibilities, but team members need to complement, not duplicate, the lead entrepreneur's capabilities and those of other team members.

Note that a by-product of forming a team may be alteration of an entry strategy if a critical gap cannot be filled. For example, a firm may find that it simply cannot assault a certain market because it cannot hire the right marketing person. But it may find it could attract a top-notch person to exploit another niche with a modified product or service.

Most important, the process of evaluating and deciding who is needed, and when, is dynamic and not a onetime event. What know-how, skills, and expertise are required? What key tasks and action steps need to be taken? What are the requisites for success? What is the firm's distinctive competence? What external contacts are required? How extensive and how critical are the gaps? How much can the venture afford to pay? Will the venture gain access to the expertise it needs through additions to its board of directors or outside consultants? Questions such as these determine when and how these needs could be filled. And answers to such questions will change over time.

The following, organized around the analytical framework introduced in Chapter 3, can guide the formation of new venture teams.

The Founder What kind of team is needed depends upon the nature of the opportunity and what the lead entrepreneur brings to the game. One key step in forming a team is for the lead entrepreneur to assess his or her entrepreneurial strategy. (The personal entrepreneurial strategy exercise in Chapter 1 is a valuable input in approaching these issues.) Thus, the lead entrepreneur needs to first consider whether the team is desirable or necessary and whether he or she wants to grow a higher potential company. He or she then needs to assess what talents, know-how, skills, track record, contacts, and resources are being brought to the table; that is, what "chunks" have been acquired. (See the managerial skills and know-how assessment in Chapter 7.) Once this is determined, the lead entrepreneur needs to consider what the venture has to have to succeed, who is needed to complement him or her, and when. The best entrepreneurs are optimistic realists and have a real desire to improve their performance. They work at knowing what they do and do not know and are honest with themselves. The lead entrepreneur needs to consider issues such as:

- What relevant industry, market, and technological know-how and experience are needed to win, and do I bring these to the venture? Do I know the revenue and cost model better than anyone?
- Are my personal and business strengths in those specific areas critical to success in the proposed business?
- Do I have the contacts and networks needed (and will the ones I have make a competitive difference), or do I look to partners in this area?
- Can I attract a "first team" of all-star partners inside and externally, and can I manage these people and other team members effectively?
- Why did I decide to pursue this particular opportunity now, and what do I want out of the business (i.e., what are my goals and my income and harvest aspirations)?
- Do I know what the sacrifices and commitment will be, and am I prepared to make these?
- What are the risks and rewards involved, am I comfortable with them, and do I look for someone with a different risk-taking orientation?

Often a student going through this process will conclude that a more experienced person will be needed to lead the venture.

The Opportunity The need for team members is something an entrepreneur constantly thinks about, especially in the idea stage before startup. What is needed in the way of a team depends on the matchup between the lead entrepreneur and the opportunity, and how fast and aggressively he or she plans to proceed. (See the Venture Opportunity Screening Exercises in Chapter 5.) While most new ventures plan to bootstrap it and bring on additional team members only as the company can afford them, the catch-22 is that if a venture is looking for venture capital or serious private investors, having an established team will yield higher valuation and a smaller ownership share that will have to be parted with. Some questions that need to be considered are:

- Have I clearly defined the value added and the economics of the business? Have I considered how (and with whom) the venture can make money in this business? For instance, whether a company is selling razors or razor blades makes a difference in the need for different team members.
- What are the critical success variables in the business I want to start, and what (or who) is needed to influence these variables positively?
- Do I have, or have access to, the critical external relationships with investors, lawyers, bankers, customers, suppliers, regulatory agencies, and so forth, that are necessary to pursue my opportunity? Do I need help in this area?
- What competitive advantage and strategy should I focus on? What people are necessary to pursue this strategy or advantage?

Outside Resources The Sarbanes-Oxley law in the United States makes governance issues even more important, even with startup enterprises.[6] Gaps can be filled by accessing outside resources, such as boards of directors, accountants, lawyers, consultants, and so forth.[7] Usually, tax and legal expertise can best be obtained initially on a part-time basis. Other expertise (e.g., expertise required to design an inventory control system) is specialized and needed only once. Generally, if the resource is a onetime or periodic effort, or if the need is peripheral to the key tasks, goals, and activities required by the business, then an alternative such as using consultants makes sense. However, if the expertise is a must for the venture at the outset and the lead entrepreneur cannot provide it or learn it quickly, then one or more people will have to be acquired. Some questions to consider are:

- Is the need for specialized, onetime, or part-time expertise peripheral or on the critical path?
- Will trade secrets be compromised if I obtain this expertise externally?

Additional Considerations

Forming and building a team is, like marriage, a rather unscientific, occasionally unpredictable, and frequently surprising exercise—no matter how hard one may try to make it otherwise! The analogy of marriage and family, with all the accompanying complexities and consequences, is a particularly useful one. Forming a team has many of the characteristics of the courtship and marriage ritual, involving decisions based in part on emotion. There may well be a certain infatuation among team members and an aura of admiration, respect, and often fierce loyalty. Similarly, the complex psychological joys, frustrations, and uncertainties that accompany the birth and raising of children (here, the product or service) are experienced in entrepreneurial teams as well.

Thus, the following additional issues need to be considered:

- *Values, goals, and commitment.* It is critical that a team be well anchored in terms of values and goals. In any new venture, the participants establish psychological contracts and climates. While these are most often set when the lead entrepreneur encourages standards of excellence and respect for team members' contributions, selection of team members whose goals and values are in agreement can greatly facilitate establishment of a psychological contract and an entrepreneurial climate. In successful companies, the personal goals and values of team members align well, and the goals of the company are championed by team members as well. While this alignment may be less exact in large publicly owned corporations and greatest in small closely held firms, significant overlapping of a team member's goals with those of other team members and the overlap of corporate goals and team members' goals is desirable. Practically speaking, these evaluations of team members are some of the most difficult to make.
- *Definition of roles.* A diligent effort needs to be made to determine who is comfortable with and who has what responsibility for the key tasks so duplication of capabilities or responsibilities is minimized. Roles cannot be pinned down precisely for all tasks, since some key tasks and problems simply cannot be anticipated

[6] Jay Lorsch, professor of Human Relations at Harvard Business School.
[7] See William A. Sahlman and Howard H. Stevenson, "Choosing Small Company Advisors," *Harvard Business Review,* March–April 1987.

and since contributions are not always made by people originally expected to make them. Maintaining a loose, flexible, flat structure with shared responsibility and information is desirable for utilizing individual strengths, flexibility, rapid learning, and responsive decision making.

- *Peer groups.* The support and approval of family, friends, and co-workers can be helpful, especially when adversity strikes. Reference group approval can be a significant source of positive reinforcement for a person's career choice and, thus, his or her entire self-image and identity.[8] Ideally, peer group support for each team member should be there. (If it is not, the lead entrepreneur may have to accept the additional burden of encouragement and support in hard times, a burden that can be sizable.) Therefore, questions of whether a prospective team member's spouse is solidly in favor of his or her decision to pursue an entrepreneurial career and the sweat equity required and of whether the team member's close friends will be a source of support and encouragement or of detraction or negativism need to be considered.

Common Pitfalls

There can be difficulties in the practical implementation of these philosophies and attitudes, irrespective of the venture opportunity and the people involved. The company may come unglued before it gets started, may experience infant mortality, or may live perpetually immersed in nasty divisive conflicts and power struggles that will cripple its potential, even if they do not kill the company.

Often, a team lacks skill and experience in dealing with such difficult startup issues, does not take the time to go through an extended "mating dance" among potential partners during the moonlighting phase before actually launching the venture, or does not seek the advice of competent advisors. As a result, such a team may be unable to deal with such sensitive issues as who gets how much ownership, who will commit what time and money or other resources, how disagreements will be resolved, and how a team member can leave or be let go. Thus, crucial early discussions among team members sometimes lead to a premature disbanding of promising teams with sound business ideas. Or in the rush to get going, or because the funds to pay for help in these areas are lacking, a team may stay together but not work through, even in a rough way, many of these issues. Such teams do not take advantage of the moonlighting phase to test the commitment and contribution made by team members. For example, to build a substantial business, a partner needs to be totally committed to the venture. The success of the venture is the partner's most important goal, and other priorities, including his or her family, come second.[9] Another advantage of using such a shakedown period effectively is that the risks inherent in such factors as premature commitment to permanent decisions regarding salary and stock are lower.

The common approach to forming a new venture team also can be a common pitfall for new venture teams. Here, two to four entrepreneurs, usually friends or work acquaintances, decide to demonstrate their equality with such democratic trimmings as equal stock ownership, equal salaries, equal office space and cars, and other items symbolizing their peer status. Left unanswered are questions of who is in charge, who makes the final decisions, and how real differences of opinion are resolved. While some overlapping of roles and a sharing in and negotiating of decisions are desirable in new venture teams, too much looseness is debilitating. Even sophisticated buy-sell agreements among partners often fail to resolve the conflicts.

Another pitfall is a belief that there are no deficiencies in the lead entrepreneur or the management team. Or a team is overly fascinated with or overcommitted to a product idea. For example, a lead entrepreneur who is unwilling or unable to identify his or her own deficiencies and weaknesses and to add appropriate team members to compensate for these, and who further lacks an understanding of what is really needed to make a new venture grow into a successful business, has fallen into this pitfall.[10]

Failing to recognize that creating and building a new venture is a dynamic process is a problem for some teams. Therefore, such teams fail to realize that initial agreements are likely not to reflect actual contributions of team members over time, regardless of how much time one devotes to team-building tasks

[8] Reference groups—groups consisting of individuals with whom there is frequent interaction (such as family, friends, and co-workers), with whom values and interests are shared, and from whom support and approval for activities are derived—have long been known for their influence on behavior. See John W. Thibault and Harold H. Kelley, *The Social Psychology of Groups* (New York: John Wiley & Sons, 1966).

[9] This has been shown, for example, by Edgar H. Schein's research about entrepreneurs, general managers, and technical managers who are MIT alumni. See the Proceedings of the Eastern Academy of Management meeting, May 1972, Boston.

[10] J. A. Timmons presented a discussion of these entrepreneurial characteristics at the First International Conference on Entrepreneurship. See "Entrepreneurial Behavior," Proceedings, First International Conference on Entrepreneurship, Center for Entrepreneurial Studies, Toronto, November 1973.

and regardless of the agreements team members make before startup. In addition, they fail to consider that teams are likely to change in composition over time. The late Richard Testa, a leading attorney whose firm has dealt with such ventures as Lotus Development Corporation and with numerous venture capital firms, recently startled those attending a seminar on raising venture capital by saying:

> The only thing that I can tell you with great certainty about this startup business has to do with you and your partners. I can virtually guarantee you, based on our decade plus of experience, that five years from now at least one of the founders will have left every company represented here today.[11]

Such a team, therefore, fails to put in place mechanisms that will facilitate and help structure graceful divorces and that will provide for the internal adjustments required as the venture grows.

Destructive motivations in investors, prospective team members, or the lead entrepreneur spell trouble. Teams suffer if they are not alert to signs of potentially destructive motivations, such as an early concern for power and control by a team member. In this context, it has been argued that conflict management is a central task for members of teams. A study of self-empowered teams found that how team members manage their conflicts could affect their self-efficacy, as well as overall team performance. Team members in this study were most effective when they recognized they wanted to resolve the conflict for mutual benefit and that the goal is to help each other get what each other really needs and values, and not to try to win or to outdo each other.[12]

Finally, new venture teams may take trust for granted. Integrity is important in long-term business success, and the world is full of high-quality, ethical people; yet the real world also is inhabited by predators, crooks, sharks, frauds, and imposters. Chapter 9 contains a detailed discussion on the importance of integrity in entrepreneurial pursuits. It is paradoxical that an entrepreneur cannot succeed without trust, but he or she probably cannot succeed with blind trust either. Trust is something that is earned, usually slowly, for it requires a lot of patience and a lot of testing in the real world. This is undoubtedly a major reason why investors prefer to see teams that have worked closely together. In the area of trust, a little cynicism goes a long way, and teams that do not pay attention to detail, such as performing due diligence with respect to a person or firm, fall into this pit.

Rewards and Incentives

Slicing the Founder's Pie

One of the most frequently asked questions from startup entrepreneurs is: How much stock ownership should go to whom? (Chapter 13 examines the various methodologies used by venture capitalists and investors to determine what share of the company is required by the investor at different rounds of investment.) Consider the recent discussions with Jed, a former student, who secured substantial early-stage funding from John Doerr of Kleiner, Perkins, Caufield & Byers. The advice for Jed and all others is the same.

First, start with a philosophy and set of values that boil down to Ewing Marion Kauffman's great principle: Share the wealth with those who help to create the value and thus the wealth. Once over that hurdle, you are less likely to get hung up on the percentage of ownership issue. After all, 51 percent of nothing is nothing. The key is making the pie as large as possible. Second, the ultimate goal of any venture-capital-backed company is to realize a harvest at a price 5 to 10 times the original investment, and up. Thus, the company will either be sold via an initial public offering (IPO) or to a larger company. It is useful to work backward from the capital structure at the time of the IPO to envision and define what will happen and who will get what. Most venture-capital-backed, smaller company IPOs during the robust capital markets of the late 1990s would have 12 million to 15 million shares of stock outstanding after the IPO. In most situations 2.5 million to 4 million shares are sold to the public (mostly to institutional investors) at $12 to $15 per share, depending on the perceived quality of the company and the robustness of the appetite for IPOs at the time. The number could be halved or doubled. Typically, the founder/CEO will own 1 million to 3 million shares after the IPO, worth somewhere between $12 million and $45 million. Put in this perspective, it is much easier to see why finding a great opportunity, building a great team, and sharing the wealth with widespread ownership in the team is far more important than what percentage of the company is owned.

Finally, especially for young entrepreneurs in their 20s or 30s, this will not be their last venture. The single most important thing is that it succeeds. Make

[11] The seminar, held at Babson College, was called "Raising Venture Capital," and was co-sponsored by *Venture Capital Journal* and Coopers & Lybrand, 1985.
[12] S. Alper, D. Tjosvold, and K. S. Law, "Conflict Management, Efficacy, and Performance in Organizational Teams," *Personnel Psychology*, 53 no. 3 (2000) pp. 625–42.

this happen, and the future opportunities will be boundless. All this can be ruined if the founder/CEO simply gets greedy and overcontrolling, keeping most of the company to himself or herself, rather than creating a huge, shared pie.

The Reward System

John L. Hayes and the late Brian Haslett of Venture Founders Corporation have made a major contribution in the area of reward systems, and the following is based on their work.

The reward system of a new venture includes both the financial rewards of a venture—such as stock, salary, and fringe benefits—and the chance to realize personal growth and goals, exercise autonomy, and develop skills in particular venture roles. Also, what is perceived as a reward by any single team member will vary. This perception will depend very much upon personal values, goals, and aspirations. Some may seek long-range capital gains, while others desire more short-term security and income.

The reward system established for a new venture team should facilitate the interface of the venture opportunity and the management team. It needs to flow from team formation and enhance the entrepreneurial climate of the venture and the building of an effective team. For example, being able to attract and keep high-quality team members depends, to a great extent, on financial and psychological rewards given. The skills, experience, commitment, risk, concern, and so forth, of these team members are secured through these rewards.

The rewards available to an entrepreneurial team vary over the life of a venture. While intangible rewards, such as opportunity for self-development and realization, may be available throughout, some of the financial rewards are more or less appropriate at different stages of the venture's development.

Because these rewards are so important and because, in its early stages, a venture is limited in the rewards it can offer, the total reward system over the life of the venture needs to be thought through very carefully and efforts need to be made to ensure that the venture's capacity to reward is not limited as levels of contribution change or as new personnel are added.

External issues also have an impact on the reward system created for a new venture. The division of equity between the venture and external investors will affect how much equity is available to team members. Further, the way a venture deals with these questions also will determine its credibility with investors and others, because these people will look to the reward system for signs of commitment by the venture team.

Critical Issues

Dividing ownership among the founding team, based on the philosophy and vision discussed earlier, is an early critical task for the lead entrepreneur. Investors may provide advice but will, more often than not, dump the issue squarely back in the lap of the lead entrepreneur, since whether and how these delicate ownership decisions are resolved often is seen by investors as an important litmus test.

Also, the process by which a reward system is decided and the commitment of each team member to deal with problems in a way that will ensure rewards continue to reflect performance are of utmost importance. Each key team member needs to be committed to working out solutions that reflect the commitments, risks, and anticipated relative contributions of team members as fairly as possible.

A good reward system reflects the goals of the particular venture and is in tune with valuations. If a venture is not seeking outside capital, outside owners need not be considered; but the same issues need to be resolved. For example, if a goal is to realize a substantial capital gain from the venture in the next 5 to 10 years, then the reward system needs to be aimed at reinforcing this goal and encouraging the long-term commitment required for its attainment.

No time-tested formulas or simple answers exist to cover all questions of how distributions should be made. However, the following issues should be considered:

- *Differentiation.* The democracy approach can work, but it involves higher risk and more pitfalls than a system that differentiates based on the value of contributions by team members. As a rule, different team members rarely contribute the same amount to the venture, and the reward system needs to recognize these differences.
- *Performance.* Reward needs to be a function of performance (as opposed to effort) during the early life of the venture and not during only one part of this period. Many ventures have been torn apart when the relative contributions of the team members changed dramatically several years after startup without a significant change in rewards. (Vesting goes a long way toward dealing with this issue.)
- *Flexibility.* Regardless of the contribution of any team member at any given time, the

probability is high that this will change. The performance of a team member may be substantially more or less than anticipated. Further, a team member may have to be replaced and someone may have to be recruited and added to the existing team. Flexibility in the reward system, including such mechanisms as vesting and setting aside a portion of stock for future adjustments, can help to provide a sense of justice.

Considerations of Timing

Division of rewards, such as the split of stock between the members of the entrepreneurial team, will most likely be made very early in the life of the venture. Rewards may be a way of attracting significant early contribution; however, it is performance over the life of the venture that needs to be rewarded.

For example, regarding equity, once the allocation of stock is decided, changes in the relative stock positions of team members will be infrequent. New team members or external investors may dilute each member's position, but the relative positions will probably remain unchanged.

However, one or more events may occur during the early years of a venture. First, a team member who has a substantial portion of stock may not perform and need to be replaced early in the venture. A key team member may find a better opportunity and quit, or a key team member could die in an accident. In each of these cases, the team will then be faced with the question of what will happen to the stock held by the team member. In each case, stock was intended as a reward for performance by the team member during the first several years of the venture, but the team member will not perform over this time period.

Several mechanisms are available to a venture when the initial stock split is so made to avoid the loss or freezing of equity. A venture can retain an option of returning stock to its treasury at the price at which it was purchased in certain cases, such as when a team member needs to be replaced. A buyback agreement also achieves this purpose.

To guard against the event that some portion of the stock has been earned and some portion will remain unearned, as when a team member quits or dies, the venture can place stock purchased by team members in escrow to be released over a two- or three-year period. Such a mechanism is called a stock-vesting agreement, and such an agreement can foster longer-term commitment to the success of the venture, while also providing a method for a civilized no-fault corporate divorce if things do not work out. Such a stock-vesting agreement is attached as a restriction on the stock certificate. Typically, the vesting agreement establishes a period of years, often four or more. During this period, the founding stockholders can "earn out" their shares. If a founder decides to leave the company before completion of the four-year vesting period, he or she may be required to sell the stock back to the company for the price originally paid for it, usually nothing. The departing shareholder, in this instance, would not own any stock after the departure. Nor would any capital gain windfall be realized by the departing founder. In other cases, founders may vest a certain portion each year, so they have some shares even if they leave. Such vesting can be weighted toward the last year or two of the vesting period. Other restrictions can give management and the board control over the disposition of stock, whether the stockholder stays or leaves the company. In essence, a mechanism such as a stock-vesting agreement confronts team members with the reality that "this is not a get-rich-quick exercise."

Other rewards, such as salary, stock options, bonuses, and fringe benefits, can be manipulated more readily to reflect changes in performance. But the ability to manipulate these is also somewhat dependent upon the stage of development of the venture. In the case of cash rewards, there is a trade-off between giving cash and the growth of the venture. Thus, in the early months of a venture, salaries will necessarily be low or nonexistent, and bonuses and other fringe benefits usually will be out of the question. Salaries, bonuses, and fringe benefits all drain cash, and until profitability is achieved, cash can always be put to use for operations. After profitability is achieved, cash payments will still limit growth. Salaries can become competitive once the venture has passed breakeven, but bonuses and fringe benefits should probably be kept at a minimum until several years of profitability have been demonstrated.

Considerations of Value

The contributions of team members will vary in nature, extent, and timing. In developing the reward system, particularly the distribution of stock, contributions in certain areas are of particular value to a venture, as follows:

- *Idea.* In this area, the originator of the idea, particularly if trade secrets or special technology for a prototype was developed or if product or market research was done, needs to be considered.
- *Business plan preparation.* Preparing an acceptable business plan, in terms of dollars and hours expended, needs to be considered.

- *Commitment and risk.* A team member may invest a large percentage of his or her net worth in the company, be at risk if the company fails, have to make personal sacrifices, put in long hours and major effort, risk his or her reputation, accept reduced salary, or already have spent a large amount of time on behalf of the venture. This commitment and risk need to be considered.
- *Skills, experience, track record, or contacts.* A team member may bring to the venture skills, experience, track record, or contacts in such areas as marketing, finance, and technology. If these are of critical importance to the new venture and are not readily available, these need to be considered.
- *Responsibility.* The importance of a team member's role to the success of the venture needs to be considered.

Being the originator of the idea or expending a great amount of time or money in preparing the business plan is frequently overvalued. If these factors are evaluated in terms of the real success of the venture down the road, it is difficult to justify much more than 15 percent to 20 percent of equity for them. Commitment and risk, skills, experience, and responsibility contribute more by far to producing success of a venture.

The above list is valuable in attempting to weigh fairly the relative contributions of each team member. Contributions in each of these areas have some value; it is up to a team to agree on how to assign value to contributions and, further, to leave enough flexibility to allow for changes.

Compensation and Incentives in High Potential Ventures

A useful technical note covering the important tax and accounting issues for stock options, incentive stock options, bonuses, phantom stock, and the like was developed by the author. "Compensation Incentives in High Potential Ventures" (HBS 9-392-035) is available through Harvard Business School Publishing, Soldiers Field Road, Boston. An excellent CD-ROM has been developed on rewards and compensation in high growth companies by The Ewing Marion Kauffman Foundation in Kansas City (800/489-4900).

Internet Impact: Team

Attracting Talent

The Internet is quickly changing the economics and capabilities of the job market. The ease and low cost of posting detailed employment openings, the extremely large databases of job seekers, and the speed of candidate response have many hiring managers and entrepreneurs devoting more time than ever before to recruiting online. The Interactive Advertising Bureau reported that just over $107 million was spent on online recruitment advertising in 2004—roughly 10 percent of all recruitment advertising in the United States.

Since employers can delimit résumé searches to specified skill sets, years of experience, and salary requirements with a few keystrokes, a single Internet site such as Monster.com can serve as a targeted recruiting engine that is equal to a dozen or more recruiters. Jeff Taylor, Monster.com's founder and CEO, commented, "Post an opening for somebody fluent in Japanese and English, and you're as apt to hear from applicants in Tokyo and Dublin as from those in Los Angeles. We get 5 million visitors a month, and in many cases, small businesses get as many as 400 responses from one posting."

Web sites representing professional associations such as Women in Technology International (http://www.witi.com) also have large databases of qualified individuals. These sites will often post job openings for a nominal fee.

Chapter Summary

1. A strong team is usually the difference between a success and a marginal or failed venture, and between a so-so and a great company.
2. Core philosophies, values, and attitudes, particularly sharing the wealth and ownership with those who create it, are key to team building.
3. The fit concept is central to anticipating management gaps and building the team.
4. Numerous pitfalls await the entrepreneur in team building and need to be avoided.
5. Compensating and rewarding team members requires both a philosophy and technical know-how, and can have enormous impact on the odds of success.

Study Questions

1. Why is the team so important in the entrepreneurial process?
2. Describe what is meant by "team" philosophy and attitudes. Why are these important?
3. What are the most critical questions a lead entrepreneur needs to consider in thinking through the team issue? Why?
4. What are some common pitfalls in team building?
5. What are the critical rewards, compensation, and incentive issues in putting a team together? Why are these so crucial and difficult to manage?
6. How does the lead entrepreneur allocate stock ownership and options in the new venture? Who should get what ownership and why?

Internet Resources for Chapter 8

http://www.fed.org *The Beyster Institute is a non-profit organization whose mission is to advance the use of entrepreneurship and employee ownership to build stronger, higher performing enterprises*

http://www.bizmove.com *Resource of small business information packed with dozens of guides and worksheets*

http://www.morebusiness.com *A comprehensive resource for small businesses, contains tips, articles, ideas, templates, worksheets, sample business plans, tools, financial benchmarks, and sample contracts*

http://www.onlinewbc.gov *SBA's Women's Business Center*

http://www.businessweek.com/smallbiz/index.html *Business Week Small Business*

http://www.ivysea.com/pages/bizon.html *Inspiration and advice on leadership, management, and organizational behavior topics*

MIND STRETCHERS

Have you considered?

1. Think about a team on which you have been a member or a captain. What leadership and coaching principles characterized the most and least successful teams?
2. What *is* a team? What is its antithesis?
3. A team may not be for everyone. How do you see the fit between you and the team concept?
4. One expert insists that the only guarantee he can make to a startup team is that in five years, at least one or two members will leave or be terminated. What causes this? Why will your team be different?
5. Ask five people who have worked with you in a team to give you feedback about your team-building skills.

Exercise
Rewards

The following exercise can help an entrepreneur devise a reward system for a new venture. In proceeding with the exercise, it is helpful to pretend to look at these issues from an investor's point of view and to imagine that the venture is in the process of seeking capital from an investor group to which a presentation was made several weeks ago and which is favorably impressed by the team and its plan for the new venture. Imagine then that this investor group would like a brief presentation (of 10 to 15 minutes) about how the team plans to reward its members and other key contributors.

Name:

Venture:

Date:

Part I

Part I is to be completed by each individual team member—*alone.*

STEP 1

Indicate who will do what during the first year or two of your venture, what contributions each has made or will make to creating a business plan, the commitment and risk involved for each, and what unique critical skills, experience, contacts, and so forth, each brings to the venture. Try to be as specific as possible, and be sure to include yourself.

Team Member	Responsibility	Title	Contribution to Business Plan	Commitment and Risk	Unique/Critical Skills, Etc.

STEP 2

Indicate below the approximate salary and shares of stock (as a percent) each member should have upon closing the financing of your new venture.

Team Member	Salary	Shares of Stock (# and %)

STEP 3

Indicate below what fringe benefits you believe the company should provide during the first year or two.

Team Member	Vacation	Holidays	Health/Life Insurance	Retirement Plan	Other

STEP 4

List other key contributors, such as members of the board of directors, and indicate how they will be rewarded.

Name	Expertise/ Contribution	Salary	Shares of Stock (# and %)	Other

Part II

Part II involves meeting as a team to reach consensus on the responsibilities of each team member and how each will be rewarded. In addition to devising a reward system for the team and other key contributors, the team will examine how consensus was reached.

STEP 1

Meet as a team and reach consensus on the above team issues and indicate the consensus solution below.

Responsibilities/Contributions

Team Member	Responsibility	Contribution to Business Plan	Commitment and Risk	Unique/Critical Skills, Etc.

Rewards

Team Member	Salary	Shares of Stock (# and %)

Rewards (continued)

Team Member	Title	Vacation	Holidays	Health/Life Insurance	Retirement Plan	Other

STEP 2

Meet as a team and reach consensus on issues involving other key contributors and indicate the consensus solution below.

Name	Expertise/ Contribution	Salary	Shares of Stock (# and %)	Other

STEP 3

Discuss as a team the following issues and indicate any important lessons and implications:

- What patterns emerged in the approaches taken by each team? What are the differences and similarities?
- How difficult or easy was it to reach agreement among team members? Did any issues bog down?
- If salaries or stock were equal for all team members, why was this so? What risks or problems might such an approach create?
- What criteria, either implicit or explicit, were used to arrive at a decision concerning salaries and stock? Why?

Case

Maclean Palmer

Preparation Questions

1. Evaluate Maclean Palmer's decision to create a new venture capital fund in 2000 and his progress to date.
2. What is your evaluation of the team?
3. Outline the major risks you see, the due diligence questions you would focus on, and whom you would contact as a pension fund analyst or prospective limited in the fund.
4. Prepare a detailed outline of what you would include in a private placement memorandum to market the fund to potential investors.
5. Who should invest in a venture capital fund?

Maclean Palmer

Maclean Palmer strode out onto a Martha's Vineyard beach to enjoy the warm sun as it set on what had proved to be a pivotal day in his quest to start up a $200 million private equity fund. That August afternoon in 2000, Palmer and his four chosen partners had made a collective decision that would, for better or for worse, change their lives forever.

In less than two months, each of the partners would quit their jobs, sell their homes, and move their families to Boston to begin crafting an offering memorandum for a private equity fund that they were certain would attract a differentiated and lucrative deal flow. With 2000 shaping up to be the largest venture fund-raising year in history, it seemed that they could not have picked a better time to strike out on their own.

The Venture Capital Investing Process

Venture capitalists and entrepreneurs engaged in a process whereby they assumed and managed the risks associated with investing in compelling new business opportunities. Their aim was long-term value creation for themselves, their companies, their communities, and other stakeholders. The process began with the conceptualization of an investment opportunity. A prospectus would then be written to articulate the strategy and outline the qualifications and track record of the investment team. Raising the money was a networking and sales undertaking that typically gained momentum only after an institutional investment advisor—known as a gatekeeper (see box)—had committed capital to the fund.

Once the money had been raised, the venture capital firm sought to add value in many ways: identifying and evaluating business opportunities, negotiating and closing the investment, tracking and coaching the company, providing technical and management assistance, and attracting additional capital, directors, management, suppliers, and other key resources (see Exhibit 1). Given the fortuitous convergence of factors (e.g., management talent, market timing, strategic vision) required for a startup to reach a profitable harvest event such as an acquisition or an IPO, home runs were very rare. In fact, historical data indicated that only about 1 out of every 15 of these investments ever realized a return of 10 times or more on invested capital. The venture capital process occurred in the context of mostly private, imperfect capital markets for new, emerging, and middle-market companies (i.e., those with $20 million to $150 million in sales).[1]

The dominant legal structure for private venture capital funds was the limited partnership, with the venture capitalist assuming the role of general partners and the investors as limited partners (see Exhibit 2). The general partners acted as organizers and investment managers

[1] William D. Bygrave and Jeffry A. Timmons, *Venture Capital at the Crossroads* (Boston: Harvard School Press, 1992). Note: middle market company figures reflect the range in the early 2000s.

This case was prepared by Carl Hedberg under the direction of Professor Jeffry Timmons, the Franklin W. Olin Distinguished Professor of Entrepreneurship at the Arthur M. Blank Center for Entrepreneurship, Babson College. Funding provided by the Franklin W. Olin Foundation.

The Gatekeepers

Institutional investors such as corporations, foundations, and pension funds invested as limited partners in hundreds of venture capital and buyout funds. Many of these investors, having neither the resources nor the expertise to evaluate and manage fund investments, delegated these duties to investment advisors with expertise in the venture capital industry. These advisors would pool the assets of their various clients and invest those proceeds on behalf of their limited partners into a venture or buyout fund currently raising capital. For this service, the advisors collected a fee of 1 percent of committed capital per annum. Since these investment experts exerted a tremendous amount of influence over the allocation of capital to new and existing venture teams and funds, they were referred to as gatekeepers.

EXHIBIT 1

Classic VC Investing Process

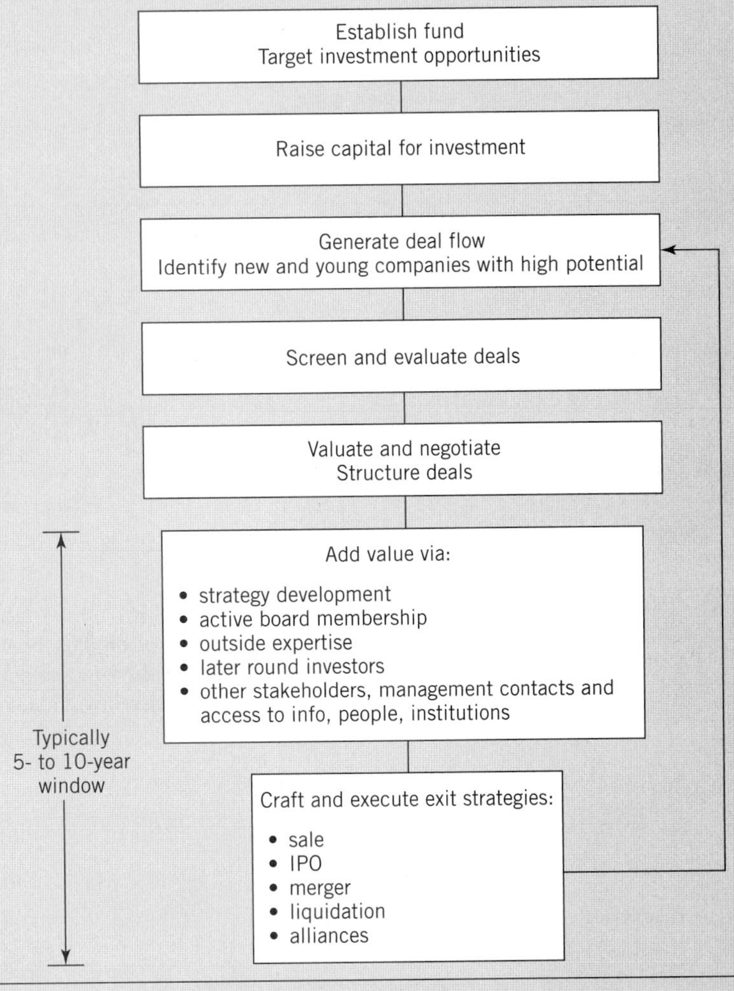

of the fund, while the limited partners enjoyed a passive role in fund management as well as limited liability for any fund activity. As compensation for their direct participation and risk exposure, general partners stood to reap substantial gains in the form of carried interest on successful portfolio companies.

This partnership structure stipulated a specific term of years for the fund. Extending that life span required the consent of the general partners and two-thirds of the limited partners. The fee structure between the general and limited partners was considerably varied and, as a result, affected the level of attraction of the fund.[2]

Between 1980 and mid-2000, there were two recessions (in 1981–1982 and in 1990–1992), and a stock market panic in late 1987 that sent share prices plummeting 22 percent in a single day in October that year. Nevertheless, according to Venture Economics—a private equity database compiler—venture investments during that time had yielded a 19.3 percent average annual return after fees and expenses. Over the same period, the S&P 500 and the Russell 2000 index of small companies generated average annual returns, respectively, of 15.7 percent and 13.3 percent. The latest five-year trends showed venture returns far ahead of lackluster buyout performance and falling U.S. blue chip prices. Fueled by these figures and the high-profile Internet boom, year 2000 was shaping up to be a record-breaking period for venture fund-raising (see Exhibit 3).

Historically, equity funds had been conceived, invested, and exited on an 8- to 12-year cycle, with preparation for follow-on funds beginning in years three and four. To a large degree, that time frame had been driven by the reality that, on average, it took five to seven years to build and harvest a successful portfolio investment.

By the late 1990s, however, the throughput time for harvesting high flyers had been slashed to the point where some companies were skipping from a first round of venture financing into a successful IPO—all in the

[2] Ibid.

EXHIBIT 2

Flows of VC

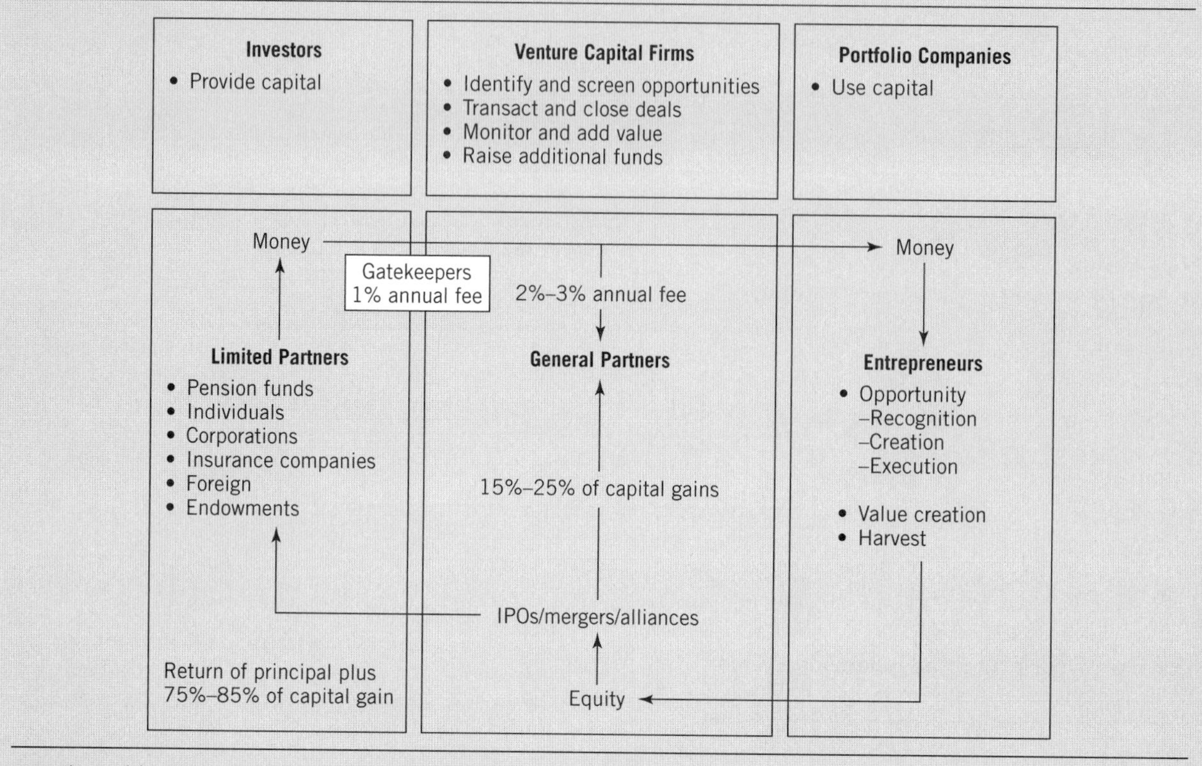

Note: These exhibits are discussed further in Chapter 13, Obtaining Venture and Growth Capital.

EXHIBIT 3

Funds, Fund Commitments, and Average Fund Size

	Venture Capital				Buyout and Mezzanine			
Year/Qtr	First Time Funds	Total Funds	Avg Fund Size ($mil)	Total Raised ($Billions)	First Time Funds	Total Funds	Avg Fund Size ($mil)	Total Raised ($Billions)
1994	25	138	56.5	7.8	31	103	202.9	20.9
1995	36	155	63.9	9.9	32	105	253.3	26.6
1996	54	163	74.2	12.1	38	112	300.9	33.7
1997	79	232	76.3	17.7	39	140	355.7	49.8
1998	82	277	109.7	30.4	42	166	386.1	64.1
1999	146	424	139.5	59.2	44	157	410.8	64.5
Q1 2000	45	165	132.1	21.8	9	42	300	12.6
Q2 2000	51	183	168.3	30.8	10	50	212	10.6

Source: National Venture Capital Association (http://www.nvca.org/nvca2_11_02.html).

space of a year or less—and typically in less than two years. While not all portfolio gems were cut loose this quickly, this new landscape had radically altered the frequency and capitalization of follow-on venture capital funds. For example, between 1994 and 2000, Spectrum Equity Investors (Boston/Menlo Park) had been able to close on four funds totaling just over $3 billion. Between 1998 and 2001, over $200 billion had been raised by venture groups—more than the total of the previous 40 years.

Concepting

With five years of direct investing experience in this heady private equity space as a principal at Point West Partners in San Francisco—along with 17 years of operating experience—venture capitalist Maclean Palmer, 40, decided in 1999 that the time was right to develop his own fund:

> As an ethnic minority, I had always been committed to minority business development, and I knew that there was a large pool of talented minority executives out there that traditional VCs weren't calling on to run portfolio companies. These executives have a tremendous amount of operating experience, and I figured there should be a way to build significant post-investment value by bridging that operating experience with a solid investing strategy. I began to ask, "What should be the profile and experience of the team that could exploit that opportunity?"

In seeking advice, one of his first calls was to Wanda Felton, a director of private equity investments at Credit Suisse First Boston. During the early 1990s, Felton had honed her due diligence skills while working at Hamilton Lane, a Philadelphia-based gatekeeper with an interest in first-time funds in the minority space. She and Palmer had initially met as judges for a Wharton business plan competition, and later, they worked together when she had assisted the Point West group in raising their fourth fund.

Outlining what she felt were important criteria for assessing first-time private equity offerings (see Exhibit 4), Felton recalled that while Palmer had some hurdles to clear, she sensed that he had come up with a salable concept:

> For a limited partner, putting money into a first-time fund has all the risks associated with a typical startup investment. On top of that, this type of deal is a 10-year-plus commitment with no ability to get out. LPs, therefore, look for groups that can demonstrate that they have worked successfully together in the past, will stay together, and have a common view of how they'll run their portfolio businesses. Since Maclean was talking about developing a new team, this collective experience was of course something his fund would not have.
>
> Still, Maclean was describing a focused, "management-centric" concept—meaning that his core strategy would be to identify and recruit top-level ethnic-minority managers from Fortune 1,000 companies to run—and add value to—his fund's investments. The other elements of the strategy included a focus on being company builders with an operating orientation, and the ability to leverage their combined operating and investing expertise to add value to their portfolio companies. This was intriguing, and it certainly differentiated him from the majority of private equity firms.

EXHIBIT 4

Due Diligence on New Funds

The Business

What is the overall strategy?

Is there a market opportunity, and can it be executed in the current market environment, and during the expected commitment period?

Has the team articulated a strategic and operating business strategy for portfolio companies?

Do they have a viable exit plan?

Probably most crucial: How has the general partner group demonstrated that they will be able to add investment value to their portfolio companies?

The Team

Do the general partner and the team have the requisite private equity investing experience and resources to execute the strategy?

Will the team have access to deal flow within the stated strategy?

Is the team stable?

Has the team worked together before?

Do they have a common view as to how they will run the businesses?

Do they have a meaningful track record in the stated strategy?

Next, Palmer contacted Grove Street Advisors (GSA) partner David Mazza, an expert in the venture executive search field, and an outspoken champion of first-time funds.

The Advocates

Back in 1997, Dave Mazza had introduced Babson MBA Palmer—then a Kauffman Fellow (see box) at Advent International in Boston—to the venture group at Point West Partners. When Palmer (see Appendix A: Team Profiles) contacted Mazza in 1999 with an idea for developing a fund that would proactively seek out talented ethnic-minority executives to back in mainstream ventures, the seasoned advisor was immediately drawn to the possibilities:

> I'm being told by the chairman of General Motors that if we could start three or four well-run ethnic-minority-owned supplier businesses, we could build them to $300 million to $400 million companies over the next four to five years—easily and profitably. That's an opportunity you don't always hear—and it's because of the minority aspect. In the automotive industry, 10 percent of all supplier contracts have to be set aside for minority businesses—that's life, and traditional venture capital firms like Kleiner, Bessemer and Sequoia can't effectively go after that market; but someone like Palmer could.

The Kauffman Fellowship

In 1993, the Ewing Marion Kauffman Foundation (www.emkf.org) established the Kauffman Fellows Program (www.kauffmanfellows.org), a program designed to educate and train emerging leaders in the venture capital process. The curriculum provided a rigorous yet flexible educational experience, enabling the Fellow to combine the theory and best practice of venture creation, while utilizing their position in venture capital as a learning laboratory. Like a medical residency, the Fellowship was an apprenticeship program that featured a structured educational curriculum, an individual learning plan, facilitated mentoring, peer learning and networking, and leadership development in specific areas of interest.

Kauffman Fellows were students of the Center for Venture Education, and could serve as either temporary or permanent full-time associates of the venture firm during the time of the Fellowship. As associates, their salary, benefits, and expenses were the responsibility of, and determined by, the firm.

Mazza added that the capabilities of nontraditional funds were something that gatekeepers like Hamilton Lane and GSA had been advocating for years:

> Traditional institutional investors always look for the same things. They think that the guys who made money before are going to make it again; that's wrong—it's a different world now. The reality is that white boys aren't the only people who know how to make money. Sure, there are still going to be the guys making money in biotech and in semiconductors, but more and more we are seeing women entrepreneurs, African-American entrepreneurs, Hispanic entrepreneurs. The trouble is, there has been no money going in that direction except for government funding programs—and those are not set up to provide critical post-money support.

GSA co-founder Clint Harris referred to his firm's detailed evaluation model (see Exhibit 5) as he explained that

EXHIBIT 5

GSA Evaluation Process

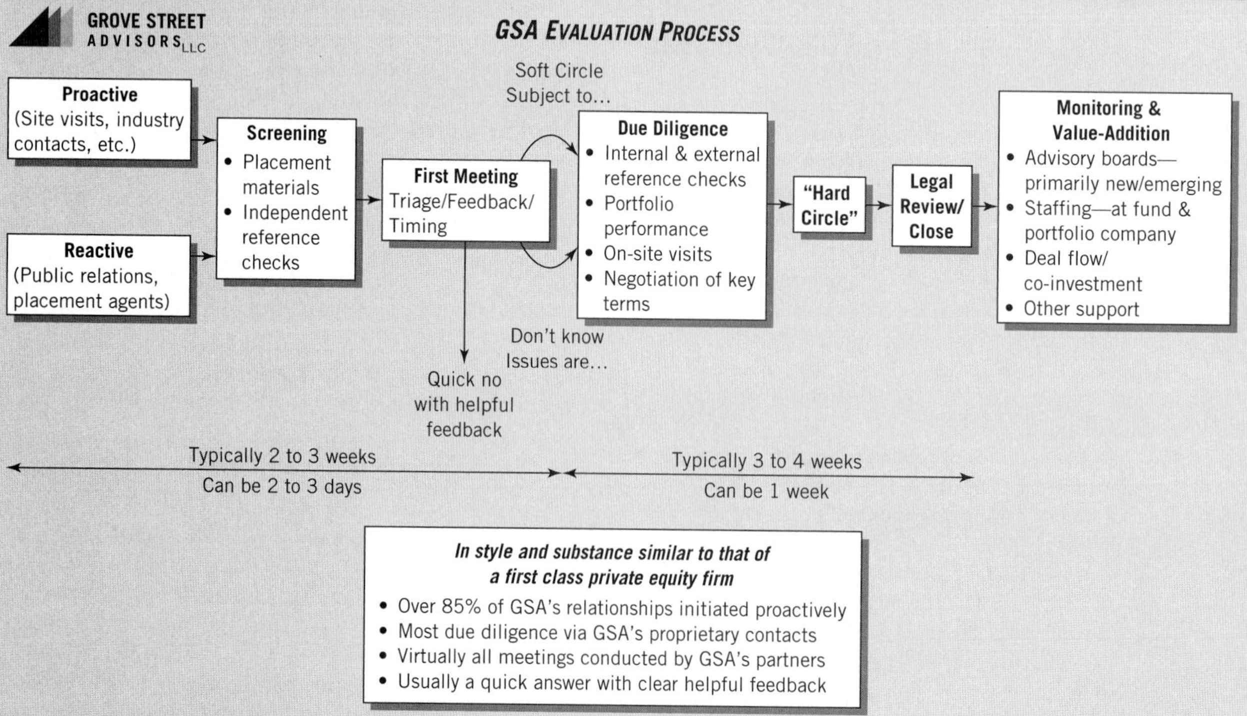

Source: Used by permission of Grove Street Advisors, LLC.

identifying and supporting emerging talent was similar to the work of assessing new venture opportunities:

> As with startups and entrepreneurs, the difference between the average investment manager and the top performers is huge. And just like with successful venture investing, we look at a lot of offerings and meet with a lot of teams. We tend to say no quickly; when we do spot talent, we start small, help them along. As they gain experience and credibility as successful investors, we write bigger and bigger checks.

Although the GSA partners felt that Palmer had the background, the drive, and the personality to lead the charge, the influential player was adamant about the need to achieve critical mass by bringing in known, experienced players. Mazza elaborated:

> I told Maclean that what he really needed to do was create an effort that became so prominent that if you were a top entrepreneur, a CEO, an Oprah, or a Steadman Graham—and you weren't part of it—you'd feel like you were out of it. That's the ideal.
>
> This would have to be a very high-profile group with private equity expertise and some buyout experience. I wanted to see some names that people could immediately identify with—either on the advisory board or in the partnership ranks.

Palmer, however, felt that far too much emphasis was being placed on the minority aspect of what he was trying to develop; and he also had his own vision about the sort of partners he needed to attract:

> GSA made it clear that if they were going to make any kind of substantial investment in my concept, then they would prefer that I focused on finding partners with lots of deal experience. That was, of course, one thing I had to look at, but I don't think that prior experience working together is necessarily the most important consideration in building a team of people who I expect to be partners with for 20 or 30 years. Although experience and track record are key, who my partners are as people is much more important to me than what they have accomplished up until now.

Recruiting an "American" Lineup

Driven by his strategy to develop a compelling investment team that would reflect the focus of the fund they would manage, Palmer tirelessly networked and thoroughly investigated dozens of potential minority candidates. His due diligence gave him a good sense of not only their investment preferences, management abilities, and track record, but their personal style as well. When asked about his first two choices, Wharton MBA Clark Pierce,[3] 38, and Harvard MBA Andrew Simon, 30, Palmer referred to their respective résumés (see Appendix A: Team Profiles), adding:

> Clark was a principal with Ninos Capital with seven years of mezzanine experience. What attracted me most about him was that we knew each other well and had complementary skill sets. He had come up through the financial side, and I had come up through the venture operating side, so the things that he liked and was most experienced and skilled with, I was less inclined toward. Andrew had excellent fundamentals and I liked the way he thought. I could sense that even though he was a young guy, he definitely had what it took.

In the spring of 1999, Wanda Felton introduced Palmer to 61-year-old Ray Turner—a newly retired senior executive at a Fortune 50 heavy industry corporation who had thus far turned down seven CEO jobs and 38 offers to serve on boards of directors. Turner recalled his first meeting with the nascent group:

> The four of us met on a Saturday morning at Logan Airport, and we spent a lot of time talking beyond just intellect. It was about character. I told them that if this was all about excellence, then I would consider playing—but if not, I didn't want to touch it. These were young, bright guys, and I was energized by how committed they were.

Felton explained that while Turner's sterling credentials (see Appendix A: Team Profiles) would help raise the profile of the group, it was his understanding of operations and his ability to connect with and evaluate senior-level managers that would add the most value to the team:

> The pool of ethnic-minority business talent—people with 20 or 30 years of experience—is something we haven't had in this country until very recently. Although there is now a huge cadre of senior managers—minority men and women who have risen to real positions of authority—they are not altogether visible since they have their heads down and they are doing their jobs. As a member of organizations like the Executive Leadership Council,[4] Ray has the ability to tap into that group.
>
> In most equity funds there are people executing the deals and there are people who are there because of who they know, and because of their wisdom, vision, and experience. The marriage of younger, hungry investors like Maclean and Clark with Ray's Rolodex and experience would be seen as a big plus for the effort.

For the position of vice president, Palmer recruited Harvard MBA Dario Cardenas, 31, a young man whose name

[3] Palmer and Pierce had first met in 1995. Seeing that they shared many of the same values and aspirations, they had kept in touch—professionally and socially.

[4] The Executive Leadership Council was an independent, nonpartisan, nonprofit corporation founded in 1986 to provide African-American executives with a network and leadership forum designed to add perspective and direction to the achievement of excellence in business, economic, and public policies for the African-American community, corporate America, and the public.

had come up on everyone's short list of the most talented Hispanic candidates in the country. Cardenas had earned that reputation in part because of his service—at just 23 years old—as the youngest elected mayor of a major U.S. city (see Appendix A: Team Profiles). Palmer explained that there was an advantage to bringing together people who were previously unknown to each other:

> One way to think about a private equity firm is that it is only as good as the combined talents and networks of its team members. For this reason, I wanted to set up a group that could bring to the table a diverse set of skills, contacts, and perspectives. What we wound up with was 57 years of operating and 25 years of private equity experience, leading deals of over $200 million, with $100 million returned on just four of 16 investments.

Clint Harris was impressed with the capable team that Palmer had recruited that year. Nevertheless, he remained concerned about their ability to evaluate and add significant value to opportunities that came their way:

> These guys had a good track record—which we verified with calls to their former colleagues, people at companies that they had invested in, and members of boards that they had served on. We could see that these were very bright and talented junior partner guys—as talented as any general partners that we had worked with—and Ray Turner was a real plus. In fact, a single half-hour call to my former suite mate at HBS—now CEO of General Motors—was all the due diligence I needed to learn that Ray would be a tremendous asset to the team, that he was totally committed, and that these young guys were top notch.
>
> That said, it takes time and investing results for anyone to learn the equity investment business, and to calibrate on their judgment and skills. These guys didn't have much of a track record, and in that respect they were on the thin edge of what we like to see.

Grove Street Advisors—Gatekeeper

Back in 1997, Clint Harris, a founder and former managing director of the Boston venture capital firm Advent International Corp., and Catherine Crocket, founder of the Gazelle Group, a state investment program advisor, moved to parlay their extensive venture capital relationships into a unique investment management practice for institutional clients.

Harris explained that the seemingly risk-averse approach of traditional fee-for-service investment advisors had served to, over time, shut their clients out of participating in top-tier funds (see Exhibits 6–8):

> Gatekeepers generally view first-time funds as too risky and therefore imprudent investments. With teams now raising new funds before they have proven track records, it becomes very difficult to evaluate a team based on their investments. By the time these teams do emerge as top-tier players, their funds are often closed to all but the people who have been supporting them all along. As an advisor and a fund of funds, the only way that we can hope to be on top 10 years from now is to identify and nurture the best new and emerging investment managers out there.
>
> The other big issue is that the gatekeepers and their large pension fund clients are not set up to make small investments. It takes much more effort and personnel on a per-dollar basis to evaluate a large number of emerging teams, negotiate 10, $10 million commitments, and then monitor those relationships than it does to put $100 million into a single large, established fund. As a result,

EXHIBIT 6

Life Cycle of Private Equity Managers

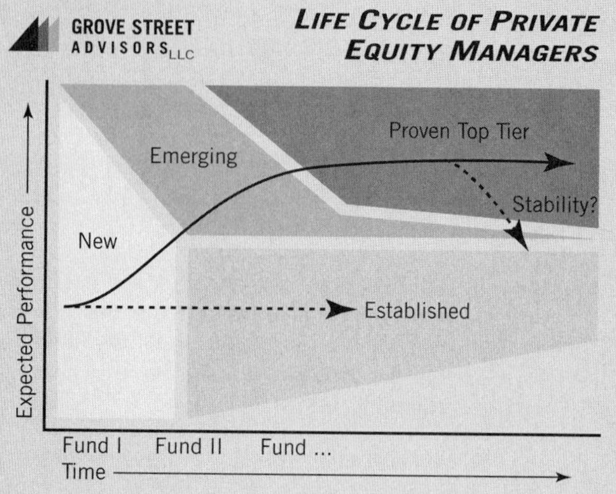

Source: Used by permission of Grove Street Advisors, LLC.

EXHIBIT 7

Gatekeeper Dilemma

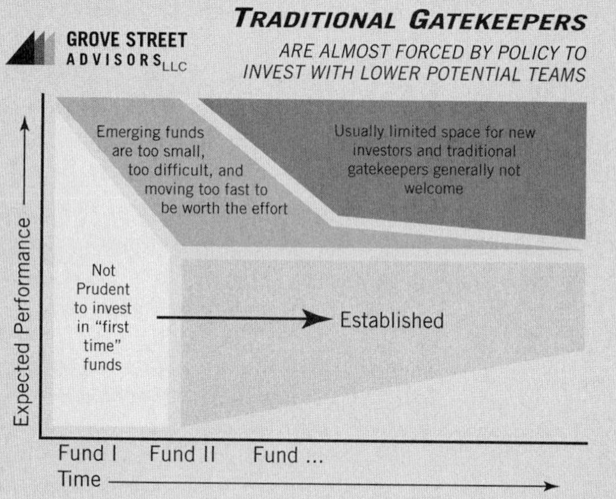

Source: Used by permission of Grove Street Advisors, LLC.

EXHIBIT 8

Critical Issues and Development Stage

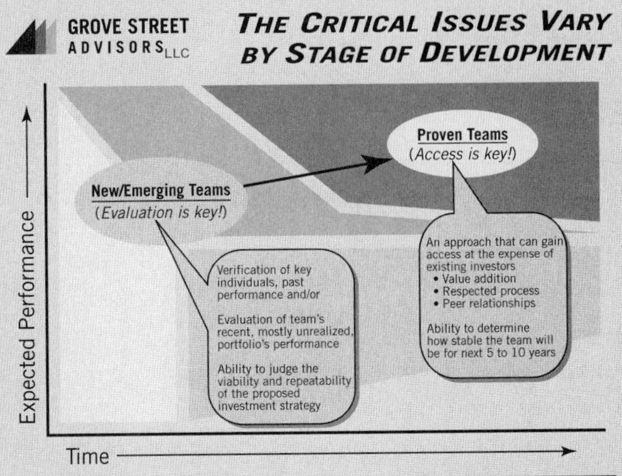

Source: Used by permission of Grove Street Advisors, LLC.

> the truly top-tier private equity funds, as well as small funds in general, are not represented or are significantly underweighted in the portfolios of most of the major state pension funds.
>
> Our idea was to offer these institutional investors a vehicle that could effectively identify, evaluate, and invest in a portfolio of very high quality new and emerging fund managers. Over time, these relationships would translate into a far higher quality core of funds in their private equity portfolios.

As a new organization with no track record, Harris and Crocket had assumed that they would start with a small client before going after a big state pension fund opportunity. Then, in the Spring of 1998, the Grove Street pair met with Barry Gonder, senior investment officer for the California Public Employees Retirement System (CalPERS). After filling out their team with the addition of Dave Mazza—founder of the largest and best-known executive search practice serving the venture capital industry—and proposing the creation of a dedicated fund of funds they would call California Emerging Ventures I (CEV I), GSA succeeded in beating out several other firms for the $350 million account.

Almost immediately, GSA began opening venture capital doors for their sole client. By early 2001, CalPERS had increased their GSA capital stake to $750 million, and the advisor group had placed CEV I money with nearly 45 top venture capital firms. Harris explained that with a third of the total investment pool earmarked for new and emerging teams, his group was naturally drawn to nontraditional niche opportunities:

> The paradox with demanding that mainstream investment standards are met is that those standards severely limit deal flow. We had our antennae up for minority and women investment opportunities, not for social reasons, but because we had the conviction that if we were able to find a strong enough team, they would attract a proprietary deal flow by way of their demographic network. We also knew that there were a lot of pension fund managers out there that were very interested in minority funding opportunities—opportunities that were being ignored by the mainstream.

At the heart of GSA's effectiveness was a broad base of business and venture capital industry contacts that enabled them to consistently conduct a level of due diligence on private equity managers that had not been seen before. Some particularly critical observers of the industry felt that quite often, institutional investors were inclined to follow lead investors, rather than conduct extensive investigations on their own.

As they had done when they were venture capitalists, GSA interviewed, reviewed, and assessed hundreds of potential new fund managers and concepts—and passed on all but a few. Three funds received backing early on: The Audax Group, a firm led by two former Bain Capital partners, Geoffrey Rehnert and Marc Wolpow; New Mountain Capital, the brainchild of ex-Forstmann Little partner Steven Klinsky; and Solera Capital, headed by Molly Ashby, a former buyout and growth-financing specialist at J.P. Morgan Capital Corporation.

Although Palmer had not recruited a senior partner with a proven return performance of "50 IRR over 20 years," the GSA group remained solidly behind his efforts. Now that the young venture capitalist had assembled a talented team that was demographically similar to the underserved and potentially lucrative entrepreneurial slice of America he aimed to target, Palmer knew that his next step was to foster a cohesive group dynamic.

Bonding the Team

Over the next few months, Palmer juggled the busy schedules of his potential partners in order to organize a number of in-depth strategy and bonding sessions (see Exhibit 9). He recalled that while these gatherings addressed issues related to the investment business that they would come together to create, the main focus was on building rapport and understanding:

> At our first get-together each of us told our whole personal and professional story. Once we had a collective sense of who we were, then we began to talk in general terms about what we wanted to build. It had to be something we all believed in—something that would last over the long term—and be able to survive economic down cycles. Then we asked, "Does the market want what we envision, and do we have the collective talent to succeed?"

In the summer of 2000, Palmer took his wife and two young children to Martha's Vineyard for his first two-week

EXHIBIT 9

Meeting Notes

Agenda- Introduction and Strategy Session

– All connected to the same Rope.

Date: **July 21, 2000**

Vilma Martinez – Roy's Contact

9:00 am	Introduction • Progress to date – Team / Research / LPs / • Team introductions – Detailed / Worst trouble...
10:30am	Discussion of fund strategy – Broaden MKT → Serve, Employ, Located / Basket for General MKT Deals • Fund size – \$150M (→ \$200M w/...) • Deal stages – Growth Equity → Buyouts • Industries – focus on ... of strong ... prospects • Geography – Midwest presence – access to deal flow MKT • Deal flow – Growth equity → Buyouts • Portfolio company management – style / 2 per BOD • Side fund – Charles Tribbett / ... of executives / Operating Affiliates → Second side fund
11:30am	Firm operating philosophy – End product ⇒ View of the firm and internal culture • Management philosophy – Open / all-hands, all-eyes / veto / No mng partner • Roles – 1-2 Admin / AH–LP, EMs, banks, etc / AH. PR resp. Fundr • Decision-making – consensus • Due diligence – set parameters / evolve over time • Partner meetings – format • Portfolio management – 1 lead, 1 backup
12:30pm	Review draft budget – startup [Timing]
12:45pm	Discussion of fund raising strategy • First close goals – • LP targets and amount for first close – who / \$ amounts • Placement agent? – see notes from Wanda
1:30pm	Open issues for the team – How do we get to a decision on whether to do this – timing / concerns / additional info needed
2:00pm	Next Steps Strategic Partner – • Decision on doing it with or without Wind Point – Financial - Startup capital – Continuity and timing of close – don't pay for what you don't use • Timing for other decisions • PPM draft- need team resumes and track record info • Side fund- executive recruitment • Pick counsel- for mgmt company, GP&LP documents • Negotiate economics – F/U w/ each individual and come back w/proposal to the group • Startup logistics – who/when/location / steps • Firm name? – Input...

vacation in 15 years. He used part of that time to further bond the team:

> I invited everyone—partners and their families—to visit with us on the island for three days. I explained to their wives why I was asking their spouses to do this. I felt that I needed to look them in the eye and tell them that there were no guarantees, that there would be hard, lean times, and that we'd be working harder than we ever had before.

The team was experienced enough to understand that success with this venture would yield a financial upside that was commensurate with the risks and challenges they would be taking on. At that time, the average total pay package—salary plus bonus—for managing general partners and senior-level partners was $1.24 million and $1.04 million, respectively. In addition, effective equity investors stood to reap even greater rewards in the form of carried interest distributions as their investments matured; managing general partners were bringing home an average of $2.5 million in carry, compared with $1.0 million by senior-level partners.[5]

Palmer's wife Emily, a patent attorney with her own practice, recalled that from the beginning, the spouses were behind the idea:

> Our husbands had outlined for us a certain timetable, and we understood that this thing was probably going to take a lot of patience and fortitude. With regard to my career, I needed to figure out whether I would try to maintain my firm, reopen something in Boston, or do something different altogether. Still, I was very excited about the venture because they had a team that could make this a success.

The team estimated that their startup expenses for one year of fund-raising would be just under $400,000 (see Exhibit 10)—funded out of pocket or through personal loans. They felt that if they could articulate an opportunity that leveraged their collective skill set (and resonated with potential investors), they could cut their fund-raising time and be in business by late fall of 2001.

EXHIBIT 10

Startup Estimates

October 2000 to October 2001	
Variable Expenses	
Salaries	90,000[1]
Legal	44,000
Travel	20,000
Rent	62,500[2]
Phone	10,000
Postage and Printing	14,000
Meals	10,000
Entertainment	20,000
	$270,500
Fixed Expenses	
Computers/Networking/Printers	40,000
Phone System	20,000
Office Supplies	5,000
Office Furniture	50,000
	$115,000
Total Startup Expenses	$385,500

[1] Salaries: Three partners @ $40,000 each. Half salary for six months.

[2] Rent: 2,500 square feet @ $25/sf.

The Opportunity

The fund that Palmer and his team were setting up would execute buyout investments in a broad range of profitable, small- to middle-market private companies that served or operated in the minority marketplace. When these portfolio companies needed to recruit or partner with talented managers, their primary strategy would be to marshal their contacts and tap into the "hidden" pool of experienced ethnic-minority executives.

While they planned to pursue and evaluate investment opportunities in the manner of any professional private equity group, the team understood that many prospective limiteds would, consciously or otherwise, align them with previous minority-focused investment efforts that had been set up and managed by groups with little or no private equity experience. Clint Harris noted that many of those funds had lost sight of what should have been their main objective:

> Minority funds in the past were often driven by political and social agendas; money got wasted and didn't do any good—and burned investors have very long memories. When this happens, it's not just the failure of the team and the fund; it's the failure of the good intentions to do social investing for the wrong reasons. Some succeeded in making money, but most of them failed to achieve investment returns that were robust enough to attract mainstream investors.

The team frequently encountered a tendency by some limited partner prospects to pigeonhole the fund as one that would, as prior funds had done, invest exclusively in existing minority enterprises. For instance, Judith Elsea, who was at that time the chief investment officer for the Ewing Marion Kauffman Foundation, noted that the challenge for some prospective limited partners would be in conducting due diligence:

> This team is proposing something different by addressing markets that are not as heavily trafficked by private equity groups. But while those markets are arguably underserved, they are also in areas where a lot of institutional investors don't have a lot of experience—or big networks where people would be easy to check out.

Palmer felt that the entire discussion was missing the point:

> I'm not worrying about what other minority firms are doing or have done, but I know that as soon as we sit down with potential investors, they are going to think we are investing exclusively in minority ventures. We are going to have to craft our presentation in a way that gets people

[5] *Venture Capital Journal*, Nov. 1, 2000; *The Compensation Game: While Opportunities Abound, Firms Entice Partner-Level VCs to Stick Around.* Data was according to a compensation survey of over 100 private equity firms, conducted by William M. Mercer Inc. Performance & Rewards Consulting.

> to stop thinking about that and instead see what we are doing as a generic way to go make money, a solid private equity strategy—no mirrors or hidden agendas. We're going to do it the old-fashioned way: back great managers, invest in fundamentally sound businesses, and then put our heads down and execute a value-creation strategy over four to six years.

Wanda Felton agreed:

> It is important to understand that this group was being set up to build and add value to a company, and then be able to sell that business to anybody. Sure, the minority angle might provide a competitive advantage on the margin in terms of proprietary deal flow, but the team needs to communicate that their business proposition will not necessarily rely on minority ownership or set-aside programs.

Since they were anticipating that much of their deal flow would involve established and later-stage opportunities, David Mazza cautioned against being too quick to initiate operations:

> I told them that a $50 million buyout fund was only going to get them into trouble. We like to see a bare minimum of $100 million, and prefer $200 million to $250 million. You can certainly have a first closing at $100 million, but you want to end up with something that has critical mass.

The Beginning

Now that he had secured a unified commitment from the team to move to Boston by the end of the summer, Palmer decided that when his partners and their families arrived in September, he'd welcome them all with a van tour of the city. Then—all assembled and all on the same page—the team would take up the challenge of crafting the offering prospectus and raising the fund.

Appendix A: Team Profiles

Maclean Palmer, Jr.

Maclean Palmer, Jr. (41) has over 5 years of *direct* private equity experience and over 17 years of operating experience. Prior to joining Forte, he was a managing director with Point West Partners from 1997 to 2000 in their San Francisco office. While at Point West, Mr. Palmer was responsible for deal origination, transaction execution, and portfolio company management and focused on growth equity and buyout investments in the telecommunications, business-to-business services, industrial manufacturing, and auto sectors. Mr. Palmer led Point West investments in 3 competitive local exchange carriers (CLECs): Cobalt Telecommunications, MBCS Telecommunications, and Concept Telephone. He continues to represent Point West on the board of directors of both MBCS and Concept Telephone.

From 1995 to 1997, Mr. Palmer was a vice president in the Boston office of Advent International. While at Advent, he focused on industrial and technology investments and led Advent's investment in ISI, a financial and business information services provider. From 1986 to 1995, Mr. Palmer worked in various management and engineering positions for three startup companies—UltraVision Inc., Surglaze Inc., and DTech Corporation—which were all financed by private equity investors. During his startup career, Mr. Palmer was involved in the development and successful market introduction of 12 new products. In addition, Mr. Palmer held engineering positions with Borg Warner Corporation from 1984 to 1986 and with the Diesel Division of a major automotive firm from 1983 to 1984.

Mr. Palmer sits on the board of JT Technologies, a minority-owned firm that develops battery and ultracapacitor technology. He also sits on the board of the Cooper Enterprise Fund, a minority focused fund based in New York; the Community Preparatory School, a private inner-city school focused on preparing middle school students for college preparatory high schools; and the Zell Laurie Entrepreneurial Institute at the University of Michigan Business School.

Mr. Palmer holds a BSME from the Automotive Institute, an MBA cum laude from Babson College, and was awarded a Kauffman Fellowship, graduating with the program's inaugural class.

Ray S. Turner

Ray S. Turner (61) has had a long and distinguished career as an operating executive at Fortune 50 companies. From October 1998 to March 2000, he was group vice president, North America Sales, Service and Marketing for a multinational heavy-industry manufacturer. From 1990 to 1998, Mr. Turner also served as vice president and general manager for North America Sales and Manufacturing at that company.

From 1988 to 1990, he served as vice president for manufacturing operations. From 1977 to 1988, Mr. Turner served in senior manufacturing management and plant manager roles for a number of assembly and manufacturing operations for the company. Prior to his career at that corporation, Mr. Turner spent several years serving in a variety of positions in engineering, materials management, manufacturing, sales, personnel, and labor relations. He serves on the board of directors of two Fortune 100 corporations.

Mr. Turner received a bachelor's degree in Business Administration from Western Michigan University. He also completed the Executive Development Program at Harvard Business School, and an Advanced International General Management Program in Switzerland.

Clark T. Pierce

Clark T. Pierce (38) has over 7 years of mezzanine and private equity experience and over 4 years of corporate finance experience. Most recently, he was a principal with Ninos Capital, a publicly traded mezzanine investment fund. While at Ninos he was responsible for leading all aspects of the investment process, including deal origination and evaluation, due diligence, deal, execution, and portfolio company management. Mr. Pierce has closed numerous transactions in various industries, including business services, distribution, manufacturing, and financial services.

From 1993 to 1995, Mr. Pierce managed Ninos Capital's Specialized Small Business Investment Company ("SSBIC"). This SSBIC was a $45 million investment vehicle directed toward minority owned and controlled companies. Prior to Ninos Capital, Mr. Pierce spent one year with Freeman Securities as a vice president in the Corporate Finance Group where he advised bondholders and companies involved in the restructuring process. From 1989 to 1991, Mr. Pierce was an associate with Chase Manhattan Bank, N.A., in the Corporate Finance Group.

Mr. Pierce served on the board of directors of Sidewalks, Inc., a social services organization for troubled teenagers, and the Orphan Foundation of America, a nonprofit agency focusing on adoption of older children.

Mr. Pierce received a BA from Morehouse College, a JD from George Washington University, and an MBA from the Wharton Business School at the University of Pennsylvania.

Andrew L. Simon

Andrew L. Simon (30) has 4 years of direct private equity experience, as well as 3 years of strategy consulting experience. During his career, Mr. Simon has worked on private equity investments in numerous industry sectors including contract manufacturing, industrial products, health care, financial services, and direct marketing. Most recently, he was a senior associate in the New York office at McCown De Leeuw & Co., Inc. ("MDC"), where he focused on growth and leveraged equity investments, including recapitalization and buy-and-build acquisitions. While at MDC, Mr. Simon played a lead role in identifying potential investments, negotiating with sellers, structuring and arranging debt financing, as well as supervising the legal documentation and closing of transactions. Post-acquisition, he played an active role in the financing and strategic direction of MDC portfolio companies and participated at board meetings.

From 1995 to 1997, Mr. Simon was an associate in the Boston office of Trident Partners ("Trident"). At Trident, Mr. Simon was responsible for evaluating, prioritizing, and analyzing potential new acquisition opportunities, as well as supporting deal teams with business and analytical due diligence. From 1992 to 1995, Mr. Simon was a senior analyst at Marakon Associates where he was responsible for valuation analysis, industry research, and strategy development. In addition, Mr. Simon has worked for Littlejohn & Co., an LBO firm focused on restructuring, Physicians Quality Care, a venture-backed health care services company, and Lotus Development.

Mr. Simon earned an AB degree from Princeton University's Woodrow Wilson School and earned his MBA, with honors, from Harvard Business School, where he was a Toigo Fellow.

Dario A. Cardenas

Most recently, Fidel A. Cardenas (31) was a managing director with MTG Ventures from 1999 to 2000. At MTG, a private equity firm focused on acquiring and operating manufacturing and service companies, Mr. Cardenas was responsible for deal origination, transaction execution, and portfolio company management. Prior to his role at MTG Ventures, Mr. Cardenas was a principal with MTG Advisors from 1992 to 1997 where he focused on strategy consulting and executive coaching. Concurrent with MTG Advisors, Mr. Cardenas was elected to two terms as mayor of Sunny Park, California, becoming, at 23, the mayor of that city. He has also served as assistant deputy mayor for Public Safety for the City of Los Angeles and as an analyst for McKinsey and Company.

Mr. Cardenas received a BA in Political Science from Harvard, cum laude, and his MBA from Harvard Business School.

9

Chapter Nine

Personal Ethics and the Entrepreneur

If you gain financial success at the expense of your integrity, you are not a success at all.

John Cullinane
Founder of Cullinet, Inc., and a 1984 Inductee, Babson Academy of Distinguished Entrepreneurs

Results Expected

Upon completion of this chapter, you will have:

1. Made decisions involving ethical issues and identified and analyzed your reason for deciding as you did.
2. Discussed with others the ethical implications of the decisions you made and identified how they might affect you, your partners, your customers, and your competitors in the contexts described.
3. Acquired a background, based on history, philosophy, and research, about the nature of business ethics and context for thinking about ethical behavior.
4. Gained an awareness of the importance of ethical awareness and high standards in an entrepreneurial career.
5. Analyzed the "Wayne Postoak" case study.

Exercise

Ethics

In this exercise, decisions will be made in ethically ambiguous situations and then analyzed. As in the real world, all the background information on each situation will not be available, and assumptions will need to be made.

It is recommended that the exercise be completed before reading the following material, and then revisited after you have completed the chapter.

Name:

Date:

Part I

STEP 1

Make decisions in the following situations.

You will not have all the background information on each situation; instead, you should make whatever assumptions you feel you would make if you were actually confronted with the decision choices described. Select the decision choice that most closely represents the decision you feel you would make personally. You should choose decision choices even though you can envision other creative solutions that were not included in the exercise.

Situation 1. You are taking a very difficult chemistry course, which you must pass to maintain your scholarship and to avoid damaging your application for graduate school. Chemistry is not your strong suit, and because of a just-below-failing average in the course, you must receive a grade of 90 or better on the final exam, which is two days away. A janitor who is aware of your plight informs you that he found the master stencil for the chemistry final in a trash barrel and saved it. He will make it available to you for a price, which is high but which you could afford. What would you do?

_______ *(a)* I would tell the janitor thanks, but no thanks.
_______ *(b)* I would report the janitor to the proper officials.
_______ *(c)* I would buy the exam and keep it to myself.
_______ *(d)* I would not buy the exam myself, but I would let some of my friends, who are also flunking the course, know that it is available.

Situation 2. You have been working on some complex analytical data for two days now. It seems that each time you think you have them completed, your boss shows up with a new assumption or another what-if question. If you only had a copy of a new software program for your personal computer, you could plug in the new assumptions and revise the estimates with ease. Then a colleague offers to let you make a copy of some software that is copyrighted. What would you do?

_______ *(a)* I would readily accept my friend's generous offer and make a copy of the software.
_______ *(b)* I would decline to copy it and plug away manually on the numbers.
_______ *(c)* I would decide to go buy a copy of the software myself for $300 and hope I would be reimbursed by the company in a month or two.
_______ *(d)* I would request another extension on an already overdue project date.

Situation 3. Your small manufacturing company is in serious financial difficulty. A large order of your products is ready to be delivered to a key customer, when you discover that the product is simply not right. It will not meet all performance specifications, will cause problems for your customer, and will require rework in the field; but this, you know, will not become evident until after the customer has received and paid for the order. If you do not ship the order and receive the payment as expected, your business may be forced into bankruptcy. And if you delay the shipment or inform the customer of these problems, you may lose the order and also go bankrupt. What would you do?

_______ *(a)* I would not ship the order and place my firm in voluntary bankruptcy.
_______ *(b)* I would inform the customer and declare voluntary bankruptcy.
_______ *(c)* I would ship the order and inform the customer, after I received payment.
_______ *(d)* I would ship the order and not inform the customer.

Situation 4. You are the cofounder and president of a new venture, manufacturing products for the recreational market. Five months after launching the business, one of your suppliers informs you it can no longer supply you with a critical raw material since you are not a large-quantity user. Without the raw material the business cannot continue. What would you do?

_______ *(a)* I would grossly overstate my requirements to another supplier to make the supplier think I am a much larger potential customer in order to secure the raw material from that supplier, even though this would mean the supplier will no longer be able to supply another, noncompeting small manufacturer who may thus be forced out of business.
_______ *(b)* I would steal raw material from another firm (noncompeting) where I am aware of a sizable stockpile.
_______ *(c)* I would pay off the supplier, since I have reason to believe that the supplier could be persuaded to meet my needs with a sizable under-the-table payoff that my company could afford.
_______ *(d)* I would declare voluntary bankruptcy.

Situation 5. You are on a marketing trip for your new venture for the purpose of calling on the purchasing agent of a major prospective client. Your company is manufacturing an electronic system that you hope the purchasing agent will buy. During the course of your conversation, you notice on the cluttered desk of the purchasing agent several copies of a cost proposal for a system from one of your direct competitors. This purchasing agent has previously reported mislaying several of your own company's proposals and has asked for additional copies. The purchasing agent leaves the room momentarily to get you a cup of coffee, leaving you alone with your competitor's proposals less than an arm's length away. What would you do?

_______ *(a)* I would do nothing but await the man's return.
_______ *(b)* I would sneak a quick peek at the proposal, looking for bottom-line numbers.
_______ *(c)* I would put the copy of the proposal in my briefcase.
_______ *(d)* I would wait until the man returns and ask his permission to see the copy.

Part II

STEP 1

Based on the criteria you used, place your answers to each of the above situations along the continuum of behavior shown below.

	Duty	Contractual	Utilitarian	Situational
Situation 1				
Situation 2				
Situation 3				
Situation 4				
Situation 5				

STEP 2

After separating into teams of five to six people, record the answers made by each individual member of your team on the form below. Record the answers of each team member in each box and the team's solution in the column on the far right.

Member Name:						Team Answer
Situation 1						
Situation 2						
Situation 3						
Situation 4						
Situation 5						

STEP 3

Reach a consensus decision in each situation (if possible) and record the consensus that your team has reached above. Allow 20 to 30 minutes.

STEP 4

Report to the entire group your team's conclusions and discuss with them how the consensus, if any, was reached. The discussion should focus on the following questions:

- Was a consensus reached by the group?
- Was this consensus difficult or easy to achieve and why?
- What kinds of ethical issues emerged?
- How were conflicts, if any, resolved, or were they left unresolved?
- What creative solutions did you find in order to solve the difficult problem without compromising your integrity?

STEP 5

Discuss with the group the following issues:

- What role do ethical issues play and how important are they in the formation of a new venture management team?
- What role do ethical issues play and how important are they in obtaining venture capital? That is, how do investors feel about ethics and how important are they to them?
- What feelings bother participants most about the discussion and consensus reached? For example, if a participant believes that his or her own conduct was considered ethically less than perfect, does he or she feel a loss of self-respect or a sense of inferiority? Does he or she fear others' judgment, and so on?

STEP 6

Define each group member's general ethical position and note whether his or her ethical position is similar to or different from yours:

Member	Position	Different/ Similar

STEP 7

Decide whom you would and would not want as a business partner based on their ethical positions:

Would Want	Would Not Want

Overview of Ethics

A good number of successful entrepreneurs believe that high ethical standards and integrity are exceptionally important to long-term success. For example, Jeffry Timmons and his colleague Howard H. Stevenson conducted a study among 128 presidents/founders attending the Harvard Business School's Owner/President Management program (OPM) in 1983.[1] Their firms typically had sales of $40 million, and sales ranged from $5 million to $200 million. These entrepreneurs were also very experienced, with the average age in the mid-40s, and about half had founded their companies. They were asked to name the most critical concepts, skills, and know-how for success at their companies at the time and what they would be in five years. The answer to this question was startling enough that the Sunday *New York Times* reported the findings: 72 percent of the presidents responding stated that high ethical standards were the single most important factor in long-term success.[*] A May 2003 study by the Aspen Institute found that MBA students are concerned that their schools are not doing enough to prepare them for ethical dilemmas they may face in the business world. Seventeen hundred MBA students from the United States, Canada, and Britain were surveyed, and the results, plus student reactions, are addressed in the May 21, 2003, issue of *Chronicle of Higher Education.* Their concern and awareness is not surprising given the recent spate of corporate scandals. Ethical lapses like those of Enron executives, for example, erode the confidence in business activity at all levels. By the middle of 2005, 33 executives had been charged: 15 pleaded guilty, 6 were convicted by a jury, 5 are on trial, 3 await trial, 3 are fighting extradition, and 1 was found not guilty.[2]

Conventional ethical disciplines have been accused of dealing with the business realm by narrowly defining the scope of inquiry so as to be able to offer a definitive answer. One author, for instance, assumed that "competitors are ethical and engaged in business, rather than jungle warfare."[3] What is ethical is not always obvious; rather, situations involving ethical issues are often ambiguous. Today, as throughout much of this century, students, businesspeople, and others have received many conflicting signals, as "first artists and intellectuals, then broader segments of the society, challenged every convention, every prohibition, every regulation that cramped the human spirit or blocked its appetites and ambitions."[4]

This discussion has also generated much controversy. For example, a provocative and controversial article published in the *Harvard Business Review* asserted that the ethics of business were not those of society but rather those of the poker game.[5] The author of the article argued, "Most businessmen are not indifferent to ethics in their private lives, everyone will agree. My point is that in their office lives they cease to be private citizens; they become game players who must be guided by a somewhat different set of ethical standards." The author further argued that personal ethics and business ethics are often not in harmony, and by either negotiation or compromise, a resolution must be reached. The article provoked a storm of response. The question remains, how are businesspeople supposed to operate in this capitalist system?

In addition, the law, which one might expect to be black and white, is full of thorny issues. Laws not only have authority but also limitations. Laws are made with forethought and with the deliberate purpose of ensuring justice. They are, therefore, ethical in intent and deserve respect. However, laws are made in legislatures, not in heaven. They do not anticipate new conditions; they do not always have the effect they were intended to have; they sometimes conflict with one another; and they are, as they stand, incapable of making judgments where multiple ethical considerations hang in the balance or seem actually to war with one another. Thus, from the beginnings of recorded history in Egypt and the Middle East, a code of laws was always accompanied by a human interpreter of laws, a judge, to decide when breaking the letter of the law did not violate the spirit or situation that the law was intended to cover. Great moments in history, religion, philosophy, and literature focus on the legal/ethical dilemma, and debating teams would wither away if the dilemma were to disappear.

Ethical Stereotypes

The 1990s ushered in the "New Era of Entrepreneurship" worldwide. The United States, now as in the past, is seen as providing an inviting and nurturing

[*] For an overview of the philosophical underpinnings of ethics and a decision-making framework, see "A Framework for Ethical Decision Making," John Leslie Livingstone et al., Babson College Case Development Center, 2003.

[1] Jeffry A. Timmons and Howard H. Stevenson, "Entrepreneurship Education in the 1980s," presented at the 75th Anniversary Entrepreneurship Symposium, Harvard Business School, Boston, 1983. *Proceedings,* pp. 115–34.

[2] www.HoustonChronicle.com/SpecialReport/Enron.

[3] Thomas Garret, *Business Ethics* (New York: Appleton-Century-Crofts, 1966), pp. 149–50.

[4] Derek Bok, "Ethics, the University, & Society," *Harvard Magazine,* May–June 1988, p. 39.

[5] Reprinted by permission of *Harvard Business Review.* An Excerpt from "Is Business Bluffing Ethical?" by Albert Z. Carr, January–February 1968, pp. 145–52. Copyright © 1967 by the President and Fellows of Harvard College.

climate for those wishing to start their own enterprises and reap the rewards. In part, this is because the federal government has encouraged, to a greater degree than in any other country, an atmosphere under which free market forces, private initiative, and individual responsibility and freedom can flourish. Legislation such as antitrust laws, laws regulating labor, and the graduated income tax have not hampered the growth of entrepreneurship in America.

These laws, enacted in response to society's changing perceptions of what constitutes ethical business practices, have had the equally desirable effect of encouraging those in many industries to develop codes of ethics—in large part because they wished to have the freedom to set their own rules, rather than to have rules imposed on them by Congress.

As the ethical climate of business has changed, so has the image of the entrepreneur. Horatio Alger personifies the good stereotype. Entrepreneurs doing business in the unfettered economic climate of the 19th century—the era of the robber barons, where acts of industrial sabotage were common—represent the ruthless stereotype. The battles of James Hill and Edward Harriman over the rights of railroads, the alleged sabotage by John D. Rockefeller of his competitors' oil refineries, the exploitation of child labor in New England's textile mills and of black labor in the Southern cotton plantations, and the promoting of "snake oil" and Lydia Pinkham's tonics leave an unsavory aftertaste for today's more ethically conscious entrepreneurs.

Yet, thoughtful historians of American entrepreneurship will also recall that regardless of standards by which they are judged or of the motivations attributed to them, certain American entrepreneurs gave back to society such institutions as the Morgan Library and the Rockefeller Foundation. The extraordinary legacy of Andrew Carnegie is another example. (Scholars are much more inclined to examine and dissect the ethical behavior of the business sector, rather than that of the clergy, or even of academia itself. In many comparisons, the behavior of the business sector would look quite pure.)

Carnegie's case is also interesting because he described the total change of attitude that came over him after he had amassed his fortune. Carnegie, the son of a Scots weaver, created a personal fortune of $300 million in the production of crude steel between 1873 and 1901. (That's $130 billion in 2005 dollars!) As Carnegie himself described, he believed that competition "insures the survival of the fittest in every department." Carnegie also felt that "the fact that this talent for organization and management is rare among men is proved by the fact that it invariably secures enormous rewards for its possessor."[6] So apparently satisfied was Carnegie with the correctness of his view, he did not try to reconcile it with the fact that British steel rails were effectively excluded by a protective tariff equaling over half the production price of each ton of steel rails.[7] That Carnegie's mind was not easy over his fortune, however, is evident from his statement, "I would as soon give my son a curse as the almighty dollar."[8] After 1901, when he sold Carnegie Steel to United States Steel under pressure from a group headed by J. P. Morgan, Carnegie personally supervised donations in the United States and Great Britain of more than $300 million. Among his gifts to humanity were over 2,800 libraries, an Endowment for International Peace, and the Carnegie Institute of Pittsburgh.

From today's perspective, the entrepreneurs above might be described as acting in enlightened self-interest. However, when the same sort of entrepreneurial generosity is demonstrated today by such people as Armand Hammer of Occidental Petroleum, Ted Turner of CNN fame, and Bill Gates of Microsoft, we are more likely to speak of their acts as philanthropy than as fulfilling their social contract.

A touch of suspicion still tinges entrepreneurial activity, and the word *entrepreneur* may still connote to some a person who belongs to a ruthless, scheming group located a good deal lower than the angels. In 1975, *Time* suggested that a businessman might make the best-qualified candidate for U.S. president but noted the "deep-rooted American suspicion of businessmen's motives."[9] Quoting John T. Conner, chairman of Allied Chemical and former head of Merck and Company, *Time*'s editors added: "Anyone with previous business experience becomes immediately suspect. Certain segments think he can't make a decision in the public interest."[10] However, in 1988, the prophecy of *Time* was fulfilled when George Bush, an oil entrepreneur, was elected president of the United States, a revealing conclusion to America's most entrepreneurial decade, and later reinforced in 2000 when his son George W. Bush, a Harvard MBA, was also elected president.

[6] "Introduction to Contemporary Civilization in the West," *The Gospel of Wealth* (New York: Century, 1900), p. 620.

[7] W. E. Woodward, *A New American History* (Garden City, NY: Garden City Publishing, 1938), p. 704.

[8] Ibid., p. 622.

[9] "Time Essay: New Places to Look for Presidents," *Time*, December 15, 1975, p. 19.

[10] Ibid.

Should Ethics Be Taught?

Just as the 1990s ushered in a new era of worldwide entrepreneurship, the world of business ethics has redefined itself, according to Andrew Stark. Stark asserts,

> Advocates of the new business ethics can be identified by their acceptance of two fundamental principles. While they agree with their colleagues that ethics and interest can conflict, they take that observation as the starting point, not the ending point, of an ethicist's analytical task. . . . Second, the new perspective reflects an awareness and acceptance of the messy work of mixed motives.[11]

The challenge facing this new group of business ethicists is to bridge the gap between the moral philosophers and the managers. The business ethicists talk of "moderation, pragmatism, minimalism"[12] in their attempt to "converse with real managers in a language relevant to the world they inhabit and the problems they face."[13] With this focus on the practical side of decision making, courses on ethics can be useful to entrepreneurs and all managers.

Ethics Can and Should Be Taught

In an article that examines the ancient tradition of moral education, the decline of moral instruction beginning in the 19th century, and the renaissance of interest in ethics in the 1960s, Derek Bok, former president of Harvard University, argues that ethics can and should be taught by educational institutions and that this teaching is both necessary and of value:

> Precisely because its community is so diverse, set in a society so divided and confused over its values, a university that pays little attention to moral development may find that many of its students grow bewildered, convinced that ethical dilemmas are simply matters of personal opinion beyond external judgment or careful analysis.
>
> Nothing could be more unfortunate or more unnecessary. Although moral issues sometimes lack convincing answers, that is often not the case. Besides, universities should be the last institutions to discourage belief in the value of reasoned argument and carefully considered evidence in analyzing even the hardest of human problems.[14]

John Shad, a former chairman of the New York Stock Exchange, gave more than $20 million to the Harvard Business School to help develop a way to include ethics in the MBA curriculum. Beginning in the fall of 1988, first-year students at the Harvard Business School are required to attend a three-week, nongraded ethics module called "Decision Making and Ethical Values." The cases discussed range from insider trading at Salomon Brothers to discrimination in employee promotions to locating a U.S. manufacturing unit in Mexico. Thomas R. Piper, associate dean, emphasizes that the role of the course is "not converting sinners . . . but we're taking young people who have a sense of integrity and trying to get them to connect ethics with business decisions."[15] J. Gregory Dees, another ethics professor at Harvard, now at Duke University, stresses that the "primary objective of the course is to get people thinking about issues that are easy to avoid. . . . What we want people to leave DMEV with is a commitment to raising these issues in other settings, other courses, and on the job, with [an acceptable] comfort level in doing so."[16]

Since John Shad made his contribution, three second-year electives ("Moral Dilemmas of Management," "Managing Information in a Competitive Context," and "Profits, Markets, and Values") have been added to Harvard's ethics program. The Wharton School has a similar course required of first-year MBA students. "Leadership Skills" is a yearlong, graded course with a four-week ethics module. The Wharton faculty hope to introduce the core literature of business ethics and corporate responsibility, to expose students to discussions, and to stimulate the students to address these moral issues in their other courses. These two programs are part of a larger effort to incorporate ethics as

> over 500 business-ethics courses are currently taught on American campuses; fully 90 percent of the nation's business schools now provide some kind of training in the area. There are more than 25 textbooks in the field and three academic journals dedicated to the topic. At least 16 business-ethics research centers are now in operation, and endowed chairs in business ethics have been established at Georgetown, Virginia, Minnesota, and a number of other prominent business schools.[17]

In addition, the 1990s saw the emergence of numerous courses on socially responsible business and entrepreneurship, and on the role of environmentally sustainable and responsible businesses.

[11] Andrew Stark, "What's the Matter with Business Ethics?" *Harvard Business Review*, May–June 1993, p. 46.
[12] Ibid., p. 48.
[13] Ibid.
[14] Derek Bok, "Is Dishonesty Good for Business?" *Business & Society Review*, Summer 1979, p. 50.
[15] John A. Byrne, "Can Ethics Be Taught? Harvard Gives It the Old College Try," *BusinessWeek*, April 6, 1992, p. 34.
[16] Chitra Nayak, "Why Ethics DMEV under the Microscope," *The Harbus* 1989.
[17] Andrew Stark, "What's the Matter with Business Ethics?" *Harvard Business Review*, May–June 1993, p. 38.

The Usefulness of Academic Ethics

The study of ethics does seem to make students more aware of the pervasiveness of ethical situations in business settings, bring perspective to ethical situations from a distance, and provide a framework for understanding ethical problems when they arise. Further, the study of ethics has been shown to affect, to some degree, both beliefs and behavior. For example, in a study of whether ethics courses affect student values, value changes in business school students who had taken a course in business ethics and those who did not were examined closely and were plotted across the multiple stages.[18]

The study used a sequence of stages, called the Kohlberg construct, developed by Kohlberg in 1967. These stages are presented in Exhibit 9.1. In the Kohlberg construct, being moral in Stage 1 is synonymous with being obedient, and the motivation is to avoid condemnation. In Stage 2, the individual seeks advantage. Gain is the primary purpose, and interaction does not result in binding personal relationships. The orientation of Stage 3 is toward pleasing others and winning approval. Proper roles are defined by stereotyped images of majority behavior. Such reciprocity is confined to primary group relations. In Stage 4, cooperation is viewed in the context of society as a whole. External laws serve to coordinate moral schemes, and the individual feels committed to the social order. One thus subscribes to formal punishment by police or the courts. In Stage 5, there is acknowledgment that reciprocity can be inequitable. New laws and social arrangements now may be invoked as corrective mechanisms. All citizens are assured of fundamental safety and equality. Cognitive structures at the Stage 6 level automatically reject credos and actions that the individual considers morally reprehensible, and the referent is a person's own moral framework, rather than stereotyped group behavior. Because most of one's fellows endorse a law does not guarantee its moral validity. When confronting social dilemmas, the individual is guided by internal principles that may transcend the legal system. Although these convictions are personal, they are also universal because they have worth and utility apart from the individual espousing them. Kohlberg's final stage thus represents more than mere conformity with state, teacher, or institutional criteria. Rather, it indicates one's capacity for decision making and problem solving in the context of personal ethical standards. In the study, those who took a course in business ethics showed a progression up the ethical scale, while those who had not taken a course did not progress.

EXHIBIT 9.1

Classification of Moral Judgment into Stages of Development

Stage	Orientation	Theme
1	Punishment and obedience	Morality of obedience
2	Instrumental relativism	Simple exchange
3	Interpersonal concordance	Reciprocal role taking
4	Law and order	Formal justice
5	Legitimate social contract	Procedural justice
6	Universal ethical principle	Individual conscience

Source: Adapted from Kohlberg (1967).[19]

Integrity as Governing Ethic

In her Harvard Business School article, Professor Lynn Paine distinguishes among avoiding legal sanctions, compliance, and the more robust standard of integrity.

> From the perspective of integrity, the task of ethics management is to define and give life to an organization's guiding values, to create an environment that supports ethically sound behavior, and to instill a sense of shared accountability among employees.[20]

Paine goes on to characterize the hallmarks of an effective integrity strategy (see Exhibit 9.2) and the strategies for ethics management (see Exhibit 9.3). Clearly, the call for ethical strategies and practices, first made in the original 1977 edition—which was the first text to do so—is being heard. That is good news for our society, our economy, and you!

Entrepreneurs' Perspectives

Most entrepreneurs also believe ethics should be taught. In the research project previously mentioned, entrepreneurs and chief executive officers attending the Owner/President Management (OPM) program at the Harvard Business School were asked

[18] David P. Boyd, "Enhancing Ethical Development by an Intervention Program," unpublished manuscript, Northeastern University, 1980.

[19] Lawrence Kohlberg was a professor at Harvard University. He became famous for his work there as a developmental psychologist and then moved to the field of moral education. His work was based on theories that human beings develop philosophically and psychologically in a progressive fashion. Kohlberg believed and demonstrated in several published studies that people progressed in their moral reasoning (i.e., in their bases for ethical behavior) through a series of six identifiable stages.

[20] L. S. Paine, "Managing for Organizational Integrity," *Harvard Business Review,* March–April 1994, pp. 105–17.

EXHIBIT 9.2

Ethical Decisions Matrix

	Possible Consequences of Each Alternative on Stakeholders				
Stakeholders	**Decision Alternative 1**	**Decision Alternative 2**	**Decision Alternative 3**	**Decision Alternative 4**	**Decision Alternative 5**
1.					
2.					
3.					
4.					
5.					
6.					
7.					
8.					

Source: John Leslie Livingstone et al., *Framework for Ethical Decision Making*, Babson College, 2003.

the question, Is there a role for ethics in business education for entrepreneurs? Of those responding, 72 percent said ethics can and should be taught as part of the curriculum. (Only 20 percent said it should not, and two respondents were not sure.)

The most prominently cited reason for including ethics was that ethical behavior is at the core of long-term business success, because it provides the glue that binds enduring successful business and personal relationships together. In addition, the responses reflected a serious and thoughtful awareness of the

EXHIBIT 9.3

Strategies for Ethics Management

Characteristics of Compliance Strategy		**Characteristics of Integrity Strategy**	
Ethos	Conformity with externally imposed standards	**Ethos**	Self-governance according to chosen standards
Objective	Prevent criminal misconduct	**Objective**	Stable responsible conduct
Leadership	Lawyer driven	**Leadership**	Management driven with aid of lawyers, HR, others
Methods	Education, reduced discretion, auditing and controls, penalties	**Methods**	Education, leadership, accountability, organizational systems and decision processes, auditing and controls, penalties
Behavioral Assumptions	Autonomous beings guided by material self-interest	**Behavioral Assumptions**	Social beings guided by material self-interest, values, ideals, peers
Implementation of Compliance Strategy		**Implementation of Integrity Strategy**	
Standards	Criminal and regulatory law	**Standards**	Company values and aspirations, social obligations, including law
Staffing	Lawyers	**Staffing**	Executives and managers with lawyers, others
Activities	Develop compliance standards, train, and communicate	**Activities**	Lead development of company values and standards Train and communicate Integrate into company systems Provide guidance and consultation Assess values performance Identify and resolve problems Oversee compliance activities
Education	Compliance standards and system	**Education**	Decision making and values Compliance standards and system

Source: Reprinted by permission of *Harvard Business Review*. From "Managing for Organizational Integrity," by Lynn Sharp Paine, March–April 1994, p. 113. Copyright ©1994 by the Harvard Business School Publishing Corporation; all rights reserved.

fragile but vital role of ethics in entrepreneurial attainment and of the long-term consequences of ethical behavior for a business. Typical comments were:

- If the free enterprise system is to survive, the business schools better start paying attention to teaching ethics. They should know that business is built on trust, which depends upon honesty and sincerity. BS comes out quickly in a small company.
- If our society is going to move forward, it won't be based on how much money is accumulated in any one person or group. Our society will move forward when all people are treated fairly—that's my simple definition of ethics. I know of several managers, presidents, etc., who you would not want to get between them and their wallets or ambitions.
- In my experience the business world is by and large the most ethical and law-abiding part of our society.
- Ethics should be addressed, considered, and thoroughly examined; it should be an inherent part of each class and course...; instead of crusading with ethics, it is much more effective to make high ethics an inherent part of business—and it is.

However, these views were not universally held. One entrepreneur who helped to found a large company with international operations warned: "For God's sake, don't forget that 90 percent of the businessman's efforts consist of just plain hard work."

There is also some cynicism. The 40-year-old head of a real estate and construction firm in the Northeast with 300 employees and $75 million in annual sales said: "There is so much hypocrisy in today's world that even totally ethical behavior is questioned since many people think it is some new negotiating technique."

It would be unfortunate if the entrepreneur did not realize his or her potential for combining action with ethical purpose because of the suspicion that the two are unrelated or inimical. There is no reason they need be considered generically opposed. Nevertheless, in analyzing ethics, the individual can expect no substitute for his or her own effort and intelligence.

Thorny Issues for Entrepreneurs

Although the majority of entrepreneurs take ethics seriously, researchers in this area are still responding to David McClelland's call for inquiry: "We do not know at the present time what makes an entrepreneur more or less ethical in his dealings, but obviously there are few problems of greater importance for future research."[21] One article outlined the topics for research (see Exhibit 9.4). Clearly, an opportunity for further research still exists.

Action under Pressure

An entrepreneur will have to act on issues under pressure of time and when struggling for survival. In addition, the entrepreneur will most likely decide ethical questions that involve obligations on many sides—to customers, employees, stockholders, family, partners, himself, or a combination of these. Walking the tightrope and balancing common sense with an ethical framework is precarious.

To cope with the inevitable conflicts, an entrepreneur should develop an awareness of his or her own explicit and implicit ethical beliefs, those of his or her team and investors, and those of the milieu within which the company competes for survival. As the successful entrepreneurs quoted above believe, in the long run, succumbing to the temptations of situational ethics will, in all likelihood, result in a tumble into the quicksand, not a safety net—just ask Steve Madden, or executives at Enron, Tyco, and Arthur Anderson.

An appreciation of this state of affairs is succinctly stated by Fred T. Allen, chairman and president of Pitney-Bowes:

> As businessmen we must learn to weigh short-term interests against long-term possibilities. We must learn to sacrifice what is immediate, what is expedient, if the moral price is too high. What we stand to gain is precious little compared to what we can ultimately lose.[22]

Different Views

Different reactions to what is ethical may explain why some aspects of venture creation go wrong, both during startup and in the heat of the battle, for no apparent reason. Innumerable examples can be cited to illustrate that broken partnerships often can be traced to apparent differences in the personal ethics among the members of a management team. So, too, with investors. While the experienced venture capital investor seeks entrepreneurs with a reputation for integrity, honesty, and ethical behavior, the definition is necessarily subjective

[21] David McClelland, *Achieving Society* (New York: Van Nostrand, 1961), p. 331.
[22] "Letter to Editor," *Wall Street Journal*, October 17, 1975.

EXHIBIT 9.4

Selected Ethical Dilemmas of Entrepreneurial Management

Dilemma: Elements	Issues That May Arise
Promoter: Entrepreneurial euphoria Impression management Pragmatic versus moral considerations	What does honesty mean when promoting an innovation? Does it require complete disclosure of the risks and uncertainties? Does it require a dispassionate analysis of the situation, with equal time given to the downside as well as the upside? What sorts of influence tactics cross the line from encouragement and inducement to manipulation and coercion? Tension between perceived obligations and moral expectations.
Relationship: Conflicts of interest and roles Transactional ethics Guerrilla tactics	Changes in roles and relationships: pre- versus post-venture status. Decisions based on affiliative concerns rather than on task-based concerns. Transition from a trust-based work environment to one that is more controlled.
Innovator: "Frankenstein's problem" New types of ethical problems Ethic of change	Side effects and negative externalities force a social reconsideration of norms and values. Heightened concern about the future impact of unknown harms. Who is responsible for the assessment of risk? Inventor? Government? Market? Breaking down traditions and creating new models.
Other dilemmas: Finders-keepers ethic Conflict between personal values and business goals Unsavory business practices	Is there a fair way to divide profits when they are the result of cooperative efforts? Should the entrepreneur take all the gains that are not explicitly contracted away? Managing an intimate connection between personal choices and professional decisions. Coping with ethical pressures with creative solutions and integrity. Seeking industry recognition while not giving into peer pressure to conform.

Source: Adapted from J. Gregory Dees and Jennifer A. Starr, "Entrepreneurship through an Ethical Lens," in *The State of the Art of Entrepreneurship,* ed. Donald L. Sexton and John D. Kasarda (Boston: PWS-Kent Publishing Company, 1992), p. 96.

and depends in part on the beliefs of the investor himself and in part on the prevailing ethical climate in the industry sector in which the venture is involved.

Problems of Law

For entrepreneurs, situations where one law directly conflicts with another are increasingly frequent. For example, a small-business investment company in New York City got in serious financial trouble. The Small Business Administration stated the company should begin to liquidate its investments, because it would otherwise be in defiance of its agreement with the SBA. However, the Securities and Exchange Commission stated that this liquidation would constitute unfair treatment of stockholders, due to resulting imbalance in their portfolios. After a year and a half of agonizing negotiation, the company was able to satisfy all the parties, but compromises had to be made on both sides.

Another example of conflicting legal demands involves conflicts between procedures of the civil service commission code and the (dates from FDR) Fair Employment Practice Acts. The code states that hiring will include adherence to certain standards, a principle that was introduced in the 20th century to curb the patronage abuses in public service. Recently, however, the problem of encouraging and aiding minorities has led to the Civil Service Commission Fair Employment Practice Acts, which require the same public agencies that are guided by CSC standards to hire without prejudice, and without the requirement that a given test shall serve as the criterion of selection. Both these laws are based on valid ethical intent, but the resolution of such conflicts is no simple matter.

Further, unlike the international laws governing commercial airline transportation, there is no international code of business ethics. When doing business abroad, entrepreneurs may find that those with whom they swish to do business have little in common with them—no common language, no common historical context for conducting business, and no common set of ethical beliefs about right and wrong and everything in between. For example, in the United States, bribing a high official to obtain a favor is considered both ethically and legally unacceptable; in parts of the Middle East, it is the only way to get things done. What we see as a bribe, those in parts of the Middle East see as a tip, like what you might give the headwaiter at a fancy restaurant in New York for a good table.

"When in Rome" is one approach to this problem. Consulting a lawyer with expertise in international business before doing anything is another. Assuming that the object of an entrepreneur's international business venture is to make money, he or she needs to figure out some way that is legally tolerable under the laws that do apply and that is ethically tolerable personally.

Examples of the Ends-and-Means Issue

A central question in any ethical discussion concerns the extent to which a noble end may justify ignoble means—or whether using unethical means for assumed ethical ends may subvert the aim in some way. As an example of a noble end, consider the case of a university agricultural extension service whose goal was to aid small farmers to increase their crop productivity. The end was economically constructive and profit oriented only in the sense that the farmers might prosper from better crop yields. However, to continue being funded, the extension service was required to provide predictions of the annual increase in crop yield it could achieve, estimates it could not provide at the required level of specificity. Further, unless it could show substantial increases in crop yields, its funding might be heavily reduced. In this case, the extension service decided, if need be, to fudge the figures because it was felt that even though the presentation of overly optimistic predictions was unethical, the objectives of those running the organization were highly ethical and even the unethical aspects could be condoned within the context of the inability of the various groups involved to speak each other's language clearly. The funding source finally backed down in its demand, ameliorating the immediate problem. But if it had not, the danger existed that the individuals in this organization, altruistic though their intentions were, would begin to think that falsification was the norm and would forget that actions that run contrary to one's ethical feelings gradually would build a debilitating cynicism.

Another example is given in the case of a merger of a small rental-service business with a midsize conglomerate, where a law's intent was in direct opposition to what would occur if the law was literally enforced. In this case, a partner in the rental firm became involved in a severe automobile accident and suffered multiple injuries shortly before the merger and was seemingly unable to return to work. The partner also knew that the outlook for his health in the immediate future was unpredictable. For the sake of his family, he was eager to seek some of the stock acquired in the merger and make a large portion of his assets liquid. However, federal law does not allow quick profit taking from mergers and therefore did not allow such a sale. The partner consulted the president and officers of the larger company, and they acquiesced in his plans to sell portions of his stock and stated their conviction that no adverse effect on the stock would result. Still unsure, the man then checked with his lawyer and found that the federal law in question had almost never been prosecuted. Having ascertained the risk and having probed the rationale of the law as it applied to his case, the man then sold some of the stock acquired in the merger to provide security for his family in the possible event of his incapacitation or death. Although he subsequently recovered completely, this could not have been foreseen.

In this instance, the partner decided that a consideration of the intrinsic purpose of the law allowed him to act as he did. In addition, he made as thorough a check as possible of the risks involved in his action. He was not satisfied with the decision he made, but he believed it was the best he could do at the time. One can see in this example the enormous ethical tugs-of-war that go with the territory of entrepreneurship.

An Example of Integrity

The complicated nature of entrepreneurial decisions also is illustrated in the following example. At age 27, an entrepreneur joined a new computer software firm with sales of $1.5 million as vice president of international marketing of a new division. His principal goal was to establish profitable distribution for the company's products in the major industrialized nations. Stock incentives and a highly leveraged bonus plan placed clear emphasis on profitability, rather than on volume. In one European country, the choice of distributors was narrowed to 1 from a field of more than 20. The potential distributor was a top firm, with an excellent track record and management, and the chemistry was right. In fact, the distributor was so eager to do business with the entrepreneur's company that it was willing to accept a 10 percent commission, rather than the normal 15 percent royalty. The other terms of the deal were acceptable to both parties. In this actual case, the young vice president decided to give the distributor the full 15 percent commission, even though it would have settled for less. This approach was apparently quite successful because, in five years, this international division grew from zero to $18 million in very profitable sales, and a large firm acquired the venture for $80 million. In describing his reasoning, the entrepreneur said his main goal was to create a sense of long-term integrity. He said further:

> I knew what it would take for them to succeed in gaining the kind of market penetration we were after. I also knew that the economics of their business definitely needed the larger margins from the 15 percent, rather than the smaller royalty. So I figured that if I offered them the full royalty, they would realize I was on their side, and that would create such goodwill that when we did have some serious problems down the road—and you always have them—then we would be able to work together to solve them. And that's exactly what happened. If I had exploited their eagerness to be our distributor, then it only would have come back to haunt me later on.

Ethics Exercise Revisited

The following statements are often made, even by practicing entrepreneurs: How can we think about ethics when we haven't enough time even to think about running our venture? Entrepreneurs are doers, not thinkers—and ethics is too abstract a concept to have any bearing on business realities. When you're struggling to survive, you're not worried about the means you use—you're fighting for one thing: survival.

However, the contemplation of ethical behavior is not unlike poetry—emotion recollected in tranquility. This chapter is intended to provide one such tranquil opportunity.

Through the decisions actually made, or not made, an individual could become more aware of his or her own value system and how making ethical decisions can be affected by the climate in which these decisions are made. However, in the exercise, participants were asked only to answer questions. They were not asked to carry out an action. Between intent and action lies a large gap, which can be filled only by confronting and acting in a number of ambiguous situations.

Chapter Summary

1. The vast majority of CEOs, investors, and entrepreneurs believe that a high ethical standard is the single most important factor in long-term success.
2. Historically, ethical stereotypes of businesspeople ranged widely, and today the old perceptions have given way to a more aware and accepting notion of the messy work of ethical decisions.
3. Many leading business schools today have incorporated ethical issues into their curricula.
4. Entrepreneurs can rarely, if ever, finish a day without facing at least one or two ethical issues.
5. Numerous ethical dilemmas challenge entrepreneurs at the most crucial moments of survival, like a precarious walk on a tightrope.

Study Questions

1. What conclusions and insights emerged from the ethics exercise?
2. Why have ethical stereotypes emerged and how have they changed?
3. Why is ethics so important to entrepreneurial and other success?
4. Why do many entrepreneurs and CEOs believe ethics can and should be taught?
5. What are the most thorny ethical dilemmas that entrepreneurs face, and why?
6. Describe an actual example of how and why taking a high ethical ground results in a good decision for business.

Internet Resources for Chapter 9

http://www.mapnp.org/library/ethics/ethxgde.htm *An Ethics Toolkit for Managers*

http://libnet.colorado.edu/Bell *Resources for Research in Business Ethics and Social Responsibility*

http://e-businessethics.com *The e-business ethics center from the University of Colorado provides a source of information on business ethics, corporate citizenship, and organizational compliance*

http://www.business-ethics.org/index.asp *An international institute fostering global business practices to promote equitable economic development, resource sustainability, and just forms of government*

http://www.epic-online.net *Ethics and Policy Integration Centre*

http://www.ethics.org *Ethics Resource Center*

MIND STRETCHERS

Have you considered?

1. How would you define your own ethics?
2. What was the toughest ethical decision you have faced? How did you handle it, and why? What did you learn?
3. How do you personally determine whether someone is ethical or not?
4. How would you describe the ethics of the president of the United States? Why? Would these ethics be acceptable to you from an investor, a partner, a spouse?

Case
Wayne Postoak

Preparation Questions

1. What roles/titles has Wayne Postoak held? What did he have to do to earn these?
2. What are the strengths and weaknesses of the entrepreneur?
3. Evaluate this business opportunity. What are the opportunities and barriers?
4. What are the critical skills and resources necessary to succeed in this business?
5. Would you invest in this business? Why, or why not?
6. What should the entrepreneur do, and why?

Wayne Postoak

In late 1983, at age 44, Wayne Postoak, a Choctaw Indian, was employed as an instructor in the Biological Science Department at Haskell Indian Junior College (now Haskell Indian Nations University) located in Lawrence, Kansas. Lawrence is approximately 40 miles west of Kansas City and is also the home of the University of Kansas. Wayne had been in the classroom since 1980, but was previously the Haskell basketball coach and recruiter since the early 1970s. During his tenure as coach, the Haskell Indians had the longest winning streak in the history of the school and even beat the JV squad of the University of Kansas. The primary reason he came to Haskell to coach was the administration's support of intercollegiate sports. Eventually the support waned and Wayne ended up teaching in the classroom.

Wayne began to wonder about remaining a teacher because there was a philosophical difference between his approach to education and his supervisor's approach. In addition to this difference was his continued discontentment with not coaching. At the time his eldest son, Darren Wayne, prompted him to consider the

This case was written in 1998 by Ms. Cheryl Chuckluck; Director, Center for Tribal Entrepreneurial Studies, Haskell Indian Nations University, Lawrence, KS. It has been contributed by, and is used with the permission of, Ms. Chuckluck and CTES. The author is most appreciative of Ms. Chuckluck, Mr. Postoak, and CTES.

future of his children. At the age of 6, Darren Wayne dreamed of becoming a medical doctor. Wayne knew that if he were to help his four children attend college, he could not do so on a teacher's salary. This was ever present in his mind each summer as he, like all other Haskell federal employees, was required to take a summer furlough. During these furloughs, Wayne would supplement his income by completing small construction jobs such as fireplaces and sidewalks.

These summer projects kept him apprised of opportunities within the Lawrence area, and a conversation with a friend in the Anadarko area office of the Bureau of Indian Affairs mentioned the plans to build 36 bridges on the four Indian reservations in Kansas. With his dissatisfaction with his job, the upcoming bridge projects, and his desire to care for his family, Wayne began to look at the possibility of starting his own construction company. At the time of his pondering, he also knew he had accumulated approximately $20,000 in his retirement that could possibly be used to start a company.

The Entrepreneur's Background

Wayne grew up the middle child of six brothers and six sisters in Ardmore, Oklahoma. He originally spoke only Choctaw. When his father was cutting his hair the week before he was to go to school, his mother cried because his beautiful hair was being cut. During his father's explanation for why he was cutting his hair, Wayne was introduced to the English language. To this day, during stressful situations, Wayne tends to translate from Choctaw to English in his mind.

One of Wayne's first role models was Mrs. Crumb, his first grade teacher. There were two Indian children in her class of 21 students. She had the other 19 students learn to say they wanted a drink or wanted to go to the restroom in Choctaw. This helped Wayne and taught him courtesy.

Wayne's father, Sam, was the main role model in his life and owned a masonry company as well as the family truck farm. Because they were below the poverty level, it was surprising to Wayne that his father had acquired over 1,200 acres of land by the time he passed away in the late 1980s.

Early on, Sam trained his sons in bricklaying. When Wayne was only 8 years old, his father gave Wayne and his brothers "assignments" to build walls made of brick. These assignments usually took them 6 to 8 hours each day, so they didn't play like the other kids did. When Sam would come home to check on their assignments, anything less than a "B" would have to be redone. If this required them to do the work at night, he would put up a light bulb for them to see. Sometimes they would finish at 2 or 3 o'clock in the morning. This taught them to do things right without supervision and gave them a skill so they could support themselves, which two of his older brothers eventually did.

Sam also taught his sons about the economy of movement. He showed them that if they laid 500 bricks and took an extra step that was 500 steps. He also showed them that if they cut off the mortar 3 times or tapped the bricks 3 times they would have to multiply that by 500 bricks. Wayne later used this knowledge to consult with other people about different ways to save movements.

Wayne also recalls that the family had to wash clothes in some of the streams nearby or in the town washers, when the weather was bad, and then hang them upon the fences near their house. During Wayne's third grade, he and his father were hanging out the clothes to dry when a big, black Chrysler drove up and scattered the clothes with dust. Sam explained to the man, a Mr. Quinn Wicker, that it was hard work to clean the clothes and that it wasn't polite for him to drive up in such a manner.

Mr. Wicker was a businessman from Ardmore who came to buy 20 acres that Sam bought after he had learned that there were plans to drill for oil nearby. Mr. Wicker's manager offered Sam a certain amount of money a couple of times, and Sam counteroffered each time with a larger figure that was only good for that day. Since the manager did not have the authority to accept a larger offer, he had to check with his boss and would come back to Sam the next day. Because Sam stuck to his principle that the offer was only good for that day, Mr. Wicker decided to negotiate directly with Sam. He pulled out a wad of money that turned out to be $3,000. Sam, sensing that Wayne was keenly observing, took Mr. Wicker off to negotiate. Sam did not accept the $3,000 because his land was for sale at $160 per acre, a vastly larger amount than what the other Indians had received for their land. Many of those Indians had unknowingly sold their land for a pittance, and he didn't want Mr. Wicker to take advantage of him. In the end, the land was in the middle of an area where plans were to build a Standard Oil Refinery, and Sam did not sell his land; and he held on to his principle.

Wayne remembers that when he was only six, his father had been an alcoholic, but he had joined a church and never drank again. Wayne understood the discipline his father had, and if he could have that kind of discipline, then he would also develop the behavior. While growing up, team sports also became very important to Wayne and his siblings. They learned how to be a team player and learned the discipline needed to get into shape. His playing ability garnered him scholarships in football, basketball, and baseball. These skills also served him well as a coach.

At the age of 11, Wayne wasn't very accomplished at the production side of construction. His father introduced him to ordering supplies for the company, and it was here that Wayne excelled. During his teenage years, he completed small construction jobs such as fireplaces on his own. Many of his brothers remained in the construction arena. Wayne also enjoyed many aspects of building fireplaces on his own, but he also knew his competencies lay elsewhere.

When he reached 17 years old, Wayne attended the Haskell Institute (now Haskell Indian Nations University) and went into the prevocational program. During his senior year, he was completing six hours of masonry and one hour of English. He also participated in on-the-job training where he could get work and also get school credit. A businessman from downtown Lawrence, Kansas, approached the masonry instructor about building a car wash. The instructor didn't have the time to perform the job, and gave a quote equal to what the business owner received from another company. Wayne's estimate was half of the other bid. With the Haskell Institute's equipment, trucks, and subcontractors who were also students, he completed the project in 22 working days (compared to the expected 60 working days) and at half the cost.

Wayne liked the feeling of sharing the work with friends and completing a project. However, the owner thought that they did the job too quickly and that a 17-year-old kid should not be able to make that kind of money. Wayne finally said he couldn't control the student laborers and student subcontractors, so if the building wasn't standing the next day the businessman would just have to build it again. The owner asked if Wayne was threatening him and he said, "I'm not saying anything, I just want to get paid and pay the subcontractors so that it might not happen." The owner paid him $2,800, and he was able to share some of the money with two of his brothers and a sister who were attending Haskell at the time. Thus the first car wash in the midwest was built near the corner of Louisiana and 23rd Street in Lawrence.

While at college Wayne was very shy and withdrew from his speech class three times in a row. He was terrified to complete the required three-minute public speech. Finally he had to complete the class in order to graduate, but with two weeks still remaining before the speech, he couldn't sleep. He did give his speech, and now 100 or so speeches later, public speaking has become easier for Wayne.

Initially, Wayne did not go into the construction industry, but completed college and went into coaching. Eventually he became the coach and recruiter at Haskell Indian Junior College. Wayne identified talent and put together winning teams from 1970 to 1980.

During his time as coach, he taught his teams several important lessons. One of these was to be courteous to others. While they dined, his teams had to say thank you to the waitresses several times and they became known as a courteous group. Those teams were always welcomed back during the following season. He also taught the teams to be courteous with other people's time. Being on time meant that if the basketball team was expected between 4:00 AM and 4:05 AM for a breakfast before a tournament, stragglers arriving after 4:06 AM would find the food line closed, and they'd go hungry. After winning their first game in the tournament, they stayed late (despite growling stomachs) to watch the team they would play the next day. Wayne then would call Don's Steakhouse in Lawrence, and ask them if they could have their meal ready at an exact time. Wayne had a group of hungry boys coming in!

Each time the team traveled, Wayne would tell the team to be ready at 5:00 AM. He went home to get himself ready, and returned at 4:55 AM to find all the students waiting on the bus! They began to check on one another so no one would be late. They learned shared responsibility, and this enhanced their teamwork.

While serving as head coach, Wayne also sold the season tickets to the basketball games to raise funds for the athletic program. At every opportunity he spoke to organizations in Lawrence, and would attempt to sell season tickets to everyone. One season he sold 2,000 tickets to anyone and everyone he could think of—businesses, organizations, and individuals—even though the building could only hold 1,400 people! He knew that not all the people would come to the games, and that the athletic program needed the funds. When he spoke to banks, he would tell them that another bank bought 50 tickets. Wayne challenged them to buy as well, and it worked.

The Industry

During 1983, Lawrence was a town of approximately 65,000 people, when the University of Kansas was in session. Interest rates were high, and reached as much as 19 percent, lessening the feasibility of new construction. Most construction firms in the area were small, and specialized in one area or another. There were only two larger general contractors that had annual sales up to $18 million. At this time there were 22 minority certified construction firms that were mostly specialized subcontractors in the entire state of Kansas. Many projects were found by attending the Association of General Contractors' monthly cocktail hour. This event was held the evening before the bid letting—mainly for Department of Transportation projects.

During this time, the Affirmative Action law had been passed and was scheduled to be implemented in January 1984. Any construction firm that obtained federal contracts had to utilize a certain percentage of minority-owned subcontractors to be in compliance. In addition to this mandate, there were 36 bridge projects in northeast Kansas available for Indian-owned construction companies because of the Buy Indian Act. [See *Exhibits A–D* for population and employment data for Douglas County, Kansas.]

The Risks

As Wayne contemplated what to do, he started to list the risks and unknowns:

- He would have no job, which meant no continuous income.

- He would be undercapitalized for a construction company—he had only $20,000.
- He would have no employees.
- He would have no equipment.
- If he considered the bridge projects, he had no bridge building experience.
- He would have no estimator.

EXHIBIT A

Douglas County, Kansas, Population

Year	Population
1980*	67,640
1981	69,574
1982	69,947
1983	69,945

*Indicates decennial census 10% population counts. Others are population estimates.
Source: U.S. Bureau of the Census.

EXHIBIT B

Douglas County, Kansas, per Capita Income

Year	Per Capita Income
1980	8,157
1981	8,939
1982	9,188
1983	9,846

Source: Bureau of Economic Analysis [REIS].

EXHIBIT C

Employment and Civilian Labor Force, Douglas County, Kansas

Year	Number Employed	Civilian Labor Force
1980	33,214	34,650
1981	33,133	34,506
1982	32,472	34,066
1983	32,421	34,103

Source: Kansas Department of Labor.

EXHIBIT D

Employment by Industry, Douglas County, Kansas

Year	Total	Nonfarm	Construction	Manufacturing	Transportation	Gov't/G Services
1980	34,655	33,604	1,681	4,908	1,345	10,326
1981	33,777	32,707	1,336	4,743	1,323	9,817
1982	33,595	32,513	1,243	4,527	1,209	9,768
1983	34,102	32,945	1,382	4,447	1,180	9,755

Source: Bureau of Economic Analysis [REIS].

IV

PART FOUR

Financing Entrepreneurial Ventures

A financing strategy should be driven by corporate and personal goals, by resulting financial requirements, and ultimately by the available alternatives. In the final analysis, these alternatives are governed by the entrepreneur's relative bargaining power and skill in managing and orchestrating the fund-raising moves. In turn, that bargaining power is governed to a large extent by the cruelty of real time. It is governed by when the company will run out of cash given its current cash burn rate.

More numerous alternatives for financing a company exist now than ever before. Many contend that money remains plentiful for well-managed emerging firms with the promise of profitable growth. Savvy entrepreneurs should remain vigilant for the warnings noted here to avoid the myopic temptation to "take the money and run." The cost of money can vary considerably.

While some of these alternatives look distinct and separate, a financing strategy probably will encompass a combination of both debt and equity capital. In considering which financial alternatives are best for a venture at any particular stage of growth it is important to draw on the experience of other entrepreneurs, professional investors, lenders, accountants, and other professionals.

In the search for either debt or equity capital, it is important that entrepreneurs take a professional approach to selecting and presenting their ventures to investors and lenders.

10

Chapter Ten

Resource Requirements

When it comes to control of resources... all I need from a source is the ability to use the resources. There are people who describe the ideal business as a post office box to which people send cash.

Howard H. Stevenson
Harvard Business School

Results Expected

Upon completion of this chapter, you will have:

1. Examined the successful entrepreneur's unique attitudes about and approaches to resources—people, capital, and other assets.
2. Identified the important issues in the selection and effective utilization of outside professionals, such as members of a board of directors, lawyers, accountants, and consultants.
3. Examined decisions about financial resources.
4. Analyzed the "Quick Lube Franchise" case study.
5. Created simple cash flow and income statements and a balance sheet.
6. Discovered the ways in which entrepreneurs turn less into more.

The Entrepreneurial Approach to Resources

Resources include (1) people, such as the management team, the board of directors, lawyers, accountants, and consultants; (2) financial resources; (3) assets, such as plant and equipment; and (4) a business plan. Successful entrepreneurs view the need for and the ownership and management of these resources in the pursuit of opportunities differently from the way managers in many large organizations view them. This different way of looking at resources is reflected in a definition of entrepreneurship given in Chapters 1 and 2—the process of creating or seizing an opportunity *and pursuing it regardless of the resources currently controlled.*[1]

Howard H. Stevenson has contributed to understanding the unique approach to resources of successful entrepreneurs. The decisions on what resources are needed, when they are needed, and how to acquire them are strategic decisions that fit with the other driving forces of entrepreneurship. Further, Stevenson has pointed out that entrepreneurs seek to use the minimum possible amount of all types of resources at each stage in their ventures' growth. Rather than own the resources they need, they seek to control them.

[1] This definition was developed by Howard H. Stevenson and colleagues at the Harvard Business School. His work on a paradigm for entrepreneurial management has contributed greatly to this area of entrepreneurship. See Howard H. Stevenson, "A New Paradigm for Entrepreneurial Management," in *Proceedings from the 7th Anniversary Symposium on Entrepreneurship, July 1983* (Boston: Harvard Business School, 1984).

Entrepreneurs with this approach reduce some of the risk in pursuing opportunities, including:

- *Less capital.* The amount of capital required is simply smaller due to the quest for parsimony. The financial exposure is therefore reduced and the dilution of the founder's equity.
- *Staged capital commitments.* The capital infusions are staged to match critical milestones that will signal whether it is prudent to keep going, and thus infuse the second stage of capital, or abort the venture. Both the founder's and investor's financial exposure, and dilution of equity ownership, are thereby reduced.
- *More flexibility.* Entrepreneurs who do not own a resource are in a better position to commit and decommit quickly.[2] One price of ownership of resources is an inherent inflexibility. With the rapidly fluctuating conditions and uncertainty with which most entrepreneurial ventures have to contend, inflexibility can be a curse. Response times need to be short if a firm is to be competitive. Decision windows are most often small and elusive. And it is extremely difficult to predict accurately the resources that will be necessary to execute the opportunity. In addition, the entrepreneurial approach to resources permits iterations or strategic experiments in the venture process—that is, ideas can be tried and tested without committing to the ownership of all assets and resources in the business, to markets and technology that change rapidly, and so forth. For example, Howard Head says that if he had raised all the money he needed at the outset, he would have failed by spending it all too early on the wrong version of his metal ski. Consider also, for example, the inflexibility of a company that commits permanently to a certain technology, software, or management system.
- *Low sunk cost.* In addition, sunk costs are lower if the firm exercises the option to abort the venture at any point. Consider, instead, the enormous upfront capital commitment of a nuclear power plant and the cost of abandoning such a project.
- *Lower costs.* Fixed costs are lowered, thus favorably affecting breakeven. Of course, the other side of the coin is that variable costs may rise. If the entrepreneur has found an opportunity with forgiving and rewarding economics, then there still will most likely be ample gross margins in the venture to absorb this rise.
- *Reduced risk.* In addition to reducing total exposure, other risks, such as the risk of obsolescence of the resource, are also lower. For example, venture leasing has been used by biotechnology companies as a way to supplement sources of equity financing.

While some might scoff at the practice, assuming erroneously that the firm cannot afford to buy a resource, in fact not owning a resource can provide advantages and options. These decisions are often extremely complex, involving consideration of such details as the tax implications of leasing versus buying, and so forth.

Bootstrapping Strategies: Marshaling and Minimizing Resources

Minimizing resources is referred to in colloquial terms as bootstrapping or, more formally, as a lack of resource intensity, defined as a multistage commitment of resources with a minimum commitment at each stage or decision point.[3] When discussing his philosophy on bootstrapping, Greg Gianforte (who retired at the age of 33 after he and his partners sold their software business, Brightwork Development Inc., to McAfee Associates for more than $10 million) stated, "A lot of entrepreneurs think they need money . . . when actually they haven't figured out the business equation."[4] According to Gianforte, lack of money, employees, equipment—even lack of product—is actually a huge advantage because it forces the bootstrapper to concentrate on selling to bring cash into the business. Thus, to persevere, entrepreneurs ask at every step how they can accomplish a little more with a little less and pursue the opportunity.

As was outlined in Exhibit 1.3, the opposite attitude is often evident in large institutions that usually are characterized by a trustee or custodial viewpoint. Managers in larger institutions seek to have not only enough committed resources for the task at hand but also a cushion against the tough times.

Build Your Brain Trust

At Babson College, we have created a yearlong Entrepreneurship Intensity Track (EIT) tailored for second-year MBA candidates who have a serious venture opportunity they want to launch. A central part of the EIT is the Babson Brain Trust (BBT). The example of Kirk Poss illustrates how this works, and why building a brain trust for your venture is a huge

[2] Howard H. Stevenson, Michael J. Roberts, and H. Irving Grousbeck, *New Business Ventures and the Entrepreneur* (Homewood, IL: Richard D. Irwin, 1985).
[3] Ibid.
[4] Emily Barker, "Start with Nothing," *INC.*, February 2002.

part of improving the "fit" vis-à-vis the Timmons Model, and managing risk and reward.

Originally, Kirk planned to go to medical school, so he found a job at Massachusetts General Hospital in Boston, one of the world's premier medical centers. While working on an imaging research project, he gained the respect of the distinguished doctor leading the project. The new imaging technology showed great promise and Mass General was willing to license the technology to a new company that Kirk and the doctor would create. In the meantime, Kirk decided to go back to Babson for an MBA and enrolled in the EIT to start the venture more quickly, more wisely, and less expensively. Enter Professor Timmons who created the Babson Brain Trust around his personal networks and trustees, faculty, and friends at Babson. After gaining an understanding of the venture and Kirk's background through a basic "Gap Analysis" and applying the Timmons Model to the venture, it became clear that two members of the BBT could potentially add enormous value during the creation, launch, and building of the company. Mike Herman spent 20 some years helping Ewing Marion Kauffman build Marion Labs into a $1 billion pharmaceutical firm as chief financial officer, and was later a president of the Kauffman Foundation. As a private investor and director, he had extensive experience working with young medical-related startups. Bob Compton was the original venture capitalist who helped launch Sofamor-Danele. Later he became its chief operating officer, building it into the leading company in the world specializing in spinal and neck injury implants and corrective devices. Medtronic acquired the company for more than $3 billion in 1999.

By introducing Kirk to these two people, he gained access to their brains, their relevant and extensive experience, and their contacts with other talent pools and capital. It was then up to Kirk, through his entrepreneurial energy, promise, and salesmanship, to capture their interest, gain their confidence, and tap into their talent. Happily, all this came together. Herman and Compton saw considerable potential in the technology, Kirk, and the market potential, enough so that they became seed-round investors and directors. Note their decision process. They recognized high potential and that each could personally make a large impact on the odds of success *because* they knew what and how they could add value to this specific opportunity. As of this writing in 2005, the company has raised over $10 million and has surpassed every projected milestone significantly ahead of schedule. More important, the company has recently closed on a valuable drug development deal. The **"Build Your Brain Trust,"** exercise at the end of the chapter will walk you through the key issues and tasks necessary to assemble a brain trust that can add maximum value to your venture.

As this example shows, the right advisors and brain trust members are very important and provide critical value to your venture. The most successful entrepreneurs think this through *before* they launch. They know what they need to fill in the gaps that exist on the team, and they ask themselves what they don't know. They focus on identifying individuals with the know-how, experience, and networks who have access to critical talent, experience, and resources that can make the difference between success and failure.

Using Other People's Resources (OPR)

Obtaining the use of other people's resources, particularly in the startup and early growth stages of a venture, is an important approach for entrepreneurs. In contrast, large firms assume that virtually all resources have to be owned to control their use, and decisions center around how these resources will be acquired and financed—not so with entrepreneurs.

Having the use of the resource and being able to control or influence the deployment of the resource are key. The quote at the beginning of the chapter illustrates this mind-set perfectly.

Other people's resources can include, for example, money invested or lent by friends, relatives, business associates, or other investors. Or resources can include people, space, equipment, or other material loaned, provided inexpensively or free by customers or suppliers, or secured by bartering future services, opportunities, and the like. In fact, using other people's resources can be as simple as benefiting from free booklets and pamphlets, such as those published by many of the old Big Six accounting firms, or using low-cost educational programs or government-funded management assistance programs. Extending accounts payable is one of the primary sources of working capital for many startups and growing firms.

How can you as an entrepreneur begin to tap into these resources? Howard H. Stevenson and William H. Sahlman suggest that you have to do "two seemingly contradictory things: seek out the best advisors—specialists if you have to—and involve them more thoroughly, and at an earlier stage, than you have in the past. At the same time, be more skeptical of their credentials and their advice."[5] A recent study found that social capital, including having an established business

[5] Howard H. Stevenson and William H. Sahlman, "How Small Companies Should Handle Advisors," in *The Entrepreneurial Venture* (Boston: Harvard Business School, 1992), p. 296. See also a *Harvard Business Review* reprint series called "Boards of Directors: Part I" and "Board of Directors: Part II" (Boston: Harvard Business Review, 1976).

EXHIBIT 10.1

Hypotheses Concerning Networks and Entrepreneurial Effectiveness

Effective entrepreneurs are more likely than others to systematically plan and monitor network activities.

- Effective entrepreneurs are able to *chart their present network* and to discriminate between production and symbolic ties.
- Effective entrepreneurs are able to *view effective networks as a crucial aspect for ensuring the success of their company.*
- Effective entrepreneurs are able to *stabilize and maintain networks* to increase their effectiveness and their efficiency.

Effective entrepreneurs are more likely than others to undertake actions toward increasing their network density and diversity.

- Effective entrepreneurs set aside time for purely random activities—things done with no specific problem in mind.
- Effective entrepreneurs are able to *check network density,* so as to avoid too many overlaps (because they affect network efficiency) while still attaining solidarity and cohesiveness.
- Effective entrepreneurs multiply, through extending the reachability of their networks, the stimuli for better and faster adaptation to change.

Source: Adapted from Paola Dubini and Howard Aldrich, "Executive Forum: Personal and Extended Networks Are Central to the Entrepreneurial Process," *Journal of Business Venturing* 6, no. 5 (September 1991), pp. 310–12. Copyright 1991, with permission from Elsevier.

network and encouragement from friends and family, is strongly associated with entrepreneurial activity.[6] In addition to networking with family, friends, classmates, and advisors, Stevenson and Sahlman suggest that the human touch enhances the relationship between the entrepreneur and the venture's advisors.[7] Accuracy in social perception, skill at impression management, skill at persuasion and influence, and a high level of social adaptability may be relevant to the activities necessary for successful new ventures.[8] Paola Dubini and Howard Aldrich have contributed to the growing body of knowledge about how these "social assets" may benefit the bottom line of a new venture; see Exhibit 10.1 for the strategic principles they have identified. However, a handful of studies have failed to demonstrate the effectiveness of networking activities on the performance of ventures.[9]

There are many examples of controlling people resources, rather than owning them. In real estate, even the largest firms do not employ top architects full-time but, rather, secure them on a project basis. Most smaller firms do not employ lawyers but obtain legal assistance as needed. Technical consultants, design engineers, and programmers are other examples. An example of this approach is a company that grew to $20 million in sales in about 10 years with $7,500 cash, a liberal use of credit cards, reduced income for the founders, and hard work and long hours. This company has not had to raise any additional equity capital.

An example of the opposite point of view is a proposed new venture in the minicomputer software industry. The business plan called for about $300,000, an amount that would pay for only the development of the first products. The first priority in the deployment of the company's financial resources outlined in the business plan was to buy outright a computer costing approximately $150,000. The founders refused to consider other options, such as leasing the computer or leasing computer time. The company was unable to attract venture capital, even though, otherwise, it had an excellent business plan. The $150,000 raised from informal private investors was not enough money to execute the opportunity, and the founders decided to give it back and abandon the venture. A more entrepreneurial team would have figured out a way to keep going under these circumstances.

Outside People Resources

Board of Directors

Initial work in evaluating the need for people resources is done when forming a new venture team (see Chapter 8). Once resource needs have been determined and a team has been selected, it will usually be necessary to obtain additional resources from outside the venture in the startup stage and during other stages of growth as well.

[6] B. Honig and P. Davidsson, *"The Role of Social and Human Capital among Nascent Entrepreneurs," Academy of Management Proceedings,* 2001, pp. 1–7.
[7] Ibid., p. 301.
[8] R. A. Baron and G. D. Markman, *(2000) "Beyond Social Capital: How Social Skills Can Enhance Entrepreneurs' Success," Academy of Management Executive* 14 no 1, pp. 106–17.
[9] O. O. Sawyerr and J. E. McGee, *The Impact of Personal Network Characteristics on Perceived Environmental Uncertainty: An Examination of Owners/Managers of New High Technology Firms,* http://www.babson.edu/entrep/fer/papers99, 1999.

The decision of whether to have a board of directors and, if the answer is yes, the process of choosing and finding the people who will sit on the board are troublesome for new ventures.[10]

The Decision The decision of whether to have a board of directors is influenced first by the form of organization chosen for the firm. If the new venture is organized as a corporation, it must have a board of directors, which must be elected by the shareholders. There is flexibility with other forms of organization.

In addition, certain investors will require a board of directors. Venture capitalists almost always require boards of directors and that they be represented on the boards.

Beyond that, deciding whether to involve outsiders is worth careful thought. This decision making starts with identifying missing relevant experience, know-how, and networks, and determining venture has current needs that can be provided by outside directors. Their probable contributions then can be balanced against the resultant greater disclosure to outsiders of plans for operating and financing the business. Also, since one responsibility of a board of directors is to elect officers for the firm, the decision whether to have a board also is tied to financing decisions and ownership of the voting shares in the company.

> The flood of Internet IPOs over the past years raises concerns because their boards are dominated by company executives and venture capitalists.[11] According to the authors of this article, at least half of a board's members should be outside directors in order to provide independent, outside viewpoints.

When Art Spinner of Hambro International was interviewed by *INC.*, he explained:

> Entrepreneurs worry about the wrong thing... that the boards are going to steal their companies or take them over. Though entrepreneurs have many reasons to worry, that's not one of them. It almost never happens. In truth, boards don't even have much power. They are less well equipped to police entrepreneurs than to advise them.[12]

As Spinner suggests, the expertise that members of a board can bring to a venture, at a price it can afford, can far outweigh any of the negative factors mentioned earlier. David Gumpert cites the crucial roles of the advisory board recruited by him and his partner for what was originally NetMarquee, an online direct marketing agency. He describes the importance of intentionally choosing a board by focusing on "holes" that need to be filled, while also being mindful of financial constraints. According to Gumpert, "The board continually challenged us—in terms of tactics, strategy and overall business philosophy." These challenges benefited their company by (1) preventing dumb mistakes, (2) keeping them focused on what really mattered, and (3) stopping them from getting gloomy.[13]

Selection Criteria: Add Value with Know-How and Contacts Once the decision to have a board of directors has been made, finding the appropriate people for the board is a challenge. It is important to be objective and to select trustworthy people. Most ventures typically look to personal acquaintances of the lead entrepreneur or the team or to their lawyers, bankers, accountants, or consultants for their first outside directors. While such a choice might be the right one for a venture, the process also involves finding the right people to fill the gaps discovered in the process of forming the management team.

This issue of filling in the gaps relates to one criteria of a successful management team, intellectual honesty; that is, knowing what you know and what you need to know (see Exhibit 1.2). In a study of boards and specifically venture capitalists' contribution to them, entrepreneurs seemed to value operating experience over the financial expertise.[14] In addition, the study reported, "Those CEOs with a top-20 venture capital firm as the lead investor, on average, did rate the value of the advice from their venture capital board members significantly higher—but not outstandingly higher—than the advice from other outside board members."[15]

Defining expectations and minimum requirements for board members might be a good way to get the most out of a board of directors.

A top-notch outside director usually spends *at least* 9 to 10 days per year on his or her responsibilities. Four days per year are spent for quarterly meetings, a day of preparation for each meeting, a day for

[10] The authors are indebted to Howard H. Stevenson of the Harvard Business School, and to Leslie Charm and Carl Youngman formerly of Doktor Pet Centers and Command Performance hair salons, respectively, for insights into and knowledge of boards of directors.

[11] J. W. Lorsch, A. S. Zelleke, and K. Pick, "Unbalanced Boards," *Harvard Business Review*, February 1, 2001, p. 28.

[12] "Confessions of a Director: Hambro International's Art Spinner Says Most CEOs Don't Know How to Make Good Use of Boards. Here He Tells You How," *INC.*, April 1991, p. 119.

[13] D. E. Gumpert, "Tough Love: What You Really Want from Your Advisory Board," http://www.entreworld.org/content/entrebyline, 2001.

[14] Joseph Rosenstein, Albert V. Bruno, William D. Bygrave, and Natalie T. Taylor, "The CEO, Venture Capitalist, and the Board," *Journal of BusinessVenturing*, 1988, pp. 99–113.

[15] Ibid., pp. 99–100.

another meeting to cope with an unanticipated issue, plus up to a day or more for various phone calls. Yearly fees are usually paid for such a commitment.

Quality directors become involved for the learning and professional development opportunities, rather than for the money. Compensation to board members varies widely. Fees can range from as little as $500 to $1,000 for a half- or full-day meeting to $10,000 to $30,000 per year for four to six full-day to day-and-a-half meetings, plus accessibility on a continuous basis. Directors are also usually reimbursed for their expenses incurred in preparing for and attending meetings. Stock in a startup company, often 2 percent to 5 percent, or options, for 5,000 to 50,000 shares, are common incentives to attract and reward directors.

As a director of 11 companies and an advisor to two other companies, Art Spinner suggested the following as a simple set of rules to guide you toward a productive relationship with your board:

- Treat your directors as individual resources.
- Always be honest with your directors.
- Set up a compensation committee.
- Set up an audit committee.
- Never set up an executive committee.[16]

New ventures are finding that, for a variety of reasons, people who could be potential board members are increasingly cautious about getting involved.

Liability Motivated by an apparent wave of corporate fraud scandals in the United States that many felt could lead to a crisis of confidence in the capital marketplace, in 2002 Congress passed the Sarbanes-Oxley Act (SOX). SOX requires companies to file paperwork with the Securities and Exchange Commission faster, create a more transparent means of collecting and posting financial data, maintain volumes of data, and test their procedures for posting accurate, timely information. The potential consequences of running afoul of this law are ominous, including prison time and huge fines for the company's chief officers.

While startups are usually not subject to the technical requirements of the act, the spirit of the law and emerging case law create higher disclosure standards for even small and growing firms. Audit committees sitting on startup boards, for example, could have real SOX-like exposure.

As well, directors of a company can be held personally liable for its actions and those of its officers. A climate of litigation exists in many areas. For example, some specific grounds for liability of a director have included voting a dividend that renders the corporation insolvent, voting to authorize a loan out of corporate assets to a director or an officer who ultimately defaults, and signing a false corporate document or report. Courts have held that if a director acts in good faith, he or she can be excused from liability. However, it can be difficult for a director to *prove* that he or she has acted in good faith, especially in a startup situation. This proof is complicated by several factors, including possibly an inexperienced management team, the financial weaknesses and cash crises that occur and demand solution, and the lack of good and complete information and records, which are necessary as the basis for action. In recent years, many states have passed what is known as the "Dumb Director Law." In effect, the law allows that directors are normal human beings who can make mistakes and misjudgments; it goes a long way in taking the sting out of potential lawsuits that are urged by ambulance chasers.

One solution to liability concerns is for the firm to purchase indemnity insurance for its directors. But this insurance is expensive. Despite the liability problems noted above, one survey mentioned found that just 11 percent of the respondents reported difficulty in recruiting board members.[17] In dealing with this issue, new ventures will want to examine a possible director's attitude toward risk in general and evaluate whether this is the type of attitude the team needs to have represented.

Harassment Outside stockholders, who may have acquired stock through a private placement or through the over-the-counter market, can have unrealistic expectations about the risk involved in a new venture, the speed at which a return can be realized, as well as the size of the return. Such stockholders are a source of continual annoyance for boards and for their companies.

Time and Risk Experienced directors know that often it takes more time and intense involvement to work with an early-stage venture with sales of $10 million or less than with one having sales of $25 million to $50 million or more, and the former is riskier.

Paying the Board The Mellon Financial Corporation's annual Board of Directors Compensation and Governance Practices Survey[18] found that new

[16] "Confessions of a Director," *INC.*, April 1991, p. 119. Reprinted with permission. © 1991 by Goldbirsh Group, Inc., 38 Commercial Wharf, Boston, MA 02110.

[17] "The *Venture* Survey: Who Sits on Your Board?" *Venture*, April 1984, p. 32.

[18] The Mellon Financial Corporation, *Board of Directors Compensation and Governance Practices Survey*, February 16, 2005.

governance practices are reshaping the boardroom of corporate America, with significant increases in director pay, responsibility, and accountability. The survey results reflect the compensation practices of more than 200 U.S.-based companies. Analysis provides information on both cash- and equity-based compensation, retainers, meeting fees, and board or committee-based leadership differentials. Key findings include:

- Median board retainer was $39,500, up 17.2 percent from the previous year.
- Median total cash compensation, including retainers and meeting fees, was up 13.1 percent to $54,385.
- Equity awards represent approximately 59 percent of total direct compensation in 2004.
- Thirty-eight percent of survey respondents require directors to own company stock.
- Twenty-three percent of companies have a nonexecutive chairman of the board; a further 48 percent have a lead director. More than 83 percent conduct meetings without corporate management present.
- Thirty-six percent of boards now conduct formal evaluations of their own members; this is more than double the findings in 2003.

Alternatives to a Formal Board

The use of advisors and quasi-boards can be a useful alternative to having a formal board of directors.[19] A board of advisors is designed to dispense advice, rather than make decisions, and therefore advisors are not exposed to personal liability. A firm can solicit objective observations and feedback from these advisors. Such informal boards can bring needed expertise, without the legal entanglements and formalities of a regular board. Also, the possible embarrassment of having to remove someone who is not serving a useful role can be avoided. Informal advisors are usually much less expensive, with honorariums of $500 to $1,000 per meeting common. Remember, however, the level of involvement of these advisors probably will be less than that of members of a formal board. The firm also does not enjoy the protection of law, which defines the obligations and responsibilities of members of a formal board.

An informal group of advisors can also be a good mechanism through which a new venture can observe a number of people in action and select one or two as regular directors. The entrepreneur gains the advantages of counsel and advice from outsiders without being legally bound by their decisions.

Attorneys

The Decision Nearly all companies need and use the services of attorneys, and entrepreneurial ventures perhaps more than most.[20] Since it is critical that entrepreneurs fully understand the legal aspects of any decisions and agreements they make, they should never outsource that knowledge to their attorney. Babson College Adjunct Professor Leslie Charm put it this way, "You must understand the meaning of any document you're considering as well as your attorneys do. That's because at the end of the day, when you close that deal, you are the one who has to live with it, not your lawyers." In addition, Charm noted that attorneys should be viewed as teachers and advisors; use them to explain legalese, articulate risk and ramifications; and in negotiations, use them to push to close the deal.

Various authors describe the importance of choosing and managing legal counsel. By following some legal basics and acquiring appropriate legal services, companies can achieve better legal health, including fewer problems and lower costs over the long term.[21] According to FindLaw, Inc., some of the legal work can be done by entrepreneurs who do not have law degrees by using self-help legal guides and preprinted forms. However, one should not rely exclusively on these materials. According to this organization, the factors to consider in choosing an attorney include availability, comfort level with the attorney, experience level and appropriateness to case, cost, and whether the lawyer knows the industry and has connections to investors and venture capital.[22]

Just how attorneys are used by entrepreneurial ventures depends on the needs of the venture at its particular stage. Size is also a factor. As company size increases, so does the need for advice in such areas as liability, mergers, and benefit plans. Contracts and agreements were almost uniformly the predominant use, regardless of the venture's size.

[19] C. O. White and G. Gallop-Goodman. "Tap into Expert Input," *Black Enterprise 30*, no. 12 (2000), p. 47.

[20] The author wishes to acknowledge the input provided by Gerald Feigen of the Center for Entrepreneurial Studies, University of Maryland, from a course on entrepreneurship and the law he has developed and teaches at George Washington University Law School; also John Van Slyke of Alta Research.

[21] J. Adamec, "A Business Owner's Guide to Preventive Law," http://www.inc.com, 1997.

[22] FindLaw, Inc., "Selecting an Attorney," http://www.findlaw.com, 2000.

Entrepreneurs will most likely need to get assistance with the following areas of the law:

- *Incorporation.* Issues such as the forgivable and nonforgivable liabilities of founders, officers, and directors or the form of organization chosen for a new venture are important. As tax laws and other circumstances change, they are important for more established firms as well. How important this area can be is illustrated by the case of a founder who nearly lost control of his company as a result of the legal maneuvering of the clerk and another shareholder. The clerk and the shareholder controlled votes on the board of directors, while the founder had controlling interest in the stock of the company. The shareholder tried to call a directors' meeting and not reelect the founder president. The founder found out about the plot and adroitly managed to call a stockholders' meeting to remove the directors first.
- *Franchising and licensing.* Innumerable issues concerning future rights, obligations, and what happens in the event of nonperformance by either a franchisee or lessee or a franchisor or lessor require specialized legal advice.
- *Contracts and agreements.* Firms need assistance with contracts, licenses, leases, and other such agreements as noncompete employment agreements and those governing the vesting rights of shareholders.
- *Formal litigation, liability protection, and so on.* In today's litigious climate, sooner or later most entrepreneurs will find themselves as defendants in lawsuits and require counsel.
- *Real estate, insurance, and other matters.* It is hard to imagine an entrepreneur who, at one time or another, will not be involved in various kinds of real estate transactions, from rentals to the purchase and sale of property, that require the services of an attorney.
- *Copyrights, trademarks, patents, and intellectual property protection.* Products are hard to protect. But pushing ahead with product development before ample protection from the law is provided can be expedient in the short term but disastrous in the long term. For example, an entrepreneur—facing the loss of a $2.5 million sale of his business and uncollected fees of over $200,000 if his software was not protected—obtained an expert on the sale, leasing, and licensing of software products. The lawyer devised subtle but powerful protections, such as internal clocks in the software that shut down the software if they were not changed.
- *Employee plans.* Benefit and stock ownership plans have become complicated to use effectively and to administer. They require the special know-how of lawyers to avoid common pitfalls.
- *Tax planning and review.* Too frequently the tail of the accountant's tax avoidance advice wags the dog of good business sense. Entrepreneurs who worry more about finding good opportunities to make money, rather than tax shelters, are infinitely better off.
- *Federal, state, and other regulations and reports.* Understanding the impact of and complying with regulations often is not easy. Violations of federal, state, and other regulations often can have serious consequences.
- *Mergers and acquisitions.* Specialized legal knowledge is required when buying or selling a company. Unless an entrepreneur is highly experienced and has highly qualified legal advisors in these transactions, he or she can either lose the deal or end up having to live with legal obligations that can be costly.
- *Bankruptcy law.* Many people have heard tales of entrepreneurs who did not make deposits to pay various federal and state taxes in order to use that cash in their business. These entrepreneurs perhaps falsely assumed that if their companies went bankrupt, the government was out of luck, just like the banks and other creditors. They were wrong. The owners, officers, and often the directors are held personally liable for those obligations.
- *Other matters.* These matters can range from assistance with collecting delinquent accounts to labor relations.
- *Personal needs.* As entrepreneurs accumulate net worth (i.e., property and other assets), legal advice in estate, tax, and financial planning is important.

Selection Criteria: Add Value with Know-How and Contacts In a survey of the factors that enter into the selection of a law firm or an attorney, 54 percent of the respondents said personal contact with a member of the firm was the main factor.[23]

[23] Bradford W. Ketchum, Jr., "You and Your Attorney," INC., June 1982, p. 52.

Reputation was a factor for 40 percent, and a prior relationship with the firm for 26 percent. Equally revealing was the fact that fees were mentioned by only 3 percent.

Many areas of the country have attorneys who specialize in new ventures and in firms with higher growth potential. The best place to start in selecting an attorney is with acquaintances of the lead entrepreneur, of members of the management team, or of directors. Recommendations from accountants, bankers, and associates also are useful. Other sources are partners in venture capital firms, partners of a leading accounting firm (those who have privately owned and emerging company groups), a bar association, or the *Martindale-Hubbell Law Directory* (a listing of lawyers). To be effective, an attorney needs to have the experience and expertise to deal with specific issues facing a venture. Stevenson and Sahlman state that hooking up with the vast resources of a large law firm or national accounting firm may be the best course, but we do not necessarily advise that strategy. You can usually get reasonable tax or estate-planning advice from a big law firm merely by picking up a telephone. The trade-off is that, if you are a small company and they have a dozen General Electrics as clients, you may get short shrift. One- or two-person firms can have an excellent network of specialists to refer to for problems outside their bailiwick. Use the specialist when you have to.[24]

As with members of the management team, directors, and investors, the chemistry also is important. Finally, advice to be highly selective and to expect to get what you pay for is sound. It is also important to realize that lawyers are not businesspeople and that they do not usually make *business* judgments. Rather, they seek to provide perfect or fail-safe protection.

Most attorneys are paid on an hourly basis. Retainers and flat fees are sometimes paid, usually by larger ventures. The amount a venture pays for legal services expectedly rises as the firm grows. Many law firms will agree to defer charges or initially to provide services at a lower than normal rate to obtain a firm's business. According to the *Massachusetts Lawyers Weekly*, legal fees fall into the following ranges: partners' hourly rates, from \$195 to \$400; associates' hourly rates, from \$80 to \$245; and paralegals' rates are between \$45 and \$165.

Bankers and Other Lenders

The Decision Deciding whether to have a banker or another lender usually involves decisions about how to finance certain needs. Most companies will need the services of a banker or other lender at some time in this respect. The decision also can involve how a banker or other lender can serve as an advisor.

As with other advisors, the banker or other lender needs to be a partner, not a difficult minority shareholder. First and foremost, therefore, an entrepreneur should carefully pick the *right banker or lender* rather than to pick just a bank or a financial institution, although picking the bank or institution is also important. Different bankers and lenders have reputations ranging from "excellent" to "just OK" to "not OK" in how they work with entrepreneurial companies. Their institutions also have reputations for how well they work with entrepreneurial companies. Ideally, an entrepreneur needs an excellent banker or lender with an excellent financial institution, although an excellent banker or lender with a just OK institution is preferable to a just OK banker or lender with an excellent institution.

For an entrepreneur to know clearly what he or she needs from a lender is an important starting point. Some will have needs that are asset-based, such as money for equipment, facilities, or inventory. Others may need working capital to fund short-term operating needs.

Having a business plan is invaluable preparation for selecting and working with a lender. Also, because a banker or other lender is a "partner," it is important to invite him or her to see the company in operation, to avoid late financial statements (as well as late payments and overdrafts), and to be honest and straightforward in sharing information.

Selection Criteria: Add Value with Know-How and Contracts Bankers and other lenders are known to other entrepreneurs, lawyers, accountants that provide general business advisory services, and venture capitalists. Starting with their recommendations is ideal. From among four to seven or so possibilities, an entrepreneur will find the right lender and the right institution.

Today's banking and financial services marketplace is much more competitive than in the past. There are more choices, and it is worth the time and effort to shop around.

Accountants

The Decision The accounting profession has come a long way from the "green eyeshades" stereotype one hears reference to occasionally. Today, virtually all

[24] Stevenson and Sahlman, "How Small Companies Should Handle Advisors," p. 297.

the larger accounting firms have discovered the enormous client potential of new and entrepreneurial ventures, and a significant part of their business strategy is to cater specifically to these firms. In the Boston area, for instance, leading accounting firms from the former Big Six located offices for their small business groups on Route 128 in the heart of entrepreneurs' country.

Accountants often are unfairly maligned, especially after the fallout of the Enron/Arthur Andersen case. The activities that accountants engage in have grown and no longer consist of solely counting numbers.[25] Accountants who are experienced as advisors to emerging companies can provide valuable services in addition to audits and taxation advice. An experienced general business advisor can be invaluable in helping to evaluate strategy, raising debt and equity capital, facilitating mergers and acquisitions, locating directors, and even balancing business decisions with important personal needs and goals.

Selection Criteria: Add Value with Know-How and Contacts In selecting accountants, the first step is for the venture to decide whether to go with a smaller local firm, a regional firm, or one of the major accounting firms. Although each company should make its own decision, in an informal survey of companies with sales between $4 million and $20 million, "More than 85 percent of the CEOs preferred working with smaller regional accounting firms, rather than the Big Six, because of lower costs and what they perceived as better personal attention."[26] In making this decision, you will need to address several factors:[27]

- *Service.* Levels of service offered and the attention likely to be provided need to be evaluated. Chances are, for most startups, both will be higher in a small firm than a large one. But if an entrepreneur of a higher potential firm seeking venture capital or a strategic partner has aspirations to go public, a national firm is a good place to start.
- *Needs.* Needs, both current and future, have to be weighed against the capabilities of the firm. Larger firms are more equipped to handle highly complex or technical problems, while smaller firms may be preferable for general management advice and assistance because the principals are more likely to be involved in handling the account. In most instances, those companies in the early stages of planning or that do not plan to go public do not require a top-tier accounting firm. However, one exception to this might be those startups that are able to attract formal venture-capital funds from day one.[28]
- *Cost.* Most major firms will offer very cost-competitive services to startups with significant growth and profit potential. If a venture needs the attention of a partner in a larger firm, services of the larger firm are more expensive. However, if the firm requires extensive technical knowledge, a larger firm may have more experience and therefore be cheaper. Many early-growth phase companies are not able to afford to hire a leading national accounting firm and therefore a small local firm is best. According to Tim McCorry of McCorry Group Inc., these firms should tell you when you are ready to move on to a larger firm that provides more extensive services.[29]
- *Chemistry.* Chemistry always is an important consideration.

The recent trend in the accounting market has lead to increased competition, spiraling capital costs, declining profit margins, and an increase in lawsuits.[30] Entrepreneurs should shop around in such a buyer's market for competent accountants who provide the most suitable and appropriate services. Sources of reference for good attorneys are also sources of reference for accountants, and trade groups are also valuable sources.

Once a firm has reached any significant size, it will have many choices. The founders of one firm, which had grown to about $5 million in sales and had a strong potential to reach $20 million in sales in the next five years and eventually go public, put together a brief summary of the firm, including its background and track record, and a statement of needs for both banking and accounting services. The founders were startled by the aggressive response they received from several banks and major accounting firms.

[25] J. Andresky Fraser, "How Many Accountants Does It Take to Change an Industry?" April 1, 1997, http://www.inc.com.

[26] Susan Greco and Christopher Caggiano, "Advisors: How Do You Use Your CPA?" *INC.*, September 1991.

[27] Neil C. Churchill and Louis A. Werbaneth, Jr., "Choosing and Evaluating Your Accountant," in *Growing Concerns,* ed. David E. Gumpert (New York: John Wiley & Sons and *Harvard Business Review,* 1984), p. 265.

[28] J. Andresky Fraser, "Do I Need a Top-Tier Accounting Firm?" http://www.inc.com/incmagazine, June 1, 1998.

[29] Ibid., p. 2.

[30] Andresky Fraser, "How Many Accountants Does It Take To Change an Industry."

The accounting profession is straightforward enough. Whether the accounting firm is small or large, it sells time, usually by the hour. Today, the hourly partner rates range between $250–$600 for Big Four firms, to $150–$300, for a small, local firm.

Consultants

The Decision[31] Consultants are hired to solve particular problems and to fill gaps not filled by the management team. There are many skilled consultants who can be of invaluable assistance and are a great source of "other people's resources." Advice needed can be quite technical and specific or general and far-ranging. Problems and needs also vary widely, depending upon whether the venture is just starting or is an existing business.

Startups usually require help with critical onetime tasks and decisions that will have lasting impact on the business. In a study of how consultants are used and their impact on venture formation, Karl Bayer, of Germany's Institute for Systems and Innovation Research of the Fraunhofer-Society, interviewed 315 firms. He found that 96 used consultants and that consultants are employed by startups for the following reasons:

1. To compensate for a lower level of professional experience.
2. To target a wide market segment (possibly to do market research for a consumer goods firm).
3. To undertake projects that require a large startup investment in equipment.[32]

These tasks and decisions might include assessing business sites, evaluating lease and rental agreements, setting up record and bookkeeping systems, finding business partners, obtaining startup capital, and formulating initial marketing plans.

Existing businesses face ongoing issues resulting from growth. Many of these issues are so specialized that rarely is this expertise available on the management team. Issues of obtaining market research, evaluating when and how to go about computerizing business tasks, deciding whether to lease or buy major pieces of equipment, and determining whether to change inventory valuation methods can be involved.

While it is not always possible to pinpoint the exact nature of a problem, sometimes a fresh, outside view helps when a new venture tries to determine the broad nature of its concern, such as whether it involves a personnel problem, manufacturing problem, or marketing problem, for example. Mie-Yun Lee of BuyerZone.com offers helpful hints for establishing an effective consultation relationship: (1) Define, define, define—invest whatever time is necessary to define and communicate the expected outcome of the project; (2) when choosing a consultant, expect a long-term relationship as it takes time to get the consultant up to speed on your business; and (3) outsourcing is not a magic bullet that relieves you of work, as communication is critical to success.[33]

Bayer reported that the use of consultants had a negative effect on sales three to five years later. Additionally, his surveys overwhelmingly reported (two-thirds of the 96) that "the work delivered by the consultants . . . [was] inadequate for the task."[34] Bayer suggests that the entrepreneur can find and adequately prepare a consultant so that gaps are filled and the firm benefits in the long run, but it takes diligence.

Selection Criteria: Add Value with Know-How and Contacts Unfortunately, nowhere are the options so numerous, the quality so variable, and the costs so unpredictable as in the area of consulting. The number of people calling themselves management consultants is large and growing steadily. By 2003, there were an estimated 75,000 to 80,000 private management consultants around the country. An estimated 2,000 or more are added annually. More than half the consultants were found to work on their own, while the remainder work for firms. In addition, government agencies (primarily the Small Business Administration) employ consultants to work with businesses; various private and nonprofit organizations provide management assistance to help entrepreneurs; and others, such as professors, engineers, and so forth, provide consulting services part time. Such assistance also may be provided by other professionals, such as accountants and bankers.

Again, the right chemistry is critical in selecting consultants. One company president who was asked what he had learned from talking to clients of the consultant he finally hired said, "They couldn't really pinpoint one thing, but they all said they would not consider starting and growing a company without him!"

[31] The following is excerpted in part from David E. Gumpert and Jeffry A. Timmons, *The Encyclopedia of Small Business Resources* (New York: Harper & Row, 1984), pp. 48–51.

[32] Karl Bayer, "The Impact of Using Consultants during Venture Formation on Venture Performance," in *Frontiers of Entrepreneurship Research 1991,* ed. Neil H. Churchill et al. (Babson Park, MA: Babson College, 1991), pp. 298–99.

[33] Mie-Yun Lee, "Finding the Right Consultant," http://www.inc.buyerzone.com, February 2, 2000.

[34] Bayer, "The Impact of Using Consultants," p. 301.

As unwieldy and risky as the consulting situation might appear, there are ways of limiting the choices. Consultants tend to have specialties; while some consultants claim wide expertise, most will indicate the kinds of situations they feel most comfortable with and skillful in handling. In seeking a consultant, consider the following:[35]

- Good consultants are not geographically bound; they will travel and can work via electronic sources.
- The best referral system is word of mouth. This point cannot be stressed enough.
- Always check references carefully. It is important to look at the past solutions consultants have utilized.
- People skills are essential and therefore should be assessed when interviewing a consultant.
- Ask about professional affiliations and call them to verify the person is in good standing.

Three or more potential consultants can be interviewed about their expertise and approach and their references checked. Candidates who pass this initial screening then can be asked to prepare specific proposals.

A written agreement, specifying the consultant's responsibilities and objectives of the assignment, the length of time the project will take, and the type and amount of compensation, is highly recommended. Some consultants work on an hourly basis, some on a fixed-fee basis, and some on a retainer-fee basis. Huge variations in consulting costs for the same services exist. At one end of the spectrum is the Small Business Administration, which provides consultants to small businesses without charge. At the other end of the spectrum are well-known consulting firms that may charge large amounts for minimal marketing studies or technical feasibility studies.

While the quality of many products roughly correlates with their price, this is not so with consulting services. It is difficult to judge consultants solely on the basis of the fees they charge.

Financial Resources

Analyzing Financial Requirements

Once the opportunity has been assessed, once a new venture team has been formed, and once all resource needs have been identified, *then* is the time for a new venture to evaluate what financial resources are required and when.

As has been noted before, there is a temptation to place the cart before the horse. Entrepreneurs are tempted to begin their evaluation of business opportunities—and particularly their thinking about formal business plans—by analyzing spreadsheets, rather than focusing first on defining the opportunity, deciding how to seize it, and then preparing the financial estimates of what is required.

However, when the time comes to analyze financial requirements, it is important to realize that cash is the lifeblood of a venture. As James Stancill, professor of finance at the University of Southern California's business school, has said: "Any company, no matter how big or small, moves on cash, not profits. You can't pay bills with profits, only cash. You can't pay employees with profits, only cash."[36] Financial resources are almost always limited, and important and significant trade-offs need to be made in evaluating a company's needs and the timing of those needs.

Spreadsheets Computers and spreadsheet programs are tools that save time and increase productivity and creativity enormously. Spreadsheets are nothing more than pieces of accounting paper adapted for use with a computer.

The origins of the first spreadsheet program, VisiCalc, reveal its relevance for entrepreneurs. It was devised by MBA student Dan Bricklin while he was attending Harvard Business School. The student was faced with analyzing pro forma income statements and balance sheets, cash flows, and breakeven for his cases. The question "*What if* you assumed such and such?" was inevitably asked.

The major advantage of using spreadsheets to analyze capital requirements is having the ability to answer what-if questions. This takes on particular relevance also when one considers, as James Stancill points out:

> Usual measures of cash flow-net income plus depreciation (NIPD) or earnings before interest and taxes (EBIT) give a realistic indication of a company's cash position only during a period of steady sales.[37]

Take cash flow projections. An entrepreneur could answer a question such as, What if sales grow at just 5 percent, instead of 15 percent, and what if only 50 percent, instead of 65 percent, of amounts billed

[35] J. Finnegan, "The Fine Art of Finding a Consultant," http://www.inc.com.incmagazine, July 1, 1997.

[36] Reprinted by permission of *Harvard Business Review*. An excerpt from "When Is There Cash in Cash Flow?" by James M. Stancill, March–April 1987, p. 38. Copyright © 1987 by the President and Fellows *of* Harvard College.

[37] Stancill, "When Is There Cash in Cash Flow?" p. 38.

are paid in 30 days? The impact on cash flow of changes in these projections can be seen.

The same what-if process also can be applied to pro forma income statements and balance sheets, budgeting, and break-even calculations. To illustrate, by altering assumptions about revenues and costs such that cash reaches zero, breakeven can be analyzed. Thus, for example, RMA assumptions could be used as comparative boundaries for testing assumptions about a venture.

An example of how computer-based analysis can be of enormous value is the experience of a colleague who was seriously considering starting a new publishing venture. His analysis of the opportunity was encouraging, and important factors such as relevant experience and commitment by the lead entrepreneur were there. Assumptions about fixed and variable costs, market estimates, and probable startup resource requirements had also been assembled. What needed to be done next was to generate detailed monthly cash flows to determine more precisely the economic character of the venture, including the impact of the quite seasonal nature of the business, and to determine the amount of money needed to launch the business and the amount and timing of potential rewards. In less than three hours, the assumptions about revenues and expenditures associated with the startup were entered into a computer model. Within another two hours, he was able to see what the venture would look like financially over the first 18 months and then to see the impact of several different what-if scenarios. The net result was that the new venture idea was abandoned because the amount of money required appeared to outweigh the potential.

The strength of computer-based analysis is also a source of problems for entrepreneurs who place the "druther" before the fact. With so many moving parts, analysis that is not grounded in sound perceptions about an opportunity is most likely to be confused.

Internet Impact: Resources

Fund-raising for Nonprofits

A dynamic online service model has emerged that is changing the way nonprofits conduct their fund-raising auctions. Charity auctions, which in 2004 accounted for $18 billion in charitable giving in the United States, often attract high-income individuals and freely donated, high-quality items. But coordinating and staffing those venues has always been a challenge, particularly since volunteer turnover requires the retraining of a majority of the workforce each time an auction is held. In addition, physical auctions are typically catered affairs that are attended by only a small percentage of an organization's support base.

cMarket, Inc., a venture-funded startup based in Cambridge, Massachusetts, has developed an online service model that allows nonprofits to promote their causes, build their donor base, provide value to corporate sponsors, and improve the results of their fund-raising programs. Jon Carson, president of the organization, noted, "Now any nonprofit—without training or in-house technical people—can hold a fund-raising event that reaches the inbox of its entire constituency."

In 2004—the company's first full year of operations—cMarket signed over 400 clients. Then in May 2005, the company announced a partnership with Network for Good. Founded in 2001 by the Time Warner Foundation and AOL, Inc., the Cisco Foundation and Cisco Systems, Inc., and Yahoo! Inc., Network for Good is an independent, nonprofit organization that works to advance nonprofit adoption of the Internet as a tool for fund-raising, volunteer recruitment, and community engagement.

Chapter Summary

1. Successful entrepreneurs use ingenious bootstrapping approaches to marshaling and minimizing resources.
2. Control of resources rather than ownership of resources is the key to a "less is more" resource strategy.
3. Entrepreneurs are also creative in identifying other people's money and resources, thereby spreading and sharing the risks.
4. Selecting outside advisors, directors, and other professionals boils down to one key criterion: Do they add value through their know-how and networks?
5. Today, access to financial and nonfinancial resources is greater than ever before and is increasing because of the Internet.
6. Building a brain trust of the right mentors, advisors, and coaches is one of the entrepreneur's most valuable "secret weapons."

Study Questions

1. Entrepreneurs think and act ingeniously when it comes to resources. What does this mean and why is it so important?
2. Describe at least two creative bootstrapping resources you know of.
3. Why will the Internet become an increasingly important gateway to controlling resources?
4. In selecting outside advisors, a board, consultants, and the like, what are the most important criteria, and why?

Internet Resources for Chapter 10

http://www.startupjournal.com *The Wall Street Journal Center for Entrepreneurs is organized with tabs on Columnists, How-To, Ideas, Franchising, Financing, Technology, and Running a Business*

http://www.businesslaw.gov *A government site providing tips and contacts for the legal aspects of starting and running a business*

http://emc.score.org *The SCORE Association is a national, nonprofit association, and a resource partner with the SBA with 11,500 volunteer members and 389 chapters throughout the United States*

http://www.businessweek.com/smallbiz/index.html *Site includes a legal guide and a Small Business Guide*

http://www.gmarketing.com *Guerilla Marketing offers creative marketing tips to help you outsmart your competition*

http://biz.findlaw.com *The most extensive guide to law sites for business*

MIND STRETCHERS

Have you considered?

1. Many successful entrepreneurs and private investors say it is just as bad to start out with too much money as it is too little. Why is this so? Can you find some examples?
2. It is said that money is the least important part of the resource equation and of the entrepreneurial process. Why is this so?
3. What bootstrapping strategies do you need to devise?

Exercise

Build Your Brain Trust

Building a cadre of mentors, advisors, coaches, and directors can be the difference between success and failure in a venture. Building this brain trust will require your professionalism, thoroughness, salesmanship, and tenacity. You gain the trust and confidence of these mentors through your performance and integrity.

This exercise is intended to provide a framework and key steps in thinking through your requirements and developing a brain trust for your ventures.

Part I: Gap and Fit Analysis vis-à-vis the Timmons Model

1. At each phase of development of a venture, different know-how and access to experience, expertise, and judgment external to the founding team are often required. A key risk-reward management tool is the gap and fit analysis using the model.

   ✓ Who has access to key know-how and resources that we do not?

   ✓ What is missing that we have to have to obtain a very good chance?

   ✓ Who can add the most value / insights / solid experience to the venture now, in the next two years; and how?

   ✓ Who are the smartest, most insightful people given what we are trying to do?

   ✓ Who has the most valuable perspective and networks that could help the venture or in an area that you know least about?

2. Break down the Timmons model to focus on each dimension.

   - Core opportunity: If they are not on your team now, who are the people who know more than anyone else on the planet about: the revenue and cost model, and underlying drivers and assumptions; how to price, get sales, marketing, customer service, and distribution; IT and e-business; the competition; the free cash flow characteristics and economics of the business?
   - Resources: Who can help you get the necessary knowledge of and access to people, networks, money, and key talent?
   - Team: Who has 10 to 20 years more experience and scar tissue than you do in building a venture from ground zero?
   - Context: Who understands the context, changes, and timing of the venture in terms of the capital markets, any key regulatory requirements, and the internal drivers of the industry / technology / market?

3. Conclusions: What and who can make the biggest difference in the venture? Usually just one to three key people or resources can make a huge difference.

Part II: Identify and Build the Brain Trust

1. Once you've figured out what and who can make the greatest difference, you need to arrange for an introduction. Faculty, family friends, roommates, and the like are good places to start.
2. If you can't get the introductions, then you have to go with your wits and creativity to get a personal meeting.

   ✓ Be highly prepared and articulate.

   ✓ Send an executive summary and advance agenda.

   ✓ Know the reasons and benefits that will be most appealing to this person.

   ✓ Follow up and follow through: send a handwritten note, not just another e-mail.

3. Ask for blunt and direct feedback to such questions as:

   ✓ What have we missed here? What flaws do you see in our team, our marketing plan, our financial requirements, our strategy, etc.?

   ✓ Are there competitors we don't know about?

   ✓ How would you compete with me?

   ✓ Who would reject and accept us for an investment? Why?

   ✓ Who have we missed?

   ✓ Who else should we talk with?

   You will gain significant insight into yourself and your venture, as well as how knowledgeable and insightful the potential brain trust member is about your business, from the questions he or she asks, and from your own. You will soon know whether the person is interested and can add value.

4. Grow the brain trust to grow the venture. Think two years ahead and add to the brain trust people who have already navigated the difficult waters you expect to travel.

Exercise

How Entrepreneurs Turn Less into More

Entrepreneurs are often creative and ingenious in bootstrapping their ventures and in getting a great deal out of very limited resources. This assignment can be done alone, in pairs, or in trios. Identify at least two or three entrepreneurs whose companies exceed $3 million in sales and are less than 10 years old and who have started their companies with less than $25,000 to $50,000 of initial seed capital. Interview them with a focus on their strategies and tactics that minimize and control (not necessarily own) the necessary resources.

1. What methods, sources, and techniques did they devise to acquire resources?
2. Why were they able to do so much with so little?
3. What assumptions, attitudes, and mind-sets seemed to enable them to think and function in this manner?
4. What patterns, similarities, and differences exist among the entrepreneurs you interviewed?
5. What impact did these minimizing bootstrapping approaches have on their abilities to conserve cash and equity and to create future options or choices to pursue other opportunities?
6. How did they devise unique incentive structures in the deals and arrangements with their people, suppliers, and other resource providers (their first office space or facility, brochures, etc.)?
7. In lieu of money, what other forms of currency did they use, such as bartering for space, equipment, or people or giving an extra day off or an extra week's vacation?
8. Can they think of examples of how they acquired (gained control of) a resource they could afford to pay for with real money and did not?
9. Many experienced entrepreneurs say that for first-time entrepreneurs it can be worse to start with too much money rather than too little. How do you see this and why?
10. Some of the strongest new companies are started during an economic recession, among tight credit and capital markets. It is invaluable to develop a lean-and-mean, make-do, less-is-more philosophy and sense of frugality and budgetary discipline. Can you think of any examples of this? Do you agree or disagree? Can you think of opposite examples, such as companies started at or near the peak of the 1990s economic boom with more capital and credit than they needed?

You will find as very useful background reading the feature articles on bootstrapping in *INC.* magazine, *Success* magazine, *Fast Company,* and others.

Case

Quick Lube Franchise Corporation (QLFC)

Preparation Questions

1. What grounds might QLFC have for filing a lawsuit against Huston?
2. Why do you think Huston has asked for a meeting with Herget?
3. What advice would you give Herget as he considers Huston's request for a meeting with QLFC?
4. As part of that advice, how much is QLFC worth?
5. Does your answer to Question 4 depend on how QLFC is harvested?

It had been a year since Huston, a major oil company, had bought 80 percent of Super Lube, Inc., the number one franchisor of quick lubrication and oil-change service centers in the United States with 1,000 outlets. As a result of that takeover, Super Lube's largest franchisee, Quick Lube Franchise Corporation (QLFC), found itself in the position where its principal supplier, lead financing vehicle, and franchisor were the same entity. Was this an opportunity or a disaster? In April 1991, Frank Herget, founder, chairman, and CEO of QLFC was faced with one of the most important decisions of his life.

Historical Background

Super Lube was the innovator of the quick lube concept, servicing the lube, motor oil, and filter needs of motorists in a specialized building with highly refined procedures. It was founded in March 1979 by Jeff Martin. Frank Herget was one of the four founding members of Martin's team. After a few years, Herget became frustrated with life at the franchisor's headquarters in Dallas. He believed that the future of Super Lube was in operating service centers. That put him at odds with founder, chairman, and CEO Jeff Martin who was passionately committed to franchising service centers as fast as possible. Martin and Herget had known each other for a long time so they sought a mutually acceptable way to resolve their differences. Their discussions quickly resulted in the decision that Herget would buy a company-owned service center in northern California by swapping his Super Lube founder's stock valued at $64,000, which he had purchased originally for $13,000. Quick Lube Franchise Corporation was founded.

Early Success and Growth

Success in his first service center inspired growth. Eventually, QLFC controlled service center development and operating rights to a geographic area covering parts of California and Washington with the potential for over 90 service centers. Herget's long-term goal was to build QLFC into a big chain of Super Lube service centers that would have a public stock offering or merge with a larger company (*Exhibits A* and *B*).

Herget financed QLFC's growth with both equity and debt (*Exhibits C* and *D*). Most of the additional equity came from former Super Lube employees who left the franchisor to join QLFC in senior management positions. They purchased stock in QLFC with cash realized by selling their stock in Super Lube. A key member of Herget's team was Mark Roberts, who had been Super Lube's CFO until 1986. He brought much needed financial sophistication to QLFC.

The primary debt requirement was for financing new service centers. In 1991, the average cost of land acquisition and construction had risen to $750,000 per service center from about $350,000 10 years earlier.

Growth was originally achieved through off-balance-sheet real estate partnerships. An Oregon bank lent about $4 million and a Texas bank lent almost $3 million. However, rapid growth wasn't possible until QLFC struck a deal with Huston Oil for $6.5 million of subordinated debt. The Huston debt was 8 percent interest—only for 5 years and then amortized on a straight line basis in years 6 through 10. The real estate developed with the Huston financing was kept in the company. QLFC was contractually committed to purchasing Huston products.

EXHIBIT A

QLFC Growth

	82	83	84	85	86	87	88	89	90	91
Service Centers	2	3	4	7	16	25	34	44	46	47
Sales ($ million)	.5	1.6	2.1	3.8	8.5	15.5	19	27	28	30

EXHIBIT B

Quick Lube Franchise Corp.: FY 1991 Budget Worksheet*

	Apr	May	Jun	Jul	Aug	Sep	Oct	Nov	Dec	Jan	Feb	Mar	Total
Sales	2,424,718	2,444,629	2,756,829	2,816,765	2,872,074	2,358,273	2,619,415	2,435,022	2,494,696	2,733,469	2,464,172	2,795,804	**31,215,866**
Cost of sales	544,689	549,348	613,728	626,809	639,126	529,542	588,628	547,137	573,063	627,574	565,836	642,144	**7,047,624**
Variable expenses†	805,251	826,956	894,782	914,080	943,260	790,276	893,236	819,709	844,626	911,313	826,811	949,576	**10,419,876**
Fixed expenses	358,640	349,858	351,828	363,917	371,498	366,260	371,988	391,686	378,485	388,381	399,375	393,974	**4,485,890**
Real estate cost	320,377	337,372	340,652	341,353	352,053	352,053	372,030	372,030	392,337	392,452	392,452	410,552	**4,375,713**
Store operating income	395,761	381,095	555,839	570,606	566,137	320,142	393,533	304,460	306,185	413,749	279,698	399,558	**4,886,763**
Overhead	255,515	261,573	245,083	241,089	263,458	278,333	258,655	274,724	277,974	269,551	279,819	275,440	**3,181,214**
Operating income	140,246	119,522	310,756	329,517	302,679	41,809	134,878	29,736	28,211	144,198	(121)	124,118	**1,705,549**
Other income	7,392	7,392	7,392	7,392	7,392	7,392	7,392	7,392	7,392	7,392	7,392	7,392	**88,704**
Dropped site expense	(8,333)	(8,333)	(8,333)	(8,333)	(8,333)	(8,333)	(8,333)	(8,333)	(8,333)	(8,333)	(8,333)	(8,333)	**(99,996)**
Minority interest	686	613	(2,610)	(3,254)	(3,145)	2,065	511	4,529	4,346	1,290	6,564	2,459	**14,054**
Interest expense	(5,495)	(5,495)	(5,495)	(5,495)	(5,495)	(5,495)	(5,495)	(5,495)	(5,495)	(5,495)	(5,495)	(5,495)	**(65,940)**
Taxable income	134,496	113,699	301,710	319,827	293,098	37,438	128,953	27,829	26,121	139,052	7	120,141	**1,642,371**
Income tax expense	54,921	47,253	119,971	126,613	115,680	17,885	53,211	17,790	16,727	58,652	6,880	51,779	**687,362**
Net income	79,575	66,446	181,739	193,214	177,418	19,553	75,742	10,039	9,394	80,400	(6,873)	68,362	**955,009**

* Budget revised March 21, 1990.

† Royalties to the franchisor equal 7% of gross sales.

EXHIBIT C

Quick Lube Franchise Corp.: Consolidated Balance Sheets

	Year Ended March 31	
	1991	**1990**
Assets		
Current Assets		
Cash	$ 740,551	$ 665,106
Accounts receivable, net doubtful accounts of $61,000 in 1991 and $44,000 in 1990	518,116	309,427
Construction advances receivable	508,168	137,412
Due from government agency		407,678
Inventory	1,093,241	1,074,513
Prepaid expenses other	407,578	401,562
Total Current Assets	3,267,654	2,995,698
Property and Equipment		
Land	351,772	351,772
Buildings	3,171,950	2,519,845
Furniture, fixtures and equipment	2,988,073	2,644,801
Leasehold improvements	242,434	183,635
Property under capital leases	703,778	703,778
Construction in progress	68,138	531,594
	7,526,145	6,935,425
Less accumulated deprec and amort	(1,290,565)	(854,473)
	6,235,580	6,080,952
Other Assets		
Area development and license agreements, net of accumulated amortization	923,970	988,314
Other intangibles, net accumulated amort	273,737	316,960
Other	151,604	208,898
	$10,852,545	$10,590,822
Liabilities and Shareholders' Equity		
Current Liabilities		
Accounts payable & accrued expenses	$ 3,085,318	$ 3,198,694
Income taxes payable	37,224	256,293
Note payable		250,000
Current portion - LTD	203,629	174,134
Current portion of capital lease	19,655	17,178
Total Current Liabilities	3,345,826	3,896,299
Long-Term Debt, less current	2,848,573	3,052,597
Capital Lease Obligations, less current	628,199	648,552
Other Long-Term Liabilities	731,783	483,534
Minority Interest	2,602	13,821
Total Long-Term Liabilities	4,211,157	4,198,504
Shareholders' Equity		
Common stock, par value $.01/share authorized 10,000,000 shares; issued 1,080,000 shares	10,800	10,800
Additional paid-in capital	1,041,170	774,267
Retained earnings	2,243,592	1,710,952
	3,295,562	2,496,019
	$10,852,545	$10,590,822

EXHIBIT D

Quick Lube Franchise Corp.: Consolidated Cash Flow

	Year Ended March 31		
Operating Activities	**1991**	**1990**	**1989**
Net Income	$ 532,640	$ 764,794	$ 524,211
Adjustments to reconcile net income to net cash provided by operating activities:			
Depreciation and Amortization	612,063	526,750	414,971
Provision for losses on accounts receivable	16,615	30,510	5,559
Provision for deferred income taxes	(15,045)	12,519	50,388
Minority interest in losses of subsidiaries	(11,217)	(129,589)	(83,726)
Loss (gain) on disposition of property and equipment	33,301	(420)	N/A
Changes in operating assets and liabilities:			
Accounts Receivable	(225,304)	(58,700)	(135,585)
Inventory	(18,728)	(273,559)	(286,037)
Prepaid expenses and other	(6,016)	(102,117)	(34,334)
Accounts payable and accrued expenses	(113,376)	559,456	1,409,042
Income taxes payable	(219,069)	404,068	(620,434)
Due from shareholders and affiliates	N/A	N/A	(43,742)
Other long-term liabilities	263,294	167,501	84,697
Net Cash Provided by Operating Activities	849,158	1,901,213	1,285,010
Investing Activities			
Purchases of property and equipment	(599,327)	(1,922,892)	(1,922,852)
Proceeds from sale of property and equipment	374,592	8,523	782,519
Acquisition of license agreements	(44,000)	(127,000)	(117,000)
Acquisition of other intangibles	(2,615)	(327,549)	(2,500)
Change in construction advance receivable	(370,756)	593,017	(601,525)
Change in other assets	43,894	(138,816)	11,908
Net Cash Used in Investing Activities	(598,212)	(1,914,717)	(1,849,450)
Financing Activities			
Proceeds from long-term borrowings and revolving line of credit	4,940,000	4,026,441	2,448,071
Proceeds from borrowings from related parties	N/A	N/A	19,600
Principal payments on long-term borrowings	(5,364,529)	(3,463,693)	(2,658,534)
Principal payments on borrowings from related parties		(19,600)	(7,216)
Principal payments on capital lease obligations	(17,876)	(38,048)	N/A
Proceeds from sale of Common Stock and capital contributions	266,903	97,201	19,600
Net Cash Provided by (Used in) Financing Activities	(175,502)	602,301	(178,479)
Increase (Decrease) in Cash	75,444	588,797	(742,919)
Cash at beginning of year	665,106	76,309	819,228

Super Lube's Relationship with Its Franchisees

Despite bridge financing of $10 million at the end of 1985 followed by a successful initial public offering, Super Lube's growth continued to outpace its ability to finance it. At the end of the 1980s, Super Lube was in technical default to its debt holders. Huston struck a deal to acquire 80 percent of the company in a debt restructuring scheme. However, during the time of Super Lube's mounting financial problems and the subsequent Huston deal, franchisees grew increasingly discontented.

A franchise relationship is governed by a contract called a license agreement. As a "business format" franchise, a franchisor offers a franchisee the rights to engage in a business system by using the franchisor's trade name, trademark, service marks, know-how, and method of doing business. The franchisee is contractually bound to a system of operation and to pay the franchisor a royalty in the form of a percentage of top-line sales.

The Super Lube license agreement called for the franchisor to perform product development and quality assurance tasks. Super Lube had made a strategic decision early in its existence to sell franchises on the basis of area development agreements. These franchisees had grown to become a group of sophisticated, fully integrated companies. As the franchisees grew with multiple outlets and became increasingly self-reliant, the royalty became difficult to justify. When the franchisor failed to perform its contractually obligated tasks as its financial problems grew more and more burdensome toward the end of the 1980s, a franchisee revolt began to surface.

The Huston Era Begins

The new owners, Huston Oil, quickly moved to replace virtually the entire management team at Super Lube. The new CEO was previously a long-term employee of a Kmart subsidiary. He took a hard-line position on how the franchise system would operate and that Huston motor oil would be an important part of it. The first national convention after the Huston takeover was a disaster. The franchisees, already frustrated, were dismayed by the focus of the franchisor on motor oil sales instead of service center-level profitability.

Herget decided to make a thorough analysis of the historical relationship between Quick Lube Franchise Corporation and Super Lube. Three months of research and documentation led to Quick Lube Franchise Corporation calling for a meeting with Huston to review the findings and address concerns.

The meeting was held at the franchisor's offices with Herget and the franchisor's CEO and executive vice president. Herget described the meeting:

> The session amounted to a three-hour monologue by me followed by Super Lube's rejection of the past as relevant to the relationship. I was politely asked to trust that the future performance of the franchisor would be better and to treat the past as sunk cost. In response to my concern that Huston might have a conflict of interest in selling me product as well as being the franchisor and having an obligation to promote service center profitability, they answered that Huston bailed Super Lube out of a mess and the franchisees should be grateful, not combative.

Litigation

The QLFC board of directors received Herget's report and told him to select a law firm and to pursue litigation against Huston. QLFC's three months of research was supplied to the law firm. A suit against Huston was filed three months after the failed QLFC/Huston "summit."

Huston denied the charges and filed a countersuit. Document search, depositions, and general legal maneuvering had been going on for about three months when QLFC's attorneys received a call from Huston requesting a meeting. Herget immediately called a board meeting, and prepared to make a recommendation for QLFC's strategic plan.

11

Chapter Eleven

Franchising

Franchising is sharing an entrepreneurial vision and working together to make it a reality. Franchisees and the franchisor must believe in their business, but more important they must believe in each other. The power of focused and dedicated partners creates a momentum of personal, business and financial growth that is limitless. It's also a lot of fun.

W. J. Hindman
Founder, Jiffy Lube International, Inc.

Results Expected

Upon completion of this chapter, you will have:

1. Examined what franchising is and the nature of the role of the franchisor and the franchisee.
2. Learned about the criteria for becoming a franchisee of an existing system and the criteria for becoming a franchisor.
3. Reviewed a basic screening method for evaluating franchises with a higher success probability.
4. Analyzed the franchise relationship model and its use as a guide for developing a franchise high potential venture.
5. Analyzed the franchise growth strategy of a young startup company, Bagelz, and the career decisions of one of its founders, Mike Bellobuono.

Introduction

In this chapter we will explore what franchising is and how well it fits the Timmons Model definition of entrepreneurship. We will consider the scope of franchising and examine the criteria for determining a franchise's stature, from the perspective of a prospective franchisee and from the perspective of an existing or prospective franchisor. We will present several templates and models that can be helpful in conducting due diligence on a franchise opportunity.

Let us consider how well franchising fits our definition of entrepreneurship from Chapters 1 and 2. Just as the focus of our definition of entrepreneurship is opportunity recognition for the purpose of wealth creation, so too is the focus of franchising. Franchising offers a thoughtful system for reshaping and executing a delivery system designed to extract maximum value from the opportunity. Just as opportunity, thought, and action are essential elements of an entrepreneurial venture, so too are they important components of a franchise opportunity. Franchising also fulfills our definition of entrepreneurship because each partner understands the expectation for wealth of the other and they work together toward that goal; their "bond" is sealed as partners in the franchise entrepreneurial alliance.

As eloquently described by Jim Hindman in the chapter's introduction, franchising is, at its core, an entrepreneurial alliance between two organizations, the franchisor and the franchisee. The successful franchise relationship defines and exploits an opportunity as a team. The franchisor is the concept innovator who grows by seeking partners or franchisees to operate the concept in local markets. A franchisor can be born when at least one company store exists and the opportunity has been *beta* tested. Once the concept is proven, the franchisor and the franchisee enter into an agreement to grow the concept based on a belief that there are mutual advantages to the alliance. The nature of these advantages is defined by the ability of the partners to execute a particular aspect of the opportunity for which each is respectively better suited than the other. The heart of franchising is entrepreneurship, the pursuit of and intent to gain wealth by exploiting the given opportunity. The unique aspect of franchising is that it brings together two parties that both have individual intentions of wealth creation through opportunity exploitation, but who choose to achieve their goals by working together. Because franchising aligns the different skill sets and capabilities of the franchisor and franchisee as a partnership, the whole of a franchise opportunity is greater than the sum of its parts.

At its most fundamental level, franchising is a large-scale growth opportunity based on a partnership rather than on individual effort. Once a business is operating successfully, then according to the Timmons Model, it is appropriate to think about franchising as a growth tool. The sum of the activities between the partners is manifest in a trademark or brand. The mission of the entrepreneurial alliance is to maintain and build the brand. The brand signals a price–value relationship in the minds of customers. Revenue is driven higher because the marketplace responds to the brand with more purchases or purchases at a higher price than the competition.

Job Creation versus Wealth Creation

As a franchise entrepreneur, we can control the growth of our franchise opportunity. For those whose life goal is to own a pizza restaurant and earn a comfortable income, the opportunity is there. Franchising allows us to do this, but it also allows us to build 30 pizza restaurants and to participate fully in the wealth-creation process. One strength of franchising is that it provides a wide breadth of options for individuals to customize opportunities to meet their financial goals and business visions, however conservative or grandiose.

The ability to create wealth in any venture starts with the initial opportunity assessment. For example, a franchise company may decide to limit its geographic territories in terms of the number of stores. Therefore, the expansion market is limited from the start for potential franchisees. Even if franchisees work hard and follow all the proven systems, they may be buying a job versus creating wealth.

But some companies are designed to reward successful franchisees with the opportunity to buy more stores in a particular market or region. Franchisees who achieve prosperity with single units are rewarded with additional stores. The entrepreneurial process is encouraged, and wealth is created.

Much of the goal of *New Venture Creation* is to increase the odds for success in a new venture and increase its scope. Franchising can be an excellent vehicle for growth.

Franchising: A History of Entrepreneurship

The franchise entrepreneurial spirit in the United States has never been more alive than today. More than 4,500 franchise businesses with 600,000 outlets populate the marketplace; these businesses make up 36 percent of all retail sales nationwide. Internationally, franchising generates as much as 10 percent of retailing in the United Kingdom, France, and Australia. The International Franchise Association expects that franchise businesses will continue to thrive and prosper, accounting for 40 percent of U.S. retail sales within five years.[1] The belief that franchising can be an exciting entrepreneurial venture is supported by the continued success of established franchise systems, the proliferation of new franchises, and the profitability reported by franchisees and franchisors.[2] These statistics hint at the scope and richness that franchising has achieved in a relatively short period. The process of wealth creation through franchising continues to evolve as we witness an increase not only in the number of multiple outlet franchisees,[3] but also in the number of franchisees that operate multiple outlets in different franchise systems.

Evidence of the success of franchising as an entrepreneurial opportunity-exploiting and wealth-creating vehicle comes from one of the largest franchisors in the world—the U.K. conglomerate Allied Domecq, which owns Dunkin' Donuts, Baskin-Robbins, and

[1] *Franchising Guide to Policy Making,* IFA, 2003.

[2] Stephen Spinelli, Jr., Benoit Leleux, Sue Birley, "An Analysis of Shareholder Return in Public Franchisors," Society of Franchising presentation, 2001.

[3] Scott Shane, "Hybrid Organizational Arrangements and Their Implications for Firm Growth and Survival: A Study of New Franchisors," *Academy of Management Journal* 39 (1996), pp. 216–34.

EXHIBIT 11.1

Franchise Facts about Some of the Largest U.S. Franchisors*

Franchise system age	21 years
Number of outlets per franchisor	2,652
Annual revenue	$871 million
Franchise fee	$28,559
Royalty rate	5.58%
Advertising rate	2.89%
License agreement term	14 years

*The average for 91 firms is used for all categories.

Togo's restaurants. Bob Rosenberg,[4] son of Dunkin' Donuts founder Bill Rosenberg, grew the Dunkin' system from a few hundred to more than 3,000 outlets before being acquired by Allied Domecq. Bob continued to operate Allied Domecq's North American retail operation for 10 years, doubling its size, until he retired in 1998. Bob believes, "Allied Domecq's franchise operation can double again in the U.S. and the potential in Europe and Asia are exponential." Clearly, franchising can be a global business model that is adaptable to most locales.

Another company that signaled the prevalence of franchising in contemporary business is Jiffy Lube International. Although most franchisors tend to think in terms of national scale, the team that grew Jiffy Lube purchased the then-small "mom-and-pop" company based in Ogden, Utah, and immediately added *International,* sensing that globalization of their business model and service offering could be successful outside the United States. When people hear the names Ray Kroc and Anita Roddick, most people certainly identify the founders of McDonald's and the Body Shop as entrepreneurs and their trademarks and brands as some of the most successful in the world. Exhibit 11.1 reveals several aspects of contemporary franchises.

Anyone considering and exploring entrepreneurial opportunities should give serious consideration to the franchising option. As franchisor or franchisee, this option can be a viable way to share risk and reward, create and grow an opportunity, and raise human and financial capital.

Franchising: Assembling the Opportunity

As we saw in earlier chapters, the Timmons Model identifies the three subsets of opportunity as market demand, market size and structure, and margin analysis. The franchise organization must understand the nature of demand both as it resides in the individual consumer and in the society. At the most fundamental level, the primary target audience (PTA) is the defining quality of the opportunity recognition process. Without a customer, there is no opportunity; without an opportunity, there is no venture; and without a sustainable opportunity, there can be no franchise.

As we discussed earlier in the chapter, our goal is to look at franchising as it presents opportunities for both franchisees and franchisors. We will now investigate several aspects of franchise opportunity recognition: PTA identification; service concept; service delivery system (SDS) design; training and operational support; field support, marketing, advertising, and promotion; and product purchase provision. Prospective franchisees should understand the nature and quality of each of these franchise components. Existing franchisors might study their offerings in light of this information. Those considering growth through franchising must pay attention to the detail of their system offering.

Primary Target Audience

Defining the target customer is essential because it dictates many diverse functions of the business. Most important, it measures the first level of demand. Once the primary target audience is defined, secondary targets may be identified. The degree of market penetration in the secondary target is less than that of the primary target. Although measuring market demand is not an exact science, a franchisor must continually collect data about its customers. Even after buying a franchise, the franchisee compares local market demographics with national profiles to decide the potential of the local market in terms of the number of outlets that can be developed. Revenue projections are made from the definition of the target audiences and the degree of market penetration that can be expected based on historical information. Three major areas of data collection can be integral to refining the PTA.

Demographic Profiles A demographic profile is a compilation of personal characteristics that enables the company to define the "average" customer. Most franchisors perform market research as a central function, developing customer profiles and disseminating the information to franchisees. That research may include current user and nonuser profiles. Typically, a

[4] Bob Rosenberg is now an adjunct professor at Babson College and teaches in the entrepreneurship division. The authors have consulted with Professor Rosenberg on a number of issues in entrepreneurship, including franchising.

demographic analysis includes age, gender, income, home address (driving or walking miles from the store), working address (driving or walking miles from the store), marital status, family status (number and ages of children), occupation, race and ethnicity, religion, and nationality. Demographics must be put into context by looking at concept-specific data such as mean number of automobiles for a Midas franchise or percentage of disposable income spent on clothes for a Gap franchise.

Psychographic Profiles Psychographic profiles segment potential customers based on social class, lifestyle, and personality traits. Economic class in America is generally divided into seven categories:

1. Upper uppers 1 percent
2. Lower uppers 2 percent
3. Upper middles 12 percent
4. Middle class 32 percent
5. Working class 38 percent
6. Upper lowers 9 percent
7. Lower lowers 7 percent

Lifestyle addresses such issues as health consciousness, fashion orientation, or being a "car freak." Personality variables such as self-confident, conservative, and independent are used to segment markets.

Behavioral variables segment potential customers by their knowledge, attitude, and use of products to project usage of the product or service. By articulating a detailed understanding of the target market and why that consumer will buy our product or service, you gain great knowledge of the competitive landscape. Why will a consumer spend their money with us instead of where they currently find value?

Geographic Profiles The scope of a franchise concept can be local, regional, national, or international. The U.S. national market is typically divided into nine regions: Pacific, Mountain, West North Central, West South Central, East North Central, East South Central, South Atlantic, Middle Atlantic, New England. Regions are divided by population density and described as urban, suburban, or rural from under 5,000 to 4 million or more.

The "smart" franchise uses the ever-growing system of franchisees and company outlets to continually gather data about customers. This helps dynamically shape the vision and therefore the opportunity. The analysis of system data must include a link to the vision of the concept and to what seems possible for the vision. For example, if we launched an earring company 10 years ago, we could have defined the target market as women ages 21 to 40, and the size of the market as the number of women in this age group in the United States. But perhaps looking beyond the existing data and anticipating the larger market that now exists can shape our vision. The target market for earrings could be defined as women and men ages 12 to 32, with an average of three earrings per individual, not two. The identification of the target market requires that we combine demographic data with our own unique vision for the venture.

The focus on PTA development as the core to franchise opportunity recognition is essential to determine the consumer appeal of a franchise and to establish validity of the opportunity. We will consider a set of criteria that will help define due diligence in assessing how a franchise has exploited the opportunity. This discussion holds value for an overall understanding of franchising for existing franchisors and potential franchisors and franchisees alike.

Theory into Practice: Market Demand
Radio Shack's Moving Target Market

Target markets are dynamic, often metamorphosing very quickly. Radio Shack had to change its business to reflect the shift in its target market. In the 1970s and 1980s, Radio Shack grew by addressing the needs of technophiles—young men with penchants for shortwave radios, stereo systems, walkie-talkies, and the like. The national retail chain supplied this audience with the latest gadgets and did very well.

Then, starting in the early 1990s, technology became more sophisticated. Personal electronic equipment began to include cell phones, handheld computers, and electronic organizers. The market for these products was expanding from a smaller group of technophiles to a larger group of middle-age males who loved gadgets and who had more disposable income. Yet Radio Shack remained Radio Shack. Its audience dwindled while the personal electronics market boomed.

In the early 1990s, Radio Shack refocused its business to target this new demographic. Its advertising addressed the needs of the 44-year-old upper-middle-class male versus the 29-year-old technophile. That 29-year-old who used to shop at Radio Shack was now 44! He was not going to make a radio, but he would buy a cell phone. Radio Shack made dramatic changes in its marketing and inventory. As a result, it has made dramatic changes in its profitability.

Evaluating a Franchise: Initial Due Diligence

Before looking at the detail of a franchise offering, the prospective franchisee must mine an offering from the 4,500 franchises in the United States. Although the next section is most appropriate for prospective franchisees, the savvy franchisor will use this information to better craft his franchise offering for potential franchisees.

Exhibit 11.2 provides a franchise screening template designed to make a preliminary assessment of the key variables that constitute a franchise. The exercise is crafted to help map the risk profile of the franchise and highlight areas that will most

EXHIBIT 11.2

Franchise Risk Profile Template

Criteria	Low Risk/Avg. Market Return 15–20%	Acceptable Risk/ Incremental 30% Return	High Risk/Marginal 40–50% Return	Extreme Risk/Large Return 60–100%
Multiple Market Presence	National	Regional	State	Local
Outlet Pro Forma Disclosed or Discerned	Yes, 90%+ apparently profitable	Yes, 80%+ apparently profitable	Yes, 70%+ apparently profitable	No, less than 70% profitable
Market Share	No. 1 and dominant	No. 1 or 2 with a strong competitor	Lower than No. 2	Lower than No. 3 with a dominant player
National Marketing Program	Historically successful creative process, national media buys in place	Creative plus regional media buys	Creative plus local media buys	Local media buys only
National Purchasing Program	More than 3%+ gross margin advantage in national purchasing contract	1–3% gross margin advantage versus independent operators	Regional gross margin advantages only	No discernible gross margin advantages
Margin Characteristics	50%+ gross margin 18%+ net outlet margin	40–50% gross margin 12–17% net outlet margin	30–40% gross margin less than 12% net outlet margin	Declining gross margin detected, erratic net outlet margin
Business Format	Sophisticated training, documented operations manual, identifiable feedback mechanism with franchisees	Initial training and dynamically documented operations manual, some field support	Training and operations but weak field support	Questionable training and field support and static operations
Term of the License Agreement	20 years with automatic renewal	15 years with renewal	Less than 15 years or no renewal	Less than 10 years
Site Development	Quantifiable criteria clearly documented and tied to market specifics	Markets prioritized with general site development criteria	General market development criteria outlined	Business format not tied to identifiable market segment(s)
Capital Required per Unit	$15,000–$25,000 working capital	Working capital Plus $50,000–$100,000 machinery and equipment	Working capital plus machinery and equipment plus $500,000–$1,000,000 real estate	Erratic, highly variable, or ill-defined
Franchise Fee and Royalties	PDV* of the fees are less than the demonstrated economic advantages (reduced costs or increased revenue) of the franchise versus stand-alone		PDV of the fees are only projected to be less than the expected economic advantages (reduced costs or increased revenue) of the franchise versus stand-alone	PDV of the fees are not discernibly less than the expected value of the franchise

*PDV is an abbreviation for present discounted value. If franchising is a risk-reduction strategy, then the discount of future revenue should be less. Concurrently, the economies of scale in marketing should increase the amount of revenue a franchise can generate versus a "stand-alone" operation.

likely need further due diligence. If the following criteria are important to the potential franchisee, then they also provide a map of the growth and market positioning objectives a stable franchisor should be pursuing.

This exercise is not designed to culminate in a "go or no go" decision. Rather, prospective franchisees should use it to help evaluate if the franchise meets their personal risk/return profile. Franchisors should also review the exercise to examine the risk signals they may be sending to prospective franchisees. It is especially important to understand this risk profile in the context of the alternative investments a prospective franchisee can make.

Franchisor as the High Potential Venture

As Ray Kroc and Anita Roddick demonstrate, becoming a franchisor can be a high potential endeavor. Growth and scale are the essence of the franchise mentality. Throughout this chapter we have taken the approach of franchising as entrepreneurship for both the franchisee and franchisor. In this section, we focus principally on franchisors and their rewards. In a study of *publicly traded franchisors*, the size and scope of the firms that achieved public capital is impressive. The capital marketplace has rewarded many franchisors, which have measured well against the criteria for a high potential venture franchise. They, in turn, have performed well vis-à-vis return to shareholders. Exhibit 11.3 illustrates the performance of public franchisors compared with the Standard and Poor's 500. This analysis of total return to shareholder (dividends and stock price appreciation) demonstrates that while the S&P index was hit hard by the downturn in the economy after 2001, the public franchisor index was not. While the stock slide following the period of irrational exuberance in the late 1990s was precipitated by dot-com valuations, the correction tended to depress share prices across the board—even blue chip stocks. The relative buoyancy

EXHIBIT 11.3

Franchisor Market Performance, 1992–2004 (total return to shareholders)

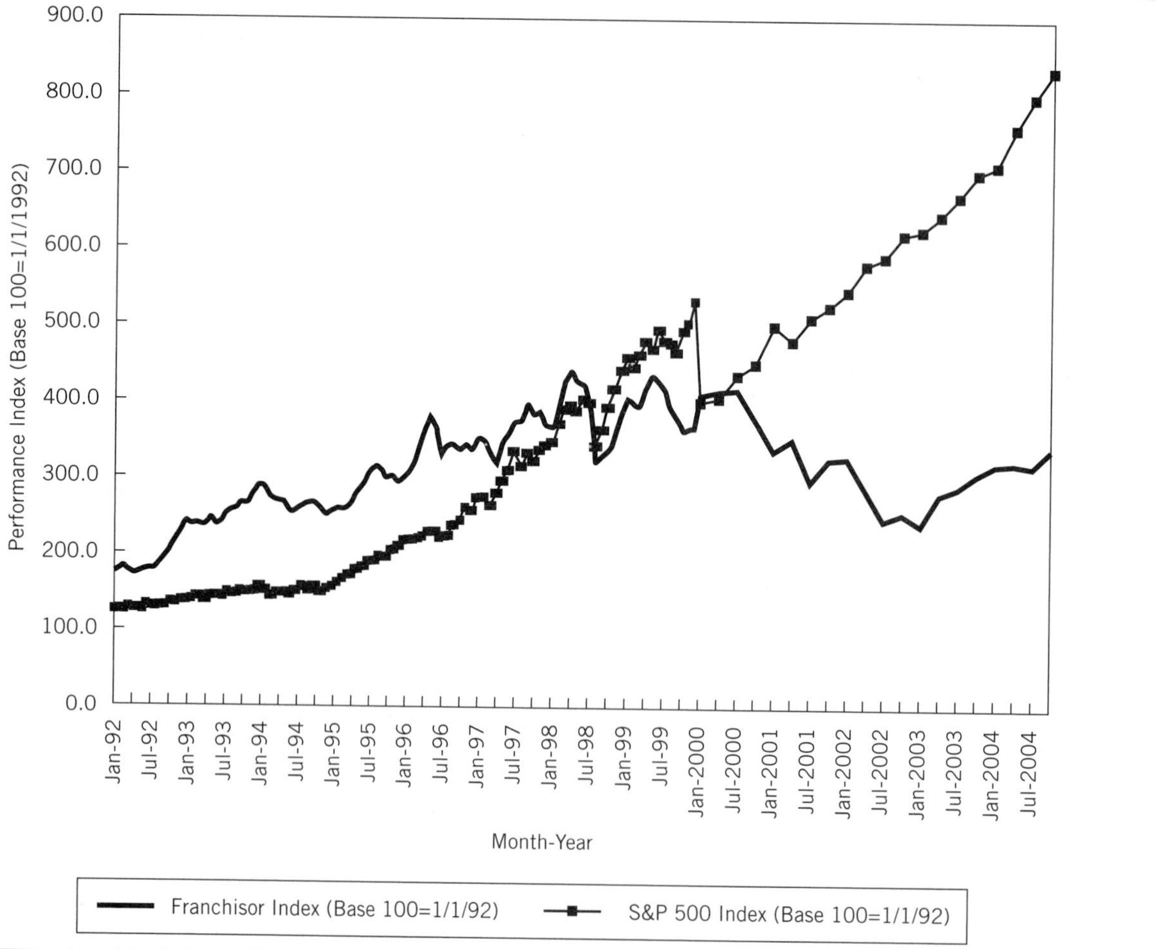

of the franchisor index can be attributed to the index being heavily weighted in the food category. During a recession, when household budgets are tight, consumers seek out dining establishments that offer the best value, the primary driver of many food-based franchise organizations.

Even more interesting are those exceptional performers among the high achieving franchisors. Take, for example, the quintessential franchise, McDonald's Corporation. McDonald's is the world's largest food service organization with more than 31,000 restaurants in 119 countries as of June 2005. Its global infrastructure includes a network of suppliers and resources that allows it to achieve economies of scale and offer great value to customers. In 2004, systemwide sales reached $30 billion, operating income was $3.5 billion, and earnings per share increased 10 percent on a constant currency basis. A local management team runs each market.

Allied Domecq's unique complementary day-part strategy combines two or three brand concepts in a single operation, attempting to optimize return-on-investment through more efficient use of resources. Launched in 1950, Dunkin' Donuts, now the world's largest coffee and donut shop chain, has grown to more than 5,000 locations throughout the United States and 37 countries. Founded in 1971, Togo's is California's fastest growing chain of sandwich eateries and is now spreading across the country. Baskin-Robbins' 31 flavors of sweet creamy treats are offered in more than 4,700 locations from California to Moscow.

Key Components of a Franchise Offering

In this section, we describe the major aspects of delivering a franchise system. It is excellence in both concept and delivery that has created wealth for the franchisors in publicly trade companies. We have analyzed the features that propel the high performance franchisor into exceptional return. The excellent franchisor supports the franchisee, and the symbiotic nature of the relationship leverages return for both partners. After prospective franchisees narrows their search for a franchise (by using the screening guide among other activities), they should begin a detailed analysis of the exact nature of a franchise. Franchisors should note the following in terms of how they might construct their offerings, knowing that prospective franchisees will conduct a detailed due diligence around these franchise components.

Service Delivery System

The road map for marshaling resources for the franchise comes from establishing the service delivery system (SDS). The opportunity dictates that we perform certain tasks to meet consumer demand. The assets put into place to meet these demands are largely the resources needed to launch the concept. In the franchise entrepreneurial alliance, the franchisor develops a method for delivering the product or service that fills customer demand. In its most basic essence, the service delivery system is the way in which resources are arrayed so that demand can be extracted from the marketplace. This service delivery system has to be well defined, documented, and tested by the company or prototype operation. The end result of the organization, execution, and transfer of the service delivery system is the firm's competitive advantage.

The Timmons Model first looks at opportunity assessment, which demands a clear understanding of the target market and customer. Next it looks at resource marshaling or, in franchising, the establishment of the service delivery system. The SDS is the fundamental means by which customers will be served, and the fashion, often proprietary in design, in which the service delivery resources are arrayed can create competitive advantage in the marketplace. In franchising, this aspect is sometimes called the *business format.* A successful SDS's form and function will reflect the specific needs of the target customer. Highly successful and visible examples of business format innovations are the drive-through in fast-food restaurants and the bi-level facilities in quick-oil-change facilities. Every franchise has a well-defined SDS, however overt or transparent it may seem to an outside observer.

Because the SDS is truly the essence of the successful franchise, the detail given to it should not be underestimated. For the concept innovator, the common phrase, "The devil is in the details," never takes on more meaning than when designing the SDS for the franchise. Steve Spinelli can corroborate this fact from experiences while expanding the Jiffy Lube franchise. One particular component of Jiffy Lube's expansion plans paints a vivid picture as to the intricacy of the development of the SDS and reveals what a great benefit this design paid over time.

Jiffy Lube franchises must meet specific location criteria: high volume of car traffic, side of the street located for inbound or outbound traffic, high profile retail area, and the far corner of any given street or block, among other requirements. Through trial and error, Jiffy Lube has determined the optimal location of the structure on any given property. Once these aspects are met, the building specifications follow. Structural specifications regarding the angle of the building and the width, depth, and angle of the entrance allow the optimal number of cars to stack in line waiting for the car in front to complete the service. On several occasions, facilities that met location criteria were failing to perform as expected. Analysis of the situation determined the bend in the driveway was too sharp, preventing customers from driving their cars completely into the line and giving the inaccurate impression that the lot was full. Driveways were adjusted to accommodate an increased number of cars waiting for service.

This same level of refinement and detail orientation is encouraged for concept innovators while looking at their conceptual and actual SDS. Unless examined under a microscope, essential components of the SDS will be missed, deteriorating the value of the franchise. Jiffy Lube's experience also reinforces the benefits of a beta site, providing a real-world laboratory that can be adjusted and modified until the outlet reaches optimal performance.

Another part of the complete Jiffy Lube SDS was the design of the maintenance bay. Considering the limitations inherent in the use of hydraulic lifts, Jiffy Lube faced the dilemma of providing 30 minutes of labor in only 10 minutes. To deliver this 10-minute service, three technicians would need to work on a car at once without the use of a lift. This quandary led to the design of having cars drive into the bay and stop above an opening in the floor. This allowed one technician to service the car from below, another to service the car underneath the hood, and a third to service the car's interior. Without developing such a disruptive system, Jiffy Lube would not have been able to succeed as it did.

The soundness of the decision to use the drive-through/bi-level system was confirmed when competitors, gas stations and car dealers, failed to deliver on offering a "quick lube" using hydraulic lifts and traditional bays. The sum of Jiffy Lube's intricately designed parts created the value of the SDS. Such is the level of detail needed for an SDS to deliver both value to the customer and cost efficiencies to the operator. In much the same way, the following example highlights the specific design components of the SDS that create value.

Theory to Practice: The Service Delivery System (SDS)
How Wendy's Used Its Business Format to Enter a "Saturated" Market

In 1972, Dave Thomas entered what many experts called a crowded hamburger fast-food market. His concept was to offer a "Cadillac hamburger" that was hot, fresh, and delivered more quickly than the competitions'. To execute Thomas's mission, Wendy's introduced the first drive-through in a national fast-food chain. Because Wendy's menu offered double and triple patties in addition to the traditional single-patty hamburger, its kitchens were designed to mass-produce hamburgers and deliver them to the front counter or drive-through window with minimal effort. To ensure a cooked just-in-time hamburger, each Wendy's restaurant included a large front window that enabled grill cooks (who were placed in clear view of the customer, not in a rear kitchen) to observe the flow of customers onto the premises.

Notwithstanding the huge market share owned by McDonald's and Burger King, Wendy's was able to successfully enter the fray because of the manner in which it arranged its resources to create a competitive advantage. In Wendy's, the sum of the intricacies—the drive-through window, the position of the cooks and kitchen, and the double and triple patties—has allowed the chain to compete and prosper in the fast-food hamburger market.

Dave Thomas's vision and personal impact on the fast-food industry were significant. When he passed away in January 2002, Wendy's received thousands of e-mails from customers expressing condolences.

Training and Operational Support

Formal franchisor training programs transfer knowledge of the SDS to the franchisees, both managers and line workers. Continuous knowledge gathering and transfer is important both before launch and on an ongoing basis. The license agreement must define the specific form in which this franchisor responsibility will be performed. It should extend significantly beyond a manual and the classroom. Training will vary with the specifics of the franchise, but it should include organized and monitored on-the-job experience in the existing system for the new franchisee and as many of the new staff members as the franchisor will allow. Established and stable franchise systems such as Jiffy Lube and Dunkin' Donuts require such operational experience in the existing system for as long as a year before the purchase of the franchise; however, this level of dedication to the franchisee's success is not the norm. Once the franchise is operational, the franchisee may be expected to do much or all of the on-site training of new hires. But as we will discuss in the next section, field support from the franchisor is often a signal of franchise stability and a reflection of the strength of the franchise partnership. Manuals, testing, training aids such as videos, and certification processes are often provided by the franchisor as part of this ongoing field support.

As discussed previously, the trade name and trademark are the most valuable assets in a franchise system. A franchisee's success rests soundly on the sales of products that are based on the brand equity and strength of the franchisor. As important as a sound service delivery system design is to the concept's foundation for success, the prospective training regimen is equally important. Without appropriately instructed individuals, an exceptional product will never reach the consumer's hands. As such, a poor training program will inevitably dilute the standardized, consistent delivery of the product and eventual erode the brand's value.

Field Support

Akin to the training program mentioned above is ongoing field support. This will take at least two forms, one in which a franchisor's representative will visit the franchisee's location in person, and the other in which the franchisor will retain resident experts in each of the essential managerial disciplines for consultation at the corporate headquarters. Ideally the license agreement will provide for scheduled visits by the franchisor's agents to the franchisee's outlet with prescribed objectives, such as performance review, field training, facilities inspection, local marketing review, and operations audit. Unfortunately, some franchisors use their field role as a diplomatic or pejorative exercise rather than for training and support. The greater the substance of the field function, the easier it is for the franchisee to justify the royalty cost. Additionally, in the litigious environment in which we presently live, a well-documented field support program will mute franchisee claims of a lack of franchisor support.

One means of understanding the franchisor's field support motive is to investigate the manner in which the field support personnel are compensated. If field staff are paid commensurate with franchisee performance and ultimate profitability, then politics will play a diminished role. Key warning signs in this regard are when bonuses are paid for growth in the number of stores versus individual store growth, or for product usage (supplied by franchisor) by franchisee. Clearly, as with the training program prescribed by the franchisor and agreed to by the franchisee, a quality field support program is another integral factor to success, and a poor support program will eventually become evident.

Marketing, Advertising, and Promotion

Marketing activities are certainly one of the most sensitive areas in the ongoing franchise relationship because they imprint the trade name and trademark in the mind of the consumer to gain awareness—the most important commodity of the franchise. If the delivery of the product validates the marketing message, then the value of the franchise is enhanced, but if it is not congruent, then there can be a detrimental effect at both the local and national level. As outlet growth continues, marketing budgets increase and spread across the growing organization, thereby optimizing the marketing program.

Generally, marketing programs are funded and implemented at three different levels: national, regional, and local. A national advertising budget is typically controlled by the franchisor and each franchisee contributes a percentage of top-line sales to the fund. The franchisor then produces materials (television, radio, and newspaper advertisements; direct-mail pieces; and point-of-sale materials) for use by the franchisees and, depending on the size of the fund, also buys media time or space on behalf of the franchisees. Because it is impossible to allocate these services equally between franchisees of different sizes across different markets, the license agreement will specify the use of "best efforts" to approximate equal treatment between franchisees. Although "best efforts" will invariably leave some franchisees with more advertising exposure and some with less, over time this situation should balance itself. This is one area of marketing that requires careful monitoring by both parties.

Regional marketing, advertising, and promotion is structured on the basis of an area of dominant influence (ADI). All the stores in a given ADI (e.g., Greater Hartford, Connecticut) would contribute a percentage of their top-lines sales to the ADI advertising cooperative.[5] The cooperative's primary function is usually to buy media using franchisor-supplied or -approved advertising and to coordinate regional site promotions. If the franchise has a regional advertising cooperative requirement in the license agreement, it should also have standardized ADI cooperative bylaws. These bylaws will outline such areas as voting rights and expenditure parameters. Often a single-store franchisee can be disadvantaged in a poorly organized cooperative, whereas a major contributor to the cooperative may find his voting rights disproportionately low in any given cooperative.

The third and final scenario for marketing is typically dubbed local advertising or local store marketing.

[5] Advertising cooperatives in franchising are common. A cooperative is a contractual agreement whereby franchisees in a geographic area are bound to contribute a percentage of their revenue to a fund that executes a marketing plan, usually including media purchases. The cooperative is typically governed by the participating franchisees and sometimes includes representation from the franchisor and advertising agency.

At this level, the franchisee is contractually required to make direct expenditures on advertising. There is often a wide spectrum of permissible advertising expenditures, depending on the franchisor guidelines in the license agreement; unfortunately, the license agreement will probably not be specific. Franchisors will try to maintain discretion on this issue for maximum flexibility in the marketplace, while franchisees will vie for control of this area. Company-owned store should have advertising requirements equal to those for the franchised units to avoid a franchisor having a free ride; in this regard, historical behavior is the best gauge of reasonableness.

The franchisor should monitor and enforce marketing expenditures. For example, the customer of a franchisee leaving one ADI and entering another will have been affected by the advertising of adjacent regions. Additionally, advertising expenditures not made are marketing impressions lost to the system. When this happens, the marketing leverage inherent in franchising is not optimized.

Supply

In most franchise systems, one major benefit is bulk purchasing and inventory control. In the license agreement, there are several ways to account for this economy of scale advantage. Because of changing markets, competitors and U.S. antitrust law make it impossible for the franchisor to be bound to best-price requirements. The franchise should employ a standard of best efforts and good faith to acquire both national and regional supply contracts.

Depending on the nature of the product or service, regional deals might make more sense than national ones. Regional contact may provide greater advantages to the franchisee because of shipping weight and cost or service requirements. The savvy franchisor will recognize this and implement a flexible purchase plan. When local advantages exist and the franchisor does not act appropriately, the franchisees will fill the void. The monthly area of dominant influence (ADI) meeting then becomes an expanded forum for franchisees to voice their appreciations and concerns. The results of such ad hoc organizations can be reduced control of quality and expansion of franchisee association outside the confines of the license agreement. Advanced activity of this nature can often fractionalize a franchise system and even render the franchisor obsolete. In some cases, the franchisor and franchisee-operated buying cooperatives peaceably coexist, acting as competitors and lowering the costs to the operator. However, the dual buying co-ops usually reduce economies of scale and dilute system resources, not to mention provide fertile ground for conflict within the franchise alliance.

For purposes of quality control, the franchisor will reserve the right to publish a product specifications list. The list will clearly establish the quality standards of raw materials or goods used in the operation. From those specifications, a subsequent list of approved suppliers is generated. This list can evolve into a franchise "tying agreement," which occurs when the business format franchise license agreement binds the franchisee to the purchase of a specifically branded product. This varies from the product specification list because brand, not product content, is the qualifying specification. The important question here is: does the tying arrangement of franchise and product create an enhancement for the franchisee in the marketplace? If so, then are arm's-length controls in place to ensure that pricing, netted from the enhanced value, will yield positive results? Unfortunately, this is impossible to precisely quantify. However, if the tying agreement is specified in the license agreement, then the prospective franchise owner is advised to make a judgment before purchasing the franchise. With this sort of decision at hand, the franchisor should prove the value of the tying agreement or abandon it.

Another subtle form of tying agreements occurs when the license agreement calls for an approved suppliers list that ultimately includes only one supplier. If adding suppliers to the list is nearly impossible, there is a de facto tying arrangement. Additionally, another tying arrangement can occur when the product specification is written so that only one brand can qualify. A franchisor should disclose any remuneration gained by the franchisor or its officers, directly or indirectly, from product purchase in the franchise system. In this case, the franchisor's market value enhancement test is again proof of a credible arrangement.

Franchise Relationship Model

Now that we have established the nature and components of the franchise relationship, we can connect these principles to the franchise relationship model (FRM), which we have developed over the past eight years (see Exhibit 11.4). The FRM takes the entrepreneurial framework provided by the Timmons Model and connects the specific processes that are unique to franchising. We have argued that franchising is a powerful entrepreneurial alliance because it fits the Timmons Model and because it creates wealth. The FRM illustrates both how a concept innovator (i.e., potential franchisor) can most efficiently construct a franchising company and how a concept implementer (i.e., potential franchisee) can determine which company to join. The FRM further

EXHIBIT 11.4

Franchise Relationship Model

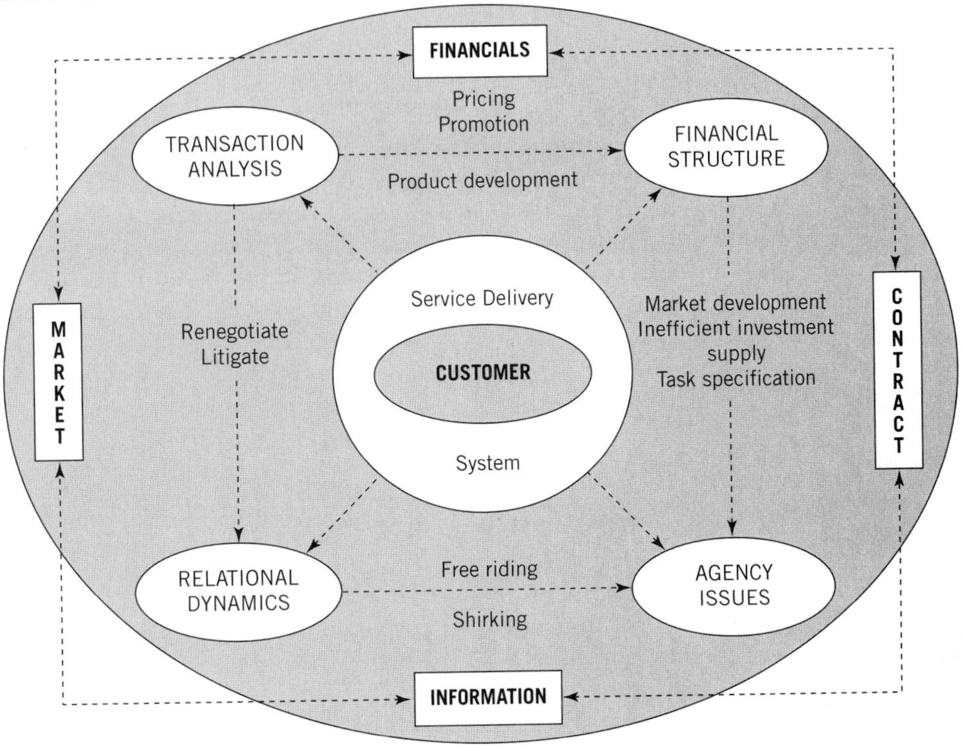

helps to distinguish between those tasks best executed under a corporate umbrella and those best done by the individual franchisee. Just as franchising is itself a risk ameliorating tool for the entrepreneur; the franchise relationship model is also a tool that both franchisors and franchisees can use to judge the efficiency or success potential of a franchise opportunity. By overlaying the FRM template onto any given franchise, we can forecast to a great extent where the bottlenecks will impede success or where improvements can be made that will offer a competitive advantage.

The FRM is a puzzle, a series of franchise principles, each of which fit into the others to form a powerful interlocking business concept that solidifies itself as the linkages are implemented more efficiently. While the process starts in the center with the customer, moves to the service delivery system and follows from there, the outer perimeter of means and mechanisms drives the competitive advantage of a franchise system. The major areas of concern other than the customer and the SDS are transaction analysis, financial structure, agency issues, and relational dynamics.

Transaction analysis considers which transactions are better served at a national level by the franchisor and which at the local level by the franchisee.[6] Typically the franchisor functions are centered on economies of scale. Franchisee functions include those that require on-site entrepreneurial capacity such as hiring and local promotion. The financial structure flows from pro forma analysis of customer demand and the cost associated with development and execution of the service delivery system. Agency issues concern delegating responsibility to a partner.[7] No franchisor can know absolutely that the franchisee is "doing the right thing" at the store level. Franchisees cannot possibly know that the franchisor is always acting in their best interest. Relational dynamics is the area that allows the partnership between franchisor and franchisee to continually change and develop as the business continues to expand.[8] Any partnership that strictly adheres to a contract will end in litigation.

[6] O. E. Williamson, "Comparative Economic Organizations: The Analysis of Discrete Structural Alternatives," *Administrative Science Quarterly* (June1991), pp. 269–288.

[7] F. Lafontaine, "Agency Theory and Franchising; Some Empirical Results," *RAND Journal of Economics* 23 (1992), pp. 263–68.

[8] I. R. Mcneil, "Economic Analysis of Contractual Relations: Its Shortfalls and Need for a 'Rich Classification Apparatus,' " *Northwestern University Law Review*, February 1980, pp. 1018–63.

The franchise relationship model (Exhibit 11.4) is dynamic—as events affect one aspect of the model, all other aspects must be reviewed in an iterative process. For example, if renegotiation of the license agreement were to result in a reduced royalty, the financial model would be altered. A change in royalty could dictate a change in the services that the franchisor provides. Any change creates a cascading effect throughout the system—a reconstruction of the puzzle.

The franchise relationship model begins with opportunity recognition and shaping (customer) and then articulates the competitive advantages and costs of the service delivery system that will extract the demand (SDS) and create a return on investment. The competitive sustainability of the franchise is embedded in the delineation of responsibilities between franchisor and franchisee and in the conscious design of the service delivery system. The franchisor's tasks are centrally executed and focus on economies of scale; the franchisee concentrates on those responsibilities that require local on-site entrepreneurial intensity (transaction analysis). The emergent financial structure is the manifestation of the interaction between the primary target customer and the service delivery system. By sharing both the burden of the service delivery system and the potential for return on investment, the franchise entrepreneurial alliance is formed.

Central to the long-term stability of the franchise system is the proper selection of partners and monitoring of key partner responsibilities (agency issues). However, even in the most stable relationship, a dynamic business environment dictates adjustments in the relationship to ensure continued competitive advantage. Understanding the partner's tolerance zone in performance and reacting to market changes can be standardized by formal review programs and kept unstructured by informal negotiations (relational dynamics). Failure to recognize the need for dynamic management of the relationship can often result in litigation, as noted.

The franchise relationship model illustrates how a concept innovator can construct a franchising company and the pathway for implementing it in the most entrepreneurial way. The model also eliminates those ideas that are best developed using another growth strategy, such as distributorships, licensing, or corporate-owned outlets.

We now understand that franchising is entrepreneurial and we understand the unique components of franchising that enable this entrepreneurial alliance.

Chapter Summary

Franchising is an inherently entrepreneurial endeavor. In this chapter we argue that opportunity, scale, and growth are at the heart of the franchise experience. The success of franchising is demonstrated by the fact that it accounts for more than one-third of all U.S. retailing. Equally important is the demonstrated performance of the top franchise companies, outperforming the Standard & Poor's 500. Franchising shares profits, risk, and strategy between the franchisor and the franchisee. A unique aspect of franchising as entrepreneurship is the wide spectrum of opportunity that exists and the matching of scale to appetite for a broad spectrum of entrepreneurs. Two tools have been provided in this chapter to help the entrepreneur. For those interested in creating a franchise, the franchise relationship model articulates the dynamic construction of the franchisor–franchisee alliance. For the prospective franchisee, the franchise risk profile helps the budding entrepreneur assess the risk–return scenario for any given franchise opportunity.

Study Questions

1. Can you describe the difference between the franchisor and the franchisee? How are these differences strategically aligned to create a competitive advantage?
2. We describe franchising as a "pathway to entrepreneurship" providing a spectrum of entrepreneurial opportunities. What does this mean to you?
3. What are the most important determinants of whether franchising is an appropriate method of rapidly growing a concept?
4. What are the five components of the franchise relationship model? Can you describe the interactive nature of these components?
5. Why do you think the public franchisors consistently outperform the S&P 500?
6. What would be the most attractive aspects of franchising to you? What is the least attractive part of franchising?

Internet Resources for Chapter 11

http://www.bison1.com *Our favorite site for franchising information*

http://www.franchise-chat.com *Franchise news stories and resource articles from around the world, as well as a chat forum for prospective/existing franchisees and franchisors*

http://www.businessfranchisedirectory.com *Lengthy list of franchise offerings*

http://www.franchise.org *The International Franchise Association (IFA)*

http://www.british-franchise.org *The British Franchise Association: Europe's most sophisticated franchise trade organization*

http://www.franchiseindex.com *Lists of franchises with capital requirements*

http://www.franchisehelp.com *Help for those looking into a franchise: how it works, and when to invest*

http://www.aafd.org *The American Association of Franchisees and Dealers*

Internet Impact: The Network Enhanced

The essence of franchising is the creation of value in a trademark. Efficiently sharing information is a key to leveraging the experiences of each franchisee for the betterment of all franchisees. Because franchising is governed (primarily) by a long term contract, the players in the system are motivated to share knowledge because enhanced performance builds the commonly held trademark.

Franchising has been a pioneer in monitoring systems and feedback loops. Most franchising organizations have invested significantly in Internet and Extranet systems. Originally (well before the Internet), these systems were primarily "policing" devices established to make sure franchisees followed the prescribed business format and then paid their royalties. Today these systems go far beyond the original control function.

McDonalds recently began testing an outsourcing of their restaurant *drive-thru* ordering systems. A McDonalds' franchisee created this system and now shares it with 300 other franchisees in a beta test. Early results show a significant increase in both speed of delivery and order accuracy.

MIND STRETCHERS

Have you considered?

1. In what ways do you think entrepreneurs have created wealth because of franchising but *not* as a franchisor or franchisee?
2. The International Franchise Association reports that 90 percent of franchises succeed. Some academic research shows failure rates to be much higher. What might be the differences in the analysis that could show such variation?
3. How would you choose a company from which to buy a franchise?
4. Can you list the top 10 franchises in the world? What criteria would you use to make your judgment?
5. Do you know anyone who owns a franchise? Do you think they work more or less hard than a "stand-alone" entrepreneur?
6. Who is franchising for and not for?

Case

Mike Bellobuono

Mike Bellobuono knew he had a lot to consider. It was a very exciting time for the bagel industry. Industry-wide sales had exploded, and his company, Bagelz, a Connecticut-based bagel chain, had established seven retail locations in three years. There was tremendous opportunity for growth, but Mike knew that the company needed to achieve growth quickly or risk being faced with an inability to compete against larger players.

The company was at the point where the four-member management team had to decide whether to begin selling franchises or to remain as a fully company-owned operation. There was a lot at stake in this decision for President Joe Amodio, Vice President Wes Becher, Territory Development Manager Jamie Whalen, and Director of Operations Mike Bellobuono. Originally, they had planned on remaining as a fully company-owned operation but then had met Fred DeLuca, who suggested franchising and offered financing. Fred, founder of Subway, a multi-million-dollar sandwich franchise, had the potential to be a tremendous asset for Bagelz. He had access to large amounts of capital, an array of resources such as advertising and legal support, and, most of all, experience: His company had more locations in the United States than any other franchiser. However, Mike knew that Joe and the team didn't want Bagelz to simply become an extension of Fred's empire. The four were used to operating as members of a small, closely knit team and weren't sure if partnering with Fred would result in their losing control of the whole operation.

If they decided to franchise, Mike wondered if they would be able to find franchisees that had the finances, motivation, and ability to successfully run a Bagelz store. He had also heard many stories about conflicts arising out of franchiser–franchisee relationships. True, some of these conflicts were preventable, but inevitably there would be difficulties, probably ending in legal challenges. This greatly concerned him; he knew that disgruntled franchisees would poorly represent the company, and he wasn't sure if accelerated growth was worth the headaches and the possibility that unhappy franchisees would damage the company's reputation. He was also worried about maintaining the high standard of operations in franchisees' stores that Bagelz had put into place in its seven company-owned stores. He knew how difficult it was to build a name and how one bad incident could destroy it beyond repair. He thought about what happened to Jack-in-the-Box, another large fast-food franchise company. In January 1993, a customer had gotten sick and died from bacteria in an undercooked hamburger. Following this incident, the company hired independent inspectors to review every single franchise and ensure that all complied with the Board of Health's regulated cooking process. Not one additional violation was found in any of the hundreds of locations but nonetheless, following this incident, franchisees experienced declines in revenues of up to 35 percent.[1]

On the other hand, if they decided not to franchise they risked being locked out of certain geographical areas by the competition. Bruegger's Bagels was opening units all over New England (Exhibit A), and Manhattan Bagel, a new industry player, had gone public giving the company access to large amounts of capital for expansion. Operating as a chain store, as Bagelz was currently doing, constrained the company's potential growth rate. If the company decided against franchising, the team wondered if Bagelz would be able to withstand the onslaught of competition that was sure to occur. They wanted to make the right decision, but there was much to consider, and the offer to partner with DeLuca would not stay on the table for long. The bagel wars were heating up and Mike knew that they had to develop a superior growth strategy.

Mike's Background

Mike graduated from Babson College with a BS in May of 1991. He was working for a lawn service, but he and his college friend Jamie Whalen were looking to find a career in a hot market. Specifically the two were looking at bagels and chicken franchises. Although neither of them had any previous food-franchise experience, as part of a class project during Mike's senior year, they had done an in-depth study of the food-service industry (Exhibit B). Based on this research, they believed that the industry would experience continued growth, and that bagels and chicken would be the next high-growth segments.

It was then that Mike first met Wes Becher and Joe Amodio. The two had opened a bagel store one year earlier by the name of Bagelz, and business had gone so well that they had opened a second store and set their sights on developing additional locations in the near future. (See Exhibit C for Bagelz's income statement.) Mike was very impressed with Bagelz's operations and the possibility of getting in on a ground-floor opportunity. After considering alternatives such as Cajun Joe's, Boston Chicken, and Manhattan Bagel, he decided

This case was prepared by Andrea Alyse with assistance from Dan D'Heilly under the direction of Professor Stephen Spinelli. Funding provided by the Ewing Marion Kauffman Foundation.

[1] "E-Coli Scare Deals Blow to Seattle Burger Sales," *Restaurant Business*, March 20, 1993; and "Fallout of E-Coli Episode Still Troubles Foodmarket," *Nation's Restaurant News*, March 20, 1995.

EXHIBIT A

Bruegger's Bagels Growth Statistics

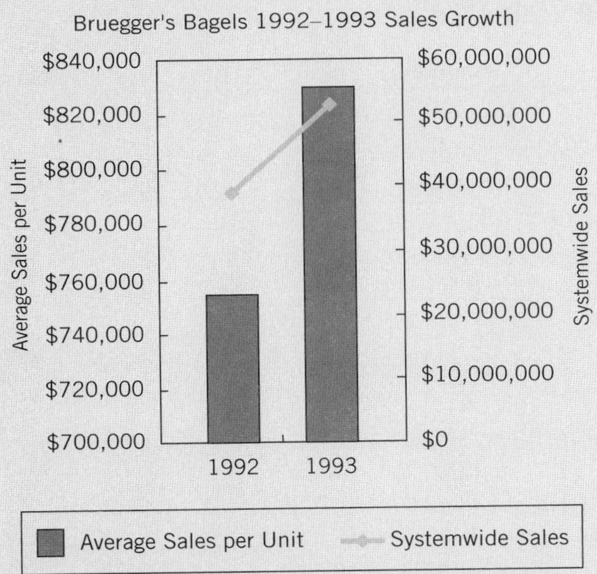

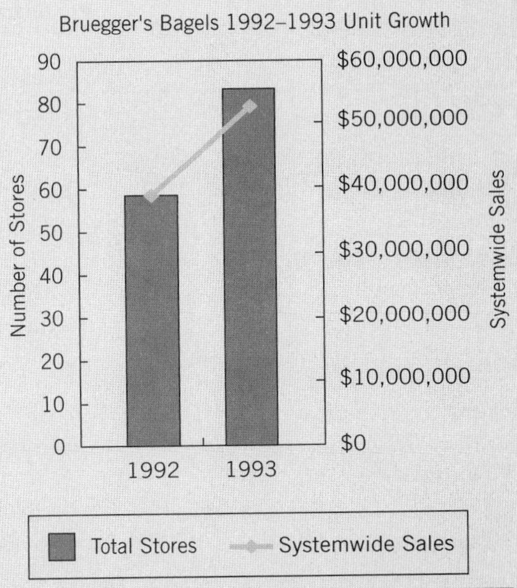

EXHIBIT B

Food-Service Industry Growth

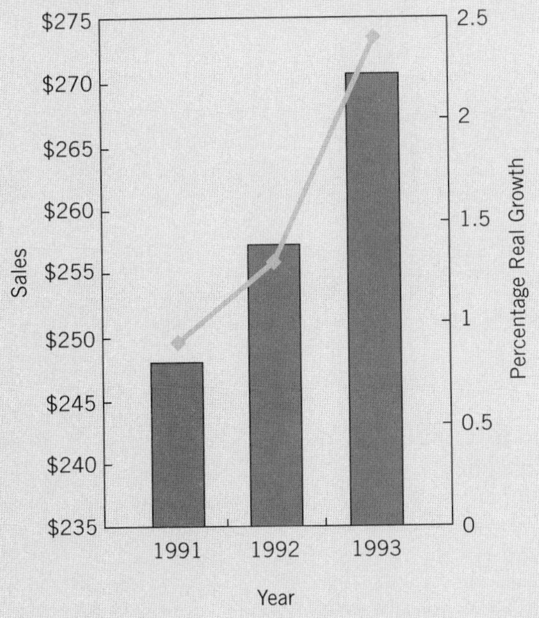

he liked both the company and the taste of Bagelz bagels best.

Jamie's father, who had originally approached Mike about the possibility of Mike becoming a partner with Jamie, was extremely supportive of the decision. Mike and Jamie had grown up in the same neighborhood and been friends as far back as they could both remember. Through the years, Mr. Whalen and Mike had become so close that Mike thought of him as his second father, and Mr. Whalen looked at Mike as the perfect business partner for Jamie. He eagerly endorsed Mike's idea and even felt that Jamie should leave school one year early to do this. Mike's father, however, was somewhat less than enthused at first:

> My father wanted me to go to law school or work for Aetna, where I had a job offer, but to me, working for someone else was never an option. When I told him about Bagelz he said, "Bagels? You went to business school and now you're going to sell bagels?" He wasn't exactly convinced that I was making the right decision, but he supported my decision anyway.

Due Diligence

Mike first approached Bruegger's about opening bagel stores in Connecticut, but the company believed that there was no market potential there. He then considered Manhattan Bagel. He liked its analysis of the bagel market, and the company also agreed that Connecticut was a viable market. However, in the end Mike decided to invest in Bagelz because he felt that Bagelz had several distinct competitive advantages. First there was Irving Stearns. Irv, Bagelz's chief bagel-maker, had been in the business for more than 20 years and knew everything there was to know about bagels. He baked a product that tasted better than any Mike had ever eaten, and he could quickly develop new products. There simply wasn't

EXHIBIT C

Bagelz Per Store Earning Claims 1993*	Weekly	Annually	Percent of Total Revenue per Store
Total Revenue per Store	$8,000.00	$416,000.00	100%
Cost of Goods Sold			
Salaries & Wages	2,000.00	104,000.00	25%
Food	1,680.00	87,360.00	21%
Beverages	800.00	41,600.00	10%
Paper Supplies	320.00	16,640.00	4%
Total C.O.G.S.	$4,800.00	$249,600.00	60%
Gross Profit on Sales	$3,200.00	$166,400.00	40%
Operating Expenses			
Payroll Tax	136.00	7,072.00	1.70%
Payroll Service	20.00	1,040.00	0.25%
Rent	480.00	24,960.00	6.00%
Connecticut Light & Power	200.00	10,400.00	2.50%
Connecticut Natural Gas	120.00	6,240.00	1.50%
Telephone	24.00	1,248.00	0.30%
Advertising	200.00	10,400.00	2.50%
Local Advertising	80.00	4,160.00	1.00%
Insurance	80.00	4,160.00	1.00%
Linen & Laundry	16.00	832.00	0.20%
Repairs & Maintenance	80.00	4,160.00	1.00%
Rubbish Removal	40.00	2,080.00	0.50%
Office Supplies	40.00	2,080.00	0.50%
Uniforms	16.00	832.00	0.20%
Professional Fees	40.00	2,080.00	0.50%
Miscellaneous	20.00	1,040.00	0.25%
Total Operating Expenses	$1,592.00	$82,784.00	19.90%
Total Income from Operations	$1,608.00	$83,616.00	20.10%

*All figures have been estimated based on industry data and do not necessarily represent the actual financial performance of a Bagelz store operation.

anyone else like Irv. Mike also liked the flexibility of Bagelz's management. They were quick to spot and react to new market trends and directions. For example, Bagelz offered customers five different kinds of flavored coffees before flavored coffees became popular—at a time when all their competitors only offered regular and decaffeinated. Finally, with Bagelz, he was on the ground floor.

Bagelz

Mike and Jamie contacted Joe and Wes about buying a franchise. They soon found out that companies that franchised were required to adhere to the U.S. Federal Trade Commission (FTC) Disclosure Rule. The rule stated that franchisers must disclose certain, specified information to all prospective franchisees, in a format approved by the FTC (Exhibit D). Most franchisers used a Uniform Franchise Offering Circular (UFOC) format to comply with FTC regulations. A UFOC document contained information including a description of the business, estimated development costs, fee schedules, franchisee and franchiser obligations, other businesses affiliated with the franchise, and pending lawsuits. Additionally, 13 states required franchisers to file a UFOC prior to selling franchises. Producing this document was an expensive and time-consuming process but without complying with the FTC's Disclosure Rule, Joe and Wes weren't legally permitted to sell franchises. However, Mike and Jamie persisted until

EXHIBIT D

U.S. Federal Trade Commission Disclosure Rule

I. Rule Overview

A. Basic Requirement: Franchisors must furnish potential franchisees with written disclosures providing important information about the franchisor, the franchised business and the franchise relationship, and give them at least 10 business days to review it before investing.

B. Disclosure Option: Franchisors may make the required disclosures by following either the Rule's disclosure format or the Uniform Franchise Offering Circular Guidelines prepared by state franchise law officials.

C. Coverage: The Rule primarily covers business-format franchises, product franchises, and vending machine or display rack business opportunity ventures.

D. No Filing: The Rule requires disclosure only. Unlike state disclosure laws, no registration, filing, review or approval of any disclosures, advertising or agreements by the FTC is required.

E. Remedies: The Rule is a trade regulation rule with the full force and effect of federal law. The courts have held it may only be enforced by the FTC, not private parties. The FTC may seek injunctions, civil penalties and consumer redress for violations.

F. Purpose: The Rule is designed to enable potential franchisees to protect themselves before investing by providing them with information essential to an assessment of the potential risks and benefits, to meaningful comparisons with other investments, and to further investigation of the franchise opportunity.

G. Effective Date: The Rule, formally titled "Disclosure Requirements and Prohibitions Concerning Franchising and Business Opportunity Ventures," took effect on October 21, 1979, and appears at 16 C.F.R. Part 436.

II. Rule Requirements

A. General: The Rule imposes six different requirements in connection with the "advertising, offering, licensing, contracting, sale or other promotion" of a franchise in or affecting commerce:

1. Basic Disclosures: The Rule requires franchisors to give potential investors a basic disclosure document at the earlier of the first face-to-face meeting or 10 business days before any money is paid or an agreement is signed in connection with the investment (Part 436.1(a)).
2. Earnings Claims: If a franchisor makes earnings claims, whether historical or forecast, they must have a reasonable basis, and prescribed substantiating disclosures must be given to a potential investor in writing at the same time as the basic disclosures (Parts 436.1(b)–(d)).
3. Advertised Claims: The Rule affects only ads that include an earnings claim. Such ads must disclose the number and percentage of existing franchisees who have achieved the claimed results, along with cautionary language. Their use triggers required compliance with the Rule's earnings claim disclosure requirements (Part 436.1(e)).
4. Franchise Agreements: The franchisor must give investors a copy of its standard-form franchise and related agreements at the same time as the basic disclosures, and final copies intended to be executed at least 5 business days before signing (Part 436.1(g)).
5. Refunds: The Rule requires franchisors to make refunds of deposits and initial payments to potential investors, subject to any conditions on refundability stated in the disclosure document (Part 436.1(h)).
6. Contradictory Claims: While franchisors are free to provide investors with any promotional or other materials they wish, no written or oral claims may contradict information provided in the required disclosure document (Part 436.1(f)).

B. Liability: Failure to comply with any of the six requirements is a violation of the Franchise Rule. "Franchisors" and "franchise brokers" are jointly and severally liable for Rule violations.

1. A "franchisor" is defined as any person who sells a "franchise" covered by the Rule (Part 436.2(c)).
2. A "franchise broker" is defined as any person who "sells, offers for sale, or arranges for the sale" of a covered franchise (Part 436.2(j)), and includes not only independent sales agents, but also subfranchisors that grant subfranchises (44 FR 49963).

III. Business Relationships Covered

A. Alternate Definitions: The Rule employs parallel coverage definitions of the term "franchise" to reach two types of continuing commercial relationships: traditional franchises and business opportunities.

B. "Traditional Franchises": There are three definitional prerequisites to coverage of a business-format or product franchise (Parts 436.2(a)(1)(i) and (2)):

1. Trademark: The franchisor offers the right to distribute goods or services that bear the franchisor's trademark, service mark, trade name, advertising or other commercial symbol.
2. Significant Control or Assistance: The franchisor exercises significant control over, or offers significant assistance in, the franchisee's method of operation.
3. Required Payment: The franchisee is required to make any payment to the franchisor or an affiliate, or a commitment to make a payment, as a condition of obtaining the franchise or commencing operations. (NOTE: There is an exemption from coverage for required payments of less than $500 within six months of the commencement of the franchise (Part 436.2(a)(3)(iii))).

(Continued)

EXHIBIT D (continued)

C. Business Opportunities: There are also three basic prerequisites to the Rule's coverage of a business opportunity venture (Parts 436.2(a)(1)(ii) and (2)):

1. No Trademark: The seller simply offers the right to sell goods or services supplied by the seller, its affiliate, or a supplier with which the seller requires the franchisee to do business.
2. Location Assistance: The seller offers to secure retail outlets or accounts for the goods or services to be sold, to secure locations or sites for vending machines or rack displays, or to provide the services of someone who can do so.
3. Required Payment: The same as for franchises.

D. Coverage Exemptions/Exclusions: The Rule also exempts or excludes some relationships that would otherwise meet the coverage prerequisites (Parts 436.2(a)(3) and (4)):

1. Minimum Investment: This exemption applies if all payments to the franchisor or an affiliate until six months after the franchise commences operation are $500 or less (Part 436.2(a)(iii)).
2. Fractional Franchises: Relationships adding a new product or service to an established distributor's existing products or services, are exempt if: (i) the franchisee or any of its current directors or executive officers has been in the same type of business for at least two years, and (ii) both parties anticipated, or should have, that sales from the franchise would represent no more than 20 percent of the franchisees sales in dollar volume (Parts 436.2(a)(3)(i) and 436.2(h)).
3. Single Trademark Licenses: The Rule language excludes a "single license to license a [mark]" where it "is the only one of its general nature and type to be granted by the licenser with respect to that [mark]" (Part 436.2(a)(4)(iv)). The Rule's Statement of Basis and Purpose indicates it also applies to "collateral" licenses [e.g., logo on sweatshirt, mug] and licenses granted to settle trademark infringement litigation (43 FR 59707–08).
4. Employment and Partnership Relationships: The Rule excludes pure employer-employee and general partnership arrangements. Limited partnerships do not qualify for the exemption (Part 436.2(a)(4)(i)).
5. Oral Agreements: This exemption, which is narrowly construed, applies only if no material term of the relationship is in writing (Part 436.2(a)(3)(iv)).
6. Cooperative Associations: Only agricultural co-ops and retailer-owned cooperatives "operated 'by and for' retailers on a cooperative basis," and in which control and ownership is substantially equal are excluded from coverage (Part 436.2(a)(4)(ii)).
7. Certification/Testing Services: Organizations that authorize use of a certification mark to any business selling products or services meeting their standards are excluded from coverage (e.g., Underwriters Laboratories) (Part 436.2(a)(4)(iii)).
8. Leased Departments: Relationships in which the franchisee simply leases space in the premises of another retailer and is not required or advised to buy the goods or services it sells from the retailer or an affiliate of the retailer are exempt (Part 436.2(a)(3)(ii)).

E. Statutory Exemptions: Section 18(g) of the FTC Act authorizes "any person" to petition the Commission for an exemption from a rule where coverage is "not necessary to prevent the acts or practices" that the rule prohibits (15 U.S.C. § 57a(g)). Franchise Rule exemptions have been granted for service station franchises (45 FR 51765), many automobile dealership franchises (45 FR 51763; 49 FR 13677; 52 FR 6612; 54 FR 1446), and wholesaler-sponsored voluntary chains in the grocery industry (48 FR 10040).

IV. Disclosure Options

A. Alternatives: Franchisors have a choice of formats for making the disclosures required by the Rule. They may use either the format provided by the Rule or the Uniform Franchise Offering Circular ("UFOC") format prescribed by the North American Securities Administrators' Association ("NASAA").

B. FTC Format: Franchisors may comply by following the Rule's requirements for preparing a basic disclosure document (Parts 436.1(a)(1)-(24)), and if they make earnings claims, for a separate earnings claim disclosure document (Parts 436.1(b)(3), (c)(3), and (d)). The Rule's Final Interpretive Guides provide detailed instructions and sample disclosures (44 FR 49966).

C. UFOC Format: The Uniform Franchise Offering Circular format may also be used for compliance in any state.

1. Guidelines: Effective January 1, 1996, franchisors using the UFOC disclosure format must comply with the UFOC Guidelines, as amended by NASAA on April 25, 1993. (44 FR 49970; 60 FR 51895).
2. Cover Page: The FTC cover page must be furnished to each potential franchisee, either in lieu of the UFOC cover page in non-registration states or along with the UFOC (Part 436.1(a)(21); 44 FR 49970–71).
3. Adaptation: If the UFOC is registered or used in one state, but will be used in another without a franchise registration law, answers to state-specific questions must be changed to refer to the law of the state in which the UFOC is used.
4. Updating: If the UFOC is registered in a state, it must be updated as required by the state's franchise law. If the same UFOC is also adapted for use in a non-registration state, updating must occur as required by the law of the state where the UFOC is registered. If the UFOC is not registered in a state with a franchise registration law, it must be revised annually and updated quarterly as required by the Rule.
5. Presumption: The Commission will presume the sufficiency, adequacy and accuracy of a UFOC that is registered by a state, when it is used in that state.

EXHIBIT D (concluded)

D. UFOC vs. Rule: Many franchisors have adopted the UFOC disclosure format because roughly half of the 13 states with franchise registration requirements will not accept the Rule document for filing. When a format is chosen, all disclosure must conform to its requirements. Franchisors may not pick and choose provisions from each format when making disclosures (44 FR 49970).

E. Rule Primacy: If the UFOC is used, several key Rule provisions will still apply:
1. Scope: Disclosure will be required in all cases required by the Rule, regardless of whether it would be required by state law.
2. Coverage: The Rule will determine who is obligated to comply, regardless of whether they would be required to make disclosures under state law.
3. Disclosure Timing: When disclosures must be made will be governed by the Rule, unless state law requires even earlier disclosure.
4. Other Material: No information may appear in a disclosure document not required by the Rule or by non-preempted state law, regardless of the format used, and no representations may be made that contradict a disclosure.
5. Contracts: Failure to provide potential franchisees with final agreements at least 5 days before signing will be a Rule violation regardless of the disclosure format used.
6. Refunds: Failure to make promised refunds also will be a Rule violation regardless of which document is used.

V. Potential Liability for Violations

A. FTC Action: Rule violations may subject franchisors, franchise brokers, their officers and agents to significant liabilities in FTC enforcement actions.
1. Remedies: The FTC Act provides the Commission with a broad range of remedies for Rule violations:
   a. Injunctions: Section 13(b) of the Act authorizes preliminary and permanent injunctions against Rule violations (15 U.S.C. § 53(b)). Rule cases routinely have sought and obtained injunctions against Rule violations and misrepresentations in the offer or sale of any business venture, whether or not covered by the Rule.
   b. Asset Freezes: Acting under their inherent equity powers, the courts have routinely granted preliminary asset freezes in appropriate Rule cases. The assets frozen have included both corporate assets and the personal assets, including real and personal property, of key officers and directors.
   c. Civil Penalties: Section 5(m)(1)(A) of the Act authorizes civil penalties of up to $10,000 for each violation of the Rule (15 U.S.C. § 45(m)(1)(A)). The courts have granted civil penalties of as much as $870,000 in a Rule case to date.
   d. Monetary Redress: Section 19(b) of the Act authorizes the Commission to seek monetary redress on behalf of investors injured economically by a Rule violation (15 U.S.C. § 57b). The courts have granted consumer redress of as much as $4.9 million in a Rule case to date.
   e. Other Redress: Section 19(b) of the Act also authorizes such other forms of redress as the court finds necessary to redress injury to consumers from a Rule violation, including rescission or reformation of contracts, the return of property and public notice of the Rule violation. Courts may also grant similar relief under their inherent equity powers.
2. Personal Liability: Individuals who formulate, direct and control the franchisor's activities can expect to be named individually for violations committed in the franchisor's name, together with the franchisor entity, and held personally liable for civil penalties and consumer redress.
3. Liability for Others: Franchisors and their key officers and executives are responsible for violations by persons acting in their behalf, including independent franchise brokers, sub-franchisors, and the franchisor's own sales personnel.

B. Private Actions: The courts have held that the FTC Act generally may not be enforced by private lawsuits.
1. Rule Claims: The Commission expressed its view when the Rule was issued that private actions should be permitted by the courts for Rule violations (43 FR 59723; 44 FR 49971). To date, no federal court has permitted a private action for Rule violations.
2. State Disclosure Law Claims: Each of the franchise laws in the 15 states with franchise registration and/or disclosure requirements authorizes private actions for state franchise law violations.
3. State FTC Act Claims: The courts in some states have interpreted state deceptive practices laws ("little FTC Acts") as permitting private actions for Rule violations.

VI. Legal Resources

A. Text of Rule: 16 C.F.R. Part 436.

B. Statement of Basis and Purpose: 43 FR 59614–59733 (Dec. 21, 1978) (discusses the evidentiary basis for promulgation of the Rule, and shows Commission intent and interpretation of its provisions—particularly helpful in resolving coverage questions).

C. Final Interpretive Guides: 44 FR 49966–49992 (Aug. 24, 1979) (final statement of policy and interpretation of each of the Rule's requirements—important discussions of coverage issues, use of the UFOC and requirements for basic and earnings claims disclosures in the Rule's disclosure format).

D. Staff Advisory Opinions: Business Franchise Guide (CCH) 6380 et seq. (interpretive opinions issued in response to requests for interpretation of coverage questions and disclosure requirements pursuant to 16 C.F.R. §§ 1.2–1.4).

Joe and Wes agreed to sell them a store as a limited partnership:

> I looked at a partnership as giving me greater control over my own destiny. If we didn't form a partnership, and I just opened up stores for them, I would have no control over any changes they decided to make; having this control was extremely important to me.

Mike and Jamie opened the Manchester store in December of 1991. Then Wes, impressed by Mike and Jamie's dedication, approached the two about becoming full partners in the company. Wes explained to Mike that, although he had several prospective investors, he was interested in offering the two a partnership because he and Joe were looking for investors who would work for the company, not simply finance it. To buy into the company, Jamie and Mike arranged financing through their fathers, and the two became full partners the next year. Mike, Wes, Jamie, and Joe handled all aspects of the partnership. Each store was visited by one of the four members of the team on a daily basis to ensure that operations were running smoothly and to solve any difficulties that arose. Wes, Jamie, and Mike focused on the day-to-day operations, and Joe on growing the company:

> Joe was the leader and a fly-by-the-seat-of-the-pants type of guy. Joe would point in a direction, and we three would make it happen. Joe had an incredible talent for salesmanship, a kind of way about him that enabled him to achieve the seemingly impossible. One Christmas we were in New York City, and we were in this restaurant. The owner was depressed because the restaurant was empty. Joe said he could fill the restaurant if the owner sat him by the window. He proceeded to put on quite a show, performing in the window, carrying on, gesturing, and waving, which drove people in who wanted to see what all the excitement was about. And you know what? He filled the restaurant in under an hour. But Joe wasn't finished yet. He then got the entire place to sing "The Twelve Days of Christmas," and when people forgot the words of a section of the song, he had them running out into the street asking people if they knew the words and could help out—I mean strangers, in the middle of New York City. It was unbelievable! Even the ending was like a fairy tale: as the crowd got to the twelfth day of Christmas, Joe was tipping his hat at the door and making his exit. To this day whenever he goes into that restaurant his dinner is free; the owner never forgot what Joe did for him.

By 1993, Bagelz had seven stores with the goal of saturating the entire state of Connecticut by the year 2000. Bruegger's wasn't there yet, and Manhattan only had a few locations, but Mike knew they were coming:

> We were Bagelz, and we wanted to make Connecticut our turf, so that you knew that if you were going to go into Connecticut, you would have to fight us.

The Bagel Industry

Although the exact origin of the bagel is not fully known, legend maintains that the first bagel was created for the king of Poland, as celebration bread, when the king's army repelled a 1683 Turkish invasion. Jewish immigrants introduced the bagel in the United States, and for decades bagels were perceived as a strictly ethnic food, with limited mass-market appeal.

Traditionally, bagels were made from water, flour, yeast, and salt, combined and formed into a ring shape. These rings were boiled in water to create the crust and shiny appearance, and then baked in brick ovens to produce a crispy outside and soft, chewy inside, considerably denser than most breads. As bagels gained mass-market acceptance across the country, the industry grew at an accelerating rate. Modern-day bakers often use machine-formed bagels and large stainless-steel ovens, complete with rotating racks for faster, more uniform baking. As competition between bagel shops has increased in the United States, the traditional bagel recipe has been adapted to increase the variety of flavors (e.g., egg, salt, garlic, onion, poppy seed, sesame seed, blueberry, chocolate chip, corn, and cheddar cheese).

Lender's, now a division of Kraft General Foods, first successfully marketed a mass-produced, frozen, supermarket bagel in 1962. Before this time, bagels had only been sold as fresh. By 1991, Lender's had grown to sales of $203 million, and Sara Lee, Lender's closest competitor, who had entered the frozen bagel market in 1985, had sales of $22.4 million.

In the 1980s, Lender's and Bagel Nosh opened bagel shops nationally but both companies failed, never able to attract enough customers. By the early 1990s, bagels were gaining mass-market acceptance across the country. However, the industry was growing most notably on the East Coast where, as of mid-1992, more than half of all bagel sales in the United States (51 percent) came from 15 East Coast cities. Frozen supermarket bagels achieved sales of $211.9 million in 1992, an increase of 4 percent over the previous year, but fresh bagels, the most rapidly growing segment, increased sales to $95 million, up 28 percent from 1991. For 1993, sales of frozen bagels were projected to increase 6 percent to $224.4 million and sales of fresh bagels were projected to increase 17 percent to $111 million. Consumer awareness and consumption of bagels had increased steadily, but most dramatically throughout the past six years (Exhibit E illustrates the increase in per capita bagel consumption for 1988 to 1993). Breakfast accounted for 65 percent of all bagel sales, and with the trend toward increased consumer-health awareness, bagels had become a natural, low-fat, high-carbohydrate alternative to other menu items, such as doughnuts and muffins.

EXHIBIT E

Bagel Consumption

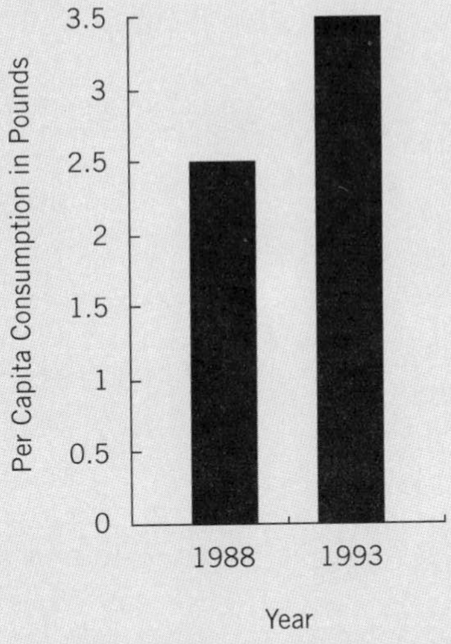

Fred DeLuca

In the spring of 1993, Fred DeLuca, founder of Subway, a large sandwich franchise, contacted the Bagelz team. A vendor that sold luncheon-meat slicers to both Bagelz and Subway had told Fred about Bagelz's operation, and Fred decided that he wanted to tour the plant and meet the team. Fred was well known in the franchise industry. While still in college, he had opened his first Subway location in 1965. Nine years later he began franchising, and by 1995, Subway had grown to more than 10,000 locations. In addition, *Entrepreneur Magazine* rated Subway the No. 1 franchise in its annual franchising 500 six times between 1988 and 1994:

> We never thought that he wanted to do business with us. We were just excited to meet him. When we realized he was interested in making a deal, we were astonished.

It was then that the team first seriously considered franchising.

To Franchise or Not to Franchise?

Fred had offered to buy into Bagelz and turn it into a world-class franchise, but first he wanted to be sure that the bagel team was fully aware of, and ready to meet, all potential difficulties involved with franchising:

> Fred wanted to know why we wanted to franchise. He said, "Do you know what you are getting yourself into? Are you sure you really want to deal with all the problems that arise from franchising?"

The team weighed both the pros and cons of becoming a franchiser. They evaluated two basic strategies: either to grow rapidly throughout Connecticut as a chain, or to franchise and grow nationally. How many stores is the right number for Connecticut? Did they have the management talent, the money, and the time?

They were afraid of losing control if they franchised, but knew it would be difficult to grow quickly without franchising. They were also afraid they wouldn't be able to lock out the competition: Manhattan Bagel planned to expand into Connecticut and Bruegger's had been named one of the 50 fastest growing U.S. restaurants (Exhibit F). Last, Mike and the team feared that DeLuca would lose interest. After all, they had already been negotiating for six months and hadn't reached an agreement. Then Subway began receiving increasing amounts of negative publicity regarding the company's support of its franchisees. One particularly disturbing article appeared in *The Wall Street Journal* by Barbara Welch, "Franchise Realities: Sandwich-Shop Chain Surges, but to Run One Can Take Heroic Effort. Investing in a Subway Outlet, Some Say, Is Just Buying a Hard, Low Paying Job. New Store Opens Next Door," *The Wall Street Journal,* 16 September, 1992, Pg. A1, and Mike and the team began to wonder if aligning with Fred could ultimately have a negative effect on Bagelz. They knew, however, that time was running out and they needed to decide the best future direction for Bagelz.

EXHIBIT F

50 Fastest Growing Restaurants, 1992–1993

Name of Restaurant	City and State	Type of Restaurant	Does the Company Franchise?	Projected 1992–1993 % Change in Systemwide Sales	Projected 1992–1993 %Change in Units	Projected 1992–1993 % Change in Average Unit Sales
1 Boston Chicken	Naperville, IL	Fast food	Y	261.0%	161.4%	9.2%
2 Lone Star Steakhouse & Saloon	Wichita, KN	Casual steakhouse	Y	136.3	95.7	3.6
3 Italian Oven	Latrobe, PA	Casual Italian dinnerhouse	Y	126.2	60.0	11.7
4 Romano's Macaroni Grill	Dallas	Casual Italian dinnerhouse	N	107.7	86.7	0.2
5 Hooters	Atlanta	Casual dinnerhouse	Y	87.2	16.0	25.0
6 Papa John's	Louisville	Delivery/take-out pizza	Y	80.4	81.8	8.7
7 Outback Steakhouse	Tampa	Casual steakhouse	Y	77.9	71.8	6.7
8 Checkers Drive-In	Clearwater, FL	Drive-through hamburgers	Y	68.1	81.2	5.2
9 Taco Cabana	San Antonio, TX	Patio-style Mexican	Y	65.1	87.7	−4.2
10 Hot 'n Now	Irvine, CA	Drive-through hamburgers	N	64.0	80.9	3.6
11 Wall Street Deli	Memphis	Self-serve deli and buffet	N	56.2	26.4	5.0
12 Mick's	Atlanta	Casual dinnerhouse	N	53.8	50.0	1.5
13 Applebee's	Kansas City, MO	Casual dinnerhouse	Y	50.5	44.4	5.3
14 Starbucks	Seattle	Coffee specialist	N	50.0	63.7	6.7
15 Grady's American Grill	Dallas	Casual dinnerhouse	N	45.1	52.6	1.2
16 Bertucci's Brick Oven Pizza	Woburn, MA	Casual Italian dinnerhouse	N	45.0	42.9	5.9
17 Fresh Choice	Santa Clara, CA	Self-serve buffet	N	44.4	63.6	4.9
18 Miami Subs Grill	Fort Lauderdale, FL	Fast food	Y	42.9	23.2	3.5
19 Stacey's Buffet	Largo, FL	Self-serve buffet	Y	39.0	50.0	−5.3
20 Longhorn Steaks	Atlanta	Casual steakhouse	Y	37.4	32.5	−2.8
21 Panda Express	South Pasadena, CA	Fast-Food Oriental	N	36.8	40.0	2.9
22 Bruegger's Bagel Bakery	Burlington, VT	Fast food	Y	36.5	44.8	9.5
23 California Pizza Kitchen	Los Angeles	Casual dinnerhouse	N	26.4	51.7	5.6
24 Old Country Buffet	Eden Prairie, MN	Self-serve buffet	N	33.7	28.6	4.3
25 Sfuzzi	Dallas	Casual Italian dinnerhouse	N	33.3	25.0	3.0
26 Claim Jumper	Irvine, CA	Dinnerhouse	N	33.3	30.0	4.3
27 Nathan's Famous	Westbury, NY	Fast food	Y	31.4	20.3	−4.0
28 Morton's of Chicago	Chicago	Upscale steakhouse	N	31.1	20.0	9.2
29 The Cheesecake Factory	Redondo Beach, CA	Casual dinnerhouse	N	29.9	60.0	1.2
30 Au Ban Pain	Boston	Bakery cafe	Y	28.8	11.0	5.5
31 Ruby Tuesday	Mobile, AL	Casual dinnerhouse	N	28.2	25.6	6.2

(Continued)

Name of Restaurant	City and State	Type of Restaurant	Does the Company Franchise?	Projected 1992–1993 % Change in Systemwide Sales	Projected 1992–1993 %Change in Units	Projected 1992–1993 % Change in Average Unit Sales
32 Schlotzsky's Deli	Austin, TX	Fast food	Y	27.0	17.7	2.9
33 Blimpie	New York	Fast food	Y	26.6	27.9	0.0
34 Cracker Barrel	Lebanon, TN	Family restaurant	N	25.1	20.7	3.7
35 The Cooker Bar & Grille	Columbus, OH	Casual dinnerhouse	N	24.5	45.0	0.0
36 Subway	Milford, CN	Fast food	Y	22.7	13.9	6.0
37 The Spaghetti Warehouse	Garland, TX	Casual Italian dinnerhouse	N	21.7	37.0	11.5
38 Dunkin' Donuts	Randolph, MA	Fast food	Y	21.3	16.6	4.5
39 Sirloin Stockade	Hutchinson, KN	Budget steakhouse	Y	21.3	7.6	15.0
40 Cinnabon	Seattle	Fast food	Y	21.2	8.6	5.2
41 T.G.I. Friday's	Dallas	Casual dinnerhouse	Y	20.2	18.3	0.0
42 Don Pablo's	Bedford, TX	Casual Mexican dinnerhouse	N	19.8	47.4	2.7
43 Rally's	Louisville	Drive-through hamburgers	Y	19.6	20.0	−4.5
44 Chili's	Dallas	Casual dinnerhouse	Y	19.0	15.5	3.2
45 Damon's-The Place for Ribs	Columbus, OH	Casual dinnerhouse	Y	18.3	4.0	2.9
46 Red Robin	Irvine, CA	Casual dinnerhouse	Y	18.1	19.0	−3.5
47 Bain's Deli	King of Prussia, PA	Fast food	Y	17.9	8.0	10.3
48 On the Border Cafe	Dallas	Casual Mexican dinnerhouse	Y	17.9	46.7	0.0
49 Bojangles	Charlotte, NC	Fast food	Y	17.2	20.3	5.7
50 Ruth's Chris Steak House	New Orleans	Upscale steakhouse	Y	17.1	8.8	4.8

Source: *Restaurant Business*, July 20, 1994.

12

Chapter Twelve

Entrepreneurial Finance

Happiness to an entrepreneur is a positive cash flow.

Fred Adler
Venture Capitalist

Results Expected

Upon completion of this chapter, you will have:

1. Examined critical issues in financing new ventures.
2. Studied the difference between entrepreneurial finance and conventional administrative or corporate finance.
3. Examined the process of crafting financial and fund-raising strategies and the critical variables involved, including identifying the financial life cycles of new ventures, a financial strategy framework, and investor preferences.
4. Analyzed the "Midwest Lighting" case study.

Venture Financing: The Entrepreneur's Achilles' Heel[1]

There are three core principles of entrepreneurial finance: (1) more cash is preferred to less cash, (2) cash sooner is preferred to cash later, and (3) less risky cash is preferred to more risky cash. While these principles seem simple enough, entrepreneurs, chief executive officers, and division managers often seem to ignore them. To these individuals, financial analysis seems intimidating, regardless of the size of the company. Even management teams, comfortable with the financial issues, may not be adept at linking strategic and financial decisions to their companies' challenges and choices. Take, for example, the following predicaments:

- Reviewing the year-end results just handed to you by your chief financial officer, you see no surprises—except that the company loss is even larger than you had projected three months earlier. Therefore, for the fourth year in a row, you will have to walk into the boardroom and deliver bad news. A family-owned business since 1945, the company has survived and prospered with average annual sales growth of 17 percent. In fact, the company's market share has actually increased during recent years despite the losses. With the annual growth rate in the industry averaging less than 5 percent, your mature markets offer few opportunities for sustaining higher growth. How can this be happening? Where do you and your company go from here? How do you explain to the board that for four years you have increased sales and market share but produced losses? How will you propose to turn the situation around?
- During the past 20 years, your cable television company has experienced rapid growth through the expansion of existing properties and

[1] This section was drawn from Jeffry A. Timmons, "Financial Management Breakthrough for Entrepreneurs."

numerous acquisitions. Your net worth reached $25 million. The next decade of expansion was fueled by the high leverage common in the cable industry and valuations soared. Ten years later, your company had a market value in the $500 million range. You had a mere $300 million in debt, and you owned 100 percent of the company. Just two years later, your $200 million net worth is an astonishing zero! Additionally, you now face the personally exhausting and financially punishing restructuring battle to survive; personal bankruptcy is a very real possibility. How could this happen? Can the company be salvaged?[2]

- At mid-decade, your company was the industry leader, meeting as well as exceeding your business plan targets for annual sales, profitability, and new stores. Exceeding these targets while doubling sales and profitability each year has propelled your stock price from $15 at the initial public offering to the mid $30s. Meanwhile, you still own a large chunk of the company. Then the shocker—at decade's end your company loses $78 million on just over $90 million in sales! The value of your stock plummets. A brutal restructuring follows in which the stock is stripped from the original management team, including you, and you are ousted from the company you founded and loved. Why did the company spin out of control? Why couldn't you as the founder have anticipated its demise? Could you have saved the company in time?
- As the chairman of a rapidly growing telecommunications firm, you are convening your first board meeting after a successful public stock offering. As you think about the agenda, your plans are to grow the company to $15 million in sales in the next three years, which is comfortable given the $5 million in sales last year, the $3.5 million of cash in the bank, and no debt on the balance sheet. Early in the meeting, one of the two outside directors asks the controller and the chief financial officer his favorite question, "When will you run out of cash?" The chief financial officer is puzzled at first, then he is indignant, if not outraged, by what he considers to be an irrelevant question. After all, he reasoned, our company has plenty of cash and we don't need a bank line. However, 16 months later, without warning from the chief financial officer, the company is out of cash and has overdrawn its $1 million credit line by $700,000 and the hemorrhaging may get worse. The board fires the president, the chief financial officer, and the senior audit partner from a major accounting firm. The chairman has to take over the helm and must personally invest half a million dollars in the collapsing company to keep it afloat. At this point, it's the bank that is indignant and outraged. You have to devise an emergency battle plan to get on top of the financial crisis. How can this be done?

Financial Management Myopia: It Can't Happen to Me

All of these situations have three things in common. First, they are real companies and these are actual events.[3] Second, each of these companies was led by successful entrepreneurs who knew enough to prepare audited financial statements. Third, in each example, the problems stemmed from financial management myopia, a combination of self-delusion and just plain not understanding the complex dynamics and interplay between financial management and business strategy. Why is this so?

Getting Beyond "Collect Early, Pay Late"

During our 35-plus years as educators, authors, directors, founders, and investors in entrepreneurial companies, we have met a few thousand entrepreneurs and managers, including executives participating in an executive MBA program, MBA students, Kauffman Fellows, company founders, presidents, members of the Young Presidents Organization, and the chief executive officers of middle-market companies. By their own admission, they felt uniformly uncomfortable, if not downright intimidated and terrified, by their lack of expertise in financial analysis and its relationship to management and strategy. The vast majority of entrepreneurs and nonfinancial managers are disadvantaged. Beyond "collect early, pay late," there is precious little sophistication and an enormous level of discomfort when it comes to these complex and dynamic financial interrelationships. Even good managers who are reveling in major sales increases and profit increases often fail to realize until it's too late the impact increased sales have on the cash flow required to finance the increased receivables and inventory.

[2] For more detail, see Burton C. Hurlock and William A. Sahlman, "Star Cablevision Group: Harvesting in a Bull Market," HBS Case 293-036, Harvard Business School Publishing.

[3] Their outcomes have ranged from demise to moderate success, to radical downsizing followed by dramatic recovery.

EXHIBIT 12.1

The Crux of It: Anticipation and Financial Vigilance

To avoid some of the great tar pits like the ones described earlier, entrepreneurs need answers to questions that link strategic business decisions to financial plans and choices. The crux of it is anticipation: *What is most likely to happen? When? What can go right along the way? What can go wrong? What has to happen to achieve our business objectives and to increase or to preserve our options?* Financially savvy entrepreneurs know that such questions trigger a process that can lead to creative solutions to their financial challenges and problems. At a practical level, financially astute entrepreneurs and managers maintain vigilance over numerous key strategic and financial questions:

- What are the financial consequences and implications of crucial business decisions such as pricing, volume, and policy changes affecting the balance sheet, income statement, and cash flow? How will these change over time?
- How can we measure and monitor changes in our financial strategy and structure from a management, not just a GAAP, perspective?
- What does it mean to grow too fast in our industry? How fast can we grow without requiring outside debt or equity? How much capital is required if we increase or decrease our growth by X percent?
- What will happen to our cash flow, profitability, return on assets, and shareholder equity if we grow faster or slower by X percent?
- How much capital will this require? How much can be financed internally and how much will have to come from external sources? What is a reasonable mix of debt and equity?
- What if we are 20% less profitable than our plan calls for? Or 20% more profitable?
- What should be our focus and priorities? What are the cash flow and net income break-even points for each of our product lines? For our company? For our business unit?
- What about our pricing, our volume, and our costs? How sensitive are our cash flow and net income to increases or decreases in price, variable costs, or volume? What price/volume mix will enable us to achieve the same cash flow and net income?
- How will these changes in pricing, costs, and volume affect our key financial ratios and how will we stack up against others in our industry? How will our lenders view this?
- At each stage—startup, rapidly growing, stagnating, or mature company—how should we be thinking about these questions and issues?

The Spreadsheet Mirage It is hard to imagine any entrepreneur who would not want ready answers to many financial vigilance questions, such as in Exhibit 12.1. Until now, however, getting the answers to these questions was a rarity. If the capacity and information are there to do the necessary analysis (and all too often they are not), it can take up to several weeks to get a response. In this era of spreadsheet mania, more often than not, the answers will come in the form of a lengthy report with innumerable scenarios, pages of numbers, backup exhibits, and possibly a presentation by a staff financial analyst, controller, or chief financial officer.

Too often the barrage of spreadsheet exhibits is really a mirage. What is missing? Traditional spreadsheets can only report and manipulate the data. The numbers may be there, the trends may be identified, but the connections and interdependencies between financial structure and business decisions inherent in key financial questions may be missed. As a result, gaining true insights and getting to creative alternatives and new solutions may be painfully slow, if not interminable. By themselves, spreadsheets cannot model the more complex financial and strategic interrelationships that entrepreneurs need to grasp. And for the board of directors, failure to get this information would be fatal and any delay would mean too little and too late. Such a weakness in financial know-how becomes life threatening for entrepreneurs such as those noted earlier, when it comes to anticipating the financial and risk-reward consequences of their business decisions. During a financial crisis, such a weakness can make an already dismal situation worse.

Time and again, the financially fluent and skillful entrepreneurs push what would otherwise be an average company toward and even beyond the brink of greatness. Clearly, financially knowledgeable CEOs enjoy a secret competitive weapon that can yield a decisive edge over less financially skilled entrepreneurs.

Critical Financing Issues

Exhibit 12.2 illustrates the central issues in entrepreneurial finance. These include the creation of value, the slicing and dividing of the value pie among those who have a stake or have participated in the venture, and the handling of the risks inherent in the venture. Developing financing and fund-raising strategies, knowing what alternatives are available, and obtaining funding are tasks vital to the survival and success of most higher potential ventures.

As a result, entrepreneurs face certain critical issues and problems, which bear on the financing of entrepreneurial ventures, such as:

- *Creating value.* Who are the constituencies for whom value must be created or added to achieve a positive cash flow and to develop harvest options?

EXHIBIT 12.2

Central Issues in Entrepreneurial Finance

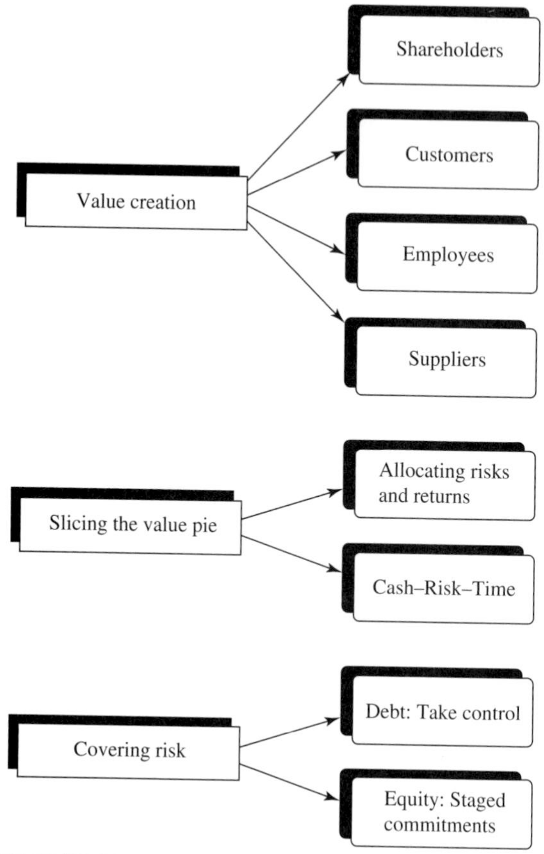

- *Slicing the value pie.* How are deals, both for startups and for the purchases of existing ventures, structured and valued, and what are the critical tax consequences of different venture structures? What is the legal process and what are the key issues involved in raising outside risk capital?
- *Selling the idea.* How do entrepreneurs make effective presentations of their business plans to financing and other sources? What are some of the nastier pitfalls, minefields, and hazards that need to be anticipated, prepared for, and responded to? How critical and sensitive is timing in each of these areas?
- *Covering risk.* How much money is needed to start, acquire, or expand the business, and when, where, and how can it be obtained on acceptable terms? What sources of risk and venture capital financing—equity, debt, and other innovative types—are available, and how is appropriate financing negotiated and obtained?
- Who are the financial contacts and networks that need to be accessed and developed?
- How do successful entrepreneurs marshal the necessary financial resources and other financial equivalents to seize and execute opportunities, and what pitfalls do they manage to avoid, and how?
- Can a staged approach to resource acquisition mitigate risk and increase return?

A clear understanding of the financing requirements is especially vital for new and emerging companies because new ventures go through financial 'hell' compared to existing firms, both smaller and larger, that have a customer base and revenue stream. In the early going, new firms are gluttons for capital, yet are usually not very debt-worthy. To make matters worse, the faster they grow, the more gluttonous is their appetite for cash.

This phenomenon is best illustrated in Exhibit 12.3 where loss as a percentage of initial equity is plotted against time.[4] The shaded area represents the cumulative cash flow of 157 companies from their inception. For these firms, it took 30 months to achieve operating breakeven and 75 months (or going into the *seventh* year) to recover the initial equity. As can be seen from the illustration, *cash goes out for a long time before it starts to come in.* This phenomenon is at the heart of the financing challenges facing new and emerging companies.

Entrepreneurial Finance: The Owner's Perspective

If an entrepreneur who has had responsibility for financing in a large established company and in a private emerging firm is asked whether there are differences between the two, the person asking will get an earful. While there is some common ground, there are both stark and subtle differences, both in theory and in practice, between entrepreneurial finance as practiced in higher potential ventures and corporate or administrative finance, which usually occurs in larger, publicly traded companies. Further, there are important limits to some financial theories as applied to new ventures.

Students and practitioners of entrepreneurial finance have always been dubious about the reliability and relevance of much of so-called modern finance theory, including the capital asset pricing model

[4] Special appreciation is due to Bert Twaalfhoven, founder and chairman of Indivers, the Dutch firm that compiled this summary and that owns the firm on which the chart is based. Mr. Twaalfhoven is also a key figure in the promotion of entrepreneurship in Europe.

EXHIBIT 12.3

Initial Losses by Small New Ventures

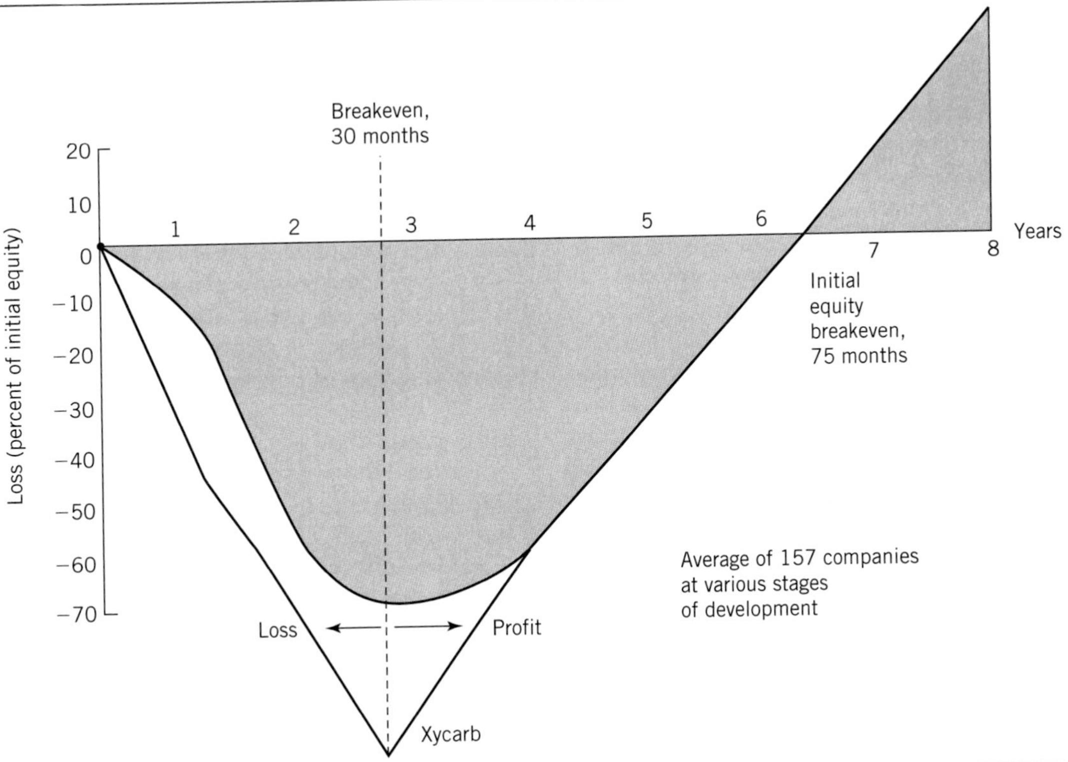

Source: Indivers.

(CAPM), beta, and so on.[5] Apparently, this skepticism is gaining support from a most surprising source, corporate finance theorists. As reported in a *Harvard Business Review* article:

> One of the strongest attacks is coming from a man who helped launch modern finance, University of Chicago Professor Eugene Fama. His research has cast doubt on the validity of a widely used measure of stock volatility: beta. A second group of critics is looking for a new financial paradigm; they believe it will emerge from the study of nonlinear dynamics and chaos theory. A third group, however, eschews the scientific approach altogether, arguing that investors aren't always rational and that managers' constant focus on the markets is ruining corporate America. In their view, the highly fragmented U.S. financial markets do a poor job of allocating capital and keeping tabs on management.[6]

Challenging further the basic assumptions of corporate finance, the author continued: "These three concepts, the efficient market hypothesis, portfolio theory, and CAPM, have had a profound impact on how the financial markets relate to the companies they seek to value. . . . They have derailed and blessed countless investment projects."[7] Nancy Nichols, concluded that "despite tidy theories, there may be no single answer in a global economy."[8]

It is especially noteworthy that even the most prestigious of modern finance theorists, prominent Nobel laureate Robert Merton of Harvard University, may have a lot to learn. His works and theories of finance were the basis for Long Term Capital Management, Inc. The total collapse of that firm in the late 1990s threatened to topple the entire financial system.

Acquiring knowledge of the limits of financial theories, of differences in the domain of entrepreneurial finance, and of understanding the implications is a core task for entrepreneurs. To begin to appreciate the character and flavor of these limits and differences, consider the following sampling.

Cash Flow and Cash Cash flow and cash are the king and queen of entrepreneurial finance.

[5] See Paul A. Gompers and William A. Sahlman, *Entrepreneurial Finance* (New York: John Wiley & Sons, 2002).
[6] Nancy A. Nichols, "In Question: Efficient? Chaotic? What's the New Finance?" *Harvard Business Review*, March–April 1993, p. 50.
[7] Ibid., p. 52.
[8] Ibid., p. 60.

Accrual-based accounting, earnings per share, or creative and aggressive use of the tax codes and rules of the Securities and Exchange Commission are not. Just ask Enron!

Time and Timing Financing alternatives for the financial health of an enterprise are often more sensitive to, or vulnerable to, the time dimension. In entrepreneurial finance, time for critical financing moves often is shorter and more compressed, the optimum timing of these moves changes more rapidly, and financing moves are subject to wider, more volatile swings from lows to highs and back.

Capital Markets Capital markets for more than 95 percent of the financing of private entrepreneurial ventures are relatively imperfect, in that they are frequently inaccessible, unorganized, and often invisible. Virtually all the underlying characteristics and assumptions that dominate such popular financial theories and models as the capital asset pricing model simply do not apply, even up to the point of a public offering for a small company. In reality, there are so many and such significant information, knowledge, and market gaps and asymmetries that the rational, perfect market models suffer enormous limitations.

Emphasis Capital is one of the least important factors in the success of higher potential ventures. Rather, higher potential entrepreneurs seek not only the best deal but also the backer who will provide the most value in terms of know-how, wisdom, counsel, and help. In addition, higher potential entrepreneurs invariably opt for the value added (beyond money), rather than just the best deal or share price.

Strategies for Raising Capital Strategies that optimize or maximize the amount of money raised can actually increase risk in new and emerging companies, rather than lower it. Thus, the concept of "staged capital commitments," whereby money is committed for a 3- to 18-month phase and is followed by subsequent commitments based on results and promise, is a prevalent practice among venture capitalists and other investors in higher potential ventures. Similarly, wise entrepreneurs may refuse excess capital when the valuation is less attractive and when they believe that valuation will rise substantially.

Downside Consequences Consequences of financial strategies and decisions are eminently more personal and emotional for the owners of new and emerging ventures than for the managements of large companies. The downside consequences for such entrepreneurs of running out of cash or failing are monumental and relatively catastrophic, since personal guarantees of bank or other loans are common. Contrast these situations with that of the president of RJR Nabisco. His bonus for signing and his five-year employment package guarantees him a total of $25 million, and he could earn substantially more based on his performance. However, even if he does a mediocre or lousy job, his downside is $25 million.

Risk-Reward Relationships While the high-risk/high-reward and low-risk/low-reward relationship (a so-called law of economics and finance) works fairly well in efficient, mature, and relatively perfect capital markets (e.g., those with money market accounts, deposits in savings and loan institutions, widely held and traded stocks and bonds, certificates of deposit), the opposite occurs too often in entrepreneurial finance to permit much comfort with this law. Some of the most profitable, highest return venture investments have been quite low-risk propositions from the outset. Many leveraged buyouts using extreme leverage are probably much more risky than many startups. Yet, the way the capital markets price these deals is just the reverse. The reasons are anchored in the second and third points noted above—timing and the asymmetries and imperfections of the capital markets for deals. Entrepreneurs or investors who create or recognize lower risk/very high-yield business propositions, before others jump on the Brink's truck, will defy the laws of economics and finance. The recent bankruptcies of Kmart and Enron illustrate this point.

Valuation Methods Established company valuation methods, such as those based on discounted cash flow models used in Wall Street megadeals, seem to favor the seller, rather than the buyer, of private emerging entrepreneurial companies. A seller loves to see a recent MBA or investment banking firm alumnus or alumna show up with an HP calculator or the latest laptop and then proceed to develop "the 10-year discounted cash flow stream." The assumptions normally made and the mind-set behind them are irrelevant or grossly misleading for valuation of smaller private firms because of dynamic and erratic historical and prospective growth curves.

Conventional Financial Ratios Current financial ratios are misleading when applied to most private entrepreneurial companies. For one thing, entrepreneurs often own more than one company at once and move cash and assets from one to another. For example, an entrepreneur may own real estate and equipment in one entity and lease it to another company. Use of different fiscal years compounds the difficulty of interpreting what the balance sheet really means and the possibilities for aggressive tax avoidance. Further, many of the most important value and equity builders in the business are off the balance sheet or are hidden assets: the excellent management team; the best scientist, technician, or designer; know-how and business relationships that cannot be bought or sold, let alone valued for the balance sheet.

Goals Creating value over the long term, rather than maximizing quarterly earnings, is a prevalent mind-set and strategy among highly successful entrepreneurs. Since profit is more than just the bottom line, financial strategies are geared to build value, often at the expense of short-term earnings. The growth required to build value often is heavily self-financed, thereby eroding possible accounting earnings.

Determining Capital Requirements

How much money does my venture need? When is it needed? How long will it last? Where and from whom can it be raised? How should this process be orchestrated and managed? These are vital questions to any entrepreneur at any stage in the development of a company. These questions are answered in the next two sections.

Financial Strategy Framework

The financial strategy framework shown in Exhibit 12.4 is a way to begin crafting financial and fund-raising strategies.[9] The exhibit provides a flow and logic with which an otherwise confusing task can be attacked. *The opportunity leads and drives the business strategy, which in turn drives the financial requirements, the sources and deal structures, and the financial strategy.* (Again, until this part of the exercise is well-defined, developing spreadsheets and "playing with the numbers" is just that—playing.)

Once an entrepreneur has defined the core of the market opportunity and the strategy for seizing it (of course, these may change, even dramatically), he or she can begin to examine the financial requirements in terms of (1) asset needs (for startup or for expansion facilities, equipment, research and development, and other apparently onetime expenditures) and (2) operating needs (i.e., working capital for operations). This

[9] This framework was developed for the Financing Entrepreneurial Ventures course at Babson College and has been used in the Entrepreneurial Finance course at the Harvard Business School.

EXHIBIT 12.4

Financial Strategy Framework

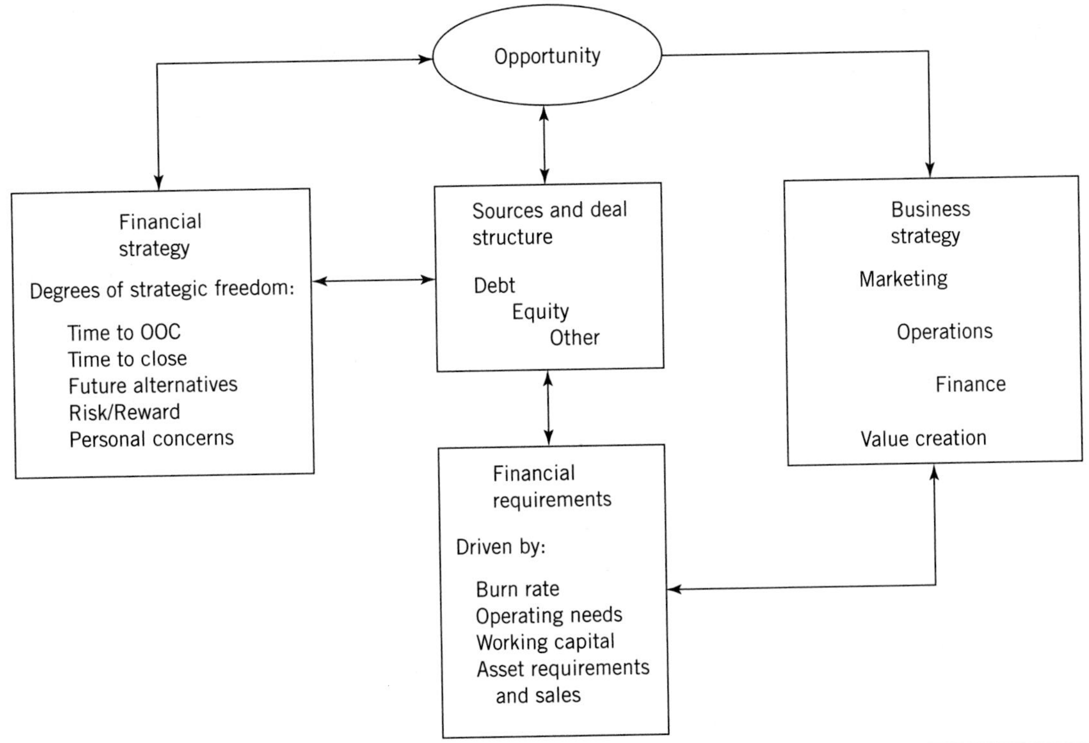

framework leaves ample room for crafting a financial strategy, for creatively identifying sources, for devising a fund-raising plan, and for structuring deals.

Each *fund-raising strategy,* along with its accompanying deal structure, commits the company to actions that incur actual and real-time costs and may enhance or inhibit future financing options. Similarly, each *source* has particular requirements and costs—both apparent and hidden—that carry implications for both financial strategy and financial requirements. The premise is that successful entrepreneurs are aware of potentially punishing situations, and that they are careful to "sweat the details" and proceed with a certain degree of wariness as they evaluate, select, negotiate, and craft business relationships with potential funding sources. In doing so, they are more likely to find the right sources, at the right time, and on the right terms and conditions. They are also more likely to avoid potential mismatches, costly sidetracking for the wrong sources, and the disastrous marriage to these sources that might follow.

Certain changes in the financial climate, such as the aftershocks felt after March 2000 and October 1987, can cause repercussions across financial markets and institutions serving smaller companies. These take the form of greater caution by both lenders and investors as they seek to increase their protection against risk. When the financial climate becomes harsher, an entrepreneur's capacity to devise financing strategies and to effectively deal with financing sources can be stretched to the limit and beyond. Also, certain lures of cash that come in unsuspecting ways turn out to be a punch in the wallet. (The next chapter covers some of these potentially fatal lures and some of the issues and considerations needed to recognize and avoid these traps while devising a fund-raising strategy and evaluating and negotiating with different sources.)

Free Cash Flow: Burn Rate, OOC, and TTC

The core concept in determining the external financing requirements of the venture is free cash flow. Three vital corollaries are the burn rate (projected or actual), time to OOC (when will the company be out of cash), and TTC (or the time to close the financing and have the check clear). These have a major impact on the entrepreneur's choices and relative bargaining power with various sources of equity and debt capital, which is represented in Exhibit 12.5. Chapter 14 addresses the details of deal structuring, terms, conditions, and covenants.

The message is clear: If you are out of cash in 90 days or less, you are at a major disadvantage. OOC even in six months is perilously soon. But if you have a year or more, the options, terms, price, and covenants that you will be able to negotiate will improve dramatically. The implication is clear: Ideally, raise money when you do not need it.

The cash flow generated by a company or project is defined as follows:

	Earnings before interest and taxes (EBIT)
Less	Tax exposure (tax rate times EBIT)
Plus	Depreciation, amortization, and other noncash charges
Less	Increase in operating working capital
Less	Capital expenditures

EXHIBIT 12.5

Entrepreneur's Bargaining Power Based on Time to OOC

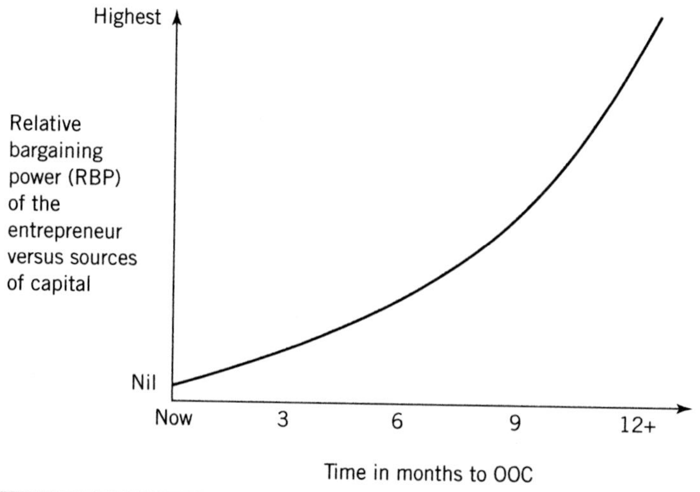

Economists call this result free cash flow. The definition takes into account the benefits of investing, the income generated, *and* the cost of investing, the amount of investment in working capital and plant and equipment required to generate a given level of sales and net income.

The definition can fruitfully be refined further. Operating working capital is defined as:

	Transactions cash balances
Plus	Accounts receivable
Plus	Inventory
Plus	Other operating current assets (e.g., prepaid expenses)
Less	Accounts payable
Less	Taxes payable
Less	Other operating current liabilities (e.g., accrued expenses)

Finally, this expanded definition can be collapsed into a simpler one:[10]

	Earnings before interest but after taxes (EBIAT)
Less	Increase in net total operating capital (FA + WC)

where the increase in net total operating capital is defined as:

	Increase in operating working capital
Plus	Increase in net fixed assets

Crafting Financial and Fund-Raising Strategies

Critical Variables

When financing is needed, a number of factors affect the availability of the various types of financing, and their suitability and cost:

- Accomplishments and performance to date.
- Investor's perceived risk.
- Industry and technology.
- Venture upside potential and anticipated exit timing.
- Venture anticipated growth rate.
- Venture age and stage of development.
- Investor's required rate of return or internal rate of return.
- Amount of capital required and prior valuations of the venture.
- Founders' goals regarding growth, control, liquidity, and harvesting.
- Relative bargaining positions.
- Investor's required terms and covenants.

Numerous other factors, especially an investor's or lender's view of the quality of a business opportunity and the management team, will also play a part in a decision to invest in or lend to a firm.

Generally, a company's operations can be financed through debt and some form of equity financing.[11] Moreover, it is generally believed that a new or existing business needs to obtain both equity and debt financing if it is to have a sound financial foundation for growth without excessive dilution of the entrepreneur's equity.

Short-term debt (i.e., debt incurred for one year or less) usually is used by a business for working capital and is repaid out of the proceeds of its sales. Longer-term borrowings (i.e., term loans of one to five years or long-term loans maturing in more than five years) are used for working capital and/or to finance the purchase of property or equipment that serve as collateral for the loan. Equity financing is used to fill the nonbankable gaps, preserve ownership, and lower the risk of loan defaults.

However, a new venture just starting operations will have difficulty obtaining either short-term or longer-term bank debt without a substantial cushion of equity financing or long-term debt that is subordinated or junior to all bank debt.[12] As far as a lender is concerned, a startup has little proven capability to generate sales, profits, and cash to pay off short-term debt and even less ability to sustain profitable operations over a number of years and retire long-term debt. Even the underlying protection provided by a venture's assets used as loan collateral may be insufficient to obtain bank loans. Asset values can erode with time; in the absence of adequate equity capital and good management, they may provide little real loan security to a bank.[13]

A bank may lend money to a startup to some maximum debt-to-equity ratio. As a rough rule, a startup may be able to obtain debt for working capital purposes that is equal to its equity and subordinated

[10] This section is drawn directly from "Note on Free Cash Flow Valuation Models," HBS 288-023, pp. 2–3.

[11] In addition to the purchase of common stock, equity financing is meant to include the purchase of both stock and subordinated debt, or subordinated debt with stock conversion features or warrants to purchase stock.

[12] For lending purposes, commercial banks regard such subordinated debt as equity. Venture capital investors normally subordinate their business loans to the loans provided by the bank or other financial institutions.

[13] The bank loan defaults by the real estate investment trusts (REITs) in 1975 and 1989–91 are examples of the failure of assets to provide protection in the absence of sound management and adequate equity capital.

debt. A startup can also obtain loans through such avenues as the Small Business Administration, manufacturers and suppliers, or leasing.

An existing business seeking expansion capital or funds for a temporary use has a much easier job obtaining both debt and equity. Sources such as banks, professional investors, and leasing and finance companies often will seek out such companies and regard them as important customers for secured and unsecured short-term loans or as good investment prospects. Furthermore, an existing and expanding business will find it easier to raise equity capital from private or institutional sources and to raise it on better terms than the startup.

Awareness of criteria used by various sources of financing, whether for debt, equity, or some combination of the two, that are available for a particular situation is central to devise a time-effective and cost-effective search for capital.

Financial Life Cycles

One useful way to begin identifying equity financing alternatives, and when and if certain alternatives are available, is to consider what can be called the financial life cycle of firms. Exhibit 12.6 shows the types of capital available over time for different types of firms at different stages of development (i.e., as indicated by different sales levels).[14] It also summarizes, at different stages of development (research and development, startup, early growth, rapid growth, and exit), the principal sources of risk capital and costs of risk capital.

As can be seen in the exhibit, sources have different preferences and practices, including how much money they will provide, when in a company's life cycle they will invest, and the cost of the capital or expected annual rate of return they are seeking. The available sources of capital change dramatically for companies at different stages and rates of growth, and there will be variations in different parts of the country.

Many of the sources of equity are not available until a company progresses beyond the earlier stages of its growth. Some sources available to early-stage companies, especially personal sources, friends, and other informal investors or angels, will be insufficient to meet the financing requirements generated in later stages if the company continues to grow successfully.

Another key factor affecting the availability of financing is the upside potential of a company. Of the 3 million-plus new businesses of all kinds expected to be launched in the United States in 2006, probably 5 percent or less will achieve the growth and sales levels of high potential firms. Foundation firms will total about 8 percent to 12 percent of all new firms, which will grow more slowly but exceed $1 million in sales and may grow to $5 million to $15 million. Remaining are the traditional, stable lifestyle firms. High potential firms (those that grow rapidly and are likely to exceed $20 million to $25 million or more in sales) are strong prospects for a public offering and have the widest array of financing alternatives, including combinations of debt and equity and other alternatives (which are noted later), while foundation firms have fewer, and lifestyle firms are limited to the personal resources of their founders and whatever net worth or collateral they can accumulate.

In general, investors believe the younger the company, the more risky the investment. This is a variation of the old saying in the venture capital business: The lemons ripen in two-and-a-half years, but the plums take seven or eight.

While the timeline and dollar limits shown are only guidelines, they do reflect how these money sources view the riskiness, and thus the required rate of return, of companies at various stages of development.

Investor Preferences

Precise practices of investors or lenders may vary between individual investors or lenders in a given category, may change with the current market conditions, and may vary in different areas of the country from time to time. Identifying realistic sources and developing a fund-raising strategy to tap them depend upon knowing what kinds of investments investors or lenders are seeking. While the stage, amount, and return guidelines noted in Exhibit 12.6 can help, doing the appropriate homework in advance on specific investor or lender preferences can save months of wild-goose chases and personal cash, while significantly increasing the odds of successfully raising funds on acceptable terms.

Internet Impact: Opportunity

International Finance and Trade

Like the global supply chains it has already fostered, the Internet has dramatically improved the facilitation and movement of financial instruments and

[14] William H. Wetzel, Jr., of the University of New Hampshire originally showed the different types of equity capital that are available to three types of companies. The exhibit is based on a chart by Wetzel, which the authors have updated and modified. See William H. Wetzel, Jr., "The Cost of Availability of Credit and Risk Capital in New England," in *A Region's Struggling Savior: Small Business in New England,* ed. J. A. Timmons and D. E. Gumpert (Waltham, MA: Small Business Foundation of America, 1979).

EXHIBIT 12.6

Financing Life Cycles

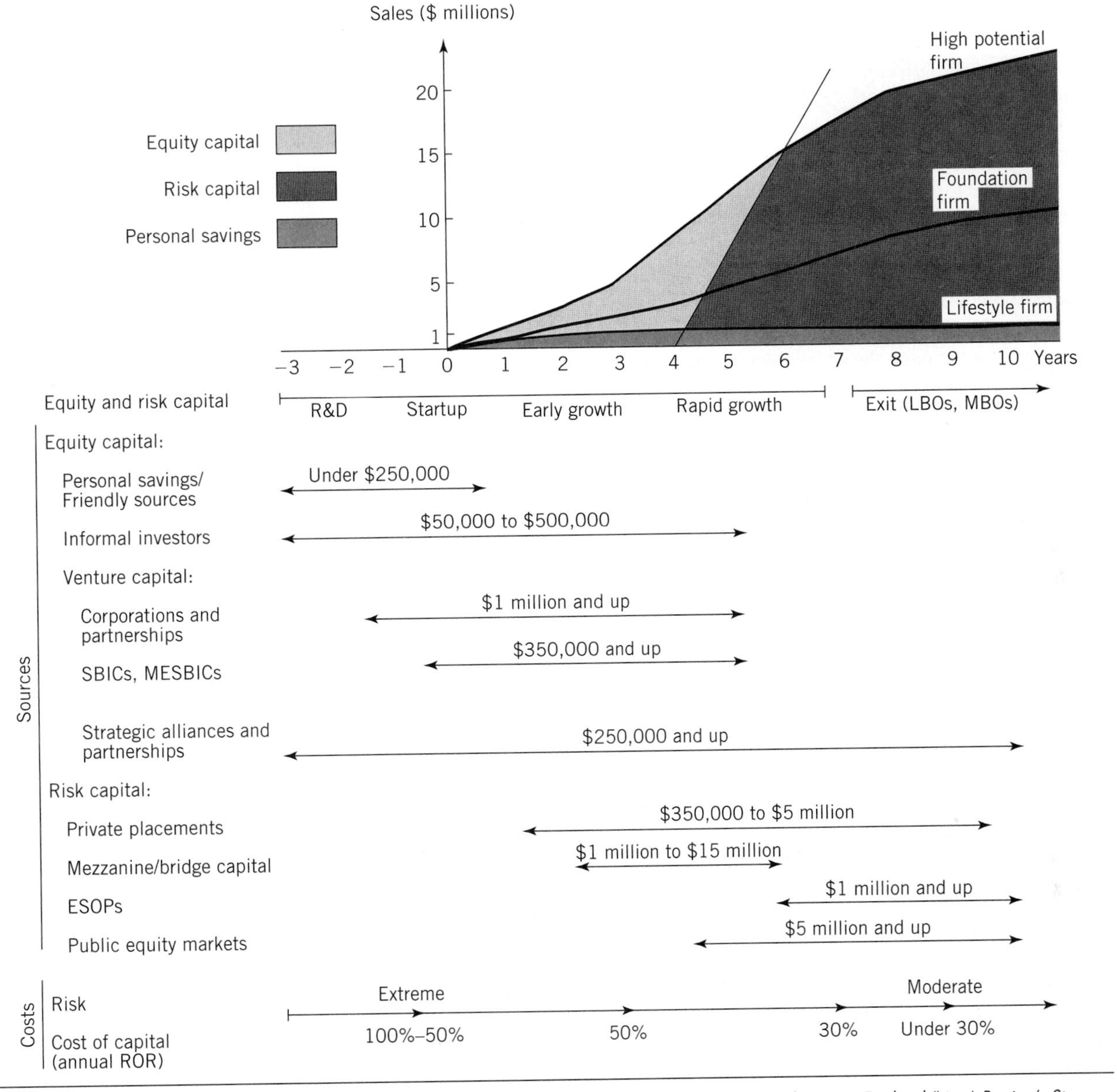

Source: Adapted and updated from W. H. Wetzel, Jr., "The Cost of Availability of Credit and Risk Capital in New England," in *A Region's Struggling Savior: Small Business in New England,* ed. J. A. Timmons, D. E. Gumpert (Waltham, MA: Smaller Business Foundation of America, 1979), p. 175.

trade documents. The result has been an acceleration of transactions and collections that have strengthened cash flow, boosted investment income, and bolstered balance sheets.

Major financial institutions now offer sophisticated trade portals that support document creation and transmission, making it possible for all parties to a transaction (exporter, importer, bank, freight forwarder, ocean carrier, cargo insurer) to exchange information through the same secure site. Letters of Credit (L/Cs), for example, frequently carry discrepancies such as misspelled names, inaccurate descriptions of products, and faulty dates. Amending those errors has typically meant additional bank fees and higher port charges (to cover delays), slower movement through overseas customs, and the possibility of failing to perform within the legal timetable of the L/C. Electronic trade documentation helps avoid discrepancies in the first place, and supports quick and easy corrections when needed.

In a similar way, the U.S. Export-Import Bank has leveraged the speed and ease of the Internet to structure stand-alone deals between their approved exporters and large finance companies that in the past worked only with regular clients. This is giving first-time and early-stage trade ventures that meet Ex-Im Bank's credit standards access to major suppliers of trade credit and insurance.

Chapter Summary

1. Cash is king and queen. Happiness is a positive cash flow. More cash is preferred to less cash. Cash sooner is preferred to cash later. Less risky cash is preferred to more risky cash.
2. Financial know-how, issues, and analysis are often the entrepreneurs' Achilles' heels.
3. Entrepreneurial finance is the art and science of quantifying value creation, slicing the value pie, and managing and covering financial risk.
4. Determining capital requirements, crafting financial and fund-raising strategies, and managing and orchestrating the financial process are critical to new venture success.
5. Harvest strategies are as important to the entrepreneurial process as value creation itself. Value that is unrealized may have no value.

Study Questions

1. Define the following and explain why they are important: burn rate, fume date, free cash flow, OOC, TTC, financial management myopia, spreadsheet mirage.
2. Why is entrepreneurial finance simultaneously both the least and most important part of the entrepreneurial process? Explain this paradox.
3. What factors affect the availability, suitability, and cost of various types of financing? Why are these factors critical?
4. What is meant by free cash flow, and why do entrepreneurs need to understand this?
5. Why do financially savvy entrepreneurs ask the financial and strategic questions in Exhibit 12.1? Can you answer these questions for your venture?

Internet Resources for Chapter 12

http://www.entreworld.org *Kauffman Foundation resources*

http://www.exim.gov *Export-Import Bank of the United States*

http://www.businessfinance.com *Business funding directory and resources*

http://www.opic.gov *The Overseas Private Investment Corporation is a U.S. government agency that helps businesses invest overseas*

http://www.sba.gov/financing/sbaloan/7a.html *The SBA's primary lending program*

http://www.sba.gov/financing/sbaloan/microloans.html *Micro loans up to $35,000 via community-based lenders*

http://www.ita.doc.gov *International Trade Administration*

http://www.export.gov *Online trade resources and one-on-one assistance for new and established international ventures*

MIND STRETCHERS

Have you considered?

1. To what extent might you be suffering from financial myopia and spreadsheet mirage?
2. People who believe that you first have to have money, in large amounts, to make money are naive and ignorant. Why is this so? Do you agree?
3. Who do you need to get to know well to strengthen the entrepreneurial finance know-how on your team?

Case

Midwest Lighting, Inc.

Preparation Questions

1. Evaluate the company. How much do you believe the company is worth? Bring to class a written bid of how much you would pay for it if you were Scott and Peterson.
2. What should they do to resolve the ownership situation?
3. How would you finance the purchase of the company?
4. Assume you do purchase the company: What specific actions would you plan to take on the first day? By the end of the first week? By the end of six months? Explain how and why.

Jack Peterson was discouraged by the continuing conflicts with his partner, David Scott, and had sought advice on how to remedy the situation from friends and associates as early as 1996. By 2005 Jack had begun to believe that he and David had just grown too far apart to continue together. Jack had to find a mutually agreeable way to accomplish a separation. One alternative was for one partner to buy the other out, but they would first have to agree on this and find an acceptable method. David seemed to have no interest in such an arrangement.

Throughout 2004, the differences between the partners had grown. The vacillations in leadership were disruptive to the operation and made the employees very uncomfortable.

By early 2005, the situation was growing unbearable. Jack recalled the executive committee's annual planning meeting in January:

> It was a total disaster. There were loud arguments and violent disagreements. It was so bad that no one wanted to ever participate in another meeting. We were all miserable.
>
> What was so difficult was that each of us truly thought he was right. On various occasions other people in the company would support each of our positions. These were normally honest differences of opinion, but politics also started to enter in.

Company Description

Midwest Lighting, Inc. (MLI), manufactured custom-engineered fluorescent lighting fixtures used for commercial and institutional applications. Sales in 2005 were approximately $5.5 million with profits of just over $144,000.

Most sales are for standard items within the nine major lines of products designed and offered by the company. Ten percent of sales were completely custom-designed or custom-built fixtures, and 15 percent of orders were for slightly modified versions of a standard product. In 2005, CFI shipped 82,500 fixtures. Although individual orders ranged from one unit to over 2,000 units, the average order size is approximately 15–20 fixtures. Modified and custom-designed fixtures averaged about 25 per order. Jack Peterson, MLI president, described their market position:

> Our product-marketing strategy is to try to solve lighting problems for architects and engineers. We design products which are architecturally styled for specific types of building constructions. If an architect has an unusual lighting problem, we design a special fixture to fit his needs. Or if he designs a lighting fixture, we build it to his specifications. We try to find products that satisfy particular lighting needs that are not filled by the giant fixture manufacturers. We look for niches in the marketplace.
>
> Having the right product to fit the architect's particular needs is the most important thing to our customer. Second is the relationship that the architect, the consulting engineer, or the lighting designer has with the people who are representing us. The construction business is such that the architect, engineer, contractor, distributor, and manufacturer all have to work as a team together on a specified project to ensure its successful completion. The architect makes a lot of mistakes in every building he designs, unless he just designs the same one over and over. Consequently, there's a lot of trading that goes on during the construction of a building, and everybody's got to give and take a little to get the job done. Then the owner usually gets a satisfactory job and the contractors and manufacturers make a fair profit. It requires a cooperative effort.
>
> Most of our bids for orders are probably compared with bids from half a dozen other firms across the country. Since a higher percentage of our orders are for premium-priced products, we are not as price sensitive as producers of more commonplace lighting fixtures. It is difficult for a small firm to compete in that market. As many as 30 companies might bid on one standard fixture job.

MLI owned its own modern manufacturing facility, located outside Pontiac, Michigan. Production consisted of stamping, cutting, and forming sheet metal; painting; and assembling the fixture with the electrical components which were purchased from outside suppliers. The company employed a total of 130 workers, with 42 people in sales, engineering, and administration, and another 88 in production and assembly.

The company sold nationwide through regional distributors to contractors and architects for new buildings and renovations. Prior to 2003, MLI sold primarily to a regional market. At that time, marketing activities were

EXHIBIT A

Historical Performance

Year	Net Sales	Profit after Tax	No. of Fixtures Shipped	Total Employees	Hourly Employees
2005	$5,515,239	$144,011	82,500	130	88
2004	4,466,974	126,266	72,500	118	73
2003	3,717,225	133,160	65,000	103	65
2002	3,669,651	79,270	67,500	103	63

broadened geographically. This was the primary reason that sales had been increasing over the last few years—even during a weak construction market. (See *Exhibit A* for historical sales, earnings, unit sales, and employment.)

Background

Midwest Lighting, Inc., was formed in Flint, Michigan, in 1956 by Daniel Peterson and Julian Walters. Each owned one-half of the company. Peterson was responsible for finance and engineering and Walters for sales and design. They subcontracted all manufacturing for the lighting systems they sold.

After several years, differences in personal work habits led Peterson to buy out Walters' interest. Daniel Peterson then brought in Richard Scott as his new partner. Scott had been one of his sheet metal subcontractors. Richard Scott became president and Daniel Peterson treasurer. Ownership was split so that Peterson retained a few shares more than half and all voting control because of his prior experience with the company.

In 1960, MLI began manufacturing and moved its operations to a multifloor 50,000-square-foot plant also located in Flint. The company grew and was quite profitable over the next decade. Peterson and Scott were quite satisfied with the earnings they had amassed during this period and were content to let the company remain at a steady level of about $1.2 million in sales and about $18,000 in profit after taxes.

Daniel Peterson's son, Jack, joined MLI as a salesman in 1983 after graduating from MIT and then Colorado Business School. Richard Scott's son, David, who was a graduate of Trinity College, became an MLI salesman in 1984 when he was discharged from the service. The two sons were acquaintances from occasional gatherings as they were growing up but had not been close friends.

In 1986, Daniel Peterson had a heart attack and withdrew from management of the business. Although he remained an interested observer and sometime advisor to his son, Daniel was inactive in company affairs after this time. Richard Scott assumed overall responsibility for the management of the company.

Jack Peterson moved inside to learn about other parts of the company in 1987. His first work assignments were in manufacturing and sales service. David Scott joined his father in the manufacturing area a year later. Jack Peterson became sales manager, David Scott became manufacturing manager, and, at Richard Scott's suggestion, another person was added as financial manager. These three shared responsibility for running the company and worked well together, but major decisions were still reserved for Richard Scott, who spent less and less time in the office.

As the new group began revitalizing the company, a number of employees who had not been productive and were not responding to change were given early retirement or asked to leave. When the man who had been Richard Scott's chief aide could not work with the three younger managers, they ultimately decided he had to be discharged. Richard Scott became so angry that he rarely entered the plant again.

For several years the three managers guided the company as a team. However, there were some spirited discussions over the basic strategic view of the company. As sales manager, Jack Peterson pressed for responding to special customer needs. This, he felt, would be their strongest market niche. David Scott argued for smooth production flows and less disruption. He felt they could compete well in the "semistandard" market.

In 1988, Jack Peterson began to work with an individual in forming a company in the computer field. The company rented extra space from MLI, and MLI provided management and administrative support, helping the new company with bidding and keeping track of contracts. Although David Scott was not active in this company, Jack split his partial ownership in this new company with David because they were partners, and because Jack was spending time away from MLI with the computer company.

In 1989, the fathers moved to restructure the company's ownership to reflect the de facto changes in management. The fathers converted their ownership to nonvoting class A stock, and then each transferred 44 percent of their nonvoting stock to their sons. Daniel Peterson decided to relinquish his voting control at that time in an effort to help things work as the new generation took over. Accordingly, Jack Peterson and David Scott were each issued 50 percent of the class B voting shares.

Due to the demands associated with the startup of the computer company, this new effort began to weaken the relationship between Jack and David. At the same time, David and the financial manager began to have strong disagreements. These seemed to arise primarily from errors in cost analysis, which led the financial manager to question some of David's decisions. There were also differences of opinion over relations with the workforce and consistency of policy. David preferred to control the manufacturing operation in his own way. Jack felt David could be more consistent, less arbitrary, and more supportive of the workforce. When the computer company was sold in 1995, the financial manager joined it as treasurer and resigned from MLI.

Growing Conflict

The departure of the financial manager led to a worsening of the relationship between Jack and David. Jack had been made company president in 1990. Jack recalled the decision:

> Richard Scott had resigned as president and the three of us were sitting around talking about who should be president. David Scott finally said, "I think you should be it." And I said, "Okay."

Yet even after Jack became president, the three managers had really operated together as a team for major decisions. Now, Jack was upset that they had lost an excellent financial manager, someone critical to the operation (partially due, in his opinion, to the disagreements with David). Also, there was no longer a third opinion to help resolve conflicts. Although the financial manager was replaced with an old classmate of David's, the new manager became one of several middle-level managers who had been hired as the company grew.

The pressure of growth created more strains between Jack and David. Sales had reached $2.3 million and had begun to tax MLI's manufacturing capacity. Jack felt that some of the problems could be alleviated if David would change methods that had been acceptable during slacker periods but hindered intense production efforts. David had different views. Both, however, agreed to look for additional space.

The transition to a new factory outside Pontiac, Michigan, in 1997 eased the stresses between the partners. A major corporation had purchased an indirect competitor to obtain its product lines and sold MLI the 135,000-square-foot plant. MLI also entered into an agreement to manufacture some of the other company's light fixtures as a subcontractor. The plant was in poor condition, and David Scott took over the project of renovating it and continuing production of the other company's lines. That was also the year that Richard Scott had died. Although he had remained chairman of the board, he had generally been inactive in the company since 1988. Daniel and Jack Peterson and David Scott were now the only directors.

Jack Peterson remained in Flint running the MLI operation alone until such time as it became possible to consolidate the entire operation in Pontiac. Jack described this interlude:

> The next year was a sort of cooling-off period. David was immersed in the project with the new factory and I was busy with the continuing operation. David had always enjoyed projects of this sort and was quite satisfied with this arrangement.
>
> Then, in 1998, we hired a plant manager to run the Pontiac plant and David came back to work in Flint. By that time, of course, a lot of things had changed. All of Flint had been reporting to me. I had somewhat reshaped the operation and the people had gotten used to my management style, which was different from David's.
>
> David's reaction was to work primarily with the design and engineering people, but he really wasn't involved very much with the daily manufacturing anymore. He developed a lot of outside interests, business and recreation, that took up much of his time.
>
> I was very happy with the arrangement because it lessened the number of conflicts. But when he did come back, the disagreements that did rise would be worse. I guess I resented his attempts to change things when he only spent a small amount of his time in the company.
>
> Then, in 2000, we made the decision to sell the Flint plant and put the whole company in Pontiac. We were both involved in that. Most of the key people went with us. David and I were very active in pulling together the two groups, and in integrating the operations.
>
> That began a fairly good time. I was spending my time with the sales manager trying to change the company from a regional company to a national one and was helping to find new representatives all over the country. David Scott spent his time in the engineering, design, and manufacturing areas. There was plenty of extra capacity in the new plant, so things went quite smoothly. In particular, David did an excellent job in upgrading the quality standards of the production force we had acquired with the plant. This was critical for our line of products and our quality reputation.
>
> This move really absorbed us for almost two years. It just took us a long time to get people working together and to produce at the quality level and rate we wanted. We had purchased the plant for an excellent price with a lot of new equipment and had started deleting marginal product lines as we expanded nationally. The company became much more profitable.

During the company's expansion, a group of six people formed the operating team. David Scott concentrated on applications engineering for custom fixtures and new product design. In addition, there was a sales manager, financial manager, engineering manager, the plant manufacturing manager, and Jack Peterson. Disagreements began again. Jack recounted the problems:

> Our operating group would meet on a weekly or biweekly basis, whatever was necessary. Then we would have monthly executive committee meetings for broader planning issues. These became a disaster. David had reached the point where he didn't like much of anything that was going on in the company and was becoming very critical. I disagreed with him, as did the other managers on most occasions. Tempers often flared and David became more and more isolated.
>
> He and I also began to disagree over which topics we should discuss with the group. I felt that some areas were best discussed between the two of us, particularly matters concerning personnel, and that other matters should be left for stockholders meetings. The committee meetings were becoming real battles.

Search for a Solution

When Jack Peterson returned from a summer vacation in August 2005, he was greeted by a string of complaints from several of MLI's sales agents and also from some managers. Jack decided that the problem had to be resolved. Jack sought an intermediary:

> I knew that David and I weren't communicating and that I had to find a mediator David trusted. I had discussed this before with Allen Burke, our accountant. He was actually far more than our accountant. Allen is a partner with a Big Six accounting firm and is active in working with smaller companies. Allen was a boyhood friend who had grown up with David. I felt he had very high integrity and was very smart. David trusted him totally and Allen was probably one of David's major advisors about things.
>
> When I first talked to Burke in March, he basically said, "Well, you have problems in a marriage and you make it work. Go make it work, Jack." He wasn't going to listen much.
>
> Then in early September, I went back to say that it wasn't going to work anymore. I asked him for his help. Allen said that David had also seen him to complain about the problems, so Allen knew that the situation had become intolerable.

Both directly and through Burke, Jack pressured David to agree to a meeting to resolve the situation. Although David was also unhappy about their conflicts, he was hesitant to meet until he had thought through his options.

Jack felt that there were several principal reasons for David's reluctance to meet. Since they couldn't seem to solve their differences, the alternative of having one of them leave the company or become a silent partner glared as a possibility. Jack knew that David's only work experience was with MLI and was limited primarily to managing manufacturing operations he had known for years. Second, Jack thought that David was very uncertain about financial analysis, in which he had little training. Because he had not been directly involved in the financial operations, he was not aware of all the financial implications of his decisions. Jack felt that this made David's task of weighing the pros and cons of alternative courses of action much more difficult. Finally, there was the emotional tie to the company and the desire to avoid such a momentous decision.

As discussion began to result in the possibility that the partners would sell the company, David's reluctance waxed and waned. Just before Thanksgiving, David called Jack, who was sick at home, and said he had decided to fire the financial manager and become the treasurer of the company. David wanted to look at the figures for a year or so, and then he would be able to make a better decision. Jack felt that the financial manager was essential and could not be discharged. He thought that this was really more of an attempt to buy time. After some discussion, Jack convinced David that the financial manager should be retained.

After another month of give and take, Jack and David realized that they had no estimate of the value of the company if it were to be sold. Both felt that this might alter the attractiveness of the alternatives that each was considering.

Valuing the Company

Before making his decision, Jack reviewed the thinking he had done since first considering the idea of buying or selling the company. He began with the company's current position. With the serious discussions going on about the buyout agreement, preparation of the financial statements for 2005 had been accelerated and they were already completed. (These are shown, together with the results of 2004 and 2003, as *Exhibits B* and *C*.)

Jack had also begun developing the bank support he might need to fund a buyout. The company's banker indicated that he would lend Jack funds secured by his other personal assets if Jack was the buyer, but that since he had not worked with David, the bank would decline to finance an acquisition with David as the buyer. In addition, the bank would continue the company's existing line of credit, which was secured by MLI's cash and accounts receivable. The maximum that could be borrowed with this line was an amount equal to 100 percent of cash plus 75 percent of receivables. Both types of borrowing would be at 1 percent over the prime rate (then about 6 percent).

Jack worked with the financial manager to develop financial projections and valuation assessments. To be conservative, Jack had made the sales projections about 10 percent lower each year than he really thought they would achieve. Because fixed costs would not rise appreciably with modest increases in sales, any improvements in sales volume would directly increase profits. He felt he should consider how these various changes would impact his financing requirements and his assessment.

EXHIBIT B

Statement of Earnings

	Year Ended December 31		
	2005	**2004**	**2003**
Net Sales	$5,515,239	$4,466,974	$3,717,225
Cost of goods sold:			
Inventories at beginning of year	928,634	741,481	520,640
Purchases	1,999,283	1,594,581	1,387,226
Freight in	24,400	33,244	26,208
Direct labor	537,693	450,710	410,609
Manufacturing expenses	1,221,536	1,002,715	842,054
	4,711,545	3,822,731	3,186,736
Inventories at end of year	1,032,785	928,634	741,481
	3,678,760	2,894,098	2,445,255
Gross Profit	1,836,479	1,572,876	1,271,970
Product development expenses	164,683	161,011	127,874
Selling and administrative expenses	1,390,678	1,143,925	926,001
	1,555,360	1,304,936	1,053,875
Operating income	281,119	267,940	218,095
Other expense (income):			
Interest expense	70,324	47,238	40,520
Payments to retired employee	12,500	12,500	25,000
Miscellaneous	(1,154)	(1,939)	(7,741)
	81,670	57,799	57,779
Earnings before income taxes	199,449	210,141	160,316
Provision for income taxes	55,438	83,875	61,250
Earnings before extraordinary income	144,011	126,266	99,066
Extraordinary income—life insurance proceeds in excess of cash surrender value			34,094
Net earnings	$ 144,011	$ 126,266	$ 133,160
Earnings per share of common stock	$ 23.94	$ 20.99	$ 16.46

(continued)

EXHIBIT B (continued)

Statement of Earnings

	Year Ended December 31		
	2005	**2004**	**2003**
Assets			
Current Assets:			
Cash	$ 64,060	$ 4,723	$ 88,150
Accounts receivable:			
Customers	750,451	538,438	397,945
Refundable income taxes	28,751		
Other		2,845	6,611
	779,203	541,283	404,556
Less allowance for doubtful receivables	4,375	4,375	4,375
	774,828	536,908	400,181
Inventories			
Raw materials	364,738	324,438	346,340
Work in progress	668,048	604,196	395,141
	1,032,785	928,634	741,481
Prepaid insurance and other	17,760	25,168	32,588
Total current assets	1,889,433	1,495,431	1,262,400
Property, plant, and equipment:			
Buildings and improvements	426,783	407,108	368,913
Machinery and equipment	263,116	216,341	169,274
Motor vehicles	40,723	40,723	36,776
Office equipment	53,583	54,881	46,186
	784,204	719,053	621,149
Less accumulated depreciation	341,605	291,805	231,519
	442,599	427,248	389,630
Land	13,876	13,876	13,876
	456,475	441,124	403,506
Other assets:			
Cash surrender value of life insurance policies (less loans of $24,348 in 2004, $24,488 in 2003, and $24,290 in 2002)	102,473	96,519	90,711
Total assets	$2,448,380	$2,033,074	$1,756,618

EXHIBIT B (continued)

Statement of Earnings

	Year Ended December 31		
	2005	**2004**	**2003**
Liabilities and Stockholders' Equity			
Current liabilities			
Current maturities of long-term debt	15,230	13,198	11,250
Note payable; bank	406,250	250,000	
Note payable; officer		37,500	48,750
Accounts payable	486,978	369,010	391,504
Amount due for purchase of treasury stock			93,750
Accrued liabilities	193,238	145,168	111,196
Total current liabilities	1,101,695	814,875	656,450
Long-term debt	220,653	236,403	244,638
Stockholders' Equity	13		
Contributed capital:			
6% cumulative preferred stock; authorized 10,000 shares of $12.50 par value: issued 2,000 shares	25,000	25,000	25,000
Common stock:			
Class A (nonvoting)			
Authorized 15,000 shares of $12.50 par value: issued 8,305 shares	103,813	103,813	103,813
Class B (voting)			
Authorized 5,000 shares of $12.50 par value: issued and outstanding 20 shares	250	250	250
	129,063	129,063	129,063
Retained earnings	1,115,495	971,484	845,218
	1,244,558	1,100,546	974,280
Less shares reacquired and held in treasury, at cost: 2,000 shares 6% cumulative preferred stock	25,000	25,000	25,000
2,308 shares Class A common stock	93,750	93,750	93,750
	118,750	118,750	118,750
	1,125,808	981,796	855,530
Total liabilities and stockholders' equity	$2,448,155	$2,033,074	$1,756,618

(continued)

EXHIBIT B (continued)

Statement of Earnings

	Year Ended December 31		
	2005	**2004**	**2003**
Statement of Changes in Financial Position			
Working capital provided:			
From operations:			
Earnings before extraordinary income	144,011	126,266	99,066
Add depreciation not requiring outlay of working capital	69,973	63,323	55,334
Working capital provided from operation	213,984	189,589	154,400
Extraordinary income from life insurance proceeds			34,094
Capitalized equipment lease obligation		6,619	
Proceeds from cash surrender value of life insurance policies			64,846
Total working capital provided	213,984	196,208	253,340
Working capital applied:			
Additions to property, plant, and equipment	85,324	100,940	58,884
Increase in cash surrender value of life insurance policies; net of loans	5,954	5,808	7,443
Reduction of long-term debt	15,750	14,854	11,244
Purchase of 2,308 shares of nonvoting Class A stock			93,750
Total working capital applied	107,028	121,601	171,320
Increase in working capital	106,956	74,606	82,020
Net change in working capital consists of:			
Increase (decrease) in current assets:			
Cash	59,338	(83,428)	81,068
Accounts receivable: net	237,920	136,726	(4,435)
Inventories	104,151	187,153	220,841
Prepaid expenses	(7,633)	(7,420)	(6,225)
	393,776	233,031	291,249

EXHIBIT B (continued)

Statement of Earnings

	Year Ended December 31		
	2005	2004	2003
Increase (decrease) in current liabilities:			
Current portion of long-term debt	2,033	1,948	625
Note payable to bank	156,250	250,000	
Note payable to officer	(37,500)	(11,250)	
Accounts payable	117,968	(22,494)	130,104
Amount due for purchase of treasury stock		(93,750)	93,750
Contribution to profit-sharing trust			(25,000)
Accrued liabilities	48,070	33,971	9,751
Total	286,820	158,425	209,230
Increase in working capital	106,956	74,606	82,019
Working capital at beginning of year	680,556	605,950	523,931
Working capital at end of year	787,513	680,556	605,950

EXHIBIT C

Pro Forma Financial Statements

Historical Percentages			Projected Percentages				Thousands of Dollars		
2003	2004	2005	2006	2007	2008		2006	2007	2008
100.00	100.00	100.00	100.0	100.0	100.0	Net sales	$6,000	$6,375	$6,750
65.80	64.79	66.70	67.0	67.0	67.0	Cost of goods sold	4,020	4,271	4,523
34.22	35.21	33.30	33.0	33.0	33.0	Gross income	1,980	2,104	2,228
28.61	29.28	28.25	28*	28.0	28.0	Operating, general, and admin.	1,680	1,785	1,890
5.61	5.93	5.05	5.0	5.0	5.0	Profit before taxes	300	319	338
38.20	39.90	27.80	39†	39.0	39.0	Taxes†	121	124	131
						Net earnings	$ 179	$ 195	$ 206

*Projected percentages reflect an assumption that one partner will leave the company, and include a $30,000 cost reduction for the reduced salary requirements of a replacement.

†Effective tax rate.

Source: Income Statement Projections (prepared by Jack Peterson).

Jack also had sought out common valuation techniques. By looking through business periodicals and talking to friends, he found that these methods were not necessarily precise. Private manufacturing companies were most often valued at between 5 and 10 times after-tax earnings. Book net asset value also helped establish business worth, but was often adjusted to reflect differences between the market value of assets and the carrying values shown on balance sheets. For MLI, this was significant because it had obtained the new plant at an excellent price. Jack felt that it alone was probably worth $250,000 more than the stated book value.

To Jack, the variations in worth suggested by these different methods not only reflected the uncertainty of financial valuation techniques but also showed that a business had different values to different people. His estimate would have to incorporate other, more personal and subjective elements.

Personal Financial Considerations

One important consideration was what amount of personal resource each could and should put at risk. Both Jack and David were financially very conservative. Neither of them had ever had any personal long-term debt—even for a house. Jack could gather a maximum of $815,000 of assets outside of MLI that could be pledged to secure borrowing. His bank had already confirmed that he could borrow against those assets. However, for him to put his entire worth at risk to purchase David's share of the company, he would want to be very comfortable that the price was a reasonable one. Jack described his feelings: "You get very protective about what you have outside the company. The problem you always have with a small company is that most of your worth is tied up in it and you may have very little to fall back on if something goes sour. We both have never been big leverage buyers or anything like that."

Besides the element of increased financial risk, several other considerations tempered Jack's willingness to pay a very high price. Since they had moved to the plant in Pontiac, the one-hour commute to work had been a bit burdensome. It would be nice not to have that drive. Jack also felt that he had good experience in the overall management of a business and his engineering undergraduate degree and MBA gave him a certain amount of flexibility in the job market. This was important because, for both financial and personal reasons, he felt he would still have to work if he was no longer associated with MLI.

On the other hand, some factors encouraged Jack to be aggressive. His father cautioned him to be reasonable, but Jack knew his father would be very disappointed if he lost the company, and Jack himself had strong emotional ties to MLI. Jack also developed a point of view that in some ways he was buying the entire company, rather than just half: "I'm sitting here with a company that I have no control over because of our disagreements. If I buy the other half share, I'm buying the whole company—I'm buying peace of mind, I could do what I want, I wouldn't have to argue. So I'd buy a 'whole peace of mind' if I bought the other half of the company."

Finally, Jack considered his competitive position versus David. Although David had not accumulated the personal resources that Jack had, he had a brother-in-law with a private company that Jack knew had the ability to match Jack's resources and might be willing to back David financially. The brother-in-law would also be giving David financial advice in evaluating his alternatives and setting a value for the company. David also probably had fewer job prospects if he sold out. His undergraduate study was in liberal arts and his entire experience was within MLI. Jack also thought David might have some doubts about his ability to manage the company on his own.

The Meeting

After another conversation with Allen Burke, David Scott called Jack Peterson at home one evening: "Jack, I realize that you're right—I can't live in this tense environment any longer. I've spoken with Allen, and he has agreed to meet with both of us to discuss our situation, and to attempt to identify some possible solutions. Would Friday at 9:00 be convenient for you?"

13

Chapter Thirteen

Obtaining Venture and Growth Capital

Money is like a sixth sense without which you cannot make a complete use of the other five.

W. Somerset Maugham
Of Human Bondage

Results Expected

At the conclusion of this chapter, you will have:

1. Examined the capital markets food chain and its implications.
2. Identified informal and formal investment sources of equity capital.
3. Learned how to find, contact, and deal with equity investors.
4. Discovered how venture capital investors make decisions.
5. Analyzed "Forte Ventures," a case about an entrepreneur's fund-raising strategies to launch and grow a new private equity business at the worst possible time in the history of the U.S. venture capital industry.

The Capital Markets Food Chain

Consider the capital markets for equity as a "food chain," whose participants have increasing appetites in terms of the deal size they want to acquire (Exhibit 13.1). This framework can help entrepreneurs identify and appreciate the various sources of equity capital at various stages of the venture's development, the amount of capital they typically provide, and the portion of the company and share price one might expect should the company eventually have an initial public offering (IPO) or trade sale.

The bottom row in Exhibit 13.1 shows this ultimate progression from R&D stage to IPO, where the capital markets are typically willing to pay $12 to $18 per share for new issues of small companies. Obviously, these prices are lower when the so-called IPO window is tight or closed, as in 2001. Prices for the few offerings that do exist (1 to 3 per week versus more than 50 per week in June 1996) are $5 to $9 per share. In hot IPO periods, 1999 for instance, offering prices reached as high as $20 per share and more. Since the last edition, the IPO markets suffered a severe decline and were basically shut down in 2001 to mid-2003. The modest revival that began in late 2003 has continued into 2005. Still, although 91 venture-capital-backed companies went public in 2004—the most annually since 2000—that was just a fraction of the boom years of 1996 and 1999.

One of the toughest decisions for the founders is whether to give up equity, and implicitly control, to have a run at creating very significant value. The row, "% company owned at IPO," shows that by the time a company goes public, the founders may have sold 70 percent to 80 percent or more of their equity. As long as the market capitalization of the company is at least $100 million or more, the founders have created significant value for investors and themselves. During the peak of the dot.com mania in the late 1990s, companies went public with market capitalizations of

EXHIBIT 13.1

The Capital Markets Food Chain for Entrepreneurial Ventures

Stage of Venture	R&D	Seed	Launch	High Growth
Company Enterprise Value at Stage	Less than $1 million	$1 million–$5 million	More than $1 million–$50 million-plus	More than $100 million
Sources	Founders High Net Worth Individuals FFF SBIR	FFF* Angel Funds Seed Funds SBIR	Venture Capital Series A, B, C . . . Strategic Partners Very High Net Worth Individuals Private Equity	IPOs Strategic Acquires Private Equity
Amount of Capital Invested	Less than $50,000–$200,000	$10,000–$500,000	$500,000–$20 million	$10 million–$50 million-plus
% Company Owned at IPO	10–25%	5–15%	40–60% by prior investors	15–25% by public
Share Price and Number†	$.01–$.50 1–5 million	$.50–$1.00 1–3 million	$1.00–$8.00 +/−5–10 million	$12–$18 + 3–5 million

*Friends, families, and fools.
†At post–IPO.

$1 billion to $2 billion and more. Founders' shares on paper were at least initially worth $200 million to $400 million and more. These were truly staggering, unprecedented valuations, which were not sustainable. Take Sycamore Networks for example. From startup to IPO in less than 24 months, founders Desh Deshpanda and Don Smith achieved paper value in the billions each.[1] By late 2004, the founders had lost more than 90 percent of the paper value of their stock.

In the remainder of the chapter, we will discuss these various equity sources and how to identify and deal with them. Exhibit 13.2 summarizes the recent venture capital food chain. In the first three rounds, series A, B, C, one can see that on average, the amount of capital invested was quite substantial: $1–4 million, $6–10 million, and $10–15 million.

EXHIBIT 13.2

The Venture Capital Food Chain for Entrepreneurial Ventures

Venture Capital Series A, B, C, . . . (Average Size of Round): Example of Three Staged Rounds

Round (Dec. 2004)*
- "A" @ $1–4 million—Startup
- "B" @ $6–10 million—Product development
- "C"+ @ $10–15 million—Shipping product

*Valuations vary markedly by industry (e.g., 2x^{s}+).
+Valuations vary by region and venture capital cycle.

Cover Your Equity

One of the toughest trade-offs for any young company is to balance the need for startup and growth capital with preservation of equity. Holding on to as much as you can for as long as you can is generally good advice for entrepreneurs. As was evident in Exhibit 12.6, the earlier the capital enters, regardless of the source, the more costly it is. Creative bootstrapping strategies can be great preservers of equity, as long as such parsimony does not slow the venture's progress so much that the opportunity weakens or disappears.

Three central issues should be considered when beginning to think about obtaining risk capital: (1) Does the venture need outside equity capital? (2) Do the founders want outside equity capital? and finally, (3) Who should invest? While these three issues are at the center of the management team's thinking, it is also important to remember that a smaller percentage of a larger pie is preferred to a larger percentage of a smaller pie. Or as one entrepreneur stated, "I would rather have a piece of a watermelon than a whole raisin."[2]

After reviewing the Venture Opportunity Screening Exercises in Chapter 5, the business plan you prepared in Chapter 6, and the free cash flow equations

[1] Alex Pham, "MassFirm Takes $14B Rocket Ride" *The Boston Globe* 10/23/1999.
[2] Taken from a lecture on March 4, 1993, at the Harvard Business School, given by Paul A. Maeder and Robert F. Higgins of Highland Capital Partners, a Boston venture capital firm.

(including OOC, TTC, and breakeven) from Chapter 12, it may be easier to assess the need for additional capital. Deciding whether the capital infusion will be debt or equity is situation specific, and it may be helpful to be aware of the trade-offs involved; see Chapter 15 for an introduction to debt capital. In the majority of the high-technology startups and early-stage companies, some equity investment is normally needed to fund research and development, prototype development and product marketing, launch, and early losses.

Once the need for additional capital has been identified and quantified, the management team must consider the desirability of an equity investment. As was mentioned in Chapter 10, bootstrapping continues to be an attractive source of financing. For instance, *INC.* magazine suggested that entrepreneurs in certain industries tap vendors' by getting them to extend credit.[3]

Other entrepreneurs interviewed by *INC.* suggested getting customers to pay quickly.[4] For instance, one entrepreneur, Rebecca McKenna, built a software firm that did $8 million in sales in 2001 with customers in the health care industry. The robustness of economic benefits to her customers justified a 25 percent advance payment with each signed contract. This upfront cash has been a major source for her bootstrap financing. These options, and others, exist if the management team members believe that a loss of equity would adversely affect the company and their ability to manage it effectively. An equity investment requires that the management team firmly believe that investors can and will add value to the venture. With this belief, the team can begin to identify those investors who bring expertise to the venture. Cash flow versus high rate of return required is an important aspect of the "equity versus other" financing decision.

Deciding *who* should invest is a process more than a decision. The management team has a number of sources to consider. There are both informal and formal investors, private and public markets. The single most important criterion for selecting investors is what they can contribute to the value of the venture—beyond just funding. Angels or wealthy individuals are often sought because the amount needed may be less than the minimum investment required by formal investors (i.e., venture capitalists and private placements). Whether a venture capitalist would be interested in investing can be determined by the amount needed and the required rate of return expected.

Yet, entrepreneurs should be cautioned that "only 30 percent to 40 percent of the companies seeking private equity actually wind up getting it at the end of the process."[5] Additionally, the fees due the investment bankers and attorneys involved in writing up the prospectus and other legal documents must be paid whether or not the company raises capital.

Timing

There are two times for a young company to raise money; when there is lots of hope, or lots of results, but never in between.

Georges Doriot

Timing is also critical. A venture should not wait to look for capital until it has a serious cash shortage. For a startup, especially one with no experience or success in raising money, it is unwise to delay seeking capital because it is likely to take six months or more to raise money. In addition to the problems with cash flow, the lack of planning implicit in waiting until there is a cash shortage can undermine the credibility of a venture's management team and negatively impact its ability to negotiate with investors.

But if a venture tries to obtain equity capital too early, the equity position of the founders may be unnecessarily diluted and the discipline instilled by financial leanness may be eroded inadvertently.

Angels and Informal Investors

Who They Are

Wealthy individuals are probably the single most important source of capital for startup and emerging businesses in America today.[6] To meet accreditation standards, angel investors are required by the Securities and Exchange Commission to have assets of at least $1 million.[7] According to the Center for Venture Research at the University of New Hampshire, there are approximately 400,000 active angels in the United States. In 2000, as tech stocks sank, U.S. angels invested an estimated $30 billion in startup financing, compared with about $50 billion from venture capitalists.[8]

New Hampshire's Bill Wetzel has found these angels are mainly American self-made entrepreneur

[3] Robert A. Mamis, "The Secrets of Bootstrapping," *INC.*, September 1992, p. 72.
[4] Ibid., p. 76.
[5] Ibid.
[6] G. Baty, "Initial Financing of the New Research Based Enterprise in New England," Federal Reserve Bank of Boston Research Report No. 25, Boston, MA, 1964; and G. Baty, *Entrepreneurship: Play to Win* (Reston, VA: Reston Publishing, 1974), p. 97.
[7] *New York Times*, July 6, 2001.
[8] Robert J. Robinson, and Mark Van Osnabrugge, *Startup Funds with Startup Companies—A Guide for Entrepreneurs, Individual Investors, and Venture Capitalists* (San Francisco: Jossey-Bass, 2000).

millionaires. They have made it on their own, have substantial business and financial experience, and are likely to be in their 40s or 50s. They are also well educated; 95 percent hold college degrees from four-year colleges, and 51 percent have graduate degrees. Of the graduate degrees, 44 percent are in a technical field and 35 percent are in business or economics. According to Scott Peters, cofounder and co-CEO of AngelSociety, 96 percent of angels are men. One growing effort to involve female entrepreneurs is Chicago-based Springboard Enterprises. Springboard provides women-led high growth companies with access to investment capital and to a community committed to helping them build lasting businesses. By mid-2005, Springboard had showcased 317 women-led businesses at 14 forums across the country. To date Springboard portfolio companies have raised $3 billion in equity capital, grants, and strategic investments.

Since the typical informal investor will invest from $10,000 to $250,000 in any one deal, informal investors are particularly appropriate for the following:[9]

- Ventures with capital requirements of between $50,000 and $500,000.
- Ventures with sales potential of between $2 million and $20 million within 5 to 10 years.
- Small, established, privately held ventures with sales and profit growth of 10 percent to 20 percent per year, a rate that is not rapid enough to be attractive to a professional investor, such as a venture capital firm.
- Special situations, such as very early financing of high-technology inventors who have not developed a prototype.
- Companies that project high levels of free cash flow within three to five years.

These investors may invest alone or in syndication with other wealthy individuals, may demand considerable equity for their interests, or may try to dominate ventures. They also can get very impatient when sales and profits do not grow as they expected.

Usually, these informal investors will be knowledgeable and experienced in the market and technology areas in which they invest. If the right angel is found, he or she will add a lot more to a business than just money. As an advisor or director, his or her savvy, know-how, and contacts that come from having "made it" can be far more valuable than the $10,000 to $250,000 invested. Generally, the evaluations of potential investments by such wealthy investors tend to be less thorough than those undertaken by organized venture capital groups, and such noneconomic factors as the desire to be involved with entrepreneurship may be important to their investment decisions. There is a clear geographic bias of working within a one-hour driving radius of the investors' base. For example, a successful entrepreneur may want to help other entrepreneurs get started, or a wealthy individual may want to help build new businesses in his or her community.

Finding Informal Investors

Finding these backers is not easy. One expert noted: "Informal investors, essentially individuals of means and successful entrepreneurs, are a diverse and dispersed group with a preference for anonymity. Creative techniques are required to identify and reach them."[10] The Internet has provided entrepreneurs with an effective method of locating such investors. Formal sources such as GarageTechnology Ventures (http://www.garage.com) and Business Partners (http://www.businesspartners.com) provide invaluable advice, assistance, and information regarding potential investors and help forge the link between investors and entrepreneurs seeking capital. Specialized assistance for women includes womenangels.net (http://www.womenangels.net) and the Center for Women & Enterprise (http://www.cweboston.org).

Invariably, financial backers are also found by tapping an entrepreneur's own network of business associates and other contacts. Other successful entrepreneurs know them, as do many tax attorneys, accountants, bankers, and other professionals. Apart from serendipity, the best way to find informal investors is to seek referrals from attorneys, accountants, business associates, university faculty, and entrepreneurs who deal with new ventures and are likely to know such people. Because such investors learn of investment opportunities from their business associates, fellow entrepreneurs, and friends, and because many informal investors invest together in a number of new venture situations, one informal investor contact can lead the entrepreneur to contacts with others.

In most larger cities, there are law firms and private placement firms that syndicate investment packages as Regulation D offerings to networks of private investors. They may raise from several hundred thousand dollars to several million. Directories of these firms are published annually by *Venture* magazine and are written about in magazines such as *INC.* Articles on angel investors can also be found in *Forbes, Fortune, Wall Street Journal (WSJ Start-up.com), BusinessWeek, Red Herring, Wired,* and their respective Web sites.

[9] Robert Harrison and Colin Mason, *Informal Venture Capital: Evaluating the Impact of Business Introduction Services,* Hemel Hempstead, Woodhead Faulkner, 1996.

[10] William H. Wetzel, Jr., "Informal Investors—When and Where to Look," in *Pratt's Guide to Venture Capital Sources,* 6th ed., Stanley E. Pratt (Wellesley Hills, MA: Capital Publishing, 1982), p. 22.

Contacting Investors

If an entrepreneur has obtained a referral, he or she needs to get permission to use the name of the person making a referral when the investor is contacted. A meeting with the potential investor then can be arranged. At this meeting, the entrepreneur needs to make a concise presentation of the key features of the proposed venture by answering the following questions:

- What is the market opportunity?
- Why is it compelling?
- How will/does the business make money?
- How soon can the business reach positive cash flow?
- Why is this the right team at the right time?
- How does an investor exit the investment?

In the post-dot.com crash era, investors throughout the capital markets food chain are returning to these fundamental basics for evaluating potential deals.

Entrepreneurs need to avoid meeting with more than one informal investor at the same time. Meeting with more than one investor often results in any negative viewpoints raised by one investor being reinforced by another. It is also easier to deal with negative reactions and questions from only one investor at a time. Like a wolf on the hunt, if an entrepreneur isolates one target "prey" and then concentrates on closure, he or she will increase the odds of success.

Whether or not the outcome of such a meeting is continued investment interest, the entrepreneur needs to try to obtain the names of other potential investors from this meeting. If this can be done, the entrepreneur will develop a growing list of potential investors and will find his or her way into one or more networks of informal investors. If the outcome is positive, often the participation of one investor who is knowledgeable about the product and its market will trigger the participation of other investors.

Evaluation Process

An informal investor will want to review a business plan, meet the full management team, see any product prototype or design that may exist, and so forth. The investor will conduct background checks on the venture team and its product potential, usually through someone he or she knows who knows the entrepreneur and the product. The process is not dissimilar to the due diligence of the professional investors (see below) but may be less formal and structured. The new venture entrepreneur, if given a choice, would be wise to select an informal investor who can add knowledge, wisdom, and networks as an advisor and whose objectives are consistent with those of the entrepreneur.

The Decision

If the investor decides to invest, he or she will have an investment agreement drafted by an attorney. This agreement may be somewhat simpler than those used by professional investors, such as venture capital firms. All the cautions and advice about investors and investment agreements that are discussed later in the chapter apply here as well.

Most likely, the investment agreement with an informal investor will include some form of a "put," whereby the investor has the right to require the venture to repurchase his or her stock after a specified number of years at a specified price. If the venture is not harvested, this put will provide an investor with a cash return.

For access to important documents for venture agreements, please see the Web site for this textbook for downloadable sample term sheets.[11]

Venture Capital: Gold Mines and Tar Pits

There are only two classes of investors in new and young private companies: value-added investors and all the rest. If all you receive from an investor, especially a venture capitalist or a substantial private investor, is money, then you may not be getting a bargain. One of the keys to raising risk capital is to seek investors who will truly add value to the venture well beyond the money. Research and practice show that investors may add or detract value in a young company. Therefore, carefully screening potential investors to determine how they might fill some gaps in the founders' know-how and networks can yield significant results. Adding key management, new customers or suppliers, or referring additional investment are basic ways to add value.

A young founder of an international telecommunications venture landed a private investor who also served as an advisor. The following are examples of how this private investor provided critical assistance: introduced the founder to other private investors, to foreign executives (who became investors and helped in a strategic alliance), to the appropriate legal and accounting firms; served as a sounding board in crafting and negotiating early rounds of investments; identified potential directors and other advisors familiar with the technology and relationships with foreign investors and cross-cultural strategic alliances.

Numerous other examples exist of venture capitalists' being instrumental in opening doors to key accounts and vendors that otherwise might not take a

[11] To access New Venture Creation online, go to http://highered.mcgraw-hill.com/sites/0072498404/information_center_view0/.

new company seriously. Venture capitalists may also provide valuable help in such tasks as negotiating original equipment manufacturer (OEM) agreements or licensing or royalty agreements, making key contacts with banks and leasing companies, finding key people to build the team, helping to revise or to craft a strategy. Norwest Venture Partners brought in Ashley Stephenson to run a portfolio company and then backed him in a second venture. "Most venture capitalists have a short list of first-class players. Those are the horses you back," says Norwest partner Ernie Parizeau.

It is always tempting for an entrepreneur desperately in need of cash to go after the money that is available, rather than wait for the value-added investor. These quick solutions to the cash problem usually come back to haunt the venture.

What Is Venture Capital?[12]

The word *venture* suggests that this type of capital involves a degree of risk and even something of a gamble. Specifically, "The venture capital industry supplies capital and other resources to entrepreneurs in business with high growth potential in hopes of achieving a high rate of return on invested funds."[13] The whole investing process involves many stages, which are represented in Exhibit 13.3. Throughout the investing

[12] Unless otherwise noted, this section is drawn from William D. Bygrave and Jeffry A. Timmons, *Venture Capital at the Crossroads* (Boston: Harvard Business School Press, 1992.), pp. 13–14. Copyright 1992 by William D. Bygrave and Jeffry A. Timmons.

[13] "Note on the Venture Capital Industry (1981)," HBS Case 285–096, Harvard Business School, 1982, p. 1.

EXHIBIT 13.3

Classic Venture Capital Investing Process

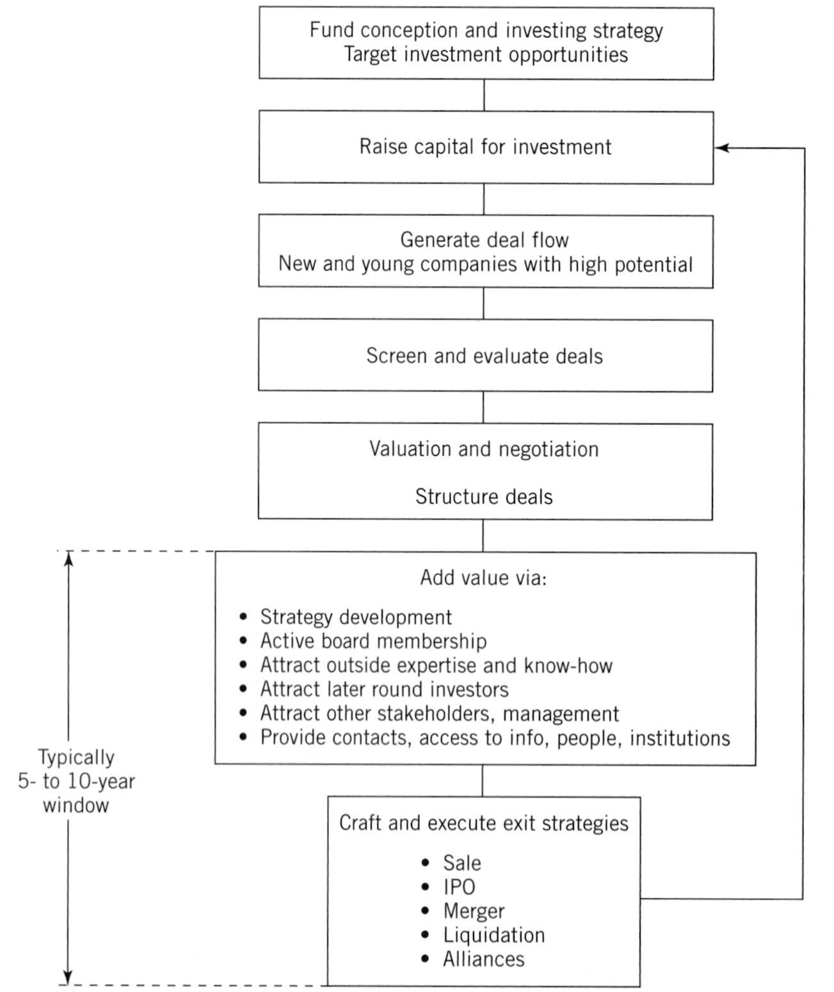

Source: Reprinted by permission of Harvard Business School Press. From *Venture Capital at the Crossroads* by W. D. Bygrave, J. A. Timmons. Boston, MA 1992. Copyright © 1992 by the Harvard Business School Publishing Corporation; all rights reserved.

process, venture capital firms seek to add value in several ways: identifying and evaluating business opportunities, including management, entry, or growth strategies; negotiating and closing the investment; tracking and coaching the company; providing technical and management assistance; and attracting additional capital, directors, management, suppliers, and other key stakeholders and resources. The process begins with the conception of a target investment opportunity or class of opportunities, which leads to a written proposal or prospectus to raise a venture capital fund. Once the money is raised, the value creation process moves from generating deals to crafting and executing harvest strategies and back to raising another fund. The process usually takes up to 10 years to unfold, but exceptions in both directions often occur.

The Venture Capital Industry

Although the roots of venture capital can be traced from investments made by wealthy families in the 1920s and 1930s, most industry observers credit Ralph E. Flanders, then president of the Federal Reserve Bank of Boston, with the idea. In 1946, Flanders joined a top-ranked team to found American Research and Development Corporation, the first firm, as opposed to individuals, to provide risk capital for new and rapidly growing firms, most of which were manufacturing and technology oriented.

Despite the success of American Research and Development, the venture capital industry did not experience a growth spurt until the 1980s, when the industry went ballistic. See Exhibit 13.4 for the capital commitments between 1969 and 2003. Before 1980, venture capital investing activities could be called dormant; just $460 million was invested in 375 companies in 1979. But at its peak in 1987, the industry had ballooned to more than 700 venture capital firms, which invested $3.94 billion in 1,729 portfolio companies. The sleepy cottage industry of the 1970s was transformed into a vibrant, at times frenetic, occasionally myopic, and dynamic market for private risk and equity capital in the 1980s. "After shrinking by an average of 25 percent a year for four years, new venture capital raised in 1992 more than doubled over 1991."[14] Yet, industry observers attributed the increase to "repeat fund raisers assembling partnerships of more than $100 million."[15]

[14] Michael Vachon, "Venture Capital Reborn," *Venture Capital Journal*, January 1993, p. 32.
[15] Ibid.

EXHIBIT 13.4
Venture Capital Fund Commitments (1969–2004)

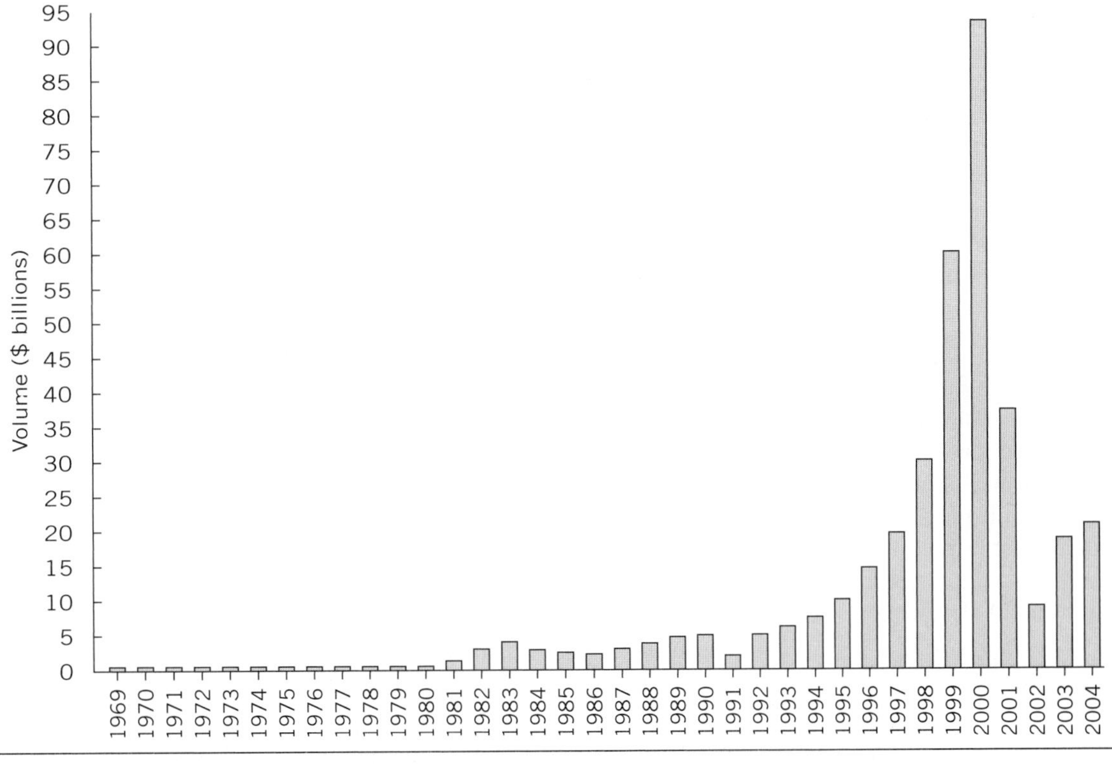

Source: *2004 National Venture Capital Association Yearbook.*

EXHIBIT 13.5

Total Venture Capital under Management

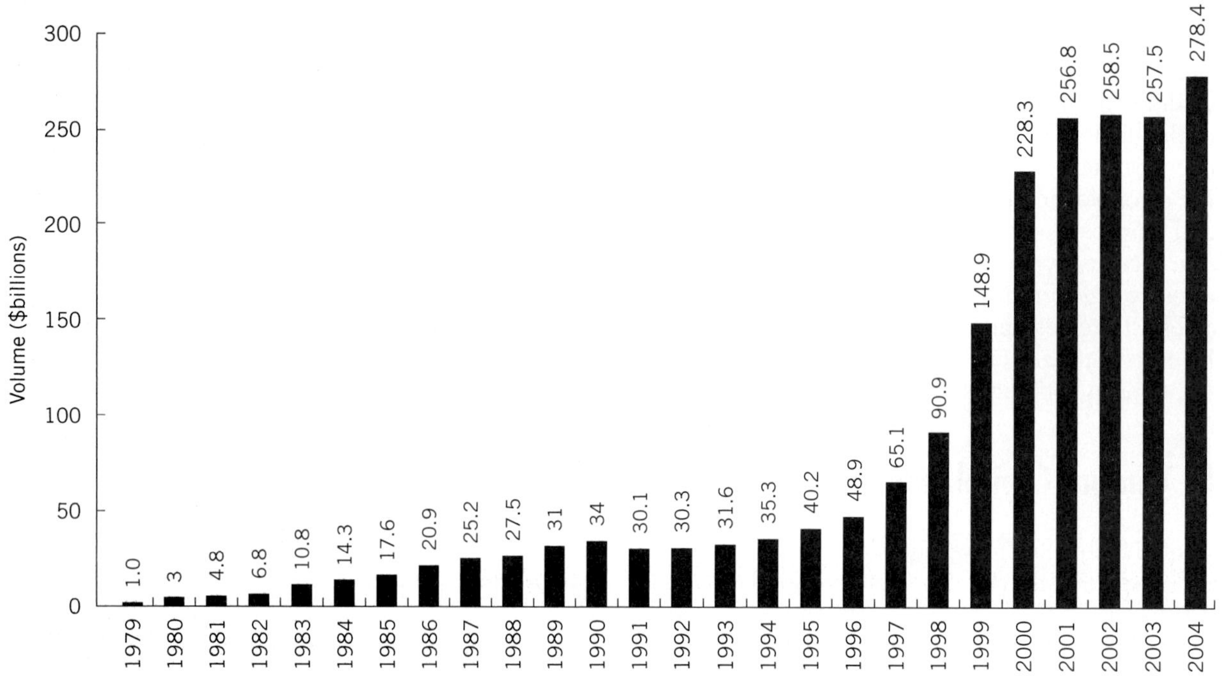

Source: *2004 National Venture Capital Association Yearbook.*

The Booming 90s

As one can see in Exhibits 13.4 and 13.5, the industry experienced an eightfold increase in the 1990s. While the absolute dollars committed and invested by 2000 were huge, the rate of increase in the 1980s was much greater, from $1 billion in 1979 to $31 billion in 1989.

By 2001, not only had the commitments changed, but also a new structure was emerging, increasingly specialized and focused. Exhibit 13.6 summarizes some of the important changes in the industry, which have implications for entrepreneurs seeking money and for those investing it. The major structural trends that emerged at the end of the 1980s continued through the 1990s. Among these patterns were:

1. The average fund size grew larger and larger and these megafunds of more than $500 million accounted for nearly 80 percent of all capital under management. High performing funds like Spectrum Equity Partners and Weston-Presidio, whose first fund just seven years earlier was in the $100 million to $200 million range, closed funds in 2000 well over $1 billion.
2. The average size of investments, correspondingly grew much larger as well. Unheard of previously, startup and early rounds of $20 million, $40 million, even $80 million were common in the dot.com and telecom feeding frenzy of the late 1990s.
3. The specialization pattern, which began in the 1980s, expanded to mainstream and megafunds. Oak Venture Partners, for instance, abandoned its longtime health care investing for information technology, along with many others.

The one significant trend that was reversed in the 1990s is especially good news for startup entrepreneurs. By 1990, as funds grew larger and larger, investing in startup and early stage ventures had performed a disappearing act. During the 1990s, startup and early stage funds experienced a major rebirth as opportunities in the Internet, software, information technology and telecommunications, and networking exploded.

Beyond the Crash of 2000: The Venture Capital Cycle Repeats Itself

The crash of the NASDAQ began in March 2000, resulting in more than a 60 percent drop in value by late summer 2001. This major crash in equity values began a shakeout and downturn in the private equity and public stock markets. The repercussions and consequences were still being felt in 2005. Many high-flying companies went public in 1998 and 1999 at high

EXHIBIT 13.6

New Heterogeneous Structure of the Venture Capital Industry

	Megafunds	Mainstream	Second Tier	Specialists and Niche Funds	Corporate Financial and Corporate Industrial
Estimated Number and Type (2005)	106 Predominantly private, independent funds	76 Predominantly private & independent; some large institutional SBICs & corporate funds	455 Mostly SBICs; some private independent funds	87 Private, independent	114
Size of Funds under Management	More than $500 million	$250–$499 million	Less than $250 million	$25–$50 million	$50–$100 million-plus
Typical Investment	Series B, C, . . . $5–25 million-plus	Series A, B, C . . . $1–$10 million	Series A, B $500,000–$5 million	Series A, B $500,000–$2 million	Series A, B, C . . . $1–$25 million
Stage of Investment	Later expansion, LBOs, startups	Later expansion, LBOs, some startups; mezzanine	Later stages; few startups; specialized areas	Seed and startup; technology or market focus	Later
Strategic Focus	Technology; national and international markets; capital gains; broad focus	Technology and manufacturing; national and regional markets; capital gains; more specialized focus	Eclectic—more regional than national; capital gains, current income; service business	High-technology national and international links; "feeder funds," capital gains	Windows on technology; direct investment in new markets and suppliers; diversification; strategic partners; capital gains
Balance of Equity and Debt	Predominantly equity	Predominantly equity; convertible preferred	Predominantly debt; about 91 SBICs do equity principally	Predominantly equity	Mixed
Principal Sources of Capital	Mature national and international institutions; own funds; insurance company and pension funds; institutions and wealthy individuals; foreign corporation and person funds; universities	Mature national and international institutions; own funds; insurance company and pension funds; institutions and wealthy individuals: foreign corporation and pension funds; universities	Wealthy individuals; some smaller institutions	Institutions and foreign companies; wealthy individuals	Internal funds
Main Investing Role	Active lead or colead; frequent syndications; board seat	Less investing with some solo investing	Initial or lead investor; outreach; shirtsleeves involvement	Later stages, rarely startups; direct investor in funds and portfolio companies	

Note: Target rates of return vary considerably, depending on stage and market conditions. Seed and startup investors may seek compounded after-tax rates of return in excess of 50 to 100 percent; in mature, later stage investments they may seek returns in the 30–40 percent range. The rule of thumb of realizing gains of 5 to 10 times the original investment in 5 to 10 years is a common investor expectation.

Source: *2001 National Venture Capital Association Yearbook.*

prices, saw their values soar beyond $150 to $200 per share, then came plummeting down to low single-digit prices. For example, Sycamore Networks went public in October 1999 at $38 per share, soared to nearly $200 per share in the first week, and was trading around $3.50 per share by the summer of 2005. The list of dot.coms that went bankrupt is significant.

Similarly, beginning in the late summer of 2000, many young telecommunications companies saw their stocks begin to decline rapidly, losing 90 percent or more of their value in less than a year. These downdrafts swept the entire venture capital and private equity markets. By mid-2001, the amount of money being invested had dropped by half from the record highs of 2000, and valuations plummeted. Down rounds—investing at a lower price than the previous round—were very common. Not since the periods 1969–1974 and 1989–1993 have entrepreneurs experienced such a downturn.

To illustrate the consequences for entrepreneurs and investors alike, in 2001 as companies burned through their invested capital and faced follow-on rounds of financing, the valuations were sagging painfully. Even companies performing on plan were seeing share prices 15 to 30 percent below the previous round a year or 18 months earlier. Where performance lagged milestones in the business plan, the down round could be 50 percent or more below the previous financing valuation. To make matters worse for entrepreneurs, the investing pace slowed significantly. Due diligence on companies was completed in 45 days or less during the binge of 1998–1999. By 2002 investors reported a six- to eight-month due diligence phase, which would be very close to the historical norm experienced before the feeding frenzy.

The stark reality of all this is that the venture capital cycle—much like real estate—seems to repeat itself. Scarcity of capital leads to high returns, which attracts an overabundance of new capital, which drives returns down. The new millennium welcomed the real "Y2K" problem. The meltdown side of the venture capital and private equity markets repeated the 1969–1974 and 1988–1992 pattern.

The Sign-Curve Lives Circa 2005

Historically, the venture capital cycle of ups and downs has had the shape of a sign-curve; an "S" on its side. Fortunately, after a period of painful losses, too much time spent working on troubled portfolio companies, and too few exits in 2002–2003, the industry began to rebound in 2004 and into 2005. In 2004, for instance, the total number of companies invested in rose for the first time since the 2000 bubble; from 2,825 to 2,873. Total investments also inched up from $18.95 billion in 2003 to $20.94 billion in 2004, and the average deal size likewise increased from $6.65 million to $7.22 million.[16] Exhibit 13.7 shows the history since 1990.

The Venture Capital Process

Exhibit 13.8 represents the core activities of the venture capital process. At the heart of this dynamic flow is the collision of entrepreneurs, opportunities, investors, and capital.[17] Because the venture capitalist brings, in addition to money, experience, networks, and industry contacts, a professional venture capitalist can be very attractive to a new venture. Moreover, a venture capital firm has deep pockets and contacts with other groups that can facilitate the raising of money as the venture develops.

The venture capital process occurs in the context of mostly private, quite imperfect capital markets for new, emerging, and middle-market companies (i.e., those companies with $5 million to $200 million in sales). The availability and cost of this capital depend on a number of factors:

- Perceived risk, in view of the quality of the management team and the opportunity.
- Industry, market, attractiveness of the technology, and fit.
- Upside potential and downside exposure.
- Anticipated growth rate.
- Age and stage of development.
- Amount of capital required.
- Founders' goals for growth, control, liquidity, and harvest.
- Fit with investors' goals and strategy.
- Relative bargaining positions of investors and founders given the capital markets at the time.

However, no more than 2 percent to 4 percent of those contacting venture capital firms receive financing from them. Despite the increase in funds in the recent boom years, observers comment that the repeat fund-raisers "stay away from seed and early-stage investments largely because those deals tend to require relatively small amounts of capital, and the megafunds, with $500 million-plus to invest, like to make larger commitments."[18] Further, an entrepreneur may give up 15 percent to 75 percent of his or her equity for seed/startup financing. Thus, after several rounds of venture financing have been completed, an

[16] *Venture Capital Journal*, February 2005, pp. 29–30.
[17] Bygrave and Timmons, *Venture Capital at the Crossroads*, p. 11.
[18] Vachon, "Venture Capital Reborn," p. 35.

EXHIBIT 13.7

U.S. Venture Capital Investment by Year (1990–2004)

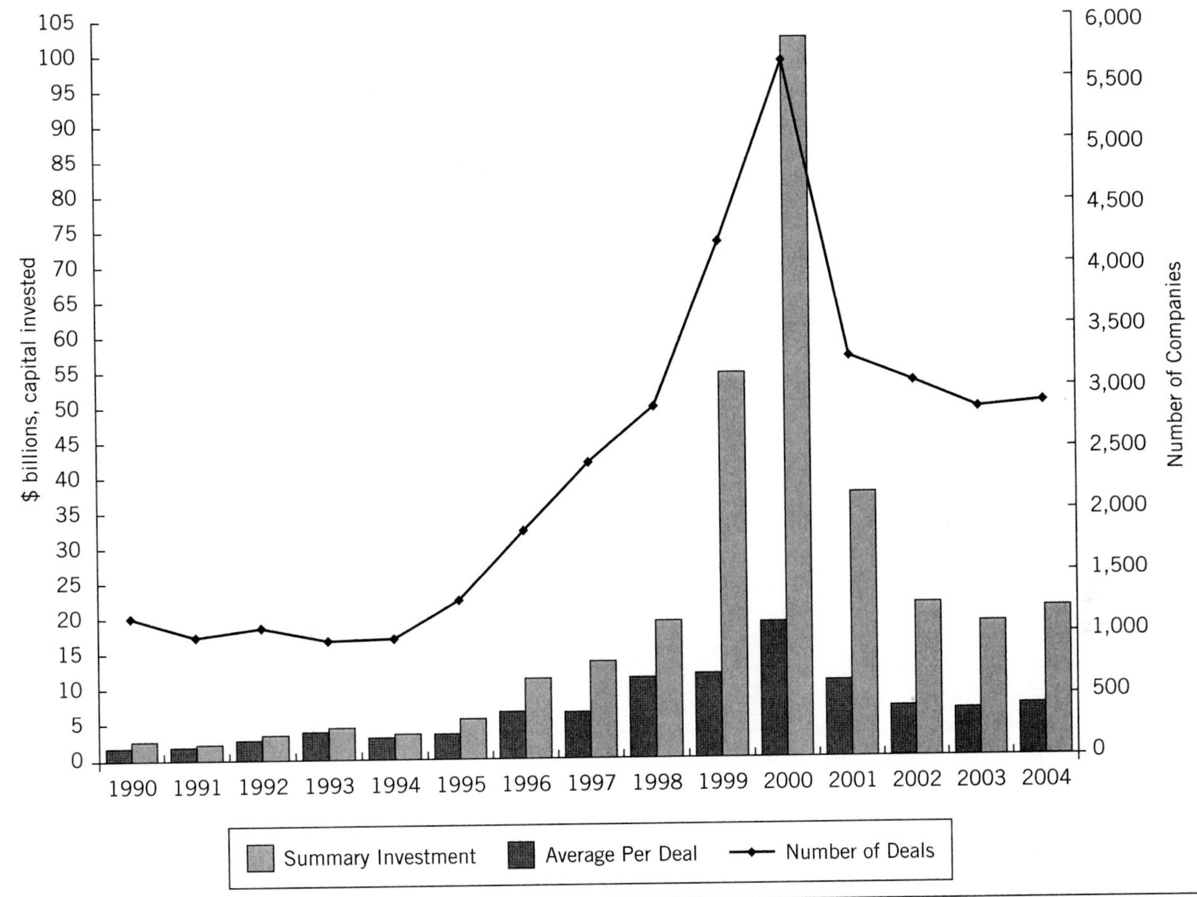

Source: PricewaterhouseCoopers/Venture Economics/National Venture Capital Association/Money Tree™ Survey of 3/28/05. Used by permission of PricewaterhouseCoopers.

entrepreneur may own no more than 10 percent to 20 percent of the venture.

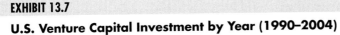

The venture capitalists' stringent criteria for their investments limit the number of companies receiving venture capital money. Venture capital investors look for ventures with very high growth potential where they can quintuple their investment in five years; they place a very high premium on the quality of management in a venture; and they like to see a management team with complementary business skills headed by someone who has previous entrepreneurial or profit-and-loss (P&L) management experience. In fact, these investors are searching for the "superdeal." Superdeals meet the investment criteria outlined in Exhibit 13.9.

Identifying Venture Capital Investors

Venture capital corporations or partners have an established capital base and professional management. Their investment policies cover a range of preferences in investment size and the maturity, location, and industry of a venture. Capital for these investments can be provided by one or more wealthy families, one or more financial institutions (e.g., insurance companies or pension funds), and wealthy individuals. Most are organized as limited partnerships, in which the fund managers are the general partners and the investors are the limited partners. Today, most of these funds prefer to invest from $2 million to $5 million or more. Although some of the smaller funds will invest less, most of their investments are in the range of $500,000 to $1.5 million. Some of the so-called megafunds with more than $500 million to invest do not consider investments of less than $5 million to $10 million. The investigation and evaluation of potential investments by venture capital corporations and partnerships are thorough and professional. Most of their investments are in high-technology businesses, but many will consider investments in other areas.

Sources and Guides If an entrepreneur is searching for a venture capital investor, a good place to start is with *Pratt's Guide to Venture Capital*

EXHIBIT 13.8

Flows of Venture Capital

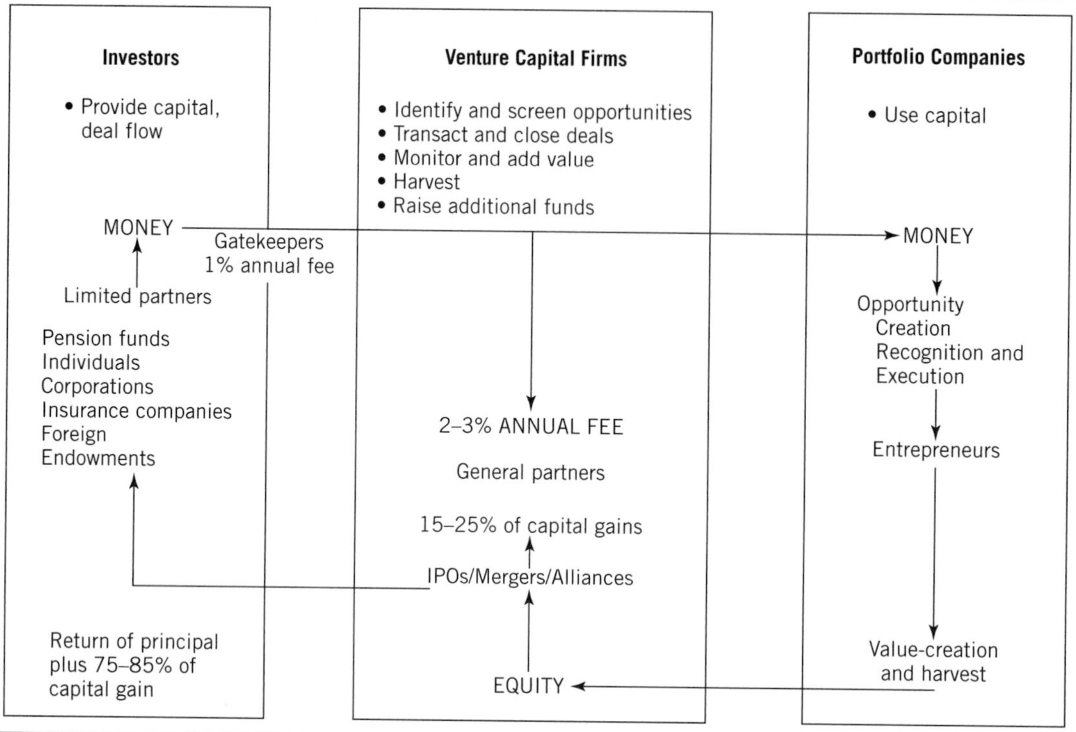

Source: Reprinted by permission of Harvard Business School Press. From *Venture Capital at the Crossroads* by W. D. Bygrave, J. A. Timmons. Boston, MA 1992. Copyright © 1992 by the Harvard Business School Publishing Corporation; all rights reserved.

Sources, published by Venture Economics, as well as the ventureone Web site http://www.ventureone.com, two of several directories of venture capital firms. Entrepreneurs also can seek referrals from accountants, lawyers, investment and commercial bankers, and businesspeople who are knowledgeable about professional investors. Especially good sources of information are other entrepreneurs who have recently tried, successfully or unsuccessfully, to raise money.

Sometimes professional investors find entrepreneurs. Rather than wait for a deal to come to them, a venture capital investor may decide on a product or technology it wishes to commercialize and then put its own deal together. Kleiner Perkins used this approach to launch Genentech and Tandem Computer Corporation, as did Greylock and J. H. Whitney in starting MassComp.

What to Look For Entrepreneurs are well advised to screen prospective investors to determine the appetites of such investors for the stage, industry, technology, and capital requirements proposed. It is also useful to determine which investors have money to invest, which are actively seeking deals, and which have the time and people to investigate new deals. Depending on its size and investment strategy, a fund that is a year or two old will generally be in an active investing mode.

Early-stage entrepreneurs need to seek investors who (1) are considering new financing proposals and can provide the required level of capital; (2) are interested in companies at the particular stage of growth; (3) understand and have a preference for investments in the particular industry (i.e., market, product, technology, or service focus); (4) can provide good business advice, moral support, and contacts in the business and financial community; (5) are reputable, fair, and ethical and with whom the entrepreneur gets along; and (6) have successful track records of 10 years or more advising and building smaller companies.[19]

Entrepreneurs can expect a number of value-added services from an investor. Ideally, the investor should define his or her role as a coach, thoroughly

[19] For more specifics, see Harry A. Sapienza and Jeffry A. Timmons, "Launching and Building Entrepreneurial Companies: Do the Venture Capitalists Build Value?" in *Proceedings of the Babson Entrepreneurship Research Conference,* May 1989, Babson Park, MA. See also Jeffry A. Timmons, "Venture Capital: More Than Money," in *Pratt's Guide to Venture Capital Sources.* 13th ed., ed. Jane Morris (Needham, MA: Venture Economics, 1989), p. 71.

EXHIBIT 13.9

Characteristics of the Classic Superdeal from the Investor's Perspective

Mission
- Build a highly profitable and industry-dominant market leading company.
- Go public or merge within four to seven years at a high price-earnings (P/E) multiple.

Complete Management Team
- Led by industry "superstar."
- Possess proven entrepreneurial, general management, and P&L experience in the business.
- Have leading innovator or technologies/marketing head.
- Possess complementary and compatible skills.
- Have unusual tenacity, imagination, and commitment.
- Possess reputation for high integrity.

Proprietary Product or Service
- Has significant competitive lead and "unfair" and sustainable or defensible advantages.
- Has product or service with high value-added properties resulting in early payback to user.
- Has or can gain exclusive contractual or legal rights.

Large, Robust, and Sustainable Market
- Will accommodate a $100 million entrant in five years.
- Has sales currently at $200 million, or more, and growing at 25 + % per year.
- Has no dominant competitor now.
- Has clearly identified customers and distribution channels.
- Possesses forgiving and rewarding economics, such as:
  —Gross margins of 40% to 50%, or more.
  —10% or more profit after tax.
  —Early positive cash flow and break-even sales.

Deal Valuation and ROR
- Has "digestible" first-round capital requirements (i.e., greater than $1 million and less than $10 million).
- Able to return 10 times original investment in five years at P/E of 15 times or more.
- Has possibility of additional rounds of financing at substantial markup.
- Has antidilution and IPO subscription rights and other identifiable harvest/liquidity options.

Source: Reprinted by permission of Harvard Business School Press. From *Venture Capital at the Crossroads* by W. D. Bygrave, J. A. Timmons. Boston, MA 1992. Copyright © 1992 by the Harvard Business School Publishing Corporation; all rights reserved.

involved, but not a player. In terms of support, investors should have both patience and bravery. The entrepreneur should be able to go to the investor when he or she needs a sounding board, counseling, or an objective, detached perspective. Investors should be helpful with future negotiations, financing, private and public offerings, as well as in relationship building with key contacts.

What to Look Out For There are also some things to be wary of in finding investors. These warning signs are worth avoiding unless an entrepreneur is so desperate that he or she has no real alternatives:

- *Attitude.* Entrepreneurs need to be wary if they cannot get through to a general partner in an investment firm and keep getting handed off to a junior associate, or if the investor thinks he or she can run the business better than the lead entrepreneur or the management team.
- *Overcommitment.* Entrepreneurs need to be wary of lead investors who indicate they will be active directors but who also sit on the boards of six to eight other startup and early-stage companies or are in the midst of raising money for a new fund.
- *Inexperience.* Entrepreneurs need to be wary of dealing with venture capitalists who have an MBA; are under 30 years of age; have worked only on Wall Street or as a consultant; have no operating, hands-on experience in new and growing companies; and have a predominantly financial focus.
- *Unfavorable reputation.* Entrepreneurs need to be wary of funds that have a reputation for early and frequent replacement of the founders or those where more than one-fourth of the portfolio companies are in trouble or failing to meet projections in their business plans.

- *Predatory pricing.* During adverse capital markets (e.g., 1969–1974, 1988–1992, 2000–2003), investors who unduly exploit these conditions by forcing large share price decreases in the new firms and punishing terms on prior investors do not make the best long-term financial partners.

How to Find Out How does the entrepreneur learn about the reputation of the venture capital firm? The best source is the CEO/founders of prior investments. Besides the successful deals, ask for the names and phone numbers of CEOs the firm invested in whose results were only moderate to poor, and where the portfolio company had to cope with significant adversity. Talking with these CEOs will reveal the underlying fairness, character, values, ethics, and potential of the venture capital firm as a financial partner, as well as how it practices its investing philosophies. It is always interesting to probe regarding the behavior at pricing meetings.

Most investors who have serious interest will have some clear ideas about how to improve your strategy, product line, positioning, and a variety of other areas. This is one of the ways they can add value—if they are right. Consequently, you need to be prepared for them to take apart your business plan and to put it back together. They are likely to have their own format and their own financial models. Working with them on this is a good way to get to know them.

Never lie. As one entrepreneur put it, "You have to market the truth, but do not lie." Do not stop selling until the money is in the bank. Let the facts speak for themselves. Be able to deliver on the claims, statements, and promises you make or imply in your business plan and presentations. Tom Huseby adds some final wisdom: "It's much harder than you ever thought it could be. You can last much longer than you ever thought you could. They have to do this for the rest of their lives!" Finally, never say no to an offer price. There is an old saying that your first offer may be your best offer.

Dealing with Venture Capitalists[20]

Don't forget that venture capitalists see lots of business plans and proposals, sometimes 100 or more a month. Typically, they invest in only one to three of these. The following suggestions may be helpful in working with them.

If possible, obtain a personal introduction from someone that is well-known to the investors (a director or founder of one of their portfolio companies, a limited partner in their fund, a lawyer or accountant who has worked with them on deals) and who knows you well. After identifying the best targets, you should create a market for your company by marketing it. Have several prospects. Be vague about who else you are talking with. You can end up with a rejection from everyone if the other firms know who was the first firm that turned you down. It is also much harder to get a yes than to get a no. You can waste an enormous amount of time before getting there.

When pushed by the investors to indicate what other firms/angels you are talking to, simply put it this way: "All our advisors believe that information is highly confidential to the company, and our team agrees. We are talking to other high quality investors like yourselves. The ones with the right chemistry who can make the biggest difference in our company and are prepared to invest first will be our partner. Once we have a term sheet and deal on the table, if you also want co-investors we are more than happy to share these other investors' names." Failing to take such a tack usually puts you in an adverse negotiating position.

Questions the Entrepreneur Can Ask

The presentation to investors when seeking venture capital is demanding and pressing, which is appropriate for this high-stakes game. Venture capitalists have an enormous legal and fiduciary responsibility to their limited partners, not to mention their powerful self-interest. Therefore, they are thorough in their due diligence and questioning to assess the intelligence, integrity, nimbleness, and creativity of the entrepreneurial mind in action. *(See Chapter 1.)*

Once the presentation and question-answer session is complete, the founders can learn a great deal about the investors and enhance their own credibility by asking a few simple questions:

- Tell us what you think of our strategy, how we size up the competition, and our game plan. What have we missed? Who have we missed?
- Are there competitors we have overlooked? How are we vulnerable and how do we compete?
- How would you change the way we are thinking about the business and planning to seize the opportunity?
- Is our team as strong as you would like? How would you improve this and when?
- Give us a sense of what you feel would be a fair range of value for our company if you invested $_____?

Their answers will reveal how much they have done and how knowledgeable they are about your industry,

[20] The authors express appreciation to Thomas Huseby of SeaPoint Ventures in Washington for his valuable insights in the following two sections.

technology, competitors, and the like. This will provide robust insight as to whether and how they can truly add value to the venture. At the same time, you will get a better sense of their forthrightness and integrity: Are they direct, straightforward, but not oblivious to the impact of their answers? Finally, these questions can send a very favorable message to investors: Here are entrepreneurs who are intelligent, open-minded, receptive, and self-confident enough to solicit our feedback and opinions even though we may have opposing views.

Due Diligence: A Two-Way Street

It can take several weeks or even months to complete the due diligence on a startup, although if the investors know the entrepreneurs, it can go much more quickly. The verification of facts, backgrounds, and reputations of key people, market estimates, technical capabilities of the product, proprietary rights, and the like is a painstaking investigation for investors. They will want to talk with your directors, advisors, former bosses, and previous partners. Make it as easy as possible for them by having very detailed résumés and lists of 10 to 20 references (with phone numbers and addresses) such as former customers, bankers, vendors, and so on, who can attest to your accomplishments. Prepare extra copies of published articles, reports, studies, market research, contract, or purchase orders, technical specifications, and the like that can support your claims.

One recent research project examined how 86 venture capital firms nationwide conducted their intensive due diligence. To evaluate the opportunity, the management, the risks, the competition, and to weigh the upside against the downside, firms spent from 40 to 400 hours, with the typical firm spending 120 hours. That is nearly three weeks of full-time effort. At the extreme, some firms engaged in twice as much due diligence.[21] Central to this investigation were careful checks of the management's references and verification of track record and capabilities.

While all this is going on, do your own due diligence on the venture fund. Ask for the names and phone numbers of some of their successful deals, some that did not work out, and the names of any presidents they ended up replacing. Who are their legal and accounting advisors? What footprints have they left in the sand regarding their quality, reputation, and record in truly adding value to the companies in which they invest? Finally, the chemistry between the management team and the general partner that will have responsibility for the investment and, in all likelihood, a board seat is crucial. If you do not have a financial partner you respect and can work closely with, then you are likely to regret ever having accepted the money.

Other Equity Sources

Small Business Administration's 7(a) Guaranteed Business Loan Program

Promoting small businesses by guaranteeing long-term loans, the Small Business Administration's 7(a) Guaranteed Business Loan Program has been supporting startup and high-potential ventures since 1953.[22] The 7(a) loan program provides 40,000 loans annually. The 7(a) program is almost exclusively a guarantee program, but under this program the Small Business Administration also makes direct loans to women, veterans of the armed forces, and minorities, as well as other small business. The program entails banks and certain nonbank lenders making loans that are then guaranteed by SBA for between 50 percent and 90 percent of each loan, with a maximum of $1 million. Eligible activities under 7(a) include acquisition of borrower-occupied real estate, fixed assets such as machinery and equipment, and working capital for items such as inventory or to meet cash flow needs.[23]

SBA programs have a noteworthy effect on the economy and entrepreneurship. The $1 million guarantees, the largest of all the SBA programs, have helped many entrepreneurs start, stay in, expand, or purchase a business. According to the SBA, in 2000, 541,539 jobs were created by SBA borrowers, and the SBA helped create 2.3 million jobs or about 15 percent of all jobs created by small businesses between 1993 and 1998.

Small Business Investment Companies

SBICs (small business investment companies) are licensed by the SBA and can obtain from it debt capital—$4 in loans for each $1 of private equity.[24] The impact of SBICs is evidenced by the many major U.S. companies that received early financing from SBICs, including Intel, Apple Computer, Staples, Federal Express, Sun Microsystems, Sybase, Inc., Callaway Golf, and Outback Steakhouse.[25] The SBIC

[21] Geoffrey H. Smart, "Management Assessment Methods in Venture Capital," unpublished doctoral dissertation, 1998 (Claremont, CA: The Claremont Graduate University), p. 109.
[22] Data were compiled from the Small Business Administration, http://www.sba.gov.
[23] Daniel R. Garner, Robert R. Owen, and Robert P. Conway, *The Ernst & Young Guide to Raising Capital* (New York: John Wiley & Sons, 1991), pp. 165–66.
[24] This section was drawn from Jeffry A. Timmons, *Planning and Financing the New Venture* (Acton, MA: Brick House Publishing Company, 1990), pp. 49–50.
[25] The National Association of Small Business Investment Companies (NASBIC), http://www.nasbic.org.

program was established in 1958 to address the need for venture capital by small emerging enterprises and to improve opportunities for growth.[26] An SBIC's equity capital is generally supplied by one or more commercial banks, wealthy individuals, and the investing public. The benefit of the SBIC program is twofold: (1) small businesses that qualify for assistance from the SBIC program may receive equity capital, long-term loans, and expert management assistance, and (2) venture capitalists participating in the SBIC program can supplement their own private investment capital with funds borrowed at favorable rates through the federal government. According to the National Association of Small Business Investment Companies, as of December 2000 there were 404 operating SBICs with more than $16 billion under management. Since 1958, the SBIC program has provided approximately $27 billion of long-term debt and equity capital to nearly 90,000 small U.S. companies.

SBICs are limited by law to taking minority shareholder positions and can invest no more than 20 percent of their equity capital in any one situation. Because SBICs borrow much of their capital from the SBA and must service this debt, they prefer to make some form of interest-bearing investment. Four common forms of financing are long-term loans with options to buy stock, convertible debentures, straight loans, and, in some cases, preferred stock. In 2000, the average financing by bank SBICs was $4 million. The median for all SBICs was $250,000.[27] Due to their SBA debt, SBICs tend not to finance startups and early-stage companies but to make investments in more mature companies.

As of this writing in 2005, the SBIC program is being phased out. The Bush administration's 2006 budget proposes to eliminate government support for SBICs.

Small Business Innovation Research

The risk and expense of conducting serious research and development are often beyond the means of startups and small businesses. The Small Business Innovation Research (SBIR) is a federal government program designed to strengthen the role of small businesses in federally funded R&D, and to help develop a stronger national base for technical innovation (http://www.sba.gov/sbir).

The SBIR program provides R&D capital for innovative projects that meet specific needs of any one of 11 federal government agencies, including the Departments of Agriculture, Commerce, Education, Energy, and Homeland Security; the Environmental Protection Agency; and the National Science Foundation. SBIR is a highly competitive, three-phase process. Phase I provides funds to determine the feasibility of the technology. During Phase II, the necessary R&D is undertaken to produce a well-defined product or process. Phase III involves the commercialization of the technology using non-SBIR funds.

An SBIR small business is defined as an independently owned and operated, for-profit organization with no more than 500 employees. In addition, the small business must be at least 51 percent owned by U.S. citizens or lawfully admitted resident aliens, not be dominant in the field of operation in which it is proposing, and have its principal place of business in the United States.

Corporate Venture Capital

During the Internet boom in the late 1990s, corporate investors were very active. In 2000 alone, large corporations invested $17 billion in small and mid-size opportunities. When the bubble burst, many of these funds scaled back or shut down entirely. But as we have seen, business investing is highly cyclical in nature. In 2004, corporate-based venture capitalists were back, investing $1.4 billion. This was an 8 percent increase over 2003, and the first increase since 2000.[28]

While corporate venture capitalists are similar to traditional VCs in that they look for promising young companies on the verge of a spike in sales, corporations tend to be more risk-averse and specialized. Since investing in a relevant technology can reduce the costs of their own research and development, fit is usually an important aspect of the funding decision. When working with corporate funding sources, make sure you consider the corporation's philosophy and culture, as well as their investment track record with small businesses before agreeing to any deal.

Mezzanine Capital

At the point where the company has overcome many of the early-stage risks, it may be ready for mezzanine capital.[29] The term *mezzanine financing* refers to capital that is between senior debt financing and common stock. In some cases it takes the form of redeemable preferred stock, but in most cases it is subordinated

[26] Small Business Administration, http://www.sba.gov.
[27] The National Association of Small Business Investment Companies (NASBIC), http://www.nasbic.org.
[28] *INC.*, May 2005, p. 48.
[29] This section was drawn from Donald P. Remey, "Mezzanine Financing: A Flexible Source of Growth Capital," in *Pratt's Guide to Venture Capital Sources*, ed. D. Schutt (New York: Venture Economics Publishing, 1993). pp. 84–86.

debt that carries an equity "kicker" consisting of warrants or a conversion feature into common stock. This subordinated-debt capital has many characteristics of debt but also can serve as equity to underpin senior debt. It is generally unsecured, with a fixed coupon and maturity of 5 to 10 years. A number of variables are involved in structuring such a loan: the interest rate, the amount and form of the equity, exercise/conversion price, maturity, call features, sinking fund, covenants, and put/call options. These variables provide for a wide range of possible structures to suit the needs of both the issuer and the investor.

Offsetting these advantages are a few disadvantages to mezzanine capital compared to equity capital. As debt, the interest is payable on a regular basis, and the principal must be repaid, if not converted into equity. This is a large claim against cash and can be burdensome if the expected growth and/or profitability does not materialize and cash becomes tight. In addition, the subordinated debt often contains covenants relating to net worth, debt, and dividends.

Mezzanine investors generally look for companies that have a demonstrated performance record, with revenues approaching $10 million or more. Because the financing will involve paying interest, the investor will carefully examine existing and future cash flow and projections.

Mezzanine financing is utilized in a wide variety of industries, ranging from basic manufacturing to high technology. As the name implies, however, it focuses more on the broad middle spectrum of business, rather than on high-tech, high-growth companies. Specialty retailing, broadcasting, communications, environmental services, distributors, and consumer or business service industries are more attractive to mezzanine investors.

Private Placements

Private placements are an attractive source of equity capital for a private company that for whatever reason has ruled out the possibility of going public. If the goal of the company is to raise a specific amount of capital in a short time, this equity source may be the answer. In this transaction, the company offers stock to a few private investors, rather than to the public as in a public offering. A private placement requires little paperwork compared to a public offering.

If the company's management team knows of enough investors, then the private placement could be distributed among a small group of friends, family, relatives, or acquaintances. Or the company may decide to have a broker circulate the proposal among a few investors who have expressed an interest in small companies. The following four groups of investors might be interested in a private placement:[30]

1. Let us say you manufacture a product and sell to dealers, franchisors, or wholesalers. These are the people who know and respect your company. Moreover, they depend on you to supply the product they sell. They might consider it to be in their interest to buy your stock if they believe it will help assure continuation of product supply, and perhaps give them favored treatment if you bring out a new product or product improvement. One problem is when one dealer invests and another does not; can you treat both fairly in the future? Another problem is that a customer who invests might ask for exclusive rights to market your product in a particular geographical area, and you might find it hard to refuse.
2. A second group of prospective buyers for your stock are those professional investors who are always on the lookout to buy a good, small company in its formative years, and ride it to success. Very often, these sophisticated investors choose an industry and a particular product or service in that industry they believe will become hot and then focus 99 percent of their attention on the caliber of the management. If your management, or one key individual, has earned a high reputation as a star in management, technology, or marketing, these risk-minded investors tend to flock to that person. (The high-tech industry is an obvious example.) Whether your operation meets their tests for stardom as a hot field may determine whether they find your private placement a risk to their liking.
3. Other investors are searching for opportunities to buy shares of smaller growth companies in the expectation that the company will soon go public and they will benefit as new investors bid the price up, as often happens. For such investors, news of a private placement is a tip-off that a company is on the move and worth investigating, always with an eye on the possibility of its going public. These investors usually have no fear of losing control or suffering their interference.
4. Private placements also often attract venture capitalists who hope to benefit when the company goes public or when the company is sold. To help ensure that happy development, these investors get seriously active at the level of the board of directors, where their skill and experience can help the company reach its potential.

[30] The following examples are drawn directly from Garner, Owen, and Conwav, *The Ernst & Young Guide to Raising Capital*, pp. 51–52.

Initial Public Stock Offerings

Commonly referred to as an IPO, an initial public offering raises capital through federally registered and underwritten sales of the company's shares. Numerous federal and state securities laws and regulations govern these offerings; thus, it is important that management consult with lawyers and accountants who are familiar with the current regulations.

In the past, such as during the strong bull market for new issues that occurred in 1983, 1986, 1992, 1996, and 1999, it was possible to raise money for an early-growth venture or even for a startup. These boom markets are easy to identify because the number of new issues jumped from 78 in 1980 to an astounding 523 in 1983, representing a sharp increase from about $1 billion in 1980 to about 12 times that figure in 1983 (see Exhibit 13.10). Another boom came three years later, in 1986, when the number of new issues reached 464. While in 1992, the number of new issues (396) did not exceed the 1986 record, a record $22.2 billion was raised in IPOs. Accounting for this reduction in the number of new issues and the increase in the amounts raised, one observer commented, "The average size of each 1983 deal was a quarter of the $70 million average for the deals done in 1992."[31] In other, more difficult financial environments, such as following the 2001 recession, the new-issues market became very quiet for entrepreneurial companies, especially compared to the hot market of 1999. As a result, exit opportunities were limited. In addition, it was very difficult to raise money for early-growth or even more mature companies from the public market. Consider the following situations that resulted from the stock market crash on October 19, 1987:

> An entrepreneur spent a dozen years building a firm in the industrial mowing equipment business from scratch to $50 million in sales. The firm had a solid record of profitable growth in recent years. Although the firm is still small by Fortune 500 standards, it was the dominant firm in the business in mid-1987. Given the firm's plans for continued growth, the entrepreneur, the backers, and the directors decided the timing was right for an IPO, and the underwriters agreed. By early 1987, everything was on schedule and the "road show," which was to present the company to the various offices of the underwriter, was scheduled to begin in November. The rest is history. Nearly two years later, the IPO was still on hold.
>
> In 1991, as the IPO market began to heat up, a Cambridge-based biotech firm was convinced by its investors and investment bankers to take the company public. In the spring, the IPO window opened as medical

[31] Thomas N. Cochran, "IPOs Everywhere: New Issues Hit a Record in the First Quarter," *Barron's*, April 19, 1993, p. 14. Though softened in 1997, the IPO market by any prior standard remains robust.

EXHIBIT 13.10

Initial Public Offerings (1980–2003)

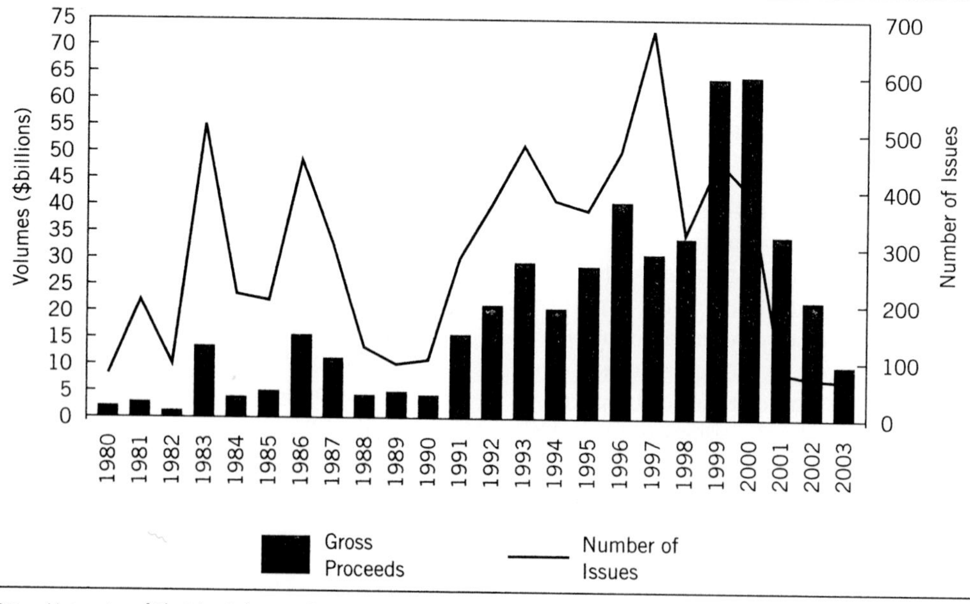

Sources: Jay R. Ritter, University of Florida, February 17, 2005, "Summary Statistics on 1975–2003 Initial Public Offerings with an Offer Price of $5.00 or more." Used by permission of the author.

Note: These numbers are slightly different than those reported in previous editions of this text, due to Ritter's exclusion of IPOs with an offer price of less than $5, American Depositor Receipts (ADRs), best efforts offers, unit offers, Regulation A offerings, real estate investment trusts, partnerships, and closed-end funds, and due to updating of numbers. However, the trends seen in this exhibit are in keeping with prior numbers.

and biotechnology stocks were the best performing of all industry groups. By May, they had the book together; in June, the road show started in Japan, went through Europe, and ended in the United States in July. As the scheduled IPO date approached, so did the United Nations deadline for Saddam Hussein. After U.S. involvement, the new issues market turned downward, as the management of the biotech company watched their share price decline from $14 to $9 per share.[32]

A classic recent example occurred in 2000, as the NASDAQ collapsed and the IPO market shut down. A company we will call NetComm had raised more than $200 million in private equity and debt, was on track to exceed $50 million in revenue, and was 18 months away from positive cash flow. It would require another $125 million in capital to reach this point. The company had completed registration and was ready for an IPO in May 2000, but it was too late. Not only was the IPO canceled, but also subsequent efforts to merge the company failed and the company was liquidated for 20 cents on the dollar in the fall of 2000! Dozens of companies experienced a similar fate during this period. As seen in Exhibit 13.11, 2002 ended with just 22 venture-backed IPOs from U.S. companies for a total offer size of $1.9 billion, down significantly from the 2000 record of $19.3 billion. A recovery was evident in 2004, when the average offer size increased to $131.5 million, and the post-offer value reached a four-year high at $61.1 million.

The more mature a company is when it makes a public offering, the better the terms of the offering. A higher valuation can be placed on the company, and less equity will be given up by the founders for the required capital.

There are a number of reasons an entrepreneurial company would want to go public. The following are some of the advantages:

- To raise more capital with less dilution than occurs with private placements or venture capital.
- To improve the balance sheet and/or to reduce or to eliminate debt, thereby enhancing the company's net worth. To obtain cash for pursuing opportunities that would otherwise be unaffordable.
- To access other suppliers of capital and to increase bargaining power, as the company pursues additional capital when it needs it least.
- To improve credibility with customers, vendors, key people, and prospects. To give the impression: "You're in the big leagues now."
- To achieve liquidity for owners and investors.
- To create options to acquire other companies with a tax-free exchange of stock, rather than having to use cash.
- To create equity incentives for new and existing employees.

Notwithstanding the above, IPOs can be disadvantageous for a number of reasons:

- The legal, accounting, and administrative costs of raising money via a public offering are more disadvantageous than other ways of raising money.
- A large amount of management effort, time, and expense are required to comply with SEC regulations and reporting requirements and to

[32] "Rational Drug Design Corporation," HBS Case 293-102. Copyright © 1992 Harvard Business School. Used by permission of Harvard Business School; all rights reserved.

EXHIBIT 13.11

Analysis of Recent IPO History

Year	Number of U.S. IPOs	Number of U.S. Venture-Backed IPOs	Total Venture-Backed Offer Size ($million)	Average Venture-Backed Offer Size ($million)	Total Venture-Backed Post-Offer Value ($million)	Average Venture-Backed Post-Offer Value ($million)
1996	771	268	$11,605.6	$43.1	$56,123.0	$208.6
1997	529	131	4,501.4	35.9	20,838.8	159.1
1998	301	75	3,515.4	48.3	16,837.4	224.5
1999	461	223	18,355.5	76.4	114,864.6	493.0
2000	340	226	19,343.0	93.3	106,324.3	470.5
2001	81	37	3,088.2	87.3	15,078.5	407.5
2002	71	22	1,908.5	86.8	8,219.6	373.6
2003	82	29	2,022.7	75.6	8,257.5	273.0
2004	246	93	11,014.9	131.5	61,087.6	699.6

Source: Thomson Venture Economics/NVCA. Used by permission.

maintain the status of a public company. This diversion of management's time and energy from the tasks of running the company can hurt its performance and growth.

- Management can become more interested in maintaining the price of the company's stock and computing capital gains than in running the company. Short-term activities to maintain or increase a current year's earnings can take precedence over longer-term programs to build the company and increase its earnings.
- The liquidity of a company's stock achieved through a public offering may be more apparent than real. Without a sufficient number of shares outstanding and a strong "market maker," there may be no real market for the stock and, thus, no liquidity.
- The investment banking firms willing to take a new or unseasoned company public may not be the ones with whom the company would like to do business and establish a long-term relationship.

Private Placement after Going Public[33]

Sometimes a company goes public and then, for any number of reasons that add up to bad luck, the high expectations that attracted lots of investors early on turn sour. Your financial picture worsens; there is a cash crisis; down goes the price of your stock in the public marketplace. You find that you need new funds to work your way out of difficulties, but public investors are disillusioned and not likely to cooperate if you bring out a new issue.

Still, other investors are sophisticated enough to see beyond today's problems; they know the company's fundamentals are sound. While the public has turned its back on you, these investors may be receptive if you offer a private placement to tide you over. In such circumstances, you may use a wide variety of securities—common stock, convertible preferred stock, convertible debentures. There are several types of exempt offerings, usually described by reference to the securities regulation that applies to them.

Regulation D is the result of the first cooperative effort by the SEC and the state securities associations to develop a uniform exemption from registration for small issuers. A significant number of states allow for qualification under state law in coordination with the qualification under Regulation D. Heavily regulated states, such as California, are notable exceptions. However, even in California, the applicable exemption is fairly consistent with the Regulation D concept.

Although Regulation D outlines procedures for exempt offerings, there is a requirement to file certain information (Form D) with the SEC. Form D is a relatively short form that asks for certain general information about the issuer and the securities being issued, as well as some specific data about the expenses of the offering and the intended use of the proceeds.

Regulation D provides exemptions from registration when securities are being sold in certain circumstances. The various circumstances are commonly referred to by the applicable Regulation D rule number. The rules and their application are as follows:

Rule 504. Issuers that are not subject to the reporting obligations of the Securities Exchange Act of 1934 (nonpublic companies) and that are not investment companies may sell up to $1 million worth of securities over a 12-month period to an unlimited number of investors.

Rule 505. Issuers that are not investment companies may sell up to $5 million worth of securities over a 12-month period to no more than 35 nonaccredited purchasers, and to an unlimited number of accredited investors. Such issuers may be eligible for this exemption even though they are public companies (subject to the reporting requirements of the 1934 Act).

Rule 506. Issuers may sell an unlimited number of securities to no more than 35 unaccredited but sophisticated purchasers, and to an unlimited number of accredited purchasers. Public companies may be eligible for this exemption.

Employee Stock Ownership Plans (ESOPs)

ESOPs are another potential source of funding used by existing companies that have high confidence in the stability of their future earnings and cash flow. An ESOP is a program in which the employees become investors in the company, thereby creating an internal source of funding. An ESOP is a tax-qualified retirement benefit plan. In essence, an ESOP borrows money, usually from a bank or insurance company, and uses the cash proceeds to buy the company's stock (usually from the owners or the treasury). The stock then becomes collateral for the bank note, while the owners or treasury have cash that can be used for a variety of purposes. For the lender, 50 percent of the interest earned on the loan to the ESOP is tax exempt. The company makes annual tax-deductible contributions — of both interest and principal—to the ESOP in an amount needed to service the bank loan. "The

[33] Garner, Owen, and Conway, *The Ernst & Young Guide to Raising Capital*, pp. 52–54.

combination of being able to invest in employer stock and to benefit from its many tax advantages make the ESOP an attractive tool."[34]

Keeping Current about Capital Markets

One picture is vivid from all this: Capital markets, especially for closely held, private companies right through the initial public offering, are very dynamic, volatile, asymmetrical, and imperfect. Keeping abreast of what is happening in the capital markets in the 6 to 12 months before a major capital infusion can save invaluable time and hundreds of thousands and occasionally millions of dollars. Below are listed the best sources currently available to keep you informed:

[34] Ibid., p. 281.

- National Venture Capital Association (www.nvca.org).
- Daniel R. Gamer, Robert R. Owen, and Robert R. Conway *The Ernst & Young Guide to Raising Capital* (New York: John Wiley & Sons, 1991).
- David Schutt, ed., *Pratt's Guide to Venture Capital Sources* (New York: Venture Economics Publishing, 1993).
- *Venture Capital Journal* (published monthly by Thomson Venture Economics).
- *Venture Finance,* "IPO Reporter."
- *INC.*
- *Red Herring,* a Silicon Valley magazine.
- *Venture One,* database and reports on venture capital from California.

Chapter Summary

1. Appreciating the capital markets as a food chain looking for companies to invest in is key to understanding motivations and requirements.
2. Entrepreneurs have to determine the need for outside investors, whether they want outside investors, and if so whom.
3. America's unique capital markets include a wide array of private investors, from "angels" to venture capitalists.
4. The search for capital can be very time consuming, and whom you obtain money from is more important than how much.
5. It is said that the only thing that is harder to get from a venture capitalist than a "yes" is a "no."
6. Fortunately for entrepreneurs, the modest revival of the venture capital industry has raised the valuations and the sources available. Entrepreneurs who know what and whom to look for—and look out for—increase their odds for success.

Study Questions

1. What is meant by the following, and why are these important: cover your equity; angels; venture capital; valuation; due diligence; IPO; mezzanine; SBIC; private placement; Regulation D; Rules 504, 505, and 506; and ESOP?
2. What does one look for in an investor, and why?
3. How can the founders prepare for the due diligence and evaluation process?
4. Describe the venture capital investing process and its implications for fund-raising.
5. Most venture capitalists say: There is too much money chasing too few deals. Why is this so? When does this happen? Why and when will it reoccur?
6. What other sources of capital are available and how are these accessed?
7. Explain the capital markets food chain and its implications for entrepreneurs and investors.

Internet Resources for Chapter 13

http://www.nvca.com *The National Venture Capital Association*

http://www.pwc.com *PricewaterhouseCoopers*

http://www.garage.com *Garage Technology Ventures*

http://www.businesspartners.com *Business Partners is an online resource connecting entrepreneurial ventures with a wide range of investors*

http://www.ventureeconomics.com *Venture Economics*

MIND STRETCHERS

Have you considered?

1. Some entrepreneurs say you shouldn't raise venture capital unless you have no other alternative. Do you agree or disagree, and why?
2. Identify a founder/CEO who has raised outside capital, and was later fired by the board of directors. What are the lessons here?
3. How do venture capitalists make money? What are the economics of venture capital as a business?

Case

Forte Ventures

Preparation Questions

1. Evaluate the situation facing the Forte founders in April 2001 and the Private Placement Memorandum (PPM) (Appendix A) prepared to convince institutional investors to invest.
2. What should Maclean Palmer and his partners do and why?
3. What are the economics of the venture capital business? Assume that Forte is a "top quartile" fund in terms of performance. What will the cumulative pay checks and distributions to the limited partners and the general partners be over 10 years?

Forte Ventures

Bite off more than you can chew, then chew it.

Roger Babson, Speech to the Empire Club of Canada, 1922

Maclean Palmer hung up the phone and took another quick glance at an article from the Web site of the Boston-based firm of Hale & Dorr:

> ***April 6, 2001: Bear Market Drives IPOs into Hibernation***
> *Further deterioration in the capital markets amidst growing concern about the health of the U.S. and global economy resulted in a dismal start to the 2001 IPO market. There has also been a reduction in the number of companies in registration as withdrawals continue to exceed new filings. Completed IPOs trailed the number of withdrawals every week during the first quarter . . .*

Roger Babson's urging was now haunting Palmer as he wondered whether he had bitten off more than he could chew in seeking to raise a first-time $200 million venture fund. Was a precipitous collapse of the venture capital and private equity markets coming at the worst possible time? Would it be best to shut down, minimize losses, and revisit the fund-raising when the markets revived? Or should they press on? As he tapped in the number for the next moneyed prospect on his list, Palmer smiled ruefully to himself.

What a difference a year makes . . .

Last winter, when he had begun to pull together a talented young private equity team from around the country, venture investments in new funds had been at an all-time high, and the capital markets were still riding the Internet wave. His partners had made the leap with him in September; they quit their jobs, sold their homes, and moved their families to Boston.

Convincing institutional investors to allocate a portion of their risk capital to a long-term, illiquid, nonrecourse investment with an unproven team was the challenge faced by all new venture groups as they set out to raise money. By the spring of 2001, however, a weakening economy had significantly increased that level of difficulty.

With IPOs in decline, and early-stage venture money being diverted to prop up existing portfolio investments, institutional investors had severely tightened their criteria as to what constituted a worthy new fund opportunity. In addition, the Forte group was encountering objections related to the very strategy that they felt gave them a distinctive edge. Dave Mazza, a partner at Grove Street Advisors (GSA), explained:

> The backdrop to all of this is that there have been a lot of African-American-led funds; they've been predominantly SBICs, and few of them have come close to the top quartile performance that we have come to expect from private equity investors. We didn't have any question about what this team's motives were, but in the minds of some limited partners, they are always going to equate the two.

Despite the harsh environment, the news wasn't all bad. The GSA group—which had been early supporters of

Palmer's concept—had recently committed $10 million to Forte, with a pledge of $15 million more once the team had garnered commitments of $50 million.

Now that the influential gatekeeper had given an official nod to the Forte group, a number of state pension funds had begun to take a closer look. Still, Palmer and his partners, who were bootstrapping this effort from their savings, understood that their targeted first closing of $100 million was likely to be a long way off.

The Offering

The team had spent the last quarter of 2000 developing their offering memorandum for a $200 million venture fund (see Appendix A). As private equity fund managers, Palmer and his partners would receive both management fees and performance-based incentives. The typical management fee was in the range of 1.5 to 2.5 percent of the total assets under management. The incentive was generally 20 percent of the investment returns in excess of a predetermined baseline—known as the preferred, or hurdle, rate.

While the plan articulated a clear preference for backing ethnic-minority managers and opportunities, the team emphasized that their core mission was wealth creation. Palmer summarized their concept:

> We have put a new spin on a very successful private equity strategy that we believe has been proven successful in good and bad markets—a fundamental long-term investing approach using a management-centric strategy. And since virtually no one is out there recruiting these seasoned ethnic-minority managers, that gives us a unique advantage.
>
> We will then partner with these managers and go out to buy a small middle-market company—but not necessarily an existing ethnic-minority-owned business or even an ethnic-minority marketplace. At the end of the day, we're going to do exactly what a firm like Point West does; it's just that we'll be tapping a different network.

What was most distinct about the Forte undertaking, though, was that unlike the venture funds of the late-90s, this group would be working to raise capital in the midst of an increasingly tenuous environment.

The Venture Capital Climate in 2001

By early April 2001, the Internet bubble had clearly burst. Despite three federal funds rate cuts designed to stimulate the slowing (or contracting) economy, all major equity indices remained in negative territory for the first three months of the year. As a result of this slowdown, many companies had pre-announced revenue and/or earnings shortfalls, declared that "future visibility was low," and issued cautious outlooks for the coming months. The year 2001 was looking to be a dismal period for venture fund-raising, and for five-year private equity fund performance as well (see Exhibits 1 and 2).

As a result of all this negative news and outlook, the equity markets had an extremely difficult first quarter as the NASDAQ, S&P 500, and S&P Technology Sector were down 12.1 percent, 25.5 percent, and 24.8 percent, respectively. There were two adverse consequences of this precipitous fall in the equity markets. The first was that the IPO market had dried up virtually overnight. Consider that while the first quarter of 2000 had produced a solid record of 142 IPOs with gross proceeds of $32.15 billion, the first three months of 2001 had generated just 20 IPOs with gross proceeds of $8.21 billion—85 percent of which had come from three offerings.

The second consequence of falling share prices was that as the aggregate portfolios of pension fund managers shrunk, the denominator (which defined the

EXHIBIT 1

Funds, Fund Commitments, and Average Fund Size

	Venture Capital				Buyout and Mezzanine			
Year/Qtr	First-Time Funds	Total Funds	Commitments ($billions)	Avg. Fund Size ($mil)	First-Time Funds	Total Funds	Commitments ($billions)	Avg. Fund Size ($mil)
Q1 1999	32	86	9.1	106	16	48	10	208
Q2 1999	27	92	9.5	103	10	40	12.9	323
Q3 1999	38	103	11.4	111	10	41	13.9	339
Q4 1999	59	194	29.6	153	12	62	25.5	411
Q1 2000	33	150	21.7	145	6	35	14.3	409
Q2 2000	56	167	29.2	175	13	42	22.8	543
Q3 2000	37	113	26.6	235	7	32	12.8	400
Q4 2000	51	147	23.8	162	8	34	20.6	606
Q1 2001	29	95	16.1	169	7	33	8.9	270

EXHIBIT 2

Five-Year Performance Trends

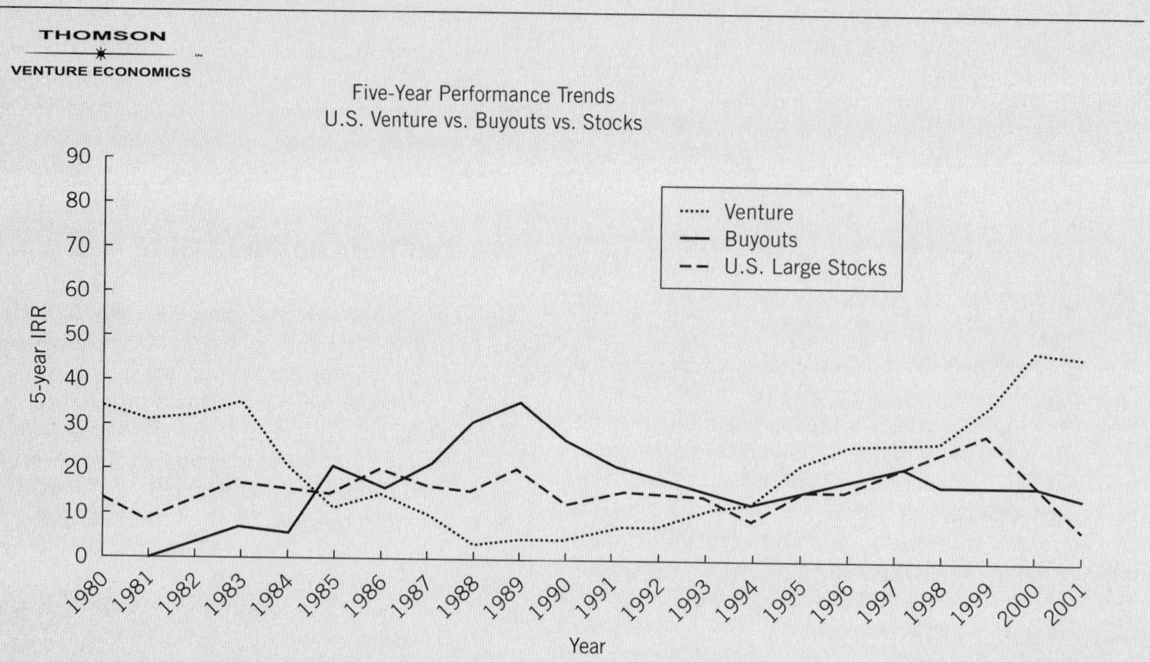

Source: Thomson Venture Economics/NVCA. Used by permission.

percentage of total investments allocated to venture capital and private equity) also shrunk. This resulted in a considerable over-allocation for that asset class. Consequently, pension fund managers had simply stopped investing their money in venture capital until the allocation percentage was back within a range set by their investing policies.

As Palmer and his partners struggled for footing in an increasingly soft market, they also needed to contend with an additional negative dynamic—unrelated to their experience, but entirely related to who they were.

Fund Raising: Perceptions and Realities

Since the Forte Ventures team had begun courting investors just as the capital markets had begun to weaken, it was hardly a revelation when pension fund managers and other prospective limited partners explained that in those increasingly uncertain times, they were unwilling to place a bet on an untested team. Palmer and his partners could appreciate why many limited partner prospects had almost no incentive to take a chance with a new fund; profitable allocations were considered part of that job, and backing what in hindsight appeared to have been a long shot could get a pension fund manager fired. Palmer said that their fund-raising pitch emphasized the team and their commitment to success:

> We were selling on the fact that we had put a lot of thought into deciding who we wanted to be partners with. We all bet on ourselves and on each other. If we were willing to do it—literally burn all the boats and move to Boston before we ever raised a dime—we figured that ought to say something about our level of confidence and dedication.

Judith Elsea, at the time the chief investment officer with the Ewing Marion Kauffman Foundation, discussed her response to their prospectus:

> What made Forte different from many minority-centric funds of the past was that they had a good deal of operating experience, so once they got the deals, they'd know what to do with them. The challenge was that many limiteds saw the team as a group whose investment activities would be outside of their sphere of contacts.

Even with the material support from GSA—as well as ongoing advice and referrals—by the spring of 2001 the team was making little headway with prospects who were watching the value of their investment portfolios decline with the falling capital markets. Mazza commented on the deteriorating fund-raising environment:

> The limited partner excuses are coming in a few flavors: the market is terrible, Forte doesn't have a senior star equity player, and we are tapped out. They are all in real bad moods because they're losing a lot of money, and even though this fund is a good bet—and certainly doesn't have anything to do with their market losses—it is just about the worst time in the world to be raising a fund.

GSA founder Clint Harris reiterated that the ability of new funds to attract investors was unfortunately closely related to market conditions:

> The bar has gone way up. If a new group like Forte had come to us a year earlier, we probably could have gotten them a check for half of the $200 million they're looking for.

The Worsening Storm

As Palmer hung up from yet another prospect that was planning to hold off on new investments for the time being, he had a hard time diverting his gaze from a tally of first-quarter market indices:

Index	1Q 2001
PVCI[1]	−31.4%
Dow Jones	−8.02%
S&P 400	−12.42%
S&P 500	−11.85
S&P 600	−6.57%
NASDAQ	−25.51%
Russell 1000	−12.56%
Russell 2000	−6.51%
Russell 3000	−12.51%

[1] The Warburg Pincus/Venture Economics Post-Venture Capital Index (PVCI) is a market cap weighted index of the stock performance of all venture-backed companies taken public over the previous 10-year period.

Appendix A

FORTE VENTURES, L.P.: PRIVATE PLACEMENT MEMORANDUM (PPM)

I. Executive Summary

Introduction

Forte Ventures, L.P. (the "Fund" or the "Partnership"), is being formed principally to make equity investments in a broad range of profitable, small to middle-market private companies that are owned or managed by ethnic minorities. The Fund will also invest in businesses that serve or operate in the minority marketplace. Forte's core investment principles are to support or recruit high quality management teams who are focused on wealth creation and to invest in businesses that, because of their strategic position, have attractive growth prospects. Forte's overriding investment thesis is to leverage its investment and operating expertise, as well as its extensive contacts and knowledge of the minority marketplace, in order to allocate capital to fundamentally sound businesses in an underserved market. Forte believes that it is uniquely positioned to execute this investment thesis and provide attractive returns to the Fund's Limited Partners.

Forte is currently offering limited partnership interests in Forte Ventures, L.P., to institutional investors and a limited number of qualified individuals with the objective of raising $200 million. The Fund will be managed by Maclean E. Palmer, Jr., Ray S. Turner, Clark T. Pierce, and Andrew L. Simon (the "Principals").

Forte's private equity transactions will take several forms, including recapitalizations, leveraged buyouts, industry consolidations/build-ups, and growth equity investments. Forte will seek investments opportunistically with particular focus on industry sectors in which the Firm's Principals have substantial prior experience. These sectors currently include auto, auto aftermarket, business-to-business services, growth manufacturing, branded consumer products, OEM industrial products, health care, information technology services, and telecommunications.

Forte's Success Factors

Forte believes the Partnership represents an attractive investment opportunity for the following reasons:

- *Experienced Team of Investment Professionals.* Messrs. Palmer, Pierce, and Simon have over 17 years of *direct* private equity experience. At their previous firms—Advent International, Point West Partners, Ninos Capital, Trident Partners, and McCown De Leeuw—Messrs. Palmer, Pierce, and Simon executed all aspects of private equity transactions. They have led investments in a variety of industries and have considerable experience in manufacturing, business services and outsourcing, health care, consumer products, financial services, and telecommunications. In addition, Messrs. Palmer and Pierce led 13 transactions for their prior firms and were co-lead on three others, investing over $169 million.
- *Operating Experience of Principals.* Forte's team brings a combined 57 years of operating experience to the firm in addition to their investing expertise. The Principals have found that this experience and insight are invaluable in assessing investment opportunities, recruiting management teams, and adding value to portfolio companies post-investment. The Principals will continue to leverage their operating experience through active involvement with portfolio management teams to develop and implement value creation strategies that will drive growth and deliver superior returns.
- *Proven Investment Track Record.* As highlighted in the following table, Mr. Palmer has fully exited three of six equity transactions returning $75.2 million on $16.4 million invested, yielding a cash on cash return of 4.7x and an internal rate of return (IRR) of 113 percent. Mr. Pierce has fully exited one of ten mezzanine transactions returning $10.6 million on $5.3 million invested, yielding a cash on cash return of 2.0x and an IRR of 23 percent. For another three transactions where values have been established but are as yet unrealized, Messrs. Palmer and Pierce have collectively generated $46.1 million on investments of $24 million for an imputed cash on cash return of 1.9x. The Principals believe there is substantial remaining value to be realized from these three unrealized investments, as well as the remaining nine unrealized investments.
- *Implementation of a Proven and Successful Strategy.* Forte will implement a proven and effective two-part strategy that has been utilized by the Principals to generate excellent investment returns:
  - Support or recruit high quality management teams with demonstrated records of success who are focused on creating shareholder value.
  - Invest in fundamentally sound businesses that, because of their strategic position, have sustainable margins and attractive growth prospects.

Summary Investment Track Record

	Number of Deals	Invested Capital ($m)	Value Realized ($m)	Value Unrealized ($m)	IRR (%)	Cash on Cash
Equity Investments						
Valuation Status						
Realized[1]	3	$16.4	$75.2		113%	4.7x
Established but Unrealized	1	$8.0		$19.1	109%	2.4x
Unrealized[1]	2	$50.0		$50.0		1.0x
Total	**6**	**$74.4**	**$75.2**	**$69.1**	**112%**	**1.9x**
Mezzanine Investments						
Valuation Status						
Realized	1	$ 5.3	$ 10.6		23%	2.0x
Established but Unrealized	2	$16.0	$ 10.5	$16.5	29%	1.7x
Unrealized[1]	7	$73.5		$68.4		0.9x
Total	**10**	**$94.8**	**$21.1**	**$84.9**	**26%**	**1.1x**

[1] Includes one investment each for which Messrs. Palmer or Pierce had significant, but not full, responsibility.

The Principals believe that the ongoing refinement of this strategy in the target marketplace will contribute to the success of the Fund's investments. In addition, Forte's strategy will utilize, where appropriate, the minority status of the firms it invests in as a means to accelerate growth. However, it should be noted that because Forte intends to invest in fundamentally sound businesses the minority status of its portfolio companies will not influence or be a substitute for the goal of building world-class operational capabilities in each portfolio company.

- *Attractiveness of Minority Companies and the Minority Marketplace.* Minority managed or controlled companies and the minority marketplace represent attractive investment opportunities for the following reasons:
  - The number of seasoned minority managers with significant P&L experience has grown appreciably over the past 15 years and provides a sizable pool from which Forte can recruit.[2,3]
  - The number of minority controlled companies with revenues in excess of $10 million has increased dramatically over the past 15 years and these companies need equity capital to continue their impressive growth rates.[4,5]
  - Rapid growth in the purchasing power of minority consumers, currently estimated at over $1.1 trillion of retail purchasing power and growing at seven times the rate of the overall U.S. population, presents an attractive investment opportunity for companies serving the minority marketplace.[6]
  - Numerous corporations have initiatives in place to increase their purchasing from minority suppliers; however, these corporations are being forced to reduce their supplier bases to remain competitive. Minority controlled companies that serve these corporations need significant equity capital in order to support the growth rates demanded by their customers. Without this capital infusion, minority suppliers will be unable to remain competitive in an environment of supplier rationalization and corporations will be unable to reach the targets they have set for their minority purchasing.[7]
  - The minority marketplace is overlooked and underserved by private equity investors. Despite the numerous investment opportunities, Forte estimates that less than 1 percent of the $250 billion in private equity capital is targeted at the minority marketplace.
- *Access to Multiple Sources of Proprietary Deal Flow.* Over their years in private equity and operating positions, the Principals have developed an extensive network for sourcing and developing potential transactions and identifying and recruiting management teams. Forte expects the majority of its opportunities will be negotiated or initiated transactions developed from the following sources:
  - Proprietary investment ideas generated by the Principals involving world-class minority management talent.
  - Growth stage opportunities led by minority management teams or companies serving the minority marketplace.
  - Traditional buyouts and corporate divestitures to minority-led management teams or companies serving the minority marketplace.

[2] July 2000 interview with senior Russell Reynolds & Associates executives.
[3] "What Minorities Really Want," *Fortune Magazine*, Vol. 142, No. 2, July 10, 2000.
[4] U.S. Census Bureau, the Survey of Minority Owned Businesses, 1997.
[5] National Minority Supplier Development Council Survey, 1999.
[6] SBA Office of Advocacy, 1997 Economic Census.
[7] National Minority Supplier Development Council Survey, 1999.

- The existing pool of minority controlled enterprises.
- Corporations seeking to increase their minority purchasing.
- Proactive calling efforts to generate proprietary deal flow that leverages the relationships of the Principals.
- Investment banks and other financial intermediaries.

- *Principals' Extensive Knowledge of the Minority Marketplace.* The Principals have direct experience sourcing and executing deals in the target marketplace through their involvement in two minority-focused funds. In addition, the Principals believe that the combination of their in-depth knowledge of the target marketplace, their operating experience, and their ability to identify and recruit exceptional management teams affords Forte a distinct competitive advantage.

II. Investment Strategy

Overview

The combined experience of Forte's Principals has helped them evolve a two-fold investment strategy:

- To support or recruit high quality management teams with demonstrated records of success and provide them the opportunity for significant equity ownership in order to align their interests with the Fund.
- To acquire or invest in fundamentally sound companies in the minority marketplace that, because of their strategic positions, have sustainable margins and attractive growth prospects.

In executing this strategy during both the pre- and post-investment stages of a transaction, Forte's Principals will consistently take the following steps:

- Maintain a disciplined approach to valuation and structuring.
- Conduct a thorough due diligence examination to identify the stress points in the business model.
- Obtain controlling equity positions, possibly with co-investors, or significant equity positions with certain super majority rights.
- Implement focused value creation plans and performance monitoring metrics.
- Align companies with strategic and corporate partners to control costs and accelerate growth and thus value creation.
- Exercise value-added operating leadership by supporting management in the development and achievement of business goals.
- Create liquidity through carefully timed and executed transactions.

Forte has developed an investment strategy that builds on the strengths of the Principals' prior experiences. It is also a strategy that has produced excellent results. The Principals expect the Fund's capital to be invested in approximately three to four years from the date of the first close. Forte will primarily seek to invest in established companies generally ranging in value from $25 million to $75 million and will typically invest $10 million to $35 million in any given investment.

Investment Focus

Forte will seek investments opportunistically with particular focus on industry sectors in which the Firm's Principals have substantial prior experience. These sectors currently include auto, auto aftermarket, business-to-business services, growth manufacturing, branded consumer products, OEM industrial products, health care, information technology services, and telecommunications. The Principals' depth of industry knowledge has led to a substantial flow of potential investments and an ability to rapidly and thoroughly evaluate proposed opportunities. It has also provided numerous industry contacts to call upon for assistance in due diligence and has been helpful in supporting management plans for growth and development. Furthermore, the Principals' industry expertise will enable Forte to be an attractive participant in corporate partnerships.

Forte's specific industry knowledge has evolved over time and new industries will be added as the firm opportunistically explores new areas for potential investment. It is expected that Forte will leverage its analytical skills and network of contacts to continue developing logical extensions of its current preferences as well as new areas of focus in which high rates of growth and outstanding management are present. The following charts are representative of the Principals' prior allocation of investment dollars by stage and industry sector as well as Forte's expected allocations for the Fund.

Types of Investment Opportunities

Forte believes that the most attractive investments generally share several important characteristics including:

- A proven and highly motivated management team that owns or wishes to acquire a significant equity interest in the company.
- A strong competitive market position or the ability to build one.
- Presence in an industry with attractive dynamics and an investment structure that supports sustainable earnings growth.
- An established track record of solid financial performance and resistance to earnings downturns during economic or industry cycles.
- The potential to increase operating earnings through focused value creation efforts.

Prior Allocations by Forte Principals ($ weighted)

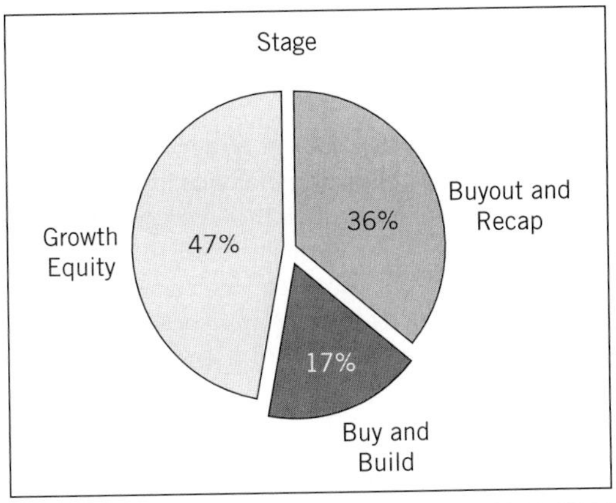

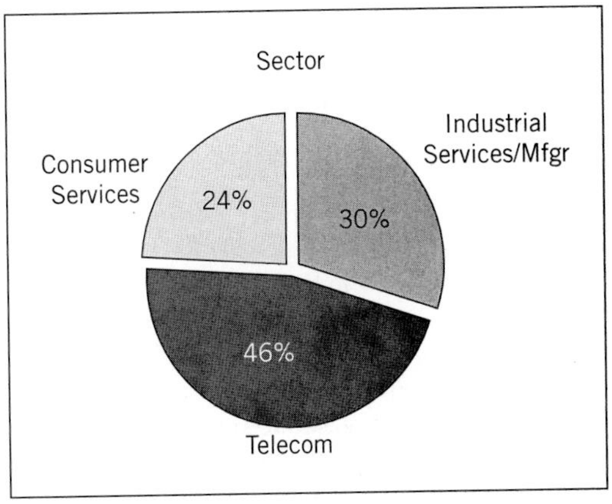

Projected Allocations in Forte Ventures ($ weighted)

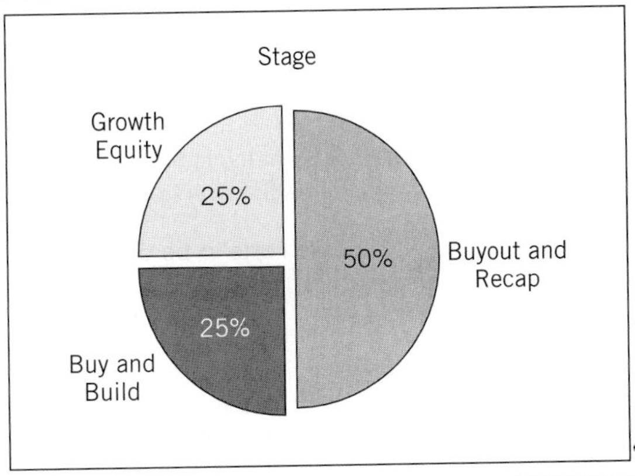

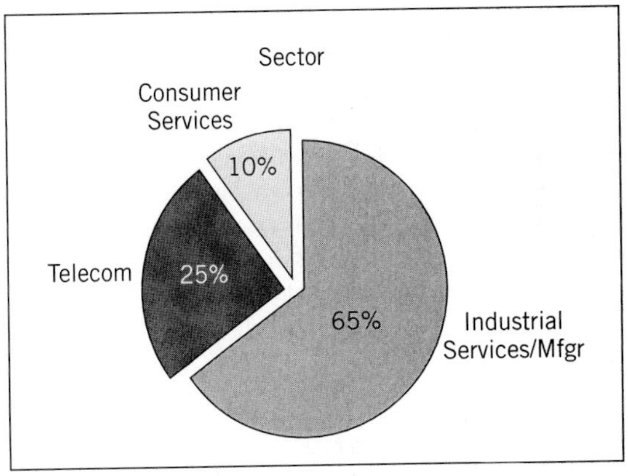

Since Forte's priorities start with the capability of the management team and a company's growth prospects, the actual form of a transaction is often secondary. Forte will seek to participate in the following types of transactions:

- *Leveraged Buyouts:* Forte will initiate LBOs and participate in buyouts organized by management and other investment partners.
- *Recapitalizations:* Forte will assist in organizing recapitalizations of businesses in which management retains significant ownership. Forte will participate as either a majority or minority partner.
- *Growth Capital Investments:* Forte will provide capital to companies in need of equity to support attractive growth opportunities.
- *Industry Consolidations/Build-Ups:* Forte will support management teams that seek to build significant companies through acquisition within fragmented industries.

The Principals' prior transactions are indicative of the mix of transactions that will be pursued: five of these prior transactions were LBOs, two were recapitalizations, three were consolidations/build-ups, and five were growth capital investments.

III. Selected Investment Summaries

Cobalt Telecommunications

The Company Cobalt Telecommunications (Cobalt or the "Company") provides small to medium-sized businesses a resold package of local, long distance, Internet, paging, and cellular telecommunications services from a variety of providers. The Company added value by aggregating the charges onto one customized bill, as well as providing one source for all customer support.

The Investment While at Point West Partners, Mr. Palmer became the lead investor in Cobalt in December 1997 with an investment of $2 million. In October 1998 he led another $2 million investment in the Company.

The Situation Cobalt was formed to capitalize on the deregulation of the local telecom marketplace. The Company's vision was to provide a higher level of customer service and a full suite of voice and data products to a neglected, but very profitable, customer segment. The Company needed financing to build its customer support and service-provisioning infrastructure, as well as recruit and support an agent-based sales channel.

Role of Forte Principal Mr. Palmer worked with Cobalt management to develop the Company's strategy of concentrating its sales activity within a focused geography in the western Boston suburbs. Mr. Palmer also identified a low cost, yet robust, billing and customer support platform that proved to be the key component of the Company's low cost and efficient back office. Mr. Palmer recruited the Company's CFO prior to the investment and he played a key role in the Company's acquisition efforts. He also worked with the Company to initiate price increases and cost reductions to improve gross margins. After recognizing weaknesses in the existing Sales VP, Mr. Palmer also identified and recruited a new VP of Sales and Marketing and worked with him to accelerate the performance of the Company's sales channels, as well as introduce a new telemarketing channel. The new sales focus enabled Cobalt to increase its sales by over 600 percent in one year.

Liquidity Event In the summer of 1999, Mr. Palmer led the effort to identify potential strategic acquirers for the Company after it was determined that an attractive purchase price could be achieved. After an intense three-month process, the Company received and accepted an offer to be acquired by Macklin USA (NASDAQ: MLD). Mr. Palmer led the negotiations with Macklin and achieved, to Forte's knowledge, the highest multiple that has been paid to date for a pure reseller of telecom services. The transaction closed in December 1999 with a return to Point West Partners valued at 4.2x cash on cash and an 83 percent IRR.

MBCS Telecommunications

The Company MBCS Telecommunications (MBCS or the "Company") is a switched-based provider of local, long distance, Internet, data, and high speed access services to small to medium-sized businesses. The Company has offices in five markets in the Ameritech region and is expanding its switch network in each of these markets.

The Investment Mr. Palmer led Point West Partners' initial $3 million investment in MBCS in July 1998, and made a follow-on investment of $5 million in March 2000.

The Situation MBCS had received a first round investment in July 1997, which was used to finance the Company's growth in long distance services and to recruit additional management. In 1998, the Company was seeking investors with telecom expertise to aid in the transition into local voice and data services.

Role of Forte Principal Mr. Palmer worked with the Company to identify and select a low cost, yet robust, billing and customer support platform that saved over $1 million in potential capital expenditures. This system has proven to be a key component in supporting MBCS's growth from 20,000 to over 70,000 customers. Mr. Palmer also played a key role in recruiting senior management team members, and advised and assisted management in two of the Company's three acquisitions. Most recently, Mr. Palmer has been a leader in the Company's fund-raising efforts, introducing the Company to senior lenders and investment bankers and guiding the management team through the selection and approval process.

Valuation Events In March 2000, MBCS received a third round of financing that was led by a new investor at a valuation that represented a 2.6x step up over the previous round (on a fully diluted basis). In September 2000, MBCS acquired a data services and high speed access provider in a stock-for-stock transaction that valued LDM at a 1.6x step up over the third round.

X-Spanish Radio

The Company X-Spanish Radio Networks, Inc. (X-Spanish or the "Company"), was built by acquiring radio stations in California, Arizona, Texas, and Illinois. These stations form a Spanish language radio network. The programming is satellite delivered from the Company's main studio located in Sacramento, California.

The Investment Mr. Pierce led Ninos Capital's $5.25 million initial investment in X-Spanish in November 1994.

The Situation X-Spanish's overall strategy was to acquire radio stations at attractive prices in desirable markets and keep operating costs low by delivering the programming via satellite to the entire network. To execute the strategy the Company needed capital to purchase additional stations. Over a four-year period X-Spanish was able to acquire 15 radio stations and build a loyal audience, which led to increasing advertising revenues.

Role of Forte Principal Mr. Pierce sourced, structured, priced, and underwrote Ninos' investment in X-Spanish. He also performed a complete due diligence review on the Company, the management team, and the Company's competitive position in each of its target markets. Mr. Pierce's due diligence review included the technical performance of the stations, the demand for advertising in the target markets, and the "stick" value of the radio stations. In his board observer role, he monitored the Company's strategic plan, operating performance, and acquisition opportunities and was involved in the strategic decisions of the Company, including potential acquisitions and capital raising.

Liquidity Event X-Spanish was sold to a financial buyer in November 1998, and this investment resulted in a 23 percent IRR to Ninos Capital.

Krieder Enterprises

The Company Krieder Enterprises, Inc. (Krieder or the "Company"), is the largest manufacturer of nail enamel in bulk in the United States. Krieder is a leading supplier of enamel to the world's leading cosmetics companies.

The Investment Mr. Pierce led Ninos Capital's $4 million initial investment in Krieder in April 1995 to finance a buyout.

The Situation To gain market share and improve its competitive position, the Company needed to build infrastructure, upgrade and improve its manufacturing facilities, strengthen its laboratory and technical capabilities, increase the level of customer service, and build an organization that could support the planned growth. The buyout allowed the Company to evolve from an entrepreneurial managed company to a professionally managed one.

Role of Forte Principal Mr. Pierce sourced, structured, priced, and underwrote Ninos' investment in Krieder. He also performed a complete due diligence review of the equity sponsor, the Company, the management team, and the Company's competitive position within its industry. In his board observer role, he evaluated and analyzed the Company's growth plans, acquisition candidates and deal structures, expansion of the manufacturing facilities, and the implementation of an MIS system.

Liquidity Event For the three-year period 1997 to 1999, the Company's revenues and EBITDA have grown at CAGRs of 20 percent and 33 percent, respectively. In January 1999, Ninos' investment was repaid along with an additional $1 million distribution. Ninos' warrant position is currently valued in excess of $3.5 million. The combination of the repayment and the warrant value yield a 29 percent IRR on this investment.

Cidran Food Service

The Company Cidran Food Services II, L.P. (Cidran or the "Company"), owned and operated 130 Burger King restaurants in Louisiana, Arkansas, and Mississippi. Cidran owned and operated over 80 percent of the Burger King restaurants in Louisiana.

The Investment Mr. Pierce led Ninos Capital's $12 million investment in Cidran in December 1998 to complete a recapitalization of the company and provide growth capital.

The Situation The Company was recapitalized to repurchase the equity interests of several minority shareholders and to allow the Company to continue execution of its strategic plan. This plan required continuously upgrading and improving restaurants, aggressively opening new restaurants, and selectively pursuing acquisitions.

Role of Forte Principal Mr. Pierce sourced, structured, priced, and underwrote Ninos' investment in Cidran. He performed a complete due diligence review on the Company, the management team, and the Company's competitive position in its markets. Through active participation in investor meetings, he evaluated and reviewed the Company's strategic planning and budgeting process, the operating performance at the store level, various advertising and marketing initiatives, new store level development, and acquisition opportunities.

Liquidity Event In June 2000, Mr. Pierce led Ninos' voluntary reinvestment in a combination of all the Cidran sister companies. The new company is called Cidran Services LLC ("Cidran Services"). As part of the reinvestment, Ninos sold its 5 percent warrant position back to Cidran in June 2000, which resulted in an IRR of 28 percent.

IV. Investment Process

Sourcing Investment Opportunities

The majority of the Principals' prior investments were originated by the Principals themselves. The Principals have developed sources and techniques for accessing quality investment opportunities, and the Principals' deal flow ability represents an important asset. Investment opportunities for the Fund are expected to emerge from a broad range of categories:

- Operating executives, entrepreneurs, board members, and other investment professionals with whom the Principals have forged relationships. The Principals have developed relationships with hundreds of potential partners and referral sources that understand the Principals' investment approach.
- Original concepts developed and implemented by the Principals.
- Service professionals (e.g., attorneys, accountants, and consultants).
- Professional financial community contacts and relationships (major investment banks, small and regional investment banks, and business brokers).

This network is maintained and developed by a combination of personal visits and telephone calls, as well as frequent mailings.

Evaluation of Investment Opportunities

The Principals possess strong analytical skills and seasoned judgment, reflecting over 17 years of collective investing experience and over 57 years of operating experience. The Principals will leverage this experience in selecting attractive investment opportunities. When considering investment opportunities, a team of Forte professionals will be assembled to conduct a thorough due diligence investigation of the target company including its history, management, operations, markets, competition, and prospects. The deal team works closely with the target company's management to develop a thorough understanding of their individual goals and objectives as well as their capabilities. Each Forte managing director will also spend considerable time interacting with the CEO. The deal team will also spend considerable time conducting extensive reference checks on the senior team, especially the CEO. If the Principals determine that the management team requires strengthening, professional searches will be initiated during due diligence.

The deal team will independently assess the market by studying available research reports, attending industry trade conferences, conducting competitive interviews, and performing original market and industry research. The deal team will also conduct customer interviews and, in most cases, participate in sales calls, both with and without company personnel. Forte will augment the efforts of the deal team with outside resources such as attorneys, accountants, and function-specific consultants as appropriate. Market research consultants may also be engaged to validate management's market forecasts.

The Principals, because of their operating experience, work with all levels of an organization to understand the capabilities of each manager as well as the internal dynamics of the organization. In the considerable amount of time devoted to the management team, the deal team develops knowledge of each manager's objectives to ensure that they can be aligned in a common strategy to maximize growth and shareholder value.

Transaction Structuring

While engaged in due diligence, the deal team simultaneously structures the transaction, which includes valuing the company, negotiating with the seller, securing the financing, and arranging management's equity participation. As in the past, the Principals will price transactions based on conservative operating assumptions and capital structures. Forte will risk adjust target rates of return for various investments based upon general industry and financial risk, as well as specific operating characteristics of individual investments. Using these risk adjustment factors, the deal team will model a variety of possible operating results and exit outcomes.

Forte only considers investments where multiple exit alternatives are clearly identified at the time of the transaction. The Principals' years of transaction experience enhance their ability to successfully negotiate outcomes that satisfy Forte's investment goals. Generally, the management team will invest its own funds on the same terms as Forte and participate in a performance-based option plan to augment their ownership interests. The management team's ownership will be carefully structured to ensure that the objectives of all the participants are aligned to the ultimate goal of maximizing the return on the investment.

Development and Implementation of a Focused Value Creation Plan

Prior to closing a transaction, Forte's Principals will work in partnership with the management team to develop a 3- to 5-year value creation plan. These plans will usually be anchored by systemic growth which is most often achieved through management team development, operating and systems improvements that enhance the company's ability to serve its customer, as well as sales force development, new customer recruitment, and new product development.

Developing and Monitoring Investments

The Principals' post-transaction activities will involve extensive interaction with each portfolio company and its management with the Value Creation Plan serving as the blueprint for increasing shareholder value. Forte believes that its strategy of investing in small to middle-market companies with growth potential necessitates the dedication of Forte management resources to a significantly greater extent than might be required if Forte were investing in larger or slower growing enterprises. The Principals' involvement will include regular communications with management, typically in the form of weekly flash reports, informal meetings and conversations, monthly or quarterly board meetings, and annual budgeting review sessions. The Principals also actively participate in strategic planning sessions and industry trade conferences. In addition, the Firm will assist each portfolio company on a project or functional basis as required. Forte will hold weekly staff meetings where each portfolio company is reviewed on at least a monthly basis to ensure full communication and input from all Forte professionals. Objectives for developing each company will be developed by Forte, and management will be encouraged to pursue activities to enhance investment value. Semiannual comprehensive reviews of the entire portfolio will also be conducted to ensure prior objectives have been met and adequate progress has been targeted for the upcoming period. The Principals will also assist portfolio companies in addressing strategic issues through the creation and effective use of a strong board of directors. Two Forte Principals will generally sit on each portfolio company board, and the Principals will augment these boards through the recruitment of outside industry-specific directors, often from the group of successful executives with whom the Principals have previously worked.

Achieving Investment Liquidity

Forte's investment strategy focuses heavily on the ultimate exit strategy at the time each investment is made. Forte will regularly consider opportunities for investor liquidity as part of its formal semiannual portfolio company planning process or as specific circumstances arise.

The Principals have successfully led the exit of four investments and achieved significant realizations from two others. The four exited investments were strategic sales, and the Principals also have direct involvement in companies that have gone public or been acquired by other equity sponsors.

Internal Planning

At the end of each year, Forte will undertake an annual planning process during which it will evaluate its investment strategy and the financial and human resources needed to execute that strategy. Several days will be set aside by the Principals to set priorities and the targets for the coming year, as well as to give consideration to longer-term trends affecting Forte's business. The output of this planning process will provide a formal agenda for a second meeting of all Forte professionals. Forte believes that an emphasis on internal planning and evaluation will result in continued refinement of its investment strategy and identification and development of new partners to provide for the Firm's long-term continuity.

V. Investment Team

Forte Ventures, L.P., will be managed by the General Partner. The Principals of the General Partner are Maclean E. Palmer, Jr., Ray S. Turner, Clark T. Pierce, and Andrew L. Simon. Two of the Principals have known each other for over five years and developed a working relationship through their prior firms' co-investment in two deals. These two Principals have demonstrated the ability to generate superior returns for investors and have experience initiating investment opportunities, structuring and negotiating investments, and actively working with portfolio company management teams to maximize returns. Two members of Forte's team also bring over 57 years of operating experience covering a broad range of industry sectors including auto and other heavy industries, high-tech electronics, and health care. The team's operating experience was garnered from Fortune 100 companies as well as startup and fast growth companies financed by private equity investors.

Managing Directors

Maclean E. Palmer, Jr. Maclean Palmer, Jr. (41), has over 5 years of direct private equity experience and over 17 years of operating experience. Prior to joining Forte, he was a managing director with Point West Partners from 1997 to 2000 in their San Francisco office. While at Point West, Mr. Palmer was responsible for deal origination, transaction execution, and portfolio company management, and focused on growth equity and buyout investments in the telecommunications, business-to-business services, industrial manufacturing, and auto sectors. Mr. Palmer led Point West investments in three competitive local exchange carriers (CLECs): Cobalt Telecommunications, MBCS Telecommunications, and Concept Telephone. He continues to represent Point West on the board of directors of both MBCS and Concept Telephone.

From 1995 to 1997, Mr. Palmer was a vice president in the Boston office of Advent International. While at Advent, he focused on industrial and technology investments and led Advent's investment in ISI, a financial and business information services provider. From 1986 to 1995, Mr. Palmer worked in various management and engineering positions for three startup companies, UltraVision Inc., Surglaze Inc., and DTech Corporation, which were all financed by private equity investors. During his startup career, Mr. Palmer was involved in the development and successful market introduction of 12 new products. In addition, Mr. Palmer held engineering positions with Borg Warner Corporation from 1984 to 1986 and with the Diesel Division of a major automotive firm from 1983 to 1984.

Mr. Palmer sits on the board of JT Technologies, a minority-owned firm that develops battery and ultra-capacitor technology. He also sits on the board of the Cooper Enterprise Fund, a minority-focused fund based in New York; the Community Preparatory School, a private inner-city school focused on preparing middle school students for college preparatory high schools; and the Zell Laurie Entrepreneurial Institute at the University of Michigan Business School.

Mr. Palmer holds a BSME from the Automotive Institute, an MBA cum laude from Babson College, and was awarded a Kauffman Fellowship, graduating with the program's inaugural class.

Ray S. Turner Ray S. Turner (61) has had a long and distinguished career as an operating executive at Fortune 50 companies. From October 1998 to March 2000, he was group vice president, North America Sales, Service and Marketing for a multinational heavy-industry manufacturer. From 1990 to 1998, Mr. Turner also served as vice president and general manager for North America Sales and Manufacturing at that company.

From 1988 to 1990, he served as vice president for manufacturing operations. From 1977 to 1988, Mr. Turner served in senior manufacturing management and plant manager roles for a number of assembly and manufacturing operations for the company. Prior to his career at that corporation, Mr. Turner spent several years serving in a variety of positions in engineering, materials management, manufacturing, sales, personnel, and labor relations.

Mr. Turner serves on the board of directors of two Fortune 100 corporations.

Mr. Turner received a bachelor's degree in Business Administration from Western Michigan University. He also completed the Executive Development Program at Harvard Business School, and an Advanced International General Management Program in Switzerland.

Clark T. Pierce Clark T. Pierce (38) has over 7 years of mezzanine and private equity experience and over 4 years of corporate finance experience. Most recently, he was a principal with Ninos Capital, a publicly traded mezzanine investment fund. While at Ninos he was responsible for leading all aspects of the investment process, including deal origination and evaluation, due diligence, deal execution, and portfolio company management. Mr. Pierce has closed numerous transactions in various industries, including business services, distribution, manufacturing, and financial services.

From 1993 to 1995, Mr. Pierce managed Ninos Capital's Specialized Small Business Investment Company ("SSBIC"). This SSBIC was a $45 million investment vehicle directed toward minority-owned and controlled companies. Prior to Ninos Capital, Mr. Pierce spent one year with Freeman Securities as a vice president in the Corporate Finance Group where he advised bondholders and companies involved in the restructuring process. From 1989 to 1991, Mr. Pierce was an associate with Chase Manhattan Bank, N.A., in the Corporate Finance Group.

Mr. Pierce served on the board of directors of Sidewalks, Inc., a social services organization for troubled teenagers, and The Orphan Foundation of America, a nonprofit agency focusing on adoption of older children.

Mr. Pierce received a BA from Morehouse College, a JD from George Washington University, and an MBA from the Wharton Business School at the University of Pennsylvania.

Andrew L. Simon Andrew L. Simon (30) has 4 years of direct private equity experience, as well as 3 years of strategy consulting experience. During his career, Mr. Simon has worked on private equity investments in numerous industry sectors including contract manufacturing, industrial products, health care, financial services, and direct marketing. Most recently, he was a senior associate in the New York office at McCown De Leeuw & Co., Inc. ("MDC") where he focused on growth and leveraged equity investments, including recapitalization and buy-and-build acquisitions. While at MDC, Mr. Simon played a lead role in identifying potential investments, negotiating with sellers, structuring and arranging debt financing, as well as supervising the legal documentation and closing of transactions. Post-acquisition, he played an active role in the financing and strategic direction of MDC portfolio companies and participated at board meetings.

From 1995 to 1997, Mr. Simon was an associate in the Boston office of Trident Partners ("Trident"). At Trident, Mr. Simon was responsible for evaluating, prioritizing, and analyzing potential new acquisition opportunities, as well as supporting deal teams with business and analytical due diligence. From 1992 to 1995, Mr. Simon was a senior analyst at Marakon Associates where he was responsible for valuation analysis, industry research, and strategy development. In addition, Mr. Simon has worked for Littlejohn & Co., an LBO firm focused on restructuring; Physicians Quality Care, a venture-backed health care services company; and Lotus Development.

Mr. Simon earned an AB degree from Princeton University's Woodrow Wilson School and earned his MBA, with honors, from Harvard Business School where he was a Toigo Fellow.

Vice President

Fidel A. Cardenas Most recently, Fidel A. Cardenas (31) was a managing director with MTG Ventures from 1999 to 2000. At MTG, a private equity firm focused on acquiring and operating manufacturing and service companies, Mr. Cardenas was responsible for deal origination, transaction execution, and portfolio company management. Prior to his role at MTG Ventures, Mr. Cardenas was a principal with MTG Advisors from 1992 to 1997 where he focused on strategy consulting and executive coaching. Concurrent with MTG Advisors, Mr. Cardenas was elected to two terms as mayor of Sunny Park, California, becoming, at 23, the mayor of that city. He has also served as assistant deputy mayor for Public Safety for the City of Los Angeles and as an analyst for McKinsey and Company.

Mr. Cardenas received a BA in Political Science from Harvard, cum laude, and his MBA from Harvard Business School.

VI. Summary of Principal Terms

The following is a Summary of Terms relating to the formation of Forte Ventures, L.P. (the "Partnership"), a Delaware limited partnership. This Summary of Terms is by its nature incomplete and subject to the terms and conditions contained in the definitive limited partnership agreement of the Partnership (the "Partnership Agreement") and certain other documents. In the event that the description of terms in this Summary of Terms or elsewhere in this Memorandum is inconsistent with or contrary to the description in, or terms of, the Partnership Agreement or related documents, the terms of the Partnership Agreement and the related documents shall control.

Purpose

The principal purpose of the Partnership is to produce long-term capital appreciation for its partners through equity and equity-related investments in companies that are owned or managed by ethnic minorities or serve or operate in the minority marketplace.

Partnership Capital

The Partnership will have a target size of $200 million (together with the General Partner Commitment) of capital commitments. Commitments in excess of this amount may be accepted at the discretion of the General Partner.

General Partner

The general partner (the "General Partner") of the Partnership will be Forte Ventures, LLC, a Delaware limited liability company formed under the laws of the State of Delaware. Maclean E. Palmer, Jr., Clark T. Pierce, Ray S. Turner, and Andrew L. Simon will be the initial members of the General Partner. The General Partner will control the business and affairs of the Partnership.

Management Company

The management company (the "Management Company") will be Forte Equity Investors, LLC, a Delaware limited liability company. The Management Company will act as investment advisor to the Partnership pursuant to the terms of the Management Agreement.

The Management Company will be responsible for identifying investment opportunities, structuring and negotiating the terms and conditions of each acquisition, arranging for all necessary financing, and, after consummation, monitoring the progress of, and arranging for the disposition of, its interest in each portfolio company. The Management Company may, at its discretion, retain other professionals, including but not limited to accountants, lawyers, and consultants to assist in rendering any services described herein. In addition, the Management Company may provide services directly to portfolio companies.

General Partner's Capital Contribution

The General Partner shall contribute an amount equal to the greater of $2 million or 1 percent of the total contributions of the Partners, at the same time and in the same manner as the Limited Partners.

Partnership Term

The Partnership term shall be 10 years from the First Closing unless extended by the General Partner for up to a maximum of three additional one-year periods to provide for the orderly liquidation of the Partnership.

Investment Period

The General Partner will generally not be permitted to make any capital calls for the purpose of making investments after the termination of the period (the "Investment Period") commencing on the First Closing and ending on the fifth anniversary thereof, other than commitments to make investments that were committed to prior to such fifth anniversary, and Follow-On Investments (occurring after the Investment Period) which will not exceed 15 percent of the committed capital of the Partnership.

Side Fund

The General Partner may establish an investment fund (the "Side Fund") for individual investors who will be assisting and/or advising the Management Company in connection with originating investment opportunities, recruiting senior management candidates, conducting due diligence, and analyzing selective industry opportunities. The aggregate capital commitments of the Side Fund shall not exceed $5 million. The Side Fund will have terms similar to the Partnership, *provided however* that the individual investors in the Side Fund will only be required to pay a nominal management fee and the profits from investments made by the Side Fund will not be subject to a Carried interest. The Side Fund will invest alongside the Partnership in each Investment of the Partnership on a pro rata basis. A percentage of each Investment equal to the Capital Commitments of the Side Fund divided by the total Capital Commitments of the Side Fund, the Partnership, or any Parallel Regulatory Vehicle shall be reserved for co-investment by the Side Fund.

Investment Limits

The Partnership will not make investments (excluding Bridge Financings as noted below) in any single or group of related portfolio companies which exceed 25 percent of committed capital, or 35 percent of committed capital when combined with Bridge Financings, of such portfolio companies. With the consent of the Limited Partners, such investment limits may be increased by up to 10 percent with respect to one portfolio company or group of related companies.

Without the approval of the Limited Partners the investments shall not include:

(i) any investment in an entity that provides for "Carried interests" or management fees to any persons other than the management of a portfolio company or the General Partner or the Management Company unless the General Partner waives its right to receive "Carried interest" distributions with respect to such investment or the General Partner makes a good faith determination that such investment is expected to (a) yield returns on investments within the range of returns expected to be provided by the equity and equity-related securities in which the Partnership was organized to invest (taking into account any management fee or Carried interest relating thereto), and (b) foster a strategic relationship with a potential source of deal flow for the Partnership, *provided however* that such investments shall not exceed 15 percent of the committed capital of the Partnership;

(ii) acquisition of control of businesses through a tender offer (or similar means) if such acquisition is opposed by a majority of the members of such business's board of directors or similar governing body;

(iii) any investment in an entity the principal business of which is the exploration for or development of oil and gas or development of real property;

(iv) investments in uncovered hedges or derivative securities; or

(v) any investment in marketable securities unless immediately after giving effect to such investment the total amount of the Partnership's investments in marketable securities does not exceed 15 percent of aggregate capital commitments of all Partners (other than an investment in marketable securities of an issuer which the General Partner intends to engage in a going private transaction on the date of such investment or in which the General Partner expects to obtain management rights).

The Partnership will not invest more than 20 percent of its committed capital in businesses which have their principal place of business outside of the United States. The Partnership will not invest in securities of entities formed outside of the United States unless it has first obtained comfort that Limited Partners of the Partnership will be subject to limited liability in such jurisdiction which is no less favorable than the limited liability they are entitled to under the laws of Delaware. The Partnership will use its reasonable efforts to ensure that Limited Partners are not subject to taxation in such jurisdiction(s) other than with respect to the income of the Partnership. The Partnership will not guarantee the obligations of the portfolio companies in an amount in excess of 10 percent of capital commitments to the Partnership at any time. The Partnership may only borrow money to pay reasonable expenses of the Partnership or to provide interim financings to the extent necessary to consummate the purchase of a portfolio company prior to receipt of capital contributions.

Bridge Financings

The Partnership may provide temporary financings with respect to any portfolio company ("Bridge Financings"). Any Bridge Financing repaid within 18 months will be restored to unpaid capital commitments.

Any Bridge Financing that is not repaid within 18 months shall no longer constitute Bridge Financing and will be a permanent investment in the portfolio company in accordance with the terms of the Partnership. Bridge Financings may not be incurred if, after giving *pro forma* effect to such incurrence, the aggregate principal amount of Bridge Financings outstanding is in excess of 10 percent (or up to 20 percent with the approval of the Limited Partners) of the Partnership's aggregate capital commitments.

Distributions

Distributions from the Partnership may be made at any time as determined by the General Partner. All distributions of current income from investments, proceeds from the disposition of investments (other than Bridge Financings and proceeds permitted to be reinvested), and any other income from assets of the Partnership (the "Investment Proceeds") from or with respect to each investment initially shall be apportioned among each partner (including the General Partner) in accordance with such Partner's Percentage Interest in respect of such investment. Notwithstanding the previous sentence, each Limited Partner's share of such distribution of Investment Proceeds shall be allocated between such Limited Partner, on the one hand, and the General Partner, on the other hand, and distributed as follows:

i. *Return of Capital and Partnership Expenses:* First, 100 percent to such Limited Partner until such Limited Partner has received distributions equal to (A) such Limited Partner's capital contributions for all Realized Investments and such Limited Partner's pro-rata share of any unrealized losses on write-downs (net of write-ups) of the Partnership's other portfolio company investments and (B) such Limited Partner's capital contributions for all Organizational Expenses and Partnership Expenses allocated to Realized Investments and write-downs of the Partnership's other portfolio company investments (the amounts discussed in clauses (A) and (B) are referred to collectively as the "Realized Capital Costs");

ii. *8 Percent Preferred Return:* 100 percent to such Limited Partner until cumulative distributions to such Limited Partner from Realized Investments represent an 8 percent compound annual rate of return on such Limited Partner's Realized Capital Costs;

iii. *General Partner Catch-Up to 20 Percent:* 100 percent to the General Partner until cumulative distributions of Investment Proceeds under this clause (iii) equal 20 percent of the total amounts distributed pursuant to clauses (ii) and (iii); and

iv. *80/20 Split:* Thereafter, 80 percent to such Limited Partner and 20 percent to the General Partner (the distributions to the General Partner pursuant to this clause (iv) and clause (iii) above are referred to collectively as the "Carried Interest Distributions").

The rate of return regarding each distribution relating to an investment shall be calculated from the date the capital contributions relating to such investment were used to make such investment to the date that the funds or the property being distributed to each Limited Partner have been received by the Partnership.

Proceeds from cash equivalent investments will be distributed to the Partners in proportion to their respective interests in Partnership assets producing such proceeds, as determined by the General Partner. Proceeds of Bridge Financings will be distributed in accordance with contributions to such Bridge Financings.

Subject, in each case, to the availability of cash after paying Partnership Expenses, as defined below, and setting aside appropriate reserves for reasonably anticipated liabilities, obligations, and commitments of the Partnership, current income earned (net of operating expenses) will be distributed at least annually, and the net proceeds from the disposition of securities of portfolio companies, other than proceeds permitted to be reinvested, shall be distributed as soon as practicable.

The General Partner may make distributions from the Partnership, as cash advances against regular distributions, to the Partners to the extent of available cash in amounts necessary to satisfy their tax liability (or the tax liability of the partners of the General Partner) with respect to their proportion of the Partnership taxable net income.

The Partnership will use its best efforts not to distribute securities in kind unless they are marketable securities or such distribution is in connection with the liquidation of the Partnership. If the receipt of such securities by a Limited Partner will violate law or if a Limited Partner does not wish to receive distributions in kind, the General Partner will make alternative arrangements with respect to such distribution.

Allocations of Profits and Losses

Profits and losses of the Partnership will be allocated among Partners in a manner consistent with the foregoing distribution provisions and the requirements of the Internal Revenue Code.

Clawback

If, following the dissolution of the Partnership, the General Partner shall have received Carried Interest Distributions with respect to a Limited Partner greater than 20 percent of the cumulative net profits (calculated as if all the profits and losses realized by the Partnership with respect to such Limited Partner had occurred simultaneously), then the General Partner shall pay over to such Limited Partner the lesser of (i) the amount of such excess or (ii) the amount of distributions received by the General Partner with respect to such Limited Partner reduced by the taxes payable by the General Partner with respect to such excess and increased by the amount of any tax benefits utilized by the General Partner as a result of such payment in the year of payment.

Management Fees

The Partnership will pay to the Management Company an annual management fee (the "Management Fee") equal to, during the Investment Period, 2 percent of the Partners' total capital committed to the Partnership and, during the period thereafter, 2 percent of the total capital contributions that were used to fund the cost of, and remain invested in, investments, which amount shall be increased quarterly by any capital contributions made during such period and decreased quarterly by amounts distributed to partners as a return of capital. The Management Fee will be payable in advance on a semiannual basis with the first payment being made on the First Closing Date and each semiannual payment thereafter occurring on the first business day of each calendar semiannual period.

Management Fees may be paid out of monies otherwise available for distribution or out of capital calls. The payments by Additional Limited Partners with respect to the Management Fee and interest thereon will be paid to the Management Company.

Other Fees

The General Partner, the Management Company, and their affiliates may from time to time receive monitoring fees, directors' fees, and transaction fees from portfolio companies or proposed portfolio companies. All such fees will be first applied to reimburse the Partnership for all expenses incurred in connection with Broken Deal Expenses (as defined below) and 50 percent of any excess of such fees will be applied to reduce the Management Fees payable to the Management Company by the Partnership.

"Break-Up Fees" shall mean any fees received by the General Partner, Management Company, or their affiliates in connection with such proposed investment in a portfolio company that is not consummated, reduced by all out-of-pocket expenses incurred by the Partnership, the General Partner, the Management Company, or their affiliates in connection with such proposed investment in the portfolio company.

Partnership Expenses

The Partnership will be responsible for all Organizational Expenses and Operational Expenses (collectively, the "Partnership Expenses").

"Organizational Expenses" shall mean third-party and out-of-pocket expenses, including, without limitation, attorneys' fees, auditors' fees, capital raising, consulting and structuring fees, and other startup expenses incurred by either of the Partnership, the General Partner, or Management Company, or any affiliates thereof in connection with the organization of the Partnership.

"Operational Expenses" shall mean with respect to the Partnership, to the extent not reimbursed by a prospective or actual portfolio company, if any, all expenses of operation of the Partnership, including, without limitation, legal, consulting, and accounting expenses (including expenses associated with the preparation of Partnership financial statements, tax returns, and K-1s); Management Fees; any taxes imposed on the Partnership; commitment fees payable in connection with credit facilities, accounting fees, third-party fees and expenses, attorney's fees, due diligence, and any other costs or fees related to the acquisition or disposition of securities or investment, whether or not the transaction is consummated; expenses associated with the Limited Partners and other advisory councils and investment committees of the Partnership; insurance and the costs and expenses of any litigation involving the Partnership; and the amount of any judgments or settlements paid in connection therewith.

"Broken Deal Expenses" mean with respect to each investment, to the extent not reimbursed by a prospective or actual portfolio company, all third-party expenses incurred in connection with a proposed investment that is not ultimately made or a proposed disposition of an investment which is not actually consummated, including, without limitation, (i) commitment fees that become payable in connection with a proposed investment that is not ultimately made; (ii) legal, consulting, and accounting fees and expenses; (iii) printing expenses; and (iv) expenses incurred in connection with the completion of due diligence concerning the prospective portfolio company.

Limited Partner Advisory Committee

The General Partner shall establish a Limited Partner Advisory Committee (the "Advisory Committee") which will consist of between three and nine representatives of the Limited Partners selected by the General Partner.

VII. Risk Factors

An investment in Forte Ventures involves a high degree of risk. There can be no assurance that Forte Ventures' investment objectives will be achieved, or that a Limited Partner will receive a return of its capital. In addition, there will be occasions when the General Partner and its affiliates may encounter potential conflicts of interest in connection with Forte Ventures. The following considerations should be carefully evaluated before making an investment in Forte Ventures. Risk factors include:

- Illiquid and long-term investments.
- General portfolio company risk.
- Reliance on the principals.
- Past performance is not indicative of future investment results.
- Lack of operating history.
- Lack of transferability of the limited partnership interests.
- Potential of contingent liabilities on dispositions of portfolio company investments.
- No separate counsel for limited partners.
- Uncertain nature of investments.
- Use of leverage increases exposure to adverse economic factor.

14

Chapter Fourteen

The Deal: Valuation, Structure, and Negotiation

Always assume the deal will not close and keep several alternatives alive.

James Hindman
Founder, CEO, and Chairman, Jiffy Lube International

Results Expected

Upon completion of this chapter, you will have:

1. Determined methodologies used by venture capitalists and professional investors to estimate the value of a company.
2. Examined how equity proportions are allocated to investors.
3. Studied how deals are structured, including critical terms, conditions, and covenants.
4. Examined key aspects of negotiating and closing deals.
5. Characterized good versus bad deals and identified some of the sand traps entrepreneurs face in venture financing.
6. Analyzed an actual deal and startup financing in the "Paul J. Tobin" case study.

The Art and Craft of Valuation

The entrepreneur's and private investor's world of finance is very different from the corporate finance arena where public companies jostle and compete in well-established capital markets. The private company and private capital world of entrepreneurial finance is more volatile, more imperfect, and less accessible than corporate capital markets. The sources of capital are very different. The companies are much younger, more dynamic, and the environment more rapidly changing and uncertain. The consequences, for entrepreneurs and investors alike, of this markedly different context are profound. Cash is king, and beta coefficients and elegant corporate financial theories are irrelevant. Also, liquidity and timing are everything, and there are innumerable, unavoidable conflicts between users and suppliers of capital. Finally, the determination of a company's value is elusive and more art than science.

What Is a Company Worth?

The answer: It all depends! Unlike the market for public companies, where millions of shares are traded daily and the firm's market capitalization (total shares outstanding times the price per share) is readily determined, the market for private companies is very imperfect.

Determinants of Value

The criteria and methods applied in corporate finance to value companies traded publicly in the capital markets, when cavalierly applied to entrepreneurial companies, have severe limitations. The ingredients to the entrepreneurial valuation are cash, time, and risk. In Chapter 12 you determined the burn rate, OOC, and the TTC for your venture, so it is not hard to infer that the amount of cash available and the cash generated will play an important role in valuation. Similarly, Exhibit 12.5 showed that time also plays an influential role. Finally, risk or perception of risk contributes to the determination of value. The old adage, "The greater the risk, the greater the reward" plays a considerable role in how investors size up the venture.

Long-Term Value Creation versus Quarterly Earnings

The core mission of the entrepreneur is to build the best company possible and, if possible, to create a great company. This is the single surest way of generating long-term value for all the stakeholders and society. Such a mission has quite different strategic imperatives than one aimed solely at maximizing quarterly earnings to attain the highest share price possible given price/earnings ratios at the time. More will be said about this in Chapter 19.

Psychological Factors Determining Value

Time after time companies are valued at preposterous multiples of any sane price/earnings or sales ratios. In the best years, such as the 1982–1983 bull market, the New York Stock Exchange Index was trading at nearly 20 times earnings; it sank to around 8 after the stock market crash of October 1987. Even 12 to 15 would be considered good in many years. By 1998 to late 2001, the S&P 500 was setting above a P/E of 30. In contrast, consider a late 1990s survey of the top 100 public companies in Massachusetts. The stocks of many of these companies were being traded at 50 or more times earnings and several were at 95 to 100 times earnings and 6 to 7 times sales! Even more extreme valuations were seen during the peak of the so-called dot.com bubble from 1998 to early 2000. Some companies were valued at 100 times revenue and more during this classic frenzy. High multiples persist in 2005 with the S&P 500 trading at 20 times earnings.

Often, behind extraordinarily high valuations is a psychological wave, a combination of euphoric enthusiasm for a fine company, exacerbated by greed and fear of missing the run up. The same psychology can also drive prices to undreamed of heights in private companies. In the late 1960s, for instance, Xerox bought Scientific Data Systems, then at $100 million in sales and earning $10 million after taxes, for $1 billion: 10 times sales and 100 times earnings! Value is also in the eye of the beholder.

A Theoretical Perspective

Establishing Boundaries and Ranges, Rather than Calculating a Number Valuation is much more than science, as can be seen from the examples just noted. As will be seen shortly, there are at least a dozen different ways of determining the value of a private company. A lot of assumptions and a lot of judgment calls are made in every valuation exercise. In one case, for example, the entrepreneur consults 13 experts to determine how much he should bid for the other half of a $10 million in sales company. The answer ranged from $1 million to $6 million. He subsequently acquired the other half for $3.5 million.

It can be a serious mistake, therefore, to approach the valuation task in hopes of arriving at a single number or even a narrow range. All you can realistically expect is a range of values with boundaries driven by different methods and underlying assumptions for each. Within that range, the buyer and the seller need to determine the comfort zone of each. At what point are you basically indifferent to buying and selling? Determining your point of indifference can be an invaluable aid in preparing you for negotiations to buy or sell.

Investor's Required Rate of Return (IRR)[1]

Various investors will require a different rate of return (ROR) for investments in different stages of development and will expect holding periods of various lengths. For example, Exhibit 14.1 summarizes, as ranges, the annual rates of return that venture capital investors seek on investments by stage of development and how long they expect to hold these investments. Several factors underlie the required ROR on a venture capital investment, including premiums for systemic risk, illiquidity, and value added. Of course, these can be expected to vary regionally and from time to time as market conditions change, because the investments are in what are decidedly imperfect capital market niches to begin with.

Investor's Required Share of Ownership

The rate of return required by the investor determines the investor's required share of the ownership, as

[1]IRR is a synonym for internal rate of return, calculated annually.

EXHIBIT 14.1

Rate of Return Sought by Venture Capital Investors

Stage	Annual ROR%	Typical Expected Holding Period (years)
Seed and startup	50–100% or more	More than 10
First stage	40–60	5–10
Second stage	30–40	4–7
Expansion	20–30	3–5
Bridge and mezzanine	20–30	1–3
LBOs	30–50	3–5
Turnarounds	50+	3–5

EXHIBIT 14.2

Investor's Required Share of Ownership under Various ROR Objectives

Assumptions:

Amount of initial startup investment = $1 million
Holding period = 5 years
Required rate of return = 50%
Year 5 after-tax profit = $1 million
Year 5 Price/earnings ratio = 15

Calculating the required share of ownership:

	Investor's Return Objective (Percent/Year Compounded)			
Price/Earning Ratio	**30%**	**40%**	**50%**	**60%**
10×	37%	54%	76%	106%
15×	25	36	51	70
20×	19	27	38	52
25×	15	22	30	42

Exhibit 14.2 illustrates. The future value of a $1 million investment at 50 percent compounded is $1 million × $(1.5)^5$ = $1 million × 7.59 = $7.59 million. The future value of the company in Year 5 is profit after tax × price/earnings ratio = $1 million × 15 = $15 million. Thus, the share of ownership required in Year 5 is:

$$\frac{\text{Future value of the investment} = \$7.59 \text{ million}}{\text{Future value of the company} = \$15.00 \text{ million}} = 51\%$$

One can readily see that by changing any of the key variables, the results will change accordingly.

If the venture capitalists require the RORs mentioned earlier, the ownership they also require is determined as follows: In the startup stage, 25 to 75 percent for investing all of the required funds; beyond the startup stage, 10 to 40 percent, depending on the amount invested, maturity, and track record of the venture; in a seasoned venture in the later rounds of investment, 10 to 30 percent to supply the additional funds needed to sustain its growth.

The Theory of Company Pricing

In Chapter 13, we introduced the concept of the food chain, which we have included here as Exhibit 14.3. This chart depicts the evolution of a company from its idea stage through an initial public offering (IPO). The appetite of the various sources of capital—from family, friends, and angels, to venture capitalists, strategic partners, and the public markets—varies by company size, stage, and amount of money invested. We argue that entrepreneurs who understand these appetites and the food chain are better prepared to focus their fund-raising strategies on more realistic sources, amounts, and valuations.

The Theory of Company Pricing is simplistically depicted in Exhibit 14.4. In the ideal scenario, a venture capital investor envisions two to three rounds, starting at a $1.00 per share equivalent, then a 4 to 5 times markup to Series B, followed by a double markup to Series C, and then doubling that $8.00 round at an IPO. This generic pattern

EXHIBIT 14.3

The Capital Markets Food Chain for Entrepreneurial Ventures

	Stage of Venture			
	R&D	**Seed**	**Launch**	**High Growth**
Company Enterprise Value at Stage	Less than $1 million	$1 million–$5 million	$1 million–$50 million-plus	More than $100 million
Sources	Founders High Net Worth Individuals FFF* SBIR	FFF* Angel Funds Seed Funds SBIR	Venture Capital Series A, B, C. . .† Strategic Partners Very High Net Worth Individuals Private Equity	IPOs Strategic Acquirers Private Equity
Amount of Capital Invested	Less than $50,000–$200,000	$10,000–$500,000	$500,000–$20 million	$10 million–$50 million-plus
% Company Owned at IPO	10–25%	5–15%	40–60% by Prior Investors	15–25% by Public
Share Price and Number‡	$.01–$.50 1–5 million	$.50–$1.00 1–3 million	$1.00–$8.00 +/– 5–10 million	$12–$18+ 3–5 million

*Friends, Families & Fools

†Venture Capital Series A, B, C, . . .(Average Size of Round)

Round (Q4 2004):
- "A" @ $3–5 million—startup
- "B" @ $5–10 million—Product Development
- "C"+ @ $10 million—Shipping Product

Valuations vary markedly by industry (e.g., 2×[5])

Valuations vary by region and VC cycle

‡ At Post–IPO

EXHIBIT 14.4

Theory of Company Pricing

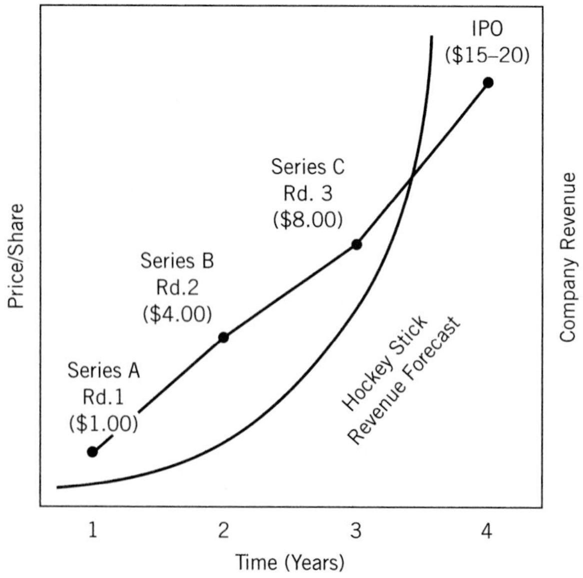

would characterize the majority of deals that succeeded to an IPO, but there are many variations to this central tendency. In truth, many factors can affect this theory.

The Reality

The past 25 years have seen the venture capital industry explode from investing only $50 million to $100 million per year to nearly $100 billion in 2000. Exhibit 14.5 shows how the many realities of the capital marketplace are at work, and how current market conditions, deal flow, and relative bargaining power influence the actual deal struck. Exhibit 14.6 shows how the dot.com explosion and the plummeting of the capital markets led to much lower values for private companies. The NASDAQ index fell from over 5000 to less than 2000, a 63 percent collapse in about nine months by year-end 2000. By 2005, the NASDAQ was barely above 2000.

EXHIBIT 14.5

The Reality

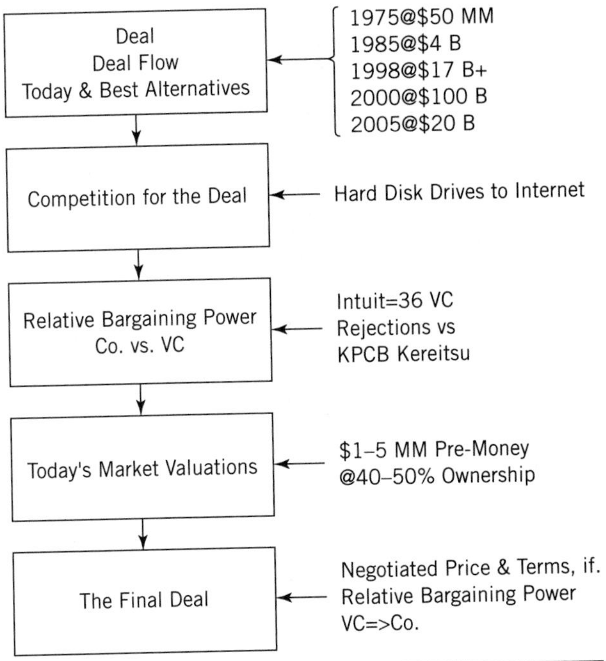

EXHIBIT 14.6

The Reality: The Down Round

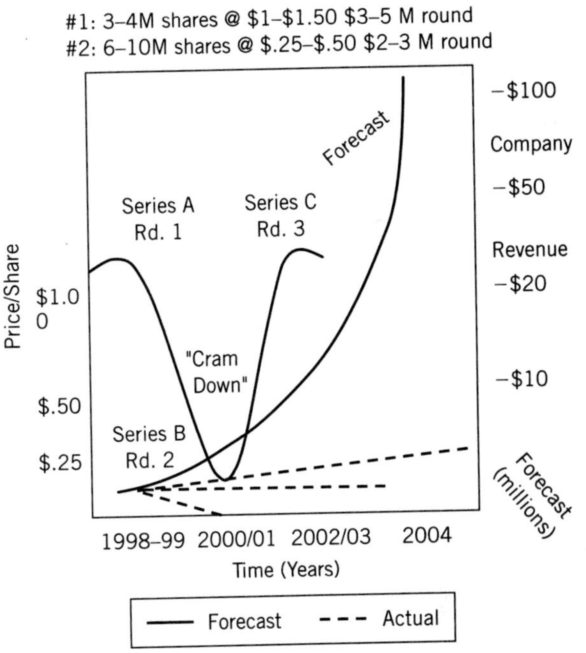

NASDAQ: peaked above 5000 in March 2000.
Dropped 63 percent by 12/31/2000.

The Down Round or Cram Down circa 2003

In this environment, which also existed after the October 1987 stock market crash, entrepreneurs face rude shocks in the second or third round of financing. Instead of a substantial four or even five times increase in the valuation from Series A to B, or B to C, they are jolted with what is called a "cram down" round: The price is typically one-fourth to two-thirds of the last round, as shown in Exhibit 14.6. This severely dilutes the founders' ownership, as investors are normally protected against dilution. Founder dilution as a result of failing to perform is one thing, but dilution because the NASDAQ and IPO markets collapsed seems rudely unfair. But that is part of the reality of valuation.

Take, for example, two excellent young companies, one launched in 1998 and one in 1999. By the fall of 2001, the first had secured two rounds of venture financing, was on target to exceed $20 million in revenue, and was seeking a $25 million round of private equity. The previous round was at $4.50 per share. The Series C round was priced at $2.88 per share, a 36 percent discount from the prior round. The second company met or exceeded all its business plan targets and was expected to achieve $25 million of EBITDA in 2001. Its prior Series B round was priced at $8.50 per share. The new Series C was set at $6.50 per share, or nearly a 24 percent discount.

In many financings in 2001 and into 2002, onerous additional conditions were imposed, such as a three to five times return to the Series C investors *before* Series A or B investors receive a dime! Both the founders and early-round investors are severely punished by such cram-down financings. The principle of the last money in governing the deal terms still prevails.

One can sense just how vulnerable and volatile the valuation of a company can be in these imperfect markets when external events, such as the collapse of the NASDAQ, trigger a downward spiral. One also gains a new perspective on how critically important timing is. Even these two strongly performing companies in the above examples were crammed down. Imagine those companies that didn't meet their plans: They were pummeled, if financed at all. What a startling reversal from the dot.com boom in 1998–1999 when companies at *concept stage* (with no product, no identifiable or defensible model of how they would make money or even break even, and no management team with proven experience) raised $20, $50, $70 million, and more *and* had an IPO with multibillion valuations. History asks: What is wrong with this picture! History also offers the answer: Happiness is still a positive cash flow!

Improved Valuations by 2005

As we saw in the last chapter, both the number of deals and average investment per deal were slowly increasing as we entered 2005. Valuations were rising, and the punishing cram down rounds with severe preferential returns had become the exception rather than the norm. There was a general sense that the capital climate was improving.

Valuation Methods

The Venture Capital Method[2]

This method is appropriate for investments in a company with negative cash flows at the time of the investment, but which in a number of years is projected to generate significant earnings. As discussed in Chapter 13, venture capitalists are the most likely professional investors to partake in this type of an investment, thus the reference to the venture capital method. The steps involved in this method are as follows:

1. Estimate the company's *net income* in a number of years, at which time the investor plans on harvesting. This estimate will be based on sales and margin projections presented by the entrepreneur in his or her business plan
2. Determine the appropriate *price-to-earnings ratio,* or P/E ratio. The appropriate P/E ratio can be determined by studying current multiples for companies with similar economic characteristics.
3. Calculate the projected *terminal value* by multiplying net income and the P/E ratio.
4. The terminal value can then be discounted to find the *present value* of the investment. Venture capitalists use discount rates ranging from 35 percent to 80 percent, because of the risk involved in these types of investments.
5. To determine the investor's *required percentage of ownership,* based on their initial investment, the initial investment is divided by the estimated present value.

To summarize the above steps, the following formula can be used:

$$\text{Final ownership required} = \frac{\text{Required future value (investment)}}{\text{Total terminal value}}$$

$$= \frac{(1+\text{IRR})^{\text{years}}\ (\text{investment})}{\text{P/E ratio (terminal net income)}}$$

6. Finally, the number of shares and the share price must be calculated by using the following formula:

$$\text{New shares} = \frac{\text{Percentage of ownership required by the investor}}{1 - \text{Percentage ownership required by the investor} \times \text{old shares}}$$

By definition, the share price equals the price paid divided by the number of shares.

This method is commonly used by venture capitalists because they make equity investments in industries often requiring a large initial investment with significant projected revenues; in addition, the percentage of ownership is a key issue in the negotiations.

The Fundamental Method

This method is simply the present value of the future earnings stream (see Exhibit 14.7).

The First Chicago Method[3]

Another alternative valuation method, developed at First Chicago Corporation's venture capital group, employs a lower discount rate, but applies it to an *expected* cash flow. That expected cash flow is the average of three possible scenarios, with each scenario weighted according to its perceived probability. The equation to determine the investor's required final ownership is:

$$\text{Required final ownership} = \frac{\text{Future value of investment} - \text{Future value of non-IPO cash flow}}{\text{Probability (Success) (Forecast terminal value)}}$$

This formula[4] differs from the original basic venture capital formula in two ways: (1) the basic formula assumes there are no cash flows between the investment and the harvest in Year 5; the future value of the immediate cash flows is subtracted from the future value of the investment because the difference between them is what must be made up for out of the terminal value; and (2) the basic formula does not distinguish between the *forecast* terminal value and the *expected* terminal value. The traditional method uses the forecast terminal value, which is adjusted through the use of a high discount rate. The formula employs the expected value of the

[2] The venture capital method of valuation is adapted from William A. Sahlman, "A Method for Valuing High-Risk, Long-Term Investment: The 'Venture Capital Method,'" Note 9-288-006, Harvard Business School 1988, pp. 2–4. Copyright © 1988 by the President and Fellows of Harvard College.
[3] This paragraph is adapted from Sahlman, "A Method for Valuing High-Risk, Long-Term Investments," p. 56.
[4] Ibid., pp. 58–59.

EXHIBIT 14.7

Example of the Fundamental Method

Hitech, Inc.

Year	Percentage Growth of Revenue	Revenue (millions)	After-Tax Margin	After-Tax Profit (millions)	Present Value Factor	PV of Each Year's Earnings ($ millions)
1	50%	$3.00	-0-	-0-	1.400	-0-
2	50	4.50	4.0%	$ 0.18	1.960	$0.09
3	50	6.75	7.0	0.47	2.744	0.17
4	50	10.13	9.0	0.91	3.842	0.24
5	50	15.19	11.0	1.67	5.378	0.31
6	40	21.26	11.5	2.45	7.530	0.33
7	30	27.64	12.0	3.32	10.541	0.32
8	20	33.17	12.0	3.98	14.758	0.27
9	15	38.15	12.0	4.58	20.661	0.22
10	10	41.96	12.0	5.03	28.926	0.17
Total present value of earnings in the supergrowth period						2.12
Residual future value of earnings stream				$63.00	28.926	2.18
Total present value of company						4.30

EXHIBIT 14.8

Example of the First Chicago Method

	Success	Sideways Survival	Failure
1. Revenue growth rate (from base of $2 million)	60%	15%	0%
2. Revenue level after 3 years	$ 8.19 million	$ 3.04 million (liquidation)	$ 2 million
3. Revenue level after 5 years	$20.97 million (IPO)	$ 4.02 million	
4. Revenue level after 7 years		$ 5.32 million (acquisition)	
5. After-tax profit margin and earnings at liquidity	15% $3.15 million	7% $ .37 million	
6. Price-earnings ratio at liquidity	17	7	
7. Value of company liquidity	$53.55 million	$ 2.61 million	$ .69 million
8. Present value of company using discount rate of 40%	$ 9.96 million	$ .25 million	$ .25 million
9. Probability of each scenario	.4	.4	.2
10. Expected present value of the company under each scenario	$ 3.98 million	$ .10 million	$ .05 million
11. Expected present value of the company		$ 4.13 million	
12. Percentage ownership required to invest $2.5 million		60.5%	

terminal value. Exhibit 14.8 is an example of using this method.

Ownership Dilution[5]

The previous example is unrealistic because in most cases, several rounds of investments are necessary to finance a high-potential venture. Take, for instance, the pricing worksheet presented in Exhibit 14.9 in which three financing rounds are expected. In addition to estimating the appropriate discount rate for the current round, the first-round venture capitalist must now estimate the discount rates that are most likely to be applied in the following rounds, which are projected for Years 2 and 4. Although a 50 percent rate is still appropriate for Year 0, it is estimated that investors in Hitech, Inc., will demand a 40 percent return in Year 2 and a 25 percent return in Year 4. The final ownership that

[5]Ibid., p. 24.

EXHIBIT 14.9

Example of a Three-Stage Financing

Hitech, Inc. (000)	Year 0 1989	Year 1 1990	Year 2 1991	Year 3 1992	Year 4 1993	Year 5 1994
Revenues	500	1,250	2,500	5,000	81,000	12,800
New income	(250)	(62)	250	750	1,360	2,500
Working capital at 20%	100	250	500	1,000	1,600	2,560
Fixed assets at 40%	200	500	1,000	2,000	3,200	5,120
Free cash flow	(550)	(512)	(500)	(750)	(440)	(380)
Cumulative external financial need	500	1,653	1,543	2,313	2,753	3,133
Equity issues	1,500	0	1,000	0	1,000	0
Equity outstanding	1,500	1,500	2,500	2,500	3,500	3,500
Cash balance	950	436	938	188	748	368
Assume: long-term IRR required each round by investors	50%	45%	40%	30%	25%	20%

Source: From "A Method for Valuing High-Risk, Long-Term Investments," by William A. Sahlman, Harvard Business School Note 9-288-006, p. 45.

each investor must be left with, given a terminal price/earnings ratio of 15, can be calculated using the basic valuation formula:

Round 1:

$$\frac{\text{Future value (Investment)}}{\text{Terminal value (Company)}} = \frac{1.50^5 \times \$1.5 \text{ million}}{15. \times \$2.5 \text{ million}} = 30.4\% \text{ ownership}$$

Round 2:

$$(1.40^3 \times \$1 \text{ million}) / (15 \times \$\ 2.5 \text{ million}) = 7.3\%$$

Round 3:

$$(1.25^1 \times \$1 \text{ million}) / (15 \times \$1.5 \text{ million}) = 3.3\%$$

Discounted Cash Flow

In a simple discounted cash flow method, three time periods are defined: (1) Years 1–5; (2) Years 6–10; and (3) Year 11 to infinity.[6] The necessary operating assumptions for each period are initial sales, growth rates, EBIAT/sales, and (net fixed assets + operating working capital)/ sales. While using this method, one should also note relationships and trade-offs. With these assumptions, the discount rate can be applied to the weighted average cost of capital (WACC).[7] Then the value for free cash flow (Years 1–10) is added to the terminal value. This terminal value is the growth perpetuity.

Other Rule-of-Thumb Valuation Methods

Several other valuation methods are also employed to estimate the value of a company. Many of these are based on similar, most recent transactions of similar firms, established by a sale of the company, or a prior investment. Such comparables may look at several different multiples, such as earnings, free cash flow, revenue, EBIT, and book value. Knowledgeable investment bankers and venture capitalists make it their business to know the activity in the current marketplace for private capital and how deals are being priced. These methods are used most often to value an existing company, rather than a startup, since there are so many more knowns about the company and its financial performance.

Tar Pits Facing Entrepreneurs

There are several inherent conflicts between entrepreneurs or the users of capital and investors or the suppliers of capital.[8] While the entrepreneur wants to have as much time as possible for the financing, the investors want to supply capital just in time or to

[6] Jeffry A. Timmons, "Valuation Methods and Raising Capital," lecture, Harvard Business School, March 1993.
[7] Note that it is WACC, not free cash flow, because of the tax factor.
[8] Jeffry A. Timmons, "Deals and Deal Structuring," lecture, Harvard Business School, February 23, 1993.

invest only when the company needs the money. Entrepreneurs should be thinking of raising money when they do not need it, while preserving the option to find another source of capital.

Similarly, users of capital want to raise as much money as possible, while the investors want to supply just enough capital in staged capital commitments. The investors, such as venture capitalists, use staged capital commitments to manage their risk exposure over 6- to 12-month increments of investing.

In the negotiations of a deal, the entrepreneur sometimes becomes attracted to a high valuation with the sentiment "My price, your terms." The investors will generally attempt to change this opinion because it is their capital. The investors will thus focus on a low valuation, with the sentiment, "My price *and* my terms."

This tension applies not only to financial transactions but also to the styles of the users versus the styles of the suppliers of capital. The users value their independence and treasure the flexibility their own venture has brought them. However, the investors are hoping to preserve their options as well. These options usually include both reinvesting and abandoning the venture.

These points of view also clash in the composition of the board of directors, where the entrepreneur seeks control and independence, and the investors want the right to control the board if the company does not perform as well as was expected. This sense of control is an emotional issue for most entrepreneurs, who want to be in charge of their own destiny. Prizing their autonomy and self-determination, many of these users of capital would agree with the passion Walt Disney conveyed in this statement: "I don't make movies to make money. I make *money* to make movies." The investors may believe in the passions of these users of capital, but they still want to protect themselves with first refusals, initial public offering rights, and various other exit options.

The long-term goals of the users and suppliers of capital may also be contradictory. The entrepreneurs may be content with the progress of their venture and happy with a single or double. It is their venture, their baby; if it is moderately successful, many entrepreneurs believe they have accomplished a lot. The investors will not be quite as content with moderate success, but instead want their capital to produce extraordinary returns—they want a home run from the entrepreneur. Thus, the pressures put on the entrepreneur may seem unwarranted to the entrepreneur, yet necessary for the investor.

These strategies contradict each other when they are manifested in the management styles of the users and providers of capital. While the entrepreneur is willing to take a calculated risk or is working to minimize or avoid unnecessary risks, the investor has bet on the art of the exceptional and thus is willing to bet the farm everyday.

Entrepreneurs possess the ability to see opportunities and, more importantly, to seize those opportunities. They possess an instinctual desire to change, to adapt, or to decommit in order to seize new opportunities. Yet the investors are looking for clear steady progress, as projected in the business plan, which leaves little room for surprises.

Finally, the ultimate goals may differ. The entrepreneur who continues to build his or her company may find operating a company enjoyable. At this point, the definition of success both personally and for the company may involve long-term company building, such that a sustainable institution is created. But the investors will want to cash out in two to five years, so that they can reinvest their capital in another venture.

Staged Capital Commitments[9]

Venture capitalists rarely, if ever, invest all the external capital that a company will require to accomplish its business plan; instead they invest in companies at distinct stages in their development. As a result, each company begins life knowing that it has only enough capital to reach the next stage. By staging capital, the venture capitalists preserve the right to abandon a project whose prospects look dim. The right to abandon is essential because an entrepreneur will almost never stop investing in a failing project as long as others are providing capital.

Staging the capital also provides incentives to the entrepreneurial team. Capital is a scarce and expensive resource for individual ventures. Misuse of capital is very costly to venture capitalists but not necessarily to management. To encourage managers to conserve capital, venture capital firms apply strong sanctions if it is misused. These sanctions ordinarily take two basic forms. First, increased capital requirements invariably dilute management's equity share at an increasingly punitive rate. Second, the staged investment process enables venture capital firms to shut down operations. The credible threat to abandon a venture, even when the firm might be economically viable, is the key to the relationship between the entrepreneur and the venture capitalists. By denying capital, the venture capitalist also signals other capital suppliers that the company in question is a bad investment risk.

[9] W. A. Sahlman, "Structure of Venture Capital Organizations," *Journal of Financial Economics* 27 (1990), pp. 506–7. Reprinted with the permission of Elsevier.

Short of denying the company capital, venture capitalists can discipline wayward managers by firing or demoting them. Other elements of the stock purchase agreement then come into play. For example, the company typically has the right to repurchase shares from departing managers, often at prices below market value, and vesting schedules limit the number of shares employees are entitled to if they leave prematurely. Finally, noncompete clauses can impose strong penalties on those who leave, particularly if their human capital is closely linked to the industry in which the venture is active.

Entrepreneurs accept the staged capital process because they usually have great confidence in their own abilities to meet targets. They understand that if they meet those goals, they will end up owning a significantly larger share of the company than if they had insisted on receiving all of the capital up front.

Structuring the Deal

What Is a Deal?[10]

Deals are defined as economic agreements between at least two parties. In the context of entrepreneurial finance, most deals involve the allocation of cash flow streams (with respect to both amount and timing), the allocation of risk, and hence the allocation of value between different groups. For example, deals can be made between suppliers and users of capital, or between management and employees of a venture.

A Way of Thinking about Deals over Time

To assess and to design long-lived deals, Professor William A. Sahlman from Harvard Business School suggests the following series of questions as a guide for deal makers in structuring and in understanding how deals evolve:[11]

- Who are the players?
- What are their goals and objectives?
- What risks do they perceive and how have these risks been managed?
- What problems do they perceive?
- How much do they have invested, both in absolute terms and relative terms, at cost and at market value?
- What is the context surrounding the current decision?
- What is the form of their current investment or claim on the company?
- What power do they have to act? To precipitate change?
- What real options do they have? How long does it take them to act?
- What credible threats do they have?
- How and from whom do they get information?
- How credible is the source of information?
- What will be the value of their claim under different scenarios?
- How can they get value for their claims?
- To what degree can they appropriate value from another party?
- How much uncertainty characterizes the situation?
- What are the rules of the game (e.g., tax, legislative)?
- What is the context (e.g., state of economy, capital markets, industry specifics) at the current time? How is the context expected to change?

The Characteristics of Successful Deals[12]

While deal making is ultimately a combination of art and science, it is possible to describe some of the characteristics of deals that have proven successful over time:

- They are simple.
- They are robust (they do not fall apart when there are minor deviations from projections).
- They are organic (they are not immutable).
- They take into account the incentives of each party to the deal under a variety of circumstances.
- They provide mechanisms for communications and interpretation.
- They are based primarily on trust rather than on legalese.
- They are not patently unfair.
- They do not make it too difficult to raise additional capital.
- They match the needs of the user of capital with the needs of the supplier.
- They reveal information about each party (e.g., their faith in their ability to deliver on the promises).
- They allow for the arrival of new information before financing is required.

[10] From "Note on Financial Contracting Deals," by William A. Sahlman, Harvard Business School Note 99-288-014, 1988, p. 1. Copyright © 1988 Harvard Business School Publishing; all rights reserved.
[11] Ibid., pp. 35–36.
[12] Ibid., p. 43.

- They do not preserve discontinuities (e.g., boundary conditions that will evoke dysfunctional behavior on the part of the agents of principals).
- They consider the fact that it takes time to raise money.
- They improve the chances of success for the venture.

The Generic Elements of Deals A number of terms govern value distribution, as well as basic definitions, assumptions, performance incentives, rights, and obligations. The deal should also cover the basic mechanisms for transmitting timely, credible information. Representations and warranties, plus negative and positive covenants, will also be part of the deal structure. Additionally, default clauses and remedial action clauses are appropriate in most deals.

Tools for Managing Risk/Reward In a deal, the claims on cash and equity are prioritized by the players. Some of the tools available to the players are common stock, partnerships, preferred stock (dividend and liquidation preference), debt (secured, unsecured, personally guaranteed, or convertible), performance conditional pricing (ratchets or positive incentives), puts and calls, warrants, and cash. Some of the critical aspects of a deal go beyond just the money:[13]

- Number, type, and mix of stocks (and perhaps of stock and debt) and various features that may go with them (such as puts) that affect the investor's rate of return.
- The amounts and timing of takedowns, conversions, and the like.
- Interest rates on debt or preferred shares.
- The number of seats, and who actually will represent investors, on the board of directors.
- Possible changes in the management team and in the composition of the board.
- Registration rights for investor's stock (in the case of a registered public offering).
- Right of first refusal granted to the investor on subsequent private placements or an IPO.
- Employment, noncompete, and proprietary rights agreements.
- The payment of legal, accounting, consulting, or other fees connected with putting the deal together.
- Specific performance targets for revenues, expenses, market penetration, and the like, by certain target dates.

Understanding the Bets

Deals, because they are based on cash, risk, and time, are subject to interpretation. The players' perceptions of each of these factors contribute to the overall valuation of the venture and the subsequent proposed deal. As was described earlier, there are a number of different ways to value a venture, and these various valuation methods contribute to the complexity of deals. Consider, for instance, the following term sheets:[14]

- A venture capital firm proposes to raise $150 million to $200 million to acquire and build RSA Cellular Phone Properties. The venture capital firm will commit between $15 million and $30 million in equity and will lead in raising senior and subordinated debt to buy licenses. Licensees will have to claim about 30 percent of the future equity value in the new company, the venture capital firm will claim 60 percent (subordinated debt claim is estimated at 10 percent), and management will get 5 to 10 percent of the future equity but only after all prior return targets have been achieved. The venture capital firm's worst-case scenario will result in 33 percent ROR to the firm, 9 percent ROR to licensees, and 0 percent for management. The noncompete agreements extend for 12 years, in addition to the vesting.
- An entrepreneur must decide between two deals:

  Deal A: A venture capital firm will lead a $3 million investment and requires management to invest $1 million. Future gains are to be split 50-50 after the venture capital firm has achieved a 25 percent ROR on the investment. Other common investment provisions also apply (vesting, employment agreements, etc.). The venture capital firm has the right of first refusal on all future rounds and other deals management may find.

  Deal B: Another venture capital firm will lead a $4 million investment. Management will invest nothing. The future gains are to be split 75 percent for the venture capital firm and 25 percent for management on a side-by-side basis. Until the venture achieves positive cash

[13] Timmons, Spinelli, and Zacharakis, "How to Raise Capital," McGraw-Hill, 2004.
[14] Timmons, "Deals and Deal Structuring."

flow, this venture capital firm has the right of first refusal on future financing and deals management may find.

- A group of very talented money managers is given $40 million in capital to manage. The contract calls for the managers to receive 20 percent of the excess return on the portfolio over the Treasury bond return. The contract runs for five years. The managers cannot take out any of their share of the gains until the last day of the contracts (except to pay taxes).

While reading and considering these deals, try to identify the underlying assumptions, motivations, and beliefs of the individuals proposing the deals. Following are some questions that may help in identifying the players' bets.

- What is the bet?
- Who is it for?
- Who is taking the risk? Who receives the rewards?
- Who should be making these bets?
- What will happen if the entrepreneurs exceed the venture capitalists' expectations? What if they fall short?
- What are the incentives for the money managers? What are the consequences of their success or failure to perform?
- How will the money managers behave? What will be their investing strategy?

Some of the Lessons Learned: The Dog in the Suitcase

A few years ago a friend, living in a New York City high-rise, called in great distress. Her beloved barkless dog had died in the middle of the night. She wanted a decent burial for the dog, but since it was the dead of winter, she did not know what to do. It was suggested that she contact a pet cemetery on Long Island and take the dog there. It would be frozen until spring, at which time it would be properly buried.

She gathered her courage, placed the dog in a suitcase, and headed down the elevator to the outdoors. As she struggled toward the nearest intersection to catch a cab, a young man noticed her struggle and offered to help. Puffing by now, she sized up the young man quickly and accepted his offer to carry the bag. In no time, she turned to find the young man sprinting down the street with her suitcase. Imagine the look on the faces of the young man and his buddies when they opened the suitcase and discovered the loot!

The moral of this story is that raising capital can have all the surprises of a dog in the suitcase for the entrepreneur. The following tips may help to minimize many of these surprises:

- Raise money when you do not need it.
- Learn as much about the process and how to manage it as you can.
- Know your relative bargaining position.
- If all you get is money, you are not getting much.
- Assume the deal will never close.
- Always have a backup source of capital.
- The legal and other experts can blow it—sweat the details yourself!
- Users of capital are invariably at a disadvantage in dealing with the suppliers of capital.
- If you are out of cash when you seek to raise capital, suppliers of capital will eat you for lunch.
- Startup entrepreneurs are raising capital for the first time; suppliers of capital have done it many times, everyday, for a living.

Negotiations

Negotiations have been defined by many experts in a variety of ways, as the following examples demonstrate. Herb Cohen, the author of *You Can Negotiate Anything,* defines negotiations as "a field of knowledge and endeavor that focuses on gaining the favor of people from whom we want things"[15] or similarly, as "the use of information and power to affect behavior within a 'web of tension.'"[16] Other experts in the field of negotiations, Roger Fisher and William Ury, assert that negotiations are a "back-and-forth communication designed to reach an agreement when you and the other side have some interests that are shared and others that are opposed."[17]

What Is Negotiable?

Far more is negotiable than entrepreneurs think.[18] For instance, a normal ploy of the attorney representing the investors is to insist, matter of factly, that

[15] Herb Cohen, *You Can Negotiate Anything* (New York: Bantam Books, 1982), p. 15.
[16] Ibid., p. 16.
[17] Roger Fisher and William Ury, *Getting to Yes* (New York: Penguin Books, 1991), p. xvii.
[18] See, for example, H. M. Hoffman and J. Blakey, "You Can Negotiate with Venture Capitalists," *Harvard Business Review,* March–April 1987, pp. 16–24.

"this is our boilerplate" and that the entrepreneur should take it or leave it. It is possible for an entrepreneur to negotiate and craft an agreement that represents his or her needs.

During the negotiation, the investors will be evaluating the negotiating skills, intelligence, and maturity of the entrepreneur. The entrepreneur has precisely the same opportunity to size up the investor. If the investors see anything that shakes their confidence or trust, they probably will withdraw from the deal. Similarly, if an investor turns out to be arrogant, hot-tempered, unwilling to see the other side's needs and to compromise, and seems bent on getting every last ounce out of the deal by locking an entrepreneur into as many of the "burdensome clauses" as is possible, the entrepreneur might want to withdraw.

Throughout the negotiations, entrepreneurs need to bear in mind that a successful negotiation is one in which both sides believe they have made a fair deal. The best deals are those in which neither party wins and neither loses, and such deals are possible to negotiate. This approach is further articulated in the works of Fisher and Ury, who have focused neither on soft nor hard negotiation tactics, but rather on principled negotiation, a method developed at the Harvard Negotiation Project. This method asserts that the purpose of negotiations is "to decide issues on their merits rather than through a haggling process focused on what each side says it will and won't do. It suggests that you look for mutual gains wherever possible, and that where your interests conflict, you should insist that the result be based on some fair standards independent of the will of either side."[19] They continue to describe principled negotiations in the following four points:

People: Separate the people from the problem.

Interests: Focus on interests, not positions.

Options: Generate a variety of possibilities before deciding what to do.

Criteria: Insist that the result be based on some objective standard.

Others have spoken of this method of principled negotiation. For example, Bob Woolf of Bob Woolf Associates, a Boston-based firm that has represented everyone from Larry Bird to Gene Shalit, states simply, "You want the other side to be reasonable, not defensive—to work *with* you. You'll have a better chance of getting what you want. Treat someone the way that you would like to be treated, and you'll be successful most of the time."[20]

The Specific Issues Entrepreneurs Typically Face[21]

Whatever method you choose in your negotiations, the primary focus is likely to be on how much the entrepreneur's equity is worth and how much is to be purchased by the investor's investment. Even so, numerous other issues involving legal and financial control of the company and the rights and obligations of various investors and the entrepreneur in various situations may be as important as valuation and ownership share. Not the least of which is the value behind the money—such as contacts and helpful expertise, additional financing when and if required, and patience and interest in the long-term development of the company—that a particular investor can bring to the venture. The following are some of the most critical aspects of a deal that go beyond "just the money":

- Number, type, and mix of stocks (and perhaps of stock and debt) and various features that may go with them (such as puts) that affect the investor's rate of return.
- The amounts and timing of takedowns, conversions, and the like.
- Interest rate in debt or preferred shares.
- The number of seats, and who actually will represent investors, on the board of directors.
- Possible changes in the management team and in the composition of the board of directors.
- Registration rights for investor's stock (in case of a registered public offering).
- Right of first refusal granted to the investor on subsequent private or initial public stock offerings.
- Stock vesting schedule and agreements.
- The payment of legal, accounting, consulting, or other fees connected with putting the deal together.

Entrepreneurs may find some subtle but highly significant issues negotiated. If they, or their attorneys, are not familiar with these, they may be missed as just boilerplate when, in fact, they have crucial future implications for the ownership, control, and financing of the business. Some issues that can be burdensome for entrepreneurs are:

- *Co-sale provision.* This is a provision by which investors can tender their shares of their stock before an initial public offering. It protects the first-round investors but can cause conflicts

[19] Fisher and Ury, *Getting to Yes,* p. xviii.
[20] Quoted in Paul B. Brown and Michael S. Hopkins, "How to Negotiate Practically Anything." Reprinted with permission *INC.* magazine (February 1989), p. 35. Copyright © 1989 by Goldhirsh Group, Inc., 38 Commercial Wharf, Boston, MA 02110.
[21] Jeffry A. Timmons, "Deals and Deal Structuring" lecture.

with investors in later rounds and can inhibit an entrepreneur's ability to cash out.

- *Ratchet antidilution protection.* This enables the lead investors to get for free additional common stock if subsequent shares are ever sold at a price lower than originally paid. This protection allows first-round investors to prevent the company from raising additional necessary funds during a period of adversity for the company. While nice from the investor's perspective, it ignores the reality that, in distress situations, the last money calls the shots on price and deal structure.
- *Washout financing.* This is a strategy of last resort, which wipes out all previously issued stock when existing preferred shareholders will not commit additional funds, thus diluting everyone.
- *Forced buyout.* Under this provision, if management does not find a buyer or cannot take the company public by a certain date, then the investors can proceed to find a buyer at terms they agree upon.
- *Demand registration rights.* Here, investors can demand at least one IPO in three to five years. In reality, such clauses are hard to invoke because the market for new public stock issues, rather than the terms of an agreement, ultimately governs the timing of such events.
- *Piggyback registration rights.* These grant to the investors (and to the entrepreneur, if he or she insists) rights to sell stock at the IPO. Since the underwriters usually make this decision, the clause normally is not enforceable.
- *Key-person insurance.* This requires the company to obtain life insurance on key people. The named beneficiary of the insurance can be either the company or the preferred shareholders.

The Term Sheet

Regardless of whether you secure capital from angels or venture capitalists, you will want to be informed and knowledgeable about the terms and conditions that govern the deal you sign. Many experienced entrepreneurs will argue that the terms and who your investor is are more important than the valuation. Today, the technical sophistication in deal structures creates an imperative for entrepreneurs and their legal counsel: if you don't know the details you will get what you deserve—not what you want.

To illustrate this point, consider the choice among four common instruments: (1) fully participating preferred stock, (2) partially participating preferred stock (4× return), (3) common preference ($1.00/share to common), and (4) nonparticipating preferred stock. Then, consider a $200 million harvest realized either through an IPO or an acquisition by another company. Why does any of this matter? Aren't these details better left to the legal experts?

Consider the economic consequences of each of these deal instruments under the two harvest scenarios in Exhibit 14.10. The graph shows there can be up to a $24 million difference in the payout received, even though, in the example, there are equal numbers of shares of common stock, typically owned by the founders, and preferred stock, owned by investors. The acquisition exit is more favorable to investors, especially since periodically the IPO market is closed to new companies.

Black Box Technology, Inc., Term Sheet

The best single presentation and discussion we have seen of the deal structure, term sheet contents, and their implications for negotiating the deal is presented in, Black Box Technology, Inc.—Term Sheet. This was developed by the former Boston law firm of Testa, Hurwitz & Thibeault, LLP. This was part of a presentation at Professor Timmons's course on venture capital on October 3, 2001, by Heather M. Stone and Brian D. Goldstein. It is included here with the permission of the firm and the authors. We highly recommend its careful reading before any negotiations with private investors and selecting very experienced counsel.

Sand Traps[22]

Strategic Circumference

Each fund-raising strategy sets in motion some actions and commitments by management that will eventually scribe a strategic circumference around the company in terms of its current and future financing choices. These future choices will permit varying degrees of freedom as a result of the previous actions. Those who fail to think through the consequences of a fund-raising strategy and the effect on their degrees of freedom fall into this trap.

While it is impossible to avoid strategic circumference completely, and while in some cases scribing a strategic circumference is clearly intentional, others

[22] Copyright © 1990 by Jeffry A. Timmons.

EXHIBIT 14.10

Considering the Economics: $200 Million IPO or Acquisition?

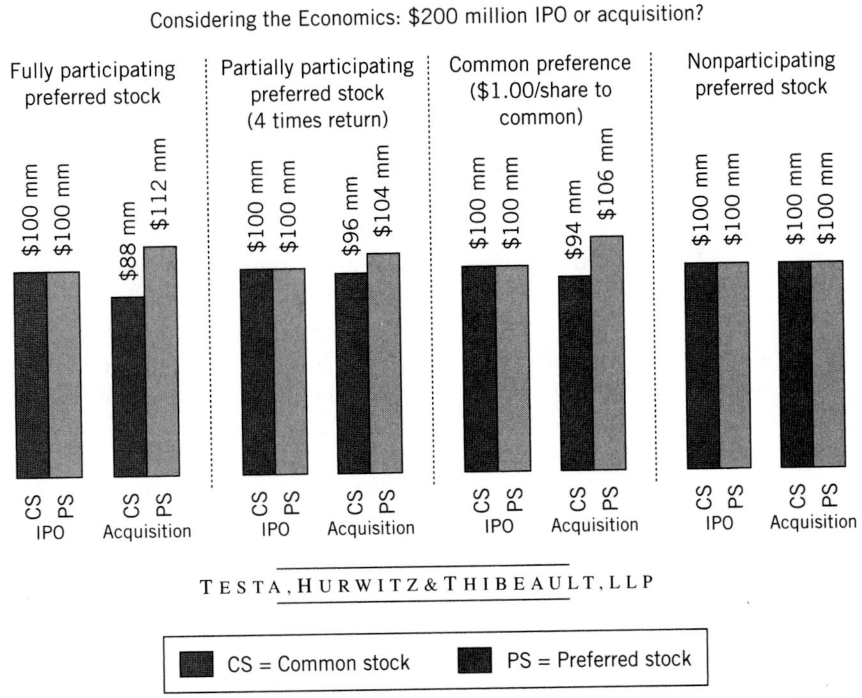

Source: Testa, Hurwitz & Thibeault, LLP, from a presentation by Heather M. Stone and Brian D. Goldstein at Babson College, October 3, 2001.

may be unintended and, unfortunately, unexpected. For example, a company that plans to remain private or plans to maintain a 1.5 to 1.0 debt-to-equity ratio has intentionally created a strategic circumference.

Legal Circumference

Many people have an aversion to becoming involved in legal or accounting minutiae. Many believe that since they pay sizable professional fees, their advisors should and will pay attention to the details.

Legal documentation spells out the terms, conditions, responsibilities, and rights of the parties to a transaction. Because different sources have different ways of structuring deals, and because these legal and contractual details come at the *end* of the fund-raising process, an entrepreneur may arrive at a point of no return, facing some very onerous conditions and covenants that are not only very difficult to live with, but also create tight limitations and constraints—legal circumference—on future choices that are potentially disastrous. Entrepreneurs cannot rely on attorneys and advisors to protect them in this vital matter.

To avoid this trap, entrepreneurs need to have a fundamental precept: "The devil is in the details." It is very risky for an entrepreneur *not* to carefully read final documents and very risky to use a lawyer who is *not* experienced and competent. It also is helpful to keep a few options alive and to conserve cash. This also can keep the other side of the table more conciliatory and flexible.

Attraction to Status and Size

It seems there is a cultural attraction to higher status and larger size, even when it comes to raising capital. Simply targeting the largest or the best-known or most-prestigious firms is a trap entrepreneurs often fall into. These firms are often most visible because of their size and investing activity and because they have been around a long time. Yet, as the venture capital industry has become more heterogeneous, as well as for other reasons, such firms may or may not be a good fit.

Take, for example, an entrepreneur who had a patented, innovative device that was ready for use by manufacturers of semiconductors. He was running out of cash from an earlier round of venture capital investment and needed more money for his device to be placed in test sites and then, presumably, into production. Although lab tests had been successful, his prior backers would not invest further because he was nearly two years behind schedule in his business plan. For a year, he concentrated his efforts on many of the largest and most well-known firms and celebrities in the venture capital business, but to no avail. With the help of outside advice, he then decided to pursue an alternative fund-raising strategy. First, he listed firms that were most likely prospects as customers for the device. Next, he sought to identify investors who already had investments in this potential customer base, because it was thought that these would be the most likely potential backers since they would be the most informed about his technology, its potential value-added properties, and any potential competitive advantages the company could achieve. Less than a dozen venture capital firms were identified (from among a pool of over 700, at the time), yet none had been contacted previously by this entrepreneur. In fact, many were virtually unknown to him, even though they were very active investors in the industry. In less than three months, offers were on the table from three of these and the financing was closed.

It is best to avoid this trap by focusing your efforts toward financial backers, whether debt or equity, who have intimate knowledge and first-hand experience with the technology, marketplace, and networks of expertise in the competitive arena. Focus on those firms with relevant know-how that would be characterized as a good match.

Unknown Territory

Venturing into unknown territory is another problem. Entrepreneurs need to know the terrain in sufficient detail, particularly the requirements and alternatives of various equity sources. If they do not, they may make critical strategic blunders and waste time.

For example, a venture that is not a "mainstream venture capital deal" may be overvalued and directed to investors who are not a realistic match, rather than being realistically valued and directed to small and more specialized funds, private investors, or potential strategic partners. The preceding example is a real one. The founders went through nearly $100,000 of their own funds, strained their relationship to the limit, and nearly had to abandon the project.

Another illustration of a fund-raising strategy that was ill conceived and, effectively, a lottery—rather than a well-thought-out and focused search—is a company in the fiber optics industry we'll call Opti-Com.[23] Opti-Com was a spin-off as a startup from a well-known public company in the industry. The management team was entirely credible, but members were not considered superstars. The business plan suggested the company could achieve the magical $50 million in sales in five years, which the entrepreneurs were told by an outside advisor was the minimum size that venture capital investors would consider. The plan proposed to raise $750,000 for about 10 percent of the common stock of the company. Realistically, since the firm was a custom supplier for special applications, rather than a provider of a new technology with a significant proprietary advantage, a sales estimate of $10 million to $15 million in five years would have been more plausible. The same advisor urged that their business plan be submitted to 16 blue-ribbon mainstream venture capital firms in the Boston area. Four months later, they had received 16 rejections. The entrepreneurs then were told to "go see the same quality of venture capital firms in New York." A year later, the founders were nearly out of money and had been unsuccessful in their search for capital. When redirected away from mainstream venture capitalists to a more suitable source, a small fund specifically created in Massachusetts to provide risk capital for emerging firms that might not be robust enough to attract conventional venture capital but would be a welcome addition to the economic renewal of the state, the fit was right. Opti-Com raised the necessary capital, but at a valuation much more in line with the market for startup deals.

Opportunity Cost

The lure of money often leads to a common trap—the opportunity cost trap. An entrepreneur's optimism leads him or her to the conclusion that with good people and products (or services), there has to be a lot of money out there with "our name on it!" In the process, entrepreneurs tend to grossly underestimate the real costs of getting the cash in the bank. Further, entrepreneurs also underestimate the real time, effort, and creative energy required. Indeed, the degree of effort fund-raising requires is perhaps the least appreciated aspect in obtaining capital. In both these cases, there are opportunity costs in expending these resources in a particular direction when both the clock and the calendar are moving.

For a startup company, for instance, founders can devote nearly all their available time for months to seeking out investors and telling their story. It may take six months or more to get a "yes" and up to a year for a "no." In the meantime, a considerable amount of cash and human capital has been flowing out, rather than in, and this cash and capital might have been better spent elsewhere.

[23] This is a fictional name for an actual company.

One such startup began its search for venture capital in 1984. A year later the founders had exhausted $100,000 of their own seed money and had quit their jobs to devote themselves full time to the effort. Yet they were unsuccessful after approaching more than 35 sources of capital. The opportunity costs are clear.

There are opportunity costs, too, in existing emerging companies. In terms of human capital, it is common for top management to devote as much as half of its time trying to raise a major amount of outside capital. Again, this requires a tremendous amount of emotional and physical energy as well, of which there is a finite amount to devote to the daily operating demands of the enterprise. The effect on near-term performance is invariably negative. In addition, if expectations of a successful fund-raising effort are followed by a failure to raise the money, morale can deteriorate and key people can be lost.

Significant opportunity costs are also incurred in forgone business and market opportunities that could have been pursued. Take, for example, the startup firm noted above. When asked what level of sales the company would have achieved in the year had it spent the $100,000 of the founders' seed money on generating customers and business, the founder answered without hesitation, "We'd be at $1 million sales by now, and would probably be making a small profit."

Underestimation of Other Costs

Entrepreneurs tend to underestimate the out-of-pocket costs associated with both raising the money and living with it. There are incremental costs after a firm becomes a public company. The Securities and Exchange Commission requires regular audited financial statements and various reports, there are outside directors' fees and liability insurance premiums, there are legal fees associated with more extensive reporting requirements, and so on. These can add up quickly, often to $100,000 or more annually.

Another "cost" that can be easily overlooked is of the disclosure that may be necessary to convince a financial backer to part with his or her money. An entrepreneur may have to reveal much more about the company and his other personal finances than he or she ever imagined. Thus, company weaknesses, ownership and compensation arrangements, personal and corporate financial statements, marketing plans and competitive strategies, and so forth may need to be revealed to people whom the entrepreneur does not really know and trust, and with whom he or she may eventually not do business. In addition, the ability to control access to the information is lost.

Greed

The entrepreneur—especially one who is out of cash, or nearly so—may find the money irresistible. One of the most exhilarating experiences for an entrepreneur is the prospect of raising that first major slug of outside capital, or obtaining that substantial bank line needed for expansion. If the fundamentals of the company are sound, however, then there is money out there.

Being Too Anxious

Usually, after months of hard work finding the right source and negotiating the deal, another trap awaits the hungry but unwary entrepreneur, and all too often the temptation is overwhelming. It is the trap of believing that the deal is done and terminating discussions with others too soon. Entrepreneurs fall into this trap because they want to believe the deal is done with a handshake (or perhaps with an accompanying letter of intent or an executed term sheet).

A masterful handling of such a situation occurred when an entrepreneur and a key vice president of a company with $30 million in sales had been negotiating with several venture capitalists, three major strategic partners, and a mezzanine source for nearly six months. The company was down to 60 days' worth of cash, and the mezzanine investors knew it. They offered the entrepreneur $10 million as a take-it-or-leave-it proposition. The vice president, in summarizing the company's relative bargaining position, said, "It was the only alternative we had left; everything else had come to rest by late last month and the negotiations with the three major companies had not reached serious stages. We felt like they were asking too much, but we needed the money." Yet the two had managed to keep this weakness from being apparent to the mezzanine. Each time negotiations had been scheduled, the entrepreneur had made sure he also had scheduled a meeting with one of the other larger companies for later that afternoon (a two-hour plane ride away). In effect, he was able to create the illusion that these discussions with other investors were far more serious than they actually were. The deal was closed on terms agreeable to both. The company went public six months later and is still highly successful today.

Impatience

Another trap is being impatient when an investor does not understand quickly, and not realizing each deal has velocity and momentum.

The efforts of one management group to acquire a firm in the cellular phone business being sold by their employers provides an example. As members of the management team, they were the first to know in May that the company was going to be sold by its owners. By early July, the investment bankers representing the sellers were expected to have the offering memorandum ready for the open market. To attempt to buy the company privately would require the team to raise commitments for approximately $150 million in three to four weeks, hardly enough time to put together even a crude business plan, let alone raise such a substantial sum. The train was moving at 140 miles per hour and gaining speed each day. The founders identified five top-notch, interested venture capital and leveraged buyout firms and sat down with representatives of each to walk through the summary of the business plan and the proposed financing. One excellent firm sent an otherwise very experienced and capable partner, but his questioning indicated just how little he knew about this business. The team knew they had to look elsewhere.

Had the group been too impatient simply because the train was moving so quickly, they would have exposed themselves to additional risk. That potential investor had a serious lack of elementary knowledge of the industry and the business model, and had not done his homework in advance. If they had waited for this investor to become knowledgeable about the business, it would have been too late.

Take-the-Money-and-Run Myopia

A final trap in raising money for a company is a take-the-money-and-run myopia that invariably prevents an entrepreneur from evaluating one of the most critical longer-term issues—to what extent can the investor add value to the company beyond the money? Into this trap falls the entrepreneur who does not possess a clear sense that his or her prospective financial partner has the relevant experience and know-how in the market and industry area, the contacts the entrepreneur needs but does not have, the savvy and the reputation that adds value in the relationship with the investor—and yet takes the money.

As has been said before, the successful development of a company can be critically affected by the interaction of the management team and the financial partners. If an effective relationship can be established, the value-added synergy can be a powerful stimulant for success. Many founders overlook the high value-added contributions that some investors are accustomed to making and erroneously opt for a "better deal."

Internet Impact: Resources

Real Estate Marketing and Sales

The Internet enables buyers and sellers of real estate to bypass agents whose function has been to collect data from many sources and make it available to end-users. In that way, online resources are quickly changing the basis for competing and creating value in the real estate industry. Gone are the days where local agents—armed with the latest proprietary Multiple Listing Service (MLS) data—were the gatekeepers and purveyors of up-to-date information on available properties, community aspects, and comparative pricing.

Instead of spending weekends with a broker—or driving around town looking for sale signs and open houses—buyers can now conduct detailed searches on MLS portals like www.realtor.com, and on sale-by-owner sites like www.isoldmyhouse.com. For buyers looking to relocate or purchase secondary properties far from their current home, the Internet has become a powerful resource.

Despite many dire predictions in the early days of the Internet, it is unlikely that these online capabilities will ever do away with the need for professional intermediaries in the complex—and often emotional—purchase of real estate. However, as their commissions shrink along with the scope of the services they are being expected to provide, the success factor for real estate agents will be in taking on a value-added consultative role in the overall process.

Chapter Summary

1. There is rarely a "fair fight" between users (entrepreneurs) and suppliers of capital (investors). Entrepreneurs need to be prepared by learning how the capital markets determine valuation risk.
2. Several valuation methods are used to arrive at value for a company, the venture capital method being the most common.
3. Investors prefer to stage their capital commitments, thereby managing and containing the risk, and preserving their options to invest further or cease.
4. Numerous potential conflicts exist between users and suppliers of capital, and these require appreciation and managing. The economic consequences can be worth millions to founders.

5. Successful deals are characterized by careful thought and sensitive balance among a range of important issues.
6. Deal structure can make or break an otherwise sound venture, and the devil is always in the details.
7. Negotiating the deal is both art and science, and also can make or break the relationship.
8. The entrepreneur encounters numerous strategic, legal, and other "sand traps" during the fund-raising cycle and needs awareness and skill in coping with them.

Study Questions

1. Why can there be such wide variations in the valuations investors and founders place on companies?
2. What are the determinants of value?
3. Define and explain why the following are important: long-term value creation, investor's required IRR, investor's required share of ownership, DCF, deal structure, and sand traps in fund-raising.
4. Explain five prevalent methods used in valuing a company and their strengths and weaknesses, given their underlying assumptions.
5. What is a staged capital commitment, and why is it important?
6. What is a company worth: explain the theory and the reality of valuation.
7. What is a "cram down" round?
8. What are some of the inherent conflicts between investors and entrepreneurs, and how and why can these affect the venture's odds for success?
9. What are the most important questions and issues to consider in structuring a deal? Why?
10. What issues can be negotiated in a venture investment, and why are these important?
11. What are the pitfalls and sand traps in fund-raising, and why do entrepreneurs sometimes fail to avoid them?

Internet Resources for Chapter 14

http://www.sia.com/capitol_hill/ *The securities Industry Association: On Capital Hill*

http://www.nacva.com/ *The National Association of Certified Valuation Analysts*

http://www.ivsc.org *The International Valuation Standards Committee is a non-government-organization (NGO) member of the United Nations that works to harmonize and promote agreement and understanding of valuation standards*

http://www.valuationresources.com/ *Resources such as business valuation publications, economic data, public market data, transaction data, and legal and tax resources*

http://www.money.cnn.com/ *Financial news*

http://www.kauffmanfollowsprogram.org

http://www.ventureone.com/ *One of the world's leading venture capital research firms*

http://www.venturewire.com/ *VentureWire Newsletters: a source of news, networking, and information about private technology companies, VC firms, and the people that manage and finance them*

MIND STRETCHERS

Have you considered?

1. Who should and should not have outside investors in their companies?
2. It is said that a good deal structure cannot turn a bad business into a good one, but many a good business has been killed by a bad deal structure. Why is this so? Find an example of each.
3. What beliefs and assumptions are revealed by the "bets" made in different deals?
4. What is a good deal? Why?

Case

Paul J. Tobin

Preparation Questions

1. Evaluate the situation and harvest options for BCGI.
2. How should Paul think about the process? What should he do with the RFQ (Exhibit N)?
3. Evaluate the deals struck in 1990 and 1992 (Exhibits H and K).
4. What do investment bankers do? How do they make money?
5. What should Paul do, and why?

Paul Tobin, founder, CEO, and chairman of Boston Communications Group, Inc. (BCGI) had already been through a venture-backed harvest, but this situation was quite different than anything he'd faced before. As he prepared for his board meeting in early November 1995, Paul wondered whether this was the right time to harvest BCGI, a provider of support services to the wireless carrier industry, and how best to handle the process. The board had enthusiastically encouraged him at its August meeting to test the waters for a possible strategic sale, but the board also believed substantial value in the company was in the future. Should he wait? Given BCGI's product lines and strategy, both the board and management felt that a cash sale to a large corporate strategic buyer probably made the most sense. Recent projections indicated that the company would exceed $100 million in revenue by the end of the decade. If this was achieved, the company could conceivably be valued in the $150–250 million range by the year 2000, but today he felt fortunate to have a prospective buyer willing to pay $60–75 million.

An eventual harvest was a given. After all, that is what an entrepreneur signs up for when accepting a venture capital investment: the only issues were when and how. One of Paul's outside directors and a founding shareholder was a professor at a nearby college widely considered the world's leading school in entrepreneurship. He suggested a dual strategy in order to maximize the company's terminal value: Create a competition among investment banks to determine whether a strategic sale or an initial public offering (IPO) made the most sense. This strategy would best enable the capital markets to value the company at its maximum while determining which harvest mechanism would be the best overall fit, given the company's strategy, stage of development, and future opportunities.

Paul's team had done it before with a venture capital-backed company in only two years: launch, grow, and harvest. This time around it had taken five years, a capital investment of nearly $12 million, major strategic changes, deal restructuring, and at least one false start in the paging business to create enough value to make the harvest attractive. By the late summer of 1995, it appeared that BCGI had become the high potential venture Paul and his partners had envisioned. The prospect for a harvest was, for the first time, becoming a reality. One corporate buyer, GTE Corp., was showing serious interest, and while initial contact was a cautious, cat-and-mouse exercise, early indications seemed to suggest a valuation of as much as $75 million for the company. There was considerable joy at this possibility among the management team, founding shareholders, and investors.

The Wireless Telecommunications Communications Industry

The consumer wireless telecommunications industry was divided into three segments: paging devices, enhanced specialized mobile radio communications (ESMR), and cellular phoning. Cellular phoning first emerged in the early 1980s when the Federal Communications Committee (FCC) granted frequency concessions for wireless telephony. After dividing the country into 734 potential geographic market segments, two frequencies per segment were granted, resulting in duopolistic competition between carriers.

In the 1980s the cellular industry underwent significant consolidation as cellular carriers sought to achieve greater market coverage and economies of scale in operations, marketing, and customer service. As of mid-1995, the majority of cellular licenses were held by a small number of companies, with the remaining cellular licenses divided between approximately 200 others (See *Appendix A* for a listing of the top 50 cellular companies.)

Between 1985 and 1995, wireless phoning was considered one of the fastest growing areas of the telecommunications industry. The Cellular Telecommunications Industry Association (CTIA) projected that the number of cellular subscribers in the United States would continue to rise dramatically: It had gone from 340,000 in 1985, to a projected 34 million in 1995, and the number of subscribers was projected to grow to 116 million by the year 2005. Aggregate annual service revenues from cellular subscribers were expected to grow from approximately $482 million in 1985 to a projected $19 billion in 1995 (see *Exhibit A* for industry forecast). A number of factors contributed to this growth, including the build-out of the cellular network infrastruc-

EXHIBIT A

Wireless Revenue Forecast ($ billions)

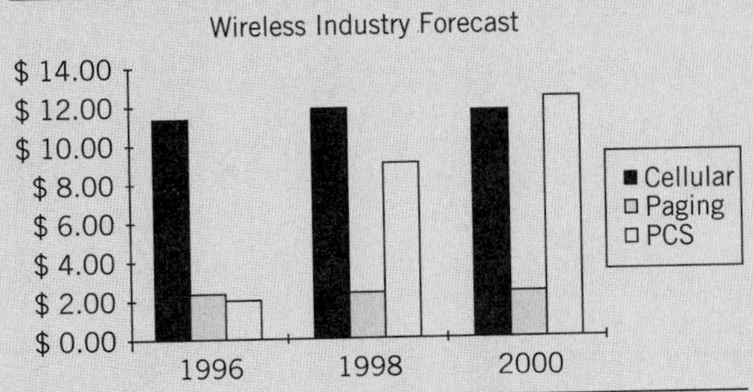

Source: BIS Strategic Division

EXHIBIT B

Cellular Industry Revenues (billions)

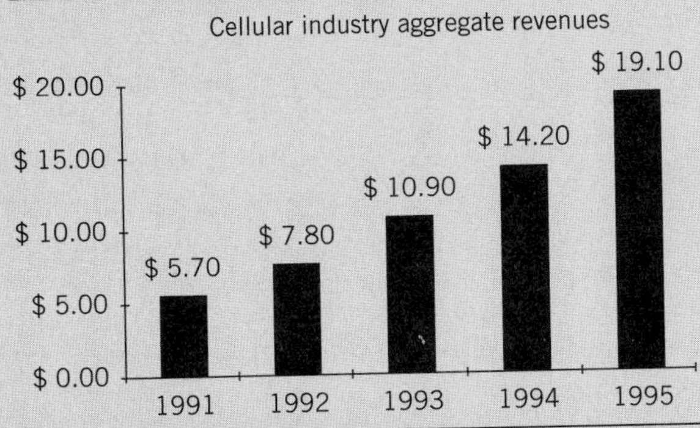

Source: CTIA

ture, the decreasing cost of cellular telephones, technological improvements in the size and battery life of cellular telephones, and greater acceptance of wireless phones.

One important source of revenues for cellular carriers was subscribers that used their phones outside their home service areas. These users, known as "roamers," were projected to be billed nearly $2.5 billion in 1995, or 13 percent of total revenues. From 1990 to 1995, roaming revenues grew at a compounded annual rate of 41 percent compared to 33 percent for aggregate wireless service revenues (see *Exhibit B*). Roaming revenues were generated when an agreement was in place between cellular carriers, and a roamer made a call from the non-home carrier's territory. Under these agreements, home carriers billed subscribers on behalf of the servicing carrier whose territory the subscriber was roaming. The home carrier often did not retain any revenues, yet still bore all collection and fraud risks associated with the call. Increasing amounts of fraud, projected at over $400 million for 1995, caused some carriers to terminate roaming agreements in markets with high incidents of fraud. In addition, both the home and the servicing carrier bore costs associated with the inter-carrier roaming agreement. These costs related primarily to managing the authorized-user databases and to validating roaming calls. No carrier had licenses or agreements in every market, so roamers were limited in their ability to place and receive cellular telephone calls.

Cellular carriers were also developing strategies to penetrate untapped market segments. Due to relatively high marketing and service costs, cellular carriers had generally only accepted subscribers who met certain credit, volume, and use standards. There were many people who didn't qualify for cellular service: people with credit problems, low-volume users, temporary subscribers, and people who wanted to authorize multiple users for one account were often denied service by both carriers in their region.

Although the subscriber base was increasing rapidly, profitability lagged. This was primarily due to a high customer turnover rate and to low revenue per customer. The average revenue per subscriber was steadily declining due to an increasing number of lower-volume cellular subscribers. Cellular carriers looked to reduce the subscriber churn rate, historically between 26 percent and 36 percent per year, through increased customer satisfaction. Customer retention was linked to a carrier's ability to respond promptly to subscriber inquiries regarding billing matters, rate plans, service problems, and other related issues, but the demands of hiring, training, and retaining a large number of customer service representatives made it difficult to provide high-quality, 24-hour, 7-day service on a cost-effective basis.

It was expected that the wireless communication industry would change significantly with the introduction of Personal Communication System (PCS) technology (see Appendix B for PCS industry overview) and the termination of the duopolistic market structure. While PCS offerings would vary by carrier, a likely set of services would include local cellular-like voice service combined with data messaging, wireless data service, and wireless office telephony. The FCC planned to auction three to six PCS licenses in most markets across the United States. Analysts predicted that the wireless industry would become increasingly fragmented with the introduction of PCS, and that market share would come to be dominated by multiple-service providers, each with a variety of service packages offered at different price points.

Acquiring Relevant Entrepreneurial Experience

Paul Tobin began his career as a securities analyst at Chase Manhattan Bank after receiving his undergraduate degree in economics from Stonehill College. He earned his MBA in marketing/finance through the full-time program at Northeastern University in 1970 and launched U.S. Glass with two partners. U.S. Glass was a middleman connecting large retail chains and franchises with reputable glaziers from New England to the mid-Atlantic region. When a window was broken, the local manager had a phone number to call for fast, reliable, and economical service.

The U.S. Glass partnership dissolved in 1978 when Paul sold his interest to his former partners. Next, Paul tried his hand at light-industrial manufacturing and chemicals brokering. Then in 1980, he joined Satellite Business Systems (a joint venture of IBM, Comsat, and Aetna) as a salesman. Paul was quickly promoted to regional sales and marketing manager at this telecom joint venture (launched with nearly $1 billion in startup capital). Then in 1984, Paul was recruited by a headhunter to interview for the position of president for Metromedia's cellular telephone operation in Boston and Worcester, Massachusetts. He got the job. Under Paul Tobin's leadership, the Boston CellularOne operation gained a 75 percent market share in a region that achieved a 1 percent market penetration in the first three years of the embryonic cellular car phone industry.

EXHIBIT C

Size-Structure of the Venture Capital Industry

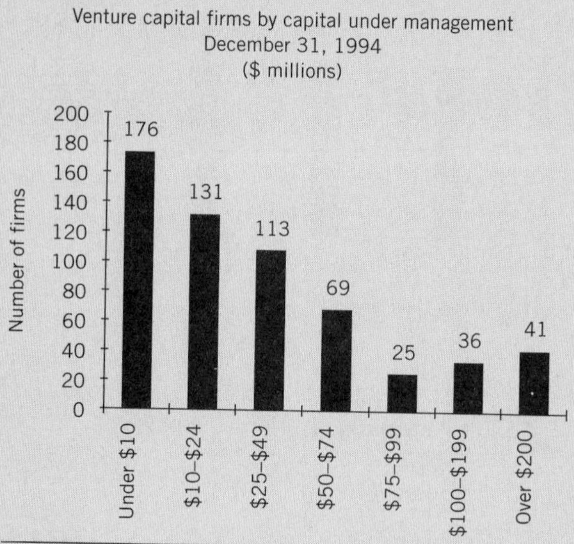

Source: Venture Economics; Inc.

Creating a Venture-Backed Wireless Company

In 1987, John Kluge, chairman of Metromedia, put his telecom holdings up for sale: cellular and paging operations in Boston, Dallas, Chicago, New York, Philadelphia, and many other markets across the country. Having led the launch and development of CellularOne in Boston, Paul knew that the market still had significant potential. He put together a team of his top executives at CellularOne, and introduced himself to the venture capital community.

After a series of meetings, Paul secured an agreement with Boston Ventures. One of a select number of firms known for doing deals of this magnitude (see *Exhibit C:* Size Structure of the VC Industry). Boston Ventures had also handled many of Kluge's telecom purchases. They had taken Metromedia public, then private through a leveraged buy-out, so they had both access and credibility. Paul presented an offer to purchase Boston CellularOne for $130 million, but SW Bell offered to acquire John Kluge's entire telecom portfolio for $1.65 billion. The game was over. However, Paul had also formed a relationship with the people at the Boston venture capital firm of Burr, Egan, Deleage, & Co., and they decided to back Paul's team in a cellular venture. Paul was concerned that SW Bell would want to put their own people into executive management at Boston CellularOne and he did not intend to wait around for the takeover.

That spring, they acquired the Portsmouth cellular license (Southern Maine and Southeastern New Hampshire) for $2 million, or $9 per pop,[1] and Paul tendered his resignation to SW Bell. However, Boston CellularOne was a model operation, and SW Bell knew that Paul would take his team with him, so instead of letting him go, they made him an unusual offer. They allowed him to stay on as president of Boston CellularOne with the stipulation that he operate Portsmouth CellularOne, located an hour and a half north of Boston, through a remote management team.

Over the next 18 months, the Boston CellularOne team successfully provided remote executive management for the Portsmouth operation. Then in 1989, Paul managed to obtain an offer for Portsmouth Cellular worth just over $37 million, or $148 per pop, at an industry seminar. The lead venture capital investor, Burr, Egan, Deleage, & Co., received proceeds of $16.9 million, for a 132.5 percent IRR (including a later-stage subordinated-debt investment of $3 million). When Paul announced his intention to create another venture in the cellular industry, they were interested in leading a syndicate to fund his next deal.

Creating Another Venture-Backed Wireless Company

Three members of the management team that built and sold Portsmouth Cellular left SW Bell and formed a new company in 1989, Boston Communications Group, Inc. Paul Tobin, Bob Sullivan, and Fritz von Mering planned to purchase cellular licenses when possible, and to pursue other wireless businesses as opportunities appeared.

[1]The industry valued cellular license based on the population—per pop—in the area under license.

EXHIBIT D

Venture Capital Resources by Type of Firm ($ millions)

Type of Firm	Average Capital/Firm		Median Size of Firm		Number of Firms	
	1990	1995*	1990	1995*	1990	1995*
Independent Private	$56.1	$ 61.0	$21.2	$29.9	514	424
Corporate Financial	67.6	103.7	22.3	16.0	68	39
Corporate Industrial	30.5	37.8	20.0	26.7	82	63
Totals	$54.1	$ 61.7	$21.0	$20.0	664	526

*projected
Source: Thomson Venture Economics/NVCA. Used by permission.

EXHIBIT E

Venture Capital Market

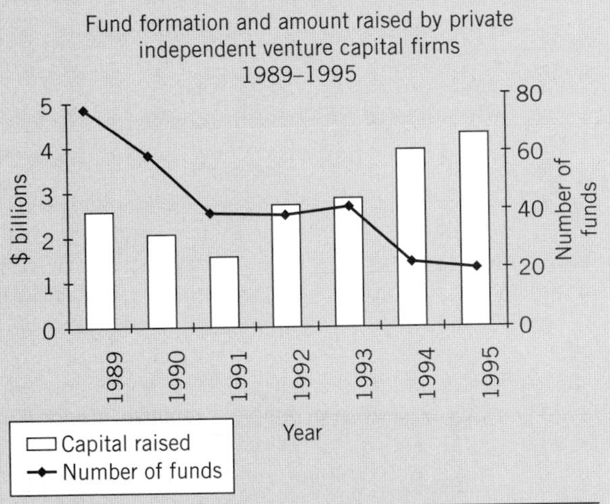

Source: Thomson Venture Economics/NVCA. Used by permission.

Paul was pleased that Brion Applegate of Burr, Egan, Deleage, & Co. was able to put together a syndicate with Highland Capital Partners. They were well-respected firms with knowledgeable partners, and he anticipated that BCGI would benefit from their contributions as members of his Board of Directors. Although pleased with the investors, Paul was not entirely pleased with the terms of the investment. The venture capital market was being squeezed in 1989: The IPO window was tight and venture capitalists were having difficulty raising new funds. (See *Exhibits D, E* and *F* for venture market information.)

However, the demand for cellular licenses peaked in 1989 (see *Exhibit G,* Price per Pop), and the most enticing opportunities in cellular were rural service areas (RSA), but even that market was overpriced. In 1990, they purchased the RSA license for Franklin county in southern Massachusetts for $6 million, or $90 per pop. BCGI paid $1.5 million in cash and the seller took paper for the rest. The Franklin county license had not been developed; Paul and his team installed an infrastructure and grew the business from the ground up.

BCGI launched three other new companies in 1990: Cellular Service of Washington DC, a sales and service company; BeeperPlus, a paging company in upstate New York; and ROAMER*plus* (aka Cellular Express), a company based in the Boston area that processed remote transactions for cellular carriers. BeeperPlus and the Franklin county license were sold in 1992, for just under a million dollars, and for $8 million ($120 per pop), respectively. In 1995, Cellular Service of Washington, D.C., was also sold for less than a million dollars. Paul recalled the situation:

> Our objective was to acquire, build and operate cellular licenses. But the price of cellular licenses skyrocketed so we had to divert our strategy and try a couple of different things.

Fortunately, ROAMER*plus* was a winner. ROAMER*plus* allowed carriers to profit from customers traveling outside of their cellular service area: These customers were called roamers. The FCC duopoly system had created a fragmented service industry, so roamers were sometimes unable to make calls. ROAMER*plus* processed calls placed by unregistered roamers.

To complete a call, the carrier simply forwarded unregistered users to BCGI's automated call processing system and the carrier was compensated directly by BCGI for the airtime. The majority of calls did not require an operator, but operators were available as needed. Carriers were attracted to this service because it provided additional revenues with little additional cost. BCGI bore a substantial collection risk and reserved 15 percent of gross revenues for uncollectible ROAMER*plus* charges. However, BCGI needed funding to build a nationwide telecom network, for working capital, and to develop the software to make it work.

Paul's investors had originally agreed to supply $10 million, but had staged the investment so that disbursements were linked to specific acquisitions (see *Exhibit H,* 1990 Term Sheet). BCGI had received $6 million for the Franklin county acquisition, starting the cellular service company, the paging company, and the roaming service.

EXHIBIT F

Trends in the IPO Market

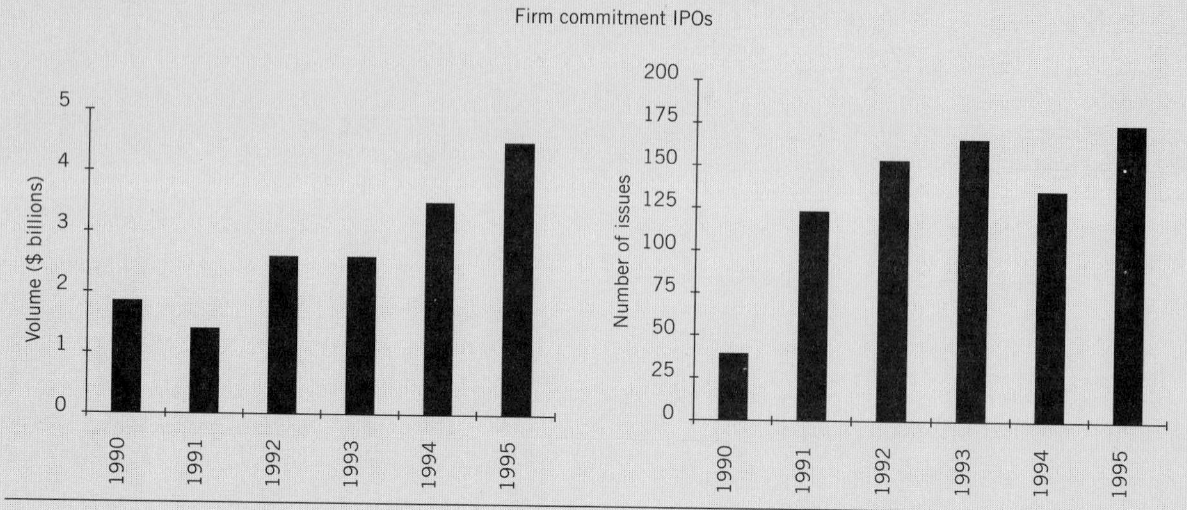

Source: Thomson Venture Economics/NVCA. Used by permission.

EXHIBIT G

Cellular License Price per Pop

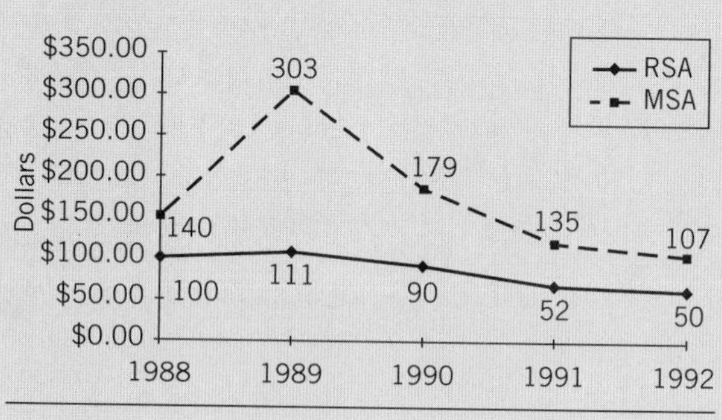

Source: Paul Kagan & Associates

The other $4 million was committed to acquire 20 ground-to-air frequencies from NYNEX, but that deal fell through when the New England wireless market weakened in 1990.

In lieu of the NYNEX deal, the investors committed to funding the purchase of a paging company in Rhode Island that had 15,000 subscribers. After weeks of negotiations, an intent to purchase agreement was executed. However, adverse developments in the credit and capital markets raised strong enough doubts that Paul decided to terminate the agreement. Final first-round funding totaled $6 million for acquisitions and working capital; unfortunately, BCGI had already spent the entire amount.

In 1990, Paul went back to his investors with a new strategy and a request for additional funding. He repositioned the company to focus on the ROAMER*plus* market, providing services to cellular carriers. Burr, Egan, Deleage, &Co. and Highland Capital Partners brought Hancock Venture Partners into the syndicate (see *Exhibit I*, Venture Firm Summaries), and renegotiated the deal with management. The syndicate invested an additional $4 million, and the management team contributed $900,000 to provide the rest of the financing. However, the recapitalization came with a price: The investors wanted a five-year put[2] clause that would rapidly transfer ownership of the company to the syndicate if BCGI could not provide liquidity. BCGI agreed, with the condition that there also be a call. Paul recalled that the investors readily agreed.

> We structured the original deal to be 50/50 after a 25 percent annual rate of return for the investors. Then we converted it to preferred and we got a 50/50 split on the returns after a 35 percent rate of return. They also got to pick three people for the board, and I only had one seat, then the four of us picked the fifth member of the board, so they had control. It sounded pretty onerous at the time, but we were in no position to argue. We could renegotiate if things went well, if not, then who cares?
>
> The put was to protect the venture guys. The terms were that they could put their interest to us at fair market value [e.g., forcing BCGI to buy back the investors' shares] as determined by a jury of three: one of theirs, one of mine, and one independent chosen by the first two, at five years. In case we were unable to come up with the capital to pay off the venture guys, their money would stay in. From then on, it would accrue at an additional 25 percent interest a year. We wanted a call because we believed in ourselves and thought it was fair. I probably should have been tougher in the negotiations.

[2] A put (called a "mandatory redemption" in the 1990 term sheet) is a contract allowing the holder to sell a given number of securities back to the issuer of the contract at a fixed price for a given period of time.

EXHIBIT H

Excerpts[3] from Summary of Terms for Proposed Private Placement, 2/27/90

Radio Telephone Systems (dba BCGI)

Current Outstanding Securities

100 shares of Common Stock (Common) sold to Burr, Egan, Deleage & Co. (BED); 100 shares of Common Stock issuable to Highland Capital Partners Limited Partnership (HCP) upon conversion of $305,000 demand convertible note; and shares of Common and/or options to purchase Common representing an aggregate of up to 28 shares issued to or reserved for issuance to Management (as defined below).

At or prior to the Closing (as defined below) each share of Common held by BED will be converted into 100 shares of Class A Common Stock (Class A Common); HCP will convert its $305,000 demand convertible note into 100 shares of Common and each such share of Common will be converted into 100 shares of Class A Common; and each share (and/or option to purchase a share of) Common held by Management will be converted into 100 shares of (and/or options to purchase 100 shares of) Class B Common Stock (Class B Common).

Investors

Entities affiliated with BED will invest an aggregate of $4,445,000; HCP will invest $4,445,000; and $2,500,000 will come from other investors. Management may invest up to $125,000 of the remaining $2,500,000 at the initial closing (the Closing), and the balance will be invested by Fidelity Ventures (Fidelity).

Type of Security and Amount of Investment

An aggregate of $10,800,000 of Non-Convertible Preferred Stock (Preferred) and an aggregate of $590,000 of Class A Common. The Preferred and the Class A Common (the Securities) will be sold in two closings. The initial Closing will involve an aggregate of approximately $4,746,000 of Securities, and will be conditioned on the obtaining of all necessary approvals for the acquisition of certain radio paging systems from NYNEX as well as on the obtaining of all necessary regulatory approvals for the change in control of the Company resulting from this financing.

	First Closing		Second Closing	
	P.S.	**Cl.A.C.S**	**P.S.**	**Cl.A.C.S**
BED	$1,781,250*	$ 70,833	$2,493,750	$ 99,166
HCP	1,781,250*	70,833	2,493,750	99,166
Others	937,500	104,167	1,312,500	145,834

*Payment will be in cash and surrender of demand notes: all other payments will be in cash.

Cellular Express, Inc.

Prior to the Closing, an accommodation will be reached among the Company, BED and HCP with respect to Cellular Express, Inc.

Bank Line of Credit

Prior to the second closing, the Company shall use its best efforts to obtain a bank line of credit in an amount of at least $2 million on terms approved by the Board. If such line of credit cannot be obtained, the Company and Investors will negotiate for the Investors to provide additional financing on mutually agreeable terms.

Post-Second Closing Capitalization

Preferred		$10,800,000
Class A Common:		39,400 shares
Class B Common:	Committed to Management	2,800 shares
	Uncommitted Shares	8,313 shares
Total		50,513 shares

Bridge Advances

Any bridge advances made by Highland prior to Closing will be structured to bring Highland's position into line with BED, subject to FCC and other regulatory requirements. Additional bridge advances will be conditioned on Management preparing cash budgets for the existing business of the Company for the approval of the Investors.

[3] The non-excerpted areas of this term sheet cover important boilerplate deal points including voting, default, liquidation, stock options, anti-dilution, key-man insurance, and other protective provisions.

(Continued)

EXHIBIT H (concluded)

Price per Share
$1,000 per share of Preferred and $30.50 per share of Class A Common.

Description of Preferred

1) Dividend Provisions: A cumulative dividend will accrue at a rate of 10 percent per annum on the original purchase price and any accrued but unpaid dividends of the Preferred. Such dividend will be payable only if (a) as, and when declared by the Board of Directors (Board) or (b) upon a Liquidation Event (as defined below) or redemption of the Preferred.

2) Mandatory Redemption: On the fifth (5th) anniversary of the Closing the Company shall redeem the Preferred by paying in cash the Preferred Liquidation Amount. If the Company fails to redeem the Preferred when due, the per annum dividend of the Preferred shall thereafter increase by $10 on the first day of each calendar quarter; provided, however, that the Preferred dividend rate shall not in any event exceed 15 percent per annum.

3) Optional Redemption: The Company may redeem the Preferred in whole or in part at any time, without penalty or premium, by paying in cash the Preferred Liquidation Amount.

Description of Class A Common

1) Dividend Provisions: A cumulative dividend on the Class A Common will accrue at the rate of $2,745 per share per annum. Such dividend will be payable only (a) if, as, and when determined by the Board or (b) upon a Liquidation Event.

2) Liquidation Preference: Upon any Liquidation Event, the holder of Class A Common will be entitled to receive in preference to the holders of Class B Common an amount per share (Class A Liquidation Amount) equal to the greater of (a) $30.50 plus any dividends accrued on the Class A Common but not paid, or (b) the amount they would have received had they converted the Class A Common to Class B Common immediately prior to such Liquidation Event.

3) Conversion: A holder of Class A Common will have the right to convert the Class A Common, at the option of the holder, at any time, into shares of Class B Common. The total number of shares of Class B Common into which the Class A Common may be converted initially will be determined by dividing by $30.50. The conversion price will be subject to adjustment as provided in paragraph (5) below.

4) Automatic Conversion: The Class A Common will be automatically converted into Class B Common, at the then applicable conversion price, in the event of an underwritten public offering of shares of the Class B Common at the public offering price per share that is not less than $90.00 in an offering of not less than $10,000,000.

5) Voting Rights: Except with respect to election of directors and certain protective provisions, the holders of Class A Common will have the right to that number of votes equal to the number of shares of Class B Common issuable upon conversion of the Class A Common. Election of directors and the protective provisions will be as described under "Board Representation and Meetings" and "Protective Provisions," respectively, below.

6) Protective Provisions: Consent of the holders of at least two-thirds of the Class A Common will be required for (i) any sale by the company of all or substantially all of its assets, (ii) any merger or consolidation of the company with another entity, (iii) any liquidation or winding up of the Company, (iv) any amendment of the Company's charter or by-laws, (v) any dividend on, or repurchase of, any security other than the Preferred or Class A Common in accordance with their respective terms, or (vi) certain other actions materially affecting the Class A Common.

Description of Class B Common

Upon a Liquidation Event, after payment of the Preferred Liquidation Amounts and the Class A Liquidation Amounts, the remaining net assets of the Company will be distributed pro-rata to the holders of Class B Common. The Class B Common shall have one vote per share on all matters presented to the stockholders of the Company generally.

Board Representation and Meetings

The charter will provide that the authorized number of directors is five. The Class A Common (voting as a class) will elect three directors; the Class B Common (voting as a class) will elect one director; and the fifth director will be elected by the Class A Common and Class B Common, voting as separate classes.

Hockey Stick Growth

By late 1992, the company was growing rapidly (see *Exhibit J* for financial statement) as ROAMER*plus* gained momentum. Bill Egan, a partner at Burr, Egan, Deleage, & Co., suggested that he would like to renegotiate the deal because the original note lacked the proper management incentives. (See *Exhibit K* for 1992 Term Sheet which governed the restructuring.) Relations with the investors had remained positive, though occasionally strained, as the company underperformed its original plan. In particular, Brion Applegate had worked closely with Paul's team since the mid-1980s and was held in the highest regard as a partner, advisor, and friend.

Another opportunity arose in 1993 when Ameritech asked for off-hour customer service support. BCGI already offered 24-hour, 7-day service for ROAMER*plus* customers; operators just needed additional training to service Ameritech customers. BCGI called this new

EXHIBIT I

Summary of Venture Firm Activities

Burr, Egan, Deleage, & Co.

Burr, Egan, Deleage, & Co., founded in 1979, is based in Boston, Massachusetts, with one additional office located in San Francisco, California. This is a private venture capital firm which invests its own capital and functions either as a deal originator or as an investor in deals created by others. Current capital under management is $600 million. The company provides financing for projects needing seed, startup, first-stage, second-stage, or mezzanine capital, and projects focused on leveraged buyouts, control-block purchases, or other, special situations. The minimum investment made is $1 million, to companies located in the United States. Industry preferences for investment from Burr, Egan, Deleage, & Co. are communications, computer-related, distribution, electronic components and instrumentation, genetic engineering, industrial products and equipment, medical and health-related, and education-related. The company will not consider investing in oil and gas exploration and production or real estate. Return on investment is the company's primary concern and there are no additional fees charged for their services.

Highland Capital Partners

Highland Capital Partners, founded in 1988, is located in Boston, Massachusetts. This private venture capital firm invests its own capital and prefers to function as a deal originator but will consider investing in deals created by others. Current capital under management is $280 million. The company provides financing for projects needing seed, research and development, startup, first-stage, second-stage, or mezzanine capital, and projects focused on control-block purchases or other, special situations. The minimum investment made is $500,000 to companies located in the United States. Industry preferences for investment from Highland Capital Partners are communications, computer-related, electronic components and instrumentation, genetic engineering, and medical and health-related. The company will not consider investing in real estate. Return on investment is the company's primary concern and there are additional closing and service fees.

Hancock Venture Partners, Inc.

Hancock Venture Partners, Inc., founded in 1982, is located in Boston, Massachusetts with one additional office located in London, United Kingdom. This venture capital subsidiary of John Hancock will function either as a deal originator or as an investor in deals created by others. Current capital under management is $2 billion. The company provides financing for projects needing first-stage, second-stage, or mezzanine capital, and projects focused on leveraged buyouts. The minimum investment made is $2 million to companies located in the United States. Industry preferences for investment from Hancock Venture Partners, Inc., are communications, computer-related, distribution, electronic components and instrumentation, energy and natural resources, industrial products and equipment, finance and insurance, and publishing. The company will not consider investing in oil and gas exploration and production or real estate. Return on investment is the company's primary concern and there are no additional fees charged for their services.

Source: Pratt's Guide to Venture Capital, 1996 Edition.

EXHIBIT J

BCGI Financials

Boston Communications Group
Pro Forma Financials
Year Ended December 31,

	1991	1992	1993	1994	1995E(5)	CAGR 1991–1994	CAGR 1994–1995
Revenues	$ 1,447	$7,557	$10,244	$21,520	$35,500	145.9%	65.0
Costs and expenses (1)	1,838	6,504	9,684	20,184	32,602		
EBITDA	(391)	1,053	560	1,336	2,898	12.6%(6)	116.9%
Depreciation and amortization (2)	629	613	681	600	926		
Income (loss from operations)	(1,020)	440	(121)	736	1,972		168.0%
Interest expense (3)	100	100	100	100	100		
Pre-tax income (loss)	(1,120)	340	(221)	636	1,872		
Assumed net income after taxes (4)	$(1,120)	$ 204	$ (221)	$ 382	$ 1,123		194.4%
Growth Rates							
Revenues	—	422.3%	35.6%	110.1%	65.0%		
EBITDA	—	NM	−46.8%	138.4%	116.9%		
EBIT	—	NM	NM	NM	168.0%		
Pre-tax	—	NM	NM	NM	194.4%		
Net income	—	NM	NM	NM	194.4%		

(Continued)

EXHIBIT J (concluded)

	1991	1992	1993	1994	1995E(5)	CAGR 1991–1994	CAGR 1994–1995
Margin Analysis							
EBITDA	−27.0%	13.9%	5.5%	6.2%	8.2%		
EBIT	−70.5%	5.8%	−1.2%	3.4%	5.6%		
Pre-tax	−77.4%	4.5%	−2.2%	3.0%	5.3%		
Net income	−77.4%	2.7%	−2.2%	1.8%	3.2%		

Source: Company's projections as of June, 1995. Pro forma to exclude discontinued operations.

(1) Corporate overhead allocated as a percentage of Cellular Express revenues
(2) Assumes all depreciation and amortization attributable to Cellular Express
(3) Assumes historical interest expense of $100,000 for Cellular Express
(4) Assumes a 40% tax rate
(5) Excludes $2,500 in revenue and $250 in operating income which is assumed to be from discontinued operations
Assumes $100,000 of interest expense attributable to continuing operations
(6) CAGR from 1992–1994

EXHIBIT K

Summary of Terms for Proposed Restructuring, 12/31/92

1. The new capital structure for Boston Communications Group (BCGI or the Company) will consist of the following:
   a. Common Stock—One vote per share.
   b. Redeemable Preferred Stock—These shares have no voting rights. The shares will be subject to redemption at the option of either the BCGI or the holder thereof on the earlier to occur of (i) 6/30/97 or (ii) the sale of BCGI's Roamer Plus business, at their purchase price, plus unpaid dividends. The shares may also be redeemed, on a pro-rata basis, with the proceeds of bank financing at any time without penalty. The shares will have an 8 percent cumulative dividend and a liquidation purchase price, plus unpaid dividends.
   c. Convertible Preferred Stock—These shares may be converted to Common Stock at any time, and the Class B may be converted to Class A at any time, subject in each case to the prior receipt of any necessary approvals of the FCC or State regulatory bodies. The holders of the Convertible Preferred will be entitled to convert their shares into 75 percent of the total Common Stock which may be outstanding from time to time at and after the date of restructuring, assuming the exercise or conversion of all options, warrants, and other securities which are convertible into or exchangeable for Common Stock. Conversion of the Class B Convertible Preferred to Class A Convertible Preferred will be on a one-for-one basis. These shares will have a liquidation preference in the amount of their purchase price, junior to the Redeemable Preferred Stock and will have no dividend. The shares will be subject to put/call provisions at fair market value following the redemption of the redeemable Preferred Stock, but not before 6/30/97. There will be two classes of Convertible Preferred Stock:

   Class A—Voting—Each share shall be entitled to that number of votes equal to the number of shares of Common Stock into which it is then convertible.

   Class B—Nonvoting.
2. The funds managed by Burr, Egan, Deleage & Company (BEDCO) will exchange the 375 shares of old Class A Common Stock for 375 shares of the new Class A Convertible Preferred Stock.
3. Highland Capital Partners L.P. (Highland) will exchange its Convertible Note (Class A Common Stock) in the principal amount of $275,000 for 275 of the new Class B Convertible Preferred Stock.
4. BEDCO, Highland, Hancock Venture Partners III and Paul Tobin (the Investors) will exchange their Convertible Notes (Class B Common Stock) in the principal amount of $400,000 for 200 shares of the new Class B Convertible Preferred Stock.
5. The management group (consisting of Paul Tobin, Robert Sullivan, Frederick von Mering, Jeffry Timmons, Clifford Tallman and Robin Leonard) (Management) will exchange their stock options to acquire 850 shares of the old Class C Common Stock for 283.3 shares of the new Common Stock, which shall constitute 25 percent of the total Common Stock which may be outstanding from time to time at and after the date of restructuring, assuming the exercise or conversion of all options, warrants, and other securities which are convertible into or exchangeable for Common Stock.
6. The holders of Senior Subordinated Notes (except the holders of the rollover notes) will exchange their notes, in the total amount of $9,991,118, plus accrued interest (for 1991) in the total amount of $1,855,900, for Redeemable Preferred Stock.
7. The holders of the rollover notes (except Kim Mayyasi) will exchange their notes in the total principal amount of $865,934, plus accrued interest (for 1991) in the total amount of $158,100, for Redeemable Preferred Stock.

(Continued)

EXHIBIT K (concluded)

8. As a result of these exchanges, the Company will be held as follows:

BEDCO	375.0	Shares of Class A Convertible Preferred Stock
BEDCO	71.0	Shares of Class B Convertible Preferred Stock
Highland	333.5	Shares of Class B Convertible Preferred Stock
Hancock	62.5	Shares of Class B Convertible Preferred Stock
Tobin	7.5	Shares of Class B Convertible Preferred Stock
Mgmt.	283.8	Shares of Common Stock
Total	1,133.3	

BEDCO	$5,991,857	Redeemable Preferred Stock
Highland	4,517,861	Redeemable Preferred Stock
Hancock	1,337,300	Redeemable Preferred Stock
Tobin	412,466	Redeemable Preferred Stock
Sullivan	171,440	Redeemable Preferred Stock
BCGI	440,128	Redeemable Preferred Stock

The Company will use its best reasonable effort to raise bank debt of $2 million to $5 million by December 31, 1992, for the purpose of redeeming the Redeemable Preferred Stock, on a pro-rata basis.

9. Upon sale of the Beeper One (New York State) paging system, the Company will pay the Senior Subordinated Note in the principal amount of $144,900 held by Kim Mayyasi in full, including any accrued interest. Following the sale of assets of the Massachusetts One RSA (Franklin County) cellular system or Beeper One, the Company shall pay the following from the net proceeds of sale, to the extent received, on a pro-rata basis:

BEDCO Redeemable Preferred	$928,100
Highland Redeemable Preferred	715,500
Hancock Redeemable Preferred	212,300
BCGI Redeemable Preferred	67,600
Tobin Redeemable Preferred	64,200
Sullivan Redeemable Preferred	26,300
BCGI Redeemable Preferred	372,528
Tobin Redeemable Preferred	348,266
Sullivan Redeemable Preferred	145,140
	$2,879,934

10. There will be no payment of accrued interest for 1992 on the Senior Subordinated Notes or the Convertible Notes.
11. Management will establish a management company to provide management services to BCGI. BCGI and the management company will enter into a management agreement, containing such terms and conditions as may be agreed upon by BCGI and the management company. The fee for the management company's services will be based upon the current BCGI G&A expenses.
12. Management will devote sufficient time, energy and skills to the proper performance of the duties of the Company.
13. Immediately following the restructuring, the board of directors shall consist of five members: Brion B. Applegate, William J. Boyce, Paul J. Tobin, Clifford P. Tallman and Jeffry A. Timmons.
14. In the event that the internal rate of return to the investors on their $12,897,018 of invested capital, as measured from January 1, 1992, exceeds 35 percent per annum at the time of any complete or partial liquidation or sale of the Company or a major portion of its assets, then the excess above 35 percent shall be divided equally between the investors and management.
15. Preemptive rights to purchase, on a pro-rata basis, new issues of securities by the Company (as in the current Articles of Organization, as amended) shall be granted to the holders of the Convertible Preferred Stock and the Common Stock.

business Carrier Support Services. This service was labor intensive and was characterized by high personnel turnover. Several carriers soon followed Ameritech and outsourced off-hour customer service activities to BCGI.

In 1994, cellular industry leader Brian Boyle (see *Exhibit L* for biographical sketches) joined the BCGI team. In the mid-1980s, Brian had founded APPEX Corporation and grew it to $16 million in annual revenues before selling to EDS for $48 million. In 1989, he founded Credit Technology, Inc., a developer of custom software for the cellular industry. Credit Technology generated approximately $10 million in 1994. Brian and Paul negotiated a merger between BCGI and Credit Technology which essentially combined the companies with a 50/50 stock split. The merger passed the BCGI board, but stalled in the Credit Technology board meeting. Brian became vice chairman in charge of developing new wireless services.

EXHIBIT L

Executive Officers and Directors

The executive officers and directors of the Company and their ages as of September 31, 1995, are as follows:

Name	Age	Position
Paul J. Tobin	53	Chairman, President, and Chief Executive Officer
Brian E. Boyle	48	Vice Chairman
Frederick E. von Mering	43	Vice President, Finance and Administration, Director
Jeffry A. Timmons	53	Director
Clifford Tallman	52	Director
Craig L. Burr	51	Director
James L. McLean	35	Director

Mr. Tobin has served as Chairman of the Board of Directors of the Company since February 1996 and served as the Company's President and Chief Executive Officer from 1990 until February 1996. Prior to joining the Company, Mr. Tobin served as President of CellularOne Boston/Worcester from July 1984 to January 1990 and as a Regional Marketing Manager for Satellite Business Systems, a joint venture of IBM, Comsat Corp. and Aetna Life & Casualty from April 1980 to June 1984. Mr. Tobin received his undergraduate degree in economics from Stonehill College and his MBA, in marketing and finance, from Northeastern University. Mr. Tobin also serves as a member of the Board of Trustees at Stonehill College.

Mr. Boyle has served as Vice Chairman of the Company since February 1996 and as Chairman, New Wireless Services of the Company from January 1994 to February 1996. From July 1990 to September 1993, Mr. Boyle served as Chief Executive Officer of Credit Technologies, Inc., a supplier of customer application software for the cellular telephone industry. Prior to 1990, Mr. Boyle founded and operated a number of ventures servicing the telecommunications industry, including APPEX Corp. (now EDS Personal Communications Division of EDS Corporation, a global telecommunications service company) and Leasecomm Corp., a micro-ticket leasing company. Mr. Boyle earned his BA in mathematics from Amherst College and his BS, MS, and Ph.D. in electrical engineering and operations research from M.I.T. Mr. Boyle is also a Director of Saville Systems PLC, a provider of customized billing solutions to telecommunications providers, as well as of several private companies.

Mr. von Mering has served as the Company's Vice President, Finance and Administration since 1989. Prior to joining the Company, Mr. von Mering served as Regional Vice President and General Manager for the paging division of Metromedia, Inc., a communications company, from 1980 to 1986. From 1975 to 1979, Mr. von Mering was employed at Coopers & Lybrand LLP. Mr. von Mering earned his BA in accounting from Boston College and his MBA from Babson College.

Dr. Timmons has served as Director of the company since 1989. He is director of CellularOne in Boston and was co-founder and director of CellularOne in both Maine and New Hampshire. He is an advisor to Ernst & Young's National Entrepreneurial Service Group, BCI Advisors, Inc., Chemical Venture Partners, and Fax International. Dr. Timmons is internationally recognized for his work in entrepreneurship and venture capital, has authored and co-authored many books, and has been a trustee of Colgate University since 1991. In 1989 he became the first to hold a joint appointment with Harvard University as the MBA Class of 1954 Professorship of New Ventures and first to hold the Frederic C. Hamilton Professorship for Free Enterprise Studies at Babson College.

Mr. Tallman has served as Director of the company since 1989. Prior to joining the Company, Mr. Tallman was an associate with Highland Capital Partners from 1984 to 1988. Mr. Tallman received his AB from Harvard College and his MBA from Harvard Graduate School of Business Administration.

Mr. Burr has served as a Director of the Company since April 1993. Mr. Burr has been a Managing General Partner of Burr, Egan, Deleage & Co., a venture capital firm, since 1979. Mr. Burr received his AB from Harvard College and his MBA from Harvard Graduate School of Business Administration. Mr. Burr is a director of several privately-held companies affiliated with Burr, Egan, Deleage & Co.

Mr. McLean has served as a Director of the Company since May 1995. Mr. McLean has been a general partner of Highland Capital Partners, Incorporated, a venture capital firm, since December 1994. From December 1993 to December 1994, he was an associate with Highland Capital Partners. Prior to that, Mr. McLean was an associate with Accel Partners, a venture capital firm, from October 1990 to December 1993. Mr. McLean received his BS from Harvard University and his MBA from the University of California, Berkeley.

Robert Sullivan, Vice President of Engineering at Boston Communications Group, is responsible for development of telecommunications systems and service supporting the cellular telephone industry. Mr. Sullivan is also technical advisor for all telephony related products and services. As a co-founder of BCGI, Mr. Sullivan came to the partnership with over 20 years experience in engineering and construction of communications systems. After graduating from Northeastern University, Mr. Sullivan was employed by Raytheon, Inc. in Norwood, MA in the Microwave Radio Delay Department. From there Mr. Sullivan took a position with ZipCall, Inc. in Boston, MA where he became a Chief Engineer and worked to develop the largest radio paging system in New England. ZipCall was sold to Metromedia Telecommunications, Inc. in 1993. At CellularOne Boston, Mr. Sullivan became Vice President of Operations and was responsible for startup construction and operation of cellular telephone systems in the Boston/Worcester, Massachusetts, and Portsmouth, New Hampshire markets.

Each officer serves at the discretion of the Board of Directors. There are no family relationships among any of the directors and executive officers of the Company.

Source: BCGI Business Plan, 9/95

BCGI, 1995

By mid-1995, BCGI provided services exclusively to cellular carriers and their subscribers. BCGI's largest source of revenue was ROAMER*plus*. This calling service was so widely used by cellular carriers, that further growth was more likely to be from general growth in the roaming market, than from the addition of new carrier clients.

A significant portion of these revenues came from a limited number of carriers. Although ROAMER*plus* served almost 100 carriers, net revenues attributable to the ten largest customers accounted for approximately 85 percent, 81 percent, and 85 percent of BCGI's total revenues in 1993, 1994, and the first half of 1995, respectively. Similarly, two carriers accounted for 75 percent of BCGI's Carrier Support Services business in the first half of 1995, with the remaining 25 percent contributed by four other carriers.

The contracts for both ROAMER*plus* and Carrier Support Services were generally for a period of one year, and except for certain support contracts, had no minimum payment obligation to BCGI. In addition to being vulnerable to fluctuations within its key-account customer base, BCGI's calling services were affected by a number of relatively unpredictable factors: The frequency of temporary suspensions of intercarrier roaming agreements, competitive developments, changes in regulations affecting the wireless industry, general economic conditions, and changes in the technological landscape.

BCGI was recognized for developing leading-edge technology and services, setting the pace of change in the wireless telephone industry. The company hired some of the best software engineers in the industry and its ability to compete was partially dependent upon proprietary technology. BCGI relied primarily on a combination of statutory and common law copyright, trademark and trade secret laws, customer licensing agreements, employee and third-party nondisclosure agreements to protect its intellectual property rights. BCGI also entered into confidentiality agreements with employees, consultants, clients, and potential clients to protect its proprietary knowledge. In spite of these precautions, all proprietary advantages had to be considered temporary due to vulnerability to reverse engineering and to the high quality R&D being conducted in the wireless communications industry. Despite these vulnerabilities, Paul was optimistic because BCGI had the plan (see *Exhibit M* for Pro Forma projections), the people, and the strategy to succeed in this industry.

EXHIBIT M

BCGI Pro Forma Financials

	Boston Communications Group Projected Financials Year Ended December 31,					CAGR	CAGR
	1995E[1]	1996E	1997E	1998E	1999E	1995–1996	1996–1998
Revenues	$35,500	$54,000	$77,000	$109,000	$153,000	52.1%	41.5%
Cost and expenses	32,602	48,530	66,740	91,776	125,226		
EBITDA	2,898	5,470	10,260	17,224	27,774	88.8%	71.9%
Depreciation and amortization	926	1,270	2,360	2,724	2,974		
Income (loss from operations)	1,972	4,200	7,900	14,500	24,800	113.0%	80.7%
Interest expense	100	300	400	500	600		
Loss (gain) on sale of furniture and equipment	—	—	—	—	—		
Pre-tax income (loss)	1,872	3,900	7,500	14,000	24,200		
Assumed net income after taxes @ 40% tax rate	$ 1,123	$ 2,340	$ 4,500	$ 8,400	$ 14,520	108.3%	83.8%
Growth Rates							
Revenues	—	52.1%	42.6%	41.6%	40.4%		
EBITDA	—	88.8%	87.6%	67.9%	61.3%		
EBIT	—	113.0%	88.1%	83.5%	71.0%		
Pre-tax	—	108.3%	92.3%	86.7%	72.9%		
Net income	—	108.3%	92.3%	86.7%	72.9%		
Margin Analysis							
EBITDA	8.2%	10.1%	13.3%	15.8%	18.2%		
EBIT	5.6%	7.8%	10.3%	13.3%	16.2%		
Pre-tax	5.3%	7.2%	9.7%	12.8%	15.8%		
Net income	3.2%	4.3%	5.8%	7.7%	9.5%		

Source: Company's projections
[1]Excludes discontinued operations

Strategy

BCGI was focused on developing, marketing and providing high quality, innovative call processing and customer support services to wireless carriers. Paul believed that wireless telephone service would continue to be one of the fastest growing segments of the telecommunications industry and that wireless carriers would be under increasing competitive pressure. As a result, he believed there would be significant opportunities to provide wireless carriers with services that enabled them to focus internal resources on their core business activities while simultaneously increasing revenues, improving service quality, and reducing costs. In addition to focusing on the wireless carrier services industry, BCGI's strategy included the following elements:

- *Identify and Develop Additional Value-Added Services*

  BCGI sought to create innovative value-added services that wireless telephone carriers either had not identified or had found difficult or uneconomical to provide on their own. It was particularly focused on developing and providing services that created incremental revenue and profit for wireless carriers, such as its ROAMER*plus* service and a new prepaid wireless service BCGI called C2C. C2C would allow carriers to offer cellular service to prospective customers who did not qualify for credit approval. Many people who wanted cellular service were turned away, but very few would be ineligible for C2C because service was prepaid. BCGI planned to introduce C2C in the fall of 1995. Paul believed that such services would be increasingly attractive to wireless telephone carriers seeking innovative ways to respond to a highly competitive and evolving industry.
- *Develop and Maintain Long-Term Customer Relationships*

  BCGI established and maintained long-term relationships with carriers to enable it to understand customer needs and continue to develop new service offerings to meet those needs. They regularly solicited feedback from customers regarding the challenges they faced in order to identify potential new service offerings. Paul's team sought to build upon its existing customer relationships and distribution channels by integrating and cross-selling its different service offerings. Paul believed that focus on building customer relationships was an important factor in developing customer loyalty and expanding existing customer relationships over time.
- *Provide Services on a Recurring Revenue Basis*

  BCGI focused on offering services that generated recurring revenues. Paul wanted to provide ongoing services to align BCGI's interests with those of its customers and maximize the potential benefit to those customers. BCGI provided its call processing and Carrier Support Services on a per-minute or per-call basis, or in combination. These pricing methods minimized up-front costs and focused on the revenue enhancement potential for the carriers.
- *Offer Premium Quality Services*

  Paul believed that providing high quality service was critical to BCGI's ability to satisfy customers. BCGI's Carrier Support Services were designed to be indistinguishable from the services provided by the cellular carrier's own customer support personnel. BCGI provided extensive in-house classroom and on-the-job training programs for its personnel, including carrier-specific training programs designed in collaboration with the applicable carrier.
- *Expand into New Wireless Telephone Markets*

  Paul believed there were significant opportunities to leverage BCGI's experience to penetrate new wireless telephone markets. First, he believed there would be opportunities for BCGI to provide services to PCS carriers similar to those which it provided to cellular carriers. Second, the management team was exploring ways to expand into new international markets, primarily through the establishment of joint ventures and strategic alliances.

By mid-1995, BCGI was on track to generate $38 million, so Paul was not surprised when GTE Sylvania approached to discuss a buyout.

> In this industry, there were a number of service providers to the cellular carriers, and there are three majors: EDS, GTE, and Cincinnati Bell. The fourth largest in terms of revenues and name recognition was BCGI. We were on a much lower tier, but we probably provided more services to more carriers than anyone. They just get more revenue out of it. So it was natural for someone who wanted to be a supplier to the cellular industry to wind up at our door pretty fast.

Determining a Harvest Strategy

Paul began considering his harvest options in mid-1995, about the time that he was approached by the acquisition group at GTE. He liked the idea of a buyout because of the intense burdens of going public (e.g., insider trading rules, competitive and personal disclosures, SEC regulations, etc.), so he was attentive to GTE's approach. However, the discussions progressed slowly.

> We had three or four meetings and each one was more aggressive than the last. The discussion went back and forth, "What do you guys think you're worth?" "I don't know, you tell me." "No, you tell me first." Over the past couple of years it had dawned on them that we were a pretty good management group, and that they didn't want to compete with us in the marketplace. They had

more money and more resources to throw at it, but we had a better reputation. Given an equal service, we were going to sell more than they would. Part of their motivation was to buy distribution, but another part was to buy out a competitor.

GTE provided a number of the same services to the wireless industry that we did. We had a great sales and marketing group; about 25 people who started in the cellular industry in 1984–1985. These people had 10-year relationships with cellular people all across the country. So our marketing strength was much better, or we like to think that it was much better, than this $20 billion corporation.

GTE's interest was part of the impetus to thinking, maybe it is time. In addition to that, we were funded by three different firms: Burr, Egan, Deleage, & Co., Highland Capital Partners, and Hancock Venture Partners. The life cycle of a venture fund is generally 10 years, then you can get a two-year extension on top of that, and maybe another year or two after that. We were the last investment in one of these funds, and they were in the two-year extension period. So there was some pressure from our venture guys to come up with liquidity because they don't like to go back and ask for another extension. A third reason we looked at GTE was that the venture guys had the put. It was time for us to start looking for liquidity.

Another option was an IPO. Paul held meetings with people familiar with the IPO process, particularly R. Douglas Kahn, a Boston-area entrepreneur whose company was the first to go public following the invasion of Kuwait in August 1990. Kahn had been remarkably thorough and perceptive in developing his approach to the harvest process.[4] Tobin was particularly intrigued with a letter sent by Kahn to "The Four Horsemen"[5] (see *Exhibit N* for a copy of the letter). This request for quotation (RFQ) posed a number of tough questions to the investment banks. Although the IPO market of late-1995 was very different than mid-1990, Paul was better able to understand the bank selection process after meeting

[4] See Jeffry A. Timmons, EASEL Corporation, *New Venture Creation, 4th edition,* 1994.

[5] The investment banking firms of Alex Brown & Sons, Donaldson, Lufkin & Jennette, Hambrecht & Quist, and Robertson, Stephens & Company.

EXHIBIT N

EASEL Corp., Request for Quotation Summary (condensed)

July 18, 1990

Dear _____ :

We appreciate the interest you have expressed in providing investment banking services to EASEL. In order to provide us with the information to help us in the investment banker selection process, we would appreciate your written response to the following questions.

I. IPO Timing

- When would be the best time, given current market conditions? Why?
- What financial performance would need to be achieved in order to feel comfortable with an IPO in the September time frame? Would you require an audit of interim financials in order to go public in 1990?
- How does your "commitment committee" operate and at what point in the process is the "commitment" obtained?

II. Pricing

- What offering price range would you select if the IPO were today? Please explain how you determined this price.
- How would you position EASEL among comparable software companies? Please indicate which companies you would add or delete from the list of companies which we believe to be comparable to EASEL.

III. IPO Process

- Please provide the names of the proposed investment banking team and describe specific involvement of each person (drafting sessions, due diligence sessions . . .)
- Which law firm would you select and who would be the lead attorney from the firm?
- Would you market the offering outside of the United States? Why or why not?
- What is your recommended mix of institutional versus retail buyers and why?
- Describe your recommended "road show" process. Please note anything unique or unusual relative to other investment banks.

IV. Research

- Who within your firm will be responsible for research? How long have they been with your firm? Is there any information that we should be aware of that would provide us comfort that this person will remain with your firm in the future? Please attach some reports developed by this individual in the past year.

(Continued)

EXHIBIT N (concluded)

- How would the analyst describe EASEL (positioning statement)? What is the analyst's opinion of the company's strategy? Will EASEL be included in the "universe" of software companies your firm tracks?
- When would you release the first research report?
- How often would research reports be released?

V. Fees

- Please provide a schedule of fees expected to be incurred.

VI. The Offering

- What percentage of shares would you feel comfortable allocating to existing investors? To management? What are your policies on selling stockholder indemnification? What are your policies on company reimbursement of selling stockholder expenses?
- What "lockup" provisions would you want to place for investors, management and employees?
- Management has received proposals from counsel as to the implementation of anti-takeover provisions prior to an IPO, including poison pill defense and a staggered board. What is your position on these provisions?

VII. Support

- Describe the scope of your trading operation and how you would support our stock in the market. Will you act as market-maker? Who else would you recommend as additional market-makers?
- What type and level of support would we receive after an IPO?

VIII. Other Information

- Please provide examples of the last five technology company IPOs you have managed or comanaged. Please provide IPO price and 30-day post IPO price. Please also provide prospectus copies, and CEO and CFO names and telephone numbers.
- Please provide any other information you would like us to consider.

We would appreciate six copies of your response to this request by April 30 which we will share with our IPO committee and Board of Directors. We may ask you to make a formal presentation to this committee at a later date.

Thank you for your continued interest and feel free to contact me if you would have any questions.

Sincerely,

John McDonough
Vice President and
Chief Financial Officer

Source: Jeffry A. Timmons, "EASEL Corporation," *New Venture Creation, 4th edition,* 1994.

with Kahn. Paul settled on a strategy and contacted investment bankers at the Four Horsemen:

> Our venture partners gave me names at each of the four firms—the people they did business with on a regular basis. So I called, and then the venture guys called them. We had a couple of meetings with each of them before they drew up their proposals.
>
> When you are talking to investment bankers, you want to project your company in the best light to get the best valuation. You need to make sure they understand your company, but everybody's selling: we're selling them, they're selling us, and both of us are trying to sell the public or a deal guy.

Generally, the bankers sent two or three guys, an analyst and a couple of salespeople called managing directors. They tell you what it costs and then they try to sell you on why they are the best. The guy from Alex Brown said, "We know a lot about communications and we can do an M&A deal, but we think it would be crazy. You're leaving too much money on the table—you should do an IPO," because that was their expertise. DLJ also does a lot of telecommunications deals. They said, "We have a good M&A department and this should be an M&A deal." It depends on the bank, but it also has a lot to do with the bias of the managing director, whether he's an M&A guy or an IPO guy.

November Board of Directors Meeting

Three of the Four Horsemen responded to Paul's request for a proposal. Working with the rest of the management, Paul prepared a summary evaluation of the bankers' proposals for the next board meeting (see *Exhibit O* for Proposal Matrix). He recalled the board's discussions.

EXHIBIT O

BCGI Evaluation of Investment Bankers: Underwriting Proposal Summaries

	Alex Brown	Donaldson, Lufkin, & Jenrette	Robertson, Stephens & Company
Strategic Alternatives	1. IPO 2. Sale to Strategic/Financial Buyer 3. Hedged Approach (approach select group of potential buyers to gauge interest) 4. Status Quo	1. IPO 2. Sale to Strategic/Financial Buyer 3. Strategic Investor/Partner	1. IPO 2. Sale of Company (partial to 100%) 3. Joint Venture/Merger 4. Recapitalization (in anticipation of acquisitions) 5. Status Quo
Recommended Pricing **Pricing Method**	$80–120 million 1–3.4x Revenues(*) 7.8–31.4x EBITDA 10.1–60.9x EBIT 17.4–105.3x NI	1. $90–$125 million Discounted Cash Flows(**) Modification of BCGI's Projections	$70–$95 million Discounted Cash Flows
Recommended Pricing **Pricing Method** **Recommended Pricing** **Pricing Method**		2. $65–$95 million Comparable Acquisitions 3. $45–$60 million Comparable Public Companies	
Pricing Comparables	Physician Billing, Inc. Genex Services, Inc. Advacare, Inc. EPS/National Card System Medical Management Resources, Inc. Consolidated Medical Services, Inc. Northwest Creditors Service, Inc. Datamedic Corporation Alpha Beta Daya Services, Inc. General Electric Information Services CyCare Systems Financial Processors, Inc. Vantage Computer Systems, Inc. Winsbury Co. LP	Cellular Technical Services Global Telecom. Solutions Midcom Communications Racotek Tel-Save Holdings Tele-Matic Corp.	Affiliated Computer Services, Inc. AMNEX, Inc. Brite Voice Systems, Inc. Business Records Corporation Holding Company Shared Technologies, Inc. Transition Network Services, Inc.

(Continued)

EXHIBIT O (concluded)

Range of Selected Market Multiples for Public Companies			
1. Transaction Processing (**)	2.3–7.4X Trailing Revenues 13.9–31.9X Trailing Cash Flow 18.7–38.6X Trailing EBIT		
2. Specialty Business Service Providers(**)	.4–5.4X Trailing Revenues 6.9–24.8X Trailing Cash Flow 10.2–28.7X Trailing EBIT		
3. Wireless Communication		(227.5)–319.6X LTM EPS 1.6–19.6X Book Value	
4. Information Processing			11.4–145.8 P/E Ratio .7–4.1Enterprise Value/Revenue (LTM) 12.7–28.1 Enterprise Value/EBIT (LTM) 20.0–35.0 Equity Value/LTM Net Income
Range of Selected Recent Transaction Multiples (***)	.5–8.4X Trailing Revenues 7.0–33.4X LTM EBITDA 8.3–53.2X LTM EBIT	9.6–54.0 IX LTM EPS 4.5–11.8X Book Value	13.1–33.3 NI/LTM 1.0–8.2 Book Value/LTM .5–3.8 Revenue/LTM 6.5–18.8 EBIT/LTM
Primary Offering Size **Preferred Strategy**	$30 million IPO to maximize value If sale, use auction among candidates. Identified 12 potential acquirers, strong on transaction processing.	Not Specified Sale with auction; should get a higher value with control premium vs. potential IPO discount. Identified 36 potential acquirers, good mix, includes most of our potentials	Not Specified Sale of 100% of the Company Sale with "controlled competitive offering"
Timing	Immediate	Not Specified	Immediate—Closing in 1996
Strengths/Weaknesses	Oriented toward equity underwriting: #1 in venture backed IPOs; strong sales & distribution channels MEDIUM focus on wireless 14 analysts for media, communications & technology	Ranked #1 in cellular underwriting 1990–1994 STRONG focus on wireless Dennis Leibowitz ranked #2 wireless analyst #1 cable; long DLJ tenure	Very focused on technology players 18 analysts in the technology sector, 4 in communication LOW focus on wireless

(*)Calculated using 1995–1997 est. Revenues, EBITDA, EBIT, and NI.
(**)Cash flow analysis is based on company projections and a 10X exit multiple discounted at 25% to 35%.
(***)An adjusted market value was calculated using the market value of equity plus total debt less cash and equivalents. Multiples are expressed in relation to this adjusted market value.

Our board thought an IPO was better money. There is a structural conflict between the venture guys and management here: On a sale everybody cashes in, but on an IPO the venture guys do better because of the lock up. Not only are they cashing in on the IPO, but then you have rule 144 restrictions.[6] So there is a potential conflict of objectives, but we always had a great relationship with our venture guys. They said, "It's your deal. Do what you think is right—here is our best advice."

To further complicate his recommendation to the board, the bankers were split on their recommendations: Alex Brown & Sons recommended an IPO (see Appendix C: Excerpts from Alex Brown Proposal), while Donaldson, Lufkin & Jenrette (see Appendix D: Excerpts from Donaldson, Lufkin & Jenrette Proposal) and Robertson, Stephens recommended a sale of the company. To his pleasant surprise, valuations also covered a higher range than Paul had expected, \$45–125 million. Clearly, BCGI had created a significant amount of value in a fairly short period of time. In addition, the robust capital and IPO markets were influencing valuations. The trick was: How long would it last? On balance, it appeared that the company might bring \$75–90 million, if one assumed the banks' more optimistic estimates were part of their own selling process. As Paul reviewed the summary of management's evaluations, he pondered his choices.

[6] Rule 144 governs securities sold through interstate commerce and mail. It is designed to prevent fraud by mandating that all securities provide adequate information to consumers. It also limits the amount and timing of securities that can be sold by individuals involved in that deal.

Table of Appendices

Appendix A: The Top 50 Wireless Operators

Appendix B: Personal Communications Services

Appendix C: Excerpts from Alex Brown Proposal

- Appendix C1: Free Cash Flow Analysis
- Appendix C2: Discounted Cash Flow Analysis
- Appendix C3: Excerpts from Valuation Summary
- Appendix C4: Excerpts from IPO Valuation Analysis
- Appendix C5: Excerpts from Selected Potential Buyers

Appendix D: Excerpts from Donaldson, Lufkin & Jenrette Proposal

- Appendix D1: Effect of Growth on Future Trading Value
- Appendix D2: The M&A Sales Process
- Appendix D3: Proposed Time Schedule
- Appendix D4: Selected M&A Transaction Multiplies Wireless Communications Industry
- Appendix D5a: Comparison of Selected Publicly Held, Value-added Companies
- Appendix D5b: Comparison of Publicly Held Wireless Communication Companies

APPENDIX A

The Top 50 Wireless Operators

	Operator Name	Mkts	Population		Operator Name	Mkts	Population
1	AT&T Wireless Services, Inc.*	142	175,296,174	**26**	Cellular Communications, Inc.	22	8,189,198
2	Nextel Communications	311	158,183,228	**27**	American Personal Communications	1	7,777,875
3	Sprint Spectrum	29	144,938,590	**28**	Comcast Cellular Com.	9	7,629,202
4	Geotek Communications	25	69,045,270	**29**	ALLTEL Mobile Communications	53	7,524,952
5	GTE Mobilnet*	127	68,704,157	**30**	Century Cellunet	37	7,333,411
6	PCS PrimeCo	11	57,191,542	**31**	Activated Com.	1	7,261,176
7	Bell Atlantic NYNEX Mobile	79	57,043,488	**32**	Vanguard Cellular Systems, Inc.	26	6,869,771
8	AirTouch Communications	100	55,228,917	**33**	SNET Mobility, Inc.	12	5,609,227
9	Southwestern Bell Mobile Systems*	72	54,576,997	**34**	CommNet Cellular, Inc.	55	4,008,766
10	BellSouth Corp.	94	47,417,568	**35**	Wireless One Network	19	3,788,988
11	Ameritech Cellular Services*	44	35,428,615	**36**	Palmer Wireless, Inc.	18	3,569,247
12	Pacific Bell Mobile Services	2	31,036,409	**37**	Centennial Cellular Corp.—PCS	1	3,522,037
13	American Portable Telecommunications	8	26,439,502	**38**	Puerto Rico Telephone Co.	12	3,522,037
14	OmniPoint Corporation	1	26,410,597	**39**	B.C. Tel Mobility Cellular, Inc.	1	3,221,600
15	Rogers Cantel Mobile, Inc.	11	26,293,388	**40**	Horizon Cellular Group	15	3,098,508
16	Western Wireless	75	24,245,556	**41**	PriCellular Corporation	19	2,858,249
17	US Cellular	136	21,034,955	**42**	Frontier Corporation	12	2,765,286
18	Cox Com	2	20,804,505	**43**	AGT Mobility, Inc.	2	2,479,956
19	Pittencrieff Communications	68	20,052,039	**44**	Cellular Com of Puerto Rico	4	2,466,350
20	360° Communications	94	19,536,870	**45**	Poka Lambro Telecommunications	5	2,218,905
21	GTE Macro Communications	4	19,366,561	**46**	Lincoln Telecommunications	13	1,706,625
22	Bell Mobility	2	16,849,800	**47**	Centennial Cellular	9	1,610,342
23	BellSouth Personal Communications	2	11,474,228	**48**	Radiofone, Inc.	4	1,504,908
24	Powertel PCS Partners, L.P.	3	8,984,235	**49**	Cellular South	11	1,407,371
25	PhillieCo	1	8,927,748	**50**	Pacific Telecom Cellular	8	1,246,908

*Market and population figures reflect the combined cellular and PCS holdings for these companies. Source: CTIA

APPENDIX B

Personal Communications Services

Personal Communications Services (PCS) are a wide range of wireless mobile technologies, including two-way paging and cellular-like calling services, which are transmitted at lower power and higher frequencies than regular cellular services. The PCS spectrum is comprised of three sections: one for operating narrowband services, one for broadband services, and a third reserved for unlicensed devices.

Narrowband: In July of 1994, the Federal Communication Commission (FCC) auctioned its first group of PCS licenses. Six companies, with combined bids totaling more than $617 million, were awarded rights to provide nationwide, narrowband PCS paging services. In late 1994, nine other companies with bids totaling $491 million, were awarded rights to provide regional, narrowband PCS services.

Broadband: In March of the following year, 18 companies bid more than $7 billion for broadband PCS licenses. Broadband PCS will consist of cellular-like services including new categories of wireless voice and data transmissions, including enhanced privacy and antifraud security features, over both local and wide areas using low power, lightweight pocket phones and hand-held computers.

Unlicensed: The area between the narrowband and broadband blocks is allocated for unlicensed PCS device use, including short-distance wireless voice and data devices (e.g., local area networks and Private Branch Exchanges). Previously, unlicensed short distance wireless voice and data applications had been relegated to industrial, scientific, or medical bands and were often plagued by interference.[1]

There are 2,074 licenses in 51 Major Trading Areas and 493 Basic Trading Areas in the United States. As of December 1995, 18 percent of these had been auctioned. Three of them were awarded to companies designated by the FCC as holders of "pioneer's preferences," a category for awarding licenses to parties that have developed new communications services and technologies.[2] The FCC also created a "designated entities" category for small, rural, women, or minority-owned businesses. Businesses in this category have race or gender-based preferences.

"The PCS industry is expected to compete with existing cellular and private advanced mobile communications services, thereby yielding lower prices for existing users of those services," according to the FCC. Additionally, PCS will promote the development of other services and devices (e.g., private branch exchanges, smaller, lighter, multi-function portable phones, multichannel cordless phones, and portable facsimiles and other imaging equipment.[3]

[1] Mathias and Rysavy, "The ABCs of PCS," *Network World*, March 1995.

[2] The pioneer's preference regulations are codified at 47 C.F.R. §§ 1.402, 5.207. *Establishment of Procedures to Provide a Preference*, Report and Order, 6 FCC Rcd 3488 (1991), 7 FCC Rcd 1808 (1992), further recon. pending.

[3] See FCC Gen Docket No. 90-314, *Amendment of the Commissions Rules to Establish New Personal Communications Services*, Second Report and Order, October 22, 1993, page 11.

APPENDIX C1

Excerpts from Alex Brown Proposal, Free Cash Flow Analysis

	Fiscal Year Ending December 31,					
($ 000s)	1995E[1]	1996E	1997E	1998E	1999E	CAGR 1995–1999
Total Revenue	$35,500	$54,000	$77,000	$109,000	$153,000	44.1%
Operating Expenses	32,602	48,530	66,740	91,776	125,226	
Operating Cash Flow	2,898	5,470	10,260	17,224	27,774	75.9%
Less: Deprec. & Amortization	926	1,270	2,360	2,724	2,974	
Operating Income	1,972	4,200	7,900	14,500	24,800	88.3%
Less: Interest Expense	100	300	400	500	600	
Pre-Tax Expense	1,872	3,900	7,500	14,000	24,200	
Income Tax Expense[2]	749	1,560	3,000	5,600	9,680	
Earnings After Tax	1,123	2,340	4,500	8,400	14,520	89.6%
Plus: Deprec. & Amortization	926	1,270	2,360	2,724	2,974	
Less: Capital Expenditures[3]	1,000	1,000	1,000	1,000	1,000	
Increase/(Decrease) in WC[4]	86	370	460	640	880	
Free Cash Flow	$ 963	$ 2,240	$ 5,400	$ 9,484	$ 15,614	100.6%
Revenue Growth	13.7%	52.1%	42.6%	41.6%	40.4%	
Operating Cash Flow Margin	8.2%	10.1%	13.3%	15.8%	18.2%	
Operating Income Margin	5.6%	7.8%	10.3%	13.3%	16.2%	
Free Cash Flow Margin	2.7%	4.1%	7.0%	8.7%	10.2%	

[1] Excludes discontinued operations

[2] Assumes a 40% tax rate

[3] Assumes annual $1,000 capital expenditure

[4] Assumes working capital = 2% of revenues

APPENDIX C2

Discounted Cash Flow Analysis from Alex Brown Proposal

Disc Rate	($000s)	1.75 X	2.00 X	2.25 X	8.0 X	10.0 X	12.0 X	22.0 X	24.0 X	26.0 X
	PV of Cash Flow	$ 19,602	$ 19,602	$ 19,602	$ 19,602	$ 19,602	$ 19,602	$ 19,602	$ 19,602	$ 19,602
	PV of Terminal Value	$138,102	157,831	177,560	114,604	143,255	171,906	164,764	179,742	194,721
18%	Total Market Value	157,705	177,434	197,163	134,206	162,857	191,509	184,366	199,344	214,323
	PV of Cash Flow	18,635	18,635	18,635	18,635	18,635	18,635	18,635	18,635	18,635
	PV of Terminal Value	129,123	147,569	166,016	107,153	133,941	160,729	154,051	168,056	182,060
20%	Total Market Value	147,758	166,204	184,651	125,788	152,576	179,364	172,686	186,691	200,695
	PV of Cash Flow	17,735	17,735	17,735	17,735	17,735	17,735	17,735	17,735	17,735
	PV of Terminal Value	120,862	138,128	155,394	100,297	125,372	150,446	144,195	157,304	170,412
22%	Total Market Value	138,597	155,863	173,129	118,032	143,107	168,181	161,930	175,039	188,147

To December 31, 1995

APPENDIX C3

Excerpts from Alex Brown Proposal Valuation Summary[1]

Firm Value* Value as a Multiple	($ mil.)	$80	$90	$100	$110	$120
Revenues						
1995E	$38.0	2.1X	2.4X	2.6X	2.9X	3.2X
1995E-Adj.	35.5	2.3	2.5	2.8	3.1	3.4
1996E	54.0	1.5	1.7	1.9	2.0	2.2
1997E	77.0	1.0	1.2	1.3	1.4	1.6
EBITDA						
1995E	$3.1	25.4X	28.6X	31.8X	34.9X	38.IX
1995E-Adj.	2.9	27.6	31.1	34.5	38.0	41.4
1996E	5.5	14.6	16.5	18.3	20.1	21.9
1997E	10.3	7.8	8.8	9.7	10.7	11.7
Equity Market Value Multiple						
Net Income						
1995E	$1.2	65.2X	73.5X	81.8X	90.2X	98.5X
1995E-Adj.	1.1	69.6	78.5	87.4	96.3	105.3
1996E	2.3	33.4	37.7	42.0	46.2	50.5
1997E	4.5	17.4	19.6	21.8	24.0	26.3

* Firm Value defined as equity value plus debt less cash and equivalents.

[1] This analysis is based upon data drawn from the following sectors: (1) transaction processing companies such as Paycheck, Inc.; (2) specialty service providers such as Mead Data Central; and (3) cellular companies like Nationwide Cellular.

APPENDIX C4

Excerpts from Alex Brown Proposal, IPO Valuation Analysis: Pro Forma Income Statement for Initial Public Offering

	Pre-IPO 1995[1]	Post-IPO 1995[1]	Post-IPO 1996
Revenues	$35,500	$35,500	$54,000
Cost and expenses	32,602	32,602	48,530
EBITDA	2,898	2,898	5,470
Depreciation and amortization	926	926	1,270
Income (loss) from operations	1,972	1,972	4,200
Pro forma interest expense[2]	100	0	0
Pro forma interest income[3]	0	1,026	966
Pro forma pre-tax income (loss)	2,838	2,998	5,166
Assumed net income @ 40% tax rate	$ 1,703	$ 1,799	$ 3,100
Growth Rates			
Revenues	—	—	52.1%
EBITDA			88.8%
EBIT			113.0%
Pre-tax			82.0%
Net income			82.0%
Margin Analysis			
EBITDA	8.2%	8.2%	10.1%
EBIT	5.6%	5.6%	7.8%
Pre-tax	8.0%	8.4%	9.6%
Net income	4.8%	5.1%	5.7%

[1] Excludes discontinued operations

[2] Assumes debt repayment of $1,000 with offering proceeds in 1995 and assumes 10% interest rate and the use of $2,000 in cash to pay down debt in 1996

[3] Assumes 6% interest rate on cash proceeds from offering

APPENDIX C5

Excerpts from Alex Brown Proposal, Selected Potential Buyers

1) Alltel Corp.
2) AT&T
3) Automatic DP
4) British Telecom.
5) Cable Data
6) Cable & Wireless
7) Cincinnati Bell
8) Concord EFS
9) EDS
10) First Data Corp.
11) First Financial Mgmt.
12) GTE Corp.
13) Nat'l. Dispatch Center

APPENDIX D

Excerpts from Donaldson, Lufkin & Jenrette Proposal

APPENDIX D1

Effect of Growth on Future Trading Value

	1996	1997	1998
Projected EBITDA	$ 5.5	$ 10.3	$ 17.2
Assumed Trading Multiple	10.0x	10.0x	10.0x
Future Trading Value	$55.0	$103.0	$172.0
Discount Rate	17.5%	20.5%	22.5%
Discounted Enterprise Value[1]	**$46.8**	**$ 70.9**	**$ 93.6**

[1] Discounted based on respective discount rates presented above.

APPENDIX D2

The M&A Sales Process

The Company. In order to properly position the Company for sale, the DLJ team will identify:

—Strengths and weaknesses of BCGI's competitive position;

—Growth opportunities; and

—Synergy and cost saving opportunities that may be available to potential purchasers.

Financial Presentation. In order to maximize the value that can be obtained for the Company, the DLJ team will:

—Develop a complete understanding of BCGI's business and financial performance; and

—Prepare adjusted financial statements for the Company which restate BCGI's performance exclusive of non-recurring charges and, if appropriate, after giving effect to the cost saving programs which have been implemented.

Potential Purchasers. DLJ will work with BCGI's management to identify the most complete universe of potential purchasers

—DLJ has well established North American and International relationships in the telecommunications industries.

—DLJ is the leading investment bank to financial buyers.

Valuation. After fully understanding the competitive position and financial performance of BCGI, DLJ will deliver a preliminary valuation of the Company in order to provide BCGI with a useful basis for analyzing offers received for the Company.

Selling Memorandum. DLJ will work with the Company's management to prepare a confidential information memorandum for delivery to potential purchasers which reflects the attractive investment opportunity that BCGI represents.

Management Presentations. DLJ will work with the management to tailor a presentation and outlook by management which presents BCGI in the most defensible and the best light.

Sale Procedures. After fully understanding the strengths and weaknesses of the Company and developing a view of the likely purchasers and valuation range, DLJ will design and implement a sale process which is designed to achieve the highest price.

—Because several potential strategic buyers exist, an auction/sale process designed to maximize price competition for the Company will likely yield the highest price.

Negotiations with Interest Parties. DLJ has negotiated over 350 transactions since 1990. Given this expertise, DLJ will work with BCGI and potential purchasers to negotiate and structure a transaction which provides the highest value to BCGI's shareholders.

APPENDIX D3

Proposed Time Schedule

Organizational Meeting

- Preliminary Valuation of the Company
- Prepare Offering Memo
- Create Buyer List

- Marketing Call Program
- Draft Purchase Agreements
- Prepare Management Presentation
- Prepare Data Room

Preliminary Indications of Interest

- Management Presentations
- Plant Visits and Due Diligence
- Supplemental Information

- Bidding Procedures Letter
- Purchase Agreement Distributed

Final Bid Date

- Evaluation of Bids & Contracts
- Contract Negotiation & Execution
- Hart-Scott[1] Filing

Close

0 2 4 6 8 10 12 14 16 18 20 22 24 weeks

[1] The Hart-Scott-Rodino Act requires notification before a merger takes place if the acquiring person will hold 15% or more of the voting securities and assets or an aggregate total of the amount of the voting securities in excess of $15,000,000.

APPENDIX D4

Selected M&A Transaction Multiples Wireless Communications Industry

Announcement Date	Target/ Acquirer	Equity Purchase Price	Adjusted Purchase Price	Last Twelve Months (LTM) Revenue	LTM EBITDA	LTM EBIT	LTM Net Income	Target Business Description
14 May 93	LDDS Communications, Inc./ Resurgens Communications Group	$ 2,044.4	$ 2,480.7	3.0x	13.6x	19.8x	35.9x	Provides telecommunications services
1 Jun. 93	OCOM Corp. International CableTel., Inc.	$ 77.6	$ 47.3	4.4x	12.1x	NM	NM	Provides radio/telephone communication services
16 Aug. 93	McCaw Cellular Communications, Inc./ AT&T	$15,229.9	$20,039.8	10.2x	26.9x	NM	NM	Largest cellular telephone company in the U.S.
19 Aug. 93	Celutel, Inc./ Century Telephone Enterprises	$ 62.3	$ 101.9	4.2x	NM	NM	NM	Provides cellular telephone services
23 Sep. 93	Telematics International, Inc./ ECI Telecom, Ltd.	$ 305.4	$ 286.8	4.1x	22.2x	35.5x	41.7x	Manufacturers high-performance networking and communication products
31 Jan. 94	Radiation Systems, Inc./ COMSTAT Corp.	$ 154.0	$ 165.5	1.5x	9.7x	12.3x	17.6x	Designs and manufactures communication systems
24 Feb. 94	Associated Communications Corp./ SBC Communications Inc.	$ 674.2	$ 440.0	0.5x	2.6x	NM	NM	Operator of six domestic cellular telephone systems
15 Mar. 94	Centex Telemanagement Inc./ MFS Communications Co. Inc.	$ 210.6	$ 189.9	1.0x	13.2x	17.6x	30.8x	Provides telecommunications services
13 Jul. 94	IDB Communications Group/ LDDS Communications, Inc.	$ 659.8	$ 829.6	1.9x	13.7x	23.0x	NM	Provider of international telecommunications services as well as specialized broadcasting services
22 Jul. 94	Keptel, Inc./ ANTEC Corp.	$ 89.2	$ 84.5	1.8x	8.8x	11.8x	20.4x	Manufacturers telecommunications and transmission equipment for residential and commercial applications
9 Aug. 94	Network Systems Corporation/ Storage Technology Corporation	$ 314.2	$ 278.8	1.2x	8.8x	32.1x	33.1x	Manufacturer of high-performance data communication systems, hubs, bridges and routers
10 Oct. 94	WCT Communications/ Rochester Telephone Corp.	$ 79.6	$ 109.3	0.9x	NM	NM	NM	Provider of telephone services
19 Jan. 95	Confertech International, Inc./ ALC Communications Corp.	$ 64.0	$ 63.2	1.5x	10.6x	24.4x	38.6x	Manufacturer of teleconferencing systems
	Summary:	High		10.2x	26.9x	35.5x	47.1x	
		Low		0.5x	2.6x	11.8x	17.6x	
		Average[1]		2.5x	13.4x	22.9x	32.4x	

[1] Average excludes high and low.

APPENDIX D5A

Comparison of Selected Publicly Held, Value-Added Companies

	AVG.	HIGH	LOW	CELLULAR TECHNICAL SERVICE	GLOBAL TELECOM. SOLUTIONS	MIDCOM COMMUNICATIONS	RACOTEK	TEL-SAVE HOLDINGS	TELE-MATIC CORP.
Fiscal Year End				12/94	12/94	12/94	12/94	12/94	7/95
Last Financial Statement				6/95	6/95	6/95	6/95	6/95	4/94
BUSINESS DESCRIPTION				Software development co. specializing in facilitating wireless communications, namely, switching, billing.	Produces, markets, and sells prepaid phone cards.	Switchless reseller, with a focus on small businesses.	Develops, markets, and supports software and related products for wireless mobile transmission.	Long-distance telecom. services to small and med.-sized businesses (reseller); now building its own network.	Specialized call processing services on a transaction fee basis for use in correctional facilities.
MARKET DATA									
Symbol/Where Traded				CTSC/OTC	GTST/OTC	MCCI/OTC	RACO/OTC	TALK/OTC	TMAT/OTC
Stock Price (10/24/95)				$17.73	$5.95	$14.25	$5.88	$13.75	$13.25
Shares Outstanding				10.0	3.1	13.5	23.8	12.6	7.6
Equity Market Capitalization				$176.7	$18.7	$192.6	$139.8	$172.6	$100.1
Enterprise Value				$167.7	$15.3	$239.6	$117.3	$162.3	$104.8
LTM Price Range				$12.25–$31.00	$3.88–$7.00	$11.25–$16.75	$3.00–$7.88	$13.75–$16.50	$7.38–$15.00
OPERATING DATA									
LTM Revenues				$14.7	$2.2	$145.6	$5.8	$135.3	$23.3
LTM Operating Cash Flow (EBDAIT)				3.9	(2.6)	5.6	(11.6)	15.8	6.3
LTM Operating Earnings (EBIT)				3.4	(2.6)	(1.5)	(12.2)	15.0	3.4
LTM EPS				$0.33	($1.05)	($0.79)	($0.51)	$1.44	$0.31
Book Value per Share				$1.49	$1.03	($0.60)	$1.30	$1.84	$2.57
1995 Projected EPS				$0.57	($0.22)	($0.41)	($0.51)	$1.62	$0.59
1996 Projected EPS				$0.64	$0.11	$0.28	($0.35)	$1.82	$0.66
MARKET CAP MULTIPLES Price/									
LTM EPS	14.4x	54.1x	9.6x	54.1x	NM	NM	NM	9.6x	43.1x
1995 Projected EPS	22.5	30.9	8.5	30.9	NM	NM	NM	8.5	22.5
1996 Projected EPS	32.8	54.0	7.6	27.5	54.0x	50.9x	NM	7.6	20.0
Book Value	6.1	11.8	4.5	11.8	5.8	NM	4.5	7.5	5.2
Enterprise Value/LTM Revenues	6.1x	20.4x	1.2x	11.4x	6.9x	1.6x	20.4x	1.2x	4.5x
LTM EBDAIT	25.6	45.6	10.3	45.6	NM	34.5	NM	10.3	16.6
LTM EBIT	31.3	49.6	10.8	49.6	NM	NM	NM	10.8	31.1
THREE YEAR AVG. MARGINS									
Gross Margin	28.2%	49.5%	12.8%	49.5%	12.8%	32.7%	40.6%	16.1%	23.5%
LTM EBDAIT	−71.1%	10.1%	−298.3%	−5.1%	−267.1%	4.2%	−298.3%	10.1%	−16.3 %
LTM EBIT	−75.7%	9.8%	−311.0%	−11.6%	−270.0%	1.4%	−311.0%	9.8%	−22.6%
Net Margin	−81.2%	9.8%	−317.5%	−7.9%	−284.2%	−1.7%	−317.5%	9.8%	−30.9 %
THREE YEAR GROWTH RATES									
LTM Revenues	111.4%	222.7%	41.8%	41.8%	222.7%	106.1%	132.5%	116.5%	90.7%
LTM EBDAIT	74.3%	160.4%	51.3%	NM	83.4%	65.2%	51.3%	160.4%	NM
LTM EBIT	157.4%	157.4%	157.4%	NM	NM	NM	NM	157.4%	NM
LTM EPS	148.5%	148.5%	148.5%	NM	NM	NM	NM	148.5%	NM

APPENDIX D5B

Comparison of Publicly Held Wireless Communication Companies

	AVG.	HIGH	LOW	PALMER WIRELESS	ROGER CANTEL	VANGUARD	VODAFONE GROUP
Last Statement/Fiscal Year End				12/94...6/95	12/94...6/95	12/94...6/95	3/95...3/95
BUSINESS DESCRIPTION				Construction/operation of cellular phone systems in Southeast; recently acquired GTE's GA cellular assets.	In Canada, largest cellular, 2nd largest paging company; chain of communications stores.	Owns/operates cellular phone systems primarily in the eastern US; under trademark of CellularOne.	UK operator of analog/digital cellular radio network; paging, value-added services.
MARKET DATA							
Symbol/Where Traded				PWIR/OTC	RCMIF/OTC	VCELA/OTC	VOD/NYSE
Stock Price (10/24/95)				$22.75	$22.38	$24.00	$41.50
Fully Diluted Shares				24.0	93.9	42.9	307.3
Equity Market Capitalization				$546.0	$2,101.0	$1,029.6	$12,753.0
LTM Price Range				$24.50–$14.25	$31.88–$22.25	$29.63–$21.50	$45.00–$41.50
OPERATING DATA							
LTM Revenues				$86.6	$711.0	$202.7	$1,866.1
LTM Operating Cash Flow (EBDAIT)				30.9	249.7	46.5	733.3
LTM Operating Earnings (EBIT)				18.0	126.9	16.9	583.9
LTM EPS				($0.10)	$0.07	($0.58)	$1.25
Book Value per Share				$12.45	($3.50)	$0.78	$4.34
1995 Projected EPS				$0.12	$0.03	($0.18)	$1.59
1996 Projected EPS				$0.51	$0.51	$0.41	$2.12
1995 Projected Cellular EBITDA				51.1	233.1	69.7	843.9
1996 Projected Cellular EBITDA				70.8	286.8	116.8	1,047.4
Subscribers at 6/30/95 (thousands)				141.9	840.7	314.0	2,040.0
Total Proportionate POPs				3.1	23.6	7.5	104.9
MARKET MULTIPLES: Price/							
LTM EPS	48.9x	319.6x	(227.5)x	(227.5)x	319.6	(41.2)x	33.3x
1995 Projected EPS	48.3	745.8	(133.3)	189.6	745.8	(133.3)	26.1
1996 Projected EPS	36.7	64.4	(11.6)	44.6	43.9	58.5	19.6
Book Value	4.2	19.6	1.6	1.8	NM	NM	9.6
Enterprise Value/LTM Revenues	7.7x	34.4x	4.3x	8.4	4.3	7.3	7.0x
LTM EBDAIT	23.3	43.5	11.8	23.3x	11.8x	30.1x	14.4x
1995 Projected Cellular EBDAIT	14.8	20.1	12.5	14.1	12.6	20.1	12.5
1996 Projected Cellular EBDAIT	10.8	12.6	10.1	10.2	10.3	12.0	10.1
Per POP/Pager	170.1x	322.6x	66.4x	232.4	124.9	186.8	100.9
LEVERAGE RATIOS							
Debt/LTM EBDAIT	5.4x	10.2x	0.4x	6.1x	3.7x	9.9x	0.4x
Debt+Preferred/LTM	5.4	15.3	0.4	6.1	3.7	9.9	0.4
Valuation							
Equity Market Capitalization				$546.0	$2,101.0	$1,029.6	$12,753.0
Plus: Long Term Debt				187.3	925.4	459.1	284.8
Less: Cash and Equivalents				(3.4)	0.0	(5.7)	(25.7)
Less: Option/Warrant Proceeds				(9.3)	0.0	(53.0)	0.0
Less: Int Value at 70% PMV				0.0	0.0	0.0	(2,077.6)
Less: Other Value at 70% PMV				0.0	(79.2)	(29.1)	(350.0)
Implied Enterprise Value				$720.6	$2,947.2	$1,400.9	$10,584.4

15

Chapter Fifteen

Obtaining Debt Capital

Leveraging a company is like driving your car with a sharp stick pointed at your heart through the steering wheel. As long as the road is smooth it works fine. But hit one bump in the road and you may be dead.

Warren Buffet

Results Expected

Market cycles impact credit availability—often creating a lack thereof—for emerging companies. After the market meltdown in early 2000, many old rules disappeared and a harsher banking climate once again appeared. This chapter aims at preparing you to cope better with the new realities in the debt capital markets. But even as debt markets improve, lessons learned here will provide important competitive advantages. Upon completion of this chapter, you will have:

1. Identified sources of debt and how to access them in today's capital markets.
2. Examined the lender's perspective and criteria in making loans, how to prepare a loan proposal, and how to negotiate a loan.
3. Gained knowledge to help you in managing and orchestrating the acquisition of debt capital.
4. Determined how lenders estimate the debt capacity of a company.
5. Identified some tar pits entrepreneurs need to avoid in considering debt.
6. Analyzed the "Bank Documents" case study.

A Cyclical Pattern: The Good Old Days Return but Fade Again

For entrepreneurs and their investors, the punishing credit crunch and stagnant equity markets of 1990–1993 gave way to the most robust capital markets in U.S. history as we approached the end of the millennium. Interest rates reached historical lows, and the credit environment was much friendlier, mimicking the heady days of pre-crash 1987. The availability of bank loans and competition among banks increased dramatically from the dormant days of the early 1990s.

The improved credit environment led to lenders' greater awareness of growth companies' potential in the new entrepreneurial economy. Bank presidents and loan officers were aggressively seeking entrepreneurial companies as prospective clients. They worked with local universities and entrepreneurial associations to sponsor seminars, workshops, and business fairs, all to cultivate entrepreneurial customers. This was a welcome change in the credit climate for entrepreneurs. A less severe credit crunch, even with extremely low interest rates, began in 2000 and increased into 2002. By 2004, banks had become more aggressive. Remember though, the availability of credit is cyclical, and the fundamentals of credit don't change that much.

The authors wish to thank Babson College colleague and longtime friend Mr. Leslie Charm for his significant contributions to the revisions on this chapter.

A Word of Caution

History suggests a favorable credit environment can and will change, sometimes suddenly. When a credit climate reverses itself, personal guarantees come back. Even the most creditworthy companies with enviable records for timely repayment of interest and principal could be asked to provide personal guarantees by the owners. In addition, there could be a phenomenon viewed as a perversion of the debt capital markets. As a credit crunch becomes more severe, banks face their own illiquidity and insolvency problems, which might result in the failure of more banks as happened in the 1990s. To cope with their own balance sheet dissipation, banks can and might call the best loans first. Thousands of high quality smaller companies can be stunned and debilitated by such actions. Also, as competition among banks lessens, pricing and terms can become more onerous as the economy continues in a period of credit tightening. Debt reduction could then become a dominant financial strategy of small and large companies alike.

The Lender's Perspective

Lenders have always been wary capital providers. Because banks may earn as little as a 1 percent net profit on total assets, they are especially sensitive to the possibility of a loss. If a bank writes off a $1 million loan to a small company, it must then be repaid an incremental $100 million in profitable loans to recover that loss.

Yet, lending institutions are businesses and seek to grow and improve profitability as well. They can do this only if they find and bet on successful, young, growing companies. Historically, points and fees charged for making a loan have been a major contributor to bank profitability. During parts of the credit cycle, banks may seek various sweeteners to make loans. Take, for instance, a lending proposal for a company seeking a $15 million five-year loan. In addition to the up-front origination fees and points, the bank further proposed a YES, or yield enhancement security, as part of the loan. This additional requirement would entitle the bank to receive an additional $3 million payment from the company once its sales exceeded $10 million and it was profitable, or if it was sold, merged, or taken public. While this practice hasn't happened frequently in the current economic climate, it could be revived, depending on the cycle.

Sources of Debt Capital[1]

The principal sources of borrowed capital for new and young businesses are trade credit, commercial banks, finance companies, factors, and leasing companies.[2] Startups have more difficulty borrowing money than existing businesses because they don't have assets or a track record of profitability and/or a positive cash flow. Nevertheless, startups managed by an entrepreneur with a track record and with significant equity in the business who can present a sound business plan can borrow money from one or more sources. Still, if little equity or collateral exists, the startup won't have much success with banks.

The availability of such debt for high-tech startups can sometimes depend on where a business is located. Debt and leases as well as equity capital can be more available to startup companies in such hotbeds of entrepreneurial activity as eastern Massachusetts and Silicon Valley in California than, say, in the Midwest. The hotbed areas also feature close contact between venture capital firms and the high-technology-focused lending officers of banks. This contact tends to make it easier for startups and early-stage companies to borrow money, although banks rarely lend to new ventures. But even in these hotbeds, very few banks are active in this startup environment.

The advantages and disadvantages of these sources, summarized in Exhibit 15.1, are basically determined by such obvious dimensions as the interest rate or cost of capital, the key terms, the conditions and covenants, and the fit with the owner's situation and the company's needs at the time.[3] How good a deal you can strike is a function of your relative bargaining position and the competitiveness among the alternatives.

Ultimately, most important is the person with whom you will be dealing, rather than the amount, terms, or institution. You will be better off seeking the right banker (or other provider of capital) than just the right bank. Once again, the industry and market characteristics, and the stage and health of the firm in terms of cash flow, debt coverage, and collateral are central to the evaluation process. Exhibit 15.2, summarizes the term of financing available from these different sources. Note the difficulty in finding sources for more than one year of financing.

Finally, an enduring question entrepreneurs ask is, What is bankable? How much money can I expect to borrow based on my balance sheet? Exhibit 15.3, summarizes some general guidelines in answer to this

[1] Jeffry A. Timmons, *Financing and Planning the New Venture* (Acton, MA: Brick House Publishing Company, 1990).
[2] Ibid., p. 68.
[3] Ibid., p. 33.

EXHIBIT 15.1

Debt Financing Sources for Types of Business

Source	Startup Company	Existing Company
Trade credit	Yes	Yes
Finance companies	Occasionally, with strong equity	Yes
Commercial banks	Rare (if assets are available)	Yes
Factors	Depends on nature of the customers	Yes
Leasing companies	Difficult, except for startups with venture capital	Yes
Mutual savings banks and savings & loans	Depends on strength of personal guarantee	Real estate and asset-based companies
Insurance companies	Rare, except alongside venture capital	Yes, depending on size

Source: Jeffry A. Timmons, *Financing and Planning the New Venture* (Acton, MA: Brick House Publishing Company, 1990), p. 34.

EXHIBIT 15.2

Debt Financing Sources by Term of Financing

	Term of Financing		
Source	**Short**	**Medium**	**Long**
Trade credit	Yes	Yes	Possible
Commercial banks	Most frequently	Yes (asset-based)	Rare (depends on cash flow predictability)
Factors	Most frequently	Rare	No
Leasing companies	No	Most frequently	Some
Mutual savings banks, savings & loans	Yes	Yes	Real estate and other asset-based companies
Insurance companies	Rare	Rare	Most frequently

Source: Jeffry A. Timmons, *Financing and Planning the New Venture* (Acton, MA: Brick House Publishing Company, 1990), p. 34.

EXHIBIT 15.3

What Is Bankable? Specific Lending Criteria

Security	Credit Capacity
Accounts receivable	70–85% of those less than 90 days of acceptable receivables
Inventory	20–70% depending on obsolescence risk and salability
Equipment	70–80% of market value (less if specialized)
Chattel mortgage*	80% or more of auction appraisal value
Conditional sales contract	60–70% or more of purchase price
Plant improvement loan	60–80% of appraised value or cost

Source: Jeffry A. Timmons, *Financing and Planning the New Venture* (Acton, MA: Brick House Publishing Company, 1990), p. 33, Table 1.

*A lien on assets other than real estate breaking a loan.

question. Because most loans and lines of credit are asset-based loans, knowing the lenders' guidelines is very important. The percentages of key balance sheet assets that are often allowable as collateral are only ranges and will vary from region to region, for different types of businesses, and for stages in the business cycle. For instance, nonperishable consumer goods versus technical products that may have considerable risk of obsolescence would be treated very differently in making a loan collateral computation. If the company already has significant debt and has pledged all its assets, there may not be much room for negotiations. A bank with full collateral in hand for a company having cash flow problems is unlikely to give up such a position to enable the company to attract another lender, even though the collateral is more than enough to meet these guidelines.

Trade Credit[4]

Trade credit is a major source of short-term funds for small businesses. Trade credit represents 30 percent to 40 percent of the current liabilities of nonfinancial companies, with generally higher percentages in smaller companies. It is reflected on the balance sheets as accounts payable, or sales payable-trade.

If a small business is able to buy goods and services and be given, or take, 30, 60, or 90 days to pay for them, that business has essentially obtained a loan of 30 to 90 days. Many small and new businesses are able to obtain such trade credit when no other form of debt financing is available to them. Suppliers offer trade credit as a way to get new customers, and often build the bad debt risk into their prices. Additionally, channel partners who supply trade credit often do so with more industry-specific knowledge than can be obtained by commercial banks.[5]

The ability of a new business to obtain trade credit depends on the quality and reputation of its management and the relationships it establishes with its suppliers. Continued late payment or nonpayment may cause suppliers to cut off shipments or ship only on a COD basis. A key to keeping trade credit open is to continually pay some amount, even it not the full amount. Also, the real cost of using trade credit can be very high; for example, the loss of discounts for prompt payment. Because the cost of trade credit is seldom expressed as an annual amount, it should be analyzed carefully, and a new business should shop for the best terms.

Trade credit may take some of the following forms: extended credit terms; special or seasonal datings, where a supplier ships goods in advance of the purchaser's peak selling season and accepts payment 90 to 120 days later during the season; inventory on consignment, not requiring payment until sold; and loan or lease of equipment.

Commercial Bank Financing

Commercial banks prefer to lend to existing businesses that have a track record of sales, profits, and satisfied customers, and a current backlog. Their concern about the high failure rates in new businesses can make banks less than enthusiastic about making loans to such firms. They like to be lower-risk lenders, which is consistent with their profit margins. For their protection, they look first to positive cash flow and then to collateral, and in new and young businesses (depending on the credit environment) they are likely to require personal guarantees of the owners. Like equity investors, commercial banks place great weight on the quality of the management team.

Notwithstanding these factors, certain banks do, rarely, make loans to startups or young businesses that have strong equity financings from venture capital firms. This has been especially true in such centers of entrepreneurial and venture capital activity as Silicon Valley, Boston, Los Angeles, Austin, Texas, and New York City.

Commercial banks are the primary source of debt capital for existing (not new) businesses. Small business loans may be handled by a bank's small business loan department or through credit scoring (where credit approval is done "by the numbers"). Your personal credit history will also impact the credit scoring matrix. Larger loans may require the approval of a loan committee. If a loan exceeds the limits of a local bank, part or the entire loan amount will be offered to "correspondent" banks in neighboring communities and nearby financial centers. This correspondent network enables the smaller banks in rural areas to handle loans that otherwise could not be made.

Most of the loans made by commercial banks are for one year or less. Some of these loans are unsecured, while receivables, inventories, or other assets secure others. Commercial banks also make a large number of intermediate-term loans (or term loans) with a maturity of one to five years. On about 90 percent of these term loans, the banks require collateral, generally consisting of stocks, machinery, equipment, and real estate. Most term loans are retired by systematic, but not necessarily equal payments over the life of the loan. Apart from real estate mortgages and loans guaranteed by the SBA or a similar organization, commercial banks make few loans with maturities greater than five years.

Banks also offer a number of services to the small business, such as computerized payroll preparation, letters of credit, international services, lease financing, and money market accounts.

There are now over 7,800 commercial banks in the United States. A complete listing of banks can be found, arranged by states, in the *American Bank Directory* (McFadden Business Publications), published semiannually.

Line of Credit Loans

A line of credit is a formal or informal agreement between a bank and a borrower concerning the maximum loan a bank will allow the borrower for a one-year period. Often the bank will charge a fee of a certain percent of the line of credit for a definite commitment to make the loan when requested.

[4] Ibid., pp. 68–80.
[5] Neelam Jain, "Monitoring Costs and Trade Credit," *Quarterly Review of Economics and Finance*, 41: 2001, pp. 89–111.

Line of credit funds are used for such seasonal financings as inventory buildup and receivable financing. These two items are often the largest and most financeable items on a venture's balance sheet. It is general practice to repay these loans from the sales and reduction of short-term assets that they financed. Lines of credit can be unsecured, or the bank may require a pledge of inventory, receivables, equipment, or other acceptable assets. Unsecured lines of credit have no lien on any asset of the borrower and no priority over any trade creditor, but the banks may require that all debt to the principals and stockholders of the company be subordinated to the line of credit debt.

The line of credit is executed through a series of renewable 90-day notes. The renewable 90-day note is the more common practice, and the bank will expect the borrower to pay off his or her open loan within a year and to hold a zero loan balance for one to two months. This is known as "resting the line" or "cleaning up." Commercial banks may also generally require that a borrower maintain a checking account at the bank with a minimum ("compensating") balance of 5 percent to 10 percent of the outstanding loan.

For a large, financially sound company, the interest rates for a "prime risk" line of credit will be quoted at the prime rate or at a premium over LIBOR. (LIBOR stands for "London Interbank Offered Rate." Eurodollars—U.S. dollars held outside the United States—are most actively traded here, and banks use Eurodollars as the "last" dollars to balance the funding of its loan portfolio. Thus, LIBOR represents the marginal cost of funds for a bank.) A small firm may be required to pay a higher rate. The true interest calculations should also reflect the multiple fees that may be added to the loan. Any compensating-balance or resting-the-line requirements or other fees will also increase effective interest rates.

Time-Sales Finance

Many dealers or manufacturers who offer installment payment terms to purchasers of their equipment cannot themselves finance installment or conditional sales contracts. In such situations, they sell and assign the installment contract to a bank or sales finance company. (Some very large manufacturers do their own financing through captive finance companies—such as the Ford Motor Company and Ford Credit. Most very small retailers merely refer their customer installment contracts to sales finance companies, which provide much of this financing, and on more flexible terms.)

From the manufacturer or dealer's point of view, time-sales finance is a way of obtaining short-term financing from long-term installment accounts receivable. From the purchaser's point of view, it is a way of financing the purchase of new equipment.

Under time-sales financing, the bank purchases installment contracts at a discount from their full value and takes as security an assignment of the manufacturer/dealer's interest in the conditional sales contract. In addition, the bank's financing of installment note receivables includes recourse to the seller in the event of loan default by the purchaser. Thus, the bank has the payment obligation of the equipment purchaser, the manufacturer/dealer's security interest in the equipment purchased, and recourse to the manufacturer/dealer in the event of default. The bank also withholds a portion of the payment (5 percent or more) as a dealer reserve until the note is paid. Since the reserve becomes an increasing percentage of the note as the contract is paid off, an arrangement is often made when multiple contracts are financed to ensure that the reserve against all contracts will not exceed 20 percent or so.

The purchase price of equipment under a sales financing arrangement includes a "time-sales price differential" (e.g., an increase to cover the discount, typically 6 percent to 10 percent) taken by the bank that does the financing. Collection of the installments may be made directly by the bank or indirectly through the manufacturer/dealer.

Term Loans

Bank term loans are generally made for periods of one to five years, and may be unsecured or secured. Most of the basic features of bank term loans are the same for secured and unsecured loans.

Term loans provide needed growth capital to companies. They are also a substitute for a series of short-term loans made with the hope of renewal by the borrower. Banks make these generally on the basis of predictability of positive cash flow.

Term loans have three distinguishing features: Banks make them for periods of up to five years (and occasionally more); periodic repayment is required; and agreements are designed to fit the special needs and requirements of the borrower (e.g., payments can be smaller at the beginning of a loan term and larger at the end).

Because term loans do not mature for a number of years, during which time the borrower's situation and fortunes could change significantly, the bank must carefully evaluate the prospects and management of the borrowing company. Even the protection afforded by initially strong assets can be wiped out by several years of heavy losses. Term lenders stress the entrepreneurial and managerial abilities of the borrowing company. The bank will also carefully consider such things as the long-range prospects of the company and its industry, its present and projected profitability, and its ability to generate the cash required to meet the loan payments, as shown by past performance. Pricing for a term loan may be higher, reflecting a perceived higher risk from the longer term.

To lessen the risks involved in term loans, a bank will require some restrictive covenants in the loan agreement. These covenants might prohibit additional borrowing, merger of the company, payment of dividends, sales of assets, increased salaries to the owners, and the like. Also, the bank will probably require financial covenants to provide early warning of deterioration of the business, like debt to equity and cash flow to interest coverage.

Chattel Mortgages and Equipment Loans

Assigning an appropriate possession (chattel) as security is a common way of making secured term loans. The chattel is any machinery, equipment, or business property that is made the collateral of a loan in the same way as a mortgage on real estate. The chattel remains with the borrower unless there is default, in which case the chattel goes to the bank. Generally, credit against machinery and equipment is restricted primarily to new or highly serviceable and salable used items.

It should be noted that in many states, loans that used to be chattel mortgages are now executed through the security agreement forms of the Uniform Commercial Code (UCC). However, chattel mortgages are still used in many places, are still used for moving vehicles (i.e., tractors or cranes), and, from custom, many lenders continue to use that term even though the loans are executed through the UCCs security agreements. The term chattel mortgage is typically from one to five years; some are longer.

Conditional Sales Contracts

Conditional sales contracts are used to finance a substantial portion of the new equipment purchased by businesses. Under a sales contract, the buyer agrees to purchase a piece of equipment, makes a nominal down payment, and pays the balance in installments over a period of from one to five years. Until the payment is complete, the seller holds title to the equipment. Hence, the sale is conditional upon the buyer's completing the payments.

A sales contract is financed by a bank that has recourse to the seller should the purchaser default on the loan. This makes it difficult to finance a purchase of a good piece of used equipment at an auction. No recourse to the seller is available if the equipment is purchased at an auction; the bank would have to sell the equipment if the loan goes bad. Occasionally, a firm seeking financing on existing and new equipment will sell some of its equipment to a dealer and repurchase it, together with new equipment, in order to get a conditional sales contract financed by a bank.

The effective rate of interest on a conditional sales contract is high, running to as much as 15 percent to 18 percent if the effect of installment features is considered. The purchaser/borrower should make sure the interest payment is covered by increased productivity and profitability resulting from the new equipment.

Plant Improvement Loans

Loans made to finance improvements to business properties and plants are called plant improvement loans. They can be intermediate and long term and are generally secured by a first or second mortgage on that part of the property or plant that is being improved.

Commercial Finance Companies

The commercial bank is generally the lender of choice for a business. But when the bank says no, commercial finance companies, which aggressively seek borrowers, are a good option. They frequently lend money to companies that do not have positive cash flow, although commercial finance companies will not make loans to companies unless they consider them viable risks. In tighter credit economies, finance companies are generally more accepting of risk than are banks.

The primary factors in a bank's loan decision are the continuing successful operation of a business and its generation of more than enough cash to repay a loan. By contrast, commercial finance companies lend against the liquidation value of assets (receivables, inventory, equipment) that it understands, knows how and where to sell, and whose liquidation value is sufficient to repay the loan. Banks today own many of the leading finance companies. As a borrower gains financial strength and a track record, transfer to more attractive bank financing can be easier.

In the case of inventories or equipment, liquidation value is the amount that could be realized from an auction or quick sale. Finance companies will generally not lend against receivables more than 90 days old, federal or state government agency receivables (against which it is very difficult to perfect a lien and payment is slow), or any receivables whose collection is contingent on the performance of a delivered product.

Because of the liquidation criteria, finance companies prefer readily salable inventory items such as electronic components or metal in such commodity forms as billets or standard shapes. Generally, a finance company will not accept inventory as collateral unless it also has receivables. Equipment loans are made only by certain finance companies and against such standard equipment as lathes, milling machines, and the like. Finance companies, like people, have items in which they are more comfortable and therefore would extend more credit against certain kinds of collateral.

How much of the collateral value will a finance company lend? Generally, 70 percent to 90 percent of acceptable receivables under 90 days old, 20 percent to 70 percent of the liquidation value of raw materials and/or finished goods inventory that are not obsolete or damaged, and 60 percent to 80 percent of the liquidation value of equipment, as determined by an appraiser, is acceptable. Receivables and inventory loans are for one year, while equipment loans are for three to seven years.

All these loans have tough prepayment penalties: Finance companies do not want to be immediately replaced by banks when a borrower has improved its credit image. Generally, finance companies require a three-year commitment to do business with them, with prepayment fees if this provision is not met.

The data required for a loan from a finance company includes all that would be provided to a bank, plus additional details for the assets being used as collateral. For receivables financing, this includes detailed aging of receivables (and payables) and historical data on sales, returns, or deductions (all known as dilution), and collections.

For inventory financing, it includes details on the items in inventory, how long they have been there, and their rate of turnover. Requests for equipment loans should be accompanied by details on the date of purchase, cost of each equipment item, and appraisals, which are generally always required. These appraisals must be made by acceptable (to the lender) outside appraisers.

The advantage of dealing with a commercial finance company is that it will make loans that banks will not, and it can be flexible in lending arrangements. The price a finance company exacts for this is an interest rate anywhere from 0 to 6 percent over that charged by a bank, prepayment penalties, and, in the case of receivables loans, recourse to the borrower for unpaid collateralized receivables.

Because of their greater risk taking and asset-based lending, finance companies usually place a larger reporting and monitoring burden on the borrowing firm to stay on top of the receivables and inventory serving as loan collateral. Personal guarantees will generally be required from the principals of the business. A finance company or bank will generally reserve the right to reduce the percentage of the value lent against receivables or inventory if it gets nervous about the borrower's survivability.

Factoring

Factoring is a form of accounts receivable financing. However, instead of borrowing and using receivables as collateral, the receivables are sold, at a discounted value, to a factor. Factoring is accomplished on a discounted value of the receivables pledged. Invoices that do not meet the factor's credit standard will not be accepted as collateral. (Receivables more than 90 days old are not normally accepted.) A bank may inform the purchaser of goods that the account has been assigned to the bank, and payments are made directly to the bank, which credits them to the borrower's account. This is called a notification plan. Alternatively, the borrower may collect the accounts as usual and pay off the bank loan; this is a nonnotification plan.

Factoring can make it possible for a company to secure a loan that it might not otherwise get. The loan can be increased as sales and receivables grow. However, factoring can have drawbacks. It can be expensive, and trade creditors sometimes regard factoring as evidence of a company in financial difficulty, except in certain industries.

In a standard factoring arrangement, the factor buys the client's receivables outright, without recourse, as soon as the client creates them, by shipment of goods to customers. Although the factor has recourse to the borrowers for returns, errors in pricing, and so on, the factor assumes the risk of bad debt losses that develop from receivables it approves and purchases. Many factors, however, provide factoring only on a recourse basis.

Cash is made available to the client as soon as proof is provided (old-line factoring) or on the average due date of the invoices (maturity factoring). With maturity factoring, the company can often obtain a loan of about 90 percent of the money a factor has agreed to pay on a maturity date. Most factoring arrangements are for one year.

Factoring can also be on a recourse basis. In this circumstance, the borrower must replace unpaid receivables after 90 days with new current receivables to allow the borrowings to remain at the same level.

Factoring fits some businesses better than others. For a business that has annual sales volume in excess of $300,000 and a net worth over $50,000 that sells on normal credit terms to a customer base that is 75 percent credit rated, factoring is a real option. Factoring has become almost traditional in such industries as textiles, furniture manufacturing, clothing manufacturing, toys, shoes, and plastics.

The same data required from a business for a receivable loan from a bank are required by a factor. Because a factor is buying receivables with no recourse, it will analyze the quality and value of a prospective client's receivables. It will want a detailed aging of receivables plus historical data on bad debts, return, and allowances. It will also investigate the credit history of customers to whom its client sells and establish credit limits for each customer. The business client can receive factoring of customer receivables only up to the limits so set.

The cost of financing receivables through factoring is higher than that of borrowing from a bank or a finance company. The factor is assuming the credit risk, doing credit investigations and collections, and advancing funds. A factor generally charges up to 2 percent of the total sales factored as a service charge.

There is also an interest charge for money advanced to a business, usually 2 percent to 6 percent above prime. A larger, established business borrowing large sums would command a better interest rate than the small borrower with a onetime, short-term need. Finally, factors withhold a reserve of 5 percent to 10 percent of the receivables purchased.

Factoring is not the cheapest way to obtain capital, but it does quickly turn receivables into cash. Moreover, although more expensive than accounts receivable financing, factoring saves its users credit agency fees, salaries of credit and collection personnel, and maybe bad debt write-offs. Factoring also provides credit information on collection services that may be better than the borrower's.

Leasing Companies

The leasing industry has grown substantially in recent years, and lease financing has become an important source of medium-term financing for businesses. There are about 700 to 800 leasing companies in the United States. In addition, many commercial banks and finance companies have leasing departments. Some leasing companies handle a wide variety of equipment, while others specialize in certain types of equipment—machine tools, electronic test equipment, and the like.

Common and readily resalable items such as automobiles, trucks, typewriters, and office furniture can be leased by both new and existing businesses. However, the startup will find it difficult to lease other kinds of industrial, computer, or business equipment without providing a letter of credit or a certificate of deposit to secure the lease, or personal guarantees from the founders or from a wealthy third party.

An exception to this condition is high-technology startups that have received substantial venture capital. Some of these ventures have received large amounts of lease financing for special equipment from equity-oriented lessors, who receive some form of stock purchase rights in return for providing the startup's lease line. Equate (of Oakland, California, with offices in Boston, New York, and Dallas) and Intertec (of Mill Valley, California) are two examples of companies doing this sort of venture leasing. Like many financing options, availability of venture leasing may be reduced significantly in tight money markets.

Generally, industrial equipment leases have a term of three to five years, but in some cases may run longer. There can also be lease renewal options for 3 percent to 5 percent per year of the original equipment value. Leases are usually structured to return the entire cost of the leased equipment plus finance charges to the lessor, although some so-called operating leases do not, over their term, produce revenues equal to or greater than the price of the leased equipment.

Typically, an up-front payment is required of about 10 percent of the value of the item being leased. The interest rate on equipment leasing may be more or less than other forms of financing, depending on the equipment leased, the credit of the lessee, and the time of year.

Leasing credit criteria are very similar to the criteria used by commercial banks for equipment loans. Primary considerations are the value of the equipment leased, the justification of the lease, and the lessee's projected cash flow over the lease term.

Should a business lease equipment? Leasing has certain advantages. It enables a young or growing company to conserve cash and can reduce its requirements for equity capital. Leasing can also be a tax advantage, because payments can be deducted over a shorter period than can depreciation.

Finally, leasing provides the flexibility of returning equipment after the lease period if it is no longer needed or if it has become technologically obsolete. This can be a particular advantage to high-technology companies.

Leasing may or may not improve a company's balance sheet, because accounting practice currently requires that the value of the equipment acquired in a capital lease be reflected on the balance sheet. Operating leases, however, do not appear on the balance sheet. Generally, this is an issue of economic ownership rather than legal ownership. If the economic risk is primarily with the lessee, it must be capitalized and it therefore goes on the balance sheet along with the corresponding debt. Depreciation also follows the risk, along with the corresponding tax benefits. Startups that don't need such tax relief should be able to acquire more favorable terms with an operating lease.

Before the Loan Decision[6]

Choosing a bank and, more specifically, a banker is one of the more important decisions a new or young business will make. Babson College Adjunct Professor Leslie Charm offers the following advice to entrepreneurs seeking to develop a constructive banking relationship:

> *Industry experience is critical.* Choose a banker who understands your particular industry. They will have other clients in the same industry and may serve as a valuable resource for networking and service professionals with relevant experience. In the case of funding requests, bankers with industry knowledge are more apt to make a quick and reasoned determination.
>
> *Understand their business model.* Every bank has different criteria with regard to working with new ventures and their lending decisions are largely based on quantitative credit scoring metrics. The entrepreneur needs to have an understanding of how a particular bank works and determine whether that model is a fit with his or her venture.
>
> *Understand who you're dealing with.* Bankers are relationship managers whose job is to support their clients—including expediting the approval of loans and credit lines that fit with their bank's lending criteria. Like a lot of good vendors, the best of them have specialized knowledge, excellent contacts, and will take a genuine interest in your business.

Much of the following discussion of lending practices and decisions applies to commercial finance company lenders as well as to banks. A good lender relationship can sometimes mean the difference between the life and death of a business during difficult times. There have been cases where one bank has called its loans to a struggling business, causing it to go under, and another bank has stayed with its loans and helped a business to survive and prosper.

Those banks that will not make loans to startups and early-stage ventures generally cite the lack of operating track record as the primary reason for turning down a loan. Lenders that make such loans usually do so for previously successful entrepreneurs of means or for firms backed by investors with whom they have had prior relationships and whose judgment they trust (e.g., established venture capital firms when they believe that the venture capital company will invest in the next round).

In centers of high technology and venture capital, the main officers of the major banks will have one or more high-technology lending officers who specialize in making loans to early-stage, high-technology ventures. Through much experience, these bankers have come to understand the market and operating idiosyncrasies, problems, and opportunities of such ventures. They generally have close ties to venture capital firms and will refer entrepreneurs to such firms for possible equity financing. The venture capital firms, in turn, will refer their portfolio ventures to the bankers for debt financing.

What should an entrepreneur consider in choosing a lender? What is important in a lending decision? How should entrepreneurs relate to their lenders on an ongoing basis? In many ways, the lender's decision is similar to that of the venture capitalist. The goal is to make money for his or her company, through interest earned on good loans. The lender fears losing money by making bad loans to companies that default on their loans. To this end, he or she avoids risk by building in every conceivable safeguard. The lender is concerned with the client company's loan coverage, its ability to repay, and the collateral it can offer. Finally, but most important, he or she must judge the character and quality of the key managers of the company to whom the loan is being made.

Exhibit 15.4 outlines the key steps in obtaining a loan. Because of the importance of a banking relationship, an entrepreneur should shop around before making a choice. The criteria for selecting a bank should be based on more than just loan interest rates. Equally important, entrepreneurs should not wait until they have a dire need for funds to try to establish a banking relationship. The choice of a bank and the development of a banking relationship should begin when you do not urgently need the money. When an entrepreneur faces a near-term financial crisis, the venture's financial statements are at their worst and the banker has good cause to wonder about management's financial and planning skills—all to the detriment of the entrepreneur's chance of getting a loan.

G. B. Baty and J. M. Stancill describe some of the factors that are especially important to an entrepreneur in selecting a bank.[7] The bank selected should be big enough to service a venture's foreseeable loans but not so large as to be relatively indifferent to your business. Banks differ greatly in their desire and capacity to work with small firms. Some banks have special small business loan officers and regard new and early-stage ventures as the seeds of very large future accounts. Other banks see such new ventures loans as

[6] Ibid., pp. 81–82.

[7] G. B. Baty, *Entrepreneurship: Playing to Win* (Reston, VA: Reston Publishing Company, 1974), and J. M. Stancill, "Getting the Most from Your Banking Relationship," *Harvard Business Review,* March–April 1980.

EXHIBIT 15.4

Key Steps in Obtaining a Loan

Before choosing and approaching a banker or other lender, the entrepreneur and his or her management team should prepare by taking the following steps:

- Decide how much growth they want, and how fast they want to grow, observing the dictum that financing follows strategy.
- Determine how much money they require, when they need to have it, and when they can pay it back. To this end, they must:
  —Develop a schedule of operating and asset needs.
  —Prepare a real-time cash flow projection.
  —Decide how much capital they need.
  —Specify how they will use the funds they borrow.
- Revise and update the "corporate profile" in their business plan. This should consist of:
  —The core ingredients of the plan in the form of an executive summary.
  —A history of the firm (as appropriate).
  —Summaries of the financial results of the past three years.
  —Succinct descriptions of their markets and products.
  —A description of their operations.
  —Statements of cash flow and financial requirements.
  —Descriptions of the key managers, owners, and directors.
  —A rundown of the key strategies, facts, and logic that guide them in growing the corporation.
- Identify potential sources for the type of debt they seek, and the amount, rate, terms, *and conditions* they seek.
- Select a bank or other lending institution, solicit interest, and prepare a presentation.
- Prepare a written loan request.
- Present their case, negotiate, and then close the deal.
- After the loan is granted, borrowers should maintain an effective relationship with the lending officer.

Source: Jeffry A. Timmons, *Financing and Planning the New Venture* (Acton, MA: Brick Housing Publishing Company, 1990), pp. 82–83.

merely bad risks. Does the bank tend to call or reduce its loans to small businesses that have problems? When it has less capital to lend will it cut back on small business loans and favor older, more solid customers? Is the bank imaginative, creative, and helpful when a venture has a problem? To quote Baty, "Do they just look at your balance sheet and faint or do they try to suggest constructive financial alternatives?"

Has the bank had lending experience in your industry? If it has, your chances of getting a loan are better, and the bank will be more tolerant of problems and better able to help you exploit your opportunities. Is there good personal chemistry between you and your prospective lending officer? Remember, the person you talk to and deal with *is* the bank. Does this person know your industry and competition? Can this officer competently explain your business, technology, and uniqueness to other loan officers? Is he or she experienced in administering loans to smaller firms? Can you count on this person consistently? Does he or she have a good track record? Does his or her lending authority meet or exceed your needs? Does he or she have a reputation for being reasonable, creative, and willing to take a sound risk?

How does an entrepreneur go about evaluating a bank? First, the entrepreneur should consult accountants, attorneys, and other entrepreneurs who have had dealings with the bank. The advice of entrepreneurs who have dealt with a bank through good and bad times can be especially useful. Second, the entrepreneur should meet with loan officers at several banks and systematically explore their attitudes and approaches to their business borrowers. Who meets with you, for how long, and with how many interruptions can be useful measures of a bank's interest in your account. Finally, ask for small business references from their list of borrowers and talk to the entrepreneurs of those firms. Throughout all of these contacts and discussions, check out particular loan officers as well as the viability of the bank itself; they are a major determinant of how the bank will deal with you and your venture.

Approaching and Meeting the Banker

Obtaining a loan is, among other things, a sales job. Many borrowers tend to forget this. An entrepreneur with an early-stage venture must sell himself or herself as well as the viability and potential of the business to the banker. This is much the same situation that the early-stage entrepreneur faces with a venture capitalist.

The initial contact with a lender will likely be by telephone. The entrepreneur should be prepared to describe quickly the nature, age, and prospects of the venture; the amount of equity financing and who provided it; the prior financial performance of the business; the entrepreneur's experience and background; and the sort of bank financing desired. A referral from a venture capital firm, a lawyer or accountant, or other business associate who knows the banker can be very helpful.

If the loan officer agrees to a meeting, he or she may ask that a summary loan proposal, description of the business, and financial statements be sent ahead of time. A well-prepared proposal and a request for a reasonable amount of equity financing should pique a banker's interest.

The first meeting with a loan officer will likely be at the venture's place of business. The banker will be interested in meeting the management team, seeing how team members relate to the entrepreneur, and getting a sense of the financial controls and reporting used and how well things seem to be run. The banker may also want to meet one or more of the venture's equity investors. Most of all, the banker is using this meeting to evaluate the integrity and business acumen of those who will ultimately be responsible for the repayment of the loan.

Throughout meetings with potential bankers, the entrepreneur must convey an air of self-confidence and knowledge. If the banker is favorably impressed by what has been seen and read, he or she will ask for further documents and references and begin to discuss the amount and timing of funds that the bank might lend to the business.

What the Banker Wants to Know[8]

You first need to describe the business and its industry. Exhibit 15.5 suggests how a banker "sees a company" from what the entrepreneur might say. What are you going to do with the money? Does the use of the loan make business sense? Should some or all of the money required be equity capital rather than debt? For new and young businesses, lenders do not like to see total debt-to-equity ratios greater than one. The answers to these questions will also determine the type of loan (e.g., line of credit or term).

1. How much do you need? You must be prepared to justify the amount requested and describe how the debt fits into an overall plan for financing and developing the business. Further, the amount of the loan should have enough

[8] This section is drawn from Timmons, *Financing and Planning the New Venture* (Action, MA: Brick House Publishing Company, 1990), p. 85–88.

EXHIBIT 15.5

How Your Banker Interprets the Income Statement

Sales	What do you sell? Whom do you sell to?
Cost of goods	How do you buy? What do you buy? Whom do you buy from?
Gross margin	Are you a supermarket or a boutique?
Selling	How do you sell and distribute the product?
G & A: General and Administration	How much overhead and support is needed to operate?
R & D	How much is reinvested in the product?
Operating margins	Dollars available before financing costs?
Interest expense	How big is this fixed nut?
Profit before taxes	Do you make money?
Taxes	Corporation or Sub S?
Profit after taxes	
Dividends / withdrawals	How much and to whom? How much money is left in The company?

Source: This exhibit was created by Kathie S. Stevens and Leslie Charm as part of a class discussion in the Entrepreneurial Finance course at Babson College, and is part of a presentation titled, "Cash Is King, Assets Are Queen, and Everybody Is Looking for an Ace in the Hole." Ms. Stevens is former chief lending officer and member of the credit committee for a Boston bank.

EXHIBIT 15.6

Sample of a Summary Loan Proposal

Date of request:	May 30, 2005	
Borrower:	Curtis-Palmer & Company, Inc.	
Amount:	$4,200,000	
Use of proceeds:	A/R, up to	$1,600,000
	Inventory, up to	824,000
	WIP, up to	525,000
	Marketing, up to	255,000
	Ski show specials	105,000
	Contingencies	50,000
	Officer loans due	841,000
		$4,200,000
Type of loan:	Seasonal revolving line of credit	
Closing date:	June 15, 2005	
Term:	One year	
Rate:	Prime plus ½ percent, no compensating balances, no points or origination fees.	
Takedown:	$500,000 at closing	
	$1,500,000 on August 1, 2005	
	$1,500,000 on October 1, 2005	
	$700,000 on November 1, 2007	
Collateral:	70 percent of acceptable A/R under 90 days	
	50 percent of current inventory	
Guarantees:	None	
Repayment schedule:	$4,200,000 or balance on anniversary of note	
Source of funds for repayment:	*a.* Excess cash from operations (see cash flow).	
	b. Renewable and increase of line if growth is profitable.	
	c. Conversion to three-year note.	
Contingency source:	*a.* Sale and leaseback of equipment.	
	b. Officer's loans (with a request for a personal guarantee).	

Source: Updated and adapted from Jeffry A. Timmons, *Financing and Planning the New Venture* (Acton, MA: Brick House Publishing Co., 1990), p. 86.

cushion to allow for unexpected developments (see Exhibit 15.6).

2. When and how will you pay it back? This is an important question. Short-term loans for seasonal inventory buildups or for financing receivables are easier to obtain than long-term loans, especially for early-stage businesses. How the loan will be repaid is the bottom-line question. Presumably you are borrowing money to finance activity that will generate enough cash to repay the loan. What is your contingency plan if things go wrong? Can you describe such risks and indicate how you will deal with them?
3. What is the secondary source of repayment? Are there assets or a guarantor of means?
4. When do you need the money? If you need the money tomorrow, forget it. You are a poor planner and manager. On the other hand, if you need the money next month or the month after, you have demonstrated an ability to plan ahead, and you have given the banker time to investigate and process a loan application. Typically, it is difficult to get a lending decision in less than three weeks (some smaller banks still have once-a-month credit meetings).

One of the best ways for all entrepreneurs to answer these questions is from a well-prepared business plan. This plan should contain projections of cash flow, profit and loss, and balance sheets that will demonstrate the need for a loan and how it can be repaid. Particular attention will be given by the lender to the value of the assets and the cash flow of the business, and to such financial ratios as current assets to current liabilities, gross margins, net worth to debt, accounts receivable and payable periods, inventory turns, and net profit to sales. The ratios for the borrower's venture will be compared to averages for competing firms to see how the potential borrower measures up to them.

For an existing business, the lender will want to review financial statements from prior years prepared or audited by a CPA, a list of aged receivables and payables, the turnover of inventory, and lists of key customers and creditors. The lender will also want to know that all tax payments are current. Finally, he or she will need to know details of fixed assets and any liens on receivables, inventory, or fixed assets.

The entrepreneur-borrower should regard his or her contacts with the bank as a sales mission and provide data that are required promptly and in a form that can be readily understood. The better the material entrepreneurs can supply to demonstrate their business credibility, the easier and faster it will be to obtain a positive lending decision. The entrepreneur should also ask, early on, to meet with the banker's boss. This can go a long way to help obtain financing. Remember you need to build a relationship with a bank, and not just a banker.

The Lending Decision

One of the significant changes in today's lending environment is the centralized lending decision. Traditionally, loan officers might have had up to several million dollars of lending authority and could make loans to small companies. Besides the company's creditworthiness as determined by analysis of its past results via the balance sheet, income statement, cash flow, and collateral, the lender's assessment of the character and reputation of the entrepreneur was central to the decision. As loan decisions are made increasingly by loan committees or credit scoring, this face-to-face part of the decision process has given way to deeper analysis of the company's business plan, cash flow drivers and dissipaters, competitive environment, and the cushion for loan recovery given the firm's game plan and financial structure.

The implication for entrepreneurs is a demanding one: You can no longer rely on your salesmanship and good relationship with your loan officer alone to continue to get favorable lending decisions. You, or the key team member, need to be able to prepare the necessary analysis and documentation to convince people (you may never meet) that the loan will be repaid. You also need to know the financial ratios and criteria used to compare your loan request with industry norms and to defend the analysis. Such a presentation can make it easier and faster to obtain approval of a loan because it gives your relationship manager the ammunition to defend your loan request.

Lending Criteria

First and foremost, as with equity investors, the quality and track record of the management team will be a major factor. Historical financial statements, which show three to five years of profitability, are also essential. Well-developed business projections that articulate the company's sales estimates, market niche, cash flow, profit projections, working capital, capital expenditure, uses of proceeds, and evidence of competent accounting and control systems are essential.

In its simplest form, what is needed is analysis of the available collateral, based on guidelines such as those shown in Exhibit 15.3, and of debt capacity determined by analysis of the coverage ratio once the new loan is in place. Interest coverage is calculated as earnings before interest and taxes divided by interest (EBIT/interest). A business with steady, predictable cash flow and earnings would require a lower coverage ratio (say, in the range of two) than would a company with a volatile, unpredictable cash flow stream, for example, a high-technology company with risk of competition and obsolescence (which might require a coverage ratio of five or more). The bottom line, of course, is the ability of the company to repay both interest and principal on time.

Loan Restrictions[9]

A loan agreement defines the terms and conditions under which a lender provides capital. With it, lenders do two things: try to assure repayment of the loan as agreed and try to protect their position as creditor. Within the loan agreement (as in investment agreements) there are negative and positive covenants. Negative covenants are restrictions on the borrower; for example, no further additions to the borrower's total debt, no pledge to others of assets of the borrower, and no payment of dividends or limitation on owners' salaries.

Positive covenants define what the borrower must do. Some examples are maintenance of some minimum net worth or working capital, prompt payment of all federal and state taxes, adequate insurance on key people and property, repayment of the loan and interest according to the terms of the agreement, and provision to the lender of periodic financial statements and reports.

Some of these restrictions can hinder a company's growth, such as a flat restriction on further borrowing. Such a borrowing limit is often based on the borrower's assets at the time of the loan. However, rather than stipulating an initially fixed limit, the loan agreement

[9] Ibid., pp. 90–94.

should recognize that as a business grows and increases its total assets and net worth, it will need and be able to carry the additional debt required to sustain its growth; however, banks (especially in tighter credit periods) will still put maximums after allowed credit as it gives them another opportunity to recheck the loan. Similarly, covenants that require certain minimums on working capital or current ratios may be very difficult, for example, for a highly seasonal business to maintain at all times of the year. Only analysis of past financial monthly statements can indicate whether such a covenant can be met.

Covenants to Look For

Before borrowing money, an entrepreneur should decide what sorts of restrictions or covenants are acceptable. Attorneys and accountants of the company should be consulted before any loan papers are signed. Some covenants are negotiable (this changes with the overall credit economy), and an entrepreneur should negotiate to get terms that the venture can live with next year as well as today. Once loan terms are agreed upon and the loan is made, the entrepreneur and the venture will be bound by them. If the bank says, "Yes, but . . ."

- Wants to put constraints on your permissible financial ratios.
- Stops any new borrowing.
- Wants a veto on any new management.
- Disallows new products or new directions.
- Prevents acquiring or selling any assets.
- Forbids any new investment or new equipment.

What follows are some practical guidelines about personal guarantees: when to expect them, how to avoid them, and how to eliminate them.

Personal Guarantees and the Loan

Personal guarantees may be required of the "lead" entrepreneur or, more likely, shareholders of significance (more than 10 percent) who are also members of the senior management team. Also, personal guarantees are often "joint and severable"—meaning that each guarantor is liable for the total amount of the guarantee.

When to Expect Them

- If you are under collateralized.
- If there are shareholder loans or lots of "due to" and "due from" officer accounts.
- If you have had a poor or erratic performance.
- If you have management problems.
- If your relationship with your banker is strained.
- If you have a new loan officer.
- If there is turbulence in the credit markets.
- If there has been a wave of bad loans made by the lending institution, and a crackdown is in force.
- If there is less understanding of your market.

How to Avoid Them

- Good to spectacular performance.
- Conservative financial management.
- Positive cash flow over a sustained period.
- Adequate collateral.
- Careful management of the balance sheet.

How to Eliminate Them (if you already have them)

- See "How to Avoid Them."
- Develop a financial plan with performance targets and a timetable.
- Negotiate elimination *upfront* when you have some bargaining chips, based on certain performance criteria.
- Stay active in the search for backup sources of funds.

Building a Relationship

After obtaining a loan, entrepreneurs should cultivate a close working relationship with their bankers. Too many businesspeople do not see their lending officers until they need a loan. The astute entrepreneur will take a much more active role in keeping a banker informed about the business, thereby improving the chances of obtaining larger loans for expansion and cooperation from the bank in troubled times.

Some of the things that should be done to build such a relationship are fairly simple.[10] In addition to monthly and annual financial statements, bankers should be sent product news releases and any trade articles about the business or its products. The entrepreneur should invite the banker to the venture's facility, review product development plans and the prospects for the business, and establish a personal relationship with him or her. If this is done, when a new loan is requested, the lending officer will feel better about recommending its approval.

[10] Baty, *Entrepreneurship: Playing to Win.*

What about bad news? Never surprise a banker with bad news; make sure he or she sees it coming as soon as you do. Unpleasant surprises are a sign that an entrepreneur is not being candid with the banker or that management does not have the business under the proper control. Either conclusion by a banker is damaging to the relationship.

If a future loan payment cannot be met, entrepreneurs should not panic and avoid their bankers. On the contrary, they should visit their banks and explain why the loan payment cannot be made and say when it will be made. If this is done before the payment due date and the entrepreneur–banker relationship is good, the banker may go along. What else can he or she do? If an entrepreneur has convinced a banker of the viability and future growth of a business, the banker really does not want to call a loan and lose a customer to a competitor or cause bankruptcy. The real key to communicating with a banker is candidly to inform but not to scare. In other words, entrepreneurs must indicate that they are aware of adverse events and have a plan for dealing with them.

To build credibility with bankers further, entrepreneurs should borrow before they need to and then repay the loan. This will establish a track record of borrowing and reliable repayment. Entrepreneurs should also make every effort to meet the financial targets they set for themselves and have discussed with their banker. If this cannot be done, the credibility of the entrepreneur will erode, even if the business is growing.

Bankers have a right to expect an entrepreneur to continue to use them as the business grows and prospers, and not to go shopping for a better interest rate. In return, entrepreneurs have the right to expect that their bank will continue to provide them with needed loans, particularly during difficult times when a vacillating loan policy could be dangerous for businesses' survival.

The TLC of a Banker or Other Lender

1. Your banker is your partner, not a difficult minority shareholder.
2. Be honest and straightforward in sharing information.
3. Invite the banker to see your business in operation.
4. Always avoid overdrafts, late payments, and late financial statements.
5. Answer questions frankly and honestly. *Tell the truth.* Lying is illegal and undoubtedly violates loan covenants.
6. Understand the business of banking.
7. Have an "Ace in the Hole."

What to Do When the Bank Says No

What do you do if the bank turns you down for a loan? Regroup, and review the following questions.

1. Does the company really need to borrow now? Can cash be generated elsewhere? Tighten the belt. Are some expenditures unnecessary? Sharpen the financial pencil: be lean and mean.
2. What does the balance sheet say? Are you growing too fast? Compare yourself to published industry ratios to see if you are on target.
3. Does the bank have a clear and comprehensive understanding of your needs? Did you really get to know your loan officer? Did you do enough homework on the bank's criteria and their likes and dislikes? Was your loan officer too busy to give your borrowing package proper consideration? A loan officer may have 50 to as many as 200 accounts. Is your relationship with the bank on a proper track?
4. Was your written loan proposal realistic? Was it a normal request, or something that differed from the types of proposals the bank usually sees? Did you make a verbal request for a loan, without presenting any written backup?
5. Do you need a new loan officer, or a new bank? If your answers to the above questions put you in the clear, and your written proposal was realistic, call the head of the commercial loan department and arrange a meeting. Sit down and discuss the history of your loan effort, the facts, and the bank's reasons for turning you down.
6. Who else might provide this financing (ask the banker who turned you down)?

You should be seeing multiple lenders at the same time so you don't run out of time or money.

Tar Pits: Entrepreneurs Beware

Modern corporate financial theory has preached the virtues of zero cash balances and the use of leverage to enhance return on equity. When applied to closely held companies whose dream is to last forever, such thinking can be extremely destructive. If you judge by the 1980s, the excessive leverage used by so many larger companies was apparently simply not worth the risk: Two-thirds of the LBOs done in the 1980s have ended up in serious trouble. The serious erosion of IBM began about the same time as the company acquired debt on its balance sheet for the very first time, in the early 1980s. This problem was manifested in the acquisition binges of the early 1990s and in the high-technology feeding frenzy of the late 1990s. Following the 2000–2003 downturn, LBOs once again emerged as a popular growth vehicle.

Beware of Leverage: The ROE Mirage

According to the theory, one can significantly improve return on equity (ROE) by utilizing debt. Thus, the present value of a company would also increase significantly as the company went from a zero debt-to-equity ratio to 100 percent, as shown in Exhibit 15.7. On closer examination, however, such an increase in debt only improves the present value, given the 2 percent to 8 percent growth rates shown, by 17 percent to 26 percent. If the company gets into any trouble—and the odds of that happening sooner or later are very high—its options and flexibility become very seriously constrained by the covenants of the senior lenders. Leverage creates an unforgiving capital structure, and the potential additional ROI often is not worth the risk. If the upside is worth risking the loss of the entire company should adversity strike, then go ahead. This is easier said than survived, however.

Ask any entrepreneur who has had to deal with the workout specialists in a bank and you will get a sobering, if not frightening, message: It is hell and you will not want to do it again.

IRS: Time Bomb for Personal Disaster

There is a much lesser known tar pit that entrepreneurs need to be aware of when considering leveraging their companies. Once the company gets into serious financial trouble, a subsequent restructuring of debt is often part of the survival and recovery plan. In such a restructuring, the problem becomes the principal and interest due to lenders may be forgiven in exchange for warrants, direct equity, or other considerations. Such forgiven debt becomes *taxable income* for the entrepreneur who owns the company and who has personally had to guarantee the loans. BEWARE: In one restructuring of a midwestern cable television company, the founder at one point faced a possible $12 million personal tax liability, which would have forced him into personal bankruptcy, or possibly worse. In this case, fortunately, the creative deal restructuring enabled him to avoid such a calamitous outcome, but many other over-leveraged entrepreneurs have not fared as well.

EXHIBIT 15.7

Total Present Value

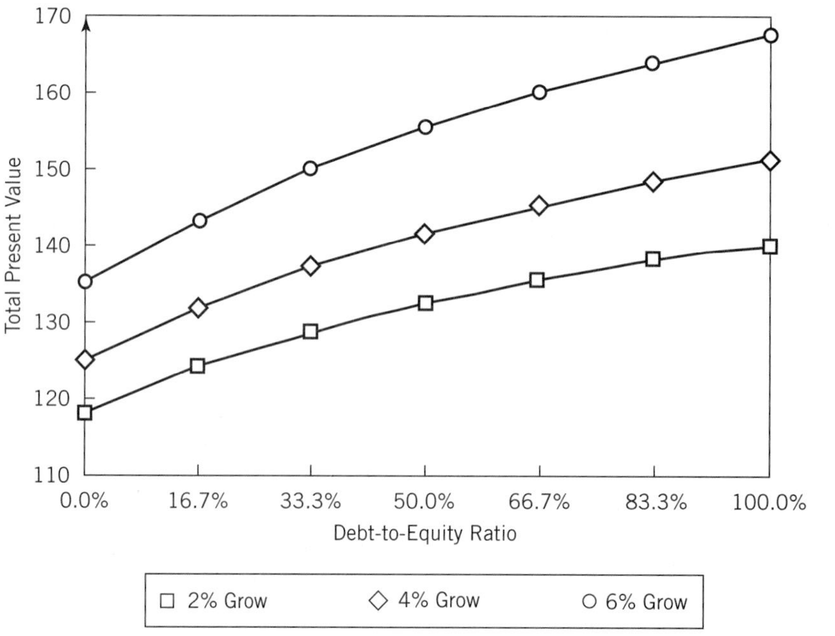

Source: William A. Sahlman, "Note on Free Cash Flow Valuation Models," HBS Note 288-023, Figure 5.

Neither a Lender nor a Borrower Be, But If You Must . . .

In Garrison Keillor's radio program, "A Prairie Home Companion," he describes the mythical town of Lake Wobegon, Minnesota. Inscribed in granite over the entrance to the Bank of Lake Wobegon is the motto "Neither a Lender nor a Borrower Be," which is actually very good advice for early-stage entrepreneurs. Thus, the following may serve as useful tips if you must borrow:

1. Borrow when you do not need it (which is the surest way to accomplish No. 2).
2. Avoid personal guarantees. Put caps and time limits on the amounts based on performance milestones, such as achieving certain cash flow, working capital, and equity levels. Also, don't be afraid in many markets to offer your guarantee and then negotiate ways to get back in whole or in part!
3. The devil is in the details. Read each loan covenant and requirement carefully—only the owner can truly appreciate their consequences.
4. Try to avoid or modify so-called hair-trigger covenants, such as: "If there is any change or event of any kind that can have any material adverse effect on the future of the company, the loan shall become due and payable."
5. Be conservative and prudent.

Chapter Summary

1. Business cycles impact lending cycles, with more or less restrictive behavior.
2. Startups are generally *not* candidates for bank credit but numerous sources of debt capital are available once profitability and a decent balance sheet are established.
3. Managing and orchestrating the banking relationship before and after the loan decision is a key task for entrepreneurs.
4. Knowing the key steps in obtaining a loan, selecting a banker—not a bank—who can add value can improve your odds.
5. Loan covenants can have a profound impact on how you can and cannot run the business. The devil is in the details of the loan agreement.
6. For the vast majority of small companies, leverage works only during the most favorable economic booms of credit availability. Leverage is a disaster if business turns sour.
7. The IRS also places a time bomb for personal disaster with every entrepreneur who borrows money: Even if your bank debt is forgiven in a restructuring it becomes *taxable income* to the borrower!
8. When the bank says no to a loan request, several key questions need to be addressed in an effort to reverse the decision or you need to seek alternative sources of credit than banks.

Study Questions

1. Define and explain the following, and why they are important: sources of debt financing, trade credit, line of credit, accounts receivable financing, time-sales factoring, commercial finance company.
2. What security can be used for a loan, and what percentage of its value do banks typically lend?
3. What are the things to look for in evaluating a lender, and why are these important?
4. What does "value-added banker" mean, and how and why is this crucial?
5. What criteria do lenders use to evaluate a loan application, and what can be done before and after the loan decision to facilitate a loan request?
6. What restrictions and covenants might a lender require, and how and why should these be avoided whenever possible?
7. What issues need to be addressed to deal with a loan request rejection?
8. Why do entrepreneurs in smaller companies need to be especially wary of leverage?
9. Why is there an IRS time bomb any time one borrows money?
10. When should a company borrow money?

Internet Resources for Chapter 15

http://www.federalreserve.gov *The Board of Governors of the Federal Reserve*

http://www.sba.gov/financing *Financing section of the Small Business Administration*

http://www.aba.com *The American Bankers Association*

http://emc.score.org *Service Corps of Retired Executives*

http://www.entrepreneur.com *Resources from* Entrepreneur *magazine*

MIND STRETCHERS

Have you considered?

1. You have been married nearly 30 years and love your spouse and family. A credit crunch leads you to defaults on your loans, and the lenders forgive $50 million of debt. The IRS tells you that you owe them $15 million. Your lawyers say you should get divorced to protect other assets. What would you do?
2. Why is Warren Buffet so wary about leverage?
3. Can you calculate the debt capacity of your proposed venture three to four years hence if it achieves positive cash flow and profitability?

Case

Bank Documents "The Devil Is in the Details"

Preparation Questions:

1. Outline the transactions. Include the flow of funds among the individuals and the corporations.
2. What specific risks was the bank trying to protect itself against? Which specific terms were intended to provide the protection?
3. What does "subordination" and "personal guarantee" mean to the respective parties?
4. What in the numbers indicate why the bank took the position it did?

The Parent Company ("TPC") had been in existence for 6 to 7 years under the control of a group of venture capitalists. The Parent Company was publicly held, two-thirds of which was held by the venture capitalists and the operating manager. It was in the business of manufacturing, under an overseas license, a product that was distributed throughout the United States. The Parent Company was running at an annual rate of $3 million to $4 million in sales and substantially all of its assets were secured under a loan agreement to Union Trust ("The Bank"). The company had a negative net worth and had not made profits during the last five years.

This company determined it needed to expand the business by acquisition. It went into a substantially different industry to accomplish this tactic. It found through investment bankers a chain of retail stores. At the same time it was doing its due diligence on The Retail Company ("TRC"), it opened discussions with the major supplier of The Retail Company, The Distribution Company ("TDC"). The Distribution Company distributed products, all of which were manufactured by others, throughout the United States to 300 customers. It distributed its products from two warehouse locations: one on the East Coast and one on the West Coast. The products sold to retailers who did a great deal of their business during the Christmas season.

The Distribution Company was the largest in its industry and was a privately held company with sales of approximately $25 million and an irregular earnings history (see Exhibit 1, The Distribution Company's audited financial statements, and Exhibit 2, the bank's analysis of the financial statements).

In November 2000, The Parent Company purchased all the stock of The Retail Company for $2.5 million in cash and $500,000 in a Non-Competition Agreement for the owner and chief operating officer, who left the business after the acquisition. This money was raised from the existing investors. The Retail Company had locations in Massachusetts, New York, and Connecticut. The Retail Company had revenues of approximately $6 million and earnings before taxes of approximately $500,000.

In August 2001, The Parent Company merged with The Distribution Company by giving the owners of The Distribution Company 20 percent of the stock of The Parent Company. In addition, The Parent Company raised approximately $3.2 million from its venture capitalists to infuse needed working capital into The Distribution Company.

In addition to receiving 20 percent of the stock of The Parent Company, the owners of The Distribution Company received a consulting contract and a Non-Competition Agreement calling for monthly payments and continuing lease payments on certain equipment used by The Distribution Company. Both the consulting contract and the lease contract called for monthly payments which would be lowered if wholesale sales decreased by more than 10 percent or certain specific extraordinary demands of The Distribution Company's cash flow occurred. In addition, the sellers had a secured note outstanding from The Distribution Company which was put on a full payout schedule. The owners and chief operating officer of The Distribution Company were not active in the business from the time of the merger.

Because of the financial markets at the time, The Parent Company needed to retain the existing bank that was lending money to The Distribution Company.

The bank was asked to finance both The Distribution Company and The Retail Company, and signed the Credit Facility Modification Agreement (see Exhibit 3). The bank also required The Parent Company and the selling shareholders to guaranty the line of credit. The bank also required the selling shareholders to pledge their 20 percent interest in The Parent Company as additional security for the loan. In addition, the sellers' secured loan was subordinated to the bank.

This case was prepared by Babson Professor Leslie Charm. Funding provided by Ewing Marion Kauffman Foundation.

EXHIBIT 1

Consolidated Balance Sheets of The Distribution Company

September 30, 1999, 1998, 1997	1999	1998	1997
Assets			
Current assets			
Cash and cash equivalents	$ 638,899	$ 1,149,730	$ 836,841
Accounts and notes receivable, net of allowance for doubtful accounts and notes (1994, $204,000; 1993, $510,000; 1992, $511,000) (Notes 2 and 7)*	5,081,489	3,279,823	2,674,876
Merchandise inventories (Notes 1 and 3)	3,831,577	3,969,947	4,180,428
Refundable income taxes	—	—	21,232
Other current assets (Notes 1 and 7)	82,251	306,775	757,031
Total Current Assets	9,634,216	8,706,275	8,470,408
Notes and receivable and other assets, noncurrent, net of allowance for doubtful notes (1994, $165,000; 1993, $640,000; 1992, $186,000) (Notes 1 and 2)	698,450	800,885	615,070
Investment in unconsolidated subsidiary, at cost, plus equity in undistributed earnings (Note 4)	669,652	641,521	601,512
Equipment and leasehold improvements at cost:			
Equipment	404,948	403,589	385,581
Leasehold improvements	123,040	213,978	192,530
	527,988	617,567	578,111
Less accumulated depreciation and amortization	(324,995)	(312,822)	(344,152)
	202,993	304,745	233,959
Total Assets (Note 5)	$11,205,311	$10,453,426	$9,920,949
Liabilities and Shareholders' Equity			
Current liabilities			
Notes payable (Notes 5 and 7)*	$4,695,000	$3,251,000	$3,010,000
Current portion of long-term debt (Note 5)	345,595	349,344	353,156
Franchise deposits	75,835	49,000	67,000
Accounts payable and accrued expenses:			
Merchandise	1,723,836	2,397,287	2,723,878
Other (Note 7)	2,415,479	2,278,073	2,154,200
Income taxes payable	—	29,271	—
Deferred income taxes	356,537	265,083	282,448
Total current liabilities	9,612,282	8,619,058	8,590,682

*The accompanying notes are an integral part of the consolidated financial statements.

EXHIBIT 1 (*Continued*)

September 30, 1999, 1998, 1997	1999	1998	1997
Liabilities and Shareholders' Equity			
Long-term debt, net of current portion (Note 5)	646,534	1,116,524	776,573
Deferred income taxes	132,000	34,600	25,670
Commitments and contingencies (Notes 6 and 7)			
Shareholders' equity			
Common stock, $.01 par value; authorized 300,000 shares; issued and outstanding 4,275 shares	43	43	43
Additional paid-in capital	940,679	940,679	940,679
Accumulated deficit	(126,227)	(257,478)	(412,698)
Total shareholder's equity	814,495	683,244	528,024
Total Liabilities and Shareholders' Equity (Note 5)	$11,205,311	$10,453,426	$9,920,949

Consolidated Statements of Operations of The Distribution Company

For the years ending September 30, 1999, 1998, 1997	1999	1998	1997
Revenues			
Merchandise sales	$19,172,938	$17,675,839	$16,050,887
Retail sales by company-owned stores	306,721	1,702,280	5,326,783
Franchise royalties and other income	5,818,428	5,356,993	4,691,235
Initial franchise and related fees	155,000	145,485	178,500
	25,453,087	24,880,597	26,247,405
Costs and expenses (Notes 6 and 7)*			
Cost of merchandise sold and distribution expenses	17,030,024	15,151,470	13,711,089
Cost of retail sales and direct operating expenses of company owned stores	317,345	1,721,405	4,972,098
Selling, general and administrative expenses	7,915,565	7,915,053	7,360,408
Net (gain) loss from store sales	(48,391)	(244,394)	25,599
	25,214,543	24,543,534	26,069,194
Income from operations	238,544	337,063	178,211
Interest expense, net (Note 5)	425,293	176,043	149,956
Income (loss) before income taxes and cumulative effect of accounting change	(186,749)	161,020	28,255
Income tax expense (benefit) (Note 8)	(18,000)	5,800	19,000
Income (loss) before cumulative effect of accounting change	(168,749)	155,220	9,255
Cumulative effect to October 1, 1987, of change in method of accounting for inventory costs, net of tax (Note 1)	300,000	—	—
Net Income	$ 131,251	$ 155,220	$ 9,255

*The accompanying notes are an integral part of the consolidated financial statements.

EXHIBIT 2

Comparative Statement of Financial Condition of The Distribution Company Prepared by The Bank

The Distribution Company
COMPARATIVE STATEMENT OF FINANCIAL CONDITION
Business: Wholesale Supply
In: $000's SIC Code: 5199

Date:	9/30/98 UNQUAL		9/30/99 UNQUAL		9/30/00 UNQUAL		8/10/01 UNQUAL	(7)	8/11/01 BEG. B.S.	(8)
1. Current Assets	8,167		8,858		9,384		4,838		4,723	
2. Current Liabilities	8,219		9,447		11,463		9,318		9,858	
3. Working Capital	(52)		(589)		(2,079)		(4,480)		(5,135)	
4. Total Long-Term Debt	1,552		1,241		321		1,744		4,157	
5. Tangible Net Worth	579		815		(473)		(3,600)		(3,590)	
6. Net Sales	24,881		25,341		25,757		19,817		0	
7. Net Profits	155		132		(1,288)		(3,127)		0	
8. Cash Generation	280		174		(1,227)		(3,089)		0	
9. Cash	1,150	11%	678	5.9%	793	7%	5	0.1%	5	0.0%
10. Marketable Securities										
11. Receivables—Net	2,907	27.8%	4,266	37.1%	4,123	36.5%	1,524	20.4%	1,063	5.8%
12. Inventory (FIFO) (1)	3,970	38%	3,832	33.3%	4,324	38.2%	3,010	40.3%	3,356	18.4%
13.										
14.										
15.										
16. Other Current Assets	140	1.3%	82	0.7%	44	1.3%	299	4%	299	1.6%
17. Prepaid Expenses										
18. Total Current Assets	8,167	78.1%	8,858	77%	9,384	83%	4,838	64.8%	4,723	25.9%
19.										
20. Net Fixed Assets	305	2.9%	203	1.8%	180	1.6%	174	2.3%	1,187	6.5%
21. Due from Affiliates	58	.6%	25	.2%	45	.4%	75	1%	75	.4%
22. Other Receivables	43	.4%	376	3.3%	295	2.6%	207	2.8%	512	2.8%
23.										
24. Notes Receivable	1,073	10.3%	2,041	17.7%	1,407	12.4%	2,168	29.1%	1,789	9.8%
25. Stores Held for Resale	63	.6%								
26. Inv. in Unconsol Subs	641	6.1%								
27. Non-Competitive Agreement									1,564	8.6%
28. Option Agreement									575	3.2%
29.										

Date:	9/30/98 UNQUAL		9/30/99 UNQUAL		9/30/00 UNQUAL		8/10/01 UNQUAL	(7)	8/11/01 BEG. B.S.	(8)
30. Intangibles (4)	104	1.0%							7,777	2.7%
31. TOTAL ASSETS	10,454	100%	11,503	100%	11,311	100%	7,462	100%	18,202	100%
32. Notes Payable	2,851	27.3%	3,645	31.7%	2,800	24.8%	2,236	30%	2,236	2.3%
33. Notes Payable	166	1.6%	598	5.2%	598	5.3%	588	7.9%	588	3.2%
34. Accounts Payable—Trade	2,397	22.9%	1,724	15%	3,261	28.8%	2,939	39.4%	2,939	6.1%
35. Accruals & Payables (Other)	2,351	22.5%	2,231	19.4%	2,864	25.3%	3,427	45.9%	3,803	0.9%
36. Current Maturities LTD	349	3.3%	390	3.4%	146	1.3%	75	1.0%	239	1.3%
37. Franchise Deposits	49	.5%	76	.7%	61	.5%	52	.7%	52	.3%
38. A/P Affiliate			233	2%	383	3.4%	1	0%	1	0%
39. N/P Affiliate	56	5%	550	4.8%	1,350	11.9%				
40.										
41.										
42. Total Current Liabilities	8,219	78.6%	9,447	82.1%	11,463	101.3%	9,318	124.9%	9,858	54.2%
43. LTD	442	4.2%	191	1.7%	71	.6%	155	2.1%	1,004	5.5%
44.									1,564	8.6%
45. Non-Competitive Agreement										
46. Deferred Items	35	.3%								
47. Subordinated LTD	1,075	10.3%	1,050	9.1%	250	2.2%	1,589	21.3%	1,589	8.7%
48. Total Liabil & Reserves	9,771	93.5%	10,688	92.9%	11,784	104.2%	11,062	148.2%	14,015	77%
49. Preferred Stock										
50. Common Stock										
51. Capital Surplus	941	9%	941	8.2%	941	8.3%	941	12.6%	4,187	23%
52. Earned Surplus	(258)	−2.5%	(126)	−1.1%	(1,414)	−12.5%	(4,541)	−60.9%		
53. Treasury Stock										
54. TOTAL NET WORTH	683	6.5%	815	7.1%	(473)	−4.2%	(3,600)	−48.3%	4,187	23%
55. TOTAL LIABIL & NET WORTH	10,454	100%	11,503	100%	11,311	100%	7,462	100%	18,202	100%
56. Annual Lease Rental	2,413	9.7%	2,444	9.6%	2,501	9.7%	2,371	12%	2,371	0%
57. Contingent Liabilities (5)	1,142	10.9%	1,174	10.2%	991	8.8%	579	7.8%	579	3.2%
58. ____________ Fin Goods										
59. INVENTORY Work Process										
60. ____________ Raw Material										
61. Land										
62. ____________ Buildings										
63. Leaseholds	214	34.6%	123	23.3%	134	23.7%	146	24.4%	96	8.1%
64. Furn. & Fixt										

(Continued)

Date:	9/30/98 UNQUAL		9/30/99 UNQUAL		9/30/00 UNQUAL		8/10/01 UNQUAL	(7)	8/11/01 BEG. B.S.	(8)
65. FIXED ASSETS Mach & Equip	404	65.4%	405	76.7%	432	76.3%	452	75.6%	1,091	100%
66. ____________ Gross F A	618	100%	528	100%	566	100%	598	100%	1,187	100%
67. ____________ Depreciation	313	50.6%	325	61.6%	386	68.2%	424	70.9%		
68. Spread Done By:	MVD	HEW		CMS		CHV		CHV		
69. Date Spread Done By:	1/21/99	2/23/00		2/22/01		2/22/02		2/22/02		
70. Net Sales	24,881	100%	25,341	100%	25,757	100%		19,817	100%	
71. Cost of Merch Sold/Distr	15,152	60.9%	17,030	67.2%	17,779	69%		12,928	65.2%	
72. Cost of Retail Sales	1,721	6.9%	317	1.3%	0			14	.1%	
73. Gross Profit	8,008	32.3%	7,994	31.5%	7,978	31%		6,875	34.7%	
74. General & Admin Expense	7,915	31.8%	7,838	30.9%	8,827	34.3%		9,750	49.2%	
75.										
76. Operating Profit	93	.4%	156	.6%	(849)	−3.3%		(2,875)	−14.5%	
77. Other Income										
78. Other Expense										
79. Earnings pre Int & Tax	473	1.9%	357	1.4%	(690)	−2.7%		(2,640)	−13.3%	
80. Interest	312	1.3%	532	2.1%	598	2.3%		487	2.5%	
81. Profit Before IncomeTax	161	.6%	(175)	−.7%	(1288)	−5%		(3,127)	−15.8%	
82. Income Taxes	6	0%	(7)	0%						
83. Extraordinary Items (7)			300	1.2%						
84. Net Profit After Tax	155	.6%	132	.5%	(1288)	−5%		(3,127)	−15.8%	
85. BEGINNING NET WORTH	528		683		815			(427)		
86. Net Income/Loss	155		132		(1,288)			(3,127)		
87. New Equity										
88.										
89.										
90.										
91. Dividends/Withdrawals										
92. Inc Treasury Stock										
93. ENDING NET WORTH	683		815		(473)			(3,600)		
94. Change in Net Worth	155		132		(1,288)			(3,127)		
95. Officers Salaries										
96. Net Profit After Taxes	155		132		(1,288)			(3,127)		
97. Depreciation	116		77		61			38		
98. Amortization										
99. Deferred Items	9		(35)		0			0		
100. SUB-TOTAL CASH GENERATION	280		174		(1,227)			(3,089)		

Date:	9/30/98 UNQUAL	9/30/99 UNQUAL	9/30/00 UNQUAL	8/10/01 UNQUAL (7)	8/11/01 BEG. B.S. (8)
101. New Long-Term Debt	0	0	0	84	
102. New Equity	0	0	0	0	
103. Decrease Intangibles	96	104	0	0	
104. Due From Affiliates	292	33	0	0	
105. Decrease other Non-Curren	0	0	715	0	
106. Inc in on-Current Liabs	0	0	0	0	
107. Inc Subordinated Debt	1,075	0	0	1,339	
108. Dec in Fixed Assets	0	25	0	0	
109.					
110. TOTAL SOURCES	1,743	336	(512)	(1,666)	
111.					
112.					
113.					
114. Repayment of LTD	335	251	120	0	
115. Capital Expenditures	187	0	38	32	
116. Dividends/Withdrawals	0	0	0	0	
117. Increase Intangibles	0	0	0	0	
118. Due from Affiliates	0	0	20	30	
119. Inc other Non-current Ass	139	597	0	673	
120. Dec Subordinated Debt	0	25	800	0	
121. Dec in Non-current Liabs	0	0	0	0	
122. Decrease in Equity	0	0	0	0	
123.					
124.					
125.					
126. TOTAL APPLICATIONS	661	873	978	735	
127. CHANGE NET WORKING CAPITAL	1,082	(537)	(1,490)	(2,401)	
128. Current Ratio	0.99	0.94	0.82	0.52	0.48
129. Quick Ratio	0.49	0.52	0.43	0.16	0.11
130. Sales/Receivables (days)	42	61	58	25	
131. Cost of Sales/Inven (days)	94	81	88	77	
132. Total Debt/Tang Net Worth	16.88	13.11	−24.91	−3.07	−3.9
133. Unsub Debt/Tang Cap Fnds	5.26	5.17	−51.72	−4.71	6.21
134. Net Profit as % Net Worth	22.69%	16.2%	272.3%	94.76%	
135. Sales/Working Capital	−478.48	−43.02	−12.39	−4.83	
136. Sales/Net Worth	36.43	31.09	−54.45	6.01	
137. COGS/Payables (days)	57	36	66	75	

(Continued)

EXHIBIT 2 (*Continued*)

Cash Flow Summary of The Distribution Company Prepared by The Bank

Date:	9/30/98 UNQUAL	9/30/99 UNQUAL	9/30/00 UNQUAL	8/10/01 UNQUAL
GROSS CASH FLOW				
1. Net Income (Loss)	155	132	(1,288)	(3,127)
2. Depreciation	116	77	61	38
3. Amortization	0	0	0	0
4. Deferred Items	9	(35)	0	0
5.				
6. TOTAL GROSS CASH FLOW	280	174	(1,227)	(3,089)
7. FLOWS FROM (FOR) WORKING ACCTS				
8. Receivables—Net	(559)	(1,359)	143	2,599
9. Inventory (FIFO) (1)	210	138	(492)	1,314
10. Accounts Payable—Trade	(327)	(673)	1,537	(322)
11. Accruals & Payables Other	790	(120)	633	563
12. Income Taxes	0	0	0	0
13. Other Current Assets	(49)	58	(62)	(155)
14. Marketable Securities	0	0	0	0
15. CASH GENER FROM OPER.	345	(1,782)	532	910
16. FLOWS FROM (FOR) NON-CUR ACCTS				
17. Net Fixed Assets	(187)	25	(38)	(32)
18. Due from Affiliates	292	33	(20)	(30)
19. Other Non-Current Assets	(139)	(597)	715	(673)
20. Intangibles (4)	96	104	0	0
21. CASH AVAIL FOR EXT	407	(2,217)	1,189	175
22. REQUIRED PMTS AND RETIREMENTS				
23. Other Cur Liab	(837)	754	935	(1,741)
24. Other Non-Current Liabs	0	0	0	0
25. Dividends/Withdrawals	0	0	0	0
26. Current Maturities LTD	(4)	41	(244)	(71)
27. INTERNAL CASH FLOW	(434)	(1,422)	1,880	(1,637)
28. FINANCING				
29. Notes Payable—UST	(159)	794	(845)	(564)

Date:	9/30/98 UNQUAL	9/30/99 UNQUAL	9/30/00 UNQUAL	8/10/01 UNQUAL
30. Notes Payable—Bank Fiveq	166	432	0	(10)
31. Long-Term Debt	(335)	(251)	(120)	84
32. Subordinated LTD	1,075	(25)	(800)	1,339
33. Equity Financing	0	0	0	0
34. INCREASE/DECREASE IN CA	313	(472)	115	(788)

Footnotes:

1. As of 10/1/98, the company changed its method of accounting for inventory to include overhead costs, which had previously been charged to expense.
   As of 8/11/01, the company changed the method of inventory valuation from LIFO to FIFO.
2. Consolidation up to and including FYE '99 did not include the finance company subsidiary. FYE 2000 financials include this subsidiary as a wholly owned subsidiary.
3. Previous to 8/10/01, the company's auditors were Cooper's & Lybrand.
4. In FYE '98, intangibles consist of unrecognized costs.
   At 8/11/97, intangibles consisted of goodwill, a noncompete agreement, and an option agreement.
5. Contingent liabilities consist of the company's guarantee on obligations of some franchisees, letters of credit with the bank, and various lawsuits about normal business.
6. Extraordinary item at FYE 2000 is the cumulative effect of the change in the method of accounting for inventory costs, net of tax effects.
7. Deloitte & Touche feels that there is substantial doubt whether the company will continue as a going concern due to historical losses and a deficiency in capital.
8. On August 11, 2001, The Parent Company acquired all the outstanding shares of The Distribution Company. Accordingly, the company's historical balance sheet at August 10, 2001, has been revalued to fair market value on the opening balance sheet of the company as of August 11, 2001.

EXHIBIT 3

Credit Facilities Modification Agreement

This is a Credit Facilities Modification Agreement made and entered into as of this 8th day of August 2001 by and among The Distribution Company, a Massachusetts corporation having a principal place of business at 385 Appleton Street, North Andover, Massachusetts ("TDC" "Borrower"); The Parent Company ("TPC"), a Delaware corporation with a principal place of business at 222 Benchley Avenue, Hartford, Connecticut; and The Retail Company ("TRC"), a Delaware corporation with principal place of business at 18 Holland Street, Hartford, Connecticut 06874; and the Bank ("Bank"), a Massachusetts banking corporation having an address at Boston, Massachusetts 02108.

Preamble

WHEREAS, on December 3, 1995, the Borrower entered into a $4,000,000.00 revolving loan facility with the Bank, as evidenced by two notes in the amounts of $1,500,000 and $2,500,000, respectively, secured by a security agreement covering all assets of the Borrower and further secured by an assignment of certain promissory notes payable to the Borrower (the Assignment); and

WHEREAS, on April 8, 1997, the Borrower executed a further "Security Agreement—Inventory, Accounts, Equipment and other Property" ("Security Agreement") securing all liabilities of the Borrower to the Bank (a true copy of which is attached hereto as Exhibit A-1); and

WHEREAS, on October 1, 1999, the Borrower executed a "Commercial Demand Note" in the amount of Three Million Five Hundred Thousand Dollars ($3,500,000.00), which Commercial Demand Note superseded the two notes dated as of December 3, 1995, and is secured by the Security Agreement (a true copy of which is attached hereto as Exhibit A-2); and

WHEREAS, on November 18, 1999, Sellers 1, 2, and 3 (S123) ("Individual Guarantors") each executed a "Limited Guaranty" of the liabilities of the Borrower (true copies of which are attached hereto as Exhibit A-3, A-4, and A-5); and

WHEREAS, on November 18, 1999, Seller, an affiliate of the Borrower, executed a Subordination Agreement in favor of the Bank in which certain notes of the Borrower held by Seller were subordinated to the Borrower's indebtedness to the Bank ("Subordination Agreement") (a true copy of which is attached hereto as Exhibit A-6); and

WHEREAS, the Individual Guarantors own all of the issued and outstanding common stock of the Borrower; and

WHEREAS, pursuant to an Agreement and Plan of Merger dated as of August 2001 ("Merger Agreement"), TDC has been merged into the Borrower so that the Borrower is now a wholly owned subsidiary of TPC and the Individual Guarantors have received Series E Preferred Stock of TPC in lieu of the common stock of the Borrower; and

WHEREAS, TRC is a wholly owned subsidiary of TPC which operates approximately nine TRCs in Massachusetts, Connecticut, and New York; and

WHEREAS, TPC, TRC, and the Borrower have requested that the existing credit facility from the Bank to the Borrower be continued and amended for the benefit of TPC and TRC, and in consideration thereof TPC and TRC have agreed to guaranty loans, the parties now wish to restate and amend the terms and conditions of the credit facility;

NOW, THEREFORE, for good and valuable consideration, the parties do hereby agree as follows:

Section 1. Definitions

Section 1.1. Acceptable Inventory. Acceptable Inventory shall mean such of the Borrower's new, unopened saleable inventory shelf for sale to others (but excluding raw materials, work in progress, and materials used or consumed in the Borrower's business) as the Bank in its sole discretion deems eligible for borrowing.

Section 1.2. Acceptable Accounts. Acceptable Accounts shall mean accounts under sixty (60) days old measured from the date of the invoice, which arose from *bona fide* outright sales of merchandise to a Person which is not a subsidiary or affiliate of the Borrower, TPC, or TRC.

Section 1.3. Accounts. "Accounts" and "Accounts Receivable" include, without limitation, "accounts" as defined in the UCC, and also all accounts, accounts receivable, notes, drafts, acceptances, and other forms of obligations and receivables and rights to payment for credit extended and for goods sold or leased, or services rendered, whether or not yet earned by performance; all inventory which gave rise thereto, and all rights associated with such inventory, including the right of stoppage in transit; all reclaimed, returned, rejected, or repossessed inventory (if any) the sale of which gave rise to any Account.

Section 1.4. Bank. The Bank, a Massachusetts banking Corporation.

Section 1.5. Base Lending Rate. The rate of interest published internally and designated by the Bank from time to time, as its Base Lending Rate.

Section 1.6. Collateral. All assets of the Borrower, tangible and intangible, as described in the Security Agreement and in the Assignment, as amended herein.

Section 1.7. Corporate Guarantors. TPC and TRC.

Section 1.8 Credit Facilities Modification Agreement. This agreement and any and all subsequent amendments thereto.

EXHIBIT 3 (*Continued*)

Section 1.9. Credit Facility. The Loans granted to or for the benefit of the Borrower pursuant to the Loan Documents.

Section 1.10. Event of Default. Any event described in Section 8 hereto.

Section 1.11. Guarantors. The Corporate Guarantors, the Individual Guarantors, and Sellers.

Section 1.12. Individual Guarantors. Sellers 1, 2, 3.

Section 1.13. Loan Documents. This term shall refer, collectively, to (i) the Commercial Demand Note, (ii) the Security Agreement, (iii) the Assignment, (iv) all UCC Financial Statements, (v) the Subordination Agreement, (vi) the Individual Guarantees, (vii) TPC Guaranty, (viii) TRC Guaranty, (ix) the Sellers Guaranty, (x) the Sellers Pledge and Security Agreement, (xi) TPC Pledge of Stock of Borrower and TRC, (xii) TPC Subordination Agreement, (xiii) the Individual Guarantor's Pledge of Preferred Stock of TPC, (xiv) TRC Security Agreement, (xv) this Credit Facilities Modification Agreement, and all amendments, modifications, and extensions thereof, and any other document or agreement pursuant to which the Bank is granted a lien or other interest as security for the Borrower's obligations to it.

Section 1.14. Loan(s). Loans or advances by the Bank to the Borrower pursuant to the Loan Documents. The Loan shall consist of a Revolving Loan of up to $2,800,000.00 as provided for in Sections 2.1 through 2.5 hereof, including any letters of credit issued by the Bank for the account of the Borrower as provided in Section 2.4 hereof. The Borrower and the Lender acknowledge that as of August 2001, the outstanding balance of the Revolving Loans was $________.

Section 1.15. Loan Review Date. July 31, 2002, or such later date to which the Loan may be extended pursuant to Section 2.5 hereof.

Section 1.16. Note. The $3,500,000.00 Commercial Demand Note dated October 1, 1999.

Section 1.17. Obligations. Those obligations described in Section 2 hereof.

Section 1.18. Person. A corporation, association, partnership, trust, organization, business, individual or government, or any governmental agency or political subdivision thereof.

Section 1.19. Sellers Debt. All loans from Sellers to the Borrower whether now existing or hereafter arising.

Section 1.20. Revolving Loan or Revolving Credit. The revolving working capital loan evidenced by the Commercial Demand Note as described in this Agreement.

Section 1.21. Subordinated Debt. The Sellers Debt and TPC Debt.

Section 1.22. Subsidiary. Means any entity that is directly or indirectly controlled by the Borrower or TPC.

Section 1.23. Capitalized terms not otherwise defined herein shall have the meanings ascribed thereto in the Loan Documents.

Section 2. Loans, Revision of Terms, Confirmation of Security Documents; Additional Security

Section 2.1 (a) *Amount of Availability of Revolving Credit.* The Bank has established a discretionary revolving line of credit in the Borrower's favor in the amount of the Borrower's Availability (as defined below), as determined by the Bank from time to time hereafter. All loans made by the Bank under this Agreement, and all of the Borrower's other liabilities to the Bank under or pursuant to this Agreement, are payable ON DEMAND.

As used herein, the term "Availability" refers at any time to the lesser of (i) or (ii) below:

(i) up to (A)Two Million Eight Hundred Thousand Dollars ($2,800,000.00) (or such other amount as the Bank may set from time to time, in the Bank's discretion),

minus . . .

(B) the aggregate amounts then undrawn on all outstanding letters of credit issued by the Bank for the account of the Borrower.

(ii) up to (A) seventy percent (70%) (or such revised percentage as the Bank may set from time to time, in the Bank's discretion) of the face amount (determined by the Bank in the Bank's sole discretion) of each of the Acceptable Accounts,

Plus...

(B) thirty percent (30%) (or such revised percentage as the Bank may set from time to time, in the Bank's discretion) of the value of the Acceptable Inventory (Acceptable Inventory being valued at the lower cost or market after deducting all transportation, processing, handling charges, and all other costs and expenses affecting the value thereof, all as determined by the Bank in its sole discretion) but not to exceed $1,200,000.

Minus...

(C) the aggregate amounts then undrawn on all outstanding letters of credit issued by the Bank for the account of the Borrower (the "Formula Amount").

The Revolving Credit is not a committed line of financing. The borrowing formula described in this Section 2.1 is intended solely for monitoring purposes.

(b) *Advances.* Advances may consist of direct advances to the Borrower payable ON DEMAND, or letters of credit issued on behalf of the Borrower. The Borrower may borrow, repay, and re-borrow Revolving Loans under this Agreement by written notice

EXHIBIT 3 (*Continued*)

given to the Bank at least two business days prior to the date of the requested advance. Each request for an advance shall be in an integral multiple of $50,000.00 and shall be subject to approval by the Bank, which approval may be granted, denied, or granted conditionally in the Bank's sole discretion.

(c) *Mandatory Reduction.* The Borrower shall reduce the outstanding balance of the Revolving Loan to $600,000.00 or less (exclusive of letters of credit) for a period of thirty (30) consecutive days between December 1, 2001, and January 31, 2002.

(d) *Availability—Overadvances.* The Borrower's Availability shall not exceed the Formula Amount (as set forth in Section 2.1 (a) (ii)), provided that the Borrower may borrow $700,000.00 in excess of the Formula Amount prior to September 30, 2001, and $300,000.00 in excess of the Formula Amount between February 28, 2002, and July 31, 2002, provided further that in no event shall outstanding advances ever exceed $2,800,000.00.

(e) *Approval of Accounts and Inventory:*

(i) *Accounts.* All account debtors shall be subject to the approval of the Bank in its sole discretion and the Bank's eligibility determinations shall be final and conclusive. The determination by the Bank that a particular account from a particular account debtor is eligible for borrowing shall not obligate the Bank to deem subsequent accounts from the same account debtor to be eligible for borrowing, nor to continue to deem that account to be so eligible. All collateral not considered eligible for borrowing nevertheless secures the prompt, punctual, and faithful performance of the Borrower's Obligations. The determination that a given account of the Borrower is eligible for borrowing shall not be deemed a determination by the Bank relative to the actual value of the account in question. All risks concerning the credit worthiness of all accounts are and remain upon the Borrower.

(ii) *Inventory.* The Bank's determinations that certain inventory is, or is not, eligible for borrowing shall be final and conclusive. No sale of inventory shall be on consignment, approval, or under any other circumstances such that such inventory may be returned to the Borrower without the consent of the Bank, except for transactions in the normal course of business. None of the inventory will be stored or processed with a bailee or other third party without the prior written consent of the Bank.

(f) *Borrowing Certificate.* Each request for an advance shall be accomplished by a borrowing certificate, in form acceptable to the Bank, which shall be signed by such person whom the Bank reasonably believes to be authorized to act in this regard on behalf of the Borrower, and shall certify that as of the date of the subject certificate, (i) there has been no material adverse change in the Borrower's and Corporate Guarantors' respective financial conditions taken as a whole from the information previously furnished the Bank; (ii) the Borrower and TPC are in compliance with, and have not breached any of, the covenants contained herein; and (iii) no event has occurred or failed to occur which occurrence or failure is, or with the passage of time or giving of notice (or both) would constitute, an Event of Default (as described herein) whether or not the Bank has exercised any of its rights upon such occurrence.

(g) *Loan Account.*

(i) An account (hereinafter, the "Loan Account") has been opened on the books of the Bank in which account a record has been, and shall be, kept of all loans made by the Bank to the Borrower under or pursuant to this Loan and of all payments thereon.

(ii) The Bank may also keep a record (either in the Loan Account or elsewhere, as the Bank may from time to time elect) of all interest, service charges, costs, expenses, and other debits owed the Bank on account of the loan arrangement contemplated hereby and of all credits against such amounts so owed.

(iii) All credits against the Borrower's indebtedness indicated in the Loan Account shall be conditional upon final payment to the Bank of the items giving rise to such credits. The amount of any item credited against the Loan Account which is charged back against the Bank for any reason or is not so paid may be added to the Loan Account, or charged against any account maintained by the Borrower with the Bank (at the Bank's discretion and without notice, in each instance), and shall be Liability, in each instance whether or not the item so charged back or not so paid is returned.

(iv) Any statement rendered by the Bank to the Borrower shall be considered correct and accepted by the Borrower and shall be conclusively binding upon the Borrower unless the Borrower provides the Bank with written objection thereto within twenty (20) days from the mailing of such statement, which such written objection shall indicate with particularly the reason for such objection. The Loan Account and the Bank's books and records concerning the loan arrangement contemplated herein shall be prima facie evidence and proof of the items described therein.

Section 2.2. Note. The Borrower has executed and delivered the Note to the Bank. The Note evidences each advance under the Loan. The Note is on a DEMAND basis and is payable as to interest in arrears on the first day of each calendar month. The Note may be prepaid at any time, in whole or in part, without penalty. Except as modified herein, the Borrower hereby ratifies and confirms the Note in every respect.

Section 2.3. Interest and Fees

(a) *Interest.* The Loans (except the letters of credit) shall bear interest at a rate which, until the Loan may be due and payable, shall be the Base Lending Rate plus one percent (1%). The rate of interest shall vary from time to time as the Base Lending Rate varies, and any change in the rate of interest shall become effective on the date of the change in the Base Lending Rate. Interest shall be computed and adjusted on a daily basis using a 360-day year. Overdue principal and interest shall bear interest at the rate of two percent (2%) per annum above the Base Lending Rate.

(b) *Balances.* The Borrower shall maintain a balance (exclusive of balances necessary to cover service charges) at all times of at least ten percent (10%) of the outstanding balance of the Revolving Loan. For each day that the Borrower shall fail to maintain

EXHIBIT 3 (*Continued*)

such balances, the Borrower shall pay to the Bank on the first day of the following month a fee to compensate the Bank for the lack of use of such funds during the previous month.

(c) *Alternative Pricing.* At its election, the Bank may transfer the Revolving Credit from the commercial lending division to the asset-based lending division in which event the interest rate may be changed to the Base Lending Rate plus one and one-half percent (1 1/2%), with two business days' clearance. In addition the Borrower shall provide such further reports and information as is customarily required of Borrowers serviced by such division.

Section 2.4. Letters of Credit. From time to time, the Bank has made loans to the Borrower in the form of letters of credit, as evidenced by the Applications for Commercial Credit as attached hereto as Exhibit B. The borrower may request that the Bank make additional loans in the form of further letters of credit provided that the total amount of Documentary Letters of Credit outstanding at any time shall not exceed $550,000.00 and the total amount of Standby Letters of Credit outstanding at any time shall not exceed $72,000.00. Each such request for the issuance of a letter of credit shall be made at least five (5) business days in advance and shall be accompanied by the Bank's standard form of "Application for Commercial Credit" and "Commercial Letter of Credit Agreement" duly executed by the Borrower. The Bank shall have the right, at its option, to limit the term of any letter of credit to the Loan Review Date. In the event the Bank elects to issue a Standby Letter of Credit, the Borrower shall pay the Bank a fee of one percent (1%) per annum of the face amount of such Standby Letter of Credit, and one-half of one percent (.5%) of the face amount of a Documentary Letter of Credit or, if different, the then standard or customary fee for the type and amount of letter of credit requested, in lieu of the interest otherwise required on the Loan. All drafts drawn on a letter of credit shall be immediately repayable in full by the Borrower without need for notice or demand, together with interest thereon at the rate of three percent (3%) above the Base Rate for each day that such draft remains outstanding.

Section 2.5. Review of Loan. Without derogating from the DEMAND nature of the Revolving Loan, the Revolving Credit facility will be subject to review on July 31, 2002. There is no obligation on the Bank to renew the Revolving Credit or to extend it beyond July 31, 2002.

Section 2.6. Subordination of Sellers Debt. Sellers, a Massachusetts general partnership controlled by the Individual Guarantors, acknowledges that the Subordination Agreement remains in full force and effect, that the Loans constitute Senior Debt under the Subordination Agreement, and that the Sellers Debt in the amount of $1,800,000.00 as evidenced by a Term Promissory Note in said amount dated as of August 8, 2001, remains subject and subordinate to the Loans as provided in the Subordination Agreement. The Term Promissory Note evidencing the Sellers Debt has this day been delivered to the Bank duly endorsed.

Section 2.7. Assignment. The Borrower hereby ratifies and confirms the Assignment, and acknowledges that the Assignment secures the Loans. A current Schedule A to the Assignment is attached hereto as Exhibit C. The notes secured by the Assignment have this day been delivered to the Bank duly endorsed. Upon payment in full of any of the assigned notes by the makers thereof and the deposit of such funds in the Borrower's account at the Bank, the Bank shall redeliver the paid note(s) to the Borrower. From time to time, the Borrower may renegotiate the terms of such notes with the makers thereof on commercially reasonable terms and conditions in the Borrower's reasonable judgment. All such amendments or renegotiated notes shall be delivered to the Bank against delivery to the Borrower of the original notes, if required by it, and shall be included in the Assignment.

Section 2.8. Guaranty; Security. (a) *Individual Guarantors.* The Individual Guarantors hereby ratify and confirm their respective Limited Guarantees in all respects and further confirm that such Limited Guarantees apply to the Loan, including, without limitations to, the various letters of credit. To secure such guarantees, the Individual Guarantors have this day pledged to the Bank their Series E Preferred Stock of TPC as set forth in the respective Pledge Agreements attached hereto as Exhibit D. The Individual Guarantors may convert their Series E Preferred Stock into common stock of TPC, in which event all shares received as a result of such conversion shall be similarly pledged to the Bank as collateral for their respective Limited Guarantees.

(b) *Corporate Guarantors.* TPC and TRC have this day guaranteed all of the Borrower's obligations to the Bank by the execution of "TPC Guaranty" and "TRC Guaranty" attached hereto as Exhibit E and F, respectively. TPC has secured TPC Guaranty by pledging to the Bank all of the Borrower's and TRC shares as set forth in the Pledge Agreement attached hereto as Exhibit G. TRC has further secured TRC Guaranty by executing and delivering to the Bank a Security Agreement on all of its assets as set forth on Exhibit H attached hereto. TRC has deposited $250,000.00 in an account at the Bank which amount may be used by TRC for working capital purposes.

(c) *Seller Associates.* Seller has this day executed a limited guaranty of the Borrower's obligations to the Bank by the execution of the "Seller's Guaranty" attached hereto as Exhibit I. Seller has secured its guaranty by the execution and delivery to the Bank of a pledge and assignment of various payments due Seller from the Borrower under (i) the Consulting and Non-Competition Agreement, and (ii) the Seller's Debt, all as set forth in the "Seller's Pledge and Security Agreement" attached hereto as Exhibit J. Except as set forth in the Seller's Pledge and Security Agreement, all payments and proceeds received by Seller pursuant to the Consulting and Non-Competition Agreement and the Seller Debt shall be immediately deposited in a separate account with the Bank and pledged to the Bank as further security for the Guarantee. Except as set forth in the Seller's Pledge and Security Agreement, no funds may be withdrawn from such account until Loan has been paid in full and the Bank has no further obligation to advance funds hereunder. In the event that the Bank shall apply any funds received by Seller under Sections 3(a), 3(c), and 3(d) of the Consulting and Non-Competition Agreement (but not the Seller debt) against the Loan, the Individual Guarantors shall receive credit against their respective Limited Guarantees for the amount so applied by the Bank.

EXHIBIT 3 (*Continued*)

Section 2.9. Security Agreement. As the security for the prompt satisfaction of all its Obligations to the Bank, the Borrower has executed and delivered the Security Agreement. The Borrower hereby ratifies and confirms the Security Agreement and acknowledges that the Security Agreement remains in full force and effect and constitutes a first and exclusive lien on the Collateral. The Collateral, together with all other property of the Borrower of any kind held by the Bank, shall stand as one general continuing collateral security for all Obligations and may be retained by the Bank until all Obligations are paid in full.

Section 2.10. TPC Debt. As of the date hereof, TPC has agreed to loan to the Borrower the sum of $2,750,000.00 ("TPC Loan") to be used as additional working capital. Of this sum, $575,000 will be advanced to Realty Trust to be applied toward the third mortgage on the property at 385 Appleton Street, North Andover, Massachusetts, and approximately $400,000 has been or will be advanced to pay (i) costs of a certain litigation settlement and (ii) accounting fees, legal fees, and closing costs incurred by the Borrower in connection with the Merger Agreement and this Loan. TPC has this day deposited the balance of TPC Loan, approximately $1,775,000, in an account to the Bank as security for the Loan as set forth in the "Pledge and Security Agreement—Cash Collateral Account" attached hereto as Exhibit K. At such time as TPC shall have restructured its loan with Union Bank & Trust as provided in Section 2.11 hereof (or otherwise restructured such debt in a manner reasonably satisfactory to the Bank), TPC may withdraw $250,000 from the Cash Collateral Account and may use such funds for its own corporate purposes. From time to time, and so long as there is not Event of Default hereunder, TPC may withdraw funds from the cash collateral account at the Bank and advance such funds to the Borrower by depositing such funds in the Borrower's account at the Bank for the purpose of implementing TPC Debt. At such time as TPC advances funds to the Borrower pursuant to TPC Debt, the Borrower shall execute one or more promissory notes to evidence TPC Debt and such note(s) shall be endorsed in favor of and delivered to the Bank. TPC Debt shall be fully subject and subordinate to the Loan, and the Bank and TPC have this day executed "TPC Subordination Agreement" in the form attached hereto as Exhibit L to evidence such subordination.

Section 2.11. Restructuring of Union Trust Debt. TPC shall restructure its existing indebtedness with Union Trust Company as follows: (a) the line of credit shall not exceed $1,000,000; (b) the maturity date thereof shall be no earlier than July 31, 2002; and (c) Union Trust shall not have received any security interest in the assets of the Borrower or TPC Loan (or the proceeds thereof). TPC shall provide written evidence of such debt restructuring in form satisfactory to the Bank on or before August 30, 2001.

Section 2.12. Confirmation of Subsidiary Debt. As of the date hereof, the Borrower shall provide written confirmation to the Bank, in form satisfactory to the Bank, that TDC debt to the Boston Five Cents Savings Bank has been extended on a term basis for not less than one year, that such debt does not exceed $598,000, that the Borrower has guaranteed the interest but not the principal thereof, and that the collateral securing the loan is set forth on a schedule submitted to and approved by the Bank.

Section 3. Use of Proceeds and Payments

Section 3.1. Use of Proceeds. The Borrower has used and shall continue to use the proceeds of the Revolving Loan for its general working capital purposes.

Section 3.2. Payment. All payments of commitment fees, fees for letters of credit, service fees, activity charges, and all payments and prepayments of principal and all payments of interest shall be made by the Borrower to the Bank in immediately available funds at the head office of the Bank in Boston, Massachusetts 02108. The Borrower hereby authorizes the Bank, without any further notice, to charge any account the Borrower maintains at the Bank for each payment due hereunder or under the Note (for interest, fees, service charges, activity charges, principal, or otherwise) on the due date thereof, provided that the Bank shall not charge any account in which the Borrower is acting as agent or trustee for any other person.

Section 3.3. Regular Activity Charges. The Borrower shall pay to the Bank, on a monthly basis, the Bank's usual activity charges for banking services which such charges may be payable by maintaining adequate balances or by payment of a deficiency fee.

Section 4. Representations and Warranties of the Borrower

The Borrower represents and warrants that:

Section 4.1. Corporate Authority.

(a) *Incorporation; Good Standing.* The Borrower is a corporation duly organized, validly existing, and in good standing under the laws of the Commonwealth of Massachusetts, and has all requisite corporate power to own its property and conduct its business as now conducted and as presently contemplated.

(b) *Authorization.* The execution, delivery, and performance of this Agreement, the Note, the Security Agreement, the Assignment, and the transactions contemplated hereby and thereby (i) are within the authority of the Borrower; (ii) have been authorized by the Board of Directors of the Borrower; and (iii) will not contravene any provision of law, or the Borrower's Articles of Organization, By-Laws, or any other agreement, instrument, or undertaking binding upon the Borrower;

Section 4.2. Governmental and Other Approvals. The execution, delivery, and performance of this Agreement, the Note, the Security Agreement, the Assignment, and the transactions contemplated hereby and thereby by the Borrower: (a) do not require any approval or consent of, or filling with, any governmental agency or authority in the United States of America or otherwise which has not been obtained and which is not in full force and effect as of the date hereof; and (b) do not require any approval or consent of any security holder of the Borrower.

EXHIBIT 3 (*Continued*)

Section 4.3. Title to Properties; Absence of Liens. The Borrower has good and valid title to all of the Collateral free from all defects, liens, charges, and encumbrances.

Section 4.4. No Default. The Borrower is not in default in any material respect under provision of its Articles of Organization, or any provisions of any material contract, agreement, or obligation, exclusive of leases (whether related to the Loans or otherwise), which default could result in a significant impairment of the ability of the Borrower to fulfill its obligations hereunder or under the Note or the Loan Documents or a significant impairment of the financial position or business of the Borrower.

Section 4.5. Margin Regulations. The Borrower is not in the business of extending credit for the purpose of purchasing or carrying margin stock (within the meaning of Regulation G or Regulation U of the Board of Governors of the Federal Reserve System) and no portion of any Loan made to the Borrower hereunder has been or will be used, directly or indirectly, by the Borrower to purchase or carry or to extend credit to others for the purpose of purchasing or carrying any margin stock.

Section 4.6. Financial Statements. The Borrower has furnished to the Bank an audited balance sheet and statement of income and changes in financial position of the Borrower for the period ended September 30, 2000 (the September 2000 Report), and an internally prepared income statement for the interim period ending May, 31 2001 (May 2001 Report), which has been certified to be true, accurate, and complete by the chief financial officer of the Borrower. The balance sheets, income statements, and statements of changes in financial position set forth in the "September 2000 Report" and the "May 2001 Report" presents fairly the financial position of the Borrower as at the date thereof.

Section 4.7. Changes. To the best of the Borrower's knowledge, since the September 2000 Report and the May 2001 Report, there has been no material change in the assets, liabilities, financial condition, or business of the Borrower which taken together would have a material, adverse effect on the net worth therein reported.

Section 4.8. Taxes Except as set forth in Schedule ___ of the Merger Agreement, the Borrower has filed all United States Federal and State income tax returns and all other state, federal, or local tax returns required to be filed and the Borrower and its Subsidiaries have paid or made adequate provision for the payment of all taxes, assessments, and other governmental charges due. The Borrower knows of no basis for any material additional assessment with respect to any fiscal year for which adequate reserves have not been established.

Section 4.9. Litigation. Except as set forth in Exhibit 3.18 of the Merger Agreement, there is no material litigation pending or, to the knowledge of its officers, threatened against the Borrower, or any of the Individual Guarantors.

Section 5. Representation and Warranties of TPC and TRC

Each of the Corporate Guarantors warrants and represents as to itself as follows:

Section 5.1. Corporate Authority.

(a) *Incorporation; Good Standing.* Each corporation is a corporation duly organized, validly existing, and in good standing under the law of Delaware and has all requisite corporate power to own its property and conduct its business as now conducted and as presently contemplated.

(b) *Authorization.* The execution, delivery, and performance of this Agreement, and the transactions contemplated hereby and thereby, (i) are within the authority of such corporation; (ii) have been authorized by the Board of such corporation; and (iii) will not contravene any provision of law, or Articles of Organization, By-Laws, or any other agreement, instrument, or undertaking binding upon such corporation;

Section 5.2. Governmental and Other Approvals. The execution, delivery, and performance of this Agreement, and the transactions contemplated hereby and thereby by the Corporate Guarantors, (a) do not require any approval or consent of, or filing with, any governmental agency or authority in the United States of America or otherwise which has not been obtained and which is not in full force and effect as of the date hereof; and (b)do not require any approval or consent of any security holder of such corporations.

Section 5.3. Title to Properties; Absence of Liens. TRC has good and valid title to all of the collateral described in the TRC Security Agreement free from all defects, liens, charges, and encumbrances. TPC has good and valid title to the shares of the Borrower described in the TPC Pledge of Stock Agreement.

Section 5.4. No Default. Such corporation is not in default in any material respect under any provision of its Articles of Organization, or any provisions of any material contract, agreement, or obligation (whether related to the Loans or otherwise), which default could result in a significant impairment of the ability of such corporation to fulfill its obligations hereunder or any of the Loan Documents or a significant impairment of the financial position or business of such corporation.

Section 5.5. Financial Statements. TPC has furnished to the Bank a copy of its audited Consolidated Balance Sheet and Consolidated Statement of Operations for the period ended December 31, 2000 (the December 2000 Report), and for the interim period ending March 31, 2001 (March 2001 Report), which have been certified to be true, accurate, and complete by the chief financial officer of the Borrower. The Consolidated Balance Sheets, and Consolidated Statement of Operations set forth in the December 2000 Report and the March 2002 Report, presents fairly the financial position of TPC as at the dates thereof.

EXHIBIT 3 (*Continued*)

Section 5.6. Changes. Since the December 2000 Report and the March 2001 Report there has been no material change in the assets, liabilities, financial condition, or business of TPC which taken together would have a material, adverse effect on the net worth therein reported except as previously reported to the Bank in the May 31, 2001, interim Report.

Section 5.7. Taxes. TRC and its Subsidiaries have filed all United States Federal and State income tax returns and all other state, federal, or local tax returns required to be filed, and TPC and its Subsidiaries have paid or made adequate provision for the payment of all taxes, assessments, and other governmental charges due. TPC knows of no basis for any material additional assessment with respect to any fiscal year for which adequate reserves have not been established.

Section 5.8. Litigation. Except as set forth in TPC Form 10K dated as of December 31, 2000, there is no material litigation pending or, to the knowledge of its officers, threatened against either of the Corporate Guarantors.

Section 6. Conditions Precedent to Loans

Section 6.1. Conditions Precedent to Each Advance. The obligation of the Bank to continue to make future Revolving Loan advances and to issue additional letters of credit shall be subject to the performance by the Borrower of all its agreements heretofore to be performed by it and to the satisfaction, prior to or at the time of making each such advances, of the following conditions ("Conditions Precedent"):

(a) *First Advance.* Prior to the Bank's making the first advance after the date hereof, the Borrower shall provide to the Bank and the Bank shall have approved (i) evidence of compliance with the provisions of Section 2.10 and 2.12 hereof; (ii) internally prepared financial statements of TPC and TRC as of May 31, 2001, certified as accurate by the chief financial officer of such corporation; (iii) copies of all documents executed in connection with the Merger Agreement, including all exhibits and schedules thereto; (iv) copies of all documents by which TPC has generated or raised the amount of TPC Debt; (v) fully executed Loan Documents; (vi) certified or original copies of all corporate votes, consents, and authorizations necessary to implement this Agreement; and (vii) such other documents, certificates, instruments, and opinions as the Bank may reasonably require.

(b) *Authorized Signatures.* The Borrower shall have certified to the Bank the name and a specimen signature of each officer of the Borrower, authorized to sign requests for loan advances, borrowing certificates, or applications for letters of credit. The Bank may rely conclusively on such certification until it receives notice in writing to the contrary from the Borrower;

(c) *Corporate Action.* The Bank shall have received duly certified copies of all votes passed or other corporate action taken by the Board of Directors of the Borrower with respect to the Loan;

(d) *No Adverse Development.* Neither the consolidated financial position nor the business as a whole of the Borrower or the Corporate Guarantors, nor any substantial portion of the properties and assets of the Borrower or the Corporate Guarantors shall have been materially adversely affected between the date of application and the date of any advanced hereunder as a result of any legislative or regulatory change or of any fire, explosion, tidal wave, flood, windstorm, earthquake, landslide, accident, condemnation, or governmental intervention, order of any court or governmental agency or commission, invalidity or expiration of any patent or patent license, act of God or of the public enemy or of armed forces, rebellion, strike, labor disturbance or embargo, or otherwise, whether or not insured against, which might impair materially the ability of the Borrower or Corporate Guarantors to fulfill punctually their obligations under this Agreement, the Note, the Loan Documents, and the Guarantee executed in connection herewith;

(e) *Legality.* The making of such Loans shall not contravene any law or rule or regulations thereunder or any Presidential Executive Order binding on the Borrower;

(f) *Representatives True; No Default or Event of Default and Compliance with Covenants.* The representations and warranties in Section 4 and 5 hereof and all other representations in writing made by or on behalf of the Borrower or the Corporate Guarantors in connection with the transactions contemplated by this Agreement shall be true in all material respects as of the date on which they were made and shall also be true in all material respects at and as of the time of the making of such Loans with the same effect as if made at and as of the time of the making of such Loans, no Event of Default or condition which with notice or the passage of time or both would constitute an Event of Default shall exist and each covenant set forth in this Agreement shall be fully compiled.

(g) *Fees and Expenses Paid.* Any expenses and other amounts due and payable in connection with the Loan prior to or on the date of such advance shall have been paid.

(h) *No Other Debt.* Except for the Subordinated Debt and trade debt incurred in the normal course of business, the Borrower shall not have incurred any additional debt.

(i) *Delivery of Assigned Notes.* All of the notes secured by the Assignment shall have been delivered to the Bank, duly endorsed, and the Borrower and the Bank shall not have been notified of any claims, offsets, or defenses to the enforceability of the notes asserted by the respective makers thereof.

(j) *Miscellaneous.* The Borrower shall have submitted to the Bank such other agreements, documents, and certificates, in form and substance satisfactory to the Bank, as the Bank in its sole discretion deems appropriate or necessary.

Section 7. Covenants

The Borrower covenants and agrees that from the date hereof and as long as the Bank has any obligation to make Loans or any indebtedness to the Bank is outstanding hereunder:

Section 7.1. Notices. It will promptly notify the Bank in writing of the occurrence of any act, event, or condition which constitutes or which after notice or lapse of time, or both, would constitute a failure to satisfy any Condition Precedent set forth in Section 6 or a breach of any Warranty or Representation contained in Section 4 or 5.

EXHIBIT 3 (*Continued*)

Section 7.2. Accuracy of Accounts. The amount of each Account shown on the books, records, and invoices of the Borrower represented as owing or to be owing by each account debtor is and will be the correct amount actually owing or to be owing by such Account Debtor. The Borrower has no knowledge of any impairment of the validity or collectibility of any of the Accounts and shall notify the Bank of any such fact immediately after the Borrower becomes aware of any such impairment.

Section 7.3. Receipt of Proceeds of Accounts

(a) All accounts receivable and all proceeds and collections therefrom received by the Borrower shall be held in trust by the Borrower for the Bank and shall not be commingled with any of the Borrower's other funds or deposited in any bank account of the Borrower other than the Loan Account.

(b) At such time as any advances made by the Bank pursuant hereto or any letters of credit are outstanding, the Borrower shall deliver to the Bank as and when received by the Borrower, and in the same form as so received, all checks, drafts, and other items which represent the Accounts and any proceeds and collections therefrom, each of which checks, drafts, and other items shall be endorsed to the Bank or as the Bank may otherwise specify from time to time and which shall be accompanied by remittance reports in form satisfactory to the Bank. In addition, the Borrower shall cause any wire or other electronic transfer of funds which constitutes the Accounts or proceeds therefrom to be directed to the Bank. The Bank may apply the proceeds thereof to the Obligations in such manner as the Bank may determine, in its direction.

(c) At the Bank's request, in the Bank's discretion, so long as any Loans are then outstanding, or so long as the Bank has any obligation to make future advances hereunder, the Borrower shall cause all checks, drafts, and other items which represent the Account and any proceeds and collections therefrom to be delivered by the Borrower's account debtors directly to a lock box, blocked account, or similar recipient over which the Bank has sole access and control. The Bank may apply the proceeds and collections so delivered to the Obligations in such manner as the Bank may determine, in its discretion.

Section 7.4. Status and Reports with Respect to Accounts Receivable and Inventory. At the Bank's request, either daily or weekly as determined by the Bank, the Borrower shall provide the Bank with a detailed report (in such form as the Bank may specify from time to time) of any of the following, and within two business days prior to the date on which such report is so provided: (i) a listing of the name and amounts of all Accounts and the aging thereof; (ii) a schedule of all inventory and the location thereof; (iii) all allowances, adjustments, returns, and repossessions concerning the Accounts, account receivables, or inventory; (iv) any downgrading in the quality of any of the inventory or occurrence of any event which has an adverse effect upon such inventory's merchantability; and

Section 7.5. Monthly Receivables and Inventory Reports. Monthly, within fifteen (15) days following the end of the previous month (unless the Bank shall request such reports on a more frequent basis), the Borrower shall provide the Bank with:

(a) A listing and aging of the Borrower's Accounts as of the end of the subject month; and

(b) A reconciliation of the Accounts with payments received as of the end of the month;

(c) A certificate listing the Borrower's inventory, in such form as the Bank may specify from time to time, as of the end of such month;

Section 7.6. Schedule of Collateral. At such intervals as the Bank may indicate from time to time by written notice given the Borrower, the Borrower shall provide the Bank with a schedule (in such form as the Bank may specify from time to time) of all Collateral which has come into existence since the date of the last such schedule.

Section 7.7. Financial Statements. It will furnish, or cause to be furnished, to the Bank:

(a) Within ninety (90) days after the end of each fiscal year, the consolidating balance sheet of the Borrower, TPC, and TRC as at the end of, and the related consolidated and consolidating statement of operations and consolidated and consolidating statement of changes in financial position for, such year certified by independent certified public accountants satisfactory to the Bank, together with a written statement by the accountants certifying such financial statements to the effect that in the course of the audit upon which their certification of such financial statements was based, they obtained knowledge of no condition or event relating to financial matters which constitutes or which with notice or the passage of time, or both, would constitute an Event of Default under this Agreement, or, if such accountants shall have obtained in the course of such audit knowledge of any such condition or event, they shall disclose in such written statement the nature and period of existence thereof, provided that the consolidating statements need not be audited and may be internally prepared and certified as accurate by the chief financial officer of TPC;

(b) Within twenty (20) days after the end of each month, the balance sheet of the Borrower, TPC, and TRC as at the end of such month, and the related statements of operations for the portion of the Borrower's, TPC's, and TRC's fiscal years then elapsed, in each case certified by the principal financial officer of the Borrower, TPC, and TRC as constituting a fair presentation of the Borrower's, TPC's, and TRC's respective financial positions as of such date;

(c) By June 30th of each year, personal financial statements of the Individual Guarantors and Seller, prepared as of May 31st of such year, satisfactory to the Bank and certified as accurate by the Individual Guarantors and by a partner of Seller.

(d) Within a reasonable period of time, and from time to time, such other financial data and information (including accountant's management letters) as the Bank may reasonably request provided that the Borrower, TPC, and TRC shall not be required to furnish any further financial data in audited form unless such materials have been prepared in audited form apart from the Lender's request thereof.

The Bank shall use reasonable care to treat such information as being confidential, but the Bank shall have the unrestricted right to use such information in all ways in the enforcement of the Bank's rights against the Borrower or TPC.

EXHIBIT 3 (*Continued*)

The financial statements referred to above in this Section shall be prepared in accordance with generally accepted accounting principles in force at the time of the preparation thereof.

Section 7.8. Legal Existence; Maintenance of Properties; Ownership of Assets. The Borrower and Corporate Guarantors will do or cause to be done all things necessary to preserve and keep in full force and effect their legal existence, rights, and franchises. The Borrower will cause all of its properties used or useful in the conduct of its business to be maintained and kept in good condition, repair, and working order and supplied with all necessary equipment and will cause to be made all necessary repairs, renewals, replacements, betterments, and improvements thereof, all as may be reasonably necessary so that the business carried on in connection therewith may be properly and advantageously conducted at all times.

Section 7.9. Conduct of Business Etc. The Borrower will continue to engage solely in the businesses now conducted by it and in businesses directly related thereto.

Section 7.10. Use of Revolver. Advances under the Revolving Loan shall be used for general working capital purposes of the Borrower, but in no event shall such advances be used to acquire Subsidiaries, to purchase new stores, or to open new company owned stores, it being expressly understood that any new stores shall be financed with additional equity; provided, however, that upon the prior written approval of the Bank which shall not be unreasonably withheld or delayed, the Borrower may use a portion of the Loan, not to exceed $25,000 per store, to purchase or repurchase existing TDC stores, up to a maximum of four stores.

Section 7.11. Deposit Account. In order to perfect the Bank's security interest in the Borrower's assets, the Borrower shall maintain its principal depository and checking accounts at the Bank, including, without limitation, the account representing the proceeds of TPC Debt, when implemented.

Section 7.12. Compliance with Franchise Agreements. The Borrower shall comply with all of the terms and conditions of its various franchise agreements.

Section 7.13. Books and Records. The Borrower shall keep true records and books of account in which full, true, and correct entries will be made of all dealings or transactions in relation to its business and affairs in accordance with generally accepted accounting principals.

Section 7.14. Negative Covenants. The Borrower does hereby covenant and agree with the Bank that, so long as any of the Obligations remain unsatisfied or any commitments hereunder remain outstanding, it will comply, and it will cause its Subsidiaries to comply, at all times with the following negative covenants, unless the Bank shall otherwise have agreed in writing:

(a) The Borrower will not change its name, enter into any merger, consolidation, reorganization, or recapitalization, or reclassify its capital stock, provided that nothing herein shall preclude the Borrower from changing the name of any of its product lines;

(b) The Borrower will not sell, transfer, lease, or otherwise dispose of all or (except in the ordinary course of business and except for obsolete or useless assets) any material part of its assets;

(c) The Borrower will not sell, lease, transfer, assign, or otherwise dispose of any of the Collateral except in the ordinary course of business (and except for obsolete or useless assets), provided that nothing herein shall preclude the Borrower from terminating unproductive or defaulting franchisees so long as the Borrower gives the Bank prior written notice of such intended action;

(d) The Borrower will not sell or otherwise dispose of, or for any reason cease operating, any of its divisions, franchises, or lines of business;

(e) The Borrower will not mortgage, pledge, grant, or permit to exist a security interest in, or a lien upon, any of its assets of any kind, now owned or hereafter acquired, except for those existing on the date hereof;

(f) The Borrower will not become liable, directly or indirectly, as guarantor or otherwise for any obligation of any other Person, except for the endorsement of commercial paper for deposit or collection in the ordinary course of business and except for guarantees of franchisees' leases in the normal course of business;

(g) The Borrower will not incur, create, assume, or permit to exist any Indebtedness except: (1) the Loan; (2) the Subordinated Debt; (3) trade indebtedness incurred in the ordinary course of business (provided, however, that the Borrower may not acquire inventory other than for cash or on open account except as expressly approved in writing and in advance by the Bank);

(h) The Borrower will not declare or pay any dividends, or make any other payment or distribution on account of its capital stock, or make any assignment or transfer of accounts, or other than in the ordinary course of business or inventory;

(i) The Borrower will not form any subsidiary, make any investment in (including any assignment of inventory or other property), or make any loan in the nature of an investment to any Person, provided that nothing herein shall prohibit the Borrower from converting franchisees' accounts receivable into term notes in which event such notes shall be endorsed in favor of and delivered to the Bank as additional Collateral hereunder.

(j) The Borrower will not make any loan or advance to any officer, shareholder, director, or employee of the Borrower, except for business travel and similar temporary advances in the ordinary course of business.

(k) The Borrower will not issue, redeem, purchase, or retire any of its capital stock or grant or issue, or purchase or retire for any consideration, any warrant, right, or option pertaining thereto or other security convertible into any of the foregoing, or permit any transfer, sale, redemption, retirement, or other change in the ownership of the outstanding capital stock of the Borrower;

EXHIBIT 3 (*Continued*)

(l) Except as permitted in the Subordination Agreement, the Borrower will not prepay any Subordinated Debt or indebtedness for borrowed money (except the Loan) or enter into or modify any agreement as a result of which the terms of payment of any of the foregoing Indebtedness are waived or modified;

(m) The Borrower will not acquire or agree to acquire any stock, in all or substantially all of the assets, of any Person; and

(n) The Borrower will not amend its lease of the premises at 385 Appleton Street, North Andover, Massachusetts, in such a way as to increase the rent or other monetary obligations due thereunder.

(o) The Borrower will not furnish the Bank any certificate or other document that will contain any untrue statement of material fact or that will omit to state a material fact necessary to make it not misleading in light of the circumstances under which it was furnished.

Section 7.15. TPC Covenants. So long as the Loan shall remain outstanding or Bank shall have any obligation to make future advances, TPC shall not (i) transfer, convey, sell, assign, hypothecate, grant a security interest in, or pledge any of the shares of the Borrower or all, or substantially all, of the assets of the Borrower; (ii) cause the Borrower to pay any dividends otherwise distribute cash or other assets to TPC, provided that TPC may cause the Borrower to distribute not more than $250,000 in the aggregate in any twelve month period by way of dividends, distributions, or salary to TPC and/or its officers and employees; or (iii)permit any transactions involving the stock of TPC which individually or in the aggregate shall cause a change of control or of management of TPC.

Section 8. Events of Default

Without derogating from the DEMAND nature of the Note and the Credit Facility, if any of the following events shall occur:

Section 8.1. If the Borrower shall fail to pay an installment of interest or of principal on the Note due hereunder on or before the due date thereof, if the Borrower shall fail to reduce the outstanding principal balance of the Loan as provided in Section 2.1 hereof, or if the full principal balance of the Note is not paid on the Loan Review Date (or such earlier date upon which such balance may become due and payable following an Event of Default) or on the making of demand by the Bank.

Section 8.2. If the Borrower shall fail in any material respect to perform within ten (10) days following written notice from the Bank any term, covenant, or agreement contained in Section 7 hereof, provided, however, that if such default is susceptible of cure but may not be cured within ten days, the Borrower shall commence to cure such default within ten days after notice thereof and shall proceed continuously and diligently to complete such cure but in any event within thirty (30) days of the date of such notice.

Section 8.3. If any representation or warranty of the Borrower in Section 4 or of the Corporate Guarantors in Section 5 hereof or in any certificate delivered hereunder shall prove to have been false in any material respect upon the date when made;

Section 8.4. If the Borrower shall fail to perform any other term, covenant, or agreement herein contained or contained in any Loan Documents, as amended, for ten (10) days after written notice of such failure has been given to the Borrower by the Bank, provided, however, that if such default is susceptible of cure but may not be cured within ten (10) days, the Borrower shall commence to cure such default with ten (10) days after notice thereof and shall proceed continuously and diligently to complete such cure but in any event within thirty (30) days of the date of such notice.

Section 8.5. If the Borrower, or any Guarantor, shall (i) apply for or consent to the appointment of, or the taking of possession by, a receiver, custodian, trustee, or liquidator of itself or of all or a substantial part of its property; (ii) admit in writing his or its inability, or generally unable, to pay his or its debts as such debts become due; (iii) make a general assignment for the benefit of its creditors; (iv) commence a voluntary case under the Federal Bankruptcy Code (as now or hereafter in effect); (v) file a petition seeking to take advantage of any other law relating to bankruptcy, insolvency, reorganization, winding-up, or composition or adjustment of debts; (vi) with respect to any Individual Guarantor, die, or become legally incompetent or incapacitated; (vii) with respect to any Corporate Guarantor dissolve or liquidate; (viii) fail to convert in a timely or appropriate manner, or acquiesce in writing to, any petition filed against the Borrower or any Corporate Guarantor in an involuntary case under such Bankruptcy Code; or (ix) take any corporate action for the purpose of effecting any of the foregoing; or

Section 8.6. If a proceeding or case shall be commenced without the application or consent of the Borrower in any court of competent jurisdiction seeking (i) the liquidation, reorganization, dissolution, winding-up, or composition or re-adjustment of debts, of the Borrower or any Corporate Guarantor; (ii) the appointment of a trustee, receiver, custodian, liquidator, or the like of the Borrower or any Corporate Guarantor or of all or any substantial part of its assets; (iii) similar relief in respect of the Borrower or any Corporate Guarantor under any law relating to bankruptcy, insolvency, reorganization, winding-up, or composition or adjustment of debts, and such proceeding or case shall continue undismissed, or an order, judgment, or decree approving or ordering any of the foregoing shall be entered or an order of relief against the Borrower or any Corporate Guarantor shall be entered in an involuntary case under such Bankruptcy Code;

Then, and in every such event (an "Event of Default"): the Commitments of the Banks hereunder (if then outstanding) shall forthwith terminate and the principal of and interest on the Loans (if any are then outstanding) shall be and become forthwith due and payable in each case all without presentment or demand for payment, notice of nonpayment, protest, or further notice or demand of any kind, all of which are expressly waived by the Borrower. No remedy herein conferred upon the holder of the Note is intended to be exclusive of any other remedy and each and every remedy shall be cumulative and shall be in addition to every other remedy given hereunder or under any other agreement or now or hereafter existing at law or in equity or by statute or any other provision of law.

EXHIBIT 3 (*Continued*)

Section 9. Miscellaneous

Section 9.1. Notices. Any notice or other communication in connection with this Agreement shall be deemed to be delivered if in writing (or in the form of a telegram) addressed as provided below and if either (a) actually delivered at said address or (b) in the case of a letter, three business days shall have elapse after the same shall have been deposited in the United States mails, postage prepaid and registered or certified:

and in any case at such other address as the addressee shall have specified by written notice. All periods of notice shall be measured from the date of delivery thereof.

Section 9.2. Costs, Expenses, and Taxes. The Borrower agrees to pay, whether or not any of the transactions contemplated hereby are consummated, the reasonable out-of-pocket costs and expenses of the Bank in connection with the preparation, execution, delivery, and enforcement of this Agreement, and any amendments, waivers, or consents with respect to any of the foregoing.

Section 9.3. Lien; Set-Off. The Borrower grants to the Bank a direct and continuing lien and continuing security interest, as security for the performance of its obligations hereunder, in and upon all deposits, balances, and other sums credited by or due from the Bank to the Borrower. Regardless of the adequacy of any other collateral, if a demand has been made for the payment of the Note and has not been withdrawn, or if the Loan has otherwise become due and payable, any such deposits, balances, or other sums credited by or due from the Bank to the Borrower may at any time or from time to time, without notice to the Borrower or compliance with any other condition precedent now or hereafter imposed by statute, rule of law, or otherwise (all of which are hereafter expressly waived), be set off, appropriated, and applied by the Bank against any or all such obligation in such manner as the Bank in its discretion may determine; and, in addition, the Bank shall have the rights of a secured party under the Uniform Commercial Code with respect thereto.

Section 9.4. Cumulative Rights; Non-Waiver. All of the rights of the Bank hereunder and under the Note, the Loan Documents, and each other agreement now or hereafter executed in connection herewith, therewith, or otherwise, shall be cumulative and may be exercised singly, together, or in such combination as the Bank may determine in its sole judgment. No waiver or condonation of a breach on any one occasion shall be deemed to be a waiver or condonation in other instance.

Section 9.5. Governing Law. This Agreement and the rights and obligations of the parties hereunder and under the Loans shall be construed, interpreted, and determined in accordance with laws of the Commonwealth of Massachusetts.

Section 9.6. Successors and Assigns. This Agreement shall be binding upon the Borrower and its successors and assigns and shall be binding upon and inure to the benefit of the Bank and its successors and assigns; provided, however, that that Borrower may not assign any of its rights hereunder.

Section 9.7. Table of Contents; Title and Headings. Any table of contents, the titles of the Articles, and the headings of the Sections are not parts of this Agreement and shall not be deemed to affect the meaning or construction of any of its provisions.

Section 9.8. Counterparts. This Agreement may be executed in several counterparts, each of which when executed and delivered is an original, but all of which together shall constitute one instrument. In making proof of this Agreement, it shall not be necessary to produce or account for more than one such counterpart.

Section 9.9. Indemnification. The Borrower hereby agrees to indemnify the Bank and hold it harmless against any and all liabilities, obligations, loans, damages, penalties, actions, judgments, costs, or expenses of any kind whatsoever (including without limitation, reasonable attorneys fees and disbursements) that may be imposed on or incurred by or asserted against the Bank in any way relating to or arising out of or in connection with any of the transactions contemplated herein.

Section 9.10. Venue; Jury Trial. The Borrower and the Guarantors hereby agree that any action or proceeding involving this Agreement or any other agreement or document referred to herein, including the Note, may be brought in, and hereby expressly submit to the jurisdiction of, all state courts located in the Commonwealth of Massachusetts. To the extent permitted by applicable law, the Borrower and the Guarantors hereby waive trial by jury in any action on or with respect to this Agreement, the Note, or any other agreement with the Bank.

Section 9.11. Conflicting Provisions. In the event that any provision, term, and condition of any of the Loan Documents shall conflict with any of the provisions, terms, and conditions of this Agreement, the provisions, terms, and conditions set forth herein shall prevail.

IN WITNESS WHEREOF, the parties hereto have executed this Agreement as of the 8th day of August, 2001, by their respective officers hereunto duly authorized.

V

PART FIVE

Startup and Beyond

Under conditions of rapid growth, entrepreneurs face unusual paradoxes and challenges as their companies grow and the management modes required by these companies change.

Whether they have the adaptability and resiliency in the face of swift developments to grow fast enough as managers and whether they have enough courage, wisdom, and discipline to balance controlled growth with growing fast enough to keep pace with the competition and industry turbulence will become crystal clear.

Entrepreneurs face enormous pressures and physical and emotional wear and tear during the rapid growth of their companies. It goes with the territory. Entrepreneurs after startup find that "it" has to be done now, that there is no room to falter, and that there are no "runners-up." Those who have a personal entrepreneurial strategy, who are healthy, who have their lives in order, and who know what they are signing up for fare better than those who do not.

Among all the stimulating and exceedingly difficult challenges entrepreneurs face—and can meet successfully—none is more liberating and exhilarating than a successful harvest. Perhaps the point is made besting one of the final lines of the musical *Oliver:* "In the end, all that counts is in the bank, in large amounts!"

Obviously, money is not the only thing, or everything. But money can ensure both independence and autonomy to do what you want to do, mostly on your terms, and can significantly increase the options and opportunities at your discretion. While value creation was the goal, the measure of success is wealth creation, and how one chooses to distribute and use that wealth. In effect, for entrepreneurs, net worth is the final scorecard of the value creation process.

Chapter Sixteen

Managing Rapid Growth: Entrepreneurship Beyond Startup

Bite off more than you can chew, and then chew it!

Roger Babson
Founder, Babson College

Results Expected

Upon completion of the chapter, you will have:

1. Examined how higher potential, rapidly growing ventures have invented new organizational paradigms to replace brontosaurus capitalism.
2. Studied how higher potential ventures "grow up big" and the special problems, organization, and leadership requirements of rapid growth.
3. Examined new research on the leading management practices that distinguish high growth companies.
4. Explored concepts of organizational culture and climate, and how entrepreneurial leaders foster favorable cultures.
5. Identified specific signals and clues that can alert entrepreneurial managers to impeding crises and approaches to solve these.
6. Analyzed the "EverNet Corporation" case study.

Inventing New Organizational Paradigms

At the beginning of this text we examined how nimble and fleet-footed entrepreneurial firms have supplanted aging corporate giants with new leadership approaches, a passion for value creation, and an obsession with opportunity that have been unbeatable in the marketplace for talent and ideas. These entrepreneurial ventures have experienced rapid to explosive growth and have become the investments of choice of the U.S. venture capital community.

Because of their innovative nature and competitive breakthroughs, entrepreneurial ventures have demonstrated a remarkable capacity to invent new paradigms of organization and management. They have abandoned the organizational practices and structures typical of the industrial giants from the post-World War II era to the 1990s. One could characterize those approaches thus: What they lacked in creativity and flexibility to deal with ambiguity and rapid change, they made up for with rules, structure, hierarchy, and quantitative analysis.

Special thanks to Ed Marram, entrepreneur, educator, and friend, for his lifelong commitment to studying and leading growing businesses and sharing his knowledge with the authors.

The epitome of this pattern is the Hay System, which by the 1980s became the leading method of defining and grading management jobs in large companies. Scoring high with "Hay points" was the key to more pay, a higher position in the hierarchy, and greater power. The criteria for Hay points include number of people who are direct reports, value of assets under management, sales volume, number of products, square feet of facilities, total size of one's operating and capital budget, and the like. One can easily see who gets ahead in such a system: Be bureaucratic, have the most people and largest budget, increase head count and levels under your control, and think up the largest capital projects. Missing in the criteria are all the basic components of entrepreneurship we have seen in this book: value creating, opportunity creating and seizing, frugality with resources, bootstrapping strategies, staged capital commitments, team building, achieving better fits, and juggling paradoxes.

Contrast the multilayered, hierarchical, military-like levels of control and command that characterize traditional capitalism with the common patterns among entrepreneurial firms: they are flat—often only one or two layers deep—adaptive, and flexible; they look like interlocking circles rather than ladders; they are integrative around customers and critical missions; they are learning- and influence-based rather than rank- and power-based. People lead more through influence and persuasion, which are derived from knowledge and performance rather than through formal rank, position, or seniority. They create a perpetual learning culture. They value people and share the wealth with people who help create it.

Entrepreneurial Leaders Are Not Administrators or Managers

In the growing business, owner-entrepreneurs focus on recognizing and choosing opportunities, allocating resources, motivating employees, and maintaining control —while encouraging the innovative actions that cause a business to grow. In a new venture the entrepreneur's immediate challenge is to learn how to dance with elephants without being trampled to death! Once beyond the startup phase, the ultimate challenge of the owner/manager is to develop the firm to the point where it is able to lead the elephants on the dance floor.

Consider the following quotes from two distinguished business leaders, based on their experiences with holders of MBAs in the 1960s–80s. Fred Smith, founder, chairman, and CEO of Federal Express: "MBAs are people in Fortune 500 companies who make careers out of saying no!"

According to General George Doriot, father of American venture capital and for years a professor at Harvard Business School, "There isn't any business that a Harvard MBA cannot analyze out of existence!"

Those are profound statements, given the sources. These perceptions also help to explain the stagnancy and eventual demise of brontosaurus capitalism. Legions of MBAs in the 1950s, 60s, 70s, and early 1980s were taught the old style model of management. Until the 1980s, virtually all the cases, problems, and lectures in MBA programs were about large, established companies.

Breakthrough Strategy: Babson's F. W. Olin Graduate School

The first MBA program in the world to break the lockstep of the prior 50 years was the Franklin W. Olin Graduate School of Business at Babson College. In 1992, practicing what they taught, faculty members discarded the traditional, functional approach to an MBA education, consisting of individual courses in accounting, marketing, finance, information technology, operations, and human resources in stand-alone sequence, with too many lectures.

A revolutionary curriculum for the first year of the MBA took its place: An entirely new and team-taught curriculum in a series of highly integrative modules anchored conceptually in the model of the entrepreneurial process from *New Venture Creation.*[1] MBAs now experience a unique learning curve that immerses them for the first year in cases, assignments, and content that has immediate and relevant applicability to the entrepreneurial process. Emerging entrepreneurial companies are the focal points for most case studies, while larger, established companies seeking to recapture their entrepreneurial spirit and management approach are examined in others. After more than five years, students, employers, and faculty have characterized the program as a resounding success. (See the Babson College Web site: www.babson.edu.)

Leading Practices of High Growth Companies[2]

In Chapter 3, we examined a summary of research conducted on fast growth companies to determine the leading practices of these firms. Now, this research

[1] See William Glavin, *The President's Report—1996* (Babson Park, MA: 1996), Babson College.
[2] Special appreciation is given to Ernst & Young LLP and The Kauffman Center for Entrepreneurial Leadership for permission to include the summary of their research here.

will likely take on new meaning to the reader. As one examines each of these four practice areas—marketing, finance, management, and planning—one can see the practical side of how fast growth entrepreneurs pursue opportunities; devise, manage, and orchestrate their financial strategies; build a team with collaborative decision making; and plan with vision, clarity, and flexibility. Clearly, rapid growth is a different game, requiring an entrepreneurial mind-set and skills.

Growing Up Big

Stages of Growth Revisited

Higher potential ventures do not stay small very long. While an entrepreneur may have done a good job of assessing an opportunity, forming a new venture team, marshaling resources, planning, and so forth, managing and growing such a venture is, a different managerial game.

Ventures in the high growth stage face the problems discussed in Chapter 7. These include forces that limit the creativities of the founders and team; that cause confusion and resentment over roles, responsibilities, and goals; that call for specialization and therefore erode collaboration; that require operating mechanisms and controls; and more.

Recall also that managers of rapidly growing ventures are usually relatively inexperienced in launching a new venture and yet face situations where time and change are compounded and where events are nonlinear and nonparametric. Usually, structures, procedures, and patterns are fluid, and decision making needs to follow counterintuitive and unconventional patterns.

Chapter 7 discussed the stages or phases companies experience during their growth. Recall that the first three years before startup are called the research-and-development (R&D) stage; the first three years, the startup stage; years 4 through 10, the early-growth stage; the 10th year through the 15th or so, maturity; and after the 15th year, stability stage. These time estimates are approximate and may vary somewhat.

Various models, and our previous discussion, depicted the life cycle of a growing firm as a smooth curve with rapidly ascending sales and profits and a leveling off toward the peak and then dipping toward decline.

In truth, however, very few, if any, new and growing firms experience such smooth and linear phases of growth. If the actual growth curves of new companies are plotted over their first 10 years, the curves will look far more like the ups and downs of a roller-coaster ride than the smooth progressions usually depicted. Over the life of a typical growing firm, there are periods of jerks, bumps, hiccups, indigestion, and renewal interspersed with periods of smooth sailing. Sometimes there is continual upward progress through all this, but with others, there are periods where the firms seem near collapse or at least in considerable peril. Ed Marram, an entrepreneur and educator for 20 years, characterizes the five stages of a firm as Wonder, Blunder, Thunder, Plunder, Asunder (see Exhibit 16.1). Wonder is the period that is filled with uncertainty about

EXHIBIT 16.1

Growth Stages

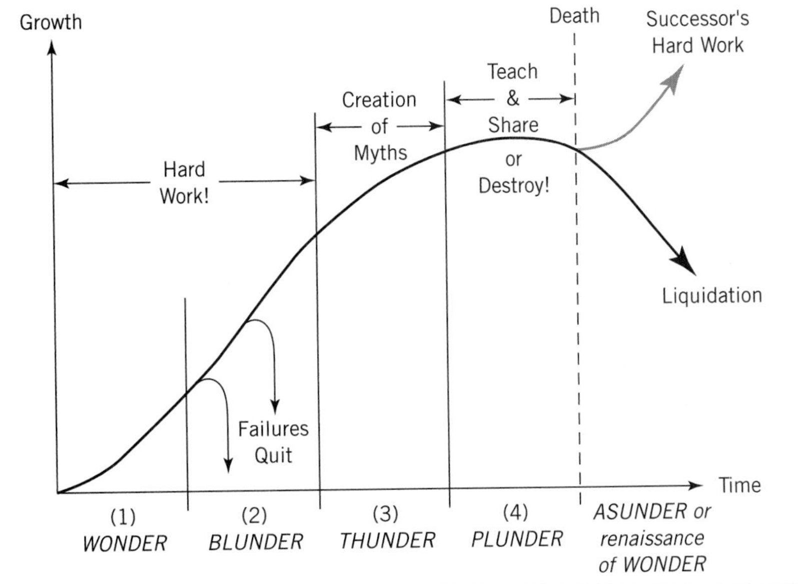

survival. Blunder is a growth stage when many firms stumble and fail. The Thunder stage occurs when growth is robust and the entrepreneur has built a solid management team. Cash flow is robust during Plunder, but in Asunder the firm needs to renew or will decline.

Core Management Mode

As was noted earlier, changes in several critical variables determine just how frantic or easy transitions from one stage to the next will be. As a result, it is possible to make some generalizations about the main management challenges and transitions that will be encountered as the company grows. The core management mode is influenced by the number of employees a firm has, which is in turn related to its dollar sales.[3]

Recall, as shown in Exhibit 7.3, that until sales reach approximately $5 million and employees number about 25, the core management mode is one of *doing*. Between $5 million and $15 million in sales and 25 to 75 employees, the core management mode is *managing*. When sales exceed $10 million and employees number over 75, the core management mode is *managing managers*. Obviously, these revenue and employment figures are broad generalities. The number of people is an indicator of the complexity of the management task, and suggests a new wall to be scaled, rather than a precise point.

To illustrate how widely sales per employee (SPE) can vary among established firms, consider Exhibit 16.2. Dell, by virtue of an online model and a tremendously effective supply chain management system, is generating over $923,000 in SPE, whereas a real estate–based service business like Sonesta is generating in the range of just $64,000 in SPE.

EXHIBIT 16.2

2004 Sales per Employee

Company	(000)
Dell	923.9
Delta Airlines	218.7
Raytheon	259.6
Home Depot	337.2
Gillette	378.0
Biogen	529.8
Costco	881.1
Nike	547.7
Sonesta International Hotels	63.7
Cisco	710.3
Juniper Networks	529.2
Yum Brands Restaurants	154.6
McDonalds	44.5
IBM	278.8
Sun Microsystems	320.3
Genentech	668.3
Bristol-Myers Squibb Co.	448.6
Citicorp	284.4
Sony Corporation	423.3
Wal Mart	171.4

Source: Capital IQ, via Yahoo! Finance. Used by permission of Capital IQ.

These numbers are boundaries, constantly moving as a result of inflation and competitive dynamics. Sales per employee (SPE) can illustrate how a company stacks up in its industry, but remember that the number is a relative measurement. In 2001 Siebel Systems' SPE was $560,532, while Sun Microsystems' SPE was $493,098. IT provider GTSI had an SPE of $1,300,871 and NVIDIA's SPE was $1,875,673.[4] Explosive sales per employee was one of the failed promises of the Internet, and to some extent the irrational dot.com valuations of the late 1990s were an anticipation of technology massively leveraging variable employee expense.

The central issue facing entrepreneurs in all sorts of businesses is this: As the size of the firm increases, the core management mode likewise *changes from doing to managing to managing managers*.

During each of the stages of growth of a firm, there are entrepreneurial crises, or hurdles, that most firms will confront. Exhibit 16.3 and the following discussion consider by stage some indications of crisis.[5] As the exhibit shows, for each fundamental driving force of entrepreneurship, a number of "signals" indicate crises are imminent. While the list is long, these are not the only indicators of crises—only the most common. Each of these signals does not necessarily indicate that particular crises will happen to every company at each stage, but when the signals are there, serious difficulties cannot be too far behind.

The Problem in Rate of Growth

Difficulties in recognizing crisis signals and developing management approaches are compounded by rate of growth itself. The faster the rate of growth, the greater the potential for difficulty; this is because of the various pressures, chaos, confusion, and loss of control. It is not an exaggeration to say that

[3] Harvey "Chet" Krentzman described this phenomenon to the authors many years ago. The principle still applies.
[4] Kim Cross, "Does Your Team Measure Up? Business 2.0" (www.business2.com), June 2001.
[5] The crises discussed here are the ones the authors consider particularly critical. Usually, failure to overcome even a few can imperil a venture at a given stage. There are, however, many more, but a complete treatment of all of them is outside the scope of this book.

EXHIBIT 16.3

Crises and Symptoms

Pre-Startup (Years −3 to −1)

Entrepreneurs:

- *Focus.* Is the founder really an entrepreneur, bent on building a company, or an inventor, technical dilettante, or the like?
- *Selling.* Does the team have the necessary selling and closing skills to bring in the business and make the plan—on time?
- *Management.* Does the team have the necessary management skills and relevant experience, or is it overloaded in one or two areas (e.g., the financial or technical areas)?
- *Ownership.* Have the critical decisions about ownership and equity splits been resolved, and are the members committed to these?

Opportunity:

- *Focus.* Is the business really user-, customer-, and market-driven (by a need), or is it driven by an invention or a desire to create?
- *Customers.* Have customers been identified with specific names, addresses, and phone numbers, and have purchase levels been estimated, or is the business still only at the concept stage?
- *Supply.* Are costs, margins, and lead times to acquire supplies, components, and key people known?
- *Strategy.* Is the entry plan a shotgun and cherry-picking strategy, or is it a rifle shot at a well-focused niche?

Resources:

- *Resources.* Have the required capital resources been identified?
- *Cash.* Are the founders already out of cash (OOC) and their own resources?
- *Business plan.* Is there a business plan, or is the team "hoofing it"?

Startup and Survival (Years 0 to 3)

Entrepreneurs:

- *Leadership.* Has a top leader been accepted, or are founders vying for the decision role or insisting on equality in all decisions?
- *Goals.* Do the founders share and have compatible goals and work styles, or are these starting to conflict and diverge once the enterprise is under way and pressures mount?
- *Management.* Are the founders anticipating and preparing for a shift from doing to managing and letting go—of decisions and control—that will be required to make the plan on time?

Opportunity:

- *Economics.* Are the economic benefits and payback to the customer actually being achieved, and on time?
- *Strategy.* Is the company a one-product company with no encore in sight?
- *Competition.* Have previously unknown competitors or substitutes appeared in the marketplace?
- *Distribution.* Are there surprises and difficulties in actually achieving planned channels of distribution on time?

Resources:

- *Cash.* Is the company facing a cash crunch early as a result of not having a business plan (and a financial plan)? That is, is it facing a crunch because no one is asking: When will we run out of cash? Are the owners' pocketbooks exhausted?
- *Schedule.* Is the company experiencing serious deviations from projections and time estimates in the business plan? Is the company able to marshall resources according to plan and on time?

Early Growth (Years 4 to 10)

Entrepreneurs:

- *Doing or managing.* Are the founders still just *doing,* or are they managing for results by a plan? Have the founders begun to delegate and let go of critical decisions, or do they maintain veto power over all significant decisions?
- *Focus.* Is the mind-set of the founders operational only, or is there some serious strategic thinking going on as well?

Opportunity:

- *Market.* Are repeat sales and sales to new customers being achieved on time, according to plan, and because of interaction with customers, or are these coming from the engineering, R&D, or planning group? Is the company shifting to a marketing orientation without losing its killer instinct for closing sales?
- *Competition.* Are price and quality being blamed for loss of customers or for an inability to achieve targets in the sales plan, while customer service is rarely mentioned?
- *Economics.* Are gross margins beginning to erode?

Resources:

- *Financial control.* Are accounting and information systems and control (purchasing orders, inventory, billing, collections, cost and profit analysis, cash management, etc.) keeping pace with growth and being there when they are needed?
- *Cash.* Is the company always out of cash—or nearly OOC, and is no one asking when it will run out, or is sure why or what to do about it?
- *Contacts.* Has the company developed the outside networks (directors, contacts, etc.) it needs to continue growth?

(Continued)

EXHIBIT 16.3 (concluded)

Crises and Symptoms

Maturity (Years 10 to 15 plus)

Entrepreneurs:

- *Goals.* Are the partners in conflict over control, goals, or underlying ethics or values?
- *Health.* Are there signs that the founders' marriages, health, or emotional stability are coming apart (i.e., are there extramarital affairs, drug and/or alcohol abuse, or fights and temper tantrums with partners or spouses)?
- *Teamwork.* Is there a sense of team building for a "greater purpose," with the founders now managing managers, or is there conflict over control of the company and disintegration?

Opportunity:

- *Economics/competition.* Are the products and/or services that have gotten the company this far experiencing unforgiving economics as a result of perishability, competitor blind sides, new technology, or off-shore competition, and is there a plan to respond?
- *Product encore.* Has a major new product introduction been a failure?
- *Strategy.* Has the company continued to cherry-pick in fast-growth markets, with a resulting lack of strategic definition (which opportunities to say no to)?

Resources:

- *Cash.* Is the firm OOC again?
- *Development/information.* Has growth gotten out of control, with systems, training, and development of new managers failing to keep pace?
- *Financial control.* Have systems continued to lag behind sales?

Harvest/Stability (Years 15 to 20 plus)

Entrepreneurs:

- *Succession/ownership.* Are there mechanisms in place to provide for management succession and the handling of very tricky ownership issues (especially family)?
- *Goals.* Have the partners' personal and financial goals and priorities begun to conflict and diverge? Are any of the founders simply bored or burned out, and are they seeking a change of view and activities?
- *Entrepreneurial passion.* Has there been an erosion of the passion for creating value through the recognition and pursuit of opportunity, or are turf-building, acquiring status and power symbols, and gaining control favored?

Opportunity:

- *Strategy.* Is there a spirit of innovation and renewal in the firm (e.g., a goal that half the company's sales come from products or services less than five years old), or has lethargy set in?
- *Economics.* Have the core economics and durability of the opportunity eroded so far that profitability and return on investment are nearly as low as that for the Fortune 500?

Resources:

- *Cash.* Has OOC been solved by increasing bank debt and leverage because the founders do not want—or cannot agree—to give up equity?
- *Accounting.* Have accounting and legal issues, especially their relevance for wealth building and estate and tax planning, been anticipated and addressed? Has a harvest concept been part of the long-range planning process?

these pressures and demands increase geometrically, rather than in a linear way (see discussion in Chapter 7).

Growth rates affect all aspects of a business. Thus, as sales increase, as more people are hired, and as inventory increases, sales outpace manufacturing capacity. Facilities are then increased, people are moved between buildings, accounting systems and controls cannot keep up, and so on. The cash burn rate accelerates. As such acceleration continues, learning curves do the same. Worst of all, cash collections lag behind, as shown in Exhibit 16.4.

Distinctive issues caused by rapid growth were considered at seminars at Babson College with the founders and presidents of rapidly growing companies—companies with sales of at least $1 million and growing in excess of 30 percent per year.[6] These founders and presidents pointed to the following:

- *Opportunity overload.* Rather than lacking enough sales or new market opportunities (a classic concern in mature companies) these firms faced an abundance. Choosing from among these was a problem.

[6] These seminars were held at Babson College near Boston in 1985 and 1999. A good number of the firms represented had sales over $1 million, and many were growing at greater than 100 percent per year.

EXHIBIT 16.4

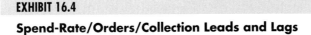

Spend-Rate/Orders/Collection Leads and Lags

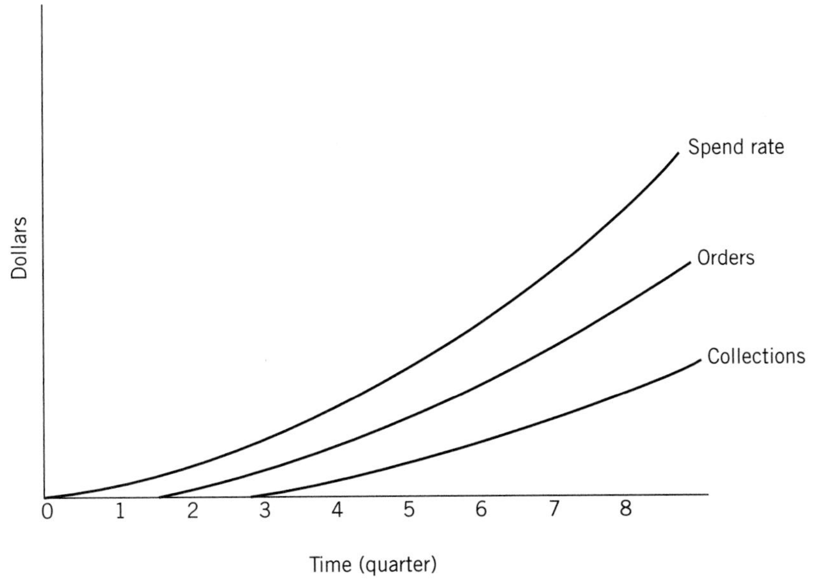

- *Abundance of capital.* While most stable or established smaller or medium-size firms often have difficulties obtaining equity and debt financing, most of the rapidly growing firms were not constrained by this. The problem was, rather, how to evaluate investors as "partners" and the terms of the deals with which they were presented.
- *Misalignment of cash burn and collection rates.* These firms all pointed to problems of cash burn rates racing ahead of collections. They found that unless effective integrated accounting, inventory, purchasing, shipping, and invoicing systems and controls are in place, this misalignment can lead to chaos and collapse. One firm, for example, had tripled its sales in three years from $5 million to $16 million. Suddenly, its president resigned, insisting that, with the systems that were in place, the company would be able to grow to $100 million. However, the computer system was disastrously inadequate, which compounded other management weaknesses. It was impossible to generate any believable financial and accounting information for many months. Losses of more than $1 million annually mounted, and the company's lenders panicked. To make matters worse, the auditors failed to stay on top of the situation until it was too late and were replaced. While the company has survived, it has had to restructure its business and has shrunk to $6 million in sales, to pay off bank debt and to avoid bankruptcy. Fortunately, it is recovering.
- *Decision making.* Many of the firms succeeded because they executed functional day-to-day and week-to-week decisions, rather than strategizing. Strategy had to take a back seat. Many of the representatives of these firms argued that in conditions of rapid growth, strategy was only about 10 percent of the story.
- *Expanding facilities and space . . . and surprises.* Expansion of space or facilities is a problem and one of the most disrupting events during the early explosive growth of a company. Managers of many of these firms were not prepared for the surprises, delays, organizational difficulties, and system interruptions that are spawned by such expansion.

Industry Turbulence

The problems just discussed are compounded by the amount of industry turbulence surrounding the venture. Firms with higher growth rates are usually found in industries that are also developing rapidly. In addition, there are often many new entrants, both with competing products or services and with substitutes.

The effects are many. Often, prices fluctuate. The turbulence in the semiconductor industry in the 1980s is a good example. From June 1984 to June 1985, the

EXHIBIT 16.5

How the Mighty Have Fallen

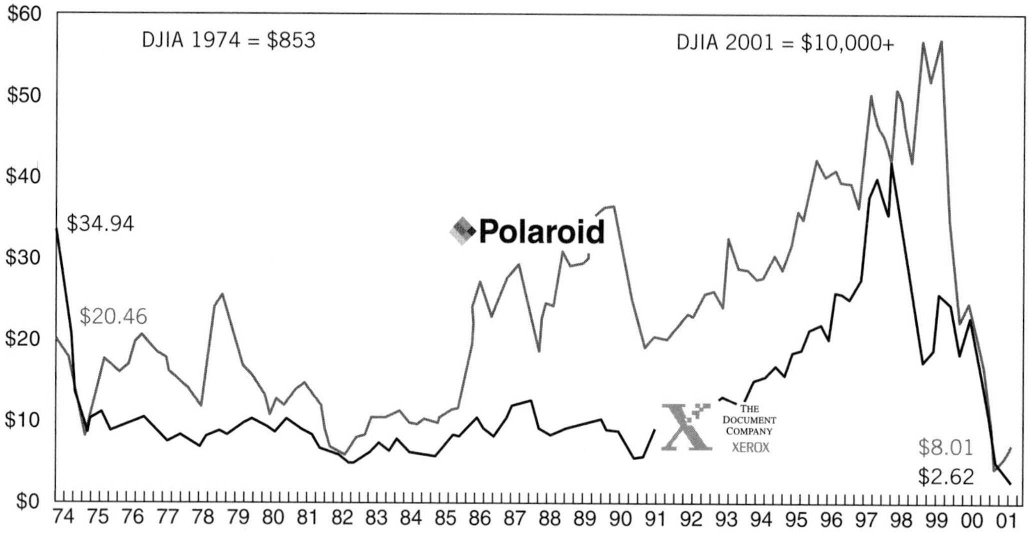

Source: The authors wish to thank Ed Marram for sharing this analysis.

price to original equipment manufacturers (OEMs) of 64K memory chips fell from $2.50 each to 50 cents. The price to OEMs of 256K chips fell from $15 to $3. The same devastating industry effect manifested in the years 2000–2002 when cellular airtime pricing plunged by more than 50 percent. Imagine the disruption this caused in marketing and sales projections, in financial planning and cash forecasting, and the like, for firms in these industries. Often, too, there are rapid shifts in cost and experience curves. The consequences of missed steps in growing business are profound. Consider the examples of Polaroid and Xerox shown in Exhibit 16.5.

The Importance of Culture and Organizational Climate

Six Dimensions

The organizational culture and climate, either of a new venture or of an existing firm, are critical in how well the organization will deal with growth. Studies of performance in large businesses that used the concept of organizational climate (i.e., the perceptions of people about the kind of place it is to work) have led to two general conclusions.[7] First, the climate of an organization can have a significant impact on performance. Further, climate is created both by the expectations people bring to the organization and by the practices and attitudes of the key managers.

The climate notion has relevance for new ventures, as well as for entrepreneurial efforts in large organizations. An entrepreneur's style and priorities—particularly how he or she manages tasks and people—are well known by the people being managed and affect performance. Recall the entrepreneurial climate described by Enrico of Pepsi, where the critical factors included setting high performance standards by developing short-run objectives that would not sacrifice long-run results, providing responsive personal leadership, encouraging individual initiative, helping others to succeed, developing individual networks for success, and so forth. Or listen to the tale of Gerald H. Langeler, the president of the systems group of Mentor Graphics Corporation, who explained what "the vision trap" was.[8] Langeler described the vision of his company's entrepreneurial climate as simply to "Build Something People Will Buy."[9] The culture of Mentor Graphics was definitely shaped by the founders' styles because "there were perhaps 15 of us at the time—we could not only share information very

[7] See Jeffry A. Timmons, "The Entrepreneurial Team: Formation and Development," a paper presented at the Academy of Management annual meeting, Boston, August 1973.
[8] Gerald H. Langeler, "The Vision Trap," *Harvard Business Review*, March–April 1992, reprint 92204.
[9] Ibid., p. 4.

quickly, we could also create a sense of urgency and purpose without the help of an articulated vision."[10]

Evidence suggests that superior teams function differently than inferior teams in their setting priorities, in resolving leadership issues, in what and how roles are performed by team members, in attitudes toward listening and participation, and in dealing with disagreements. Further, evidence suggests that specific approaches to management can affect the climate of a growing organization. For example, gains from the motivation, commitment, and teamwork, which are anchored in a consensus approach to management, while not immediately apparent, are striking later. At that time, there is swiftness and decisiveness in actions and in follow-through, since the negotiating, compromising, and accepting of priorities are history. Also, new disagreements that emerge generally do not bring progress to a halt because there is both high clarity and broad acceptance of overall goals and underlying priorities. Without this consensus, each new problem or disagreement often necessitates a time-consuming and painful confrontation and renegotiation simply because it was not done initially.

Organizational climate can be described along six basic dimensions:

- *Clarity.* The degree of organizational clarity in terms of being well organized, concise, and efficient in the way that tasks, procedures, and assignments are made and accomplished.
- *Standards.* The degree to which management expects and puts pressure on employees for high standards and excellent performance.
- *Commitment.* The extent to which employees feel committed to the goals and objectives of the organization.
- *Responsibility.* The extent to which members of the organization feel responsibility for accomplishing their goals without being constantly monitored and second-guessed.
- *Recognition.* The extent to which employees feel they are recognized and rewarded (nonmonetarily) for a job well done, instead of only being punished for mistakes or errors.
- *Esprit de corps.* The extent to which employees feel a sense of cohesion and team spirit, of working well together.

Approaches to Management

In achieving the entrepreneurial culture and climate described above, certain approaches to management (also discussed in Chapter 7) are common across core management modes.

[10] Ibid., p. 5.

Leadership No single leadership pattern seems to characterize successful ventures. Leadership may be shared, or informal, or a natural leader may guide a task. What is common, however, is a manager who defines and gains agreements on who has what responsibility and authority and who does what with and to whom. Roles, tasks, responsibilities, accountabilities, and appropriate approvals are defined.

There is no competition for leadership in these organizations, and leadership is based on expertise, not authority. Emphasis is placed on performing task-oriented roles, but someone invariably provides for "maintenance" and group cohesion by good humor and wit. Further, the leader does not force his or her own solution on the team or exclude the involvement of potential resources. Instead, the leader understands the relationships among tasks and between the leader and his or her followers and is able to lead in those situations where it is appropriate, including managing actively the activities of others through directions, suggestions, and so forth.

This approach is in direct contrast to the commune approach, where two to four entrepreneurs, usually friends or work acquaintances, leave unanswered such questions as who is in charge, who makes the final decisions, and how real differences of opinion are resolved. While some overlapping of roles and a sharing in and negotiating of decisions are desirable in a new venture, too much looseness is debilitating.

This approach also contrasts with situations where a self-appointed leader takes over, where there is competition for leadership, or where one task takes precedence over other tasks.

Consensus Building Leaders of most successful new ventures define authority and responsibility in a way that builds motivation and commitment to cross-departmental and corporate goals. Using a consensus approach to management requires managing and working with peers and with the subordinates of others (or with superiors) outside formal chains of command and balancing multiple viewpoints and demands.

In the consensus approach, the manager is seen as willing to relinquish his or her priorities and power in the interests of an overall goal, and the appropriate people are included in setting cross-functional or cross-departmental goals and in making decisions. Participation and listening are emphasized.

In addition, the most effective managers are committed to dealing with problems and working problems through to agreement by seeking a reconciliation of viewpoints, rather than emphasizing differences, and by blending ideas, rather than playing the role of hard-nose negotiator or devil's advocate to force their own solution. There is open confrontation of differences of opinion and a willingness to talk out differences, assumptions, reasons, and inferences. Logic and reason tend to prevail, and there is a willingness to change opinions based on consensus.

Communication The most effective managers share information and are willing to alter individual views. Listening and participation are facilitated by such methods as circular seating arrangements, few interruptions or side conversations, and calm discussion versus many interruptions, loud or separate conversations, and so forth, in meetings.

Encouragement Successful managers build confidence by encouraging innovation and calculated risk-taking, rather than by punishing or criticizing what is less than perfect, and by expecting and encouraging others to find and correct their own errors and to solve their own problems. Their peers and others perceive them as accessible and willing to help when needed, and they provide the necessary resources to enable others to do the job. When it is appropriate, they go to bat for their peers and subordinates, even when they know they cannot always win. Further, differences are recognized and performance is rewarded.

Trust The most effective managers are perceived as trustworthy and straightforward. They do what they say they are going to do; they are not the corporate rumor carriers; they are more open and spontaneous, rather than guarded and cautious with each word; and they are perceived as being honest and direct. They have a reputation of getting results and become known as the creative problem solvers who have a knack for blending and balancing multiple views and demands.

Development Effective managers have a reputation for developing human capital (i.e., they groom and grow other effective managers by their example and their mentoring). As noted in Chapter 7, Bradford and Cohen distinguish between the heroic manager, whose need to be in control in many instances actually may stifle cooperation, and the post-heroic manager, a developer who actually brings about excellence in organizations by developing entrepreneurial middle management. If a company puts off developing middle management until price competition appears and its margins erode, the organization may come unraveled. Linking a plan to grow human capital at the middle management and the supervisory levels with the business strategy is an essential first step.

Entrepreneurial Management for the 21st Century: Three Breakthroughs

Three extraordinary companies have been built or revolutionized in the past two decades: Marion Labs, Inc., of Kansas City; Johnsonville Sausage of Cheboygan, Wisconsin; and Springfield Remanufacturing Corporation of Springfield, Missouri. Independently and unbeknown to each other, these companies created "high standard, perpetual learning cultures," which create and foster a "chain of greatness." The lessons from these three great companies provide a blueprint for entrepreneurial management in the 21st century. They set the standard and provide a tangible vision of what is possible. Not surprisingly, the most exciting, faster growing, and profitable companies in America today have striking similarities to these firms.

Ewing Marion Kauffman and Marion Labs

As described in Chapter 1, Marion Laboratories, founded in Ewing Marion Kauffman's garage in 1950, had reached $2.5 billion in sales by the time it merged with Merrill Dow in 1989. Its market capitalization was $6.5 billion. Over 300 millionaires and 13 foundations including the Ewing Marion Kauffman Foundation, were created from the builders of the company. In sharp contrast, RJR Nabisco, about 10 times larger than Marion Labs at the time of the KKR leveraged buyout, generated only 20 millionaires. Clearly, these were very different companies. Central to Marion Labs' phenomenal success story was the combination of a high potential opportunity with management execution based on core values and management philosophy ahead of its time. These principles are simple enough, but difficult to inculcate and sustain through good times and bad:

1. Treat everyone as you would want to be treated.
2. Share the wealth with those who have created it.
3. Pursue the highest standards of performance and ethics.

As noted earlier, the company had no organizational chart, referred to all its people as associates, not employees, and had widespread profit-sharing and stock participation plans. Having worked for a few years now with Mr. K and the top management that built Marion Labs and then ran the foundation, the authors can say that they are genuine and serious about these principles. They also have fun while succeeding, but they are highly dedicated to the practice of these core philosophies and values.

Jack Stack and Springfield Remanufacturing Corporation

The truly remarkable sage of this revolution in management is Jack Stack; his book, *The Great Game of Business,* should be read by all entrepreneurs. In 1983, Stack and a dozen colleagues acquired a tractor engine remanufacturing plant from the failing International Harvester Corporation. With an 89-to-1 debt-to-equity ratio and 21 percent interest, they acquired the company for 10 cents a share. In 1993, the company's shares were valued near $20 for the employee stock ownership plan, and the company had completely turned around with sales approaching $100 million. What had happened?

Like Ewing Marion Kauffman, Jack Stack created and implemented some management approaches and values radically opposite to the top-down, hierarchical, custodial management commonly found in large manufacturing enterprises. At the heart of his leadership was creating a vision called *The Big Picture: Think and act like owners, be the best we can be, and be perpetual learners. Build teamwork as the key by learning from each other, open the books to everyone, and educate everyone so they can become responsible and accountable for the numbers, both short and long term.* Stack puts it this way:

> We try to take ignorance out of the workplace and force people to get involved, not with threats and intimidation but with education. In the process, we are trying to close the biggest gaps in American business—the gap between workers and managers. We're developing a system that allows everyone to get together and work toward the same goals. To do that, you have to knock down the barriers that separate people, that keep people from coming together as a team.[11]

At Springfield Remanufacturing Corporation, everyone learns to read and interpret all the financial statements, including an income statement, balance sheet, and cash flow, and how his or her job affects each line item. This open-book management style is linked with pushing responsibility downward and outward, and to understanding both wealth creation (i.e., shareholder value) and wealth sharing through short-term bonuses and long-term equity participation. Stack describes the value of this approach thus: "The payoff comes from getting the people who create the numbers to understand the numbers. When that happens, the communication between the bottom and the top of the organization is just phenomenal."[12] The results he achieved in 10 years are astounding. Even more amazing is that he has found the time to share this approach with others. More than 150 companies have participated in seminars that have enabled them to adopt this approach.

Ralph Stayer and Johnsonville Sausage Company[13]

In 1975, Johnsonville Sausage was a small company with about $5 million in sales and a fairly traditional, hierarchical, and somewhat custodial management. In just a few years, Ralph Stayer, the owner's son, radically transformed the company through a management revolution whose values, culture, and philosophy are remarkably similar to the principles of Ewing Marion Kauffman and Jack Stack.

The results are astonishing: By 1980, the company had reached $15 million in sales; by 1985, $50 million; and by 1990, $150 million. At the heart of the changes he created was the concept of a *total learning culture: Everyone is a learner, seeking to improve constantly, finding better ways. High performance standards accompanied by an investment in training, and performance measures that made it possible to reward fairly both short- and long-term results were critical to the transition.* Responsibility and accountability was spread downward and outward. For example, instead of forwarding complaint letters to the marketing department, where they are filed and the standard response is sent, they go directly to the front-line sausage stuffer responsible for the product's taste. The sausage stuffers are the ones who respond to customer complaints now. Another example is the interviewing, hiring, and training process for new people. A newly hired woman pointed out numerous shortcomings with the existing process and proposed ways to improve it. As a result, the entire responsibility was shifted from the traditional human resources/personnel group to the front line, with superb results.

As one would guess, such radical changes do not come easily. Consider Stayer's insight:

> In 1980, I began looking for a recipe for change. I started by searching for a book that would tell me how to get people to care about their jobs and their company.

[11] Jack Stack, *The Great Game of Business* (New York: Currency/Doubleday Books, 1991), p. 5.
[12] Ibid., p. 93.
[13] For an excellent discussion of this transformation, see "The Johnsonville Sausage Company," HBS Case 387-103, rev. June 27, 1990. Copyright © 1990 by the President and Fellows of Harvard College. See also Ralph Stayer, "How I Learned to Let My Workers Lead," *Harvard Business Review,* November–December 1990. Copyright © 1990 by the President and Fellows of Harvard College.

EXHIBIT 16.6

Summary of the Johnsonville Sausage Company

The critical aspects of the transition:

1. Started at the top: Ralph Stayer recognized that he was the heart of the problem and recognized the need to change—the most difficult step.
2. Vision was anchored in human resource management and in a particular idea of the company's culture:
   - Continuous learning organization.
   - Team concept—change players.
   - New model of jobs (Ralph Stayer's role and decision making).
   - Performance- and results-based compensation and rewards.
3. Stayer decided to push responsibility and accountability downward to the front-line decision makers:
   - Front-liners are closest to the customer and the problem.
   - Define the whole task.
   - Invest in training and selection.
   - Job criteria and feedback = development tool.
4. Controls and mechanisms make it work:
   - Measure performance, not behavior, activities, and the like.
   - Emphasize learning and development, not allocation of blame.
   - Customize to you and the company.
   - Decentralize and minimize staff.

> Not surprisingly, the search was fruitless. No one could tell me how to wake up my own workforce; I would have to figure it out for myself. . . . The most important question any manager can ask is: "In the best of all possible worlds what would I really want to happen?"[14]

Even having taken such a giant step, Stayer was ready to take the next, equally perilous steps:

> Acting on instinct, I ordered a change. "From now on," I announced to my management team, "you're all responsible for making your own decisions." . . . I went from authoritarian control to authoritarian abdication. No one had asked for more responsibility; I had forced it down their throats.[15]

Further insight into just how challenging it is to transform a company like Johnsonville Sausage is revealed in another Stayer quote:

> I spent those two years pursuing another mirage of well-detailed strategic and tactical plans that would realize my goals of Johnsonville as the world's greatest sausage maker. We tried to plan organizational structure two to three years before it would be needed. . . . Later I realized that these structural changes had to grow from day-to-day working realities; no one could dictate them from above, and certainly not in advance.[16]

Exhibit 16.6 summarizes the key steps in the transformation of Johnsonville Sausage over several years. Such a picture undoubtedly oversimplifies the process and understates the extraordinary commitment and effort required to pull it off, but it does show how the central elements weave together.

The Chain of Greatness

As we reflect on these three great companies, we can see that there is clearly a pattern here, with some common denominators in both the ingredients and the process. This chain of greatness becomes reinforcing and perpetuating (see Exhibit 16.7). Leadership that instills across the company a vision of greatness and an owner's mentality is a common beginning. A philosophy of perpetual learning throughout the organization accompanied by high standards of performance is key to the value-creating entrepreneurial cultures at the three firms. A culture that teaches and rewards teamwork, improvement, and respect for each other provides the oil and glue to make things work. Finally, a fair and generous short- and long-term reward system, as well as the necessary education to make sure that everyone knows and

[14] Stayer, "How I Learned to Let My Workers Lead," p. 1.
[15] Ibid., pp. 3–4.
[16] Ibid., p. 4.

EXHIBIT 16.7

The Chain of Greatness

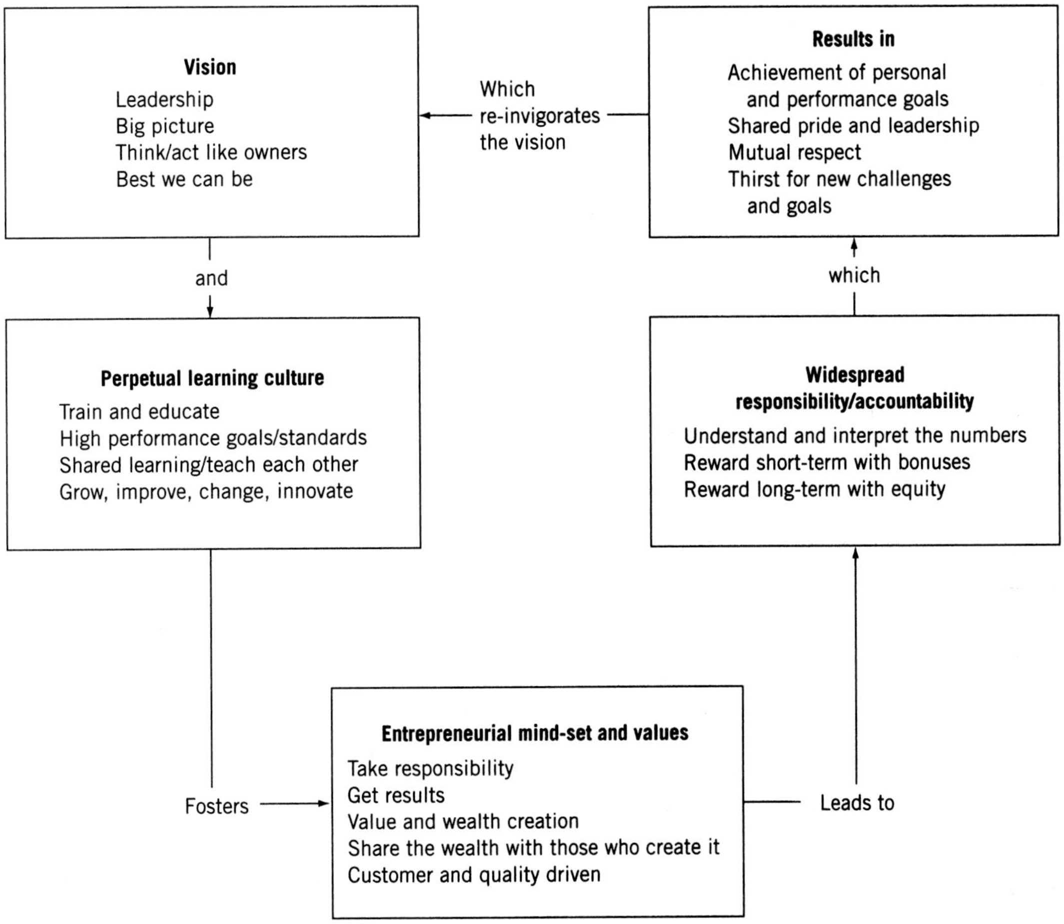

can use the numbers, creates a mechanism for sharing the wealth with those who contributed to it. The results speak for themselves: extraordinary levels of personal, professional, and financial achievement.

Internet Impact: Resources

Supply Chain Management

By increasing the quantity and expanding the richness of information in real time to many more participants, the Internet has raised the importance and value of information in supply chain management. Online communication extends the scope of management options across all firms in the supply chain and contributes to reductions in costs and improvements in service.

Dell Computer, for example, is at the forefront of global businesses in leveraging online capabilities to support its 100 percent build-to-order business model. The company continues to improve its demand-planning and factory-execution accuracy, reduce order-to-delivery time, and enhance real-time customer service. Using the Internet, Dell has been able to adapt more quickly to rapidly changing technologies, and therefore maintain its position as a high-performance operation.

For entrepreneurial companies, the ability to share progress data and information in real time can significantly cut the cost of collaborative projects, in addition to improving communications with companies downstream. In the case of setbacks, a manufacturer is now able to alert everyone instantly—and coordinate corrective measures. The best part is that while the speed and quality of these enabling technologies continue to improve, the overall cost of global networking and communication continues to fall.

Chapter Summary

1. The demands of rapid growth have led to the invention of new organizational paradigms by entrepreneurs.
2. The entrepreneurial organization today is flatter, faster, more flexible and responsive, and copes readily with ambiguity and change. It is the opposite of the hierarchy, layers of management, and the more-is-better syndrome prevalent in brontosaurus capitalism.
3. Entrepreneurs in high growth firms distinguish themselves with leading entrepreneurial practices in marketing, finance, management, and planning.
4. As high-potential firms "grow up big" they experience stages (Wonder, Blunder, Thunder, Plunder, Asunder or Wonder redux), each with its own special challenges and crises, which are compounded the faster the growth.
5. Establishing a culture and climate conducive to entrepreneurship is a core task for the venture.
6. A chain of greatness characterizes some breakthrough approaches to leadership and management in entrepreneurial ventures.

Study Questions

1. Why have old hierarchical management paradigms given way to new organizational paradigms?
2. What special problems and crises can new ventures expect as they grow? Why do these occur?
3. Explain the stages many ventures experience and why these are unique.
4. What role does the organizational culture and climate play in a rapidly growing venture? Why are many large companies unable to create an entrepreneurial culture?
5. What is the chain of greatness and why can entrepreneurs benefit from the concept?
6. Why is the rate of growth the central driver of the organization challenges a growing venture faces?

Internet Resources for Chapter 16

http://finance.yahoo.com *Stock market news and research engine*

http://www.entreworld.org *EntreWorld provides a selective review guide to Web sources for the entrepreneur*

http://edge.lowe.org *Peerspectives from the Edward Lowe Foundation is a peer-learning community for growing companies*

http://biz.findlaw.com *FindLaw is an extensive guide to law sites for business*

MIND STRETCHERS

Have you considered?

1. Many large organizations are now attempting to reinvent themselves. What will be the biggest challenge in this process, and why?
2. How fast should a company grow? How fast is too fast, organizationally and financially?
3. In your ideal world, how would you describe what it is like to live and work within the perfect entrepreneurial organization?
4. Who should *not* be an entrepreneur?

Case

EverNet Corporation

Preparation Questions

1. Evaluate what Kenefick has accomplished with his new company, EverNet.
2. Examine Jim's leadership skills and strategies for EverNet.
3. What is your assessment of EverNet's financing strategies, deal structures, and progress to date?
4. What is your assessment of the investment opportunity in EverNet as a private equity investor in mid-1999?
5. What should Kenefick do now, and why?

June 1999 brought a crisis to Jim Kenefick. While business was going great, he had hit a dead end in fund-raising and needed help, fast. EverNet was out of cash and Kenefick was no closer to securing additional funding. Vendors were demanding payment. Kenefick needed to act, and act quickly. A telecommunications startup, EverNet had reached $20 million in annualized revenue, but with major construction bills coming in from the installation of the networks added to the cost of opening the company's new headquarters and a payroll for almost 350 people, EverNet's appetite for cash was voracious. The national direct sales force was expanding by the month, taking advantage of the booming market for integrated broadband access of local, Internet, and long-distance services.

Starting Over

On January 9, 1995, 31-year-old Jim Kenefick had sold his first telecommunications venture, Keystone Corporation, after an unexpected breach with his partner that had ended in legal action.[1] Kenefick had profited enough from the sale that his only immediate obligations were sailing and enjoying his free time. He had not expected to be retired and single at this point in his life. After several months of "playing" on his sailboat, skiing, and traveling, Kenefick decided to systematically review his options for the future. He was enjoying serving on the board of directors for EPOCH Networks, an ISP (Internet service provider) started by a Young Entrepreneurs Organization (YEO) friend, but was not satisfied. "I wasn't happy with the life of leisure," he explains. " I knew I had to get back into business." Kenefick was 31 years old.

The Opportunity

Telecommunications seemed to be a segment of the market with great opportunity due to the Telecommunications Act of 1996, which created competition in the

[1] See "James Kenefick: Making of an Entrepreneur" case study for background on Keystone Corporation.

 Funding provided by the Ewing Marion Kauffman Foundation.

This case was adapted and edited by Nancy C. Godfrey, based on the James Kenefick (D) and (E) cases by Jesseca P. Timmons, M.Ed. These cases were prepared under the supervision of Professor Jeffry A. Timmons, Franklin W. Olin Distinguished Professor of Entrepreneurship, Babson College, Wellesley, MA, as a basis for class discussion rather than to illustrate either effective or ineffective handling of an entrepreneurial situation. In loving memory of William Joseph Kenefick, an inspiring man whose family dedication and actions spoke louder than words. With Love, Your son, Jamie.

The Telecommunications Act of 1996 (Excerpt)

The Telecommunications Act of 1996, enacted on Feb. 8, 1996, departs from prior legislation in the industry by establishing local exchange competition as a national policy through the removal of state regulatory barriers to competition and the preemption of laws restricting competition in the local exchange market. The Act mandates that each LEC [local exchange carrier] must I) permit the resale of their services on reasonable and nondiscriminatory terms; II) interconnect their networks to those of other carriers; III) allow customers to retain the same telephone number when they switch local providers; IV) ensure that an end user does not have to dial any more digits to reach the customers of local competitors; V) establish reciprocal compensation arrangements for the transport and termination of telecommunications traffic; and VI) permit access to poles, ducts, conduits and rights-of-way. In addition to the above-mentioned duties, each LEC must also I) permit resale of their retail services at wholesale rates; II) permit interconnection by competitors at any technical feasible point that is at least equal in quality to that which the LEC provides to itself and on rates and terms that are reasonable and nondiscriminatory; and III) unbundle their network elements at any technical feasible point on rates and terms that are reasonable and nondiscriminatory in a manner that allows carriers to combine such elements in order to provide telecommunications services.

EXHIBIT A

Web Hosting Services Projected to Grow Dramatically

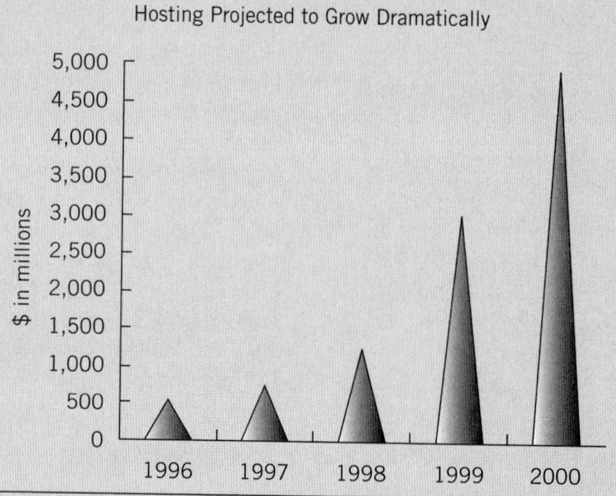

residential and hospitality markets and the exploding Internet service market (see Exhibit A).

The rapid opening of local markets to competition, accelerated growth in local traffic related to increases in Internet access, and the demand from small and medium businesses for a "one-stop" provider of integrated services presented a significant opportunity for new entrants to achieve substantial penetration of the large, established, local service market. According to industry sources, revenues generated by the U.S. telecommunications industry have grown 8.5 percent annually over the past four years, totaling $212 billion in 1998.

Kenefick knew that Internet access service was one of the fastest growing segments of the global telecommunications services market. IDC, an independent research firm, estimated that the number of Internet users worldwide had reached 69 million in 1997, and would grow to over 320 million by the year 2002. Forrester Research reported that ISP revenues should continue to grow exponentially, adding that over 50 percent of households and 50 percent of businesses in the United States would be online by the year 2002. One powerful underlying driver of all the opportunities in this market was the recurring revenue character of the business. Once a customer signed up, the continuous revenue stream began just as it had previously in the cellular phone and cable TV industries.

Within the ISP industry, the small- to medium-sized business market was among the most rapidly growing market segments. According to *Residential and Small Business Telecom,* published by Insight Research in 1997, "Small to medium sized businesses are the fastest growing part of our economy and they have real money to spend—over $60 billion for telecom services and products in 1997 alone."

The local and long-distance telecommunications markets were still highly concentrated. AT&T, Sprint, and MCI WorldCom together accounted for approximately 66 percent of the small to medium business market, and 78 percent of the total long-distance market. Although long-distance revenues had grown at an average annual rate of 7.0 percent, market penetration for new entrants had increased by more than 20 percent. Local telecommunications markets were even more concentrated, with the local exchange carriers (LECs) dominating their markets. Industry sources reported that in 1999 Competitive Local Exchange Carriers (CLECs) had less than 5 percent market penetration; however, their market share as a group is expected to increase to 15 percent by 2002.

Kenefick had telecommunications experience, first with Keystone and later as a founding shareholder and board member at EPOCH Networks. As he was considering options for his next startup, Kenefick met Wally Arhol,[2] a venture capitalist and longtime friend of Kenefick who had started several successful telecommunications companies. Arhol had financed the "10-10-257" startup, one major European telecom company, and Mid Atlantic Telecom. The meeting was to prove important to Kenefick. Arhol would serve as a crucial advisor and investor to what would become EverNet.

Starting Over: EverNet Corporation

Jim Kenefick was now poised to reenter telecommunications with the aim of building a high-growth venture, using his skills from past experiences. He would name his new venture EverNet Corporation. His first priorities

[2] Name has been changed.

would be hiring the best team he could find, establishing a set of guiding principles for the company, and installing the corporate culture. "I knew I needed three things: a business plan, a professional management team, and funding in place," says Kenefick. Kenefick saw the high-growth potential in voice and data services and knew that was where he wanted to go with his business: he wanted to start a high-growth venture in telecommunications.

Kenefick felt that the 1996 Telecommunications Act paved the way for new companies to provide residential and commercial long-distance services to smaller and medium-sized businesses in selected markets across the United States that were currently ignored or underserved. From his analysis and experience, he characterized these customers as follows:

- Underserved by major carriers.
- Lacking dedicated, in-house telecommunications professionals.
- Respond well to consultative sales approach.
- Higher margin segment of the market.

Kenefick knew EverNet would be a high-growth venture that would create a significant company with serious harvest potential through an IPO or a strategic sale. He also knew that rather than vacations and weekends off, EverNet would bring him nonstop work. "I wanted to build a company that was going to really work," says Kenefick. "Not just financially successful but a real company, with a good corporate culture."

Entry Strategy

EverNet entered the market as an integrated communications provider carrier offering residential and commercial long-distance (IXC) telephone services and local and long-distance combined Internet services (CLEC) primarily to medium size, small and small office/home office business customers in selected markets across the United States. EverNet Corporation began carrying traffic in December 1996 and initially marketed "casual calling" services primarily through multiple sales channels, while also offering 800 and 888 service, international long-distance, calling cards, conference calling, T-1 and Internet connect services. EverNet marketed its comprehensive communications services through direct mail, including a direct sales force of approximately 150 sales professionals in 12 offices nationwide. The company would plan to provide its customers dedicated and switched long-distance services, dedicated Internet connections, and value-added services, presented on a single integrated bill.

EverNet was incorporated on February 9, 1996. Business began on June 15, 1996, with a $500,000 investment from Kenefick. After four months of operation, the company received $1 million in startup funding from Wally Arhol's firm, Palmer and Moore.[3] This capital structure resulted in Kenefick retaining control of the new company. Next, Kenefick hired two employees. He licensed the name EverNet and the company became a carrier with network products. The first product, a casual calling service called Dial Around, was launched in the Ameritech service area.

Of the earliest days of EverNet, Kenefick states, "Startups are no fun. This time I included a legal governance plan . . . the startup *always* takes longer than you think." During 1996, EverNet completed the process of becoming an interexchange carrier (IXC), loading its carrier identification code (CIC) in every major end-office in the country and filing for state certification/ regulatory and tariffs throughout the country. This process took over 13 months and consumed approximately $1 million.

By December of 1996, EverNet had revenues reaching $3.5 million. Having been through one startup and advised another, Kenefick had a clearer vision for the future and how to handle rapid growth.

The Approach

EverNet began marketing casual long-distance services in 1997 to residential customers in the Ameritech region. In early 1998, the company began marketing its services to businesses through the three primary sales channels: the direct sales force, the independent agents, and the "branchisors."

A "branchise" is a cooperative relationship between EverNet and an independent, experienced telecommunications sales professional who builds a sales team exclusively to sell EverNet's services in exchange for operational support, advanced payments, and sales commissions. EverNet recruits qualified "branchisees" to complement the direct sales force. Branchisors enable the company to reach customers cost-effectively in regions that may not justify an EverNet direct sales office.

Kenefick's approach to this opportunity was to simplify the services offered by bundling local, Internet, and long-distance services, believing this offered much greater market potential (see Exhibits B and C). This integrated communications solution was dubbed, "The EverNet Difference: One Company. One Network. One Bill. One Solution."

In January 1998, the company began utilizing direct sales and "branchising," or assigning sales territory to captive agents with a quota who operated independently, but worked exclusively for EverNet. During 1998, the company hired an experienced direct sales force of about 200 sales professionals and managers. Eight "branchises" were also established to complement the company's direct sales efforts by focusing on businesses primarily in secondary and tertiary markets, and established

[3] Name has been changed.

EXHIBIT B

Average Monthly Spending on Local, Long Distance, and Internet

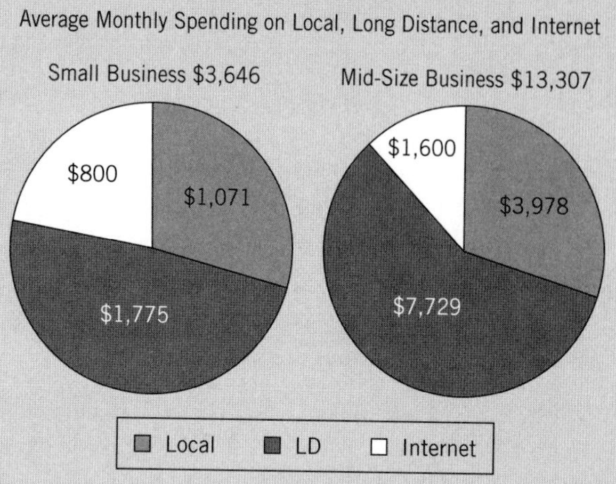

EXHIBIT C

The EverNet Approach

- Long distance
- Internet access
- Local dial-tone
- Value-added services

- Multiple sales channels
- IP / ATM network design
- State-of-the-art OSS
- Integrated billing

EXHIBIT D

Multiple Sales Channels

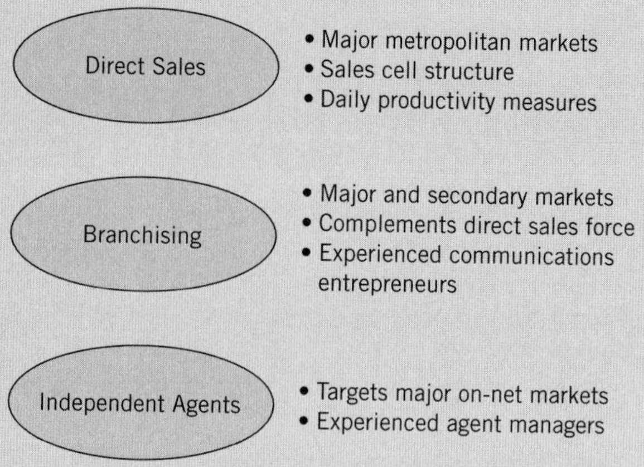

Direct Sales
• Major metropolitan markets
• Sales cell structure
• Daily productivity measures
Branchising
• Major and secondary markets
• Complements direct sales force
• Experienced communications entrepreneurs
Independent Agents
• Targets major on-net markets
• Experienced agent managers

EXHIBIT E

Utility Communications Application Provider

Sales	Direct Branchise Agent
Utility Applications/ Middleware	Utilities: Internet Access, Local, LD Middleware: *EverNet eApplications*, ePayment, eBilling, eHosting, eCommerce, eConferencing/Messaging
Network Elements	IP / ATM Backbone, Frame Relay Nortel DMS500 switches, Cisco routers

an independent agent program by recruiting over 100 independent agents nationwide (see Exhibits D and E).

Kenefick describes this as a period of tremendous change and transformation and, for EverNet, a period that would forever change the company and its approach to the market. "We hired 200 people practically overnight—in three weeks we went from 18 employees to 220. I knew this was a crucial moment." EverNet now had an experienced sales force in place and was focused on the midsize-business market. Palmer and Moore then provided another $10 million in funding.

Creating a Corporate Culture

Kenefick knew he had to establish a corporate culture to make the company succeed. He also knew how he wanted his new employees to be treated. "I saw all these other companies which were successful but miserable," he says. "There was no corporate culture. They weren't happy places to work."

In January 1998, Kenefick brought his new senior management team, along with a professional facilitator, to the Washington, D.C., Ritz-Carlton for a two-day retreat. The group's goal was to create a set of guiding values and principles for the fledgling company. The group came up with the slogan "Right Things Right" to define the philosophy and goals of EverNet. Everyone agreed that EverNet was to be the *opposite* of "all things to all people"—instead, it would be only the *right* things to the *right* people. The slogan defines EverNet's goal of focusing on providing the best services available to the specifically targeted group of customers (midsize companies), thereby providing the "right things" and getting them done "right." In addition, the phrase refers to "right"

EXHIBIT F

Right Things Right

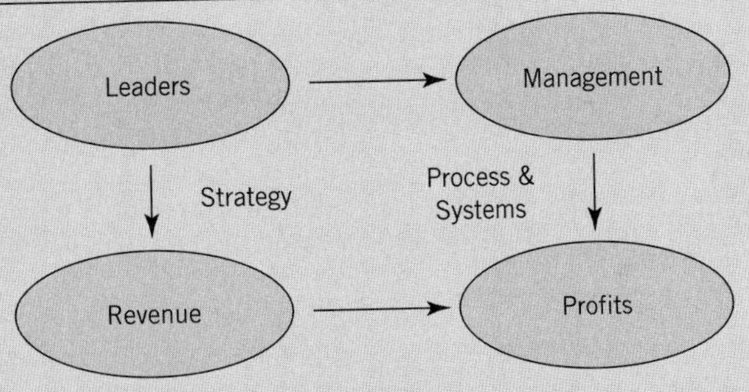

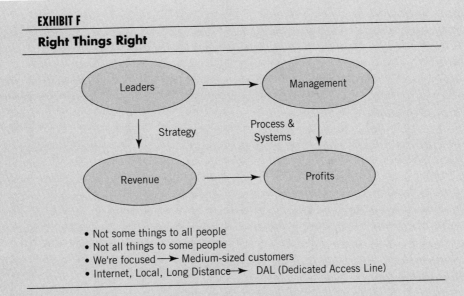

- Not some things to all people
- Not all things to some people
- We're focused → Medium-sized customers
- Internet, Local, Long Distance → DAL (Dedicated Access Line)

management of the company's revenue stream by carefully chosen leadership (see Exhibit F).

Together, the management team expanded the philosophy to a list of principles, starting with "Treat others as you want to be treated." Kenefick attributes this inspiration to the teachings of Ewing Marion Kauffman. The Kauffman Foundation, in which Kenefick had been involved for several years, operates by the same principle, starting with the "Golden Rule."

EverNet's Culture and Philosophy: *Right Things Right*

- Treat others as you want to be treated.
- Conduct every action with integrity.
- Share the wealth with those who have helped produce the revenue and profits.
- Embrace proven, leading edge vs. bleeding edge technologies.
- Do it right and with pride the first time.
- Maintain a sense of humility and a sense of humor.
- Take five minutes out of every day to do something nice for someone.

Kenefick also came up with a theme for the mission of the new management team: Operation Geronimo. T-shirts, buttons, and cards were printed for the members of the management team. "Geronimo endured against all odds, and against all conditions," Kenefick explains. "He didn't necessarily win every battle, but he was totally committed and he prevailed in the war. He was the last Native American chief to surrender to the U.S. Cavalry. We all committed to work together and beat the odds in running a successful startup. We all knew how hard it would be."

Planning for Growing Pains

While EverNet officially began doing business in June of 1996, Kenefick did not offer any stock options until January of 1998. "I realized that companies grow faster than people," says Kenefick. "We were bringing new people in and had to give them all stock options. I knew that my controller now might not be my controller in a year, and that the controller's share of the stock options might have been gone with the first guy." Kenefick set aside 15 percent of the company's stock by way of options for people who would come later. EverNet had no entitlement options—everyone was paid by performance. It was the "FEAST" strategy—*F*eed your *E*agles *A*nd *S*tarve your *T*urkeys. Everyone was expected to check the ego at the door—Kenefick included. Employees knew they would be rewarded by performance with stock options and bonuses. In the spring of 1998, employees were given shares worth about 17 cents. In mid-1999, EverNet stock was worth $6.73 a share. A hundred EverNet employees retain original stock options.

EverNet established an intensive 8- to 10-week training program for all salespeople, covering corporate culture and core ideologies, selling techniques, the company's product and service offerings, and the company's OSS (operational support service) functions. All other employees go through two three-day orientation programs. Corporate employees are eligible for semiannual bonuses based on improved individual, department, and company results, and 100 percent of all employees receive stock options. EverNet has also developed a compensation plan specifically for its direct sales employees, which is designed to encourage both individual and group success.[4]

EverNet's goal: "To deliver integrated broadband customer centric experience for mid-sized business throughout the United States." That goal would be pursued through the following slogans:

- Encourage a learning environment.
- Thoughtful and decisive.
- Be proactive.
- The customer is king.
- If it's going to be, it's up to me.
- Together everyone achieves more.
- That which is measured is improved.
- Attitude is everything.
- Do them all with speed!

Building the Business Infrastructure

In late 1997 and early 1998, EverNet was providing long-distance and Internet service nationwide. The direct sales force was established in 12 cities. The company's distribution channels were now immense, with new sales offices opening regularly, new leases being signed, and new employees being hired at a rapid rate. Kenefick knew EverNet had to get its own network for providing service in place rather than relying on other carriers. Leasing network access from other carriers would be a temporary solution to the company's needs, but EverNet's growth required a permanent networking solution.

After solving the significant space issue at EverNet's D.C. corporate headquarters by moving into a larger facility in the Georgetown area of the city, Kenefick began to focus on getting EverNet's switches in place for the network. He decided on a roll-up strategy, planning to acquire small networks all over the country and to put all the networks under one management and operation. Valuations of these companies in the spring of 1998 were far higher than Kenefick anticipated, and later turned out to be inflated. The inflated prices steered Kenefick away from widespread acquisitions.

Kenefick referred back to his business plan and realized that the roll-up strategy allowed EverNet no control over the speed and span of acquisitions. The best option for EverNet would be to build its own IPM/ATM voice and data network.

Kenefick rebuilt EverNet's business plan after determining the cost, timing, and location of building a new IP/ATM (Internet protocol / asycrones transfer mode) network that would provide exclusive service to EverNet's customers. The network would take advantage of current voice and data capabilities available through the newest technology. Kenefick studied competitors such as Lucent and Nortel to create the network plan. Kenefick emphasizes his need as CEO to be "working on the business instead of working in the business," or not losing sight of the company's priorities at crucial moments. He made sure the company's balance sheet was leveraged to start the process of building a billion-dollar infrastructure.

In developing the strategy for the building of the network, Kenefick returned to the company's basic principles: the network would be built right the first time, as quickly as possible, and with the best technology available. A four-hour Saturday meeting was convened with management, network engineering, experts from other competitors, and representatives from the sales force. Kenefick describes the meeting: "I told them, we're not leaving this meeting until we have an OSS [operational support service] strategy." Many companies spend days or weeks figuring this stuff out. Although Kenefick's employees thought he was crazy, they did reach a decision by the end of the meeting. EverNet would use the IBM AS 400 E with an IX/Plus billing platform from EDS. This would be the core delivery system for EverNet's trademarked services, SIMIS (Seamless Integrated Management Information Systems). The network would enable EverNet to provide one bill for all services provided, which would be a cornerstone of EverNet's niche in the market.

While the new network was being built, the sales force began to have problems selling services over Teleglobe, a factor EverNet couldn't control. The sales reps had to sell services based on the network under construction while using a leased network to provide them. Kenefick knew the sales force needed constant training to keep up with new services being created, such as Internet service, then the fastest growing segment of the telecommunications industry. The sales force needed to understand the new network being built, since what they were selling was actually evolving with the new network. Kenefick explains,

> It was a bloodbath getting the thing built. We saw five other companies fail trying to do the same thing at the same time. They didn't integrate the new network from the top down or the whole company didn't buy into it. But we did it.

In March of 1998, EverNet signed a deal with EPOCH Networks, where Kenefick and Wally Arhol were still on the board of directors. EPOCH would allow EverNet to resell its IP network and market and develop new products. By August, EverNet was EPOCH's largest Internet access customer. The initial process took 105 days, with an additional two to three months of personnel training. EverNet emerged as a first-tier Internet provider with long-distance service with its own network in place.

Early Results

EverNet's revenue during 1997 was primarily derived from the sale of "casual calling" residential long-distance services. Casual calling revenue declined from 98 percent

[4] EverNet confidential investment prospectus, May 1999.

of total revenue by the end of 1997 to 38 percent of revenue by December 1998. While casual calling revenue was expected to continue to grow, this service was expected to contribute less than 15 percent of revenues in 1999 and 2000. Approximately 90 percent of EverNet's 1998 revenues were generated from long distance, the remaining 10 percent comprised of revenues from data services. The U.S. telecommunications market is expected to grow significantly to $296 billion in 2002, representing a compounded annual growth rate of 8.7 percent. Local access is estimated to increase to over $200 billion in 2002, while long-distance revenues net of access charge are projected to increase 5.7 percent annually, reaching approximately $80.9 billion in 2002. Internet and broadband revenues are projected to grow from approximately $7.0 billion in 1998 to roughly $30.0 billion in 2002. This increase demonstrates a 43.9 percent compounded annual growth rate and results in a contribution of over 10 percent of total 2002 telecommunications revenues as compared to only 3 percent in 1998.

Coping with Growth: Organization and Outsourcing

By the end of 1998, EverNet had agreed to sell long-distance service from Frontier Network as the new EverNet network was being built. Jim Kenefick had believed that EverNet needed to build its own network rather than assemble a network through piecemeal roll-up in order to deliver services most effectively. In November 1998, construction began on three major switch sites: in Chicago, Los Angeles, and New York City. The company had also just invested in a new billing system, IX Plus by EDS; a new accounting system; and a much larger office space for the national headquarters. Also in November, Palmer and Moore, the venture capital firm represented by EverNet board member Wally Arhol, extended EverNet's credit line to $12 million at 12 percent interest.

Needing someone with strong financial skills for the upcoming fund-raising, Kenefick brought on fellow Babson alumni Craig Bandes in early fall 1998. Bandes had experience in corporate development and finance and had gone through training at Salomon Brothers bank. EverNet's existing $20 million in equity, the $12 million credit line, and the recent jump to 220 employees impressed Bandes. A new marketing vice president and CFO were also hired at EverNet, but neither person proved to be an appropriate fit with EverNet. The entry and exit of both managers slowed the organizational development of the company, and EverNet was no closer to securing the financing it needed.

Kenefick began to prioritize EverNet's needs. Constant reorganization of employees was taking the company's time and energy away from concentrating on the infrastructure. By January, the challenge was keeping EverNet's corporate culture intact despite the rapid addition of so many new employees to the business. Constant reorganization could not keep up with the demands of the business. Kenefick decided to outsource some departments "before they got out of control." He felt that outsourcing would avoid burnout and enable the team to focus on issues that mattered more to the company. Departments outsourced at EverNet would include corporate communications, including writing and producing the company's prospectus, and customer care (Level 1 support), where a professional customer care firm was contracted for EverNet's customer service. Technical support and "dialing help" for local and wide area network questions for employees were also centralized. The last department to be outsourced was collections. With outsourcing eliminating many organizational problems within the company, Kenefick was free to focus on raising funds and increasing EverNet's credit line.

The Search for Funding

Early in 1999 Kenefick and his team decided to seek out the large investment banks such as Lehman, Bear Stearns, and CIBC that they had approached in the past for the company's financing. Kenefick had found his first experience with the large banks unnerving, and recalls having to sit under bright lights in the conference rooms of various banks and be grilled in a manner that he compared to being on trial. Even as founder and CEO, he was uncertain he knew the answer to every single query about EverNet. However, Kenefick had passed the test and was now more comfortable with the road show process.

In early winter, Kenefick selected CIBC to provide funds for EverNet. CIBC was at the time the largest provider of the type of sub-debt capital EverNet needed. Kenefick then chose Legg Mason, a D.C. area capital firm, as partner in the deal to pursue the LBO/mezzanine financing market. Together, they assembled a private placement memorandum for EverNet to raise a $40 million high-yield offering in spring of 1999. The high-yield market was increasingly receptive to such offerings.

While negotiations for Nortel switching equipment were under way, Kenefick saw the decreasing price erosion in the long-distance marketplace continue to fall. AT&T's "One Rate Plan" was 15 cents/minute in January of 1999, and only 7 cents/minute by June. Kenefick knew that leasing fiber capacity would not help keep EverNet competitive. He knew EverNet would have to buy fiber optics to compete, but the company didn't have the cash to undertake such a major initiative. After studying the amount of local, long-distance, and Internet traffic the company was projected to need in the next three years (9000 of OC-3 155 mbs of bandwidth), EverNet was ready to make a proposal.

"Now we had an opportunity to leverage, and it was time to go out there and buy some fiber," Kenefick recalls. What Kenefick needed was a partner to finance and sell fiber, or the cable that carries the service, to EverNet. He called colleagues and contacts at industry leaders such as Nortel Networks, Qwest, Williams, and Frontier, and found that while they were used to leasing and selling fiber, they were not accustomed to selling and financing fiber. None of the vendors seemed to understand Kenefick's proposal at first. After convincing contacts what he needed and why, Kenefick put out an informal proposal for equity or sub-debt financing for fiber. Though very few precedents existed for such an arrangement, Kenefick believed his suppliers could be good potential sources to finance further development of the switches, network, and working capital. The senior management of vendors, including Nortel Networks, would attend an industry trade show in February 1999 and Kenefick thought this could provide the opportunity to propose a new financial partnership with one or more of these vendors. After all, he reasoned, the CIBC/Legg Mason high-yield offering was limited to only $40 million, and it was not cheap money. The terms of one deal included warrants for shares of EverNet's stock, as well as a $2.5 million investment-banking fee.

A New Strategy for a New Vision

Thus began a parallel fund-raising strategy whereby Kenefick, directly and independently of any investment banks, would attempt to meet his coming capital requirements by securing vendor financing while continuing to work with CIBC on the $40 million offering. "I think CEOs need to get out and do that more than they do," he says. "Entrepreneurs need to think about . . . working *on* the business as opposed to just working in the business. I sat down with the vendors face to face, businessman to businessman, not engineer to engineer, and told them what we needed."

Kenefick found Nortel Networks initially eager to participate in the funding of EverNet's network. He asked that Nortel Network's engineering teams complete out the network strategy, give a "third party blessing" to EverNet's network deployment, and asked Nortel Networks to finance the equipment and put a working capital line along with it. Nortel began considering Kenefick's offer.

Throughout March and into April 1999, Kenefick continued the institutional road show with CIBC/Legg Mason, meeting with the participating investment banks six to eight hours a day for their grueling due diligence interrogations. A total of 23 institutional investment teams visited with EverNet's management. "If that isn't disruptive, I don't know what is," Kenefick says. "They challenge everything, your ability to lead, your management style, everything—they really try to trip you up."

Waiting for Action

After 60 days of negotiating with Nortel Networks and the investment banks, Kenefick was frustrated. In addition to running EverNet day to day, he was devoting every spare moment to fund-raising, and knew that his senior management team was also getting distracted. In early May 1999, Kenefick called Nortel directly and said he felt things were "taking way too long." A few days later, Kenefick happened to sit next to Richard Smith, then the president of global services for Nortel, at an industry event. He took advantage of the opportunity to present EverNet's case personally, sharing the EverNet "Right Things Right: Technology Counts, People Matter" corporate philosophy.

After Kenefick had vented his frustration over the slow pace of the process, Nortel sent its senior vice president of global services, Jim Banter, to EverNet to expedite the investment process. By fortunate coincidence, Banter happened to be a dog lover, and the meeting started off on a positive note when Banter met Kenefick's yellow lab, Baron, who spends his days in Kenefick's office. "He just fell to his knees when he saw Baron," says Kenefick. "I knew this was going to be great."

Kenefick took advantage of the moment to point out to Banter that teams from Williams Communications were in the EverNet conference room at that very moment, hammering out their funding agreement. Kenefick made it clear that Williams had acted quickly and decisively at his proposal.

Kenefick had approached Tulsa-based Williams Telecommunications for funding at the same time he had contacted Nortel Networks and the other vendors, but Williams had agreed to back EverNet after only a 30-minute presentation. The process was expedited by the fact that one of the key players at Williams was a friend of Kenefick's whom Kenefick met while on the EPOCH board. EverNet was able to buy 9,000 miles of OC-3 (155mb) fiber for $29 million, receiving $10 million in equity infusion and paying $5 million down on the fiber. As this process, too, slowed, Kenefick called and asked for the financing to be put in place as soon as possible. Williams asked Kenefick for his valuation of the company. Kenefick said the company valuation would be priced later, claiming: "If this is a true strategic partnership, we can price it later. If the entire $40 million deal falls through, then the company's valuation is the last valuation of a year ago at $100 million." Kenefick also insisted that the team from Williams remain at EverNet until the deal was finalized, which they did, for five days. Kenefick was able to use the swift action of the Williams team as an example to point out to other vendors, spurring Nortel Networks and Allied Capital to bring their support.

With a connection established with the vice president from Nortel, the deal finally began to take shape. Nortel management apologized for the slow process and disorganization Kenefick had seen in the previous months. Nortel flew a team of people from headquarters in Dallas to EverNet to initiate the due diligence process necessary for funding EverNet's network. Finally, in May of 1999, Nortel Networks agreed to provide $150 million for vendor financing and working capital. The size of the marketing team was tripled and the Chicago, Los Angeles, and New York switches were turned up.

Meanwhile, the investment banks stated that they needed a $15 million lead equity investor in EverNet for the $40 million private placement memorandum before they could get the other institutional investors to follow. Nortel Networks had put up an unprecedented $20 million in equity, but it declined to lead the deal. Allied Capital had committed to $5 million in equity and $10 million in debt and Williams Communications to $10 million in equity and $15 million in debt; but EverNet still lacked a leading firm willing to commit $15 million. Kenefick asked for a one-week extension from the investment banks to find a lead funder. He returned to Palmer and Moore, who had supported EverNet since startup days, and secured an $8 million credit line. By May of 1999, EverNet was burning through $4 million a month.

Out of Cash

By June of 1999, EverNet was out of cash and looking for a lead partner in the funding deal. "We were in the middle of the fire," Kenefick says. "We had all these construction bills, and we didn't have enough cash flow." Kenefick went back to Palmer and Moore and asked for another $8 million bridge loan, proposing that EverNet would get the funds back from the $150 million Nortel financing. Palmer and Moore agreed. In July, the portion of funds from Williams finally closed. Kenefick realized that with the $8 million already committed by Palmer and Moore, the firm could potentially become the lead partner. Kenefick approached Williams, Nortel, Allied Capital and asked if they would agree to Palmer and Moore becoming the lead partner with a $15 million commitment. All three companies said yes. With just another $7 million committed to EverNet, Kenefick convinced Palmer and Moore to become the lead equity investor, turning the $8 million in debt into equity.

Next, Kenefick received the term sheets from the investment bank. The brokers were asking a $ 2.5 million commission, plus warrants, for raising the $40 million from the institutional investors. They were not, however, aware that Allied, Nortel, Williams, and Palmer and Moore had already committed to provide all the financing EverNet needed.

Surprise!

When Kenefick's one-week extension period ended at 5:00 PM on a Friday afternoon in August 1999, Kenefick called CIBC to discuss terms for the deal. Having closed on the cash from Williams, Kenefick had all the financing he needed, and he let the bankers know the terms of their deal with EverNet were not acceptable. The institutional investors represented by CIBC wanted two seats on the EverNet board of directors and an additional 5 percent dilution with a "clawback" clause allowing the investors to recoup enough stock to raise their internal rate of return to match the target value. The investors, Kenefick told the bankers, would need to restructure the financing deal on EverNet's terms.

"I had them against the wall," Kenefick says. "There was this shocked silence on the phone!" The investment bankers in turn brought the institutional investors in on the call to ask if the investors would consider changing the terms of the deal to accommodate EverNet's requests. With no warning from the bankers, in the 11th hour of the negotiations, the investors were dumbfounded.

Kenefick gave the astounded investment bankers until 5:00 PM the following Monday to restructure the terms of the deal. When they were unable to come to a compromise by the deadline, the deal was off. Kenefick did agree to pay the firm several hundred thousand dollars in fees for the work it had done on the deal, pointing out, "We're here to build bridges, not burn them."

On August 2, the last of the wires were brought in, and the deal was complete. Kenefick planned a public announcement in the *Washington Post* and *The Wall Street Journal* after Labor Day 1999. Nortel Networks had now pledged a $130 million senior secured loan with $20 million in equity; Williams, $15 million in debt and $10 million in equity financing; Allied Capital, $5 million in equity and $10 million in debt; and Palmer and Moore, $15 million in equity investment. EverNet was back on its feet. The company's new balance sheet was revealing—instead of $40 million in new capital obtained at a cost through investment bankers, EverNet had corralled a stunning $210 million in new financing from its own vendors.

With this war chest in place, Kenefick and his team barely had time to catch their breath before racing onward. Kenefick wondered whether and how this financing would affect the company's future, its strategy, its competitors, and his own priorities. One thing was clear: EverNet's financial strength had taken a giant leap forward.

In other departments, the decision had to be made on how to keep up with the growth.

EverNet is now organized into three management teams: executive, operational, and organizational. Each team meets bimonthly and national teams meet together at quarterly retreats. Retreats and meetings often focus on team building, the company mission, mission strategy, and customer-centric focus. Sessions include case studies such as Dell Computer/Netscape vs. Microsoft to analyze the evolving role of strong teamwork in a venture. Teams also focus on organizational growth, comparing their phase of organizational growth with that of other departments, which may be in a completely different phase.

"We break up the teams into groups and ask them which phase their team is in—collaborative, creative, delegative, or collective. It's funny to hear the results, because all of a sudden you have the groups coming back, and they all say a different phase. The answer is they're *all* right—the company is in several different phases at once," Kenefick says. Just as employees are asked to evaluate their role within the constantly changing company, groups and teams are asked to evaluate the stages and phases of their departments in terms of the long-term development of the business.

As he did with "Operation Geronimo" at the launch of EverNet, Kenefick plans new initiatives around themes, either targeting certain departments or for the entire company. In September of 1999, EverNet was launching "Mission Go-T" to focus on operational excellence and organize the process of installing millions of dollars worth of new software systems in the company, as well as assimilating a large number of new Internet, voice and T-1 circuits. Kenefick defines Mission Go-T as "a communitywide effort in operational excellence." As part of the effort, Kenefick believes in "putting together goals and roles for every single person in the company."

Underlying every decision at EverNet is the company's slogan "Technology Counts, People Matter." Meetings start with a "good news" story about an individual in the company, both on a professional and a personal level. Employees are encouraged to "take five minutes every day" to do something nice for somebody that they might not otherwise do. Meetings are an opportunity for all employees to talk about where things stand and to share ideas or concerns with others.

"People look at business seriously—it's civilized warfare. We either win or lose the battle every day," Kenefick reflects. "But it's not just about the destination. It's about the journey. You have to enjoy the process of the journey."

James Kenefick feels that the success of EverNet depends on the competence and confidence of its employees and their ability to market and sell the company's products and services better than the company's many competitors. EverNet is today a rapidly growing integrated communications provider focused on providing a core set of communications services primarily to medium-sized and small business customers.

The Future: So Many Rivers . . .

Norman Maclean is author of the now famous fly-fishing tales of his Montana youth, captured in Robert Redford's film by the same title *A River Runs Through It*. One of the more memorable quotes from his father, a Presbyterian minister, circumscribed the essence of the passion of fly-fishing: "At the final judgement, God does not subtract from a man's life those days spent fly-fishing for trout." For James Kenefick and his EverNet team, the future opportunities seem boundless. Like Maclean, they faced a parallel dilemma: so many rivers, so little time. And for EverNet we could add: so little cash.

By mid-1999 the company had made substantial progress on all fronts. Revenues in 1998 exceeded $13 million, were expected to reach $40 million in 1999, and should surge to $100 million in 2000.

Change Is Inevitable

The technological and competitive environment surrounding EverNet in 1999 was turbulent, rapidly changing, and not very predictable (see Exhibit G). Forces of exponential growth pummeled the company, its competitors, and the global economy (see Exhibit H). The cumulative and chaotic impact of these exponential forces on both the computer and telecommunications industries were and continued to be profound, as seen in Exhibits I through K.

EXHIBIT G

Change Is Inevitable

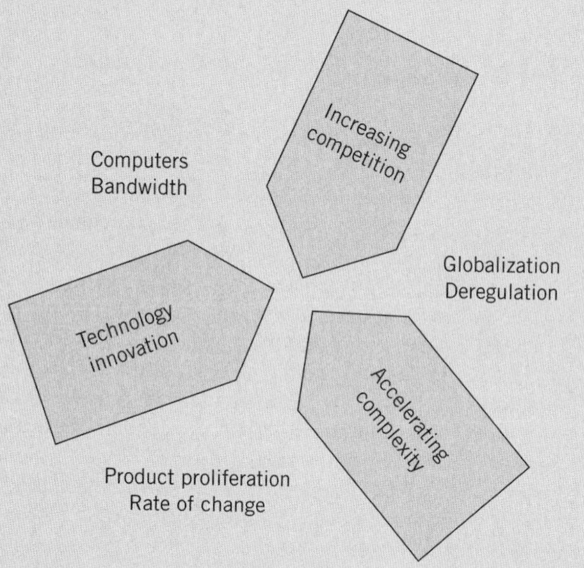

EXHIBIT H

Forces of Exponential Growth

Metcalfe's Law:	The value of a network is equal to the square of the number of users on the network
Gilder's Law:	Bandwidth capacity will triple every 12 months
Internet Fact:	The number of people and computers connected to the Internet doubles every 12 months
Moore's Law:	The computing power of transistors will double every 18 months

EXHIBIT I

Evolution of the Computer Industry

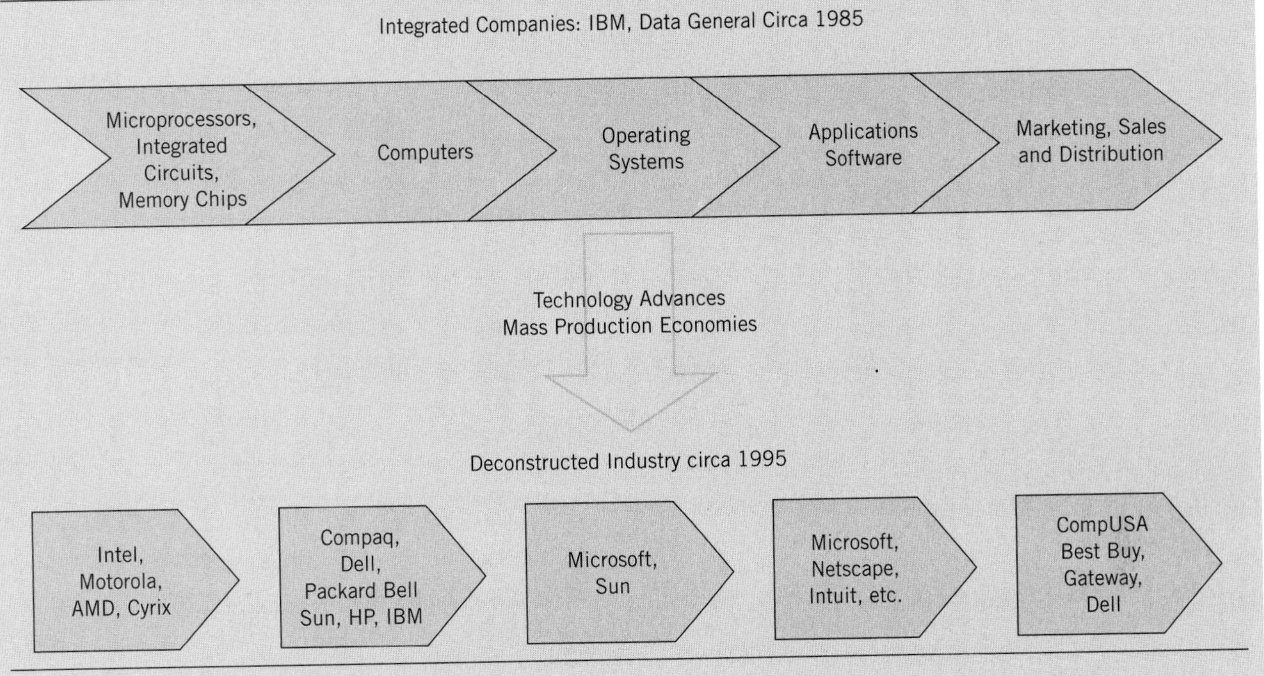
Integrated Companies: IBM, Data General Circa 1985
Microprocessors, Integrated Circuits, Memory Chips
Computers
Operating Systems
Applications Software
Marketing, Sales and Distribution
Technology Advances
Mass Production Economies
Deconstructed Industry circa 1995
Intel, Motorola, AMD, Cyrix
Compaq, Dell, Packard Bell Sun, HP, IBM
Microsoft, Sun
Microsoft, Netscape, Intuit, etc.
CompUSA Best Buy, Gateway, Dell

EXHIBIT J

Evolution of the Telecom Industry

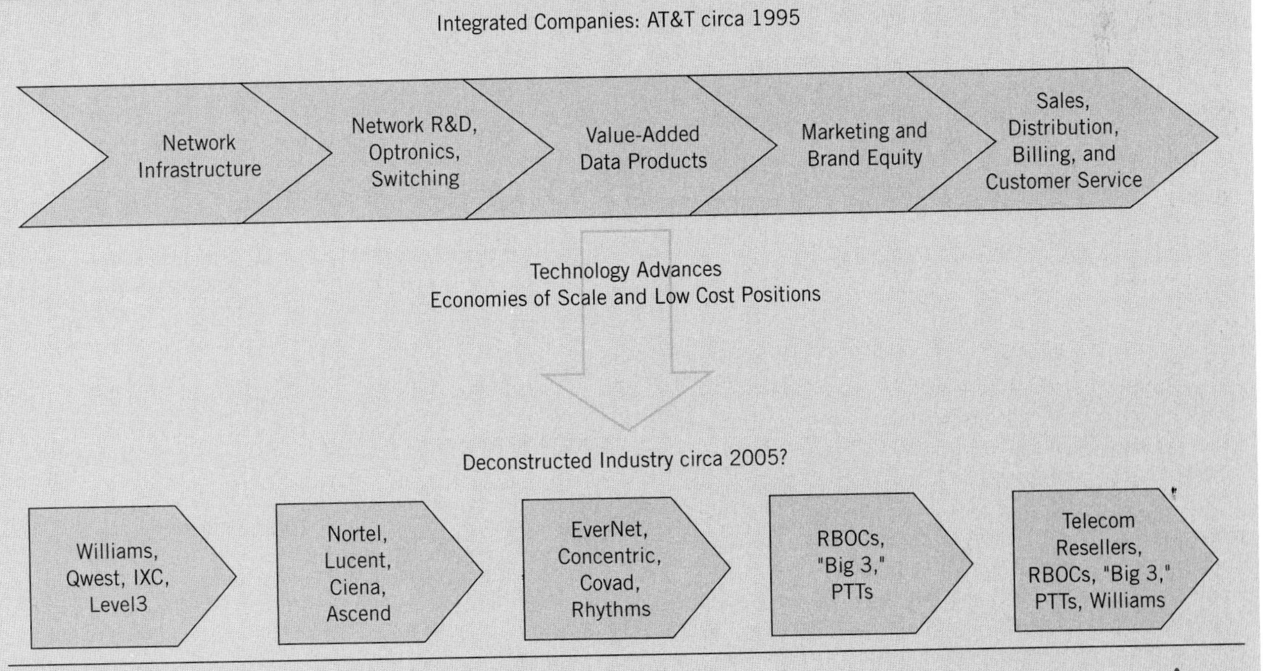
Integrated Companies: AT&T circa 1995
Network Infrastructure
Network R&D, Optronics, Switching
Value-Added Data Products
Marketing and Brand Equity
Sales, Distribution, Billing, and Customer Service
Technology Advances
Economies of Scale and Low Cost Positions
Deconstructed Industry circa 2005?
Williams, Qwest, IXC, Level3
Nortel, Lucent, Ciena, Ascend
EverNet, Concentric, Covad, Rhythms
RBOCs, "Big 3," PTTs
Telecom Resellers, RBOCs, "Big 3," PTTs, Williams

EXHIBIT K

Deconstruction Continues: Long-Distance Market Share

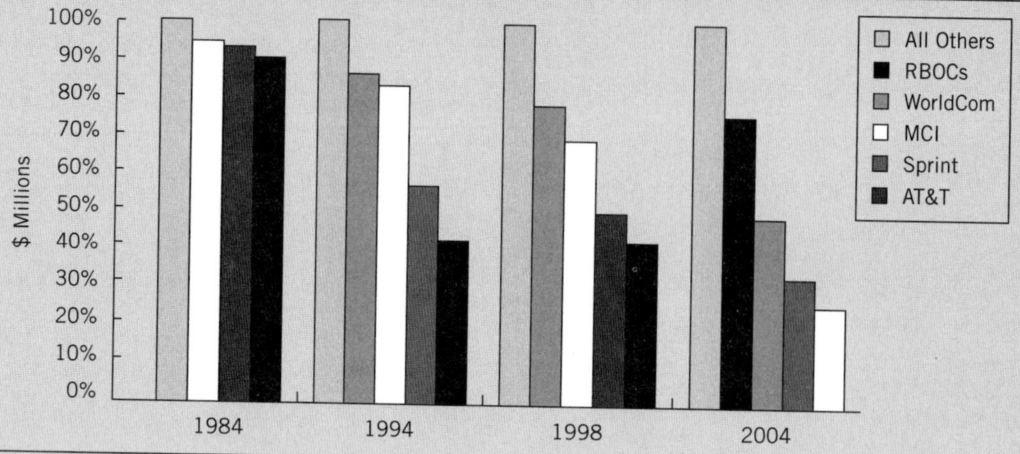

EXHIBIT L

The EverNet Opportunity

- 71% of midsize businesses are interested in **bundled** local and long-distance services
- 90% of midsize businesses are interested in **bundled** Internet services

Benefits of Bundling Communications Services:

To EverNet	To Customers
Increase revenue	Greater simplicity
Improve relations	Price savings
Reduce churn	Improved service
Network efficiencies	Accountability
Reduce costs	

Source: The Yankee Group, 1999, and EverNet, 1999.

EXHIBIT M

Venture Capital Disbursements, 1993–1998

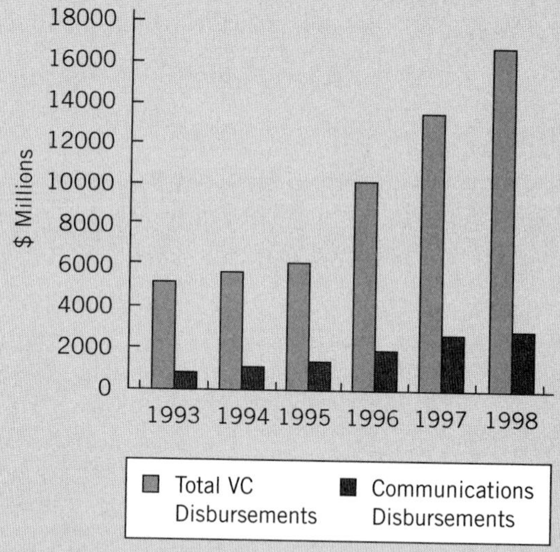

The net result of all this in EverNet's view was an "enormous telecommunications opportunity," as summarized in Exhibit L. This translated into significant monthly expenditures by small and medium-size businesses in the United States (see Exhibit J), as well as compounded annual growth rate now exceeding 25 percent (see Exhibit K). Forrester Research estimated that the $43 billion market for business-to-business electronic commerce in 1998 would grow to a staggering $1.3 trillion in 2003, representing 9 percent of total business sales. Indeed, similar growth was anticipated in all businesses and consumer trade affected by the World Wide Web.

Capital Markets Context

The capital markets continued their robustness by mid-1999. Private equity and venture capital funds were headed for what would be another record-setting year, exceeding the $85 billion and $18 billion, respectively, that poured into these funds in 1998 (see Exhibits M–O).

The IPO markets for telecom and Internet service providers were also strong. It was hoped such an environment would make Jim Kenefick's fund-raising challenge less daunting.

EXHIBIT N

Venture Capital Financed IPOs—Communications Sector

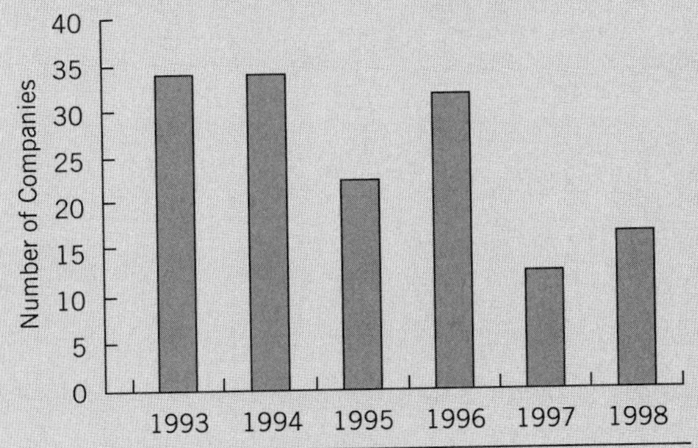

Financial Implications: Insatiable Appetite for Cash

Kenefick and his management team envisioned profound financial implications from these enormous opportunities. For one thing, the growth potential for the company seemed equally enormous. The new five-year financial projections were very robust, and management believed they were attainable, with revenue expected to reach $564 million in 2003 (see Exhibit P). For another, such hypergrowth would create a voracious appetite for new capital, judging by the negative cumulative free cash flows projected through 2003 in excess of $150 million (see Exhibit P).

EverNet had traversed the last three years at what seemed to James Kenefick and his team nothing short of warp speed. Few startup companies journey so far so quickly. There were many reasons for joy and celebration at EverNet. Yet, one harsh reality confronted the company: EverNet was out of cash and there was no funding in sight.

EXHIBIT O

Venture Capital-Backed Communication IPOs

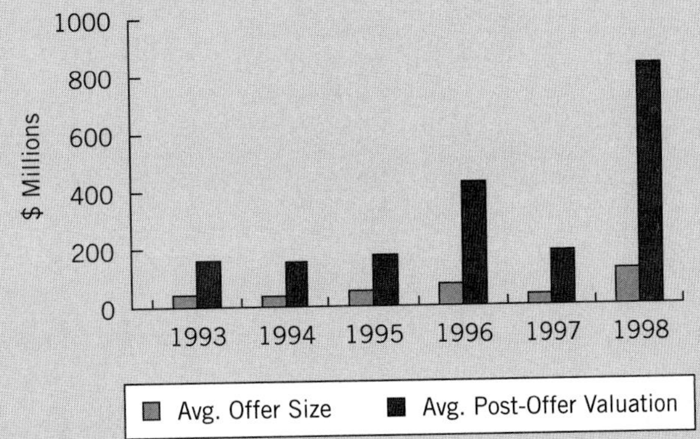

EXHIBIT P

EverNet Communications, Inc., Summary Projected Financial Data

	For the Year Ended December 31, ($000)				
	1999	**2000**	**2001**	**2002**	**2003**
Statement of Operations Data:					
Revenue					
Dedicated long distance	$ 11,224	$ 38,415	$ 68,423	$ 99,795	$ 132,115
Switched long distance	28,723	56,992	93,936	142,724	221,686
Internet access	8,375	27,757	48,439	69,629	91,173
Local dial tone	1,400	26,615	60,556	94,753	129,067
Total revenue	49,721	149,779	271,354	406,901	574,041
Cost of revenue	31,836	86,657	156,857	235,611	327,449
Gross margin	36%	42%	42%	42%	42%
Operating expenses:					
Selling, general and administrative	36,654	53,138	75,926	105,636	142,230
Depreciation	626	3,476	6,621	10,536	16,348
Total operating expenses	37,280	56,614	82,547	116,172	158,578
EBIT	(19,395)	6,437	31,950	55,119	78,014
Interest expense (income)	7,986	25,162	32,658	36,712	41,294
Net income	$ (27,381)	$ (18,725)	$ (708)	$ 18,407	$ 36,720
Other Financial Data:					
EBITDA	$ (18,769)	$ 9,914	$ 38,571	$ 65,654	$ 94,361
Capital expenditures	28,644	48,091	42,455	63,809	101,206
Change in working capital	(8,917)	(11,238)	(12,637)	(13,312)	(15,989)
Free cash flow	$ (56,330)	$ (49,415)	$ (16,521)	$ (11,467)	$ (22,834)
Other Operating Data (at period end)					
Direct sales representatives	198	246	294	342	390
Direct sales offices	16	19	22	24	25
Branchise offices	17	23	29	35	41
Commercial lines (000s)					
Dedicated	0.5	1.2	2.0	2.7	3.5
Switched	71	126	187	253	322
Residential lines (000s)	166	341	655	1,319	2,688
Commercial customers (000s)	15	31	52	76	97
Avg. revenue per commercial customer	$3,063	$4,475	$4,902	$4,899	$5,052
Avg. revenue per total line					
Dedicated	$72	$108	$121	$127	$131
Switched	$34	$38	$42	$47	$55

	For the Year Ended December 31, ($000)				
	1999	**2000**	**2001**	**2002**	**2003**
Balance Sheet Data:					
Cash and restricted cash	$166,591	$173,408	$134,679	$95,720	$30,659
Property, plant and equipment, net	32,720	77,335	113,169	166,442	251,301
Total assets	214,927	287,819	309,292	351,348	405,291
Total l-t debt (exc. current portion)	169,200	225,200	225,200	225,200	225,200
Total stockholders' equity	(26,601)	(46,744)	(51,274)	(39,131)	(20,975)

17

Chapter Seventeen

The Family as Entrepreneur

Whoever thought that safeguarding the brands, assets, and customers that made your company a success would constitute risky behavior? But these days it is—if it is all your company is doing. By conserving resources and honing operational efficiencies, established companies try to guarantee that there is never an unexpected downside. In so doing they often miss out on the real action in today's economy—capitalizing on the upside potential of new ideas.

Gary Hamel[1]

Results Expected

Upon the completion of this chapter, you will have:

1. Understood the significant economic and entrepreneurial contribution families make to communities and countries worldwide.
2. Examined the different roles families play as part of the entrepreneurial process.
3. Developed a definition of family enterprising and transgenerational entrepreneurship.
4. Assessed your family on the mindset and methods continua for family enterprising and identified key issues for family dialogue.
5. Explored key questions on the six dimensions for family enterprising.
6. Plotted your family's resources and capabilities on the "familiness F+ F− assessment continuum" in order to understand their advantages and constraints.

Families, Entrepreneurship, and the Timmons Model

The tension among generations in families can often revolve around the aggressive younger executives seeking to explore new and exciting deals and the older executive who seeks to march forward on the pathway that created the family's fortune. The purpose of this chapter is to help families (and those working with families!) understand that opportunity recognition and balance in the Timmons Model helps guide the family's decision-making process. By encouraging the discussion toward the model, we ask, "What is the richest opportunity?" and "Are the opportunity, team, and resources well balanced?" Families have special knowledge, experience, and often resources that bring competitive advantages. We aspire to leverage these special factors to create a "familiness" advantage that creates value.

The concepts and models presented in this chapter are based on the research and writing of Timothy Habbershon and colleagues, including T.G. Habbershon and M.L. Williams, "A Resource Based Framework for Assessing the Strategic Advantages of Family Firms," *Family Business Review*, 12, 1999, pp. 1–25; T.G. Habbershon, M. Williams, I.C. MacMillan, "A Unified Systems Perspective of Family Firm Performance," *Journal of Business Venturing*, 18(4), 2003, pp. 451–465; T.G. Habbershon and J. Pistrui, "Enterprising Families Domain: Family-Influenced Ownership Groups in Pursuit of Transgenerational Wealth," *Family Business Review*, XV(1), 2002, pp. 223–237.

[1] Gary Hamel, "Bringing Silicon Valley Inside," *Harvard Business Review*, September–October 1999, Vol. 77, Issue 5, p. 70.

Building Entrepreneurial Family Legacies[2]

When we hear the phrase *family business,* images of high-flying, harvesting entrepreneurs are not usually the first thoughts that come to our mind. We more often think of the small mom-and-pop businesses, or the large business family fights that hold the potential for reality TV. It is fair to say that family businesses do not always look and act entrepreneurially. They can focus on serving local markets, sustaining the family's lifestyle or providing jobs to family members. They are often conflicted due to family dynamics, constrained by nepotism, or limited by their conservative risk profile.

But these realities should be held in tension with the corresponding truth that families comprise the dominant form of business organization worldwide and provide more resources for the entrepreneurial economy than any other source. We must be careful that we do not form mental caricatures about either family businesses or entrepreneurs that might keep us from exploring the link between entrepreneurship and family or, more important, keep us from understanding the significance the linkage holds for social and economic wealth creation in our communities and countries worldwide.

The purpose of this chapter is to deepen our understanding of entrepreneurship in the family context. We will explore the entrepreneurial commitments, capabilities, and contributions of families and their businesses. To describe families who leverage the entrepreneurial process in the family context we use the phrase *family enterprising.* As enterprise refers to economic activity, enterprising is the action of generating economic activity. Consistent with earlier definitions of entrepreneurship, families who are enterprising generate new economic activity and build long-term value across generations. We refer to this outcome as *transgenerational entrepreneurship and wealth creation* and it is how to build entrepreneurial family legacies. This chapter will provide families with three sets of assessment and strategy tools to assist them in knowing how to become enterprising and build their family legacy.

Large Company Family Legacies

We must first begin by understanding the economic and entrepreneurial significance of families. It is difficult to walk into a Marriot Hotel, see the father and son picture of J. Willard Marriott Jr. and Sr., and not think about entrepreneurial family legacies. From a small root beer concession stand, who would have expected the emergence of a $10 billion and 133,000 employee company? The Marriotts are now operating in their third generation of family leadership and are just one example of the many U.S. companies and branded products that are synonymous with family names and legacies.

Ford Motor Company celebrated 100 years of making cars in 2003. Henry Ford's original company is in its fifth-generation with fourth-generation leader William (Bill) Clay Ford, Jr., as the chairman and CEO. The Ford family still controls about 40 percent of the voting shares in the $170 billion-plus company, and board member Edsel B. Ford II said that they are interested in creating a new generation of entrepreneurs.

Walgreen Co. began when Chicago pharmacist and entrepreneur Charles Walgreen borrowed $2,000 from his father for a down payment on his first drugstore in 1901. Today the company is in its fourth generation of Walgreen family involvement with Charles R. Walgreen III as the chairman emeritus of the board of directors and his son Kevin Walgreen is a vice president. It has grown through the generations to over 4,800 stores with $37.5 billion in annual revenue. It has fewer stores than its rival CVS, but still beats them in annual sales.

Cargill is the largest privately held corporation in the United States generating more than $62 billion in annual revenues across a diversified group of food, agricultural, and risk management businesses around the globe. One hundred and forty years after its inception, the founding Cargill and MacMillan families still own 85 percent of the company.

While it is often assumed that family companies cannot play in the technology and telecommunications arena, father and son team Ralph and Brian Roberts have grown the Comcast cable company into the largest in the United States. Even with a $54 billion takeover of AT&T Broadband in 2002, the Roberts family still maintains 33 percent of the voting shares and top leadership positions.[3]

Families also dominate many of the leading financial services and banking institutions worldwide. In Boston, Fidelity and the Johnson family are a leading business family. The Johnsons control 49 percent of the largest mutual fund company in the world. They have more than $1 trillion under management. Ned Johnson continues to lead the company as CEO and chairman, while his daughter is president of the fastest growing Retirement Services Unit.

Many of the popular branded product companies are controlled by families including Tyson Foods, an

[2] Primary financial, performance, and ownership data from Hoovers Online.
[3] "A New Cable Giant," *BusinessWeek,* November 18, 2002, p. 108.

Arkansas-based $26 billion company in which the family controls 80 percent and the grandson of the founder is the current chairman and CEO. Mars is still 100 percent family owned and the $20 billion company has multiple generations of family members at all levels of top leadership. Cosmetic, fragrance, and skin care products company Estee Lauder generates nearly $6 billion in revenues with the founding family controlling approximately 88 percent of its voting shares with six members in top management bearing the Lauder name. Wrigleys gum, a $3.6 billion company currently run by the founder's great-grandson, William Wrigley Jr., far outperforms its rivals with a 20.3 percent return on assets. Smucker's Jam—"With a name like Smucker's, it has to be good"—has sales of over $2 billion with brothers Tim and Richard continuing to grow the 100-year-old company.

Another interesting category of entrepreneurial family involvement is the investment-holding company. Warren Buffet may be one of the most famous examples. Buffet's company, Berkshire Hathaway, owns many recognizable companies such as GEICO Insurance, Fruit of the Loom, and Dairy Queen. For over 37 years, Buffet's investments in companies have provided an average annual return of 22.6 percent and have increased the value of Berkshire by over 195,000 percent since 1965. His 38 percent stake in the $74 billion Berkshire gives him an estimated net worth of $41 billion and makes him the second-richest person in the world, behind only Bill Gates.[4] Warren's son, Howard G. Buffet, is a director at several Berkshire subsidiaries and currently sits on the board at Berkshire. While succession planning at Berkshire is highly secretive, it is anticipated that Howard Buffet will take over as chairman of the board.

Minnesota-based Carlson Companies is a lesser known company, but CEO Marilyn Carlson Nelson took over her family holding company and grew it 25 percent in 2004 to $26 billion in revenues. The 100 percent family-owned company is predominately in hospitality and travel, owning companies such as the TGI Friday's restaurant chain, Radisson, Regent International Hotels, and Park Plaza Hotels & Resorts.

There are many smaller family investment-holding companies such as the Berwind Group in Philadelphia, Pennsylvania, that fly under the radar in our cities. The multi-billion-dollar fifth-generation family company invested more than $900 million in acquisitions during their most recent three-year planning cycle, including the acquisition of Elmer's Products.

In keeping with this picture of family legacy contributions, a recent study showed that 35 percent (177) of 2003 Fortune 500 companies are controlled and or managed by families. These family-influenced companies consistently outperform non-family businesses on annual shareholder return, return on assets, and both annual revenue and income growth.[5] But these large family companies only begin to tell the story of the entrepreneurial and economic contribution made by business families. (See Exhibit 17.1.)

WAL-MART: A GROWTH-ORIENTED FAMILY ENTERPRISE

Whether one loves or hates Wal-Mart, the Walton family tops the list of family wealth creation legacies. The family still controls nearly 40 percent of the largest company in the world with $288 billion in annual revenue. The family fortune totals $100 billion—more than Bill Gates and Warren Buffet combined, or more than the GDP of Singapore. There are five Walton family members[6] in the top 10 of the list of richest Americans[7] and they contributed more than $700 million in charitable giving with 80 percent of their donations to education since 1998. The visible link between the company and the family is Wal-Mart Chairman Rob Walton, who is commended by *Fortune* magazine as one of "the most knowledgeable non-executive chairmen in American business." Rob's father, Sam Walton, had a vision to allow ordinary folks to buy what only rich people could once buy. This aspiration was translated into the company slogan "everyday low prices." Chairman Rob Walton makes clear that the Walton vision is alive and well, proclaiming that "Wal-Mart is still a growth company."[8]

Smaller and Mid-Size Family Legacies

In many regards, the real heart and often overlooked segment of the U.S. economy and entrepreneurial activity is the smaller and mid-size companies. This segment is substantively controlled by families, and they are not all your typical "mom and pop" operations.

Cardone manufacturing in Philadelphia, Pennsylvania, is a prime example. Founded by a father and son team in 1970, it is the largest non-government employer in the city and the largest privately held remanufacturer of car parts in the United States. The founding son, Michael Cardone and his third-generation children

[4] "Forbes 400 List," September 24, 2004, *Forbes*, http://www.forbes.com/400richest/.
[5] Joseph Weber, et. al., "Family Inc.," *BusinessWeek*, November 10, 2003.
[6] On June 27, 2005, John Walton, son of Sam Walton, tragically died in a crash of his ultralight plane near Jackson Hole, Wyoming. John was tied for fourth richest person according to *Forbes* with a net worth of $18 billion. It is still unsure what will be done with his remaining fortune.
[7] "Forbes 400 List," September 24, 2004, *Forbes*, http://www.forbes.com/400richest/.
[8] Andy Serwer, et. al., "The Waltons: Inside America's Richest Family," *Fortune*, November 15, 2004, Vol. 150, Issue 10, p. 86.

EXHIBIT 17.1

Performance Comparison

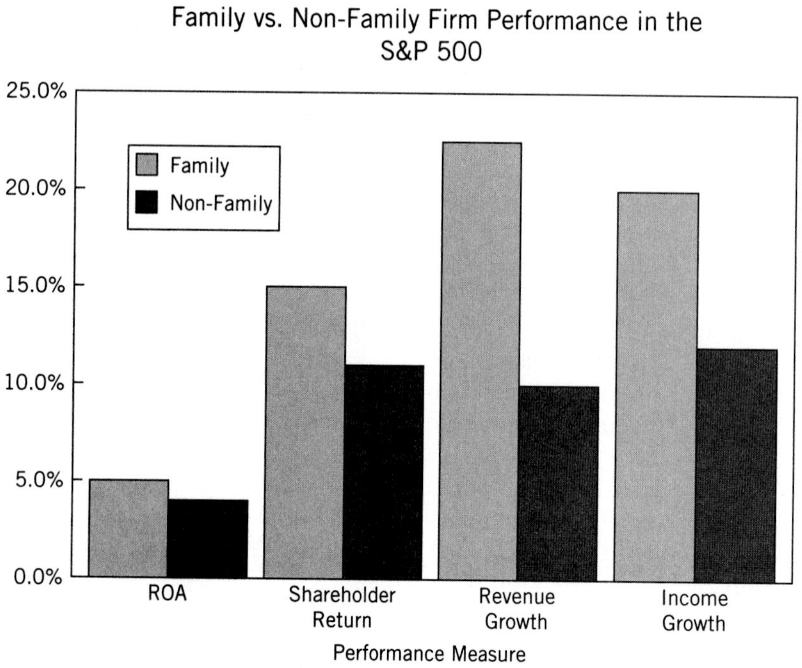

Source: "Family Inc.," *BusinessWeek*, November 10, 2003. Used by permission of the McGraw-Hill Companies, Inc.

are continuing their entrepreneurial legacy by expanding the multi-hundred-million-dollar company into Europe and China, while moving into the new car parts arena.

The largest privately held hair salon chain in the United States was founded by a husband and wife. The Ratner Company has a strong top leadership team and is training its second generation of family members. They outperform their larger public rival, Regis, and continue to act entrepreneurially. With nearly 1,000 company stores in their largest brand, Hair Cuttery, they are moving into franchising, expanding their upscale brands, and establishing strategic partnerships to continue their global expansion. While co-founder Dennis Ratner could be resting on his accomplishments, he is committed to family enterprising, telling his children "You either eat or get eaten."

Many family companies may not have brand names consumers recognize, but they are dominant in their industries because they play in the supply chains of large multinationals. Bloomer Chocolates in Chicago, Illinois, is known as the company that makes Chicago smell like chocolate. The third-generation multi-hundred-million-dollar company is the largest roaster of chocolate beans in the United States. They have taken a low-margin commodities business that large chocolate companies have outsourced and created a profitable niche. Many of the chocolate products from companies such as Hershey's and Nestlé are made from chocolate produced by Bloomer.

The list of these "everyday" family entrepreneurs is endless. In Boston, Gentle Giant is the largest regional moving company. The entrepreneurial vision of this $20 million company sets the standard for the moving industry, and they plan to replicate it in other cities. The largest distributor of IAMS pet food on the East Coast has a third generation of entrepreneurs at the helm. Having recently bought the business from their father, two brothers are next-generation entrepreneurs, growing Pet Food Experts and diversifying it to lessen the risk of being a dedicated distributor. In the ski industry, dominated by large public resort companies, Tim and Diane Mueller stand out as successful family entrepreneurs. Since 1982 they have grown the run-down Vermont ski resort they purchased to a $100 million company and have acquired a resort in Denver. CarSense is a new concept car dealership that has grown to $100 million in sales in seven years after the second-generation entrepreneur sold the families' traditional car dealerships to innovate for the future. Majestic Athletic, a sports apparel company in eastern Pennsylvania, run by the Capobianco family, makes the uniforms for all of Major League Baseball. Many critics felt Major League Baseball was crazy to choose a small family-run company instead of a large apparel maker, but the hands-on quality approach of the family has been a big hit for the company and the league.

In this montage of families we have not even mentioned the nascent entrepreneurs and smaller companies that will become the next-generation Marriot, Smucker's, or Ratner family company. Nor have we considered the children in existing family firms who will become nascent entrepreneurs. In a recent undergraduate class on family entrepreneurship at Babson College, more than 80 percent of the students said that they wanted to start *their own company* as an extension of their family company. They were not just looking to run their family company. Students like Toby Donath created a business plan to move his mother's business, Backerhaus Veit, from manufacturing and wholesaling to retailing and branded products. Brothers Colby and Drew West are starting a technology company with their parents as "support investors" based on a new technology developed by Drew. Student Jonathan Gelpey has a plan to commercialize a product for which his grandfather holds the patent. All of these young entrepreneurs fulfill our vision for next-generation entrepreneurship and family enterprising.

The Family Contribution and Roles

It is clear from our descriptions of family companies that families still dominate the U.S. economy and even more fully the economies of other countries worldwide. The most recent economic impact study in the United States reported that 89 percent of all business tax returns and 60 percent of all public companies had family participation and strategic control. That is more than 24 million businesses and represents nearly $6 trillion in gross domestic product (64 percent of GDP) and 82 million jobs (62 percent of workforce).[9] Worldwide, the economic numbers are similar to those in countries like Italy, reporting 93 percent of their businesses are family controlled, and Brazil, 90 percent.[10] (See Exhibits 17.2 and 17.3.)

Once we acknowledge the economic relevance of families we can better understand the significant pool

[9] Joseph H. Astrachan and Melissa Carey Shanker, "Family Businesses' Contribution to the U.S. Economy: A Closer Look," *Family Business Review*, September 2003, Volume 16, Issue 3, p. 211.

[10] "IFERA. Family Businesses Dominate," *Family Business Review*, December 2003, Volume 16, Issue 4, p. 235.

EXHIBIT 17.2

Family Businesses' Economic Contribution

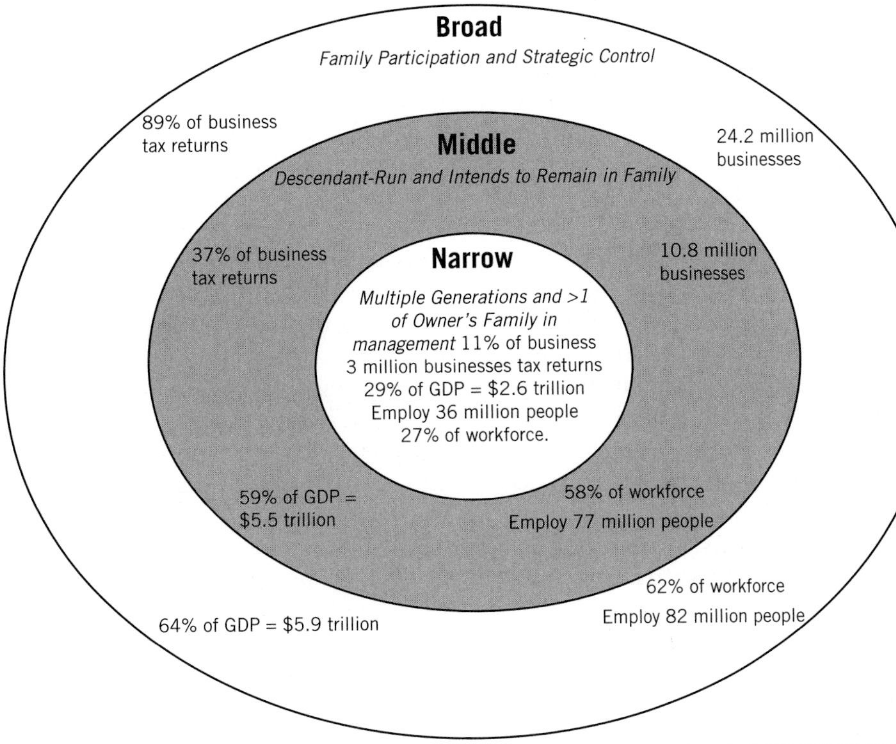

Source: Joseph H. Astrachan, Melissa Carey Shanker, "Family Businesses' Contribution to the U.S. Economy: A Closer Look," *Family Business Review*, September 2003, Vol. 16, Issue 3, p. 211. Copyright 2003 Blackwell Publishing. Used by permission.

EXHIBIT 17.3

Worldwide Highlights of Family Businesses

Country	Definition	% of FBs	GNP
Brazil	Middle	90%	63%
Chile	Broad	75%	50–70%
USA	Broad	96%	40%
Belgium	Narrow	70%	55%
Finland	Narrow	80%	40–45%
France	Broad	>60%	>60%
Germany	Middle	60%	55%
Italy	Broad	93%	
Netherlands	Narrow	74%	54%
Poland	Broad	Up to 80%	35%
Portugal	Broad	70%	60%
Spain	Narrow	79%	
UK	Middle	70%	
Australia	Narrow	75%	50%
India	Broad		65%

of resources and potential they represent for entrepreneurial activity. There was a day when "business" meant "family" because the family was understood to be foundational to all socioeconomic progress.[11] Today, however, we must more intentionally categorize the roles families play economically and entrepreneurially. Exhibit 17.4 presents five different roles families can play in the entrepreneurial process and distinguishes between a formal and informal application of these roles.

In this regard the categories are both descriptive and prescriptive. They describe what role families play and how they play them, but also hint at a prescription for a more formal approach to entrepreneurship in the family context. By "formal" we mean establishing individual and organizational disciplines and structure of the entrepreneurial process. We do not mean "bureaucratic." Many family entrepreneurs, particularly senior generation entrepreneurs, embrace the myth that any formalization will constrain their entrepreneurial behavior. Nothing could be further from the truth. With informed intuition, disciplined processes, clear financial benchmarks, and organizational accountability, family teams can generate higher potential ventures and get the odds in their favor for transgenerational entrepreneurship and wealth creation.

The first and dominant role families play is what we call *family-influenced startups*. Data from the GEM report indicated that there were 25 million "new family firms" started in 2002 worldwide.[12] Because families are driven by social forces of survival, wealth creation, and progeny, it is natural that startup businesses think family first. Family-influenced startups are new businesses where the family ownership vision and/or leadership influence impacts the strategic intent, decision making, and financial goals of the company. They may have family involvement in the beginning, intend to have family involvement, or end up having family involvement during the formative stages of the company. Some families begin their collective entrepreneurship experience with a more formal vision and planning process that delineates how the family will capture a new opportunity. This approach often clarifies the role family members will play in the startup and puts them on a faster path for successfully meeting their family and financial goals.

The *family corporate venturing* category is when an existing family company or group starts new businesses. Families are often, and quite naturally, portfolio entrepreneurs who build numerous businesses under a family umbrella. While they may not always grow each of the businesses to their fullest potential, the new businesses are often synergistic, create jobs for a community, and grow the net worth of the family. Often they are started so that family members have their own business to run. The more formal approach to family corporate venturing makes the new business process part of an overall strategic plan for growing family wealth while leveraging the resources and capabilities of family members.

Family corporate renewal is where the family's entrepreneurial activity is focused on creating new streams of value within the business or group through innovation and transformational change activities. Companies that launch new products or services, enter new markets, or establish new business models are renewing their strategies for the future. This type of strategic or structural renewal is particularly prevalent during family generational transitions or when a family realizes their legacy business can no longer compete. A more formal approach to corporate renewal is proactive, continuous, and institutionalized versus waiting for transitions or competitive triggers to start the renewal processes.

One of the primary roles families play is to provide *family private cash* to family members who want to start a business. More than 63 percent of businesses in the planning stage and up to 85 percent

[11] Howard E. Aldrich and Jennifer E. Cliff, "The Pervasive Effects of Family on Entrepreneurship: Toward a Family Embeddedness Perspective," *Journal of Business Venturing*, September 2003, Volume 18, Issue 5, p. 573.
[12] GEM 2002, Special Report on Family Sponsored New Ventures.

EXHIBIT 17.4

Roles Families Play in the Entrepreneurial Process

	Family-Influenced Startups	Family Corporate Venturing	Family Corporate Renewal	Family Private Cash	Family Investment Funds
Formal	An entrepreneur with no legacy assets/ existing business, but who formally launches a new business with family and/or intending to involve family	Family holding companies or businesses that have formal new venture creation and/or acquisition strategies, plans, departments, or capabilities	Family-controlled companies with a formal strategic growth plan for creating new streams of value through change in business strategy, model, or structure	Startup money from family member or business with a formal written agreement for market-base ROI and or repayment	Stand-alone professional private equity or venture capital fund controlled by family and/or using family generated capital
Informal	An entrepreneur with no legacy assets/ existing business who happens to start a new business out of necessity and it begins to involve family members	Family holding companies or businesses that grow through more informal, intuitive, and opportunistic business startup and acquisitions	Intuitive growth initiatives that result in a change in business strategy, model, or structure and new streams of value for the family company	Startup money or gift from family member or business with no agreement or conversation about ROI or repayment	Internal capital and/or funds used by family owners to invest in real estate, passive partnerships, or seed new businesses

of existing new ventures used family funding. Between 30 percent and 80 percent of all informal (non-venture capital) funding comes from family. In the United States this amounts to nearly .05 percent of GDP and as high as 3 percent of GDP in South Korea.[13] Most often the family cash is given based upon altruistic family sentiments rather than having more formal investment criteria. While providing seed capital whether it is forma or informal is clearly a significant role in the entrepreneurial process, having some formal investment criteria can avoid future confusion or conflict among family members. It also creates more discipline and accountability for family entrepreneurs, which is a good thing. (See Exhibit 17.5.)

Family investment funds are pools of family capital that families use for entrepreneurial activities. These family funds, both formal and informal, are becoming increasingly more common as families find themselves flush with cash. Most often, the formal family investment funds are created after a family has liquidated all or part of their family group. These funds are generally formed in conjunction with a family office. Informal family investment funds are pools of money, generally from cash flows, that family leaders invest in entrepreneurial activities as a way to diversify their family portfolios and/or have fun. They often invest within their network of peers and the investments are usually non-operating investments in businesses or real estate deals. These investments are often significant portions of their total wealth.

EXHIBIT 17.5

Distribution of Businesses with Family Venture Backing

	Planning Stage Startups	New Firms	Established Firms
Number of Cases	1,425	1,594	3,743
Family-Sponsored Ventures	63%	76%	85%

Source: *Family Sponsored Ventures.* Astrachan, Joseph H., Shaker A. Zahra, and Pramodita Sharma. Publication for The Entrepreneurial Advantage of Nationals: First Annual Global Entrepreneurship Symposium, United Nations Headquarters. April 29, 2003; based on findings from the Global Entrepreneurship Monitor 2002 sponsored by Babson College, London Business School and the Kauffman Foundation.

When we catalog the wide range of informal and formal roles families can play in the entrepreneurial process, we see the contribution they are capable of making to the entrepreneurial economy. We believe business families who are interested in transgenerational entrepreneurship and wealth creation must cultivate the more formal approach to entrepreneurship. The remainder of this chapter assists families in formalizing their entrepreneurship roles. We present three strategy frames that are based on the Timmons Model introduced in Chapter 3. The frames focus on the controllable components of the entrepreneurial processes that can be assessed, influenced, and altered.

13 Ibid.

Frame One: The Mindset and Method for Family Enterprising

Families who are enterprising are a particular type of family and *not* just a family who is in business. Enterprising families understand that today's dynamic and hypercompetitive marketplace requires families to act entrepreneurially. That is, they must generate new economic activity if they intend to survive and prosper over long periods of time. The Timmons Model shows us that at the heart of the entrepreneurial process is the opportunity. Those families who intend to act entrepreneurially must be opportunity focused. Consistent with this focus, enterprising is seen as the decision that leaders and organizations make to investigate opportunity and seek growth "when expansion is neither pressing nor particularly obvious."[14] The enterprising decision to search for opportunity precedes the economic decision to capture the opportunity. It is when families are faced with a decision (knowingly or unknowingly) to continue along their existing path, versus to expend effort and commit resources to investigate whether there are higher potential opportunities that are not yet obvious, that the "spirit of enterprising" is evidenced. We thus define enterprising as the proactive and continuous search for opportunistic growth.

TWELVE CHALLENGES TO FAMILY ENTERPRISING

Like the gravitational pull that keeps us bound to the earth, families face a number of inherent challenges that may keep them bound to past strategies rather than pursuing new opportunities.

1. Families assume that their past success will guarantee their future success.
2. Family members attribute "legacy value" to their businesses or assets, but that value does not translate into a market value or advantage.
3. Families want a "legacy pass" in the market—"We are 50 years old and we deserve another 50 years since we have been such good citizens."
4. Leaders try to balance the risk profile (risk and reward expectations) of their shareholders with the risk and investment demands of the marketplace.
5. Senior and successor generations have different risk profiles and goals for how the business should grow in the future.
6. Families find it hard to pass the entrepreneurial commitments and capabilities from the senior generation to a less "hungry" successor generation.
7. Families build their first-generation businesses on the founder's intuition, but the business never establishes more intentional entrepreneurial processes to keep the entrepreneurial contributions alive.
8. Families will not use many of the financial strategies that entrepreneurs use to grow businesses—i.e., debt, equity capital, strategic alliances, and partnerships.
9. Families do not "shed" unproductive assets and underperforming businesses to reallocate resources to more productive places.
10. Successor generation family members feel entitled to get a business rather than seek next-generation entrepreneurial opportunity.
11. Senior leaders communicate to the next generation that business planning and entrepreneurial analysis is a waste of time.
12. Family members are given a business to run as part of their legacy and that is viewed as entrepreneurship in the family.

Enterprising families institutionalize the opportunity seeking processes in the mindset and methods of both their family ownership group and their business organizations. Those families who simply try to maintain their local advantage, safeguard their brands, assets, and customers, or hone their operational efficiencies put themselves at a competitive risk in the shorter run. In the longer run, if their strategic planning is mainly focused on how to pass their business from one generation to the next, rather than developing people and strategies for creating new streams of value, their future may be limited. We would certainly not describe these types of families as enterprising or assume that they are transgenerational.

Enterprising Mindset and Methods

The first assessment and strategy frame for family enterprising is the Mindset and Methods Model (Exhibit 17.6). The model shows that family enterprising is the combination of a financial ownership mindset and entrepreneurial strategic methods. The purpose of the model is to ensure that families talk about both the ownership *and* management requirements for carrying out the entrepreneurial process in their family and business. The mindset and methods

[14] Judith E. Penrose, *The Theory of the Growth of the Firm*, 3rd ed., Oxford University Press, New York. 1995.

EXHIBIT 17.6

Mindset and Methods Enterprising Model

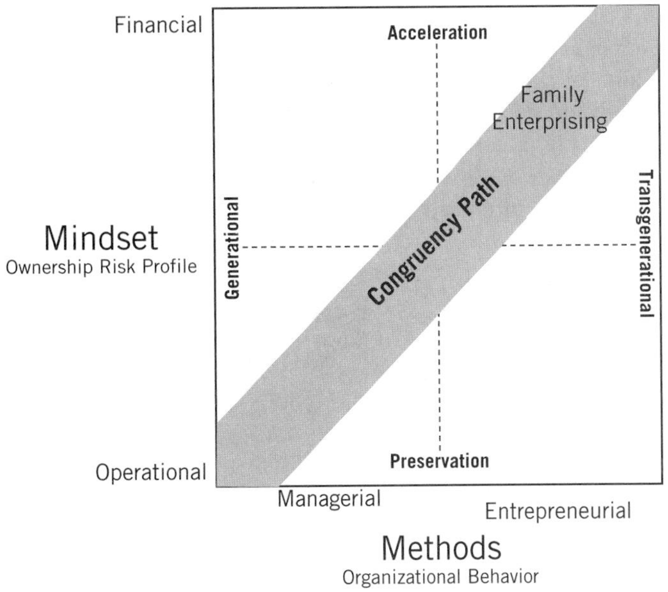

Source: © Habbershon and Pistrui.

assessment instruments[15] at the back of this chapter will enable families to determine their level of congruence on the two dimensions. It will also allow them to have a strategic conversation about where they currently are and how they might need to change in order to become more enterprising.

WHAT ENTERPRISING IS NOT

It is often useful in defining a concept to understand *what it is not*. Judith Penrose takes this approach by contrasting the concept of enterprising with three categories of firms that are not necessarily enterprising.[16]

"Just grew firms"—The "just grew" category are those that were in the right place at the right time. They were on the wave of an expanding market and they had to expand to keep up with demand. The decision to grow was automatic, and because they were able to capitalize on the circumstances, they grew. The situation may continue for a long period of time, but because markets do not expand indefinitely and competitors fill the opportunity gap, firm growth and the firm will come to an end.

"Comfort firms"—This category is often referred to as lifestyle firms. There are firms who refrain from taking full advantage of opportunities for expansion because it would increase their effort and risk. Firms that are comfortable with their income and position have no incentive to grow beyond their acceptable level of profits. These are firms where the goals of the owners to be comfortable are closely aligned with the goals of the firm. Like "just grew firms," comfort firms may continue for decades, but in the end meeting the comfort needs of the owners is not a driver for advantage or renewal.

"Competently managed firms"—Many firms are competently managed and consequently are able to find normal returns for relatively long periods of time by maintaining their operational efficiencies. Competently managed firms are often striving to sustain the entrepreneurial efforts of a founder. They may be competing in more traditional, less dynamic circumstances, have a distinctive market niche, or maintain a regional advantage as a favored business. While these are exploitable strategies, they are not inherently sustainable and may quickly disappear.

[15] The content and questions from the Mindset and Methods inventories are based upon the following literature:
Jeffrey, G. Covin and Dennis P. Slevin, "Strategic Management in Small Firms in Hostile and Benign Environments," *Strategic Management Journal*, 1989, 10(1), pp. 75–87.
Rita Gunther McGrath, and Ian. MacMillan, *The Entrepreneurial Mindset: Strategies for Continuously Creating Opportunity in an Age of Uncertainty*, 2000, Harvard Business School Press Boston, MA.
Daniel L. Mconaughy, Charles H. Matthews, and Anne S. Fialko, "Founding Family Controlled Firms: Performance, Risk, and Value." *Journal of Small Business Management*, January 2001, Volume 39, Issue 1, p. 31.
Danny. Miller, "The Correlates of Entrepreneurship in Three Types of Firms," *Management Science*, 1983, Vol. 29, Issue 7, 770.
Danny Miller and Peter H. Friesen, "Innovation in Conservative and Entrepreneurial Firms: Two Models of Strategic Momentum," *Strategic Management Journal*, January–March 1982, Volume 3, Issue 1, p. 1.
Shaker Zahra, "Entrepreneurial Risk Taking in Family Firms," *Family Business Review*, March 2005, Volume 18, Issue 1, p. 23.

[16] Judith E. Penrose, *The Theory of the Growth of the Firm*, 3rd ed., Oxford University Press, New York 1995.

The *mindset continuum* is primarily a measure of the financial risk profile of the family owners-shareholders. In general, it reflects the financial premise that entrepreneurial leaders gain strategic advantage and find above normal rents by deploying their resources to points of highest return and by developing strategies that exploit new opportunity. Family leaders who have an operational mindset predominately focus on management strategies, operational efficiencies, and the perpetuity of a *particular* business. A financial mindset moves beyond the operational focus to an investor focus with a view toward the overall capital strategy of the family, creating new streams of value and finding a return on the *totality* of their assets. While the operational mindset is a requirement for running an efficient business, the financial focus is a requirement for transgenerational entrepreneurship and wealth creation.

The financial mindset for enterprising includes the following characteristics[17]

- A proclivity for higher risk and above normal returns.
- A willingness to sell and redeploy assets to seek higher returns.
- A desire to grow by creating new revenue streams with higher returns.
- A commitment to generating next-generation entrepreneurship.
- A willingness to continuously revisit the existing business model.
- An assumption that a percentage of the business will become obsolete.
- A willingness to leverage the business to grow and find higher returns.
- A desire to reinvest versus distribute capital.
- A willingness to enter into partnerships and alliances to grow.
- A strategy to manage the family's wealth for a total return.
- A commitment to innovation in business strategies and structures.
- A belief that bold, wide-ranging acts are necessary to achieve investment objectives in today's environment.

The *methods continuum* is a measure of the entrepreneurial orientation and actions in the business organizations. It assumes that enterprising organizations are taking bold, innovative market leading actions in order to seek a competitive advantage and generate new streams of value. It also reflects the premise that to be enterprising (proactively and continuously seeking new opportunities for growth) organizations must have a collection of individuals who act like an entrepreneur and not just a single leader or small group of family leaders. A single leader acting entrepreneurially might generate entrepreneurial actions in the business during their generation, but it will not create a transgenerational family business or group. Enterprising organizations move beyond managerial methods that focus on maintaining the existing and implementing incremental change. They are seeking and creating "the new" and establishing entrepreneurial renewal processes. While entrepreneurial methods do not replace the need for managerial actions, managerial actions are not sufficient conditions for enterprising and transgenerational wealth creation.

The entrepreneurial methods for enterprising include the following characteristics:[18]

- Allocating disproportionate resources to new business opportunities.
- Systematically searching for and capturing new investment opportunities.
- Seeking new opportunities beyond the core (legacy) business.
- Creating a core competency in innovation at the business unit level.
- Making significant change in products, services, markets, and customers.
- Initiating competitive change to lead our market.
- Investing early to develop or adopt new technology and processes.
- Typically adopting an "undo the competitor" posture in our markets.
- Having institutionalized the entrepreneurial process in the organization.
- Having formal routines for gathering and disseminating market intelligence.
- Having people at every level in the organization "think like competitors."
- Typically adopting a bold, aggressive posture in order to maximize the probability of exploiting potential investment opportunities.

Creating the Dialogue for Congruence

The Mindset and Methods Model helps families fulfill key process conditions for family enterprising and transgenerational wealth creation:

[17] Jeffrey, G. Covin and Dennis P. Slevin, "Strategic Management in Small Firms in Hostile and Benign Environments," *Strategic Management Journal*, 1989, Vol. 10, No. 1, p. 75.
[18] Ibid.

EXHIBIT 17.7

Backerhaus Veit Analysis

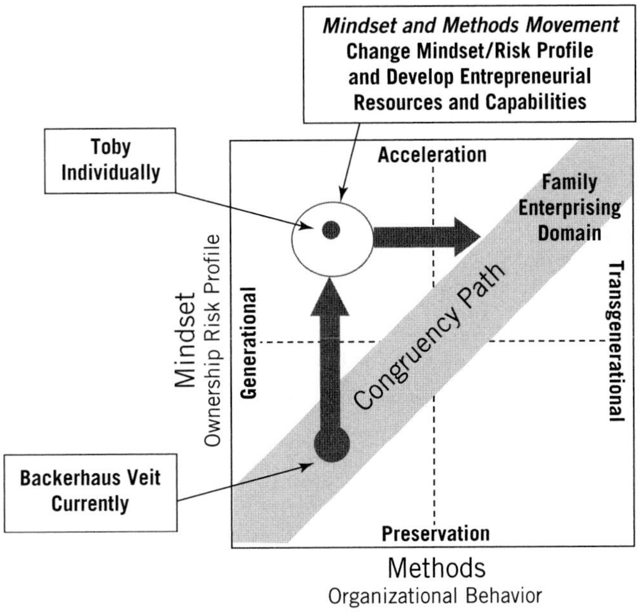

Creating a healthy *dialogue* in the family ownership group and organization around the mindset and methods issues.

Establishing *congruence* between the mindset of the owner-shareholder group and the methods of the business organization(s).

One of the major differences between family enterprising and entrepreneurship as it is normally envisioned is that by definition the team includes the family. Family entrepreneurs are either currently working with family members or planning to work with family members; they are either multigenerational teams or hope to be a multigenerational team; they either have multiple family member shareholders and stakeholders or will have them as they go through time. This inherent familial condition requires families to cultivate effective communication skills to build relationship capital for family enterprising. Families know that it takes financial capital for entrepreneurial activity, but they do not always know that it also requires relationship capital. Relationship capital allows families to have healthy dialogue and find congruence around the mindset and methods for enterprising.

Sabine Veit, founder of Backerhaus Veit in Toronto, Canada, realized the importance of dialogue and congruence when her son came home from college toting a business plan for aggressive growth. She had built her artisan bread manufacturing company into a $20 million (U.S.) force in the industry. When her son Toby won Babson's business planning competition she was definitely proud, but she also knew she was in trouble. The plan was to grow *her* business. Sabine loved the thought of working with Toby and he definitely shared her passion for artisan breads. In fact, during college Toby took every class with the artisan bread industry in mind. How could a parent hope for anything more?

But Toby didn't want to just run her company someday. He wanted to move the business beyond manufacturing and wholesaling into branded products and retailing, and he wanted to do it now. On the Mindset and Methods Model (Exhibit 17.7), Backerhaus Veit was on the congruency path as an operationally focused, managerially sound business. Sabine had a self-defined lifestyle firm that was competitive in her niche with a clear harvest strategy. But Toby was committed to family enterprising and wanted to be a growth firm. This meant moving beyond their current niche and lifestyle expectations. Clearly Toby had a mindset for much higher risk than Sabine.

On the methods continuum, Backerhaus Veit did not have the entrepreneurial methods to exploit Toby's plan. Sabine individually had the capabilities and Toby believed he did, but the entrepreneurial team and organization would have to be built. There was clearly significant incongruence as a family and business. The challenge for Sabine and Toby is to establish a plan and process for aligning their mindset and methods if they want to capture the new opportunity and become an enterprising family.

SUCCESSFUL NEXT GENERATION ENTREPRENEURSHIP

The challenge for multigenerational family teams like Toby and Sabine is to "keep it in dialogue" rather than letting it turn into a debate or disconnect. Debates become personal and disconnect cuts off opportunity. When family members turn the situation into right and wrong, good and bad, winning or loosing, there is very little listening, give-and-take, or changing one's position. In contrast, the word *dialogue* actually means "talking through" an issue. It assumes the ability to challenge each other's assumptions, to keep an open mind, and to test different options. It looks at the big picture, considers the long-term perspective, and discusses the process for getting there. Most important, dialogue does not follow hierarchical roles like parent-child, boss-employee, or the one who owns the business versus the one who does not. The goal of dialogue is to find solutions that are not constrained by the boundaries of either of the original positions.

There are a number of things Toby and Sabine need to do in order to ensure they are an enterprising family. First, they need to develop communication skills to have an effective dialogue. Most families assume they are able to carry on a dialogue simply because they are a family. In actuality the familiarity of a family can make it very difficult to challenge assumptions and talk about differing views. Often families need a facilitator to help them develop communication skill and have a dialogue.

Second, they need to make sure their views of the future are the same. Families often have a vague notion of "working together" and they assume that they will figure the details out over time. This is a clear formula for future discontent and conflict. In reality, Toby and Sabine had very different visions for their futures. Sabine's vision was to enjoy her passion for breads while balancing growth with her lifestyle interests. Toby's vision was to exploit his passion for breads by building new businesses on the family's reputation and skills.

Third, Toby and Sabine had very different risk profiles. What Sabine was willing to risk for future returns was very different from what Toby was willing to risk and the returns he desired. It is not surprising that the successor generation is willing to risk more than the senior generation. The key is to keep talking until you understand each other's perspective. Once you understand each other you can create a business model and structures that accommodate the risk profiles of both generations. Locking into one generational perspective or the other undermines the collective strengths of a multigenerational team.

Fourth, remember that timing is everything. Usually for the successors the time is *now* and for the seniors the time is *someday*. Chances are that both generations will end up out of their comfort zones a little. Toby and Sabine realized that timing was really a strategy question of how they would proceed, not just if or when they would proceed.

Fifth, get creative. Your can be sure that the final outcome will not look exactly like either of you envisioned. Through dialogue it became clear to Toby and Sabine that the range of options was fairly extensive. We often tell family members to "remember their algebra" when it comes to dialogue. Just because "a equals b" it doesn't mean that "a" might not equal "c, d, or even e, f, and g." The point is that once you start a true dialogue, you may find many more options than you originally envisioned.

Frame Two: The Six Dimensions for Family Enterprising

The second assessment and strategy frame for family enterprising addresses the team component of the Timmons Model. In family enterprising "team" is a much broader and complex concept. It encompasses the family ownership group and the family and non-family entrepreneurial capabilities. The entrepreneurial process cannot occur unless there is alignment in the team's ownership mindset and entrepreneurial methods as described above. When the entrepreneurial leader is a family member there is potentially another layer of team complexity around issues such as parent-child relationships, altruistic versus entrepreneurial decision making, nepotism and competency, family versus personal equity and compensation, and success measures. In essence, the family as team can create more perfect balance in the Timmons Model or can cause imbalance. One key is to stay focused on the opportunity and stress that the team is in support of exploiting that opportunity.

The six dimensions for family enterprising provide family teams with six areas that they can address to assist them in aligning their mindset and methods and moving up the congruency path toward the enterprising domain. The six dimensions and the corresponding strategic questions apply key entrepreneurial considerations to the family context. As family owners and leaders answer the questions they are creating unity within the team for entrepreneurial action. The six dimensions are as follows:

Leadership
Relationship
Vision

Strategy
Governance
Performance

There is an internal logic and order to the six dimensions. We begin with the *leadership dimension* because leaders are the catalyst for organizational behavior and have the responsibility for creating the team. Leaders also set the tone for the relationship commitments and culture in the family and organization. The *relationship dimension* is often overlooked, but it is the foundation for organizational effectiveness and health, especially in family teams and enterprising. The *strategy dimensions* flow out of the leadership and relationship dimensions. At the end of the day, strategy and planning are simply extended organizational conversations. Organizational strategy is only as effective as the leadership and relationships in the family and organization. Governance structures and policies simply enable organizations to carry out their strategies. The *governance dimension* must, therefore, follow both ownership and business strategy formulation. In an interesting way, the *performance dimension* is the last dimension because it is an organizational outcome, but it is also feedback that leaders use to frame their leadership actions.

Leadership Dimension—Does Your Leadership Create a Sense of Shared Urgency for Enterprising and Transgenerational Wealth Creation?

Entrepreneurial leaders create a sense of shared urgency in the organization. The goal is to have everyone, from the owners to those carrying out tasks, thinking and acting like competitors.[19] Families are traditionally and systemically hierarchical in nature—parent-child, older-younger siblings, male-female—and their family organizations often embody these hierarchies in their leadership models. A transgenerational commitment requires families to move beyond the "great leader" model to the "great group."[20] Family leaders who strive to turn their families into a team based upon the great group philosophy overcome many of the negative caricatures often associated with family business leadership and empower the family and organization to be enterprising.

Leadership Dimension Diagnostic Questions

Do family leaders understand the requirements to be transgenerational?

Do they develop next-generation leadership?

Do they move the family beyond the "great leader" model?

Do they promote a sense of openness and mutuality?

Do they encourage participation by family members at all levels in the family and organization?

Do they lead others to think and act like entrepreneurs?

Do they help the family grow beyond a hierarchical model of leadership to become the "great group"?

Relationship Dimension—Does Your Family Have the Relationship Capital to Sustain Their Transgenerational Commitments?

Effective teams are built upon healthy relationships. We describe healthy relationships as those that build relationship capital and allow efficient interpersonal interactions in the team. Relationship capital is the reserve of attributes such as trust, loyalty, positive feelings, benefit of the doubt, goodwill, forgiveness, commitment, and altruistic motives. Relationship capital is a necessary condition for long-lasting teams and transgenerational families. Now here are two opposite but simultaneously true statements: Families have the natural potential to build relationship capital better than other social groups *and* families have the natural potential to destroy relationship capital more ruthlessly than any other social group. Is this good news or bad news for family enterprising? It depends. Those families who intentionally gain the skills and strive to build relationship capital leverage the natural advantage of family teams. But those families who assume they will always have relationship capital or take their relationships for granted open themselves up to potentially destructive tendencies of families. Families who have relationship capital reserves are more likely to create the dialogue that moves them up the congruence path to the family enterprising domain.

Relationship Dimension Diagnostic Questions

Is your family intentionally building relationship capital?

[19] Rita Gunther McGrath and Ian MacMillan, *The Entrepreneurial Mindset: Strategies for Continuously Creating Opportunity in an Age of Uncertainty*, Harvard Business School Press, Boston, MA 2000.

[20] Duane R. Ireland and Michael A. Hitt, "Achieving and Maintaining Strategic Competitiveness in the 21st Century: The Role of Strategic Leadership," *The Academy of Management Executive*, February 1999, Volume 13, Issue 1, p. 43.

Are you investing in the communication and relationship building skills you need to build relationship capital?

Are there healthy relationships between family siblings, branches, and across generations?

Does your family have formal family meetings to discuss family ownership and relationship issues?

Do you experience synergy in your family relationships?

Do you have a positive vision for working together as a family?

Do family members see relationship health as part of their competitive advantage?

Do all family members share in the rewards from the vision?

Vision Dimension—Does Your Family Have a Compelling Multigenerational Vision That Energizes People at Every Level?

A compelling vision is what creates the shared urgency for family enterprising and mobilizes people to carry out the vision. By compelling we mean that it "makes sense" to people in light of tomorrow's marketplace realities. Often a vision might make sense for the moment, but it does not make sense of the future. For enterprising families, the vision must describe how the family will collectively create new streams of wealth that allow them to be transgenerational. It also has to be multigenerational. It is easy for the different generations to craft their personal visions for the future. Transgenerational families must craft a vision that is compelling to all generations and in a sense transcends generational perspectives. This multigenerational necessity also underscores the importance of establishing participatory leadership and building relationship capital.

Vision Dimension Diagnostic Questions

Does your family have a vision that makes sense of tomorrow's marketplace?

Would all generations describe the vision as compelling?

Was the vision developed by everyone in the family?

Does the vision have relevance for your decision making and lives?

Does your family regularly review and test the vision as an ownership group?

Is the vision transgenerational?

Is the vision larger than the personal interests of the family?

Does the vision mobilize others to create new streams of value?

Strategy Dimension—Does Your Family Have an Intentional Strategy for Finding Their Competitive Advantage as a Family?

We have already said that there is a more intentional and formal application of the entrepreneurial process within the family context. Part of that formal approach is developing strategies for both cultivating and capturing new business opportunities. But for families it means much more. The family's strategic thinking and planning should be based on determining how to exploit their unique family-based resources and capabilities to find advantages in enterprising. While we will address this more specifically in the next section, it includes things like finding synergies with current assets, leveraging their networks of personal relationships, cultivating next-generation entrepreneurs, and extending the power of their family reputation. Because families tend to take their family-influenced resources and capabilities for granted they often fail to see the opportunities they represent for providing them with a long-term advantage for enterprising.

Strategy Dimension Diagnostic Questions

How does your family provide you with an advantage in entrepreneurial wealth creation?

What resources and capabilities are unique to your family?

Does your family have a formal planning process to direct their enterprising?

Does your organization have form systems for cultivating and capturing new opportunities?

Does your family mentor next-generation family members to become entrepreneurs?

Does your strategic thinking and planning empower your family to fulfill their transgenerational vision?

What role does your family play in the strategy process?

Governance Dimension—Does Your Family Have Structures and Policies That Stimulate Change and Growth in the Family and Organization?

Few family leaders would consider that governance structures and policies could actually stimulate growth and change. Most would equate the word *governance* with bureaucracies and, at best, acknowledge that structures and policies are a necessary evil to be tolerated and minimized. But we offer two different perspectives. First the lack of effective governance structures and policies creates significant ambiguity in families and constrains enterprising. Second, when entrepreneurial processes are institutionalized through the governance structures and policies it promotes growth and change activities. For example, when ownership, equity, or value realization is unclear or undiscussable it disincentivizes family entrepreneurs. But when financial conversations are part of the professional culture and there is transparent ownership structures, family entrepreneurs are clear on the rules of the game. Governance structures are thus critical to transgenerational entrepreneurship and wealth creation.

Governance Dimension Diagnostic Questions

Does your family view governance as a positive part of their family and business lives?

Are your governance structures static or fluid?

Do your structures and policies promote family unity?

Do your governance structures and policies give an appropriate voice to family members?

Do your governance structures and policies assist you in finding your family advantage?

Do you have formal processes that institutionalize the entrepreneurial process in your family and businesses?

Do your governance structures and policies promote next-generation involvement and entrepreneurship?

Performance Dimension—Does Your Performance Meet the Requirements for Transgenerational Entrepreneurship and Wealth Creation?

The performance dimension is where families clarify whether or not they are really committed to family enterprising. Families who are enterprising are market driven and seek to accelerate their wealth creation through their opportunistic entrepreneurial actions. They have clear financial benchmarks and information for assessing their performance against the market. Lifestyle firms often assume that they are performing well because they are sustaining their lifestyles. Enterprising also implies a process of matching the organization's core competencies with external opportunities in order to create new streams of value. Enterprising families do not rely on past performance as an indicator that they will perform well in the future, nor do they define success by the preservation of an asset. Their success measures are their ability to fulfill their transgenerational vision for social and economic wealth creation.

Performance Dimension Diagnostic Questions

Does your family talk openly about financial performance issues or are finances secretive?

Are you in lifestyle or enterprising mode?

Are your performance and strategies driven by a clear market orientation?

Do family owners agree on their risk and return expectations?

Are performance expectations clear to next-generation entrepreneurs?

Are there clear transparency and accountability structures in relation to meeting performance expectations?

Is there family dialogue about performance expectations—growth, dividends, reinvestment, ROE?

Frame Three: The Familiness Advantage for Family Enterprising

All entrepreneurial success and the opportunity to capture above-average returns is premised upon finding an advantage over your competitors. Correspondingly, the potential for finding an advantage is rooted in the distinctive resources and capabilities that an organization possesses. The "resources" aspect of the Timmons Model is where enterprising can get exciting for families. Because every family is unique, they can generate very idiosyncratic bundles of resources and capabilities that can give them an advantage in the entrepreneurial process if they know how to identify and leverage them. We refer to this idiosyncratic bundle of resources and capabilities as their *familiness*.

The Family Systems Model in Exhibit 17.8 shows how the familiness bundle of resources and capabilities is generated. As the vision, history, and capabilities of the collective family interact with the goals, skills, and commitments of the individual family members, and they both in turn interact with the organizational history, culture, and resources of the business entities, it creates this familiness effect or the "f factor" of resources_f and capabilities_f. If we think of the four resource categories in Chapter 11—

EXHIBIT 17.8

Familiness Systems Model

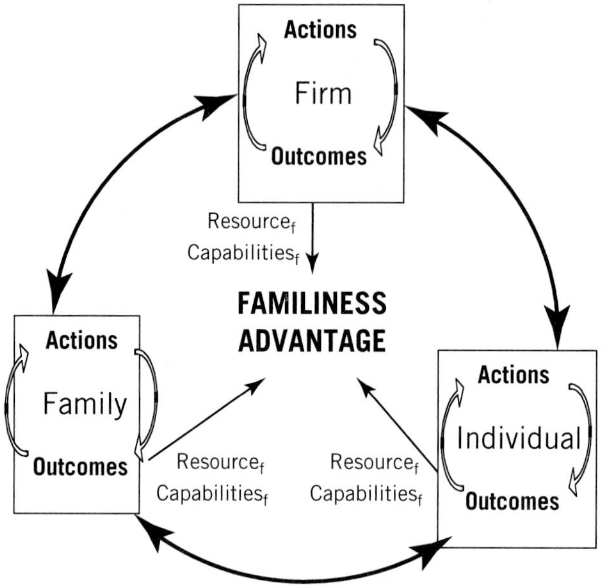

people, financial, assets, and plan—we can explore how the systemic family influence impacts, changes, or somehow reconfigures the properties of the resource. We identify familiness resources and capabilities with a subscript "f" such as capital$_f$, leadership$_f$, networking$_f$, knowledge$_f$, reputation$_f$.

The familiness assessment frame helps families become realists. What we mean is the assessment process leads families to realistically evaluate where their family influence might be positive and where it might be negative. One of the key insights from this model is the understanding that family cannot be characterized as either good or bad. Rather, family influence must be viewed as one of the inputs that entrepreneurs need to intentionally manage. As family leaders manage the actions and outcomes within the subsystems—family unit, individuals, and business entities—and between the subsystems, they are managing their bundle of resources$_f$ and capabilities$_f$.

When these familiness resources$_f$ and capabilities$_f$ lead to a competitive advantage for the family we refer to them as "distinctive familiness" or an "f+." When they constrain the competitive enterprising ability of the family we refer to them as "constrictive familiness" or "f−." Exhibit 17.9 allows families to place their resources and capabilities on an assessment continuum. The job of families who desire to be enterprising is to determine how to generate and exploit their distinctive familiness and to minimize or shed their constrictive familiness. When families begin assessing and planning based upon their distinctive and constrictive familiness, they move from an intuitive and informal to the intentional and formal mode of family enterprising.

To better understand familiness let's return to the family enterprising decision that Toby and Sabine have to make in regard to Backerhaus Veit (BV). If we analyze the distinctive (f+) and constrictive (f−) familiness in their situation we can bring significant focus to the dialogue and move them along the mindset and methods congruence path.

Exhibit 17.10 is their familiness resource and capabilities continuum as it relates to the new venture opportunity. When you see the f+ f− assessment it is a comprehensive and revealing picture of their individual and organizational contribution to the new venture. But it is not only the final picture that is useful to families. The conversation to identify the resources and capabilities and to determine where they should be placed is the real learning outcome.

First, you will notice that there are clear resources and capabilities specifically associated with the senior and successor generations and others that are mixed. The white boxes picture those that are tied to Sabine, the grey boxes to Toby, and the blended boxes are found in both. While Toby's successor drive is an f+ his business capabilities and lack of

EXHIBIT 17.9

f+ f− Familiness Advantage

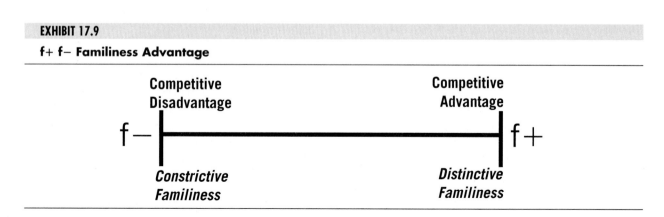

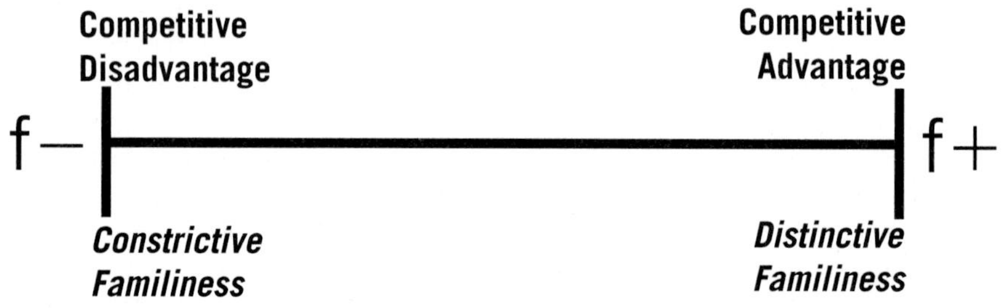

EXHIBIT 17.10

Backerhaus Veit f+ f− Analysis

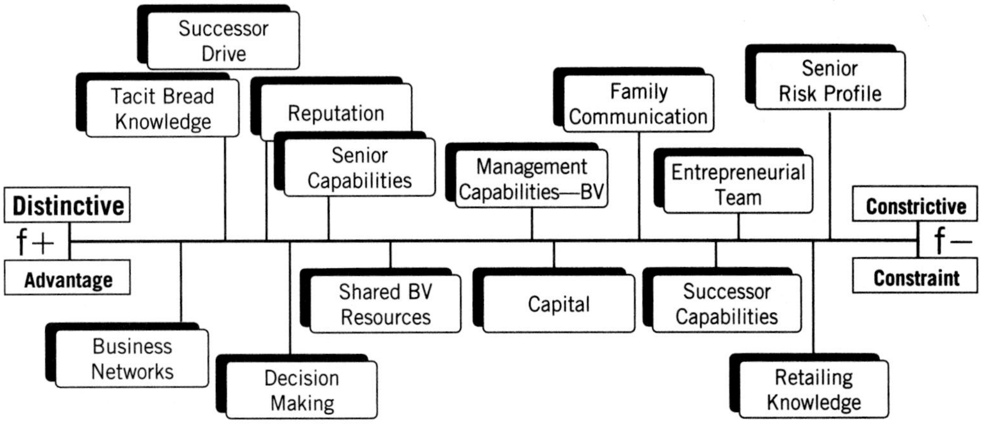

experience are an f−. Sabine readily admits that without Toby's drive she would never consider this opportunity. But Sabine's advisors are concerned that Toby may overestimate his capabilities and contribution. This discussion is very natural in next-generation entrepreneurship and families should "normalize" it and not allow it to become personal. Conversely, Sabine's senior capabilities, business networks, and reputation are an f+ for Toby's new venture. Toby readily admits that Sabine's role makes his business plan a much higher potential venture. On the other hand, Sabine's risk profile and lifestyle goals are a significant f− and constraint to enterprising. But we need to remember that they fit very well for her current strategy.

Second, there are resources and capabilities associated with BV, but we put them in white boxes because in many ways BV *is* Sabine. Toby's business plan calls for BV to provide valuable shared resources such as wholesale bread supply, bookkeeping, used equipment, repair services, and the like. This opportunity creates a very significant resource advantage that we would call "plan$_{f+}$" because only family members with existing businesses could incorporate these into their plan. The existing management team capabilities are also an f+, but because the existing team is not entrepreneurial (in fact, they see the new venture as a drain on the existing business), we have to give an f− to entrepreneurial team.

Third, there are certain resources pictured in the blended boxes that are associated with both Sabine and Toby. Most important is the f+ for tacit bread knowledge. They both know bread making, but the particularly interesting point is to see how advanced Toby is as a young person because he grew up in the bread industry. Correspondingly, the f− for retailing is significant. While Sabine grew up in the retail bread industry (her family has 70 retail bakeries in Germany), she does not know the casual dining bread industry (like Panera Bread Company) and this is the target for Toby's plan. While decision making is an f+, family communication is an f−. The family has great relationships, but in the business setting, they sometimes communicate like mother and son rather than business peers.

The f+ f− continuum makes Toby's and Sabine's "pre-launch" work very clear. Managing the f+ and f− continuum is how families build their resources and capabilities bundle as part of formalizing the entrepreneurial process. It is a critical step in getting the odds more in their favor. Toby and Sabine now need to create a work plan for each of the constraining resources in order to move them to a point of neutrality or advantage.

An additional realization from this analysis is to see the potential synergy between the successor and senior generations for family enterprising. Four things are immediately clear from the analysis. First, as we already noted, Sabine would never explore and/or capture this opportunity if it were not for Toby driving the process. Second, Toby does not have the synergistic familiness resources and capabilities if he tries to do the business on his own. Fourth, while there are positive reasons to do it together, there are also constraints that must be addressed. Fourth, family enterprising is when they decide to do it together as a family, rather than not doing it, or Toby doing it on his own. That is not to say that one way is right or wrong, but simply that doing it together is a family enterprising approach.

We will provide a final assessment of Sabine and Toby using the Timmons Model to discuss fit and balance. Clearly the opportunity for Backerhaus Veit to

EXHIBIT 17.11

Timmons Model for Backerhaus Veit

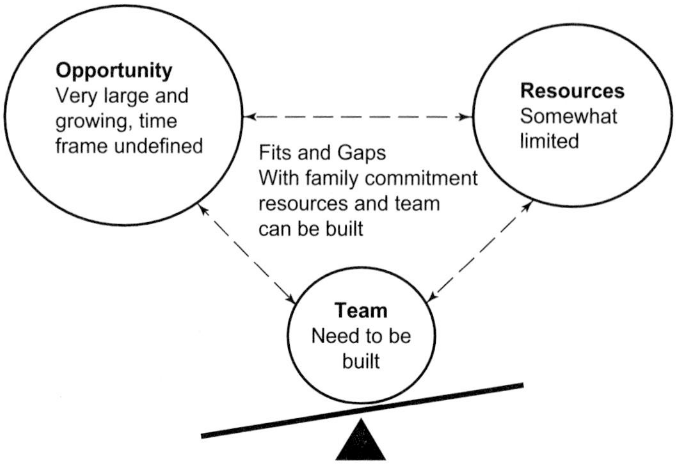

move into the retail fast-casual-eating market is very large and growing. In fact, the opportunity is probably greater than the current resources and capabilities of BV, Toby, and Sabine to meet them without outside resources. Currently, the weakest link in the model is the team. While Toby and Sabine have great bread knowledge, they do not have the entrepreneurial team for the retailing initiative. Further the BV leaders and advisors are strongly committed to managing their current assets, rather than launching an entrepreneurial business. Exhibit 17.11 shows that the model is "out of balance" and reaffirms the conclusions from our previous assessment that there is significant pre-launch work to be done to ensure a "fit." If they do this pre-launch work and can get the Timmons Model into balance, however, they have a great high potential venture for the family.

Conclusion

For those business families who would like to act more entrepreneurially and become an intentional enterprising family that has multiple generations seeking higher potential opportunities we suggest that there are four strategic shifts that may need to occur:

- From lifestyle firm that has the goal of personal comfort to an enterprising family committed to transgenerational entrepreneurship and wealth creation.
- From an intuitive family business that "kicks around" (as one family entrepreneur described it) to see what new opportunities turn up to an intentional entrepreneurial process that seeks to generate and capture new opportunities.
- From a senior-generation entrepreneur who does it to a successor-generation entrepreneurial process and team that create opportunities for others to do it.
- From a "low potential" entrepreneurial family that creates one-off businesses as they can to a "higher potential" entrepreneurial family that mobilizes resources to create transgenerational wealth.

Chapter Summary

1. We began by demonstrating the significant contributions families make to the economy and entrepreneurial process. It is often overlooked that the majority of the businesses worldwide are controlled and managed by families, including many of the very largest businesses that we normally do not associate with family.
2. Families play a diverse number of formal and informal roles in the entrepreneurial process. We described them as (a) the family-influenced startup, (b) family corporate venturing, (c) family corporate renewal, (d) family private cash, and (e) family investment funds.

3. Family enterprising was defined as the proactive and continuous search for opportunistic growth when expansion is neither pressing nor particularly obvious. The outcome of family enterprising is transgenerational entrepreneurship and wealth creation through balance in the Timmons Model.
4. The mindset continuum assesses the family's risk profile and those interested in enterprising move from an operational to a financial investor strategy. The methods continuum assesses the organizational behavior of leaders and organizations and requires a move from managerial to entrepreneurial strategies for enterprising.
5. There are six dimensions for family enterprising that were described as antecedents from the entrepreneurship literature: leadership, relationship, vision, strategy, governance, and performance. The chapter presented key questions on each dimension to assist families in becoming more enterprising.
6. We defined the familiness of an organization as the unique bundle of resources and capabilities that result from the interaction of the family and individual family members with the business entities. Families can have positive and negative family influence, which we described as an f+ or f−.

Study Questions

1. What are the entrepreneurial implications of not appreciating or understanding the role and contribution of families to the economies of our communities and countries?
2. Describe the advantages of a more formal approach on each of the roles families play in the entrepreneurial process. Give a few contrasting examples from a family firm with which you are familiar.
3. Define family enterprising, familiness, and relationship capital and relate each of them to the Timmons Model of the entrepreneurial process.
4. Choose a family firm with which you are familiar and plot them on the Mindset and Methods Model. Describe the firm in light of the mindset and method definition. Make six recommendations for what they could do to become more enterprising.
5. How do the six dimensions for family enterprising relate to one another? How do they enhance family enterprising? Describe how the six dimensions can be used to stimulate positive family dialogue.
6. If a family is trying to find their competitive advantage, how can the familiness assessment approach help them? How is the familiness approach a more formal application of the entrepreneurial process? How can the familiness approach change the family dialogue?
7. Given the familiness assessment of Backerhaus Veit in the chapter, describe why Sabine should or should not partner with Toby to implement his business plan. Describe the familiness action steps that they should take if you say they should launch the business. Describe the familiness reasons for why they possibly should not launch the business.
8. Assess a family firm with which you are familiar on the familiness resource and capabilities continuum. Describe what action steps they need to take to enhance their competitive advantage as a family organization.

Internet Resources for Chapter 17

http://www.familybusinessmagazine.com/ *The Family Business Library is a searchable archive covering a wide array of topics on family business.*

http://www.ffi.org/ *The Family Firm Institute (FFI) is an international professional membership organization that provides interdisciplinary education and networking opportunities for family business advisors, consultants, educators, and researchers.*

http://www.fbn-i.org/ *The Family Business Network is the world's leading network of business owning families, promoting the success and sustainability of family business.*

http://knowledge.insead.edu *INSEAD Knowledge is a free Internet service aimed at making INSEAD research as widely available as possible. For cases and research on family business, see the section Entrepreneurship & Family Business.*

http://www.gemconsortium.org *The Global Entrepreneurship Monitor (GEM) is the world's largest and longest-standing study of entrepreneurial activity.*

www3.babson.edu/eship/ife *Institute for Family Enterprising at Babson College*

Research and Resources:

- *GEM 2002 Special Report on Family Sponsored New Ventures*
- *American Family Business Survey with MassMutual*
- *Women in Family-Owned Businesses*
- *Improving the Long-Run Survival of Family Firms—LEADS Research Project*

MIND STRETCHERS

Have you considered?

1. Like a bumble bee that should not be able to fly, it is said that family businesses should not be able to compete. Why might this be a true statement? Why are families so economically dominant worldwide if they are like the bumble bee?
2. How can a lifestyle firm be both a fine choice for a family and a dangerous choice for a family at the same time?
3. Give 10 reasons why dialogue can be harder for families than non-families even though families are suppose to have closer relationships.
4. If you were a Marriot successor-generation family member, what expectations would you have about your future?
5. Watch the DVD "Born Rich" by Jamie Johnson (HBO Documentary). What did you learn about wealth and entrepreneurship?

(Resource Note: The DVD "Born Rich" by Jamie Johnson can be purchased on Amazon.com. Additional questions to consider for "Born Rich": Are wealthy families the same as entrepreneurial families? Is Jamie Johnson entrepreneurial? Is Paris Hilton entrepreneurial? Is this the same as family enterprising? What are their family legacies?)

Exercises

Determine where your family is on the mindset and methods continuum and what familiness advantage you might have for enterprising. Fill out the assessment surveys, plot your family group on the Family Enterprising Model, and fill out the resources and capabilities continuum.

Mindset Continuum

The mindset continuum establishes the family's financial risk and return expectations and their competitive posture in relation to the marketplace. There are no right and wrong answers. The point of the assessment is to surface family members' beliefs and fuel the family dialogue.

Using the assessment continuums, have the family member shareholders and future shareholders answer the questions on the mindset continuum listed below. Circle the number between the two statements that best reflects the strength of your belief about the family as a shareholder group. Total scores are between 12 and 84 reflecting views from the most traditional to the most enterprising.

In general, family member shareholders . . .

Have a strong proclivity for low-risk businesses and investment opportunities (with normal and certain returns).	1 2 3 4 5 6 7	Have a strong proclivity for high-risk business and investment opportunities (with chances for high returns).
Would sacrifice a higher return to preserve the family's legacy business.	1 2 3 4 5 6 7	Are willing to sell and redeploy their assets to find a higher return in the market.
Tend to think about cultivating our current businesses for current returns.	1 2 3 4 5 6 7	Desire to grow by creating new revenue streams with higher possibilities for returns.
Have a commitment to operating the business and providing job opportunities for family.	1 2 3 4 5 6 7	Have a commitment to mentoring next-generation entrepreneurs to create new streams of value.
Feel we have a good business model that will take us into the future.	1 2 3 4 5 6 7	Feel we should continuously revisit the assumptions of our business model.
Feel that our current businesses and products will serve us well in the future.	1 2 3 4 5 6 7	Assume that a significant percentage of our businesses will become obsolete.
Desire to avoid debt and grow with internally generated cash as they can.	1 2 3 4 5 6 7	Are willing to leverage the businesses to grow and find higher returns in the market.
Desire to increase their financial ability to provide distributions and/or liquidity.	1 2 3 4 5 6 7	Desire to reinvest more aggressively for faster growth and higher returns.

Desire to grow within our current financial and equity structures in order to ensure control over our destiny.	1 2 3 4 5 6 7	Are willing to use alliances, partnerships, share equity, or dilute share positions in order to grow.
Would describe themselves more as a conservative company meeting their family's financial and personal goals.	1 2 3 4 5 6 7	Would describe themselves as a risk taking group seeking higher total returns for the family as investment group.
Would describe our business models and strategy as making us steady rather than opportunistic.	1 2 3 4 5 6 7	Are willing to be innovative in our business models and structures in order to be opportunistic.
Believe that a steady and consistent approach will allow us to fulfill our family's vision and goals for the future.	1 2 3 4 5 6 7	Believe that bold, wide-ranging acts are necessary to achieve our family investment objectives in today's environment.

TOTAL:

Methods Continuum

The methods continuum establishes the organization's entrepreneurial orientation and actions. It reflects the beliefs of the shareholders and stakeholders on how the leaders incite entrepreneurship in the organization.

Using the assessment continuums, have the family member shareholders and future shareholders answer the questions on the methods continuum listed below. Circle the number between the two statements that best reflects the strength of your belief about the family as a shareholder group. Total scores are between 12 and 84 reflecting views from the most traditional to the most enterprising.

In general, senior leaders in our family organization(s) . . .

Spend their time nurturing the existing businesses.	1 2 3 4 5 6 7	Pay a disproportionate amount of attention to new business opportunities.
Place a strong emphasis on pursing returns by reinvesting in tried and true businesses.	1 2 3 4 5 6 7	Place a strong emphasis on searching for and capturing new business investment opportunities.
Have pursued no new investment opportunities outside of our core operating arena (in last 5 years).	1 2 3 4 5 6 7	Have pursued many new investment opportunities beyond our core operating arena (in the last 5 years).
Believe our core competency is in managing efficient businesses.	1 2 3 4 5 6 7	Believe our core competency is in innovating for opportunistic growth.
Have made minor changes in our businesses, products, services, markets, or business units during the current generation of leaders.	1 2 3 4 5 6 7	Have made significant changes in our products, services, markets, or business units as the market required it.
Typically respond to actions that competitors or the market initiates.	1 2 3 4 5 6 7	Typically initiate actions and competitive change to lead the market and competitors.
Are generally moderate to slow in adopting new technologies and technological processes in our industry.	1 2 3 4 5 6 7	Are often early in investing to develop or adopt new technologies and technological processes in our industries.
Tend to avoid competitive clashes preferring friendly "live and let live" competition.	1 2 3 4 5 6 7	Typically adopt a competitive "undo-the-competitor" posture when making investment decisions.
Are more intuitive and informal in how the organization thinks seeking or capturing new opportunities.	1 2 3 4 5 6 7	Have established formal structures and policies to institutionalize the entrepreneurial process in the organization.
Rely on family leaders to know the markets and customers and get the information to the organization.	1 2 3 4 5 6 7	Have more formal plans and approaches to how they gather and disseminate market intelligence.
Rely on family leaders to set the tone and ensure that the organization is competitive through time.	1 2 3 4 5 6 7	Encourage and empower people at every level of the organization to think and act like competitors.
Typically adopt a cautious "wait and see" posture in order to minimize the probability of making costly investment decisions.	1 2 3 4 5 6 7	Typically adopt a bold, aggressive posture in order to maximize the probability of exploiting potential investment opportunities.

TOTAL

Family Enterprising Model

Plot your score totals from the mindset and methods assessment surveys above. The lowest possible score is a 12 and the highest possible score is an 84. Plotting the scores provides you with a visual basis for your family dialogue. Does the plotted score rightly describe your family? Is your family on the "congruence path"? Does everyone agree on where your family is on the model? Develop strategies to move your family on the model if necessary.

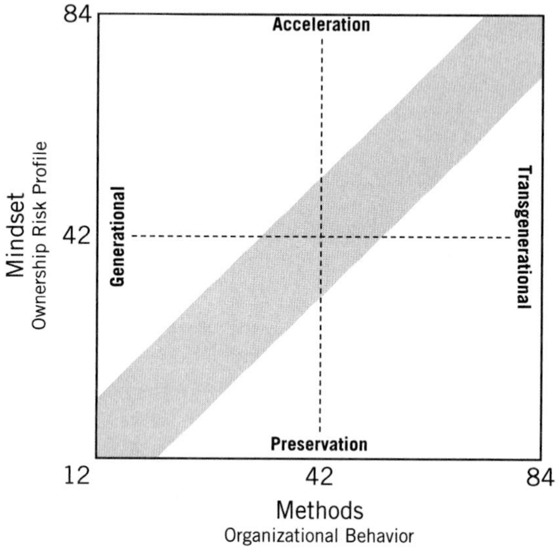

Familiness f+ f− Continuum

Identify where the family influences on your resources and capabilities are part of a competitive advantage (f+) and a competitive constraint (f−). You can conduct this analysis on many levels. The "meta" analysis would be of the larger family group as a whole, while the "micro" analysis would be of a particular business unit, or in relation to a specific innovation or new venture (such as the Backerhaus Veit example in the chapter). Identify the unit of analysis you are assessing and list the f+ and f− resources and capabilities.

Identify Unit of Analysis	
Resources and Capabilities (f+)	**Resources and Capabilities (f−)**

Plot the f+ and f− resources and capabilities from the chart on the continuum below. Place them in position relative to one another so that you see a picture of how the resources and capabilities are related.

A list of potential resources and capabilities to choose from:

Successor Leadership	Experienced leadership	Entrepreneurial processes	Team
Land	Treatment of employees	Firm specific knowledge	Patient capital
Location	Conflict resolution	Firm specific skills	Debt structure
Cash	Effective communication	Leadership development	Strategic alliances
Access to Capital	Decision making	Managerial talent	Compensation
Distribution Systems	Learning environment	Employee productivity	Strategy making and planning
Intellectual Property	Openness to ideas	Network of relationships	Information flow
Raw Materials	Cross functional communication	Employee commitment	Organizational culture
Contracts/Alliances	Reputation of company	Personal values	Unified beliefs and goals
Manufacturing Processes	Market intelligence gathering	Flexible work practices	Time horizons
Innovation Processes	Reporting structures	Trustworthiness	Brand name
Reputation of Company	Coordination and control	Training	Governance structure

Case
Indulgence Spa Products

Preparation Questions

1. Is this family and case about "family business" or "family enterprising"? How would you delineate the differences? Why does this distinction matter for understanding the case?
2. Assess the Dawson business/family using the Mindset and Methods Model for family enterprising.
3. How well is Jimella prepared to successfully grow Indulgence Spa? What are her strengths and weaknesses? Identify what resources and capabilities she represents to the family group and to her startup business.
4. What are the differences in market demand that Indulgence will face versus the Dawson Products target market? How will these differences affect the Indulgence business model? Does the new target market change the resource and capabilities requirements?
5. Craft a series of recommendations to Jimella for how she can grow "her" entrepreneurial business while advancing a family enterprising strategy. Are the two mutually exclusive? How do your recommendations address the succession and family legacy issues in the case?

Jimella, the youngest of the Dawson children, smiled as she peeked into her mother's office.

"Good Morning, Mom! Do you have a minute?"

"Sure, come in. I'm just preparing for a meeting. You're early this morning, Jimella. I thought I was the only one here."

Ulissa wasn't really surprised to see her daughter. Jimella, age 32, liked to work hard. Jimella had learned every aspect of the family personal care products business—from filling and capping containers on the line to working with markets, spas, and salons. She had started selling products door-to-door when she was 11. After completing her undergraduate degree at Wharton and receiving her MBA from Duke, she was now Dawson's chief marketing officer. Soon after taking that position, she orchestrated a clean sweep of the department—a bold move that required the transfer of a well-liked 45-year-old worker, and the firing of a number of employees that she determined had lazy and nonproductive work habits. Up until then, the company had developed a reputation for being a nurturing, family-oriented place where workers—even unproductive ones—could feel confident of long-term employment. Not only did Jimella's aggressive new management style send a wake-up call to marginal employees, but her initiative cut the marketing budget by a third and doubled profits—just like her spreadsheets had said they would.

Ulissa had come to expect this type of proactive, exceptional performance from her daughters (Angela, 39, was Dawson's COO). Now that her husband and co-founder, Robert Dawson, had begun spending much of his time speaking and teaching throughout the country about the need for African Americans to become economically self-sufficient, Jimella and Angela had become key figures in the growth trajectory of their family enterprise. And here her youngest was again, looking

This case was prepared by Sandra Sowell-Scott. © Copyright Babson College, 2005.

as if she was preparing to take another bold step. Ulissa was intrigued.

"What's on your mind, Jimella?"

"I'm going in some new directions with my plans for Indulgence Spa Products and I'd like your opinion."

"Sure."

"First of all, I'm changing my marketing strategy. My target market will be all women—not just women of color. These products are outstanding, and Indulgence is limiting its growth by not positioning itself as a company that creates luxury spa products for all women."

"Sounds interesting, Jimella. But how do you plan to do this?"

Jimella's pause increased her mother's curiosity.

"My main marketing method will be direct sales—the same basic strategy that we have recently begun using at Dawson's Cosmetics. I'm going to build a national team of independent beauty advisors who will sell primarily through home calls and Indulgence house parties."

This time Jimella's pause had Ulissa more concerned than curious.

"And?"

"And to do that right, I'll need to make Indulgence a separate company from Dawson Products.

"Mom," Jimella added as gently as the could, "I've decided to go off on my own."

A Family Enterprise

In 1959 Robert Dawson invested $10 in a Fuller Products Sales Kit and began selling that line of personal care products door-to-door in Brooklyn, New York. Three years later he met Ulissa Moser, who was selling the same line of products to earn money for college tuition. They fell in love and were married in 1963. A few years later the couple opened a Fuller Products Distributorship in Chicago, Illinois. The branch quickly became the top producing distributorship of Fuller Products. In 1971, when their mentor S. B. Fuller was hit hard by a national boycott (see Appendix A), the Dawsons moved quickly to establish their own manufacturing capabilities—initially out of their kitchen. They packaged their products in used containers they obtained from local hairdressers, supplemented with whatever they could find, including old jelly and mayonnaise jars.

By 1978, the company had expanded to include the Dawson Beauty School and a chain of beauty supply stores throughout the Midwest. Robert Dawson served as president and Ulissa assumed a significant role in the administrative and manufacturing areas. From an early age, their two girls had participated in the business and learned how to sell door-to-door by developing their own small businesses selling products such as popcorn, baked goods, fruit, and even panty hose.

Robert and Ulissa very much wanted their children and the employees to understand that building and running a business was about hard work and discipline. They regularly brought Angela and Jimella to the office after school, and the girls were given specific tasks to perform. This not only helped instill a powerful work ethic but also provided a common mission that brought the family together.

In 1988, they opened a 37,000-square-foot corporate headquarters and manufacturing facility south of Chicago. The children continued to learn all aspects of the business from sales and marketing to manufacturing. In 1991, they opened the Dawson Cosmetology Center (DDC) at the site. The DDC became an important facility for training employees interested in working for the Dawson Beauty Schools. In 1997, Dawson's corporate and manufacturing divisions moved nearby into an 80,000-square-foot state-of-the-art facility.

By the new millennium, the company manufactured and marketed a line of over 400 professional and retail hair care and personal care products designed primarily for African-American consumers.[1] The Dawson campus included a travel agency, a hotel, and a convention center. Their overall goal continued to be to empower people and aid in their education and provide opportunities for self-sufficiency and economic development. In 2004 revenues were just over $32 million, and Dawson employed a total workforce of nearly 500 people, most of whom were outside sales representatives.

The Cosmetics Division

In 1993, after she had completed Harvard Law School, Jimella's older sister Angela had officially joined the family business as legal counsel. A year later, the company acquired a cosmetics manufacturing firm as a means of building a Dawson Cosmetics line. Angela developed the business and became president of the division, as well as Dawson's chief operating officer. As with all Dawson products, the cosmetic line was not sold in retail stores. Rather, their products were sold through salon owners, who subsequently sold them to customers. This gave salon owners the opportunity to make money on a proprietary brand product without having to compete directly with retail stores. Although Dawson sales representatives (those who contacted and sold products to the salon owners) occasionally sold door-to-door in the manner of the Fuller business model, this represented a very small portion of total sales.

Jimella came on board as marketing director in 1998. Her reorganization initiatives caused a stir among rank-and-file employees, but the resounding support from her parents quelled those rumblings. In 2000,

[1] Many African-American hair products were specially formulated. For example, Caucasian hair products took oil out, while African-American products put oil in. Dawson offered different products based on hair texture and style. (Examples of styles were Naturals, Dreads, Straight styles, and all of the preceding including color.)

she launched a new product development strategy within the cosmetics division. This line of luxury spa products—named Indulgence—was initially sold alongside other Dawson products. As demand for the line grew,[2] however, Jimella began formulating a plan to more effectively capitalize on that popularity.

In the spring of 2003, Jimella instituted a major redesign of the work and compensation structure for the cosmetology division. Instead of using salaried sales representatives, Dawson Cosmetics would be sold using a multilevel marketing sales model, also known as direct selling. Sales representatives would now be independent distributors whose purpose was to sell the product and to recruit and mentor new representatives.[3] Companies such as Mary Kay, The Pampered Chef, and Tupperware had used this "Party Plan" method to build successful businesses. Jimella felt that direct selling strongly supported the company mission of creating economic self-sufficiency within the African-American community.

Parental Support

Until that morning, Ulissa had been assuming that Jimella would follow in her sister's path and become one of the directors of Dawson Products. Along with that, she had assumed that the new Indulgence line would remain in the division. Ulissa got up from her mahogany desk and walked to the window. From her office, she had an excellent view of a good portion of the Dawson complex—now the city's third largest employer. She looked out at the "Dawson University Inn" and the Manors Convention Center and Dawson Cosmetology University. She thought about how hard they had worked to create this enterprise. Like a proud mother, Ulissa had loved watching this special child develop and grow. Although she and her husband were not nearly ready to relinquish control, this move of Jimella's would upset a succession plan that they had been asking for granted.

[2] There was an explosion of personal care/spa products in the United States. Many consumers who had difficulty "justifying" spa treatments were instead turning to comparable products that they could self-administer in the home. In fact, as quality personal care products continued to proliferate, spas were having an increasingly difficult task creating a significantly value-added experience. (Source: *The ISPA 2004 Consumer Trends Report*—Executive Summary.)

[3] The multilevel compensation plan paid representatives/distributors based not only on their personal production but on the product sales of their "downline"—the people they had brought into the business. In turn, as those downline representatives established their own network, a portion of their commissions would flow back up to the original sponsor. This multitiered commission structure was most appropriate with proprietary, premium-priced, consumable products. In 2003, there were approximately 13.3 million people involved in direct selling—90 percent operated their business part time. Products were sold primarily through in-home product demonstrations, parties, and one-on-one selling. The Direct Selling Association (www.dsa.org) estimated that more than 55 percent of the American public had purchased goods or services through direct selling.

"With a dad like Robert Dawson," she mused to herself, "the world's greatest salesman and entrepreneur—we've raised them to dream big and not take the easy path." They had taught their daughters to be self-sufficient when they were young and now they were bright, energetic, and independent. It seemed that instilling them with that entrepreneurial spirit and drive had led directly to this situation. So how could she not support Jimella in her quest to strike out on her own?

At that moment Jimella walked in. Ulissa turned to face her youngest.

"Jimella, are you sure this is what you want? Running a business is tough, you know."

"Yes, I'm confident that I can make it work—you and Dad prepared me for challenges like this. I'm used to working long hours and I can make tough choices. When we were growing up and working in the business, you taught us to expect at least one problem a week. Learning to anticipate challenges and planning for the unexpected has helped me tremendously. I guess I just have good genes. I know I'm ready."

"How do you plan to finance this move?"

"I've been saving for several years and I have enough to make a reasonable start."

"That's good."

Ulissa smiled. She had tried to teach her children the importance of saving. Jimella had always been frugal. By the time she was ready to attend undergraduate school, she had saved $25,000 to put toward her first-year tuition.

"However, I am going to need some additional working capital."

Ulissa wasn't surprised. She knew her daughter.

"I could go to a bank," Jimella continued, "but before I do that I wanted to discuss this with you and Dad. I'd like to see if we could make an arrangement to have Dawson Products help fund Indulgence."

"That sounds reasonable to me, and I'm sure your father will be willing to listen."

Jimella walked around the desk and hugged her mother. Ulissa, normally very perky, responded slowly. Jimella sensed that her Mom was not really excited about the idea. Her parents had raised her and her sister to run the family business, not to go out on their own. Jimella didn't want to hurt them or Dawson Products, but she needed her independence. She wanted to think for herself and make her own decisions. She knew that as long as she was at Dawson, her parents would continue to make all of the important decisions for her. Her father had made this clear one day when she was suggesting a change in policy. "I don't pay you to think," he had said teasingly. He had always admired her assertiveness, but he wanted her to be clear who the boss was. She had found this so frustrating that she knew she had to be out on her own. Nothing would change as long as her parents were running the business. Jimella realized that although her parents were past retirement age, they were not even close to being ready to slow down.

"Thanks, Mom. I've got to run. I have a staff meeting. I'll speak with you and Dad together later this week when he gets back."

Jimella's "Indulgence"

It took three weeks and many hours of conversation to develop a plan that provided Jimella with the capital support and independence she sought—without putting a strain on the parent company. The arrangement was that Jimella would continue to work at Dawson and handle special projects. In return for her contributions to the family business, Dawson would loan Indulgence Spa Products $250,000 and allow Jimella to use the Dawson business infrastructure to support her venture and manufacture most of her products.

One of Jimella's responsibilities was to manage the company hotel. Realizing that her continued support for Indulgence would be related to her performance at Dawson, she worked hard. She increased Dawson Hotel's profitability by raising prices (they were well below market rates) and by increasing the number of outside events.

Jimella had tried to use every resource available to assist her in her Indulgence project. She became active with the Direct Selling Association.[4] Her parents were sustaining members so she took advantage of its educational programs and used it to develop helpful contacts and mentors. She met the leaders of Mary Kay, Avon, and other companies with door-to-door operations. She toured the Avon facility and received some top-level advice.

She began to create competitive marketing strategies. She determined that her major direct competitor was The Body Shop at Home—a new division of The Body Shop. She believed her other direct competitor to be Warm Spirits, which was a new venture owned by a white male chemist and a black female. She didn't consider the other large health and beauty care companies to be competitors because they did not specialize in spa products.

Jimella designed a product guide that featured women of all races using the spa products. On its opening page, the product guide stated that "the company was founded on the belief that women can be better friends, mothers, and wives when they take a moment to refresh and rejuvenate their inner spirit." She also expanded the product line to include luxury linens and a monthly flower club.

[4] The Direct Selling Association (DSA) was the national trade association of the leading firms that manufactured and distributed goods and services sold directly to consumers. In the early 2000s, more than 150 companies were members of the association, including many well-known brand names. DSA provided educational opportunities for direct selling professionals and worked with Congress, numerous government agencies, consumer protection organizations, and others on behalf of its member companies.

Jimella traveled and presented her products at numerous holiday bazaars, trade shows, and other events. As Jimella talked with prospective distributors and customers, some people openly questioned her age, while others were polite and moved on when they learned that she owned the company.

She advertised in national publications and was slowly developing a national group of independent beauty advisors. Laura Michaels—a top producer—had joined the company after responding to one of the ads. As a middle-aged white woman with lots experience in direct sales, Laura represented the precise demographic that Jimella was certain Indulgence needed to appeal to. Laura's enthusiasm and capability had been a real boost to the enterprise, but despite that distributor's success in building a base of white clients, most Indulgence recruits were African American.

Jimella had set aggressive growth goals for her venture. She planned to attract 100 beauty advisors, $100,000 in monthly sales, and profitability by the end of fiscal year 2006 (see Exhibit 1). She was off to a good start. After just seven weeks in business, she had contracted with 28 beauty consultants and had reached $15,000 in monthly sales.

Parent Company Concerns

By the spring of 2005, Ulissa noted that Jimella was appearing quite satisfied with the arrangement with Dawson Products, and with the progress of the Indulgence venture. Still, Ulissa felt pulled in two directions; she truly hoped that Jimella succeeded, but she also wanted to make sure that Dawson Products could remain a successful, growing family business. Earlier that week, she had confided to a close friend:

"What makes Dawson Products so successful is not the bottles or jars that contain our products. It's not even the products themselves, because many of our competitors have similar things It's our spirit that makes us number one. We have always known how to take what we've got and make what we want of it.

"In time Robert and I will start focusing on leaving this business to our daughters, but now we might have to re-craft our succession strategy. If Jimella leaves and Angela is in charge, we'll certainly have to hire an executive support staff. Even if most of those hires come from within the company, I wonder whether or not the employees would have the same loyalty to Angela as they have had toward us all these years. Would old-timers be constantly questioning new ideas and procedures?

"Robert and I feel strongly that Dawson products must always remain a family business. We treat all of our employees like family. Many have several children and family members that work for Dawson. We will always try to take care of them—they believe in us and our mission."

EXHIBIT 1

Pro Forma Profit and Loss, FY 2005–2009

	2005	2006	2007	2008	2009
Sales	**$585,271**	**$869,755**	**$1,561,976**	**$2,829,716**	**$5,158,227**
Direct Costs of Goods	$169,831	$195,417	$340,731	$603,346	$1,081,017
Fulfillment Payroll	$0	$12,500	$12,500	$75,000	$100,000
Fulfillment	$18,729	$27,832	$49,983	$90,551	$165,063
Cost of Goods Sold	**$188,560**	**$235,749**	**$403,214**	**$768,897**	**$1,346,080**
Gross Margin	**$396,712**	**$634,006**	**$1,158,762**	**$2,060,819**	**$3,812,147**
Operating Expenses					
Sales and Marketing Expenses:					
Sales and Marketing Payroll	$52,000	$75,000	$165,000	$240,000	$280,000
Advertising/Promotion	$15,000	$26,093	$62,479	$141,486	$257,911
National Trade Shows and Distributor Rallies	$50,000	$75,000	$100,000	$125,000	$150,000
Total Sales and Marketing Expenses	**$117,000**	**$176,093**	**$327,479**	**$506,486**	**$687,911**
General and Administrative Expenses					
General and Administrative Payroll	$73,000	$90,000	$120,000	$152,500	$180,000
Commissions and Overides	$92,000	$156,556	$281,156	$622,538	$392,721
Depreciation	$24,123	$36,720	$45,580	$63,328	$79,992
Rent	$7,500	$12,000	$25,000	$35,000	$50,000
Utilities	$3,000	$3,600	$3,600	$3,600	$5,000
Insurance	$16,749	$21,756	$27,599	$44,039	$58,075
Payroll Taxes	$21,900	$26,625	$44,625	$70,125	$84,000
Legal Fees	$8,000	$14,000	$35,000	$50,000	$75,000
Total General and Administrative Expenses	**$246,272**	**$361,256**	**$582,560**	**$1,041,130**	**$1,924,788**
Purchase of Indulgence Assets	$75,000	$0	$0	$0	$0
Total Operating Expenses	**$438,272**	**$537,349**	**$910,039**	**$1,547,616**	**$2,612,699**
Profit Before Interest and Taxes	($41,560)	$96,657	$248,723	$513,204	$1,199,447
Interest Expense	$12,924	$12,373	$10,392	$8,288	$6,054
Taxes Incurred	$0	$31,185	$88,183	$186,819	$441,556
Net Profit	**($54,484)**	**$53,099**	**$150,149**	**$318,097**	**$751,838**
Net Profit/Sales	**−9.31%**	**6.11%**	**9.61%**	**11.24%**	**14.58%**

Ulissa and Robert had another, more global, reason for wanting to keep the company private. Dawson was one of a very few African-American personal care businesses that had managed to avoid a spate of corporate buyouts by white-controlled multinationals (see Appendix B). One particularly painful sale had involved their close friends, the Johnsons.

Johnsons Products had been a premier African-American-owned hair-care company. In the early 1990s, George and Joan Johnson had gotten divorced after 35 years of marriage. Looking to avoid a messy court battle, George had transferred all of his stock to his wife. Their son, Eric, became president and began to grow the company. Under his able control, profits rose 50 percent. Unfortunately, Eric deeply offended his sister Joanie by offering her a position in the family business that she felt was beneath her. Joanie retaliated and convinced her mother, who was chairman of the board, to oust Eric. Soon after, things began to fall apart. When Eric resigned in 1993, the company was sold to IVAC, a majority-owned Florida-based generic drug company, for $61 million.[5]

Ulissa certainly understood why the Johnson saga had caused such a controversy within the African-American community. Although she and her husband had been approached to sell on several occasions, they had always refused. They were dedicated to keeping Dawson Products an African-American family-owned business—a role model for the community and a driving force in helping African Americans become "job makers" instead of "job takers."

Ulissa looked at her watch. Curiously, Jimella was late for their usual lunch date.

[5] K. Springer and L. Reibstein, "So Much for Family Ties," *Newsweek*, March 23, 1992, Vol. 119, Issue 12, p. 49.

A Hard Truth

Although Jimella had continued to work aggressively, charging full speed ahead, Indulgence sales for fiscal year 2005 had fallen short of expectations (see Exhibit 2). As she set these actuals against her pro formas, she realized that to stay on track, she would have to increase sales dramatically in the coming weeks (see Exhibits 3 and 4).

Just as Jimella rose from her desk to head over for lunch with her Mom, she was compelled to sit down with a phone call from Laura Michaels, her perpetually upbeat, enthusiastic, and talented Indulgence representative.

"Jimella, I don't understand what happened."

"Laura, what are you talking about?"

"My cousin Patricia was ready to sign up, and then she called back and told me she had changed her mind. I had been so excited about her potential—she has a lot of friends who would love these products. She would have been an excellent distributor—with a lucrative downline in the white market."

Jimella paused. She knew that building a base of white customers would be tough, but she hadn't anticipated that it would be this difficult. It wasn't that she hadn't been warned. When she had presented her business idea at a local university, the graduate students questioned whether a black female could be successful in a white-dominated, competitive market. And white bias wasn't the only problem. Jimella also knew that many blacks resented the fact that she was using the Spa Indulgence line to "cross over" into the white market. This group included many employees of Dawson Products.

"It will be okay; things like this always happen in direct sales," Jimella said, trying hard but failing to sound encouraging.

Laura had caught the faltering tone.

"You know, I'm usually really good at spotting potential distributors. I hate to say it, Jimella, but my cousin's attitude changed when I told her that a young black female owned the company. Lately, I'm sensing that kind of attitude more and more. I really don't understand it. How can people be so narrow-minded?"

"I don't know, Laura. Or maybe, it's just that I don't want to know."

EXHIBIT 2

Actuals, FY 2005

	$5,500	$6,750	$10,000	$15,000	$25,000	$50,000	$60,000	$70,000	$75,000	$80,000	$90,000	$100,000	$587,250
	Jun	**Jul**	**Aug**	**Sep**	**Oct**	**Nov**	**Dec**	**Jan**	**Feb**	**Mar**	**Apr**	**May**	**2005**
Sales	**$5,500**	**$6,750**	**$9,813**	**$14,961**	**$24,665**	**$46,020**	**$34,199**	**$36,172**	**$46,195**	**$55,330**	**$62,293**	**$67,383**	**$409,281**
Direct Costs of Goods	$1,670	$2,055	$2,836	$4,359	$6,999	$12,398	$9,807	$10,459	$13,441	$16,084	$18,431	$20,223	$118,763
Fulfillment Payroll	$0	$0	$0	$0	$0	$0	$0	$0	$0	$0	$0	$0	$0
Fulfillment	$176	$216	$314	$479	$789	$1,473	$1,094	$1,158	$1,478	$1,771	$1,993	$2,156	$13,097
Cost of Goods Sold	**$1,846**	**$2,271**	**$3,150**	**$4,837**	**$7,788**	**$13,870**	**$10,902**	**$11,617**	**$14,920**	**$17,854**	**$20,425**	**$22,380**	**$131,860**
Gross Margin	**$3,654**	**$4,479**	**$6,662**	**$10,124**	**$16,877**	**$32,150**	**$23,297**	**$24,556**	**$31,276**	**$37,475**	**$41,868**	**$45,003**	**$277,421**
Operating Expenses:													
Sales and Marketing Expenses:													
Sales and Marketing Payroll	$3,500	$3,500	$3,500	$3,500	$3,500	$3,500	$3,500	$5,000	$5,000	$5,000	$5,000	$5,000	$49,500
Advertising/Promotion	$165	$230	$294	$449	$740	$1,381	$1,026	$1,085	$1,386	$1,660	$1,869	$2,021	$12,278
National Trade Shows	$0	$0	$15,000	$10,000	$0	$0	$0	$15,000	$0	$0	$3,500	$3,500	$47,000
Total Sales and Marketing Expenses	**$3,665**	**$3,703**	**$18,794**	**$13,949**	**$4,240**	**$4,881**	**$4,526**	**$21,085**	**$6,386**	**$6,660**	**$10,369**	**$10,521**	**$108,778**
General and Administrative Expenses:													
General and Administrative Payroll	$5,666	$5,666	$5,666	$5,666	$5,666	$5,666	$5,666	$5,666	$5,666	$5,666	$5,666	$5,670	$67,996
Commissions and Overides	$990	$1,215	$1,766	$2,693	$4,440	$8,284	$6,156	$6,511	$8,315	$9,959	$11,213	$12,129	$73,671
Depreciation	$1,271	$1,271	$1,271	$1,757	$1,757	$1,757	$2,507	$2,507	$2,507	$2,507	$2,507	$2,507	$24,123
Rent	$0	$0	$750	$750	$750	$750	$750	$750	$750	$750	$750	$750	$7,500
Utilities	$0	$0	$300	$300	$300	$300	$300	$300	$300	$300	$300	$300	$3,000
Insurance	$642	$645	$1,550	$1,259	$690	$729	$708	$1,701	$819	$1,797	$2,560	$3,649	$16,749
Payroll Taxes	$1,375	$1,375	$1,375	$1,375	$1,375	$1,375	$1,375	$1,600	$1,600	$1,600	$1,600	$1,601	$17,624
Legal Fees	$0	$2,500	$2,500	$0	$0	$0	$0	$1,000	$0	$1,000	$0	$1,000	$8,000
Total General and Administrative Expenses	**$9,945**	**$12,672**	**$15,180**	**$13,801**	**$14,978**	**$18,860**	**$17,461**	**$20,035**	**$19,957**	**$23,579**	**$24,595**	**$27,605**	**$218,664**
Purchase of Indulgence Assets	$0	$75,000	$0	$0	$0	$0	$0	$0	$0	$0	$0	$0	$75,000
Total Other Expenses	**$9,944**	**$12,671**	**$15,178**	**$13,800**	**$14,978**	**$18,860**	**$17,461**	**$20,035**	**$19,957**	**$23,579**	**$24,595**	**$27,605**	**$218,664**
Total Operating Expenses	**$13,609**	**$91,374**	**$33,972**	**$27,749**	**$19,218**	**$23,741**	**$21,987**	**$41,120**	**$26,343**	**$30,239**	**$34,964**	**$38,127**	**$402,442**
Profit Before Interest and Taxes	($9,955)	($86,895)	($27,310)	($17,625)	($2,341)	$8,409	$1,310	($16,564)	$4,933	$7,236	$6,905	$6,876	($125,021)
Interest Expense	$0	$1,238	$1,225	$1,213	$1,200	$1,188	$1,175	$1,163	$1,150	$1,137	$1,124	$1,111	$12,924
Taxes Incurred	$0	$0	$0	$0	$0	$0	$0	$0	$0	$0	$0	$0	$0
Net Profit	**($9,955)**	**($88,132)**	**($28,535)**	**($18,838)**	**($3,541)**	**$7,221**	**$135**	**($17,727)**	**$3,783**	**$6,099**	**$5,781**	**$5,765**	**($137,945)**
Net Profit/Sales	**181.01%**	**1305.67%**	**290.81%**	**125.91%**	**14.36%**	**15.69%**	**0.39%**	**49.01%**	**8.19%**	**11.02%**	**9.28%**	**8.56%**	**33.20%**

EXHIBIT 3

Indulgence Actual and Projected Cash Flows

	Actual Fiscal Year				
Cash Received	**2005**	**2006**	**2007**	**2008**	**2009**
Cash from Operations:					
Cash Sales	$409,281	$869,755	$1,561,976	$2,829,716	$5,158,227
Cash from Receivables	$0	$0	$0	$0	$0
Subtotal Cash from Operations	**$409,281**	**$869,755**	**$1,561,976**	**$2,829,716**	**$5,158,227**
Additional Cash Received					
Sales Tax, VAT, HST/GST Received	$30,696	$65,232	$117,148	$212,229	$386,867
Dawson Loan Proceeds	$250,000	$0	$0	$0	$0
Sales of Long-Term Assets	$689,977	$934,987	$1,679,124	$3,041,945	$5,545,094
Subtotal Cash Received					
Expenditures	**2005**	**2006**	**2007**	**2008**	**2009**
Expenditures from Operations:					
Cash Spending	$117,496	$177,500	$297,500	$467,500	$560,000
Payment of Accounts Payable	$336,763	$547,641	$973,793	$1,836,107	$3,462,894
Subtotal Spent on Operations	**$454,260**	**$725,141**	**$1,271,293**	**$2,303,607**	**$4,022,894**
Additional Cash Spent					
Sales Tax, VAT, HST/GST Paid Out	$25,905	$65,232	$117,148	$212,229	$386,867
Principal Repayment of Dawson Loan	$27,776	$32,027	$34,008	$36,112	$38,346
Purchase Long-Term Assets	$40,950	$75,000	$85,000	$125,000	$150,000
Subtotal Cash Spent	**$548,891**	**$897,400**	**$1,507,450**	**$2,676,948**	**$4,598,107**
Net Cash Flow	**$141,086**	**$37,586**	**$171,674**	**$364,997**	**$946,987**
Cash Balance	**$161,086**	**$198,672**	**$370,346**	**$735,344**	**$1,682,331**

EXHIBIT 4

Indulgence Actual and Projected Balance Sheets

	Actual Fiscal Year				
Assets	**2005**	**2006**	**2007**	**2008**	**2009**
Current Assets					
Cash	$161,086	$198,672	$370,346	$735,344	$1,682,331
Accounts Receivable	$0	$0	$0	$0	$0
Inventory	$75,000	$100,000	$125,000	$200,000	$300,000
Other Current Assets	$0	$0	$0	$0	$0
Total Current Assets	**$236,086**	**$298,672**	**$495,346**	**$935,344**	**$1,982,331**
Long-Term Assets					
Long-Term Assets	$65,950	$140,950	$225,950	$350,950	$500,950
Accumulated Depreciation	$0	$60,843	$106,423	$169,751	$249,743
Total Long-Term Assets	**$65,950**	**$80,107**	**$119,527**	**$181,199**	**$251,207**
Total Assets	**$302,036**	**$378,779**	**$614,873**	**$1,116,542**	**$2,233,538**
Liabilities and Capital	**2005**	**2006**	**2007**	**2008**	**2009**
Accounts Payable	$70,924	$150,718	$270,672	$490,356	$893,860
Dawson Loan Balance	$222,224	$190,196	$156,188	$120,076	$81,730
Other Current Liabilities	$4,791	$4,791	$4,791	$4,791	$4,791
Subtotal Current Liabilities	**$297,938**	**$345,706**	**$431,651**	**$615,223**	**$980,381**
Long-Term Liabilities	$0	$0	$0	$0	$0
Total Liabilities	**$297,938**	**$345,706**	**$431,651**	**$615,223**	**$980,381**
Paid-in Capital	$0	$0	$0	$0	$0
Retained Earnings	$138,000	$55	$53,154	$203,303	$521,400
Earnings	($119,404)	$53,099	$150,149	$318,097	$751,838
Total Capital	**$18,596**	**$53,154**	**$203,303**	**$521,400**	**$1,273,238**
Total Liabilities and Capital	**$316,534**	**$398,860**	**$634,954**	**$1,136,624**	**$2,253,619**
Net Worth	**$4,097**	**$33,073**	**$183,222**	**$501,319**	**$1,253,157**

Appendix A

S. B. FULLER (1905–1988)

It is contrary to the laws of nature for man to stand still; he must move forward, or the eternal march of progress will force him backward. This the Negro has failed to understand; he believes that the lack of civil rights legislation, and the lack of integration have kept him back. But this is not true. . . .

S. B. Fuller

Samuel B. Fuller was one of the wealthiest and most successful black entrepreneurs in mid-20th-century America. His Chicago-based business empire included Fuller Products, which manufactured health and beauty aids and cleaning products; a $3 million ownership in real estate, including the famous Regal Theater, comparable to Harlem's Apollo Theater; the South Center (later changed to Fuller) Department Store and Office Building; a New York Real Estate Trust, the Fuller Guaranty Corporation; the *Pittsburgh Courier,* the largest black newspaper chain; and the Fuller Philco Home Appliance Center; as well as farm and livestock operations.

Fuller was born into rural poverty in Ouachita Parish, Louisiana, in 1905. From an early age, he gained a reputation for reliability and resourcefulness. After coming to Chicago in 1920, he worked in a wide range of menial jobs, eventually rising up to become manager of a coal yard. Although he had a secure job during the depression, he struck out on his own preferring "freedom" to "security." Starting with $25, he founded Fuller Products in 1934.

By 1960, at the height of his business success, with sales of $10 million, there were 85 branches of his Fuller Products Company in 38 states. His employees, black and white, included 5,000 salespeople and some 600 workers in his office and factory, who produced and sold the 300 different products manufactured by Fuller. In 1947 Fuller secretly purchased Boyer International Laboratories, a white cosmetic manufactory, which opened a southern white consumer-based market. Fuller also held interest in the Patricia Stevens Cosmetic Company and J. C. McBrady and Company.

Fuller Products gave training to many future entrepreneurs and other leaders. Post–World War II black millionaires John H. Johnson, publisher, George Johnson, hair products manufacturer, and Robert Dawson, hair products manufacturer, have all acknowledged Fuller as their role model. He had little patience for race baiters, black or white. "It doesn't make any difference," he declared, "about the color of an individual's skin. No one cares whether a cow is black, red, yellow, or brown. They want to know how much milk it can produce."

Fuller was a leading black Republican, although he always had an independent streak. He promoted civil rights and briefly headed the Chicago South Side NAACP. Along with black Birmingham businessman A. G. Gaston, he tried to organize a cooperative effort to purchase the segregated bus company during the Montgomery Bus Boycott. He told Martin Luther King, Jr. "The bus company is losing money and is willing to sell. We should buy it." King was skeptical of the idea, and not enough blacks came forward to raise the money. Despite his belief in civil rights, however, Fuller's emphasis had always been on the need for blacks to go into business. In 1958, he blasted the federal government for undermining free enterprise and fostering socialism. He feared that it was "doing the same thing today as was done in the days of Caesar—destroying incentive and initiative." He argued that wherever "there is capitalism, there is freedom."

In the early 1960s Fuller's financial empire collapsed. Southern whites discovered his ownership in Boyer International Laboratories. A 100 percent white boycott of the company's products resulted in an abrupt drop of 60 percent of the Fuller Product Line. In addition, Fuller Products suffered severe reverses after S. B. Fuller gave a controversial speech to the National Association of Manufacturers in 1963. In his speech, Fuller charged that too many blacks were using their lack of civil rights as an excuse for failure. Many of his comments were reported out of context. Major national black leaders reacted angrily and called for a boycott of Fuller Products.

Despite a record of remarkable business success, Fuller was unable to raise professional capital to offset losses. Attempts to generate funds by selling stock in Fuller Products failed. In 1964, the Securities and Exchange Commission charged Fuller with sale of unregistered securities. He was forced to pay $1.5 million to his creditors, including black salespeople who also filed claims. Fullers sold off various enterprises to meet his debts.

After bankruptcy, but with six-figure financial support in gifts and loans from leading Chicago black business people, Fuller Products was reorganized in 1972 but never recovered as a major black business. Fuller continued manufacturing a line of cleaning products and cosmetics, with sales through distributorship franchises: $1,000 for Fuller Products valued at $26,000. In 1975, Fuller showed sales of almost $1 million. S. B. Fuller died in 1988.

Source: Juliet E. K. Walker and S. B. Fuller, *Encyclopedia of African American Business History,* (Westport CT: Greenwood Press, 1999).

Appendix B

THE ETHNIC HEALTH AND BEAUTY CARE INDUSTRY

Overview

The ethnic health and beauty care industry (HBC) consisted of hair and skin products and cosmetics, designed for and sold to minority groups. The three largest minority groups in the United States were African Americans, Hispanics, and Asians. Of these three minority groups, African Americans were by far the biggest purchasers of ethnic HBC products. For this reason, the vast majority of ethnic HBC products were directed toward African-American consumers. This lucrative and fertile industry was once the domain of African-American companies. When major manufacturers realized the potential of the ethnic HBC industry, they moved in rapidly and eventually captured all but a small fraction of the market.

In 2004, the combined retail market for ethnic hair care, color cosmetic, and skin care products was valued at $1.6 billion, and was estimated to grow to $1.9 billion by2006. The largest HBC category was hair care, 72 percent of the total at $1.124 billion, then cosmetics at $327 million or 20 percent, and skin care at $110 million or 7 percent. Products not sold through traditional retail chains (such as products used by professional stylists, Indulgence Spa and Dawson Products) are not reflected in these retail figures.

African Americans Are the Largest Consumers of HBC Products

Various studies indicated that African Americans spent 3 to 5 times more on HBC products than the general population. According to AHBAI (American Health and Beauty Aids Institute), a trade group representing African-American hair care manufacturers, African Americans buy 19 percent of all health and beauty aids and 34 percent of all hair care products while accounting for approximately 12 percent of the overall population. In 2005, the purchasing power of the African-American population exceeded $688 billion.

The Growth and Development of the Ethnic Health and Beauty Care Industry

African Americans founded and built what we today call the ethnic health and beauty care industry. The founding pioneers of the ethnic industry, Madame C. J. Walker, S. B. Fuller, and George E. Johnson, were among the first to see the great potential in creating businesses catering to the hair and skin care needs of the African-American man and women.

During their time, there were virtually no hair and skin care products designed for African Americans and for a very long period, and ethnic industry was ignored by mainstream manufacturers who did not see the value in producing ethnic products. Up until the late 19th century, the ethnic market consisted mainly of products manufactured by African Americans, for African Americans.

Madame C. J. Walker, America's first black self-made female millionaire, set the pace with the development, manufacturing, and selling of hair care products she created herself. She also developed innovations to the pressing comb, which gave rise to an entire industry. Following in her footsteps was S. B. Fuller (see Appendix A). One of Fuller's many disciples, George E. Johnson, heeded the call and pioneered the modern ethnic health and beauty care industry. Johnson Products was a company that established many "firsts" in the industry. From their legacy came Dawson Products, Bronner Brothers, Pro-Line, Soft Sheen, Luster, and many others.

The Role African-American Hair Companies Played in the African-American Community

The handful of African-American health and beauty care companies existing during Madame C. J. Walker's time would grow to nearly 20 over the next three decades. As the industry developed, thousands of jobs were created within the African-American community.

During the segregation period in America there was much turmoil and unrest among African Americans who had grown weary of the unequal treatment they were receiving from white society. Many African Americans felt that developing strong businesses in the African-American community was the only way to achieve freedom, justice, and equality. For that reason, African-American entrepreneurs were hailed as heroes, leaders, and examples in their communities. They represented black success, and their presence in the community fostered racial pride and self-esteem among African Americans.

Following desegregation, many black-owned businesses began losing market share to white companies. Black-owned banks, hotels, and corner stores soon disappeared. The only black businesses making big profits serving blacks were black hair care companies, and by the 1970s, they began to face serious challenges by mainstream corporations.

The Movement of Non-African-American Companies into the Ethnic Health and Beauty Care Industry

In the early 1970s, mainstream companies began to see abundant opportunities in the ethnic market. Prior to that, the handful of African-American hair companies in existence at the time were growing and thriving. In the late 1970s, the ethnic market received a tremendous boost with the enormous popularity of the Jheri Curl—one of the hottest styles of the time. Many companies experienced skyrocketing profits—some exceeding 40 percent.

The Jheri Curl was a product of the International Playtex Corporation—a white-owned company. Customer demand for the Jheri Curl was fueled when celebrities like Michael Jackson began sporting the glossy curls. An ample number of products were needed to achieve and maintain the Jheri Curl look, and many African-American hair care companies reaped tremendous revenues from it. According to a 1986 *Newsweek* article the Jheri Curl "spurred industry growth at a 32 percent rate."

The soaring profits reaped by African-American hair care companies from this popular style did not go unnoticed by mainstream manufacturers. Corporate giants like Alberto-Culver and Revlon entered the market. Following in their footsteps, Gillette entered the market in the middle 1980s with the purchase of Lustrasilk.

How the Changes in Ownership Affected African Americans' Companies

Many African-American health and beauty care companies, not having the capital to compete with these billion-dollar corporations, either sold, merged, or went bankrupt. Black-owned companies that did survive lost significant market share.

The shake-up shifted the balance of power to non-African-American companies. For example, Johnson Products, the modern industry pioneer, controlled 80 percent of the relaxer market in 1976. In 1977, the FTC ordered Johnson Products to put warning labels on its lye-based relaxer. This action gave Johnson Products a negative public image, and it cost the company customers. Revlon, a corporate giant, avoided a similar FTC ruling for almost two years. Eventually Revlon complied, but not until it had captured a significant portion of the relaxer market through its Realistic and Fabulaxer products. Carson Products, makers of Dark & Lovely Relaxers, cornered the market in the late 1970s when it introduced its no-lye relaxer product. Atlanta-based M&M, Inc., maker of Sta-Sof-Fro, sold over $47 million of products in 1983, but was out of business by 1990. Johnson Products later acquired the assets of M&M.

By the 1980s African-American health and beauty care companies were in serious trouble. Once controlling 80 percent of the total market, their share was estimated by industry analysts to be as low as 48 percent.

The Founding of the American Health and Beauty Aids Institute

In response to competition in the industry, the American Health and Beauty Aids Institute (AHBAI) was formed in 1981. AHBAI is a national nonprofit organization of black-owned companies that produce hair care and cosmetic products specifically for black consumers. AHBAI created the "Proud Lady" logo (a black woman in silhouette featuring three layers of hair). The logo was stamped on the back of all manufacturing members' products, printed materials, and packing and promotional materials. The mission of AHBAI was to make consumers aware of products that were manufactured by African-American-owned companies.

The Revlon Pronouncement

While African-American hair care companies were facing dwindling revenues and threats of corporate acquisitions, mergers, and takeovers, Irving Bottner, a high-ranking Revlon official, was quoted in the October 1986 issue of *Newsweek* magazine as having said: "In the next couple of years, the black owned businesses will disappear. They'll all be sold to the white companies."

In the same article, Mr. Bottner went on to criticize AHBAI, the trade organization representing black manufacturers, saying that AHBAI's campaign to encourage black consumers to purchase products from black companies was unfair to white business: "They're making a social issue out of a business issue. When you produce what the consumer wants, loyalties disappear."

Mr. Bottner also stated that black companies tend to offer "poorer grade" products: "We are accused of taking business away from the black companies, but black consumers buy quality products—too often their black brothers didn't do them any good." In response, Jesse Jackson launched a boycott against Revlon, demanding that Revlon divest in South African operations hire more black managers, and use more black suppliers. Black publications such as *Essence, Ebony,* and *Jet* temporarily stopped carrying Revlon advertisements. In response, Revlon sponsored a $3 million advertising campaign, announcing that money spent with black businesses supports the black community.

The situation escalated in the 1990s. Company by company, mergers and acquisitions dismantled black-owned health and beauty care businesses. In 1993, majority-owned IVAX, a Florida-based generic drug company, acquired Johnson Products Co., the maker of Afro-Sheen and Ultra-Sheen. IVAX also purchased Flori Roberts Cosmetics, a majority-owned line of cosmetics for women of color. In 1998, L'Oreal bought Soft Sheen. Ownership of Johnson Products changed hands that same year from IVAX to Carson Inc., a mainstream company based in Savannah, Georgia. In March 2000, Alberto-Culver, a $1.6 billion personal-care products manufacturing company in Melrose Park, Illinois, bought Pro-Line, the third largest black-owned manufacturer, for an undisclosed amount.

In 2000, L'Oreal acquired Carson. As a result, the top two black-owned hair care companies (Johnson Products and Soft Sheen) were joined under the L'Oreal umbrella. Based in France, L'Oreal was the world's dominant manufacturer of ethnic health and beauty care products, with Soft Sheen/Carson brands such as Dark & Lovely and Optimum Care as its top sellers. Soft Sheen/Carson was the name L'Oreal had given to the newly merged Soft Sheen Products and Carson Products businesses.

Lafayette Jones, president and CEO of Segmented Marketing Services, estimated that the 2004 sales of L'Oreal's ethnic market divisions were in the range of $1 billion, and those of Alberto-Culver were around $100 million. Jones is also publisher of *Urban Call,* a trade magazine for urban retailers and businesses, and *Shades of Beauty,* a magazine for multicultural salons. Alfred Washington, chairman of the American Health and Beauty Aids Institute, said in 2004, "The combination of L'Oreal's massive marketing power plus the acquired brands of Soft Sheen and Carson will work to squeeze black manufacturers from the retail shelf."

For a better understanding of the impact of the sales of many prominent African-American-owned HBC product manufacturers, see "Bad Hair Days" in *Black Enterprise Magazine* (November2000).

18

Chapter Eighteen

The Entrepreneur and the Troubled Company

Yes, I did run out of time on a few occasions, but I never lost a ball game!

Bobby Lane
Great Quarterback in the 1950s and 1960s of the Detroit Lions and the Pittsburgh Steelers

It's OK to go bankrupt, but not on your last deal.

John W. Altman
Entrepreneur and Professor

Results Expected

Upon completion of this chapter, you will have:

1. Examined the principle causes and danger signals of impending trouble.
2. Discussed both quantitative and qualitative symptoms of trouble.
3. Examined the principle diagnostic methods used to devise intervention and turnaround plans.
4. Identified remedial actions used for dealing with lenders, creditors, and employees.
5. Analyzed the "Lightwave" case study.

When the Bloom Is off the Rose

This chapter is about the entrepreneur and the troubled company. It traces the firm's route into and out of crisis and provides insight into how a troubled company can be rescued by a turnaround specialist.

Many times in the history of the United States, companies have experienced times of economic troubles. The most recent period was 2000–2003. Both corporate and personal bankruptcies increased during this period, and managers needed a new and special set of skills to lead through the shoals.

There is a saying among horseback riders that the person who has never been thrown from a horse probably has never ridden one! Jim Hindman, founder of Jiffy Lube, is fond of saying, "Ultimately it is not how many touchdowns you score but how fast and often you get up after being tackled." These insights capture the essence of the ups and downs that can occur during the growth and development of a new venture.

Special credit is due to Robert Bateman, Scott Douglas, and Ann Morgan for contributing material in this chapter. The material is the result of research and interviews with turnaround specialists and was submitted in a paper as a requirement for the author's Financing Entrepreneurial Ventures course in the MBA program at Babson College.

The authors are especially grateful to two specialists, Leslie B. Charm, who along with his partner has owned three national franchise companies, an entrepreneurial advisory and troubled business management company, and a venture capital company, AIGIS Ventures, LLC; and Leland Goldberg of Coopers & Lybrand, Boston, who contributed enormously to the efforts of Bateman, Douglas, and Morgan and to the material.

Getting into Trouble—The Causes

Trouble can be caused by external forces not under the control of management. Among the most frequently mentioned are recession, interest rate changes, changes in government policy, inflation, the entry of new competition, and industry/product obsolescence.

However, those who manage turnarounds find that while such circumstances define the environment to which a troubled company needs to adjust, they are rarely the sole reason for a company failure. External shocks impact all companies in an industry, and only some of them fail. Others survive and prosper.

Most causes of failure can be found within company management. Although there are many causes of trouble, the most frequently cited fall into three broad areas: inattention to strategic issues, general management problems, and poor financial/accounting systems and practices. There is striking similarity between these causes of trouble and the causes of failure for startups given in Chapter 3.

Strategic Issues

- *Misunderstood market niche.* The first of these issues is a failure to understand the company's market niche and to focus on growth without considering profitability. Instead of developing a strategy, these firms take on low-margin business and add capacity in an effort to grow. They then run out of cash.
- *Mismanaged relationships with suppliers and customers.* Related to the issue of not understanding market niche is the failure to understand the economics of relationships with suppliers and customers. For example, some firms allow practices in the industry to dictate payment terms, when they may be in a position to dictate their own terms.
- *Diversification into an unrelated business area.* A common failing of cash-rich firms that suffer from the growth syndrome is diversification into unrelated business areas. These firms use the cash flow generated in one business to start another without good reason. As one turnaround consultant said, "I couldn't believe it. There was no synergy at all. They added to their overhead but not to their contribution. No common sense!"
- *Mousetrap myopia.* Related to the problem of starting a firm around an idea, rather than an opportunity, is the problem of firms that have "great products" and are looking for other markets where they can be sold. This is done without analyzing the firm's opportunities.
- *The big project.* The company gears up for a "big project" without looking at the cash flow implications. Cash is expended by adding capacity and hiring personnel. When sales do not materialize, or take longer than expected to materialize, there is trouble. Sometimes the "big project" is required by the nature of the business opportunity. An example of this would be the high-technology startup that needs to capitalize on a first-mover advantage. The company needs to prove the product's "right to life" and grow quickly to the point where it can achieve a public market or become an attractive acquisition candidate for a larger company. This ensures that a larger company cannot use its advantages in scale and existing distribution channels, after copying the technology, to achieve dominance over the startup.
- *Lack of contingency planning.* As has been stated over and over, the path to growth is not a smooth curve upward. Firms need to be geared to think about what happens if things go sour, sales fall, or collections slow. There need to be plans in place for layoffs and capacity reduction.

Management Issues

- *Lack of management skills, experience, and know-how.* As was mentioned in Chapter 7, while companies grow, managers need to change their management mode from doing to managing to managing managers.
- *Weak finance function.* Often, in a new and emerging company, the finance function is nothing more than a bookkeeper. One company was five years old, with $20 million in sales, before the founders hired a financial professional.
- *Turnover in key management personnel.* Although turnover of key management personnel can be difficult in any firm, it is a critical concern in businesses that deal in specialized or proprietary knowledge. For example, one firm lost a bookkeeper who was the only person who really understood what was happening in the business.
- *Big-company influence in accounting.* A mistake that some companies often make is to focus on accruals, rather than cash.

Poor Planning, Financial/Accounting Systems, Practices, and Controls

- *Poor pricing, overextension of credit, and excessive leverage.* These causes of trouble are not surprising and need not be elaborated.

Some of the reasons for excess use of leverage are interesting. Use of excess leverage can result from growth outstripping the company's internal financing capabilities. The company then relies increasingly on short-term notes until a cash flow problem develops. Another reason a company becomes overleveraged is by using guaranteed loans in place of equity for either startup or expansion financing. One entrepreneur remarked, "[The guaranteed loan] looked just like equity when we started, but when trouble came it looked more and more like debt."

- *Lack of cash budgets/projections.* This is a most frequently cited cause of trouble. In small companies, cash budgets/projections are often not done.
- *Poor management reporting.* While some firms have good financial reporting, they suffer from poor management reporting. As one turnaround consultant stated, "[The financial statement] just tells where the company has been. It doesn't help *manage* the business. If you look at the important management reports—inventory analysis, receivables aging, sales analysis—they're usually late or not produced at all. The same goes for billing procedures. Lots of emerging companies don't get their bills out on time."
- *Lack of standard costing.* Poor management reporting extends to issues of costing, too. Many emerging businesses have no standard costs against which they can compare the actual costs of manufacturing products. The result is they have no variance reporting. The company cannot identify problems in process and take corrective action. The company will know only after the fact how profitable a product is.

  Even when standard costs are used, it is not uncommon to find that engineering, manufacturing, and accounting each has its own version of the bill of material. The product is designed one way, manufactured a second way, and costed a third.
- *Poorly understood cost behavior.* Companies often do not understand the relationship between fixed and variable costs. For example, one manufacturing company thought it was saving money by closing on Saturday. In this way, management felt it would save paying overtime. It had to be pointed out to the lead entrepreneur by a turnaround consultant that, "He had a lot of high-margin product in his manufacturing backlog that more than justified the overtime."

  It is also important for entrepreneurs to understand the difference between theory and practice in this area. The turnaround consultant mentioned above said, "Accounting theory says that all costs are variable in the long run. In practice, almost all costs are fixed. The only truly variable cost is a sales commission."

Getting Out of Trouble

The major protection against and the biggest help in getting out of these troubled waters is to have a set of advisors and directors who have been through this in the past. They possess skills that aren't taught in school or in most corporate training programs. An outside "vision" is critical. The speed of action has to be different; control systems have to be different; and organization generally needs to be different.

Troubled companies face a situation similar to that described by Winston Churchill, in *While England Slept,* "Descending inconstantly, fecklessly, the stairway which leads to dark gulf. It is a fine broad stairway at the beginning, but after a bit the carpet ends, a little farther on there are only flagstones, and a little farther on still these break beneath your feet."

Although uncontrollable external factors such as new government regulations do arise, an opportunity-driven firm's crisis is usually the result of management error. Yet in these management errors are found part of the solution to the troubled company's problems. It is pleasing to see that many companies—even companies that are insolvent or have negative net worth or both—can be rescued and restored to profitability.

Predicting Trouble

Since crises develop over time and typically result from an accumulation of fundamental errors, can a crisis be predicted? The obvious benefit of being able to predict crisis is that the entrepreneur, employees, and significant outsiders, such as investors, lenders, trade creditors—and even customers—could see trouble brewing in time to take corrective actions.

There have been several attempts to develop predictive models. Two are presented below and have been selected because each is easy to calculate and uses information available in common financial reports. Because management reporting in emerging companies is often inadequate, the predictive model needs to use information available in common financial reports.

Each of the two approaches below uses easily obtained financial data to predict the onset of crisis as much as two years in advance. For the smaller public

EXHIBIT 18.1

Net-Liquid-Balance-to-Total-Assets Ratio

Net-Liquid-Balance-to-Total-Assets Ratio = NLB/Total Assets
Where
NLB = (Cash + Marketable securities) − (Notes Payable + Contractual obligations)

Source: Joel Shulman, "Primary Rule for Detecting Bankruptcy: Watch the Cash," *Financial Analyst Journal,* September 1988.

company, these models can be used by all interested observers. With private companies, they are useful only to those privy to the information and are probably only of benefit to such nonmanagement outsiders as lenders and boards of directors.

The most frequently used denominator in all these ratios is the figure for total assets. This figure often is distorted by "creative accounting," with expenses occasionally improperly capitalized and carried on the balance sheet or by substantial differences between tangible book value and book value (i.e., overvalued or undervalued assets).

Net-Liquid-Balance-to-Total-Assets Ratio

The model shown in Exhibit 18.1 was developed by Joel Shulman, a Babson College professor, to predict loan defaults. Shulman found that his ratio can predict loan defaults with significant reliability as much as two years in advance.

Shulman's approach is noteworthy because it explicitly recognizes the importance of cash. Among current accounts, Shulman distinguishes between operating assets (such as inventory and accounts receivable) and financial assets (such as cash and marketable securities). The same distinction is made among liabilities, where notes payable and contractual obligations are financial liabilities and accounts payable are operating liabilities.

Shulman then subtracts financial liabilities from financial assets to obtain a figure known as the net liquid balance (NLB). NLB can be thought of as "uncommitted cash," cash the firm has available to meet contingencies. Because it is the short-term margin for error should sales change, collections slow, or interest rates change, it is a true measure of liquidity. The NLB is then divided by total assets to form the predictive ratio.

Nonquantitative Signals

In Chapter 16 we discussed patterns and actions that could lead to trouble, indications of common trouble by growth stage, and critical variables that can be monitored.

Turnaround specialists also use some nonquantitative signals as indicators of the possibility of trouble. As with the signals discussed in Chapter 16, the presence of a single one of these does not necessarily imply an immediate crisis. However, once any of these surfaces and if the others follow, then trouble is likely to mount.

- Inability to produce financial statements on time.
- Changes in behavior of the lead entrepreneur (such as avoiding phone calls or coming in later than usual).
- Change in management or advisors, such as directors, accountants, or other professional advisors.
- Accountant's opinion that is qualified and not certified.
- New competition.
- Launching of a "big project."
- Lower research and development expenditures.
- Special write-offs of assets and/or addition of "new" liabilities.
- Reduction of credit line.

The Gestation Period of Crisis

Crisis rarely develops overnight. The time between the initial cause of trouble and the point of intervention can run from 18 months to five years. What happens to a company during the gestation period has implications for the later turnaround of the company. Thus, how management reacts to crisis and what happens to morale determine what will need to happen in the intervention. Usually, a demoralized and unproductive organization develops when its members think only of survival, not turnaround, and its entrepreneur has lost credibility. Further, the company has lost valuable time.

In looking backward, the graph of a company's key statistics shows trouble. One can see the sales growth rate (and the gross margin) have slowed considerably. This is followed by an increasing rise in expenses as the company assumes that growth will continue. When the growth doesn't continue, the company still allows the growth rate of expenses to remain high so it can "get back on track."

The Paradox of Optimism

In a typical scenario for a troubled company, the first signs of trouble (such as declining margins, customer returns, or falling liquidity) go unnoticed or are written off as teething problems of the new project or as the ordinary vicissitudes of business. For example, one entrepreneur saw increases in inventory and receivables as a good sign, since sales were up and the current ratio had improved. However, although sales were up, margins were down, and he did not realize he had a liquidity problem until cash shortages developed.

Although management may miss the first signs, outsiders usually do not. Banks, board members, suppliers, and customers see trouble brewing. They wonder why management does not respond. Credibility begins to erode.

Soon management has to admit that trouble exists, but valuable time has been lost. Furthermore, requisite actions to meet the situation are anathema. The lead entrepreneur is emotionally committed to people, to projects, or to business areas. Further, to cut back in any of these areas goes against instinct, because the company will need these resources when the good times return.

The company continues its downward fall, and the situation becomes stressful. Turnaround specialists mention that stress can cause avoidance on the part of an entrepreneur. Others have likened the entrepreneur in a troubled company to a deer caught in a car's headlights. The entrepreneur is frozen and can take no action. Avoidance has a basis in human psychology. One organizational behavior consultant who has worked on turnarounds said, "When a person under stress does not understand the problem and does not have the sense to deal with it, the person will tend to replace the unpleasant reality with fantasy." The consultant went on to say, "The outward manifestation of this fantasy is avoidance." This consultant noted it is common for an entrepreneur to deal with pleasant and well-understood tasks, such as selling to customers, rather than dealing with the trouble. The result is that credibility is lost with bankers, creditors, and so forth. (These are the very people whose cooperation needs to be secured if the company is to be turned around.)

Often, the decisions the entrepreneur does make during this time are poor and accelerate the company on its downward course. The accountant or the controller may be fired, resulting in a company that is then flying blind. One entrepreneur, for example, running a company that manufactured a high-margin product, announced across-the-board cuts in expenditures, including advertising, without stopping to think that cutting advertising on such a product only added to the cash flow problem.

Finally, the entrepreneur may make statements that are untrue or may make promises that cannot be kept. This is the death knell of his or her credibility.

The Bloom Is off the Rose—Now What?

Generally, when an organization is in trouble some telltale trends appear.

- Ignore outside advice.
- The worse is still yet to come.
- People (including and usually, most especially, the entrepreneur) have stopped making decisions and also have stopped answering the phone.
- Nobody in authority has talked to the employees.
- Rumors are flying.
- Inventory is out of balance. That is, it does not reflect historical trends.
- Accounts receivable aging is increasing.
- Customers are becoming afraid of new commitments.
- A general malaise has settled in while a still high-stressed environment exists (an unusual combination).

Decline in Organizational Morale

Among those who notice trouble developing are the employees. They deal with customer returns, calls from creditors, and the like, and they wonder why management does not respond. They begin to lose confidence in management.

Despite troubled times, the lead entrepreneur talks and behaves optimistically or hides in the office declining to communicate with either employees, customers, or vendors. Employees hear of trouble from each other and from other outsiders. They lose confidence in the formal communications of the company. The grapevine, which is always exaggerated, takes on increased credibility. Company turnover starts to increase. Morale is eroding.

It is obvious there is a problem and that it is not being dealt with. Employees wonder what will happen, whether they will be laid off, and whether the firm will go into bankruptcy. With their security threatened, employees lapse into survival mode. As an organizational behavior consultant explains:

> The human organism can tolerate anything except *uncertainty*. It causes so much stress that people are no longer capable of thinking in a cognitive, creative manner. They focus on survival. That's why in turnarounds you see so much uncooperative, finger-pointing behavior. The only issue people understand is directing the blame elsewhere [or in doing nothing].

Crisis can force intervention. The occasion is usually forced by the board of directors, lender, or a lawsuit. For example, the bank may call a loan, or the firm may be put on cash terms by its suppliers. Perhaps creditors try to put the firm into involuntary bankruptcy. Or something from the outside world fundamentally changes the business environment.

The Threat of Bankruptcy

Unfortunately the heads of most troubled companies usually do not understand the benefits of bankruptcy law. To them, bankruptcy carries the stigma of failure; however, the law merely defines the priority of creditors' claims when the firm is liquidated.

Although bankruptcy can provide for the liquidation of the business, it also can provide for its reorganization. Bankruptcy is not an attractive prospect for creditors because they stand to lose at least some of their money, so they often are willing to negotiate. The prospect of bankruptcy also can be a foundation for bargaining in a turnaround.

Voluntary Bankruptcy

When bankruptcy is granted to a business under bankruptcy law (often referred to as Chapter 11), the firm is given immediate protection from creditors. Payment of interest or principle is suspended, and creditors must wait for their money. Generally the current management (a debtor in possession) is allowed to run the company, but sometimes an outsider, a trustee, is named to operate the company, and creditor committees are formed to watch over the operations and to negotiate with the company.

The greatest benefit of Chapter 11 is that it buys time for the firm. The firm has 120 days to come up with a reorganization plan and 60 days to obtain acceptance of that plan by creditors. Under a reorganization plan, debt can be extended. Debt also can be restructured (composed). Interest rates can be increased, and convertible provisions can be introduced to compensate debt holders for any increase in their risk as a result of the restructuring. Occasionally, debt holders need to take part of their claim in the form of equity. Trade creditors can be asked to take equity as payment, and they occasionally need to accept partial payment. If liquidation is the result of the reorganization plan, partial payment is the rule, with the typical payment ranging from zero to 30 cents on the dollar, depending on the priority of the claim.

In April 2005, President George Bush signed legislation that makes it more difficult for Americans with large credit card and medical bills to erase their obligations. The bill, which represents the most significant change to the nation's bankruptcy laws in 25 years, will make it harder for individuals to file Chapter 7 bankruptcy, which eliminates most debts. Individuals whose earnings exceed their state's median income will be required to file Chapter 13, which sets up a court-ordered repayment plan. The law is scheduled to take effect in the fall of 2005.

Involuntary Bankruptcy

In involuntary bankruptcy, creditors force a troubled company into bankruptcy. Although this is regarded as a rare occurrence, it is important for an entrepreneur to know the conditions under which creditors can force a firm into bankruptcy.

A firm can be forced into bankruptcy by any three creditors whose total claim exceeds the value of assets held as security by $5,000, and by any single creditor who meets the above standard when the total number of creditors is less than 12.

Bargaining Power

For creditors, having a firm go into bankruptcy is not particularly attractive. *Bankruptcy, therefore, is a tremendous source of bargaining power for the troubled company.* Bankruptcy is not attractive to creditors because once protection is granted to a firm, creditors must wait for their money. Further, they are no longer dealing with the troubled company but with the judicial system, as well as with other creditors. Even if creditors are willing to wait for their money, they may not get full payment and may have to accept payment in some unattractive form. Last, the legal and administrative costs of bankruptcy, which can be substantial, are paid before any payments are made to creditors.

Faced with these prospects, many creditors conclude that their interests are better served by negotiating with the firm. Because the law defines the priority of creditors' claims, an entrepreneur can use it to determine who might be willing to negotiate.

Since the trade debt has the lowest claim (except for owners), these creditors are often the most willing to negotiate. The worse the situation, the more willing they may be. If the firm has negative net worth but is generating some cash flow, the trade debt creditors should be willing to negotiate extended terms or partial payment, or both, unless there is no trust in current management.

However, the secured creditors, with their higher priority claims, may be less willing to negotiate. Many factors affect the willingness of secured creditors to negotiate. Two of the most important are the strength of their collateral and their confidence in management. Bankruptcy is still something they wish to avoid for the reasons cited above.

Bankruptcy can free a firm from obligations under executory contracts. This has caused some firms to file for bankruptcy as a way out of union contracts. Since bankruptcy law in this case conflicts with the National Labor Relations Act, the law has been updated and a good-faith test has been added. The firm must be able to demonstrate that a contract prevents it from carrying on its business. It is also possible for the firm to initiate other executory contracts such as leases, executive contracts, and equipment leases. If a company has gradually added to its overhead in a noneconomic fashion, it may be able to reduce its overhead significantly using bankruptcy as a tool.

Intervention

A company in trouble usually will want to use the services of an outside advisor who specializes in turnarounds.

The situation the outside advisor usually finds at intervention is not encouraging. The company is often technically insolvent or has negative net worth. It already may have been put on a cash basis by its suppliers. It may be in default on loans, or if not, it is probably in violation of loan covenants. Call provisions may be exercised. At this point, as the situation deteriorates more, creditors may be trying to force the company into bankruptcy, and the organization is demoralized.

The critical task is to quickly diagnose the situation, develop an understanding of the company's bargaining position with its many creditors, and produce a detailed cash flow business plan for the turnaround of the organization.To this end, a turnaround advisor usually quickly signals that change is coming. He or she will elevate the finance function, putting the "cash person" (often the consultant himself) in charge of the business. Some payments may be put on hold until problems can be diagnosed and remedial actions decided upon.

Diagnosis

Diagnosis can be complicated by the mixture of strategic and financial errors. For example, for a company with large receivables, questions need to be answered about whether receivables are bloated because of poor credit policy or because the company is in a business where liberal credit terms are required to compete.

Diagnosis occurs in three areas: the appropriate strategic posture of the business, the analysis of management, and "the numbers."

Strategic Analysis This analysis in a turnaround tries to identify the markets in which the company is capable of competing and decide on a competitive strategy. With small companies, turnaround experts state that most strategic errors relate to the involvement of firms in unprofitable product lines, customers, and geographic areas. It is outside the scope of this book to cover strategic analysis in detail. (See the many texts in the area.)

Analysis of Management Analysis of management consists of interviewing members of the management team and coming to a subjective judgment of who belongs and who does not. Turnaround consultants can give no formula for how this is done except that it is the result of judgment that comes from experience.

The Numbers Involved in "the numbers" is a detailed cash flow analysis, which will reveal areas for remedial action. The task is to identify and quantify the profitable core of the business.

- *Determine available cash.* The first task is to determine how much cash the firm has available in the near term. This is accomplished by looking at bank balances, receivables (those not being used as security), and the confirmed order backlog.
- *Determine where money is going.* This is a more complex task than it appears to be. A common technique is called subaccount analysis, where every account that posts to cash is found and accounts are arranged in descending order of cash outlays. Accounts then are scrutinized for patterns. These patterns can indicate the functional areas where problems exist. For example, one company had its corporate address on its bills, rather than the lockbox address at which checks were processed, adding two days to its dollar days outstanding.
- *Calculate percent-of-sales ratios for different areas of a business and then analyze trends in*

costs. Typically, several of the trends will show flex points, where relative costs have changed. For example, for one company that had undertaken a big project, an increase in cost of sales, which coincided with an increase in capacity and in the advertising budget, was noticed. Further analysis revealed this project was not producing enough in dollar contribution to justify its existence. Once the project was eliminated, excess capacity could be reduced to lower the firm's break-even point.

- *Reconstruct the business.* After determining where the cash is coming from and where it is going, the next step is to compare the business as it should be to the business as it is. This involves reconstructing the business from the ground up. For example, a cash budgeting exercise can be undertaken and collections, payments, and so forth determined for a given sales volume. Or the problem can be approached by determining labor, materials, and other direct costs and the overhead required to drive a given sales volume. What is essentially a cash flow business plan is created.
- *Determine differences.* Finally, the cash flow business plan is tied into pro forma balance sheets and income statements. The ideal cash flow plan and financial statements are compared to the business's current financial statements. For example, the pro forma income statements can be compared to existing statements to see where expenses can be reduced. The differences between the projected and actual financial statements form the basis of the turnaround plan and remedial actions.

The most commonly found areas for potential cuts/improvements are these: (1) working capital management, from order processing and billing to receivables, inventory control, and, of course, cash management; (2) payroll; and (3) overcapacity and underutilized assets. More than 80 percent of potential reduction in expenses can usually be found in workforce reduction.

The Turnaround Plan

The turnaround plan not only defines remedial actions but, because it is a detailed set of projections, also provides a means to monitor and control turnaround activity. Further, if the assumptions about unit sales volume, prices, collections, and negotiating success are varied, it can provide a means by which worst-case scenarios—complete with contingency plans—can be constructed.

Because short-term measures may not solve the cash crunch, a turnaround plan gives a firm enough credibility to buy time to put other remedial actions in place. For example, one firm's consultant could approach its bank to buy time with the following: By reducing payroll and discounting receivables, we can improve cash flow to the point where the firm can be current in five months. If we are successful in negotiating extended terms with trade creditors, then the firm can be current in three months. If the firm can sell some underutilized assets at 50 percent off, it can become current immediately.

The turnaround plan helps address organizational issues. The plan replaces uncertainty with a clearly defined set of actions and responsibilities. Since it signals to the organization that action is being taken, it helps get employees out of their survival mode. An effective plan breaks tasks into the smallest achievable unit, so successful completion of these simple tasks soon follows and the organization begins to experience success. Soon the downward spiral of organizational morale is broken.

Finally, the turnaround plan is an important source of bargaining power. By identifying problems and providing for remedial actions, the turnaround plan enables the firm's advisors to approach creditors and tell them in very detailed fashion how and when they will be paid. If the turnaround plan proves that creditors are better off working with the company as a going concern, rather than liquidating it, they will most likely be willing to negotiate their claims and terms of payment. Payment schedules can then be worked out that can keep the company afloat until the crisis is over.

Quick Cash Ideally, the turnaround plan establishes enough creditor confidence to buy the turnaround consultant time to raise additional capital and turn underutilized assets into cash. It is imperative, however, to raise cash quickly. The result of the actions described below should be an improvement in cash flow. The solution is far from complete, however, because suppliers need to be satisfied.

For the purpose of quick cash, the working capital accounts hold the most promise.

Accounts receivable is the most liquid noncash asset. Receivables can be factored, but negotiating such arrangements takes time. The best route to cash is discounting receivables. How much receivables can be discounted depends on whether they are securing a loan. For example, a typical bank will lend up to 80 percent of the value of receivables that are under 90 days. As receivables age past the 90 days, the bank needs to be paid. New funds are advanced as new receivables are established as long as the 80 percent and under-90-day criteria are met. Receivables under

90 days can be discounted no more than 20 percent, if the bank obligation is to be met. Receivables over 90 days can be discounted as much as is needed to collect them, since they are not securing bank financing. One needs to use judgment in deciding exactly how large a discount to offer. A common method is to offer a generous discount with a time limit on it, after which the discount is no longer valid. This provides an incentive for the customer to pay immediately.

Consultants agree it is better to offer too large a discount than too small a one. If the discount is too small and needs to be followed by further discounts, customers may hold off paying in the hope that another round of discounts will follow. Generally it is the slow payers that cause the problems and discounting may not help. By getting on the squeaky-wheel list of the particular slow-pay customer, you might get attention. A possible solution is to put on a note with the objective of having the customer start paying you on a regular basis; also, adding a small additional amount to every new order helps to work down the balance.

Inventory is not as liquid as receivables but still can be liquidated to generate quick cash. An inventory "fire sale" gets mixed reviews from turnaround experts. The most common objection is that excess inventory is often obsolete. The second objection is that because much inventory is work in process, it is not in salable form and requires money to put in salable form. The third is that discounting finished-goods inventory may generate cash but is liable to create customer resistance to restored margins after the company is turned around. The sale of raw materials inventory to competitors is generally considered the best route. Another option is to try to sell inventory at discounted prices to new channels of distribution. In these channels, the discounted prices might not affect the next sale.

One interesting option for the company with a lot of work-in-process inventory is to ease credit terms. It often is possible to borrow more against receivables than against inventory. By easing credit terms, the company can increase its borrowing capacity to perhaps enough to get cash to finish work in process. This option may be difficult to implement because, by the time of intervention, the firm's lenders are likely following the company very closely and may veto the arrangements.

Also relevant to generating quick cash is the policy regarding current sales activity. Guiding criteria for this needs to include increasing the total dollar value of margin, generating cash quickly, and keeping working capital in its most liquid form. Prices and cash discounts need to be increased and credit terms eased. Easing credit terms, however, can conflict with the receivables policy described above. Obviously, care needs to be taken to maintain consistency of policy. Easing credit is really an "excess inventory" policy. The overall idea is to leverage policy in favor of cash first, receivables second, and inventory third.

Putting all accounts payable on hold is the next option. Clearly, this eases the cash flow burden in the near term. Although some arrangement to pay suppliers needs to be made, the most important uses of cash at this stage are meeting payroll and paying lenders. Lenders are important, but if you do not get suppliers to ship goods you are out of business. Getting suppliers to ship is critical. A company with negative cash flow simply needs to "prioritize" its use of cash. Suppliers are the least likely to force the company into bankruptcy because, under the law, they have a low priority claim.

Dealing with Lenders The next step in the turnaround is to negotiate with lenders. To continue to do business with the company, lenders need to be satisfied that there is a workable long-term solution.

However, at the point of intervention, the company is most likely in default on its payments. Or, if payments are current, the financial situation has probably deteriorated to the point where the company is in violation of loan covenants. It also is likely that many of the firm's assets have been pledged as collateral. To make matters worse, it is likely that the troubled entrepreneur has been avoiding his or her lenders during the gestation period and has demonstrated that he or she is not in control of the situation. Credibility has been lost.

It is important for a firm to know that it is not the first ever to default on a loan, that the lender is usually willing to work things out, and that it is still in a position to bargain.

Strategically, there are two sources of bargaining power. The first is that bankruptcy is an unattractive result to a lender, despite its senior claims. A low margin business cannot absorb large losses easily. (Recall that banks typically earn 0.5 percent to 1.0 percent total return on assets.)

The second is credibility. The firm that, through its turnaround specialist, has diagnosed the problem and produced a detailed turnaround plan with best-case/worst-case scenarios, the aim of which is to prove to the lender that the company is capable of paying, is in a better bargaining position. The plan details specific actions (e.g., layoffs, assets plays, changes in credit policy, etc.) that will be undertaken, and this plan must be met to regain credibility.

There are also two tactical sources of bargaining power. First, there is the strength of the lender's collateral. The second is the bank's inferior knowledge of aftermarkets and the entrepreneur's superior ability to sell.

The following example illustrates that, when the lender's collateral is poor, it has little choice but to look to the entrepreneur for a way out without incurring a loss. It also shows that the entrepreneur's superior knowledge of his business and ability to sell can get himself and the lender out of trouble. One company in turnaround in the leather business overbought inventory one year, and, at the same time, a competitor announced a new product that made his inventory almost obsolete. Since the entrepreneur went to the lender with the problem, the lender was willing to work with him. The entrepreneur had plans to sell the inventory at reduced prices and also to enter a new market that looked attractive. The only trouble was he needed more money to do it, and he was already over his credit limit. The lender was faced with the certainty of losing 80 percent of its money and putting its customer out of business or the possibility of losing money by throwing good money after bad. The lender decided to work with the entrepreneur. It got a higher interest rate and put the entrepreneur on a "full following mechanism," which meant that all payments were sent to a lockbox. The lender processed the checks and reduced its exposure before it put money in his account.

Another example illustrates the existence of bargaining power with a lender who is undercollateralized and stands to take a large loss. A company was importing look-alike Cabbage Patch dolls from Europe. This was financed with a letter of credit. However, when the dolls arrived in this country, the company could not sell the dolls because the Cabbage Patch doll craze was over. The dolls, and the bank's collateral, were worthless. The company found that the doll heads could be replaced, and with the new heads, the dolls did not look like Cabbage Patch dolls. It found also that one doll buyer would buy the entire inventory. The company needed $30,000 to buy the new heads and have them put on, so it went back to the bank. The bank said, if the company wanted the money, key members of management had to give liens on their houses. When this was refused, the banker was astounded. But what was he going to do? The company had found a way for him to get his money, so it got the $30,000.

Lenders are often willing to advance money for a company to meet its payroll. This is largely a public relations consideration. Also, if a company does not meet its payroll, a crisis may be precipitated before the lender can consider its options.

When the situation starts to improve, a lender may call the loan. Such a move will solve the lender's problem but may put the company under. While many bankers will deny this ever happens, some will concede that such an occurrence depends on the loan officer.

Dealing with Trade Creditors In dealing with trade creditors, the first step is to understand the strength of the company's bargaining position. Trade creditors have the lowest priority claims should a company file for bankruptcy and, therefore, are often the most willing to deal. In bankruptcy, trade creditors often receive just a few cents on the dollar.

Another bargaining power boost with trade creditors is the existence of a turnaround plan. As long as a company demonstrates that it can offer a trade creditor a better result as a going concern than it can in bankruptcy proceedings, the trade creditor should be willing to negotiate. It is generally good to make sure that trade creditors are getting a little money on a frequent basis. Remember trade creditors have a higher gross margin than a bank, so their getting paid pays down their "risk" money faster. This is especially true if the creditor can ship new goods and get paid for that, and also get some money toward the old receivables.

Also, trade creditors have to deal with the customer relations issue. Trade creditors will work with a troubled company if they see it as a way to preserve a market.

The relative weakness in the position of trade creditors has allowed some turnaround consultants to negotiate impressive deals. For example, one company got trade creditors to agree to a 24-month payment schedule for all outstanding accounts. In return, the firm pledged to keep all new payables current. The entrepreneur was able to keep the company from dealing on a cash basis with many of its creditors and to convert short-term payables into what amounted to long-term debt. The effect on current cash flow was very favorable.

The second step is to prioritize trade creditors according to their importance to the turnaround. The company then needs to take care of those creditors that are most important. For example, one entrepreneur told his controller never to make a commitment he could not keep. The controller was told that, if the company was going to miss a commitment, he was to get on the phone and call. The most important suppliers were told that if something happened and they needed payment sooner than had been agreed, they were to let the company know and it would do its best to come up with the cash.

The third step in dealing with trade creditors is to switch vendors if necessary. The lower priority suppliers will put the company on cash terms or refuse to do business. The troubled company needs to be able to switch suppliers, and its relationship with its priority suppliers will help it to do this, because they can give credit references. One firm said, "We asked our best suppliers to be as liberal with credit references as possible. I don't know if we could have established new relationships without them."

The fourth step in dealing with trade creditors is to communicate effectively. "Dealing with the trade is as simple as telling the truth," one consultant said. If a company is honest, at least a creditor can plan.

Workforce Reductions With workforce reduction representing 80 percent of the potential expense reduction, layoffs are inevitable in a turnaround situation.

A number of turnaround specialists recommend that layoffs be announced to an organization as a one-time reduction in the workforce and be done all at once. They recommend further that layoffs be accomplished as soon as possible, since employees will never regain their productivity until they feel some measure of security. Finally, they suggest that a firm cut deeper than seems necessary to compensate for other remedial actions that may be difficult to implement. For example, it is one thing to set out to reduce capacity by half and quite another thing to sell or sublet half a plant.

Longer-Term Remedial Actions

If the turnaround plan has created enough credibility and has bought the firm time, longer-term remedial actions can be implemented.

These actions will usually fall into three categories:

- *Systems and procedures.* Systems and procedures that contributed to the problem can be improved, or others can be implemented.
- *Asset plays.* Assets that could not be liquidated in a shorter time frame can be liquidated. For example, real estate could be sold. Many smaller companies, particularly older ones, carry real estate on their balance sheet at far below market value. This could be sold and leased back or could be borrowed against to generate cash.
- *Creative solutions.* Creative solutions need to be found. For example, one firm had a large amount of inventory that was useless in its current business. However, it found that if the inventory could be assembled into parts, there would be a market for it. The company shipped the inventory to Jamaica, where labor rates were low, for assembly, and it was able to sell very profitably the entire inventory.

As was stated at the beginning of the chapter, many companies—even companies that are insolvent or have negative net worth or both—can be rescued and restored to profitability. It is perhaps helpful to recall another quote from Winston Churchill: "I have nothing to offer but blood, toil, tears, and sweat."

Internet Impact: Opportunity

Consumer Power

The Internet has begun to profoundly after the relationship between buyers, vendors, and producers. Online consumers expect convenience, speed, straightforward comparative information, best prices, and around-the-clock service.

Empowered with blocking software and the click of a mouse, customers are increasingly able to select and control the commercial content they view. Tolerance for hype is therefore very low. Flashy ads, flagrant pop-ups, and banal messages are eschewed in favor of hard content like independent reviews, vendor-specific information, and community forums where customers can garner feedback from people who have no vested interest in the product or service in question.

The Internet is fostering the creation of a real-time, global marketplace where transactions are coordinated, consummated, and fulfilled 24/7. Using sophisticated service platforms, e-vendors such as Amazon, Expedia, Drugstore.com, and Campmor have been able to partner with a wide variety of producers whose product data, fulfillment processes, and finances are linked together behind the scenes of customer-friendly portals.

What customers get is the ability to create a personal account with stored billing, payment, purchase history, and preference data. From there they can browse merchandise, order product, and choose shipping and other fulfillment options. From hotel rooms to camping supplies, online vendors are fighting for market share the old-fashioned way, by offering their customers excellent service and value.

Chapter Summary

1. An inevitable part of the entrepreneurial process is that firms are born, grow, get ill, and die.
2. Numerous signals of impending trouble—strategic issues, poor planning and financial controls, and running out of cash—invariably point to a core cause: top management.
3. Crises don't develop overnight. Often it takes 18 months to five years before the company is sick enough to trigger a turnaround intervention.
4. Both quantitative and qualitative signals can predict patterns and actions that could lead to trouble.

5. Bankruptcy, usually an entrepreneur's nightmare, can actually be a valuable tool and source of bargaining power to help a company survive and recover.
6. Turnaround specialists begin with a diagnosis of the numbers—cash, strategic market issues, and management—and develop a turnaround plan.
7. The turnaround plan defines remedial action to generate cash, deal with lenders and trade creditors, begin long-term renewal, and monitor progress.

Study Questions

1. What do entrepreneurs need to know about how companies get into and out of trouble? Why?
2. Why do most turnaround specialists invariably discover that it is management that is the root cause of trouble?
3. Why is it difficult for existing management to detect and to act early on signals of trouble?
4. What are some key predictors and signals that warn of impending trouble?
5. Why can bankruptcy be the entrepreneur's ally?
6. What diagnosis is done to detect problems, and why and how does cash play the central role?
7. What are the main components of a turnaround plan and why are these so important?

Internet Resources for Chapter 18

http://www.turnaround.org *The Turnaround Management Association*

http://www.hg.org/bankrpt.html *Information on bankruptcy from Hieros Gamos, a comprehensive site for legal resources*

http://www.nationalbankruptcyconference.org *A voluntary organization composed of persons interested in the improvement of the Bankruptcy Code and its administration*

http://www.abiworld.org *The American Bankruptcy Institute*

MIND STRETCHERS

Have you considered?

1. In the 1970s, IBM had more cash on its balance sheet than the total sales of the rest of the computer industry. Why, and how, did IBM get into so much trouble 10 years later?
2. Talk in person to an entrepreneur who has personal loan guarantees and has been through bankruptcy. What lessons were learned?
3. Can Microsoft become a troubled company? When, and why?

Case

Lightwave Technology, Inc.

Preparation Questions

1. In anticipation of an IPO, should the co-founders move forward with an additional round of bridge financing and why?
2. How would you structure and price this round, and why?
3. What should Kinson and Dr. Weiss do to grow their company?
4. How should the company evaluate and decide on whether to pursue an IPO at this time? How do they go about planning and managing that process?

The success of light-emitting diodes (LEDs) lies in their longevity (LEDs outlast incandescent lamps by a factor of 10), energy efficiency, durability, low maintenance cost, and compact size. Replacing conventional lamps with LEDs in the United States alone will bring energy benefits of up to $100 billion by 2025, saving up to 120 gigawatts of electricity annually.

Light Emitting Diodes 2002; Strategic Summit for LEDs in Illumination

In the summer of 2003, seasoned entrepreneurs George Kinson and Dr. Schyler Weiss were evaluating, once again, whether or not to pursue an initial public offering (IPO) for their young and dynamic illumination company, Lightwave Technology.

The first time they had considered such a path was back in 2001, just before the Internet bubble burst. In the months following that dramatic reversal in the capital markets, the partners were instead forced to implement a restructuring plan to reorganize their operations. In addition to a painful write-off, the ensuing economic downturn thwarted the company's efforts to take full advantage of their leadership position in this emerging market. Nevertheless, their turnaround was successful—in large part due to Lightwave's unique and proprietary capabilities. Within just a couple of years, the company was back on track.

Since the IPO market in 2003 was still quite soft—and nobody would hazard a guess as to when it might recover—Kinson had to wonder whether it would be better to remain private until they had achieved even better numbers, as well as a greater dominance in a number of key illumination market segments. On the other hand, a successful IPO would provide capital and the high profile in the industry that could have a significant impact on their ability to do just that.

Traditional Illumination Products

The light bulb was one of the most important inventions of the late 19th century. It revolutionized the way people lived, worked, and conducted business. Several improvements to Thomas Edison's original invention, including ductile tungsten filaments and fluorescent tubes, had modified the lighting industry, but the standard screw-in light bulb remained the focus. The lighting market was divided into two segments: lamps (the bulbs and tubes) and fixtures (the plastic, metal, and glass housings for the lamps). In 2001, the illumination industry represented a $79 billion market: $17 billion in lamps and $62 billion in fixtures.[1] More than one-third of that market involved indoor lighting, with lamps and outdoor lighting being the next largest segments. In 2001, the United States represented 26 percent of the world market.

The illumination industry was dominated by a small group of very large, established multinationals. The major players in commercial lighting included General Electric Lighting, Philips Lighting, and OSRAM Sylvania, Inc., which together controlled 90 percent or more of the U.S. lamp market share and supplied 60 percent of the world lamp market.[2] Each major lighting manufacturer had a wide range of products for residential and commercial applications, and was involved in the research and development of new products modified from existing traditional lighting technology.

Solid-State Lighting

Light-emitting diodes (LEDs)—small semiconductors encased in an epoxy material that gave off light when electrically charged—had been around since the 1960s. By varying the structure of the semiconductor, or the bandgap, the energy level of the LED changed to produce a colored light, typically either a red or a green (Exhibit 1). The first practical lighting applications of these LEDs were blinking clocks and indicators on such appliances as VCRs, microwaves, and stereos.

As solid-state lighting (SSL), LEDs exhibited theoretical quantum efficiencies (i.e., volume of light generated per unit of electrical input) of 60 to 70 percent. Legacy incandescent and fluorescent lamps had topped out at around 5 percent and 20 percent, respectively.[3] The

[1] Freedonia Group, Inc., www.freedoniagroup.com.

[2] Paul Thurk, "Solid State Lighting: The Case for Reinventing the Light Bulb," in fulfillment of the requirements of a Kauffman Fellows Program grant, July 2002, p. 7.

[3] Paul Thurk, "Solid State Lighting: The Case for Reinventing the Light Bulb," research paper in fulfillment of the requirements of a Kauffman Fellows Program, July 2002, pp. 4–5.

EXHIBIT 1

How an LED Emits Colored Light

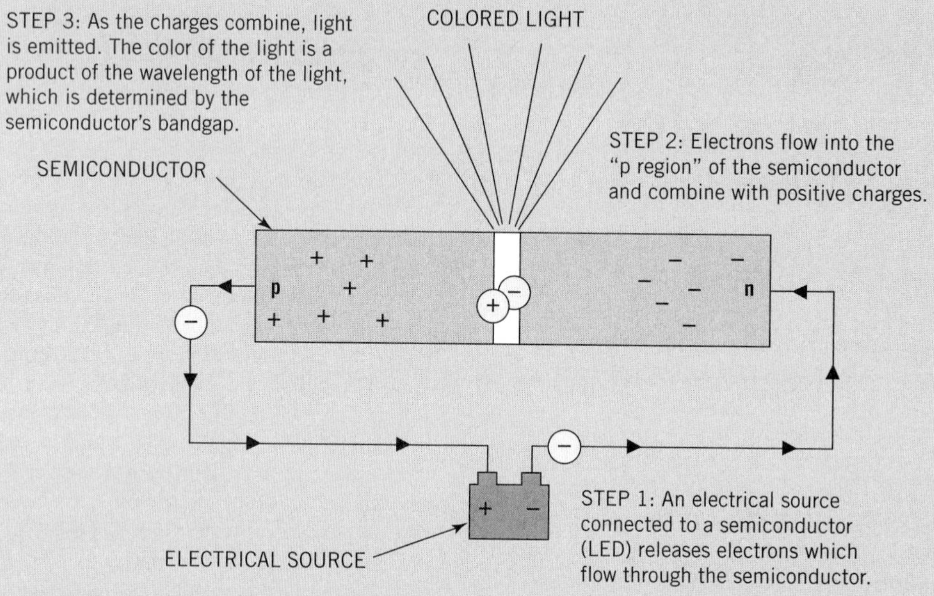
STEP 3: As the charges combine, light is emitted. The color of the light is a product of the wavelength of the light, which is determined by the semiconductor's bandgap.
COLORED LIGHT
SEMICONDUCTOR
STEP 2: Electrons flow into the "p region" of the semiconductor and combine with positive charges.
p
n
ELECTRICAL SOURCE
STEP 1: An electrical source connected to a semiconductor (LED) releases electrons which flow through the semiconductor.

balance of electricity used by typical light bulbs was converted to heat, which limited the useful life by degrading the active elements of the light source. SSL energy efficiencies were particularly acute with respect to colorized lighting. Unlike traditional fixtures where light passed through a colored filter, SSL generated colors directly—from the emission itself. Color filters could tax the luminous output of standard lamps by as much as 70 to 80 percent.

Ultraviolet (UV) radiation from regular lights could damage or discolor many products and materials, and had been shown to cause skin and eye conditions in humans. LEDs used for illumination emitted all of their light in the visible part of the color spectrum and, therefore, produced virtually no UV radiation.

Rather than burn out like incandescent bulbs, SSL faded over time. This attribute—in addition to long lifetimes, flexible form factors, low UV output, and strong color contrast—had begun to stimulate creative design across a range of industrial, architectural, and retail businesses. For example, the low heat, fast turn-on times, and small feature sizes of SSL had attracted automobile manufacturers, who were using the technology for their brake, accent, and console illumination.

Disruptive Ideas

George Kinson and Dr. Schyler Weiss had met while they were attending Carnegie Mellon University in the early 1990s. Kinson—outspoken and assertive—was a research engineer at the Field Robotics Center at the university and attended classes in their Graduate School of Industrial Administration. As an undergraduate in 1993, he earned a dual major in electrical and computer engineering, with a minor in fine art.

Schyler Weiss was the more reserved half of the pair. He received his undergraduate, master's and PhD degrees in electrical and computer engineering from Carnegie Mellon. His PhD thesis involved low-power digital circuitry. In the early 1990s, Weiss and Kinson tinkered a lot with LEDs as a hobby—enough to conclude that the technology was the future of illumination. Specifically, they were anticipating the advent of a blue LED—a color they knew could be digitally "blended" with existing red and green hues to create a full spectrum of colors.

By 1994 the pair had diverged; Kinson had cofounded what would become a successful online securities portal, and Weiss had started up Weiz Solutions, developer of a mass spectrometry data acquisition software package. Despite their separate pursuits, when a Japanese group announced in 1996 that they had come up with the coveted blue LED, Kinson recalled that he and his friend were more than ready to charge ahead:

> We had always figured that the development of a blue light-emitting diode would change the way that people used LEDs. It just so happened that the one they created was a very bright blue LED, and that brought about tremendous change very quickly. We realized that this new, high intensity technology was perfect for illumination, and we had done enough research on this boring, old, complacent industry to know how slow they would

react to any sort of disruptive technology.[4] They were offering a commodity—brass, glass, and gas—not really technology at all. Even though we felt we had a pretty big window of opportunity, we wanted to move fast.

The engineers immediately got to work to develop a digital palette to "blend" the primaries. In the process, they pioneered a new industry: intelligent semiconductor illumination technologies. In the spring of 1997, Kinson left his position at his online information company and, with Weiss's help, began developing the business model, writing a business plan, and perfecting their initial prototypes for what was to be their new venture.

Lightwave Technology, Inc.

During the summer of 1997, Kinson used his savings and credit cards to finance the initial business development. After racking up $44,000 in credit card debt and seeing his savings account shrivel to $16, he incorporated Lightwave in the summer of 1997 and filed for patent protection on their color mixer.

By linking red, green, and blue LEDs to a microprocessor that controlled the combination and intensity of those primaries, Lightwave could, with a very small device, tremendously expand the color-producing capabilities of conventional lighting. In fact, each string of LEDs linked to a microprocessor could generate up to 24-bit color (16.7 million colors) and numerous dramatic effects, such as color washing and strobe lighting. They used the first successful prototype to secure more funding and build additional prototypes.

Believing that their business would grow up around the demands and imagination of a range of clients in industries from architecture to entertainment, they decided to take the bold move of demonstrating their new capabilities at one of the top lighting forums in the world.

Affirmation

The International Lighting Exposition in Las Vegas was where many lighting companies debuted their new lighting products. The small Lightwave team secured a booth and immediately became the talk of the show—as much for their innovative, colorful products as for their flashy, youthful personalities. Kinson said that the show was an affirmation that they had discovered a means to reinvent the illumination market:

> Schyler and I, accompanied by four MIT Sloan School students, flew out to this trade show with two backpacks full of prototypes. This was the first time we had shown these in public, and then we win Architectural Lighting Product of the Year—the top award. That's a pretty good statement from the industry that intelligent semiconductor illumination technology was a significant opportunity.

As the entrepreneurs had suspected, Lightwave's new lighting capabilities had immediate appeal—particularly in the retailing markets. Output and coloration adaptability had far-reaching applications, since a tiny Lightwave microprocessor system could replace existing lighting setups that often required numerous color-filtered bulbs, as well as large mechanical controls.

Besides an expanded range of color and aesthetics, Lightwave's technology had functional benefits over conventional lighting technology. The lower heat and lack of UV emissions generated by LEDs meant that SSL could be used in many applications where conventional hot lights could not, such as in retail displays and near clothing and artwork. Since Lightwave products could be designed to complement existing technologies, they could be used alongside conventional lighting products.

The team also envisioned significant economic and environmental benefit from expanding LED technologies. While conventional color lighting products had an average life of hundreds or thousands of hours, the source life of LEDs was estimated to be around 100,000 hours (equivalent to 24 hours a day for just over 11 years). Since lighting was a large user of energy (approximately 20 percent of the estimated $1 trillion spent annually on electricity[5]), SSL had the potential to produce significant savings. It was thought that for general bright white illumination for residences, hospitals, businesses, and the like, the gains from moving to SSL would lead to global annual savings of over $100 billion in electricity costs, and to a reduction in carbon emissions of 200 million tons. In addition, the gains would alleviate the need for an estimated $50 billion in new electrical plant construction.[6]

The efficiency of the technology was attracting institutional users as well. California, for instance, had begun offering subsidies of up to 50 percent of the purchase price to municipalities that converted traffic signals to SSL alternatives. The state was also offering subsidy packages that could total up to 100 percent of the purchase price for businesses that switched their signage from neon to SSL.

While the SSL segment was a small portion of the overall illumination market, the total LED segment had increased at a rate of 11 percent over the previous seven years to almost $2.3 billion in 1999. Signage lighting—which included a host of applications such as full-color outdoor displays, highway signs, and traffic signals—accounted for the largest sector of the LED market at 23 percent, or about $530 million. More narrowly, the

[4] Disruptive technologies was an idea developed by Clayton Christensen of the Harvard Business School. In his book, *The Innovator's Dilemma*, Christensen defined a disruptive technology as an innovation that disrupted performance trajectories and resulted in the failure of the industry's leading firms.

[5] Bergh, Craford, Duggal, and Haitz, "The Promise and Challenge of Solid-State Lighting," *Physics Today*, December 2001, pp. 42–47.

[6] Tsao, Nelson, Haitz, Kish (Hewlett-Packard), "The Case for a National Research Program on Semiconductor Lighting," presented at the 1999 Optoelectronics Industry Development Association forum in Washington DC, October 6, 1999.

EXHIBIT 2

Haitz's Law: LED Light Output Increasing/Cost Decreasing

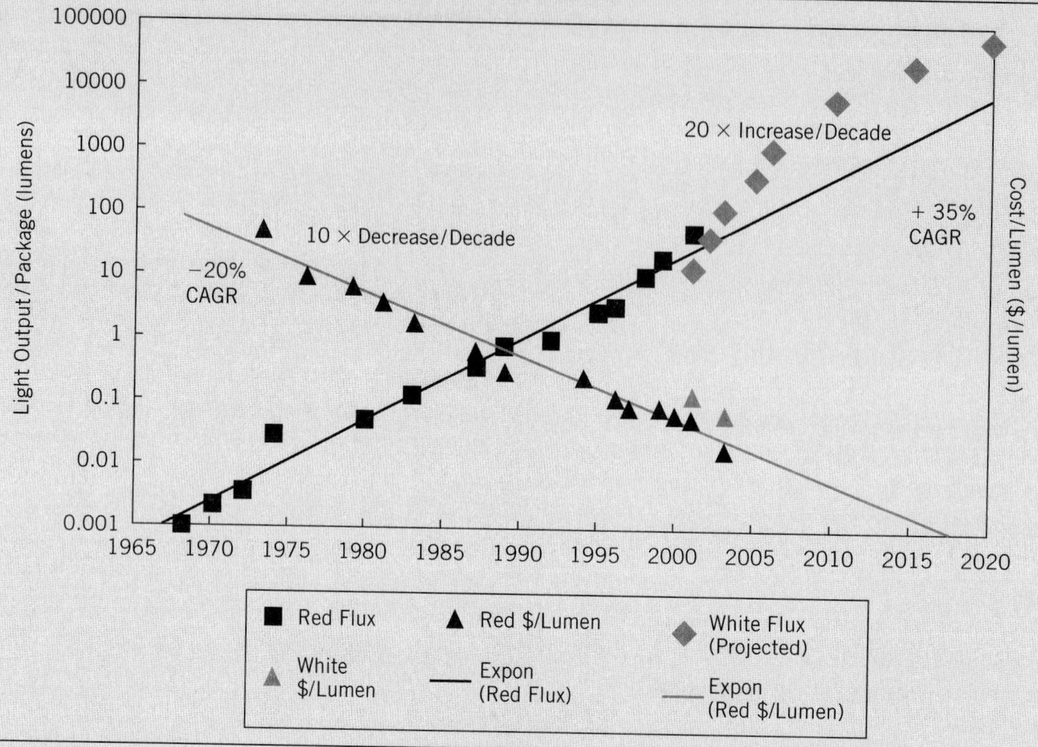

Source: Roland Haitz & Lumileds.

market for full-color LED outdoor display sign lighting grew at almost 78 percent per year from 1995 to about $150 million in 1999.

Display applications on communications equipment were the second largest sector at 22 percent of the market, closely followed by displays for computers and office equipment at 21 percent. The remainder of the market was divided among consumer applications with 15 percent of the market, automotive displays and lighting with 11 percent, and industrial instrumentation with 8 percent.[7] Of this total LED market, high-brightness LEDs—crucial to the illumination industry—had a market size of $680 million in 1999 (a nearly 500 percent growth from 1995 when the market size was $120 million). This number was projected to continue to grow to almost $1.75 billion by 2004.[8]

Despite all the proof and research and development progress that was being made at the turn of the century, illumination industry experts were very slow to embrace the use of LEDs for professional applications. Kinson explained that while there were still hurdles to overcome, he was sure that advances in SSL technology would eventually force lighting companies to redefine the way they did business:

> Similar to other disruptive technologies, LEDs are hitting an incumbent market by surprise and therefore are frequently discredited due to the traditional metrics that apply to the old market—in our case, illumination intensity and price. But what's fascinating is that while traditional "brass, gas, and glass" technology is not seeing dramatic growth, Haitz's Law (see Exhibit 2) shows that LEDs are exhibiting dramatic increases in intensity and longevity while the cost of making them is rapidly decreasing. Sure, low price and brightness are still not there for the white light market, but that will come. So everybody who works with or uses lighting in their business needs to look at what is going on here; if they don't change, they're going to be left behind.

Pioneering

Following the success at the lighting convention, Kinson finished out a financing round of $842,347 from angel investors. It had been no easy task, however. To close the round, Kinson had spoken with over 150 prospective investors and called the head of a leading lighting manufacturer 35 times before getting a response. Kinson noted, "You need to have persistence, and don't

[7] Data Source: Strategies Unlimited, *High-Brightness LED Market Overview and Forecast*, February 2000.

[8] Data Source: Strategies Unlimited, *High-Brightness LED Market Overview and Forecast*, February 2000.

take 'No' for an answer; just keep 'smiling and dialing.' Raising money is an art."

The partners rented out space across the hall from Kinson's apartment. Bootstrapping every step of the way, Kinson built the company's first computer server on a desktop computer using a Linux platform. The mail server, Web site, domain name, and office network all ran through a single desktop computer—accessed through a dial-up connection. In January 1998, they hired their first outside employee, Daniel Murdock, as vice president of finance.

As a pioneer in full spectrum SSL technology intent on gaining a sizable lead on established players in the industry, Lightwave aggressively patented their technology and applications. The partners believed their revolutionary technology and strong intellectual property portfolio had wide-ranging market and licensing opportunities in a number of markets (see Exhibit 3). Kinson commented on this aspect of their mission:

> One of our primary strategies is to file for all the intellectual property that we can, because we realize this will be a huge market in the future. We plan to have a war chest of patents to protect our interest in the market—and quite a few of those patents will be applicable in the emerging white light segment. Our intellectual property portfolio is probably going to be the strongest asset in our company.

Lightwave shipped its first order in September 1998. The company managed a huge growth surge during the next two years, moving to a large office space in downtown Boston and expanding to over 75 employees. They continued to develop new products and applications for various markets at a frenetic pace.

In May 2000, the company opened a European sales office in London, England, and in December of that year, Lightwave established a joint venture Japanese distributor in Tokyo. The venture's selling channel partners included lighting product distributors, manufacturers' representatives, and original equipment manufacturers (OEMs). Marketing efforts involved industry analyst updates, industry conferences, trade shows, Web promotions, news articles, electronic newsletters, print advertising, and speaking engagements. The marketing department also provided a variety of customer requirements, pricing, and positioning analysis for existing and new product offerings. In addition, they produced extensive material for distribution to potential customers, including presentation materials, customer profiles, product books, data sheets, product user guides, white papers, and press releases.

Determined to stay flexible and lean, the company outsourced all of its manufacturing and had no plans to develop a production capability in the future. The team developed supply agreements with a number of LED manufacturers, which allowed them to procure LEDs at favorable pricing with short lead times. Finished products and control systems were manufactured by companies in the United States and China, with the latter sup-

EXHIBIT 3

Target Markets (Excerpted from the Lightwave Offering Memorandum)

The markets for our lighting systems include the traditional markets for color-changing lighting such as theater and entertainment venues. However, many applications for this technology exist in numerous additional markets. Our lighting systems have been installed in thousands of end-user sites worldwide, in applications such as the following:

Commercial and Civic Architecture Our lighting systems are used to differentiate and accentuate architectural elements in a wide variety of corporate offices, public spaces, bridges, monuments, fountains, government facilities, churches, schools, universities, and hospitals.

Hospitality Hotels, casinos, cruise ships, restaurants, bars, and nightclubs add entertainment elements to their properties to attract and retain patrons. Dynamic lighting is an effective tool because much of this industry's business comes alive in the evening hours.

Retail and Merchandising Retailers competing for customer attention add entertainment value to the shopping experience by using dynamic lighting in their overall store design, in visual merchandising programs, and in store window displays.

Entertainment, Events, and Theatrical Production Theaters, concert halls, amusement parks, themed environments, and producers of live performances and events make extensive use of dramatic theatrical lighting and appreciate the enhanced dynamic that lighting adds to set design, stage lighting, and themed displays.

TV Production Studio-based television news programs, game shows, and talk shows use dynamic lighting to add excitement, glamour, and identity to show set designs and fill lighting.

Electronic Signage and Corporate Identity Signage and point-of-purchase designers and fabricators use dynamic lighting in projects such as backlit and uplit displays, glass signs, interior or exterior signs, and channel letters.

Residential Architecture Specialty and accent lighting are used in residential projects for applications such as cove, cabinet, undercounter, and landscape lighting, and home theaters.

Exhibits, Display, and Museums Dynamic lighting is used in trade show booths and museum displays to highlight featured areas or to add impact and entertainment value to the overall display.

plying the high-volume, low-priced items. Kinson had never stopped raising investment capital to support these efforts, and by early 2001, Lightwave had secured just over $31 million in four rounds of investment funding.[9]

Their success had certainly not gone unnoticed in the industry. Major lighting industry players had clearly begun to reevaluate the possibilities of LED technology. Since 1999, several ventures had been created between large traditional illumination companies and young, technologically advanced LED companies. Philips Lighting had joined up with Agilent Technologies to form a solid-state lighting venture called LumiLeds. Similarly, GE Lighting formed GELcore with the semiconductor company EMCORE, and OSRAM was working with LEDs in a subsidiary of Siemens in Germany. In addition, researchers from Agilent and Sandia National Laboratories in Albuquerque, New Mexico, were pressing the federal government for a $500 million, 10-year national research program on semiconductor lighting.

Kinson and his team felt that in light of these competitive tactics by multinational players, an IPO was their best strategy. They reasoned that going public would enhance their international exposure and would provide them with a significant base of capital to support rapid adoption of their products across a wide range of industries. Certain that the timing was right, they planned their public offering for the summer of 2001.

Pulling Back

Even before the terrorist attacks in September 2001, it had become painfully evident that the capital markets were softening. The Internet-driven boom had ended, and Lightwave, like many other companies, had to put on hold indefinitely its aspirations for an IPO. In the months following 9/11, the company struggled against a precipitous drop in orders and a recession-driven lack of interest by potential customers to pursue new and innovative projects. The company was forced to terminate 11 employees and abandon a large portion of a noncancelable operating lease at their new facility in Boston.

Despite a restructuring charge of nearly $3.9 million that year, and their dashed hopes for a public offering, Lightwave continued to make progress in their core markets of architecture and entertainment. By the summer of 2003 the company had stabilized, and it appeared that Lightwave would achieve cash flow breakeven in the coming year (see Exhibits 4–6).

[9] Series A—$842,347 for 1,020,285 shares; Series B—$4,354,994 for 3,956,208 shares; Series C—$13,020,880 for 3,355,897 shares; and Series D—$12,944,178 for 2,725,377 shares.

EXHIBIT 4

Income Statements

				Internal Company Projections	
	2000	**2001**	**2002**	**2003**	**2004**
Revenues					
Lighting Systems	15,080,547	18,037,552	26,197,034	34,435,012	47,040,012
OEM and Licensing	1,485,653	2,128,806	2,651,466	5,714,988	5,714,988
Total Revenues	16,566,200	20,166,358	28,848,500	40,150,000	52,755,000
Cost of Revenues					
Lighting Systems	10,556,540	11,224,786	13,285,688	16,777,212	23,012,000
OEM and Licensing	1,013,804	1,448,029	1,489,807	3,072,788	3,138,000
Total Cost of Revenues	11,570,344	12,672,815	14,775,495	19,850,000	26,150,000
Gross Profit	4,995,856	7,493,543	14,073,005	20,300,000	26,605,000
Operating Expenses					
Selling and Marketing	9,345,322	7,847,764	7,615,145	8,515,000	11,191,000
Research and Development	2,810,842	2,826,032	2,465,599	3,510,000	3,510,000
General and Administrative	3,706,739	4,494,364	4,607,946	6,750,000	6,750,000
Restructuring	3,887,865		161,413		
Total Operating Expenses	19,750,768	15,168,160	14,850,103	18,775,000	21,451,000
Operating Income (Loss)	(14,754,912)	(7,674,617)	(777,098)	1,525,000	5,154,000
Interest Income (Expense), Net	48,283	124,922	46,782	518,000	680,000
Equity in Earnings of Joint Venture (Japan)	24,415	85,232	3,350	300,000	395,000
Net Income (Loss)	(14,682,214)	(7,464,463)	(726,966)	2,343,000	6,229,000

A Pivotal Time

With the recession apparently winding down, the air at Lightwave Technology was charged with possibility and mission. As pioneers of a clearly disruptive technology, Kinson, Weiss, and their team were in position to influence the course of the entire lighting industry into the next century. The question was how best to position their company for the next big push forward.

EXHIBIT 5

Cash Flow Statements

	2000	2001	2002
Cash Flows from Operating Activities			
Net Loss	(14,682,214)	(7,464,463)	(726,966)
Adjustment to reconcile net loss to cash from operating activities:			
Depreciation and amortization	863,874	828,083	873,138
Stock-based compensation	150,000		76,449
Write-off of leasehold improvements in connection with restructuring	592,200		
Equity in earnings of joint venture (Japan)	(24,415)	(85,232)	(3,350)
Changes in current assets and liabilities			
Accounts receivable	329,027	443,049	(899,192)
Inventory	(1,588,379)	2,834,707	(1,502,304)
Prepaid expenses and other current assets	(44,526)	(62,983)	(113,144)
Restricted cash	480,848	(612,017)	676,436
Accounts payable	(675,949)	(475,901)	(41,502)
Accrued expenses	1,158,172	(757,473)	465,226
Deferred revenue	86,728	91,582	180,832
Accrued restructuring	1,956,152	(111,145)	(385,491)
Cash Flows from Operating Activities	(11,398,482)	(5,371,793)	(1,399,868)
Cash Flows from Investing Activities			
Investment in joint venture (Japan)	(165,260)		
Purchase of property and equipment	(1,085,427)	(467,181)	(519,197)
Cash Flows from Investing Activities	(1,250,687)	(467,181)	(519,197)
Cash Flows from Financing Activities			
Payments under equipment note payable and line of credit	(359,958)	(1,669,999)	(100,000)
Borrowings under line of credit	1,650,000		
Proceeds from the exercise of stock options	11,345	20,940	13,055
Proceeds from issuance of redeemable convertible preferred; net of issuance costs	17,095,382	6,883,266	
Cash Flows from Financing Activities	18,396,769	5,234,207	(86,945)
Effect of Exchange Rate Changes on Cash			3,719
Increase (Decrease) in Cash and Equivalents	5,747,600	(604,767)	(2,002,291)
Cash and Equivalents; Beginning of Year	2,545,908	8,293,508	7,688,741
Cash and Equivalents; End of Year	8,293,508	7,688,741	5,686,450

EXHIBIT 6

Balance Sheets

Assets	**2001**	**2002**
Current Assets		
Cash and equivalents	7,688,741	5,686,450
Restricted cash	1,055,748	479,312
Accounts receivable	3,450,919	4,284,529
Allowance for doubtful accounts	(469,000)	(270,000)
Accounts receivable from related parties	163,217	29,799
Inventory	3,522,002	5,024,306
Prepaid expenses and other current assets	315,304	428,448
Total Current Assets	15,726,931	15,662,844
Property and Equipment; at Cost		
Computer equipment	1,334,784	1,503,046
Furniture and fixtures	640,105	624,899
Tooling	541,899	873,961
Leasehold improvements	996,882	996,882
LESS: Accumulated depreciation and amortization	(2,094,333)	(2,933,392)
Property and Equipment; net	1,419,337	1,065,396
Investment in Joint Venture	285,082	288,432
Restricted Cash; Long-term portion	1,200,000	1,100,000
Total Assets	18,631,350	18,116,672
Liabilities & Stockholders' Equity (Deficiency)		
Current Liabilities		
Current portion of equipment note payable	100,000	
Accounts payable	1,546,392	1,483,324
Accounts payable to related party		21,566
Accrued expenses	911,956	811,970
Accrued compensation	760,567	1,471,202
Accrued restructuring	434,135	425,692
Accrued warranty	549,014	403,591
Deferred revenue	205,831	386,663
Total Current Liabilities	4,507,895	5,004,008
Accrued Restructuring	1,410,872	1,033,824
Redeemable Convertible Preferred Stock	41,115,602	41,115,602
Stockholders' Equity (Deficiency)		
Common stock, $0.001 par value; authorized 34,000,000 shares; issued and outstanding 2,781,419 and 2,804,325 shares in 2001 and 2002, respectively (12,130,979 shares pro forma)	2,781	2,804
additional paid-in capital	214,869	304,350
Accumulated other comprehensive income	10,177	13,896
Accumulated deficit	(28,630,846)	(29,357,812)
Total Stockholders' Equity (Deficiency)	(28,403,019)	(29,036,762)
Liabilities and Stockholders' Equity	**18,631,350**	**18,116,672**

19

Chapter Nineteen

The Harvest and Beyond

And don't forget: Shrouds have no pockets.

The Late Sidney Rabb
Chairman Emeritus, Stop & Shop, Boston

Results Expected

Upon completion of this chapter, you will have:

1. Examined the importance of first building a great company and thereby creating harvest options.
2. Examined why harvesting is an essential element of the entrepreneurial process and does not necessarily mean abandoning the company.
3. Identified the principal harvest options, including going public.
4. Analyzed the "Boston Communications Group" case study.

A Journey, Not a Destination

A common sentiment among successful entrepreneurs is that it is the challenge and exhilaration of the journey that gives them the greatest kick. Perhaps Walt Disney said it best: "I don't make movies to make money. I make money to make movies." It is the thrill of the chase that counts.

These entrepreneurs also talk of the venture's incredibly insatiable appetite for not only cash but also time, attention, and energy. Some say it is an addiction. Most say it is far more demanding and difficult than they ever imagined. Most, however, plan not to retire and would do it again, usually sooner rather than later. They also say it is more fun and satisfying than any other career they have had.

For the vast majority of entrepreneurs, it takes 10, 15, even 20 years or more to build a significant net worth. According to the popular press and government statistics, there are more millionaires than ever in America. In 2004 there were an estimated 2.7 million people in the United States with a net worth of over $1 million. Sadly, a million dollars is not really all that much money today as a result of inflation, and while lottery and sweepstakes winners become instant millionaires, entrepreneurs do not. The number of years it usually takes to accumulate such a net worth is a far cry from the instant millionaire, the get-rich-quick impression associated with lottery winners or in either fantasy or "reality" TV shows.

The Journey Can Be Addictive

The total immersion required, the huge workload, the many sacrifices for a family, and the burnout often experienced by an entrepreneur are real. Maintaining the energy, enthusiasm, and drive to get across the finish line, to achieve a harvest, may be exceptionally difficult. For instance, one entrepreneur in the computer software business, after working alone for several years, developed highly sophisticated software. Yet, he insisted he could not stand the computer business for another day. Imagine trying to position a company for sale effectively and to negotiate a deal for a premium price after such a long battle.

Some entrepreneurs wonder if the price of victory is too high. One very successful entrepreneur put it this way:

> What difference does it make if you win, have $20 million in the bank—I know several who do—and you are a basket case, your family has been washed out, and your kids are a wreck?

The opening quote of the chapter is a sobering reminder and its message is clear: Unless an entrepreneur enjoys the journey and thinks it is worthy, he or she may end up on the wrong train to the wrong destination.

First Build a Great Company

One of the simplest but most difficult principles for nonentrepreneurs to grasp is that wealth and liquidity are results—not causes—of building a great company. They fail to recognize the difference between making money and spending money. Most successful entrepreneurs possess a clear understanding of this distinction; they get their kicks from growing the company. They know the payoff will take care of itself if they concentrate on proving and building a sustainable venture.

Create Harvest Options

Here is yet another great paradox in the entrepreneurial process: Build a great company but do not forget to harvest. This apparent contradiction is difficult to reconcile, especially among entrepreneurs with several generations in a family-owned enterprise. Perhaps a better way to frame this apparent contradiction is to keep harvest options open and to think of harvesting as a vehicle for reducing risk and for creating future entrepreneurial choices and options, not simply selling the business and heading for the golf course or the beach, although these options may appeal to a few entrepreneurs. To appreciate the importance of this perspective, consider the following actual situations.

An entrepreneur in his 50s, Nigel reached an agreement with Brian, a young entrepreneur in his 30s, to join the company as marketing vice president. Their agreement also included an option for Brian to acquire the company in the next five years for $1.5 million. At the time, the firm, a small biscuit maker, had revenues of $500,000 per year. By the end of the third year, Brian had built the company to $5 million in sales and substantially improved profitability. He notified Nigel of his intention to exercise his option to buy the company. Nigel immediately fired Brian, who had no other source of income, had a family, and a $400,000 mortgage on a house whose fair market value had dropped to $275,000. Brian learned that Nigel had also received an offer from a company for $6 million. Thus, Nigel wanted to renege on his original agreement with Brian. Unable to muster the legal resources, Brian settled out of court for less than $100,000. When the other potential buyer learned how Nigel had treated Brian, it withdrew the $6 million offer. Then, there were no buyers. Within two years, Nigel drove the company into bankruptcy. At that point, he called Brian and asked if he would now be interested in buying the company. Brian suggested that Nigel go perform certain unnatural anatomical acts on himself!

In a quite different case, a buyer was willing to purchase a 100-year-old family business for $100 million, a premium valuation by any standard. The family insisted that it would never sell the business under any circumstances. Two years later, market conditions changed and the credit crunch transformed slow-paying customers into nonpaying customers. The business was forced into bankruptcy, which wiped out 100 years of family equity.

It is not difficult to think of a number of alternative outcomes for these two firms and many others like them, who have erroneously assumed that the business will go on forever. By stubbornly and steadfastly refusing to explore harvest options and exiting as a natural part of the entrepreneurial process, owners may actually increase their overall risk and deprive themselves of future options. Innumerable examples exist whereby entrepreneurs sold or merged their companies and then went on to acquire or to start another company and pursued new dreams:

- Robin Wolaner founded *Parenting* magazine in the mid-1980s and sold it to Time-Life.[1] Wolaner then joined Time and built a highly successful career there, and in July 1992, she became the head of Time's Sunset Publishing Corporation.[2]
- Right after graduate school, the two brothers described in the Securities Online case in Chapter 4 launched the company Kurt had worked on creating as a MBA student. That company rapidly became quite successful and

[1] This example is drawn from "Parenting Magazine," Harvard Business School case study 291–015.
[2] Lawrence M. Fisher, "The Entrepreneur Employee," *New York Times*, August 2, 1992, p. 10.

was sold in early 2000 for more than $50 million. About three years into the startup, younger brother John decided he would pursue his own startup. He left Securities Online on the best of terms and created ColorKinetics, Inc., in Boston. That company, by early 2003, had raised over $48 million of venture capital and would soon exceed $30 million in sales as the leading firm in LED lighting technology. These will not be either Kurt's or John's last startup, we predict.

- Craig Benson founded Cabletron in the 1980s, which became a highly successful company. Eventually he brought in a new CEO and became involved as a trustee of Babson College, and then began teaching entrepreneurship classes with a focus on information technology and the Internet. He was later elected governor of New Hampshire, as another way of giving back to society and to pursue his new dreams.
- While in his early 20s, Steve Spinelli was recruited by his former college football coach, Jim Hindman (see the Jiffy Lube case series), to help start and build Jiffy Lube International. As a captain of the team, Steve had exhibited the qualities of leadership, tenacity, and competitive will to win that Hindman knew was needed to create a new company. Steve later built the largest franchise in America, and after selling his 49 stores to Pennzoil in 1993, he returned to his MBA alma mater to teach. So invigorated by this new challenge, he even went back to earn his doctorate. Steve then became director of the Arthur M. Blank Center for Entrepreneurship at Babson, first division chair of the very first full-fledged Entrepreneurship Division at any American university, and then vice-provost.
- After creating and building the ninth largest pharmaceutical company in the United States, Marion Laboratories, Ewing Marion Kauffman led an extraordinary life as philanthropist and sportsman. His Kauffman Foundation and its Center for Entrepreneurial Leadership became the first and premier foundation in the nation dedicated to accelerating entrepreneurship. He brought the Kansas City Royals baseball team to that city and made sure it would stay there by gifting the team to the city, with the stipulation that it stay there when the team was sold. The $75 million proceeds of the sale were also donated to charitable causes in Kansas City.
- Jeff Parker built and sold two companies, including Technical Data Corporation,[3] by the time he was 40. His substantial gain from these ventures has led to a new career as a private investor who works closely with young entrepreneurs to help them build their companies.
- In mid-1987, George Knight, founder and president of Knight Publications,[4] was actively pursuing acquisitions to grow his company into a major force. Stunned by what he believed to be exceptionally high valuations for small companies in the industry, he concluded that this was the time to be a seller rather than a buyer. Therefore, in 1988, he sold Knight Publications to a larger firm, within which he could realize his ambition of contributing as a chief executive officer to the growth of a major company. Having turned around the troubled divisions of this major company, he is currently seeking a small company to acquire and to grow into a large company.

These are a tiny representation of the tens of thousands of entrepreneurs that build on their platforms of entrepreneurial success to pursue highly meaningful lives in philanthropy, public service, and community leadership. By realizing a harvest, such options become possible, yet the vast majority of entrepreneurs make these contributions to society while continuing to build their companies. This is one of the best-kept secrets in American culture: The public has very little awareness and appreciation of just how common this pattern of generosity is of their time, their leadership, and their money. One could fill a book with numerous other examples. The entrepreneurial process is endless.

A Harvest Goal

Having a harvest goal and crafting a strategy to achieve it are what separate successful entrepreneurs from the rest of the pack. Many entrepreneurs seek only to create a job and a living for themselves. It is quite different to grow a business that creates a living for many others, including employees and investors, by creating value—value that can result in a capital gain.

Setting a harvest goal achieves many purposes, not the least of which is helping an entrepreneur get after-tax cash out of an enterprise and enhancing substantially his or her net worth. Such a goal also can create high standards and a serious commitment

[3] For TDC's business plan, see "Technical Data Corporation Business Plan," Harvard Business School case 283-973. Revised November 1987. For more on TDC's progress and harvest strategy, see "Technical Data Corporation," Harvard Business School case 283-072. Revised December 1987.
[4] For a detailed description of this process, see Harvard Business School case 289-027, revised February 1989.

to excellence over the course of developing the business. It can provide, in addition, a motivating force and a strategic focus that does not sacrifice customers, employees, and value-added products and services just to maximize quarterly earnings.

There are other good reasons to set a harvest goal as well. The workload demanded by a harvest-oriented venture versus one in a venture that cannot achieve a harvest may actually be less and is probably no greater. Such a business may be less stressful than managing a business that is not oriented to harvest. Imagine the plight of the 46-year-old entrepreneur, with three children in college, whose business is overleveraged and on the brink of collapse. Contrast that frightful pressure with the position of the founder and major stockholder of another venture who, at the same age, sold his venture for $15 million. Further, the options open to the harvest-oriented entrepreneur seem to rise geometrically in that investors, other entrepreneurs, bankers, and the marketplace respond.

There is great truth in the old cliché that "success breeds success."

There is a very significant societal reason as well for seeking and building a venture worthy of a harvest. These are the ventures that provide enormous impact and value added in a variety of ways. These are the companies that contribute most disproportionately to technological and other innovations, to new jobs, to returns for investors, and to economic vibrancy.

Also, within the harvest process, the seeds of renewal and reinvestment are sown. Such a recycling of entrepreneurial talent and capital is at the very heart of our system of private responsibility for economic renewal and individual initiative. Entrepreneurial companies organize and manage for the long haul in ways to perpetuate the opportunity creation and recognition process and thereby to ensure economic regeneration, innovation, and renewal.

Thus, a harvest goal is not just a goal of selling and leaving the company. Rather, it is a long-term goal to create real value added in a business. (It is true, however, that if real value added is not created, the business simply will not be worth much in the marketplace.)

Crafting a Harvest Strategy: Timing Is Vital

Consistently, entrepreneurs avoid thinking about harvest issues. In a survey of the computer software industry between 1983 and 1986, Steven Holmberg found that 80 percent of the 100 companies surveyed had only an informal plan for harvesting. The rest of the sample confirmed the avoidance of harvest plans by entrepreneurs—only 15 percent of the companies had a formal written strategy for harvest in their business plans and the remaining 5 percent had a formal harvest plan written after the business plan.[5] When a company is launched, then struggles for survival, and finally begins its ascent, the farthest thing from its founder's mind usually is selling out. Selling is often viewed by the entrepreneur as the equivalent to complete abandonment of his or her very own "baby."

Thus, time and again, a founder does not consider selling until terror, in the form of the possibility of losing the whole company, is experienced. Usually, this possibility comes unexpectedly: New technology threatens to leapfrog over the current product line, a large competitor suddenly appears in a small market, or a major account is lost. A sense of panic then grips the founders and shareholders of the closely held firm, and the company is suddenly for sale—for sale at the wrong time, for the wrong reasons, and thus for the wrong price. Selling at the right time, willingly, involves hitting a strategic window, one of the many strategic windows that entrepreneurs face.

Entrepreneurs find that harvesting is a nonissue until something begins to sprout, and again there is a vast distance between creating an existing revenue stream of an ongoing business and ground zero. Most entrepreneurs agree that securing customers and generating continuing sales revenue are much harder and take much longer than they could have imagined. Further, the ease with which those revenue estimates can be cast and manipulated on a spreadsheet belies the time and effort necessary to turn those projections into cash.

At some point, with a higher potential venture, it becomes possible to realize the harvest. It is wiser to be selling as the strategic window is opening than as it is closing. Bernard Baruch's wisdom is as good as it gets on this matter. He has said, "I made all my money by selling too early." For example, a private candy company with $150 million in sales was not considering selling. After contemplating advice to sell early, the founders recognized a unique opportunity to harvest and sold the firm for 19 times earnings, an extremely high valuation. Another example is that of a cellular phone company that was launched and built from scratch and began operations in late 1987. Only 18 months after purchasing the original rights to build and operate the system, the founders decided to sell the company, even though the future looked extremely bright. They sold because the sellers' market they faced at the time had resulted in a premium

[5] Steven R. Holmberg, "Value Creation and Capture: Entrepreneurship Harvest and IPO Strategies," in *Frontiers of Entrepreneurship Research: 1991*, ed. Neil Churchill et al. (Babson Park, MA: Babson College, 1991), pp. 191–205.

valuation—30 percent higher on a per capita basis (the industry valuation norm) than that for any previous cellular transaction to date. The harvest returned over 25 times the original capital in a year and a half. (The founders had not invested a dime of their own money.)

If the window is missed, disaster can strike. For example, at the same time as the harvests described previously were unfolding, another entrepreneur saw his real estate holdings rapidly appreciate to nearly $20 million, resulting in a personal net worth, on paper, of nearly $7 million. The entrepreneur used this equity to refinance and leverage existing properties (to more than 100 percent in some cases) to seize what he perceived as further prime opportunities. Following a change in federal tax law in 1986 and the stock market crash of 1987, there was a major softening of the real estate market in 1988. As a result, by early 1989, half of the entrepreneur's holdings were in bankruptcy and the rest were in a highly precarious and vulnerable position. The prior equity in the properties had evaporated, leaving no collateral as increasing vacancies and lower rents per square foot turned a positive cash flow into a negative one.

This very same pattern happened again in 2000–2003 after the dot.com bubble burst and the NASDAQ began to crash, losing 63 percent of its value from its high of over 5000 to under 1100. California's Silicon Valley was particularly hard hit by the rapid downturn. Technology and Internet entrepreneurs who had exercised their stock options when their company's stock was soaring in the $80 to $100 range, on the hope that such escalation would continue for a long time, faced a rude a awakening. As the stock plummeted to single-digit prices, they still faced a huge capital gain tax on the difference between the cost of their options and the price at which their stock was acquired.

Shaping a harvest strategy is an enormously complicated and difficult task. Thus, crafting such a strategy cannot begin too early. In 1989–91, banking policies that curtailed credit and lending severely exacerbated the downturn following the October 1987 stock market crash. One casualty of this was a company we shall call Cable TV. The value of the company in early 1989 exceeded $200 million. By mid-1990, this had dropped to below zero! The heavy debt overwhelmed the company. It took over five years of sweat, blood, tears, and rapid aging of the founder to eventually sell the company. The price: about one-quarter of the peak value of 1989!

This same pattern was common again in 2001 and 2002, as major companies declared bankruptcy in the wake of the dot.com and stock market crash, including luminaries such an Enron, Kmart, Global Crossing, and dozens of lesser known but larger telecommunications and networking-related companies. This is one history lesson that seems to repeat itself. While building a company is the ultimate goal, failure to preserve the harvest option, and utilize it when it is available, can be deadly.

In shaping a harvest strategy, some guidelines and cautions can help:

- *Patience.* As has been shown, several years are required to launch and build most successful companies; therefore, patience can be invaluable. A harvest strategy is more sensible if it allows for a time frame of at least 3 to 5 years and as long as 7 to 10 years. The other side of the patience coin is not to panic as a result of precipitate events. Selling under duress is usually the worst of all worlds.
- *Realistic valuation.* If impatience is the enemy of an attractive harvest, then greed is its executioner. For example, an excellent, small firm in New England, which was nearly 80 years old and run by the third generation of a line of successful family leaders, had attracted a number of prospective buyers and had obtained a bona fide offer for more than $25 million. The owners, however, had become convinced that this "great little company" was worth considerably more, and they held out. Before long, there were no buyers, and market circumstances changed unfavorably. In addition, interest rates skyrocketed. Soon thereafter, the company collapsed financially, ending up in bankruptcy. Greed was the executioner.
- *Outside advice.* It is difficult but worthwhile to find an advisor who can help craft a harvest strategy while the business is growing and, at the same time, maintain objectivity about its value and have the patience and skill to maximize it. A major problem seems to be that people who sell businesses, such as investment bankers or business brokers, are performing the same economic role and function as real estate brokers; in essence, their incentive is their commissions during a quite short time frame, usually a matter of months. However, an advisor who works with a lead entrepreneur for as much as five years or more can help shape and implement a strategy for the whole business so that it is positioned to spot and respond to harvest opportunities when they appear.

Harvest Options

There are seven principal avenues by which a company can realize a harvest from the value it has created. Described on the next pages, these most commonly seem to occur in the order in which they are listed. No attempt is made here to do more than briefly describe each avenue, since there are entire books written on each of these, including their legal, tax, and accounting intricacies.

Capital Cow

A "capital cow" is to the entrepreneur what a "cash cow" is to a large corporation. In essence, the high-margin profitable venture (the cow) throws off more cash for personal use (the milk) than most entrepreneurs have the time and uses or inclinations for spending. The result is a capital-rich and cash-rich company with enormous capacity for debt and reinvestment. Take, for instance, a health care–related venture that was started in the early 1970s that realized early success and went public. Several years later, the founders decided to buy the company back from the public shareholders and to return it to its closely held status. Today the company has sales in excess of $100 million and generates extra capital of several million dollars each year. This capital cow has enabled its entrepreneurs to form entities to invest in several other higher potential ventures, which included participation in the leveraged buyout of a $150 million sales division of a larger firm and in some venture capital deals. Sometimes the creation of a capital cow results in substantial real estate holdings by the entrepreneur, off the books of the original firm. This allows for greater flexibility in the distribution of cash flow and the later allocation of the wealth.

Employee Stock Ownership Plan

Employee stock ownership plans have become very popular among closely held companies as a valuation mechanism for stock for which there is no formal market. They are also vehicles through which founders can realize some liquidity from their stock by sales to the plan and other employees. And since an ESOP usually creates widespread ownership of stock among employees, it is viewed as a positive motivational device as well.

Management Buyout

Another avenue, called a management buyout (MBO), is one in which a founder can realize a gain from a business by selling it to existing partners or to other key managers in the business. If the business has both assets and a healthy cash flow, the financing can be arranged via banks, insurance companies, and financial institutions that do leveraged buyouts (LBOs) and MBOs. Even if assets are thin, a healthy cash flow that can service the debt to fund the purchase price can convince lenders to do the MBO.

Usually, the problem is that the managers who want to buy out the owners and remain to run the company do not have the capital. Unless the buyer has the cash up front—and this is rarely the case—such a sale can be very fragile, and full realization of a gain is questionable. MBOs typically require the seller to take a limited amount of cash up front and a note for the balance of the purchase price over several years. If the purchase price is linked to the future profitability of the business, the seller is totally dependent on the ability and integrity of the buyer. Further, the management, under such an arrangement, can lower the price by growing the business as fast as possible, spending on new products and people, and showing very little profit along the way. In these cases, it is often seen that after the marginally profitable business is sold at a bargain price, it is well positioned with excellent earnings in the next two or three years. As can be seen, the seller will end up on the short end of this type of deal.

Merger, Acquisition, and Strategic Alliance

Merging with a firm is still another way for a founder to realize a gain. For example, two founders who had developed high-quality training programs for the rapidly emerging personal computer industry consummated a merger with another company. These entrepreneurs had backgrounds in computers, rather than in marketing or general management, and the results of the company's first five years reflected this gap. Sales were under $500,000, based on custom programs and no marketing, and they had been unable to attract venture capital, even during the market of 1982–1983. The firm with which they merged was a $15 million company that had an excellent reputation for its management training programs, had a Fortune 1000 customer base, had repeat sales of 70 percent, and had requests from the field sales force for programs to train managers in the use of personal computers. The buyer obtained 80 percent of the shares of the smaller firm, to consolidate the revenues and earnings from the merged company into its own financial statements, and the two founders of the smaller firm retained a 20 percent ownership in their firm. The two founders also obtained employment contracts, and the buyer provided nearly $1.5 million of capital advances during the first year of the new business. Under a put arrangement, the founders will be able to realize a gain on their 20 percent of the company, depending upon performance of the venture over the next few years.[6] The two founders now are reporting to the president of the parent firm, and one founder of the parent firm has taken a key executive position with the smaller company, an approach common for mergers between closely held firms.

In a strategic alliance, founders can attract badly needed capital, in substantial amounts, from a large company interested in their technologies. Such arrangements often can lead to complete buyouts of the founders downstream.

Outright Sale

Most advisors view outright sale as the ideal route to go because up-front cash is preferred over most stock, even though the latter can result in a tax-free exchange.[7] In a stock-for-stock exchange, the problem is the volatility and unpredictability of the stock price of the purchasing company. Many entrepreneurs have been left with a fraction of the original purchase price when the stock price of the buyer's company declined steadily. Often the acquiring company wants to lock key management into employment contracts for up to several years. Whether this makes sense depends on the goals and circumstances of the individual entrepreneur.

Public Offering

Probably the most sacred business school cow of them all—other than the capital cow—is the notion of taking a company public.[8] The vision or fantasy of having one's venture listed on one of the stock exchanges arouses passions of greed, glory, and greatness. For many would-be entrepreneurs, this aspiration is unquestioned and enormously appealing. Yet, for all but a chosen few, taking a company public, and then living with it, may be far more time and trouble—and expense—than it is worth.

After the stock market crash of October 1987, the market for new issues of stock shrank to a fraction of the robust IPO market of 1986 and a fraction of those of 1983 and 1985, as well. The number of new issues and the volume of IPOs did not rebound; instead, they declined between 1988 and 1991. Then in 1992 and into the beginning of 1993 the IPO window opened again. During this IPO frenzy, "small companies with total assets under $500,000 issued more than 68 percent of all IPOs."[9] Previously, small companies had not been as active in the IPO market. (Companies such as Lotus, Compaq, and Apple Computer do get unprecedented attention and fanfare, but these firms were truly exceptions.)[10] The SEC tried "to reduce issuing costs and registration and reporting burdens on small companies, and began by simplifying the registration process by adopting Form S-18, which applies to offerings of less than $7,500,000, and reduced disclosure requirements."[11] Similarly, Regulation D created exemptions from registration up to $500,000 over a 12-month period.[12]

This cyclical pattern repeated itself again during the mid-1990s into 2002. As the dot.com, telecommunications, and networking explosion accelerated from 1995 to 2000, the IPO markets exploded as well. In June 1996, for instance, nearly 200 small companies had initial public offerings, and the pace remained very strong through 1999, even into the first two months of 2000. Once the NASDAQ began its collapse in March 2000, the IPO window virtually shut. In 2001, there were months when not a single IPO occurred and for the year it was well under 100! Few signs of recovery were evident in 2002. The lesson is clear: Depending upon the IPO market for a harvest is a highly cyclical strategy, which can cause both great joy and disappointment. Such is the reality of the stock markets. Exhibits 19.1(A) and 19.1(B) show this pattern vividly.

There are several advantages to going public, many of which relate to the ability of the company to fund its rapid growth. Public equity markets provide access to long-term capital, while also meeting subsequent capital needs. Companies may use the proceeds of an IPO to expand the business in the existing market or to move into a related market. The founders and initial investors might be seeking liquidity, but SEC restrictions limiting the timing and the amount of stock that the officers, directors, and

[6] This is an arrangement whereby the two founders can force (the put) the acquirer to purchase their 20 percent at a predetermined and negotiated price.
[7] See several relevant articles on selling a company in *Growing Concerns*, ed. David E. Gumpert (New York: John Wiley & Sons, 1984), pp. 332–98.
[8] The Big Five accounting firms, such as Ernst & Young, publish information on deciding to take a firm public, as does NASDAQ. See also Richard Salomon, "Second Thoughts on Going Live with Wall Street," *Harvard Business Review*, reprint No. 91309.
[9] Seymour Jones, M. Bruce Cohen, and Victor V. Coppola, "Going Public," in *The Entrepreneurial Venture*, ed. William A. Sahlman and Howard H. Stevenson (Boston: Harvard Business School Publishing, 1992), p. 394.
[10] For an updated discussion of these issues, see Constance Bagley and Craig Dauchy, "Going Public," in *The Entrepreneurial Venture*, 2nd ed. W. A. Sahlman and H. H. Stevenson (Boston: Harvard Business School Publishing, 1999), pp. 404–40.
[11] Jones et al., p. 395.
[12] Ibid.

EXHIBIT 19.1(A)

Number of Recent IPOs

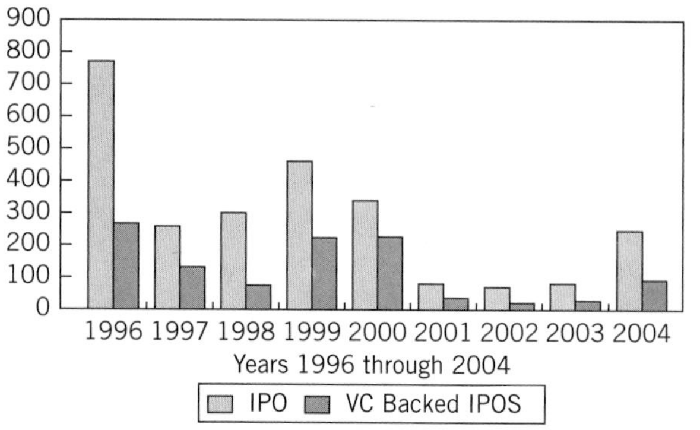

Source: Thomson Venture Economics/NVCA. Used by permission.

EXHIBIT 19.1(B)

Recent IPO ($millions)

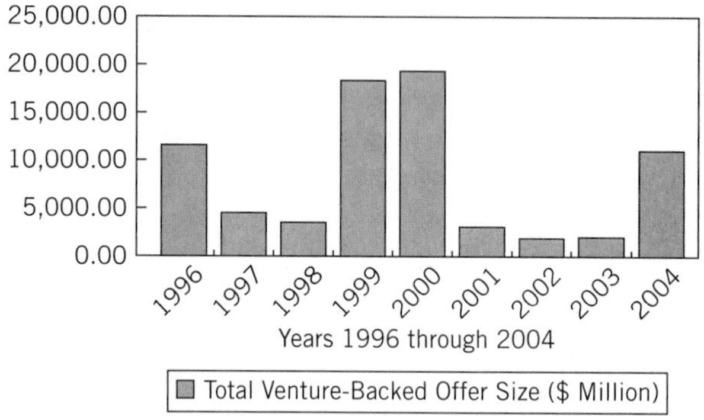

Source: Thomson Venture Economics/NVCA. Used by permission.

insiders can dispose of in the public market are increasingly severe. As a result, it can take several years after an IPO before a liquid gain is possible. Additionally, as Jim Hindman believed, a public offering not only increases public awareness of the company but also contributes to the marketability of the products, including franchises.

However, there are also some disadvantages to being a public company. For example, 50 percent of the computer software companies surveyed by Holmberg agreed that the focus on short-term profits and performance results was a negative attribute of being a public company.[13] Also, because of the disclosure requirements, public companies lose some of their operating confidentiality, not to mention having to support the ongoing costs of public disclosure, audits, and tax filings. With public shareholders, the management of the company has to be careful about the flow of information because of the risk of insider trading. Thus, it is easy to see why companies need to think about the positive and negative attributes of being a public company. When considering this decision, you may find it useful to review the Boston Communications Group case at the end of the chapter to identify the key components of the IPO process and to assess which investment bankers, accountants, lawyers, and advisors might be useful in making this decision.

Wealth-Building Vehicles

The 1986 Tax Reform Act severely limited the generous options previously available to build wealth within a private company through large deductible contributions to a retirement plan. To make matters worse, the administrative costs and paperwork necessary to comply with federal laws have become a nightmare. Nonetheless, there are still mechanisms that can enable an owner to contribute up to 25 percent of his or her salary to a retirement plan each year, an amount that is deductible to the company and grows tax free. Entrepreneurs who can contribute such amounts for just a short time will build significant wealth.

Beyond the Harvest

A majority of highly successful entrepreneurs seem to accept a responsibility to renew and perpetuate the system that has treated them so well. They are keenly aware that our unique American system of opportunity and mobility depends in large part upon a self-renewal process.

There are many ways in which this happens. Some of the following data often surprise people:

- *College endowments.* Entrepreneurs are the most generous regarding larger gifts and the most frequent contributors to college endowments, scholarship funds, and the like. At Babson College, for example, one study showed that eight times as many entrepreneurs, compared to all other graduates, made large gifts to their colleges.[14] On college and university

[13] Holmberg, "Value Creation and Capture," p. 203.
[14] John A. Hornaday, "Patterns of Annual Giving," in *Frontiers of Entrepreneurship Research, 1984,* ed. J. Hornaday et al. (Babson Park, MA: Babson College, 1984).

campuses across America, a huge number of dorms, classroom buildings, arts centers, and athletic facilities are named for the contributor. In virtually every case, these contributors are entrepreneurs whose highly successful companies enabled them to make major gifts of stock to their alma mater. Earlier at MIT, more than half of the endowment was from gifts of founders' stock. Today that figure is probably even higher.

- *Community activities.* Entrepreneurs who have harvested their ventures very often reinvest their leadership skills and money in such community activities as symphony orchestras, museums, and local colleges and universities. These entrepreneurs lead fund-raising campaigns, serve on boards of directors, and devote many hours to other volunteer work. One Swedish couple, after spending six months working with venture capital firms in Silicon Valley and New York, was "astounded at the extent to which these entrepreneurs and venture capitalists engage in such voluntary, civic activities." The couple found this pattern in sharp contrast to the Swedish pattern, where paid government employees perform many of the same services as part of their jobs.
- *Investing in new companies.* Postharvest entrepreneurs also reinvest their efforts and resources in the next generation of entrepreneurs and their opportunities. Successful entrepreneurs behave this way since they seem to know that perpetuating the system is far too important, and too fragile, to be left to anyone else. They have learned the hard lessons. As angel investors, experienced entrepreneurs are the key source of capital for startup firms.

The innovation, the job creation, and the economic renewal and vibrancy are all results of the entrepreneurial process. Government does not cause this complicated and little understood process, though it facilitates and/or impedes it. It is not caused by the stroke of a legislative pen, though it can be ended by such a stroke. Rather, entrepreneurs, investors, and hardworking people in pursuit of opportunities create it.

Fortunately, entrepreneurs seem to accept a disproportionate share of the responsibility to make sure the process is renewed. And, judging by the new wave of entrepreneurship in the United States, both the marketplace and society once again are prepared to allocate the rewards to entrepreneurs that are commensurate with their acceptance of responsibility and delivery of results.

The Road Ahead: Devise a Personal Entrepreneurial Strategy

Goals Matter—A Lot!

Of all the anchors one can think of in the entrepreneurial process, two loom above all the rest:

1. A passion for achieving goals.
2. A relentless competitive spirit and desire to win, and the will to never give up!

These two habits drive the quest for learning, personal growth, continuous improvement, and all other development. Without these good habits, most quests will fall short. Chapter 1 includes an exercise on Crafting a Personal Entrepreneurial Strategy. Completing this lengthy exercise will help you develop these good habits.

Values and Principles Matter—A Lot!

We have demonstrated, in numerous places throughout the book, that values and principles matter a great deal. We have encouraged you to consider those of Ewing M. Kauffman and to develop your own anchors. This is a vital part of your leadership approach, and who and what you are:

- Treat others as you would want to be treated.
- Share the wealth with those high performers who help you create it.
- Give back to the community and society.

We would add a fourth principle in the Native American spirit of considering every action with the seventh generational impact foremost in mind:

- Be a guardian and a steward of the air, land, water, and environment.

One major legacy of the coming generations of entrepreneurial leaders can be the sustainability of our economic activities. It is possible to combine a passion for entrepreneurship with love of the land and the environment. The work of such organizations as the Conservation Fund of Arlington, Virginia, the Nature Conservancy, the Trust for Public Land, the Henry's Fork Foundation, the Monadnock Conservancy in New Hampshire, and dozens of others is financially made possible by the contributions of money, time, and leadership from highly successful entrepreneurs. It is also one of the most durable ways to give back. Practicing what he preaches, Professor Timmons and his wife recently made a permanent gift of nearly 500 acres of their New Hampshire farm to a conservation easement. Other neighbors joined in for a combined total of over 1,000 acres of land preserved forever, never to be developed. This has led to a regional movement as well, which involves landowners from a dozen surrounding towns.

Seven Secrets of Success

The following seven secrets of success are included for your contemplation and amusement:

1. There are no secrets. Understanding and practicing the fundamentals discussed here, along with hard work, will get results.
2. As soon as there is a secret, everyone else knows about it, too. Searching for secrets is a mindless exercise.
3. Happiness is a positive cash flow.
4. If you teach a person to work for others, you feed him or her for a year, but if you teach a person to be an entrepreneur, you feed him or her, and others, for a lifetime.
5. Do not run out of cash.
6. Entrepreneurship is fundamentally a human process, rather than a financial or technological process. You can make an enormous difference.
7. Happiness is a positive cash flow.

Chapter Summary

1. Entrepreneurs thrive on the challenges and satisfactions of the game: It is a journey, not a destination.
2. First and foremost, successful entrepreneurs strive to build a great company: wealth follows that process.
3. Harvest options mean more than simply selling the company, and these options are an important part of the entrepreneur's know-how.
4. Entrepreneurs know that to perpetuate the system for future generations, they must give back to their communities and invest time and capital in the next entrepreneurial generation.

Study Questions

1. Why did Walt Disney say, "I don't make movies to make money. I make money to make movies"?
2. Why is it essential to focus first on building a great company, rather than on just getting rich?
3. Why is a harvest goal so crucial for entrepreneurs and the economy?
4. Define the principal harvest options, the pros and cons of each, and why each is valuable.
5. Beyond the harvest, what do entrepreneurs do to "give back," and why is this so important to their communities and the nation?

Internet Resources for Chapter 19

http://www.nvca.com *The National Venture Capital Association*

http://www.ventureeconomics.com *Venture Economics*

http://www.nasdaq.com

http://biz.yahoo.com/reports/ipo.html *Recent IPO news*

http://www.entreworld.org *Kauffman Foundation: Resources for the entrepreneur*

Books of Interest

Tom Ashbrook, *The Leap*

Randy Komisar, *The Monk and the Riddle*

Jerry Kaplan, *Startup*

Joel Shulman, *Getting Bigger by Growing Smaller*

MIND STRETCHERS

Have you considered?

1. The Outdoor Scene company became the largest independent tent manufacturer in North America, but eventually went out of business. The founder never realized a dime of capital gain. Why?
2. When Steve Pond sold his company in the late 1980s, he wrote checks for hundreds of thousands of dollars to several people who had left the company up to several years previously, but who had been real contributors to the early success of the company. What are the future implications for Steve? For you?
3. Dorothy Stevenson, the first woman to earn a ham radio license in Utah, said, "Success is getting what you want. Happiness is wanting what you get." What does this mean? Why should you care?

Case

Boston Communications Group, Inc.

Preparation Questions

1. Evaluate the investment bank proposals and options facing the company in early February 1996.
2. What should be the company's valuation? Why ?
3. Which underwriter would you select? Why?
4. As a venture capital director, what would you do?
5. As a founder? As an outside director?
6. What will happen?

As Paul Tobin headed across Boston's Nahant Causeway on the cold morning of February 6, 1996, for a breakfast meeting with a director on his board, he reviewed his agenda for the board meeting afterward. Two things stuck in his mind: one was a surprise, the other was not. First, the best harvest option at this point was clearly an IPO. But what had been a substantial, albeit most pleasant, surprise was the new valuations (See "Paul J. Tobin" case study in Chapter 14.) Instead of the $50 million to $90 million range originally suggested by the investment bankers known as the four Horsemen, they now concluded that the company might have a postmoney IPO market cap as high as $290 million, and at least $200 million. Assuming the board voted later this morning to pursue an IPO, the major decision now was: Who should be the underwriter?

In the discussion over breakfast, the director confirmed what Paul had suspected all along; he would step down from the board this morning, as he had a personal policy of not being on the board of new public companies.

Strategic Revelations: The Paradox of Dry Powder[1]

The delicate balancing act between optimistic versus conservative financial forecasts in a business plan can be befuddling for entrepreneurs and investors alike. The more aggressive the business plan, the less likely the management team will be able to achieve it, and as a consequence of underperforming, the company will likely suffer dilution. On the other hand, the more conservative the estimates, the more likely management will achieve its business plan projections, but may fail to attract investors at all since the company just won't be large enough or profitable enough. Further, at the harvest window overly conservative estimates lead to the ultimate" dry powder paradox" as the depressed values come bake to haunt the conservative estimator.

Paul Tobin faced this paradox of dry powder, since one of his core entrepreneurial philosophies had always been: "Commit to a business plan you know you can make or exceed. Make it aggressive, but make sure you achieve the plan." He had consistently demonstrated his

 Funding Provided by the Ewing Marion Kauffman Foundation.

[1] "Dry powder" is an expression from the colonial days of flintlock muskets, which were fired by pouring a small charge of gun powder into a flashpan which would ignite from the sparks of the flint striking a metal piece once the trigger was pulled. If one's powder become damp the musket would not fire. Thus, having a cushion or backup reserve of "dry powder" was a must for survival. Having "dry powder" in business plan forecasts simply describes a conservative philosophy of estimating.

EXHIBIT A

Data of Selected Telecommunications Companies

	1995 Average Price	1994 Average Price	Common Shares Out (mil)	Total Debt ($ mil)	1995 Revenues ($ mil)	1994 Revenues ($ mil)	1995 EPS	1994 EPS	Market Cap ($ mil)	Multiple
Airtouch Communications	29.80	25.25	498.57	1,075	1,619	1,235	0.27	0.20	14,857	9
MFS Communications	20.65	15.55	130.26	1,334	583	286	1.21	2.21	2,690	5
Mobile Telephone Technology	27.60	20.45	54.13	364	246	148	1.19	0.76	1,494	6
Nextel Communications	15.60	30.05	193.55	2,285	225	83	2.31	1.25	3,019	13
U.S. Cellular	32.15	28.85	82.97	359	492	332	0.52	0.21	2,667	5
Vanguard Cellular	24.70	23.65	41.31	542	236	168	0.17	0.36	1,020	4

Source: The Value Line Investment Survey. Used with permission.

capacity to do this in building Cellular One in eastern Massachusetts from the launch to $100 million in sales in five years, and again in Maine and New Hampshire with Portsmouth Cellular. This had been a key to creating long-term credibility with potential investors, and had enabled him both to attract venture capital and to negotiate favorable terms, given the capital market conditions at the time. Further, this same philosophy, backed by performance, had enabled him to renegotiate the BCGI deal in 1992 and significantly improve management's ownership position. Ironically, his strategy of preserving their ambitious R&D plans for the new C2C prepaid service targeted at the antifraud market as dry powder (which would have been appropriate if preparing for a future round of venture capital) resulted in a quite different set of comparable companies and valuation analysis by the investment bankers.

It was just this paradoxical situation that had revealed itself to Paul over the past three months. Fortunately, he was able to show the investment bankers that the company's future services—not just R&D, but a product already in trials—would significantly change both how one would perceive the company's future and the fundamental strategic businesses it was pursuing. BCGI was not a plain vanilla transaction processing company, such as defined in one valuation report, but rather a company whose future business also encompassed the antifraud/antitheft arena.

How does the entrepreneur discover such things? In the case of BCGI, one outside board member was uncomfortable with the initial valuations and the profile of the company articulated in the valuation reports. In seeking to understand possible misconceptions embedded in the valuation studies, he talked to Janet Green, who headed up Ernst & Young's Corporate Finance activities. A brief discussion revealed that, based on the hundreds of telecommunications transactions over the past year that she was familiar with, companies in the cellular-related antifraud arena were often valued at 5 to10 times revenue, and some outliers commanded as much as 15 to 20 times trailing revenues (see *Exhibit A*). This was a stunning contrast to everything the company had heard up to this point. The director immediately put Paul in touch with Janet. This resulted in a quite different view of the business, a new five-year business plan, and some significantly more robust valuations from the investment bankers.

A New Service, A New Valuation

BCGI launched C2C, a prepaid wireless telephone carrier support service, In the fall of 1995. Although prepaid calling was relatively new to North America, many parts of the world depended upon it. For example, Japan's NTT[2] sold over 2 billion prepaid phone cards between 1985 and 1995. Annual revenues for the prepaid wireless market in the United States were $1 billion in 1995; however, this market was still considered to be in its infancy. BCGI created a nationwide service that benefited from the expertise developed with ROAMER*plus* and found rapid market acceptance. BCGI anticipated that at least four of the regional Bell operating companies would be C2C clients by the end of the first quarter of 1996.

The synergy between ROAMER*plus* and C2C was considerable. ROAMER*plus* was in 1,100 markets nationwide, and C2C could be rolled out using much of the same infrastructure and many of the same relationships. As a result, BCGI would be the only company able to offer a national prepaid roaming service in early 1996.

Providing prepaid services had many advantages over offering credit-based services for wireless vendors. One of the biggest expenses in credit operations was fraud Losses from wireless fraud in the United States ran at over $1 million a day. Prepaid services almost eliminated this cost (see *Exhibit B*).

A New Business Plan

The revised business plan did not show a major increase in projected revenues and profits (see *Exhibit C* for new projections), but rather conveyed a new strategic definition and positioning of BCGI's products and services. Paul still wanted to hold back some dry powder. The difference was that the bankers used a different set of comparable companies to determine BCGI's marketability.

The new comparables provided a rationale for the investment bankers to offer higher valuation estimates: One bank thought the company could be worth as much as $290 million, post-IPO, and all thought it would reach or exceed $200 million. This was about three to

EXHIBIT B

Relative Prepaid vs. Credit Cost Model*

Post-Paid Billing $$ Cost	Prepaid Service $ Cost
Fraud Losses	Usage Inquiry
Fraud Staff	C2C Service
Uncollectible Accounts	Card Production
Collection Agencies	Access Facilities
Collection Staff	
Billing Inquiry (Customer Service)	
Postage	
Billing Staff	
Billing System	

*Not drawn to scale

Source: Boston Communications Group, Inc. Used by permission.

[2] NTT was the largest telecommunications company in the world in 1996.

EXHIBIT C

Five-Year Financial Plan (February 1, 1996) (000s)

Revenues:	**1991**	**1992**	**1993**	**1994**	**1995(e)**	**1996**	**1997**	**1998**	**1999**	**2000**
Cellular Express, Inc.										
Call Processing Services	$1,001	$7,557	$9,786	$18,712	$29,896	$34,200	$41,707	$50,056	$59,109	$68,660
Carrier Support Services			458	2,330	8,774	13,650	17,745	22,536	28,170	34,650
Network Services						3,198	15,747	36,405	62,214	98,381
Other Services	446									
Total Cellular Express	1,447	7,557	10,244	21,042	38,670	51,048	75,199	108,995	149,493	201,691
Cellular Services of WA	5,433	7,642	7,556	9,455	1,000					
Franklin County Cellular, Inc.	11	440	646	717						
Radio Telephone Systems, Inc.	737	228	544							
Total Revenue	7,628	15,867	18,990	31,214	39,670	51,048	75,199	108,995	149,493	201,691
Direct Operating Income:										
Cellular Express Inc.	−225	1,461	1,247	2,305	4,283	4,787	14,382	29,657	47,415	70,370
Cellular Services of WA	331	−187	317	337	−110					
Franklin County Cellular, Inc.	−78	182	406	455						
Radio Telephone Systems, Inc.	−97	−295	509							
Corporate	−873	−856	−1,273	−1,503	−1,267					
Total Operating Income	−942	305	1,206	1,594	2,906	4,787	14,382	29,657	47,415	70,370
Depreciation and Amortization	629	613	681	588	907	1,660	3,180	4,020	5,000	6,120
Interest Exp. (net of income)	2,361	526	590	558	142	54				
Other	346	103	359	−1,402	45					
Income (Loss) Before Taxes	−4,278	−937	−424	1,850	1,812	3,073	11,202	25,637	42,415	64,250
Income (Loss) After Taxes	($4,278)	($937)	($424)	$1,795	$1,726	$2,923	$7,281	$16,664	$27,570	$41,763

four times greater than the valuation offered at the last board meeting in November, just two-and-a-half months earlier.

Paul hoped that his next business plan would have another important addition: A new CEO, George Hertz. Paul wanted to step down before BCGI became a public company. George had been in the wireless and paging business in various capacities since 1982. He was currently serving as president of Advanced MobilComm, Inc., a wholly owned subsidiary of Fidelity Investments. George previously worked at Zip-Call, Inc., where he developed a nationwide multi-city paging program utilizing radio frequencies and worked on cellular license applications for four major New England markets. From 1979 to 1982 he served as budget director for the commonwealth of Massachusetts. George earned both his undergraduate and graduate degrees from the University of Massachusetts.

Paul and George had been friends for over a decade, and when it became apparent that an IPO would be the preferred harvest strategy, Paul contacted him immediately. By the time of the board meeting, George's appointment was ensured. An agreement had been reached between the principals over the preceding months. George's experience managing a cellular company in a public environment would be invaluable in both growing the business and operating as a public company. The board would vote to offer George the position of president immediately following the vote to go public.

Selecting An Underwriter

Three of the Four Horsemen were enthusiastic about taking BCGI to market. Hambrecht and Quist didn't respond with much enthusiasm and were quickly eliminated from consideration. Paul had to make a recommendation to the board as to which one to hire (see Exhibits D.1 and D.2 for ratings of investment bankers). Paul and his team had spent most of January reviewing the proposals (see Exhibit E for typical proposal terms), comparing track records (see *Exhibits F.1* and *F.2* for 1995 IPOs managed by Robertson, Stephens, and Alex Brown), and talking to advisors.

The most important factors for Paul were the recommendations of his board. Paul reasoned that they had experience with IPOs and he had none, so he was careful to heed their advice; however, the board was not unanimous. While all favored a rigorous examination of quantitative and qualitative data, it was common for venture capitalists to form close working relationships with investment bankers. On the BCGI Board, Highland had a long-standing relationship with DLJ, and Burr Egan Deleage with Alex Brown. Both these firms came highly recommended.

A complicating factor arose when Alex Brown lost its key wireless analyst, Mark Roberts, to competitor Montgomery Securities. This was a difficult decision. Fritz described the dilemma.

> When Burr Egan recommended Alex Brown, Paul decided they would take us public. But when they lost Mark Roberts to Montgomery, it was a big loss.

The IPO Environment

Timing was another crucial issue. The IPO market, though decidedly uncertain at year-end, was holding up reasonably well through January 1996. (See *Exhibits G.1, G.2,* and *G.3* for IPO aftermarket data.) In January, 32 small companies had succeeded with new issues (see *Exhibits H* and *I* for examples of IPO registration announcements). This nearly 400-per-year pace would be considered a very strong year, even though it might not match the extremely robust IPO markets of 1993–1995. (See *Exhibits J* and *K* for stock performance by industry.) The trick was, given the four- to five-month lead time required from the filing to the offering, would the IPO window stay open, and how robust would it be when the day arrived? (See *Exhibit L* for VC-backed companies in registration.) No one claimed much predictive capacity to provide accurate answers to such elusive matters.

Decision Time: The February 1996 Board Meeting

Paul knew his board would in all likelihood accept his recommendation to pursue on IPO and would honor his recommendation as to which underwriter to hire, so the burden of decision was squarely on his shoulders. He had occasional nagging thoughts about the risks of an IPO versus a sale to a strategic buyer. He also worried about timing. Although the signs of an improving IPO market looked good for the moment, the IPO window could slam shut in short order, such as in mid-1983 and after the stock market crash of 1987. (See *Exhibit M* for annual IPO data.) The risks were significant: $500,000 or so in out-of-pocket expenses, a demoralizing impact on the company, and, potentially, a long delay before the market would be favorable again. He also knew that picking the right underwriter for the company was a subtle task, and the outcome could make a major difference in the company's future.

These and other thoughts circled his mind as he entered the Callahan tunnel for his office next to Quincy Market.

EXHIBIT D.1

Analyst Rankings

Overall Rankings

Firm	1993	1994	1995
Bear Stearns	16	15	11
C.J. Lawrence/Deutsche Bank Securities	16	18	20
Cowen & Co.	18	16	12
CS First Boston	6	7	7
Dean Witter Reynolds	15	14	16
Donaldson, Lufkin & Jenrette	4	3	2
Gerald Klauer Mattison	—	—	20
Goldman Sachs	2	1	3
Kidder Peabody	11	—	—
Lehman Brothers	1	9	13
Merrill Lynch	1	2	1
Montgomery Securities	19	18	—
Morgan Stanley	5	6	6
NatWest Securities	20	—	—
Oppenheimer & Co.	14	17	15
Paine Webber	8	8	5
Prudential Securities	9	10	8
Salomon Brothers	10	4	6
Sanford C. Bernstein	13	11	10
Smith Barney	7	5	—
Wertheim Schroder	12	13	—

1995 All American Research Team Rankings

Rank	Telecommunications Equipment
1	Joseph Bellace, Merrill Lynch
2	Anthony Langham, NatWest Securities
3	James Kedersha, Cowen & Co.
4	Mary Henry, Goldman Sachs
	Telecommunications Services
1	Daniel Reingold, Merrill Lynch
2	Jack Grubman, Salomon Brothers
3	Frank Governali, CS First Boston
4	Charles Schelke, Smith Barney
	Wireless Communications
1	Linda Runyon, Merrill Lynch
2	Dennis Leibowitz, DLJ
3	Susan Passoni, Cowen & Co.
4	Barry Kaplan, Goldman Sachs

1994 Information Tech./Software and Data Services Analyst Rankings

First-Team	Richard Sherlund, Goldman Sachs
Second-Team	Stephen McClellan, Merrill Lynch
Third-Team	Scott Smith, Donaldson, Lufkin & Jenrette

Source: *Institutional Investor*, October 1995.

EXHIBIT D.2

Most Active Lead Managers, 1995 Venture-Backed IPOs

Underwriter	No. of Companies Managed	Total Co. Offering Size($ mil)	Avg. Price Change*	No. of Issues That Increased	No. of Issues That Decreased
Alex Brown & Sons	33	$1,681	72%	28	5
Hambrecht & Quist	36	1294	73	27	8
Robertson Stephens & Co.	28	1059	57	21	7
Cowen & Co.	27	946	48	20	7
Montgomery Securities	21	945	62	17	4
Morgan Stanley	15	891	91	12	3
Smith Barney	16	814	30	11	5
DLJ	13	796	42	12	1
Goldman, Sachs	15	771	83	13	2
CS First Boston	9	643	26	7	2
Volpe, Welty & Co.	15	531	55	12	3
Needham & Co.	16	498	36	12	4
Wessels, Arnold	12	445	78	10	2
Merrill Lynch & Co.	7	395	10	3	4
Bear Stearns	6	369	70	3	2

*From date of IPO to December 31, 1995.

Source: Thomson Venture Economics/NVCA. Used by permission.

EXHIBIT E

Details of a Typical Proposal

Valuation Matrix

NI = $1.22 million

Calendar Year 1995 P/E Multiple	Implied Post Offering Valuation ($ millions)Valuation
65.2	80.0
73.5	90.0
81.8	100.0
90.2	110.0
98.5	120.0

Written Reports

- Memo/Internal Report (2–6 pages)
  After quiet period expires
  After each quarter's results are announced (8 per 24 months)
- Spot Report (2–6 pages)
  As appropriate (4 per 12 months)
- Full Company Report
  Approximately every 12 months after IPO
  Investor contact (beyond reports)
- Sales Force
  Regular updates from analyst at daily capital market reports
  Direct access by management
  Software focus, experience, and credibility
- Analysts Contracts
  Interactive relationship with investment community
  Media and trade press exposure
- Investor Meetings
  Informal road shows arranged by underwriter
  Sponsorship at New York Society of Securities Analysts
- High-Tech Company Conferences
  Institutional investor attendance
  Breakout sessions for detailed question and answer
  Company-sponsored dinners
  Exposure to other corporate clients

EXHIBIT F.1

Public Offerings Managed By Robertson Stevens & Co.

Issue[a]	Date	Managing Underwriters[b]	Total Dollar Value of Underwriting[c]	Number of Shares[c]	Offer Price per Share
Enterprise Systems, Inc.*	10/9	**RS & Co.,** Volpe Welty, Wessels Arnold	$38,800,000	2,425,000	$16.00
Platinum Technology, Inc.	10/18	**DLJ,** H&Q, RS & Co	182,500,000	10,000,000	18.25
Tegal Corporation*	10/18	**Merrill Lynch,** RS & Co., Soundview Financial	49,200,000	4,100,000	12.00
Alteon, Inc.	10/17	**RS & Co.,** Lehman, Montgomery	18,000,000	2,000,000	9.00
Logic Works, Inc.*	10/16	**Morgan Stanley,** H&Q, RS & Co.	35,200,000	3,200,000	11.00
VTEL Corp.	10/16	**Piper Jaffray,** RS & Co., Cowen	60,000,000	3,000,000	20.00
Intertape Polymer Group	10/10	**First Marathon,** Dean Witter, RS & Co., RBC Dominion First Analysis, Midland Weyland	43,800,000	1,500,000	29.20
Microwave Power Devices*	9/29	**RS & Co.,** J.P. Morgan	31,200,000	3,900,000	8.00
Supreme International Corp.	9/28	**Oppenheimer,** RS & Co., Josephthal	24,700,000	1,300,000	19.00
Spectrum Holobyte, Inc.[d]	9/26	**RS & Co.,** Jeffries, Piper Jaffray	50,000,000	50,000	100.00
Cannondale Corp.	9/20	**Hambrecht & Quist,** Montgomery, RS & Co.	43,987,500	2,550,000	17.25
Information Storage Devices	9/19	**Alex Brown,** RS & Co.	63,000,000	3,150,000	20.00
Alkermes, Inc.	9/19	**RS & Co.,** Cowen	14,000,000	2,000,000	7.00
CBT Group, PLC	9/13	**Alex Brown,** RS & Co.	91,579,500	2,070,000	44.25
Opta Food Ingredients, Inc.	8/24	**Wessels,** RS & Co., Adams, Harkness & Hill	30,000,000	2,000,000	15.00
P-COM, Inc.	8/18	**RS & Co.,** Paine Webber	49,875,000	1,500,000	33.25
Mackie Designs, Inc.*	8/17	**Piper Jaffray, RS & Co.**	30,000,000	2,500,000	12.00
Neurogen Corporation	8/17	**Smith Barney,** RS & Co., Pacific Growth	40,000,000	2,500,000	16.00
Gilead Sciences, Inc.	8/17	**RS & Co.,** Hambrecht & Quist	81,956,250	3,525,000	23.25
The Vantive Corporation*	8/14	**Hambrecht & Quist,** RS & Co.	24,000,000	2,000,000	12.00
Northfield Laboratories, Inc.	8/10	**RS & Co.,** Alex Brown	51,918,750	2,925,000	17.75
Trimble Navigation, Limited	8/3	**Smith Barney,** Needham, RS & Co.	57,750,000	2,000,000	28.88
The Men's Warehouse, Inc.	8/3	**Bear Stearns,** Montgomery, Paine Webber, RS & Co.	64,000,000	2,000,000	32.00
Cephalon, Inc.	8/1	**Cowen,** Hambrecht & Quist, RS & Co.	74,508,998	3,311,511	22.50
ON Technology Corporation*	8/1	**RS & Co.,** Wessels	42,000,000	2,800,000	15.00
U.S. Office Products Company	7/28	**RS & Co.,** Furman Selz, Rodman & Renshaw	49,875,000	3,500,000	14.25
Ascend Communications, Inc.	7/27	**Morgan Stanley,** RS & Co., Wessels	222,956,250	3,162,500	70.50
PRI Automation, Inc.	7/15	**RS & Co.,** Hambrecht & Quist	42,550,000	1,150,000	37.00
Exogen, Inc.*	7/20	**RS & Co.,** Cowen, Piper Jaffray	31,625,000	2,875,000	11.00
Project Software & Development, Inc.	7/13	**RS & Co.,** Montgomery, First Albany	43,470,000	2,070,000	21.00
Legato Systems, Inc.*	7/6	**RS & Co.,** Hambrecht & Quist, Punk, Siegel & Knoell	43,700,000	2,300,000	19.00
Discreet Logic Inc.*	6/30	**RS & Co.,** Volpe Welty	74,865,000	3,565,000	21.00
Metra Biosystems, Inc.*	6/30	**RS & Co.,** Cowen, Furman Selz	34,500,000	3,450,000	10.00
Applied Materials, Inc.	6/28	**Morgan Stanley,** Lehman, Cowen, Needham, RS & Co.	333,068,750	4,025,000	82.75
Tower Semiconductor Ltd.	6/27	**Bear Stearns,** RS & Co., Furman Selz	92,958,050	3,205,450	29.00
PhyCor, Inc.	6/23	**Alex Brown,** RS & Co., Smith Barney, Equitable	122,687,500	3,250,000	27.75
Spine-Tech, Inc.*	6/22	**RS & Co.,** Piper Jaffray	36,225,000	4,025,000	9.00
HNC Software, Inc.*	6/20	**Morgan Stanley,** RS & Co.	36,225,000	2,587,500	14.00
Datalogix International, Inc.*	6/15	**RS & Co.,** Alex Brown, UBS Securities	64,515,000	3,795,000	17.00
TransSwitch Corporation*	6/14	**RS & Co.,** Hambrecht & Quist	28,875,000	2,875,000	9.00
American Oncology Resources*	6/13	**Alex Brown,** RS & Co., Volpe Welty	114,712,500	5,462,500	21.00

(Continued)

EXHIBIT F.1 (concluded)

Public Offerings Managed By Robertson Stevens & Co.

Issue[a]	Date	Managing Underwriters[b]	Total Dollar Value of Underwriting[c]	Number of Shares[c]	Offer Price per Share
ResMed, Inc.*	6/2	**RS & Co.,** William Blair, Nomura	$ 37,950,000	3,450,000	11.00
Eltrom International, Inc.	5/31	**RS & Co.,** Cruttenden Roth	42,000,000	2,000,000	21.00
Computer Learning Centers, Inc.*	5/31	**RS & Co.,** Piper Jaffray	18,320,000	2,290,000	8.00
Number Nine Visual Technology Corporation*	5/25	**RS & Co.,** Cowen, Unterberg Harris	45,712,635	3,047,509	15.00
ITI Technologies, Inc.	5/24	**Piper Jaffray,** RS & Co., Dain Bosworth	82,800,000	3,450,000	24.00
Nexgen, Inc.*	5/24	**Paine Webber,** Alex Brown, RS & Co.	53,250,000	3,550,000	15.00
VideoServer, Inc.*	5/24	**Goldman Sachs,** RS & Co.	49,725,000	2,925,000	17.00
ADFlex Solutions, Inc.	5/24	**RS & Co.,** Paine Webber	61,582,500	2,415,000	25.50
Finlay Enterprises*	4/6	**Goldman Sachs,** DLJ, RS & Co.	36,610,000	2,615,000	14.00
Pairgain Technologies, Inc.	3/20	**H & Q,** Lehman, RS & Co., Furman Selz	88,977,656	3,766,250	23.63
PacificCare Health Systems, Inc.	3/16	**Dean Witter,** Salomon, Dillon Read, Lehman, RS & Co.	351,900,000	5,175,000	68.00
Horizon Mental Health Management, Inc.*	3/13	**RS & Co.,** Raymond James	23,920,000	2,392,000	10.00
National Instruments Corporation*	3/13	**RS & Co.,** Lehman	56,695,000	3,910,000	14.50
Tivoli Systems, Inc.*	3/10	**Goldman Sachs,** RS & Co.	40,652,500	2,903,750	14.00
McAfee Associates, Inc.	3/8	**RS & Co.,** Bear Stearns, Alex Brown	64,009,000	2,909,500	22.00
P-COM, Inc.*	3/2	**RS & Co.,** Paine Webber	29,325,000	1,955,000	15.00
Software Artistry, Inc.*	3/2	**RS & Co.,** Cowen	30,348,500	2,167,750	14.00
Information Storage Devices, Inc.*	2/9	**Alex Brown,** RS & Co.	34,500,000	2,300,000	15.00
TheraTx, Inc.	2/9	**RS & Co.,** DLJ, Morgan Stanley	100,000,000	100,000	100.00

[a] Asterisk indicates company's initial public offering.
[b] Bold lettering indicates managing underwriter who handled the books.
[c] Total amounts reflect the over-allotment option in the offerings in which it was exercised.
[d] A private placement of securities.
Note: All numbers reflect 6.5% convertible subordinated notes due September 15, 2002.

EXHIBIT F.2

Alex Brown & Sons, 1995 IPOs

Issue[a]	Date	Managing Underwriters[b]	Total Dollar Value of Underwriting[c]	Number of Shares[c]	Offer Price per Share
Discreet Logic, Inc.*	6/30	**RS & Co.,** Volpe Welty	$ 74,865,000	3,566,000	$21.00
Metra Biosystems, Inc.*	6/30	**RS & Co.,** Cowen, Furman Selz	34,500,000	3,450,000	10.00
Applied Materials, Inc.	6/28	**Morgan Stanley,** Lehman, Cowen, Needham, RS & Co.	333,068,750	4,025,000	82.75
Tower Semiconductor Ltd.	6/27	**Bear Stearns,** RS & Co., Furman Selz	92,958,050	3,205,450	29.00
PhyCor, Inc.	6/23	**Alex Brown,** RS & Co., Smith Barney, Equitable	122,687,500	3,250,000	27.75
Spine-Tech, Inc.*	6/22	**RS & Co.,** Piper Jaffray	36,225,000	4,025,000	9.00
HNC Software, Inc.*	6/20	**Morgan Stanley,** RS & Co.	36,225,000	2,587,500	14.00
Datalogix International, Inc.*	6/15	**RS & Co.,** Alex Brown, UBS Securities	64,515,000	3,795,000	17.00
TransSwitch Corporation*	6/14	**RS & Co.,** Hambrecht & Quist	28,875,000	2,875,000	9.00
American Oncology Resources, Inc.*	6/13	**Alex Brown,** RS & Co. Volpe Welty	114,712,500	5,462,500	21.00
ResMed, Inc.*	6/2	**RS & Co.,** William Blair, Nomura	37,950,000	3,450,000	11.00
Eltrom International, Inc.	5/31	**RS & Co.,** Cruttenden Roth	42,000,000	2,000,000	21.00
Computer Learning Centers, Inc.*	5/31	**RS & Co.,** Piper Jaffray	18,320,000	2,290,000	8.00
Number Nine Visual Technology Corporation*	5/25	**RS & Co.,** Cowen, Unterberg Harris	45,712,635	3,047,509	15.00
ITI Technologies, Inc.	5/24	**Piper Jaffray,** RS & Co., Dain Bosworth	82,800,000	3,450,000	24.00
Nexgen, Inc.*	5/24	**Paine Webber,** Alex Brown, RS & Co.	53,250,000	3,550,000	15.00
VideoServer, Inc.*	5/24	**Goldman Sachs,** RS & Co.	49,725,000	2,925,000	17.00
ADFlex Solutions, Inc.	5/24	**RS & Co.,** Paine Webber	61,582,500	2,415,000	25.50
Firefox Communications, Inc.*	5/4	**RS & Co.,** Montgomery, Cowen	47,610,000	2,645,000	18.00
Photronics, Inc.	4/18	**RS & Co.,** Prudential, Needham	29,400,000	1,400,000	21.00
CBT Group PLC*	4/13	**Alex Brown,** RS & Co.	42,320,000	2,645,000	16.00
Finlay Enterprises*	4/6	**Goldman Sachs,** DLJ, RS & Co.	36,610,000	2,615,000	14.00
Pairgain Technologies, Inc.	3/20	**H&Q,** Lehman, RS & Co., Furman Selz	88,977,656	3,766,250	23.63
McAfee Associates, Inc.	3/8	**RS & Co.,** Bear Stearns, Alex Brown	64,009,000	2,909,500	22.00
P-COM, Inc.*	3/2	**RS & Co.,** Paine Webber	29,325,000	1,955,000	15.00
Software Artistry, Inc.*	3/2	**RS & Co.,** Cowen	30,348,500	2,167,750	14.00
Information Storage Devices, Inc.*	2/9	**Alex Brown,** RS & Co.	34,500,000	2,300,000	15.00
TheraTx, Inc.	2/9	**RS & Co.,** DLJ, Morgan Stanley	100,000,000	100,000	100.00

[a] Asterisk indicates company's initial public offering.
[b] Bold lettering indicates managing underwriter who handled the books.
[c] Total amounts reflect the over-allotment option in the offerings in which it was exercised.
Note: All numbers reflect 6.5% convertible subordinated notes due September 15, 2002.

EXHIBIT G.1

A Review of the IPO Aftermarket

Company/Location	Offering Date	Offering Size ($ mil)	Offering Price per Share	Closing Price 12/31/95	Price Change (%)	Post Offering Valuation ($ mil)
AMISYS Managed Care, Rockvill, MD	12/20/95	29.0	$14.5	$19	31%	106.2
Adept Technology, San Jose, CA	12/15/95	22.8	71.3	9.5	10.5%	57.5
BENCHMARQ, Dallas, TX	12/1/95	8.0	8	8.125	18.9%	51.4
CapMAC Holding, New York, NY	12/31/95	74.2	20	25.125	25.6%	309.6
Cardiovascular, Raleigh, NC	12/11/95	23.4	11	11	0 %	70.9
Castelle, Santa Clara, CA	12/19/95	7.0	7	7.75	10.7%	24.3
Celeritek, Santa Clara, CA	12/20/95	15.0	7.5	10.625	41.7%	49.6
Citrix, Coral Springs, FL	12/7/95	37.5	15	32.5	116.7%	170.9
DeltaPoint, Greenville, SC	12/20/95	6.6	6	8.75	45.8%	12.2
Ergo Science, Charlestown, MA	12/14/95	22.5	9	14.25	58.3%	87.9
Fuisz Technologies, Chantilly, VA	12/14/95	33.0	12	15.25	27.1%	144.3
META Group, Stamford, CT	12/1/95	43.2	18	30.625	70.1%	90.0
Mecon, San Ramon, CA	12/6/95	33.2	13	15.875	22.1%	71.9
MetaTools, Carpinteria, CA	12/12/95	43.2	18	26	44.4%	202
Molecular Devices, Sunnyvale, CA	12/12/95	25.3	11	10.5	4.5%	95.2
Pharmacopeia, Princeton, NJ	12/5/95	41.6	16	24.25	51.6%	154.4
Physio-Control, Redmond, WA	12/12/95	135.4	14.5	17.875	23.3%	242.9
Raytel Medical, San Mateo, CA	12/1/95	20.0	8	8.5	6.3%	58.0
Schlotzsky's, Austin, TX	12/15/95	24.8	11	10.25	6.8%	60.7
Spacehab, Arlington, VA	12/20/95	45.0	12	12.25	2.1%	128.4
Synaptic Pharmaceutical, Paramus, NJ	12/13/95	20.5	12.5	13.25	6 %	91.6
United TransNet, Roswell, GA	12/14/95	56.9	14.5	15.125	4.3%	125.8
Visioneer, Palo Alto, CA	12/11/95	48.0	12	22.25	85.4%	217.6

Source: Thomson Venture Economics/NVCA. Used by permission.

EXHIBIT G.2

Communications Equipment and Service IPO Aftermarket

Company	P/E Ratio	60-Month High	60-Month Low	11/30/95 Close or Bid Price	Change from 10/31/95
Brooktree	18	21 3/4	5 3/4	13 1/8	1 1/8
CMC Industries	d	10 1/2	2	4 7/16	3/16
Global Village Communication	40	24 1/8	5 3/4	22 3/4	5 3/4
LCI International	100	45 1/2	13 1/2	18 1/2	1/2
Metricom	d	33 3/4	4	15 3/4	−7/8
Microcom	40	26 5/8	1 17/32	25 1/4	3 3/8
Octel Communications	24	42 1/8	10 1/2	32 7/8	−1 1/4
PairGain Technologies	58	50 3/8	7	50 3/8	7 5/8
Racotek	d	14	3/16	5 3/4	−3/8
Signal Technology	94	10	2 7/8	5 5/8	5/8
Tricord Systems	d	29 1/8	2 7/8	3 1/8	−5/8
Trimble Navigation	31	35	6 3/4	20 3/8	5/8
Xircom	d	27 3/4	7 1/4	12 1/4	3 1/4

d = Deficit

Source: Thomson Venture Economics/NVCA. Used by permission.

EXHIBIT G.3

Venture-Backed IPOs, December 1995

Company Location	Offering Date	Size	Offering Price	Bid Price (per share)	Post Offering Valuation	Earnings per Share	Period	Underwriters	Business
Benchmarq Micro (Dallas, TX)	12/1/95	$ 8M	$ 8	$ 8.13	$ 51.3M	$ 0.35	12 Months 12/31/94	Needham & Co.	Integrated Circuits
Meta Group (Stamford, CT)	12/1/95	$43.2M	$18	$30.63	$ 91.69M	$(0.99)	12 months 12/31/94	RS & Co. DLJ	Market Assessment Services
Raytel Medical (San Mateo, CA)	12/1/95	$20M	$ 8	$ 8.50	$ 57.89M	$ 0.69	12 months 9/30/94	Vector Securities Van Kasper & Co.	Cardiovascular Heathcare Services
Pharmacopeia (Princeton, NJ)	12/5/95	$41.6M	$16	$24.25	$154.42M	$(3.15)	12 months 3/31/94	Alex Brown & Sons Cowen & Co. UBS Securities	Drug Discovery Technologies
Mecon (San Ramon, CA)	12/6/95	$33.15M	$13	$15.88	$ 71.94M	$(0.06)	12 months 3/31/95	Montgomery Securities Cowen & Co.	Health care Information Systems
Citrix (Coral Springs, FL)	12/7/95	$37.5M	$15	$32.50	$170.86M	$ 0.02	12 months 12/31/94	Hambrecht & Quist RS & Co	Multi-User Server Products
Visioneer (Palo Alto, CA)	12/7/95	$48M	$12	$22.25	$217.57M	$(0.76)	12 months 12/31/94	RS & Co Montgomery Securities Paine Webber	Paper Input Systems
Cardiovascular Diagnostic (Raleigh, NC)	12/7/95	$ 23.38M	$11	$11.00	$ 70.92M	$(0.35)	12 months 12/31/94	Bear Stearns & Co. Scott & Stringfellow	Cardiovascular Diagnostic Test System

Source: Thomson Venture Economics/NVCA. Used by permission.

EXHIBIT H

IPOs in Registration, Celeritek, Inc.—Actual

SANTA CLARA, Calif.—Celeritek, which makes transceivers, completed an initial public offering on December 20, 1995. The company sold two million shares at $7.50 per share. The shares priced well below the company's $10 to $12 filing range.

Selling shareholders sold 400,000 of the total shares offered. Venture investors Sutter Hill Ventures, Greylock Management, Venrock Associates, and Mayfield Fund V did not reduce their positions in the offering. Venture investors Burr, Egan, Deleage & Co. and Technology Funding sold shares.

Oppenheimer & Co. and Needham & Co. served as underwriters of the initial public offering. The IPO left 6,608,035 shares outstanding.

The company plans to use a portion of the funds to pay debt. Remaining proceeds are slated for working capital.

Founded in 1984, Celeritek has been profitable every year since 1991, according to its prospectus. It earned $0.06 per share for the year ending March 31, 1995.

Celeritek makes transceivers for military and wireless communications applications. The company's devices operate via its integrated circuit and proprietary gallium arsenide process technologies.

William Younger, general partner of Sutter Hill Ventures, and Charles Waite, general partner of Greylock Management, have served on Celeritek's board since 1984.

Celeritek Inc.—Selected Financials*

(in thousands, except per share amounts)

	Year ending March 31					Six Months Ended Sept 30	Six Months Ended Sept 30
	1991	**1992**	**1993**	**1994**	**1995**	**1994**	**1995**
Sales	$18,016	$22,476	$30,751	$36,029	$32,667	$16,614	$16,734
NI (Loss)	1,944	3,851	1,836	1,925	284	205	599
NI per share	0.40	0.74	0.36	0.36	0.06	0.04	0.11

*Unaudited

Source: Thomson Venture Economics/NVCA. Used by permission.

EXHIBIT I

IPOs in Registration, CSG Systems International—Projected

ENGLEWOOD, Colo.—CSG Systems International, a provider of services to communication companies, plans to go public on February 28, 1996. CSG Systems plans to sell 2.9 million shares at $12 to $14 per share.

The initial public offering is being underwritten by Alex Brown & Sons and Hambrecht & Quist. The IPO will leave 25 million shares outstanding.

The Company plans to use approximately $40 million of the IPO's proceeds to reduce its debt and pay dividends on its preferred stock.

CSG Systems was formed in October 1994 to acquire First Data Corp.'s Cable Services Group division. The purchase price was approximately $137 million, according to the Company's filing document.

Although CSG's revenue was a record $96.4 million at year-end December 31, 1995, it lost $0.86 per share during that period, according to its prospectus.

The company's software and support services enable its clients to manage such functions as billing, sales and order processing, invoice production, management reporting, and customer analysis.

Morgan Stanley Capital Partners III, its affiliate Morgan Stanley Venture Partners II, and Trident Capital Partners Fund I are the venture investors.

Frank Sica, a vice chairman of Morgan Stanley Capital Partners, Robert Loarie, vice president of Morgan Stanley Venture Partners, Rockwell Schnabel, co-chairman of Trident Capital, and Donald Dixon, president of Trident Capital, all have served as board members since CSG's inception. Andrew Cooper, also a vice president of Morgan Stanley Venture Partners, became a director of the company in November 1994.

CSG Systems International Inc.—Selected Financials

(In thousands, except per share amounts)

	Predecessor				Company	
	1991*	1992	1993	Eleven Months Ended Nov. 30, 1994	One Month Ended Dec. 31, 1994	Year Ended Dec. 31, 1995
Revenue	$65,206	$71,258	$75,578	$76,081	$7,757	$96,404
NI	3,609	6,727	8,347	8,610	(40,704)	(19,180)
NI per share	-	-	-	-	(1.81)	(.86)

*Unaudited

Source: Thomson Venture Economics/NVCA. Used by permission.

EXHIBIT J

1994–1995 Venture-Backed IPO Performance by Industry

Industry	1995 No.	1995 %	1994 No.	1994 %	5-Year Total No.	5-Year Total %
Computer Software & Services	56	31.0%	17	11.9%	131	16.7%
Medical/Health-related	27	14.9%	27	18.9%	149	19.0%
Other Electronics-related	23	12.7%	15	10.5%	80	10.1%
Telephone & Data Com.	16	8.9%	21	14.7%	85	10.9%
Other	15	8.3%	21	14.7%	66	8.4%
Biotechnology	12	6.6%	10	7.0%	91	11.6%
Consumer-related	12	6.6%	10	7.0%	77	9.8%
Computer Hardware	8	4.4%	9	6.3%	49	6.3%
Industrial Machines & Eqpt.	6	3.3%	8	5.6%	31	4.0%
Industrial Automation	3	1.7%	2	1.4%	9	1.2%
Commercial Communications	2	1.0%	3	2.0%	9	1.2%
Energy-related	1	0.6%	0	0.0%	6	0.8%
TOTAL	181	100.0%	143	100.0%	783	100.0%

Source: Thomson Venture Economics/NVCA. Used by permission.

EXHIBIT K

Telecommunications Stock Market Indices

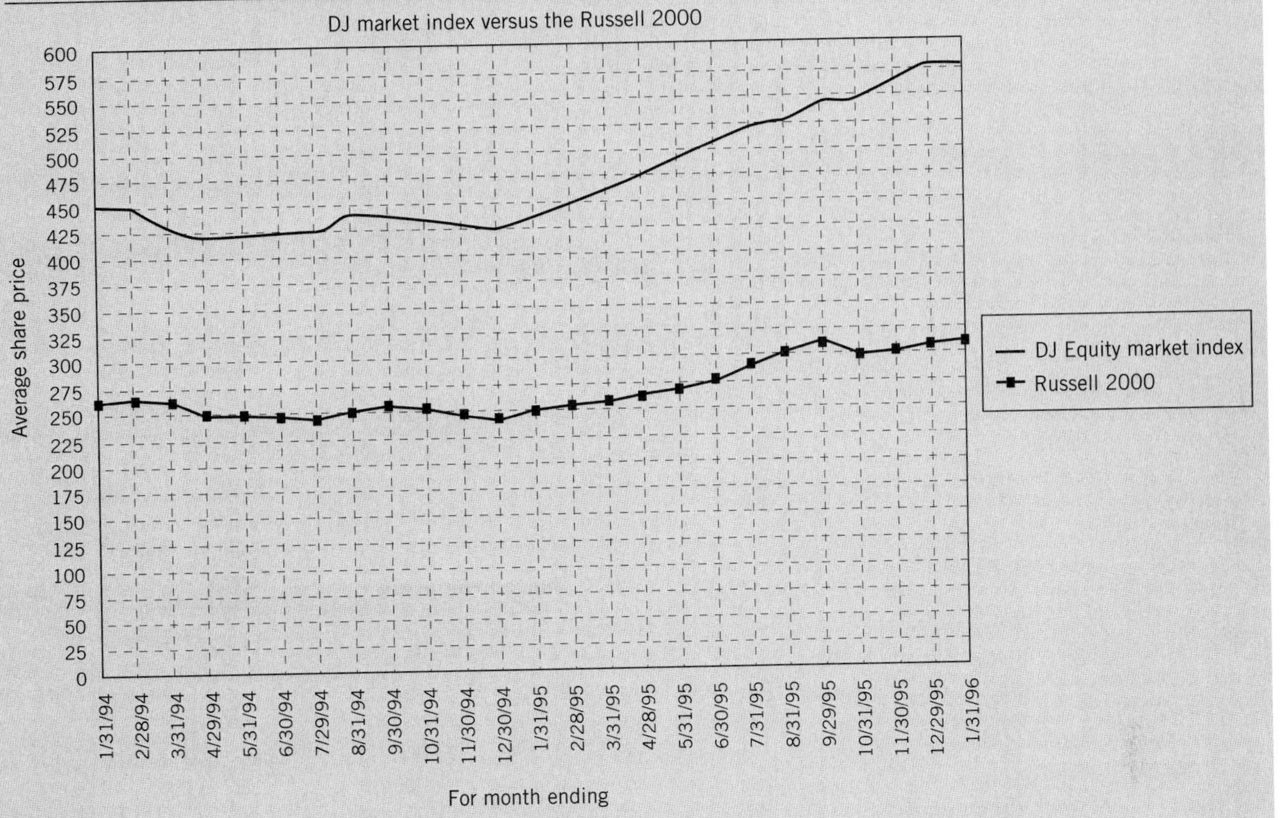

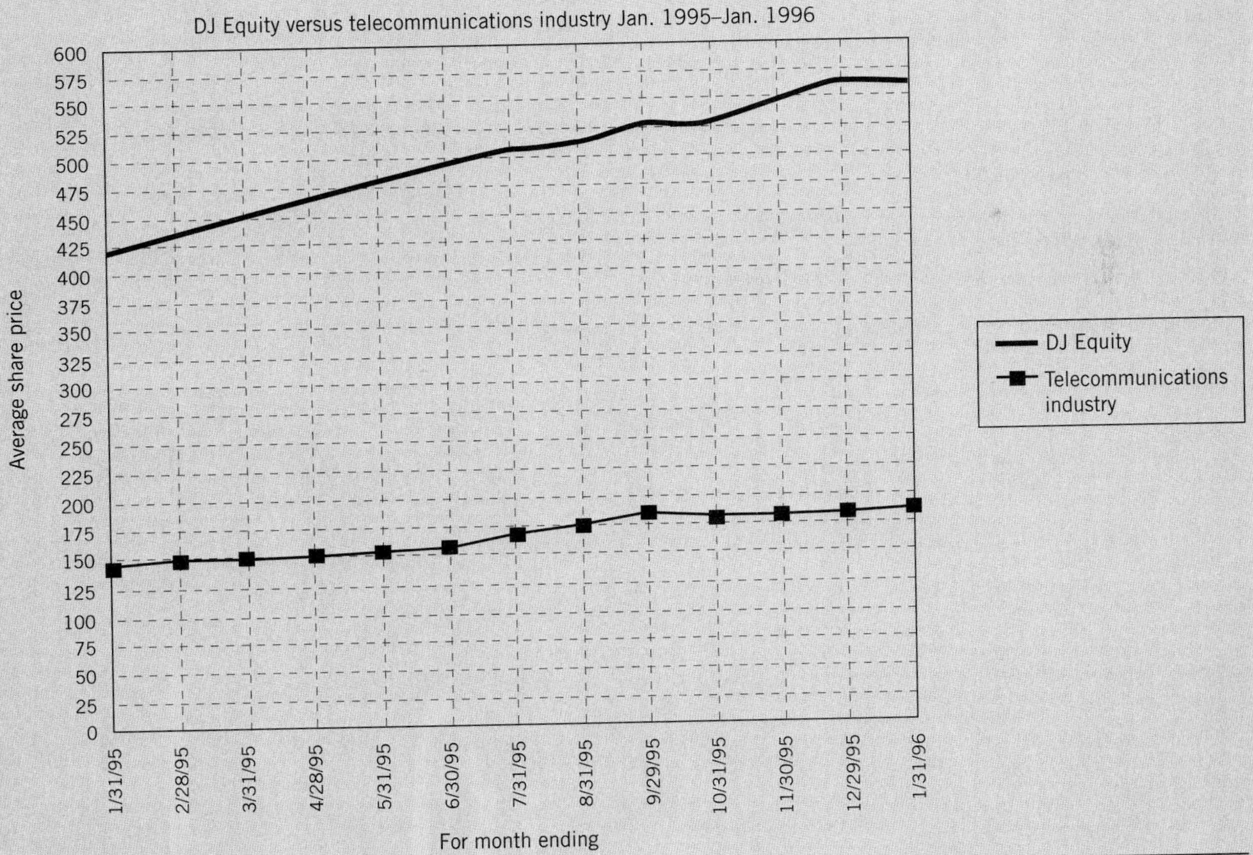

Source: Dow Jones Equity Index.

EXHIBIT L

Venture-Backed Companies in Registration, 12/29/95

Date	Filed Issuer	Low Filing Price	High Filing Price	Shares Filed	Book Manager
9/8/95	RAC Financial Group	13.00	15.00	3,000,000	Bear Stearn
9/11/95	Grand Junction Network*	12.00	14.00	3,000,000	Goldman Sachs
9/27/95	Red Brick Systems	8.00	10.00	1,800,000	Morgan Stanley
10/26/95	IC Works	7.00	9.00	3,500,000	Prudential
10/27/95	Pharmavene	10.00	12.00	2,000,000	Lehman Brothers
11/2/95	Impath	11.00	13.00	1,950,000	Salomon Brothers
11/06/95	Hybridon	9.00	11.00	2,500,000	Lehman Brothers
11/7/95	Advanta Systems	11.50	13.50	2,000,000	ABS
11/7/95	Fast Multimedia	7.00	9.00	2,500,000	ABS
11/13/95	Aavid Thermal Technologies	10.00	12.00	2,300,000	Montgomery Securities
11/22/95	TresCom International	11.00	13.00	4,166,667	Morgan Stanley
11/22/95	Wilmar Industries	10.00	12.00	4,000,000	ABS
12/1/95	Heartstream	—	13.00	3,000,000	UBS
12/1/95	Iron Mountain	16.00	18.00	4,800,000	Prudential Securities
12/1/95	Optical Sensors	11.00	13.00	2,500,000	ABS
12/4/95	Associated Building, Systems	12.00	13.00	2,100,000	George K. Baum
12/5/95	K&G Men's Center	11.00	13.00	1,700,000	Robinson-Humphrey
12/8/95	Connective Therapeutics	11.00	13.00	2,500,000	Smith Barney
12/8/95	Digital Generation Systems	—	—	3,000,000	Hambrecht & Quist
12/12/95	Platinum Entertainment	12.00	14.00	2,650,000	DLJ
12/14/95	Arthrocare	11.00	13.00	2,000,000	RS & Co
12/15/95	Caribiner International	15.00	17.00	3,000,000	Merrill Lynch
12/18/95	EndoVascular Technologies	11.00	13.00	2,000,000	Hambrecht & Quist
12/18/95	Preferred Networks	14.00	16.00	3,300,000	Paine Webber
12/18/95	Premiere Technologies	12.00	14.00	650,000	ABS
12/18/95	Trident	15.00	17.00	2,700,000	Prudential
12/19/95	Micro Enhancement	5.00	7.50	1,000,000	J.E. Liss
12/21/95	Gensym	9.00	11.00	2,000,000	Hambrecht & Quist
12/21/95	Landec	11.00	13.00	2,500,000	Smith Barney
12/21/95	Neose Technology	12.50	14.50	2,250,000	Smith Barney
12/22/95	Diacrin	14.00	16.00	2,500,000	Paine Webber
12/22/95	Health VISION	12.00	14.00	3,850,000	Montgomery

*Has agreed to be acquired by Cisco Systems

Source: Thomson Venture Economics/NVCA. Used by permission.

EXHIBIT M

Venture-Backed IPOs, 1985–1995

Year of IPO	No. of IPOS	Total Offered ($ mil)	Average Offering Size ($ mil)	Median Offering Size ($ mil)	Average Offering Valuation ($ mil)	Median Age of Co. at IPO (years)
1985	47	$843	$17.9	$15.2	$69.7	3
1986	98	2,128	21.7	16.3	86.7	5
1987	81	1,840	22.7	17.6	85.1	5
1988	36	789	21.9	17.0	91.8	5
1989	39	996	25.5	16.5	100.0	5
1990	42	1,188	28.3	23.8	109.3	6
1991	127	3,732	29.4	25.4	110.0	6
1992	160	4,317	26.9	23.1	98.7	6
1993	172	5,034	29.3	23.0	97.7	7
1994	243	3,582	25.1	22.8	87.8	7
1995	282	6,737	37.2	32.0	136.0	7

Source: Thomson Venture Economics/NVCA. Used by permission.

INDEX

A

B

C

D

E

F

G

H

N

O

P

Q

R

S

T

U

V